AF895444

Networks in the Hellenistic World

According to the pottery in the Eastern Mediterranean and beyond

Edited by

Nina Fenn
Christiane Römer-Strehl

BAR International Series 2539
2013

Published in 2016 by
BAR Publishing, Oxford

BAR International Series 2539

Networks in the Hellenistic World

ISBN 978 1 4073 1157 9

© The editors and contributors severally and the Publisher 2013

The authors' moral rights under the 1988 UK Copyright,
Designs and Patents Act are hereby expressly asserted.

All rights reserved. No part of this work may be copied, reproduced, stored, sold, distributed, scanned, saved in any form of digital format or transmitted in any form digitally, without the written permission of the Publisher.

BAR Publishing is the trading name of British Archaeological Reports (Oxford) Ltd. British Archaeological Reports was first incorporated in 1974 to publish the BAR Series, International and British. In 1992 Hadrian Books Ltd became part of the BAR group. This volume was originally published by Archaeopress in conjunction with British Archaeological Reports (Oxford) Ltd / Hadrian Books Ltd, the Series principal publisher, in 2013. This present volume is published by BAR Publishing, 2016.

Printed in England

BAR
PUBLISHING

BAR titles are available from:

BAR Publishing
122 Banbury Rd, Oxford, OX2 7BP, UK
EMAIL info@barpublishing.com
PHONE +44 (0)1865 310431
FAX +44 (0)1865 316916
www.barpublishing.com

TABLE OF CONTENTS

Preface

This volume contains papers presented at the international conference 'Networks in the Hellenistic world – according to the pottery in the Eastern Mediterranean and beyond' which took place at the universities of Cologne and Bonn 23rd–26th February 2011. The organizers Nina Fenn (Cologne), Christiane Römer-Strehl (Bonn) and Patricia Kögler (Frankfurt), all specialists in Hellenistic pottery of different regions in the Eastern Mediterranean, invited participants working from the Adriatic Sea to Asia Minor and up to Central Asia to consider their material according to the common platform of networks and exchange systems.

The participants came from the following nations: Albania, Australia, Austria, Belgium, Denmark, Egypt, France, Germany, Great Britain, Greece, Poland, Switzerland and the USA. The overwhelming response to our first call for papers reflected the huge interest in such a conference. We thank the audience for lively and inspiring discussions. We are indebted to those who chaired sessions (Andrea Berlin, Pia Guldager Bilde, Stella Drougou, Zoi Kotitsa, Elizabeth Langridge-Noti, John Lund, Bertille Lyonnet, Annette Peignard-Giros, Jeroen Poblome and Susan I. Rotroff) for helping us through the programme and keeping an eye on the time-table. We want to thank the departments of classical archaeology of the Universities of Cologne (Michael Heinzelmann) and Bonn (Martin Bentz) as well as the Akademisches Kunstmuseum Bonn (Wilfried Geominy) for their hospitality and support. We owe a great deal to our student assistants at Köln - Lisa Berger and Katharina Jungnickel - and at Bonn - Hannah Godeke, Robinson Peter Krämer, Stefanie Ostendorf, Ruth Schnittker, Klaus Maximilian Jo Schuster, Anne Segbers, Birte Semke and Natalie Wagner. We give sincere thanks to them all.

The concept found favour with the Deutsche Forschungsgemeinschaft (DFG) and we wish to thank them for their invaluable assistance in funding the conference. For the organization of the project our thanks goes to Liselotte Theil (Cologne). The rector's offices of both universities generously backed the catering.

The layout of the conference material as well as the formatting of the papers is thanks to Markus Brückle. We are grateful to BAR for agreeing to publish the proceedings within their British Archaeological Reports, International Series, and we must personally thank Gerry Brisch and David Davison.

Cologne and Bonn, May 2013
Nina Fenn & Christiane Römer-Strehl

Aims of the Conference

The main goal of our meeting was the examination of networks in the Hellenistic East. We believe that economic and cultural networks are reflected in material culture, and we regard Hellenistic pottery as the most widespread and sensitive category of material evidence. The period extends from the time of Alexander the Great until the incorporation of Egypt as a Roman colony. The geographical frame ranges from the Aegean to the Indian Ocean, and from the Black Sea to the Nile River.

Each region certainly contained its own network and until now the evidence of pottery has been investigated primarily from a regional perspective. In this context we want to mention the initiatives of the Greek meetings on Hellenistic pottery, the Centre for Black Sea Studies, and the workshop at Izmir in October 2010 on Hellenistic ceramics in Anatolia. Supra-regional approaches have been few, though here we can mention the Frankfurter Kolloquium and the 'Trade relations'.[1] In no case, however, has the Near East been taken into consideration, which means that our knowledge of Hellenistic pottery in the East is quite fragmented. It is time to open a wider perspective.

In this context the following questions are of interest: What is the character of the trade relations between political centres? What is the nature of economic development in minor cities and rural areas? Are some regions cut off from trade routes and thus characterized by a more restricted spectrum of local pottery? Which places traded their pottery globally? Whose pottery was copied, and by whom? Can the repertoire of forms reflect the adoption of specific customs?

Our first step towards the investigation of 'The networks in the Hellenistic world - according to the pottery in the Eastern Mediterranean and beyond' was to bring the speakers together. The second step is now to connect our knowledge of the material from the various find spots and regions where we work. The third step will be to detect and define economic and social networks in the Hellenistic world by means of ongoing discussions, and so to achieve a trans-regional perspective.

A conference with this range and number of contributions had never been held. Its international character is reflected in the participation of scientists from thirteen nations. Each one represented a specific place or region, which was necessary for the overall picture. Unfortunately, it was beyond our abilities to also include the Hellenistic pottery of the western Mediterranean.[2]

The geographical sectors of the Hellenistic networks along with their research focus and regional peculiarities were represented in the conference according to the following divisions:

- Greece, including the important cities of Athens and Eretria as well as the cultural landscapes of Western Greece, Laconia and Macedonia.
- Albania, the most western region taken into consideration. The southern part, represented by the historic landscape of Epirus, and the northern region both received influences from mainland Greece and areas to the east.
- The Aegean island of Delos, which is of special importance as a trading port

---

1 Herfort-Koch, M., Mandel, U. and Schädler, U. (eds.). 1996. *Hellenistische und kaiserzeitliche Keramik des östlichen Mittelmeergebietes*. Kolloquium Frankfurt 24.–25. April 1995. Frankfurt, University press; Berg Briese, M. and Vaag, L. E. 2005. *Trade relations in the eastern Mediterranean from the late Hellenistic period to late Antiquity: the ceramic evidence*. Acts from a Ph.-D.-seminar for young scholars, Sandbjerg Manorhouse, 12–15 February 1998. Odense, University Press of Southern Denmark.

2 It has been the topic of the conference 'Immensa aequora' organized by Gloria Olcese in January 2011.

not only for ordinary freight but also for fine pottery.
- Asia Minor, including supra-regional production centres such as Pergamon and Ephesos, but also beyond these centres to central Anatolia.
- Cyprus, whose strategic position between the Aegean and Egypt acts as the bridge to the Levant.
- Egypt, including Upper Egypt, the Fayoum and Marmarica. Mediterranean contacts are indicated throughout by the export of transport amphorae and their contents as well as the polychrome painting technique.
- The Seleucid kingdom, including the Levant, Mesopotamia and the Persian Gulf. Included here are contributions from specialists working in Israel, Jordan, Syria, Turkmenistan and Central Asia.
- The Black Sea region, which was a recipient of pottery in this period and so was a direct partner in its networks.
- Finally, there were general presentations on sigillata, scientific analyses, shipwrecks and coin circulation.

At the conference Pia Guldager Bilde represented the Black Sea region with two brilliant papers:
Pia Guldager Bilde, Networking élites and the emulation of precious metal vessels in clay
Pia Guldager Bilde, Innovation, networks, and the success of the mouldmade bowl[3]

Her premature death in January 2013 left a tragic gap among her family, friends and colleagues. It also left a gap in the research of this region and in this volume.

The following participants delivered oral presentations at the conference but for various reasons their papers are not included in this volume:

Barbara Böhm, The oasis of Siwa;
Krysztof Domzalski, Late Hellenistic fine pottery imports and local products from a deposit on the slopes of Mithridates Hill in Pantikapaion;
Patricia Kögler, Beyond the centres – between the centers: the imported and not imported fine ware from Lissos[4];
Sabine Ladstätter, Ptolemaic pottery from Upper Egypt. A contribution to the Hellenistic periphery;
Elizabeth Langridge-Noti, Looking outside: Recognizing material relationships between Hellenistic Laconia and the world outside;
Bernd Liesen, Malgorzata Daszkiewicz and Gerwulf Schneider, Typology and provenance studies of Hellenistic and roman pottery from Gadara/UmmQais[5];
Edyta Marzec, Hellenistic Unguentaria from Cyprus. The issue of trade and local imitations;
Hans-Christoph Noeske, Städteprägungen als Indikatoren für alltägliche Kommunikationsräume? Aktuelle Evidenz und Perspektiven;
Matthias Recke, Ein Bothros von der Akropolis in Perge. Zusammensetzung, Datierung und Funktion;
Gerwulf Schneider and Malgorzata Daszkiewicz, Production and distribution of Hellenistic and roman fine ware in the Eastern Aegean – Chemical data of pottery between Pergamon and Knidos[6].

---

3 The two papers were to form part of her monograph: Guldager Bilde, P. *Mouldmade bowls of the Black Sea region and beyond: from prestige object to an article of mass consumption*, Black Sea Studies 17. Odense, University Press of Southern Denmark. The volume was in preparation in 2012 and we hope it will be published in due course.

4 Kögler, P. 2011. Abseits der Zentren - zwischen den Zentren : die importierte und nicht importierte Feinkeramik aus Lissos. Eine Studie zu den ökonomischen und kulturellen Beziehungen der Stadt im späten Hellenismus. *Iliria* 34, 2009.2010, 77–89.

5 Daszkiewicz, M., Liesen, B. and Schneider, G. in press. Provenance study of Hellenistic, Roman and Byzantine kitchen wares from the Theatre-Temple Area of Umm Qes/Gadara, Jordan. In: *Roman pottery in the Levant: local production and regional trade*", RLAMP volume 3. Oxford, BAR Publishing.

6 Schneider, G. and Daszkiewicz, M. in press. Current state of the WD-XRF database of Hellenistic and Roman Fine Wares in the Levant. In: *Roman pottery in the Levant: local production and regional trade*, RLAMP volume 3. Oxford, BAR Publishing.

Greece

'Small things remembered': the under-theorized domestic material culture of Hellenistic Greece

D. Graham J. Shipley

Abstract

This paper argues that the material culture of hellenistic Greece, particularly the domestic, small-scale material culture of 'Old Greece' (the Greek homeland), is urgent need of being viewed synoptically by archaeologists and historians in the light of developments in material culture theory that are being applied to other periods and places. Where the archaeological evidence permits, artefacts should be interpreted in the context of the assemblages of which they form part, in order to begin to understand the value and meaning they held for those who used them. Imaginative reconstruction, such as that attempted by Deetz, may also be of value[1].

Keywords: material culture, Hellenistic history, domestic assemblages, meaning, fictional reconstruction, Greek social history

Narratives

Samos, c. 275 BC

Zopyrion watched as his mother prepared the evening meal in the two-roomed mudbrick house that was their home, overlooking the harbour. The warships of Ptolemy had arrived that day, disgorging sailors from all over the Inner Sea. They had brought a mix of Egyptian gifts to smooth their way in the taverns of the waterfront. Zopyrion's mother, perhaps against her better judgement, had bought a clay figurine of the god Sarapis, latterly so popular. Now it stood on a high shelf in the corner of the main room. Zopyrion wondered what the sailors would take back with them to Alexandria: perhaps pots of Samian honey for their girlfriends and wives, or pieces of the newfangled red-slipped pottery which his uncle Rhoikos had started making in his workshop at the back of the city.

Aï Khanum, c. 260 BC

Banabelos sighed as the horse slowed, sensing the stable was near. It had been a tiresome journey all the way from Babylon to this outpost of Antiochos's realm. He couldn't even remember the place's Greek name. But the sight of the grand buildings woke him from his lethargy, and he turned to admire the theatre and colonnades, teeming with all manner of men engaged in their trades – here a copper-beater, there a shoemaker – offering the latest fashions direct from Alexandria, or so they said. Why do we have to have shoes from that sink of corruption, Ptolemy's capital, thought Banabelos. But at least he would be in comfortable lodgings tonight and could spend time in the new gymnasium tomorrow.

Sparta, c. 240 BC

Hybrion watched as the new king rode past. He had little interest in who the king was, but recent events had made all the helots conscious that life was changing. Hadn't the aristocrats even strung up one of the kings last year? He turned back to his lathe and resumed the tedious job of fashioning arrows for the army. The weather was unseasonably cold for October, so he called his niece to put more wood chips on the brazier. The girl picked up the brazier, protecting her hands with two of the cloth bags in which Hybrion kept his tools, and brought it closer to her uncle. 'Get yourself a drink, my dear', said his uncle, and the girl, tired from a long morning helping in the workshop, picked a leather beaker off the table and went to the great jar of water in the corner. She scooped a few mouthfuls up with the clay ladle and poured them into her beaker, removed a few stray basil leaves out, and dropped them back in the water.

Those familiar with the scholarship on material culture will recognize that I am paying tribute to the historical archaeologist James Deetz (1930–2000). The phrase 'small things forgotten', used in the title of his most famous

[1] The original from which this paper derives, somewhat distantly, was presented at the Swedish Institute in Athens in 2007, a shorter version being given at the Köln–Bonn conference. I am grateful to the organizers for accepting my paper, and for their hospitality and editorial improvements. I also thank other participants in the conference for their comments, particularly Jeroen Poblome, Susan Rotroff, and Mark van der Enden; and colleagues with whom I have had encouraging exchanges both earlier and more recently, including Penelope Allison, Jennifer Baird, Patricia Baker, Elizabeth Bollen, Glenn Bugh, Duncan Campbell, Jonas Eiring, Vincent Gabrielsen, Lisa Hannestad, Kerstin Höghammar, Lars Karlsson, Sandra Karlsson, Elizabeth Langridge-Noti, Jane Masséglia (*née* Anderson), Gary Reger, Susan Rotroff, Sarah Scott, and Jenni Wallensten. None of the above is responsible for any eccentricities in the views offered.

book[2], derives from a New England house inventory. My imaginative reconstructions imitate those with which he opens the work. They also find interesting resonance in a recent discussion of how ancient historians can liberate themselves from a Eurocentric view of Greece. Prompted by the gravestone of a metic woodcutter in fifth-century Athens, Vlassopoulos asks: How would our Phrygian converse with his Athenian mates, while serving in his Athenian regiment? What would a low-class Athenian think while he was reading this epigram, while passing by going to work in his workshop[3]?

I often ask students, as a stimulus to imagination and a corrective to scholarly abstraction, what they think was actually happening in the Athenian *agora* (or some other place) on a wet Tuesday morning in a particular season of such-and-such a year. Who was selling what to whom? What sorts of background noises could be heard? Who was plotting his next political move with whom and trying not to be noticed? What goods for sale were lying about on temporary booths, or on the ground? And so on. These essays in reasoned picture-building relate strongly to the way in which we study material culture[4].

A gap in research

One of the most glaring gaps in scholarly literature on the hellenistic period, particularly from the point of view of a historian, is a book-length overview of its material culture. There are, in fact, very few publications on the hellenistic period in whose titles the phrase 'material culture' occurs[5], Rotroff's seminal chapter being the most notable exception[6]. By an overview I do not mean, of course, a comprehensive typological study of artefacts and chronology, but a synthetic treatment of part or parts of the hellenistic *oikoumene* addressing questions about social and ideological change.

Major handbooks exist, of course. They cover such classes of artefacts as terracottas[7], jewellery[8], coins[9], architecture[10], and above all (I mean in the largest numbers) sculpture[11] – to mention but a few. It is perhaps symptomatic of traditional concerns that the standard handbook on what its title refers to as hellenistic 'art' is in fact almost entirely about sculpture, with brief excursuses into mosaics, architecture, and (in passing) other pictorial representations such as wall-paintings and relief ceramics[12]. The same is broadly true of a recent, and brilliant, developmental analysis of the Greek influence on Roman art, though its authors choose to put painting first[13].

There are many important volumes – too many to list here – on the pottery (usually fine wares) and other classes of finds from specific excavations, such as Athens and Corinth. There are catalogues of exhibitions and museum collections[14]. Professor Drougou has organized eight Scientific Meetings on Hellenistic Pottery (Επιστημονικές Συναντήσεις για την Ελληνιστική Κεραμική) so far[15], in which over 500 papers, posters, and abstracts have been presented; of those, only about one in ten takes a view wider than a particular site or locality[16], though in many cases this only means analysing the development or distribution of a particular ceramic form across the wider Greek world. A still smaller number of the studies in these excellent volumes attempt to characterize a regional society, economy, or culture; or to examine the meanings which artefacts had for ancient users, the use contexts in which they are found, or the assemblages of disparate objects of which they formed part[17].

Some classes of artefacts, such as jewellery or figurines, are treated in substantial volumes often covering the whole of Greek, or even the whole of Greco-Roman, antiquity. These and other so-called 'minor arts' are even less likely than fine pottery to receive synthetic and contextual treatment, and in excavation reports they are all too likely to be relegated to a catch-all chapter called 'Small finds'[18], whether they are individually small or not. Coarse and unpainted pottery often receives only summary treatment. In her recent studies of classical and hellenistic furnishings, Andrianou makes similar points about the misrepresentation of so-called minor objects[19]. And all of these points could be made with redoubled force for the hellenistic period, since few overviews of artefact types are specifically focused on this period, let alone on the social background to the artefacts in question[20].

---

2 Deetz 1996.
3 Vlassopoulos 2007 (quotation from 237).
4 Key works on approaches to material culture include Bradley 1990; Chapman 2000; Cumberpatch and Blinkhorn 1997b; Deetz 1996; Garwood *et al.* 1991; Gosden 1999; Hill 1995; Moore 1982; Richards and Thomas 1984; Shanks 1996; Sterner 1989; Wells 1999.
5 One is to do with households in Greco-Roman Delos, with particular reference to early Christian times: Trümper 2003. The 'cluster' of papers in *TAPhA* 137. 2 (2007) collectively entitled 'Literary and material culture in hellenistic Greece' (introduction in Miller 2007) is important, but they focus variously on the materiality of inscriptions (Champion 2007) and of books of epigrams (Höschele 2007), the theft of statues from Sicily by Verres (Rosenmeyer 2007), and the relationship between poetry and painting (Gurd 2007) – not on settlement archaeology.
6 Rotroff 2006.
7 e.g. Higgins 1963.
8 e.g. Boardman 2001.
9 Overview in Davis and Kraay 1973.
10 e.g. Wycherley 1978; Lauter 1986; Lawrence 1996.
11 Classic works include Smith 1988; Smith 1991.
12 Pollitt 1986.
13 Beard and Henderson 2001.
14 e.g. Pfrommer 1993; Pfrommer 2001 (but see criticisms of Rotroff 2002).
15 1st Hellenistic Pottery Meeting in Ioannina 1986 (published 1989); 2nd Hellenistic Pottery Meeting in Rhodes 1989 (published 1990); 3rd Hellenistic Pottery Meeting in Thessaloniki 1991 (published 1994); 4th Hellenistic Pottery Meeting in Mytilene 1994 (published 1997); 5th Hellenistic Pottery Meeting in Chania 1997 (published 2000); 6th Hellenistic Pottery Meeting in Volos 2000 (published 2004); 7th Hellenistic Pottery Meeting inAigio 2005 (published 2011); 8th Hellenistic Pottery Meeting in Ioannina (forthcoming).
16 (Figures based on the first seven meetings.) I do not include the general discussions and conclusions at the end of each conference.
17 Examples, all from the later conferences, include Doulgeri-Intzesiloglou 2000; Morel 1997; Rizakis 2004; Rizakis and Touratsoglou 2011; Rotroff 1997.
18 As remarked by Allison 1997.
19 Andrianou 2009, esp. 3–4.
20 On hellenistic art see now Burn 2005 with Gorrie's review in

A welcome exception to the above generalizations appears to reside in Tal's synthesis of the material culture (in its widest sense) of hellenistic Palestine[21], though he is apparently seeking to answer broad questions of cultural continuity between periods, rather than to understand individual (public or domestic) environments. Art and architecture can also be used to address questions of culture contact[22]. Equally welcome is Andrianou's emphasis upon the use and depositional context of Greek furniture, marking a contrast with many earlier studies of artefacts, which are rarely if ever presented in their context of discovery. They are typically divided between specialists whose task is to establish – as is indeed necessary – a chronology and typology of their own material by invoking comparanda from other sites, rather than to go further and contribute to an elucidation of the social or economic features of the society that occupied a site. In a complete site report the project directors may write a synthetic chapter, usually quite brief, drawing general conclusions but not systematically showing by what methods the finds, let along 'small finds', have been analysed to produce those conclusions[23]. In some respects the authors of field survey volumes have done better in this respect, starting from compartmentalized study of types but teasing out (usually in period-specific sections) diachronic social change from the variation in surface assemblages recovered; for example the field surveys of Keos[24], Laconia[25], Methana[26], and so on.

Conversely, the work of hellenistic historians – even those who use quantitative and other data from excavations to investigate economies (such as in the Liverpool volumes)[27] – usually stands at a remove from the work of archaeologists. Two recent historical surveys of the hellenistic period in English are noticeably short on archaeology, including material culture[28]; conversely, overviews of Greek archaeology tend to focus on archaic and classical and to underplay the hellenistic. This is not just a problem of the hellenistic subfield. Even a session on 'Material histories and textual archaeologies' at the Theoretical Archaeology Group conference in 2000[29], an event normally attended by at least some ancient historians, attracted an audience made up entirely of archaeologists[30]. The work of Sauer in explicitly bridging the gap between ancient history and classical archaeology, based on a session at the 2001 TAG[31], seems to have had limited impact as far as hellenistic studies are concerned[32]. Efforts to provide more sophisticated theoretical underpinnings for classical archaeology as a whole have gathered pace with important publications[33], but this, too, has so far had a limited impact on hellenistic studies. Most historians of this period remain uninterested in the hands-on process of interpreting individual artefacts, or even in the compiled quantitative data regarding classes of artefact, and hence in the rules of evidence which a rigorous engagement with archaeology imposes; conversely, classical archaeologists (at least in the English-speaking world) often rely on outdated historical analyses or fail to offer sufficiently complex historical explanations or to problematize those they do offer. As always, there are opportunities to go forward, such as that provided by the imminent 'Theory in Greek Archaeology' conference[34], though at the time of writing none of the titles of papers so far announced appears to focus on the hellenistic period as such.

Hellenistic studies were not always so strongly compartmentalized between historians and archaeologists. Consider the wealth of archaeological evidence exploited by Tarn in his work on Baktria[35]; or, again, consider how Rostovtzeff's *Social and Economic History of the Hellenistic World* (originally published in 1941)[36] is decorated with photographs of scores of artefacts of many different categories – portrait sculptures, coin portraits, bronze copies of busts, relief carvings, ceramic and metal vases, gravestones, terracottas, faience statuettes, mosaics, wall-paintings (from Pompeii), glassware, jewellery, paintings representing textiles, bronze figurines, and so on. What Rostovtzeff does not do – understandably, given the era in which he was working – is to 'read' artefacts systematically, and with strict rules of engagement, in order to get history and society out of them. His aim seems to be, rather, that of illustrating the rapidly changing, multicultural nature of the hellenistic world whose economies are his central concern. Many of his artefacts are given no context in terms of an assemblage – indeed, they may have lacked such a context in the first place, especially those in museum collections. Nevertheless, one is grateful for the mind-broadening range of his expertise and the stimulus he gives us if we wish to conjure up imaginatively the aspects of life about which sources and inscriptions do not tell us. I should like to pay tribute, too, to another volume – somewhat neglected, I judge, since I have rarely if ever

Bryn Mawr Classical Review 2005.07.40 (http://bmcr.brynmawr.edu/2005/2005-07-40.html, last visited on 11 Oct. 2012); on figurines and networks, see Langin-Hooper 2007.

21 Tal 2006, in Hebrew; I know it only through reviews, e.g. Lehmann 2008 and Rappaport 2007.

22 On Greek-non-Greek interaction through art and architecture, see Colledge 1987; Colledge1990.

23 For similar views, see Allison 1997. On the artificiality of the distinction between small finds and others (or 'bulk finds'), see Cumberpatch and Blinkhorn 1997a, v.

24 Cherry *et al.* 1991.

25 Cavanagh *et al.* 1996; Cavanagh *et al.* 2002.

26 Mee and Forbes 1997.

27 i.e. the (so far) three volumes of papers from the conferences on hellenistic economies: Archibald *et al.* 2001; Archibald *et al.* 2005; Archibald *et al.* 2011. Note also chapters elsewhere by Davies 2006; Manning 2007; Oliver 2006; and more fully Oliver 2007 on Attica; Reger 2007.

28 Shipley 2000; and the excellent multi-authored historical survey Erskine 2003.

29 Oxford, 18–20 Dec. 2000.

30 P. A. Baker, pers. comm.

31 Dublin, 13–15 Dec. 2001.

32 Sauer 2004. Note the 10th anniversary colloquium organized by D. R. Stewart at Leicester, 19 Nov. 2011 (proceedings forthcoming).

33 e.g. Alcock and Osborne 2007; Whitley 2001.

34 Ann Arbor, Mich., 4–5 May 2012 (see http://sitemaker.umich.edu/tiga/home, last accessed 6 Feb. 2012).

35 e.g. Tarn 1938.

36 Rostovtzeff 1941 (2nd edn Rostovtzeff 1953, revised by P. M. Fraser).

seen it cited – which makes a bold attempt to integrate artefacts with history. I have in mind the *Plates* volume to the *Cambridge Ancient History* volume vii part 1, edited by Ling[37]; particularly his own chapters on 'Houses and life', 'Sport and education', 'Theatre', 'Religion', and 'Death and burial'.

With very few comparable exceptions, it seems that when either archaeologists or historians do attempt to do justice to hellenistic material culture, they do not always follow through very convincingly. Stamped amphora handles, for example, may be used as a measure of trade volume and direction, but not of culture. The former is a perfectly valid way of addressing certain questions, and I am certainly not saying the same one person should practise both; rather, I am urging that both should be done. Again, drinking vessels and the manner in which wine was consumed are typically interpreted on the basis of the Attic *symposion*, not that of wider consumption practices; yet we now know taverns existed in Greece, and that the *symposion* was the exception, not the rule[38]. Studies have shown that existing typologies of divided domestic space, such as those involving the notions of the *andron* and *gynaikonitis* (the male room and the female room), are too schematic, and that rooms at Olynthos and elsewhere had multiple uses. In other studies, regrettably, pottery styles that draw on iconographic elements from multiple sources, or different styles of pottery occurring together, are sometimes taken simply as evidence of migration and the co-existence of different ethnic groups. Scholars may even fall into the trap of estimating the proportion of each ethnic group in a population from the proportions of different pottery styles. There is an additional problem of combining sources of different kinds: for example, representations of women, such as figurines, are sometimes compared with literary texts, such as Menander[39], rather than interpreted as possible evidence of changes in social relations in their own right – let alone interpreted alongside the objects with which they were found. Cultural analysis does not always get further than treating, for example, apparent borrowings from classical styles, or from the culture of Old Greece, as expressions of a Hellenism beleaguered in a sea of barbarian culture.

Great men and others

My particular interest in raising these issues is born of a desire to know more about the everyday, small-scale material culture of the hellenistic period, for most aspects of which there are, as far as I am aware, no synthetic treatments. I have in mind not only the so-called minor arts – figurines, coins, metalwork, jewellery, and so on – but also pottery assemblages, where the data are available. In a chapter in an edited survey of the period, Rotroff gives a wonderful list of the kinds of things that must have existed, of which I quote a part: utilitarian objects and structures that, were we walking through a Hellenistic environment, we might not particularly notice, but which nonetheless carry important messages about life in that environment. . . . in the house, aside from the house itself and its fittings (doors, locks, paving, walls and their decoration, roof tiles, water pipes), furniture, domestic tools (looms, washtubs), textiles, baskets, wineskins, the pottery for storage, cooking, serving, eating, drinking, washing, and bathing, equipment for the household shrine, toilet items and secular ornaments; on ancient bodies, clothing, footwear, and items of personal adornment; in public buildings, ballots and voting machines, public measures, tokens and nametags, inscriptions, papyrus rolls, writing tablets; in the workshop, the potter's wheel, sculptor's tools, kilns, furnaces; on the farm, hoes, plows, grindstones, harnesses, beehives; in the gymnasium and the bath, athletic and bathing paraphernalia (jumping weights, discus, balls, strigils); and at shrines, votive pottery and figurines, offering tables, and sacrificial equipment. Out on the borders, soldiers on patrol would present another collection (armor, weaponry) and the unlucky victims of a siege could view from their walls the approaching material culture of the enemy in the form of siege machines. At sea, the ship, perhaps the most complex piece of material culture of its time, laden with its cargo of commodities and material culture, was also crammed with the nets, knives, cooking pots, crockery, gaming pieces, and navigational devices that sustained the crew and the passengers throughout the voyage[40]

One of the goals at which history should surely aim is the reconstruction of daily life and personal relationships, particularly when written sources are virtually silent on these matters. It is not as if politics is divorced from personal relations. John Arnold, in his splendid book *History: A Very Short Introduction*, argues compellingly that cataclysmic events happen not merely because of great men but precisely *because of* the non-great – not to mention women, including great ones[41]. The English civil war, for example, or the colonization of America, or the Reformation could not have happened without the mass (not an undifferentiated mass!) of ordinary and middling folk who were prepared to follow others, often into danger. There have been plenty of potentially charismatic leaders who never led anyone. Luther was not the first to nail theses to a church door, but he found a response others had not. And so on. One could make a similar point about Alexander the Great: his conquest would not have taken place without the tens of thousands of people willing to follow him. Their material culture, I suspect, has not been of much interest to ancient historians, even historians of ancient art.

37 Ling 1984.
38 Kelly-Blazeby 2008; also Kelly-Blazeby 2001.
39 Again, the work of Andrianou marks a significant step forward in the sophistication with which archaeological and literary evidence are combined.
40 Rotroff 2006, 136–137.
41 Arnold 2000.

The first part of Rotroff's imaginative list is perhaps the most tantalizing. Artefacts relating to technology, political-military life, or commerce relate to areas of ancient society that have tended to dominate research in any case. How much more urgent to look for evidence of value and meaning in the artefacts from domestic contexts! This sphere, it seems to me, offers the greatest potential for innovation. It might be objected that the amount of meaningful comparison we can make is limited by the differential preservation of different kinds of data in the conditions of the eastern Mediterranean, as well as by the inadequate recording practices of older excavations; but excavation and publication practice has changed, and we surely have a wide enough of range of small artefacts – sometimes even assemblages in context – to make the attempt worthwhile.

Reasons for neglect?

Why has the small-scale material culture of the period not been synoptically viewed or adequately theorized?

One undoubted reason is the relative decline of interest in hellenistic history during much of the twentieth century, at least in the English-speaking world. 'Classical archaeology' in its Greek embodiment has tended to mean the archaeology of the archaic and, as the name suggests, classical periods, the hellenistic often being appended or subsumed in studies of artefact categories such as jewellery, fine pottery, and sculpture. Happily, the level of interest in hellenistic history has revived since the 1980s, and one may hope that this carries over into the study of archaeology.

Another explanation, superficially attractive, could be that, as with archaic and classical Greece, it takes a huge effort just to make sense of, and in particular to date, the vast amount of material remains. To put it less charitably, the quantity of finds gives us plenty to keep us at work, so that we are not under too much pressure to devise theoretical models. One step in rebutting that view would be to point to the post-Winckelmann aestheticism that was, until recently, dominant in all quarters of classical archaeology and that still has great influence, perhaps particularly in the USA. This approach either admires what it selects as 'art' or 'arts' and marginalizes other classes of artefacts, or actually regards hellenistic art as second-rate in comparison with classical, compounding the problem.

A more convincing explanation for our failure to develop a strongly social approach to hellenistic material culture is that this period, like the classical, is one for which we have written sources, so that we tend to think we have all the necessary reference points to understand society and ideology – or, better, societies and ideologies. One could respond, however, not only that the sources for the period are very gappy[42], but also that material culture theory has been most actively developed precisely in the study of literate societies such as early colonial America. And it is clearly not the case that Greek sources, or sources for any period, tell us all we would like to know about social relationships and attitudes.

New work

On the positive side, some studies have attempted to move in the direction indicated. All those I know of are by archaeologists rather than historians. One of the few explicit considerations of hellenistic material culture is Rotroff's chapter, already mentioned[43]. It contains valuable pointers to what might be done, though given the introductory character of the volume of which it forms part, it understandably does little more than that. Rotroff does make telling points about the non-correspondence of datable artefact types either with the conventional limits of the period or, indeed, with each other. So-called hellenistic lamps, for example, continue into Flavian times, while Attic kraters cease around 175 BC. Changes in drinking pottery, such as the new lagynos shape, perhaps intended for a single drinker's portion of wine, can attest changes in drinking practices. Amphoras are valuable interpretative tools not only when they have stamped handles: some 90 per cent probably had no stamp, and these too must be considered. The use of rooms in elite houses, she remarks, becomes more flexible in this period. Greek cooking ware shapes are adopted in new places, helping to define a hellenistic *koine*. At a certain stage Italian cooking wares enter on the scene. Some pottery styles may be described as hybrid (combining ostensibly Hellenic and non-Hellenic elements), and the interplay between conservatism, innovation, and fusion may illuminate cultural change. Material culture may tell us even more about non-Greek cultures than about Greek cultures not described in the sources. Changes in the representation of women may be the basis for a study of ideological changes. Finally, the design, use, and location of artefacts may reflect the importance of memory and 'spirit of place' (if I may foist upon Rotroff a term popularized, though not invented, by Lawrence Durrell), such as the attempt to claim a heroic past, discussed in Alcock's classic paper on late classical–early hellenistic cult at Bronze Age tombs[44]. Residue analysis may further elucidate the physical uses to which ceramic artefacts were put.

To Rotroff's general methodological statement one may juxtapose a few detailed studies that engage with issues of context and interpretation[45]. Houby-Nielsen has argued that the abandonment of sculpted grave monuments in Athens, under and after the regime of Demetrios of Phaleron, was

42 See general discussion in Shipley 2000, ch. 1.
43 Rotroff 2006.
44 Alcock 1991.
45 Houby-Nielsen 1997.

not the result of his sumptuary law but part of a wider trend (already proposed in her earlier paper on the Kerameikos)[46] towards (*a*) equal treatment of men and women and (*b*) the conscious placing of grave markers against a background of earlier, still visible sculptural monuments meaning that people had a certain sense of landscape, of the placing of new monuments in a context that evoked a vision of the past; she uses the term 'romantic' at one point. Her earlier study calls to mind one of the few attempts I have seen to tease out the implications for social attitudes from art: Sutton's study of fifth-century vase iconography, which argues for a softening of gender opposition at Athens and a greater willingness to permit women's sexuality to be represented iconographically[47]. Zanker's study of sculptural reliefs from Smyrna is another such attempt[48]; while the work of Masséglia represents the most comprehensive attempt yet to reassess the notion of individualism in hellenistic figurative sculpture[49].

Clearly the methodological climate is slowly changing, and some site publications now acknowledge the need for more synoptic analysis. Thus Eiring, in his excellent study of graves at Aitolian Chalkis – from which comes the cover photo on the relevant volume of *Proceedings of the Danish Institute at Athens*, showing a selection of finds all from one tomb – declares as his ultimate goal a synthetic study of West Greek burial customs[50].

I should not of course neglect to mention complementary historical studies which attempt to characterize certain classes of social relationships in great detail, for example Gabrielsen's outstanding work on Rhodian associations[51]. Nor would I rule out, as irrelevant to the study of everyday material culture, studies of economies and trade patterns based on the evidence of pottery and other finds. Elsewhere I have argued on the basis of studies of particular sites and localities that the stylistic analyses of early hellenistic pottery in the Peloponnese allow us to identify at least two different 'Peloponneses'[52]. Some regions are characterized by the pottery experts as conservative and inward-looking: Eleia, the small *poleis* of Achaia and Arkadia, and the *polis* of Messene; while others show more active links with the wider world: Corinth, Dyme, coastal Messenian towns, and, perhaps surprisingly, inland Laconia including Geronthrai. It is also possible to divide the Peloponnese into a northern and north-western zone where pottery styles are apparently influenced more by Corinth, with other areas such as Laconia and coastal Messenia displaying stronger stylistic links with Magna Graecia and the eastern Mediterranean, particularly Alexandria. It would be interesting to tie this in with possible social and ideological developments in different areas.

46 Houby-Nielsen 1998.
47 Sutton 1992.
48 Zanker 1993.
49 Masséglia 2102; Masséglia forthcoming.
50 Eiring 2004, esp. 155.
51 Gabrielsen 1997; Gabrielsen 2001.
52 Shipley 2008, 62–64.

While networks are vital to understand, we must not shirk the attempt to go beyond them and comprehend the social relations that underlay them.

A new agenda?

When Michael Shanks published his provocative book on Greek archaeology[53], he highlighted the need for a sociologically and anthropologically informed approach to artefacts. What, then, is it possible to aspire to do for the hellenistic period, and how feasible is the task?

To turn an earlier point on its head: hellenistic archaeology is extremely well placed to move forward into a new phase of study informed by material culture theory, precisely because the material record is relatively rich. To formulate telling questions, however, it will be necessary to draw upon methods applied by archaeologists to other cultures, as well as upon sociological and anthropological discourses.

In an encyclopaedia article, Morphy emphasizes, first, artefacts as 'indices of cultural boundaries and markers of social categories'; second, as evidence of transformations in the value and meaning of objects as they move from context to context, either as part of local exchange systems or global trading processes. Material objects frequently outlast their maker; thus they are both sources of evidence about previous lifeways and objects to be reflected on by the generations who succeed their makers. [. . .] people make meaningful objects but they can also change the meaning of objects[54].

This formulation, while not exhausting the interpretative possibilities, does seem helpful, above all in its stress on *value* and *meaning* – notions I have rarely seen attached to the hellenistic 'minor' arts. The relative values we place on material items are not always predictable or consistent. When my family and I moved house a few years ago, we left behind (temporarily, since our old house was not yet sold) some of our most valuable silver-plated utensils because we didn't have room for them. Among the things we took great care *not* to leave behind were a number of rather tired-looking mugs, some well-worn soft toys, and a very old, handmade table of rather ordinary pine, which we valued for its utility.

The term 'historical archaeology' carries a special meaning in the English-speaking context, namely the post-colonization archaeology of North America. Deetz's classic study of early modern American life includes extensive discussion of ceramic finds, and prompts one to formulate questions about the hellenistic period. First, can we do more with the function and use of particular vessel shapes, for example to extract information about

53 Shanks 1996, esp. ch. 6.
54 Morphy 2004 (quotations from pp. 620 and 621).

regional differences in foodways or dining customs?[55] As far as I am aware, most of what has been written about foodways in Greek times has been based on literary texts and iconography[56]. Second, where did pottery stand in relation to other items of technology? How widely used, for example, were non-ceramic implements? Third, is it possible to correlate different kinds of pottery with different social classes? Fourth, did some pottery have a non-functional role, for example what Binford (according to Deetz) called socio-technic and, on another level, ideo-technic (such as cultic) roles? A vase may be displayed rather than used.

Others will wish be able to devise areas for investigation, but one specific aspect that should be of wide interest to historians is ideology. Deetz argues that intellectual changes among the elite take a long time to have any impact on ordinary men and women, but may eventually do so, perhaps after hundreds of years[57]. He has in mind the Renaissance and Enlightenment, and he undoubtedly over-schematizes, writing under the influence of Structuralism: we may be sceptical about his insistence on the essentially tripartite mental schemes characteristic of humanistic Renaissance thought, and the suggestion that modern babies' food bowls divided into three compartments are conditioning our children into Renaissance ways of thinking. While we can certainly formulate more relevant questions today, it seems vital to pose such questions and discuss them. For example, can we make any link at all between, on the one hand, the work of Aristotle and the early Stoics, the discoveries of the explorer Pytheas, the geographical research of Eratosthenes, and other intellectual advances in the late fourth century and the first half of the third; and, on the other hand, changes in intimate social relationships, domestic practice, diet and consumption, even religious belief and practice? It is a large gap to bridge, but such links have sometimes been posited – plausibly, though usually without detailed argumentation – by finding, for example, reflections of philosophical developments in imaginative literature of the period, such as the social comedies of Menander or the epic of Apollonios Rhodios. Those writers were themselves members of an elite, and thus in touch with intellectual innovations; on the other hand, we must not make the mistake of thinking that their attitudes were typical of Greeks in their age, or indeed that Greek attitudes did not vary extremely widely across the eastern Mediterranean and western Asia.

All these perspectives may be enriched by the study of excavated artefacts. I suggest that, given the right kind of data, we can use the surviving domestic material culture of the hellenistic period to explore social relations and ideology in greater depth.

Of course, it is a moot point whether there is a distinctively hellenistic material culture, or even cultures, as opposed to 'categories of material evidence that happen to be datable within certain chronological limits'[58]. Equally, we must keep an open mind about the extent to which there was such a thing as a hellenistic material culture *koine* and, if so, when it existed and where, and when and where it did not. The interplay between *koine*, region, and locality must also be borne in mind[59]. Given the quality of recent excavations from urban sites outside Old Greece – for example at Tell Anafa in Israel[60], Failaka off Kuwait[61], and Jebel Khalid in Syria[62] – it may well be that the most fruitful areas for investigation small-scale material culture lie in the 'new' Greek lands of western Asia. On the other hand, the intensity with which material from Greece itself has been studied may also lend itself to contextual investigation.

We are of course at the mercy of older excavation methods, as well as of delayed publication or even the failure to publish – what might be called 'un-publication'. Above all we are at the mercy of preservation of data, or the lack of it. The imagined sketches at the beginning of this paper may be thought of, in some respects, as shopping lists for what we would like to know rather than drawing on what we do know or even what we can hope to know. Zopyrion's self-interrogation about the harbour at Samos is predicated on Ptolemaic naval control of the island in the third century and the presumption that the fleet was manned by a cosmopolitan mix of well-travelled sailors; despite their officially military preoccupations, they 'surely would have' acted as long-distance purveyors of acculturation in several directions (Samian honey to Egypt is just one plausible object of trade)[63]. But would a family whose mother had no slave to cook for her necessarily live in a relatively generously proportioned building? Only a probabilistic case can be made, and it would need to be made on the basis of the best current knowledge and theory. The fiction, consciously un-grounded in direct evidence, asks questions; it does not seek to provide authoritative answers. Neither do those about the craftsmen at Aï Khanum (whose Greek name is indeed uncertain) who are aware of Egyptian fashion (which seems wholly likely), and about the Laconian helot (helots, too, have families)[64] who works at his house but lives in relative comfort[65].

---

55 Cf. Deetz 1996, 75.
56 e.g. Dalby 1996; Davidson 1997; Wilkins 2000; Wilkins and Hill 2006 (with some mention of archaeology).
57 Deetz 1996, 59.

58 J. Baird, pers. comm. (2007).
59 See now Colvin 2010 and, in the same volume, Erskine 2010, for sceptical remarks about notions of a linguistic or cultural *koine* in the hellenistic period.
60 Berlin and Slane 1997.
61 Hannestad 1983.
62 Jackson 2006 (figurines); Jackson 2011 (housing); Jackson and Tidmarsh 2011 (pottery); Jackson 2000 (lamps); Wright 2011. Cf. also study of Dura-Europos by Downey 1993.
63 Cf. Shipley 1987, 18 and 269, for circumstantial evidence that Samos then, as now, produced noted honey. Cf. the multifarious island goods imported into Alexandria in 259 BC (Austin 2006, no. 298 = Austin 1981, no. 237 = *P. Cairo Zen.* 59.012)
64 e.g. Hodkinson 2000, ch. 4.
65 A Hybrion was commemorated near the perioikic town of Sellasia: Shipley 1996, 214 no. 2; see also http://www.csad.ox.ac.uk/laconia/Inscription02.html (last visited on 11 Oct. 2012). To what social class he belonged remains unknown; Spartiates who died in battle

We may never know whether Greek children would take water from a pithos using a ceramic ladle, but if we do not present such scenes – and alternatives – to our imagination we may struggle to get closer to both the functions of everyday objects and the meanings they held for people.

While we may not find the data to answer all our questions, I believe that we must ask those questions. If we do not, we impoverish our understanding of life in hellenistic Greece.

D. G. J. Shipley
School of Archaeology & Ancient History
University of Leicester
University Road
Leicester
GB-LE1 7RH
gjs@le.ac.uk

Bibliography

Alcock, S. E. 1991. Tomb cult and the post-classical polis. *American Journal of Archaeology* 95, 447–467.

Alcock, S. E. and Osborne, R. G. (eds.) 2007. *Classical Archaeology*. Oxford, Blackwell.

Allison, P. M. 1997. Why do excavation reports have finds' catalogues?, in C. G. Cumberpatch and P. W. Blinkhorn (eds.), *Not So Much a Pot, More a Way of Life: Current Approaches to Artefact Analysis in Archaeology*, 77–84. Oxford, Oxbow.

Andrianou, D. 2009. *The Furniture and Furnishings of Ancient Greek Houses and Tombs*. Cambridge, Cambridge University Press.

Archibald, Z. H., Davies, J., Gabrielsen, V., and Oliver, G. J. (eds.) 2001. *Hellenistic Economies*. London–New York, Routledge.

Archibald, Z. H., Davies, J. K., and Gabrielsen, V. (eds.) 2005. *Making, Moving and Managing: The New World of Ancient Economies, 323–31 BC*. Oxford, Oxbow.

Archibald, Z. H., Davies, J. K., and Gabrielsen, V. (eds.) 2011. *The Economies of Hellenistic Societies: Third to First Centuries BC*. Oxford, Oxford University Press.

Arnold, J. H. 2000. *History: A Very Short Introduction*. Oxford–New York, Oxford University Press.

Austin, M. M. 1981. *The Hellenistic World from Alexander to the Roman Conquest (A Selection of Ancient Sources in Translation)*. Cambridge, etc., Cambridge University Press.

Austin, M. M. 2006. *The Hellenistic World from Alexander to the Roman Conquest (A Selection of Ancient Sources in Translation)*, 2nd edn. Cambridge, Cambridge University Press.

Beard, M. and Henderson, J. 2001. *Classical Art: From Greece to Rome*. Oxford, Oxford University Press.

Berlin, A. and Slane, K. W. 1997. *The Hellenistic and Roman Pottery*. Ann Arbor, Kelsey Museum of Archaeology.

were allegedly commemorated with a gravestone (Plut. *Lyc.* 27. 1), and the battlefield of Sellasia is close by, but the lettering may be Classical. His name is oddly derogatory and the carving, to all appearances, not that of a professional letter-cutter.

Boardman, J. 2001. *Greek Gems and Finger Rings*, new & expanded edn. London, Thames & Hudson.

Bradley, R. 1990. *The Passage of Arms: An Archaeological Analysis of Prehistoric Hoards and Votive Deposits*. Cambridge, Cambridge University Press.

Burn, L. 2005. *Hellenistic Art from Alexander the Great to Augustus*. Los Angeles, Getty Publications.

Cavanagh, W. G., Crouwel, J., Catling, R. W. V. and Shipley, D. G. J. 2002. *Continuity and Change in a Greek Rural Landscape: The Laconia Survey*, i: *Methodology and Interpretation*. London, British School at Athens.

Cavanagh, W. G., Crouwel, J. H., Catling, R. W. V. and Shipley, D. G. J. 1996. *Continuity and Change in a Greek Rural Landscape: The Laconia Survey*, ii: *Archaeological Data*. London, British School at Athens.

Champion, C. B. 2007. Empire by invitation: Greek political strategies and Roman imperial interventions in the second century BCE. *Transactions of the American Philological Association* 137 (2), 255–275.

Chapman, J. 2000. *Fragmentation in Archaeology: People, Places and Broken Objects in the Prehistory of South Eastern Europe*. London–New York, Routledge.

Cherry, J. F., Davis, J. L. and Mantzourani, E. 1991. *Landscape Archaeology as Long-term History: Northern Keos in the Cycladic Islands from Earliest Settlement until Modern Times*. Los Angeles, Institute of Archaeology, University of California.

Colledge, M. A. R. 1987. Greek and non-Greek interaction in the art and architecture of the hellenistic east, in A. Kuhrt and S. M. Sherwin-White (eds.), *Hellenism in the East: The Interaction of Greek and Non-Greek Civilizations from Syria to Central Asia after Alexander*, 134–162. London/Berkeley, Duckworth/University of California Press.

Colledge, M. A. R. 1990. Some observations on Greek art in western Asia after Alexander's conquest. In J.-P. Descoeudres (ed.), *Greek Colonists and Native Populations*, 323–328. Oxford, Clarendon Press.

Colvin, S. 2010. The koine: a new language for a new world, in A. Erskine and L. Llewellyn-Jones (eds.),

Creating a Hellenistic World, 31–45. Swansea, Classical Press of Wales.

Cumberpatch, C. G. and Blinkhorn, P. W. 1997a. Introduction, in C. G. Cumberpatch and P. W. Blinkhorn (eds.), *Not So Much a Pot, More a Way of Life: Current Approaches to Artefact Analysis in Archaeology*, v–vi. Oxford, Oxbow.

Cumberpatch, C. G. and Blinkhorn, P. W. (eds.) 1997b. *Not So Much a Pot, More a Way of Life: Current Approaches to Artefact Analysis in Archaeology*. Oxford, Oxbow.

Dalby, A. 1996. *Siren Feasts: A History of Food and Gastronomy in Greece*. London–New York, Routledge.

Davidson, J. 1997. *Courtesans and Fishcakes: The Consuming Passions of Classical Athens*. London/New York, HarperCollins/Harper.

Davies, J. K. 2006. Hellenistic economies. In G. R. Bugh (ed.), *The Cambridge Companion to the Hellenistic World*, 73–92. New York, Cambridge University Press.

Davis, N. and Kraay, C. M. 1973. *The Hellenistic Kingdoms: Portrait Coins and History*. London, Thames & Hudson.

Deetz, J. 1996. *In Small Things Forgotten: An Archaeology of Early American Life*, Revised and expanded edn. New York, Anchor Books/Random House.

Doulgeri-Intzesiloglou, A. 2000. Οικιακοί αποθέτες: μικρά "κλειστά" στρωματογραφικά σύνολα ελληνιστικής εποχής. In *Ε΄ Επιστημονική Συνάντηση για την ελληνιστική κεραμική*. Χανιά 1997, 329–332. Athens, TAP.

Downey, S. B. 1993. Hellenistic, local, and Near Eastern elements in the terracotta production of Dura-Europos, in A. Invernizzi and J.-F. Salles (eds.), *Arabia Antiqua*, 129–145. Rome, Instituto Italiano per il Medio ed Estremo Oriente.

Eiring, J. 2004. Death in Aetolia: the hellenistic graves at Aetolian Chalkis. *Proceedings of the Danish Institute at Athens* 4, 93–166.

Erskine, A. (ed.) 2003. *A Companion to the Hellenistic World*. Malden, Mass.–Oxford, etc., Blackwell.

Erskine, A. 2010. Between philosophy and the court: the life of Persaios of Kition, in A. Erskine and L. Llewellyn-Jones (eds.), *Creating a Hellenistic World*, 177–194. Swansea, Classical Press of Wales.

Gabrielsen, V. 1997. *The Naval Aristocracy of Hellenistic Rhodes*. Aarhus, Aarhus University Press.

Gabrielsen, V. 2001. The Rhodian associations and economic activity, in Z. H. Archibald, J. Davies, V. Gabrielsen, and G. J. Oliver (eds.), *Hellenistic Economies*, 215–244. London–New York, Routledge.

Garwood, P., Jennings, D., Skeates, R. and Toms, J. (eds.) 1991. *Sacred and Profane: Proceedings of a Conference on Archaeology, Ritual and Religion*. Oxford, Oxford University Committee for Archaeology.

Gosden, C. 1999. *Anthropology and Archaeology: A Changing Relationship*. New York–London, Routledge.

Gurd, S. A. 2007. Meaning and material presence: four epigrams on Timomachus's unfinished Medea. *Transactions of the American Philological Association* 137 (2), 305–331.

Hannestad, L. 1983. *The Hellenistic Pottery from Failaka: With a Survey of Hellenistic Pottery in the Near East*. 2 vols. Aarhus, Jysk Archæologisk Selskab.

Higgins, R. 1963. *Greek Terracottas*. London, Methuen.

Hill, J. D. 1995. *Ritual and Rubbish in the Iron Age of Wessex: A Study on the Formation of a Specific Archaeological Record*. Oxford, BAR Publishing/British Archaeological Reports.

Hodkinson, S. J. 2000. *Property and Wealth in Classical Sparta*. London/Swansea, Duckworth/Classical Press of Wales.

Höschele, R. 2007. The traveling reader: journeys through ancient epigram books. *Transactions of the American Philological Association* 137 (2), 333–69.

Houby-Nielsen, S. 1997. Grave gifts, women, and conventional values in hellenistic Athens, in P. Bilde, T. Engberg-Pedersen, L. Hannestad and J. Zahle (eds.), *Conventional Values of the Hellenistic Greeks*, 220–262, pls. 8–14. Aarhus, Aarhus University Press.

Houby-Nielsen, S. 1998. Revival of archaic funerary practices in the hellenistic and Roman Kerameikos. *Proceedings of the Danish Institute at Athens* 2, 127–145 (acknowledgements, 126).

Jackson, H. 2000. Terracotta lamps of a hellenistic housing insula at Jebl Khalid, North Syria. *Rei Cretariae Romanae Fautorum Acta* 36, 11–17.

Jackson, H. 2006. *The Terracotta Figurines*. Sydney, Meditarch.

Jackson, H. 2011. A late Seleucid housing insula at Jebel Khalid in North Syria: archaeological evidence for chronology and lifestyle, in K. Erickson and G. C. Ramsey (eds.), *Seleucid Dissolution: The Sinking of the Anchor*, 133–148. Wiesbaden, Harrassowitz.

Jackson, H. and Tidmarsh, J. 2011. *The Pottery*. Sydney, Meditarch.

Kelly-Blazeby, C. F. 2001. Tavernas in ancient Greece c. 475–146 BC: an archaeological perspective. *Assemblage*, 6. http://assemblage.group.shef.ac.uk/issue6/Kelly_web.htm (last visited 12 Oct. 2012)

Kelly-Blazeby, C. F. 2008. *Kapeleion: casual and commercial wine consumption in classical Greece*. PhD thesis, University of Leicester.

Langin-Hooper, S. M. 2007. Social networks and cross-cultural interaction: a new interpretation of the female terracotta figurines of hellenistic Babylon. *Oxford Journal of Archaeology* 26 (2), 145–165.

Lauter, H. 1986. *Die Architektur des Hellenismus*. Darmstadt, Wissenschaftliche Buchgesellschaft.

Lawrence, A. W. 1996. *Greek Architecture*, 6th edn. Harmondsworth, Penguin.

Lehmann, G. 2008. Review of O. Tal, *The Archaeology*

of Hellenistic Palestine, in *Journal of Hebrew Scriptures* 8 (http://jhsonline.org/reviews/reviews_new/reviews317.htm, last visited 27 May 2013).

Ling, R. (ed.) 1984. *The Cambridge Ancient History*, 2nd edn, vii. 1: *Plates*. Cambridge, Cambridge University Press.

Manning, J. G. 2007. Hellenistic Egypt, in W. Scheidel, I. Morris and R. Saller (eds.), *The Cambridge Economic History of the Greco-Roman World*, 434–59. Cambridge, Cambridge University Press.

Masséglia, J. E. A. 2012. Emotions and archaeological sources: a methodological introduction. In A. Chaniotis (ed.), *Unveiling Emotions: Sources and Methods for the Study of Emotions in the Greek World*, 131–50/49. Wiesbaden, Steiner.

Masséglia, J. E. A. forthcoming: *Gestures, Postures and Body Actions: Body Language in Hellenistic Art and Society*. Oxford, Oxford University Press.

Mee, C. B. and Forbes, H. A. (eds.) 1997. *A Rough and Rocky Place: The Landscape and Settlement History of the Methana Peninsula, Greece (Results of the Methana Survey Project Sponsored by the British School at Athens and the Universitiy of Liverpool)*. Liverpool, Liverpool University Press.

Miller, P. A. 2007. Literary and material culture in hellenistic Greece. *Transactions of the American Philological Association* 137 (2), 253–254.

Moore, H. L. 1982. The interpretation of spatial patterning in settlement residues. In I. Hodder (ed.), *Symbolic and Structural Archaeology*, 74–79. Cambridge, Cambridge University Press.

Morel, J.-P. 1997. Η ελληνιστική κοινή: κλασική παράδοση και τοπικές ιδιαιτερότητες. In *Δ΄ Επιστημονική Συνάντηση για την ελληνιστική κεραμική*. Μυτιλήνη 1994, 405–415. Athens, Ypourgeio Politismou.

Morphy, H. 2004. Material culture, in A. Kuper and J. Kuper (eds.), *The Social Science Encyclopedia*, 3rd edn, 619–621. London–New York, Routledge.

Oliver, G. J. 2006. Hellenistic economies: regional views from the Athenian polis. In R. Descat (ed.), *Approches de l'économie hellénistique*, 215–256. Musée Archéologique de Saint-Bertrand-de-Comminges.

Oliver, G. J. 2007. *War, Food and Politics of Early Hellenistic Athens*. Oxford, Oxford University Press.

Pfrommer, M. 1993. *Metalwork from the Hellenized East: Catalogue of the Collections*. Malibu, Calif., J. Paul Getty Museum.

Pfrommer, M. 2001. *Greek Gold from Hellenistic Egypt*. Los Angeles, J. Paul Getty Museum.

Pollitt, J. J. 1986. *Art in the Hellenistic Age*. Cambridge, Cambridge University Press.

Rappaport, U. 2007. Review of O. Tal, *The Archaeology of Hellenistic Palestine*, in *American Journal of Archaeology Online Book Review* 111.4. http://www.ajaonline.org/online-review-book/522 (last visited 11 Oct. 2012).

Reger, G. 2007. Hellenistic Greece and western Asia Minor, in W. Scheidel, I. Morris and R. Saller (eds.), *The Cambridge Economic History of the Greco-Roman World*, 460–486. Cambridge, Cambridge University Press.

Richards, C. and Thomas, J. 1984. Ritual activity and structured deposition in later Neolithic Wessex, in R. Bradley and J. Gardiner (eds.), *Neolithic Studies: A Review of Some Current Research*, 189–218. Oxford, BAR Publishing.

Rizakis, A. D. 2004. Οικονομία και οικονομικές δραστηριότητες των ελληνικών πόλεων από την Πύδνα έως το Άκτιον. In *ΣΤ΄ Επιστημονική Συνάντηση για την ελληνιστική κεραμική*. Βόλος 2000, 17–28. Athens, TAP.

Rizakis, A. D. and Touratsoglou, G. 2011. Η οικονοία της Πελοποννήσου κατά την ελληνιστική περίοδο. In *Ζ΄ Επιστημονική Συνάντηση για την ελληνιστική κεραμική*. Αίγιο 2005, 17–34. Athens, TAP.

Rosenmeyer, P. A. 2007. From Syracuse to Rome: the travails of Silanion's Sappho. *Transactions of the American Philological Association* 137 (2), 277–303.

Rostovtzeff, M. 1941. *The Social and Economic History of the Hellenistic World*. 3 vols. Oxford, Clarendon Press.

Rostovtzeff, M. 1953. *The Social and Economic History of the Hellenistic World*, 2nd edn. 3 vols. Oxford, Clarendon Press.

Rotroff, S. I. 1997. Εργαστήρια και παράγοντες για τη διαμόρφωση του τοπικού χαρακτήρα. In *Δ΄ επιστημονική συνάντηση για την ελληνιστική κεραμική*. Μυτιλήνη 1994, 401–404. Athens, Ypourgeio Politismou.

Rotroff, S. I. 2002. Review of M. Pfrommer, *Greek Gold from Hellenistic Egypt*, in *Bryn Mawr Classical Review* 2002.05.14.

Rotroff, S. I. 2006. Material culture. In G. R. Bugh (ed.), *The Cambridge Companion to the Hellenistic World*, 136–157. New York, Cambridge University Press.

Sauer, E. W. (ed.) 2004. *Archaeology and Ancient History: Breaking Down the Boundaries*. London–New York, Routledge.

Shanks, M. 1996. *Classical Archaeology of Greece: Experiences of the Discipline*. London–New York, Routledge.

Shipley, D. G. J. 1987. *A History of Samos 800–188 BC*. Oxford, Clarendon Press.

Shipley, D. G. J. 1996. The epigraphic material, in W. Cavanagh, J. Crouwel, R. W. V. Catling and D. G. J. Shipley, *Continuity and Change in a Greek Rural Landscape: The Laconia Survey*, ii. *Archaeological Data*. BSA Supplementary Volumes 27, 213–234. London, British School at Athens.

Shipley, D. G. J. 2000. *The Greek World after Alexander: 323–30 BC*. London–New York, Routledge.

Shipley, D. G. J. 2008. Approaching the Macedonian Peloponnese. In C. Grandjean (ed.), *Le Péloponnèse d'Épaminondas à Hadrien*, 53–68. Bordeaux/Paris, Ausonius/De Boccard.

Smith, R. R. R. 1988. *Hellenistic Royal Portraits*. Oxford, Clarendon Press.

Smith, R. R. R. 1991. *Hellenistic Sculpture: A Handbook*. London, Thames & Hudson.

Sterner, J. 1989. Who is signalling whom? Ceramic style, ethnicity and taphonomy among the Sirak Bulahay. *Antiquity* 63 (240), 451–459.

Sutton, R. F., Jr. 1992. Pornography and persuasion on Attic pottery. In A. Richlin (ed.), *Pornography and Representation in Greece and Rome*, 3–35. New York–Oxford, Oxford University Press.

Tal, O. 2006. *The Archaeology of Hellenistic Palestine: Between Tradition and Renewal [in Hebrew]*. Jerusalem, Bialik Institute.

Tarn, W. W. 1938. *The Greeks in Bactria and India*, 1st edn. Cambridge, Cambridge University Press.

Trümper, M. 2003. Material and social environment of Greco-Roman households in the east: the case of hellenistic Delos, in D. L. Balch and C. Osiek (eds.), *Early Christian Families in Context: An Interdisciplinary Dialogue*. Grand Rapids, Mich., William B. Eerdmans.

Vlassopoulos, K. 2007. *Unthinking the Greek Polis: Ancient Greek History beyond Eurocentrism*. Cambridge, Cambridge University Press.

Wells, P. S. 1999. *The Barbarians Speak: How the Conquered Peoples Shaped Roman Europe*. Princeton, Princeton University Press.

Whitley, A. J. M. 2001. *The Archaeology of Ancient Greece*. Cambridge, Cambridge University Press.

Wilkins, J. M. 2000. *The Boastful Chef: The Discourse of Food in Ancient Greek Comedy*. New York, Oxford University Press.

Wilkins, J. M. and Hill, S. 2006. *Food in the Ancient World*. Malden, Mass., Blackwell.

Wright, N. L. 2011. The last days of a Seleucid city: Jebel Khalid on the Euphrates and its temple, in K. Erickson and G. C. Ramsey (eds.), *Seleucid Dissolution: The Sinking of the Anchor*, 117–132. Wiesbaden, Harrassowitz.

Wycherley, R. E. 1978. *The Stones of Athens*. Princeton, Princeton University Press.

Zanker, P. 1993. The hellenistic grave stelai from Smyrna: identity and self-image in the polis, in A. Bulloch, E. S. Gruen, A. A. Long and A. Stewart (eds.), *Images and Ideologies: Self-definition in the Hellenistic World*, 212–230. Berkeley–Los Angeles–London, University of California Press.

Bion International: Branch pottery workshops in the Hellenistic Age

Susan I. Rotroff

Abstract

The Workshop of Bion produced moldmade bowls in Athens in the last quarter of the 3rd and the first third of the 2nd century BC and may have been responsible for the invention of the type. One of the bowls produced in this workshop bears the signature *Argeiou*, suggesting a connection to the city of Argos in the Peloponnese. Such a connection is borne out by shared stamps used for minor elements of decoration on bowls of both the Workshop of Bion at Athens and the Monograph Workshop at Argos, and I argue that the Argive shop was founded by the proprietor of the Workshop of Bion in Athens, who may have had personal connections to the Peloponnesian city. Stamps characteristic of both Argos and Athens on Corinthian moldmade bowls suggest that the shop may also have extended its operations to Corinth. Finally, a large number of shared motifs suggest that a workshop on the island of Lemnos represents yet another enterprise of the Athenian shop, founded after Lemnos became an Athenian klerouchy in the wake of the Third Macedonian War. Thus at least one Hellenistic pottery workshop expanded its operation by the establishment of branch enterprises, in the same way that Roman potters would do over a century later.

Keywords: Argos, Athens, Corinth, Hephaistia, Lemnos, moldmade, workshop

Analysis of moldmade relief bowls from the Athenian Agora has revealed the existence of two major workshops active at the beginning of production. In this paper, I will argue that one of these – the Workshop of Bion – also exerted a significant influence on bowls produced elsewhere: at Argos, at Corinth, and on the island of Lemnos. The nature of the influence cannot be determined with certainty, but it is possible that some of these secondary industries represent 'branch offices' of the original Athenian enterprise.

Athens

The story begins with a fragment of a moldmade bowl from the Agora Excavations bearing the signature Ἀργείου (**Fig. 1**)[1]. It was found in the building fill of the Middle Stoa, dated by stamped amphora handles to before about 170 BC[2]. The signature had been inscribed lightly in the mold, in the genitive, as is usual in the few signed instances of Athenian bowls. On the basis of several stamps on the fragment, the bowl can be attributed securely to the Workshop of Bion, named from signatures (in a different hand) on two fragments at the Agora (**Fig. 2**)[3]. Among characteristic stamps shared by the Argeios fragment and bowls from Bion's Workshop are a bird flying to the left, a frond with a diamond-shaped tip (**Figs. 2, 3**), and a simplified guilloche rim pattern crowned by paired double spirals and palmettes[4]. Less common in that oeuvre, but significant in the context of the present inquiry, are a frontal Nike (her right wing and arm survive at the right edge of the sherd; for the full stamp, see **Fig. 3**)[5], and a hovering Eros, facing right; they will reappear later on in my account.

About 100 inventoried bowls in the Agora collection come from this shop; there are hundreds more among uninventoried pottery, and still more among published bowls from other excavations. Fragments found in deposits dated by amphora handles show that the shop was active by *c.* 220 BC, placing it very near the beginning of the production of moldmade bowls. It is even possible that it is in this workshop that the moldmade bowl was invented, as I will argue below.

The probable location of the workshop is indicated by two cisterns on the lower slopes of the Areopagus, just south of the agora square, both of them filled with potters' debris. The easternmost contained two layers of such material[6]. The lower stratum, with only two fragments of moldmade bowls, was deposited before the end of the 3rd century. The upper layer, probably deposited around 170 BC, contained fragments of at least 26 moldmade bowls and two molds;

1 Lawall *et al.* 2002, 428–430.

2 See Rotroff 2006a, 362, under H–K 12–14 for a recent summary of evidence for the dating and further references.

3 For the shop, see Rotroff 1982a, 26–27; the signed fragments are Rotroff 1982a, 62, 64, nos. 154 and 168, pls. 28, 31, 78, 95 (Agora P 7001, P 20190a).

4 For these stamps on other bowls of Bion's Workshop, see, for instance, Rotroff 1982a, 59, 62, 64, nos. 125, 130 (rim), 152 (calyx, bird), 154 (calyx, bird), 168 (calyx), 171 (calyx, bird), pls. 24, 25, 28, 31, 78, 79.

5 Edwards 1956, 93, no. 5, pl. 35; cf. also Rotroff 1982a, 62, no. 152, pls. 28, 78.

6 The Satyr Cistern (N 21:4). Rotroff 1994, with fig. 1 illustrating the stratigraphy. See Rotroff 2006a, 369, under N 21:4, for the latest assessment of the dating of the two layers.

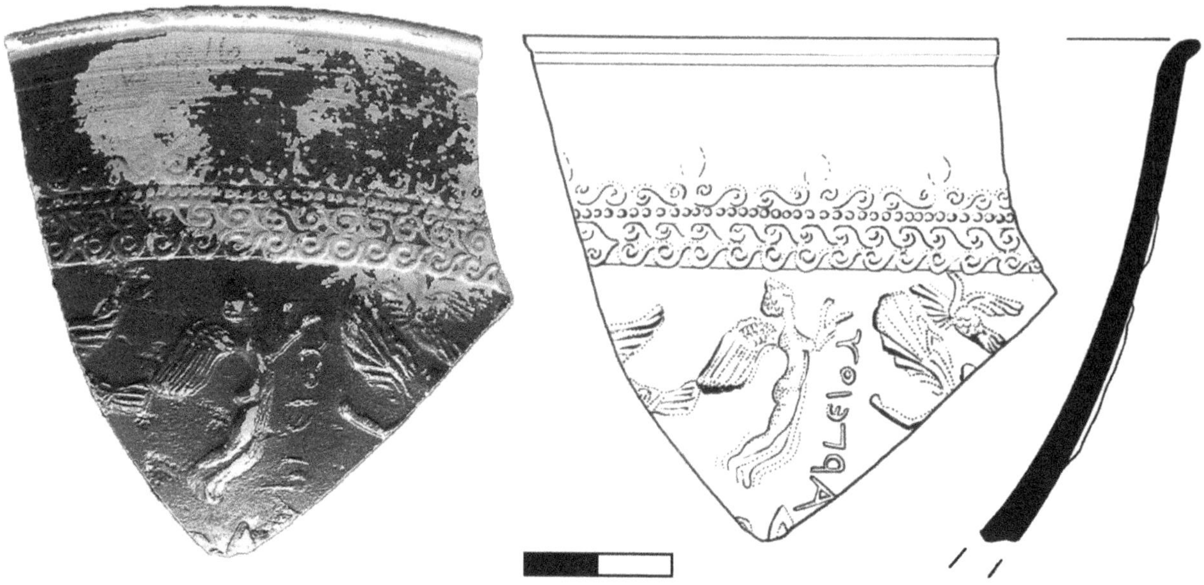

Fig. 1. Fragment of a moldmade bowl signed by Argeios (Agora P 31702). Photograph, author; drawing, A. Hooton

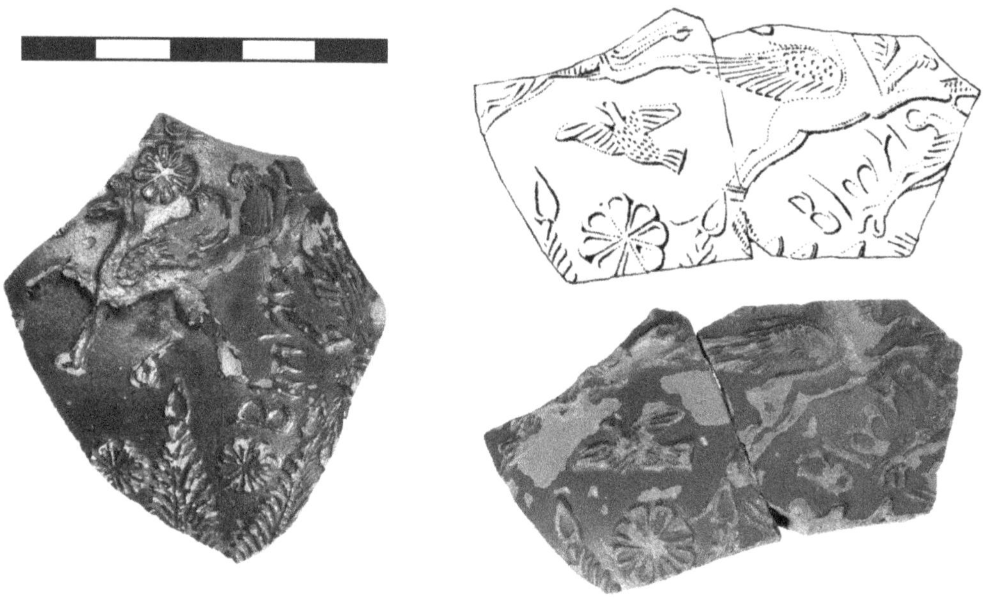

Fig. 2. Fragments of two bowls signed by Bion (Agora P 7001, P 20190; Rotroff 1982a, nos. 154, 168). Photographs and drawing, Agora Excavations

all that could be attributed were manufactured by the Workshop of Bion. The second cistern, located some 20 meters to the west, was filled at about the same time (*c.* 170 BC).[7] It contained fragments of at least 183 moldmade bowls, and 88 percent of those that could be attributed are products of the Workshop of Bion.

All in all, the remarkable concentration of moldmade bowls from the shop in this area suggests that the pottery establishment was located here. Although later construction has completely destroyed the structures that these water sources served, the two layers of the Satyr Cistern indicate that the shop functioned at this location for some time. The potters' waste of its lower fill consisted primarily of black glaze and West Slope ware characteristic of the middle to the third quarter of the 3rd century, with only two fragments of moldmade bowls.

7 The Komos Cistern (M 21:1), Rotroff 1982a, 103, under M 21:1; for stratigraphy and the most recent dating, see Rotroff 2005, 17–20 and Rotroff 2006a, 365–366.

Fig. 3. Moldmade bowl from the Workshop of Bion, found on the Pnyx (Pnyx P 354; Edwards 1956, no. 5). Photograph, Agora Excavations.drawing, Agora Excavations

Fig. 4. Gorgoneion medallion on a bowl from the Workshop of Bion (Agora P 18641; Rotroff 1982a, no. 170). Photograph, Agora Excavations

Fig. 5. Athena Parthenos medallion on a bowl from the Workshop of Bion (Agora P 18663). Photograph, Agora Excavations

One of them is of particular interest, because it belongs to the rare class of bowls that were made in molds taken directly from metal originals[8]. I have postulated that these are the first of the type to be produced, before the standard method of making molds with stamps was developed[9]. The presence of this bowl in debris from Bion's Workshop constitutes an argument that this workshop was the originator of the type and that it is from thisvery spot that this significant invention spread outward.

The bowls of the Workshop of Bion are distinctive in terms of shape, motifs, and composition. Like other Attic bowls, they present a flattened hemisphere in profile, with a high outturned rim and a scraped and miltosed groove just below the lip. The shop's most obvious earmark is the medallion, often either a Medusa of the 'beautiful gorgon' type or a frontal bust of the Athena Parthenos (**Figs. 4, 5**). Preferred rim patterns include a simplified guilloche and a stumpy ovolo, and rim registers and medallions are usually framed by beading[10]. Figured decoration is preferred, with stamps placed side by side around the upper wall, above a calyx of stylized leaves or imbricate petals.

The Argeios who signed the mold that produced the bowl illustrated in **Fig. 1** was not the same man as Bion, for his handwriting is different. He must have been a second member of the personnel of the shop, though whether contemporary, earlier, or later we cannot know. Like Bion, he was probably the artisan who made the mold, but there is no way to know whether he (or Bion) was the proprietor, a free employee, or a slave. His name is intriguing, however. Whether it is a proper name or an ethnic, it points to a special relationship with Argos. Perhaps the man was an Argive metic, or a member of a family that marked its close relationship with the city by naming a son in this

8 Rotroff 1994, 20, pl. 1:η; Rotroff 2006b, 369, fig. 7.
9 For discussion of this class of bowls, see Rotroff 1982b, 332–333; see Rotroff 2006b, 372–373 for the process of development as I envision it.

10 Characteristic medallion and rim stamps are pictured on Rotroff 1982a, pl. 98.

Fig. 6. Fragment of a bowl from the Argive Monogram Workshop (Nauplion, Maison de la Citadelle 11.367; 54.522A). After Siebert 1978, M.50, pl. 28, reproduced by permission of G. Siebert

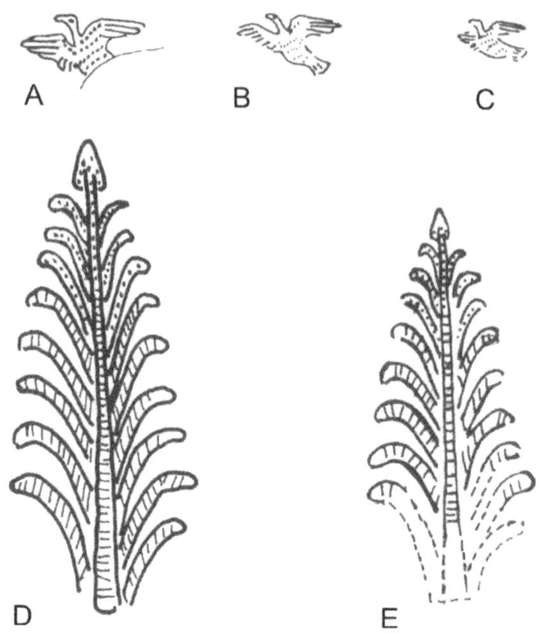

Fig. 7. Bird and frond stamps from Attic (A), Argive (B, D), and Corinthian bowls (C, E). After Edwards 1986, p. 397, fig. 1, courtesy of the Trustees of the American School of Classical Studies at Athens

manner, as Kimon had named his son Lakedaimonios centuries earlier.

Argos

The intrigue deepens when we examine the moldmade bowls of Argos, where Gérard Siebert has identified several workshops. Among these, one stands out for its close similarities to Attic production, and especially to the bowls manufactured by the Workshop of Bion. Some of its products are signed with a complex monogram that cannot be read with certainty; for convenience I will refer to it as the Argive Monogram Workshop[11]. Similarities to the Workshop of Bion are many. Compositionally, both shops favor a row of figures above a leafy calyx, in contrast to other Argive products, where figures often alternate with floral motifs, or where the calyx is set off from the wall by a horizontal ridge. Most of the figures on the Argive Monogram bowls are also found on Athenian bowls, but many of these belong to a koiné of mythological motifs that recur in many industries, and their appearance at both Athens and Argos may not be meaningful[12]. Similarities in one of the space-filling stamps commonly used by the two shops, however, are more significant. The stamp in question is a small bird flying to the left, which occurs as a filling ornament both on bowls of Bion (**Figs .1–3**) and products of the Argive Monogram workshop (**Fig. 6**)[13], but is not found on the products of other Argive workshops. The stamps are identical in all details: the widely spread wings, the stippling on the body, the parallel lines on wings and tail, the triangular head with dot eye, and the lower profile of the stamp, like a bent bow. Charles Edwards was able to examine Attic and Argive instances of the flying bird motif side by side, on bowls found at Corinth in the fill of a water reservoir excavated in 1926. His observations confirmed the close similarity of the stamps, and measurement showed that the Attic examples were larger, indicating that the Argive stamp (**Fig. 7,** B) had been created by mechanical copying of the motif on an Attic bowl (**Fig.** 7, A)[14]. The smaller size, of course, is the familiar result of the shrinkage of the clay in the process of *surmoulage*. One would expect shops to craft their own original stamps for such inconsequential filling devices, and the close similarities observed here indicate instead either copying or the use of common stamps. No other comparisons are as compelling, but the figures of the rampant goats in both productions are closely similar in the position of the hind legs, the stubby tail, the shaggy outline,

11 Siebert 1978, 50–63.

12 For example, both Athenian bowls and those of the Argive Monogram Workshop favor four mythological vignettes found also on terracotta altars (Dionysiac trio, Poseidon and Amymone, woman wreathing a trophy, Apollo and Leto), but these stamps also occur on bowls ranging from the Black Sea through the Western Coast of Asia Minor to the Greek mainland (Siebert 1978, 240–246; Rotroff 1982a, 20–21).

13 Siebert 1978, 53, 354–356, 359, nos. M.45, M.50, M.55, M.87, pls. 27, 28, 30.

14 Edwards 1986, 397–398, fig. 1.

and the horns that run straight back from the forehead[15]. In addition, both shops favor a neat, simplified guilloche as a rim pattern. It is not an unusual pattern, but the careful circularity of the spirals in the two is similar, and in both cases the points are usually directed towards the right. This guilloche is common on the Monogram bowls, but is found only infrequently on other Argive bowls[16].

Siebert concluded that the Monogram Workshop was the earliest of the Argive shops, and he placed its beginnings about 220 BC, making it closely contemporary with the Workshop of Bion. Unfortunately, evidence for an absolute date is slight[17]. The only well-dated context in which its products have been found is the Corinthian reservoir deposit alluded to above, which was probably laid down between 175 and 165 BC. Five Argive fragments were found there, attributed to the Monogram shop by stamps of the rim and calyx and a figure of Nike driving a biga[18].

We can thus conclude only that the shop was in operation by 175–165 BC, but how much earlier production began is impossible to say. The shop was also active well after that date, however, for it manufactured long-petal bowls of the developed, flat-petaled form that is probably to be placed in the 150s BC and later[19]. Either the workshop was remarkably long-lived[20], or it began production later than Siebert estimated, some time during the first half of the 2nd century, thus later than the earliest production of the Workshop of Bion. The chronological indications do not, in any event, contradict the evidence of the bird stamp concerning the dependency of the Argive motifs on an Athenian model, and they support the conclusion that the Argive workshop derives from the Athenian one and not the other way around. We can therefore discard what might seem the most obvious hypothesis: that Argeios was a citizen of Argos who, having established a pottery in the city, then set up a branch workshop in Athens. The surviving evidence shows that influence flowed the other way.

The Argive shop is atticizing, but not slavishly. Many of its stamps are not paralleled in Athens, and its overall output is hardly a carbon copy of Attic production. Since even the closely similar motifs were not made with imported stamps, but mechanically copied from Attic models, there need not have been any formal business connection between the two producers. Perhaps the simple truth is that the Argive Monogram Workshop is indeed the earliest of the moldmade bowl workshops at Argos, as Siebert maintained, and was directly inspired by imports from Athens. But the similarities between the Attic and the Argive shops and the marked differences between products of the Argive Monogram Workshop and other Argive production remain tantalizing, as is the fact that a man named 'Argive' worked in the Athenian one. A craftsman with Argive connections, having established his business with some success in Athens, may then have used those connections to set up another in the Peloponnesian city.

Corinth

Moldmade bowls made in Corinth, easily recognizable from their pale yellow fabric and flaking black gloss, add further complexity to the picture. Siebert observed that many Corinthian bowls carried stamps associated with the Argive Monogram Workshop. He characterized the resemblances as 'astonishing', as though, he said, the production of a single workshop was simultaneously distributed to the two sites[21]. Examining this phenomenon further, Charles Edwards was able to identify a Corinthian workshop that combined stamps borrowed from both Argos and Athens with its own original repertoire[22]. Measurements of the familiar bird stamp, which appears here as well, showed that the Corinthian motif was the smallest (**Fig. 7**, C), betraying its dependence on Argive models (**Fig.** 7, B), and the same relationship was demonstrated by a second motif, a tall, floppy frond (**Fig. 7,** D [Argive], 7, E [Corinthian]). A possible Attic model for the frond occurs on a bowl from the Pnyx (**Fig. 3**), identified as a product of Bion's workshop by the characteristic bird and the same frontal Nike whose right wing is preserved on the Argeios sherd (**Fig. 1**). The mechanics of the relationship are somewhat clearer here, for at Corinth there is evidence of imported molds. Edwards identified a number of bowls made of the distinctive pale Corinthian fabric, but that shared every motif with the Argive Monograph Workshop[23]. He concluded that these bowls had been made in Argive molds imported to Corinth, and he was also able to point to an Argive mold found there and identified as such by

15 Compare Rotroff 1982a, 56, no. 105, pls. 18, 75 (Athens, Workshop of Bion) with Siebert 1978, 57, 357, M.67, M.68, pl. 29 (Argos, Monogram Workshop).

16 Many examples from the Monogram Workshop are illustrated on Siebert 1978, 52, pls. 22–29. Among Argive bowls from other workshops illustrated by Siebert, it occurs only in the workshop of Demetrios-Iason (DI.1, DI.29, DI.41, DI.68, DI.75, DI.90), with points oriented to the left, not the right.

17 The only potentially helpful archaeological context at Argos is the destruction debris of a Hellenistic building southeast of the Odeion. Siebert (1978, 161–165) describes its contents at some length and places the deposit in the first quarter of the 2nd century. The only evidence for an absolute date is a group of 20 coins (all but one apparently bronze), but they cannot be dated with any precision. The types of the majority have been placed in the 3rd to 2nd century BC by Kroll (Siebert, 164, nos. 4–16; BMC Greek Coins 10, Peloponnesus, 146–147, nos. 125–135, 140–142; Kroll 1993, 242, nos. 783–785). A long-petal bowl fragment in Siebert's catalogue also comes from this building (Siebert 1978, 364, An.6), but no indication of its stratigraphic position in the building is given; if it comes from the destruction debris, it would pull the date down into at least the second quarter of the 2nd century BC.

18 Edwards 1986, 391, 416, nos. 38–40, pls. 88–89.

19 Siebert 1978, 350, M.9, pl. 23, with the monogram medallion.

20 There is no reliable way to estimate the likely lifespan of a workshop, but bowls clearly recognizable as products of the Workshop of Bion and Workshop A at Athens are largely confined to deposits laid down over about a fifty-year period.

21 Siebert 1978, 73, 77–80, with a table listing Corinthian bowls bearing stamps from the Argive Monogram workshop (with critique and corrections by Edwards 1981, 202, note 64).

22 Edwards 1986, 399–402, 417–419.

23 Edwards 1986, 402–403, pl. 90 (CP-3209). Others are illustrated in Edwards 1975, 170, no. 843, pl. 73 (C-48-14); Edwards 1981, 194, Group II, pls. 42, 43 (C-69-149, C-1980-132). Characteristic motifs are the rim pattern, the left-flying bird, and the acanthus leaf and large frond of the calyces.

Fig. 8. Argive mold found at Corinth (Corinth MF-1985-81). Photograph, Corinth Excavations

Fig. 9. Corinthian bowl made in Attic mold (Corinth C-28-74). Photograph, Corinth Excavations

the leafy acanthus of its calyx (**Fig. 8**)[24]. There is also at least one instance of a bowl of unambiguous Corinthian fabric with the gorgoneion medallion and beading that are hallmarks of the Workshop of Bion, and which was probably made in an Attic mold (**Fig. 9**)[25]. It appears, then, that molds from both the Argive Monogram Workshop and the Athenian Workshop of Bion were imported to Corinth and used there to produce moldmade bowls locally, though Corinthian potters soon developed their own distinctive repertoire of stamps, as Argive potters had earlier.

Lemnos

A final intriguing connection joins Athens and the island of Lemnos, where Italian excavations at Hephaistia have uncovered extensive remains of a Hellenistic pottery enterprise that functioned in the first half of the 2nd century. Rich deposits of debris from its kilns revealed that its chief product was the moldmade bowl, and hundreds of fragments of both bowls and molds have been published by Morella Massa in a well-illustrated monograph[26]. Without personal examination it is not possible to identify stamps identical to those used in Athens, but the general similarity of the material to Athenian products is very clear from the illustrations, and underlined by the parallels to the Athenian material cited throughout the publication. The simplified guilloche, with pairs of double spirals and a crowning palmette above, standard for the Workshop of Bion, is also common on Lemnos[27], as are the gorgoneion and Athena Parthenos medallions that are hallmarks of the Athenian shop[28]. The Parthenos image is particularly striking, because it preserves the tiny dots left of the head that are found also on the Athenian medallion (**Fig. 5**)[29]. Many figured stamps also crop up in both workshops. The hovering Eros on a Lemnian mold (**Fig. 10**, left) is the same as the central stamp on the Attic bowl made in a mold signed by Argeios (**Fig. 1**)[30]. A clearer impression on another Athenian bowl explains the odd position of Eros's arms; he is playing the double pipes, and on Athenian bowls is he usually paired with an antithetical Eros playing a lyre[31]. A similarly positioned Nike, hovering and with her arms outstretched, occurs on three Lemnian bowls (always facing right), and again as antithetical pairs on bowls of

24 Edwards 1986, 402, pl. 90 (MF-1985-81).
25 Edwards 1986, 403, pl. 90 (C-28-74). See also Rotroff 1982a, 88, no. 371, pl. 65, of clay that appears to be Corinthian, but with the miltosed scraped groove below the rim that is characteristically Athenian.
26 Massa 1992.
27 E.g., Massa 1992, pls. 74–76.
28 E.g., Massa 1992, 164, 180–181, C 305, C 421, C 422, M 428, M 429, pl. 67, 69.
29 See Rotroff 1982a, pl. 98, no. 104.
30 Massa 1992, 268, Eros, tipo a; 145, M 170, pls. 30, 95. Measurements of published drawings suggest that the hovering Eros on the Lemnian mold is the same size as that on the Athenian bowl. The figure on a bowl made in that mold would therefore have been smaller than the Athenian one, an indication of the dependence of the Lemnian industry on the Athenian one.
31 Rotroff 1982a, 70, no. 212, pl. 82. Cf. also two later examples: Rotroff 1982a, 61, no. 145, pl. 27; Thompson 1934, 378–379, D 34, fig. 65.

Fig. 10. A mold (left) and a fragment of a bowl (right) from Hephaistia (Hephaistia E-1667, E-1798b-c). After Massa 1992, no. M 170, pl. 95 and no. C 135, pl. 93, reproduced by permission of M. Massa and L'Erma di Bretschneider

Fig. 11. Moldmade bowl probably from the Workshop of Bion (Agora P 26037; Rotroff 1982a, no. 211). Drawing, Agora Excavations

Fig. 12. Fragment of an Athenian bowl with a griffin stamp, probably from the Workshop of Bion (Agora P 31703). Photograph, Agora Excavations

Bion's workshop[32]. As a filling element, a frontal baby Eros with wide-spread legs, holding a torch and displaying only one wing, is found both at Lemnos (**Fig. 10**, right) and on Bion's Athenian bowls (**Fig. 11**)[33]. The Athenian and Lemnian industries also share a highly unusual stamp, a sturdy griffin walking in a stately manner with one front paw raised (**Figs. 10** [Lemnos], **11**, **12** [Athens]). The same distinctive patterning of the wing, the horn-like protrusion on the top of the head, the crest of the arched neck, and the loop of the tail can be observed in the clearest of the stamps at both sites[34]. On one Lemnian mold, the animal appears together with the hovering Eros described above, though the tail has been reworked as a zigzag (**Fig. 10**). The Attic bowls may come from the Workshop of Bion; note the characteristic beaded rim pattern on the fragment illustrated in **Fig. 12**[35]. Another unusual shared stamp is a partially draped woman who bends to the right; the full stamp (preserved at Lemnos but not at Athens) indicates she is offering a drink to an animal (a swan?), and she may represent Leda[36]. The single Athenian bowl on which this rare stamp is known has been tentatively ascribed to Workshop A, not the Workshop of Bion; it may be that this stamp, like the Dionysiac trio, Poseidon and Amymone, and other mythological motifs, was shared by both workshops. Additional filling ornaments of the Lemnian repertoire are also paralleled at Athens on bowls made in several different workshops: for example, an Eros with a tambourine flying to the left and a kore mask[37]. Perhaps most striking, however, is the scraped groove just below the rim on many of the Lemnian bowls[38]. This feature occurs without fail on all Attic bowls (regardless of workshop) where, painted with miltos, it adds an accent of color. Either these Lemnian fragments are unrecognized Attic imports (only clay analysis could settle that question), or at least one potter at Hephaistia was steeped in Attic production procedures.

This detail adds weight to Moralla Massa's suggestion that the shop may have owed its origin to an émigré Athenian potter[39], and given the pattern of motifs, it is most likely that that potter had connections with the Workshop of Bion. History provides another hint as tantalizing as the name Argeios, for in the wake of the Third Macedonian War in 168 BC, Athens regained control of her former kleruchy Lemnos[40]. The substantial dumps of workshop debris in the cisterns on the slopes of the Areopagus at Athens suggest that the Workshop of Bion may have experienced damage at just about this time. What better time to look for a new opportunity abroad?

Conclusion

There is thus substantial evidence that 'Bion' – if I may refer thus to the generations of craftsmen who lie behind the workshop that I have christened with his name – was an international entrepreneur. A craftsman in the

32 Massa's Nike, tipo b; e.g., Massa 1992, 141, 157, nos. C 139, M 257, pls. 24, 44, 93, 98, 112:2. Cf. Rotroff 1982a, 60–61, 64, 73–74, nos. 139, 140, 170, 238, pls. 26, 31, 46, 77 (among others). The same peculiar splitting of the lower drapery that appears on the Lemnian stamp can be seen on the drawings of the Attic motif (Thompson 1934, 354–356, C 21, C 22, figs. 39, 40).

33 Massa 1992, 268, Eros, bambino, tipo f (dadoforo). Compare, for example, Massa 1992, 140–141, C 135–C 138, C 140, pls. 24, 93 with Rotroff 1982a, 68, 70, nos. 197, 211, pls. 37, 41, 80, 81. Stamps on the Attic bowls appear to be larger.

34 Compare for example Massa 1992, 142, 145, 156, 165, 178, C 146–C 148, M 170 (with the tail retooled), M 247, C 308, M 404, pls. 30, 43, 52, 65, 95, 98 with Rotroff 1982a, 64, 65, 70, nos. 169, 180, 211, pls. 31, 33, 41, 79, 81. The second two are not attributed in Rotroff 1982a, but probably come from the Workshop of Bion. Insofar as measurements can be assessed from drawings and photographs, the Lemnian stamps are smaller than the Attic ones.

35 Rotroff 1982a, no. 169 is a small fragment, tentatively attributed to the workshop. No. 180 is highly unusual and cannot be associated with any shop on the basis of its stamps, but the rampant goats, kraters, and torch-bearing Eros of no. 211 are closely similar to stamps on bowls from Bion's workshop.

36 Massa 1992, 161, nos. 278, M 280–M 285, pls. 47, 48, 116:3; Rotroff 1982a, 71, no. 223, pl. 43 (Workshop A?). Cf. perhaps Courby 1922, 346, no. 31:b, fig. 72. For the identification of the figure as Leda, see Massa 1992, 95–96.

37 For a good drawing of the Eros type see Courby 1922, 342-343, fig. 69:12g; it is best attested at Athens on a bowl from Workshop A (Rotroff 1982a, 54, no. 87, pl. 15). For the figure on a Lemnian bowl see Massa 1992, 153, no. C 229, pl. 38. That same Lemnian bowl has an Odysseus figure paralleled on bowls of the Workshop of Bion (cf. Rotroff 1982a, 54–55, 67, nos. 91, 190, 191, pls. 15, 35, 80) and, as part of the rim pattern, a kore mask found in several Athenian workshops (e.g., Rotroff 1982a, nos. 103, 163 [Workshop of Bion], no. 114 [Workshop A?], no. 109 [M Monogram Class], no. 143 [Class 1]). For a good drawing of the kore mask, see Courby 1922, 340, fig. 68:21.

38 E.g., Massa 1992, 121, 124, 153, nos. C 12, C 27, C 229, pls. 6, 9, 38.

39 Massa 1992, 244.

40 Polybios 30.20; Habicht 1997, 217–218.

shop probably invented the moldmade bowl; some time thereafter, but before *c.* 165 BC, the proprietor set up a branch workshop in Argos, with further connections to Corinth, and, perhaps just after 168 BC, established a pottery on Lemnos as well. Whether this was the work of a single talented and energetic artisan/businessman or the development of several generations of craftsmen we will not know until our abilities to date these objects and contexts has been honed to greater precision. But the evidence is that Hellenistic potters, like their Roman colleagues later on, looked beyond their own localities in the development of their enterprise.

Susan I. Rotroff
Departments of Classics and of Art History and Archaeology
Campus Box 1050
Washington University in Saint Louis
Saint Louis, MO 63130

Bibliography

Courby, F. 1922. *Les vases grecs à reliefs*. Paris, De Boccard.

Edwards, C. M. 1981. Corinth 1980: Moldmade Relief Bowls. *Hesperia* 50, 189–210.

Edwards, C. M. 1986. Corinthian Moldmade Bowls: The 1926 Reservoir. *Hesperia* 55, 389–419.

Edwards, G. R. 1956. Hellenistic Pottery. In *Small Objects from the Pnyx: II*. Hesperia Supplement 10, 79–112. Princeton, NJ., American School of Classical Studies.

Edwards, G. R. 1975. *Corinthian Hellenistic Pottery*. Corinth VII.iii. Princeton, NJ., American School of Classical Studies at Athens.

Habicht, C. 1997. *Athens from Alexander to Antony*. Cambridge, MA., Harvard University Press.

Kroll, J. H. 1993. *The Greek Coins*. The Athenian Agora XXVI. Princeton, NJ., American School of Classical Studies at Athens.

Lawall, M. L., Jawando, A., Lynch, K. M., Papadopoulos, J. K. and Rotroff, S. I. 2002. Notes from the Tins 2: Research in the Stoa of Attalos. *Hesperia* 71, 425–433.

Massa, M. 1992. *La ceramica ellenistica con decorazione a rilievo della Bottega di Efestia*. Monografie della scuola archeologica di Atene e della missioni italiane in oriente V. Rome, L'Erma di Bretschneider.

Rotroff, S. I. 1982a. *Hellenistic Pottery: Athenian and Imported Moldmade Bowls*. The Athenian Agora XXII. Princeton, NJ., American School of Classical Studies at Athens.

Rotroff, S. I. 1982b. Silver, Glass, and Clay: Evidence for the Dating of Hellenistic Luxury Tableware. *Hesperia* 51, 329–337.

Rotroff, S. I. 1994. The Satyr Cistern in the Athenian Agora. In *Γ' επιστημονική συνάντηση για την ελληνιστική κεραμική*. Θεσσαλονίκη 1991, 17–22. Athens, Archetai.

Rotroff, S. I. 2005. Four Centuries of Athenian Pottery, in V. F. Stolba and L. Hannestad (eds.), *Chronologies of the Black Sea Area in the Period c. 400–100*, 11–30. Aarhus, Aarhus University Press.

Rotroff, S. I. 2006a. *Hellenistic Pottery: The Plain Wares*. The Athenian Agora XXXIII. Princeton, NJ., American School of Classical Studies at Athens.

Rotroff, S. I. 2006b. The Introduction of the Moldmade Bowl Revisited: Tracking a Hellenistic Innovation. *Hesperia 75*, 357–378.

Siebert, G. 1978. *Recherches sur les ateliers de bols à reliefs du Péloponnèse à l'époque hellénistique*. Bibliothèque des Écoles Française d'Athènes et de Rome CCXXXIII. Athens, École française d'Athènes.

Handelswege. Das Warenspektrum einer Werkstatt frühhellenistischer Zeit im Demos Kerameis

Norbert Eschbach

Abstract

In 2010, the author had the opportunity to examine material found in a small rescue excavation in the area of the Demos Kerameis in 1966. More than 100 vases and thousands of fragments had been collected at that time from a sealed pit of a potter's workshop. A certain range of typical defects is visible which leads to the conclusion that all the vases had been discarded after accidents during the production process. Their date is clearly limited to the end of the 4th century BC, therefore all the vases should come from one or maybe two collapsed kilns. Three dominant types of pottery were produced for three different groups of customers: Athenian officials, normal citizens and for export. Of special interest are the late red figure Pelikai – examples of our workshop have been found not only in northern Greece, but in South Russia and – via western Crete – in Lybia, too.

Keywords: Abfallgrube, Töpferwerkstatt, Handel, Panathenäische Preisamphora, Polemon (312/1 v. Chr.)

In einem knappen Bericht über eine kleine Notgrabung 1966 nördlich des Kerameikos auf einem Grundstück an der Kreuzung der Straßen Odos Achilleos und Odos Plataion (**Abb. 1**, Nr. 12)[1] erwähnte Olga Alexandri[2] eine Abfallgrube mit Gefäßen der schwarzgefirnißten und rotfigurigen Ware – und zwei Gefäßen einer bestimmten Gattung, die mich seit 1980, zur Zeit der Materialaufnahme für die Dissertation besonders interessierten[3]. Ich kam damals allerdings nicht an das Material, erst sehr viel später ergab sich die Gelegenheit[4].

Im Frühjahr 2010 fand die erste Materialaufnahme statt, dabei stellte sich heraus, das die von Alexandri genannten Anzahl der Gefäße aus der Grube (29) nur einen sehr kleinen Ausschnitt des tatsächlich geborgenen Materials darstellte. Insgesamt handelt es sich um 70 ganze oder teilrestaurierte Gefäße, hinzu kommen 18 große Kisten im Magazin, randvoll, mit ca. 6500 Fragmenten. Das Material wurde im September 2010 aufgearbeitet, mein Beitrag ist daher ein vorläufiger Werkstattbericht. Angesichts der zahlreichen Fragmente von Brennstützen verschiedenen Formats und des grundsätzlichen Erscheinungsbildes der Keramik war klar, daß es sich um den Abfall einer Töpferwerkstatt des späteren 4. Jhs. v. Chr. handeln mußte. Die ersten Fragen sind: Welches Formenspektrum ist zu beobachten, wie ausgedehnt genau war der Zeitraum der Nutzung dieser Grube, und: Gibt es die Möglichkeit einer genaueren zeitlichen Eingrenzung? Darüber hinaus natürlich: Wie ist die Werkstatt innerhalb der attischen Keramikproduktion positioniert?

Angesichts der riesigen Anzahl von attischen Töpfern und Vasenmalern, die wir vom 6. bis in das späte 4. Jh. v. Chr. nach über 100 Jahren Vasenforschung scheiden können, ist es schon erstaunlich, wie wenig konkrete (meint auch: publizierte) Informationen wir über den Produktionsprozeß und noch weniger über die Werkstätten, ihre genauen Orte und ihre Organisation haben. Das Material aus Athen und Attika ist kürzlich zusammengestellt worden[5]; Athen, speziell das Gebiet des Kerameikos bis zur Akademie des Platon, ist 1994 etwas detaillierter behandelt worden[6]. Nur in drei Fällen sind anhand der Keramik in Abfallgruben die Werkstätten wichtiger Maler des 5. bis frühen 4. Jhs. v. Chr. erkannt, bzw. publiziert, nur in einem lokalisiert, es fehlt jeweils ein verwertbarer Kontext:

1. **Abb. 1**, Nr. 9a: Odos Marathonos 2 (1967): Drei Gruben der Werkstatt des Brygos-, Briseis-, Triptolemos-Malers[7].
2. **Abb. 1**, nahe Nr. 10: unter einem Haus in der Ermou (1853): Werkstattabfall hauptsächlich des Jena-Malers[8].
3. **Abb. 1**, nahe Nr. 11: ‚bei der Metrostation am Theseion' (vor 1904): Werkstattabfall vor allem des Dinos-Malers[9].

---

1 Plan und Zählung Abb. 1 auf der Basis von Baziotopoulou-Valavani 1994, 46 Abb. 1, erweitert um die Mindestausdehnung des Demos Kerameis nach Steffelbauer 2007, 239 Abbildung 2 und das Areal der Akademie nach Travlos 1971, 318 Abb. 415. – Eine Kartierung für ganz Athen mit Trennung nach Abfallgruben und Werkstätten: Bentz *et al.* 2010, 128 Abb. 34.

2 Alexandri 1967, 36 f. Abb. 1 (Plan) Stelle 16; 58 Taf. 73 α. β.

3 Eschbach 1986, 2 mit Anm. 17.

4 Ich danke O. Tzachou-Alexandri für die Überlassung des Materials und der Ephorin der 3. Ephorie der Prähistorischen und Klassischen Altertümer, N. Valakou-Divari sowie ihrer Stellvertreterin, E. Baziotopoulou-Valavani, für die Genehmigung. Ohne die Hilfe der Mitarbeiter der Magazine der 3. Ephorie in der Odos Drakontos und in der Odos Melidoni wäre die Aufarbeitung nicht möglich gewesen; mein besonderer Dank gilt E. Servetopoulou, L. Bournias und K. Sarris. Das Deutsche Archäologische Institut Athen leistete großzügige technische Unterstützung. Besonderer Dank gilt auch der Gerda Henkel Stiftung, die das Unternehmen für ein Jahr finanzierte.

5 Monaco 2000, 34–56. 59–80. 167–238.

6 Baziotopoulou-Valavani 1994, 45–54.

7 Baziotopoulou-Valavani 1994, 47 mit Anm. 13; Maffre 1984, 113–118; Monaco 2000, 211–213 D II.

8 Baziotopoulou-Valavani 1994, 51; Monaco 2000, 201–206 B II; Paul-Zinserling 1994; Bentz *et al.* 2010, bes. 128-150 (K. Kathariou).

9 Baziotopoulou-Valavani 1994, 47 mit Anm. 16 f.; Monaco 2000,

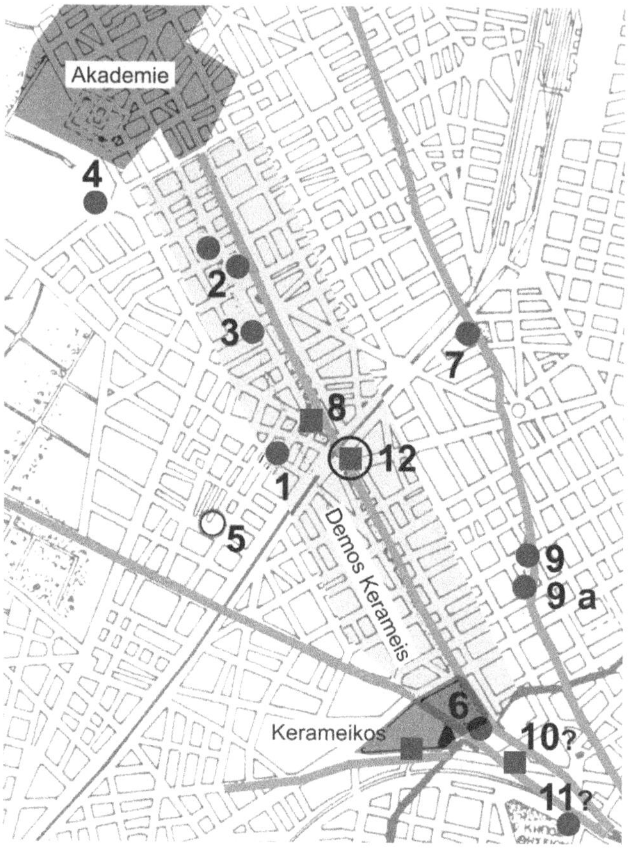

Abb. 1. Töpferwerkstätten zwischen Kerameikos und Akademie: (●) des 5. Jhs. v. Chr., teils bis in das frühe 4. Jh. v. Chr.; (■) des 4. Jhs. v. Chr. (Anm. 1)

In allen übrigen Fällen im Demos Kerameis zwischen den Stadtmauern und bis hin zum Territorium der Akademie sind die Abfallgruben der Töpferwerkstätten über einen größeren Zeitraum hinweg beschickt worden und sind die Inhalte der Gruben nicht oder nur sehr geringfügig publiziert. Dazu werden sie, und auch die der oben genannten Fundstellen 1–3, über die vorgefundene Keramik, und nicht über außerkeramische Befunde datiert. Einen eng eingrenzbaren Befund für die zweite Hälfte des 4. Jhs. v. Chr. gibt es bisher nicht.

Zurück zu unserer Grabung[10]: Durch ungenehmigte Baumaßnahmen waren die Befunde auf dem Grundstück zerstört – mit Ausnahme eines nordöstlichen Bereichs. Dort fanden sich ca. 1.50m unter dem modernen Laufniveau Teile eines Raumes mit Estrich. Direkt unter dem Fußboden wurde eine rechteckige Grube, 3,25m lang und 2,75m breit, maximal 35cm tief, angeschnitten. Die Tatsache, daß der Estrich direkt auf die Erdabdeckung der Grube angelegt wurde, deutet darauf hin, daß hier ein Bau in zeitlich enger Folge über der Abfallgrube errichtet wurde. Die eingefüllte Keramik ist in drei große Gruppen einzuteilen: 1. die schwarzgefirnißte, nicht figürlich dekorierte Keramik; 2. die rotfigurige Ware, und 3. attisch schwarzfigurige Gefäße einer speziellen Gattung: Panathenäische Preisamphoren[11].

Die schwarzgefirnißten Gefäße

Die Schwarzfirnisware deckt ein engeres Formenspektrum ab. Geschlossene Formen sind sehr selten, offenen Formen stellen den Hauptanteil. Zahlreich sind Teller, henkellose Schalen, Fischteller und Kantharoi. Große Formen sind ebenfalls selten. Hinsichtlich Datierung und Laufzeit spätklassischer und hellenistischer Keramik von der Mitte des 4. bis in das 1. Jh. v. Chr. stützen wir uns bekanntlich auf einer ganzen Reihe von geschlossenen Kontexten, die durch nichtkeramische Funde (etwa Münzen) oder historische Beobachtungen fest datiert werden können. Für die zweiten Hälfte des 4. Jhs. v. Chr. sind sie jedoch rar[12]. Einzig das kürzlich publizierte Fundmaterial des Bau Z vom Kerameikos[13] bietet für einige Formen unseres Depots das Kontrollmaterial.

Das Formenspektrum: Flache Teller kommen in vier Größen vor: Das besterhaltene Beispiel der größten Variante (vier Exemplare) hat fast einen halben Meter Durchmesser (42cm, Inv. 3880, **Abb. 2**). Unabhängig von der Größe sind die Profile stets gleich. Dekorelemente sind kleine handgezogene offene Kreise innen um den Mittelpunkt, Schraffurkreise und seltener asymmetrische Rankensterne mit sieben Palmettenspitzen. Das von zwei flachen Rillen gerahmte Band aus sieben Schraffurkreisen auf A 3880 ist eher ungewöhnlich. Die nächsten Parallelen zu unseren Exemplaren finden sich im Material der Agora, sie datieren in das ‚späte 4.', das ‚letzte Jahrzehnt des 4. Jhs. v. Chr' oder um 300'[14] – allerdings variieren dort die Dm zwischen 13 und 25cm – unsere beiden großen Varianten kommen nicht vor.

Das Schadensbild bei allen Tellern und fast der gesamten Keramik aus der Grube ist gleich: Die Gefäße sind teils stark verzogen, die Ränder mitunter eingedellt. Die Färbung des Firnis ist außerordentlich variabel – aber kaum einmal schwarz. Einzelne Fragmente legen Risse während des Brennprozesses nahe. Meist sind leicht asymmetrische Kreisflächen auf der Tellerfläche zu beobachten, die in den Maßen den Fußdurchmessern der jeweiligen Größenklasse entsprechen. Die Teller waren demnach – wie auch über 70 henkellosen Schalen, die ebenfalls in drei Größen

195-201 B 1a/b/c; Bentz *et al.* 2010, bes. 150-169 (J. M. Müller; Füllung der Grube: 440–400 v. Chr.).

10 Für die detaillierte Darstellung sei auf die Gesamtpublikation verwiesen. Die Daten des Grabungstagbuches erlauben die Rekonstruktion der Arbeiten einschließlich der Abfolge und Verortung der meisten Fundgruppen.

11 Zur Gattung der Panathenäischen Preisamphoren umfassend Bentz 1998, passim.

12 Zu den datierten Kontexten s. Rotroff 1997, 18–36.

13 Hier besonders die Befunde zu Bau Z 3, errichtet spätestens gegen 320, zerstört etwa um 307 v. Chr.: Knigge 2005, 49–79.

14 Vgl. Rotroff 1997, 142 f. mit Anm. 1; bes. 310 Kat. Nr. 645–649. bes. 646. 648 Abb. 46.

Abb. 2. Inv. A 3880, großer Teller (N. Eschbach)

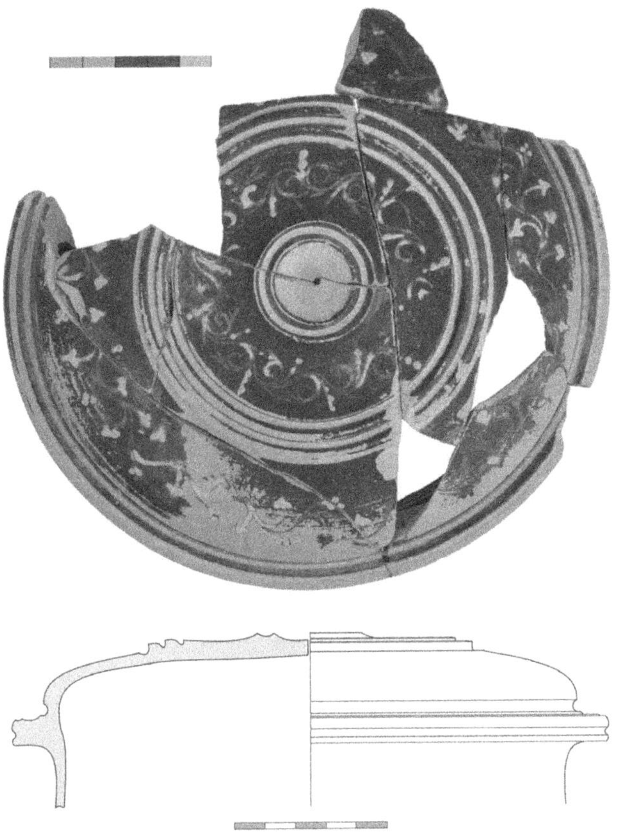

Abb. 4. Inv. A 3810, Stülpdeckel einer Pyxis (N. Eschbach)

Abb. 3. Inv. A 3870, Becken (N. Eschbach)

vorkommen –, ineinandergestapelt im Ofen abgelegt. Dies gilt auch für die Fischteller: ca. 330 Fragmente stammen von mindestens 40 Fischtellern, drei verschiedene Größen liegen vor. Zwei Exemplare mit 42cm Dm erreichen die Klasse der Riesenteller. Ihre Zeitstellung entspricht jener der Teller[15].

Ca. 500 Fragmente stammen von mindestens 40 glattwandigen oder reliefierten Kantharoi. Erstere lassen vier Größenklassen erkennen. Die Profilierung von Lippen und Füßen variiert in engem Rahmen ein und dasselbe Schema, ihre Zeitstellung entspricht jener der Teller[16].

Eine recht ungewöhnliche Form ist mit ca. sechs Beispielen vertreten (**Abb. 3**), es sind große Becken, zwischen 24 und 25cm hoch und mit einem Durchmesser der Mündung von ca. 45cm. Ein profilierter Fuß – offenbar der Standardfuß für Glockenkratere der Werkstatt[17] – trägt ein fast halbkugeliges Becken. Halbkreisförmige Griffschalen bilden die Henkel. S. Rotroff vermutete den Beginn der Formentwicklung vorsichtig vielleicht ab dem 3. Viertel

---

15 Vgl. Rotroff 1997, 146–148 mit Anm. 11; 315 f. Kat. Nr. 709–715 Abb. 50.
16 Vgl. z. B. Rotroff 1997, 83–94. bes. 85. 245 f. Kat. Nr. 38 f. Abb. 6.
17 Vgl. u. Abb. 6.

Abb. 5. Peliken. Links: a) Inv. A 3875. Mitte: b) Inv. A 3781. Rechts oben: c) Inv. A 3782. Rechts unten: d) Inv. A 3789 (N. Eschbach)

Abb. 6. Inv. A 3868, Glockenkrater (N. Eschbach)

Abb. 7. Inv. A 3867, Glockenkrater (N. Eschbach)

des 3. und eine Laufzeit bis in das frühe zweite Jahrhundert hinein[18]. Nach Ausweis unserer Beispiele erscheint die Form wohl bereits im späteren letzten Viertel des 4. Jhs. v. Chr.

Unter der golddekorierten Schwarzfirnisware fällt der Stülpdeckel einer Pyxis auf (**Abb. 4**, Inv. A 3810, Dm ca. 20 cm). Ihr und allen Beispielen dieser Technik fehlt der auf dem plastisch in Ton aufgesetzten Dekor nachträglichaufgelegte Goldüberzug[19] – ein Hinweis darauf, daß die Gefäße nicht mehr für die aufwendige Nachbehandlung infrage kamen. Die ausgeprägte Gliederung der Form durch Wulstringe und Rillen findet nur wenige Vergleichsbeispiele. Am nächsten stehen einige Fragmente vom Kerameikos aus dem letzten Viertel des 4. Jhs. v. Chr[20].

Festzuhalten ist: Die Schwarzfirnisware aus der Grube erweist eine intern genormte Massenproduktion für alltägliche Gebrauchskeramik. Keines der Gefäße ist nach Ausweis der Vergleiche vor 320 oder nach 300 v. Chr. anzusetzen – die meist mit Vorsicht gegebenen Daten vergleichbarer Beispiele weisen eher geschlossen in das letzte Jahrzehnt des 4. Jhs. v. Chr. Das Schadensbild der Waren ist einheitlich.

Die rotfigurige Keramik

Das rotfigurige Fundmaterial besteht hauptsächlich aus Peliken und Glockenkrateren, einige Fragmente gehören zu Lekanisdeckeln. Ca. 1000 Fragmente stammen von Peliken in wohl nur zwei verschiedenen Größen. Die Bilder der Vorderseite variieren in der Hauptsache zwei Themenbereiche, auf den Peliken der ersten Gruppe erscheinen Greifen mit oder gegen Krieger und/oder mazonen (**Abb. 5 a–b**). Auf den Rückseiten sind in sehr nachlässiger Zeichenweise zumeist zwei, mitunter auch drei Manteljünglinge ‚im Gespräch' abgebildet[21].

Das zweite Hauptthema bietet Frauenköpfe in unterschiedlichen Kombination (**Abb. 5 c–d**): z. B. zwischen zwei Greifen (c), allein mit Pferd (d), oder mit Greif und Pferd[22]. Das Schadensbild – Dellen und krasse Verfärbungen der Oberflächen mit überproportionalem Abrieb in den heller verfärbten Bereichen – ist hier wie bei den folgenden Krateren identisch mit den Beobachtungen an der schwarzgefirnißten Ware. Die Zeichenweise läßt bislang mindestens drei Malerhände erkennen, die ihre Parallelen sämtlich unter den Gefäßen der spätesten Gruppe G[23] finden, einer von ihnen ist der Amazonen-Maler[24]. Von 18 Glockenkrateren haben sich zum Teil größere Frgt.-Gruppen erhalten; das vollständigste und hinsichtlich der Oberfläche besterhaltene Beispiel stammt von der Hand des Amazonen-Malers (Inv. A 3868, **Abb. 6**). Das Gefäß ist stark verzogen, die Mündung eingedellt und die Rückseite fehlt. Der Fußstiel war am Beckenansatz nicht abgeschlagen sondern abgeplatzt, wie dies für alle Krateren aus der Grube mit derartigen Schäden zu gelten scheint[25]. Die Maße der Kratere sind fast einheitlich; sie sind zwischen 30 und 32cm hoch, der Dm der Mündungen liegt zwischen 32 und 34cm.

Die genaue Bedeutung der bildlichen Darstellung ist hier (**Abb. 6**) – wie bei vielen Bildern der späteren Gefäße der Gruppe G – nicht eindeutig zu bestimmen[26]. Das Themenspektrum der Kratere aus unserer Werkstatt ist nur unwesentlich breiter als jenes der Peliken: Neben den Kampfszenen mit Greifen erscheinen dionysische Reigen, Männer und Frauen mit Greifen oder auch Darstellungen des Symposions. In das weitere Umfeld des Dionysos gehört das Bild auf dem Krater A 3867 (**Abb. 7**): ein Mann greift nach einer Frau mit einem Thyrsosstab in der Linken. Überraschend ist allerdings die Gestalt am r. Bildrand: Es ist eindeutig Pan, der Waldgott, mit zotteligem Ziegenfell an den Oberschenkeln und Hufen – die m. W. späteste Darstellung des Gottes in der att. Vasenmalerei[27].

Betrachtet man die Fundorte der Gruppe G – und vor allem derjenigen Gefäße aus dem späten 4. Jh. v. Chr. – so stammt die Mehrzahl aus dem südrussischen Raum, aus Libyen und aus Nordgriechenland, nur wenige aus Athen selbst[28]. Neuere Untersuchungen sichern den Handel mit Peliken der Gruppe auch auf Westkreta, auf dem Weg in die Cyrenaika; Peliken derselben Maler aus unserer Abfallgrube erweisen den Anteil der Werkstatt an diesem Handel[29].

---

18 Vgl. Rotroff 1997, 137–139. 304 Kat. Nr. 590–594 Abb. 42 f.

19 Zur golddekorierten Schwarzfirnisware grundsätzlich Kopcke 1964, passim. – Aus der Grube stammen neben der Pyxis noch drei große Kelchkratere mit feiner Kettenverzierung, der ebenfalls die Vergoldung fehlt.

20 Kopcke 1964, 27 Nr. 12 (Athen, Kerameikos 2330 ‚320–310 v. Chr.'; Dm ca. 24 cm). Nr. 13 (Athen, Kerameikos 2339, ‚310–300 v. Chr.'; Dm ca. 22 cm). 70–72 Beil. 13, 1–2

21 Eine nächste Parallele zu A 3875 (Abbildung 5 a) und wohl von derselben Hand ist eine Pelike in Rethymnon, leider unbekannter Herkunft: Tzanakaki 1997, 20 f. Abb. 1 a. b (Mus. Rethymnon Inv. P 759).

22 Eine nächste Parallele zur Pelike A 3789 (Abbildung 5 d) und von derselben Hand stammt ebenfalls aus Kreta, eine Pelike, aus einem Grab bei Phalasarna, Tzanakaki 1997, 30 f. Abb. 8 a. b (Mus. Rethymnon P 2228). Zu Pelike A 3782 (Abbildung 5 c) vgl. eine Pelike aus einem Grab in Vergina. Drougou 2005, 83 f. Nr. 4 Abb. 78–79; FO: Toumba, Grab II (1979).

23 Zur Gruppe G grundsätzlich: ARV[2] 1462–1471. 1694 f. 1708; Para 494 f.; Add[2] 380.

24 Zum Amazonen-Maler grundsätzlich: ARV[2] 1478–1480; Para 496; Add[2] 381.

25 Typisch ist die Trennung beider Gefäßteile exakt in der Ansatznaht, sodaß die Vorbereitungen zur Verbindung außen am Beckenboden (eingetiefte spiralförmige Rillen, Firnis als Haftmittel) sichtbar sind. Die Bruchkanten am Verstrich auf den Stiel- und Beckenpartien sind sehr scharf. Soweit Fußstiele und Becken zusammengebracht werden können, sind an beiden Teilen keine Schlagspuren erkennbar, die auf eine gewaltsame Zerstörung hinweisen könnten. Auch der Krater A 3867 (Abbildung 7) zeigt diese technischen Merkmale.

26 Für den Problemkreis ‚Darstellung – Deutung – Chiffre – Identifikation' sei an dieser Stelle auf Frederike Fless verwiesen, die die verschiedensten Modell diskutiert: Fless 2002, 90–93. 99 f.

27 Zu Pan s. LIMC VIII (1997) Suppl. 923–941 s. v. Pan (J. Boardman).

28 Athener Funde: Thompson 1934, 333 f. zu den Peliken B 1 (P 1104) und B2 (P 1105); 427–429. – Moore 1997, 131. 143 Kat. Nr. 64 (P 1104). 65 (P 1105) Taf. 14; 214 Kat. Nr. 521 (P 19346) Taf. 55. Vgl. auch Moore 1997, 143 Kat. Nr. 59 Taf. 13 mit entschieden zu früher Dat. (‚2. Viertel des 4. Jhs.').

29 s. o. zu Anm. 21 f.; mit weiteren Beispielen s. Skodrou 2000, 36–61.

Abb. 8. Inv. A 3889, Panathenäische Preisamphora, Vorderseite (N. Eschbach)

Abb. 9. Inv. A 3889, Panathenäische Preisamphora, Rückseite (N. Eschbach)

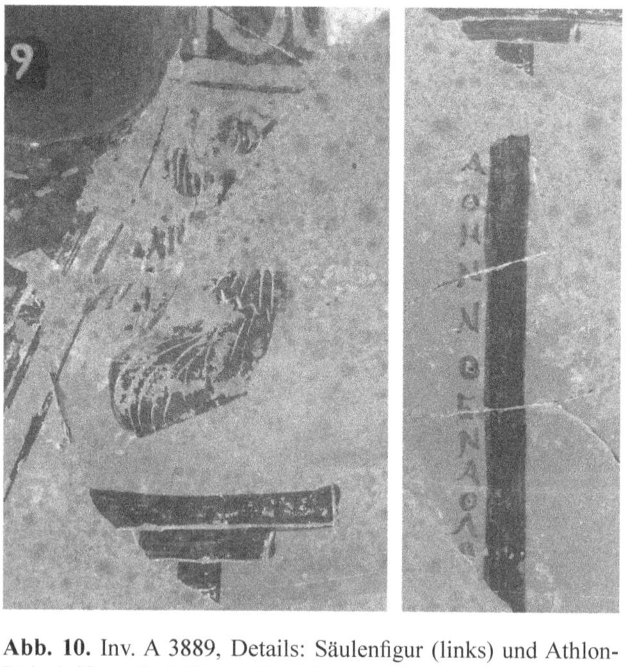

Abb. 10. Inv. A 3889, Details: Säulenfigur (links) und Athlon-Beischrift (rechts) (N. Eschbach)

Die Qualität der Bemalung kann mit Fless und Langner[30] nicht das Kriterium den Verkaufserfolg, die Importe in den genannten Regionen gewesen sein; mit Sicherheit bedient die Thematik ein Identitätsformat einer aus Griechen und unterschiedlichen indigenen Bevölkerungsgruppen zusammengesetzten Gesellschaft mit teils stark lokal geprägten Sitten und Gebräuchen. So scheinen die Peliken erforderlicher Bestandteil der Beigabenausstattung auch weniger reicher Gräber (und nicht nur in Südrußland) gewesen zu sein. Die Glockenkratere dagegen stehen offenbar mit den am Grab vollzogenen Riten in Verbindung[31].

Die schwarzfigurige Keramik

Nach dem Bericht von O. Alexandri[32] beinhaltete die Grube nur zwei, nach einem etwas späteren Hinweis von J. Frel[33] dann ca. acht Panathenäische Preisamphoren eines

30 Fless 2002, 88–93, bes. 90; Langner 2005, bes. 61–65.
31 Fless 2002, 84–86.
32 Alexandri 1967, 58 Taf. 73 α (= A 3889).
33 Frel 1972, 289 Anm. 2.

des Archonten Polemon aus dem Amtsjahr 312/1 v. Chr.; nach der Revision der Fragmentgruppen sind es jedoch mindestens 12 und maximal 15 Preisamphoren dieses Jahrgangs[34]. Nur wenig war von diesem Jahrgang bislang bekannt: Ein Frgt. mit Teilen der Namensbeischrift fand sich schon 1895 im Gymnasium von Eretria, eine kleine Frgt.-Gruppe stammt vom Kerameikos[35].

Da eine ausführliche Publikation der Gefäße in Vorbereitung ist, seien hier nur einige wesentliche Charakteristika des Jahrgangs hervorgehoben. Das am vollständigsten erhaltene Exemplar (Inv. A 3889, **Abb. 8–10**) zeigt – wie bei Gefäßen der Schwarzfirnisware und der rotfigurigen Keramik beobachtet – einen verzogenen Körper, Tongrund und Firnis sind stark verfärbt. Nur Teile der Preisbeischrift (**Abb. 10**) sind erhalten, die Zugehörigkeit zum Jahrgang ist über die übrigen Preisamphoren, u. a. mit der Zeichenweise der Athena, dem Duktus der Schrift und über die Säulenfiguren (**Abb. 10**)[36] gesichert. Ergänzt man die Amphora um die hier verlorenen, aber bei anderen Beispielen aus der Grube erhaltenen Teile, dann erreichte sie mit Deckel eine Höhe von ca. 1, 15m – und ist damit die größte bislang bekannte Preisamphora[37]. Ausgesprochen einheitlich ist die Gestaltung des Gewandes und der sonstigen Ausstattung der Göttin, hervorzuheben sind die Angabe der Ägis und die S-förmige Zeichnung des in Weiß aufgemalten Helmbuschständers. Überraschend ist die hohe Qualität der Zeichnung der Rückseitenbilder (**Abb. 9**): Ausgesprochen sicher proportionierte Körper mit reicher Binnenzeichnung und Bewegungsmotiven, Die Panathenäischen Preisamphoren setzen einen zeitlichen die an Bilder erinnern, die der Marsyas-Maler fast zwei Generationen früher auf seinen Preisamphoren bietet[38].

Fixpunkt für den gesamten in die Grube eingefüllten Keramikbestand. Die Werkstatt, die hier, an der Οδός Αχιλλέως und Πλαταιών, möglicherweise *einen* kompletten Ofeninhalt entsorgte, war offenbar mit genügend Personal ausgestattet und professionell genug für einen staatlichen Großauftrag, der Produktion von Panathenäischen Preisamphoren, die für das Panathenäenfest um 310/9 v Chr. benötigt wurden. Sie hatte neben der Herstellung von ständig benötigter alltäglicher Gebrauchskeramik auch einen größeren Anteil an der Produktion von Peliken und Glockenkrateren, die über den Fernhandel als Beigabensets für den sepulkralen Kontext nachgefragt wurden – wenn sie nicht sogar darauf spezialisiert war. Daneben stellte sie auf besonderen Kundenwunsch auch anspruchsvollere Gefäße her.

Norbert Eschbach
Justus-Liebig-Universität Giessen
Professur für Klassische Archäologie
Philosophikum I / D
Otto-Behaghel-Str. 10
D-35394 Giessen
norbert.eschbach@archaeologie.uni-giessen.de

Bibliographie

Alexandri, O. 1967. Γ' Εφορεία Κλασσικών Αρχαιοτήτων. *Αρχαιολογικόν Δελτίον* 22 B' 1, 37–130.

Baziotopoulou-Valavani, E. 1994. Ανασκαφές σε αθηναϊκά κεραμικά εργαστήρια των αρχαϊκών και κλασικών χρόνων, in W. D. E. Coulson, O. Palagia, T. L. Shear, Jr., H. A. Shapiro und F. J. Frost (Hrsg.), *The Archaeology of Athens and Attica under the Democracy*, 45–54. Oxford, Oxbow.

Bentz, M. 1998. *Panathenäische Preisamphoren. Eine athenische Vasengattung und ihre Funktion vom 6.-4. Jh. v. Chr.* Basel, Vereinigung der Freunde Antiker Kunst.

Bentz, M., Geominy, W. und Müller, J. M. (Hrsg.) 2010. *TonArt. Virtuosität antiker Töpfertechnik.* Petersberg, Imhof.

Drougou, St. 2005. *Βεργίνα. Τα πήλινα αγγεία της μεγάλης τούμπας.* Athen.

Eschbach, N. 1986. *Statuen auf Panathenäischen Preisamphoren des 4. Jh. v. Chr.* Mainz, Zabern.

Fless, F. 2002. *Rotfigurige Keramik als Handelsware. Erwerb und Gebrauch attischer Vasen im mediterranen und pontischen Raum während des 4. Jhs. v. Chr.* Rahden, Leidorf.

Frel, J. 1972. Quelques noms d'archontes sur les amphores panathénaiques. *Revue archéologique*, 285–290.

[34] Neben den 12 gesicherten Preisamphoren gibt es Frgt.-Gruppen dreier B-Seiten, die nicht mit absoluter Sicherheit an vorhandene ‚freie' A-Seiten angeschlossen werden können; nach Zeichenweise und technischen Merkmalen gehören sie allerdings sicher zu dem Jahrgang des Polemon.

[35] Eretria: Woolsley Heermance 1896, 331–334 Abb. 1; Bentz 1998, 180 Kat. 4.129. – Kerameikos: Frel 1972, 288 f. mit Abb. 3. (irrtümlich: Archont Hegemon 327/6 v. Chr, Korrektur: Valavanis 1984, 203 f.; vgl. Eschbach 1986, 145 mit Anm. 680a). – Über die Preisamphoren der Grube sind weitere Fragmente aus dem Bestand des Kerameikos dem Jahrgang zuzuweisen, hierzu demnächst der Autor. Die späte Preisamphora in Malibu 76.AE.5, Bentz 1998, 180 Kat. 4.130 mit leider abgeriebener Archontenbeischrift ist nach Ausweis der Säulenfiguren und (u. a.) der Zeichenweise der Athena ebenfalls dem Jahrgang des Polemon zuzuweisen.

[36] Bei acht Preisamphoren sind die Säulenfiguren erhalten, stets ist es die auf Athena zufliegende Nike mit dem noch offenen Kranz, d. h. sie präsentiert der Göttin in beiden vorgestreckten Händen einen Blattzweig. Auf sieben Beispielen ist die Archontenbeischrift erhalten, in nur zwei Fällen ist auch die Athlonbeischrift gesichert.

[37] erh. H: 72,5 cm, ergänzt man Mündung (6cm), Fuß und Fußstiel (ca. 12cm) = ca. 90cm – damit die größte erh. PA des 4. Jhs.; mit Deckel (25cm) = 1,15m – Die bislang größte PA ohne Deckel: London B 607 mit 83, 1cm; Jahrgang Pythodelos 336/5 v. Chr., Bentz 1998, 176 Kat. 4.086 Taf. 119 f.

[38] Zu seinen Preisamphoren aus dem Jahrgang des Kallimedes von 360/59 v. Chr.: Bentz 1998, 172- Kat. Nr. 4.050–4.051 Taf. 110. 112; Kat. 4.054 Taf. 114.

Knigge, U. 2005. *Der Bau Z.* Kerameikos. Ergebnisse der Ausgrabungen XVII. München, Hirmer.

Kopcke, G. 1964. Golddekorierte attische Schwarzfirniskeramik des vierten Jahrhunderts v. Chr. *Mitteilungen des Deutschen Archäologischen Instituts. Athenische Abteilung* 79, 28–84.

Langner, M. 2005. Barbaren griechischer Sprache? Die Bildwelt des Bosporanischen Reiches und das Selbstverständnis seiner Bewohner, in F. Fless und M. Treister (Hrsg.), *Bilder und Objekte als Träger kultureller Identität und interkultureller Kommunikation im Schwarzmeergebiet*. Kolloquium in Zschortau/Sachsen vom 13. 2. – 15. 2. 2003, 53–66. Rahden, Leidorf.

Maffre, J. J. 1984. Fragments inédits de skyphoi attiques à figures rouges des années 480. In H. A. G. Brijder (Hrsg.), *Ancient Greek and related pottery: Proceedings of the International Vase Symposium in Amsterdam.* Allard Pierson Series 5, 113–118. Amsterdam, Allard Pierson Museum.

Monaco, M. C. 2000. *Ergasteria. Impianti artigianali ceramici ad Atene ed in Attica dal protogeometrico alle soglie dell'Ellenismo.* Rom, L'Erma di Bretschneider.

Moore, M. B. 1997. *Attic red-figured and white-ground pottery.* The Athenian Agora XXX. Princeton, NJ., The American School of Classical Studies.

Paul-Zinserling, V. 1994. *Der Jena-Maler und sein Kreis. Zur Ikonologie einer attischen Schalenwerkstatt um 400 v. Chr.* Mainz, Zabern.

Rotroff, S. I. 1997. *Hellenistic Pottery. Athenian and imported wheel made Table Ware and related Pottery.* The Athenian Agora XXIX. Princeton, NJ., The American School of Classical Studies.

Skordou, M. 1997. Ύστατες ερυθρόμορφες πελίκες από την επαρχία Κισάμο. In L. Kypraiou (Hrsg.), *Ελληνιστική Κεραμική από την Κρήτη*, 36–61. Chania.

Steffelbauer, I. 2007. Lage und Grenzen des Demos Kerameis und des Kerameikos von Athen. *Mitteilungen des Deutschen Archäologischen Instituts, Athenische Abteilung* 122, 229–261.

Stroszeck, J. 2003. Horos Kerameikou. Zu den Grenzsteinen des Kerameikos in Athen. *Polis* 1, 53–85.

Travlos, J. 1971. *Bildlexikon zur Topographie des antiken Athen.* Tübingen, Wasmuth.

Tzanakaki, K. 1997. Ερυθρόμορφες πελίκες στο Μουσείο Ρεθύμνου. In L. Kypraiou (Hrsg.), *Ελληνιστική Κεραμική από την Κρήτη*, 19–35. Chania.

Valavanis, P. D. 1984. Hégémon (327/6). *Hόρος. Ἕνα Ἀρχαιογνωστικὸ Περιοδικό* 2, 203–204.

Woolsley Heermance, Th. 1896. Fragment of a dated Panathenaic Amphora. *American Journal of Archaeology and of the History of the Fine Arts (1. Serie)* 11, 331–334.

Reliefkeramik aus dem Athena-Heiligtum von Eretria. Kontakte einer Stadt Euböas zum zentralen und nördlichen Griechenland

Guy Ackermann

Abstract

A large deposit of pottery dated from the first half of the 2nd century BC was found nearby the sanctuary of Athena on top of the acropolis of Eretria (Euboea). This paper focuses on the imported moldmade pottery (bowls and plates). Attic workshops are represented by several moldmade bowls, whereas productions from Corinth and Northern Greece are attested respectively by a bowl and an Homeric bowl. This is in sharp contrast with Ionian bowls which are not evidenced in Eretria before the middle of the 2nd century, except by their local imitations. A moldmade plate decorated with a frieze of Galatian and Macedonian shields allows us to discuss the presence of a Macedonian garrison stationed on the acropolis of Eretria under the ruling of Antigonos Gonatas until the liberation of the city by the Romans in 198 BC[1].

Keywords: Eretria, Reliefbecher, Reliefteller, Makedonische Schilde

Zum Andenken an Ingrid R. Metzger

Eine hellenistische Schuttablagerung auf der Akropolis von Eretria

Auf dem Gipfel der Akropolis der Stadt Eretria konnten in fünf Grabungskampagnen der Schweizerischen Archäologischen Schule in Griechenland (ESAG) eine prähistorische Siedlung und Überreste eines Athena-Heiligtums, das auf das Ende des 7. Jhs. v. Chr. zurückgeht, freigelegt werden[2]. Die Architektur der früheren Kultstätte ist fast unbekannt, einerseits wegen des Einsturzes der Befestigungsmauer, die ebenso zum Stützen der Terrassen diente, andererseits wegen des Umbaus des Heiligtums während der hellenistischen Epoche. Dieser Periode gehört eine 30 Meter lange Terrasse an, die zum einen Teil in den Felsen gehauen und zum anderen mittels einer Planierungsschicht nach Westen verlängert wurde. Einige Meter südöstlich unterhalb dieser Esplanade wurden im Jahre 2007 unter der Leitung von S. Huber in einem Schnitt dicke Aufschüttungen ausgegraben (Sektor E, S28). Diese bestehen aus einer Art Schuttablagerung[3]. Im Rahmen der Problematik der ‚Networks in the Hellenistic World' wird diese kleine Studie auf die Importe begrenzt[4]. Die Reliefkeramik bildet die beste Gruppe, um Kontakte mit anderen Regionen der griechischen Welt zu beobachten. Insgesamt bilden die Reliefscherben weniger als fünf Prozent der eingesammelten Keramik. Es handelt sich meistens um halbkugelförmige Reliefbecher (nur einige Beispiele werden vorgestellt), aber man konnte auch eine Scherbe eines kleinen Kraters (hier nicht besprochen) und zwei Reliefteller erfassen.

Die Reliefbecher

*Reliefbecher aus Athen (**Abb. 1–6**)*

Unter den Reliefbechern stammen viele Scherben von attischen Importen, die man leicht an ihrem schwarzen Glanzton, an ihrem feinen Ton, an ihrem Profil mit einer oft mit rotem *Miltos* eingeriebenen Kerbe und an ihren Verzierungen erkennt. Diese unterscheiden sich von den lokalen Produkten in der Qualität. Von den 55 Reliefbechern unseres Fundkontextes stammen 16 sicher aus attischen Werkstätten, die man nach Verzierungen in drei Gruppen einordnen kann: zwei attische Reliefbecher sind mit schuppenförmig angeordneten Blättern verziert (‚*imbricate bowls*') und lassen sich nach ihren Parallelen aus der Athener Agora in die erste Hälfte des 2. Jhs. v. Chr. datieren:

---

[1] Diese Kommunikation ist ein Teil der Ergebnisse einer Masterarbeit an der Universität von Lausanne unter der Leitung von Prof. Dr. Karl Reber. Ich bedanke mich bei Prof. Dr. Sandrine Huber der Université de Lorraine für die Überlassung des Materials und für ihr Vertrauen, bei Dr. Kristine Gex für ihre Hilfe bei der Redaktion, bei Prof. Dr. Stephan G. Schmid der Humboldt-Universität zu Berlin für seine Expertise, bei Prof. Dr. Susan I. Rotroff, die mich während eines Aufenthaltes in Eretria über die Reliefkeramik beraten hat, und bei PD Dr. Ingrid R. Metzger. Diese Masterarbeit wurde durch die Schweizerische Archäologische Schule in Griechenland (ESAG) und durch ein Stipendium der Société académique vaudoise (SAV) unterstützt.

[2] Siehe die Grabungsberichte: Friedemann 1994, Friedemann 1995, Müller 1996, Huber 2007 und Huber 2008.

[3] Huber 2008, 151–152. Insgesamt wurden mehr als 240kg Keramik gefunden in einem Schnitt von ca. 41m^2.

[4] Die meisten Scherben dieses Kontextes finden keine Parallelen ausserhalb von Eretria: der grösste Teil der Keramik wurde demnach in lokalen (oder regionalen) Werkstätten hergestellt.

Abb. 1-6. Reliefbecher aus Athen (G. Ackermann)

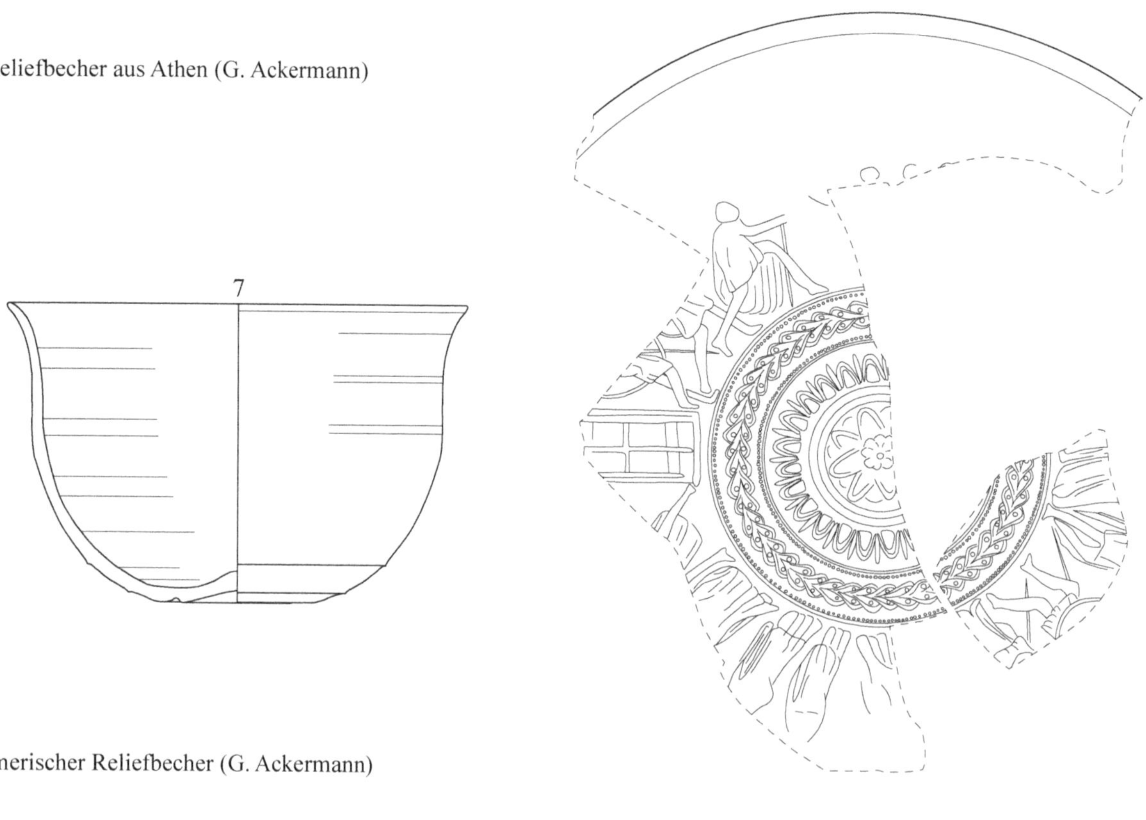

Abb. 7. Homerischer Reliefbecher (G. Ackermann)

1 (F100-AKR07-FK804+885 / V4715). Attischer Reliefbecher aus feinem Ton (5YR 6/6) mit metallischem, schwarzem Glanzton. Dm. 15.5cm. S. Rotroff 1982, 48, Nr. 28 und 31, Taf. 5 und 6 (Nr. 28: ca. 175–150 v. Chr.; Nr. 31: Becher des *Workshop A*, ca. 225–175 v. Chr.) und Metzger 1969, 62, Nr. V 1, Taf. 22 und 42.

2 (F100-AKR07-FK885+887+893+995 / V4716). Attischer Reliefbecher aus feinem Ton (5YR 6/6) mit metallischem, schwarzem Glanzton. Dm. ca. 14cm. S. Rotroff 1982, 46, Nr. 14, Taf. 3 (ca. 225–200 v. Chr.).

Die Gruppe der Becher mit pflanzlicher Verzierung (,*floral bowls*'), deren Herstellung nach der Mitte des 2. Jhs. v. Chr. endet[5], ist so stark vertreten wie die erste:

3 (F100-AKR07-FK772+804+891 / V4718). Attischer Reliefbecher aus feinem Ton (5YR 6/6) mit metallischem, schwarzem Glanzton. Dm. 12cm. S. Rotroff 1982, 52, Nr. 66, Taf. 11 (ca. 225–175 v. Chr.).

4 (F/100-AKR07-FK885 / V4719). Attischer Reliefbecher aus feinem Ton (5YR 6/6) mit glänzendem, schwarzem Glanzton. Dm. des Medaillons: 2.3cm. S. Rotroff 1982, 51, Nr. 63, Taf. 11 (Becher des *Workshop A?*, ca. 225–175 v. Chr.).

Wie für die vorangehende Gruppe endet die Herstellung der Reliefbecher mit figürlicher Verzierung (,*figured bowls*') um die Mitte des 2. Jhs. v. Chr.[6]:

5 (F/100-AKR07-FK772+804+998 / V4720). Attischer Reliefbecher aus feinem Ton (7.5YR 7/4) mit glänzendem, schwarzem Glanzton. Dm. des Medaillon: 3.5cm. S. z. B. Rotroff 1982, 57, Nr. 110, Taf. 19 (Becher der *M Monogram Class*, ca. 175–150 v. Chr.).

6 (F/100-AKR07-FK884+885+996 / V4721). Attischer Reliefbecher aus feinem Ton (5YR 6/6) mit glänzendem, schwarzem Glanzton. Dm. 14cm. S. Rotroff 1982, 70–71, Nr. 216, Taf. 43 und 82 (Becher des *Workshop A*, ca. 225–175 v. Chr.): diese zwei Becher könnten aus der gleichen Matrize hergestellt sein.

Die attischen Reliefbecher unseres Fundkontextes lassen sich nach den Parallelen der Athener Agora immer vor der Mitte des 2. Jhs. v. Chr. datieren. Man trifft die bekannten Werkstätten Athens dieser Zeit, wie die Werkstatt von Bion, die ,*M Monogram Class*' oder die ,*Workshop A*'.

5 Rotroff 1982, 18.
6 Rotroff 1982, 19.

*Homerischer Reliefbecher (**Abb.** 7)*

7 (F/100-AKR07-FK766+769+804+885 / V4722). Homerischer Reliefbecher aus feinem, leicht glimmerhaltigem Ton (10B–5PB 6/1) mit einigen weissen mineralischen Einschlüssen und hellgrauem, mattem Glanzton. Dm. 12.5cm.

Ein Reliefbecher aus grauem Ton weist um das Medaillon Verzierungen auf, die man auf mehreren homerischen Bechern findet[7]. Auf dem Fries ist eine narrative Szene zu sehen: man erkennt eine Tür, mehrere bewaffnete männliche und drapierte weibliche Figuren, mit wahrscheinlich einer bewaffneten Athena. Keine Inschrift erlaubt uns, diese mythologische Szene sicher zu bestimmen. Mehrere Figuren gleichen jedoch jenen auf zwei veröffentlichten homerischen Bechern mit Szenen des thebanischen Zyklus (Kampf des Eteokles und Polyneikes)[8] oder des trojanischen Zyklus (Opferung der Iphigenia in Aulis)[9].

Nach U. Sinn sind die homerischen Becher Produkte aus Makedonien oder Thessalien[10]: die homerischen Becher, die im südlichen Griechenland in Chalkis, Theben, im Piräus, in Korinth oder in der Elis gefunden wurden, seien materielle Zeugnisse der Präsenz von makedonischen Garnisonen in diesen Städten[11]. Eretria wurde von den Makedonern zwischen 268/7 und 198 v. Chr. besetzt[12], so dass man annehmen könnte, die homerischen Becher aus unserem Fundkontext stünden mit den Makedonen in Verbindung. Die These von U. Sinn wurde aber in Frage gestellt[13], auch in Eretria: zwei homerische Becher, die aus einem Brunnen des Apollon-Heiligtums stammen, lassen sich nach ihrem Fundkontext ins zweite Viertel des 2. Jhs. v. Chr. datieren, das heisst nach dem Ende der makedonischen Besetzung der Stadt[14]. Diese Reliefbecher sehen dem Becher Nr. 7 nicht ähnlich, so dass es sich um lokale oder regionale Produkte handeln könnte. Der homerische Becher Nr. 7, mit seinem grauen Ton und Glanzton und mit seinen Verzierungen um das Medaillon, gehört aber bestimmt zur Gruppe der grauen homerischen

7 Mindestens sechs homerische Becher des Corpus von U. Sinn tragen genau die gleichen Verzierungen um das Medaillon: Sinn 1979, Nr. MB3 (=Hausmann 1959, Nr. HB7), MB8 (=HB6), MB48 (=HB3a), MB51 (=HB23), MB64/65 (=HB8) und MB130. Diese Verzierungen treten auch getrennt auf mehreren Bechern aus Makedonien oder Thessalien auf. Ein homerischer Becher in Eretria hat die gleiche Verzierung wie Nr. 7 (Metzger 1987, 40–41 und 50, Nr. 140; Metzger 1984–1985, Taf. 4, Nr. 9).
8 Sinn 1979, 108, Nr. MB48, Taf. 18–20 (=Hausmann 1959, 52, Nr. HB3a, Taf. 11).
9 Sinn 1979, 109–110, Nr. MB52, Taf. 1 und 22–23 (=Hausmann 1959, 53, Nr. HB11, Taf. 23–24).
10 Sinn 1979, 27–30.
11 Sinn 1979, 31–36.
12 Am Anfang des chremonideischen Krieges wurde die Stadt Eretria durch Antigonos Gonatas erobert (zur Datierung dieses Ereignisses siehe Knoepfler 1993) und eine makedonische Garnison auf der Akropolis eingesetzt, die dort bis zu der Befreiung Eretrias durch die Römer unter der Leitung von L. Quinctius Flamininus im Jahr 198 v. Chr. existierte.
13 So z. B. der homerische Becher aus dem Piräus, der im Jahre 229/8 v. Chr. von der makedonischen Garnison befreit wurde, das heisst vor der Erfindung der Reliefbecher durch die athenischen Töpfer (Siehe Rotroff 1986).
14 Schmid 2006, 19 und 33–36, Nr. A2 und A3, Abb. 8–16 S. 112–115.

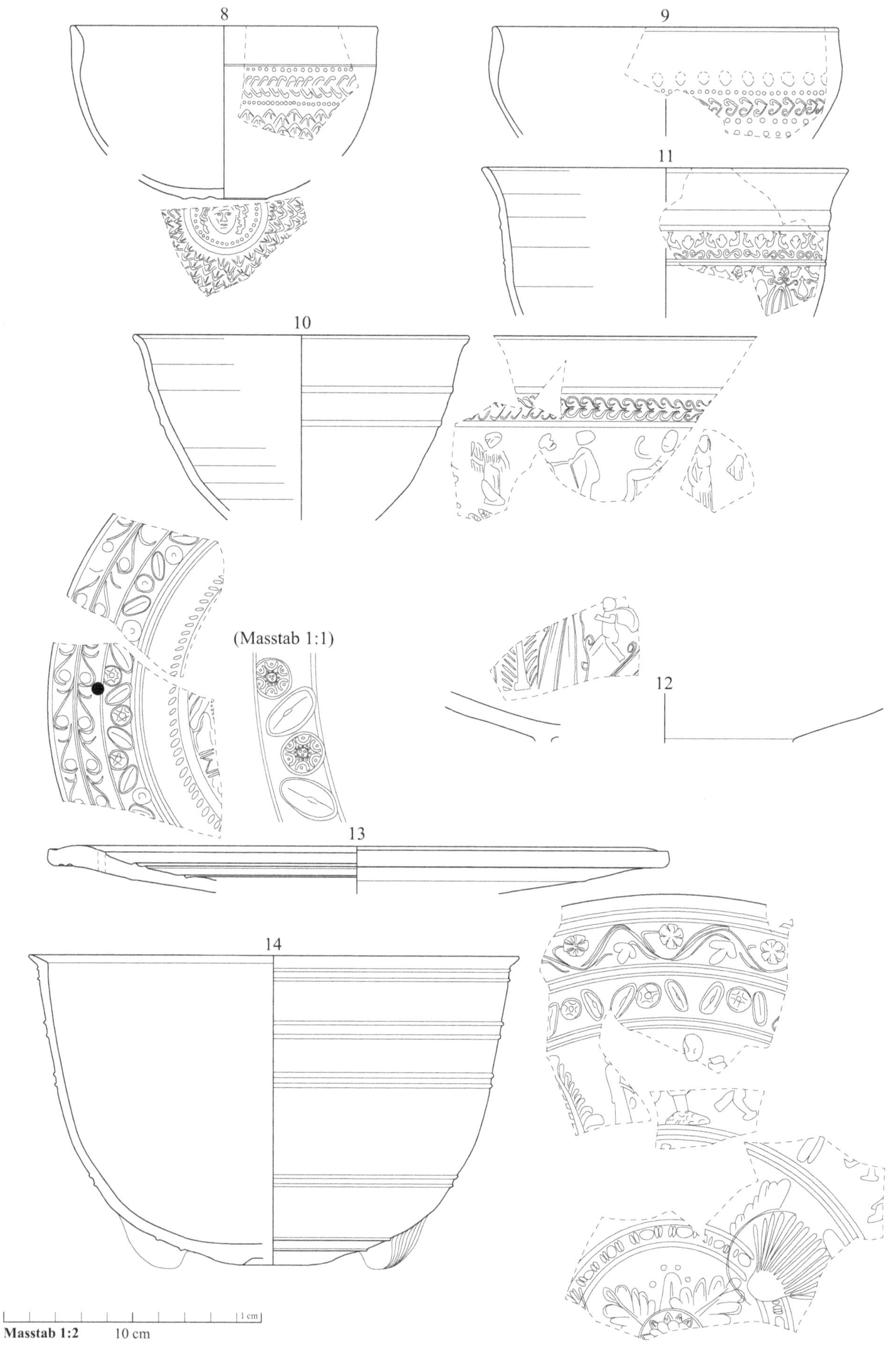

Abb. 8-9. Ionische Reliefbecher - **Abb. 10.** Korinthischer Reliefbecher - **Abb. 11.** Lokal hergestellter Reliefbecher - **Abb. 12-13.** Reliefteller - **Abb. 14.** Reliefbecher (G. Ackermann)

Becher aus Nordgriechenland, deren Herstellung sich gegen das Ende des 3. Jhs. und ins erste Drittel des 2 Jhs. v. Chr. datieren lässt.

*Ionische Reliefbecher (**Abb. 8–9**)*

Aus demselben Kontext des Apollon-Heiligtums stammen kurz vor der Mitte des 2. Jhs. v. Chr. die ersten Importe von ionischen Bechern in Eretria[15]. Nur zwei Reliefbecher unseres Fundkontextes haben das typische Profil der ionischen Becher und einen feinen glimmerhaltigen Ton:

8 (F/100-AKR07-FK765+766+767+804+835+891+994 / V4723). Reliefbecher mit ionischem Profil, aus feinem, glimmerhaltigen Ton, mit einigen weissen mineralischen Einschlüssen (7.5YR 6/6) und rotbraunem, mattem Glanzton. Dm. 12cm. Dm. des Medaillons ca. 3.2cm. Höhe ca. 6.6cm.

9 (F/100-AKR07-FK884 / V4724). Reliefbecher mit ionischem Profil, aus feinem, glimmerhaltigem Ton, mit einigen weissen mineralischen Einschlüssen (7.5YR 6/6) und braunschwarzem, mattem Glanzton. Dm. 13cm.

Die Suche nach Parallelen für ihre Verzierungen in den Keramikpublikationen von Ephesos, Delos, usw. erweist sich als erfolglos, so dass man am ionischen Ursprung dieser zwei Reliefbecher zweifeln kann[16]. Es könnte sich um lokale Nachahmungen von ionischen Produkten handeln, was I. R. Metzger schon für andere Reliefbecher mit ionischem Profil aus dem Westquartier von Eretria vorgeschlagen hat[17].

*Ein Reliefbecher aus Korinth (**Abb. 10**)*

10 (F/100-AKR07-FK804+885+893/V4725). Korinthischer Reliefbecher aus feinem Ton (7.5YR 6/6) und orangem, mattem Glanzton. Dm. 13cm. S. z. B. in Korinth: Edwards 1975, 168, Nr. 810, Taf. 37 und 69 = Siebert 1978, 74–75, Nr. Co.1, Taf. 44–45; in Kenchreai: Adamsheck 1979, 16, Nr. Gr. 36, Taf. 3; in Perachora: Cook 1962, 365–366, Nr. 3918–3919, Taf. 152.

Parallelen zum Becher Nr. 10 stammen aus der Umgebung von Korinth. Alle Vergleichsstücke, wie eine korinthische Parallele von Athen[18], lassen sich in die erste Hälfte des 2. Jhs. v. Chr. datieren.

*Lokal hergestellte Reliefbecher (**Abb. 11**)*

Ungefähr 40 Prozent der Reliefbecher können als Importe bestimmt werden. Der Rest, ohne Parallelen ausserhalb Eretrias, ist als ‚lokal' einzustufen und wird hier nicht vorgestellt, ausser einem Becher, der typische athenische Verzierungen trägt (Spiralen mit Palmetten und Delphinen)[19], der aber keine Charakteristika der attischen Becher im Profil, Ton und Glanzton aufweist. Diese Scherben zeigen den Einfluss der attischen Werkstätten auf die Töpfer Eretrias, die schnell Nachahmungen von attischen Bechern hergestellt haben.

11 (F/100-AKR07-FK810+834 / V4726). Reliefbecher aus feinem Ton, mit einigen winzigen Einschlüssen (7.5YR 6/4) und schwarzem, mattem Glanzton. Dm. ca. 14cm.

Datierung des Kontextes und die importierte Reliefkeramik in Eretria

Unser Fundkontext hat 18 Scherben von Zungenbechern geliefert (d. h. weniger als zwei Prozent der gesamten Reliefkeramik), die gegen die Mitte des 2. Jhs. v. Chr. auftreten. Vier Füsse der 25 *Unguentaria* lassen sich in die zweite Hälfte des 2. Jhs. v. Chr. datieren und stammen aus der oberen Schicht unserer Schuttablagerung, die noch zwei Tellerscherben aus östlicher Sigillata A (ESA) geliefert hat. Ausser dieser Schicht mit späterer Keramik, lassen sich die meisten Scherben unseres Fundkontexts vor der Mitte des 2. Jhs. v. Chr. datieren, wie die importierten Reliefbecher, aber auch andere Tischgefässe beweisen[20]. Was die importierte Keramik betrifft, spielt Athen in der ersten Hälfte des 2. Jhs. v. Chr. eine bedeutende Rolle mit 16 Reliefbechern (ca. 30% des Corpus). Erstaunlicherweise stammen vermutlich nur fünf andere Vasen unseres Fundkontexts aus Athen[21]: die Eretrier haben wahrscheinlich von attischen Werkstätten meistens Innovationen wie Reliefkeramik bezogen und die lokalen Töpfer ahmten diese neuen Produkte dann nach, wie der Becher Nr. 11 beweist. Vor der Mitte des 2. Jhs. v. Chr. bleiben ionische Importe selten oder kommen gar nicht vor, wenn die Becher Nr. 8 und 9 als lokale Produkte einzustufen sind. Eretria scheint in dieser Periode mehr dem zentralen und nördlichen Griechenland zugewandt gewesen zu sein, wie die Gegenwart von mehreren attischen, einem homerischen und einem korinthischen Becher beweisen.

---

15 Schmid 2006, 20–21, 37 und 98, Nr. A8, A9 und A10, Abb. 29–32 S. 121–122.

16 Die geflochtenen Girlanden sind allerdings sehr selten auf ionischen Bechern und treten nach meiner Kenntnis nie mit Perlenlinien auf, so wie die Gorgonenköpfe im Medaillon, die auch sehr selten sind (ausser bei der Werkstatt der ‚Belles Méduses') und nie mit einer Perlenlinie umrahmt auftreten.

17 Metzger 1997, 37.

18 Rotroff 1982, 89, Nr. 382, Taf. 66 und 88.

19 Siehe den attischen Becher Nr. 6.

20 Eine Bronzemünze aus Eretria (Magistrat Biotos), die nach ca. 180 v. Chr. geprägt wurde, drei Amphorenstempel sowie Lampenfragmente bestätigen diese Chronologie. Ich bedanke mich bei Marguerite Spoerri Butcher (Warwick University), Marek Palaczyk (Universität Zürich) und Solange Gürtler (Universität Basel) für diese Hinweise.

21 Unter den wenigen Importen aus Athen zählt man eine Scherbe einer Tischamphora mit Westabhangverzierung und fünf Teller, darunter zwei kleine, die in Athen meistens aus *Pyrai* stammen (Rotroff 1997, Vol. I, 151). Diese attischen Gefässe gehören der Periode zwischen der Mitte des 3. und der Mitte des 2. Jhs. v. Chr. an und wurden in Eretria also wahrscheinlich zur gleichen Zeit wie die Reliefbecher verkauft.

Fundkontext	F100 S.28 (Schuttablagerung des Athenaheiligtums)		G300 (Zisterne der Akropolis)		E600 (Sullanische Schichten)
Datierung	**ca. 200–150 v. Chr.**		**ca. 150–50 v. Chr.**		**ca. 100–86 v. Chr.**
Panel	**NR: 400**	**NMI: 55**	**NR: 258**	**NMI: 79**	**NI: 163**
Athen	22,00%	29,09%	3,10%	2,53%	9,20%
Nordgriechenland	5,00%	5,45%	0,00%	0,00%	0,00%
Ionien (sicher)	0,00%	0,00%	5,04%	7,59%	3,68%
Ionien (?)	4,50%	3,64%	2,33%	0,00%	22,09%
Korinth (?)	3,50%	1,82%	0,00%	0,00%	6,13%
Eretria (?)	65,00%	60,00%	89,53%	89,88%	58,90%
Total	*100,00%*	*100,00%*	*100,00%*	*100,00%*	*100,00%*

Tab. 1. Herkunft der Reliefkeramik von drei Fundkontexten in Eretria

Unseren Fundkontext der mittleren hellenistischen Epoche auf der Akropolis kann man mit zwei anderen Kontexten späthellenistischer Zeit in Eretria vergleichen. In der unteren Stadt hat S. G. Schmid Keramik aus sullanischen Zerstörungsschichten vom Anfang des 1. Jhs. v. Chr. veröffentlicht[22]. Der Autor untersuchte zudem die Keramik aus der Zisterne der Akropolis (Mitte des 2. Jhs. – Mitte des 1. Jhs. v. Chr.)[23]. Man beobachtet in diesen späteren Kontexten zunächst die riesige Menge von Zungenbechern, die in unserem Kontext fast nicht auftreten. Die Reliefbecher mit schuppenförmig angeordneten Blättern werden im späten 2. und frühen 1. Jh. v. Chr. selten, wie auch die figürlichen Becher. Wenn man jetzt die Importe untersucht, bemerkt man eine starke Abnahme der attischen Importe nach der Mitte des 2. Jhs. v. Chr. und eine Zunahme der ionischen Becher, was als Indiz für die Datierung dienen kann (**Tab. 1**)[24].

Die Reliefteller

*Zwei Reliefteller (**Abb. 12–13**)*

12 (F/100-AKR07-FK891+994 / V4728). Reliefteller aus feinem, leicht glimmerhaltigem Ton (10YR 5/1), mit einigen weissen mineralischen Einschlüssen und blauschwarzem, mattem Glanzton. Dm. des Fusses 10cm.

13 (F/100-AKR07-FK885 / V4727). Reliefteller aus feinem, leicht glimmerhaltigem Ton (10YR 5/1), mit einigen weissen mineralischen Einschlüssen und grauschwarzem, mattem Glanzton. Dm. 24cm.

Unser Fundkontext der Akropolis liefert vier Scherben mit inneren Reliefverzierungen, die zu zwei verschiedenen Tellern gehören. Der Teller Nr. 13 trägt ein Loch, das zwei Interpretationen zulässt: es könnte sich um eine Reparatur aus Blei oder um ein Loch für das Aufhängen der Keramik, ähnlich wie bei einem *Pinax,* handeln. Die feine innere Reliefverzierung verunmöglicht es, diese Teller als Gebrauchskeramik zu interpretieren. Es handelt sich mit grösserer Wahrscheinlichkeit um dekorative Objekte, die als Opfergabe der Göttin Athena geweiht wurden. Im östlichen Mittelmeerraum bleiben die hellenistischen Teller mit innerer Reliefverzierung sehr selten[25]. Der Ton und der Glanzton dieser Teller sehen dem homerischen Becher Nr. 7 sehr ähnlich, so dass es sich um Importe aus Makedonien oder Thessalien handeln könnte. Unter anderem erkennt man auf dem Teller Nr. 13 eine Verzierung, die uns vielleicht eine Antwort über seine Herkunft gibt: es handelt sich um eine Serie von ovalen galatischen und runden makedonischen Schilden.

Makedonische Schilde sind charakterisiert durch eine runde Form und unterschiedliche Schildzeichen, die von gebogenen Linien mit Perlen und oft mit Sternen umgeben sind. K. Liampi zeigte die enge Verbindung zwischen diesem Typ von Bewaffnung und Makedonien, wo er als Wappen der makedonischen Heere und als ethnisches Erkennungszeichen für das makedonische Volk diente[26]. Die Feinde der Antigoniden greifen seit der Mitte des 3. Jhs. v. Chr. auf dieses makedonische Symbol als Siegesdenkmal zurück, so etwa bei den Römern nach der Schlacht von Pydna im Jahre 168 v. Chr.

22 Schmid 2004.
23 Siehe die Grabungsberichte: Friedemann 1993 und Friedemann 1996.
24 Mit dem Begriff NMI (‚nombre minimum d'individus') meinen wir die minimale Anzahl von Gefässen (mit Randscherben nach dem Kleben der Fragmenten gezählt) und NR (‚nombre de restes') die Anzahl von Scherben. Zu dieser Methode siehe Arcelin und Truffeau-Libre 1998. Mit dem Begriff NI (‚nombre d'individus') meinen wir die Anzahl von Gefässen (‚In the statistics [...] fragments belonging to the same bowl were counted as one entry. However, it can not be ruled that fragments belonging to the same spécimen were not always recognised and therefore counted separately' [Schmid 2004, 500, N. 18]).

25 Siehe Mitsopoulos-Leon 1996, Fig. 8 und 9, 187–188 und im Nationalmuseum von Athen (Ath. MN inv. 2139, aus Kreta).
26 Siehe Liampi 1998 für Beispiele.

Makedonische Schilde in Eretria und die makedonische Besatzung der Stadt

Wie ist dieses Symbol mit unterschiedlichen Bedeutungen auf einem Teller zu verstehen, der auf der Akropolis zum Vorschein kam? Haben die makedonische Schilde eine direkte Beziehung zu den Makedonen, weil die Antigoniden die Stadt Eretria während der zwei letzten Drittel des 3. Jhs. v. Chr. besetzen? Oder wurden sie als antimakedonisches Propagandamittel nach der Befreiung der Stadt im Jahre 198 v. Chr. benutzt?

Im Westen der Akropolis liegt ein makedonisches Grab: C. Huguenot interpretierte es als Gruft einer makedonischen Familie, die in der euböischen Stadt während der zwei letzten Drittel des 3. Jhs. v. Chr. lebte[27]. In der Grabkammer wurden unter anderem Miniaturschilde des makedonischen Typs aus Ton gefunden[28], die mit dem Teller Nr. 13 zu einer Serie von Gegenständen gehören könnten, die in Verbindung mit den in Eretria wohnenden Makedonen stehen. Nach einer Inschrift aus Rhamnous und dem Zeugnis des römischen Historikers Livius war auf der Akropolis von Eretria eine makedonische Garnison bis im Jahre 198 v. Chr. stationiert[29]. Sie musste den strategisch wichtigsten Platz der Stadt besetzen: auf dem Gipfel der Akropolis könnte also das Athena-Heiligtum der Garnison verbunden sein oder ganz zu ihr gehören[30]. Die makedonischen Soldaten und ihre Söldner nahmen wahrscheinlich in den zwei letzten Dritteln des 3. Jhs. am Kult der Athena als Beschützerin der Stadt teil. Der Reliefteller Nr. 13 mit seinen Schilden könnte also als Opfergabe der Makedonen für Athena interpretiert werden, und der homerische Becher Nr. 7 könnte als Zeugnis der makedonischen Gegenwart in Eretria dienen, wie U. Sinn es für andere Städte im zentralen und südlichen Griechenland vorgeschlagen hat.

Diese historische Interpretation ist mit einem Datierungsproblem konfrontiert: S. I. Rotroff hat in der Athener Agora eine lange Zeitspanne zwischen der Erfindung der Reliefbecher im letzten Viertel des 3. Jhs. v. Chr. und ihrem Auftreten in athenischen geschlossenen Kontexten um 180 v. Chr. beobachtet[31]. Wenn man den gleichen Zeitraum für die Reliefkeramik (Becher und Teller) unseres Fundkontexts postuliert, können der homerische Becher Nr. 7 und der Reliefteller Nr. 13 nicht mehr als Zeugnisse der makedonischen Garnison gelten, da die Stadt Eretria schon im Jahre 198 v. Chr. befreit wurde. Die makedonischen Schilde könnten dann als antimakedonisches Symbol interpretiert werden und der Becher Nr. 7 wäre ein einfaches Zeichen von Handelsbeziehungen zwischen Euböa und Makedonien oder Thessalien am Anfang des 2. Jhs. v. Chr.[32].

Zwei kürzliche Entdeckungen im Museum von Eretria erlauben mir, diese Frage, die ich am *Workshop* in Köln offen gelassen hatte, wieder aufzunehmen: es handelt sich erstens um eine Serie von Lampen des 2. Jhs. v. Chr., die mit einem makedonischen Schild in Relief verziert sind[33], und zweitens um einen Reliefbecher (**Abb. 14**), der unter anderem die gleichen Friese von ovalen galatischen und runden makedonischen Schilden trägt.

14 (G/300-FK035 / V4729). Reliefbecher aus feinem, leicht glimmerhaltigem Ton (10GY 5/1 – N 6/1), mit einigen weissen mineralischen Einschlüssen und hellgrauem, mattem Glanzton. Dm. 19cm. Höhe 11.8cm.

Dieser grosse Becher stammt aus der Zisterne der Akropolis die zwischen dem Ende des 3. Jhs. und dem Anfang des 2. Jhs. v. Chr. gebaut wurde. Die grosse Mehrheit der gefundenen Keramik, die der Unterzeichnete untersucht, lässt sich von der Mitte des 2. Jhs. bis zur Mitte des 1. Jhs. v. Chr. datieren, so dass der Reliefbecher Nr. 14 klar mehrere Jahrzehnte nach 198 hergestellt wurde. Auf diesen beiden Gefässen des späten Hellenismus ist klar, dass die Schilde des makedonischen Typs als Siegesdenkmal oder als antimakedonisches Symbol zu interpretieren sind, wenn nicht nur als einfaches Ornament. Was der Ursprung betrifft, zeugen die Reliefteller Nr. 12 und 13, die wahrscheinlich nach Ton und Glanzton aus Makedonien oder Thessalien stammen, und der homerische Becher Nr. 7 von Wirtschaftsbeziehungen zwischen Nordgriechenland und der befreiten Stadt Eretria.

Guy Ackermann
Institut d'archéologie et des sciences de l'Antiquité (IASA)
Université de Lausanne
Quartier UNIL-Dorigny, bâtiment Anthropole 4024
CH-1015 Lausanne
guy.ackermann@unil.ch

[27] Huguenot 2008, Vol. I, 248–251. Siehe Vol. I, 240–248 über die archäologischen und historischen Zeugnisse der makedonischen Gegenwart in Eretria.

[28] Huguenot 2008, Vol. I, 167–169; Vol. II, 15, Nr. 46–49, Taf. 29 Nr. 5, 79 Nr. 1.

[29] Pouilloux 1954, Nr. 15, 129–132, Linie 17–18; Livius, XXXII, 16, 10–17. Siehe auch Knoepfler 2001, 271 und 296 Fussnote 179 und Huguenot 2008, Vol. I, 243–244.

[30] Im Norden des Heiligtums wurde ein Schnitt am nördlichen Turm der Akropolis angelegt, der Bauwerke in Verbindung mit Soldatenbarackenlager zutage gebracht hat (siehe den Grabungsbericht: Fachard 2007). Im Athena-Heiligtum wurde auch eine Situla aus Ton gefunden, eine Keramikform die man fast ausschliesslich in Makedonien in Gräbern findet (kommende Veröffentlichung in Zusammenarbeit mit S. Huber).

[31] Rotroff 2006.

[32] Es bleibt aber nicht unmöglich, dass der Übergang zwischen der Erfindung der Reliefbecher und dem Auftreten der Reliefkeramik in archäologischen Schichten auf der Akropolis von Eretria schneller ging als in der Athener Agora, da die Makedonier sicher sehr schnell die Stadt verlassen mussten.

[33] Siehe z. B. Metzger 1993, 137, Nr. 179, Abb. 273 S. 138. Ich danke Solange Gürtler für diesen Hinweis.

Bibliographie

Adamsheck, B. 1979. *Kenchreai, Eastern Port of Corinth IV. The Pottery*. Leiden, E. J. Brill.

Arcelin, P. und Truffeau-Libre, M. (Hrsg.) 1998. *La quantification des céramiques. Conditions et protocole.* Actes de la table ronde du Centre archéologique européen du Mont Beuvray (Glux-en-Glenne, 7–9 avril 1998). Glux-en-Glenne, Centre archéologique européen.

Cook, J. M. 1962. Hellenistic and Roman Wares. In T. J. Dunbabin (Hrsg.), *Perachora II*, 364–367. Oxford, Clarendon Press.

Edwards, G. R. 1975. *Corinthian Hellenistic Pottery*. Corinth VII, Part III. Cambridge, Harvard University Press.

Fachard, S. 2007. Les fortifications dans le secteur de la tour Nord. *Antike Kunst* 50, 129–134.

Friedemann, P. 1993. Un établissement hydraulique sur le flanc Est de l'acropole d'Erétrie. *Antike Kunst* 36, 132–136.

Friedemann, P. 1994. De la «carrière» au sanctuaire: investigations archéologiques sur l'acropole d'Erétrie. *Antike Kunst* 37, 93–99.

Friedemann, P. 1995. Nouvelles données sur la préhistoire d'Erétrie: l'apport des investigations 1994 sur l'acropole. *Antike Kunst* 38, 108–119.

Friedemann, P. 1996. L'établissement hydraulique sur le flanc Est de l'acropole: investigations 1995. *Antike Kunst* 39, 112–116.

Hausmann, H. 1959. *Hellenistische Reliefbecher aus attischen und böotischen Werkstätten*. Stuttgart, W. Kohlhammer.

Huber, S. 2007. Un mystère résolu: Athéna sur l'acropole d'Erétrie. *Antike Kunst* 50, 119–129.

Huber, S. 2008. Fouilles dans le sanctuaire d'Athéna sur l'acropole d'Erétrie. *Antike Kunst* 51, 148–153.

Huguenot, C. 2008. *La tombe aux Erotes et la tombe d'Amarynthos*. Eretria. Fouilles et recherches XIX. Gollion, Infolio.

Knoepfler, D. 1993. Les *Kryptoi* du stratège Epicharès à Rhamnonte et le début de la guerre de Chrémonidès. *Bulletin de Correspondance Hellénique* 117, 338–340.

Knoepfler, D. 2001. *Décrets érétriens de proxénie et de citoyenneté.* Eretria. Fouilles et recherches XI. Lausanne, Payot.

Liampi, K. 1998. *Der makedonische Schild.* Bonn, R. Habelt.

Metzger, I. R. 1969. *Die hellenistische Keramik in Eretria.* Eretria. Fouilles et recherches II. Bern, Francke.

Metzger, I. R. 1984–1985. Die Keramik von Eretria. *Αρχείον Ευβοϊκον Μελετών* 26, 221–252.

Metzger, I. R. 1987. Hellenistische Reliefkeramik in Eretria. *Ανθρωπολογικά και αρχαιολογικά Χρονικά* 2, 35–62.

Metzger, I. R. 1993. Keramik und Kleinfunde, in P. Ducrey, I. R. Metzger und K. Reber, *Le Quartier de la Maison aux mosaïques.* Eretria. Fouilles et recherches VIII, 97–143. Lausanne, Payot.

Metzger, I. R. 1997. Die Keramik aus dem Raum B von Gebäude I in Eretria. In L. Kypraiou (Hrsg.), *Δ΄ Επιστημονική Συνάντηση για την Ελληνιστική Κεραμική*. Μυτιλήνη 1994, 32–40. Athens, Ypourgeio Politismou.

Mitsopoulos-Leon, V. 1996. Krateriskoi und ein Teller mit Reliefdekor: eine Gefässgruppe aus Lousoi. *Jahreshefte des Österreichischen Archäologischen Instituts* 65, 185–206.

Müller, S. 1996. Fouilles de l'acropole d'Erétrie 1995. *Antike Kunst* 39, 107–111.

Pouilloux, J. 1954. *La forteresse de Rhamnonte.* Paris, De Boccard.

Rotroff, S. I. 1982. *Hellenistic Pottery. Athenian and Imported Moldmade Bowls.* The Athenian Agora XII. Princeton, NJ., American School of Classical Studies at Athens.

Rotroff, S. I. 1986. Bericht über Sinn 1979. *Gnomon* 58, 472–475.

Rotroff, S. I. 1997. *Hellenistic Pottery: Athenian and Imported Wheelmade Table Ware and Related Material.* The Athenian Agora XXIX. Princeton, NJ., American School of Classical Studies.

Rotroff, S. I. 2006. The Introduction of the Moldmade Bowl Revesited: Tracking a Hellenistic Innovation. *Hesperia* 75, 357–378.

Schmid, S. G. 2004. Some Reflections on Recently Found Mouldmade and Relief Decorated Pottery from Eretria. In *ΣΤ' Επιστημονική Συνάντηση για την ελληνιστική κεραμική.* Βόλος 2000, 495–504. Athens, TAP.

Schmid, S. G. 2006. *Boire pour Apollon. Céramique hellénistique et banquets dans le sanctuaire d'Apollon Daphnéphoros.* Eretria. Fouilles et recherches XVI. Gollion, Infolio.

Siebert, G. 1978. *Recherches sur les ateliers de bols à reliefs du Péloponnèse à l'époque hellénistique.* Athènes, Ecole française d'Athènes.

Sinn, U. 1979. *Die homerischen Becher: Hellenistische Reliefkeramik aus Makedonien.* Berlin, Gebr. Mann.

Western Greece and West Slope pottery: A Reversible Lid from Chalkis Aitolias

Elizabeth Bollen

Abstract

The production of glazed and over-painted decoration, commonly referred to as 'West Slope ware' occurred across the Eastern Mediterranean. Given the relative simplicity of the production techniques, local productions were able to largely fulfil local demand. There was no one dominant city production and trade in wheel-made pottery was limited. This situation allowed for potter's to reflect regional tastes and prepare vessels for regional practices. Through the pottery regional preferences and inter-regional connections can be revealed.

By focussing on a reversible lid with West Slope decoration, recovered during the Danish-Greek excavations at Chalkis Aitolias, some characteristics of and connections between different regions of the Greek world in the 3rd and 2nd centuries BC will be revealed. The productions in Aitolia share characteristics with their regional neighbours: with the lid and its decoration drawing parallels in Northern and Central Greece, Epiros, the Ionian Islands and the northern Peloponnese[1].

Keywords: West Slope Ware, Aitolia, Chalkis Aitolias, Reversible lid, Lekanis, Pyxis

Introduction

The site of Chalkis Aitolias is nestled between the two impressive mountains, Kolkova and Varassova on the northern coast line of the western reaches of the Corinthian Gulf. The Greek-Danish excavations 1995–2000, uncovered a series of eight rooms, strung below the Archaic/Classical terrace wall that surrounds the Acropolis during the in the June-July seasons of 1997, 1998, 1999 and 2000 and in an additional October season in 2000. The rooms provide evidence of the Hellenistic occupation of the site. The coins recovered from the excavations suggest that the site was abandoned in the early 2nd century BC. Well-preserved examples of Hellenistic fine, plain, cooking and coarse wares, were preserved beneath tile smashes in a number of the rooms.

The Reversible Lid from Chalkis Aitolias

Arguably the most impressive West Slope vessel found in the Greek-Danish excavations at Chalkis Aitolias is a Reversible Lid **(Figs. 1, 2 and 3)** which was recovered in numerous fragments from inside one of the rooms in section III[2]. An examination of this piece in light of other West Slope productions, will indicate the ties of this small trading outpost with its region and the wider traditions of the Hellenistic world.

Reversible lids have been found in Hellenistic graves where they cover a lekanis (continuing the tradition of the 4th century BC when they often held figured decoration in Athens and in South Italian productions). The two resting surfaces (rim and knob) allow the shape to have dual purpose. It can function as a lid, when it stands on the rim, or as a bowl, or palette, with broad relatively flat wall, when it rests on the knob. The decoration, however, is only visible when it functions as a lid. When coupled with a lekanis the function of the shape clearly overlaps with the pyxis[3]. The lekanis provides a storage area for jewelry or cosmetics and the lid provides a decorative cover. However, some lids were produced as stand alone items, probably functioning in a toiletry context as a palate for cosmetics.

The Chalkis Aitolias lid has a broad, sloping wall, offset from the sharp junction with the inclined rim by a groove. The stem of the knob is concave. The knob has a squared outer profile and a resting surface moulded by a deep groove on its upper face.

The decorative zones on the Chalkis lid are defined by grooves on the wall of the lid. The outer zone is decorated with concentric rectangles and checkerboard, the lines of both are incised. Alternate squares of the checkerboard

1 I would like to thank Søren Dietz and Lazaros Kolonas for allowing me to study the ceramic material of Chalkis Aitolias, and for support during my research. The project at Chalkis Aitolias ran under the auspices of the Danish Institute at Athens and the 6th Ephorate at Patras, with funding from the Counsul General Enbom's Foundation. My thanks to the members of the Greek-Danish team. Drawing by the author, inked by Amanda Dusting. Photographs by Ingrid Sofianou.

2 Houby-Nielsen *et al.* 2000, 245, fig. 32; see Bollen forthcoming, no. 323 (Chalkis bag no. 679; F97–2019, T6NA/5b).

3 In Athens, the decoration of the two shapes indicates a close relationship: Rotroff 1997, 192. Interestingly in Northern Greece, where the pyxis is a common find in graves, there are few published reversible lids.

Fig. 1. Reversible Lid, no. 679, view from top (Photo I. Sofianou)

display the remains of paint. The next zone carries an egg and dart pattern. Incised eggs are filled with fugitive painted dots. The darts are painted in the shape of tripartite leaves. The eggs appear suspended from a groove that boarders the decorative zone. Four light, glazed grooves are set up the wall from the egg and dart pattern. The upper wall is undecorated. Directly below the junction with the knob is another deep groove shape and suspended from this is a spearhead necklace with incised arcing chain and painted pendants. Within the knob a star flower is painted.

It is by no means certain that this piece was made at Chalkis Aitolias. The clay is quite similar to what is understood to be the local fabric, but the standard of decoration is beyond the norm.

Reversible lids with moulded knobs

The moulded knob that is set on a stem differentiates the lid from the majority of West Slope reversible lids. This version of the lid with moulded and stemmed knob, often identified as a lekanis lid, is typical of the West Slope production of Central Greece[4].

In Thessaly at Lamia, a reversible lid is preserved with its partner lekanis body[5]. The knob is a tall and moulded ring foot, with a conical interior depression (unlike the solid knob from Chalkis). The vertical rim is inclined (as at Chalkis). The mid-wall is decorated with an incised ivy wreath that crosses over double incised grooves. A similar 3rd century BC example, with partnering lekanis, was recovered from a grave at Phthiotic Thebes. Again the knob is hollow and sits on a short stem. The rim is inclined and the mid wall carries an undulating wreath of elongated leaves[6]. A lid with moulded high foot/knob was excavated at Naxos[7], and 3rd century BC examples from Ephesos also have a high, hollow foot[8].

There is an example of this lekanis-type knob from Athens dated 270–215 BC. Here lekanis lids are identified with much smaller diameter than the more numerous reversible lids and while some have a ring foot/knob, one example has a low solid stem and knob with scraped groove[9]. The wall is decorated with bunches of grapes that alternate with torches and double cornucopia.

An example from Pella is described as a 'lekanis lid' and allows for the possibility that the moulded knob variety was also produced in Northern Greece, however, the published photograph does not make this clear[10]. It is decorated with an ivy wreath.

The closest parallel for the Chalkis Aitolias lid comes from the neighbouring Aitolian site of Kallipolis[11]. On this lid, dated to the first half of the 2nd century BC, the knob is solid and stemmed. The outer face of the knob is moulded (unlike the Chalkis example). The interior of the knob is concave, rising to a central point. The walls of the lid are slightly convex and the junction with the rim is smooth and rounded. The decoration occurs in bands on the body, including a wavy dot garland and a band of rays. The zones are separated by a thick white band and clay-ground grooves. Overall the Chalkis lid has a more angular profile than the lid from Kallipolis.

Reversible lids with a low ring foot/knob

A reversible lid with a low ring foot/knob is more widely produced[12]. This is the typical form of the lid at Athens. The 3rd century BC form has a fairly flat wall and inclined or vertical rim and the knob is low and broad. In the late 2nd and 1st century BC the walls of the lid become much higher and the lid is dome-like, sometimes with a concave, bell-shaped profile. The shape is one of the few to be decorated after the Sullan sack, and the decoration on these examples links them closely to the worship of Isis[13]. In the Peloponnese, a lid and lekanis were excavated at Argos[14]. But here the lid has a simple ring foot knob

4 The form is also found in Campanian pottery: Morel 1981, nos. 4711a.1 and 4713a.1.

5 Lamia: Papakonstantinou 1997, 52 pl. 36a, c.

6 Adrimi-Sismani 2000, 143 fig. 9.

7 Zafeiropoulou and Kolia 1997, 285 pl. 208a.

8 Mitsopoulos-Leon 1991, 54 B142 pl. 62; 54 B143 pl. 61.

9 Rotroff 1997, 370 no. 1308 fig. 82 pl. 100 (Rotroff 1991, 78 no. 41 pl. 24).

10 Touratsoglou 1996, 158–159 no. 196 (Ypourgeio Politismou 1988 326, no. 286).

11 Baziotopoulou-Valavani 1994, 53 pl. 24a.

12 Of course there are additional examples of reversible lids at other productions, but in some only the rim and wall are preserved so they cannot be assigned to either group.

13 Rotroff 1997, 192 and 194. There is a series of reversible lids in the late production of Athens that hold unusual motifs of the Isis knot, sistrum, and scroll. Both the imagery and the find spot suggest that these vessels were used in the worship of Isis.

14 Argos: Bruneau 1970, 482 no. 81.4 figs. 125, 126.

Fig. 2. Reversible Lid, no. 679, profile (Photo I. Sofianou)

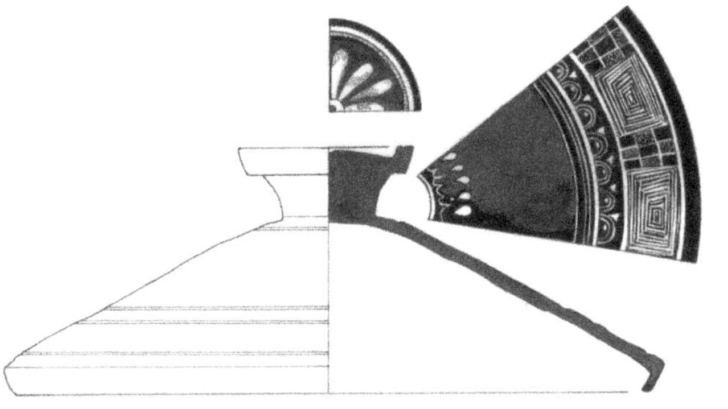

Fig. 3. Reversible Lid, no. 679 (Drawing E. Bollen and A. Dusting)

(indicating that the knob itself is not enough to distinguish a lekanis lid from an unpartnered reversible lid). It has a broad flat wall that is decorated with an elongated leaves motif set between grooves.

At Ephesos, in addition to those mentioned above, an example with a low ring foot is dated to the 3rd century BC[15]. The shape is also recorded in the late 2nd century BC but no knob profiles are preserved[16]. At Rhodes examples are of the 2nd century BC and, when preserved have a low ring foot[17].

At Pergamon the reversible lid is identified in deposits dating after the mid 2nd century BC, well after the Chalkis Aitolias piece[18]. The form has a relatively tall vertical rim, convex or straight wall and the low, broad knob can have a grooved resting surface, a moulded outer profile and often a clay-ground groove on its inner surface. The lids are decorated in incised post-West Slope decoration. Related examples are identified at Beşik Tepe and at Miletus[19].

The decoration of reversible lids

The Chalkis Aitolias lid carries the following motifs: checkerboard, concentric rectangles, egg and dart (with tripartite leaves) and a star flower. Other examples of the reversible lid at Chalkis Aitolias are fragmentary and retain only the angular junction of rim and wall and the exterior lid to identify them as reversible lids. One fragment is decorated with a lattice motif and ivy wreath[20], the other with an egg and dart pattern[21].

The decoration on the Chalkis piece is not typical. I have found no other examples of reversible lids with checkerboard and only one other example with concentric rectangles, an Athenian example dated 200–175 BC[22]. Egg and dart is more common, found on a reversible lid fragment from Eretria[23], three late 2nd century examples from Asia Minor[24], and on a lid from Lamia[25]. Star flowers only appear in the knobs of lids from Athens[26] and from Central Greece – Thebes, Lamia and Kallipolis[27]. The Chalkis Aitolias fragment with lattice motif also proves an unusual combination of shape and motif with no identified parallel.

The reversible lid functioned alongside the pyxis and overlapped in function both in the living world and as a grave gift. The geometric motifs of the concentric rectangles, checkerboard and lattice that decorate the reversible lids of Chalkis Aitolias regularly decorate

15 Mitsopoulos-Leon 1991, 54 B144 pl. 62.
16 Mitsopoulos-Leon 1991, 51 B100 pl. 49; 54 B140 pl. 62; 54 B148 pl. 63.
17 Rhodes: Patsiada 1989, 146 no. 12 fig. 5 pl. 50e; 196 no. 192 pl. 77d.
18 Pergamon (where the examples are dated from the end of the 2nd century to the middle of the 1st century BC and have a ring foot often with a moulded profile): Behr 1988, 161 no. 74 fig. 17; 162 nos. 78 and 79 fig. 18; 164 nos. 87 and 88 fig. 20; 167 nos. 89 and 90 fig. 20; Pinkwart and Stammnitz 1984, 126 K 38 pls. 24, 36; Uncertain profile Schäfer 1968, 60 D20 pl. 12.
19 Beşik Tepe, Troad: Hübner 1984, 180 fig. 6; Miletus: Pfrommer 1985, 57 no. 45 fig. 45.
20 Bollen forthcoming, no. 8 (Chalkis, Bag no. 2000: 1 O26BD/3).
21 Bollen forthcoming, no. 324 (Chalkis, Bag no. 1406: 3 T6NA/5b).
22 Rotroff 1997, 366, no. 1272 fig. 78 pl. 94.
23 Metzger 1998, 191 no. 254 (where no full profiles were preserved –or clearly published – to allow discussion of shape).
24 Ephesos: Mitsopoulos-Leon 1991, 54 B140 pl. 62; Pergamon: Behr 1988, 162 no. 75 fig. 17; 164 no. 85 fig. 19.
25 Papakonstantinou-Katsouni 1990, 61 pl. 65a (the photograph does not make it clear if this lid is from a reversible lid or pyxis).
26 Rotroff 1997, 365–368, nos. 1267–1270, 1273, 1275, 1276, 1278, 1279, 1280, 1283–1291, figs. 78–80, pls. 94–98; 368–370, nos. 1292, 1295, 1300, 1305, 1306 figs. 81–82, pls. 99–100; Vogeikoff-Brogan 2000, 314 nos. 50, 54, 55 figs. 18–19; Vogeikoff 1993, 149 D30; 150 D37; Thompson 1934, 402 E63 fig. 90.
27 Thebes: Heimberg 1982, 131 no. 151 pls. 10, 50:20; Lamia: Papakonstantinou-Katsouni 1990, 61 pl. 65a; Kallipolis: Baziotopoulou-Valavani 1994, 53 pl. 24a.

pyxides produced in Northern and Central Greece, Epiros, the Ionian islands and in the northern Peloponnese[28]. The form of pyxides produced across these regions have been found to show a similar pattern of connection[29]. The person who decorated the Chalkis lid, was working within the decorative traditions of North-Western Greece.

Conclusion

The reversible lid from Chalkis Aitolias displays ties to other productions of West Slope pottery. Its stemmed knob set it apart from many reversible lids decorated with West Slope ware which have low ring foot/knobs. The geometric motifs of concentric rectangles and checkerboard that decorate the Chalkis piece are quite unusual for the shape. Parallels can be found with occasional pieces in Athens, at Aegean and Asia Minor sites. However, there is stronger evidence, in its shape and choice of decoration, to tie the Chalkis reversible lid to the productions of Central Greece. More broadly the lid highlights connections between the productions of Northern Greece, Epiros, the Ionian islands and the northern Peloponnese.

Elizabeth Bollen
Nicholson Museum
A14 University of Sydney
AU-NSW 2006
elizabeth.bollen@sydney.edu.au

Bibliography

Agallopoulou, P. 1977. Λεύκας Σπασμένη Βρύση Καρυωτών. *Αρχαιολογικόν Δελτίον* 27, 486–492.

Adrimi-Sismani, B. 2000. Ταφικά σύνολα από το Δυτικό νεκροταφείο των Φθιωτίδων Θηβών. In L. Kypraiou (ed.), *Ελληνιστική Κεραμική από τη Θεσσαλία*, 133–146. Athens, Greek Ministry of Culture.

Anderson-Stojanović, V. R. 1997. A Third Century B.C. Deposit from the South Slope Cistern in the Rachi Settlement at Isthmia. In *Δ' Επιστημονική Συνάντηση για την ελληνιστική κεραμική*. Μυτιλήνη 1994, 13–19. Athens, Ypourgeio Politismou.

Anderson-Stojanović, V. R. 2000. Corinthian West Slope Pottery from Isthmia, in *Ε' Επιστημονική Συνάντηση για την ελληνιστική κεραμική*. Χανιά 1997, 381–385. Athens, TAP.

Andreou, I. 1994. Σύνολα ελληνιστικής κεραμικής από τα νεκροταφεία της αρχαίας Λευκάδος. In *Γ' Επιστημονική Συνάντηση για την ελληνιστική κεραμική*. Θεσσαλονίκη 1991, 196–204. Athens, Archetai.

Baur, P. V. C. 1922. *Catalogue of the Rebecca Darlington Stoddard Collection of Greek and Italian Vases in Yale University*. New Haven, Yale University Press.

Baziotopoulou-Valavani, E. 1994. Ἀπο τήν ελληνιστική κεραμική της αιτωλικής Καλλιπόλεως. In *Γ' Επιστημονική Συνάντηση για την ελληνιστική κεραμική*. Θεσσαλονίκη 1991, 46–55. Athens, Archetai.

Behr, D. 1988. Neue Ergebnisse zur pergamenischen Westabhangkeramik. *Istanbuler Mitteilungen* 38, 97–178.

Bollen, E. A. forthcoming. The Pottery in Section IIIA. In S. Dietz (ed.), *Chalkis Aitolias III, Monographs of the Danish Institute at Athens*. Athens, Danish Institute at Athens.

Bollen, E. A. 2011. West Slope pottery: some observations on comparative sequences. In *Ζ' Επιστημονική Συνάντηση για την ελληνιστική κεραμική*. Αίγιο 2005, 651–660. Athens, TAP.

Bruneau, P. 1970. 'Tombes d'Argos'. *Bulletin de correspondance hellénique* 94, 437–531.

Drosinou, P. 2000. Αγγεία από ελληνιστικούς τάφους στη Ρόκκα Κισάμου, in *Ε' Επιστημονική Συνάντηση για την ελληνιστική κεραμική*. Χανιά 1997, 37–43. Athens, TAP.

Drougou, St. and Touratsoglou, I. 1980. *Ελληνιστικοί Λαξευτοί Τάφοι Βέροιας*. Archaiologikon Deltion Suppl. 28. Athens, Greek Ministry of Culture.

Gravani, K. 1986. Die Keramik von Kassope. Ein vorläufiger Überblick, in W. Hoepfner and E. L. Schwandner (eds.), *Haus und Stadt im klassischen Griechenland*, 123–134. Munich, Deutscher Kunstverlag.

Heimberg, U. 1982. *Die Keramik des Kabirions*. Das Ka-

[28] Concentric rectangles and checkerboard: Thessaloniki: Ninou 1986, 108 fig. 96 (Kotitsa 1996, 115 M II figs. 98, 135 pl. 39); Kotitsa 1996, 114 M I figs. 97, 135, 136 pl. 38; Beroia: Drougou and Touratsoglou 1980, 75 fig. 31 pls. 51, 69 (Kotitsa 1996, 118 M VI figs. 101, 135 pl. 43); Thurreion: Zafeiropoulou 1979, 541 no. 19 pl. 366 bi–ii (Kotitsa 1996, 16 HKAk1g pl. 7) – also with star flower; Leukada: Ntouzougli 1999, 390 pl. 129c – also with star flower; Patras: Kiriakou 1994, 192–193 pls. 138, 141 (Kotitsa, 1996, 203 Pe I*) – also with star flower; 192–193 pls. 138, 141 (Kotitsa 1996, 203 Pe II*a); Aigio: Papakosta 2005, 77 P111 fig. 5; Also at Rhodes: Patsiada 1989, 201 no. 207 pl. 79a. and Athens: Vierneisel 1964, 456 fig. 50 left. Concentric rectangles: Thessaloniki: Tasia *et al.* 1998, 205 fig. 13ii ; Tasia *et al.* 1998, 205 fig. 13iii; Corinth: Anderson-Stojanovic 2000, 385; Anderson-Stojanovic 1997, 16 pl. 8c. Checkerboard and lattice:Leukada: Andreou 1994, 202 pl. 146b, top centre (Kotitsa 1996, 201 HKLeu2a.b); Ntouzougli 1999, 390 pl. 129b; Kassope: Gravani 1986, 126 fig. 129.7; And also from Crete: Rokka: Drosinou 2000, 41 pl. 19 d–e; 41 pl. 20 a, c; Chania: Baur 1922, 240 no. 506 fig. 105 (Kotitsa, 1996, 156 Kr1* pl. 57) – all Cretan examples are very like each other and are decorated with a large, incised star flower. Lattice: Leukada: Agallopoulou 1977, 490 pl. 418e left (Kotitsa 1996, 54–55 Leu2 pl. 27); Pella: Lilibaki-Akamati 1994, 131 no. 46 pl. 4 (Kotitsa 1996, 109 HKM I, fig. 135 pl. 34); 167 no. 220 pl. 26 (Kotitsa 1996, 109 HKM III fig. 135); 187 no. 321 pl. 38 (Kotitsa 1996, 153 M5*a); Pentaplatanos (Northern Greece): Korti-Konti 1987, 417 no. 1 pl. 82.1–2 (Kotitsa 1996, 117 M IVd fig. 99, 135 pl. 42).

[29] Bollen 2011.

birenheiligtum bei Theben III, Berlin, De Gruyter.

Houby-Nielsen, S., Moschos, I. and Gazis, M. 2000. Excavations on the Hill of Haghia Triadha, in S. Isager and I. Nielsen (eds.), *Proceedings of the Danish Institute at Athens* III, 229–249.

Hübner, G. 1984. Beşik-Tepe 1982. Hellenistische Keramik und Kleinfunde. *Archäologischer Anzeiger* 99, 177–183.

Kyriakou, D. 1994. Ελληνιστική κεραμική από τα νεκροταφεία της Πάτρας. In *Γ' Επιστημονική Συνάντηση για την ελληνιστική κεραμική*. Θεσσαλονίκη 1991, 185–195. Athens, Archetai.

Korti-Konti, S. 1987. Finds from a tomb in Pentaplatanos (near Jiannitsa), in M. A. Tiverios, St. Drougou and Ch. Saatsoglou-Paliadelē (eds.), *Αμητός: τιμητικός τόμος για τον καθηγητή Μανόλη Ανδρόνικο*, 417–427. Thessaloniki, Panepistēmio.

Kotitsa, Z. 1996. *Hellenistische Tonpyxiden. Untersuchung zweier hellenistischer Typen einer Keramikform*. Mainz, Zabern.

Lilibaki-Akamati, M. 1994. *Λαξευτοί Θαλαμωτοί Τάφοι της Πέλλας*. Αρχαιολογικόν Δελτίον Suppl. 53. Athens.

Metzger, I. 1998. Keramik und Lampen. In K. Reber, *Die klassischen und hellenistischen Wohnhäuser im Westquartier*. Eretria. Ausgrabungen und Forschungen X, 173–227. Lausanne, Payot.

Mitsopoulos-Leon, V. 1991. *Die Basilika am Staatsmarkt in Ephesos. Kleinfunde, I. Teil Keramik hellenistischer und römischer Zeit*. Forschungen in Ephesos 9, 2/2. Vienna, Verlag der Österreichischen Akademie der Wissenschaften.

Morel, J.-P. 1981. *Céramique campanienne: Les formes*. Bibliothèque des Écoles françaises d'Athènes et de Rome 244. Rome, École Française de Rome.

Ntouzougli, A. 1999. Νόμος Λεφκάδας. *Αρχαιολογικόν Δελτίον* 49 B1, 388–391.

Ninou, Aik. 1986. *Οδηγός της Έκθεσης Θεσσαλονική από τα Προϊστορικά μέχρι τα Χριστιανικά Χρόνια*. Athens, Greek Ministry of Culture.

Papakonstantinou, M.-F. 1997. Ελληνιστική κεραμική από τη Λαμία. In *Δ' Επιστημονική Συνάντηση για την ελληνιστική κεραμική*. Μυτιλήνη 1994, 50–58. Athens, Ypourgeio Politismou.

Papakonstantinou-Katsouni, M. 1990. Οδός Θερμπύλων. *Αρχαιολογικόν Δελτίον* 41 B, 59–61.

Papakosta, L. 2005. Ελληνιστική κεραμική από το Αίγιο. In L. Kypraiou (ed.), *Ελληνιστική κεραμική από την Πελοπόννησο*, 73–82. Athens, Greek Ministry of Culture.

Patsiada, B. 1989. Κεραμική του τυπου της «Δυτικής Κλιτύος» απο τη Ρόδο. *Αρχαιολογικόν Δελτίον* 38, 105–210.

Pfrommer, M. 1985. Milet 1983–1984: 2a. Klassische und hellenistische Keramik aus dem Heroon III. *Istanbuler Mitteilungen* 35, 39–76.

Pinkwart, D. and Stammnitz, W. 1984. *Peristylhäuser Westlich der Unteren Agora*. Altertümer von Pergamon 14. Berlin, de Gruyter.

Rotroff, S. I. 1991. Attic West Slope Vase Painting. *Hesperia* 60, 59–102.

Rotroff, S. I. 1997. *Hellenistic Pottery: Athenian and Imported Wheelmade Table Ware and Related Material*. The Athenian Agora XXIX. Princeton, NJ., American School of Classical Studies at Athens.

Schäfer, J. 1968. *Hellenistische Keramik aus Pergamon*. Pergamenische Forschungen 2. Berlin, de Gruyter.

Tasia, A., Lola, Z., Bachlas, A. and Stagkos, A. 1998. Κεραμική Ελληνιστικών Χρόνων από την Ανασκαφή της Πλατείας Διοικητηρίου. *Athens Annals of Archaeology* 23–28, 199–210.

Thompson, H. A. 1934. Two Centuries of Hellenistic Pottery. *Hesperia* 3, 311–480.

Touratsoglou, I. 1996. *Macedonia: History. Monuments. Museums*. Athens, Ekdotike Athenon.

Vierneisel, K. 1964. Die Ausgrabungen im Kerameikos: Die Grabung in der Nekropole, 1962. *Archäologischer Anzeiger* 79, 420–467.

Vogeikoff, N. 1993. *Hellenistic Pottery from the South Slope of the Acropolis*. Unpublished PhD thesis, Bryn Mawr College.

Vogeikoff-Brogan, N. 2000. Late Hellenistic Pottery in Athens: A New Deposit and Further Thoughts on the Association of Pottery and Societal Change. *Hesperia* 69, 293–333.

Ypourgeio Politismou 1998 *Ancient Macedonia*. Athens, Greek Ministry of Culture.

Zafeiropoulou, F. 1979. Αιτωλοακαρνανία. Θυρρείον. *Αρχαιολογικόν Δελτίον* 29 B2, 539–542.

Zafeiropoulou, F. and Kolia, E.-I. 1997. Ελληνιστική Κεραμική από τη Νάξο. In *Δ' Επιστημονική Συνάντηση για την ελληνιστική κεραμική*. Μυτιλήνη 1994, 283–290. Athens, Ypourgeio Politismou.

Die hellenistische Keramik Makedoniens außerhalb des Landes

Stella Drougou & Ioannis Touratsoglou

Abstract

The recent studies of the rich ceramic material from the late classic-early Hellenistic Macedonian kingdom, based on the dating by coins and lamps, tends to accept that the main morphological characteristics of the Macedonian Hellenistic pottery were established around the middle of the 3rd century BC.

Furthermore it is clear that in the first half of the 2nd century BC novelties in the field of shapes made their appearance, which was at least in some cases after the fall of the kingdom. These new forms – products of specialised Macedonian workshops under the patronage of the last two Antigonids – reflect both political tendencies of a rebirthed nation with centrifuged masterplans (especially after 197–188 BC) as well as cultural aspirations of a deeplysophisticated court. To the new repertoire belong the tripodic pyxides – to a certain extent inspired by vases in precious metal – the so called 'homeric' cups and generally pottery with iconography from the literary works of the past, in high relief decoration; and finally the Macedonian shield bowls. The new tendencies characterize in a lesser degree and other shapes such as unguentaria, amphoras and lamps. Concerning the distribution of the former, vases of the new era circulate either within the Macedonian kingdom itself or in regions under the Macedonian protectorate, such as Thessaly, and in strongholds with garnisons, such as Corinth, or finally, beyond the Aegean, in areas of Macedonian interest and presence.

Keywords: Makedonien, Pyxiden Typ B, ‚Homerische' Becher, Makedonische Schildbecher, Unguentaria, Amphoren.

Einleitung

Die neuesten Untersuchungen der Beispiele der spätklassischen und frühen hellenistischen Keramik, die mit Hilfe von Münzen und Lampen gut zu datierenden Keramikeinheiten aus Makedonien zusammengestellt worden sind, lässt die Meinung zu, dass die wichtigsten Charakteristika der hellenistischen Keramik des makedonischen Königreichs sich höchstwahrscheinlich um die Mitte des 3. Jahrhunderts v. Chr. herauskristallisiert haben[1]. Zu diesem Zeitpunkt scheint der Vorrat an Beispielen der klassischen Tradition in den hellenistischen Werkstätten längst erschöpft gewesen zu sein.

Ohne die großen oder kleinen Abänderungen in den Formen der Keramik der früheren Perioden aus dem 4. und 3. Jahrhundert v. Chr. zu übersehen, wird deutlich, dass im 2. Jahrhundert v. Chr. und insbesondere in der ersten Hälfte offenkundige Novitäten mit bleibendem Wert im Bereich der Keramik stattfinden. Dieses Phänomen lässt sich vor allem in der Form einer Reihe besonderer Gefäße und Vasen erkennen. Darunter fallen u.a. dreifüßige Pyxiden (**Abb. 2–4**) und ‚homerische' Reliefbecher (**Abb. 5–6**), die mit Hilfe von Matrizen produziert wurden[2].

Eine vergleichbare Entwicklung lässt sich aber auch bei den Amphoren (**Abb. 9–10**), Lampen (**Abb. 11–12**) und Unguentaria feststellen. Doch erweist sich hier allerdings die Forschung als komplex und vielschichtig, da sie geographisch die gesamte hellenistische Welt mit allen ihren lokalen Eigenarten umfassen muss. Dazu kommt die Tatsache, dass die Datierung auch eine signifikante Anzahl von inhärenten Schwierigkeiten beinhaltet. Allerdings behindert die Erscheinung von ‚Novitäten' die parallel verlaufende und durchaus reichhaltige Produktion – mit entsprechendem Vertrieb von bekannten Formen und Kategorien – nicht im Geringsten[3].

Die Frage, die sich im Rahmen der folgenden Diskussion stellt, betrifft die Verbreitung dieser Keramikgattungen außerhalb Makedoniens und die Voraussetzungen und auch die Gründe dieser spezifischen ‚Ausbreitung'. An diesem Punkt sei eine allgemeine Feststellung erlaubt, die sich aus einer Gesamtbetrachtung der hellenistischen Keramik

---

1 Drougou und Touratsoglou 1991, 13–15; Drougou 1991, 21-33. Ebenfalls die Akten der Wissenschaftlichen Treffen für die Hellenistische Keramik (1–8, 1986–2008). Die Frage zu den Grenzen zwischen der ausgehenden klassischen und der beginnenden hellenistischen Zeit wurde des Öfteren kontrovers diskutiert, da die Kriterien dieser Forschung noch nicht definiert wurden, auch wenn das Ende des 4. Jhs. v. Chr. als der am besten dokumentierte Eingangszeitpunkt der hellenistischen Epoche bleibt, vgl. Drougou 1992, 104 –105, Kotitsa 2006, 20–26 .

2 Siehe oben Anmerkung 1.

3 Die Novitäten sind schon während des 3. Jahrhunderts v. Chr. erkennbar und auch mehrere, wenn auch nicht so vielfältig wie im 4. Jahrhundert v. Chr. Die kleinformatigen ‚μυροδοχεία'/unguentaria können als gutes Beispiel dafür gelten. Die Abbildung der Mythen tritt zurück. Stattdessen herrschen die verschiedenen Ornamente vor, während in der gleichen Zeit neue Formen eingeführt worden sind, auch wenn nicht so intensiv wie in vorigen Jahrhunderten. Siehe Rotroff 1982, 6–13.

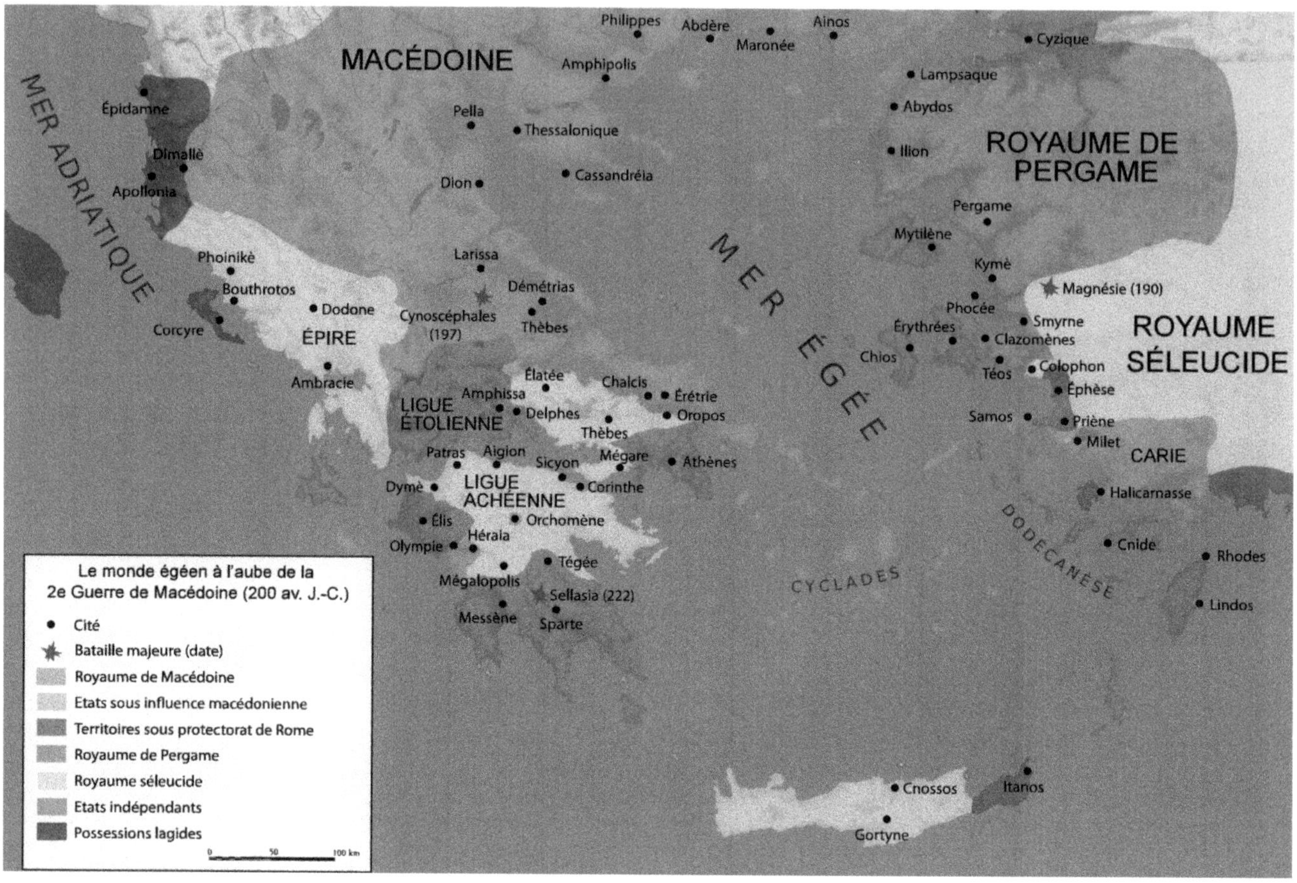

Abb. 1. Die Griechischen Staaten in der Zeit des Königs Philip V. (Ιστορία 1974, 10–11)

des 3. und 2. Jahrhunderts v. Chr. ergibt. Man kann mit großer Wahrscheinlichkeit behaupten, dass die Produktion der makedonischen Werkstätten nie als wichtiger Handelsfaktor betrachtet wurde. Vielmehr war sie ein Nebenprodukt politischer bzw. militärischer Tätigkeit der makedonischen Könige und der dazugehörigen Armee und das vor allem außerhalb der traditionellen Grenzen des Staates[4].

Eine Darstellung der signifikantesten makedonischen Formen könnte zu interessanten Schlüssen führen. Doch da dies hier nicht näher ausgeführt werden kann, werden wir uns in diesem Band mit einer Auswahl begnügen müssen[5].

Pyxis Typ B

Die Pyxis des Typs B – auch als dreifüßige Pyxis bekannt – erscheint zu einem Zeitpunkt, als noch die sehr beliebte und in großen Zahlen produzierte Pyxis des Typs A mit konischem Boden und stufenförmiger Basis in Umlauf ist (**Abb. 2–4**)[6].

Als ein herausragendes Merkmal der Pyxiden des Typs B kann ihre Größe angesehen werden. In manchen Fällen sind sie bis zu 50cm hoch. Da aber auch die Größe die Nutzung beeinflusst, bedarf es hier einer neuen Interpretation. Eines Kommentars würdig sind auch jene Funde – insbesondere aus der Region von Veroia – bei denen die Form einen komplexeren Charakter erlangt. Durch Anhängen oder Hinzufügen von kleinen Miniaturgestalten in Relief (Appliqués) wie z.B. Pyxiden und Unguentaria, werden Formen gewonnen, die in gewisser Weise an die komplexen Formen von Kernoi erinnern. Erwähnenswert ist auch der Gebrauch von aufgesetzter weißer Farbe in Kombination mit bunten Ornamenten wie z.B. Girlanden oder Palmetten. Die große Anzahl dieser Beispiele fügt die Forschung der Kategorie der Gefäße mit Malerei auf weißem Hintergrund hinzu[7].

Die Kategorie der Pyxiden des Typs B trifft man fast ausschließlich im sog. breiteren Raum des makedonischen

---

4 Touratsoglou 2010, 54. Siehe auch Anmerkung 15.
5 Siehe unten die Diskussion über Pyxiden, Reliefbecher usw.
6 Allamani und Tzanavari 1990, 151–158; Allamani und Tzanavari 1994, 90–103; Barr-Sharrar 1987, 9–11; Drougou und Touratsoglou 1980, 140–148. Kotitsa 1996, 99–107; Miller 1993, 68–77.
7 Allamani und Tzanavari, s.o. (Anm. 6); Drougou und Touratsoglou 2012. Vgl. die unpublizierten großen Pyxiden im Museum von Veroia, aus Kammergräbern in der Region. Siehe auch Drougou und Touratsoglou 1994, 128; Sokolovska 1994, Taf. 165 (2. Jh. v. Chr.). Farben und Relief-Ornamente in der hellenistischen Keramik stellen eine besondere Forschungsfrage, die schon in 4. Jh. v. Chr. erkennbar wird: siehe darüber Kyriakou 2008, 169–202.

Abb 2. Makedonien. Hellenistische Keramik. Pyxis Typus B. Veroia Museum (Drougou and Touratsoglou 1980, 145 Taf. 25)

Abb. 4. Böotien. Hellenistische Keramik. Pyxis Typus B (Kotitsa 1996, Taf. 62)

Abb. 3. Thessalien. Hellenistische Keramik. Pyxis Typus B. Volos Museum, Demetrias (Kotitsa 1996, Taf. 49; Θεσσαλία 2000, 53)

Abb. 5. Makedonien. Hellenistische Keramik. Reliefbecher (‚Homerischer Becher'). Pella Museum (Akamatis 1993, Taf. 16, 20)

Königreichs und im angrenzenden, politisch wie kulturell abhängigen Thessalien (**Abb. 1**)[8]. Sie wurden dort vorwiegend in Grabzusammenhängen gefunden. Die Münzzeugnisse der chronologisch relativ geschlossenen Funde bestimmen die Grabbeilegung um die Jahre 166–65 v. Chr. oder kurz danach[9]. Die Produktion der Pyxiden des Typs B muss unmittelbar davor stattgefunden haben. Leider gibt es keine chronologisch geschlossenen Funde für die 2. Hälfte des 2. Jahrhunderts v. Chr., so dass die Dauer der Produktion der dreifüßigen Pyxiden nicht vor, sondern eher am Ende des 2. Jahrhunderts v. Chr. festgelegt werden sollte[10].

Obwohl in der Entstehung der dreifüßigen Pyxis ältere und auch bekanntere Formen – wenn auch teilweise – leicht zu identifizieren sind, fällt die Antwort auf Grund der Grabnutzung und der Produktion im 3. Jahrhundert v. Chr. in Makedonien nicht leicht, denn es fehlen praktisch die zuverlässigen Daten[11]. In begrenzter Zahl wurden dreifüßige Pyxiden in Regionen Thessaliens (z.B. Demetrias)[12], in Böotien[13] und auf der nordöstlichen Peloponnes (Patras) erhalten und ihre zeitliche Einordnung in das 2. Jahrhundert v. Chr. scheint wahrscheinlich zu sein. Wichtig ist, dass alle diese Regionen. in denen dieser Pyxis Typ B auftaucht, die militärische Präsenz Makedoniens kannten. Sie waren zum größten Teil Schauplatz kriegerischer Auseinandersetzungen des makedonischen Könighauses, unter denen Philipp V. eine besondere Bedeutung zukommt[14].

Abb. 6. Thessalien. Hellenistische Keramik. Reliefbecher (‚Homerischer Becher'). Demetrias, Volos Museum (Sinn 1979, Taf. 30)

---

8 Θεσσαλία 2000, 20 Abb. II (Demetrias). Allgemein Anm. 1, Add. Siehe auch Schmid 2006 ,42–44

9 Drougou und Touratsoglou 1980 s.o. (Anm.6). Kotitsa 1994 s.o. (Anm.6). Mitrevski 2005, 74 f. Abb. 70h (Münzen von makedonischen Städten: 186–168 v. Chr.).

10 Drougou und Touratsoglou 2012 (Anm. 4); Drougou und Touratsoglou 1991, 13–15 (Anm. 1).

11 Vor einigen Jahren galten in der Forschung zu den Vasen die Form und teilweise auch die Ornamentik als Datierungskriterien. Heute sind auch andere Methoden notwendig.

12 Siehe oben Anm. 8. Zur Geschichte, Helly 2009, 339.

13 Siehe Schmid 2006 (Anm. 8).

14 Siehe Gehrke 2000, 178–180. Hannestad 2011, 9–15. Meloni 1953; Shipley 2000, 152; Walbank 1940.

Abb. 7. Makedonien. Hellenistische Keramik. Reliefbecher mit dem Motiv des makedonischen Schildes: a) Vergina (unpubliziert) - b) Vardarski Rid (Skopje Museum, S. Blazevska)

Reliefbecher/Skyphoi mit Erzählungsdarstellungen

Die jüngste Forschung ist sich darüber einig, dass Reliefbecher/Skyphoi (**Abb. 5–6**), die mit Hilfe von Matrizen produziert und mit Erzählungsdarstellungen auf der Außenseite versehen wurden, ein Produkt makedonischer Werkstätten sind – oder mindestens in Regionen, in denen der makedonische Einfluss überwog, hergestellt wurden. Der Versuch, die Entstehung dieser Kategorie im 3. Jahrhundert v. Chr. anzusetzen, kann von den Ausgrabungsfunden her nicht belegt werden. Diese Position wurde vor allem von Ulrich Sinn vertreten, der sich als erster damit beschäftigte[15].

Die geographische Ausbreitung der Reliefbecher mit Erzähldarstellungen entspricht vor allem dem Gebiet, das dem makedonischen Königreich entspricht, so z.B. Aiani [Elimeia], Aghios Panteleimon [Orestis], Amphipolis [Edonis und Pieris], Demir Kapija/Stenai [Paionia], Florina, Isar Marvinci/Idomenai [Amphaxitis], Lefkopetra [Bottiaia], Lychnidos/Ochris [Dassaritis], Pella, Prespes/ Lyke, Vergina/Aigai[16]. Doch trifft man sie auch in den angegliederten Regionen an, z.B. Thessalien (Demetrias, Phthiotis, Theben), sowie an Orten und Städten in denen eine große makedonische Militärpräsenz zu finden war, wie z.B. in Attika (Athen/Peiraeus), in Böotien, auf Euböa (Eretria), Lokris und auf der Peloponnes (Korinth)[17].

Das Umfeld, in denen Skyphoi, bzw. Reliefbecher dieser Kategorie zu finden sind, ist in der Regel eine Siedlung. Die Erzähldarstellungen beziehen sich auf epische Texte oder Theaterstücke großer Klassiker wie z.B. Aischylos, Sophokles und insbesondere Euripides, sowie zeitgenössische Liebesdichtung[18].

Abb. 8. Thessalien. Hellenistische Keramik. Reliefbecher mit dem Motiv des makedonischen Schildes. Larisa Museum M89/32 (Θεσσαλία 2000, Taf. 25)

15 Akamatis 1993; Hausmann 1959; Rotroff 1982 (Anm. 3); Rotroff 2000, 496–501; Sinn 1979 (ältere Bibliographie).

16 Faklaris 1983, 211–238. Neuendeckte Fragmente aus dem Metroon in Vergina/Aigai, vgl. Drougou und Touratsoglou 2000, 307–319 (2. Jh. v. Chr.). Adam-Veleni 1990, 309–311; Karamitrou-Mentesidou 1996, 52.

17 Edwards 1978, 182–185.

18 Sinn 1979, 117–120.

Trotz der fragmentarischen Informationslage verleitet das Material der genau datierten Funde dazu, den Beginn dieser Reliefbecher mit Erzähldarstellungen der ersten Hälfte des 2. Jahrhunderts v. Chr. zuzuschreiben und deren Produktion bis circa in das erste Jahrzehnt des 1. Jahrhunderts v. Chr. anzunehmen[19]. Die vorherrschenden Rahmenbedingungen im Königreich Philipps V., insbesondere nach 197–188 v. Chr., unterstützten das Bedürfnis der Hervorhebung einer glorreichen Vergangenheit. Es ist gut möglich, dass in der Endphase die Produktionsstätten Makedoniens, nachdem Reliefgefäße im gesamten griechischen Raum anerkannt wurden, eine ‚eigene' Ikonographie, aus rein ‚privaten' Gründen, adoptierten. Die Datierung der Reliefbecher/ Skyphoi mit Erzähldarstellungen sollte im Moment noch als Forschungsobjekt angesehen werden. Doch muss der Anfang der Produktion in der Mitte des 2. Jahrhunderts v. Chr. angenommen werden.

Reliefbecher mit makedonischem Schild

Die Reliefbecher, deren Ornamentik als Motiv den makedonischen Schild haben[20], sind nicht nur zahlenmäßig sehr groß (**Abb. 7–8**), sondern auch in Hinblick auf ihre Produktion und ihre Entstehung sehr problematisch. Besonders schwierig stellen sich auch die Bestimmung der Zeitspanne, sowie der Vertrieb dieser Skyphoi heraus. Die Ausgrabungsergebnisse, basierend auf den stratigraphischen Hinweisen, sollen dokumentiert und klar sein (s. Agora von Athen, Kerameikos, Korinth,Thessalien)[21]. Die Tatsache, dass Produkte dieser Kategorie auch außerhalb der griechischen Halbinsel gefunden wurden, nämlich im westlichen Kleinasien, wie z.B. in Pergamon, Ephesos und Tarsos[22], ist ein Phänomen, das der besonderen Forschung bedarf. Nach unserer Meinung dürfte es mit den Beziehungen, welcher Art auch immer, des makedonischen Königreichs der letzten Antigoniden und den hellenistischen Herrschern in Kleinasien zusammenhängen. Sicher aber wird es auch mit der Expansionspolitik der makedonischen Könige in der östlichen Ägäis zusammenhängen[23]. Die Existenz von Gefäßen mit makedonischem Schilddekor, in Ausgrabungen jenseits des helladischen Raumes – nach der Hälfte des 2. Jahrhunderts v. Chr. und sicher nach dem Ende des makedonischen Reiches – kann auch auf ‚Überbleibsel/ Restbestände' zurückzuführen sein, die einfach deren Entstehungsdatum bzw. Situation überlebten.

Der größte Teil der Ausgrabungsfunde in Kleinasien scheint die Periode zwischen der Mitte des 2. Jahrhunderts v. Chr. und dem Anfang des 1. Jahrhunderts v. Chr. für die Datierung nahezulegen. Diese zeitliche Einordnung ist für die Entstehung dieses Typs im makedonischen Raum nicht anzunehmen. Umso wichtiger ist bei einer Erstellung eines Gesamtbilds der Ausbreitung dieser Gefäßtypen die vorherrschende Stellung Makedoniens, die bei der Interpretation der Funde aus Kleinasien stärker hervorzuheben ist, als es bisher getan wurde. Als Beweis können die identifizierten Funde angeführt werden, wobei einige davon immer noch nicht ausführlich publiziert worden sind, z.B., Pella, Petres/Kelle (?), Ochris/ Lychnidos, Styberra und Vardarski Rid, Vergina/Aigai[24].

Makedonische Amphoren

Die so genannten makedonischen Amphoren (**Abb. 9–10**) findet man in einer großen Anzahl in Makedonien[25]. Die meisten wurden ins 2. Jahrhundert v. Chr. datiert. Außerhalb Makedoniens sind sie in Variationen nur noch in Thessalien und Lamia zu finden[26]. Wobei zu den interessantesten Funden außerhalb Makedoniens die hellenistischen Amphoren des Friedhofs von Lamia gehören. Der größte Teil der Gräber kann in das 3. und 2. Jahrhundert v. Chr. datiert werden. Es ist bekannt, dass die Stadt seit dem 4. Jahrhundert v. Chr. unter makedonischem Einfluss stand. Während der hellenistischen Periode tritt das bei den lokalen Produkten deutlich hervor.

Mit geringen Abweichungen stehen die makedonischen' Amphoren Lamias in einer eindeutigen, morphologischen Verwandtschaft zu den makedonischen Vorbildern. In dieses Bild passen sowohl die Keramikfunde der Gräber des 2. und 1. Jahrhunderts v. Chr. aus der Nekropole von Echinos[27], der antiken Stadt NÖ von Lamia, als auch die Funde aus den Städten Eretria und Chalkis. Offensichtlich ist die Existenz schon seit dem 4. Jahrhundert v. Chr. von Gräbern des ‚makedonischen' Typs auf dasselbe Phänomen zurück zuführen, das die Präsenz der Makedonier um die Bucht des Maliakos hervorbrachte. Ähnliches gilt auch für die Gewölbegebäude im 2. und 1. Jahrhundert v. Chr. im Tal des Sperchios.

Zusammenfassung

Die Diskussion über die Beziehungen der lokalen Keramikwerkstätten mit den entsprechenden Werkstätten Makedoniens könnte auch noch in Hinblick auf andere Kategorien und Vasenformen, speziell des 2. Jahrhunderts

19 Akamatis 1993.
20 Callaghan 1978, 54–58; Liampi 1998, 27–41; Rotroff 1982, 38–39 (Anm. 3).
21 Edwards 1978, 182–184 (Anm. 17); Rotroff 1982, 91 Nr. 400 (Anm. 3); Siehe auch Anm. 27.
22 Pergamon: Courby 1922, Abb. 87, 13, 27; De Luca und Ziegenhaus 1968, 49, 256. Kyme: Bouzek 1974, Abb. 5. Tarsos: Goldman 1950, 223–225. Ephesos: Mitsopoulos-Leon 1991, 73 Nr. D48 Taf. 85; Günay Tuluk 2001, 51–52 . Taf.42–43.
23 Siehe Anm. 23; Buraselis 1982; Shipley 2000, 151 (Anm. 14).
24 Vergina: Drougou 2009, 130 und 227–230 (Tsakiridis-Grundstück). Vardarski Rid: Blaževska und Slamkov 2005, 209 –211 Nr. 15 Abb. 12b . Für andere Beispiele s. Charziagellakis 2004, 137 f. Taf. 35–40; Liampi 1998, 85–89; Zauri und Melliou 2000, 94 Taf. 7. Andere Darstellungen s. Liampi 1998, 5–8 Beispiele aus der Großplastik: Christodoulou 2000, 76–80; Kähler 1965, 5–6.
25 Drougou und Touratsoglou 1980, 117–120 (Anm. 6).
26 Papakonstantinou 2000,193 f. (mit Bibliographie).
27 Bougia 2004, 15–17 Dakoronia 1986, 147–180; Papakonstantinou 2000a, 204–206.

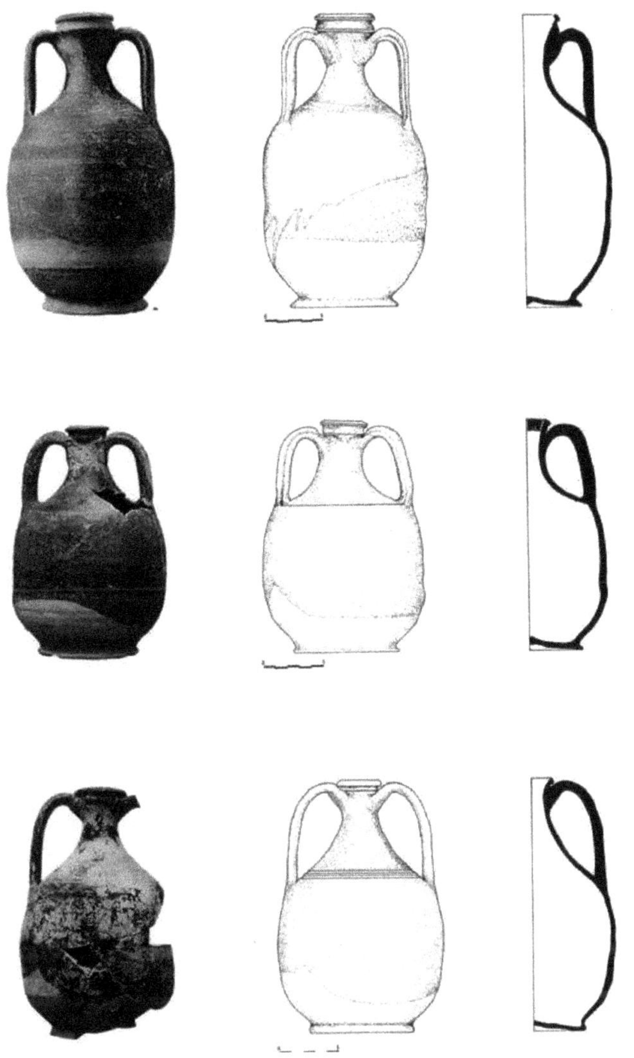

Abb. 9. Makedonien. Hellenistische Keramik. ‚Makedonische' Amphora. Veroia Museum (Drougou und Touratsoglou 1980, 117 Taf. 18, 19)

Abb. 10. Phthiotis. Hellenistische Keramik. ‚Makedonische' Amphora. Amphoren von der SO-Nekropole von Lamia (Papakonstantinou 2000, 201)

v. Chr. wie z.B. spindelförmige Unguentaria[28] und Tonlampen[29] (**Abb. 11–12**) erweitert werden.

Soweit die Ausgrabungsergebnisse glaubwürdig erscheinen und die geographische Aufteilung zweifelsfreie Informationen liefert, diente die Spezialisierung der Keramikproduktion im hellenistischen Makedonien in der ersten Hälfte des 2. Jahrhunderts v. Chr. mit dem Vertrieb von neuen Formen von Gefäßen und Vasen entweder bestimmten Ritualen und Grabpraktiken – wahrscheinlich bei dreifüßigen Pyxiden – oder Symposionsbedürfnissen, im Falle von Reliefbecher mit Erzähldarstellungen. Es wäre nicht ungewöhnlich für diese Epoche, wenn diese Gattung als eine Art Monopol verstanden wird, um die normierten Bedürfnisse der militärischen Ausrüstung im Inland und Ausland wahrzunehmen. In diesem Zusammenhang sprechen wir die Skyphoi an, deren Verzierung der makedonische Schild ist. Es geht dabei nicht nur um eine zu erwartende Entwicklung im Bereich des Keramikgewerbes, die mit dem Vorschreiten der Zeit und der Sitten zu erklären wäre. Es müsste eher als ein wichtiger Beweis der Umsetzung einer ganz bestimmten Politik von Seiten einer Führungsschicht angesehen werden.

Auf Grund der archäologischen Funde könnte man behaupten, dass die Produktion der makedonischen Werkstätten nie das Objekt eines systematischen Außenhandels war. In Wirklichkeit passt sie sich immer – und gleichzeitig drückte sie dies auch aus – den Bedürfnissen des internen Marktes und den Traditionen der makedonischen Gesellschaft an. Die archäologischen Funde der Zeit zeugen von keiner besonderen Präsenz dieser Produkte im Rahmen der großen hellenistischen

[28] Zu Ungentaria allgemein: Anderson-Stojanoviç 1987, 105; Drougou und Touratsoglou 1980, 123–129; Lilimpaki-Akamati 1994, 241

[29] Zu Lampen siehe Anm. 39, 40, 41. Drougou 1992, 16; Drougou und Touratsoglou 2012 (Anm. 7); Lilimpaki-Akamatis 1994, 238–239 (Anm. 29).

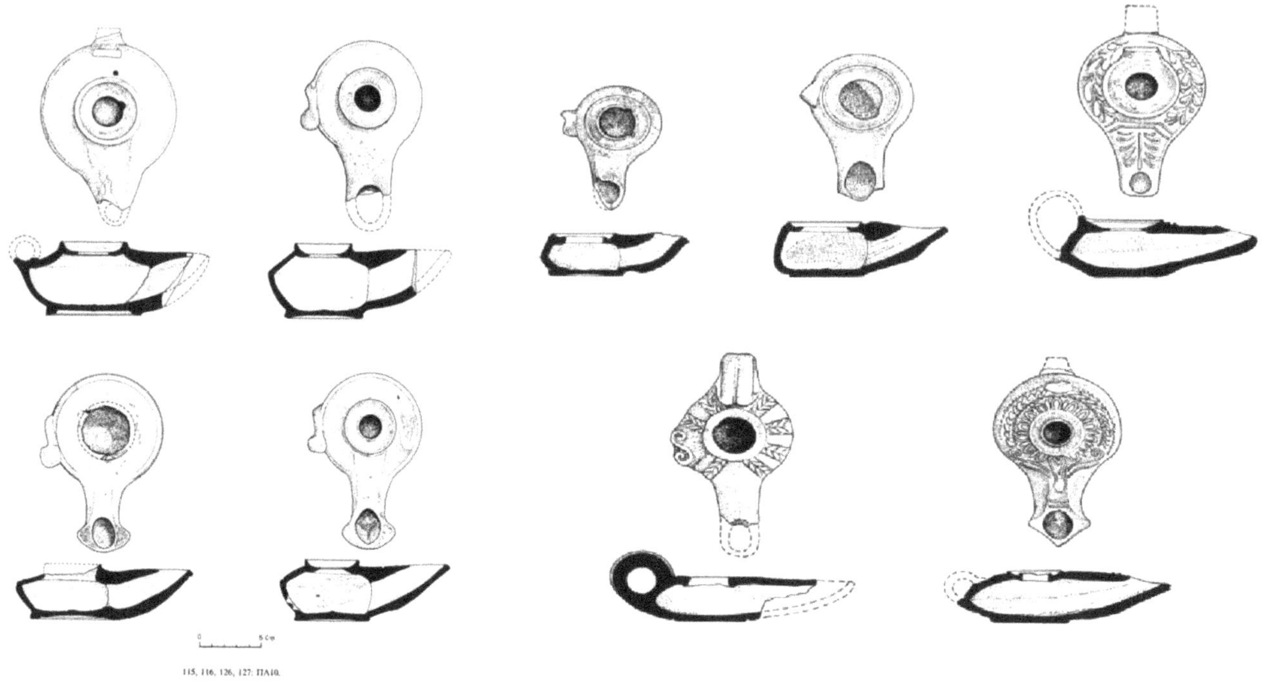

Abb. 11. Makedonien. Hellenistische Keramik. Lampen-Typen. Veroia Museum (Drougou und Touratsoglou 1980, 134–135)

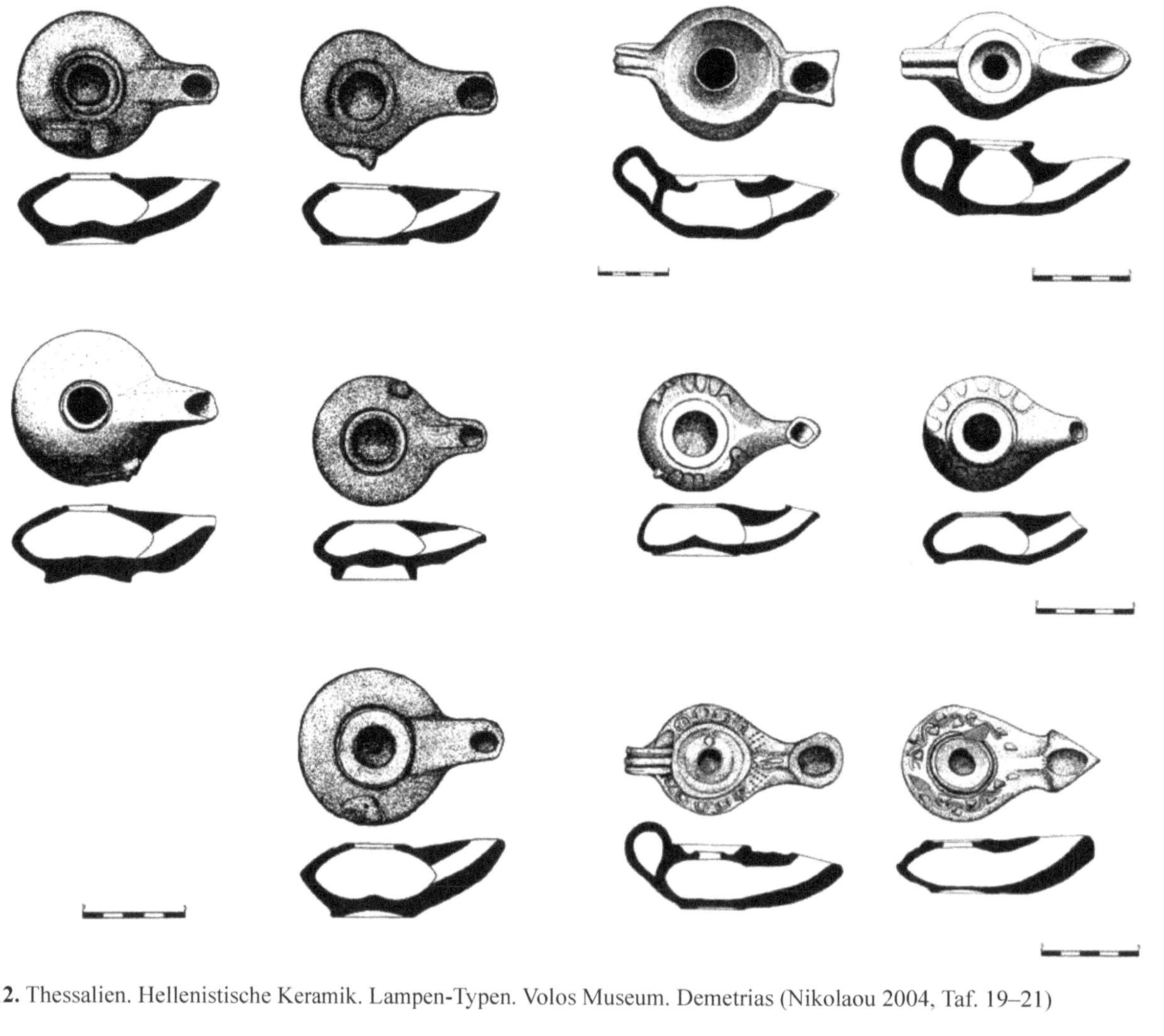

Abb. 12. Thessalien. Hellenistische Keramik. Lampen-Typen. Volos Museum. Demetrias (Nikolaou 2004, Taf. 19–21)

Handelszentren. Das Bild ändert sich radikal in den griechischen Gegenden, wo sich makedonische Militärgarnisonen niedergelassen. Dies wird besonders deutlich während der Regierungszeit Philipp V. wie z.B. in Thessalien und Epiros. Beide Regionen grenzten an Makedonien. Ein größerer Einfluss ist deutlich zu erkennen, was sich u.a. im Fundmaterial aus Pherrai und Demetrias wiederspiegelt, so dass politische Beziehungen vorausgesetzt werden können[30]. Dabei handelt es sich nicht nur um importierte Ware, sondern sehr oft um Produkte aus lokalen Werkstätten, die nach importierten Vorbildern hergestellt wurden. Die militärischen Unternehmungen Philipp V. in den Regionen von Sperchios, Böotien und der Nordpeloponnes haben einen Ausnahmezustand im griechischen Raum hervorgerufen. Letzteres muss auch mit der immanenten römischen Gefahr zusammen gesehen werden.

Trotz allem sind diese politisch-militärischen Unruhen auch der Anlass für einen bemerkenswerten Umschlag von den unterschiedlichsten Produkten und Gewohnheiten bis in das 1. Jahrhundert v. Chr. hinein.

Trotz existierender Unterschiede ist das Bild dieser Epoche für Thrakien und die NW-Küste Kleinasiens sehr ähnlich. Die archäologischen Funde dieser Region sind allerdings noch unklar und bedürfen einer genaueren Analyse.

Die Summe unserer Bemerkungen erweist sich letztlich als besonders ‚unhandlich', da sie im Rahmen einer koine bzw. ‚internationalen' hellenistischen Keramik und einesweit verbreiteten Welthandels artikuliert wurde[31]. Wie schon erwähnt, finden insbesondere im 2. Jahrhundert v. Chr. politische Änderungen in rasendem Tempo statt. Neue Produkte italienischer und orientalischer Herkunft erscheinen im griechischen Raum (terra sigillata, Eastern Sigillata A etc.), so dass oft das Alte mit dem Neuen nebeneinander einhergeht, um zusammen die ‚Einführung/Einleitung' einer ‚neuen'(!) aufkommenden Zeit hervorzubringen[32].

Stella Drougou
Marathonos-Str. 7
GR-54638 Thessaloniki
drougou@hist.auth.gr

Ioannis Touratsoglou
Kyvelis-Str. 5
GR-10682 Athen
ioannis.touratsoglou@gmail.com

Bibliographie

Adam-Veleni, P. 1990. Eine Werkstatt für Reliefgefässe in Petres, West-Makedonien, in *Akten des 13. Internationalen Kongresses für klassische Archäologie, Berlin*, 309–311. Mainz, Zabern.

Akamatis, I. 1993. *Πήλινες μήτρες αγγείων από την Πέλλα*. Athen, TAP.

Allamani, B. und Tzanavari, A. 1990. Πήλινες πυξίδες από τη Βέροια. Χρονολογικές ενδείξεις. In *Β' Επιστημονική Συνάντηση για την Ελληνιστική Κεραμική*. Ρόδος 1989, 151–159. Athen, TAP.

Allamani, B. und Tzanavari K. 1994. Σχήματα αγγείων της πρώιμης ελληνιστικής εποχής από ταφικά σύνολα της Βέροιας. In *Γ' Επιστημονική Συνάντηση για την Ελληνιστική Κεραμική*. Θεσσαλονίκη 1991, 90–103. Athen, Archetai.

Anderson-Stojanovic, V. 1987. The Chronology and Function of ceramic Unguentaria. *American Journal of Archaeology* 91, 105–122.

Archibald, Z. H. 2005. Markets and Exchange: the structure and scale of economic behavior in the Hellenistic Age, in Z. Archibald, J. Davis und V. Gabrielsen (Hrsg.), *Making, Moving and Managing. The new world of ancient economies*, 1–26. Oxford, Oxbow.

Barr-Sharrar, B. 1987. *The Hellenistic and early Imperial decorative Bust*. Mainz, Zabern.

Blaževska S. und Slamkov, E. 2005. Housing from the 4th to the 1st Century BC in the Ancient Town at Vardarski Rid, in S. Ladstätter und V. Scheibelreiter (Hrsg.), *Städtisches Wohnen im östlichen Mittelmeerraum 4. Jh. v. Chr. –1. Jh. n. Chr.* Akten des internationalen Kolloquiums vom 24.–27. Oktober 2007 an der Österreichischen Akademie der Wissenschaften, 363–388. Wien, Verlag der Österreichischen Akademie der Wissenschaften.

Bougia, P. 2004. Πήλινα κτερίσματα από το ελληνιστικό νεκροταφείο στον Αχινό. In *Στ' Επιστημονική Συνάντηση για την Ελληνιστική Κεραμική*. Βόλος 2000, 149–160. Athen, TAP.

Bouzek, J. (Hrsg.) 1974. *Megarian Bowls, Anatolian Collection of Charles University*. Prag, University Press.

Buraselis, K. 1982. *Das Hellenische Makedonien und die Ägäis. Forschungen zur Politik des Kassandros und der drei ersten Antigoniden im ägäischen Meer und im Westkleinasien.* Münchner Beiträge zur Papyrusforschung und der antiken Rechtsgeschichte

30 Siehe Anm. 27.

31 Archibald 2005, 1–12.

32 Robinson 1969; Hayes 2008, 1-11; Meyer-Schlichtmann 1988,205–211; Lund 2005, 233–240 (Anm. 32).

73. München, C. H. Beck.

Callaghan, P. J. 1978. Macedonian Shields, Shield Bowls and Corinth. A Fixed point of the Hellenistic Ceramic Chronology. *Αρχαιολογικά Ανάλεκτα εξ Αθηνών* 11, 53–60.

Chatziagelakis, A. 2004. Ανάγλυφοι σκύφοι από τη Δυτική Θεσσαλία. In *ΣΤ' Επιστημονική Συνάντηση για την Ελληνιστική Κεραμική*. Βόλος 2000, 137–148. Athen, TAP.

Christodoulou, P. 2000. *Ελληνιστική Ζωοφόρος στο Δίον*. Unpublizierte Dissertation, Universität Thessaloniki.

Courby, R. 1922. *Les vases grecs à reliefs*. Bibliothèque des ècoles Francaises d' Athènes et de Rome. Paris, De Boccard.

Dakoronia, F. 1986. Τάφοι «μακεδονικού» τύπου στην κοιλάδα του Σπερχειού, in *Ancient Macedonia* IV, Papers read at the fourth International Symposium held in Thessaloniki, September 21.–25. 1983, 147–158. Thessaloniki, Etaireia Makedonikon Spoudon.

De Luca, G. und Ziegenhaus, O. 1968. *Das Asklepieion. Der südliche Temenosbezirk in hellenistischer und frührömischer Zeit*. Altertümer von Pergamon 11, 1. Berlin, W. de Gruyter.

Drougou, S. (Hrsg.) 1991. *Ελληνιστική Κεραμική από τη Μακεδονία*. Thessaloniki, Aristoteles University Thessaloniki-Editions.

Drougou, S. 1992. *Ανασκαφή της Πέλλας 1957–1964. Οι πήλινοι λύχνοι*. Athen, Archetai.

Drougou, S. 2009. Βεργίνα. Η εικόνα του τέλους της πόλης των Αιγών. Πρώτες σημειώσεις από μια νέα ανασκαφική απόπειρα. *Εγνατία* 13, 121–132.

Drougou, S. und Touratsoglou, I. 1980. *Ελληνιστικοί Λαξευτοί τάφοι της Βέροιας*. Athen, TAP.

Drougou, S. und Touratsoglou, I. 1991. Hellenistische Keramik aus Makedonien. Chronologische Indizien. *Antike Kunst* 34, 13–21.

Drougou, S. und Touratsoglou, I. 1994. Τα χρονολογημένα σύνολα ελληνιστικής κεραμικής από τη Μακεδονία. In *Γ' Επιστημονική Συνάντηση για την Ελληνιστική Κεραμική*. Θεσσαλονίκη 1991, 128–137. Athen, Archetai.

Drougou, S. und Touratsoglou, I. 2000. *Το Ιερό της Μητέρας των Θεών στη Βεργίνα. Νομισματικές ενδείξεις και κεραμεική*. Οβολός 4. Thessaloniki, University Studio Press.

Drougou, S. und Touratsoglou, I. 2012. Η ελληνιστική Κεραμική στον Μακεδονικό χώρο. Είκοσι έτη μετά. *Threpteria'*, 241–274. Thessaloniki, Aristoteles University Thessaloniki-Editions.

Edwards, G. R. 1975. *Corinthian Hellenistic Pottery*. Excavations of Corinth VII, 3. Princeton, NJ., American School of Classical Studies at Athens.

Faklaris, P. 1983. Πήλινες μήτρες και ανάγλυφα αγγεία από τη Βεργίνα. Αρχαιολογικον Δελτιον 18, 211–238.

Gehrke, H.-J. 2000. Ιστορία του Ελληνιστικού Κόσμου. Athen, Ekdotiki Athinon.

Goldman, H. (Hrsg.) 1950. *Tarsus I, Excavation at Gözlü Kule I*. Princeton, University Press.

Günay Tuluk, G. 2001. Hellenistische Reliefbecher im Museum in Ephesos. In F. Krinzinger (Hrsg.), *Studien zur hellenistischen Keramik in Ephesos*. Ergänzungsheft zu den Jahresheften des Österreichischen Archäologischen Instituts, 51–69. Wien, Akademie der Wissenschaften.

Hannestad, L. 2001. Greek Pottery and Greek Identity. In Ch. Scheffer (Hrsg.), *Ceramics in Context*. Proceedings of the internordic colloquium on ancient pottery held at Stockholm 13–15 June 1997, 9–16. Stockholm, Almquist & Wiksell International.

Hausmann, U. 1959. *Hellenistische Reliefbecher aus attischen und böotischen Werkstätten*. Stuttgart, Kohlhammer.

Hayes, J. W. 2008. *Roman Pottery, Fine Ware Imports*. Athenian Agora XXXII. Princeton, NJ., American School of Classical Studies at Athens.

Helly, B. 2009. La Thessalie au 3e siecle av. J. C. *To Αρχαιολογικό Έργο Θεσσαλίας και Στερεάς Ελλάδας* 2, 339–368.

Ιστορία 1974. *Ιστορία του ελληνικού έθνους 5. Ελληνιστικοί χρόνοι: Περίοδος 201–30 π.Χ.* Athen, Εκδοτική Αθηνών.

Kähler, H. 1965. *Der Fries vom Reiterdenkmal des Aemilius Paullus in Delphi*. Berlin, Gebr. Mann.

Karamitrou-Mentesidi, G. 1996. *Αιανή*. Athen.

Kotitsa, Z. 1996. *Hellenistische Tonpyxiden: Untersuchung zweier hellenistischer Typen einer Keramikform*. Mainz, Zabern.

Kotitsa, Z. 2006. *Αιγίνιο Πιερίας, Κεραμική από το Νεκροταφείο στη θέση «Μελίσσια»*. Thessaloniki, K. Sfakianaki-Editions.

Kyriakou, A. 2008. *Η στενόμακρη τούμπα της Βεργίνας*. Thessaloniki, K. Sfakianaki-Editions.

Liampi, K. 1998. *Der makedonische Schild*. Bonn, Habelt.

Lilimpaki-Akamatis, M. 1994. *Λαξευτοί τάφοι της Πέλλας*. Athen, TAP.

Lund, J. 2005. An Economy of Consumption. The Eastern Sigillata A. Industry in the late Hellenistic period, in Z. H. Archibald, J. K. Davies und V. Gabrielsen (Hrsg.), *Making, Moving and Managing. The New World of Ancient Economies 323–31 BC*, 233–252. Oxford, Oxbow.

Meloni, P. 1953. *Perseo e la fine della Monarchia Macedone*. Roma, L'Erma di Bretschneider.

Meyer-Schlichtmann, C. 1988. *Die pergamenische Sigillata aus der Stadtgrabung von Pergamon*. Pergamenische Forschungen 6. Berlin, de Gruyter.

Miller, S. 1993. *The Tomb of Lyson and Kallikles. A Painted Macedonian Tomb*. Mainz, Zabern.

Mitsopoulos-Leon, V. 1991. *Die Basilika am Staatsmarkt in Ephesos, Teil I. Keramik hellenistischer und römischer Zeit*. Forschungen in Ephesos 9, 2.2 Wien, Akademie der Wissenschaften.

Nikolaou, E. 2004. Πήλινοι λύχνοι από το Βόρειο Νεκροταφείο της αρχαίας Δημητριάδος. In *Στ` Επιστημονική Συνάντηση για την Ελληνιστική*

Κεραμικη, Βόλος 2000, 47–60. Athen, TAP.

Papakonstantinou, M.-F. 2000, «Μακεδονικού τύπου» αμφορείς από το νοτιοανατολικό νεκροταφείο της Λαμίας. In *H' Ελληνιστική Κεραμικη από τη Θεσσαλία*, 193–203. Athen, TAP.

Papakonstantinou, M.-F. 2000a. Echinos. In *H' Ελληνιστική Κεραμική από τη Θεσσαλία*, 204–214. Athen, TAP.

Robinson, P. S. 1959. *Pottery of the Roman Period.* Athenian Agora V. Princeton, NJ., American School of Classical Studies at Athens.

Rotroff, S. I. 1982. *Hellenistic Pottery. Athenian and Imported Moldmade Bowls*. Athenian Agora XXII. Princeton, NJ., American School of Classical Studies at Athens.

Rotroff, S. I. 2000. Molds: Productions and Preparations – Use and spread. In *E' Επιστημονική Συνάντηση για την Ελληνιστική Κεραμική*. Χανιά 1997, 496–501. Athen, TAP.

Schmid, S. G. 2006. B*oire pour Apollon. Céramique hellénistique et banquets dans le sanctuaire d' Apollon Daphnéphoros*. Eretria 16. Gollio, Infolio.

Shipley, G. 2000. *The Greek World after Alexander 323–30 B.C.* Oxford, Routledge.

Sinn, U. 1979. *Homerische Becher: Hellenistische Reliefkeramik aus Makedonien*. Beihefte zu den Mitteilungen des Deutschen Archäologischen Institut, Athenische Abteilung 7. Berlin, Gebr. Mann.

Sokolovska, V. 1994. Some Pottery Finds from Isar Marvinci. In *Γ' Επιστημονική Συνάντηση για την Ελληνιστική Κεραμική*. Θεσσαλονίκη 1991, 215–217. Athen, Archetai.

Touratsoglou, I. 2010. *Συμβολή στην Οικονομική Ιστορία του βασιλείου της Μακεδονίας. A Contribution to the Economic History of the Kingdom of Ancient Macedonia (6th–3rd century BC)*. Athen, SEMA.

Tsantila, V. 2004. *Ανάγλυφοι σκύφοι από την Ανασκαφή των νεωσοίκων των Οινιαδών* in II Intern. Congress Aetoloakarnania. Agrinio.

Walbank, F. W. 1940. *Philip V of Macedon*. Cambridge, University Press.

Zauri, A. und Melliou, E. 2000. Ελληνιστική Κεραμική από τα νεκροταφεία της Λάρισας. In *Ελληνιστική Κεραμική από τη Θεσσαλία*, 82–110. Athen, TAP.

Hellenistic Kantharoi. Their production centers and their distribution in the Eastern Mediterranean

Chrysanti Kallini

Abstract

The aim of this paper is the outlook for the Hellenistic pottery on the occasion of the study of a specific vase shape, that of the kantharos. The Kantharos was the most popular drinking vessel during the late Classical and the whole Hellenistic period in the Eastern Mediterranean, and as such its study can add to the discussion of dating Hellenistic contexts and relationships between different regions of the Hellenistic world. All the examples used in this research derive from closed archaeological contexts, so that the dating of the materials is as secure as possible. There are four main types of Hellenistic kantharoi. Three of them derive from the Athenian Classical pottery. There are a lot of local variations of the Hellenistic types that show the diversity of the form and the free expression of the Hellenistic pottery workshops.

Keywords: Kantharos, Drinking cup, Eastern Mediterranean, Workshops, Typology

Introduction

The Kantharos was the most popular drinking cup through the whole Hellenistic period in the Eastern Mediterranean[1]. For the early Hellenistic period different types of kantharoi have been recognized, which can be distinguished twofold: firstly, the varieties which derived from the Classical Attic pottery[2] and continued to be manufactured in the Hellenistic period, and secondly the pure Hellenistic type[3].

The Classical kantharos, the cup-kantharos, and the bowl-kantharos appertain to the first group, while the Hellenistic type appeared in the end of the 4th century BC and survived throughout the whole Hellenistic period, until the end of the 2nd/ beginning of the 1st century BC, in several varieties depending on the production area.

Classical Kantharoi

The varieties of Classical kantharoi were distributed all over the Eastern Mediterranean, but – until the last decades of the 4th century BC – the majority of them were produced in Attic workshops. In the early Hellenistic years the pottery workshops outside Attica began to imitate the Attic imports, in some cases with success and in some others very unskillfully[4]. The origin of the ceramic products can be localized by applying diverse methods, such as the clay analyses, the existence of pottery kilns, and the particular vase shapes in each area. Comparison among the shapes of kantharoi found outside Attica and the examples from Athens indicates that the majority of the 4th century BC examples were Attic and only the examples dated to the last decades of the 4th or to the 3rd century BC were local products[5].

Classical kantharoi with molded rim

Among the three classical varieties mentioned above, the most popular throughout the 4th century BC is the Classical kantharos and this is why we chose to focus primarily on this type. The subtype with molded rim appeared in the second quarter of the 4th century BC in Attica and survived until the first decades of the 3rd century BC[6]. The examples of Classical kantharoi with molded rim, which date to the 4th century BC, have been manufactured in Attic workshops, despite the fact that they have been found in several places outside Attica.

A characteristic example is that of a kantharos found in a tomb in Mesokomi Serron (Macedonia). This vessel is dated c. 330–320 BC according to the coins found in the grave (3 bronze coins of Phillip II, which are dated to the period 359–336 BC)[7] **(Fig. 1)**. The relationship in shape and quality with a kantharos found in Athens, in Menon's Cistern, dated c. 335–325 BC[8], indicates the Attic provenance of the kantharos from Serres.

1 Kallini 2007; Rotroff 1997, 83.
2 Rotroff 1997, 83–91.
3 Rotroff 1997, 97–105.

4 For specific examples see below.
5 Nevertheless, the progress in research on the regional pottery of Macedonia indicates a quite earlier date of the beginning of imitating the attic prototypes to ca. mid-4th century BC at least. Unfortunately, there are not yet enough published contexts with kantharoi, in order to support the local production of kantharoi from that date (mid-4th c. BC or even earlier).
6 Kallini 2007, 266–269; Rotroff 1997, 85; Sparkes and Talcott, 1970, 122.
7 Poulios, 1987, 450, pl. 261.
8 According to Miller 1974, 200, 229, pl. 30:1, this kantharos can be dated to the third quarter of the 4th century BC. But S. Rotroff in: Rotroff 1997, 245, n. 36, suggests a chronology to c. 335–325 BC, which is widely accepted.

Fig. 1. Mesokomi Serron (Poulios 1987, 450 pl. 261)

Fig. 2. Pella (Akamatis 1993, 184 pl. 4)

Fig. 3. Afitis (Misailidou-Despotidou 1999, 311–313 pl. 9)

Fig. 4. Kabyle (Bozkova 1994, 124 pl. 90)

Another example found in Isthmia, in the South Slope Cistern in the Rachi settlement, is dated some years later, c. 300 BC. This kantharos is considered to be Attic[9], based on the comparison with a similar one found in Athens, in the Cistern System H6:9, which dates into the same period[10].

The examples from Pella and Tenos presented below document that in the first decades of the 3rd century BC the local workshops adopted and began to produce the Classical kantharos with molded rim.

The material found in a well/ deposit of a pottery workshop on the Agora of Pella included three kantharoi[11] (**Fig. 2**). These vases are dated to the end of the 4th/ beginning of the 3rd century BC according to the coins found in the same context (coins of Cassander). Taking under

[9] Anderson-Stojanovic 1997, 15, pl. 3.
[10] Rotroff 1997, 246, pl. 5:45.

[11] Akamatis 1993, 184, pl. 4.

Fig. 5. Poulios 1994, 116 pl. 66a

Fig. 6. Nikolaiodou-Patera 1994, 108 pl. 50

Fig. 7. Drougou and Touratsoglou 1980, 100 pl. 66.

consideration the context of the find we can pertain to their local provenance.

The vessel from Tenos, found in a deposit in the sanctuary of Poseidon and Amphitrite, is dated c. 280–260 BC according to the pottery and lamps found in the same context[12]. This vessel was made in a local workshop as the clay analysis indicates. The example from Tenos imitates Attic imports, as deduced by the comparison between this example and a kantharos from the Athenian Agora, dated some years earlier[13].

Classical kantharoi with plain rim

The Classical kantharos with plain rim appeared in the Attic workshops in the middle of the 4th century BC and lasted until the end of the 3rd/ beginning of the 2nd century BC[14]. As with the Classical kantharos with molded rim, the majority of the examples with plain rim, which date until the end of the 4th century BC, are considered to be Attic, too. A kantharos found in the debris of a house in Afitis in Chalkidike is dated, according to the context (coins and pottery), c. 325 BC[15] (**Fig. 3**). The vessel from Afitis could be Attic as the comparison with a kantharos found in a well (F11:2) in the Tholos Debris on the Athenian Agora shows, which is dated into the same period[16].

The kantharoi with plain rim found in Isthmia, in the South Slope Cistern in the Rachi settlement, are dated to the end of the 4th century BC[17]. These examples are considered to be Attic, according to the comparison with contemporary attic examples, as the one found in the Cistern E3:1 on the Athenian Agora[18].

The local imitations of Attic prototypes in northern Greece can be dated from the last quarter of the 4th century BC,

[12] Etienne and Braun, 1986, 211, pl. 114.

[13] Rotroff 1997, 246, pl. 5:45.
[14] Kallini 2007, 269–277; Rotroff 1997, 84–85.
[15] Misailidou-Despotidou 1999, 311–313, pl. 9.
[16] Rotroff 1997, 242, pl. 1:1.
[17] Anderson-Stojanovic 1997, 15, pl. 2–3.
[18] Rotroff 1997, 243, pl. 1:10.

Fig. 8. Doulgeri-Intzesiloglou 1997, 63–65 pl. 48b–c

Fig. 9. Kaltsas 1983, 35–36 pl. 9a

Fig. 10. Nikolaiodou-Patera 1994, 110 pl. 53a

as examples from Aiginion[19] and Thasos[20] indicate. Attic kantharoi were distributed to ancient Thrace until the first half of the 3rd century BC, as the example found in tomb 2 of the Eastern necropolis at Kabyle indicates. This example is dated c. 300–280 BC according to the context (a coin of Lysimachus)[21]. From the middle of the 3rd century BC the Thracian pottery workshops adopted the type and began to imitate the imported Attic kantharoi. An example found in a tomb at Kabyle dated to the third quarter of the 3rd century BC according to a posthumous silver drachm of Alexander III demonstrates this unskillful attempt[22] (**Fig. 4**). The same attempt is recognized on a kantharos found in a tomb at Serres, which dates to the same period (c. 250–239 BC) according to a treasure of 13 coins[23] (**Fig. 5**).

Local production of kantharoi is recognized in others areas of northern Greece, too, as for example the pottery material found in the destruction layer of a house in Hiona, dated to the second quarter of the 3rd century BC[24] (**Fig. 6**). This material can be considered as the production of a non-Attic workshop, probable from the neighbor region. These attempts of local workshops in ancient Thrace and Eastern Macedonia are quite unskillful and the same characteristics are recognized, such as the awkward profile with very thin body and the big handles with steeply raising spurs. The size and shape of the handles, with lower proportions of the body, are characteristic for two kantharoi found in a tomb in Veroia, dated to the end of the 3rd/ beginning of the 2nd century BC[25] (**Fig. 7**). These two examples from Veroia signal the end of production of the Classical kantharos. The phenomenon of imitating the Attic Classical kantharoi can be traced also on Aegean islands, such as Lemnos[26], Chios[27], Tenos[28], even Crete[29] and Rhodes[30].

Hellenistic kantharoi

The Hellenistic kantharos appeared at Athens c. 300 BC. It is a deep vessel with two handles and without foot. In the beginning the profile was straight-walled whereas from

19 Kotitsa 2007, 39–43.
20 Blonde 2007, 133–134, pl. 12.
21 Bozkova 1997, 124, pl. 89b, 90a, 92a:1.

22 Bozkova 1997, 124, pl. 90b, 92a:5.
23 Poulios 1994, 116, pl. 66a.
24 Nikolaidou-Patera 1994, 108, pl. 51–52.
25 Drougou and Touratsoglou 1980, 95, 100, 152–153, pl. 66.
26 Savona *et al. 1997, 223–224, pl. 142–143.*
27 Anderson 1954, 148, pl. 10c.
28 Etienne and Braun 1986, 208–211, pl. 113–114.
29 Egglezou 2005, 95, pl. 10b, 81c (420).
30 Gianikouri *et al. 1986, 174, pl. 87c.*

Fig. 11. Georgiadou 2005, 122 pl. 58

Fig. 12. Xatziaggelakis 2000, 182–183, 186 pl. 11

the middle of the 3rd century BC became angular[31]. The origins of the Hellenistic kantharos can be located outside Attica, maybe in Boiotia[32]. Its probable predecessor is the Kabeiric kantharos or skyphos which firstly appeared in Boiotia in the 5th century BC and survived at least until the middle of the 3rd century BC. The Hellenistic kantharos constitutes the main drinking cup in the Eastern Mediterranean from the beginning of the 3rd century BC onwards. Hellenistic kantharoi occur in various forms such as the straight-walled, the angular, the kantharos with S profile[33] and the kantharos with molded rim in several varieties according to the place of production.

The straight-walled shape was introduced at the same time (c. 300 BC) in other areas outside Attica like Thessaly[34]. The local production of kantharoi in Thessaly in the 3rd century BC is certified by an example found in a deposit of a local pottery workshop dated into the second half of the 3rd century BC[35] (**Fig. 8**). In the Peloponnese the straight-walled kantharos appeared in the end of the 4th century BC, too[36] (**Fig. 9**). The local production of this shape can be documented based on the special features of these Peloponnesian vessels, such as the shape of the body and the decoration[37]. Hellenistic straight-walled kantharoi continued to be manufactured in the Peloponnese until the middle of the 3rd century BC. In the same area and at the same time the 'cyma' kantharos or kantharos with S profile appeared[38]. This shape survived until the last quarter of the 3rd century BC and influenced the pottery production of other areas, such as Macedonia[39]. Kantharoi found in the debris of a house in Hiona (in Macedonia) are dated into the second quarter of the 3rd century BC[40] (**Fig. 10**). These vessels must have been made in a local workshop, maybe in the same one where the local Classical kantharoi, we already discussed, were manufactured. The example of Hiona is evidential of the diversity of the Hellenistic kantharoi, since a lot of varieties are represented in this context: the angular kantharos, the kantharos with S profile and the kantharos with molded rim.

Fig. 13. Egglezou 2005, 95, 98 pl. 81d (422)

31 Rotroff 1997, 97–105.
32 Kallini 2007, 291–292; Rotroff 1997, 97–98.
33 According to Edwards 1975, 76–82, the kantharos with S profile is also called 'cyma kantharos'.
34 Triantafyllopoulou 2000, 61–62, fig. 2.
35 Doulgeri-Intzesiloglou 1997, 63–65, pl. 48b, c.
36 Edwards 1975, 74–76; Kaltsas 1983, 8–10, 35–36, pl. 9a, 11a.
37 Edwards 1975, 9–11.
38 Edwards 1975, 76–82.
39 See below the example from Hiona, Nikolaiodou-Patera 1994, 110, 53a.
40 Nikolaiodou-Patera 1994, 104–114.

Fig. 14. Rotroff 1997, 273 pl. 30:301

Fig. 15. Tsakos 1994, 162 pl. 6

Variations of the Hellenistic kantharoi

In the transitional period of the 3rd century BC, special variations of Hellenistic kantharoi appeared in several places. In some other cases Classical shapes from the 4th century BC continued to be manufactured through the early Hellenistic years. A variant of kantharos called 'heliakos', existed in Helis in northern Peloponnese, from the 4th century BC onwards[41] (**Fig. 11**).

This Classical shape was formed in the first half of the 4th century BC[42] and survived in northern Peloponnese, in South-Western Greece (Aitolia[43] and Naupaktos[44]) and in ancient Epirus (Phoinike[45]) until the beginning of the 3rd century BC. From the area of Thessaly derives a variation with deep body in S profile, downturned rim, and round handles, dated to the middle of the 3rd century BC [46] (**Fig. 12**). This variant survived in western Greece, in the area of Ambrakia[47] and Corfu[48] until the middle of the 2nd century BC. A special group of Hellenistic kantharoi comes from Crete and is called the 'Cretan type'[49]. This variety appeared after the middle of the 3rd century BC and survived for just a short time, until the end of the century BC (**Fig. 13**). The Hellenistic kantharos with molded rim appeared in several places including Athens[50] (**Fig. 14**) and Peloponnese[51] from the second half of the 3rd century BC and survived until the end of the 2nd century BC. The majority of these examples were undecorated and carelessly made. The kantharoi dated to the 2nd and 1st century BC represent the last phase of the development of the Hellenistic kantharoi. The pottery of the Greek mainland and much more from the Aegean islands is influenced from the pottery of Asia Minor, as an example found in a deposit in the Pythagoreion in Samos shows[52] (**Fig. 15**). This kantharos is dated in the second half of the 2nd century BC according to coins found in the same context. The kantharoi found on Delos[53] mark the end of the production of Hellenistic kantharoi.

Conclusion

On the occasion of the study of Hellenistic kantharoi we remark that until the end of the 4th century BC the most famous pottery workshops were in Attica, and particularly in Athens. Attic ceramic products were distributed all over the Eastern Mediterranean and the Attic workshops played a very significant role to the formation of the characteristics of Greek Classical pottery.

Starting at the last decades of the 4th century BC, Athens is no longer the focal place in the development of Greek pottery. The local workshops outside Attica begin to adopt and imitate the Attic prototypes and gradually diverge from the Attic influence.

In the middle of the 3rd century BC several varieties of the Hellenistic kantharos appeared in the local pottery of the Eastern Mediterranean. The origins of these varieties can be traced in the Attic angular kantharos and the Corinthian kantharos in S profile.

41 Georgiado 2005, 122, pl. 37, 58.
42 Kyriakou 1994, 190, pl. 133.
43 Zapheiropoulou 2000, 324, pl. 163a.
44 Kolia 2004, 536, 542, pl. 257b.
45 Gamberini 2009, 90–91, fig. 7:8–10.
46 Xatziaggelakis 2000, 182–183, 186, fig. 11.
47 Aggeli 2009, 168–169, fig. 11.
48 Riginos *et al. 2009, 181–182, fig. 6, 184–186, fig. 12.*
49 Egglezou 2005, 95, 98, pl. 81d (422).
50 Rotroff 1997, 273, pl. 30:301.
51 Katsas 1983, 20–21, pl. 28a.
52 Tsakos 1994, 162, fig. 6.
53 Zafeiropoulou and Xatzidakis 1994, 244, pl. 195c.

From the 3rd century BC on local workshops formed, according to their pottery tradition, new vase-shapes or local variations, such as the kantharoi of the 'Cretan type' or continued to manufacture Classical shapes like the 'heliakoi kantharoi'. In most of the cases, these products were used to cover the local needs of each area. The local variations show the diversity of the Hellenistic pottery but also the political and economic relationships among different areas.

Chrysanthi Kallini
Aristotle University of Thessaloniki
Department of Archaeology
Thessaloniki 54124
kallini@hist.auth.gr

Bibliography

Aggeli, A. 2009. Ελληνιστική κεραμική από το δυτικό νεκροταφείο της Αμβρακίας,. In *Ελληνιστική κεραμική από την αρχαία Ήπειρο, την Αιτωλοακαρνανία και τα Ιόνια νησιά*, 163–178. Athens, Archaeological Receipts Fund.

Akamatis, I. 1993. Η Αγορά της Πέλλας κατά το 1993. *Το Αρχαιολογικό Έργο στη Μακεδονία και Θράκη* 7, 183–194.

Anderson, J. K. 1954. Excavations on the Kofina ridge, Chios. *The Annual of the British School at Athens* 49, 123–182.

Anderson-Stojanovic, V. 1997. A third century BC Deposit from the South Slope Cistern in the Rachi Settlement at Isthmia. In *Δ' Επιστημονική Συνάντηση για την Ελληνιστική Κεραμική*. Μυτιλήνη 1994, 13–19. Athens, Ypourgeio Politismou.

Blondé, F. 2007. *Les ceramiques d'usage quotidien a Thasos au IVe siecle avant J.-C.* Athens, École française d'Athènes.

Bozkova, A. 1997. La ceramique des necropolis hellenistiques de Cabyle. In *Δ' Επιστημονική Συνάντηση για την Ελληνιστική Κεραμική*. Μυτιλήνη 1994, 123–127. Athens, Ypourgeio Politismou.

Doulgeri-Intzesiloglou, A. 1997. 'Κλειστό' σύνολο φεραϊκής κεραμικής ελληνιστικής εποχής από σωστική ανασκαφή στο οικόπεδο Θ. Ντόντου στο Βελεστίνο. In *Δ' Επιστημονική Συνάντηση για την Ελληνιστική Κεραμική*. Μυτιλήνη 1994, 59–78. Athens, Ypourgeio Politismou.

Drougou, S. and Touratsoglou, I. 1980. *Ελληνιστικοί λαξευτοί τάφοι Βέροιας*. Athens, Ministry of Culture.

Edwards, G. R. 1975. *Corinthian Hellenistic Pottery.* Corinth VII,3. Princeton, NJ., American School of Classical Studies.

Egglezou, M. 2005. *Ελληνιστική κεραμική Κρήτης: Κεντρική Κρήτη*. Athens, Archaeological Receipts Fund.

Etienne, R. and Braun, J.-P. 1986. *Le Sanctuaire de Poseidon et d'Amphitrite. Tenos I.* Paris, École française d'Athènes.

Gamberini, A. 2009. Le prime fasi di vita della citta di Phoinike (Albania Meridionale): La stratigrafia del vano L nella 'Casa dei due peristili'. In *Ελληνιστική κεραμική από την αρχαία Ήπειρο, την Αιτωλοακαρνανία και τα Ιόνια νησιά*, 87–96. Athens, Archaeological Receipts Fund.

Georgiadou, A. 2005. *Totenkult und elische Grabkeramik spätklassischer und hellenistischer Zeit.* Thessaloniki, University Studio Press.

Gianikouri, A., Patsiada, V. and Filimonos, M. 2000. Ταφικά σύνολα από τις νεκροπόλεις της αρχαίας Ρόδου. In *Α' Επιστημονική Συνάντηση για την Ελληνιστική Κεραμική*. Ιωάννινα 1986, 63–117. Ioannina, Panepistimio Ioanninon.

Kallini, Chr. 2007. *Ο ελληνιστικός 'κάνθαρος'. Συμβολή στη μελέτη της ελληνιστικής κεραμικής*. PhD thesis, Aristotle University of Thessaloniki. www.digital.lib.auth.gr/record/79364.

Kaltsas, N. 1983. Από τα ελληνιστικά νεκροταφεία της Πύλου. *Αρχαιολογικόν Δελτίον Μελεται* 38, 1–77.

Kolia, E. I. 2004. Ταφικά σύνολα από τη Ναύπακτο. In *ΣΤ' Επιστημονική Συνάντηση για την Ελληνιστική Κεραμική*. Βόλος 2000, 535–546. Athens, TAP.

Kotitsa, Z. 2007. *Αιγίνιο Πιερίας. Κεραμική από το νεκροταφείο στη θέση 'Μελίσσια'.* Thessaloniki, Kornilia Sfakianaki Press.

Kyriakou, D. 1994. Ελληνιστική κεραμική από τα νεκροταφεία της Πάτρας. In *Γ' Επιστημονική Συνάντηση για την Ελληνιστική Κεραμική*. Θεσσαλονίκη 1991, 185–195. Athens, Archetai.

Miller, St. G. 1974. The Menon's Cistern. *Hesperia* 43, 194–245.

Misailidou-Despotidou, V. 1999. Ανασκαφική έρευνα στην αρχαία Άφυτη. *Το Αρχαιολογικό Έργο στη Μακεδονία και Θράκη* 13, 305–316.

Nikolaidou-Patera, M. 1994. Σύνολο Ελληνιστικής Κεραμικής από τα περίχωρα της Ηιόνας. In *Γ' Επιστημονική Συνάντηση για την Ελληνιστική Κεραμική*. Θεσσαλονίκη 1991, 104–114. Athens, Archetai.

Poulios, V. 1987. *Αρχαιολογικόν Δελτίον Χρονικα* 42, 449–451.

Poulios, B. 1994. Χρονολογημένη Ελληνιστική Κεραμική από την Ανατολική Μακεδονία. In *Γ' Επιστημονική Συνάντηση για την Ελληνιστική Κεραμική*. Θεσσαλονίκη 1991, 115–127. Athens, Archetai.

Riginos, G., Georgiadou, G. and Adamopoulou, R.

2009. Κεραμική ελληνιστικών χρόνων από τη βόρεια νεκρόπολη της αρχαίας Κέρκυρας. In *Ελληνιστική κεραμική από την αρχαία Ήπειρο, την Αιτωλοακαρνανία και τα Ιόνια νησιά*, 179–190. Athens, Archaeological Receipts Fund.

Rotroff, S. I. 1997. *Hellenistic Pottery. Athenian and Imported wheelmade table ware and Related Material.* The Athenian Agora XXIX. Princeton, NJ., American School of Classical Studies.

Poggesi, G., Savona, S., Monaco, M.-Ch. and Monaco, M. C. 1997. Un deposito di ceramiche tardoclassische ed ellenistische del Cabirio di Lemno: Analisi delle forme. In *Δ' Επιστημονική Συνάντηση για την Ελληνιστική Κεραμική*. Μυτιλήνη 1994, 220–231. Athens, Ypourgeio Politismou.

Sparkes, B. A. and Talcott, L. 1970. *Black and Plain Pottery of the 6th, 5th and 4th centuries BC. T*he Athenian Agora XII. Princeton, NJ., American School of Classical Studies.

Triantafyllopoulou, P. 2000. Νεκροταφείο των Αμφανών. Οι πρώιμοι ελληνιστικοί τάφοι, in S. Drougou, E. Zervoudaki, A. Doulgeri-Intzesiloglou and G. Touratsoglou (eds.), *Ελληνιστική Κεραμική από τη Θεσσαλία*, 60–69. Volos, Ministry of Culture.

Tsakos, K. 1994. Pottery from a Late Hellenistic Samian Deposit, in A. Archontidou, S. Drougou, L. Marangou, G. Touratsoglou and E. Zervoudaki (eds.), *Ελληνιστική κεραμική από το Αιγαίο*, 146–163. Mytilene, Ministry of Culture.

Xatziaggelakis, L. P. 2000. Το ανατολικό νεκροταφείο της Αργιθέας, in S. Drougou, E. Zervoudaki, A. Doulgeri-Intzesiloglou and G. Touratsoglou (eds.), *Ελληνιστική Κεραμική από τη Θεσσαλία*, 180–191. Volos, Ministry of Culture.

Zafeiropoulou, F. and Xatzidakis, P. 1994. Δήλος – Κεραμική από τον δρόμο βόρεια του Ανδήρου των Λεόντων. In *Γ' Επιστημονική Συνάντηση για την Ελληνιστική Κεραμική*. Θεσσαλονίκη 1991, 235–248. Athens, Archetai.

Zapheiropoulou, F. 2000. Τάφοι στο Τριχόνιο Αιτωλίας. In *Ε' Επιστημονική Συνάντηση για την Ελληνιστική Κεραμική*. Χανιά 1997, 323–328. Athens, TAP.

Frühhellenistische Keramik aus Pydna: Hinweise auf regionale und überregionale Kontakte

Zoi Kotitsa

Abstract

The aim of this paper is to examine contacts of the ancient city of Pydna to other centers of the Early Hellenistic world through the pottery from grave contexts of the northern cemetery of the city. Significant in this respect are on the one hand imports, which lead to Athens, Corinth and the nearby Pella, on the other hand, affinities between ceramics found in Pydna and products from other near or distant regions. Aiginio, Aigai / Vergina, Veroia and Aiani are places in the wider region of the city, where ceramic workshops seem to share a kind of ceramic Koine with those in Pydna. Thrace, the Black Sea area, Egypt, Rhodes, Cyprus share also some forms with the Macedonian port, while new data regarding tin-foiled pottery permit to question a possible relationsship with southern Italy and Etruria. Those affinities can be explained as results either of direct trade or of mutual influence of workshops, or of use of common models; they could be also due to the mobility of individuals. In the case of Pydna is unfortunately hardly possible, in the present state of research, to decide between these options. An aggravating factor to be considered in this task is the so called pseudo-Attic pottery detected in our material, which leads to a reconsideration of the primary role of Attic potters in the invention and distribution of some forms.

Keywords: Scherbentyp, Nachahmung, Koine, pseudo-attisch, attisierend, Import, Auswanderung, Handelsbeziehungen.

In diesem Beitrag werden ‚Netzwerke' zur Diskussion gestellt, die aus der Erforschung der frühhellenistischen Keramik aus der Nordnekropole von Pydna hervorgehen[1]. Regionale und überregionale Kontakte werden durch Betrachtung einerseits von Importen, andererseits von Affinitäten zwischen den in Pydna gefundenen Keramikprodukten und denjenigen anderer Regionen aufgespürt.

Überregionale Kontakte

Betrachtet man zunächst die durch die Keramik bezeugten bzw. angedeuteten überregionalen Kontakte von Pydna, wird man gleich zum großen Keramikzentrum Athen geleitet. Die Handelsbeziehungen zwischen den beiden Städten bestanden bereits seit dem 5. Jh. v. Chr., wie die zahlreichen Funde attischer Keramik in den pydnäischen Nekropolen bezeugen[2], und setzten sich bis zum Ende des 4./Anfang 3. Jhs. v. Chr. fort[3]. Außerdem dürfte das für Athen wertvolle makedonische Schiffbauholz, vor allem nach der Einnahme und der Räumung von Methone durch Philipp II. im Jahr 354 v. Chr., vom pydnäischen Hafen verschifft gewesen sein.

Der Umfang der attischen Importe nach Pydna scheint jedoch im Laufe der 2. Hälfte des 4. Jhs. v. Chr. deutlich abzunehmen. An ihrer Stelle treten Produkte auf, die attische Formen bis ins letzte Detail nachahmen und nur bei näherer Betrachtung von den attischen unterschieden werden können. Der Scherben dieser Gefäße ist farblich von demjenigen attischer Keramik kaum auseinander zu halten (2.5YR 7/6 bis 5YR 6/6) aber entweder ungleichmäßig gebrannt, oder weniger dicht, oder seifig bzw. speckig. Der Glanzton ist von guter Qualität, hat manchmal olivegrüne ‚Flecken' und erscheint insgesamt weniger ‚gesättigt' als derjenige der meisten attischen Exemplare[4]. Den Formen dieser Produkte fehlen bei genauerer Untersuchung die klare Artikulation und die präzise Ausführung attischer Gefäße, so dass man sich an die Bewertung von Sparkes und Talcott, dass ‚…the attic workshops differed from the others not in practice but in precision…', erinnert fühlt[5] (**Abb. 1**). Die frappierende Ähnlichkeit dieser Gefäße mit den attischen Erzeugnissen hat uns veranlasst, sie als ‚pseudo-attisch' zu bezeichnen, im Gegensatz zu den Glanztongefäßen aus deutlich nicht-attischem Scherbentyp[6], die sich in der Formgebung an die

[1] Die Untersuchung der spätklassischen und hellenistischen Keramik aus der Nordnekropole von Pydna durch die Verfasserin erfolgte im Rahmen eines durch die DFG geförderten Forschungsprojektes an der Philipps-Universität Marburg, dessen Publikation sich in Vorbereitung befindet. Ich möchte an dieser Stelle dem Ausgräber M. Bessios für das Überlassen des Materials und seine Hilfsbereitschaft zu jeder Zeit herzlich danken. Genauso gilt mein Dank H. Froning-Kehler (Philipps-Universität Marburg), die das Projekt unterstützte und mir mit Rat und Tat zur Seite stand.

[2] Bessios und Pappa o. J. 48–61; Bessios 2010, 122–123. 140–162 passim und für attische Funde aus der erweiterten Region von Pydna S. 261–267.

[3] Kotitsa 2004, 196–199.

[4] Es gilt auch für Pydna die bildhafte zutreffende Beschreibung und Unterscheidung zwischen attischen und ‚attisierenden' Oberflächen von Berlin und Lynch 2002, 171: ‚The difference is akin to that between the surface of an ice rink and a swimming pool. Both are the same medium, but in the former light is reflected back and the surface has a hard, opaque quality, whereas in the latter light appears to be absorbed and the surface has a soft translucent look'.

[5] Sparkes und Talcott 1970, 17.

[6] Für den deutschen Begriff ‚Scherbentyp', der den englischen ‚fabric'

Abb. 1. Pseudo-attischer Kantharos Py 1224, 320–300 v. Chr. H 7,8cm (mit Henkeln), Photo: Grabungsarchiv von Pydna

Abb. 2. Attisierende Hydria Py 2322, 320–305 v. Chr. H 13,2cm, Photo: Grabungsarchiv von Pydna

attischen Produkte orientieren, ohne sie jedoch detailgetreu nachzuahmen, und deshalb als ,attisierend' zu bezeichnen sind (**Abb. 2**)[7].

Hinter der Herstellung der pseudo-attischen Gefäße sind höchstwahrscheinlich ausgewanderte attische Töpfer zu vermuten. Denn Pydna wäre sicherlich als wichtigster Hafen Makedoniens, genauso wie Aigai und Pella als Hauptstädte der neuen politischen Macht in Griechenland, ein attraktiver Auswanderungsziel für Töpfer im 4. Jh. v. Chr., die dort nach besseren Chancen für ihr Handwerk aufsuchen konnten[8]. Die große Blüte der Stadt im 5. Jh. v. Chr., als sie über eine Fläche von mehr als 250.000m^2 verfügte und dadurch bis in die Regierungszeit von Philipp II. die größte Stadt des makedonischen Königreiches war[9], hätte außerdem bereits früher, wie z. B. in den Wirren des peloponnesischen Krieges, attische Töpfer dazu veranlassen können, sich hierhin niederzulassen[10].

Die attisierenden Gefäße sind wiederum entweder als Ergebnis eines durch die seit langem nach Pydna ankommenden attischen Gefäße mittelbaren Einflusses oder als Resultat der ,Schulung' einheimischer Töpfer durch ausgewanderte ,Kollegen' aus Athen zu interpretieren, die dann ihre eigenen Werkstätten gründeten und gemäß ihren Fähigkeiten, Ambitionen und den zur Verfügung stehenden Tonsorten attisch-orientierte Gefäße produzierten[11].

Mit den Begriffen ,pseudo-attisch' und ,attisierend' fällt man natürlich in der ,Falle' eines ,Athenocentrism', wie Elizabeth Pemberton die Tendenz bezeichnet hat, Entwicklungen in der Keramik im Allgemeinen auf Athen zurückführen zu wollen[12]. Dennoch greifen auch im Fall der pydnäischen Keramik die Gründe, die Pemberton selbst für die Erklärung dieses Phänomens angeführt hat, nämlich der fortgeschrittene Forschungsstand und die Qualität der attischen Keramik. Die nachgewiesenen wirtschaftlichen Beziehungen zwischen Athen und Pydna dürften zudem als ,reale' Gründe für eine attische Orientierung der pydnäischen Keramikproduktion eine wichtige Rolle gespielt haben[13], während die kurze athenische Besatzung der Stadt zwischen 364/3 und 357 v. Chr.[14] sicherlich zu einem verstärkten Austausch zwischen den beiden Seiten beigetragen hat.

Die Herstellung pseudo-attischer und qualitätsvoller attisierender Keramik verkompliziert allerdings enorm das Bild der Handelsverflechtungen und erschwert bedeutend den Versuch, Netzwerke anhand von Keramikfunde zu

wiedergibt, s. Gassner 2003, 26.

7 Mit Ausnahme von Py 1978 und Morel 1995, 369 wird bislang in der Forschung nur der Begriff ,attisierend' verwendet. s. z. B. Berlin und Lynch 2002; Cook 1965, 143; Furtwängler 1990, 49 mit Lit.; Herda und Sauter 2009, 80–84; Kopcke 1964, 25; Kowalleck 2008, 92–98; Missailidou-Despotidou 1999, 776–777. Die durchgeführten zerstörungsfreien m-XRF-Analysen, deren Auswertung im Cultural and Educational Technology Institute in Xanthi/Nordgriechenland noch nicht abgeschlossen ist, konnten jedoch keine klare Abweichung der pseudo-attischen und attisierenden Gefäße von den attischen aufzeigen; vgl. Furtwängler 1990, 52.

8 Zur Auswanderung attischer Töpfer in spätklassischer-frühhellenistischer Zeit s. Furtwängler 1990, 49–50 mit Lit.; Morel 2000, 16. 18; Robertson 1992, 268. 294–295; s. zudem auch die Anwesenheit verschiedener Künstler bereits seit dem späten 5. Jh. v. Chr. in der makedonischen Hauptstadt: Papakonstantinou-Diamantourou 1971, 68–69.

9 Bessios 1993, 1113–1114; Bessios und Pappa 1995, 5–6; Bessios 1997, 59; Bessios 2010, 114.

10 Vgl. McDonald 1981, 159–163. Für die Anwesenheit athenischer Töpfer in Makedonien bereits im späten 6. Jh. v. Chr. s. Karamitrou-Mentessidi und Kefalidou 1999, 538.

11 Vgl. Furtwängler 1990, 52–53; McDonald 1981, 164.

12 Pemberton 2003, 167–168.

13 Vgl. Furtwängler 1997, 399, der in diesem Sinne von einer attischen Formen-,Koine' im späten 4. und frühen 3. Jh. v. Chr. im ägäischen Raum spricht und bemerkt: ,Oft sind es Bereiche, auf die Athen schon während des zweiten attischen Seebundes größten Einfluss ausübte, Plätze, die traditionell dem kulturellen Einfluss der attischen Metropole ausgesetzt waren.'

14 Für einen kurzen historischen Überblick zu Pydna s. Bessios 2010 passim; Hatzopoulos 2004, 806 s. v. Pydna.

Abb. 3. Attischer ‚Salznapf' Py 344, um 350 v. Chr. H 4,9cm, Photo: Z. Kotitsa

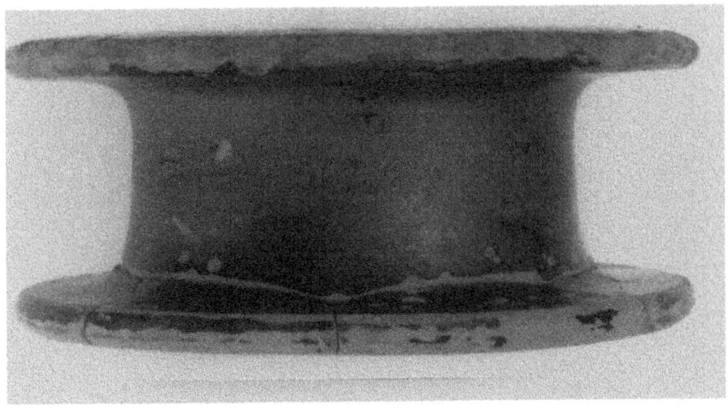

Abb. 5. Attischer(?),Salznapf' Py 5155, 320–305 v. Chr. H 3,9cm, Photo: Grabungsarchiv von Pydna

Abb. 4. Attischer(?) Salznapf Py 2592 (Mitte) und pseudo-attische ‚Salznäpfe' (von l. nach r.: Py 2452, Py 2467), 330–315 v. Chr, Photo: Z. Kotitsa

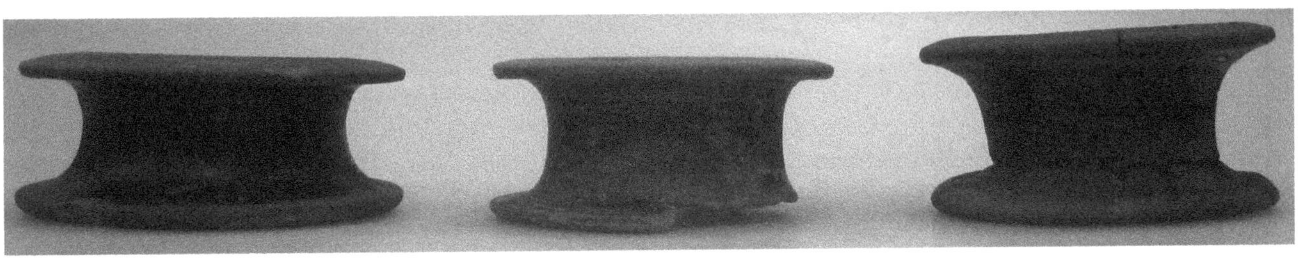

Abb. 6. Lokale/regionale ‚Salznäpfe' (von l. nach r.: Py 5201, Py 2681, Py 8167), 320–305 v. Chr., Photo: Z. Kotitsa

erkennen, da man feine, meistens an attische Vorbilder orientierte Glanztonkeramik aus verschiedenen Gebieten zu erwarten hat[15]. Die Unterscheidung von pseudo-attischen und attisierenden Gefäßen führt außerdem dazu, die angenommene führende Rolle Athens in der Erfindung bzw. Verbreitung von Formen der Glanztonkeramik zu hinterfragen[16]. In Pydna lässt sich dies durch die Fundsituation bezüglich einer charakteristischen Form, des spulenförmigen Salznapfes, demonstrieren, die als Erzeugnis attischer Werkstätte mit einer Lebensdauer zwischen 325 und 295 v. Chr. gilt[17]. In einem pydnäischen Grab aus der Mitte des 4. Jhs. v. Chr. wurde allerdings ein attischer Salznapf gefunden, der bereits Merkmale der

[15] s. exemplarisch Kalliga 2004, 294 und vor allem die Situation in Kleinasien: Trinkl 2006, 215–220. Morel 2000, 15–16 bemerkt zutreffend: ‚Le problème considérable de l'imitation, de la véritable imitation … risque de vicier notre connaissance de la production et de la diffusion de la céramique attique à vernis noir. A la racine de ce problème, une constatation : il n'est pas toujours facile d'affirmer qu'un vase « attique » à vernis noir vient bien d'Athènes. Les plus experts hésitent parfois à ce propos.' Unter diesem Aspekt ist zu fragen, ob manche als ‚attisch' deklarierte oder postulierte Gefäße nicht vielleicht Importe aus anderen Orten waren. Zur Behandlung dieser Frage wären zunächst einige realitätstreue Farbfotos in den Publikationen von großer Hilfe. So z. B. scheint ein spätklassisches Näpfchen aus Apollonia Pontike, Hermary 2010, 102. 224 Kat. VN 100 Taf. 32d;102e, im Scherbentypus und in Glanztonqualität identisch mit pseudo-attischen spätklassischen und frühhellenistischen Exemplaren aus Pydna zu sein.

[16] Vgl. Lawall 2004, 467: ‚Perhaps the assumed dominance and influence of Attic potters should be reconsidered'. s. allerdings auch die Kommentare von Sparkes und Talcott 1970, 2–3 zur Unterscheidung zwischen Siedlungs- und Grabkeramik.

[17] Rotroff 1984; Rotroff 1997, 166.

Abb. 7. Pseudo-attischer Kelchbecher Py 2139, 320–310 v. Chr. H 8cm, Photo: Grabungsarchiv von Pydna

neuen Form aufweist (**Abb. 3**)[18]. Obwohl es dem älteren konkaven Salznapftypus verpflichtet ist, zeigt es einen deutlichen oberen Kragrand und einen Ansatz für einen unteren auf, so dass man den Zusammenhang zwischen der konkaven und der neuen Variante nicht anzweifeln kann. Die eigentliche spulenförmige Variante erscheint jedoch in pydnäischen Grabkontexten von *ca.* 330–315 v. Chr., d. h. fast gleichzeitig wie in Athen, mit drei Exemplaren (**Abb. 4**), wovon nur ein mit großer Wahrscheinlichkeit attisch sein kann (**Abb. 4,** Mitte), während die anderen beiden aufgrund des Scherbentyps als ‚pseudo-attisch‘ zu bezeichnen sind. Ihre typologische Stufe ist früher als die der attischen Exemplare aus der Agora, die eher mit einem weiteren, wohl attischen Salznapf aus einem pydnäischen Grabkontext von *ca.* 315–300 v. Chr. zu vergleichen sind (**Abb. 5**). In Grabkontexten des späten 4. Jhs. v. Chr. wurden außerdem auch drei Salznäpfe aus lokalen/regionalen Scherbentypen gefunden (**Abb. 6**), von denen zumindest ein als grobe Nachahmung eines Exemplars aus der athenischen Agora wirkt[19].

Die geschilderte Fundsituation wirft folgende Fragen auf: Handelt es sich um eine in Athen erfundene Form, die die lokalen/regionalen Werkstätten durch Importe oder ausgewanderte Töpfer kennengelernt und anschließend produziert haben? Oder geht es vielleicht um eine makedonische Erfindung als ‚Entwicklung‘ des konkaven Typus, die danach auch in Athen bekannt und hergestellt wurde? Zusätzlich zu den relativ frühen pseudo-attischen spulenförmigen Salznäpfen, spricht auch die Fundverteilung der bislang bekannten Exemplare dieser Form eher für letztere Möglichkeit, denn sie stammen hauptsächlich aus Makedonien (Vergina, Aiginio, Akanthos, Aiani)[20], während ein makedonischer Einfluss bzw. eine makedonische Präsenz in den restlichen Fundorten (Thrakien, Eretria, Böotien, Ägypten, Ras-Shamra, Samaria)[21] seit dem ausgehenden 4. Jh. v. Chr. aus historischen Gründen naheliegend ist. Leider sind die vorhandenen Abbildungen der meisten Exemplare aus Makedonien nicht für eine Stellungnahme zu ihrer Herkunft hilfreich und eine persönliche Untersuchung war nicht immer möglich, aber zumindest für einen Salznapf aus Aiginio und alle Exemplare aus Aiani ist eine attische Provenienz eher auszuschließen. Das zeitliche Verhältnis zu den Exemplaren aus Athen ist außerdem nur für zwei Salznäpfe, aus Aiginio und Akanthos, klar, die aus dem letzten Viertel des 4. und dem frühen 3. Jh. v. Chr. stammen[22], d. h. mit den attischen Exemplaren zeitgleich sind. Für die restlichen Gefäße kennt man entweder noch keine Kontexte, wie im Fall von Aiani, oder ihre Kontexte werden noch kontrovers diskutiert, wie im Fall der Salznäpfe aus dem ‚Philippsgrab‘ von Vergina[23].

Eine makedonische Herkunft der Form erscheint außerdem durch eine Information in einer Masterarbeit über hellenistische Keramik aus Pella in der Abguss-Sammlung der Universität Thessaloniki noch wahrscheinlicher. Dort wird berichtet, dass spulenförmige Salznäpfe in den untersten Schichten der Agora von Pella, im Süden der südlichen Stoa, gefunden wurden, die wahrscheinlich mit der dortigen Nekropole klassischer Zeit zusammenhängen und demnach früher als die bekannten Exemplare aus Athen sind[24]. Wenn dies zutrifft und keine Verwechslung

---

18 Die Datierung des angeblich früheren Salznapfes aus Stryme ist gewiss sowohl aufgrund der Fundsituation als auch der in letzter Zeit geäußerten Anzweiflung der Identifizierung des Fundortes mit der antiken Stryme zu revidieren: Kotitsa 2007, 31; Loukopoulou und Psoma 2008, 55–86.

19 Vgl. hier **Abb. 6** (rechts) und Rotroff 1997, Nr. 1068 Abb. 65 Taf. 78.

20 Daux 1961, 773. 782 Abb. 5. 16; Drougou 2005, 42–43 Abb. 24–26; Karamitrou-Mendessidi 2004, 215 Taf. 72a; Karamitrou-Mendessidi 2007, 40. 44 Abb. 3. 10; Keramopoullos 1932, 64 Abb. 19, 3; Kotitsa 2007, 130 Nr. 26 Zeichn. 1 Taf. 13; Trakossopoulou-Salakidou 2004, 176 Taf. 50a; Vatali 2004, 233 Taf. 75, 7; 76, 2; 77, 1; 79, 2. Unpublizierte Exemplare des späten 4./frühen 3. Jhs. v. Chr. aus Aiani sind im dortigen Archäologischen Museum ausgestellt: s. Karamitrou-Mendessidi 2008, 142 Abb. 243. 245; zudem hat G. Karamitrou-Mendessidi im 8. Wissenschaftlichen Treffen für die hellenistische Keramik (Ioannina, April 2009) die Form als ‚sehr beliebt‘ für die Präfekturen von Kozani und Grevena in Westmakedonien bezeichnet.

21 s. gesammelt in Rotroff 1997, 166 mit Anm. 71; dazu s. Čičikova 1984, 80 Nr. III. 117 Taf. XXIV(‚pyxis‘). Drei weitere, nicht attische Salznäpfe stammen aus alten ägyptischen Grabungen in Schedia (genauer Fundkontext unbekannt), 30km südöstlich von Alexandria, und sind heute im Depot in Mustafa Kamel aufbewahrt. Ich bin für diese Information Chr. Römer-Strehl zu Dank verpflichtet.

22 Kotitsa 2007, 130 Nr. 26 Zeichn. 1 Taf. 13; Trakossopoulou-Salakidou 2004, 176 Taf. 50a.

23 Zur Chronologie dieses Kontextes s. zuletzt einerseits Daumas 2009, besonders 139–165, Drougou 2005 und Hatzopoulos 2008, die für eine frühe Datierung im 3. Viertel des 4. Jhs. bzw. um 336 v. Chr. plädieren, andererseits Borza und Palagia 2007 und Gill 2008, die eine spätere Einordnung vertreten, da sie eine Zuweisung des Grabs an Philipp III. Arrhidaios und seiner Gemahlin Adea Euridike vorschlagen. In Zusammenhang mit der Frage des Inhabers und somit der Datierung dieses Grabes vgl. auch die Ausführungen von Touloumakos 2010, der sich gegen eine Identifizierung von Vergina mit Aigai ausspricht.

24 Pappas 2001, 228 Anm. 41. Ein im Archäologischen Museum von Pella ausgestelltes (attisches? / pseudo-attisches?) Exemplar stammt zusammen mit einer kleinen, mit einer Palmette dekorierten Hydria

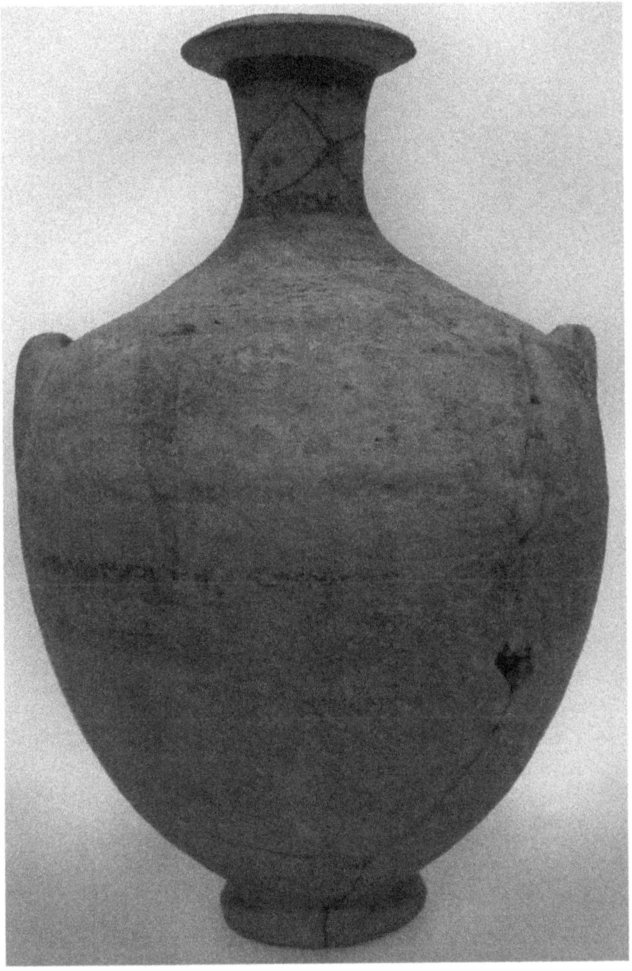

Abb. 8. Korinthisches(?) Unguentarium Py 2633, 325–315 v. Chr. H 17,2cm, Photo: Z. Kotitsa

Abb. 9. Attisierendes Unguentarium Py 9659, 330–320 v. Chr. H 11,2cm, Photo: Z. Kotitsa

mit der konkaven Variante vorliegt, wären diese Salznäpfe früher als die pydnäischen Gefäße und dadurch wäre eine Entstehung der Form in der makedonischen Hauptstadt sehr wahrscheinlich.

Eine wechselseitige und erklärungsbedürftige Beeinflussung zwischen Athen und Pydna offenbaren auch die attischen Vertreter einer anderen Form, des hohen achämenidischen Bechers. Sie tauchen in Pydna in Grabkontexten des letzten Viertels des 4. Jhs. v. Chr., d. h. früher als in Athen, auf und werden umgehend nachgeahmt. Drei attische Exemplare stammen aus Aiginio und Palaiokatachas in der Region von Pydna, ein pseudo-attisches Exemplar ist in der Nordnekropole von Pydna gefunden (**Abb. 7**), zwei weitere (attische? / pseudo-attische?) hohe Becher kamen in Aigai/Vergina vor[25]. Für die in Athen gefundenen Exemplare hat man hingegen eine Datierung ins frühe 3. Jh. v. Chr. angenommen, da man die Form als Entwicklung der niedrigen Becher angesehen hat[26]. Wenn die Datierung der Becher aus Athen stimmt, könnte man das Auftauchen der früheren attischen Exemplare im griechischen Norden auf den Einfluss von Metallexemplaren zurückführen, die wohl aus Makedonien nach Athen exportiert wurden und den dortigen Töpfern als Anregung für eigene, für einen Export nach Norden viel versprechende Produkte gedient haben. Allerdings sind die erhaltenen hohen ‚achämenidischen' Becher aus Metall später als die keramischen Erzeugnisse zu datieren[27], so dass man eher einen Einfluss durch die niedrigen Metallbecher zu postulieren hat, die sowieso als Inspirationsquelle für die niedrigen Tonexemplare der Form betrachtet werden[28].

aus einem Grab des wohl frühen letzten Viertels des 4. Jhs. v. Chr. Für ein weiteres, späteres, dekoriertes Exemplar aus einem Brunnen der pellischen Agora mit den Abfällen einer Töpferwerkstatt s. Lilibaki-Akamati *et al.* 2011, 82.

25 Zuletzt Alexandropoulou 2007, 138 Abb. 18.

26 Rotroff 1997, 92. Pfrommer 1987, 68–73 spricht von einem separaten ‚hohen Typus' von Kelchbechern, Zimmermann 1998, 36 betrachtet die hohen Kelchbecher als spätere Variante eines und desselben Typus.

27 Settis und Parra 2005, 415 Nr. III.205; Sideris 2000, 17 Abb. 20. 21; Thraker 2004, 146 Nr. 199; Zafiropoulou 2004, 685 Taf. 330b (Aitolien); Zimmermann 1998, 161 Nr. BM18. 19.

28 Rotroff 2003, 214–215. Im Gegensatz dazu kennt man bislang nur ein der Form der spulenförmigen Salznäpfe nahe stehendes silbernes Exemplar aus Trichonio/Aitolien, das in einem Grab des frühen 2.

Abb. 10. Pseudo-attisches Kännchen Py 4466, 340–325 v. Chr. H 8cm, Photo: Grabungsarchiv von Pydna

Abb. 11. Pseudo-attisches(?) Kännchen Py 8283, 320–310 v. Chr. H 8,7cm, Photo: Grabungsarchiv von Pydna

Eine andere Gefäßform, das Unguentarium, weist auf einen Bezug von Pydna nicht nur zu Athen sondern auch zu Korinth hin[29]. Ein Exemplar mit Pseudohenkeln und dem charakteristischen pflanzlichen Dekor der sog. pseudozyprischen Amphoren aus einem pydnäischen Grabkontext des frühen letzten Viertels des 4. Jhs. v. Chr. (325–315 v. Chr.) besteht aus dem Scherbentyp des sog. Blister Ware, das als korinthische Produktion gilt (**Abb. 8**)[30]. S. Rotroff hat zuletzt diesen Scherbentyp als wichtiges Argument für den Vorschlag der Entstehung der sog. pseudo-zyprischen Amphoren in Korinth verwendet, die als Vorbilder für die Form der Unguentaria gedient haben[31]. Die Vermutung der Entstehung dieser Formen in Korinth unterstützt inzwischen auch ein bauchiges ovales Unguentarium aus einer antiken Siedlung am Korinthischen Golf, nordwestlich vom antiken Aigeira, d. h. im Einflussbereich von Korinth, dessen aufwendiger Palmettendekor auf Motive der korinthischen ‚conventionalizing Pottery' zurückzuführen ist[32]. Die unmittelbaren Parallelen zu seiner Form führen nicht nur zu Unguentaria aus Korinth und Isthmia aus dem 3. Viertel des 4. Jhs. v. Chr.[33], sondern auch zum pydnäischen, allerdings leicht späteren Exemplar. Zudem findet sich der charakteristische plastische Ring unter dem Rand des Unguentariums aus Pydna bei einem Halsfragment eines korinthischen Unguentariums in ‚Blister Ware' bzw. aus ‚Blister Ware'-ähnlichem Scherbentyp[34].

Das wohl früheste Unguentarium aus der pydnäischen Nordnekropole aus einem Grabkontext von 330–320 v. Chr. (**Abb. 9**) besteht jedoch aus einem besonders feinen Scherbentyp und zeigt durch seine Form erneut einen Bezug zu Athen, da es bis auf die Randform unmittelbar mit einem Exemplar aus einem Brandgrab von *ca.* 340 im Kerameikos zu vergleichen ist[35]. Der schmale, leicht konvexe, abfallende Rand des pydnäischen Gefäßes findet sich jedoch ebenfalls unter den frühen attischen Unguentaria mit oder ohne Pseudohenkel aus dem Kerameikos, die aufgrund der Stratigraphie zwischen 338 und *ca.* 317 v. Chr. einzuordnen sind[36]. Ein weiteres ähnliches Glanztonexemplar mit schmalerem Fuß stammt aus einem attischen Grab des letzten Viertels des 4. Jhs. v. Chr., wo es zusammen mit einem grauen Exemplar gefunden wurde[37]. Da es sich beim pydnäischen Unguentarium bislang um ein Einzelstück handelt, erscheint die Vermutung eines in Pydna oder Umgebung arbeitenden Töpfers aus Athen sehr verlockend.

Eine weitere Form, die in Pydna einerseits ein überregionales Netzwerk offenbart und andererseits

Jhs. v. Chr. wohl als Erbstück deponiert wurde: Zaphiropoulou 2000, 326 Taf. 165a; Zaphiropoulou *et al.* 2011, 88 Kat. 28. Die silbernen Exemplare aus dem Grab B von Derveni (Themelis und Touratsoglou 1997, 67–68 Nr. B20, B21 Taf. 70) und dem ‚Prinzengrab' in Vergina (Andronikos 1984, 209, heute im Museum der Königsgräber von Aigai in Vergina ausgestellt) gehören hingegen zu der früheren konkaven Variante.

29 Ausführlich s. Kotitsa im Druck. Für mögliche Beziehungen zwischen Makedonien und Korinth im 4. Jh. v. Chr. s. auch Trakosopoulou 2004, 175.

30 Zuletzt s. Rotroff 2006, 135.

31 Rotroff 2006, 144–145; vgl. auch in diesem Band den Beitrag von L. Trakatelli.

32 Kolia 2007–2008, 55–57 Anm. 32 Abb. 25.

33 Broneer 1962, 25 Nr. 22 Taf. 11b; Williams und Fisher 1972, 161 Nr. 45 Taf. 27.

34 Pemberton 1989 Nr. 134 Taf. 99 mit einer wohl zu späten Datierung ins frühe 3. Jh. v. Chr. Die durchgeführten Tonanalysen mit m-XRF konnten leider für das Unguentarium aus Pydna eine korinthische Herkunft weder bestätigen noch ausschließen.

35 Kovacsovics 1990, 114 Nr. 110, 1 Taf. 49, 5 (Amphoriskos).

36 Schlörb-Vierneisel 1966, 85 Nr. 144, 1; 87–88 Nr. 150, 1; 89 Nr. 154, 1 Beil 53, 6; 55, 3.

37 Threpsiadis 1932, 8 Abb. 4 (rechts).

die oft postulierte Vorreiterrolle attischer Töpfer selbst in den Fällen, wo die Formen in Athen keine Parallelen aufweisen, hinterfragen lässt, ist die eines dünnwandigen, fein modellierten Kännchens. Bislang stammen die meisten Beispiele aus der Region von Pydna, zwei Exemplare aus der Nordnekropole (**Abb. 10, 11**) und ein aus einem Grab in Palaiokatachas[38]. Darunter ist auch der bislang früheste Vertreter dieser Form, aus einem Grab von 340–325 v. Chr., zu finden (**Abb. 10**), dessen Scherbentyp demjenigen der pseudo-attischen Gefäße entspricht. Für ein leicht späteres Exemplar aus der Nordnekropole (**Abb. 11**) lässt sich wiederum eine attische Herkunft aufgrund des Scherbentyps nicht ausschließen. Weitere derartige Kännchen sind vereinzelt aus verschiedenen anderen Orten Makedoniens wie Vergina und Derveni[39], aus der Westküste des Schwarzmeergebiets (Enisala)[40], aus der Krim (Panskoje)[41], aus Alexandria[42], Zypern[43] und wahrscheinlich aus Rhodos (Schiff von Kyrenia) bekannt[44]. Ein einfacher Blick auf einigen Fotos dieser Kännchen wie der Exemplare aus Alexandria oder Rhodos reicht um zu verstehen, dass man allein aufgrund der Ausführung der Form nicht mit einem einzelnen Produktionszentrum dieser Gefäße zu tun hat. Eine lokale Produktion der Form mit Dekor im ‚Westabhangstil' ist zudem für Thessalien nachgewiesen.[45] Darüber hinaus existieren zwei derartige Silberkännchen aus Makedonien (dem sog. Philippsgrab in Vergina)[46] und Thrakien (Gornjane)[47], wobei ersteres eine andere Henkelform aufweist, während letzteres henkellos ist. Aus Thrakien (Zlokučene) stammt auch ein geriefeltes bronzenes Exemplar[48].

Die geschilderte Fundsituation legt die Vermutung nahe, dass Makedonien bzw. Pydna als Ausgangspunkt für die Herstellung und Verbreitung der Form gedient hat. Dabei bleibt allerdings unklar, wie genau diese Keramikform-‚Koine' entstand, solang die Keramikproduktion der verschiedenen Fundorte nicht umfangreich untersucht ist. Die Fundorte erlauben jedoch im Norden eine Bewegung von Pydna über Thrakien bis zum Krim anzunehmen, während im Süden womöglich Alexandria oder/und Rhodos als Umschlagplätze fungierten.

Eine ähnliche Problematik über die Entstehung eines überregionalen Netzwerks wirft auch die Verbreitung der verzinnten Keramik auf, die bekanntlich im griechischen Raum auf zahlreichen spätklassischen-frühhellenistischen Gefäßen hauptsächlich in der Region von Pydna mit naturwissenschaftlichen Methoden festgestellt wurde[49]. Einige Erwähnungen in der Fachliteratur, persönliche Untersuchung von Exemplaren aus anderen Orten sowie Bilder von Gefäßoberflächen bzw. ihre Beschreibung lassen jedoch keinen Zweifel daran, dass es sich um ein breites Phänomen handelt[50]. Dabei dürfte Pydna, wo die frühesten Vertreter der Technik bereits im späten 5. Jh. v. Chr. festgestellt wurden[51], eine wichtige Rolle für ihre Verbreitung gespielt haben. Ein zusätzlicher Hinweis darauf liefern zwei verzinnte Miniaturexemplare, ein Kelchkrater und eine Situla, aus dem letzten Viertel des 4. Jhs. v. Chr., die von der Verfasserin vor nicht all zulange Zeit im publizierten Material von der athenischen Agora makroskopisch festgestellt wurden[52]. Dabei weist der Scherbentyp des Kelchkraters deutliche Ähnlichkeiten mit demjenigen von verzinnten, zum Teil pseudo-attischen Gefäßen aus Pydna auf[53], so dass man von einem, wohl aus Makedonien nach Athen importierten bzw. mitgebrachten Exemplar ausgehen darf, zumal die beiden Miniaturen Weihgeschenke sein könnten[54]. Im Fall der Miniatur-Situla spricht die Form für eine makedonische Herkunft, da sie ihre nächsten Parallelen bei verzinnten Exemplaren aus dieser Region findet (Aineia, Amphipolis, Pella)[55]. Solang man jedoch keine zuverlässigen Tonanalysen durchführen kann, lässt sich nicht die reizvolle Vorstellung ausschließen, dass diese Miniaturgefäße einen ersten Hinweis für eine bislang nicht festgestellte Verwendung der Verzinnung in

38 Bessios 1991, 45 mit Abb.

39 Drougou 2005, 129–130 Abb. 149 (320–300 v. Chr.); Themelis und Touratsoglou 1997, 105–106 Nr. D22 Taf. 118. Wahrscheinlich stammt ein vergoldetes Exemplar aus dem Kunsthandel ebenfalls aus Makedonien: Williams 2003, 230–231 Abb. 1 (als attisch bezeichnet).

40 Teleaga 2008, 405 Nr. 639 Taf. 30, 4; 137, 10.

41 Hannestad *et al.* 2002, 130. 145 Nr. B 187 Taf. 67. 74 mit weiteren Beispielen aus dem Schwarzmeergebiet.

42 Breccia 1912, 53 Nr. 107–110 Taf. 49, 75; 51, 92.

43 Hayes 1984 Nr. 154 (3.–2. Jh. v. Chr.); Vessberg und Westholm 1956, 60 Abb. 23, 16; 24, 6. Ein weiteres unpubliziertes Exemplar befindet sich im Museum von Lemessos und stammt aus der Sammlung Lanitis.

44 Womer Katzev 2007, 291. 298 Abb. 22.

45 Adrimi-Sismani 2000, 136 Abb. 4; Adrimi-Sismani und Alexandrou 2004, 76 Taf. 15a. b: als Askoi besprochen, mit dementsprechend unzutreffenden Vergleichen.

46 Vokotopoulou 1996, 162. 161 mit Abb.

47 Gold 1987, Kat. 413.

48 Teleaga 2008, 446 Nr. 980 Taf. 123, 2; 201, 8.

49 Kotitsa und Schüssler 2002 und zuletzt Kotitsa 2012, 112–116. Mit naturwissenschaftlichen Analysen wurde die Verzinnung ansonsten nur in Vergina, Aineia und Thessalien festgestellt: Karapanou und Katakouta 2004, 119–120; Kotitsa und Nazlis 2007; Kyriakou 2008, 130–131. s. auch Dakoronia 2000, 216, Abb. 36. Inzwischen wurde auch die von der Verfasserin vermutete Verzinnung eines Exemplars aus einem Mädchengrab in Eretria (Martin Pruvot et al. 2010, 304 Nr. 317) naturwissenschaftlich nachgewiesen wie C. Huguenot dankenswerterweise mich informiert hat. Für weitere vermutlich verzinnte Exemplare aus Makedonien s. Kotitsa 2007, 29, Anm. 25 und darüber hinaus Bonias 2000, 205–206, Abb. 14; Drougou 2005, 478 Abb. 5; Kaltsas 1998, 117 Taf. 131b (nach persönlicher makroskopischer Untersuchung); Skarlatidou 2007, 82. 86.

50 Arapogianni 1984, 115 Zeichn. 22 Taf. 42d; Breccia 1912, 82; Dakoronia 1977, 107 (Lamia); Kallintzi 2003; Maaß 1996, 142 Abb. 16; 186 Nr. 113. 114; Martin Pruvot *et al.* 2010, 244 Kat. 239 (die drei rechts auf der Abb. 239, S. 245, nach makroskopischer Untersuchung); 304 Kat. 317; Pologiorgi 1981, 172–174 Nr. 5383. 5421. 5418 Abb. 11 (links); 12 (rechts); Pruglo 1974, 70 Abb. 3. 4, 1–3; 13; Themelis 1999, 104 Taf. 59b; 61d (antike Messene); Tsatsopoulou 1987, 473, Abb. 8.
Nach makroskopischer Untersuchung dürften ebenfalls spätklassische/frühhellenistische Alabastra aus der Nekropole von Amphipolis verzinnt gewesen sein. Ich möchte K. Rhomiopoulou für ihre Erlaubnis, diese Gefäße genauer zu studieren, danken.

51 Kotitsa und Schüssler 2002, 76–77.

52 Rotroff 1997 Nr. 1372.1373 Abb. 84 Taf. 104. Mein Dank gilt an dieser Stelle J. Jordan für ihre Hilfsbereitschaft während meines Aufenthalts in den Magazinen der American School of Classical Studies in Athen.

53 Zum Scherbentyp s. Rotroff 1997, 203: ‚soft fabric associated with votives'.

54 Rotroff 1997, 203 zögert aufgrund des Glanztones, den sie auf diesen Gefäßen zu sehen glaubte, von Weihgeschenken zu sprechen. Die Verzinnung hingegen wäre eine passende Oberflächenbehandlung für Weihgeschenke; vgl. zwei unpublizierte Miniatur-Lekaniden aus dem Demeterheiligtum in Dion: Kotitsa 2007, 30 Anm. 37.

55 Kotitsa und Nazlis 2007, 274 mit Lit. Das Exemplar aus Pella ist unpubliziert aber im dortigen Archäologischen Museum ausgestellt.

Abb. 12. Unguentarium aus Pella(?), Py 1601, 280–270 v. Chr. H 14,7cm, Photo: Grabungsarchiv von Pydna

Abb. 13. Unguentarium aus Pella(?) mit Dekor im Westabhangstil, Py 1266, 280–270 v. Chr. H 13,8cm, Photo: Z. Kotitsa

Athen selbst liefern[56]. Wenn das allerdings zutreffen sollte, hätte es erhebliche Konsequenzen auf die Beurteilung der Entstehung und Verbreitung des Phänomens sowie auf die Arbeitsweise der Töpfer und die Mechanismen des Handels[57].

Eine unpublizierte verzinnte Miniaturhydria des letzten Viertels des 4. Jhs. v. Chr. aus Ambrakia, im westlichen Griechenland[58], erlaubt wiederum zum ersten Mal konkret nach der Beziehung zwischen der verzinnten Keramik des griechischen Festlandes, vor allem Nordgriechenlands bzw. Makedoniens, und der sog. ceramica argentata zu fragen, die in der zweiten Hälfte des 4. und im 3. Jh. v. Chr. in Unteritalien und Etrurien hergestellt wurde[59]. Ein einzelnes Exemplar reicht natürlich nicht aus um einer solchen Frage ernsthaft nachzugehen, aber wenn tatsächlich ein Netzwerk existiert hat, sprechen die bislang zur Verfügung stehenden chronologischen Daten der verzinnten Keramik zweifellos für eine Entfaltung des Phänomens von Osten nach Westen.

Regionale Kontakte Pydna-Westmakedonien

Die untersuchte frühhellenistische Keramik aus der Nordnekropole von Pydna liefert einige interessante

56 Vgl. die festgestellte, nur partielle Verzinnung in einer Schale des Villa Giulia Malers: Kotitsa und Schüssler 2002, 66.

57 Es wäre z. B. zu überlegen, ob die frühen attischen verzinnten Gefäße in Pydna doch nicht verzinnt exportiert wurden!

58 Gesehen auf dem Poster von Th. Kirkou, Ελληνιστική Κεραμική από το ανατολικό νεκροταφείο της Αμβρακίας, auf der Konferenz 8. Wissenschaftliches Treffen zur hellenistischen Keramik, Ioannina 2009. Anschließend konnte ich dank der Großzügigkeit von G. Riginos und A. Angeli, denen ich an dieser Stelle meine Dankbarkeit aussprechen möchte, das Exemplar persönlich in den Magazinen des Museums von Arta überprüfen und mich von seiner Verzinnung vergewissern.

59 Für Etrurien s. Michetti 2003. Für Apulien s. Canosa 2005, 78. 86 (3. Viertel des 4. Jhs. v. Chr.); Kotitsa, 1998, 145–146; Lo Porto 1990, 110–113 Taf. 42. 44–46 (‚kurz vor der Mitte des 4. Jhs. v. Chr.‘).

Hinweise über die Kontakte der Hafenstadt mit anderen Orten in ihrem erweiterten Umland. Dabei kann man allerdings kaum konkrete Ergebnisse präsentieren sondern lediglich Beobachtungen ausführen und Fragen bzw. Arbeitshypothesen formulieren, da man weder über umfangreiche Veröffentlichungen aus dieser Region mit entsprechenden Fragestellungen, noch ausreichende publizierte Farbfotos von regionaler Keramik verfügt, noch einen leichten Zugang zum entsprechenden Material für eine persönlichen Untersuchung bekommt.

Zunächst scheinen nur die Beziehungen mit der makedonischen Hauptstadt Pella auf einer relativ soliden Basis zu stehen. Nachdem die Verfasserin dort die Gelegenheit hatte, lokale Keramik persönlich zu untersuchen[60], war es möglich eine Gefäßgruppe aus der Nordnekropole von Pydna abzusondern, deren Scherbentyp makroskopische Ähnlichkeiten mit pellischen Produkte aufweist. Der Scherben dieser Gefäße ist meistens orangefarbig (5YR 7/6 oder 6/6), hart gebrannt und hat winzige, durch Kalkaussprengungen entstandene Hohlräume. Die m-XRF-Analysen bestätigten in diesem Fall deutlich die Besonderheit der Gruppe, wobei man einräumen muss, dass keine Referenzstücke aus Pella zur Verfügung standen, die den endgültigen Beweis für einen Import aus dieser Stadt liefern würden.

Abb. 14. Kantharos aus Pella(?), Py 1580, 280–265 v. Chr. H 13,7cm, Photo: Grabungsarchiv von Pydna

Die Formen und der Dekor der Gefäße dieser Gruppe finden jedoch ihre nächsten Parallelen ebenfalls unter den bislang publizierten Gefäßen aus Pella, wie z. B. die Form eines Unguentariums aus Grabkontexten zwischen *ca.* 300 und *ca.* 270 v. Chr. (**Abb. 12**) mit kugeligem Körper, verdünntem weißlichem Überzug und dunklem Streifendekor, der sich auf allen Exemplaren, nicht nur aus Pydna sondern auch aus dem benachbarten Aiginio, auf die gleiche Art und Weise verteilt[61]. Ein weiteres Beispiel für einen Import aus der Hauptstadt bietet ein Glanztonunguentarium aus einem Grab von 280–270 v. Chr., der fast spindelförmig ist und Pseudohenkel aufweist, auf deren Höhe Westabhangdekor zwischen zwei Rillen aufgetragen wurde (**Abb. 13**). Die nächsten Parallelen sowohl für die Form als auch für das Dekorkonzept lassen sich in Pella nachweisen[62]. Das gleiche Dekormotiv der Volutenranke mit dreifingrigen Blättern findet sich außerdem etwas vereinfacht auch auf einem Westabhangkantharos des 2. Viertels des 3. Jhs. aus der Nordnekropole von Pydna, der ebenfalls zur Gruppe der ‚pelläischen' Gefäße gehört (**Abb. 14**) sowie auf einer pelläischen Pyxis aus der östlichen Stoa der Agora[63]. Die Verwandtschaft mit Pella bezeugt im Fall des Kantharos auch ein Vergleich des Gefäßes mit den wenigen bekannten Kantharoi aus der Agora der Stadt[64]. Er teilt mit ihnen die scharfe Artikulation des Fußes, die ausgeprägte Schulterpartie, den nach oben eingezogenen Körper und den gleichen Verlauf der dünnen Bandhenkel mit den angehobenen Daumenplättchen.

Weniger klar ist die Situation in Bezug auf eine Gefäßgruppe aus Gräbern der Nordnekropole zwischen *ca.* 310 und 280 v. Chr., die aus einem grau bis braun gebrannten (10YR 6/2 bis 4/4) glimmerhaltigen Scherben besteht und mit schwarzem bis grau-braunem, stumpfem, dünnem Glanzton bedeckt ist. Die verschiedenen zum Teil außergewöhnlichen Formen (**Abb. 15, 16**) weisen in den Rillen eine rote Füllung auf, die der attischen *Miltos* ähnlich ist. Die unmittelbaren Parallelen in den technischen Details, insbesondere in der Qualität des Glanztones und der Verwendung von Rot auch *über* dem Glanzton, lassen sich bislang nur in Aiani in Obermakedonien nachweisen[65]. Zum Scherbentyp ist allerdings keine Äußerung möglich, da die Verfasserin keine Möglichkeit hatte, die Gefäße aus Aiani eingehend zu untersuchen. Da die größte Anzahl derartiger Gefäße bislang anscheinend aus diesem Ort stammt, das Formenrepertoire jedoch in Pydna zum Teil unterschiedlich ist[66] und die m-XRF-Tonanalysen keine

[60] Ich danke an dieser Stelle I. M. Akamatis und M. Lilibaki-Akamati für die Möglichkeit, sowohl publiziertes als auch unpubliziertes Material aus Pella näher zu untersuchen. Am wichtigsten war für die hier behandelte Frage der regionalen Beziehungen unpubliziertes Material aus einem Brunnen der Agora der Stadt, der u.a. misslungene Keramikprodukte der Töpferwerkstätten enthielt.

[61] Dazu zuletzt Kotitsa 2007, 60–61 mit Lit.

[62] Vgl. Lilibaki-Akamati 1989–91, 111. 129–130 Zeichn. 61 Taf. 40a.b; 48e; Lilibaki-Akamati 1994 Nr. 310. 364 Zeichn. 75 Taf. 36: manche dieser Exemplare zeigen eine identische Eingrenzung einer undekorierten Zone durch bemalte Streifen; für die Ausformung des Fußes vgl. besonders das Unguentarium Lilibaki-Akamati 1989–91 Taf. 40b.

[63] Kotitsa 1996, 88 und bes. 14–15 Kat. HKM2a, Abb. 131 Taf. 4.

[64] Lilibaki-Akamati *et al.* 2011, 83; Makedonia 1988, 279. 283. 284.

[65] Die entsprechenden Exemplare sind im Archäologischen Museum von Aiani ausgestellt; s. ein Beispiel in Karamitrou-Mendessidi 2008, 133 Abb. 219.

[66] Man findet z. B. viele Askoi in Aiani (Karamitrou-Mendessidi 2008,

Abb. 15. Lokale/regionale (Aiani?) Tasse Py 1188, 300–285 v. Chr. H 7,8cm, Photo: Grabungsarchiv von Pydna

Abb. 16. Lokaler/regionaler (Aiani?) Kantharos Py 2670, 300–285 v. Chr. H 10,1cm, Photo: Grabungsarchiv von Pydna

klare Differenzierung zwischen dieser pydnäischen Gefäßgruppe und den restlichen lokalen analysierten Gefäßen aus Pydna ergeben haben, kann man einen unmittelbaren Import aus Obermakedonien nicht behaupten[67]. Handelt es sich eventuell um Töpfer aus Aiani, die ihre Werkstätten in Pydna etabliert hatten und für dessen Bevölkerung ansprechende Formen anfertigten oder sind vielmehr die Produkte von Aiani Importe aus Pydna bzw. von dorthin ausgewanderten pydnäischen Töpfern hergestellt? Oder sollte man doch ein drittes Produktionszentrum postulieren, das beide Orte belieferte? Zurzeit würde jeder Versuch diesen Fragen nachzugehen nur zu Spekulationen führen.

Schließlich legen makroskopische Beobachtungen von Keramik aus dem Gebiet von Veroia die Vermutung nahe, dass viele pseudo-attische sowie attisierende frühhellenistische Gefäße aus Pydna, die aus einem besonders feinen Scherben bestehen, möglicherweise aus denselben Werkstätten wie einige Gefäße aus Veroia stammen, die vielleicht um die alte Hauptstadt Aigai situiert waren[68]. Eine derartige Annahme erscheint umso plausibel, wenn man die Wahrscheinlichkeit vor Augen hält, dass sich athenische Töpfer bereits im späten 5. Jh. v. Chr. sowohl in der alten Hauptstadt als auch am größten Hafen Makedoniens niederlassen hätten können.

Nach diesen Ausführungen erscheint Pydna in frühhellenistischer Zeit, sich in einem breiten Beziehungsgeflecht einzufügen, wobei die einzelnen Stationen sowie die Verbindungsmechanismen noch zum großen Teil unklar sind. Weitere koordinierte Forschungen im Hinblick auf diese Fragestellung werden hoffentlich diese Situation ändern und zum besseren Verständnis der antiken wirtschaftlichen Beziehungen und somit auch der sozialen und kulturellen Verflechtungen dieser makedonischen Stadt beitragen.

Zoi Kotitsa
Philipps-Universität Marburg
Archäologisches Seminar
Biegenstr. 11
D-35032 Marburg
zoiko@web.de

136 Abb. 230), die in Pydna selten und in dieser Warengruppe gar nicht vorkommen. Andererseits gehören zwei von den drei ‚lokalen' pydnäischen spulenförmigen Salznäpfen, einer in Aiani äußerst beliebten Form (Karamitrou-Mendessidi 2008, 142 Abb. 243), ebenfalls zu dieser Gefäßgruppe.

67 Zu den Handelswegen zwischen Ober- und Untermakedonien s. Karamitrou-Mentessidi 1998; Karamitrou-Mendessidi und Kefalidou 1999, 551; Rizakis und Touratsoglou 2000, 240. 246

68 Ich möchte I. Graikos und G. Mallios für ihre Großzügigkeit, mir unpubliziertes Material aus den Ausgrabungen in Veroia zu zeigen, und für ihre Bereitschaft, es mit mir zu besprechen, herzlich danken. Darüber hinaus hat mich A. Kyriakou auf die makroskopische Ähnlichkeit des feinen Scherbentyps von Pydna mit demjenigen von Gefäßen aus Aigai/Vergina aufmerksam gemacht, darunter mit demjenigen einer vielleicht pseudo-attischen Eichellekythos, Kyriakou 2008, 138–140. 202–205. Ich danke ihr ebenfalls an dieser Stelle für unsere aufschlussreichen Gespräche.

Bibliographie

Adrimi-Sismani, V. 2000. Ταφικά σύνολα από το Δυτικό νεκροταφείο των Φθιωτίδων Θηβών. In *Ελληνιστική Κεραμική από τη Θεσσαλία*, 133–146. Athen, TAP.

Adrimi-Sismani, V. und Alexandrou, St. 2004. Ταφικά σύνολα από το νεκροταφείο των Φθιωτίδων Θηβών. In *Στ΄ Επιστημονική Συνάντηση για την Ελληνιστική Κεραμική*. Βόλος 2000, 73–88. Athen, TAP.

Alexandropoulou, A. 2007. Η κεραμική των υστεροκλασικών και ελληνιστικών χρόνων από τη νεκρόπολη των Αιγών: πρώτες εκτιμήσεις. *Το Αρχαιολογικό Έργο στη Μακεδονία και Θράκη* 21, 35–142.

Andronikos, M. 1984. *Vergina. The royal tombs and the ancient city*. Athen, Ekdotiki Athinon.

Arapogianni, X. 1984. Τάφοι από την αρχαία Άμβροσσο. *Αρχαιολογικόν Δελτίον* 39, 77–118.

Berlin, A . M. und Lynch, K. 2002. Going Greek: Atticizing Pottery in the Achaemenid World. *Studia Troica* 12, 167–178.

Bessios, M. 1993. Μαρτυρίες Πύδνας. Το ψήφισμα του Απόλλωνος Δεκαδρύου, in *Ancient Macedonia* 5, 2. Papers read at the fifth international symposium held in Thessaloniki, October 10–15, 1989, Manolis Andronikos in memoriam, 1111–1119. Thessaloniki, Institute for Balkan Studies.

Bessios, M. 1997. Πύδνα. *Αρχαιολογία* 63, 56–63.

Bessios, M. 2010. *Πιερίδων Στέφανος: Πύδνα, Μεθώνη και οι αρχαιότητες της βόρειας Πιερίας*. Katerini, Ekdoseis A. Ph. E.

Bessios, M. und Pappa, M. *Πύδνα* (o. O., o. J.).

Bonias, Z. 2000. Τάφοι Αμφιπόλεως. In P. Adam-Veleni (Hrsg.), *ΜΥΡΤΟΣ. Μνήμη της Ιουλίας Βοκοτοπούλου*, 199–217. Thessaloniki, Aristoteleio Panepistimio Thessalonikis.

Borza, E. N. und Palagia, O. 2007. The Chronology of the Macedonian Royal Tombs at Vergina. *Jahrbuch des Deutschen Archäologischen Instituts* 122, 81–124.

Breccia, E. 1912. *La necropoli di Sciatbi*. Kairo, Imprimerie de l'Institut Français d'Archéologie Orientale.

Broneer, O. 1962. Excavations at Isthmia 1959–1961. *Hesperia* 31, 1–25.

Canosa, M. G. 2005. La tomba n° 33 di Timmari, in M. Denoyelle, E. Lippolis, M. Mazzei und Cl. Pouzadoux (Hrsg.), *La céramique apulienne. Bilan et perspectives*. Actes de la Table Ronde organisée par l'École française de Rome en collaboration avec la Soprintendenza per i Beni Archeologici della Puglia et le Centre Jean Bérard de Naples, Naples, Centre Jean Bérard 30 novembre – 2 décembre 2000, 77–87. Neapel, Centre Jean Bérard.

Čičikova, M. 1984. Ancient Pottery, in D. P. Dimitrov, M. Čičikova, A. Balkanska und L. Ognenova-Marinova, *Seuthopolis* I, 18–114. Sofia, Publishing House of the Bulgarian Academy of Sciences.

Cook, J. M. 1965. Old Smyrna: Fourth-Century Black Glaze. *The Annual of the British School at Athens* 60, 143–153.

Dakoronia, F. 1977. Εφορεία προϊστορικών και κλασικών αρχαιοτήτων Λαμίας. Ανασκαφικές εργασίες. *Αρχαιολογικόν Δελτίον* 32 B, 104–110.

Dakoronia, F. 2000. Ασυνήθιστοι τύποι ελληνιστικών αγγείων από την κοιλάδα του Σπερχειού. In *Ελληνιστική Κεραμική από τη Θεσσαλία*, 214–220. Athen, TAP.

Daumas, M. 2009. *L'or et le pouvoir. Armement scythe et myths grecs*. Paris, Presses universitaires de Paris ouest.

Daux, G. 1961. Chronique des fouilles et découvertes achéologiques en Grèce en 1960. *Bulletin de Correspondance Hellénique* 85, 601–953.

Drougou, St. 2005. *Βεργίνα. Τα πήλινα αγγεία της Μεγάλης Τούμπας*. Athen, TAP.

Furtwängler, A. 1990. Demetrias, ein Produktionsort "attischer" Keramik? In *Β΄ Επιστημονική Συνάντηση για την Ελληνιστική Κεραμεική*. Ρόδος 1989, 49–53. Athen, TAP.

Furtwängler, A. 1997. Μεθοδολογικά προβλήματα χρονολόγησης. In *Δ΄ Επιστημονική Συνάντηση για την Ελληνιστική Κεραμική*. Μυτιλήνη 1994, 396–400. Athen, Ypourgeio Politismou.

Gassner, V. 2003. *Materielle Kultur und kulturelle Identität in Elea in spätarchaisch-frühklassischer Zeit*. Archäologische Forschungen 8, Velia-Studien 2. Wien, Verlag der Österreichischen Akademie der Wissenschaften.

Gill, D. W. J. 2008. Inscribed Silver Plate from Tomb II at Vergina. Chronological Implications. *Hesperia* 77, 335–358.

Gold 1987. *Gold of the Thracian Horsemen. Treasures from Bulgaria*. Ausstellungskatalog Montreal. Montreal, Ed. de L'Homme.

Hannestad, L., Stolba, V. F. und Blinkenberg Hastrup, H. 2002. Black-glazed, red-figure, and grey ware pottery, in L. Hannestad, V. F. Stolba und A. N. Ščeglov (Hrsg.), *Panskoye I*, 127–149. Aarhus, Aarhus University Press.

Hatzopoulos, M. B. 2004. Makedonia, in M. H. Hansen und T. H. Nielsen (Hrsg.), *An Inventory of Archaic and Classical Poleis*, 794–809. Oxford, Oxford University Press.

Hayes, J. W. 1984. *Greek and Italian Black-Gloss Wares and Related Wares in the Royal Ontario Museum*. Toronto, Royal Ontario Museum.

Herda A. und Sauter, E. 2009. Karerinnen und Karer in Milet. Zu einem spätklassischen Schüsselchen mit karischem Graffito aus Milet. *Archäologischer Anzeiger* 2, 51–112.

Hermary, A. (Hrsg.) 2010. *Apollonia du Pont (Sozopol). La nécropole de Kalfata (Ve–IIIe s. av. J.-C.). Fouilles franco-bulgares (2002–2004)*. Paris, Éditions Errance.

Kalliga, K. 2004. Anchialos-Sindos Double Trapeza. Pit C: observations on the painted and black-glazed pottery of local fourth-century BC workshops. *The Annual of the British School at Athens* 99, 291–313.

Kallintzi, K. 2003. Αλάβαστρα από το νεκροταφείο των αρχαίων Αβδήρων. *Peri Thrakis* 3, 11–42.

Kaltsas, N. E. 1998. *Άκανθος I. Η ανασκαφή στο νεκροταφείο κατά το 1979*. Athen, TAP.

Karamitrou-Mentessidi, G. 1998, Από την Ελιμιώτιδα στην Κάτω Μακεδονία. Σύγχρονες πορείες και αρχαίες διαβάσεις. In M. Lilimbaki-Akamati (Hrsg.), *Μνείας χάριν*. Festschrift M. Siganidou, 103–114. Thessaloniki, TAP.

Karamitrou-Mendessidi, G. 2004. Αιανή Ελληνιστικοί τάφοι στη βασιλική νεκρόπολη. In *Στ΄ Επιστημονική Συνάντηση για την Ελληνιστική Κεραμική*. Βόλος

2000, 207–218. Athen, TAP.
Karamitrou-Mendessidi, G. 2007. Αιανή 2007: η έρευνα στο Ανατολικό Νεκροταφείο. *Το Αρχαιολογικό Έργο στη Μακεδονία και Θράκη* 21, 37–46.
Karamitrou-Mendessidi, G. 2008. *Αιανή. Αρχαιολογικοί χώροι και Μουσείο.* Aiani, Ipourgio Politismou, Archaiologiko Mouseio Aianis.
Karamitrou-Mentessidi, G und Kefalidou, E. 1999. Τοπικά εργαστήρια αρχαϊκής και κλασικής κεραμικής από την Αιανή και τον νομό Κοζάνης, in *Ancient Macedonia* 6, 2. Papers read at the sixth international symposium held in Thessaloniki 15.–19.10.1996, 537–562. Thessaloniki, Idrima Meleton Chersonisou tou Aimou.
Karapanou, S. und Katakouta, St. 2004. Ευρήματα από τα νεκροταφεία του Πελινναίου. In *Στ΄ Επιστημονική Συνάντηση για την Ελληνιστική Κεραμική.* Βόλος 2000, 111–126. Athen, TAP.
Keramopoullos, A. D. 1932. Ανασκαφαί και έρευναι εν τη Άνω Μακεδονία. *Αρχαιολογική Εφημερίς*, 48–133.
Kolia, E. 2007–2008. Παράκτιος οικισμός της Κλασικής Εποχής στην Ανατολική Αιγιάλεια. *Αρχαιολογικά Ανάλεκτα εξ Αθηνών* 40–41, 41–60.
Kopcke, G. 1964, Golddekorierte attische Schwarzfirniskeramik des vierten Jahrhunderts v. Chr. *Mitteilungen des Deutschen Archäologischen Instituts, Athenische Abteilung* 79, 22–84.
Kotitsa, Z. 1996. *Hellenistische Tonpyxiden.* Mainz, Zabern.
Kotitsa, Z. 1998. *Hellenistische Keramik im Martin von Wagner Museum der Universität Würzburg.* Würzburg, Ergon.
Kotitsa, Z. 2004: Πρώιμη ελληνιστική κεραμική από κλειστά ταφικά σύνολα της αρχαίας Πύδνας. In *Στ΄ Επιστημονική Συνάντηση για την Ελληνιστική Κεραμική.* Βόλος 2000, 193–206. Athen, TAP.
Kotitsa, Z. 2007. *Αιγίνιο Πιερίας. Κεραμική από το νεκροταφείο στη θέση „Μελίσσια".* Thessaloniki, K. Sfakianaki.
Kotitsa, Z. 2012. Metal-coated pottery in Macedonia in Late Classical and Hellenistic period, in S. Drougou und I. Touratsoglou (Hrsg.), *Topics on Hellenistic pottery in ancient Macedonia,* 108–125. Athen, TAP.
Kotitsa, Z. im Druck. Τυπολογία, χρονολόγηση και χρήση μυροδοχείων: ενδείξεις από τη Βορεια Πιερία. In *Η΄ Επιστημονική Συνάντηση για την Ελληνιστική Κεραμική*, Ioannina 2009.
Kotitsa, Z. und Schüssler, U. 2002. Zinn auf Keramik: Entstehung und Verwendung eines Statussymbols in Makedonien. *Archäologischer Anzeiger* 2, 65–84.
Kotitsa, Z. und Nazlis, I. 2007. Ο τάφος ΙΙΙ του τύμβου Α της Αίνειας: Επανεξετάζοντας τα δεδομένα. *Το Αρχαιολογικό Έργο στη Μακεδονία και Θράκη* 21, 269–276.
Kovacsovics, W. K. 1990. *Die Eckterrasse an der Gräberstrasse des Kerameikos.* Kerameikos XIV. Berlin, de Gruyter.
Kowalleck, I. 2008. Attische und attisierende Keramik, in M. Kerschner, I. Kowalleck und M. Steskal, *Archäologische Forschungen zur Siedlungsgeschichte von Ephesos in geometrischer, archaischer und klassischer Zeit. Grabungsbefunde und Keramikfunde aus dem Bereich von Koressos.* Ergänzungshefte zu den Jahresheften des Österreichischen Archäologischen Institutes in Wien 9, 75–107. Wien, Österreichisches Archäologisches Institut.
Kyriakou, A. 2008. *Η στενόμακρη Τούμπα της Βεργίνας. Ταφικές πρακτικές στη Μακεδονία του 4ου αι. π.Χ.* Thessaloniki, K. Sfakianaki.
Lawall, M. L. 2004. Rezension: L. E. Vaag, V. Nørskov und J. Lund, The Pottery: Ceramic Material and Other Finds from Selected Contexts, The Maussolleion at Halikarnassos, Reports of the Danish Archaeological Expedition to Bodrum 7 (Aarhus 2002). *American Journal of Archeology* 108, 466–467.
Lilibaki-Akamati, M. 1989–91. Ανατολικό νεκροταφείο Πέλλας. Ανασκαφή 1989. *Αρχαιολογικόν Δελτίον* 44–46, 73–152.
Lilibaki-Akamati, M. 1994. *Λαξευτοί θαλαμωτοί τάφοι της Πέλλας.* Athen, TAP.
Lilibaki-Akamati, M., Akamatis, I. M., Chrysostomou, A. und Chrysostomou, P. 2011. *The Archaeological Museum of Pella.* Athen <www. latsis-foundation. org/gr/elibrary>.
Lo Porto, F. G. 1990. Oria I. Ritrovamento di tombe nel rione Maddalena. *Studi di antichità* 6, 101–117.
Loukopoulou, L. D. und Psoma, S. 2008. *Maroneia and Stryme Revisited: Some Problems of Historical Topography.* Thrakika Zetemata I, Μελετήματα 58. Athen, Kentron Ellinikis kai Romaikis Archaiotitos.
Maaß, M. (Hrsg.) 1996. *Delphi, Orakel am Nabel der Welt.* Ausstellungskatalog Karlsruhe, Sigmaringen, Thorbecke.
Makedonia 1988. *Archaia Makedonia.* Ausstellungskatalog Melbourne. Athen, Ypourgeio Politismou.
Martin Pruvot, Ch., Reber, K. und Theurillat, Th. (Hrsg.) *2010. ausgegraben! Schweizer Archäologen erforschen die griechische Stadt Eretria.* Ausstellungskatalog Basel. Basel, Schwabe.
McDonald, B. R. 1981. The Emigration of Potters from Athens in the Late Fifth Century B.C. and its Effect on the Attic Pottery Industry. *American Journal of Archaeology* 85, 159–168.
Michetti, L. M. 2003. *Le ceramiche argentate e a rilievo in Etruria nella prima età ellenistica*, Accademia Nazionale dei Lincei, Monumenti Antichi, Serie Miscellanea VIII. Roma, Giorgio Bretschneider.
Missailidou-Despotidou, V. 1999. Χρονολογικά στοιχεία από ταφικά σύνολα του 4ου αι. π.Χ. από τη Ν. Φιλαδέλφεια, in *Ancient Macedonia* 6, 2. Papers read at the sixth international symposium held in Thessaloniki 15.–19.10.1996, 771–785. Thessaloniki, Idrima Meleton Chersonisou tou Aimou.

Morel, J.-P. 1995. Observations sur les céramiques à vernis noir d'Alexandrie, in N. Bonacasa, C. Naro, E. Ch. Portale und A. Tullio (Hrsg.), *Alessandria e il mondo ellenistico-romano*. I Centenario del Museo Greco-Romano, Alexandria, 23–27 November 1992, Atti del II Congresso Internazionale Italo-Egiziano, 368–376. Rom, L'Erma di Bretschneider.

Morel, J.-P. 2000. La céramique attique à vernis noir du IVe siècle: position des problèmes. In B. Sabattini (Hrsg.), *La céramique attique du IVe siècle en Méditerranée occidentale*. Actes du colloque international organisé par le Centre Camille Jullian, Arles 7–9 Dezember 1995, 11–21. Neapel, École Française de Rome.

Papakonstantinou-Diamantourou, D. 1971. *Πελλα Ι. Ιστορική επισκόπησις και μαρτυρίαι*. Athen, Archetai.

Pappas, N. V. 2001. *Ελληνιστική κεραμική από την Αγορά της Πέλλας και την περιοχή της στο Μουσείο Εκμαγείων του Α.Π.Θ.* Unpubl. Masterarbeit an der Aristoteles Universität Thessaloniki.

Pemberton, E. G. 1989. *The Sanctuary of Demeter and Kore. The Greek Pottery*. Corinth XVIII 1. Princeton, NJ., American School of Classical Studies at Athens.

Pemberton, E. G. 2003. Classical and Hellenistic Pottery from Corinth and its Athenian Connections, in Ch. K. Williams II und N. Bookidis (Hrsg.), *Corinth, The Centenary 1896–1996*. Corinth XX, 167–179. Athens, American School of Classical Studies at Athens.

Pologiorgi, M. 1981. Υστεροκλασικός τάφος στην Κίσαμο. *Αρχαιολογικά Ανάλεκτα εξ Αθηνών* 14, 162–179.

Pruglo, V. I. 1974. K voprosu o date kurgana bolschaja Blisniza. *Sovetskaja archeologija* 3, 64–77.

Py, M. 1978. Une production massaliète de céramique pseudo-attique à vernis noir. *Rivista di studi liguri* 44, 175–198.

Rizakis, A. und Touratsoglou, I. 2000. Mors macedonica. Ο θάνατος στα επιτάφια μνημεία της Άνω Μακεδονίας. *Αρχαιολογική Εφημερίς*, 237–281.

Robertson, M. 1992. *The art of vase-painting in classical Athens*. Cambridge, Cambridge University Press.

Rotroff, S. I. 1984. Spool Saltcellars in the Athenian Agora. *Hesperia* 53, 343–354.

Rotroff, S. I. 1997. *Hellenistic Pottery. Athenian and Imported Wheelmade Table Ware and Related Material*. The Athenian Agora XXIX. Princeton, NJ., American School of Classical Studies at Athens.

Rotroff, S. I. 2003. Minima macedonica, in O. Palagia und S. V. Tracy (Hrsg.), *The Macedonians in Athens 322–229 B.C.*, 213–225. Oxford, Oxbow Books.

Rotroff, S. I. 2006. *Hellenistic Pottery. The Plain Wares*. The Athenian Agora XXXIII. Princeton, NJ., American School of Classical Studies at Athens.

Schlörb-Vierneisel, B. 1966. Eridanos-Nekropole, I. Gräber und Opferstellen. *Mitteilungen des Deutschen Archäologischen Instituts, Athenische Abteilung* 81, 4–111.

Settis, S. und Parra, M. C. (Hrsg.) 2005. *Magna Grecia. Archeologia di un sapere*. Ausstellungskatalog Catanzaro. Mailand, Electa.

Sideris, A. 2000. Les tombes de Derveni: quelques remarques sur la toreutique. *Revue archéologique*, 3–36.

Skarlatidou, E. 2007. *Thermi: The ancient cemetery beneath the modern town*. Athen, Municipality of Thermi / 16th Ephorate of Prehistoric and Classical Antiquities.

Teleaga, E. 2008. *Griechische Importe in den Nekropolen an der unteren Donau, 6. Jh. – Anfang des 3. Jhs. v. Chr.* Marburger Studien zur Vor- und Frühgeschichte 23. Rahden/Westf., Leidorf.

Themelis, P. 1999. Ανασκαφή Μεσσήνης. *Πρακτικά της εν Αθήναις Αρχαιολογικής Εταιρείας*, 79–113.

Themelis, P. G. und Touratsoglou, G. P. 1997. *Οι τάφοι του Δερβενίου*. Athen, TAP.

Thraker 2004. *Die Thraker. Das goldene Reich des Orpheus*. Ausstellungskatalog Bonn 2004 (Hrsg. Kunst- und Ausstellungshalle der Bundesrepublik Deutschland GmbH). Mainz, Zabern.

Threpsiadis, I. 1932. Μικρά σκαφή παρά την Αγ. Παρασκευήν. *Αρχαιολογική Εφημερίς, Χρονικά*, 6–12.

Touloumakos, J. 2010. Die historische Problematik der Gräber von Vergina. *Ancient Society* 40, 15–50.

Trakossopoulou-Salakidou, E. 2004. Άκανθος: Ελληνιστική κεραμική. In *Στ΄ Επιστημονική Συνάντηση για την Ελληνιστική Κεραμική*. Βόλος 2000, 173–184. Athen, TAP.

Trinkl, E. 2006. Schwarzfirniskeramik klassischer Zeit aus den Agoragrabungen, in P. Scherrer und E. Trinkl, *Die Tetragonos Agora in Ephesos*. Forschungen in Ephesos 13/2, 177–245. Wien, Verlag der Österreichischen Akademie der Wissenschaften.

Tsatsopoulou, Tz. 1987. Αιγαιακή Μεσημβρία. Η ανασκαφική έρευνα στο χώρο της αρχαίας πόλης κατά το 1987. *Το Αρχαιολογικό Έργο στη Μακεδονία και Θράκη* 1, 469–478.

Vatali, M. 2004. Πολύμυλος Κοζάνης: Ταφικά σύνολα ελληνιστικών χρόνων. In *Στ΄ Επιστημονική Συνάντηση για την Ελληνιστική Κεραμική*. Βόλος 2000, 219–235. Athen, TAP.

Vessberg O. und Westholm, A. 1956. *The Hellenistic and Roman Periods in Cyprus*. The Swedish Cyprus Expedition IV 3. Lund, The Swedish Cyprus Expedition.

Vokotopoulou, J. 1996. *Führer durch das Archäologische Museum Thessaloniki*. Athen, Editions Kapon.

Williams, D. 2003. Gilded pottery and golden jewellery, in O. Palagia und S. V. Tracy (Hrsg.), *The Macedonians in Athens 322–229 B.C.*, 226–235. Oxford, Oxbow.

Williams, Ch. K. und Fisher, J. E. 1972. Corinth 1971: Forum Area. *Hesperia* 41, 143–184.

Womer Katzev, S. 2007. The Ancient Ship of Kyrenia beneath Cyprus seas, in P. Valavanis, V. Petrakos und A. Delivorrias, *Great Moments in Greek Archaeology*, 286–299. Los Angeles, Getty

Publications.
Zaphiropoulou, F. 2000. Τάφοι στο Τριχόνιο Αιτωλίας. In *Ε΄ Επιστημονική Συνάντηση για την Ελληνιστική Κεραμική*. Χανιά 1997, 323–328. Athen, TAP.
Zaphiropoulou, F., Stavropoulou-Gatsi, M. und Stamatis, G. 2011. *Τριχόνειον – Άκραι – Μέταπα. Αιτωλών πόλεις*. Athen, Sima.
Zimmermann, N. 1998. *Beziehungen zwischen Ton- und Metallgefäßen spätklassischer und frühhellenistischer Zeit*. Rahden/Westf., Leidorf.

The category of the so called pseudo-Cypriot amphoras and their distribution in Cyprus, Greece and the Black Sea

Lydia Antonia Trakatelli

Abstract

This paper examines the category of the so called pseudo-Cypriot amphoras and their distribution in Greece, Cyprus and the Black Sea Region. The category of pseudo-Cypriot vessels holds a lot of interest since is not widely known and regards topics of production centers and relationships between different regions of the Hellenistic world.

Keywords: pseudo-Cypriot, amphoras, amphorisques, unguentaria, Cyprus, Greece, Black Sea

Hellenistic pottery has always been considered to have a somewhat different character that distinguishes it from classical pottery. A lot have been said and written about the special traits of Hellenistic pottery and the new techniques regarding its manufacture and decoration. However that is not always the case and a few categories seem to be directly linked to previous forms of pottery or even intentionally imitate older shapes. One such case is the category of pseudo-Cypriot vessels (**Figs. 1–3**). This paper focuses on two different networks regarding the production and distribution of this kind of pottery. The first network pre-dating Hellenistic times and thus briefly mentioned here, concerns the Cypriot amphoras and their introduction in other regions, mainly Greece. The second network established in the early Hellenistic period, refers to the distribution of pseudo-Cypriot pottery within Greece and in the Black Sea region. To put it simply the questions that need answering are how does a type of pottery produced in Cyprus in the geometric period and onwards suddenly appears in the late classical early Hellenistic period in various sites of Greece and in the Black Sea? And where was it produced during the Hellenistic period?

The term pseudo-Cypriot was firstly used for some amphoras (**Fig. 1**) that seemed to have a lot in common with Cypriot vases[1] but were not produced in Cyprus[2]. Originally these vessels were called Cypriot-amphoras but since it soon became clear that they were only imitations the term pseudo-Cypriot was chosen. However as research has shown this type of pottery does not only include amphoras, but amphorisques (**Fig. 2**) and unguentaria (**Fig. 3**) as well[3]. So the term pseudo-Cypriot pottery refers to a particular kind of side-handled amphora, small amphorisques with horizontal handles and unguentaria with pseudo-handles that all bear the same specific floral decoration in the area between the handles and various sized red, black and white bands on the neck, shoulder and belly[4].

The Cypriot amphoras and amphorisques predate the ones found in Greece[5] and are more numerous[6] (**Fig. 4**). In Cyprus this shape, probably influenced by earlier Mycenaean prototypes[7] appears in the geometric period and continues to be produced until the 4th century BC. In the 4th century BC examples of this kind of amphoras are limited and most of the known vessels derive from Larnaca (**Fig. 5**), while the production seems to come to an end in the middle of the same century[8]. Although the finds of the 4th century BC seem to bridge the chronological gap between the production of Cypriot and pseudo-Cypriot vases, the geographical distance between Greece and Cyprus and the question of how these particular vessels were made known from one area to another still remains. One could argue that the permanent settlements of Cypriot metics in different regions of Greece and especially the Greek islands, even before the 7th century BC played an important part in the distribution of the pseudo-Cypriot pottery[9]. With the islands' colonies in Chalcidiki and the

---

1 The term pseudo-Cypriot amphoras was applied to this kind of pottery because of the common traits between vessels found in Greece and other parts of the Mediterranean and pottery from Cyprus, Drougou 2005, 165–167. The resemblance between the Cypriotic vases and the ones found outside Cyprus was so strong that originally archaeologists believed that all the pottery originated from Cyprus, Andronikos 1969, 28.

2 Rotroff 2006, 144.

3 Trakatelli 2009, 133–166.

4 For amphorisques see Akkaya 1997, 131–132; Drougou 2005, 62, 190; Giannikouri *et al.* 1989, 69 pl. 12; Markoulaki and Niniou-Kindeli 1982, 89–90 fig. 38 pl. 25; Papachristodoulou 1980, 543; Vokotopoulou 1990, 25; Williams 1969, 58 ff. For unguentaria with vestigial handles see Lilimpaki-Akamati 1991, 73–152 pl. 49a; Sparkes and Talcott 1970, 191–192 pl. 63; Touratsoglou 1986, 637; Williams 1969, 58 ff. For unguentarium see Broneer 1962, 25.

5 Gjerstad (1960, 120) considers that the shape originated from Mycenaean prototypes. For examples of geometric amphoras see e.g. Christou 1974, 174–185; Lempesi 1996, 739 pl. 245d. For examples of Cypro-Archaic I see Christou 1973, 98 pl. XIV, 2 and Christou 1978, 138, 143, no. 3, 52; Nikolaou 1964, 131–185.

6 Gjerstad 1935, tomb 84 no. 18, Gjerstad 1948, 74–75 pl. LV no. 1, 3, 6 and for the linear decoration Deshayes 1963, 216–225; Pieridou 1965, 108–109; Yon 1984, 234–238.

7 Chatzidimitriou 2005, 41; Gjerstad 1948, 282 ff. and 286; Karageorghis and Iakovou 1982, 131; Pieridou 1964, 128.

8 Rotroff 2006, 144 note 59. I consider that the last example of this particular category is an amphora exposed in the museum in Nicosia that according to its shape should probably be dated around 350 BC. To my knowledge in burials of the 3rd century BC from the cemetery in Amathous and Marion no such vessel has been found.

9 Cypriotic pottery of the geometric and archaic period has been found

Fig. 1. Olynthus, inv.number 551

Fig. 2. Aineia, inv.number 7567

wider northern region of Greece, Cycladic pottery becomes known and in a way influences local pottery production. It is also possible that the islanders were accompanied by Cypriots who in the 4th century BC introduced the pseudo-Cypriot amphoras in mainland Greece, but this is only speculation. What is a fact is that Cypriot amphoras and amphorisques were not unknown in Greece although the exact network of their introduction from Cyprus to Greece remains a mystery. The only known examples of Cypriot amphoras in mainland Greece have been found in Ambracia and can be dated in the 4th century BC[10]. It is worth mentioning that along with these Cypriot amphoras, vases of the 4th century BC that most likely come from Macedonia were also discovered there.

Generally speaking pseudo-Cypriot vessels constitute a specific type of early Hellenistic pottery. The oldest shape of the group is that of the side-handled amphora (**Fig. 1**). Pseudo-Cypriot amphoras from Greece have been found in Macedonia[11], Epirus[12], Central Greece[13], Peloponnese[14] and the Cyclades[15], while other examples derive from sites of the Black Sea such as Pontic Apollonia[16] and Theodosia[17].

In the 4th century BC the shape of the pseudo-Cypriot amphora can be characterized by the ring or disc base, a spherical, plump body and a flaring neck that ends with a simple, straight rim or sometimes a rim shaped like a kalyx[18] (**Figs. 6–7**). Gradually the shape evolves and after the middle of the same century according to safely dated contexts, the body transforms to ovoid, the neck is almost vertical and the rim is downward-slopping[19] (**Fig. 8**).

in several places in northern Greece,, Tiverios 2004, 299–300 and note 33.

10 Museum of Arta inv. no. 6657 and two more vessels without inventory number both from the same part of the cemetery (Dimou field), from the small graves number 2 and 34.

11 Andronikos 1953, 150 ff. fig. 17; Andronikos 1969, 28 pl. 135; Drougou 2005, 37, 43–45, 102–104, 189–190; Drougou 2006, 231 fig .1; Lilimpaki-Akamati 2007, 100 pl. 61; Robinson 1933, 34–35, 43 pl. 32–33, 39; Robinson 1950, 51, 192 pl. 10; Skarlatidou 1993, 328–334 pl. 100B; Themelis and Touratsoglou 1997, 37–38, 77, 131, 165 pl. 45, 147; Tzanavari 2000, 606–607 fig. 7.

12 Aggeli 1996, 387; Gravani 1988/89, 100–101 pl. 2; Meliades 1926, 63–77; Touchais *et al.* 1999, 720–721 fig. 78; Touchais *et al.* 2001, 884–885; Tsirivakos 1965, 355–360.

13 Andriomenou 1960, 150 pl. 130b; Rotroff 2006, 287–288 fig. 60 pl. 50–51; Sparkes and Talcott 1970, 339–340 pl. 63.

14 Williams 1969, 57–58 fig. 8 pl. 18c; Williams 1970, 5 ff.

15 Daux 1967, 761; Zafiropoulos 1966, 135–138 fig. 140.

16 Panayotova 2005, 545–547 pl. 3–4.

17 Reports of two more vessels from the Kertch region are published by Šurgaja and Aĭbabin 1978, 83, note 12.

18 Andronikos 1969, 280 pl. 135; Drougou 2005, 102–104 fig. 109; Rotroff 2006, 287–288 fig. 60 pl. 50; Sparkes and Talcott 1970, 339–340 pl. 63; Williams 1969, 57–58 fig. 8.

19 Aggeli 1996, 387 pl. 104b; Drougou 2005, 43–45, 189–190; Lilimpaki-Akamati 2007, 100 pl. 61; Sparkes and Talcott 1970, 340 pl. 63; Themelis and Touratsoglou 1997, 37–38, 77, 131, 165; Tzanavari 2000, 606–607 fig. 7; Williams 1969, 58; Williams 1970, 5 ff.

Fig. 3. Pydna, inv.number Πυ7301, unpublished

Fig. 5. Cyprus, MLα 1023 (T1/1)

Fig. 4. Cyprus, LM 1314/28 (T214/28)

The pseudo-Cypriot amphoras from Ambracia have a somewhat different shape and evolution that the rest (**Figs. 9–10**). Vases from the second half of the 4th century BC have a fairly squat angular or ovoid body, ring or disc base and a very tall and wide neck that meets the sloping shoulder at a sharp angle[20]. In the first half of the 3rd century BC a low foot can be seen[21] while on the second half of the same century the size of the amphoras seems to be reduced and their body is rendered angular[22]. Besides the differences in the shape the pseudo-Cypriot amphoras from Epirus are differentiated from the others in the decoration and fabric as well. Generally speaking pseudo-Cypriot amphoras either from Epirus or the rest of the sites are produced until the end of the 3rd century BC.

Pseudo-Cypriot amphorisques appear at the same time as the amphoras and examples have been unearthed in Macedonia[23], Thessaly[24], Central Greece[25], Peloponnese[26] and the Aegean[27], while one solitary find was located in the

20 E.g. the unpublished vases kept in the Archaeological Museum in Arta no. 3014, 3406, 3410 and 6657.
21 Aggeli 1996, 387 pl. 104a; Meliades 1926, 63–77 fig. 5.
22 Meliades 1926, 63–77 fig. 5–6; Tsirivakos 1965, 355–360 pl. 423a.
23 Akamatis 2008, 618 fig. 1; Drougou 2005, 62, 65–66, 190; Drougou 2006, 231; Lilimpaki-Akamati 2007, 99 pl. 61; Vokotopoulou 1990, 25.
24 Theocharis and Chourmouziadis 1970, 205 fig. 3.
25 Rotroff 2006, 288 fig. 60–61 pl. 51.
26 Williams 1969, 57–58 fig. 8.
27 Giannikouri *et al.* 1989, 69 pl. 11–12; Markoulaki and Niniou-Kindeli 1982, 89–90 fig. 38 pl. 25; Papachristodoulou 1980, 543.

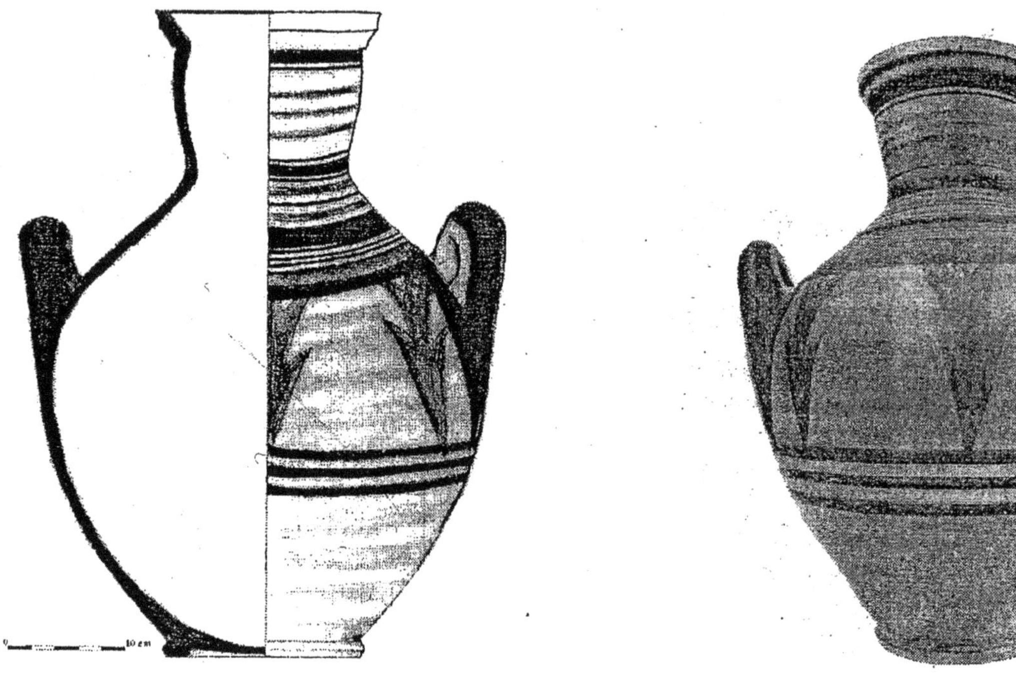

Fig. 6. Apollonia, inv.number 2787, Panayotova 2005, 547 pl. 4:5, 6

black sea region of Asia Minor[28] and one in the Western Mediterranean.

Amphorisques basically constitute a smaller version of the regular sized amphoras[29]. The reduced size is most proably connected with their usage[30]. The first examples appear around the third quarter of the 4th century BC[31] and the amphorisques seem to be produced until the middle of the 3rd century BC[32].

Pseudo-Cypriot amphorisques can be divided into two different variations according to their shape. In the earliest chronological variation (**Fig. 2**) the amphorisques' shape can be related to unguentaria with ovoid body without a foot[33]. The earliest examples have a height that can reach up to 23cm and the following morphological characteristics: low ring base, spherical or ovoid body, narrow, conical neck, downturned rim, small handles that form a high arc[34]. In the last quarter (**Fig. 11**) of the 4th century BC the height of the amphorisques surpasses the 24cm[35]. Examples have small disc base, slightly concave on the underside, ovoid body, slightly conical neck, downturned rim and small horizontal handles.

Chronological evidence for the dating of pseudo-Cypriot amphorisques derives from secure contexts[36] and is verified by comparisons with contemporary unguentaria. Parallels, for the earliest pseudo-Cypriot amphorisques can be found in the Eridanos cemetery[37], while for the later ones similar shaped vases occur in graves at Aiginio[38], Rhodes[39] and Naupaktos[40].

In the second variation (**Fig. 12**) of pseudo-Cypriot amphorisques are sorted those that can be compared to unguentaria with foot, the earliest version of fusiform unguentaria[41]. These amphorisques are characterized by a

28 Akkaya 1997, 131–132.

29 For the shapes origin from the amphoras see Hübner 2006, 30; Kotitsa 2007, 53; Markoulaki and Kindeli 1994, 208, 220 fig. 1; Rotroff 1984, 258; Rotroff 1997, 177; Rotroff 2006, 142–144. For unguentaria made from glass see Triantafillidis 2005.

30 For the connection between shape and usage see Hübner 2006, 27.

31 For completely or partially black-glazed amphorisques and amphorisques with banded decoration see Krstić 2004, 589 pl. 294a.

32 However amphorisques generally continue even after the middle of the 3rd century BC, Bitrakova-Grozdanova 1990, 70 pl. 35b; Krstić 2004, 589 pl. 294a; Themelis 2005, 100–101 fig. 5;Tolstikov and Zhuravlev 2004, 274 pl. 97:9.

33 Drougou and Touratsoglou (Drougou, 1994, 135) point to the similarities between spherical unguentaria and amphorisques and comment on the parallel evolution of the two shapes from the end of the 4th century BC and onwards. Also see Rotroff 1997, 177–178. We must however point out that pseudo-cypriot amphorisques predate the unguentaria. Rotroff 2006, 150–151.

34 Giannikouri *et al. 1989, 69 pl. 12; Papachristodoulou 1980, 543; Vokotopoulou 1990, 25; Williams 1969, 57–58 fig. 8 and also the unpublished vases from Pydna Π3286, Π3287 and Π3288.*

35 Akamatis 2008, 618, fig. 1; Drougou 2005, 62, 66, 190 fig. 57.

36 E.g. Pydna tomb 5, tomb 12; Alikes Kitrous tomb 13; Drougou 2005; Giannikouri *et al. 1989, 69 pl. 12; Markoulaki and Niniou-Kindeli 1982, 89–90 fig. 38 pl. 25; Rotroff 1997, 434; Sparkes and Talcott 1970, 397; Vokotopoulou 1990, 25.*

37 3rd quarter of the 4th century BC. Schlörb-Vierneisel 1966, 83 fig. 53,6, 85, fig. 55,3 and 90 fig. 53,5.

38 Unguentarium no. 131, Kotitsa 2007, 63 fig. 17 pl. 30.

39 Giannikouri and Patsiada 1994, 304 pl. 236a.

40 Mastrokostas 1961/62, 183–184 pl. 210b.

41 Akkaya 1997, 131–132; Giannikouri *et al. 1989, 69 pl. 11; Markoulaki and Niniou-Kindeli 1982, 89–90 fig. 38 pl. 25; Rotroff 2006, 288 fig. 60–61 pl. 51; Theocharis and Chourmouziadis, 1970, 205 fig. 3.*

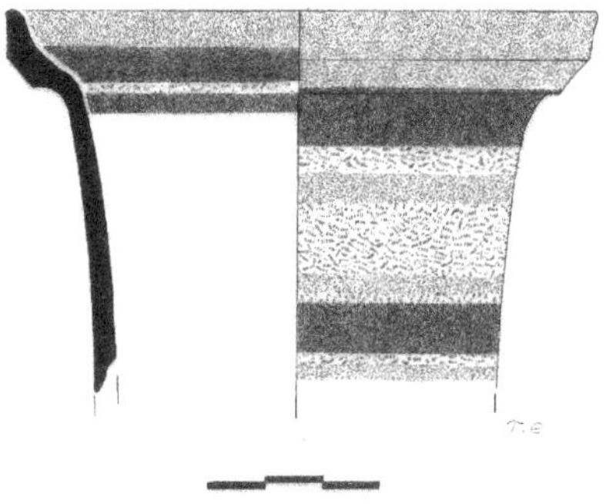

Fig. 7. Vergina, unpublished

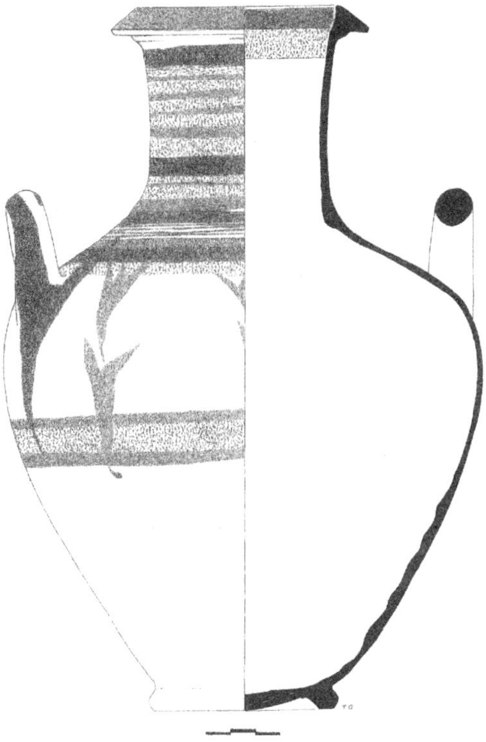

Fig. 8. Vergina, tomb II, number 2

Fig. 9. Ambracia, inv.number 5489

disc base, with a flat or slightly concave underside and a shallow groove in the juncture of the base with the foot foot relatively wide and narrow, spherical body, tall and thin neck with downward-slopping rim and handles that form a small arch and are turned a little bit outwards. The dating of these vases is based on chronological evidence from secure contexts and is verified by comparisons with contemporary unguentaria found in graves in the Kerameikos[42], the Opountioi Lokroi[43] and Thessaloniki[44].

The last shape of pseudo-Cypriot pottery is that of the unguentarium with vestigial handles (**Fig. 3**). This kind of unguentarium has been found in Thrace[45], Macedonia[46], Athens[47] and the Peloponnese[48]. Pseudo-Cypriot unguentaria are small vessels that basically have the same morphological characteristics with the rest of the unguentaria that don't have this particular floral and banded decoration. In the third quarter of the 4th century BC their height can reach up to 16,7cm and have ring, disc or even conical base, ovoid or spherical to ovoid body with the widest diameter higher than the middle of the vase, sloping

[42] Knigge 1976, 159 no. 358 pl. 67, 4.
[43] Onasoglou 1994, 62–63 pl. 28a–b, 29a.
[44] Drougou 1988, 82–83 fig. 5–6; Tsimpidou-Avloniti 1994, 82 pl. 38b, also see the unguentaria on pl. 38e.

[45] Triantafillos 1992, 499 pl. 138c.
[46] Kotitsa 2007, 64–65, 150 fig. 17 pl. 30, Lilimpaki-Akamati 1991, 133 pl. 49a; Misailidou-Despotidou 1990, 129 and note 20 fig. 9; Misailidou-Despotidou 1999, 310–311 fig. 8; Skarlatidou 2007, 82; Touratsoglou 1986, 637.
[47] Sparkes and Talcott 1970, 191–192, 340 pl. 63.
[48] Broneer 1962, 25 pl. 11b; Williams 1969, 58 ff.; Williams 1972, 161 pl. 27.

Fig. 10. Ambracia, inv.number 1824

shoulder, short, slightly flaring neck and a downward-sloping rim or one in the form of a kalyx [49] (**Fig. 13**). By the end of the same century the size of the pseudo-Cypriot unguentaria increases and their height reaches 20,9cm[50] (**Fig. 3**). In the last quarter of the 4th century BC the unguentaria have conical, ring or disc base, angular body with the widest diameter in the shoulder's height, or more seldom ovoid body, sloping shoulder that sometimes meets the belly at a sharp angle, neck much taller and narrower than the previous examples and downturned rim[51].

The vestigial handles in all of the unguentaria of the 4th century BC are relatively small and shaped like a small arch. They are placed quite high on the vessel's belly and covered with color. An unguentarium from Isthmia (**Fig. 14**) constitutes a unique find since it is the only example from Greece that has no pseudo-handles and is considered part of the pseudo-Cypriot category[52].

Chronological evidence for the pseudo-Cypriot unguentaria derives either from their context or by comparisons with unguentaria from graves e.g. in Akanthos[53] and the Eridanos cemetery[54] for the earliest ones and Akanthos[55], Alos[56] and the cemetery of Amphanes[57] for the vases placed in the last quarter of the 4th century BC.

After the presentation of the different shapes belonging in pseudo-Cypriot pottery we return to the second question we posed in the beginning of this paper. Where was this kind of pottery produced during the Hellenistic period? The logical approach to answer this question is the examination primarily of the fabric, but also that of the decoration of all the vessels found in Greece. Surprisingly all known vessels so far do not display considerable variations. Macroscopic analysis of the fabric sorted the vases into two basic groups and a few variations, regardless of where they were found. In the first group and its variations, according to my research, forty-three amphoras, nine amphorisques and eleven unguentaria can be placed. The fabric in this group is hard, mostly fine or with medium sized grains, containing white and black inclusions of variable sizes. Sometimes in addition to these inclusions, there are also red ones, quite large sized. The outer surface, which has been wet-smoothed before the placement of the vessel in the kiln, bears multiple small voids and on the larger vessels the outer surface is a little ruff and lumpy, in most cases covered with a cream colored wash.

The second group includes mainly amphorisques. The fabric is fine, red, especially compact and hard and has few to none small inclusions and sparkling inclusions. Pseudo-Cypriot vases belonging to Group B were probably placed in very high temperatures in the kiln, since the fabric is more solid than that of Group A and the outer surface is smooth without any voids and most times turns grey resembling the standard gray unguentarium fabric.

To sum up we have to observe that pseudo-Cypriot pottery found within Greece, can be sorted into two major groups. It seems that it is a special type of pottery that could very likely be produced in one or two geographical areas and then distributed in the other sites. If that is the case then we have to try to find out where exactly was their original source. The theory that there were all made in Cyprus has long ago been put aside. Newest theories included Rhodes, East Greece, Syria, Corinth, Athens and Macedonia as the

[49] Kotitsa 2007, 64–65, 150; Misailidou-Despotidou 1990, 129 and note 20 fig. 9; Touratsoglou 1986, 637.
[50] Pydna Π7301.
[51] Lilimpaki-Akamati 1991, 133 pl. 49a; Skarlatidou 2007, 82, 86.

[52] Broneer 1962, 25.
[53] Trakosopoulou-Salakidou 2004, 175–176 pl. 49c.
[54] Unguentaria of the 3rd quarter of the 4th century BC, Schlörb-Vierneisel 1966, 83 fig. 53, 6, 85, fig. 55, 3 and 90 fig. 53, 5.
[55] Trakosopoulou-Salakidou 2004, 175–176 pl. 49c, 50a–b.
[56] Malakasioti 2004, 106–107 fig. 6.
[57] Triantafillopoulou 2004, 62–63 pl. 13d, 14e.

Fig. 11. Vergina, number of publication 3

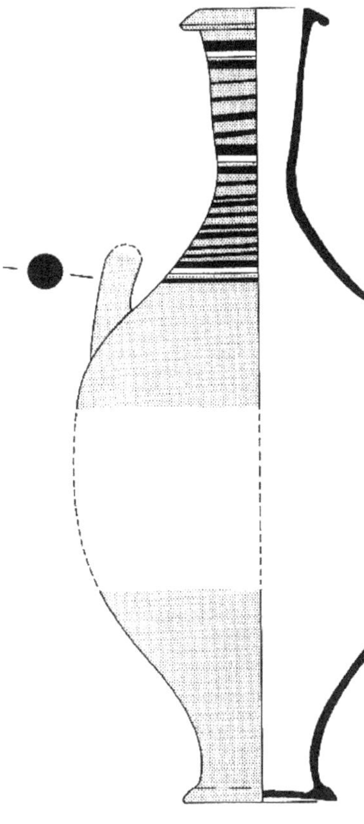

Fig. 12. Athens, inv.number P 30948, P 30950, Rotroff 2006, 288 fig. 61 pl. 51

Fig. 13. Aiginio, inv.number Πυ 1308

Fig. 14. Isthmia, inv.number IP 2822

Fig. 15. Corinth, inv.number C-69-111

Fig. 16. Vergina, inv.number BΠ4791

production center for the earliest examples, the pseudo-Cypriot amphoras.

However, according to our research the most qualified candidates seem to be either Corinth or Macedonia[58] (**Figs. 15–16**). The similarities between the Group A fabric and blister ware, the large numbers of pseudo-Cypriot amphoras found there, and a long tradition as a producer of perfumed oil point towards a Corinthian origin[59]. However the fact that the Macedonian assemblage demonstrates wider variety in size and shape than Corinth, combined with the fact that the earliest known safely dated examples of pseudo-Cypriot amphoras derive from the so-called tomb of Eurydice in Macedonia and the fact that particularly the fabric of Group A is not uncommon there, makes it more likely that pseudo-Cypriot amphoras were made in a Macedonian workshop. A Macedonian origin based on their technical characteristics and their fabric has been suggested from time to time by various archaeologists[60]. Generally speaking it is quite obvious that vases from Corinth and Macedonia share a lot of common traits, especially when it comes to decoration. Both areas use three colors (black-red-white) to decorate the vases and the inside of the vase's rim is covered by black or white and black band, while the upper surface is usually red. The decoration of the shoulder usually begins with a red and a black band and ends with lines alternating red, black and white. Regarding the amphorisques and unguentaria from Corinth the poor condition of the remaining material and the relatively small number of examples are not sufficient to prove the existence of a workshop specializing in their production[61]. The fact that some of the vases have a lot in common with pottery from northern Greece may suggest that these vessels were imported in Corinth and not made there. This suggestion seems to be sustained by the fact that out of a total of 18 unguentaria all but five examples have been found in Pydna. If indeed Pydna is where the workshop was located, or if it was located in another area of northern Greece is a matter that still remains undetermined.

The distribution of pseudo-Cypriot pottery in Corinth and other parts of Greece can be interpreted with two very different explanations: either the vases were imported

58 Trakatelli 2009, 207–209, 289–299.
59 Rotroff 2006, 145, 149.
60 Drougou 2005, 189–190; Markoulaki and Niniou-Kindeli 1982, 91 note 220; Panti 2008, 233–234; Robinson 1950, 4–7; Robinson 1933, 45 ff.; Themelis and Touratsoglou 1997, 37–38, 77, 131, 165 according to them the mica and the poor firing constitute strong indications that the amphoras were made in a local workshop; Vokotopoulou 1990, 25 and note 36.

61 Rotroff suggests that the amphorisques and unguentaria were made locally in the places where the pseudo-cypriot amphoras were exported. Rotroff 2006, 149.

to the Peloponnese, Attica and the various islands from Macedonia, or they are local imitations using a very similar fabric. Although we are not really aware of the precise time when the vases appeared in southern Greece and the Aegean, a possible date at least for their appearance in Corinth could be 338 BC after the battle of Chaeronea when Corinth was chosen by Philipp II as a locale for the great conference he called to decide the future relationships between the Greek cities and himself[62]. The result was known as the league of Corinth and since then and up to 243 BC a Macedonian garrison was permanently placed there[63]. So it is quite possible that with the presence of Macedonians in southern Greece in the third quarter of the 4th century BC the category of pseudo-Cypriot pottery became widely known. The appearance of Macedonian pseudo-Cypriot amphoras in Corinth's colony Ambracia, in the last quarter of the 4th century BC, reinforces this theory. However this is only a suggestion that only specialized microscopic examination of the fabric may support.

Regarding the introduction of the pseudo-Cypriot amphoras in Apollonia, it seems more possible that they constitute local production and they are manufactured there and not imported. If it was made by Cypriot potters living there, by Macedonians or by locals who were aware of this kind of pottery remains unknown.

Lydia Antonia Trakatelli
toniatrak@yahoo.gr

Bibliography

Aggeli, A. 1996. Οδός Κομμένου. *Αρχαιολογικόν Δελτίον Χρονικα* 51, 387–389.

Aĭbabin, A. И. 1978. *АНТИУНОЕ ПОГРЕБЕНИЕ В ФЕОДОСИИ*, КРАТКИЕ СООБЩЕНИЯ 156, 80–84.

Akamatis, I. 2008. Πανεπιστημιακή ανασκαφή αγοράς Πέλλας 2006. *Το Αρχαιολογικό Έργο στη Μακεδονία και Θράκη* 20, 615–626 fig. 1.

Akkaya, M. 1997. Mezardaki Pontos Hazinesi 'Pontos treasury in a tomb. *ATLAS* 48, 130–133.

Andriomenou, A, 1960. Εύβοια, Νέα Λάμψακο. *Αρχαιολογικόν Δελτίον Χρονικα* 16, 150.

Andronikos, M, 1953. Ανασκαφή νεκροταφείου Βεργίνη. *Πρακτικά*, 141–158.

Andronikos, M, 1969. *Βεργίνα Ι: το νεκροταφείο των τύμβων*. Athens, Archaeological Society at Athens.

Bengston, H, 1991. *Ιστορία της αρχαίας Ελλάδος*. Athens, Melissa publications (2nd ed).

Bitrakova-Grozdanova, V, 1990. Les caractéristiques de la céramique Hellénistique de la region d'Ohrid et de Prespa. In *Β΄ Επιστημονική Συνάντηση για την Ελληνιστική Κεραμεική*. Ρόδος 1989, 66–73. Athens, TAP

Broneer, O, 1962. Excavations at Isthmia 1959–196, *Hesperia* 31, 1–25.

Chatzidimitriou, K. 2005. *History of Cyprus*. Cyprus, private publisher.

Christou, D. 1973. Νέαι αρχαιολογικαί μαρτυρίαι εκ της. νεκροπόλεως των Σόλων. *Report of the Department of Antiquities, Cyprus*, 91–102.

Christou, D. 1974. Pottery types from a new necropolis at Kato Dheftera. *Report of the Department of Antiquities, Cyprus*, 174–185.

Christou, D. 1978. Amathus Tomb 151. *Report of the Department of Antiquities, Cyprus*, 132–148.

Daux, G. 1967. Chronique des Fouilles 1966, Théra. *Bulletin de correspondance hellénique* 91, 623–889.

Deshayes, J. 1963. *La nécropole de Ktima: Mission Jean Bérard 1953–1955*. Paris, P. Geuthner.

Drougou S. and Touratsoglou I. 1994. Τα χρονολογημένα σύνολα Ελληνιστικής Κεραμικής από τη Μακεδονία. In *Γ΄ Επιστημονική Συνάντηση για την Ελληνιστική Κεραμική*. Θεσσαλονίκη 1991, 128–137. Athens, Archetai.

Drougou, S. 1988. Τα πήλινα κτερίσματα του μακεδονικού τάφου στην πλατεία Συντριβανίου Θεσσαλονίκης. *'Αρχαιολογική Εφημερίς 127, 71–93.*

Drougou, S. 2005. *Βεργίνα. Τα πήλινα αγγεία της μεγάλης τούμπας*. Athens, Archaeological Society at Athens.

Drougou, S. 2006. Βεργίνα 2004–2005. *Egnatia* 10, 231–238.

Gehrke, H.-J. 2000. Ιστορία του ελληνιστικού κόσμου. Athens, National Bank of Greece Cultural Foundation (MIET).

Giannikouri, A. and Patsiada V. 1994. Σύνολα κεραμικής από τη νεκρόπολη της Ρόδου. Συμβολή στην ελληνιστική κεραμική. In *Ελληνιστική Κεραμική από το Αιγαίο*, 102–125. Mytilene, Ministry of Culture.

Giannikouri, A., Patsiada, V. and Filimonos, M. 1989. Ταφικά σύνολα από τις νεκροπόλεις της αρχαίας Ρόδου. In *Α΄ συνάντηση για την ελληνιστική κεραμεική*. Ιωάννινα 1986, 63–117. Ioannina, Panepistimio Ioanninon.

Gjerstad, E. 1960. Pottery types, Cypro-geometric to Cypro-classical. *Opuscula Atheniensia* 3, 105–122.

Gjerstad, E. 1935. *The Swedish Cyprus Expedition: finds and results of the excavation in Cyprus 1927–1931*, vol. 2. Stockholm, Swedish Cyprus Expedition Press.

62 Bengston 1991, 293 ff.
63 Gehrke 2000, 25; Hammond 1999, 226–227.

Gjerstad, E. 1948. *The Swedish Cyprus Expedition: the Cypro-geometric, Cypro-archaic and Cypro-classical periods*, vol. 4. 2. Stockholm, The Swedish Cyprus Expedition Press.

Gravani, K. 1988/89. Κεραμική των ελληνιστικών χρόνων από την Ήπειρο. *Ηπειρωτικά Χρονικά* 29, 89–132.

Hammond, N. G. L. 1999. *Το μακεδονικό κράτος: γένεση, θεσμοί και ιστορία*. Athens, Papazisis Press.

Hübner, G. 2006. Hellenistic and Roman unguentaria: Function-related aspects of the shapes, in D. Malfitana, J. Poblome and J. Lund, *Old pottery in a new century: innovating perspectives on Roman pottery studies*. Atti del convegno internazionale di studi, Catania, 22–24 aprile 2004, C.N.R. 1, 27–39. Catania, Monografie dell'Istituto per I Beni Archeologici e Monumentali.

Karageorghis, V. and Iakovou, M. 1982. Cypro-Geometric Material from Palaepaphos. *Report of the Department of Antiquities, Cyprus, 123–137.*

Knigge, U. 1976. *Der Südhügel*. Kerameikos 9. Berlin, de Gruyter.

Kotitsa, Z. 2007. *Αιγίνιο Πιερίας: Κεραμική από το Νεκροταφείο στη θέση «Μελίσσια»*. Thessaloniki, Kornilia Sfakianaki Press.

Krstić, V. 2004. Hellenistic pottery from Budva from the Greek collection of the National Museum of Belgrade. In *ΣΤ΄ Επιστημονική Συνάντηση για την Ελληνιστική Κεραμική*. Βόλος 2000, 585–592. Athens, TAP.

Lempesi, A. 1996. Εφορεία αρχαιοπωλείων και ιδιωτικών συλλογών. *Αρχαιολογικόν Δελτίον Χρονικα* 51, 739–741.

Lilimpaki-Akamati, M. 1991. Ανατολικό νεκροταφείο Πέλλας. *Αρχαιολογικόν Δελτίον Μελεται* 44–46, 73–152.

Lilimpaki-Akamati, M. 2007. *Πέλλης: κιβωτιόσχημος τάφος με ζωγραφική διακόσμηση από την Πέλλα*. Thessaloniki, Ministry of Culture.

Malakasioti, Z. 2004. Ελληνιστικά λυχνάρια της Άλου. In *ΣΤ΄ Επιστημονική Συνάντηση για την Ελληνιστική Κεραμική*. Βόλος 2000, 89–109. Athens, TAP.

Markoulaki, S. and Kindeli, V. 1994. Αντιπροσωπευτικές ομάδες ελληνιστικής κεραμικής από ταφικά σύνολα του νομού Χανίων. In *Ελληνιστική Κεραμική από το Αιγαίο*, 208–221. Mytilene, Ministry of Culture.

Markoulaki, S. and Niniou-Kindeli, V. 1982. Ελληνιστικός λαξευτός τάφος Χανίων: ανασκαφή οικοπέδου Μαθιουλάκη. *Αρχαιολογικόν Δελτίον Μελεται* 37, 7–118.

Mastrokostas, E. 1961/62. Αρχαιότητες και μνημεία Αιτωλοακαρνανίας. *Αρχαιολογικόν Δελτίον Χρονικα 17, 183–184.*

Meliades, G. 1926. Αμβρακίας Τάφοι. *Αρχαιολογικόν Δελτίον* 10, 63–77.

Misailidou-Despotidou, V. 1990. Από το Νεκροταφείο της Αρχαίας Μίεζας. *Το Αρχαιολογικό Έργο στη Μακεδονία και Θράκη 4, 127–135.*

Misailidou-Despotidou, V. 1999. Ανασκαφική έρευνα στην αρχαία Άφυτη. *Το Αρχαιολογικό Έργο στη Μακεδονία και Θράκη* 13, 305–316.

Nikolaou, K. 1964. Ανασκαφή τάφων εις Μάριον. *Report of the Department of Antiquities, Cyprus* 1964, 131–185.

Onasoglou, A. 1994. Νεκροταφείο των Οπουντίων Λοκρών στην Τριανταφυλλιά Λειβανατών. Οι ελληνιστικοί τάφοι. In *Γ΄ Επιστημονική Συνάντηση για την Ελληνιστική Κεραμική*. Θεσσαλονίκη 1991, 55–70. Athens, Archetai.

Panayotova, K. 2005. Amphorae of the so-called "Cypriot" type from Apollonia Pontica, in M. Milčeva (ed.), *Stephanos Archaeologicos in honorem Professoris Ludmili Getov*, 540–554. Sofia, Universitetsko Izdatelstvo Sv. Kliment Ochidski.

Panti, A. 2008. *Τοπική κεραμική από τη Χαλκιδική και το μυχό του Θερμαϊκού κόλπου (Άκανθος, Καραμπουρνάκι, Σίνδος)*. Thessaloniki, City Publish.

Papachristodoulou, I. C. 1980. Οικόπεδο Ιω. Διακοδημητρίου. *Αρχαιολογικόν Δελτίον Χρονικα* 35, 527–546.

Pieridou, A. 1964. A Cypro-geometric cemetery at "vathyrkakas" Karavas. *Report of the Department of Antiquities, Cyprus, 114–129.*

Pieridou, A. 1965. An early Cypro-geometric tomb at Lapethos. *Report of the Department of Antiquities, Cyprus*, 75–111.

Robinson, D. M. 1933. *Mosaics, Vases, and Lamps of Olynthus*. Excavations at Olynthus 5. London, Oxford University Press.

Robinson, D. M. 1950. *Vases Found in 1934 and 1938*. Excavations at Olynthus 13. London, Oxford University Press.

Rotroff, S. I. 1984. The origins and chronology of Hellenistic gray unguentaria. *American Journal of Archaeology* 88, 258.

Rotroff, S. I. 1997. *Hellenistic Pottery and wheelmade tableware.* The Athenian Agora XXIX. Princeton, NJ., American School of Classical Studies.

Rotroff, S. I. 2006. *Hellenistic Pottery. The plain Wares*. The Athenian Agora XXXIII. Princeton, NJ., American School of Classical Studies.

Schlörb-Vierneisel, B. 1966. Eridanos-Nekropole 1. Gräber und Opferstellen hS 1–204. *Mitteilungen des Deutschen Archaologischen Instituts, Athenische Abteilung* 81, 4–111.

Skarlatidou, E. 1993. Οικόπεδο 315β (οδός Χαλκιδικής). *Αρχαιολογικόν Δελτίον Χρονικα* 48, 328–334.

Skarlatidou, E. 2007. *Θέρμη, το αρχαίο νεκροταφείο κάτω από τη σύγχρονη πόλη*. Athens, Olkos.

Sparkes, B. A. and Talcott, L. 1970. *Black and Plain Pottery of the 6th, 5th and 4th Centuries BC*. The Athenian Agora XII. Princeton, NJ., American School of Classical Studies.

Themelis, P. 2005. Η ελληνιστική κεραμική της Μεσσήνης. In *Ελληνιστική Κεραμική από την Πελοπόννησο*, 95–106. Aigio, Archaeological Receipts Fund.

Themelis, P. and Touratsoglou, I. 1997. *Οι τάφοι του Δερβενίου*. Athens, Ministry of Culture and

Archaeological Receipts Fund.

Theocharis, D. and Chourmouziadis, G. 1970. Ανασκαφή τάφων Φθιώτιδων Θηβών. *Αρχαιολογικά Ανάλεκτα εξ Αθηνών* 3, 204–207.

Tiverios, M. 2004. Οι πανεπιστημιακές ανασκαφές στο Καραμπουρνάκι Θεσσαλονίκης και η παρουσία των φοινίκων στο Βόρειο Αιγαίο, in N. Stambolidis and A. Giannikouri (eds.), *Το αιγαίο στην πρώιμη εποχή του σιδήρου*, 295–306. Athens, University of Crete and Archaeological Institute of Aegean Studies.

Tolstikov, V. and Zhuravlev, D. 2004. Hellenistic pottery from two cisterns on the acropolis of Panticapaeum. In *ΣΤ' Επιστημονική Συνάντηση για την Ελληνιστική Κεραμική*. Βόλος 2000, 269–276. Athens, TAP.

Touchais, G., Huber, S. and Philippa-Touchais, A. 2001. Chroniques fouilles et découvertes archéologiques en Grèce en 1998. *Bulletin de correspondance hellénique* 125, 635–848.

Touratsoglou, I. 1986. Το ξίφος της Βέροιας: Συμβολή στη Μακεδονική οπλοποιία των ύστερων κλασικών χρόνων, in *Ancient Macedonia 4*. Papers read at the fourth Internationale Symposium held at Thessaloniki September 21.–25., 1983, 611–651. Thessaloniki, Institute for Balkan Studies.

Trakatelli, L. A. 2009. *Οι 'ψευδοκυπριακοί' αμφορείς. Συμβολή στη μελέτη της πρώιμης ελληνιστικής κεραμικής*. Unpublished PhD thesis, Aristotle University of Thessaloniki.

Trakosopoulou-Salakidou, E. 2004. Άκανθος: Ελληνιστική κεραμική. In *ΣΤ' Επιστημονική Συνάντηση για την Ελληνιστική Κεραμική*. Βόλος 2000, 173–184. Athens, TAP.

Triantafillidis, P. 2005. Η ελληνιστική κοινή: το γυαλί και ο πηλός. In *Ζ' Επιστημονική Συνάντηση για την Ελληνιστική Κεραμική*. Αίγιο 2005, 661–672. Athens, TAP.

Triantafillopoulou, P. 2004. Νεκροταφείο των Αμφανών: οι πρώιμοι ελληνιστικοί τάφοι. In *ΣΤ' Επιστημονική Συνάντηση για την Ελληνιστική Κεραμική*. Βόλος 2000, 61–66. Athens, TAP.

Triantafillos, D. 1992. Παραδόσεις αρχαίων. *Αρχαιολογικόν Δελτίον* 47, 498–499.

Tsimpidou-Avloniti, M. 1994. Σύνολα κεραμικής από το ελληνιστικό νεκροταφείο της Θεσσαλονίκης. In *Γ' Επιστημονική Συνάντηση για την Ελληνιστική Κεραμική*. Θεσσαλονίκη 1991, 80–89. Athens, Archetai.

Tsirivakos, I. 1965. Ανασκαφή εν Αμβρακία. *Αρχαιολογικόν Δελτίον Χρονικα* 20, 355–360.

Tzanavari, K. 2000. Ο μακεδονικός τάφος του τύμβου του Δερβενίου. Επαναπροσδιορισμός της ταυτότητας ενός παλιού ευρήματος. In P. Adam-Veleni (ed.), *Μύρτος, Μελέτες στη μνήμη της Ιουλίας Βοκοτοπούλου*, 593–617. Thessaloniki, Ministry of Culture.

Vokotopoulou, I. 1990. *Οι ταφικοί τύμβοι της Αίνειας*. Athens, Archaeological Receipts Fund.

Williams, C. K. and Fisher, J. E. 1972. Corinth 1971: Forum Area. *Hesperia* 41, 143–184.

Williams, C. K. 1969. Excavations at Corinth, 1968. *Hesperia* 38, 36–63.

Williams, C. K. 1970. Corinth 1969: Forum Area. *Hesperia* 39, 1–39.

Yon, M. 1984. Céramiques greques et imitations chypriotes. In H. A. Brijde (ed.), *Ancient Greek and Related Pottery*: proceedings of the international vase symposium in Amsterdam, 12–15 April, 234–238. Amsterdam, Allard Pierson Museum.

Zafiropoulos, N. S. 1966. Ανασκαφή Θήρας. *Πρακτικά*, 135–138.

Attische und attisierende Gefäß- und Verzierungstypen aus Demetrias.
Ein Produktionsort hellenistischer Keramik im Spiegel seiner Wirtschaftsbeziehungen

Horst Seilheimer

Abstract

Immediately after the foundation of Demetrias in the years 294–288 B.C. starts an extensive import of predominantly attic table wares in westslope technique. The fact, that the enormous requirements for these table wares in relation of the size of this planned city was filled from Athens may be connected – besides of the very favourable transport possibilities over the sea – with the long established workshop traditions there, which were able of a certain mass production in fine pottery. Also there was surely a very great popularity of attic shapes and decoration motifs, which were at this time on the Mainland of Greece *en vogue*. But very soon as local pottery production was initiated, again above all in attic-like westslope style, because this was clear in the main interest of the new settled customers in the city. On this new market may have set the immigrated attic craftsmen their hopes, because their products a very hardly to distinguish from the imported pieces in quality. It is true there is a certain, but very insignificant modifying of the original attic shapes and some new motif combinations in the decoration, but the origins stay clearly visible. Remarkable is the point, that many ceramic types and single decoration motifs after their introducing in the surroundings of the Macedonian capital here seemed to be produced very longer than in Athens. But the obvious mass production in Demetrias which starts in the second half of the 3rd. Century B.C. results to an clear carelessness in the glossy slip and in the making of the decoration motifs, which degenerates very fast to more simpler forms of the original, in the most case vegetable motifs of the westslope decoration; there is also significant an increasing using of incised line decoration and a common careless putting of barbotine slip or par example of white colour on the surface. Besides of the attic influences it seems that above all some initiations for the Hellenistic pottery of Demetrias came also from Asia Minor, the Black Sea region, Southern Russia, Egypt (Alexandria), but as well from the mainland of Greece. To what extinct the wares manufactured in Demetrias itself were also exported is very hard to say at the moment, but most probably there were some delivering to the settlements in the nearest area around the city, like New Halos. This conclusion seems to be very convincing instead of the fact that Demetrias was also an innovative production place of Hellenistic pottery with new combinations of shape and decoration, but most likely of new developed types too, like the Homeric bowls.

Keywords: Demetrias, Attisierende Gefäße, Attische Importe, Westabhang, innovativ neu kombinierte Gefäß-/ Dekorkombinationen, makedonisch, Thessalien

Demetrias und die Chronologie der hellenistischen Keramik

Demetrias wurde um 294–288 v. Chr. von Demetrios Poliorketes als Hauptstadt des makedonischen Reiches gegründet[1]. Vor allem die Fundamentierungsschichten des ‚Anaktoron' lieferten umfangreiche Funde hellenistischer Keramik. Größere Mengen stammen auch aus dem westlich anschließenden Zitadellenkomplex[2]. Bei dem ‚Anaktoron' von Demetrias handelt es sich allerdings wohl nicht um den makedonischen Palast der Residenzstadt[3]. Fortifikatorisch in die Stadtbefestigung integriert, ist in dem nicht vollendeten Bau wohl eine Art Stadtkastell zu vermuten, während der eigentliche Palast wohl eher in den ungleich größeren Gebäudekomplexen auf der so genannten Südwest-Terrasse zu suchen ist. Aufgrund der Grabungsergebnisse kann das Gebäude Philipp V. und damit dem Zeitraum zwischen 192 und 168 v. Chr. zugewiesen werden. Allerdings bietet der Baubeginn im ersten Viertel des 2. Jhs. v. Chr. lediglich einen *t.a.q.* für die allgemeine Chronologie der dort vertretenen hellenistischen Keramik, da sich die gesamte Stratigraphie des Anaktoronkomplexes aus lagenweise eingefüllten Aufschüttungs- und Planierungsschichten für die Fundamentierung des Gebäudes zusammensetzt. Dass es sich hierbei um einen kontinuierlichen Bauprozess handelt,

1 Marzolff 1996, 148–159.

2 Bei der Bearbeitung der hellenistischen Keramik konnte dankenswerterweise auf umfangreichste Vorarbeiten und Textkompartimente von A. Furtwängler zurückgegriffen werden, die er großzügig zur Verfügung gestellt hat. Das Forschungsprojekt ‚Demetrias' wurde u.a. von der Deutschen Forschungsgemeinschaft, dem Deutschen Archäologischen Institut, der Gerda Henkel-Stiftung und vom Verfasser finanziert.

3 Seilheimer 2006, 295–316.

belegen anpassende Gefäßfragmente aus verschiedenen Arealen und über alle Auffüllschichten hinweg. Die mit dem übrigen Füllmaterial in die Planierungsschichten des Gebäudes eingebrachte Keramik gehört überwiegend dem 3. Jh. v. Chr. an und stammte folglich aus älteren Stadtgebieten. Demnach bietet das Anaktoron trotz einer mangelnden Feinstratigraphie die Möglichkeit einer chronologischen Einordnung sowohl für die aus Attika, aber auch aus anderen Regionen des Mittelmeerraumes stammenden Importwaren, ebenso für die lokal oft attisierende Produktion.

Letztere setzte offensichtlich nur wenig nach der Stadtgründung bereits im frühen 3. Jh. v. Chr. ein, da der zunehmende Bedarf an Feinkeramik dieser riesigen Stadtanlage bald nicht mehr alleine von den Importen gedeckt werden konnte. Dass diese vorwiegend aus Attika stammten, dürfte einerseits mit den günstigen Transportwegen, der seit langem in Athen etablierten Keramikindustrie mit entsprechend großem Output an Stückzahlen, aber auch mit ‚modischen' Vorlieben und der damit verbundenen Beliebtheit attischer Keramik zu erklären sein, denn immerhin handelte es sich ja bei Demetrias um die makedonische Hauptstadt und die attische Keramik war zu dieser Zeit aufgrund der dort zu beobachtenden innovativen Strömungen sozusagen *en vogue*. Hierzu passt die Beobachtung, dass sich viele einheimische Werkstätten vorwiegend an attischen Vorbildern orientierten, die vom Westabhangstil geprägt wurden. Die charakteristischen Einzelmotive, bzw. Motivkombinationen erscheinen unter weitgehender Beibehaltung der Gefäßformen manchmal als derart genaue Replik, dass sie – verbunden mit einer entsprechend sorgfältigen Herstellungsweise – lediglich durch die Verwendung lokaler Tonlagerstätten von originalen attischen Beispielen zu unterscheiden sind. Parallel dazu kommt es aber auch bei der Mehrzahl der Gefäße zu einer selektiven Neugruppierung, bzw. Abwandlung der attischen Dekormotive und schließlich etwa ab der zweiten Hälfte des 3. und dann vor allem im 2. Jh. v. Chr. zu einer zunehmenden Degeneration der jetzt oftmals geritzten Verzierungselemente, aber auch einem gewissen Qualitätsverlust, der mit dem meist nur flüchtig und partiell aufgetragenen Glanztonauftrages einhergeht. Diese Entwicklung ist wohl einer gewissen Massenproduktion geschuldet, aber auch der Tatsache, dass bestimmte keramische Formen, ebenso die damit verbundenen Verzierungsmotive in der attischen Produktion zu diesem Zeitpunkt bereits aufgegeben oder zumindest stark zurückgefahren bzw. abgewandelt worden waren, während sie sich in den demetriadischen Werkstätten immer noch großer Beliebtheit und einer deutlich längeren Laufzeit erfreuten.

Besonders wichtig erscheint hier die Korrelation mit den auf der Athener Agora identifizierten Werkstätten[4]. Zunächst ist hier die sog. Bracket Leaf Group anzuführen (280–250 v. Chr.), deren Erzeugnisse in Aigina, Kalymnos, Samos, Demetrias[5], Pella, der Nordküste des Schwarzen Meeres verbreitet waren. Die zweite Werkstatt mit dem Kombinationsnamen Edwards/Dikeras-Group, lässt sich ebenfalls recht eng fixieren (die Edwards Group von 275–265 v. Chr.[6], sowie die Dikeras-Group von 270–260 v. Chr.[7]). Der starke Einfluss attischer Waren erklärt sich aber wohl nicht nur durch die Vorbilder der Importe, sondern auch durch tatsächlich zugewanderte attische Töpfer, die möglicherweise aufgrund eines zunehmenden Konkurrenzdruckes in Athen und auf der Suche nach einem neuen Absatzmarkt ihre Formen und Verzierungsmotive in der bekannten Qualität nun mit einheimischem Ton produzierten. Gleichzeitig wurden auf diese Weise natürlich weitere Anregungen an einheimische Töpfer weitergegeben, aber auch andere Gebiete des Mittelmeerraumes bis hin zum kleinasiatischen Raum beeinflussten die Keramikproduktion in Demetrias. Es ist wohl selbstverständlich damit zu rechnen, dass die hier nun aus diesem Konglomerat verschiedener Werkstattströmungen entstandenen Formtypen und Dekormotive nun wiederum in anderen keramischen Zentren reflektiert wurden.

Damit im Zusammenhang steht die Frage nach Exporten aus Demetrias, die jedoch durchaus schwierig zu beantworten ist und plausibel nur mit Hilfe einer Kombination von Form, Dekor und Tonanalysen entschieden werden kann. Da die naturwissenschaftliche Analyse der Keramik aus Demetrias ohnehin nur an vergleichsweise wenigen Stücken durchgeführt wurde erscheint ein direkter Vergleich zu anderen Fundorten schwierig. Zusätzlich erschwert wird diese Frage noch dadurch, dass Töpferton in der Antike wohl auch direkt in andere Werkstattzentren geliefert wurde, bis hin zu einer Sekundärverwendung als Schiffsballast[8]. Es darf allerdings vermutet werden, dass zumindest – entsprechend dem anzunehmenden Absatzmarkt einer durchschnittlich besetzten Töpferwerkstatt – die in der Nähe liegenden kleineren Städte, wie z. B. New Halos beliefert wurden[9]. Mit dieser Frage korreliert auch die für Demetrias als Herstellungsort postulierte Genese der homerischen Becher, auf die hier allerdings nicht näher eingegangen werden kann[10]. Demgegenüber scheinen die megarischen Becher vorwiegend attischer Provenienz zu sein, dennoch kann man aufgrund der Tonkonsistenz zumindest bei einigen Stücken auch eine lokale Herkunft annehmen. Die eigenständige Produktion von Keramik lässt sich in Demetrias bis in die späthellenistisch-römische Zeit weiterverfolgen, dann allerdings unter dem zunehmend dominanter werdenden Einfluss der Eastern Sigillata.

4 Rotroff 1991, 65–78; dies. 1997

5 Furtwängler 1990, 50 Taf. 15 b; Rotroff, 1991, 65. 69 Abb. 1 Taf. 14

6 Furtwängler 1990, 51 Taf. 15 c; vgl. Rotroff, 1991, 71 Abb. 5 mit Katalog; zur unteren Grenze dieser Werkstatt um 265 v. Chr.: Kotitsa 1996, 93 mit Anm. 824.

7 Rotroff 1991, 72–80.

8 Enklaar 1985, 109 Anm. 14; vgl. auch Negev 1986, Er kam für die Eastern Terra Sigillata zu ähnlichen Schlussfolgerungen.

9 Reinders (1988).

10 Sinn 1979. Kritisch zur Lokalisierung der homerischer Becher in Makedonien: Rogl 1997.

Abb. 1

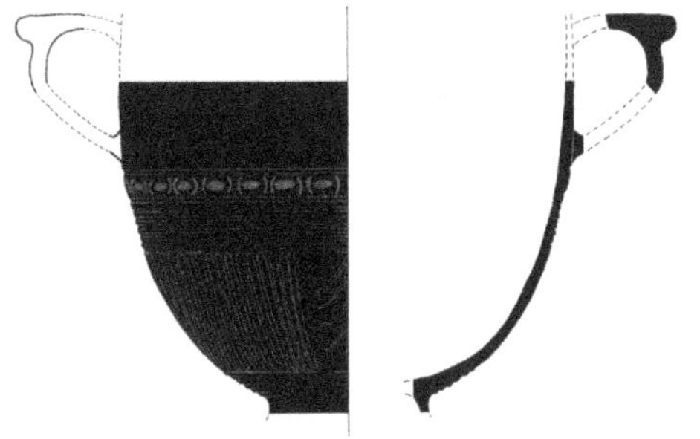

Abb. 2

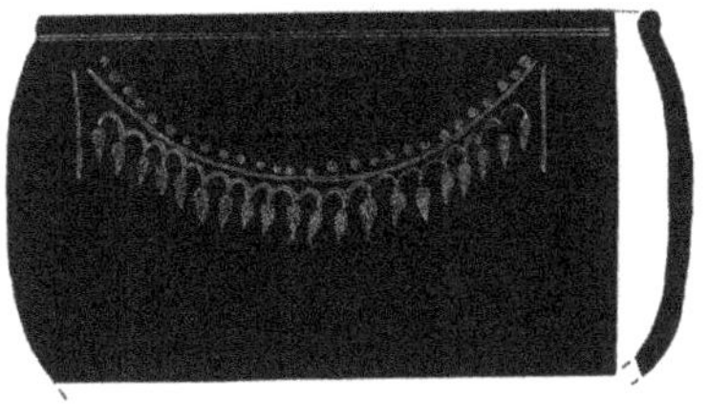

Abb. 3

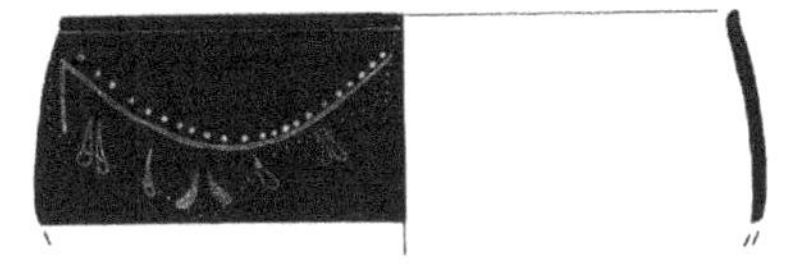

Abb. 4

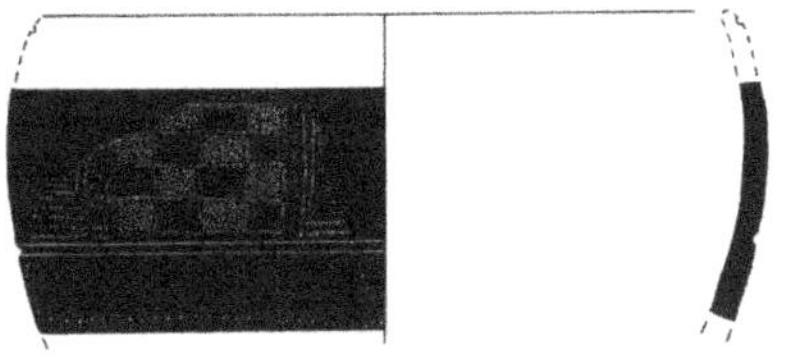

Abb. 5

Abb. 1-5. Skyphoi mit gerundetem Profil und einbiegendem Rand (1. Museum Volos, Inv. K 3443 - 2. DP 76 S XII 23 VII A/E - 3. DP 78 R XI 49 III F - 4. DP 76 V XII 13 II - 5. DP 73 R XII 16 III)

Die lokale Keramikproduktion von Demetrias und der Westabhangstil

In den 80iger Jahren des 3. Jhs. v. Chr. setzte ein intensiver Import attischer Feinkeramik nach Demetrias ein, doch nahmen bereits kurze Zeit später die lokalen Werkstätten ebenfalls die Produktion auf[11]. Qualitativ hochwertige einheimische Erzeugnisse gehören entsprechend ihres gelblich-beigen Tones der ‚gelben Ware' an und werden der ‚GW-Werkstatt' zugeordnet[12]. Gleichzeitig lässt das keramische Fundspektrum in Demetrias auf weitere lokale Werkstätten schließen, die als ‚LD-Werkstätten' angesprochen werden sollen[13]. Der Umbruch im Formen- und Verzierungsrepertoire vollzieht sich dabei im zweiten Viertel des 3. Jhs. v. Chr. Ab der zweiten Hälfte des 2. Jhs. v. Chr. gewinnt dann italischer Import zunehmend Einfluss in Demetrias wie auch in anderen Fundstätten des Mittelmeerraumes, während gleichzeitig eine gewissen Nachlässigkeit attischer Keramik in Form, Technik und Dekor stattfindet. Diese Importe verstärken sich auch in Demetrias im 1. Jh. v. Chr. durch das Aufkommen der ESA-Ware, die bereits am Ende des 2. Jhs. v. Chr. die Märkte zunehmend dominiert, während nur noch wenige Formen des ursprünglichen Formenkataloges weiterproduziert werden.

Gefäßtypen und Verzierungsweisen aus dem keramischen Fundgut von Demetrias

Die Schwierigkeiten in der typologischen und chronologischen Analyse der hellenistischen Keramik wurden noch einmal von A. Furtwängler kurz zusammengefasst[14]. Für die Beurteilung der Handelbeziehungen von Demetrias sind Fragen nach attischem Import, nach attisierender Nachahmung entweder durch lokale oder zugewanderte Töpfer, ferner nach einheimischer, aber nicht unbedingt attisierender Produktion zu stellen. Zudem ist es auch notwendig zu klären, wie der Einfluss aus anderen keramischen Zentren z.B. Kleinasien sich in der lokalen Produktion niederschlägt. Schließlich ist auch die Frage nach Exporten in andere Gebiete zu stellen.

Für die Beurteilung der Handelsbeziehungen von Demetrias bewegt sich die typologische und chronologische Analyse um die Frage nach attischem Import, nach attisierender Nachahmung entweder durch lokale oder zugewanderte Töpfer, einheimischer, aber nicht unbedingt attisierender Produktion, dem Einfluss aus anderen keramischen Zentren und schließlich um die Frage nach Exporten in andere Gebiete.

---

11 Furtwängler 1990, 51–53 Taf. 16a–e; Eiwanger, postulierte diese lokale Produktion: Eiwanger 1981, ‚Ware IV B', II. Taf. 71, IV H 209–223; 80–107 ‚Ware IV H': vgl. auch ebenda die Waren II Db; II E; III D; IV B/C.

12 Furtwängler 1990, 52 Taf. 17f.; zur teilweise langen Laufzeit hellenistischer Keramikformen: Morel 1990, 17-32; ders. 1997, 405-415; Smetaner-Scherrer 1982, 68–76.

13 Kotitsa 1996, 76–84; 139 Rotroff 1991; 1997; vgl. auch dies. 1992; 2006 mit Abb. Vor allem den Untersuchungen Rotroffs sind hier in jüngster Zeit ausführliche Beschreibungen der Charakteristika hellenistischer Keramik und der Westabhangtechnik zu verdanken.

14 Furtwängler 1997, 396-400.

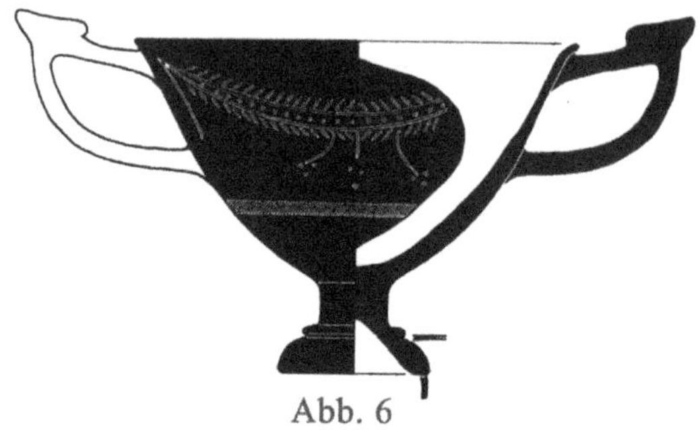

Abb. 6

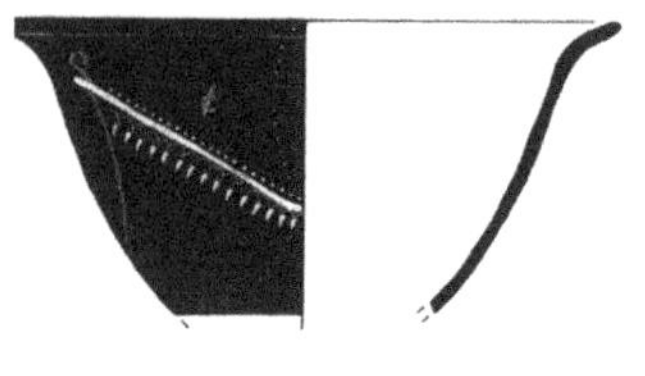

Abb. 7

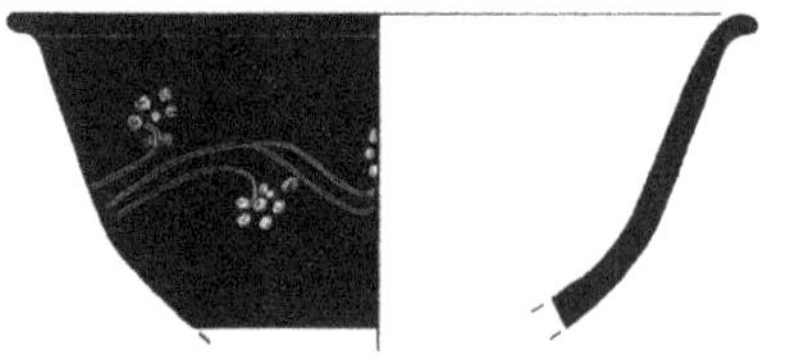

Abb. 8

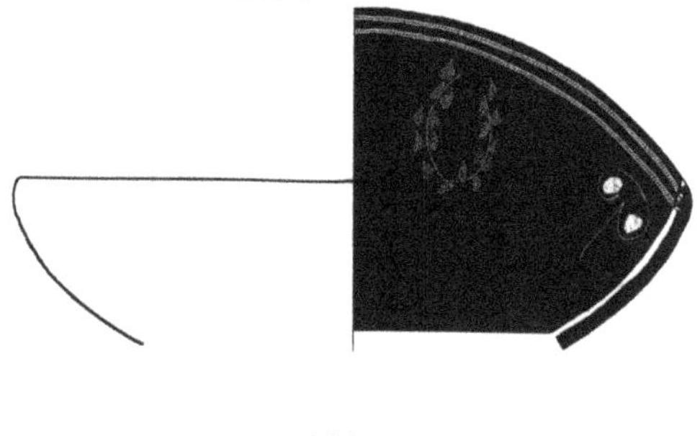

Abb. 9

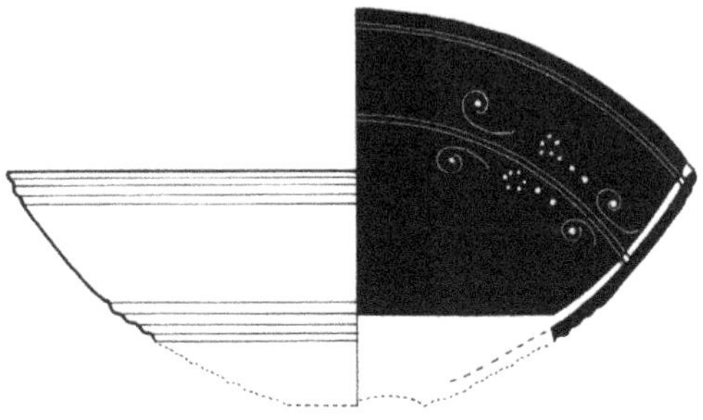

Abb. 10

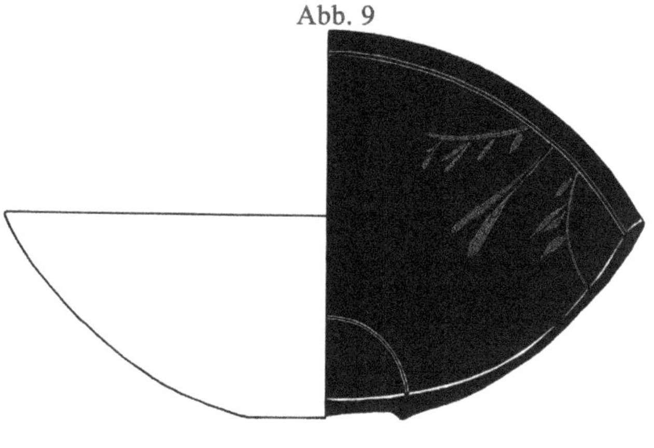

Abb. 11

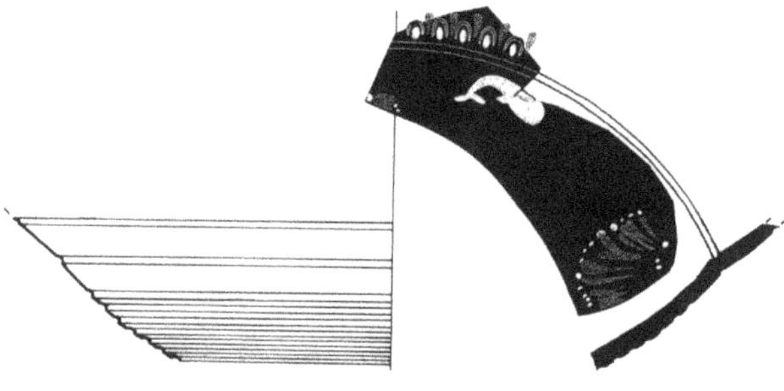

Abb. 12

Abb. 6-8. Kylikes mit ausbiegendem Rand (6. kein Herkunftsnachweis in den Unterlagen - 7. S XII 59 II B+52 III B - 8. kein Herkunftsnachweis in den Unterlagen) **Abb. 9-12.** Kalottenschalen (9. DP 76 S XII 31 VI A+21 V C - 10. DP 76 S XII 52 II A - 11. kein Herkunftsnachweis in den Unterlagen - 12. DP 73 R XII 36 VI) (F. Knauss, P. Marzolff, A. Slawisch, H. Seilheimer)

Im Folgenden sollen daher kurz einige charakteristische Typen der von der attischen Westabhangkeramik beeinflussten Feinkeramik von Demetrias vorgestellt werden, um besonders das Verhältnis zwischen Importen und lokalen Produkten näher zu beleuchten. Obwohl es hier durchaus leichte Abwandlungen in der Grundform der jeweiligen Typen bei der Rezeption in der lokalen Keramik gibt, sollen in dieser Studie vor allem die Verzierungselemente im Mittelpunkt stehen.

Skyphoi mit gerundetem Profil und einbiegendem Rand

Die Skyphoi mit gerundetem Profil und einbiegendem Rand bilden in diesem Materialkomplex die größte Gruppe von Trinkgefäßen, allerdings kommt die Form in Attika selbst in der 1. Hälfte des 3. Jhs. v. Chr. nur selten vor. Die entsprechenden Vergleiche verweisen hier nach Kleinasien, der Schwarzmeerküste und Mittelgriechenland[15]. Bevorzugt werden Vertikalhenkel mit Eufeublattappliken, nur die GW-Werkstatt stattet ihre Gefäße mit Theatermasken aus (**Abb. 1**; Museum Volos Inv. K. 3443). Aufgrund seinem qualitativen Glanzton, seiner horizontalen und vertikalen Riefen, sowie dem gerahmten tonfarbenem Eierstab-Motiv sticht **Abb. 2** als besonderes Importstück hervor. Unter den verschiedenen Verzierungsmotiven stellen die Bommelkette (**Abb. 3**)[16] und die Doppelblattkette (**Abb. 4**) den größten Anteil. Demgegenüber erreicht das Exemplar **Abb. 5** aus dem zweiten Drittel des 3. Jhs. v. Chr. mit seinem Schachbrett-/ Rechteckmuster eine derart gute Qualität, dass nicht

15 Jones 1951, 219 Nr. 112 Abb. 124; 170 B; Ephesos, Sardes: Mitsopoulos-Leon 1975, 502 Abb. 2 C; Pergamon: Schäfer 1968, Taf. 9 D 26; Böotien: Heimberg 1982, Taf. 8, 130; Euböa: Metzger 1969, IV, 47.

16 Furtwängler 1990, Taf. 18 b.

unterschieden werden kann zwischen attischen Import und einem einheimischen attisierenden Produkt. Andere beliebte Verzierungsmotive der lokalen Ware sind das Myrtenmotiv und ab dem zweiten Jahrhundertdrittel das nach attischen Vorbildern gemalte, bzw. geritzte Schleifen/ Lorbeerkranzmotiv. In der zweiten Hälfte des 3. Jhs. v. Chr. ersetzen oft Schlickerbemalung und Ritzung den qualitativen Weißauftrag. Mit der Zeit degeneriert das Bommelkettenmotiv zu flüchtigen Tropfensträngen, wie bei **Abb. 1** (2. Jh. v. Chr.). Die jüngsten Skyphoi des 2. und 1. Jhs. v. Chr. sind schließlich nur noch mit einem geritzten Eierstab verziert.

Kylikes mit ausbiegendem Rand

Kylikes mit ausbiegendem Rand sind ein primär attisches Produkt, das offensichtlich im ersten Viertel des 3. Jhs. v. Chr. weite Verbreitung fand[17]. **Abb. 7** als lokales Erzeugnis der GW-Werkstatt weist in ihrer hohen Qualität auf einen eingewanderten attischen Töpfer hin. Dagegen gehört **Abb. 8** der gängigen demetriadischen Produktion an, allerdings lassen sowohl die Qualität der Töpferarbeit als auch die geritzte Blütenranke eine zunehmende Degeneration der attischen Vorbilder erkennen[18]. **Abb. 6**, die ansonsten wiederum den attischen Vorbildern des zweiten Drittels des 3. Jhs. v. Chr. entspricht, findet u.a. Vergleichsbeispiele in Südrußland[19].

Bemalte und reliefverzierte Kalottenschalen – ‚Medaillonschalen'

Bemalte und reliefverzierte Kalottenschalen lassen sich in etlichen Produktionszentren vom Pontos über Kleinasien, Griechenland und Ägypten bis nach Italien nachweisen. Die frühesten Exemplare aus Athen gehören in das zweite Viertel des 3. Jhs. v. Chr.[20]. In Demetrias wurden die formal unterscheidbaren Typen A als Standardform, B als eine frühe (erstes Drittel des 3. Jhs. v. Chr.) Variante der Form A einer attischen oder attisierenden Werkstatt, die möglicherweise aus Kleinasien stammt[21], und C als Grundtypus produziert, wobei die Verzierung von geritzten Eierstäben mit Blüten in Schlickerauftrag, Efeuranken, Lorbeerkränzen und dem Tänienschleifen-Motiv[22] bestimmt ist (**Abb. 9**, Form A). **Abb. 10** (Form A) zeigt hingegen ein einfaches Doppelspiralband mit Punktrosetten als loser, umlaufender Wandungskranz. Die große Schale **Abb. 11** (Form A) mit ihrer schematisch gemalten Halskettengirlande gehört offensichtlich zu den spätesten lokalen Erzeugnissen. Die in anderen Fundorten eher seltene Form C kommt in Demetrias als größte Gruppe der Schalen noch vor der Mitte des 3. Jhs. v. Chr. in Mode. Das mit Ritzstreifen abgesetzte Randfeld ist mit Efeuranken, Blatteierstäben, Hakenwellenmustern, Palmetten und Delphinen (**Abb. 12,** Form C, aus der GW-Werkstatt)[23] verziert, wobei die letzten beiden als Einzelmotive gegenüber den vegetabilen[24] und geometrischen Motiven erscheinen[25]. Die meisten Emblemata lassen dionysische Themen erkennen; einige Beispiele bieten Hinweise auf weitere verstreute Werkstätten neben Demetrias, z. B. in Alexandria, auf Kreta, in Korinth, auf Sizilien, in Olbia und auf der Krim[26], die sich indirekt ohne konkreten Handelsaustausch beeinflussten[27].

Bauchige Kantharoi mit abgesetzter Randzone

Offenbar haben die demetriadischen Töpfer kleinasiatische Anregungen zur Nachahmung von bauchigen Kantharoi mit abgesetzter Randzone aufgenommen, wie vergleichbare Beispiele in südrussischen Fundzusammenhängen belegen[28] und **Abb. 14** erkennen lässt[29]. Der Verzierungsduktus entspricht demjenigen anderer demetriadischer Gefäße der 2. Jahrhunderthälfte. Die Dekormotive sind stets in etwas nachlässiger Mischtechnik (Ritzung/Tonschlicker) aufgetragen, typisch sind wieder Efeublattranken (so bei **Abb. 13**, aufgrund seiner eher flüchtigen Bemalung erste Hälfte des 2. Jhs. v. Chr. und **Abb. 14**).

Bauchkantharoi

Attische Vergleiche zu den demetriadischen Beispielen von Bauchkantharoi, die bis ins 2. Jh. reichen, finden sich bereits im frühen 3. Jh. v. Chr.[30]. Zum Ende des 3. Jhs. v. Chr. wurde allerdings in Attika offensichtlich die Produktion dieses Typs eingestellt[31], diente aber zum Vorbild in attisierende Werkstätten bis nach Thrakien und dem Schwarzen Meer[32]. Die GW-Werkstatt führt die nun schärfer profilierte Form weiter. Das qualitätvolle Exemplar **Abb. 15** bietet die typische Lorbeergirlande in kombinierter Ritz- und Schlickerauftragtechnik. Häufiger ist jedoch die Bommelkette, die mit begleitendem Band und weißen Punktreihen ergänzt wird (**Abb. 16**); darüber hinaus gibt es auch Kombinationen aus Halsketten und Blattgirlanden, wie **Abb. 17-18** belegen. Seltener finden sich der Lorbeerkranz- oder Schleifendekor (**Abb. 19**) und das Efeuwellenband.

---

17 Miller 1974, 209 f. Taf. 30 Nr. 14.
18 Furtwängler 1990, Taf. 15 a; 17 c.
19 Pharmakowsky 1903, 90 Nr. 88 Taf. 4, 2; Kopcke 1964, Beil. 46, Abb. 8 (Olbia).
20 Thompson 1934, 350 Abb. 31 (C 12); 371 D 14 Abb. 56; 376 D 28 Abb. 62; Braun 1970, Nr. 85 Taf. 56, 5; vgl. Grace 1974, 199; Rotroff 1982, 109–112: ca. 270/50 v. Chr.).
21 Sinn 1976, 181 f.; vgl. Mitsopoulos-Leon 1978, Taf. 41,10 (aus Ephesos).
22 Sinn 1976, Taf. 43, 2.
23 z. B. Watzinger 1901, 80 f. Nr. 28–29 (form C).
24 vgl. auch Walter-Karydi *et al.* 1982, 74 Nr. 556 Taf. 42.
25 Athen: Watzinger 1901, 80 Nr. 24.
26 Siebert 1978, 93 (Argos); 129 (attisch); Walter-Karydi *et al.* 1982, Taf. 50, 665 f.
27 Vgl. Sinn 1976, 182 Nr. 2–3 Taf. XIX, 2–3 Inv. 7037.
28 Belin de Ballu 1972, Taf. 42, 6; Kossatz 1985, Nr. 15 Abb. 23, S 13–346 III 30.
29 Isler 1978, Taf. 57, 265; 210 Nr. 228 Taf. 55, Beil. 8; Mitsopoulos-Leon 1975, 502 Abb. 2 B.
30 Rotroff 1997, 100–123 Nr. 195-199 Taf. 18 Abb. 13: 275–250 v. Chr.
31 Braun 1970, Taf. 79, 4; Walter-Karydi *et al.* 1982, Taf. 42, 561; Watzinger 1901, 79 Nr. 26.
32 Braun 1970, Taf. 56 Nr. 80/81; Mesambria: Ognenova 1960, 229 Abb. 8.

Abb. 13

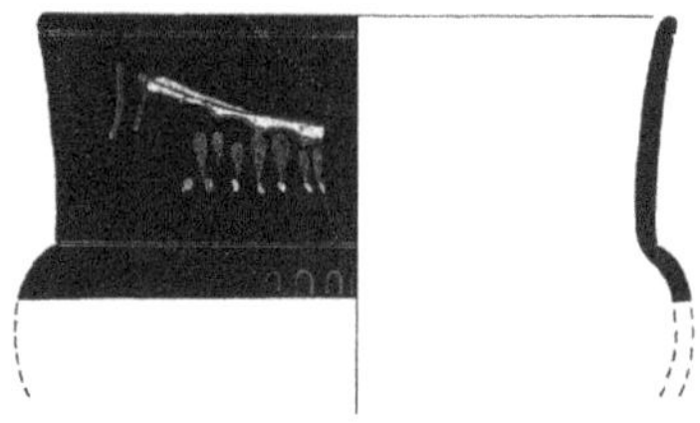
Abb. 14

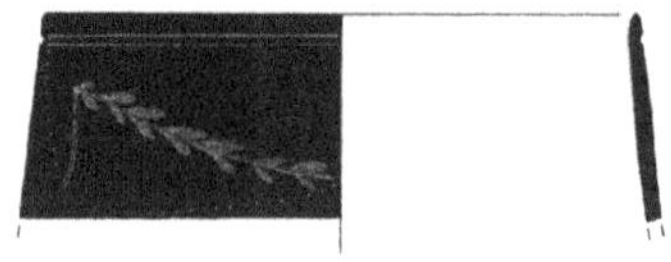
Abb. 15

Abb. 16

Abb. 17

Abb. 18

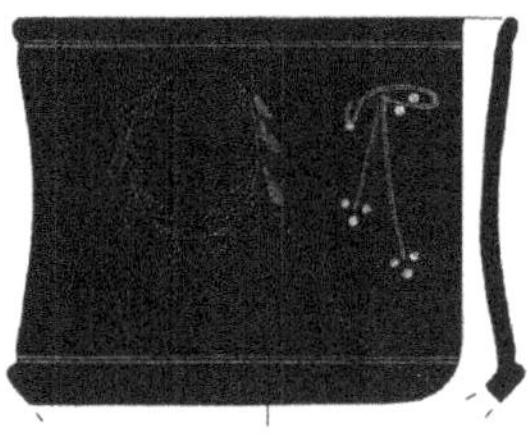
Abb. 19

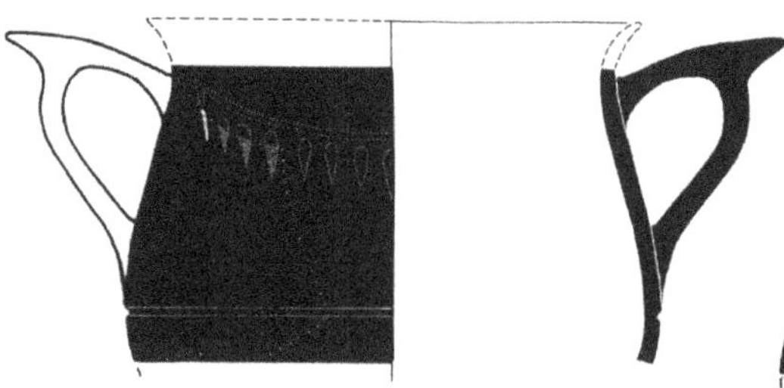
Abb. 20

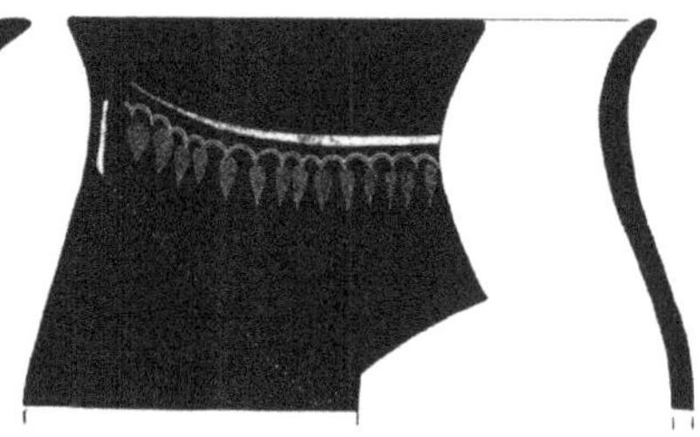
Abb. 21

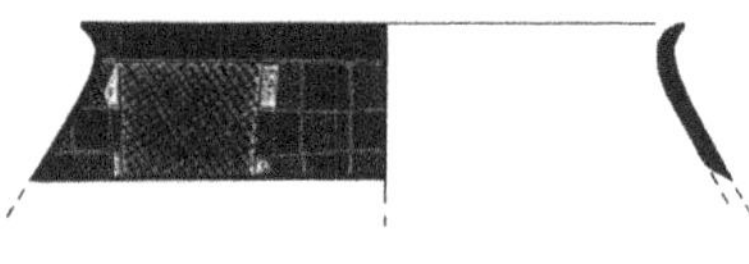
Abb. 22

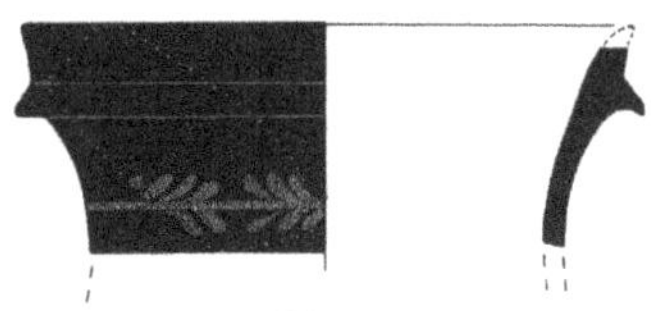
Abb. 23

Abb. 24

Abb. 25

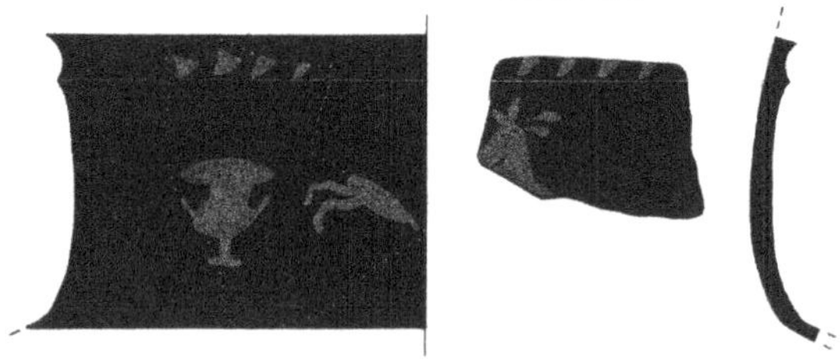
Abb. 26

Abb. 13-14. Kantharoi mit abgesetzter Randzone (13. Museum Volos, Inv. K 17 - 14. DP 73 R XII 17 I C) **Abb. 15-19.** Bauchkantharoi (15. DP ? V XII 10 I B (Nachweis in den Unterlagen unvollständig) - 16. Museum Volos, Inv. K 23 - 17. DP ? ? XII 26 III (Nachweis in den Unterlagen unvollständig) - 18. DP 76 R XII 46 III E/F - 19. DP 73 RXII 18 III A) **Abb. 20-22.** Bauchige Becher (20. ? V XII 7, 17 I E (Nachweis in den Unterlagen unvollständig) - 21. DP 73 R XII 17 III A - 22. DP 76 R XII 36 III) **Abb. 23-26.** Schulterkantharoi (23. DP 76 R XII 45 III B - 24. Museum Volos, Inv. K 105 - 25. Museum Volos, Inv. K 2980 - 26. DP 76 S XII 52 III C) (F. Knauss, P. Marzolff, A. Slawisch, H. Seilheimer)

Bauchige Becher

Obwohl der Formtypus der bauchigen Becher wiederum aus Attika übernommen wurde, lässt die demetriadische-thessalische Alternative erneut lokale Abweichungen im Detail erkennen[33]. Obwohl vorwiegend vom Schwarzmeergebiet über Thrakien und Troas bis nach Ionien verbreitet[34], stammen einige Exemplare auch aus Alexandria[35]. Die Stücke **Abb. 20; 21** stellen die frühesten Importe dar aus dem ersten Jahrhundertdrittel dar. **Abb. 20** findet Entsprechungen z. B. in Ephesos[36], **Abb. 21** in pergamenischen Produktionen. Wohl aus einer bötischen Werkstatt stammt **Abb. 22** mit seinem flüchtigen Schachbrett-Rechteckfries[37].

Schulter-Kantharoi

Der Schulterkantharos entwickelt sich im 4. Jh. v. Chr. in Athen[38] und wird bereits zu Beginn des 3. Jhs. v. Chr. nach Demetrias exportiert (**Abb. 23**)[39]; weit verbreitet ist das Olivenmotiv[40]. Nach der Aufnahme in das keramische Repertoire der demetriadischen Werkstätten als Kantharosform mit glattem Rand (**Abb. 26**)[41] in Demetrias lässt auch diese Form eine deutlich längere Laufzeit erkennen als in Athen[42]. Neben den typischen Elementen des Westabhangdekors kommen aber auch konkrete Gegenstände, wie ein Glockenkrater oder makedonischer Helm (**Abb. 26**) vor. In Demetrias greift jetzt die Werkstatt der ‚gelben Ware' die hochqualitative Produktion auf (**Abb. 24**)[43], allerdings gibt es auch deutlich schlechtere Exemplare mit gleicher Verzierung[44]. Die Form wurde offensichtlich wurde bis kurz nach der Mitte des 3. Jhs. v. Chr. produziert (**Abb. 25**)[45].

Schalen-Kantharoi – Cup-Kantharos

Der Schalen- (Cup-)Kantharos **Abb. 27** aus Demetrias belegt einen bereits um 290/85 v. Chr. beginnenden Import[46]. Ebenfalls von hervorragender Qualität ist **Abb. 28** mit ihren minutiös gezeichnet Weinrankenmotiven mit Punkttrauben, die wohl auch vom selben Maler stammten, wobei der Kantharostyp der Bracket Leaf-Group zugerechnet werden kann (275-260 v. Chr.), als dieser auf der Agora bereits zu Ende ging[47]. **Abb. 29**, der zwei antithetisch angeordneten, springenden Delphine über einem spiraligen Wellenmotivauf dem Halsfeld zeigt, findet ebenfalls Parallelen auf verschiedenen Gefäßtypen der Agora und stammt wahrscheinlich aus dem Repertoire eines bestimmten Malers[48]. Weil auch **Abb. 30**, mit dem dieser Typus in Demetrias seinen Abschluss findet, wohl ein Importstück darstellt, liegt der Schluss nahe, dass er nicht von den örtlichen Töpfern übernommen wurde[49]. Ganz anders im nahe gelegenen Theben (Phtiotis), wo Schalenkantharoi produziert und vertrieben wurden[50].

Stülpdeckel- und flachzylindrische Pyxiden

Hellenistische Stülpdeckel- und flachzylindrische Pyxiden sind in Demetrias vor allem durch den Typus I nach Z. Kotitsa vertreten[51]. Stülpdeckelpyxiden setzen offensichtlich im letzten Viertel des 4. Jhs. v. Chr. ein und weisen das typische Dekormotiv des Speerspitzencolliers mit begleitenden weißen Punktreihen auf, in der Regel gepaart mit Efeuranken. Eine Variante sind die im 3. Jh. v. Chr. auftretenden Amulettcolliers[52]. Pyxiden der erwähnten Form kommen bereits im 1. Viertel des 3. Jhs. v. Chr. mit typischem Westabhangdekor auf der athenischen Agora auf[53]. Das Beispiel **Abb. 32** aus Demetrias gehört Typus I an, den man der Dickeras-Group (270–260 v. Chr.) zuweisen kann. Nach Kotitsa[54] lehnen sich auch die Pyxiden aus Demetrias an die frühen attischen Pyxiden des 3. Jhs. v. Chr. an, wobei sie allerdings bereits im 2. Jh. v. Chr. formal denjenigen aus dem makedonischen Raum entsprechen. Typus I erfreute sich außerordentlich großer Beliebtheit in Athen; entsprechende Importe lassen sich in Makedonien bereits im 3. Jh. v. Chr. nachweisen; neben Südrussland, Rhodos und Eretria weist darüber hinaus vor allem Thessalien die meisten Importe auf[55]; im 2. Jh. v. Chr. treten zudem kleinasiatische Einflüsse in Erscheinung[56]. Ton, Dekor und Glanzton weisen bei

33 Der Typus erlangte auf der Agora im 3. Viertel des 3. Jhs. v. Chr. seine größte Verbreitung und reicht bis um 200 v. Chr. hinab. Rotroff 1997, 102 f. Nr. 219; 221; 222; 224; 226; 229; 230 Taf. 20 Abb. 15 f.; 267 Nr. 232 (und nachfolgende Varianten). Abb. 16 (260–225 v. Chr.); Abb. 17 Nr. 252 (225–210 v. Chr.).

34 Levi 1964, 222 Ab. 23, 2; Belin de Ballu 1972, Taf. 42; Ognenova 1960, 229 Abb. 8; Schäfer 1968, 49 Taf. 14-16; Abb. 18 (Pergamon); Ephesos: Mitsopoulos-Leon 1975, 502, D.

35 z. B. Pagenstecher 1923, 27 Abb. 34, 6. 8. 11.

36 Mitsopoulos-Leon 1975, 502 C; formentsprechend bei Schäfer 1968, D 61.

37 Vergleiche mit Böotien: Sinn 1976, 105 Nr. 79 u. Taf. XVIII, 9.

38 vgl. Braun 1970, 166 f. Taf. 79, 1; Hausmann 1996, 29 Anm. 109; 30; Miller 1974, 229 f. Nr. 1-7 Taf. 30; Thompson 1934, 338 B 20; 320 A27-29 (‚West Slope Krater').

39 Kopcke 1964; Sparkes–Talcott 1970, 122 f. Taf. 29.

40 Miller 1974, Taf. 48, 17. 19; Thompson 1934, 342, B 36; Watzinger 1901, 75 Nr. 20. 72 Nr. 10; aus Ephesos aufgegriffen und nachgeahmt: Mitsopoulos-Leon 1978, Taf. 42, 14.

41 Rotroff 1997, 83–91. 252 Taf. 10 Abb. 10 Nr. 103 (325–300 v. Chr.); Drougou-Touratsoglou 1991 Kantharos Form A (vor der Mitte des 3. bis zum Beginn des 3. Viertel des 3. Jhs. n. Chr.).

42 Dies gilt auch z. B. für Ephesos, vgl. Mitsopoulos-Leon 1978, 114 Taf. 40, 2. 4, 41, 7 f.

43 Braun 1970, Taf. 79 Abb. 1, 100; Furtwängler 1990, Taf. 17 a; Rotroff 1984, 265, 28.

44 Sinn 1976, Taf. 41, 2, zur Herkunft aus Demetrias hin tendierend.

45 Sinn 1976, Taf. 41, 4; Rotroff 1997, 243 Abb. 4 Taf. 2 Nr. 13 (290–275 v. Chr.).

46 Aus dem frühen 2. Jh. v. Chr. (?): Rotroff 1997, 86–89. 249 Nr. 73 Taf. 7 Abb. 8: ca. 275 v. Chr.; Bozkova, 123 f. Taf. 92 1.2-4.5 ; vgl. auch die Exemplare: Φ. Ζαφειροπουλου – Ε.-Ι. Κύχια, Ελληνιστιή κεραμική από τη Νάξο, in: Δ' ΕλλΚερ, 283-290 mit Taf. 203. 207. 208 NZ 194. 201; NZ 198. 200. 205.

47 Rotroff 1997, 88 f. 251 Nr. 89 Abb. 9; Thompson 1934, 338 B 20. 339 B 23; B 35.

48 Rotroff 1984, 176 Abb. 2 a-b: Athen, Agora Amphora P 505; vgl. auch ebenda Abb. 3.

49 Hierzu: Thompson 1934. 338 Abb. 18 B 17; Miller 1974, 202 Nr. 8 f. Taf. 30.

50 Theochares und Chourmousiadis 1970, Abb. 2, 3.

51 Kotisa 1996.

52 Kotitsa 1996, 39 f. 79-88 mit insbes. Anm. 773; 777 f., Hinweis auf Sinn 1976, Taf. 18,7; 38,8.

53 Kotitsa 1996, 9 f. mit Anm.; vgl. Rotroff 1991, Bracket Leaf-Group (280-250 v. Chr.).

54 Kotitsa 1996, 52 f. Th1: Taf. 27; Abb. 62 mit Anm. 472; Th2: Taf. 27; Abb. 63 mit Anm. 474, Th3 mit Anm. 475.

55 Drougou – Touratsoglou 1991, unterscheidet hier Typ I (= Pyxis Typ A, Mitte 3.-3. Viertel 2. Jh. v. Chr.), und Typ II (= Pyxis Typ B, 90iger Jahre des 2. Jhs. bis zum 3. Viertel des 2. Jhs. v. Chr.).

56 Kotitsa 1996, 179 f. mit Lit.

Abb. 27

Abb. 28

Abb. 29

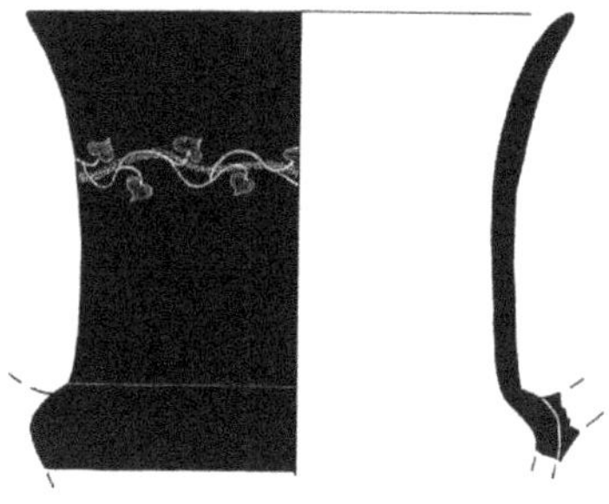
Abb. 30

Abb. 31

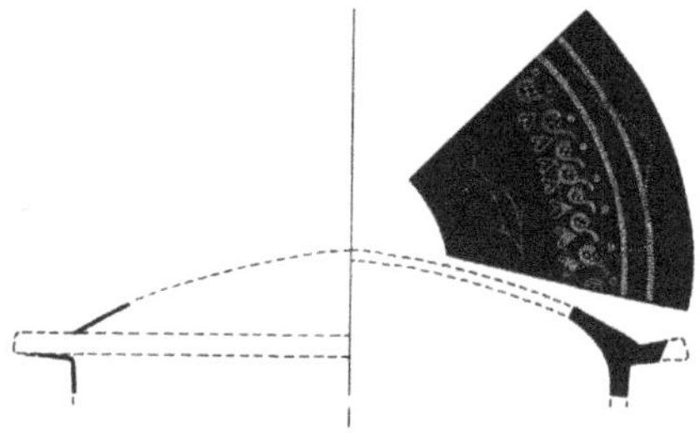
Abb. 32

Abb. 33

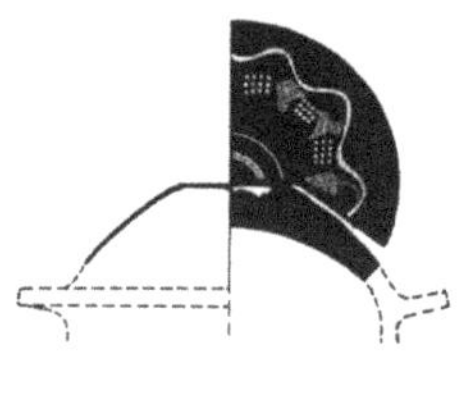
Abb. 34

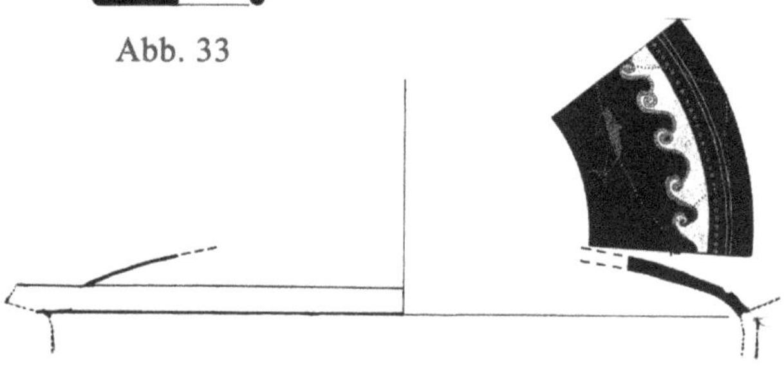
Abb. 36

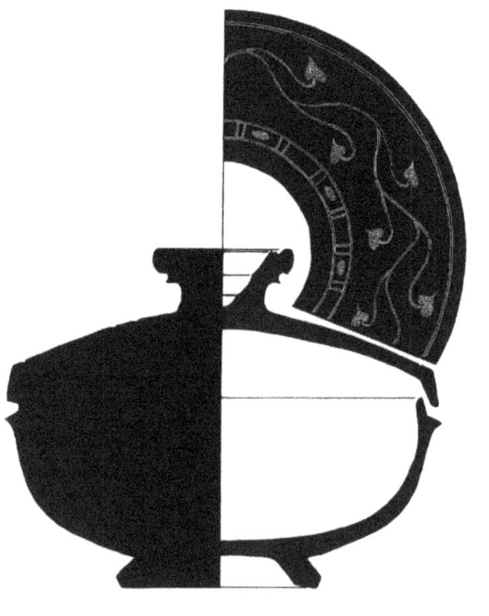
Abb. 35

Abb. 27-30. Schalen-Kantharoi – Cup-Kantharoi (27. Museum Volos, Inv. K2945 - 28. DP 73 R XII 18 III A - 29. DP 73 R XII 18 III+38 VI B - 30. DP 76 S XII 12 VI F) **Abb. 31-34.** Stüldeckelpyxiden (31. Museum Volos, Inv. K 461 - 32. kein Herkunftsnachweis in den Unterlagen - 33. Museum Volos, Inv. K 46 - 34. kein Herkunftsnachweis in den Unterlagen) **Abb. 35.** Flachzylindrische Pyxis (Museum Volos, Inv. K 2951) **Abb. 36.** Stüldeckelpyxis (DP ? R XI 98 III D (Nachweis in den Unterlagen unvollständig) (F. Knauss, P. Marzolff, A. Slawisch, H. Seilheimer)

allen hier vorgestellten Gefäßen auf eine einheimische Produktion, für die **Abb. 31** ein besonders qualitätvolles Beispiel bietet. Die Kombination zwischen Schachbrett- und Quadratmuster auf dem Deckel und der Bommelgirlande auf der Wandung erinnert erneut an den für Demetrias charakteristischen attisierenden Verzierungsmodus, wobei dieses Muster bereits im 2. Viertel des 3. Jhs. v. Chr. in attischen Werkstätten erscheint[57] und sich dort bis zum frühen 1. Jh. v. Chr. verfolgen lässt [58]. Während **Abb. 33** mit seinem Kymation auf der Deckelwölbung noch einen veritablen Dekor bietet, zeigt **Abb. 34** bereits nur noch eine alternierende Folge von Einzelblättern der ehemaligen Girlande. Neben den altbekannten Blattranken (**Abb. 35**) erscheint hier allerdings das in Demetrias bekannte Motiv des über ein Wellenband hinweg springenden Delphins (**Abb. 36**).

Zusammenfassung

Unmittelbar nach der Stadtgründung in den Jahren 294–288 v. Chr. setzte in Demetrias ein umfangreicher Import vorwiegend attischer Westabhangkeramik ein. Der Umstand, dass der bei der Größe dieser Planstadt umfangreiche Bedarf an Feinkeramik gerade aus dieser Richtung gedeckt wurde, dürfte, abgesehen von den günstigen Transportwegen übers Meer, mit der bereits lange etablierten Werkstatttradition und den dort ansässigen Betrieben, die zu einer gewissen Massenproduktion fähig waren, zusammenhängen. Hinzu kommt sicher noch die Beliebtheit der attischen Formen und Dekormotive, die zu dieser Zeit auf dem griechischen Festland tonangebend waren. Bereits sehr früh setzte aber auch eine ausgeprägte lokale Produktion ein, wiederum vorwiegend im attisierenden Westabhangstil, weil dies offenkundig dem primären Interesse der sich neu ansiedelnden Käuferklientel entsprach. Auf diese als Absatzmarkt hofften wohl auch die zugewanderten attischen Handwerker, deren Erzeugnisse kaum von importierten Stücken zu unterscheiden sind. Hierbei kam es zwar zu einer gewissen, eher geringfügigen Abwandlung der attischen Ursprungsformen und zu neuen Motivkombinationen in der Verzierung, doch sind die Ursprünge klar erkennbar. Auffallend ist allerdings die Tatsache, dass viele keramische Formen und Dekormotive nach der Etablierung im Umfeld der makedonischen Hauptstadt wesentlich länger produziert wurden als im Ursprungsgebiet. Allerdings führte die offenkundige Massenproduktion, die ab der zweiten Hälfte des 3. Jhs. v. Chr. einzusetzen scheint, zu einer deutlich wahrnehmbaren Nachlässigkeit in der Ausführung vor allem des Glanztonauftrages und der Einzelmotive, die zunehmend nur noch vereinfachte Derivate der ursprünglichen, in der Regel vegetabilen Verzierungselemente des Westabhangdekors darstellen. Auffallend sind hier ebenfalls der verstärkte Einsatz von Ritzungen, sowie ein allgemein flüchtiger Auftrag des Malschlickers oder Deckweiß. Über die attischen Einflüsse hinaus scheinen auch vor allem Anregungen aus Kleinasien, dem Schwarzmeergebiet, Südrußland, Ägypten (Alexandria), sowie auch aus Mittelgriechenland in den heimischen Werkstätten ihren Niederschlag gefunden zu haben. Dies belegen die hier vorgestellten Beispiele und andere Exemplare lokaler Feinkeramik, auf die hier nicht näher eingegangen werden kann, die aber an anderer Stelle vorgelegt werden sollen. Inwieweit die in Demetrias hergestellten Produkte wiederum exportiert wurden, ist zum derzeitigen Forschungsstand schwer zu sagen. Höchstwahrscheinlich wurden zumindest die umliegenden größeren Siedlungen, wie z.B. New Halos, beliefert[59]. Dies erscheint umso mehr plausibel, da auch Demetrias selbst wohl innovativer Produktionsort neu kombinierter Gefäß-/Dekorkombinationen war, aber wahrscheinlich auch eigene Formen entwickelte, wie z. B. die homerischen Becher.

Horst Seilheimer
Im Kirschgrund 31
D-66133 Saarbrücken
Seilheimer2001@aol.com

Bibliographie

Anderson, J. K., Hood, M. S. F. und Boardman, J. 1954. Excavation on the Kophinà Ridge, Chios. *The Annual of the British School at Athens* 49, 123–182.

Bovon, A. und Bruneau, Ph. 1966. Huiliers hellenistique. *Bulletin de correspondance hellénique* 90, 131–148.

Bozkova, A. 1997. La céramique des nécropoles hellénistiques de Cabylé. In *Δ' Επιστημονική Συνάντηση για την Ελληνιστική Κεραμική*. Μυτιλήνη 1994, 123–127. Athen, Ypourgeio Politismou

Braun, K. 1970. Kerameikos-Bericht. Der Dipylon-Brunnen B 1. Die Funde. *Mitteilungen des Deutschen Archäologischen Instituts, Athenische Abteilung* 85, 129–169.

Bruneau, Ph. 1970. Tombes d'Argos. *Bulletin de correspondance hellénique* 94, 437–531.

Bruneau, Ph., Rolley, C. und Vatin, C. 1976. *Médéon de Phocide V. Tombes hellénistiques. Objets de métal, monnaies.* Paris, De Boccard.

Belin de Ballu, E. 1972. *Olbia, cité antique du littorial*

[57] Vgl. Rotroff 1997, 188 ff. Nr. 1224, 1229 (zweite Hälfte 4. bis erstes Viertel 1. Jh. v. Chr.).
[58] Kotisa 1996, 141 mit Anm. 1269–1273.
[59] Hierzu muss allerdings die Materialvorgabe abgewartet werden; meines Wissens ist diesbezügliche eine Dissertation in Arbeit.

nord de la mer Noire. Leiden, E. J. Brill.

Enklaar, A. 1985. Chronologie et peintres des hydries de Hadra. *Bulletin antieke beschaving* 60, 106–146.

Eiwanger, J. 1981. *Keramik und Kleinfunde aus der Damokratia-Basilika in Demetrias. Die Deutschen Ausgrabungen in Demetrias.* Demetrias 4. Bonn, Habelt.

Drougou, S. und Touratsoglou, I. 1980. *Ἑλληνιστικοί λαξευτοί τάφοι Βεροίας.* Αρχαιολογικόν Δελτίον Suppl. 28. Athen, TAP.

Drougou, S. und Touratsoglou, I. 1991. Hellenistische Keramik aus Makedonien: Chronologische Indizien. *Antike Kunst* 34, 13–21.

Furtwängler, A. E. 1990. Demetrias, ein Produktionsort "attischer" Keramik? In *Β' Επιστημονική Συνάντηση για την Ελληνιστική Κεραμική.* Ρόδος 1989, 9–53. Athen, TAP.

Furtwängler, A. E. 1997. Μεθοδολογικά προβλήματα χρονολόγησης. In *Δ' Επιστημονική Συνάντηση για την Ελληνιστική Κεραμική.* Μυτιλήνη 1994, 396–400. Athen, TAP.

Grace, V. R. 1974. Revisions in Early Hellenistic Chronology. *Mitteilungen des Deutschen Archäologischen Instituts, Athenische Abteilung* 89, 193–203.

Hausmann, U. 1996. *Hellenistische Keramik. Eine Brunnenfüllung nördlich von Bau C und Reliefkeramik verschiedener Fundplätze in Olympia.* Olympische Forschungen 27. Berlin, de Gruyter.

Heimberg, U. 1982. *Die Keramik des Kabirions.* Das Kabirenheiligtum bei Theben 3. Berlin, de Gruyter.

Hellström, P. 1965. *Labraunda. Pottery of Classical and later Date, Terracotta Lamps and Glass.* Swedish excavations and researches, 2, 1. Lund, C. W. K. Leerup.

Isler, H.-P. und Kalpaxis, T. E. 1978. *Das archaische Nordtor und seine Umgebung im Heraion von Samos.* Samos 4. Bonn, Habelt.

Jones, F. F. 1950. The Pottery. In H. Goldman (ed.), *Excavations at Gözlü Kule*, Tarsus 1, 149–296. Princeton, University Press

Kossatz A.-U. 1985. Beşik-Tepe Vorbericht über die Ergebnisse der Grabung von 1983. Zur hellenistischen Keramik. *Archäologischer Anzeiger*, 182-194.

Kotitsa, Z. 1996. *Hellenistische Tonpyxiden. Untersuchung zweier hellenistischer Typen einer Keramikform.* Mainz, Zabern.

Levi, E. I. 1964. A pottery complex of the IIIrd-IInd cent. B. C. from the excavations of the Olbian Agora, in *Ol'vija. Temenos i Agora* 225–280. Moskva-Leningrad, Nauka.

Marzolff, P. 1996. Der Palast von Demetrias. In W. Hoepfner und G. Brands (Hrsg.), *Basileia. Die Paläste der hellenistischen Könige.* Internationales Symposion in Berlin vom 16.12. bis 20.12.1992, 148–159. Mainz, Zabern.

Metzger, I. R. 1969. *Die hellenistische Keramik in Eretria.* Eretria. Ausgrabungen und Forschungen XX. Bern, Francke.

Miller, S. G. 1974. Menon's cistern. *Hesperia* 43, 194–245.

Morel, J.-P. 1990. L'apport des foullies de carthage à la chronologie des céramiques hellénistiques. In *Β' Επιστημονική Συνάντηση για την Ελληνιστική Κεραμική.* Ρόδος 1989, 17–32. Athen, TAP.

Morel, J.-P. 1997. Η ελληνιστική κοινή: κλασική παράδοση και τοπικές ιδιαιτερότητες. In *Δ' Επιστημονική Συνάντηση για την Ελληνιστική Κεραμική.* Μυτιλήνη 1994, 405–415. Athen, Ypourgeio Politismou.

Negev, A. 1986. *The late Hellenistic and early Roman pottery of Nabatean Oboda Final Report.* Quedem 22. Jerusalem.

Kopcke, G. 1964. Golddekorierte attische Schwarzfirniskeramik des vierten Jahrhunderts v. Chr. *Mitteilungen des Deutschen Archäologischen Instituts, Athenische Abteilung* 79, 22–84.

Mitsopoulos-Leon, V. 1972–1975. Grabungen in Ephesos von 1960-1969, bzw. 1970. Keramik aus Basilika und Prytaneion. Ein Überblick. *Jahreshefte des Österreichischen Archäologischen Institutes in Wien* 50, Beiblatt, 495–524.

Mitsopoulos-Leon, V. 1978. Hellenistische Keramik mit Schlickerdekor aus Ephesos und ihr Verhältnis zur attischen Westabhang-Keramik, in G. Schwarz und E. Pochmarski (Hrsg.), *Classica et provincialia.* Festschrift Eva Diez, 113–123. Graz, Akademische Druck- und Verlagsanstalt.

Ognenova, L. 1960. Les fouilles de Mésambria. *Bulletin de correspondance hellénique* 84, 221–232.

Pagenstecher, R. 1913. *Expedition Ernst von Sieglin: Ausgrabungen in Alexandria 2. Die griechisch-ägyptische Sammlung Ernst von Sieglin 3. Die Gefässe in Stein und Ton, Knochenschnitzereien.* Leipzig, Giesecke & Devrient.

Pharmakowsky, B. 1903. *Izvestija Imperatorskoj Archeologičeskoj Komissii* 8.

Reinders, R. 1988. The investigation of the hellenistic city of Halos. 1987 campaign. *Newsletter of the Netherlands Institute at Athens* 1, 24–27.

Robinson, D. M. 1950. *Excavations at Olynthus, Vases found in 1934 and 1938.* Olynthus 13. Baltimore, Johns Hopkins Press.

Rogl, Ch. 1997. Homerische Becher aus der Stadt Elis. In *Δ' Επιστημονική Συνάντηση για την Ελληνιστική Κεραμική.* Μυτιλήνη 1994, 317–328. Athen, Ypourgeio Politismou.

Rotroff, S. I. 1982. *Hellenistic Pottery. Athenian and imported moldmade bowls.* The Athenian Agora XXII. Princeton, NJ., American School of Classical Studies at Athens.

Rotroff, S. I. 1984. Ceramic Workshops in Hellenistic Athens. Ancient Greek and related Pottery. In H. A. G. Brijder (Hrsg.), *Ancient Greek and related pottery.* Proceedings of the International Vase Symposium in Amsterdam 12-15 April, 1984. Allard Pierson Series 5, 173–177. Amsterdam,

Allard Pierson Museum.

Rotroff, S. I. 1991. Attic West Slope Vase Painting. *Hesperia* 60, 59–102.

Rotroff, S. I. 1997. *Hellenistic Pottery: Athenian and imported wheelmade table ware and related material.* The Athenian Agora XXIX. Princeton, NJ., American School of Classical Studies at Athens.

Rotroff, S. I. 2006. *The Plain Wares*. The Athenian Agora XXXIII. Princeton, NJ., American School of Classical Studies at Athens.

Schäfer, J. 1968. *Hellenistische Keramik aus Pergamon.* Pergamenische Forschungen 2. Berlin, de Gruyter.

Seilheimer, H. 2006. Die Palastareale von Seuthopolis und Demetrias. Allgemeine Betrachtungen zu befestigten hellenistischen Residenzen. In S. Conrad (Hrsg.), *Pontos Euxeinos. Beiträge zur Archäologie und Geschichte des antiken Schwarzmeer- und Balkanraumes Festschrift Manfred Oppermann*, 295–316. Langenweissbach, Beier+Beran.

Siebert, G. 1978. *Recherches sur les ateliers de bols à reliefs du Péloponnèse à l'époque hellénistiques.* Bibliothèque des Ecoles françaises d'Athènes et de Rome 233. Paris, De Boccard.

Sinn, U. 1976. Grabungen am Anaktoron von Demetrias 1970, in V. Milojcic und D. Theocharis (Hrsg.), *Die Deutschen Archäologischen Ausgrabungen in Thessalien*. Demetrias I, 59144. Bonn, Habelt.

Sinn, U. 1979. *Die homerischen Becher. Hellenistische Reliefkeramik aus Makedonien.* Mitteilungen des Deutschen Archäologischen Instituts, Athenische Abteilung, Beih. 7. Berlin, Gebr. Mann.

Sparkes, B. A. und Talcott, L. 1970. *Black and Plain Pottery of the 6th, 5th and 4th centuries B. C.* The Athenian Agora XII. Princeton, NJ., American School of Classical Studies at Athens.

Theochares, D. und Chourmouziades, G. 1970. Ανασκαφή τάφων φθιωτίδων Θηβών. *Αρχαιολογικά Ανάλεκτα εξ Αθηνών* 3, 208-212.

Thompson, H. P. 1934. Two Centuries of Hellenistic Pottery. *Hesperia* 3, 311-480.

Walter-Karydi, E., Felten, W. und Smetana-Scherrer, R. 1982. *Spätklassische und hellenistische Keramik.* Alt-Ägina 2,1. Mainz, Zabern.

Watzinger, C. 1901. Vasenfunde aus Athen. *Mitteilungen des (kaiserlich) deutschen Archäologischen Institutes, Athenische Abteilung*, 26, 50–103.

Zapheiropoulou, Ph. und Kolia, E.-I. 1997. Ελληνιστκή κεραμική από τη Νάξο. In *Δ' Επιστημονική Συνάντηση για την Ελληνιστική Κεραμική*. Μυτιλήνη 1994, 283–290. Athen, Ypourgeio Politismou.

Albania

Überblick über die hellenistischen Transportamphoren von Lissos/Albanien

Bashkim Lahi

Abstract

The transport amphorae found in the excavations of 2006–2011 at Lissos, Albania, are datable between the 3rd and 1st centuries BC; around 95% come from the Apennine peninsula and about 5% from Greek sources. The typology of the vessels, the characteristics of the clay and a few amphora stamps are indicative of manufacture in modern Italy – Apulia, Campania and Picenum – and in the Greek world – Corinth, Rhodes, Knidos, Kos and Thasos. Over 95% of the finds are wine amphorae and only 4–5% belong to oil containers. Both the quantity and density of the finds from the Lissos context (some 9000kg of amphora sherds were recovered from an area of about 700sqm) make this an exceptional find, both for Albania and further afield.

Keywords: Albanien, Südillyrien, Lissos, Lezha, Transportamphoren.

Einführung

Die im 4. Jh. v. Chr. gegründete illyrische Stadt Lissos mit dem heutigen Namen Lezha liegt am Ufer des Flusses Drini, an einem nahe gelegenen Hügelabhang mit einer Fläche von ca. 20ha. Sie bestand aus einer Unter-, Mittel- und Oberstadt und lag im Zentrum eines Handelsstraßensystems (**Abb. 1–2**). Sie spielte eine wichtige Rolle in der Geschichte des illyrischen Königreichs. Nach dessen Niedergang wurde sie unter Caesar zu einem römischen *municipium*[1]. Frühere archäologische Ausgrabungen fanden in Lissos in mehreren Phasen statt. Die Forschungen vor dem zweiten Weltkrieg zeigen einen oberflächlichen Charakter und beschäftigten sich vorrangig mit der Stadtidentifizierung und der Stadtgeschichte auf der Basis der historischen Quellen[2]. Die zweite Phase geht in die siebziger-achtziger Jahre des vergangenen Jahrhunderts zurück und beschäftigte sich hauptsächlich mit der gut erhaltenen Stadtbefestigung[3]. Im Jahre 2006 wurden die Ausgrabungen in Lissos wieder aufgenommen, diesmal als Zusammenarbeit zwischen dem Archäologischen Institut Albaniens und dem Deutschen Archäologischen Institut (DAI), und mit der neuen Zielsetzung: ‚Lissos. Urbanistik Polis in Illyrien'. Die Grabungen wurden seither intensiv vorangetrieben und auf das ganze Stadtgebiet ausgedehnt. Die neuen Untersuchungen haben viele neue Belege zur Stadtgeschichte in hellenistischer Zeit erbracht. Unter den vielen archäologischen Funden wollen wir hier die Transportamphoren betrachten.

Fragmente von importierten hellenistischen Transportamphoren trifft man überall im heutigen Albanien[4], die Funde von Lissos/Lezha aber sind nach ihrer Dichte und Häufigkeit einzigartig in Albanien. Allein in den Grabungsbereichen A und B (**Abb. 3–4**), auf einer Fläche von etwa 700m², sind etwa 9 Tonnen (9000 kg)! Amphoren-Scherben zutage gefördert worden, die vom Ende des 4./Anfang des 3. Jhs. v. Chr. bis ins 1. Jh. v. Chr. zu datieren sind und uns über verschiedene Handelsbeziehungen und über Transformationsprozesse im Alltagsleben Auskunft geben können. Bis jetzt konnten wir zwei Hauptrichtungen feststellen, aus welchen die Transportamphoren importiert wurden: die griechische Welt und die Apenninen-Halbinsel.

Griechische Transportamphoren

Etwa 5% der ausgegrabenen Transportamphoren bestehen aus Importen aus der griechischen Welt. Von Korinth haben wir nur zwei Randfragmente des korinthischen Typs A (**Taf. I, 1**), die typologisch mit den am Ende des 4. Jhs. v. Chr. – erste Hälfte des 3. Jhs. v. Chr. zu datierenden Funden in Albanien[5] sehr gut vergleichbar sind.

Die rhodischen Amphoren sind mit vier Exemplaren vertreten, drei Randfragmente und ein Amphorenfuß. Die Amphore LI 2010, B-298, 4 trägt auf dem Henkel einen beschädigten Stempel und vielleicht eine Weintraube als begleitendes Symbol (**Abb. 5**)[6]. Der zweite gestempelte Amphorenhenkel LE. 1970, 7997 (**Taf. I, 2**) zeigt auf der ersten Zeile den Namen ΕΠΙ ΣΥΜΜΑΧΟΥ, der als Eponym in den Zeitraum 188–186 v. Chr. nach Grace[7]

1 Historische Quellen über die antike Stadt Lissos, Polyb. II 12,3; III 16, 3; IV 16,6; VIII 13,1 und 3, 4, 8 und 9; XXVIII 8,4. Caes. B. civ. III 26,3; 29, 1 und 3; 40, 5; 42,4 ; 78, 5. Liv. XLIII 20,2; XLIV 30,6 und 7. Diod. XV 13,4; 14,2. Strab. VII 316. Plin. NH III 23. Ptolem. II 16, 3. App. Illyr. 7. TP Miller IR col. 462–471; 555–559. Steph. s.v. Lissos. Hierocl. XVII 656, 6. Rav. IV 15; V 14.

2 Praschniker und Schober 1919, 14–28.

3 Prendi und Zheku 1972, 215–244; Prendi 1975, 149–163.

4 Lahi 2009.

5 Lahi 2009, 165, tab. I, 1, 3.

6 Grace 1952, pl. XXIII, 27, 28.

7 Grace 1985, 9.

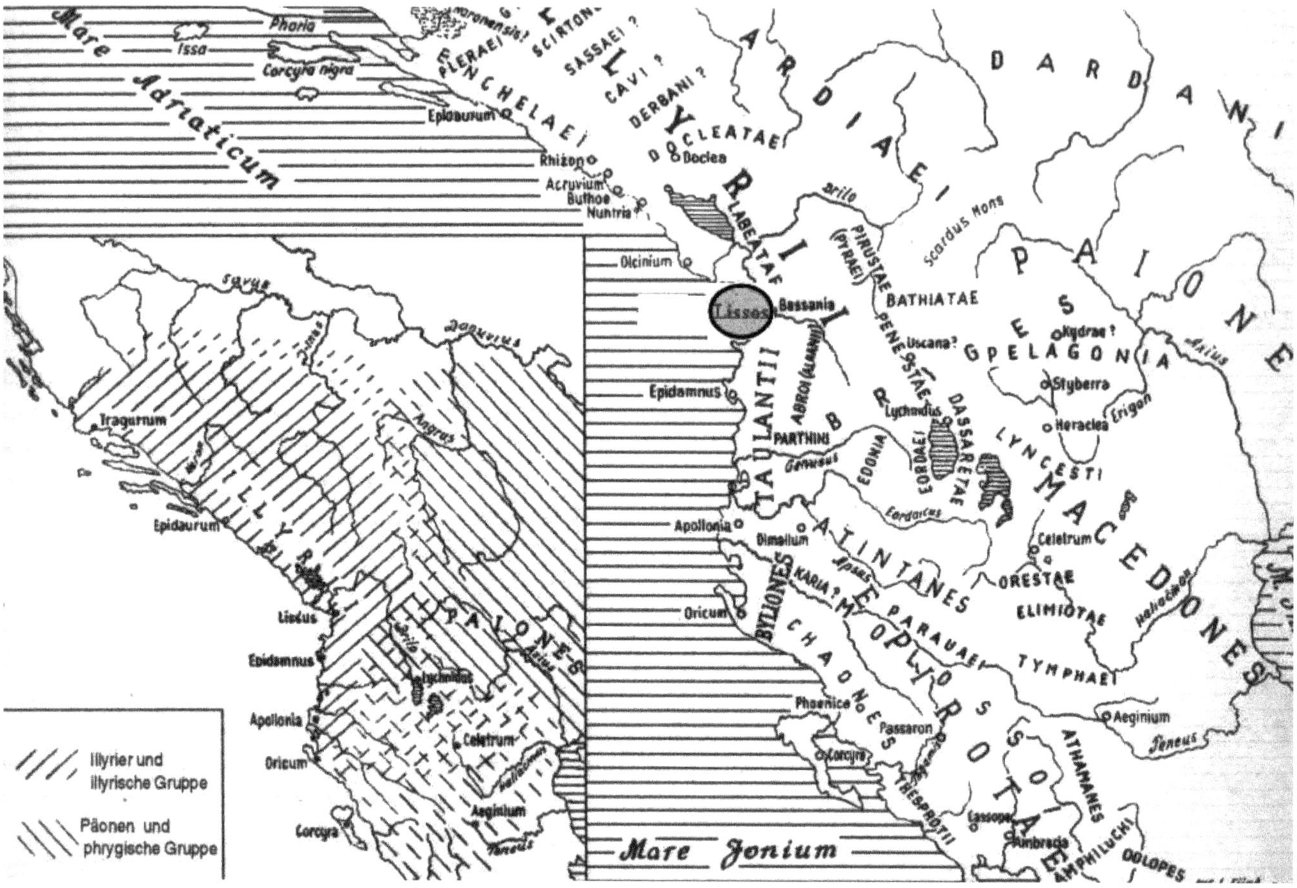

Abb. 1. Karte der Illyrischen Siedlungen (Pajakowski 2000, Karte 2)

Abb. 2. Blick auf die Akropolis von Lissos (B. Lahi)

gehört. In der zweiten Zeile des gleichen Stempels sieht man nur den obersten Teil des beschädigten Buchstabens Δ (?), den ersten Buchstaben des rhodischen Monats Δαλιος[8]. Die anderen Funde sind Amphoren von Thasos (?) (LI.2009, A-426, 2, **Taf. I, 3**), Kos (LI-A-182, 2, **Taf. I, 4**) und von Knidos (LI. 2010, B-298, 1 und 3). Eine der knidischen Amphoren trägt auf dem Henkel einen viereckigen Stempel mit den Namen von zwei Magistraten –'Α[ρτ]έμων und 'Α[ρι]στοκλη(ς) , die ihr Amt in der Duumvirenzeit, zwischen den Jahren 97 und 88 v. Chr.[9] ausgeübt haben. In der zweiten Reihe sehen wir eine Doppelaxt als begleitendes Symbol (**Tafel I, 5**).

[8] Samuel 1972, 108.

[9] Grace und Petropoulakou 1970, E 97b; E 101; E 107; E 109; E 131.

Abb. 3. Grabungsbereich A, nach Osten (B. Lahi)

Abb. 4. Grabungsbereich B, nach Westen (B. Lahi)

Transportamphoren von der Apenninen-Halbinsel

Die von der Apenninen-Halbinsel importierten Transportamphoren machen etwa 95% der gesamten Amphorenfunde aus, von denen die meisten im Grabungsbereich A angetroffen wurden[10]. Die ältesten sind vom graeco-italischen Typ Will a/MGS V, die fast überall im ganzen Stadtgebiet gefunden wurden (LI-A-395, 1, **Taf. I, 6**) und mit den am Ende des 4. Jhs./der ersten Hälfte des 3. Jhs. v. Chr. zu datierenden Amphoren von anderen Siedlungen in Albanien und außerhalb von Albanien sehr gut vergleichbar sind[11]. Momentan ist es schwierig, über die Herstellungsorte etwas Genaueres zu sagen, weil wir keine petrographischen Analysen durchgeführt haben. Leider haben wir auch keine gestempelten Amphoren, die uns die nötigen Informationen geben könnten. Wir mussten uns mit der Beobachtung durch das Mikroskop (40x vergrößert) begnügen, durch die wir vor allem Apulien (Tarent?) als Hauptherstellungsgebiet der importierten Amphoren Typ Will a/MGS V annehmen[12]. Der Auftritt von Typ Will a/ MGS V auf dem Markt von Lissos läuft parallel mit der Fundsituation in anderen illyrischen Städten und könnte belegen, dass die Importe dieser Form mit ihrem Inhalt[13] kurz nach dem Beginn der Exporte – zumindest an der südillyrischen Küste und ihrer näheren Umgebung – intensiv gewesen sein müssen.

Die graeco-italischen Amphoren Typ Will c/d/MGS VI wurden in den Grabungsbereichen A, B und M gefunden. Der gestempelte Amphorenhenkel LI. 2006, A-45, 159 (**Taf. I,** 7) gehört zum Typ Will c/MGS VI und kommt von einem gewissen Tr (ebios) Loisio von Neapel[14], der im letzten Viertel des 3. Jhs. v. Chr. tätig war[15]. Wir haben diesen Stempel damit erstmals an der östlichen Adriaküste festgestellt, was uns hilft, seine Verbreitungskarte markant zu verbreitern[16]. Sehr interessant sind auch die unter dem Dachversturz gefundenen Amphoren vom Typ Will d/ MGS VI. Sie fanden sich direkt unter dem wegen eines Brandes – vermutlich im Krieg – verstürzten Dach, deshalb können wir sie an das Ende des 3. Jhs. v. Chr. als die Stadt von Philipp von Makedonien erobert wurde (213–209 v. Chr.)[17], oder aber in das Jahr 168 v. Chr. während des dritten Krieges zwischen Illyrern und Römern datieren[18].

Wahrscheinlich kommen diese Funde aus dem Gebiet von Tarent oder Brindisi[19], wie der sandige Ton mit Schamotten, Glimmer, gelben, grauen und weißen Partikeln und fossilisierten Muscheln nahelegt.

Der größte Teil der gefundenen Amphoren gehört zu den Typen Dressel 1 und Lamboglia 2, die ein starkes Vorkommen auf dem ganzen Stadtgebiet zeigen. Die große Fundmenge ist wahrscheinlich von einem erheblichen Weinkonsum abhängig, den wir als Beleg für Veränderungen in der Lebensweise[20] und in den sozialen Strukturen während der zwei letzten Jahrhunderte werten[21].

---

10 Die neuen Ausgrabungen beweisen, dass die Unterstadt kurz nach dem Bürgerkrieg planiert wurde und durch die vor allem mit Amphorenscherben vermischte Erde etwa um 1 m erhöht wurde. Diese Füllung im Grabungsbereich A besteht zu einem großen Teil aus Amphoren. Es scheint, dass diese Baumaßnahme vor allem mit dem Kampf gegen die Feuchtigkeit und gegen die Überschwemmungen des nahe liegenden Flusses zu erklären ist.

11 Lahi 2009, 81–82 und die zitierte Fachliteratur; Lahi und Fiedler 2010, 213–255.

12 Vandermersch 1994, 79–80.

13 Der graeco-italische Typ Will a/MGS V wurde zum Weintransport benutzt, Olcese 2004, 173–192.

14 Manacorda 1981, Nr. 90; Will 1982, 350; Olcese 2004, 180; Vandermersch 1994, 85.

15 Olcese 2004, 179.

16 Zur Verbreitung dieser Stempel siehe: Empereur und Hesnard 1987, 25; Desy 1989, 23 Nr. 24, 25, 27–31; Manacorda 1989, 446; Blanc-Bijon *et al.* 1998, 22 Nr. 489.

17 Islami 1972, 354. Die Eroberung war mit Zerstörungen und Bränden verbunden, wie man dem Bericht von Polyb. VIII 14, 9 entnehmen kann.

18 Momentan ist es schwierig, eine präzise Datierung für die Zerstörung dieses Hauses zu geben, weil die Fundbearbeitung, die der Münzen eingeschlossen, noch nicht beendet ist.

19 Sciarra 1966, 123; Cuomo 1992, 73; Bruno 1995, 88.

20 Während des 2./1. Jhs. v. Chr. wurde der Weinkonsum für die Illyrer zu einem wichtigen Bestandteil des Alltagslebens s. Lahi 2009, 137.

21 Nach Liv. XL, 42,4 gab es in der Zeit des Genthius in Illyrien viele römische und latinische Bürger. Siehe auch: Papageorgiadou-Banis 1999, 115–116. Die neuen Ansiedler werden ihre eigene Lebensweise und ihren eigenen Weingeschmack mitgebracht haben.

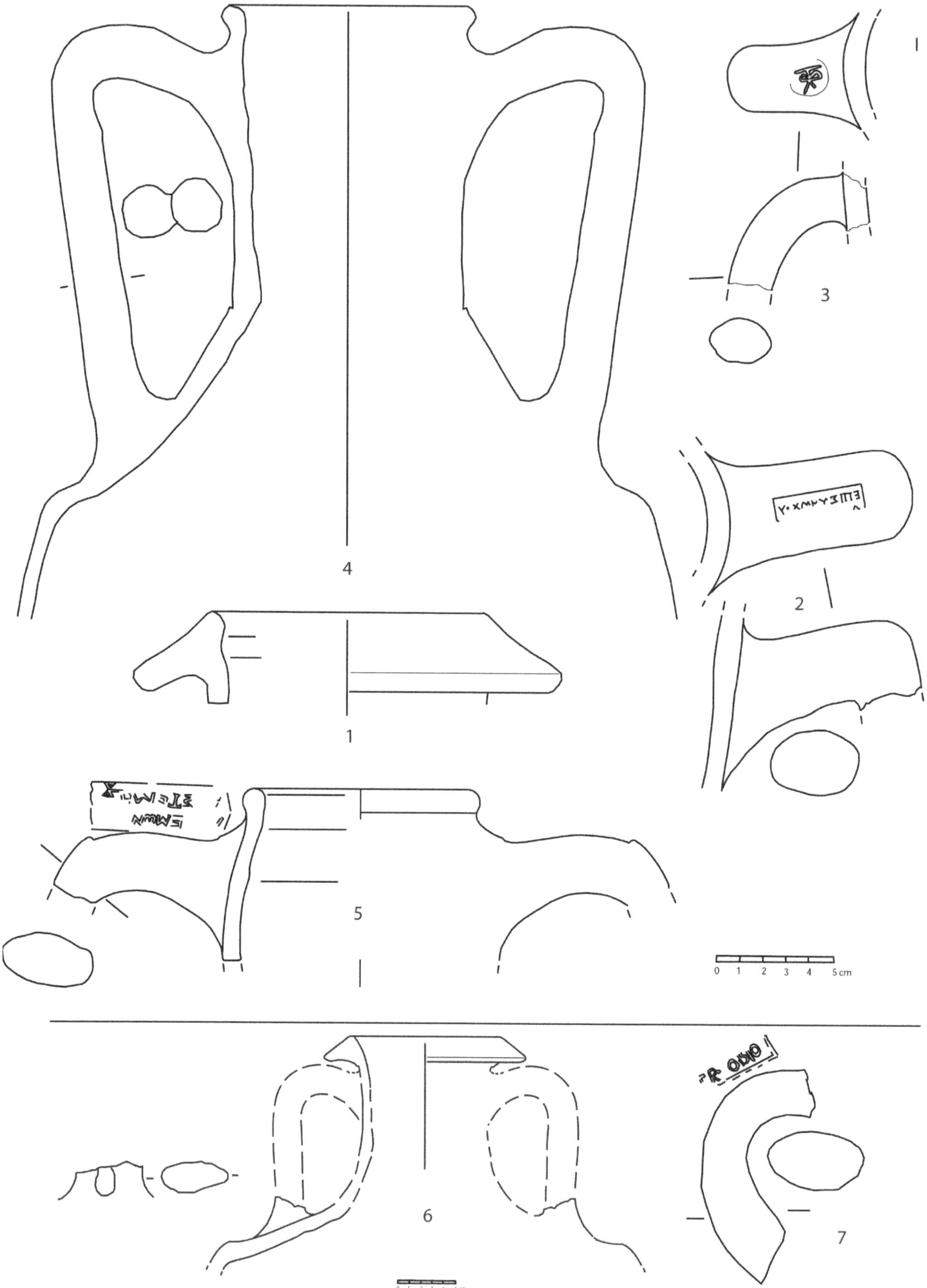

Taf. I. 1. Randfragmente des korinthischen Typs A - **2.** Gestempelter Amphorenhenkel mit dem Namen ΣΥΜΜΑΧΟΥ - **3.** Henkel einer Amphora von Thasos (?) - **4.** Amphora von Kos - **5.** knidische Amphora mit gestempelten Namen Α[ρτ]έμων und ’Α[ρι]στοκλη(ς) - **6.** Graeco-italische Amphora, Typ Will a/MGS V - **7.** Amphora Typ MGS VI gestempelt von Tr (ebios) Loisio (B. Lahi)

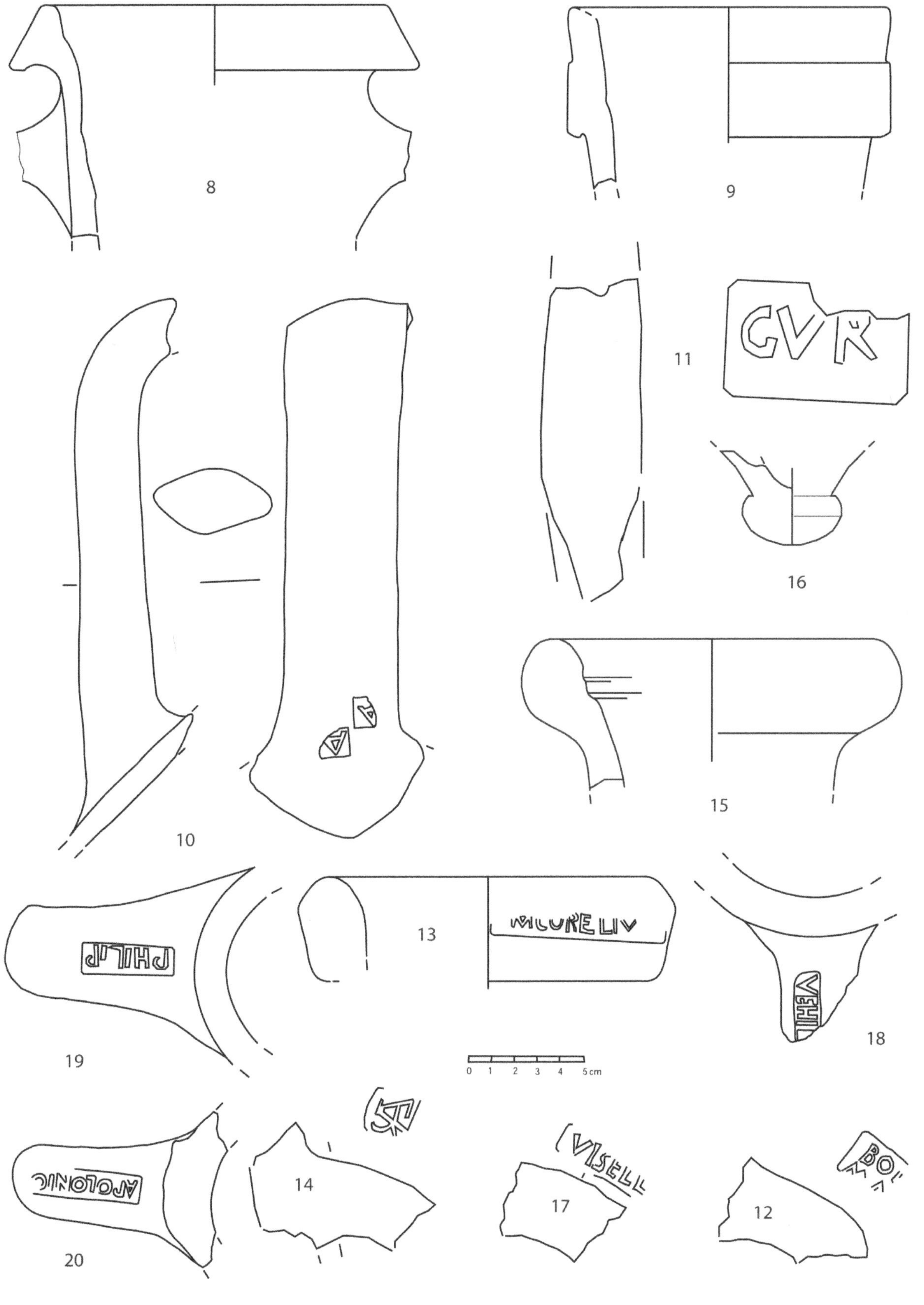

Taf. II. 8. Amphora Typ Dressel 1A - **9.** Amphora Typ Dressel 1B - **10.** Henkel von Typ Dr. 1A mit gestempeltem Großbuchstaben A. - **11.** Amphora von Typ Dr. 1B mit Stempel GVR - **12.** Frag. Henkel von Typ Lamb. 2 gestempelt von BO[ISCVS] MA[LLEOLI] - **13.** Frag. Rand von Typ Lamb. 2, gestempelt von M CORELI V[ITVLI] - **14.** Frag. Henkel von Lamb. 2 gestempelt von LTAR - **15.** Amphorenrand vom Typ Brindisi - **16.** Amphorenfuss vom Typ Brindisi - **17.** Frag. Henkel vom Typ Brindisi gestempelt von VISELL[I] - **18.** Frag. Henkel vom Typ Brindisi gestempelt von VEHIL[I] - **19.** Frag. Henkel vom Typ Brindisi gestempelt von PHILIP - **20.** Frag. Henkel vom Typ Brindisi gestempelt von APOLONIO (B. Lahi)

Abb. 5. Rhodischer Stempel auf dem Henkel (B. Lahi)

Abb. 6. Amphora Lamb. 2 mit Stempel [ALEXA]NDER (B. Lahi)

Abb. 7. Amphora Lamb. 2 mit Stempel APELE (B. Lahi)

Abb. 8. Amphora Lamb. 2 mit Stempel SVRVS (B. Lahi)

Innerhalb des Typs Dressel 1 gehören die meisten Funde zum Typ Dressel 1A (LI-A-496, 1, **Taf. II, 8**), während man den Typ Dressel 1B (LI-B-208, 2, **Taf. II, 9**) seltener antrifft. Bis jetzt haben wir nur zwei Amphorenstempel, einen auf dem Henkel des Typs Dressel 1A - LE 12124, wo der Großbuchstabe A zweimal gegeben ist (**Taf. II, 10**) und der zweite, vom Typ Dressel 1B - LI. 2006, A-53, 203, wo auf der Außenseite des Randes in einem viereckigen Rahmen 2.5cm x 3.8cm die Buchstabenfolge GVR eingestempelt ist (**Taf. II, 11**). Die Datierung des Typs Dressel 1 würden wir allgemein innerhalb seiner Umlaufzeit, also von der zweiten Hälfte des 2. Jhs. v. Chr. bis zum 1. Jh. v. Chr. suchen[22].

Der größte Teil der Amphoren vom Typ Lamboglia 2 ist auf dem Henkel oder auf der Außenseite des Randes mit einem, zwei oder drei Namen gestempelt. Von den bis jetzt etwa 120 gefundenen Stempeln wollen wir die folgenden vorlegen: [ALEXA]NDER[23] (**Abb. 6**; zwei Exemplare), APELE[24] (**Abb. 7**; zwei Expl.), SVRVS[25] (**Abb. 8**; vier Expl.), alles Hersteller aus Brundisium; BO[ISCVS] MA[LLEOLI] (**Taf. II, 12**; zwei Expl.) – Hersteller aus dem Saluntium[26]; M CORELI V[ITVLI] (**Taf.. II, 13**; drei Expl.) – Hersteller vielleicht aus Picenium[27]; LTAR (Lartius Tarius Rufius) (**Taf. II, 14**; fünf Expl.), Senator im Jahr 73 v. Chr. – Hersteller aus Dalmatien, der seine Aktivität in Picenium ausgeübt hat[28] und VEVIUS (**Abb. 9**), Weinhersteller in Picenium im letzten Viertel des 1. Jhs. v. Chr.[29].

Durch die gefundenen Stempel kann man die Herkunft von Amphoren verstehen und auch, wie sich die Handelsachsen ab dem zweiten Viertel des 1. Jhs. v. Chr. und besonders ab der Mitte dieses Jahrhunderts verändert haben. Wir

[22] Für die Umlaufzeit von Typ Dr. 1 siehe: Tchernia 1986, 42, 44, 320 und die von ihm zitierte Literatur.
[23] Baldacci 1972, 126.

[24] Cipriano und Carre 1989, 96; Manacorda *et al.* 1994, 280, 282; Nonnis 2001, 475 Anm. 40.
[25] Prendi 1975, 158–159; Desy 1983, 184 Anm. 32; Buora 2003, 45.
[26] Manacorda 1989, 453–454; Blanc-Bijon et al. 1998, 66 Nr. 650 Taf. I.
[27] Maier-Maidl 1992, 96; Bezeczky 1998, 220 Anm. 20; Nonnis 2001,488 Anm. 96.
[28] Cipriano und Carre 1989, 86, 88, 93, 99; Zaccaria 1989, 475, 481, 483; Bruno 1995, 224–225; Bezeczky 1998, 228.
[29] Tchernia et al. 1978, 36–37, 41–42; Cipriano und Carre 1989, 77.

Abb. 9. Amphora Lamb. 2 mit Stempel T.PVE (B. Lahi)

nehmen an, dass der Markt von Lissos in dieser Zeit begonnen hat, sich von den traditionellen süditalischen Handelsbeziehungen zu lösen und sich nach den neuen Handelsbeziehungen in Nordostitalien zu orientieren, was wir auch in den anderen illyrischen Siedlungen bemerkt haben[30].

Die Amphoren vom Typ Brindisi wurden vor allem in Kontexten angetroffen, die ins 1. Jh. v. Chr. datiert werden (LI-09 A 407,3, **Taf. II, 15** und B 253, 2, **Taf. II, 16**). Die begleitenden Stempel sind auf dem Henkel angebracht und tragen einen Namen, der wie im Fall von VISELL[I][31] (**Taf. II, 17**; zwei Expl.) und VEHIL[I][32] (**Taf. II, 18**; zwei Expl.) die Werkstattbesitzer, oder wie PHILIP[33] (**Taf. II, 19**), APOLONIO[34] (**Taf. II, 20**) etc. den Töpfernamen bezeichnet. Sie wurden als Öltransportamphoren im Gebiet von Brindisi hergestellt und in der ersten Hälfte des 1.Jhs. v. Chr. nach Lissos eingeführt, wie die Form und die Namen beweisen[35].

In der Typologie hellenistischer Transportamphoren folgen nun zwei andere Typen, der Typ Dressel 2-4 und Typ Dressel 6A, die beide in kleinen Mengen in Kontexten angetroffen wurden, die in die zweite Hälfte des 1. Jhs. v. Chr. datiert werden.

Zusammenfassung

Die gefundenen Transportamphoren liefern Belege für verschiedene Handelspartner, mit denen die Stadt Lissos während der hellenistischen Zeit in unterschiedlicher Intensität gehandelt hat. Die seltenen Funde von Korinth, Thasos, Rhodos, Kos und Knidos sagen mehr aus über die Handelsorientierungen als über feste Handelsbeziehungen zwischen Lissos und der griechischen Welt. Von Korinth wurde Olivenöl und von Thasos, Rhodos, Kos und Knidos die sehr bekannten Weinsorten eingeführt. Die Funde beweisen, dass ab Ende des 4./Anfang des 3. Jhs. v. Chr. der Hauptlieferant für die Stadt Lissos nicht die griechische Welt, sondern der neue römische/republikanische Markt war. Das war die Zeit, als die illyrische Gesellschaft versuchte, Schritt für Schritt mit den neuen Partnern über das Meer starke und regelmäßige Handelsbeziehungen herzustellen[36], was man auch in Lissos sehen kann.

In diesem Rahmen sind chronologisch zuerst die Beziehungen mit Apulien zu erwähnen, wo wir Tarentium und Brundisium[37] hervorheben möchten. Daneben stehen die Importe aus Kampanien, die erst am Ende des 3. Jhs. v. Chr. auf dem Markt auftauchen. Und die dritte Handelslinie gehört zum Gebiet von Picenium und begann vielleicht erst am Anfang des 1. Jhs. v. Chr. Von diesen drei Hauptgebieten hat Lissos vor allem Wein und nur in kleinen Mengen Olivenöl importiert.

Bashkim Lahi
Instituti i Arkeologjisë
Qëndra e Studimeve Albanologjike
Sheshi Nënë Tereza
Tiranë-Albanien
E-mail: bashkim_lahi@yahoo.de

Bibliographie

Baldacci, P. 1972. Le principali correnti del commercio di anfore romane nella Cisalpina. In *I problemi della ceramica romana di Ravenna, della valle padana e dell'alto Adriatico*. Atti del convegno internazionale, Ravenna, 10–12 Maggio 1969, 103–131. Bologna, Arnaldo Forni Editore.

Bezeczky, T. 1998. Amphora types of Magdalensberg. *Archeološki Vestinik 49, 225–242.*

Blanc-Bijon, V., Carre, M.-B., Hesnard, A. and Tchernia, A. 1998. *Recueil de timbres sur amphores romaines II*. Aix-en-Provence, Publications de l'Université de Provence.

Bruno, B. 1995. *Aspetti di storia economica della Cisalpina romana. Le anfore di tipo Lamboglia 2 rinvenute in*

30 Lahi 2009, 135, 160.
31 Bekannter Hersteller in Giancola im ersten Viertel des 1. Jhs. v. Chr. s. Panella 1973, 495; Manacorda 1995, 144–145.
32 Bekannter Hersteller in Apani und La Rosa (Brindisi), erste Hälfte des 1. Jhs. v. Chr. s. Palazzo 1993, 229; Manacorda 1994, 11–12.
33 Töpfer in La Rosa s. Palazzo 1990, 144–145.
34 Palazzo 1993, 229; Manacorda 1994, 11–12.
35 Zu diesem Typ s. Sciarra 1964, 39–43; Tchernia 1986, 54; Volpe 1987, 113–115; Desy 1989, 14–16; Manacorda 1995, 143–145.

36 Lahi 2009, 133, 159.
37 Daran erinnert uns der berühmte Ausdruck von Varro, der schrieb, dass aus dem Gebiet von Brundisium Olivenöl und Wein über das Meer transportiert wurden, Varro, RR II, 6,5.

Lombardia. Studi e ricerche della Gallia Cisalpina 7. Roma, Quasar.

Buora, M. 2003. Sui rapporti tra alto Adriatico e costa albanese (I secolo a.C. –I secolo d.C.), in M. Buora und S. Santoro (Hrsg.), *Progetto Durrës. L'indagine sui beni culturali albanesi dell'antichità e del medioevo. Tradizioni di studio a confronto*. Atti del primo incontro scientifico Parma-Udine, 19–20 aprile 2002 Antichità Altoadriatiche LIII, 39–56. Triest, Editreg.

Cipriano, M. T. und Carre, M. B. 1989. Production et typologie des amphores sur la côte adriatique de l'Italie, in *Amphores romaines et histoire économique: dix ans de recherche*. Actes du colloque de Sienne, 22–24 mai 1986, 67–104. Rom, École française de Rome.

Cuomo, N. 1992. Les ateliers de potiers en Grande Grèce: quelques aspectes techniques, in F. Blondé und J. Y. Perreault (Hrsg.), *Les ateliers de potiers dans le monde grec aux époques géométrique, archaïques et classique*. Actes de la table ronde organisée à l'École Française d'Athènes, 2–3 octobre 1987, *69–85*. Paris, De Boccard.

Desy, Ph. 1983. Réflexions sur l'économie et le commerce de Sallentine hellénistique. À propos d'amphores inédites de Gallipoli e d'Ugento. *L'antiquité classique 52, 175–194.*

Desy, Ph. 1989. *Les timbres amphoriques de l'Apulie républicaine: documents pour une histoire économique et sociale*. British Archaeological Reports 554, 5–213. Oxford, BAR Publishing.

Empereur, J.-Y. und Hesnard, A. 1987. Les amphores hellénistiques du bassin occidental de la méditerranée, in P. Lévêque und J.-P. Morel (Hrsg.), *Céramiques hellénistiques et romaines II*, 24–41. Paris, Belles Lettres.

Grace, V. 1952. Timbres amphoriques trouvés à Délos. *Bulletin de Correspondance Hellénique* 76, 514–540.

Grace, V. 1985. The Middle Stoa dated by amphora stamps. *Hesperia* 54, 1–54.

Grace, V. R. und Savvatianou-Petropoulakou, M. 1970. Les timbres amphoriques grecs, in Ph. Bruenau *et al.*, *L'îlot de la maison des comédiens*, Exploration archéologique de Délos XXVII, 277–382. Paris, De Boccard.

Islami, S. 1972. Prerjet monetare të Skodrës, Lisit e Gentit. *Iliria* 2, 351–376.

Lahi, B. 2009. *Amfora transporti të shekujve 3–1 pr. Kr. në Shqipëri (mit einer ausführlichen Zusammenfassung in deutscher Sprache)*. Tiranë, Instituti i Arkeologjisë.

Lahi, B. und Fiedler, M. 2010. Ausgrabungen im Zentrum von Apollonia (Albanien). Vorläufige Ergebnisse zu Untersuchungen zu der sog. Amphorenmauer und ihrer Umgebung. *Mitteilungen des Deutschen Archäologischen Instituts, Römische Abteilung* 116, 213–255.

Maier-Maidl, V. 1992. *Stempel und Inschriften auf Amphoren von Magdalensberg: wirtschaftliche Aspekte*. Kärntner Museumsschriften 73. Klagenfurt, Verlag des Landesmuseum für Kärnten.

Manacorda, D. 1981. Produzione agricola, produzione ceramica e proprietari nell'ager Cosanus nel I a.C., in A. Giardina und A. Schiavone (Hrsg.), *Società romana e produzione schiavistica, 2. Merci, mercati e scambi nel Mediterraneo*, 3–54. Bari, Laterza.

Manacorda, D. 1989. Le anfore dell'Italia repubblicana. Aspetti economici e sociali, in *Amphores romaines et histoire économique: dix ans de recherches*. Actes du colloque de Sienne, 22–24 mai 198., Collection de l'École Française de Rome 114, 443–467. Rom, École Française de Rome.

Manacorda, D. 1994. Produzione agricola, produzione ceramica e proprietà della terra nella Calabria Romana tra Repubblica e Impero, Epigrafia della produzione e della distribuzione, in *Epigrafia della produzione e della distribuzione*. Actes de la VIIe rencontre franco-italienne sur l'épigraphie du monde romain, Rome, 5–6 juine 1992, Collection de l'École Française de Rome 193, 3–59. Rom, Ecole française de Rome.

Manacorda, D. 1995. Sulla proprietà della terra nella Calabria romana tra repubblica e impero, in *Du latifundium au latifondo: un héritage de Rome, une création médiévale ou moderne?* Actes de la table ronde internationale du CNRS organisée à l'Université Michel de Montaigne - Bordeaux III, les 17–19 décembre 1992. Publication du centre Pierre Paris 25, 143–189. Paris, De Boccard.

Manacorda, D., Olcese, G. und Patterson, H., 1994. Le anfore di Giancola (BR): Archeologia, archeometria, storia. In G. Olcese (Hrsg.), *Ceramica romana e archeometria. Lo stato degli studi.* Atti delle Giornate internazionali di studio, Castello di Montegufoni (Firenze), 26–27 aprile 1993, 277–284. Firenze, All'Insegna del Giglio.

Nonnis, D. 2001. Appunti sulle anfore adriatiche d'età repubblicana: aree di produzione e di commercializzazione. In C. Zaccaria (Hrsg.), *Strutture portuali e rotte marittime nell'Adriatico di età romana.* Atti della 29 Settimana di studi aquileiesi, 20–23 maggio 1998, 467–500. Triest, Centro di Antichità Altoadriatiche.

Olcese, G. 2004. Anfore greco-italiche: Alcune osservazioni sull'origine e sulla circolazione alla luce di recenti ricerche archeologiche ed archeometriche, in E. C. De Sena und H. Dessales (Hrsg.), *Metodie approcciar archeologici: l'industria e il commerci o nell'Italia antica.* British Archaeological Reports 1262, 173–192. Oxford, BAR Publishing.

Pajakowski, W. 2000. *Die Illyrer: Illyri proprie dicti: Geschichte und Siedlungsgebiete: Versuch einer Rekonstruktion.* Poznań, Wydawnictwo Naukowe UAM.

Palazzo, P. 1990. Brindisi. Località La Rosa: i riperti anforari. *Taras. Rivista di archeologia* 10, 141–156.

Palazzo, P. 1993. Anse con bollo rinvenute in Localita La

Rosa (Brindisi). *Taras. Rivista di archeologia* 13, 227–236.

Panella, C. 1973. Anfore. In C. Ampolo *et al.* (Hrsg.), *Ostia III, parte seconda. Le Terme del nuotatore, scavo dell'ambiente V e di un saggio nell'area SO.* Studi Miscellanei 21, 463–633. Roma, De Luca.

Papageorgiadou-Banis, Ch. 1999. La diffusion de monnayage romain dans l'Epire. In P. Cabanes (Hrsg.), L' *Illyrie méridionale et l'Épire dans l'Antiquité, III.* Actes du IIIe colloque international de Chantilly, 16–19 octobre 1996, 115–118. Paris, De Boccard.

Praschniker, C. und Schober, A., 1919. *Archäologische Forschungen in Albanien und Montenegro.* Schriften der Balkankommission, Antiquarische Abteilung VIII, Wien, Hölder.

Prendi, F. 1975. Aspects de la vie sociale, économique et culturelle de Lissus (jusqu'au Ier siècle avant notre ère), in *Utverdena Ilirska Naselja.* Mostar, 24–26. oktobar 1974, 149–163. Sarajevo.

Prendi, F. und Zheku, K. 1972. Qyteti ilir i Lissit. Origjina dhe sistemi fortifikues i tij. *Iliria* 2, 215–244.

Samuel, A. E. 1972. *Greek and roman chronology: calendars and years in classical antiquity.* München, Beck.

Sciarra, B. 1964. Un primo saggio di scavi ad Apani, riassunto del giornale degli scavi. *Ricerche e studi. Museo Francesco Ribezzo. Brindisi* 1, 39–43.

Sciarra, B. 1966. Alcuni bolli anforari brindisini. *Epigraphica* 28, 122–134.

Tchernia, A. *1986. Le vin de l'Italie romaine: Essai d'histoire économique d'après les amphores.* Bibliothèque des Écoles Françaises d'Athènes et de Rome 261. Rom, De Boccard.

Tchernia, A., Pomey, P. und Hesnard, A. 1978. *L'épave romaine de la Madrague de Giens (Var): (Campagnes 1972-1975.) Fouilles de l'Institut d'Archéologie Méditerranéenne.* Gallia Suppl. 34. Paris, Éditions du Centre National de la Recherche Scientifique.

Volpe, G. 1987. Le anfore della tomba 6 di Ascoli Satriano. *Ricerche e Studi. Museo Francesco Ribezzo, Brindisi* 13, 105–120.

Vandermersch, Ch. 1994. *Vins et amphores de grande Grèce et de Sicile Ive-IIIe s. avant J.-C.* Neapel, Berard.

Will, E. L. 1982. Greco-Italic Amphoras. *Hesperia* 51, 338–356.

Zaccaria, C. 1989. Per una prosopografia dei personaggi menzionati sui bolli delle anfore romane dell'Italia nord-orientale, in *Amphores romaines et histoire économique, dix ans de recherche.* Actes du colloque de Sienne (22–24 mai 1986), Collection de l'École française de Rome 114, 469–488. Rom, École française.

Processus d'imitation dans les productions illyriennes d'époque hellénistique: le cas des lécythes de l'Artemision de Dyrrhachion

Eduard Shehi & Anne Tichit

Abstract

The miniature lekythoi discovered at the Artemision of Dyrrhachion allow us to get a better understanding of the organization of the local workshops, based on the analysis of modules, shapes and stylistic groups. There is a clear influence of Attic but also Italian productions. However, local potters only picked some of the possibilities offered by their models. This resulted in a standardization of the production, particularly perceptible in the lekythoi of the Agrinion group. This set of vases is of special interest since the influence they reflect may have originated on the same coast, south of the city. Except at Dyrrhachion, similar vases were found mainly at Apollonia and in Epirus (Ambrakia, Ioannina, and Agrinion). The finds from Dyrrhachion add a new element to the debate about the exact location of the production center: we think that they were indeed local products. This implies two possibilities: either Dyrrhachion workshops were the exclusive producers and exporters of these vases, or there were several production centers in the area and we have to consider that a close relationship existed between them.

Keywords: Dyrrhachion, squat lekythos, workshops, imitations, influences, Agrinion group

En 1970–1971, Vangjel Toçi mettait au jour, sur une colline au nord-ouest de Durrës (**Fig. 1**), nom moderne de l'antique Épidamne – Dyrrhachion, un très riche ensemble de terres cuites et de vases fragmentaires, qu'il interprétait comme le dépôt d'offrandes d'un Aphrodision. Depuis 2002, ces trouvailles sont étudiées par une mission franco-albanaise: l'analyse du répertoire des offrandes a abouti à l'identification d'un Artémision[1], confirmée ensuite par la découverte de quelques dédicaces[2]. L'étude de la céramique – environ 1500kg de tessons – a été engagée en 2006: elle en est encore dans sa phase préliminaire.

Les datations des vases rejoignent celles des terres cuites votives et permettent d'établir la période de fréquentation du sanctuaire. Elle commence dès la période archaïque, représentée par un très petit nombre de vases corinthiens. La grande masse des tessons, cependant, appartient à des vases des périodes classique et hellénistique: principalement des lécythes à figures rouges, des coupelles miniatures en nombre impressionnant – près de 50% des individus –, des vases à 'vernis' noir, des bols à reliefs et des assiettes. Il s'agit manifestement en majorité d'une production locale. Le lécythe est la forme la plus représentée parmi les vases à parfum, pour ne pas dire la seule puisqu'il n'est concurrencé que par cinq exemplaires de balsamaires de production commune locale et de dimensions réduites. Les exemplaires de lécythes, peu variés, sont surtout des lécythes aryballisques (*squat lekythos*). Dans l'état actuel de notre inventaire, un seul possède des dimensions normales, tous les autres sont de dimensions réduites[3].

Pour aborder la question du processus d'imitation des productions de céramique dans cette partie de l'Illyrie et, en particulier, le cas de la production de Dyrrhachion, nous avons choisi de concentrer notre propos sur les seuls lécythes aryballisques miniatures, présents en assez grand nombre dans le sanctuaire et dont certains appartiennent au groupe d'Agrinion. Nous avons étudié en détail 24 vases ou fragments significatifs provenant du sanctuaire et procédé à des comparaisons avec les lécythes de même type découverts dans d'autres contextes locaux (environ 200 exemplaires provenant des nécropoles de la ville)[4].

Traits techniques

Les vases sont décorés selon la technique de la figure rouge. Leur état de conservation est très mauvais, si bien que les scènes sont de lecture difficile. Le 'vernis'[5], en effet, de couleur brun-noir et peu brillant, à quelques exception près, a disparu partiellement ou entièrement (**Fig. 2**).

1 Muller et Tartari 2006, 65–92.
2 Voir sur l'une de ces dédicaces, peinte avant cuisson sur le vase, Muller-Dufeu et Shehi 2009.

3 Nous ne prenons pas en compte ici une catégorie originale de lécythes à figures rouges et décors à reliefs, d'assez grandes dimensions, sans doute d'imitation attique, dont l'étude n'est pas encore aboutie et qu'il serait trop long d'aborder ici.
4 Certains sont illustrés par Hidri 2005, 101–106, cat. 94–128.
5 Le terme de 'vernis' pour désigner l'engobe recouvrant les parois des vases grecs est reconnu aujourd'hui comme impropre puisqu'il s'agit d'une couche d'argile très épurée, qui prend sa couleur noire lors du processus de cuisson. On continue cependant de l'employer très largement par habitude, mais entre guillemets, convention que nous adoptons ici.

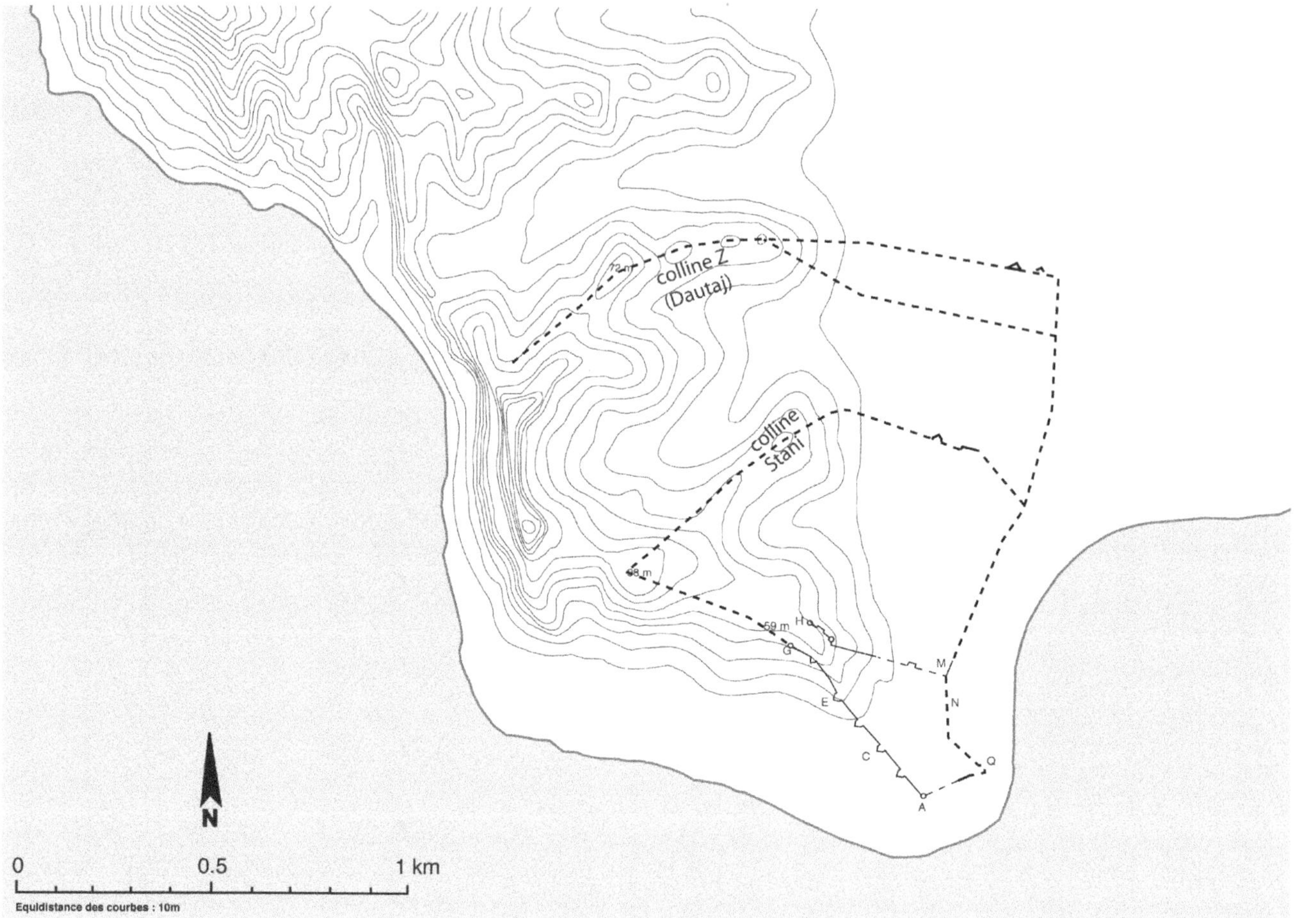

Fig. 1. plan général, d'après Shehi et Shkodra-Rrugia 2008, 332, fig. 6

Une sorte d'engobe, ou barbotine, rouge foncé est parfois conservée, le plus souvent comme fond pour le motif de godrons du col ou de quelques volutes. Ce même trait a été repéré sur les productions italiotes comme attiques: posé après l'esquisse du dessin préparatoire, il servait peut-être à masquer les différences de couleur que présente l'argile naturelle et à donner une couleur de fond homogène au décor[6].

Les détails des figures (œil, plis des vêtements, etc.), apparemment dessinés sur un engobe blanc fragile, conservé dans quelques rares cas, ne sont jamais visibles. Des résidus d'engobe blanc sont parfois aussi observables sur les volutes (**Fig. 3**). On rencontre la même technique avec la même conséquence sur des lécythes de fabrication attique du dernier quart du IVe s. av. J.-C.[7]. La présence de cet engobe est remarquée par I. McPhee concernant le groupe d'Agrinion[8]. Le mauvais état de conservation est sans doute dû à la technique de fabrication, que nous n'avons pas encore pu déterminer précisément. Il peut s'agir d'un problème de cuisson ou de qualité d'engobe adhérant mal à l'argile. La qualité de l'argile, très pulvérulente, a dû jouer un rôle.

La pâte, observée à la loupe binoculaire, est de couleur rose orangé à brun orangé[9]. Elle est généralement fine et homogène, très sableuse avec de nombreuses inclusions fines. Ce sont là les caractéristiques observées sur la majorité des productions céramiques, vases ou terres cuites figurées, recueillies lors des fouilles du sanctuaire et que nous supposons celles des productions de la ville. En réalité, deux pâtes, de natures légèrement différentes, sont reconnaissables. L'une possède de nombreuses inclusions, de couleur rouge, qui peuvent être petites ou grandes, et brun foncé, avec une faible quantité de quartz blancs de moyenne dimension. Les inclusions de mica y sont peu nombreuses. L'autre possède de nombreuses inclusions de petits coquillages, mais très peu d'inclusions rouges. Des analyses sont en cours qui permettront de donner une description plus fine et de préciser des groupes.

6 C'est l'explication donnée récemment par Hildebrandt et Hurschmann 2009, 318–319, qui récapitule les autres hypothèses proposées.
7 Voir par exemple, Van de Put 2006, pl. 208 et 209.
8 McPhee 1979, 160.
9 La couleur varie, selon le *Munsell* (édition 2009) du rose orangé, 7.5YR8/4, parfois 5YR8/4, pour la grande majorité, au brun orangé 5YR7/6, pour quelques-uns.

Fig. 2. lécythe inv. 10508. (© G. Naessens, Halma-Ipel – UMR 8164)

Fig. 3. lécythe inv. 11082. (© G. Naessens, Halma-Ipel – UMR 8164)

Les modules

Ces lécythes sont de dimensions réduites. Leur hauteur restituée se situe entre 12 et 15cm. À partir du diamètre du pied et de la hauteur de la panse, on a distingué trois modules de vases. Chacun correspond à un schéma décoratif spécifique, en fonction de l'espace dont le peintre disposait.

Premier module (M1)

Il correspond aux dimensions suivantes:

- diamètre du pied: de 4 à 5,3cm;
- hauteur de la panse: de 5,9 à 7,4cm.

Ce module regroupe le plus grand nombre de vases, 14 au total[10].

Le col. On ne trouve qu'un seul type de décor sur le col: des languettes pendantes sur fond rouge. Les lignes entre les languettes ne sont pas toujours dessinées. Lorsqu'elles existent, leurs extrémités chevauchent souvent les bandes horizontales qui séparent la partie basse du col de la zone décorée de la panse.

La panse. Les figures sont encadrées de chaque côté par une volute de trois spirales, dont celle du centre est toujours tournée dans le sens inverse des deux autres. Ces volutes peuvent être symétriques par rapport à un axe central ou, plus rarement, être identiques et présenter la même orientation. La volute reste de même type des deux côtés d'un même vase.

La figure centrale de ces lécythes est toujours une femme drapée. Généralement assise, elle n'est représentée debout, courant vers un oiseau, que sur un seul exemplaire[11]. Le visage est représenté toujours de profil et le corps de trois-quarts ou de profil. La tête peut être tournée ou non vers l'arrière. Sur quatre vases seulement, le corps est tourné vers la gauche; dans ce cas, le visage regarde aussi vers la gauche.

---

[10] Inv. 7161 (**Fig. 4**); 7163 (**Fig. 5**); 9371 (**Fig. 6**); 10200; 10508 (**Fig. 2**); 10706 (**Fig. 7**); 10890; 11082 (**Fig. 3**); 11086; 11218, 11475; 11575; 11693 (**Fig. 8**); 11706 (**Fig. 9**).

[11] Inv. 9371 (**Fig. 6**). On trouve une composition proche mais avec la figure de Niké sur un lécythe dans Smith 1925, IV D c, pl. 4, 11: Niké courant vers une oie, et la base avec un bande d'oves, et sur un alabastron du style de Gnathia, dans Romanelli 1930, IV D s, pl. 6, 3–4: Niké penchée en avant pour attraper un cygne.

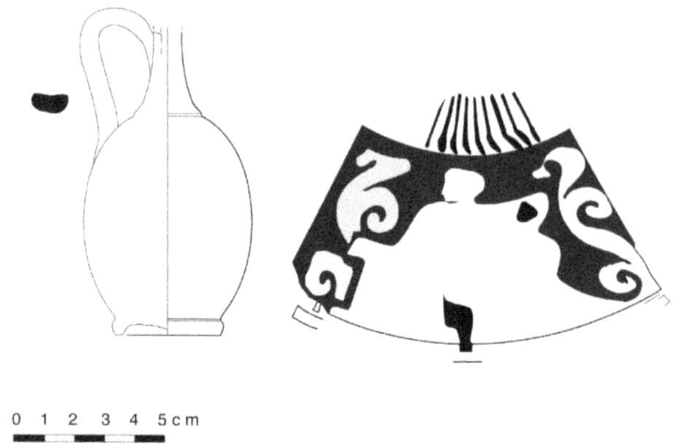

Fig. 4. lécythe inv. 7161. (E. Shehi)

Fig. 6. lécythe inv. 9371. (E. Shehi)

Fig. 5. lécythe inv. 7163. (E. Shehi)

Fig. 7. lécythe inv. 10706. (E. Shehi)

Les femmes sont généralement assises dans de larges sièges, à l'exception d'un seul vase[12], où elle est assise sur une large vasque, incongrue dans ce contexte mais fréquente sur les vases italiotes[13]. Elles portent à la main un objet: plateau d'offrande ou phiale (trois vases), un coffre (deux vases), un miroir (ou un tympanon? un vase), et peut-être une fleur (un vase, **Fig. 2**), ou sont représentées dans le geste du dévoilement, pinçant leur vêtement à la hauteur de l'épaule (au moins trois vases). Entre la femme et les palmettes, un objet aux contours peu précis et difficile à identifier est parfois dessiné dans le champ.

La base de la panse. La partie inférieure du décor connaît deux variantes pour ce premier module: un décor d'oves, portant encore parfois des traces d'engobe rouge, est présent sur tous les vases à l'exception d'un, sur lequel une bande rectangulaire est réservée, recouverte de rouge et décorée d'une ligne de points noirs[14].

En combinant tous ces détails, les peintres ont eu recours à 9 schémas décoratifs différents pour ces lécythes, à partir de variantes sur des possibilités restreintes dans chaque zone du vase.

Un fragment de lécythe, inv. 20461 (**Fig. 10**), doit faire partie du premier module mais présente une forme, avec une épaule très bombée, et une iconographie particulières. L'état de conservation est aussi exceptionnel[15].

Deuxième module (M2)

Il correspond aux dimensions suivantes:

- diamètre du pied de 3,5 à 3,7cm;
- hauteur de panse: entre 3,9 et 4,9cm.

Ce module comprend sept vases[16].

Le col. Le décor du col ne connaît qu'une variante avec des languettes pendantes. Les lignes entre les languettes

[12] Inv. 11693 (**Fig. 8**).

[13] Il serait inutile de répertorier toutes les scènes avec vasques. Pour avoir un aperçu de leur fréquence: Schauenburg 2010, péliké no 29,30 et 33, lécythes no 31, Hydrie no 32.

[14] Inv. 11706 (**Fig. 9**).

[15] Voir infra, Groupe 6.

[16] Inv. 7165 (**Fig. 13**); 8929 (**Fig. 11**); 9212; 10542; 10698 (**Fig. 14**); 10906; 10567.

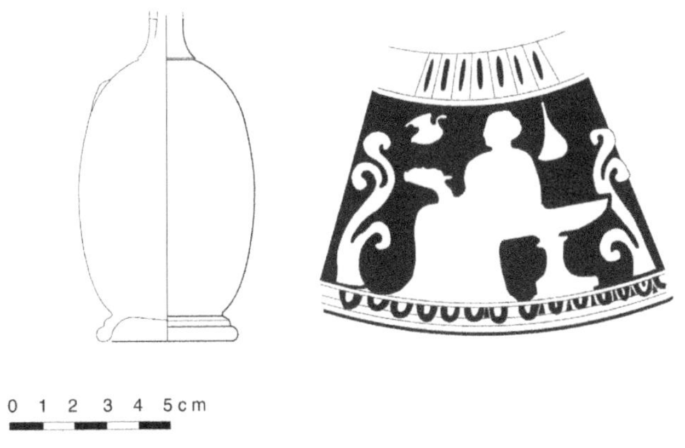

Fig. 8. lécythe inv. 11693. (E. Shehi)

Fig. 9. lécythe inv. 11706. (E. Shehi)

ne sont pas toujours dessinées. Seul le vase inv. 8929 (**Fig. 11**) présente encore des traces d'engobe rouge.

La panse. Les volutes qui encadrent la figure connaissent quatre formes différentes. Trois exemplaires[17] portent une volute très élaborée. Les autres portent une simple ligne verticale, légèrement ondulée et arquée dans la partie sommitale[18] ou une volute simple avec une unique spirale enroulée vers l'intérieur et une légère courbe au sommet[19]. La quatrième variante est semblable à celle du premier module. Les vases de ce groupe portent un décor de protomé féminine de profil (trois vases) ou d'une Niké assise (deux vases). La chevelure des protomés est relevée en arrière, des mèches ondulées tombant le long du cou. Aucun détail du visage n'est préservé. Les Nikés sont assises sur un rocher ou un amas de petites roches, le corps de trois-quarts et la tête de profil, vers la gauche. L'une, entre deux volutes, pince son vêtement, sans doute dans le geste du dévoilement, les ailes déployées dans le dos. L'autre, face à une volute unique, porte dans la main un objet rond difficile à interpréter. Malgré l'unité thématique, les styles de ces deux vases sont clairement différents: ils sont la production de deux peintres distincts.

La base. Les vases portant des figures de Nikés possèdent à la base de leur panse une frise d'oves dont l'une est plus soignée[20]: les contours des oves ne débordent pas sur les bandes qui encadrent la frise.

Les vases portant des têtes féminines ont sur leur base un décor simple d'alternance de filets réservés et noirs, d'épaisseur variable.

Troisième module (M3)

Il correspond aux dimensions suivantes:
- diamètre du pied de 2,4 à 3,4cm;
- hauteur de panse: de 3,3 à 4,3cm.

Jusqu'à présent, seuls quatre vases appartiennent à ce module[21]. Il présente un seul motif, au centre de la vasque: une palmette, un canard, ou des croisillons. Nous ne sommes pas certains que les vases de ce module soient tous des productions des ateliers de la ville. Dans le cadre de cet article, nous n'irons pas plus loin dans l'analyse.

Les formes

Tous les lécythes aryballisques possèdent des caractéristiques morphologiques identiques, que l'on ne distingue que par des détails indiquant l'intervention d'un potier différent. Aucun n'a conservé son embouchure, mais d'après les exemplaires du musée qui sont mieux conservés, ces vases possèdent une embouchure de profil concave très évasé, à bord large. Leur panse globulaire possède un profil continu. Un petit ressaut marque la transition entre le col et l'épaule. L'anse verticale s'attache au bas de l'épaule et à mi-hauteur de col. Le pied annulaire est large et bas.

On note des variations de détails dans les proportions de la panse et dans la forme du pied, qui peut-être mouluré ou en tore. Nous avons donc établi un classement typologique des vases en fonction de ces variations, qui sont l'indice de l'intervention d'autant de potiers dans les ateliers de la ville.

Forme 1 (F1)

Appartiennent à ce groupe les vases inv. 10508 (**Fig. 2**) ; 10906; 11086; 11218; 11475; 11706 (**Fig. 9**). Le vase inv. 7163 (**Fig. 5**) est proche mais pas exactement identique.

Caractéristiques: Pied bas mouluré, dont les deux anneaux de profil anguleux possèdent le même diamètre. Fond externe plat ou légèrement convexe. Panse assez élancée, de forme plutôt ovale.

17 Inv. 10698 (**Fig. 14**); 10906; 8929 (**Fig. 11**).
18 Inv. 10542.
19 Inv. 7165 (**Fig. 13**).

20 Inv. 10986.
21 Inv. 7164 (**Fig. 12**); 8558; 10501; 10570.

Fig. 10. lécythe inv. 20461. (© G. Naessens, Halma-Ipel – UMR 8164)

Le vase inv. 7163 (**Fig. 5**), dont les anneaux du pied sont de profil arrondi et de diamètres légèrement différents, peut correspondre au travail d'un même potier.

Modules concernés: M1 à l'exception de 10906 de M2.

Forme 2 (F2)

Appartiennent à ce groupe les vases inv. 7161 (**Fig. 4**); 10200; 10542; 10567 et 11082 (**Fig. 3**). Le vase inv. 10890 est proche mais pas exactement identique.

Caractéristiques: Pied bas en tore présentant une face externe et interne courbe; fond externe convexe. Le pied est généralement oblique mais le vase inv. 7161 (**Fig. 4**) présente un pied plus vertical.

Le lécythe inv. 10890 est différent dans la mesure où le tore est plus large et présente un angle dans sa partie haute. Sa panse est aussi plus trapue.

Modules concernés: M1 sauf M2 pour inv. 10542.

Forme 3 (F3)

Appartiennent à ce groupe les vases inv. 9212; 11575; 11693 (**Fig. 8**).

Caractéristiques: Pied haut et mince mouluré sur deuxniveaux dont les tores sont de diamètres différents, ce qui lui donne un profil en escalier. Fond externe plat ou légèrement convexe. Panse allongée avec des parois moins rondes.

Modules concernés: M1 (11693, **Fig. 8**) et M2 (9212).
Chacune des formes qui suivent n'est représentée que par un seul vase mais trouve parfois un ou des parallèle(s) parmi les exemplaires du musée provenant des nécropoles ou d'autres sites de la ville.

Forme 4 (F4)

Il s'agit du vase inv. 10706 (**Fig. 7**).

Caractéristiques: Pied bas, avec une moulure de profil concave et évasé, formant un sillon bien marqué au niveau de la transition avec la panse. Fond externe presque plat. Panse très arrondie et trapue.

Module concerné: M1.

Forme 5 (F5)

Il s'agit du vase inv. 7165 (**Figure 13**).
Caractéristiques: Pied bas en tore. Fond externe concave. La surface de pose est très petite en raison de l'angle interne du pied. Panse large, arrondie et trapue.

Module concerné: M2.

Forme 6 (F6)

La forme du vase inv. 9371 (**Fig. 6**) ne connaît, pour le moment, aucun parallèle dans le matériel de Dyrrhachion.

Caractéristiques: Pied bas mouluré dont le tore supérieur est plus large et plus haut que le tore inférieur. Panse allongée avec l'épaule plus large que la base (l'épaule est donc l'endroit le plus large du vase et non le milieu de la panse comme sur les autres vases). Un sillon, et non un ressaut, marque la transition entre le col et l'épaule.

Module concerné: M1.

Forme 7 (F7)

Il s'agit du vase inv. 10698 (**Fig. 14**).

Caractéristiques: Pied bas de profil triangulaire, très légèrement mouluré: un sillon peu profond passe juste au-dessus de l'arête centrale du pied. Fond externe du pied presque plat. Panse peu arrondie. Sa base constitue, de manière exceptionnelle, la partie la plus large du vase.

Module concerné: M2.

Fig. 11. lécythe inv. 8929. (© G. Naessens, Halma-Ipel – UMR 8164)

Fig. 12. lécythe inv. 7164. (© G. Naessens, Halma-Ipel – UMR 8164)

Les groupes stylistiques

L'état de conservation des scènes figurées se révèle un obstacle à la compréhension des détails qui permettent souvent la distinction des mains de peintre. On peut toutefois tenter un travail de comparaison, en ajoutant au corpus les lécythes miniatures conservés dans le musée de Durrës, qui proviennent des nécropoles ou de sites *intra-muros*. À cause de l'état de conservation, il est indispensable de s'appuyer davantage sur les éléments secondaires du décor pour tenter d'identifier les peintres ou ateliers.

Groupe 1 (G1)

Peuvent appartenir à ce groupe les vases inv. 7161 (**Fig. 4**); 11082 (**Fig. 3**) ; 9371 (?) (**Fig. 6**); 1437; 1771 (musée).

Le vase inv. 10200 est proche sans être exactement du même groupe.

Principales caractéristiques:

- Les volutes latérales: la première volute, à gauche de la scène, s'enroule vers la gauche. Seuls quatre vases du sanctuaire[22] et un exemplaire du musée[23] ont cette particularité.

Fig. 13. lécythe inv. 7165. (© G. Naessens, Halma-Ipel – UMR 8164)

[22] Ces trois vases et inv. 10906.
[23] Inv. 2658.

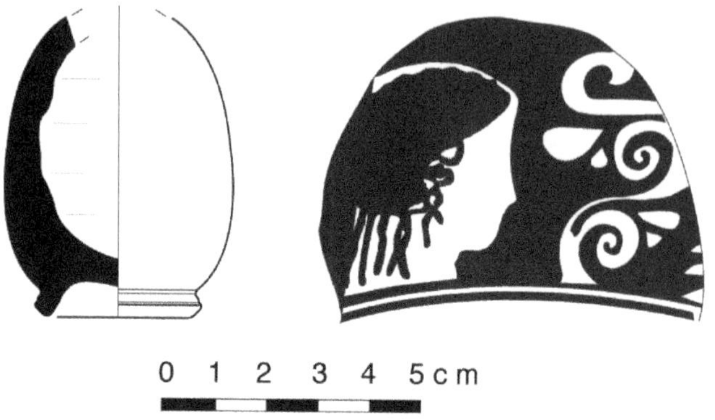

Fig. 14. lécythe inv. 10698. (E. Shehi)

- Les oves de la frise décorative au bas de la panse, d'un dessin assez peu soigné, débordent largement le cadre de la frise.
- Les languettes sur le col ne possèdent pas de ligne de séparation entre chacune d'elles et débordent sur le ressaut entre le col et l'épaule.
- Les femmes sur les vases inv. 7161 (**Fig. 4**) et 11082 (**Fig. 3**) sont dans une position identique: le corps tourné vers la droite mais la tête en arrière, vers la gauche, dans le geste du dévoilement (elles pincent leur vêtement à l'épaule). La position de la femme assise sur le vase du musée inv. 1437 est la même mais celle-ci tient dans sa main un miroir (?).
- À l'exception du lécythe inv. 11082 (**Fig. 3**), les scènes figurées débordent de l'espace délimité par les volutes qui se trouvent entremêlées au vêtement, au fauteuil ou à l'oiseau.

Cette attribution n'est pas sans poser problème. Le vase inv. 7161 (**Fig. 4**) porte à la base de sa panse une bande réservée et non une frise d'oves, mais l'exemplaire du musée inv. 1437 la présente aussi. Ces deux vases partagent aussi le fait que la scène principale vient mordre sur la volute latérale. Le vase inv. 9371 (**Fig. 6**) possède une forme sans parallèle à Dyrrhachion (F6). Enfin, les fauteuils des femmes ne sont pas représentés de la même manière sur les vases inv. 11082 (**Fig. 3**) et 7161 (**Fig. 4**).

La forme des vases de ce groupe est de deux types différents (F2 et F6): on aurait donc affaire à deux potiers travaillant avec le même peintre. Le vase inv. 10200 a sans doute été tourné par le même potier que les vases inv. 7161 (**Fig. 4**) et 11082 (**Fig. 3**).

Groupe 2 (G2)

Peuvent appartenir à ce groupe les vases inv. 8929 (**Fig. 11**); 10698 (**Fig. 14**); 13724 (musée). Le vase inv. 10906 est proche sans être exactement du même groupe.

Principale caractéristique: Les volutes très élaborées avec des pétales partant des ondulations de la tige principale. Le lécythe inv. 10906 possède sur son col des languettes de modèle différent. Ces trois vases sont du deuxième module.

Il semble que le lécythe inv. 13734, provenant de la nécropole, soit bien de la même main, malgré son très mauvais état de conservation. Il porte une volute, conservée partiellement, très proche de celles des vases inv. 10698 (**Fig. 14**) et 8929 (**Fig. 11**). Le profil féminin qui décore sa panse semble de même style que celui du vase inv. 10698 (**Fig. 14**), avec un menton large, des mèches ondulées retombant sur la nuque et des boucles sur la tempe. Le profil du pied cependant est différent.

Ce groupe reste incertain en raison de la mauvaise conservation des scènes figurées. Ces lécythes sont de formes différentes. Nous serions donc dans le même cas de figure que pour le groupe 1: plusieurs potiers collaborant avec le même peintre.

Groupe 3 (G3)

Peuvent appartenir à ce groupe les vases inv. 7163 (?) (**Fig. 5**); 9212; 11693 (**Fig. 8**) et le lécythe du musée inv. 9849 (?). Le vase inv. 11706 (**Fig. 9**) est proche sans être exactement du même groupe.

Principales caractéristiques:
- Une ligne réservée entre la scène figurée et la frise d'oves: cinq vases du sanctuaire possèdent cette ligne mais les deux vases non compris dans ce groupe[24] présentent des volutes plus élaborées et des variantes de décor rares.
- Les languettes sur le col sont fines et bien dessinées. Le vase inv. 11693 (**Fig. 8**), mieux conservé, présente à la base du col une frise de languettes courtes encadrée de filets réservés, comme le lécythe inv. 10706 (**Fig. 7**), qui pourtant doit être exclu du groupe, les languettes n'étant pas de même facture.
- Les volutes des vases inv. 9212 et 11693 (**Fig. 8**), avec des tiges fines et de petites spirales, sont presque identiques.
- Les oves en bas de la panse, dessinés au vernis dilué, débordent de leur cadre avec un arc central épais.
- Les femmes sont dans des positions identiques, avec la tête et le corps vers la gauche, ce qui est assez rare.
- Les lécythes inv. 7163 (**Fig. 5**) et 11693 (**Fig. 8**) ont dans le champ un élément de forme proche, difficilement identifiable cependant. L'organisation de la scène centrale est aussi très proche avec un élément 'volant' au-dessus du plateau tendu par la femme, dans un cas clairement un oiseau, dans l'autre un cercle (?), et un autre qui pend derrière la tête, peut-être des bandelettes rituelles d'après les parallèles italiotes.

Mais quelques obstacles peuvent mettre en cause ce regroupement:

[24] Inv. 10986 et 10706 (**Fig. 7**).

- Les sièges des femmes sont de formes variées.
- Les vases eux-mêmes sont de formes différentes, ce qui impliquerait une très grande structure d'atelier.
- Le très mauvais état de conservation du vase inv. 7163 (**Fig. 5**) limite l'interprétation et rend incertaine son appartenance au groupe.

Les formes de ces vases sont proches mais le vase inv. 7163 (**Fig. 5**) est de forme 2 alors que les autres sont de forme 3. Les vases appartiennent à deux modules différents (M1 et 2). Les lécythes inv. 11693 (**Fig. 8**) et 9212 sont vraisemblablement la production d'un même atelier, voire du même artisan si on envisage le cas d'un potier qui serait aussi peintre.

Le lécythe conservé dans les réserves du musée, inv. 9849, semble proche du lécythe inv. 11693 (**Fig. 8**), mais son très mauvais état de conservation interdit toute certitude. La forme du pied de ces deux vases est identique.

Groupe 4 (G4)

Peuvent appartenir à ce groupe les vases inv. 10706 (**Fig. 7**) et les vases du musée, inv. 1755; 1772 et 9844.

Principales caractéristiques:
- Les volutes fines aux contours précis. Les vases inv. 10706 (**Fig. 7**) et 1772 (musée) portent des petits triangles irréguliers réservés le long du rinceau des volutes. Cet aspect n'apparaît pas sur les lécythes inv. 9844 et 1755, alors que la forme générale des rinceaux est très proche.
- La présence d'une ligne réservée de démarcation avec la scène principale, bien délimitée par de minces traits de pinceau, d'un noir plus dense.
- Les personnages féminins ont la même position: la tête et le corps tournés vers la droite, ils tiennent un objet dans la main, de formes différentes. Le vase inv. 9844 montre une femme dans la même attitude mais pinçant aussi son vêtement à l'épaule droite dans le geste du dévoilement. Cette combinaison des gestes est extrêmement rare et ne se rencontre aussi que sur le vase inv. 11475, pourtant du groupe 5.
- Le fauteuil des trois femmes (ou ce qui leur sert d'appui) est représenté de façon identique par un long rectangle aux grands côtés légèrement arrondis.
- Les deux exemplaires du musée présentent le même objet de forme triangulaire, dans le champ, derrière le personnage.
- Les vases inv. 1772, 10706 (**Fig. 7**) et 9844 possèdent la même forme, alors que celle du lécythe inv. 1755 est tout à fait unique avec un pied discoïdal surélevé.

Les formes des vases de ce groupe sont de types différents. Il paraît clair toutefois que les vases inv. 1772 et 10706 (**Fig. 7**) sortent du même atelier.

Groupe 5 (G5)

Peuvent appartenir à ce groupe les vases inv. 10508 (**Fig. 2**), 11475 et peut-être 1338 (musée).
Principales caractéristiques:
- La forme des volutes qui sont relativement fines et soignées.
- Les femmes occupent largement l'espace de la scène centrale, assises sur un fauteuil de forme identique pour ce qui est des vases inv. 10508 (**Fig. 2**) et 11475. Mais le lécythe inv. 11475 est le seul à présenter un mélange des deux positions, à la fois celle du dévoilement et celle de la présentation de l'objet.
- Les oves sont larges avec un cœur en vernis plus clair mais au trait plus épais que leur contour.

Le vase inv. 1338 présente en réalité des caractéristiques intermédiaires entre ce groupe et le groupe 4, dont il ne possède pas la ligne réservée entre la scène et la frise d'oves: il permet donc d'établir un lien entre le groupe 4 et le groupe 5.

Groupe 6 (G6)

Le fragment de lécythe inv. 20461 (**Fig. 10**) est d'un style unique parmi les vases de l'Artémision et présente un intérêt particulier en ce qui concerne les importations et imitations. La figure centrale, une jeune femme, debout, de trois-quarts et tournée vers la droite, est très délicatement détaillée. Elle est représentée en train d'accomplir un rituel, avec un plateau à offrandes dans la main gauche et une œnochoé à panse côtelée, vraisemblablement métallique, dans la main droite. Elle porte un fin chiton sans manche et ceinturé sous les seins, avec replis ondulés sur les hanches et décoré de petits ronds et croix éparses. Elle a un bracelet à chaque poignet et un collier de perles autour du cou. Le visage est détaillé: un grand œil largement ouvert, vu de profil et la bouche boudeuse. La chevelure ondulée tombe en deux mèches sur l'épaule droite, seules les boucles qui encadrent le visage sont détaillées. Le plateau à offrandes d'où dépasse un cône entouré de deux petites branches est tenu un peu en-dessous de l'épaule. La volute, partiellement conservée à gauche de la figure, est complexe avec des pétales partant des spirales.

En raison du degré de détails du dessin et de l'état de conservation, il est vraisemblable qu'il s'agit d'une production d'Italie du Sud qui a pu servir de modèle (parmi d'autres) aux ateliers de Dyrrhachion. On trouve des similitudes avec la figure d'une ménade d'un vase attribué à l' 'Underworld Painter'[25], par le dessin des yeux, du vêtement, des bijoux et l'utilisation d'un plateau à offrandes semblable. Un cratère à l'iconographie proche de celle de notre lécythe a été découvert dans la nécropole de Fusco à Syracuse[26].

---

25 Trendall et Cambitoglou 1982, pl. 199.
26 Arias 1941, IV E, pl. 9 (inv. 36332).

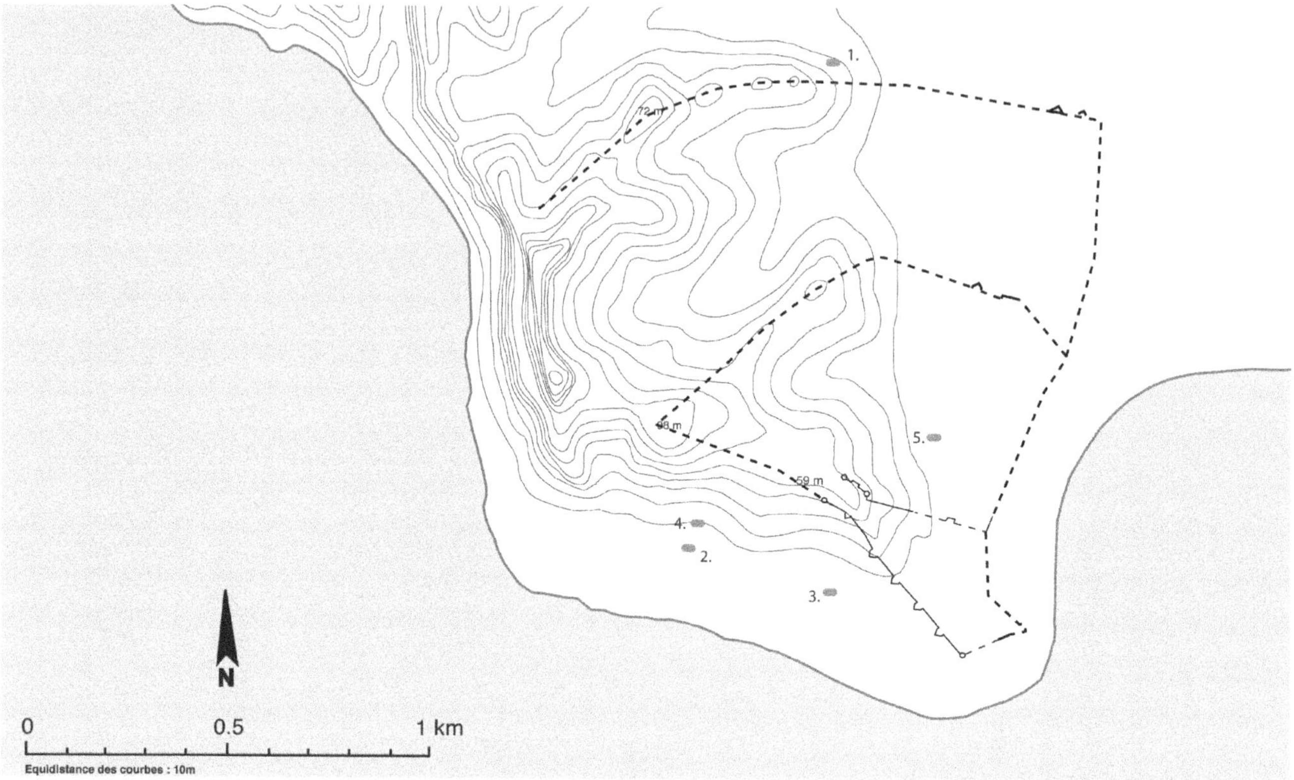

Fig. 15. plan de répartition des ateliers dans la cité, d'après Shehi 2010, 56, fig. 2

Que peut-on en déduire sur les structures des ateliers locaux?

Nous considérons ces lécythes comme des productions des ateliers de Dyrrhachion dont l'existence ne peut être mise en doute, même si leurs productions sont encore peu connues. Des découvertes dans la ville de Durrës ont en effet révélé la présence de plusieurs ateliers de céramique (**Fig. 15**). En 1976, a été mis au jour un dépotoir de ratés de cuisson, dans lequel la production principale était celle de bols à reliefs[27]. Des moules pour la production de ces mêmes vases, mais de provenance inconnue, sont, par ailleurs, exposés au musée. En 1986, un four de potier, dont la production n'a pas été précisée, a été fouillé[28]. Des découvertes plus récentes[29] témoignent de la présence d'ateliers de céramique vraisemblablement de la période hellénistique dans deux autres sites de la ville[30].

L'existence d'une production locale non seulement de bols à relief, exportés jusqu'en Dalmatie[31], mais aussi de grands vases à figures rouges d'imitation[32] est donc bien attestée. Le classement des lécythes aryballisques par groupes de formes et de styles donne les premiers indices sur la composition des ateliers de la ville. Il y a eu à Dyrrhachion des ateliers avec des structures simples: un potier et un peintre qui peuvent être le même homme. C'est, par exemple, le cas des vases 7161 (**Fig. 4**) et 11082 (**Fig. 3**) qui ont été tournés par le même potier (F2) et décorés par le même peintre (G1), tout comme les vases inv. 9212, 11693 (**Fig. 8**) (F3; G3) et 1772, 10706 (**Fig. 7**) (F1; G4). Il semble avoir existé des structures plus complexes. Premier cas de figure: un potier est en relation avec plusieurs peintres (G1 et G2). Le potier de la forme 2, par exemple, a aussi collaboré avec d'autres peintres que celui déjà mentionné. Un deuxième cas de figure est possible: un peintre collabore avec plusieurs potiers. Le peintre reconnu à travers le groupe 1 a travaillé sur deux vases avec le potier de la forme 2 mais aussi peut-être avec le potier qui a tourné la forme 6. Le peintre du groupe 2 lui aussi a travaillé avec plusieurs potiers (au moins F1 et F6). Il est difficile de savoir si cela correspond à des structures fixes ou à des collaborations ponctuelles.

Certains peintres partagent des caractéristiques stylistiques (G4 et G5), si bien que des liens entre eux sont envisageables: transmission de maître à élève ou simple collaboration au sein d'un même atelier. Il est pour le moment difficile d'être plus précis.

Les peintres cependant semblent spécialisés dans un type de décor, travaillant toujours sur des vases de module 1 ou 2 (à l'exception du peintre du groupe 3). Le peintre procède visiblement par étapes assez systématiques. Il

27 Hidri 1976, 245–258.
28 Pani et Papajani 1986, 15–24.
29 Dans le cadre de fouilles rapides, préalables à des travaux de construction qui ont détruit les vestiges.
30 Shehi 2010, 55–59.
31 Šešelj 2010, 105.
32 D'Andria 1986, 49.

devait commencer par l'esquisse des éléments de décor secondaire, d'abord les volutes, puis la base et le col, pour déterminer l'espace disponible pour la scène figurée. Les contours préliminaires des volutes changent souvent au moment où le peintre contourne les motifs au 'vernis' noir. Les vases inv. 7161 (**Fig. 4**), 7163 (**Fig. 5**), 11475, 11693 (**Fig. 8**) et 11706 (**Fig. 9**) présentent des scènes qui débordent sur les volutes: le peintre a pris tout de même le soin de bien dessiner le contour de la figure centrale, faisant disparaître les parties de volutes qui gêneraient la lecture de la figure principale.

Il faut cependant rester prudent sur ces interprétations en raison des lacunes de notre documentation: en particulier, peu de vases encore sont attribués et les formes des vases conservés dans le musée n'ont pas pu encore être étudiées dans le détail.

Influences et traits particuliers de la production

La céramique attique et italiote

Les influences semblent venir de la production attique et des productions d'Italie du Sud, plus particulièrement de l'Apulie, située juste en face de la cité. La forme des lécythes aryballisques, en particulier, est exactement copiée des modèles italiotes[33], mais les potiers de Dyrrhachion ont choisi de ne retenir que les formes miniatures, sans doute en relation avec l'usage que l'on faisait localement de ces vases.

Les décors, bien qu'inspirés des productions importées, présentent des traits propres. On constate une sélection parmi les multiples possibilités de motifs, principaux et secondaires, offerts par la production italiote. Les peintres de Dyrrhachion n'ont retenu que certaines combinaisons: les cols sont systématiquement recouverts de languettes, les volutes sont presque toujours constituées de trois rangs de spirales, les bases plus fréquemment décorées d'une frise d'oves. Sur les lécythes aryballisques apuliens, les bandes d'oves à la base des figures ne sont pas courantes[34], alors qu'elles sont presque la règle dans les productions de Dyrrhachion. De ces choix des peintres locaux, difficilement explicables, résulte de fait une standardisation de la production, qu'elle soit volontaire – recherche de productivité – ou non – conséquence d'un manque de soin des artisans.

Parmi les vases italiotes, ceux d'Apulie possèdent le plus de points communs avec les productions de Dyrrhachion[35]: une plus grande fréquence des scènes de dévoilement[36], leur prédilection pour les vases à protomé féminine ou la présence de bandelettes dans le champ (s'il s'agit bien de bandelettes sur nos lécythes). Le groupe de Cleveland, de la production apulienne tardive (2e moitié du IVe s. av. J.-C.), en particulier, a produit une série de lécythes aryballisques avec des scènes similaires[37]. Sur les vases à protomé, les modèles de Dyrrhachion se différencient des modèles italiotes dans la mesure où les femmes portent toujours les cheveux relevés en chignon mais ne portent jamais de cécryphale ou bandeau autour de la tête. Il est rare sur les vases italiotes que, comme sur nos modèles, des mèches tombent sur la nuque.

On constate une certaine unité sur le choix des figures, avec un souci de variation obtenue grâce aux détails, comme l'objet tenu, la forme du siège ou les éléments dans le champ ainsi que la position de la tête par rapport au corps. La prédilection pour les personnages féminins est très nette. La scène principale la plus commune représente une femme assise de trois-quarts.

Elle est fréquente en Apulie, mais possède ici des caractéristiques peu courantes sur les lécythes d'Italie du Sud: les structures des scènes sont en général simples et les femmes le plus souvent seules, avec un objet dans la main. Ces lécythes présentent donc une sorte 'd'extrait' des scènes italiotes, dont on reconnaît la même thématique rituelle par les objets qu'elles portent (bandelettes, coffres et phiales)[38].

Le groupe d'Agrinion

En 1979, I. McPhee isolait un petit groupe de 26 lécythes aryballisques, qu'il nommait d'après le musée où le plus grand nombre était conservé[39]. Il les caractérise par leur petite taille et leur système décoratif reposant sur une seule figure entourée de volutes, à partir des exemplaires des musées d'Agrinion et Ioannina, en signalant leur présence dans les Balkans, en Italie et en Suisse. L'ensemble de lécythes de Dyrrhachion[40], qui correspondent parfaitement à la définition qu'il donne de la forme comme du décor[41], vient considérablement augmenter sa liste et force est de

[33] Voir par exemple, le profil de lécythe aryballisque campanien, présenté dans Cassimatis 1999, 98.

[34] Les scènes encadrées par des frises d'oves sont relativement courantes mais pas sur les lécythes. Dans la bibliographie consultée, on a rencontré des bases identiques: Schauenburg 2010, fig. 2; Schauenburg 2008, fig. 21; Schauenburg 2006, fig. 9; Rivière 2009, 121: le vase est daté du premier quart du IVe s. av. J.-C.; D'Amicis *et al.* 1997, 366: 137.2, lécythe attique à figures rouges attr. au peintre Meidias (?) et daté de 410–400 av. J.-C.; p. 380: 151.1, lécythe lucanien à figures rouges attr. à l'atelier du peintre de Créuse; p. 382: 153.1, lécythe lucanien à figures rouges du 'grupe direggi', dat. 410–390; p. 396: 173.2, lécythe apulien à figures rouges; Denoyelle 1998, pl. 61, pl. 49 attr. au peintre de Sydney 46.48, daté de 380–370 av. J.C.; Romanelli 1930, I 4.

[35] C'est aussi à cette conclusion qu'arrivait I. McPhee pour le groupe d'Agrinion, par le biais d'autres comparaisons, voir McPhee 1979, 161.

[36] Trendall et Cambitoglou 1978, I, pl. 138, 3–4; II, pl. 34, 2; pl. 382, 3 et 4; pl. 384, 3; pl. 385, 4 et 6. Ce dernier présente un geste de dévoilement très proche de nos exemplaires.

[37] Les scènes de dévoilement sont proportionnellement plus courantes dans les productions de Dyrrhachion. Pour les productions du groupe de Cleveland, cf. Trendall et Cambitoglou 1978, II, pl. 306–307.

[38] Voir par exemple, la coupe du musée national de Madrid, Schauenburg 2008, no 74, présentant l'ensemble des éléments caractéristiques de ce type de scène.

[39] McPhee 1979.

[40] Dix-sept vases, parmi ceux présentés ici, appartiennent au groupe et plusieurs dizaines d'autres ont été repérées dans les réserves du musée de Durrës.

[41] McPhee 1979, 161.

constater que leur présence n'a rien d'anecdotique. On les date aujourd'hui communément de la deuxième moitié du IVe s. av. J.-C.

La question du lieu de production est au cœur de l'étude du groupe depuis qu'il a été isolé: I. McPhee rejette tout de suite l'origine attique et suggère une aire de production dans le nord-ouest de la Grèce à partir de leur contexte de découverte[42]. Plus récemment, J. K. Papadopoulos[43] complète la liste de vases établie par I. McPhee[44] et fait le point sur cette question. À partir de la carte de distribution des lécythes, il propose trois cités comme lieu de production probable du groupe: Ambracie, Apollonia et Épidamne, avec une préférence pour la première[45]. I. D'Andréou, dans sa publication sur les vases de la nécropole de Dourouti (Ioannina), envisage, quant à elle, les régions d'Ambracie, d'Apollonia d'Illyrie et de Leucade, dans la mesure où un nombre important de vases du groupe y a été trouvé[46]. Chaque auteur appuie donc sa démonstration sur le nombre de vases recueillis localement. Or l'ensemble numériquement important de Dyrrhachion modifie le jeu des proportions de vases dans les divers lieux de trouvaille. Pour notre part, nous pensons que les exemplaires trouvés dans la ville sont des productions des ateliers de Dyrrhachion, en raison de la proximité de la pâte avec celles des autres productions céramiques – vases de production commune ou figurée, terres cuites architecturales ou figurines – recueillies dans les fouilles du sanctuaire d'Artémis. La pâte décrite par J. K. Papadopoulos ne correspond d'ailleurs pas tout à fait à celle que nous observons: il signale l'absence de mica[47] pourtant présent, en petite quantité, dans les vases de Dyrrhachion. Néanmoins, leur très grande ressemblance avec les exemplaires du musée de Ioannina[48], considérés comme des productions locales, tout comme la proximité des pâtes de Dyrrhachion et de Corfou, observées à l'œil nu, restent des éléments troublants. Nous espérons que les résultats des analyses de pâtes demandées permettront de confirmer notre hypothèse et que nous offrirons ainsi un élément ferme sur lequel appuyer ce débat. Nous ne pouvons qu'appeler de nos vœux la réalisation d'analyses des pâtes des autres lécythes du groupe. En effet, dans l'état actuel de nos connaissances, il ne faut sans doute pas exclure l'existence de plusieurs centres de production[49]. Deux cas de figure sont donc envisageables. Les ateliers de Dyrrhachion sont seuls à produire et à exporter ces vases: les influences restent alors à chercher sur la côte opposée de l'Adriatique, en Apulie et en Italie du Sud de manière générale. Plusieurs centres sont responsables de la production dans l'ensemble de la région, au sens large du terme: il faut alors envisager des relations assez étroites entre eux et les ateliers de Dyrrhachion appartiendraient à un réseau plus large d'influences, aussi bien en Italie du Sud que sur la même côte, plus au sud.

Eduard Shehi
Muzeu Arkeologjik
Shetitorja «Taulantia»
Durres
Albania
eduardshehi@hotmail.com

Anne Tichit
École française d'Athènes
Didotou 6
GR-10680 Athènes
anne.tichit@wanadoo.fr

Bibliographie

Arias, P. E. 1941. *Corpus Vasorum Antiquorum Italia 17. Siracusa, Museo Archeologico Nazionale 1*. Rome, Libreria dello Stato.

Cassimatis, H. 1999. *Les vases Italiotes*. Bulletin des musées et monuments lyonnais 1–2. Lyon, Association des amis du Musée des beaux-arts.

D'Amicis, A., Giboni, G., Lippolis, E., Maruggi, G. A., et Masiello, L. 1997. *Catalogo del Museo Nazionale Archeologico di Taranto, I, 3, Atleti e guerrieri: Tradizioni Aristocratiche a Taranto tra VI e V sec. a. C.* Catalogo della mostra, Taranto, Museo Nazionale Archeologico, 9 aprile 1994. Tarente, La Colomba.

D'Andréou, I. 2009. Κεραμική από το νεκροταφείο Δουρούτης Ιωαννίνων, dans *Ελληνιστική κεραμική από την αρχαία Ηπειρο, την Αιτωλοακαρνανία και τα Ιόνια νησιά*, 123–144. Athènes, TAP.

D'Andria, F. 1986. Nuovi dati sulle relazioni tra gli Illirie le popolazioni dell'Italia méridionale. *Iliria* 1, 43–55.

Denoyelle, M. 1998. *Corpus Vasorum Antiquorum France 38. Paris, Musée du Louvre 25*. Paris, Union

42 McPhee 1979, 161.
43 Papadopoulos 2009, 235–238.
44 Il signale à cette occasion quelques lécythes exposés au musée de Durrës, voir Papadopoulos 2009, 236.
45 Papadopoulos 2009, 237–238.
46 D'Andréou 2009, 137 dresse une liste de vases trouvés dans ces lieux et récemment publiés. Sur les trouvailles qui y sont faites, voir généralement *Ελληνιστική κεραμική* 2009.
47 Papadopoulos 2009, 236. La couleur ne semble pas correspondre mais malgré l'existence du *Munsell*, ce critère reste subjectif et dépendant des variations d'éclairage.
48 Dont beaucoup proviennent de la nécropole de Dourouti, voir D'Andréou 2009, en particulier les trouvailles de la tombe 80, 130–132.
49 C'est aussi l'opinion de D'Andréou 2009, 137 et de Papadopoulos 2009, 238.

Académique Internationale.

Hidri, H. 1976. Gjurmë të një punishteje qeramike në Dyrrah (avec résumé en français). *Iliria* 6, 245–258.

Hidri, H. 2005. *Vazot antike të Dyrrahut (Antique vases of Durrah)*. Tirana, Globus R.

Hildebrandt, F. et Hurschmann, R. 2009. Form und Bemalung. Arbeitsweisen unteritalischer Vasenmaler am Beispiel der Gefäße des Museums für Kunst und Gewerbe Hamburg. *Bulletin de Correspondance Hellénique* 133, 287–344.

McPhee, I. 1979. The Agrinion group. *The Annual of the British School of Athens* 74, 159–162.

Muller-Dufeu, M. et Shehi, E. 2009. Skyphoi avec dédicaces peintes de l'Artémision d'Épidamne-Dyrrhachion. *Bulletin de Correspondance Hellénique* 133, 99–112.

Muller, A. et Tartari, F. 2006. L'Artémision de Dyrrhachion: offrandes, identification, topographie. *Académie des inscriptions et belles-lettres. Comptes rendus des séances de l'année*, 65–92.

Pani, G. et Papajani, L. 1986. Një furrë antike në Durrës dhe probleme të zhvendosjes së saj. *Monumentet* 1, 15–24.

Papadopoulos, J. K. 2009. The Relocation of Potters and the Dissemination of Style: Athens, Corinth, Ambrakia, and the Agrinion Group, dans J. H. Oakley et O. Palagia (éd.), *Athenian Potters and Painters*, vol. II. Oxbow Monograph 67, 232–240. Oxford, Oxbow.

Romanelli, P. 1930. *Corpus Vasorum Antiquorum Italia* 4. *Lecce, Museo Provinciale* 1. Rome et Paris, Champion, sans date (vers 1930).

Schauenburg, K. 2006. *Studien zur unteritalischen Vasenmalerei*, Band IX/X. Kiel, Ludwig.

Schauenburg, K. 2008. *Studien zur unteritalischen Vasenmalerei*, Band XI/XII. Kiel, Ludwig.

Schauenburg, K. 2010. *Studien zur unteritalischen Vasenmalerei*, Band XIII. Kiel, Ludwig.

Šešelj, L. 2010. The influence of the Dyrrachium pottery workshops in central and south Dalmatia. *Rei Cretariae Romanae Fautorum Acta* 41, 105–112.

Shehi, E. 2010. Kilns in Albania: an overview. *Rei Cretariae Romanae Fautorum Acta* 41, 55–59.

Shehi, E. et Shkodra-Rrugia, B. 2010. Le front nord des fortifications de Dyrrhachium. Données nouvelles et hypothèses, dans J.-L. Lamboley et M. P. Catiglioni (éd.), *L'Illyrie méridionale et l'Épire dans l'antiquité* V (8–11 octobre 2008), 325–336. Paris, De Boccard.

Smith, A. H. 1925. *Corpus Vasorum Antiquorum Great Britain* 1. *London, British Museum* 1. Londres, Union Académique Internationale.

Rivière, Y. (dir.) 2009. *De la Grèce à Rome. Tarente et les lumières de la Méditerranée*. EPCC-Abbaye de Daoulas, Sépia.

Trendall, A. D. et Cambitoglou, A. 1978. *The Red-figured Vases of Apulia*, vol. I : *Early and middle Apulian*. Oxford, Clarendon Press.

Trendall, A. D. et Cambitoglou, A. 1982. *The Red-figured Vases of Apulia*, vol. II: *Late Apulian*. Oxford, Clarendon Press.

van de Put, W. D. J., Bootsman, M. et Dekker, A. 2006. *Corpus Vasorum Antiquorum Netherlands* 10. *Amsterdam, Allard Pierson Museum, Université d'Amsterdam* 4, *Red-figure and white-ground Lekythoi*. Amsterdam, Allard Pierson Museum.

Bitumenrückstände an Keramik aus der griechisch-illyrischen Stadt Apollonia

Manuel Fiedler & Gregor Döhner

Abstract

In the centre of the ancient city Apollonia (Albania) numerous pottery fragments with traces of bitumen were found during excavations at the theatre and at the so-called amphora-wall close to the Hellenistic agora. The contexts of the ampora-wall can be dated from the 5th to mid-3rd century BC, those of the theatre from the 3rd to the 1st century BC. All of the approximately one thousand fragments belong to plain or cooking ware pottery. Four categories of ceramics can be distinguished: transport-amphoras, plain-ware pottery (like jars etc.), pithoi etc. and cooking wares. Often only rims and necks bear traces of bitumen, but frequently body sherds are covered with bitumen as well so that in these cases originally the entire body of the vessel must have been in contact with bitumen.

The use of bitumen in the central Mediterranean area during antiquity is not well known. Apollonia was famous for its petroleum resources which represent the largest oil deposits in the central and western Mediterranean furnishing high quality bitumen. Written sources mention a (not yet localized) nymphs' sanctuary and oracle near Apollonia. Apollonia's coins with depiction of nymphs dancing around a never-extinguishing fire testify to the importance of these resources for the polis as well.

The pottery has apparently been used for several purposes. To seal vessels and protect the content, often the vessel rims were coated with bitumen. Bitumen was transported and stored in large and small quantities in transport and storage vessels of different sizes. Some of the ceramics may have been used during the processing of the bitumen.

Keywords: Apollonia, Illyrien, Albanien, Bitumen.

Keramik von Apollonia – wie auch von Orten in Apollonias Umgebung – weist in nicht zu übersehender Größenordnung ein ungewöhnliches Merkmal auf: Sie trägt häufig eine Bitumenauflage oder Rückstände von Bitumen. Dies verwundert zunächst nicht, da Erdölquellen östlich und südöstlich von Apollonia existieren, die die größten Erdölvorkommen im zentralen und westlichen Mittelmeer darstellen und hochqualitativen Bitumen liefern. Aus Schriftquellen geht hervor, dass Apollonia in der Antike für diese Vorkommen berühmt war[1]. Für die Stadt waren sie offensichtlich von einiger Bedeutung, denn sie prägte Münzen mit Darstellung eines an den Quellen flammenden Feuers, um das die Nymphen tanzen[2]. Das Orakel und Nymphenheiligtum bei Apollonia, das bislang noch nicht lokalisiert werden konnte[3], war in der antiken Welt weithin bekannt.

Die Erforschung der antiken Bitumen- und Erdölnutzung im Mittelmeerraum steht, anders als die des Vorderen Orients, noch fast am Anfang. Warum also sind Bitumenspuren an der Keramik anzutreffen? Im Folgenden soll erstmals ein systematischer Überblick das Phänomen charakterisieren und die Frage geklärt werden, welche Art von Keramik Bitumenspuren aufweist und welchen Charakter diese Spuren haben. Welche Hintergründe des Gebrauches von Bitumen lassen sich also an der Keramik ablesen?

Die untersuchte Keramik stammt von zwei Grabungsplätzen in Apollonia, von der sog. Amphorenmauer auf einer Terrasse oberhalb der hellenistischen Agora[4] und aus dem Theater[5]. Sie fanden sich zumeist in Verfüll- und Nivellierungsschichten in sekundärer Lage. Die Scherben von der ersten Stelle gehören aufgrund der Fundkontexte dem 5. Jh. bis mittleren 3. Jh. v. Chr. an, das Material aus dem Theater ist in der Regel etwas jünger und stammt überwiegend aus hellenistischer Zeit. Mit wenigen Ausnahmen ist das Material stark zerscherbt. Da es sich zudem fast immer um tongrundige Keramik handelt, können die Stücke oft nur durch den Fundkontext datiert werden.

Generell lassen sich Unterschiede im Auftrag und der Erhaltung des Bitumens feststellen. Der Bitumen kann vollflächig die keramischen Oberflächen bedecken, wie

---

1 Die Schriftquellen sind zusammengestellt: Atlas Archéologique 2007, 42–44. 57–58; Forbes ²1964, 44; Grewe 2005; 217–219; Morris 2006, 95–97.

2 Ein Neufund vom Herbst 2012 verdeutlicht ebenfalls einen Zusammenhang religiöser Riten mit Bitumen: Unter der Schwelle eines klassischen Wohnhauses in der Oberstadt Apollonias hatte man ein Bauopfer niedergelegt und während der Zeremonie flüssigen Bitumen auf den Boden gegossen (Veröff. durch die Verf. in Arbeit).

3 Selenica oder Frankull (südlich von Levan) werden aufgrund von heutigen Erdölquellen und den überlieferten Entfernungsangaben angenommen, wofür es aber noch keine archäologischen Belege gibt. Vgl. Larson 2001, 162–163; Moustakis 2006, 180–182 Anm. 639. 642 mit Verweise auf Leake, Patsch, Ugolini, Praschniker, Hammond etc.

4 Vgl. Lahi und Fiedler 2010.

5 Vgl. Angelinoudi und Bäuerlein 2008; Fiedler *et al.* 2011; von Hesberg und Eck 2008.

Abb. 1. Apollonia. Kännchen mit Bitumenauflage im Inneren (a,d. M. Fiedler, b-c. M. Fiedler/S. Zabehlicky-Scheffenegger)

Abb. 2. Apollonia. a) mit Bitumen homogen versiegelte Oberfläche; b) netzartige Rißstruktur der Bitumenauflage; c) durch Bitumen verfärbte keramische Oberfläche mit Netzstruktur (Bitumen abgeplatzt) (M. Fiedler)

ein gut erhaltenes Kännchen vor Augen führt (**Abb. 1a-b**), oder eine flüchtige und dünne Auflage bilden. Bei einem zweiten Kännchen (**Abb. 1c-d**) weist der untere Teil des Gefäßes im Inneren einen dünnen Überzug auf, während Spuren heruntergelaufenen Bitumens im oberen Teil und im Halsbereich sichtbar sind. Bitumen-Spritzer (**Abb. 4c**), -Tropfen (**Abb. 1a, rechts**) und heruntergelaufene ‚Nasen' (**Abb. 5f**) sind häufige Phänomene an der Keramik von Apollonia. Oft beträgt die Stärke der Bitumenauflage 1 bis 2 mm, die die Oberfläche homogen versiegelte (**Abb. 2a**). Die keramische Oberfläche verfärbte sich bei längerem Kontakt mit Bitumen grau-schwarz. Schnelles Abkühlen des Bitumens führte zu einer netzartigen Rißstruktur (**Abb. 2b**). Häufig platzte der Bitumen teilweise oder komplett ab, so dass nur noch die grau-schwarze Färbung des Scherbens und die ehemalige Rißstruktur die ursprüngliche Bitumenauflage dokumentieren (**Abb. 2c**).

Das erstgenannte Kännchen ist aufgrund des Dekores bemerkenswert (**Abb. 1a-b**). Das Stück weist einen bauchigen Körper mit fließendem Übergang zu einem engen Hals auf, von dem ein Bandhenkel auf den Körper reicht. Die Machart und ein Glanzton-Dekor sind flüchtig. Der Dekor umläuft den Körper und besteht in einer oberen Zone aus einem Dreiecksmuster – einem Dreieck mit drei Punkten im Inneren – und einer unteren Zone aus einer von dem Dreieck herunterhängenden Schlaufe. Innen weist das Gefäß eine dicke Bitumenauflage vom Hals bis zum Boden auf, und außen sitzt ein Bitumenspritzer auf der Schulter. Es handelt sich bislang um ein Einzelstück, für das Vergleiche in Dekor und Form noch weitgehend fehlen. Bei den übrigen Stücken von den beiden Grabungen handelt es sich fast immer um einzelne Scherben, derzeit etwa 1000 Fragmente[6]. Dabei können vier Kategorien von Keramik unterschieden werden[7]:

Die erste Kategorie betrifft Transportamphoren (**Abb. 3-4**) mit Bitumenresten im Inneren. Hierbei ist zu unterscheiden, dass das Gefäßinnere vollflächig mit Bitumen überzogen gewesen sein kann, wie zahlreiche Wandungsscherben (**Abb. 3e-g**) und Böden (**Abb. 3h-i**) bezeugen. Oft sind allerdings lediglich die Hälse bedeckt (**Abb. 4a**), wobei der Bitumen dann innen die Schulter hinunterlaufen (**Abb. 4b**) oder in den Körper tropfen konnte (**Abb. 4c-d**). Den beiden Varianten liegt folglich ein unterschiedlicher Gebrauch des Bitumens zugrunde.

In der zweiten Kategorie sind geschlossene tongrundige Gefäße zusammengefasst, die nicht der Gruppe der Transportamphoren angehören. Oft sind die genauen Formen nicht rekonstruierbar, doch lassen sich darunter kleine, enghalsige Krüge (**Abb. 5a-c**) – hierzu zählen auch die erstgenannten Stücke (**Abb. 1a-d**) – und größere Krüge mit weitem Rand (**Abb. 5e-i**) identifizieren. Wiederum sind hier Stücke mit einer partiellen Bitumenauflage vertreten: An einem Fragment (**Abb. 5h**) ist Bitumen vom Rand heruntergelaufen, bei einem anderen (**Abb. 5g**) nur das Halsinnere mit Bitumen überdeckt. Anders als bei den Transportamphoren scheinen die meisten dieser Gefäße allerdings eine vollflächige Auflage besessen zu haben.

Selten trifft man Bitumenspuren bei weitmundiger Schwerkeramik an (**Abb. 6**)[8]. Ein Randstück mit einem Durchmesser von 35cm gehörte zu einem pithosartigen Gefäß (**Abb. 6a**), und zwei weitere Stücke mit Randdurchmessern von über 50cm könnten Vorratstöpfe oder große Schüsseln gewesen sein (**Abb. 6b-c**). Jeweils ist die innere Randzone komplett mit Bitumen behaftet, oben der innere Rand sorgfältig bestrichen, während das Gefäß- und Randäußere tongrundig belassen blieben.

In der vierten Kategorie sind die Kochwaren zusammengefasst (**Abb. 7**). Das zerscherbte Material lässt eine sichere Identifizierung als *chytrai, lopades* etc. nicht

[6] Stand Okt. 2011. Im Museum von Apollonia und in den Depots befinden sich einige vollständige pithosartige Gefäße mit Bitumenauflagen, die aus den Nekropolen stammen.

[7] Der fragmentarische Zustand des Materials verbietet meist eine exakte Formenzuweisung und Datierung.

[8] Unter der Grabkeramik Apollonias finden sich vollständig überlieferte Beispiele; s. Anm. 6.

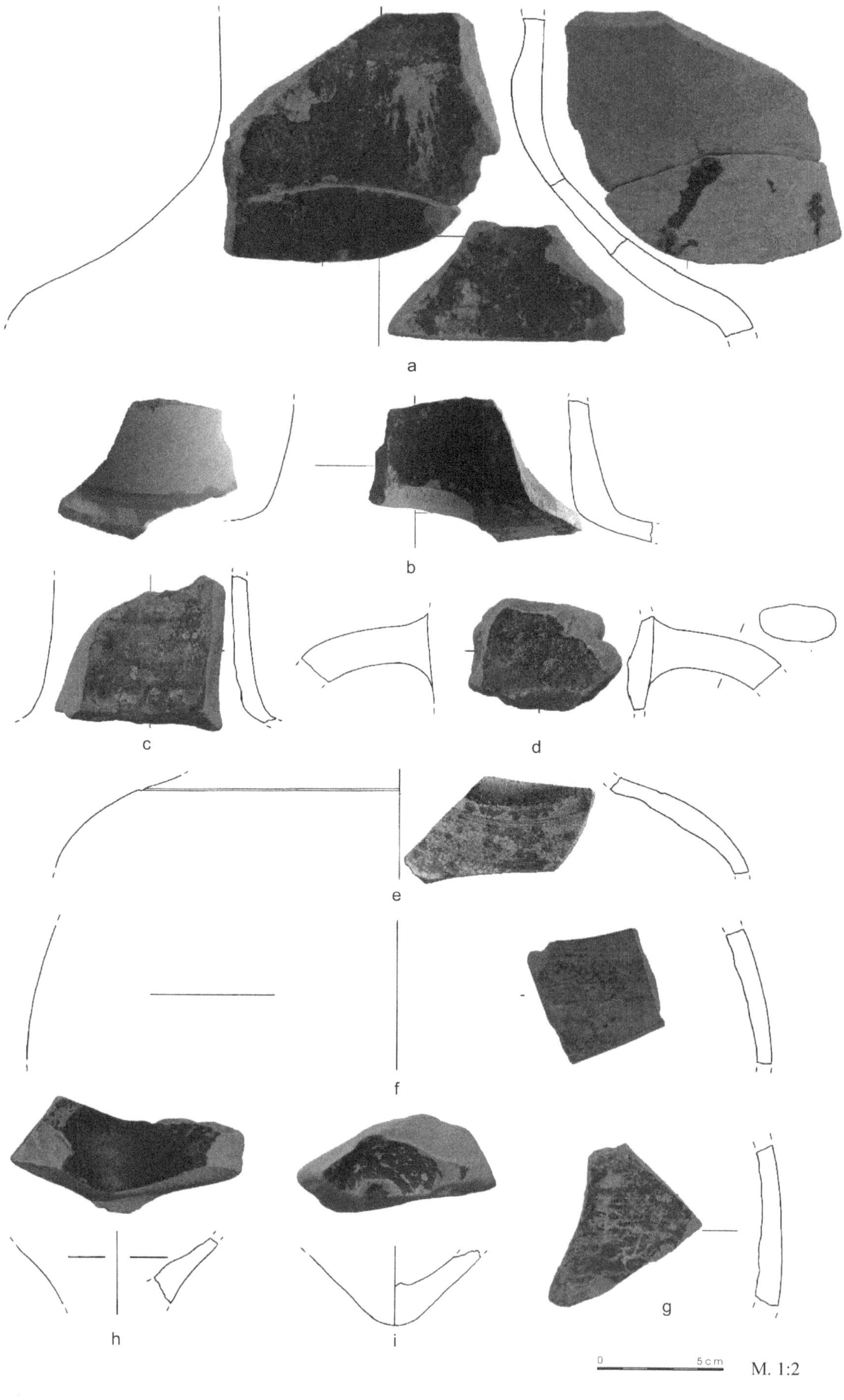

Abb. 3. Apollonia. Transportamphoren (M. Fiedler)

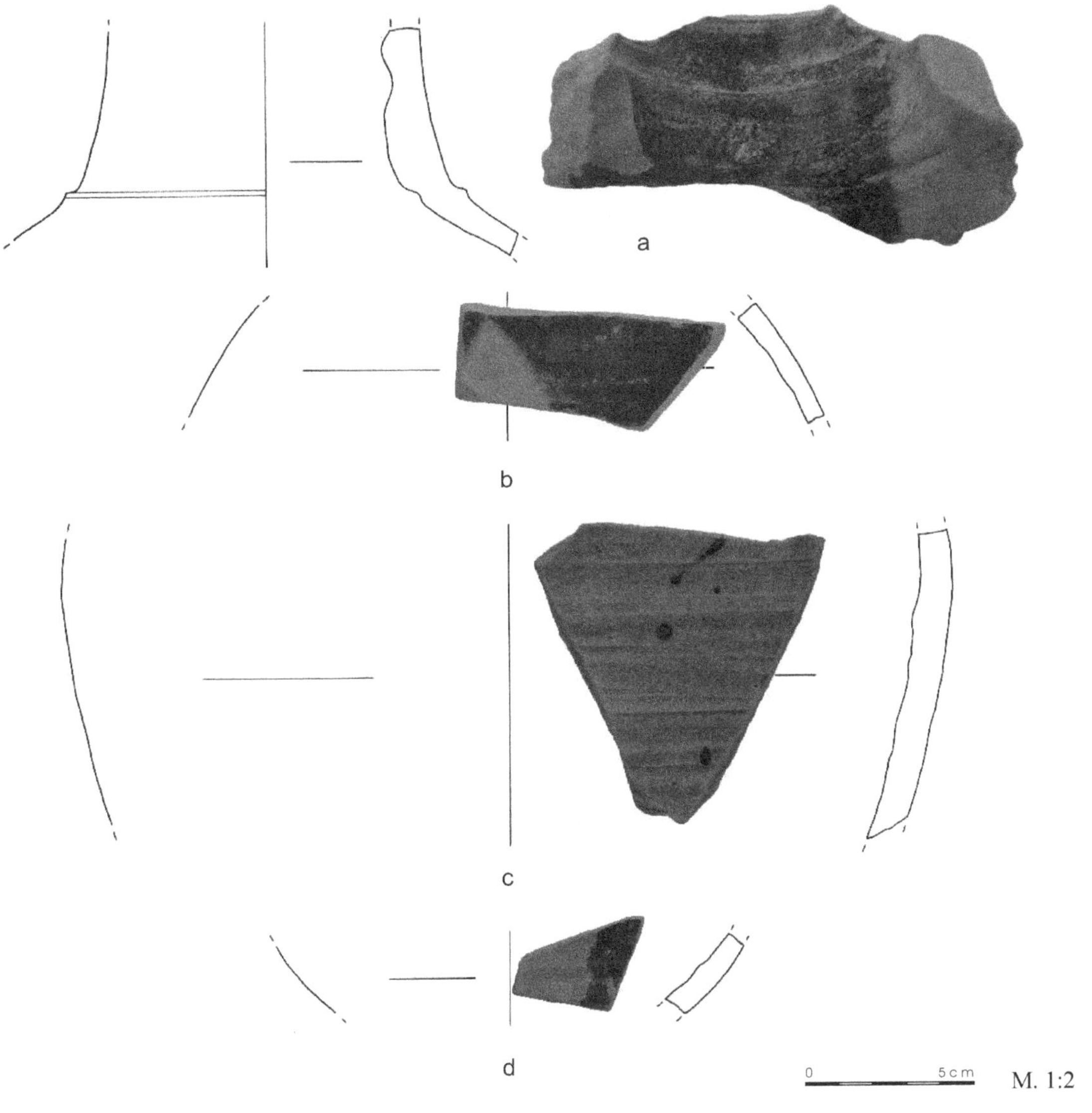

Abb. 4. Apollonia. Transportamphoren (M. Fiedler)

immer zu. Hinzu kommt eine Kanne mit Kleeblattrand (**Abb. 7a**).

Gefäße mit einer äußeren Bitumenbeschichtung (**Abb. 7b-f**), die zuweilen mit dem Pinsel aufgetragen wurde (**Abb. 7d**), lassen sich von Stücken mit einer inneren Bitumenbeschichtung unterscheiden (**Abb. 7g-k**). Da sich der Bitumen beim Erhitzen verflüssigte, können die Gefäße nicht mehr als Kochgeschirr gedient haben, sondern müssen in sekundärer Funktion gestanden haben. Den verschiedenen Mustern und Keramikgattungen muss ein unterschiedlicher Gebrauch bzw. Umgang des Bitumens zugrunde liegen, bei der die Keramik in unterschiedlicher Art zum Einsatz kam.

Bitumen stellt eine klebrige, isolierende und nicht flüchtige Verbindung dar, bestehend aus hochmulekolaren Kohlenwasserstoffen, die nur in unpolaren Lösungen teilweise bis vollständig löslich ist[9]. Als hydrophobe Verbindung ist Bitumen im Wasser unlöslich und verhält sich gegenüber nichtoxidierenden Basen und Säuren resistent. Die Verarbeitung und Anwendung von Bitumen stellt kein (oder nur ein sehr geringes) Gesundheitsrisiko dar, es ist im festen Zustand geruchlos und verhält sich lebensmittelneutral. Bei höheren Temperaturen entflammt Bitumen und zersetzt sich langsam. Dabei gehört es zu den thermoplastischen Stoffen, die keinen definierten Schmelzpunkt, sondern einen Schmelzbereich besitzen.
Aufgrund seiner Viskosität verändert Bitumen durch Temperatureinwirkung seine Eigenschaften bezüglich des Aggregatzustandes. Bei Minusgraden und bei Raumtemperatur ist es spröde bis hart und durchläuft bei Erwärmung stufenlos alle Zustände von zäh- bis dünnflüssig. Bitumen kommt in der Natur nur selten in

[9] Bitumen ist z.B. in Benzol und Toluol löslich.

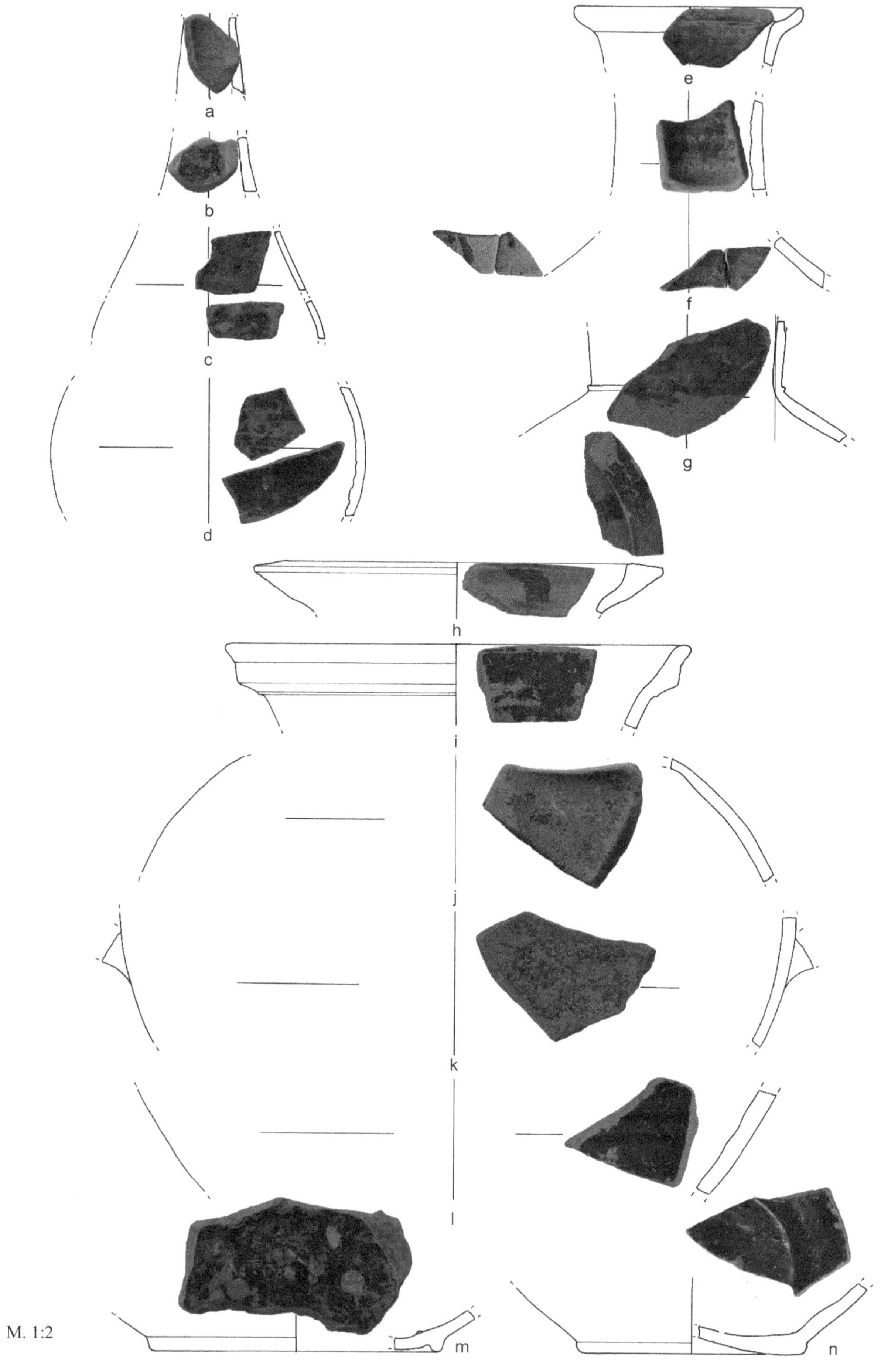

Abb. 5. Apollonia. Tongrundige Keramik (vor allem Krüge) (M. Fiedler)

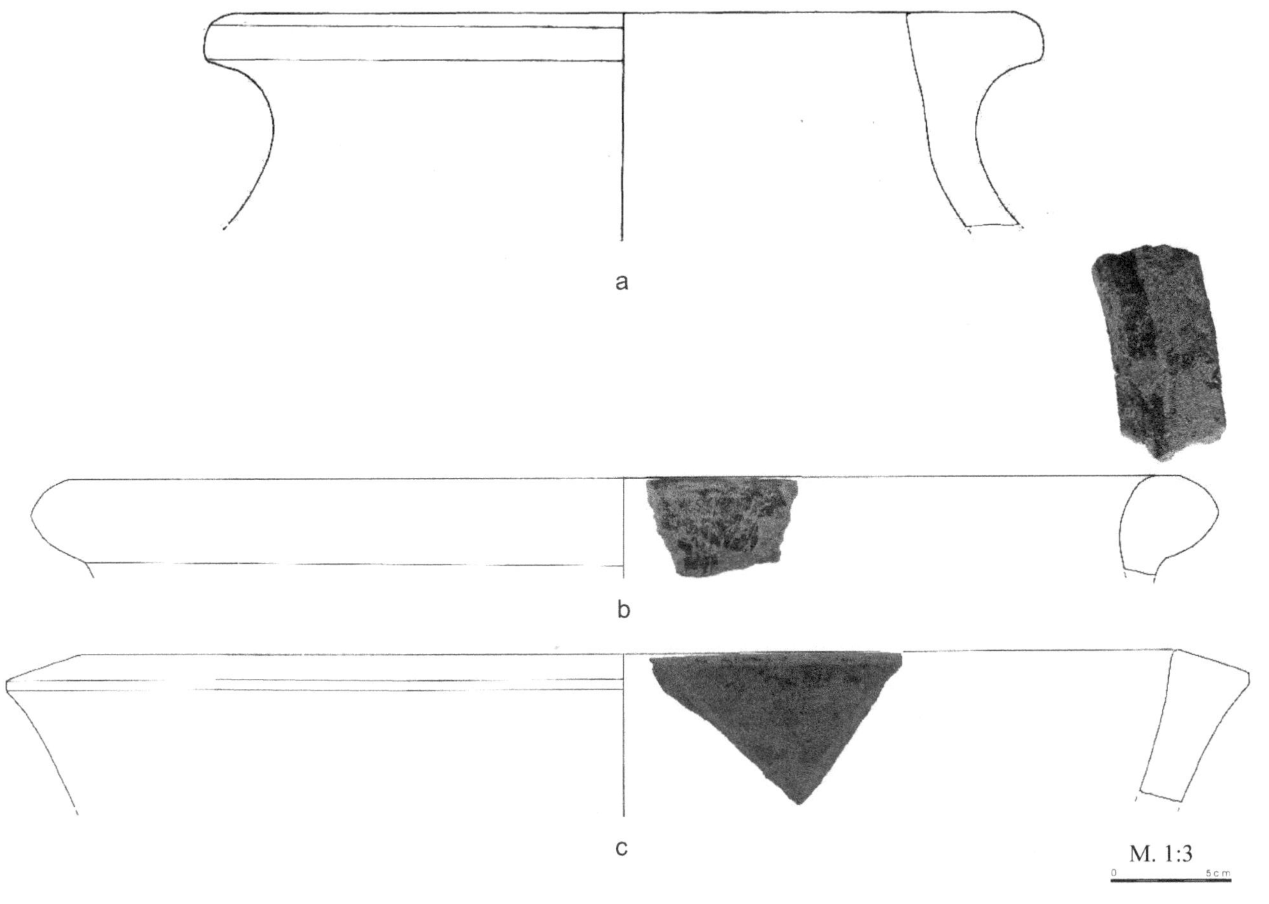

Abb. 6. Apollonia. Schwerkeramik (a. K. Sídó; b,c. C. Höpken)

reiner Form vor; meist sind mineralische Anteile und Schwefel beigemengt, so dass man gleichermaßen von Asphalt und Naturasphalt sprechen kann. Die natürlichen oder künstlich beigemengten Zuschlagstoffe beeinflussen die materialspezifischen Eigenschaften[10].

Der Abbau des Rohstoffes fand in der Antike an obertägig austretenden Stellen statt. Ob die Verarbeitung des gewonnenen Rohstoffes am Abbauort oder andernorts erfolgte, bleibt solange unklar, bis entsprechende Arbeitsplätze mit Feuerstellen, Gruben (zur Lagerung des Stoffes und weiteren Aufbereitung) etc. archäologisch nachzuweisen sind. Plinius gibt für die Aufbereitung von Asphalten das Einfüllen in kupferne Kessel an, um die Masse zu erhitzen und Essig (!) als Gerinnungsmittel beizugeben[11]. Dass Keramikgefäße bei der Aufbereitung, etwa beim Beimengen verschiedener Zuschlagstoffe oder der Entnahme aus Gruben, eine Rolle spielten, steht außer Frage.

So wenig wir über die Produktionsprozesse wissen, so lückenhaft ist auch unsere Kenntnis zur Verwendung und Nutzung des Bitumens in der Antike. Am besten sind wir über den Vorderen Orient informiert[12], wo die Verwendung von Bitumen und Asphalt eine lange Tradition aufweist. Hier wird die Vielfalt der Anwendungsmöglichkeiten vor Augen geführt: Archäologische oder schriftliche Quellen bezeugen die Nutzung z.B. im Haus- und Straßenbau, als Isoliermaterial etwa für Wasserbecken, Baderäume oder die Kanalisation. Schilfboote wurden zur Abdichtung mit Asphalt beschichtet[13]. Beliebt war Bitumen als Klebstoff. Werkzeuggriffe wurden aus Asphalt gefertigt oder mit Bitumen fixiert. In der Bildhauerei setzte man farbige Steine, z.B. für Augen, mit Bitumen ein. Für militärische Zwecke konnten mit Erdölen brennende und nur schwer zu löschende Geschosse gefertigt werden[14]. Auch in der Medizin fand Bitumen Anwendung: So wurde empfohlen, bei Magenbeschwerden ein Bitumen-Wein-Gemisch einzunehmen. Die Linderung der Beschwerden ist auf die desinfizierende Wirkung von Bitumen zurückzuführen.

[10] Der Grund liegt im niedrigen Schmelzbereich von Bitumen, in reiner Form findet eine Erweichung schon ab 40°C statt. Mineralische Zuschlagstoffe setzen den Schmelzbereich herauf und ermöglichen eine Verarbeitung.

[11] Plinius nat. 2, 235. Der Essig dürfte aber bei der Aufbereitung keine Rolle gespielt haben, da er nicht zu den unpolaren Lösungen gehört.

[12] Blümner 1887, 30–32; Forbes ²1964; Krishnan und Rajagopal 2003.

[13] McGrail 2004, 59–68.

[14] Plinius nat. 2, 235; vgl. Partington 1999, 1–5.

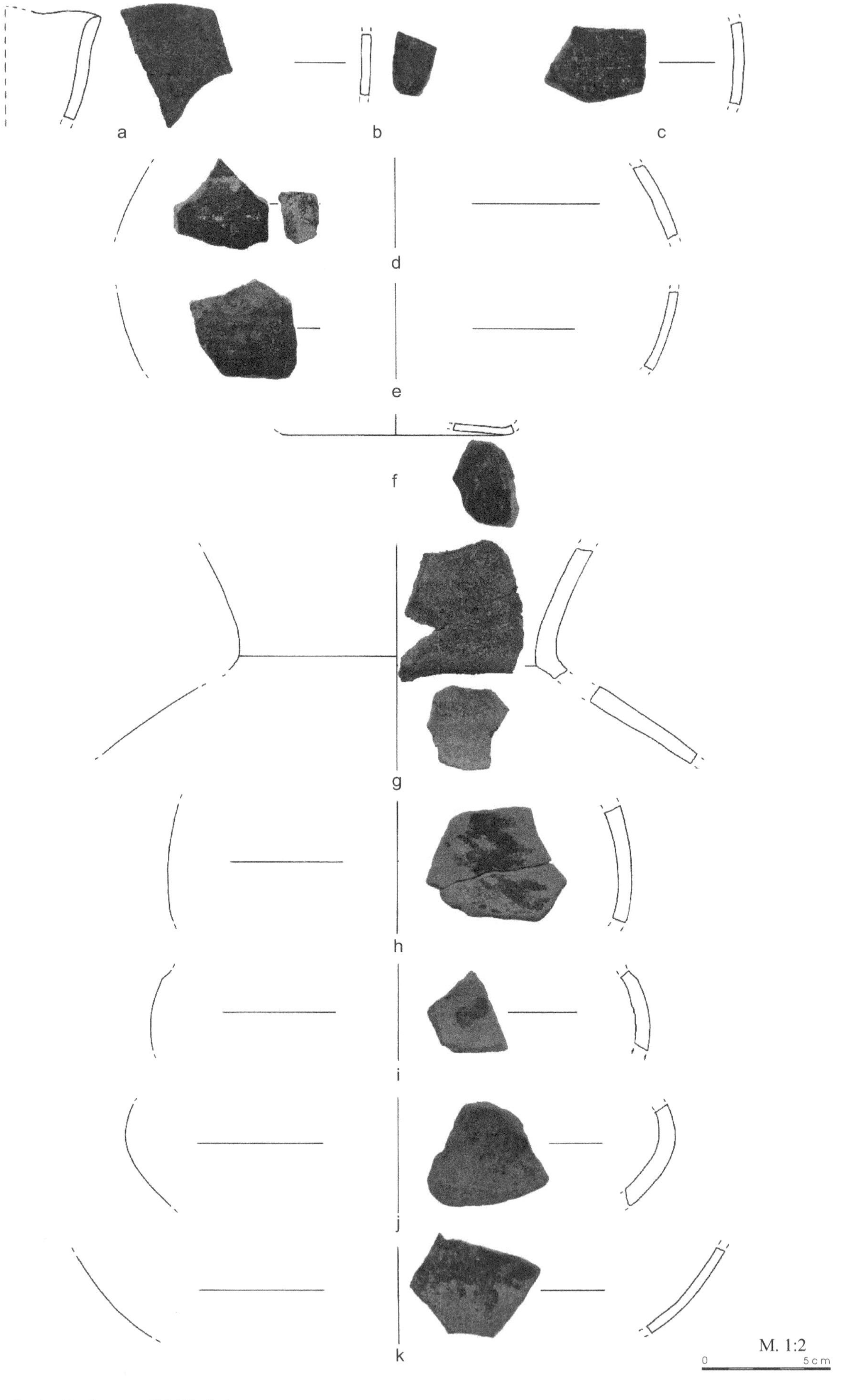

Abb. 7. Apollonia. Kochwaren (M. Fiedler)

Da die ergiebigen Bitumenvorkommen des Nahen Ostens außerhalb der griechischen Welt lagen, war im antiken Mittelmeerraum die Bitumen- und Erdölnutzung offensichtlich wesentlich weniger verbreitet. Zur Verfügung standen die seltenen, qualitativ sehr unterschiedlichen eigenen Ressourcen, bei Apollonia, auf Zakynthos, Rhodos oder bei Agrigent. Die bitumenhaltige Erde von Rhodos (Ampelitis) lohnte nicht für die Gewinnung von Bitumen, sondern wurde in den Weinbergen gegen Schädlingsbefall an Rebstöcken eingesetzt[15]. Kleinere Erdölfraktionen in Sizilien konnten vermutlich als Lampenöl – ‚sizilisches Öl' – genutzt werden[16], allerdings eigneten sich dafür nur die nahezu rußfrei verbrennenden Erdöle. Obgleich die im Osten bekannten Anwendungsmöglichkeiten auch im zentralen und westlichen Mittelmeergebiet geläufig gewesen sein dürften, fällt auf, dass die Quellenlage hier noch sehr dürftig ist. Die Anwendung beim Schiffsbau müsste systematisch untersucht werden; die Nemi-Schiffe waren beispielsweise mit einem Bitumengemisch kalfatert. Als Klebstoff lässt sich Bitumen mehrfach nachweisen: So wurden zwei rotfigurige Gefäße im apulischen Ascoli Satriano, die als Fehlbrand den Ofen verließen, mit Bitumen repariert und als Grabbeigabe verwendet[17]. Bei bronzenen Greifenprotomen in Delphi konnte eine Reparatur mit Bitumen nachgewiesen werden, ebenso wie bei weiteren Protomen in Olympia, Milet und Praeneste[18]. Unterschiedliche Materialen konnten miteinander fixiert werden, wie eine Glas-Amphora aus Olbia belegt[19]. Aus Apollonia sind Skulpturen bekannt, die mit Bitumen geklebt wurden. Nach Plinius wurden Bronzestatuen zuweilen mit Bitumen bestrichen[20], um Oberflächen zu schützen und zum Glänzen zu bringen.

Im zentralen Mittelmeergebiet dürften die Bitumenvorkommen in Illyrien qualitativ und quantitativ am wirtschaftlichsten gewesen sein. Bereits im Neolithikum wurde der Rohstoff hier verwendet[21]. Die Funde im Grabhügel von Löfkend bezeugen seine große Bedeutung in der Region während der frühen Eisenzeit[22].

Wenn auch die konkreten Anwendungen in Apollonia weitgehend unklar bleiben, so lässt sich allein aus der Menge der überlieferten Bitumen-Keramik der große Wert des Stoffes erkennen. Alle vorgestellten Stücke gehören den tongrundigen Waren an; ein Dekor mittels Bitumen, wie es in anderen Kulturen überliefert ist[23], lässt sich bei der Gefäßkeramik von Apollonia nicht nachweisen. Die Transportamphoren, die innen vollflächig Reste der Auflage zeigen, dürften primär zum Transport großer Bitumenmengen genutzt worden sein. Ob sie von den Quellen und den Aufbereitungsplätzen in die Stadt transportiert wurden, oder die Aufbereitung in Apollonia selbst stattfand und die Amphoren zum Export vorgesehen waren, bleibt ungewiß. Kleinere Behältnisse mit vollflächigen Auflagen im Inneren, wie einige der Kannen, bezeugen den Gebrauch des Stoffes innerhalb der Stadt. Sie dienten dem Transport, der Aufbewahrung und Nutzung kleinerer Mengen. Zu fragen ist sogar, ob das eigenartige Kännchen mit dem Dreiecksmuster (**Abb. 1a**) eine speziell für den Bitumengebrauch gefertigte ‚Bitumenkanne' darstellte.

Einige der Stücke könnten als Schöpfgefäße oder für die Aufbewahrung gedient haben, wie etwa die Töpfe.

Auffällig häufig sind an Transportamphoren, Kannen und der Schwerkeramik die lediglich mit Bitumen bestrichenen Gefäßränder. Die desinfizierende Wirkung des Bitumens war bekannt; folglich können wir davon ausgehen, dass hier die Gefäßinhalte durch Verpichung der Ränder geschützt werden sollten. Die Gefäße könnten mit Deckeln geschlossen und mittels Bitumen versiegelt worden sein. Inwieweit Bitumen von Apollonia überregional exportiert wurde, kann derzeit nicht festgestellt werden, da Bitumenfunde oder Gegenstände mit Bitumenspuren selten Beachtung fanden und es an naturwissenschaftlichen Untersuchungen mangelt. Den Anstoß hierfür möchte dieser kurze Überblick geben.

Manuel Fiedler
Wilhelm-Waldeyer- Str. 2
D-50937 Köln
mfiedler1999@yahoo.com

Gregor Döhner
Bizetstrasse 104
D-13088 Berlin
mail@archaeofakt.de

15 Plinius nat. 35, 194. Rhodische Amphoren sind im Übrigen häufig mit Baumharz ausgekleidet, frdl. Hinweis Chr. Römer-Strehl.
16 Plinius nat. 15, 25–26.
17 Reyer-Völlenklee 2005. Im Museum von Brindisi ist eine Transportamphorenscherbe mit Reste von Bitumen ausgestellt.
18 Rolley *et al.* 2004–2005, mit weiteren Beispielen S. 58–59.
19 Platz-Horster 1995, 40.
20 Plinius nat. 34, 15.
21 Klebungen an neolithischer Keramik von Cakran: Korkuti 1995, 145 Taf. 56, 32.
22 Morris 2006; Papadopoulos *et al.* 2007, 121. 123–124. 130 Abb. 20. 23.
23 Kalicz 2006 für neolithische Keramik im ungarischen Raum. Das Phänomen müßte auch für Albanien untersucht werden.

Bibliographie

Angelinoudi, A. und Bäuerlein, J. 2008. Das Theater von Apollonia (Albanien). Ein Vorbericht. *Mitteilungen des Deutschen Archäologischen Instituts, Römische Abteilung* 114, 17–29.

Atlas Archéologique 2007. Dimo, V., Lenhardt, Ph. und Quantin, F. (Hrsg.), *Apollonia d'Illyrie 1. Atlas Archéologique et historique*. Athen/Rom. Écoles françaises de Rome et d'Athènes.

Blümner, H. 1887. Technologisches. In *Festschrift zur Begrüssung der vom 28. September bis 1. Oktober 1887 in Zürich tagenden XXXIX. Versammlung deutscher Philologen und Schulmänner, dargeboten von der Universität Zürich*, 23–39. Zürich, Zürcher & Furres.

Fiedler, M., Franz, St., Gjongecaj, Sh., von Hesberg, H., Hinz, V., Lahi, B., Pánczél, Sz.-P., Quantin, F., Shehi, E., Shkodra-Rrugia, B. 2011. Neue Forschungen zum hellenistisch-römischen Theater von Apollonia (Albanien). *Mitteilungen des Deutschen Archäologischen Instituts, Römische Abteilung* 117, 55–200.

Forbes, R. J. ²1964. Bitumen and Petrolium in Antiquity. In R. J. Forbes, *Studies in Ancient Technology* I, 1–124. Leiden, E. J. Brill.

Grewe C.-V. 2005, *Untersuchung der naturwissenschaftlichen Fragmente des stoischen Philosophen Poseidonios und ihrer Bedeutung für seine Naturphilosophie*. Unveröffentlichte Dissertation, Universität Hannover.

von Hesberg, H. und Eck, W. 2008. Reliefs, Skulpturen und Inschriften aus dem Theater von Apollonia (Albanien). *Mitteilungen des Deutschen Archäologischen Instituts, Römische Abteilung* 114, 31–97.

Kalicz, N. 2006. Die Bedeutung der schwarzen Gefäßbemalung der Lengyeé-Kultur aus Aszód (Kom. Pes, Ungarn), *Analele Banatului* S.N. 14/1, 135–158.

Korkuti, M. 1995. *Neolithikum und Chalkolithikum in Albanien*. Internationale Interakademische Kommission für die Erforschung der Vorgeschichte des Balkans. Monographie 4. Mainz, Zabern.

Krishnan, J. M. und Rajagopal, K. R. 2003. Review of the uses and modeling of bitumen from ancient to modern times. *American Society of Mechanical Engineers, Applied Mechanics Reviews* 56, 149–214.

Lahi, B. und Fiedler, M. 2010. Ausgrabungen im Zentrum von Apollonia (Albanien). Vorläufige Ergebnisse zu der sog. Amphorenmauer und ihrer Umgebung. *Mitteilungen des Deutschen Archäologischen Instituts, Römische Abteilung* 116, 213–255.

Larson J. 2001. *Greek Nymphs: Myth, Cult, Lore*. Oxford, University Press.

McGrail, S. 2004. *Boats of the World: From the Stone Age to Medieval Times*. Oxford, University Press.

Morris, S. P. 2006. Illyrica Pix. The Exploitation of Bitumen in Ancient Albania, in L. Bejko, und R. Hodges (Hrsg.), *New Directions in Albanian Archaeology. Studies presented to Mustafer Korkuti*, 94–106. Tirana, International Centre for Albanian Archaeology.

Moustakis, N. 2006. *Heiligtümer als politische Zentren. Untersuchungen zu den multidimensionalen Wirkungsgebieten von polisübergreifenden Heiligtümern im antiken Epirus*. München, Herbert Utz.

Partington, J. R. 1999. *A History of Greek Fire and Gunpowder*. Baltimore, The Johns Hopkins University Press.

Papadopoulos, J. K., Bejko, L. und Morris, S. P. 2007. Excavations at the Prehistoric Burial Tumulus of Lofkënd in Albania. A Preliminary Report for the 2004–2005 Seasons. *American Journal of Archaeology* 111, 105–145.

Platz-Horster, G. 1995. Die Berliner Glasamphora aus Olbia. *Journal of Glass Studies* 37, 35–50.

Reyer-Völlenklee, S. 2005. Antike Flickungen aus bituminöser Masse an apulisch-rotfiguriger Keramik, in G. Grabherr, B. Kainrath, A. Larcher und B. Welte (Hrsg.), *Vis imaginum*. Festschrift für Elisabeth Walde zum 65. Geburtstag, 399–404. Innsbruck, Institut für Klassische und Provinzialrömische Archäologie der Universität Innsbruck.

Rolley, C., Langlois, J., Balcar, N. und Regert, M. 2004–2005. Du bitume à la résine: à propos du remplissage d'une oreille de griffon de Delphes. *Bulletin de correspondance hellénique* 128–129, 55–65.

Greek Islands

La céramique hellénistique à Délos: Essai de quantification des productions dans le matériel des fouilles de L'aphrodision des Stèsiléos

Jean-Sébastien Gros

Abstract

The aim of the paper is to show the relative importance the major productions imported in Delos. After reviewing each production we examine quantification data from well stratified assemblages from the Aphrodision of Stesileos. For the Moldmade Bowls it appears that Asia Minor productions are not necessarily present in majority. Also, the analyse allows us to minimize the economical impact of the most well know productions like, Campanian black glaze, thin walled, ESA, or Cnidian.

Keywords: Delos, Aphrodision, quantification, imports, Moldmade Bowl, ESA

Introduction

Durant la période hellénistique, Délos a bénéficié d'une place privilégiée dans le commerce méditerranéen. Son sanctuaire panhellénique, sa situation géographique au centre des Cyclades, son indépendance puis, plus encore, l'institution du port franc sous le contrôle d'Athènes en 166 av. J.-C. sont autant d'exceptions qui ont favorisé la circulation des biens sur l'île sacrée. Les productions majeures de l'ensemble du bassin méditerranéen sont attestées à Délos. Il est cependant délicat d'estimer les quantités ou les proportions de chacune des importations de ce faciès céramique riche et hétéroclite. C'est cet aspect quantitatif que nous souhaitons ici sonder. Nous nous proposons de confronter les résultats obtenus jusqu'à présent aux données récentes de la fouille de l'Aphrodision.

Cadre de la recherche

Une part importante des données céramologiques est fournie par l'étude des amphores. Les travaux de V. Grace[1], suivis par ceux de J.-Y. Empereur, ont mis en évidence la présence majoritaire de timbres amphoriques rhodiens avant le deuxième quart du IIe siècle av. J.-C., puis leur graduelle diminution pendant la période postérieure à 166 av. J.-C. Les anses timbrées cnidiennes[2] sont alors les plus nombreuses, mais le phénomène le plus remarquable est l'émergence des estampilles latines jusqu'aux catastrophes de 88 et 69 av. J.-C.[3] Ces premières observations semblent correspondre parfaitement à une histoire économique délienne où les années postérieures à l'institution du port franc en 166 av. J.-C. voient le déclin de l'influence rhodienne ainsi qu'une présence romaine de plus en plus marquée. Toutefois, J.-Y. Empereur met en garde contre une interprétation trop rapide des chiffres. Puisque les anses timbrées ne sont pas directement représentatives de la circulation des amphores, il convient d'adopter une approche quantitative raisonnée. Bien que l'étude des timbres soit particulièrement enrichissante, de nombreuses difficultés se présentent dès que des analyses quantitatives sont mises en oeuvre. La publication de la totalité des amphores découvertes dans des ensembles homogènes permettrait de rectifier l'effet du prisme réducteur que constituent les seuls timbres. Pour les contextes typiquement 'déliens' de la fin du IIe et de la première moitié du Ier siècle av. J.-C., la publication du mobilier céramique de l'îlot de la Maison des Comédiens ne peut qu'éveiller notre curiosité en dévoilant seulement deux amphores Lamboglia 2 sans révéler l'identification des 10 autres amphores entières retrouvées[4].

C'est à cette période et essentiellement pendant le premier tiers du Ier siècle av. J.-C. qu'ont été observées les modifications du faciès céramique les plus marquantes. Ces modifications concernent en premier lieu l'influence romaine. J.-P. Morel a, le premier, orienté ses recherches sur le petit mobilier céramique susceptible d'accompagner les amphores italiques. Son expérience de la céramique campanienne lui a permis d'identifier quelques 150 fragments à Délos[5]. Il s'agit du lot le plus important de cette production retrouvé dans l'Orient méditerranéen; il reflète, sans aucun doute, les particularités de la situation délienne. Mais les éléments de comparaison manquent. Nulle part n'est précisée la proportion de cette production par rapport au reste du matériel. Il semble par ailleurs que différents points de vue s'affrontent au sujet de l'importance de cette

1 Grace 1952.

2 Empereur 1982, 224–225.
3 Empereur 1982, 224–225.
4 Bruneau *et al.* 1970, pl. 45; voir aussi Chatzidakis 1997.
5 Morel 1986, 486.

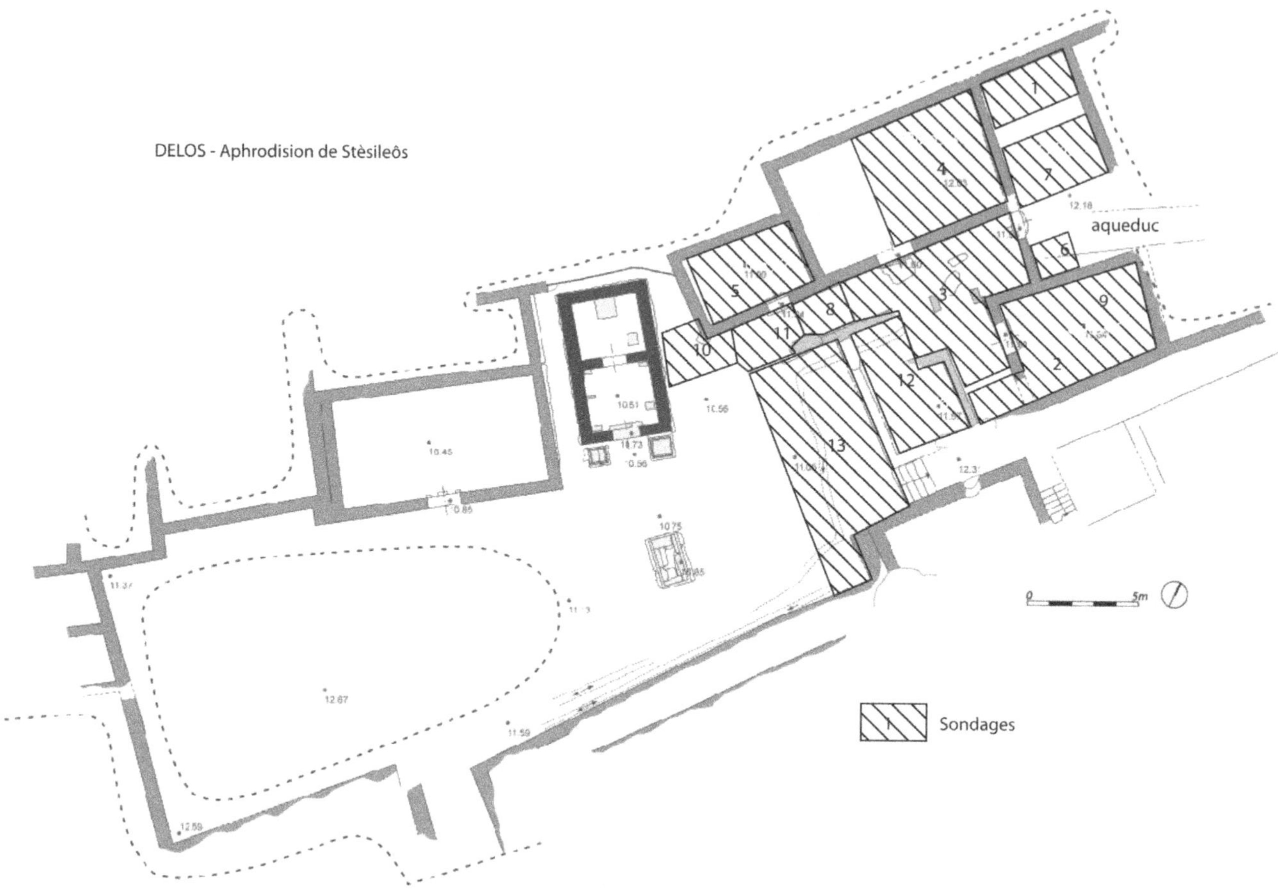

Fig. 1. plan de l'Aphrodision de Stésiléos (EfA)

production dans l'Orient méditerranéen. Elle a d'abord été considérée comme anecdotique[6]; mais une récente étude postule, au contraire, que les 'céramiques campaniennes A [...] sont bien représentées sur les sites portuaires de Méditerranée orientale'[7], mentionnant Alexandrie, Beyrouth et Thasos[8]. Cependant, dans ce cas encore, les arguments quantitatifs ne sont soutenus par aucune estimation chiffrée[9].

Même au regard des 150 fragments de Délos, il est certain que la céramique campanienne ne constituait, en fin de compte, qu'un modeste complément de charge des cargaisons d'amphores italiques à destination de l'Est. Peut-être le phénomène de complément est-il plus distinct à Délos pour d'autres productions italiques? C'est ce que semblent suggérer les comptages réalisés dans le mobilier céramique de la Maison des Sceaux. A. Peignard-Giros estime à environ 13% les vases et fragments de types occidentaux[10], dont une part essentielle est représentée par les productions à paroi fine et une part plus modeste par les plats à *orlo bifido* ou à revêtement interne rouge pompéien[11]. Ainsi l'influence italienne serait-elle fortement ressentie à Délos. Pourtant, dans ce cas encore, les éléments de comparaison manquent, ce qui exclut toute certitude dans les hypothèses émises. A. Peignard-Giros concède même que la présence des productions occidentales pourrait ne pas être particulière à Délos[12].

Les 13% évoqués pour les productions occidentales laissent entendre l'existence d'autres productions, *a fortiori* orientales, au moins aussi importantes. Ce sont les productions de céramiques fines qui apportent le plus de renseignements sur ces importations dans les contextes déliens de la fin du IIe et du début du Ier siècle av. J.-C. La publication qui offre la meilleure vue d'ensemble du mobilier céramique est celle de l'îlot de la Maison des Comédiens. Ph. Bruneau y soulignait déjà la place prépondérante dans le matériel céramique des

6 Morel 1986, 487.
7 Elaigne 2007, 537.
8 Elaigne 2007, 526.
9 La prise en compte de Thasos dans cette étude est-elle justifiée par les quatre seuls fragments énumérés? (Elaigne 2007, 533). Si c'est le cas, Tinos doit aussi être mentionnée avec les exemplaires de céramique campanienne retrouvés dans les groupes Cd, (Etienne and Braun 1986, 214 ; Ea, 221 ; Eb, 222).

10 Peignard-Giros 2007, 214.
11 Peignard-Giros 2000.

12 Peignard-Giros 2007, 216, s'appuyant pour les *orlo bifido* et plats à engobe rouge pompéien sur Hayes 2000, 291.

importations orientales[13]. Depuis, les identifications des productions ont progressé et c'est à A. Peignard-Giros que l'on doit la plupart des rectifications et précisions[14]. Les principaux centres de production mentionnés sont ceux d'Éphèse, de Cnide, et tout particulièrement celui de Pergame. D'autres études proposent de nouvelles identifications de céramiques provenant des grands centres de production du le bassin égéen[15]. Dans ces cas encore les arguments quantitatifs sont sans cesse invoqués comme preuve de relations commerciales entre Délos et les cités hellénistiques. Pourtant, il est rare qu'une analyse systématique du matériel soutienne l'argumentation.

Abordons maintenant le cas d'un ensemble particulièrement important à Délos, celui des bols à reliefs. Là aussi, la suprématie ionienne semble s'affirmer[16]. Mais si A. Laumonier livre quelques éléments de statistiques par contextes[17], les proportions par rapport aux autres types font défaut[18]. Il serait cependant particulièrement intéressant d'étudier les bols à reliefs attiques pour la période postérieure à 166 av. J.-C., qui correspond à la fois à l'apogée de la production et au retour de la domination athénienne sur l'île.

Les études conduites jusqu'à présent ont donc sans conteste permis de mettre en lumière le caractère éclectique du faciès céramique délien, que caractérisent notamment les importations à grande échelle. Mais elles ont aussi révélé leurs limites. Elles conduisent à relativiser les interprétations concernant la circulation et le commerce de la céramique à Délos. Ces problématiques, intimement liées aux aspects quantitatifs, peuvent et doivent bénéficier de nouvelles observations basées sur le matériel de fouilles récentes.

C'est donc en connaissance de cause que l'étude du mobilier des fouilles de l'Aphrodision a été entreprise avec comme principale problématique la quantification des importations.

L'Aphrodision de Stèsiléos

L'Aphrodision de Stèsiléos est un sanctuaire privé de Délos situé à une centaine de mètre au Nord du théâtre (**Fig. 1**). Un petit temple aptère de marbre blanc s'ouvre vers le Sud, face à un autel à frontons. Autour s'organisent cinq *oikoi* qui délimitent l'espace du sanctuaire lors de sa plus grande emprise. La chronologie du sanctuaire est particulièrement bien connue. Son établissement date de

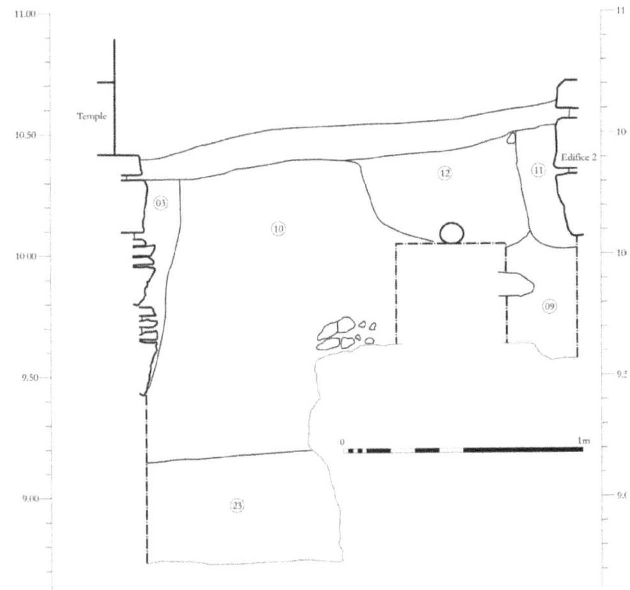

Fig. 2. paroi Nord du sondage 10 (B. Vergniaud)

la toute fin du IVe siècle av. J.-C.[19] et son activité perdure jusqu'aux catastrophes de 88 et 69 av. J.-C. Le secteur est ensuite laissé dans un état d'abandon que trouble seule la construction d'un aqueduc, peut-être au IIIe siècle ap. J.-C.[20]

Plusieurs opérations archéologiques ont eu lieu dans le secteur, en 1912, puis à nouveau en 1957 et 1958[21]. Quelques sondages profonds sont mentionnés mais les fouilleurs se sont généralement arrêtés soit sur les derniers sols antiques (Oikos 5) soit aux premières assises de fondation des murs. A l'occasion du projet de publication de l'ensemble du sanctuaire par C. Durvye, la fouille de l'Aphrodision a été reprise en 2005 et se poursuit en alternant chaque année opérations de terrain et missions d'étude. A présent, le mobilier céramique mis au jour compte plus de soixante mille fragments répartis chronologiquement entre le VIIIe et le Ier siècle av. J.-C., mais dont l'immense majorité date de la période hellénistique.

Afin d'évaluer quantitativement les proportions des céramiques importées, nous nous sommes d'abord concentrés sur les ensembles stratigraphiques d'un sondage restreint. La zone 10, située entre le temple et l'oikos 2, n'a malheureusement pas révélé de couche d'occupation ou d'abandon; mais la relation stratigraphique avec le temple des remblais qui y ont été fouillés fournit un précieux *terminus ante quem* de 304 av. J.-C. pour les couches

13 Bruneau *et al.* 1970, 240.
14 Présentées dans sa thèse de doctorat sur le matériel de la Maison des Sceaux (Peignard 1993) ainsi que dans les différents articles qui ont suivi.
15 Voir par exemple Elaigne 2007 sur les importations rhodiennes.
16 Cette catégorie était autrefois identifiée comme une production délienne en raison de son abondance sur l'île sacrée: Courby 1922, 378.
17 Laumonier 1977, 7–10.
18 Bruneau 1970, 240–242, confirme que la catégorie des bols à reliefs de profil ionien sont les plus nombreux.

19 Durvye 2006, 95.
20 La stratigraphie montre que l'aqueduc a été construit bien après l'abandon du secteur. Malheureusement, cette phase de construction n'est accompagnée par aucun artefact datable postérieur au Ier siècle av. J.-C., ni dans le sondage réalisé sur son tracé, ni dans l'ensemble du sanctuaire. Pour une proposition de datation de l'aqueduc, voir Moretti, Fincker 2011, 167–169.
21 Salviat, 1958, 821; Salviat 1959, 787.

Fig. 3. céramique fine de l'US 100100005 (J.-S. Gros)

antérieures à la construction du sanctuaires (**Fig. 2**). Les fouilles de F. Salviat dans cette zone ont décapé les sols de circulation jusqu'à l'assise de réglage, mais la partie inférieure préservée de la tranchée de fondation a pu être fouillée. Elle correspond à deux unités stratigraphiques équivalentes, US3 et US6, dont le matériel céramique assez pauvre est très fragmentaire. La céramique fine permet de se rendre compte sans peine du caractère très hétérogène de cet ensemble, avec des datations comprises entre le VIIème et le IVème siècle av. J.-C.

Zone/ US 10.3 + 10.6	*NR*	**NMI**
céramique commune	130	1
céramique culinaire	19	1
céramique fine	88	8
Total	237	10

Les tessons archaïques sont particulièrement nombreux. On reconnaît parmi eux des productions de Corinthe, de Paros, ou encore un bol à oiseau ionien. Les productions de l'époque classique sont représentées par des céramiques à vernis noir, dont deux à décor de godrons en relief. Rien dans cet ensemble ne permet de suggérer une date postérieure à 304 av. J.-C.[22] Une image similaire peut être observée dans la tranchée de fondation probablement contemporaine de l'oikos 2 (US11), mais ces ensembles sont trop hétérogènes et trop restreints en nombre d'individus pour qu'il soit possible de pratiquer sur eux une étude des provenances. La diversité des productions est notable; il est possible que cela corresponde à la fréquentation internationale de Délos dès les périodes archaïque et classique, mais, étrangement, aucun fragment de céramique fine n'est attribuable aux ateliers attiques. La même observation peut être faite pour un matériel plus conséquent dans cette même zone. La

[22] Excepté, peut être, un énigmatique tesson à pâte orange et revêtement non grésé rouge (inventaire 10.3.2).

Fig. 4. bols à reliefs 90080025 (J.-S. Gros)

tranchée de fondation du temple est creusée dans les US2 et 10 qui constituent un important remblai de terrassement préalable à l'installation du sanctuaire[23].

US *US2 + 10 + 5 + 13*	*NR*	**NMI**
amphores	232	7
céramique commune	694	8
céramique culinaire	150	9
céramique fine	258	38
Total	1334	62

Bien que la chronologie soit mixte – la céramique identifiée date des Ve et IVe siècles – il est intéressant d'observer la proportion de la céramique attique dans un ensemble correspondant à une phase antérieure à l'Indépendance. Seule une dizaine de fragments sont probablement attiques, respectivement 3 et 2 dans les US2 et 5, alors que l'US10 (**Fig. 3**), un peu plus importante, contient 3 fragments de panse de canthare dont la paroi est décorée de godrons en relief. Cette même US contient un fragment de canthare de la technique *West slope* dont la pâte orangée et poreuse exclut une identification attique. Le décor est composé d'une ligne incisée ondulée formant une boucle contenant le rehaut blanc[24].

L'ensemble de ce matériel antérieur au temple relativise sévèrement la place des importations attiques. Il apparaît clairement que la production athénienne constitue une part marginale de la céramique fine et une part insignifiante de la totalité des catégories.

Bol à reliefs

Qu'en est il pour la période postérieure à 166 av. J.-C.? Les bols à reliefs constituent un corpus particulièrement révélateur sur cette question. La production attique s'identifie aisément par sa pâte, son revêtement grésé, mais surtout par son profil particulier et la récurrence d'un sillon externe sous la lèvre ou sous la base, peint en rouge au miltos ou au cinabre. Le second critère de sélection de ce corpus est la synchronie évoquée entre l'acmé de la production des bols à reliefs attiques et la période de domination athénienne à Délos.

Nous avons déjà remarqué que la suprématie des bols à reliefs 'ioniens' est incontestée à Délos[25]. Les comptages

[23] Le comptage de ces ensembles révèle un coefficient de fragmentation important caractéristique d'un remblai remanié. Il est encore possible de leur ajouter le matériel de deux autres US équivalentes, US5 et US13.

[24] La présence de ce fragment est troublante dans ce contexte antérieur au IIIe siècle, alors que cette production se rencontre dans les contextes bien avancés de ce même siècle (Rotroff 1991, 60).

[25] On peut y ajouter un ensemble de 140 bols à reliefs découverts récemment dont tous les individus publiés ou illustrés sont de profil ionien: Chatzidakis 1997, Chatzidakis 2003, 271.

Fig. 5. bols à reliefs 90030012 (J.-S. Gros)

réalisés sur le matériel de l'Aphrodision confirment et chiffrent ces proportions. Pour un total proche de 850 fragments de bols à reliefs, seule une cinquantaine est attique. Cette faible représentation de la production attique paraît en contradiction avec la situation politique de Délos. Les importations de céramique attique, et plus particulièrement de bols à reliefs, seraient-elles totalement indépendantes de la domination athénienne? Et si, comme il est vraisemblable, il existe un lien entre la situation politique et les importations de céramique, comment expliquer ce déséquilibre en faveur des bols à reliefs 'ioniens'?

Afin de relativiser ces chiffres, il est utile d'observer le cas d'autres sites voisins. A Naxos, la publication d'ensembles de la basse époque hellénistique permet de noter l'importation massive de bols à reliefs ioniens, mais aussi d'identifier une production locale qui adopte des profils identiques à ces derniers[26]. Une image similaire s'observe à Tinos où la majorité des bols à reliefs sont de type ionien[27]. Là encore, la production locale de bols du même type est attestée, mieux même qu'à Naxos, tant par les analyses en laboratoire que par les fragments de moules retrouvés[28].

Ces exemples montrent qu'une présence majoritaire de bols à reliefs de type ionien dans les contextes hellénistiques cycladiques est courante. Le cas de Délos semble ne pas être particulier. Mais il faut espérer que des comptages précis permettront une comparaison plus fine: différences de proportions, même légères, pourraient être significatives. Les cas de Tinos et de Naxos mettent en lumière la diversité des centres de production des bols à reliefs de type ionien. Il est, en effet, bien établi que cette catégorie a été produite dans plusieurs centres non seulement sur les côtes ioniennes mais aussi dans les Cyclades. Il faut donc interpréter les proportions des bols à reliefs attiques en connaissance de cause: ils sont minoritaires face à la production de plusieurs et non pas d'une seule cité concurrente.

26 Kolia 2006, 102–103.

27 Ils sont accompagnés de quelques exemplaires attiques: voir par ex. Etienne et Braun 1986, 216.

28 Etienne et Braun 1986, 224 pl. 111.

Fig. 6. bol à relief attique 90080025 (J.-S. Gros)

Fig. 7. fragment de proto ESB 130940016 (J.-S. Gros)

Pour que l'analyse soit complète, il serait, bien entendu, indispensable de distinguer la proportion des bols à reliefs de chaque centre de production. C'est chose impossible pour le matériel fragmentaire de l'Aphrodision; mais il est possible de se baser sur les statistiques établies par A. Laumonier pour l'ensemble très riche des bols à reliefs déliens qu'il a étudiés[29]. Il apparaît que certains ateliers sont mieux représentés que d'autres, tout particulièrement les ateliers éphésiens avec en premier lieu celui 'du monogramme' qui fournit environ le quart de la collection. On peut supposer des répartitions plus ou moins similaires pour la présence des productions ioniennes parmi les bols à reliefs de l'Aphrodision.

Afin de mieux saisir la place de la production attique parmi les bols à relief de l'Aphrodision, nous avons réalisé un comptage précis du materiel provenant du secteur de l'Oikos 5.

Oikos 5	*'IONIENS'*		*ATTIQUE*		**AUTRES**	
Zone/ US/ Inv.	NR	NMI	NR	NMI	NR	NMI
2.2.21	10	1				
9.3.12	5	2	9	2	2	1
2.3.5	11	1	1		1	
2.4.12	4	2	1		1	
2.2.26					3	
9.1.4	2		1			
2.2.27	18	4	3	2	1	
9.2.25	16	6	11	4	2	1
TOTAL	66	16	26	8	10	2
%	64,7	61,5	25,5	30,8	9,8	7,7

Ce comptage fait apparaître une présence plus marquée des bols attiques alors qu'ils sont, par exemple, totalement absents d'un autre contexte clos que nous évoquerons plus bas, celui du comblement d'un puits désaffecté au Ier siècle av. J.-C. Nous n'expliquons pas encore cette disparité contextuelle, même si un facteur d'ordre chronologique est envisageable. Par contre, ces chiffres révèlent sans ambages l'importance que peuvent avoir les bols à reliefs attiques (**Fig. 4, 5**) à Délos. Même s'ils sont trop fragmentaires pour que soient systématiquement identifiés les ateliers[30], il est indéniable que l'ensemble est au moins aussi important que le mieux représenté des ateliers ioniens.
Cette observation rétablie de façon indubitable la place de la production attique à Délos et relativise l'apparente hégémonie des bols à reliefs de type 'ionien'. Mais il ne s'agit là que d'une vision très partielle du mobilier céramique et il reste à établir les proportions des autres grandes productions de céramiques fines.

Le puits

La fouille d'un contexte clos de l'Aphrodision permet d'analyser ces productions. Il s'agit d'un puits situé dans l'angle Sud-Est du sanctuaire[31]. L'ouverture était scellée par une plaque de schiste; le remplissage et le scellement de ce puits ont dû être réalisés pendant la dernière phase d'activité sur le secteur, c'est-à-dire entre 88 et 69 av. J.-C. si l'on en juge par la présence de fragments d'assiettes en proto-ESB (**Fig. 7**).

29 Laumonier 1977, 7–11.

30 On notera seulement la présence probable de 'l'atelier de Bion' (**Fig. 6**).

31 La fouille a été réalisée en plusieurs passes techniques (US13.90 à 13.99) avec pour seule distinction stratigraphique un comblement un peu plus dense sous l'US 13.95. La fouille a été interrompue à une profondeur de 4m sous le niveau du sol, la présence de l'eau et l'étroitesse du puit n'ayant pas permis d'atteindre le fond.

Les principales productions connues à Délos se retrouvent dans ce matériel dans des proportions variées. En premier productions indéterminées est le plus conséquent. De fait, lieu, il est important de souligner que le groupe des ce groupe représente généralement une grande part du mobilier, mais en tant'qu 'indéterminé', il n'est souvent que brièvement commenté dans les publications d'ensembles.

De plus, il faut considérer que ce comptage ne fait état que de la céramique fine, qui est plus aisément identifiable que le reste du matériel: les céramiques communes et culinaires n'offrent pas autant de caractéristiques permettant de distinguer les différentes productions. Il faut donc se résoudre à composer avec ce facteur d'indétermination lors de l'analyse, et en premier lieu, ne pas hésiter à fournir les chiffres de notre ignorance.

céramique fine du puits	**fragments**	**fragments de bord**
sigillée chypriote?	2	1
coupes carénées cnidiennes	23	3
ESA	70	9
céramique à fond blanc	45	0
bols à reliefs 'ioniens'	44	11
paroi fine	4	0
'pergaménienne'	15	4
plat à paroi oblique	21	4
proto-ESB	6	2
unguentaria	6	0
vernis noir	24	10
grey ware	4	0
west slope	12	2
productions indéterminées	124	31

Dans la céramique fine, la sigillée orientale A est la mieux représentée[32]. Il s'agit essentiellement d'assiettes forme 4, accompagnées d'un exemplaire de chaque forme 22, 23 (**Fig. 8**) et 17. Si l'origine exacte de cette production est encore discutée, elle semble être limitée à la région syro-palestinienne[33].

céramique du puits	**fragments**	**fragments de bord**
amphores	3386	36
céramiques communes	1620	84
céramiques culinaires	646	93
céramiques fines	401	75

Les bols à reliefs sont ensuite les plus nombreux; comme nous l'avons mentionné plus haut, il s'agit uniquement de bols à profil ionien. Les ateliers n'ont pas été identifiés, mais il est très probable qu'une partie de ce matériel provient des ateliers de la région cycladique, Naxos, Tinos ou Amorgos. L'absence des productions attiques est ici intéressante puisqu'elle pourrait s'expliquer par notre datation du remplissage aux environs ou immédiatement après 69 av. J.-C.[34]

La céramique à fond blanc est représentée par un fragment de *thymiaterion* et des fragments de deux *lagynoi* de fabriques différentes. Plusieurs centres de production existent, mais malgré les tentatives menées sur le matériel de Délos[35], l'origine de ces objets reste difficile à identifier[36].

Le groupe dont l'origine est sans doute la mieux connue est celui des bols carénés cnidiens. Non seulement la forme, mais aussi la pâte fine le plus souvent grise et le revêtement partiel sur la partie supérieure de la coupe sont autant de critères pour l'identification.

Les coupes à décor de guillochis, forme VIA[37], comptent parmi les autres importations cnidiennes régulièrement rencontrées à Délos (**Fig. 9**)[38], mais sont absentes du puits.

La céramique fine à vernis noir est encore très présente. Les fragments ont une pâte et un revêtement de qualités très diverses qui représentent autant de centres de production. Si ces derniers n'ont pu être identifiés, il semble encore une fois que la production attique soit absente, ainsi, de façon plus surprenante, que la céramique 'campanienne'. Seul un fragment de fond, dans le lot 93.14, présente une pâte et un revêtement métallescent bleuté proche de la campanienne B, mais sa forme n'est pas répertoriée. De même, le fond du lot 97.9 a une pâte proche de la campanienne B et un décor de trois bandes de guillochis, mais les cercles concentriques caractéristiques de cette production lui font défaut. Il faut donc en conclure que si le nombre absolu de céramiques campaniennes identifiées à Délos est bien plus important que sur les autres sites de l'Orient méditerranéen[39], il ne s'agit malgré tout que d'une importation très marginale.

Le matériel du puits présente encore un exemple d'importation chypriote (**Fig. 8 130910015**)[40]. Cette identification est intéressante car inédite à Délos mais l'isolement du vase coupe court à toute tentative d'interprétation. Quant aux autres groupes de la céramique fine retrouvée dans le puits, comme les *unguentaria* ou la céramique *west slope*, leur étude est rendue malaisée par

[32] Les exemplaires appartiennent tous à la sous-classe b à pâte chamois claire.
[33] Hayes 2009, 13.

[34] Un examen partiel du matériel amphorique par N. Badoud (EFA) a révélé la présence de timbres datés entre 88 et 69 av. J.-C.
[35] Elaigne 2007, 521.
[36] Kolia 2006, 108.
[37] Kögler 2011.
[38] Au moins 9 individus pour les seules fouilles de l'Aphrodision.
[39] Morel 1986, 486–487.
[40] Hayes 1991, no. 36 pl. XIX.

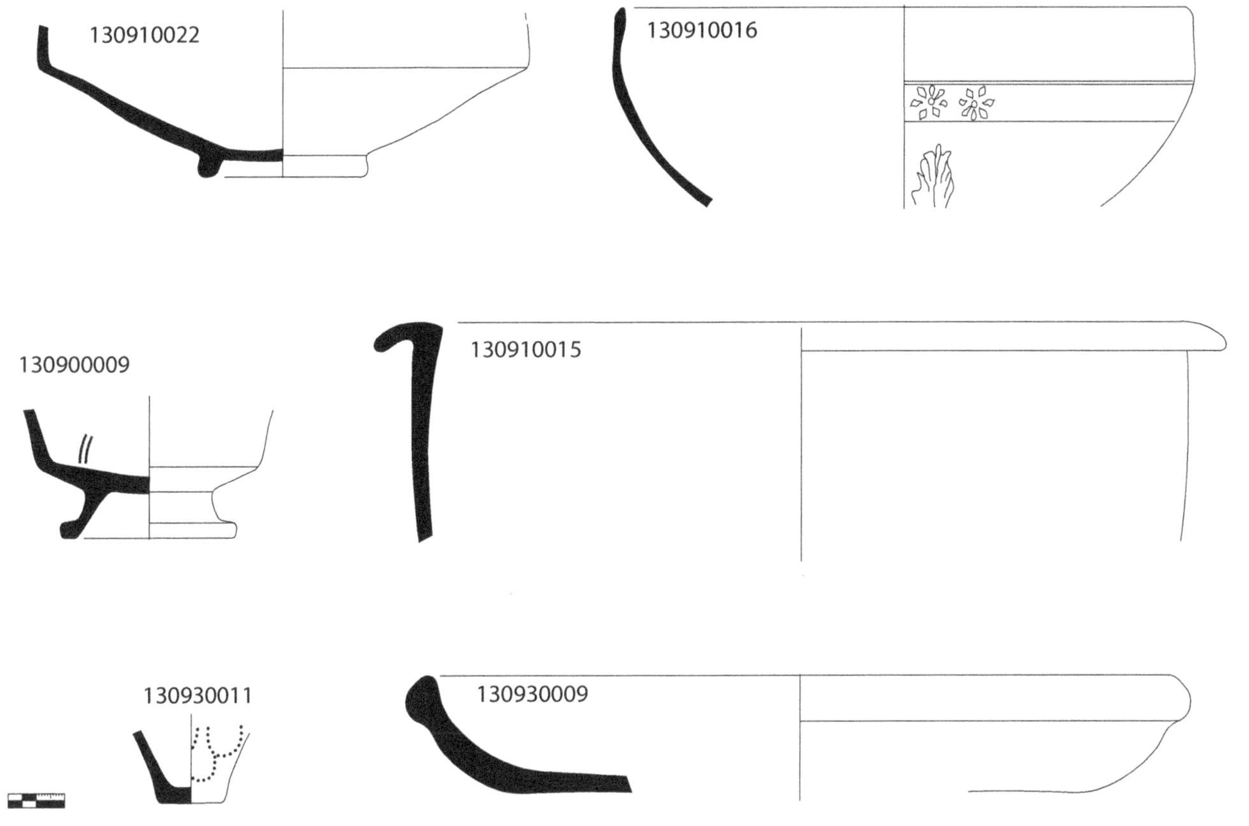

Fig. 8. céramique importée du puits (J.-S. Gros)

les incertitudes qui demeurent sur la localisation de leurs centres de production, dans la mesure où ils sont produits simultanément dans plusieurs centres. Dans ces cas, il est impossible d'établir des statistiques d'importations précises.

Conclusion

Les importations de céramique sont particulièrement intéressantes à observer dans le contexte spécifique délien, et ce pour deux raisons. D'une part Délos était le centre d'un important réseau de circulation entretenu par la fréquentation panhellénique du sanctuaire autant que par les conditions commerciales privilégiées offertes par le port franc; d'autre part il n'y avait pas sur l'île de production céramique d'importance pour répondre à la demande locale. De ce fait, la présence de productions originaires de tout le bassin méditerranéen n'est pas surprenante; les Déliens sont même parmi les premiers à importer la céramique italique ou la sigillée orientale. L'analyse quantitative vient cependant tempérer cette vision d'une céramique cosmopolite, l'importance des productions les mieux connues étant très relative. L'ESA, championne des exportations méditerranéenne dans la première moitié du Ier siècle av. J.-C., ne représente finalement qu'une très faible part de l'ensemble de la céramique. Il faut aussi garder à l'esprit qu'une grande part de la vaisselle devait

Fig. 9. fragment de bol cnidien à guillochis 90010004 (J.-S. Gros)

être produite dans des ateliers régionaux, c'est-à-dire probablement dans des ateliers cycladiques. Malgré nos efforts, il est vain de vouloir obtenir une quantification précise de toutes les productions. Les analyses en laboratoire montrent que les identifications à l'œil nu sont sujettes à caution[41].

[41] Et ce même pour les productions les mieux connues: pour la cérami-

Pour établir des statistiques précises, il faudrait procéder à l'analyse en laboratoire de la totalité des individus d'un ensemble conséquent. A supposer que cela soit possible, il faudrait encore que nous disposions de bases de références complètes, répertoriant et localisant un nombre indéfini de productions. Malgré ces restrictions, l'analyse quantitative est loin d'être vaine, puisque l'étude d'ensembles homogènes apporte des informations précieuses, permettant par exemple de mettre en évidence la faible proportion des 'grandes' productions, ou, à l'inverse, de rendre leur importance à d'autres productions sous-estimées.

Jean-Sébastien Gros
19, rue M. Cerdan
FR-92300 Levallois
jsgros3@hotmail.com

Bibliography

Blondé, F. 2007. *Les céramiques d'usage quotidien à Thasos au IVe siècle avant J.-C.*. Études thasiennes XX. Athènes, École française d'Athènes.

Bruneau, P., Vatin, C., Siebert, G., Lévy, E., et Grace, V. 1970. *L'îlot de la Maison des Comédiens*, Exploration archéologique de Délos XXVII. Paris, De Boccard.

Chatzidakis, P. 1997. Κτίριο νότια του 'Ιερού του Προμαχώνος' Μια taberna vinaria στη Δήλο. In *Δ΄ Επιστημονική Συνάντηση για την Ελληνιστική Κεραμική*. Μυτιλήνη 1994, 291–307. Athènes, Ypourgeio Politismou.

Chatzidakis, P. 2003. *Δήλος*. Athènes, Olkos.

Courby, F. 1922. *Les vases grecs à reliefs*, Bibliothèque des écoles françaises d'Athènes et de Rome CXXV. Paris, De Boccard.

Durvye, C. 2006. Aphrodite à Délos : culte privé et public à l'époque hellénistique. *Revue des Études Grecques* 119, 83–113.

Elaigne, S. 2007. La circulation des céramiques fines hellénistiques dans la région égéenne: un aperçu à partir du mobilier de Délos et de Thasos. *Bulletin de Correspondance Hellénique* 131, 515–557.

Empereur, J.-Y. 1982. Les Anses d'amphores timbrées et les amphores: aspects quantitatifs. *Bulletin de Correspondance Hellénique* 106, 219–233.

Etienne, R., et Braun, J.-P. 1986. *Ténos I: le sanctuaire de Poséidon et d'Amphitrite, Bibliothèque des Ecoles françaises d'Athènes et de Rome. 1ère série 263.* Athènes, École française d'Athènes; Paris, De Boccard.

Grace, V. 1952. Timbres amphoriques trouvés à Délos. *Bulletin de Correspondance Hellénique* 76, 514–540.

Hayes, J. W. 1991. *The Hellenistic and Roman pottery.* Paphos 3. Nicosia, Department of antiquities.

Hayes, J. W. 2000. From Rome to Beirut and beyond. Asia Minor and eastern Mediterranean trade connections. *Rei Cretariae Romanae Fautorum acta* 36, 285–297.

Hayes, J. W. 2009. *Roman Pottery: The Fine Ware Import – Typology*. The Athenian Agora XXXII. Princeton, NJ., American School of Classical Studies at Athens.

Kögler, P. 2011. *Feinkeramik aus Knidos vom mittleren Hellenismus bis in die mittlere Kaiserzeit (ca. 200 v.Chr. bis 150 n.Chr.)*. Wiesbaden, Reichert.

Kolia, E.-I. 2006. *Ελληνιστική κεραμική από τη Νάξο.* Athènes, TAP.

Laumonier, A. 1977. *La Céramique hellénistique à reliefs. 1. Ateliers « ioniens »*. Exploration archéologique de Délos XXXI. Paris, De Boccard.

Meyza, H., et Peignard-Giros, A. 2009. Analyses de tessons de « sigillées pergaméniennes » de Délos. *Bulletin de Correspondance Hellénique* 133, 227–240.

Morel, J.-P. 1986. Céramiques à vernis noir d'Italie trouvées à Délos. *Bulletin de Correspondance Hellénique* 110, 461–493.

Moretti, J.-C. and Fincker, M. 2011. Les réseaux d'eau courante à Délos. In C. Abadie-Reynal (ed.), *Les réseaux d'eau courante dans l'antiquité*, 159–172. Rennes, Presse universitaire.

Peignard-Giros, A. 2000. Habitudes alimentaires grecques et romaines à Délos à l'époque hellénistique : le témoignage de la céramique. *Pallas* 52, 209–220.

Peignard-Giros, A. 2007. Hellénisation et romanisation en Méditerranée orientale à l'époque hellénistique: l'exemple de la céramique. *Pallas* 73, 203–219.

Peignard, A. 1993. *La Céramique de la Maison des sceaux à Délos*. Unpublished PhD thesis, University of Paris IV.

Rotroff, S. I. 1991. Attic West Slope Vase Painting. *Hesperia* 60, 59–102.

Salviat, Fr. 1958. Délos, Aphrodision de Stésiléos. *Bulletin de Correspondance Hellénique* 82, 821.

Salviat, Fr. 1959. Délos, Aphrodision de Stésiléos. *Bulletin de Correspondance Hellénique* 83, 787.

que 'pergaménienne', voir Meyza et Peignard-Giros 2009; pour la céramique attique, Blondé 2008.

Importations et imitations de céramiques occidentales à Délos à la fin de l'époque hellénistique tardive

Annette Peignard-Giros

Abstract

In the destruction layers of the insulae dated 88 BC or 69 BC in Delos, many western shapes were indentified, especially cooking pans (orlo bifido and Pompeian Red Wares) and thin walled wares. These two series show that the inhabitants of Delos were familiar with italian food and drink consumption habits. The cooking pans were imported from central Italy, but no eastern imitation can be attested within the pottery used in the Delos houses before their destruction. The thin walled ware vases are also well represented in the Delos contexts. Three series of shapes were used by the inhabitants of Delos: the beaker – traditional italian shape – the kantharos, and the mug-jug. Some beaker fragments bear decorations which show that they were most probably produced in Asia Minor – e.g. white dots –, maybe from Pergamene origin. Some of the jugs may have been produced in Pergamon, too. Some fragments bear decoration patterns which must be dated later than the 69 BC destruction (pine cone decoration, thumb decoration, thorn decoration, ...). The kantharoi are present in the pre-69 BC contexts; the thin walled ware version was probably inspired by fine wares shapes of Western Asia Minor, with black or red glaze, and then transferred to the thin walled ware workshops in Italy and Spain. Eventhough it is difficult to precise when exactly the Asia Minor workshops started to produce thin walled wares counterparts to the glazed kanharoi, several different fabrics of thin walled ware vases were identified in Delos, which clearly show that the workshops were numerous, and at least some of them can be considered as eastern imitations of the western products.

Keywords: Delos, Asia Minor pottery, Pergamenian pottery, cooking pots, thin walled wares, orlo bifido pan, Pompeian Red Ware.

La céramique mise au jour dans les fouilles de l'Ecole Française d'Athènes n'a fait l'objet d'aucune publication d'envergure depuis le chapitre consacré par Ph. Bruneau en 1972 au matériel de l'Îlot des Comédiens[1]. L'étude de la céramique de la Maison des Sceaux, dont j'ai présenté les premières conclusions en 1997, m'a conduite à m'interroger sur la présence importante de céramiques d'origine occidentale, surtout d'Italie centrale, dans les habitations déliennes détruites en 88 et en 69 av. J.-C[2]. Cette question a fait l'objet d'un article[3] dans lequel j'entendais démontrer que le cas de Délos était particulier, et que la présence d'un nombre important de vases italiques s'expliquait par l'importance de la communauté des commerçants italiens.

Mais les publications parues au cours de la dernière décennie m'ont conduite à réexaminer cette question, et la spécificité du cas de Délos ne me paraît plus si sûre. La synthèse publiée en 2000[4] par J. Hayes tend à montrer que l'importation des céramiques occidentales sur les sites de Méditerranée orientale présente le même aspect qu'à Délos: les plats à cuire de type « orlo bifido » ou à engobe rouge pompéien, les céramiques campaniennes, et les vases à parois fines sont répandus dans tous les contextes de la fin IIe–début Ier s. av. J.-C.

Dans les couches de destruction datables de 69 av. J.-C. à Délos, la quantité de céramiques occidentales est plus importante que sur les autres sites analysés par J. Hayes, mais la céramique des dépôts déliens est particulièrement abondante, pour toutes les catégories de vases.

La présente étude s'attachera à deux séries: les céramiques culinaires (plats à orlo bifido et plats à engobe rouge pompéien), et les vases à paroi fine. Ces deux catégories de vases présentent un intérêt particulier, d'une part parce qu'elles sont un indicateur de l'adoption, dans le courant du Ier s. av. J.-C., d'habitudes alimentaires romaines à Délos, mais aussi dans de nombreux autres sites de Méditerranée orientale, y compris de taille modeste, comme Tel Anafa[5]; l'idée d'un facies exceptionnel de Délos paraît donc à reconsidérer. D'autre part, ces deux séries posent le problème des imitations orientales des prototypes italiques, et de la date où commencent ces imitations; les ensembles déliens fournissent, en particulier pour les vases à parois fines, quelques informations utiles.

1 Seules diverses sélections de céramiques provenant de fouilles plus récente ont été publiées; Chatzidakis 1994; Chatzidakis 1997; Zapheiropoulou and Chatzidakis 1994a; Zapheiropoulou and Chatzidakis 1994b; Peignard 1997; Peignard-Giros 2000.

2 Sur les destructions de Délos lors des attaques de 88 et 69, Bruneau 1968, 658–691; Bruneau *et al.* 1996, 34–50.

3 Peignard-Giros 2000, 209–220.

4 Hayes 2000, 285–297.

5 Berlin 1993, 35–44; Berlin 1997, 106.

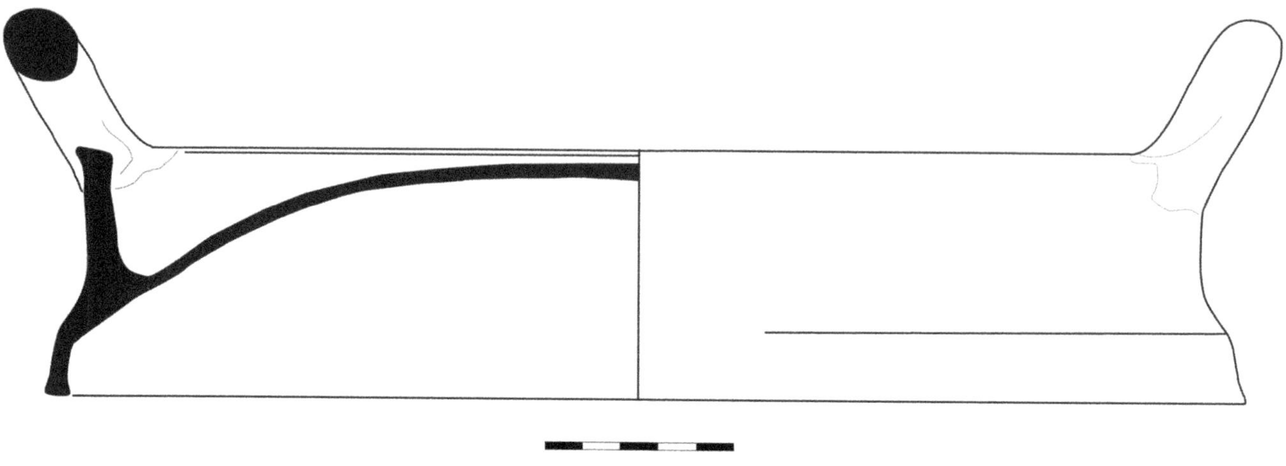

Fig. 1. Clibanus de la Maison des sceaux (dessin N. Sigalas, Ecole Française d'Athènes)

L'essentiel du matériel présenté ici provient d'habitations détruites lors du sac de 69 av. J.-C. Dans le secteur de Skardhana[6], les maisons ont été habitées pendant une courte période, entre leur construction à l'extrême fin du IIe s. av. J.-C., et leur destruction en 69 av. J.-C., et les traces de réoccupations dans ce quartier sont très sporadiques. Le second contexte analysé est celui de la Maison des stucs, et des magasins voisins, situés au Nord-Est du quartier du théâtre[7]; ce secteur, situé à l'intérieur du « mur de Triarius », a été plus densément réoccupé après le sac de 69.

Plats à four italiques

Parmi les céramiques de cuisine, les plats italiques se distinguent nettement, sur le plan morphologique, des séries de marmites de tradition hellénique. Les plats à orlo bifido[8] et les plats à engobe rouge pompéien[9], sont caractéristiques de l'adoption, dans les régions orientales du bassin méditerranéen, de nouvelles habitudes culinaires: l'alimentation intègre des galettes de céréales, à côté des traditionnelles bouillies[10].

J. Hayes a récemment souligné la place des plats à engobe rouge pompéien, avec les sigillées italiennes et les gobelets à parois fines, comme indicateur de la diffusion d'un mode de vie « à l'italienne » dans des régions éloignées[11]. A Délos, la situation est un peu différente, dans la mesure où un grand nombre des habitants de l'île à la fin de l'époque hellénistique étaient d'origine italienne, ou avaient vécu un certain temps en Italie, dans le cas des affranchis. L'utilisation de plats de cuisson italiques ne constituait donc pas, pour eux, une révolution dans leur mode de vie, mais simplement la continuation, sous d'autres cieux, des habitudes qu'ils avaient dans leur région d'origine.

La question qui peut être soulevée, mais pas résolue dans l'état actuel de nos connaissances, est celle du rôle que Délos a pu jouer, en raison du rayonnement international de son emporion, dans la diffusion de ces nouvelles coutumes en Méditerranée orientale. Les fragments de plats à engobe rouge pompéien trouvés dans la Maison des sceaux appartiennent au premier ou au deuxième groupe d'argiles défini par D. P. S. Peacock[12], considérés tous deux comme des fabriques d'Italie centrale. A Athènes, le plus ancien plat à engobe rouge interne est daté du début du Ier s. av. J.-C.[13].

Les habitations déliennes ont livré un nombre non négligeable d'exemplaires complets, qui montrent que ces plats étaient couramment en usage avant les destructions

6 Le quartier est composé de plusieurs *insulae*: Îlot des comédiens (Bruneau 1970, 239–262); Îlot des bijoux, Îlot des bronzes, Maison des sceaux et Cour à l'épée (Siebert 2001).

7 La publication de ce secteur est à paraître prochainement. Présentation des résultats de la fouille: Daux 1959, 785–786; Daux 1960, 854–856.

8 Bruneau *et al.* 1970, 259, n° D 222 pl. 49; Chatzidakis 2000, 120 fig. 3 n° 23, et 78, γ, à gauche; Chatzidakis 2004, 653 pl. 319, γ pl. 320, 9.

9 Chatzidakis 2000, 120 fig. 3, n 46 (improprement classé dans les céramiques de table) ; Peignard 1997, 310 pl. 231, a.

10 Dernière synthèse sur la question: Rotroff 2006, 193. Voir également Peignard-Giros 2000, 211–213 pour le cas de Délos.

11 Hayes 2008, 119–120.

12 Peacock, 1977, 147–161: groupe 1: 149–153; groupe 2: 153–154 Le groupe 1 (149–153) est caractérisé par une argile dure, brun-rouge, contenant des inclusions noires de taille moyenne, et parfois blanches, et où les particules de mica sont rares. La terre du groupe 2 est très voisine de la précédente, mais plus claire et très micacée ; la distinction entre les deux pâtes n'est pas toujours aisée. Peacock suggérait une origine égéo-anatolienne pour la fabrique 2, majoritaire, selon lui, dans le matériel de l'Agora d'Athènes, mais J. Hayes (Hayes 2008, 120 n° 12 et 13) suggère plutôt une origine italienne pour ce groupe aussi.

13 Hayes 2008, 121: bien qu'il ait été trouvé dans un contexte plus récent, J. Hayes le relie aux destructions de Sylla. La période de fabrication et de circulation des plats à engobe rouge pompéien s'étend, selon J. Hayes, entre 100 av. J.-C. et 100 ap. J.-C., et ils sont régulièrement exportés pendant toute cette période.

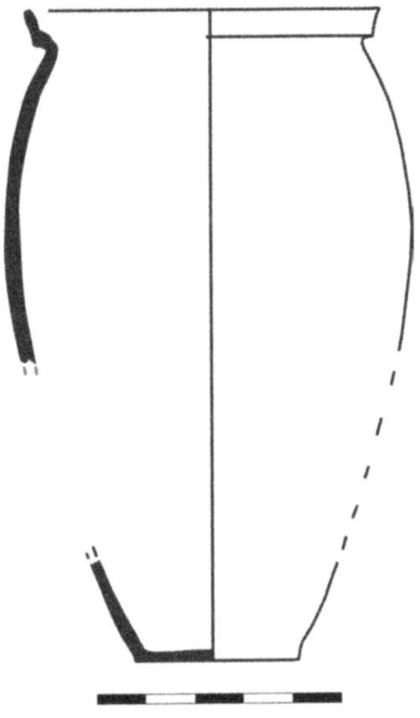

Fig. 2. Gobelet à paroi fine de la Maison des sceaux (forme Ricci I/1) (dessin S. Sorin, Hisoma)

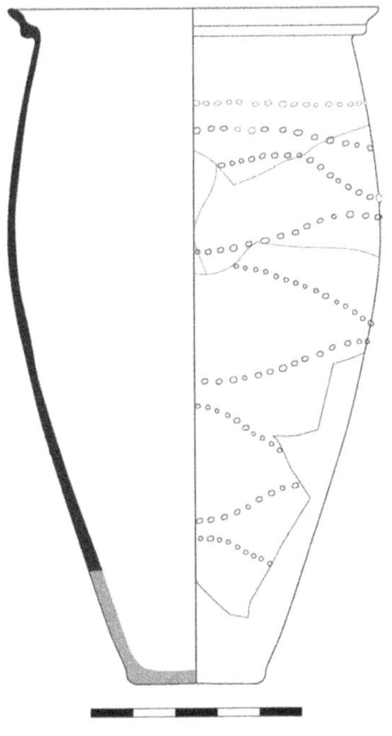

Fig. 3. Gobelet de l'Îlot des Bronzes (forme Ricci I/1) (dessin S. Sorin, Hisoma)

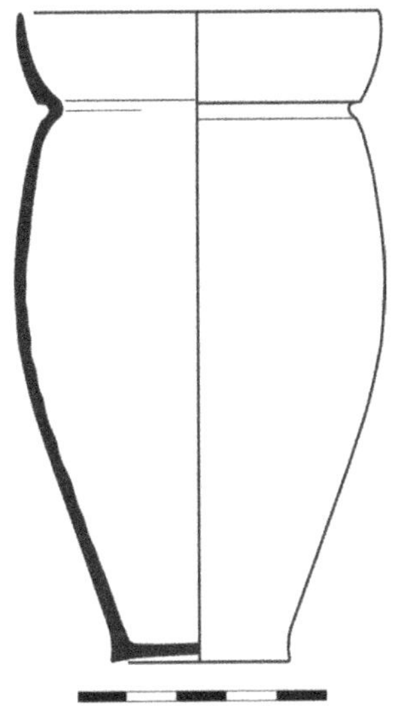

Fig. 4. Gobelet de forme I/362 (provenance inconnue) (dessin S. Sorin, Hisoma)

de 69 av. J.-C. L'existence d'imitations dès cette période semble peu probable.

Les plats à orlo bifido font eux aussi partie de la batterie de cuisine usuelle dans toutes les maisons[14]. Ce type de plat apparaît vraisemblablement en Italie aux alentours de 125 av. J.-C. S. Rotroff signale, sur l'Agora d'Athènes, la présence à la fois d'exemplaires importés et d'imitations locales dans les contextes de destructions de Sylla[15]. L'existence d'imitations orientales à Tel Anafa et à Beyrouth est attestée également, mais dans des contextes plus tardifs que ceux des habitations déliennes. Dans la Maison des stucs, quatre fragments attestent l'usage de ces plats juste avant ou juste après 69 av. J.-C.[16]. Une origine micrasiatique est probable pour au moins trois d'entre eux, mais les informations stratigraphiques manquent pour les dater d'avant ou après le sac de 69 av. J.-C.

L'influence de la cuisine italienne sur les habitudes alimentaires des habitants de Délos se manifeste aussi par un type d'ustensile original, dont plusieurs exemplaires sont attestés dans divers contextes[17]. Il s'agit d'un clibanus, utilisé pour la cuisson des aliments sub testu (**Fig. 1**). En dehors de Délos, aucun parallèle n'est attesté jusqu'à présent. L'argile de ces clibani est identique à celle d'une série de grandes lopades à flanc vertical, originaires du bassin égéen. On a affaire ici à un objet fabriqué dans la région égéenne, mais sur le modèle d'un ustensile italien, et pour un usage en lien avec un mode de cuisson occidental.

L'ensemble des céramiques culinaires mises au jour dans les quartiers d'habitation délien fournit quelques informations chronologiques sur la circulation et l'imitation des plats de cuisson italiques dans le bassin oriental de la Méditerranée.

Ces plats se développent en Italie à partir du dernier quart du IIe s. av. J.-C. Avec la création de la province romaine d'Asie, et l'afflux de nombreux Italiens en Asie Mineure, la céramique italique accompagne ces nouveaux venus, et influence les pratiques alimentaires de populations locales. La demande croissante de plats à four suscite la création d'ateliers micrasiatiques et égéens, pour satisfaire cette demande croissante. Le matériel mis au jour à Délos confirme les indices chronologiques suggérés par les contextes athéniens: dès la fin du IIe s. av. J.-C., en un très court laps de temps, les plats italiques sont importés

14 La céramique culinaire italique n'est cependant pas majoritaire : dans la Maison des Sceaux, elle représente moins d'un tiers de la totalité des vases de cuisson.

15 Rotroff 2006, 193. D'après elle, les importations de plats à orlo bifido se seraient nettement ralenties après le sac de 86, et les imitations auraient cessé aussi. Cette observation ne s'applique pas à la situation délienne.

16 La céramique mise au jour dans ce secteur a drastiquement triée au moment de la fouille, et seuls les fragments de bords ou de fonds ont été conservés. Il est donc impossible de dire si ces plats étaient complètement conservés ou non.

17 Sur la forme et l'usage de cet objet, Peignard 2000, 213–214 et pl. 19 fig. 7. Autre exemplaire, provenant de l'Agora des Italiens : Chatzidakis 2000, 127–128 pl. 77, b.

Fig. 5. Fragments de gobelets à décor de points blancs – Îlot des bijoux (photo A. Peignard-Giros)

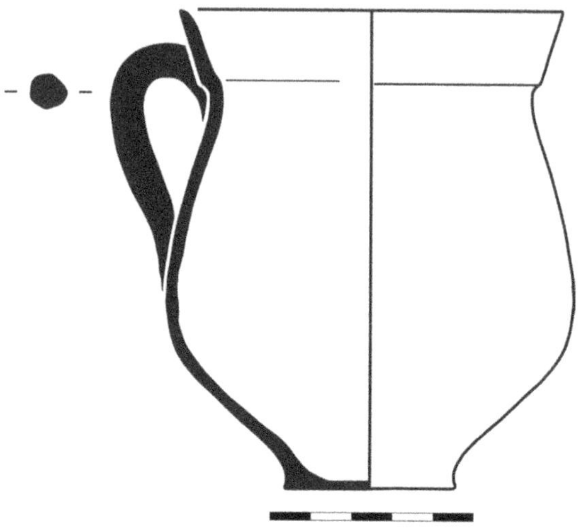

Fig. 6. Gobelet à une anse verticale (provenance inconnue) (dessin S. Sorin, Hisoma)

d'Italie, puis imités en Orient. Des fragments de plats italiens et de leurs imitations orientales sont attestés dans tous les contextes déliens, autour de 69 av. J.-C.

Vases à parois fines

Les vases à parois fines constituent également une catégorie bien représentée dans les habitations déliennes. Deux grandes séries de formes sont attestées, des gobelets et des canthares, à quoi s'ajoute un groupe de cruches-gobelets à une anse (parfois appelés « mugs » dans les publications anglo-saxonnes). Ces séries témoignent d'influences réciproques entre les productions occidentales et les productions orientales; elles sont également présentes dans des contextes antérieurs à 69 av. J.-C.

La forme la plus courante est le gobelet de forme Ricci I/1[18], qui est fabriquée en Italie centrale (Etrurie sans doute) entre le second et le troisième quart du IIème siècle av. J.-C. (**Fig. 2**). Le décor le plus répandu comprend des guirlandes de points de barbotine, combinées ou non à des lignes parallèles sous le bord ou près du fond[19] (**Fig. 3**). On peut mettre émettre l'hypothèse que l'usage de ces points blancs est une innovation orientale, sans doute La seconde forme attestée à Délos est le gobelet de type I/362 (**Fig.4**). Le début de la production de ces gobelets à haut bord arrondi et légèrement renflé se situe vers le début du Ier siècle av. J.-C. en Italie centrale[20]. Cette forme est largement attestée en Méditerranée orientale. Un exemplaire complet provenant de l'Îlot des Comédiens a été publié par Ph. Bruneau[21]: comme la majorité de la céramique, il provient de l'impasse au Sud de l'insula, et peut dater de la destruction des maisons, en 88 av. J.-C. selon Ph. Bruneau.

Certains fragments de gobelets de forme I/1 ou I/362 présentent des décors de points de barbotine blanche, contrastant fortement avec la couleur de l'argile, généralement rouge ou grise (**Fig. 5**). Cette couleur inhabituelle du décor se retrouve sur quelques tessons à Pergame et à Athènes[22]. Le fragment d'Athènes est daté par J. Hayes de la période postérieure au sac de Sylla (probablement vers 50–20 av. J.-C.) et il suggère une origine micrasiatique. La présence de ce décor à Pergame aussi pourrait indiquer une fabrication pergaménienne. Seulement quatre fragments à décor de points blancs ont été mis au jour dans l'Îlot des Comédiens, et plusieurs autres dans l'Îlot des Bijoux[23].

On peut mettre émettre l'hypothèse que l'usage de ces points blancs est une innovation orientale, sans doute micrasiatique, inspirée des prototypes à points de barbotine

[18] Ricci 1985, 231–358. Les gobelets de forme I/1 présentent une lèvre moulurée, un profil plus ou moins tendu, et un fond plat ou légèrement concave (243–244 pl. 78, 1 et 2).

[19] C'est le type de décor I de Ricci 1985, pl. 105, 4.

[20] Ricci 1985, 248 pl. 79, 6 et 7.

[21] Bruneau 1970, D179, 257, pl. 47; D180, l'autre gobelet à paroi fine publié, est très proche de la forme I/ 172, mais sans bord évasé.

[22] Pergame: Japp 1999, 328 n° 102 pl. 28; Athènes: un fragment de fond (n 1502, Hayes 2008, 97, 259 fig. 46), semble être fait d'une argile identique à celle des exemplaires déliens.

[23] Siebert 2001, plan I. L'un des fragments a été trouvé sur le sol de la pièce A-A" de l'habitation I de l'*insula*, et faisait donc partie du matériel en usage lors de la destruction de 69 av. J.-C.

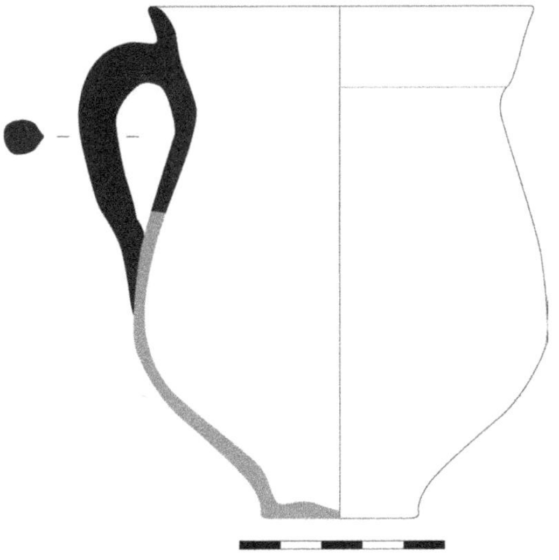

Fig. 7. Gobelet à une anse verticale de l'Îlot des Bronzes (67E1190) (dessin N. Sigalas, École Française d'Athènes)

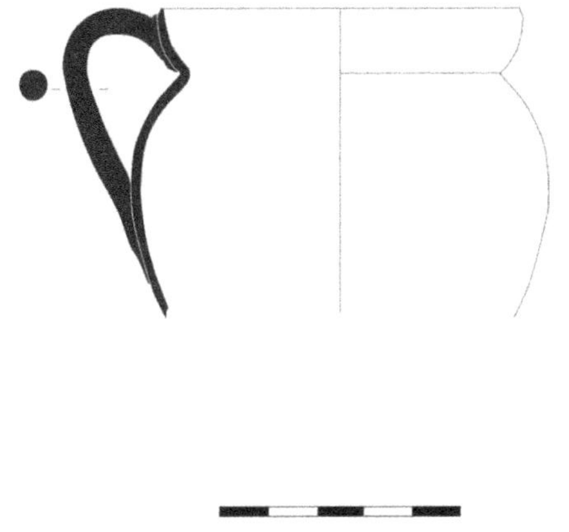

Fig. 8. Fragment de gobelet du secteur de la Maison des stucs (59M499) (dessin S. Sorin, Hisoma)

importés d'Italie, qui apparaît dans le premier tiers du Ier s. av. J.-C., peut-être à Pergame[24].

La série des cruches-gobelets à une anse verticale, avec une lèvre oblique ou légèrement rentrante, séparée de la panse par un étranglement marqué, est attestée à Athènes comme à Pergame (**Fig. 6**). Selon J. Hayes[25], une partie de ces vases au moins était fabriquée à Phocée, entre la fin du Ier s. et la fin du IIe s. ap. J.-C.

La forme est cependant déjà présente à Pergame dans des contextes plus anciens[26]. A Délos, le n° 67E1190[27] (**Fig. 7**) est très proche des exemplaires pergaméniens.

Le type Y/A de Pergame, daté du Ier av. J.-C., a également des parallèles à Délos, le mieux conservé étant le n 59M499[28] (**Fig. 8**), provenant du magasin K, à l'ouest de la Maison des Stucs[29].

Dans ces deux cas, non seulement les profils, mais également les caractéristiques de l'argile sont très proches. Deux fragments présentent une variante non attestée à Pergame, avec une anse torsadée[30]. Plusieurs fragments de gobelets portent des décors postérieurs au sac de 69 av. J.-C.: décors d'épines, décor de pétales imbriqués (type « pomme de pin », « pine cone decoration »), et décor de dépressions (« thumb decoration »). La comparaison avec le matériel de l'agora d'Athènes confirme cette datation[31]: les épines apparaissent vers la fin de l'époque républicaine et le début du règne d'Auguste[32], sur une forme fermée, et deux fragments de canthares. Un fragment de gobelet de forme I/362 portant ce type de décor est attesté à Ephèse[33].

---

24 Japp 2003, 246 suppose que la production de vases à parois fines a commencé à Pergame vers la fin du Ier ou le début du IIe s. av. J.-C.

25 Hayes 2008, 102 n° 53. Des fragments de bords similaires au numéros 1597 à 1600 (267, et fig. 50) ont été identifiés à Délos dans plusieurs contextes ; ces vases sont datés à Athènes entre le dernier quart du Ier s. et le milieu du IIe s. ap. J.-C.

26 Japp 1999, 318: Le type intermédiaire entre cruches de type X et de type Y est caractérisé par un bord oblique, surmontant une panse plus ou moins marquée vers l'extérieur. Voir également Japp, 2003, 245–246.

27 Parallèle le plus proche: n° 25 de Pergame, Japp 1999, 317 fig. 2 et 318. Le fragment a été trouvé sur le sol de la pièce ET de l'habitation I de l'Îlot des Bronzes, et appartient à la céramique en usage dans la dernière phase d'occupation. Mais ce secteur a connu plusieurs remaniements et réoccupations après 69 av. J.-C., comme le montre la construction des fours, dont la date n'a pas pu être précisée. Ce « type intermédiaire », sur la base des trouvailles des citernes de Pergame, peut se dater entre la fin Ier s. av. J.-C. et le Ier s. ap. J.-C.

28 Parallèle à Pergame : Japp 1999, 317, 319 n° 33 fig. 2.

29 Ce secteur de magasins a livré une très abondante quantité de céramique, parmi laquelle on a aussi des exemples de vases à paroi fine avec décor de dépression, sans doute postérieurs à 69 av. J.-C.

30 Le n° 66D2927 provient de la pièce AP de l'habitation VI de l'Îlot des Bijoux, et le n° 68E3248 a été trouvé sur le sol de la place au Nord de l'Îlot des Bronzes, dans un secteur de dépotoir. L'habitation VI de l'Îlot des Bijoux ne montre pas de trace de réoccupation après les destructions de 69. Mais la place et les boutiques qui la bordent, au Nord de l'Îlot des Bronzes, ont été réoccupés, cf. Siebert 2001, 103–105. L'argile du fragment de la place Nord de l'Îlot des bronzes pourrait correspondre à la fabrique phocéenne décrite par Hayes, en revanche celui de l'Îlot des Bijoux présente une paroi plus mince, et une argile plus fine et plus brun-orangée. Pour aucun de ces deux fragments, la datation ne peut être précisée.

31 Hayes 2008, 95–104.

32 Hayes 2008, 97 n° 16. Les trois exemples de l'agora d'Athènes se trouvent non pas sur des gobelets, mais sur des canthares et sur une forme fermée, le n°1577, p. 45 et fig. 49. Datation proposée par J. Hayes: 50–30 av. J.-C. J. Hayes considère ce dernier fragment comme un exemple précoce de ce décor, et il provient d'un contexte qui pourrait être pré-augustéen. Les deux canthares se datent dans la même fourchette chronologique (n° 1535, 262, fig 47 vers 50–10 av. J.-C.; n° 1537, 262 fig. 48: époque augustéenne).

33 Rogl 2007, 181–193.

Fig. 9. Fragment de gobelet à décor d'écailles (Îlot des bijoux)

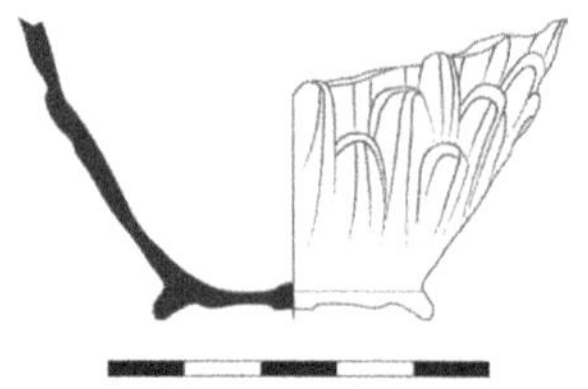

Fig. 10. Fragment de gobelet à décor d'écailles imbriquées de l'Îlot des bijoux (65D1935)

Fig. 11. Fond de gobelet à décor à dépressions (provenance inconnue)

Le décor en « écailles de pomme de pin » est bien connu sur les bols à reliefs d'époque hellénistique[34], mais aussi sur les gobelets à parois fines d'Occident, où il dérive du décor d'épines[35]. À Athènes, ce décor apparaît vers le milieu du Ier s. av. J.-C[36].

Dans les fouilles des maisons déliennes, deux fragments ont été identifiés: l'un provient de l'Îlot des Bijoux, mais sans provenance plus précise, et l'autre de l'habitation III du même Îlot, mais il n'y a pas d'information stratigraphique sur sa position dans les décombres, et aucune trace d'occupation postérieure à 69 n'a été observée dans ce secteur. Le premier tesson (**Fig. 9**) est un fragment de bord en amande et de panse, dans une argile grisâtre, certainement pas italienne; la pâte est légèrement micacée, et la présence de quelques paillettes de mica doré pourrait évoquer une origine pergaménienne. Le second fragment est un fond complet de gobelet (**Fig. 10**), pour lequel un parallèle peut être identifié à Pergame[37], mais l'argile semble moins fine que sur l'exemplaire délien.

Pour ce qui concerne les décors à dépressions, ils sont surtout fréquents sur les canthares, mais un fragment de fond montre que ce décor se trouvait parfois, mais plus rarement, sur des gobelets[38] (**Fig. 11**).

Deux bases de canthares sans fond annulaire, portant ce décor, sont attestés dans le magasin J, à l'Ouest de la Maison des Stucs; ils présentent deux argiles très différentes, fine et grise à ocre pour l'un, avec une base plate (**Fig. 12**), et

[34] Le rapprochement avec les bols à reliefs à décor d'écailles pourrait donner à penser que ce motif est typique de la partie orientale du bassin méditerranéen, et les fragments athéniens paraissent plus anciens que les exemples recensés par A. Ricci en Occident, mais il faudrait pouvoir établir une chronologie beaucoup plus précise de l'apparition de ce décor en Orient et en Occident.

[35] Ricci 1985, 329, décors 10, 99, 100, 226; pl. 107, 13–15. Aucun exemple n'est antérieur au début de notre ère. Autres décors de même type: décor 98, p. 329 pl. 107, 16: attesté à Cosa, à partir du règne de Tibère, jusqu'à celui de Claude. C'est le plus proche parallèle pour les fragments déliens.

[36] Hayes 2008, 259 n° 1500 fig. 46: le lieu de production de ce gobelet pourrait être Rome ou Naples, d'après Hayes; le dépôt est daté des années 50–25 avant notre ère. Le fond annulaire n°1548, p. 263 fig. 48, présente des écailles encore proches des types « épines », disposées en diagonales, et non imbriquées. Hayes date ce fragment des années 40–10 av. J.-C., le contexte du dépôt étant plus tardif, postérieur à 50, mais avec des inclusions d'époque augustéenne. J. Hayes suppose qu'il s'agit d'une importation d'Italie, sans exclure l'hypothèse d'une origine cnidienne. Le bord de gobelet n°1525, p. 259 fig. 47, peut-être d'Italie du Nord, se trouve dans un contexte du début du Ier s. de notre ère. Les fragments 1525–1527 se placent dans les années 40–70 ap. J.-C. (Hayes 2008, 98–99), et le gobelet le mieux conservé de la série, n° 1526, p. 261 fig. 47 pl. 74, est daté avec prudence par J. Hayes (« perhaps Claudian period ? »); il provient du même contexte que le gobelet globulaire à anse verticale n° 1564 (p. 264 fig. 49), plus tardif (vers 40–70 ap. J.-C.).

[37] Le profil du pied se retrouve sur les numéros 76, 79, Japp 1999, 323 fig. 3, daté simplement du Ier s. av. J.-C.

[38] La provenance de ce fragment est inconnue, mais il fait partie du matériel des fouilles anciennes de Délos, donc de secteurs où une réoccupation postérieure au milieu du Ier s. av. J.-C. est plus probable. Un très petit fragment de fond plat de gobelet, avec la trace d'une dépression en bas de la panse a été trouvé sur le sol du magasin b au Nord de l'Îlot des Bronzes.

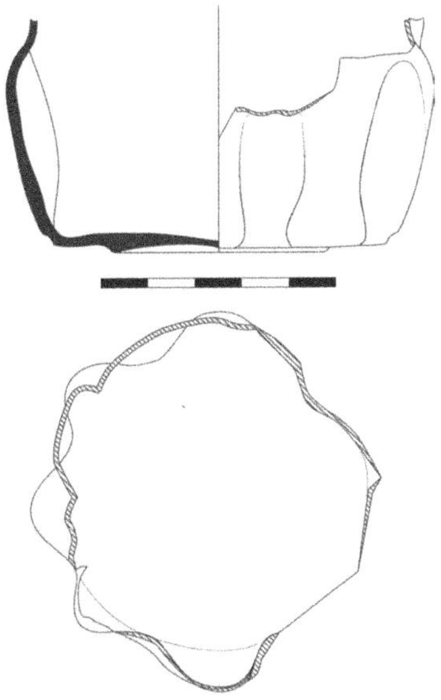

Fig. 12. vase à décor à dépression du secteur de la Maison des stucs (dessin S. Sorin, Hisoma)

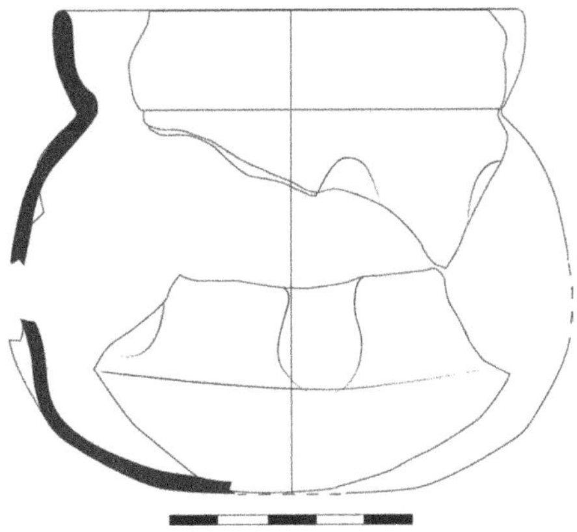

Fig. 13. vase à décor à dépression du secteur de la Maison des stucs (dessin S. Sorin, Hisoma)

Fig. 14. pot à décor d'épines et de cordes (provenance inconnue) (photo A. Peignard-Giros)

plus rouge brunâtre et plus grossière pour l'autre, avec un fond arrondi[39] (**Fig. 13**).

Les parallèles en parois fines se trouvent à Pergame[40], et surtout parmi les productions cnidiennes, mais ces dernières, en dépit de la ressemblance formelle, sont certainement d'origine différente, car elles portent un engobe, à la différence des exemplaires déliens[41]. Elles sont datées de l'époque augustéenne, ce qui est probablement aussi le cas des deux exemplaires de la Maison des Stucs.

Le seul vase complet de cette époque mis au jour à Délos est un grand gobelet, sans provenance précise (**Fig. 14**). Il présente une décoration typique de cette période, avec une combinaison de « cordes » et d'épines ou pétales imbriqués[42]. Plusieurs fragments publiés par P. Kögler présentent un bord de forme très proche[43]. La question posée par P. Kögler de l'usage de ces « gobelets » est particulièrement intéressante: si la forme rappelle, en effet, les premières séries de gobelets à parois fines, l'absence d'engobe intérieur, selon elle, exclut leur usage comme vase à boire[44]. J'ajouterais que la taille de l'exemplaire complet de Délos rend cet usage encore plus improbable[45]. L'utilisation comme vase de stockage, suggérée par P. Kögler, paraît très vraisemblable.

Autre forme typiquement romaine, le « modiolus » est attesté en très petite quantité[46] (**Fig. 15**), comme sur

[39] Le profil du fond pourrait suggérer une chytra, mais le décor de dépression paraît peu probable sur un vase de cuisson. J. Hayes signale, à Athènes, un exemplaire très proche, dans une fabrique cnidienne, mais avec un vernis rouge-orangé, datant du début du Ier s. de notre ère (Hayes 2008, 269 n° 1617 fig. 51).

[40] Japp 1999, 326–327 n° 95 fig. 4.

[41] Kögler 2010, 347–349: coupe carénée G149 (Fundkomplex G) avec décor de dépressions, fig. 43; Kn 412–417 fig. 65 pl. 63.

[42] L'argile est gris-ocre, et la présence d'un engobe n'est pas exclue. Le vase a été sans doute endommagé par le feu, et l'intérieur en a été totalement recouvert de plâtre à la restauration.

[43] Ces fragments présentent, en haut de la panse, des décors de points et une lèvre à bourrelet: G151 à G155, Kn 448, p. 354–357. P. Kögler signale, p. 355, un parallèle à Ephèse daté de la fin du Ier s. av. J.-C. C'est la datation la plus vraisemblable aussi pour le vase de Délos.

[44] Kögler 2010, 356–357.

[45] Le vase fait environ 17 cm de haut.

[46] Il y a au moins trois fragments de fonds identifiés : 59M62 a et b, proviennent du magasin J, à l'ouest de la Maison des Stucs, et un fragment de l'Îlot des Bijoux: 64D282 (habitation II, pièces I-J). Un modiolus presque complet a été trouvé dans les fouilles de Cl. Hasenohr sur l'Agora des Compétaliastes (ce matériel est actuellement étudié par Chr. Mitsopoulou).

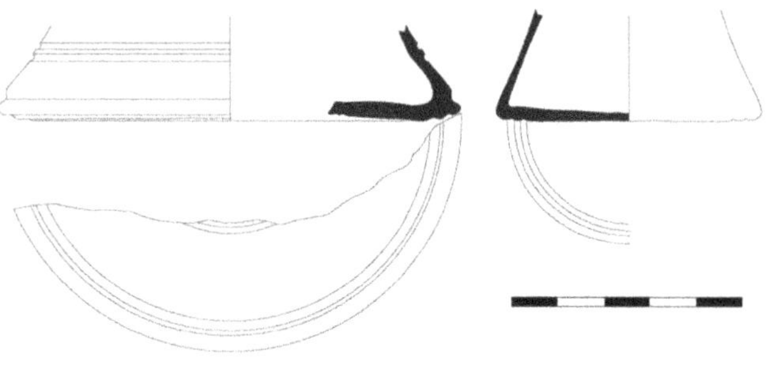

Fig. 15. fragments de fonds de modiolus, secteur de la Maison des stucs (dessin S. Sorin, Hisoma)

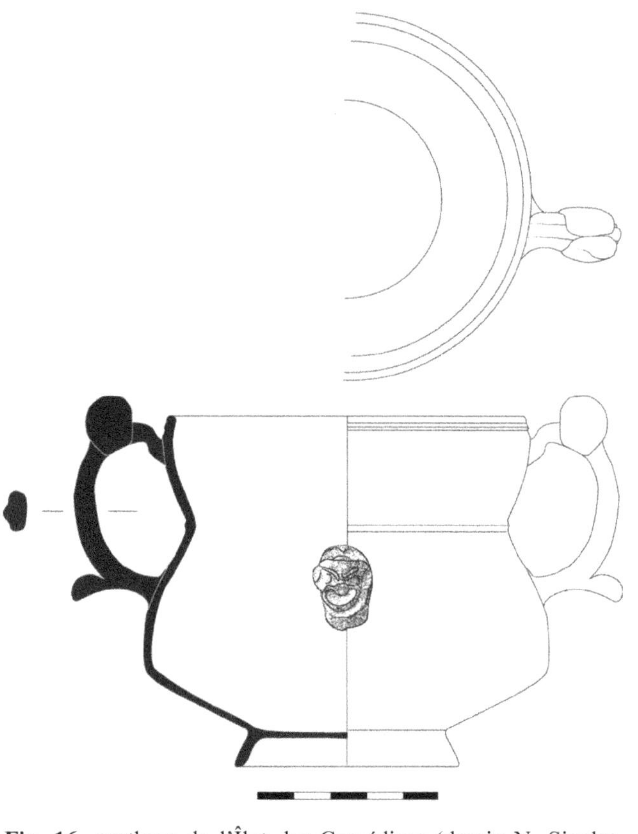

Fig. 16. canthare de l'Îlot des Comédiens (dessin N. Sigalas, Ecole Française d'Athènes)

l'Agora d'Athènes, où J. Hayes la date du dernier quart du Ier s. av. J.-C.[47]

L'influence de prototypes métalliques, visible sur la forme du « modiolus », apparaît également sur la série des canthares, dotés d'anses à pastilles latérales et d'une petite corne en dessous. Un exemplaire complet a été mis au jour dans l'Îlot des Comédiens et publié par Ph. Bruneau; il porte un décor appliqué de masques[48] (**Fig. 16**).

Le plus grand nombre de ces canthares a un profil globulaire, des anses en ruban avec deux pastilles latérales en haut, et un pied annulaire, parfois avec des moulurations sous la base. L'influence de modèles métalliques est évidente, et l'inspiration hellénique, sans doute micrasiatique, très nette aussi[49]. Ces formes de vases à boire appartiennent en effet à un répertoire et une tradition différents de celui des gobelets, plus liés aux types italiques. Les fragments publiés par J. Hayes datent du milieu du Ier s. ap. J.-C., mais la série est déjà attestée au début du Ier s. av. J.-C. en Occident[50]. Les exemplaires de Délos sont sans doute parmi les plus anciens. Si le canthare complet avec les masques appliqués est bien antérieur à la destruction de l'Îlot des Comédiens, il pourrait dater d'avant 88 av. J.-C.[51]

La présence de ces objets, et de plusieurs autres dans d'autres secteurs, incite à penser que cette forme est déjà bien présente dans le répertoire des céramiques à parois fines dans le bassin égéen vers le milieu du Ier s. av. J.-C. La popularité de ce type de canthare dans les productions d'Asie Mineure, en particulier les séries pergaméniennes, rendent plausible l'hypothèse d'un transfert de la forme du répertoire des vernis rouges d'Asie Mineure vers les séries à parois fines « égéennes », avec, ensuite, une imitation en Occident. La distinction entre une influence plus « occidentale », plus « italienne », pour les différentes variantes de gobelets, et une série plus « grecque », plus «micrasiatique » pour les canthares paraît claire.

Même s'il est bien difficile, en l'état actuel de nos connaissances sur les productions à parois fines en Orient, de préciser nettement dans quel sens et à quel date les transferts ont eu lieu, il faut souligner aussi la grande diversité des argiles utilisées dans la fabrication des vases à parois fines mis au jour à Délos.

Il m'a paru possible de distinguer, pour le matériel délien, au moins 6 fabriques différentes:
celle des gobelets importés d'Italie;
la « fabrique 2 », dans une argile plus rouge, avec une surface extérieure portant un engobe noir très lisse, avec des volutes ou d'autres motifs de points de barbotine plutôt que des festons comme sur les prototypes italiques;
la « fabrique 3 », rouge orangée, bien lissée, avec souvent des reflets ocres en surface;
la « fabrique 4 », grise à gris violacé, très fine;
la « fabrique 5 », probablement phocéenne, des gobelets à une anse verticale;
et enfin la « fabrique 6 », aisée à identifier et sans doute micrasiatique (vallée du Méandre?), caractérisée par une surface grise et une très grande quantité de paillettes de mica blanc[52].

---

47 Hayes 2008, 99, 261 n° 1530 fig. 47 pl. 74; Contexte des années 25–1 av. J.-C. L'auteur suggère une fabrique micrasiatique pour cet objet.

48 Bruneau 1970, 242 n° D28 = 63D1509 fig. 124 pl. 41; ce vase provient de la pièce AI', latrines de la Maison des Tritons.

49 Sur les liens entre les produits en métal, verre, etc... et en céramique, voir les remarques de Hayes 2008, 11–12. Sur la forme du canthare en céramique à paroi fine, *ibid.*, 99, 261–262 n° 1531–1536.

50 Hayes 2008, 99 note 33.

51 Plusieurs fragments d'anses et de fonds proviennent de l'Îlot des Bijoux, dont certains sur le sol des habitations ou dans l'égoût de la rue des Bijoux, et donc datables d'avant 69 av. J.-C.

52 Il se peut qu'il y ait deux variantes de cette fabrique, l'une tirant plus

A l'exception des fabriques italique et phocéenne, le lieu d'origine d'aucune d'entre elles n'est établi. Mais il y a de bonnes chances pour qu'elles soient caractéristiques des productions de parois fines en Asie Mineure, et leur présence parmi les céramiques mises au jour dans les maisons de Délos indique que ces productions ont sans doute commencé autour du milieu du Ier siècle av. J.-C., et peut-être même plus tôt.

Si le matériel délien, mis au jour sur un site d'importation et de consommation, ne peut nous donner des informations fiables et précises sur la chronologie exacte du début des imitations orientales des productions italiques, il fournit cependant certains indices: les plats de cuisson italiques arrivent entre 125 et 100 av. J.-C., donc très vite après l'apparition du type en Italie. Ces plats sont sans doute apportés par les commerçants italiens, qui les rendent populaires en Orient vers la fin IIe–début Ier s. av. J.-C. Les imitations orientales de ces plats semblent plus tardives, et il serait tentant d'imaginer que le développement de ces productions locales est lié à la fin de l'activité commerciale de Délos. L'emporion aurait joué, jusqu'en 69, un rôle redistributeur de ces produits en Orient, et avec la chute de son commerce, la nécessité de répondre à la demande aurait suscité le démarrage d'une fabrication plus près des consommateurs.

Dans le cas des céramiques à parois fines, la chronologie est encore plus difficile à éclairer, car les mouvements de transferts de formes et de modèles décoratifs sont à double sens. Les formes de canthares d'Asie Mineure semblent copiées en Occident, sans doute dès le début du Ier siècle av. J.-C. Il n'est pas exclu que le prototype, populaire dans les séries à vernis rouge, ait été « emprunté » par les toreutes, puis les fabricants de vase à parois fines en Occident, avant d'être repris dans les nouveaux ateliers qui fabriquaient des parois fines sur la côte d'Asie Mineure. Le type aurait ainsi effectué un voyage « aller-retour » entre Orient et Occident.

A. Peignard-Giros
Université de Lyon
Université Lumière – Lyon 2
HiSoMA – Maison de l'Orient et de la Méditerranée
7 rue Raulin.
FR-69365 LYON cedex 07
Annette.Giros-Peignard@univ-lyon2.fr

Bibliographie

Berlin, A. M. 1993. Italian Cooking Vessels and Cuisine from Tel Anafa. *Israel Exploration Journal* 43, 35–44.

Berlin, A. M. 1997. S.C. Herbert, *Tel Anafa II, 1. The Hellenistic and Roman Pottery. The Plain Wares.* Journal of Roman Archaeology Suppl. 10 / 2 / 1. Ann Arbor, MI, Kelsey Museum.

Bruneau, Ph. 1968. Contribution à l'histoire urbaine de Délos à l'époque hellénistique et à l'époque impériale. *Bulletin de Correspondance Hellénique* 92, 658–691.

Bruneau, Ph., Vatin, Cl., Bezerra de Meneses, U., Donnay, G., Lévy, E., Bovon, A., Siebert, G., Grace, V., Savvatianou-Pétropoulakou, M., Lyding-Will, E. and Hackens, T. 1970. *L'Îlot de la Maison des comédiens*, Exploration Archéologique de Délos XXVII. Paris, De Boccard.

Bruneau, Ph., Brunet, M., Farnoux, A., and Moretti, J.-Ch. 1996. *Délos île sacrée et ville cosmopolite.* Paris, CNRS Editions.

Chatzidakis, P. 1994. Οικία της Λίμνης, νότιο πηγάδι του αιθρίου / House of the Lake, South Well in the Atrium. In *Ελληνιστική Κεραμική απο το Αιγαιο*, 46–73. Mytilène, K' Ephorate of Prehistoric and Classical Antiquities, Region of North Aegean.

Chatzidakis, P. 1997. Κτίριο νότια του Ιερού του Προμαχώνος, μία taberna vinaria στη Δήλο. In *Δ' Επιστημονική Συναντησή για τήν Ελλενιστική Κεραμική*. Μυτιλήνη 1994, 291–307. Athènes, Ypourgeio Politismou.

Chatzidakis, P. 2000. Οψοποιικά σκευή απο τη Δήλο. In *E'Επιστημονική Συναντησή για τήν Ελλενιστική Κεραμική*. Χανιά 1997, 115–130. Athènes, TAP.

Chatzidakis, P. 2004. Τα μαγειρικά σκεύη στος αρχαίους ἕλληνες κωμωδιογράφους και στη Δήλο. In *ΣΤ' Επιστημονική Συναντησή για τήν Ελλενιστική Κεραμική*. Βόλος 2000, 641–654. Athènes, TAP.

Daux, G. 1959. Chronique des fouilles en Grèce en 1958. *Bulletin de Correspondance Hellénique* 83, 785–786.

Daux, G. 1960. Chronique des fouilles en Grèce en 1959. *Bulletin de Correspondance Hellénique* 84, 854–856.

Hayes, J. 2000. From Rome to Beirut and beyond: Asia Minor and Eastern Mediterranean Trade Connections. *Rei Cretariae Romanae Fautorum acta* 36, 285–297.

Hayes, J. 2008. *Roman Pottery: Fine-Ware Imports.* The Athenian Agora XXXII. Princeton, NJ., American School of Classical Studies.

Japp, S. 1999. Frührömische dünnwandige Hartware von Pergamon. *Istanbuler Mitteilungen* 49, 301–331.

Japp, S. 2003. Sigillata und dünnwandige H artware aus Pergamon, Bemerkungen zu westlichen Importen

sur l'ocre, l'autre avec un coeur rose à rouge, mais il est possible que cette différence d'aspect ne soit que le résultat d'une différence de cuisson.

und stilisticher Einflussnahme. *Rei Cretariae Romanae Fautorum acta* 38, 243–246.

Kögler, P. 2010. *Feinkeramik aus Knidos vom mittleren Hellenismus bis in die mittlere Kaiserzeit (ca. 200 v.Chr. bis 150 n.Chr.)*. Wiesbaden, Reichert Verlag.

Peignard, A. 1997. La vaisselle de la Maison des Sceaux, Délos. In *Δ΄ Επιστημονική Συναντησή για τήν Ελλενιστική Κεραμική*. Μυτιλήνη 1994, 308–316. Athènes, Ypourgeio Politismou.

Peignard-Giros, A. 2000. Habitudes alimentaires grecques et romaines à Délos à l'époque hellénistique: le témoignage de la céramique. *Pallas* 52, 209–220.

Ricci, A. 1985. Ceramica a parete sottili, in *Enciclopedia dell'Arte Antica, Atlante delle forme ceramiche nel bacino mediterraneo (tardo ellenismo e primo impero)*, 231–358. Rome, Istituto della Enciclopedia italiana.

Rogl, Chr. 2007. Späthellenistische Keramik im Osten des Reiches. Ephesos – Delos – Samos – Pergamon im Vergleich. In M. Meyer (ed.), *Neue Zeiten – Neue Sitten. Zu Rezeption und Integration römischen und italischen Kulturguts in Kleinasien*. Wiener Forschungen zur Archäologie 12, 181–193. Vienne, Phoibos.

Rotroff, S. I. 2006. *Hellenistic Pottery, The Plain Wares*. The Athenian Agora XXXIII. Princeton, NJ., American School of Classical Studies.

Siebert, G. 2001. *L'Îlot des bijoux: l'Îlot des bronzes: la Maison des sceaux. 1: Topographie et Architecture*. Exploration Archéologique de Délos XXXVIII. Paris, De Boccard.

Zapheiropoulou, Ph. and Chatzidakis, P. 1994. Δήλο, Κεραμική απο τον δρόμο βόρεια του Ανδήρου των Λεόντων. In *Γ΄ Επιστημονική Συναντησή για τήν Ελλενιστική Κεραμική*. Θεσσαλονίκη 1991, 235–248. Athènes, Archetai.

Zapheiropoulou, Ph. and Chatzidakis, P. 1994. Αγορά των Ιταλων, κόγχη Ποπλίου Σατρικανίου/ Agora of the Italians, Niche of Publius Satricanius, in *Ελλενιστική Κεραμική απο το Αιγαιο*, 28–45. Mytilène, Ministry of Culture.

Turkey

Pottery production in Pergamon - a short overview

Sarah Japp

Abstract

In Pergamon, a major city in Asia Minor, pottery production was already existent in the Bronze Age. After some disruption it was revived in the 3rd century BC with the manufacture of Table Ware that not only satisfied the wishes of the Pergamenian inhabitants but was also exported especially to the Aegean and Black Sea Region. Such production is proven by the find of potters' workshops in the Ketios Valley near the city and through archaeometric analysis. In the beginning local fabrication was adapted from Attica as most of the shapes and decoration types document. From the 2nd century BC an indigenous development commenced that lead to unique inventions such as Appliqué Ware. During the early Roman period new influences can be observed that changed the repertoire again. Together with Pitane/Çandarlı Pergamon produced Eastern Sigillata C Ware that was found across the whole eastern Mediterranean and in South Russia and along the North African coast. Pergamenian pottery is a good example of a production operating inside a wider network. On the one hand existing shapes and decorations were adopted and sometimes adjusted according to contemporary fashion. On the other hand new forms and adornments were invented that influenced other customers and production centres.

Keywords: Pergamon, local pottery production, Eastern Sigillata C, archaeometric analysis, Attic models

Introduction

The ancient city of Pergamon is situated on the western coast of modern Turkey. The area was settled from prehistoric times onwards[1]. During the Hellenistic period the city became capital of the Attalid kingdom. After the death of the last Attalid ruler the Pergamenian realm was integrated into the Roman province of Asia. Pergamon continued to be a powerful and prosperous city expanding towards the southern plain adjoining the citadel hill. However, during the early Byzantine period the city declined, only partially regaining its wealth in late Byzantine times. After the Ottoman conquest in the early 14th century the hillside location was abandoned and only the plain was resettled. Excavations in Pergamon concentrated during the first years on the acropolis and its buildings such as the Athena temple[2], the theatre[3] and the palaces[4]. Later on private dwellings were likewise uncovered, including the *peristyle* houses west of the lower Agora[5]. During the *Stadtgrabung* conducted by the German Archaeological Institute between 1973 and 1993 living quarters with private houses as well as public and semi-public buildings were excavated and provided a lot of relevant stratigraphic data[6].

Pergamenian Pottery Production

Local production of ancient Fine Ware in Pergamon was confirmed by the existence of a potters' quarter in the valley of the river Ketios that is situated at the eastern foot of the citadel hill[7]. The workshops were found during rescue excavations in the 1970s, before the area was covered by a modern water reservoir. Unfortunately the results of the excavations were published only in short preliminary reports[8]. Therefore it is unknown, whether Table Ware was produced exclusively or Coarse Ware as well. The complete vessel repertoire is also unknown. Moreover, scholarly opinion differs concerning the duration of the production. S. Erdemgil places the production between the 3rd/2nd century BC and the 4th century AD with one production location in a side arm of the Ketios River in operation until the 6th century AD[9]. Two different phases are supported by O. Bounegru, but with a different chronology[10]. His first phase lasts from the mid-3rd until the end of the 1st century BC. During this phase relief bowls, appliqué vessels and Sigillata were manufactured. The second phase starts in the 4th century AD after an interruption, during which a necropolis was installed in the area. In the 5th and the 1st

1 Radt 1999, 23–51 with bibliography.

2 Bohn 1885.

3 Bohn 1896.

4 Kawerau and Wiegand 1930.

5 Pinkwart and Stammnitz 1984.

6 See preliminary reports in *Archäologischer Anzeiger* since 1974.

7 In addition a kiln from the Hellenistic period was excavated in the area south-east of the Gate of Philetairos on the hill (Hepding 1952, 49–117; Radt 1999, 111), but is now completely lost. The production areas of the Bronze Age and of the Byzantine period, which undoubtedly had been extant in Pergamon, are undiscovered as yet. Only a workshop of the Ottoman period was brought to light in the area of the Red Hall (Mania 2006).

8 Bounegru and Erdemgil 1998; Erdemgil 1980; Erdemgil 1981a; Erdemgil 1981b; Erdemgil and Ozenir 1982; Poblome *et al.* 2001.

9 Erdemgil 1980; Erdemgil and Ozenir 1982.

10 Bounegru 2003.

Fig. 1. Different slip types of Pergamenian pottery (S. Japp)

half of the 6th century the workshops produced pottery of good quality with red slip and stamped decoration. A selected study of diagnostic ESC fragments placed their production between 150 BC and 150 AD with the majority falling into the time span of 50 BC and 75 AD[11]. As long as the pottery types are not entirely published all these assumptions stay unconfirmed[12].

Designation of vessels as Pergamenian products is still mainly based on observation using visual impressions of clay, its colour and temper, the treatment of the vessel's surface and on the knowledge of the form repertoire in Pergamon. Typical Pergamenian fabric displays carefully levigated and slightly micaceous clay which sometimes has a few white inclusions[13]. The colour can be described as light orangish brown or light orangish red, less often it is light brown or reddish brown. The slip of Pergamenian Table Ware has colours ranging from black to dark brown, reddish brown to orange red and red[14]. Obviously it turns from black in the early Hellenistic period over brown, reddish brown to red and orangish red, the latter already starting in the 2nd century BC. Grey-slipped vessels were produced in smaller numbers. From the late 2nd century BC until the early 1st century AD in particular, bi-coloured vessels with red- and black-coloured slip can be observed. Nevertheless, overlaps have to be kept in mind within this rough chronological order. In general the slip shows two different qualities: dense and slightly shining or less dense, irregular and matt. Within these two slip types several variations appear as a result of the production process or firing; there exist completely or partly covered, double-dipped as well as mottled and blotted vessels. Hellenistic vessels with black and brown slip often show a metallic shine.

Local fabrication of pottery in Pergamon started early. A beginning in the middle to late Bronze Age is now in discussion[15]. While in the Archaic period several types were produced locally, during the Classical period imports predominated presumably coming from Greece[16].

---

11 Poblome *et al.* 2001, 156–158.

12 The thesis that between the early 1st century and the 4th century AD no pottery was produced in the Ketios Valley workshops seems to be problematic as the archaeometric analysis classified pieces from the Hellenistic to the late Roman period into two main groups (see below). Vessel fragments are extant in those groups that are said to belong to the workshop material (Japp 2009, 200).

13 The clay source of Pergamenian vessel production is still unidentified. A. Conze (1912, 123) assumed an area near the Kybele sanctuary of Kapıkaya nearby the Attalid capital. The Ketios valley is reported to have available clay raw material (Erdemgil and Özenir 1982; Poblome *et al.* 2001, 150). During a research project conducted by U. Outschar and R. Sauer (Ephesos excavation, *Österreichisches Archäologisches Institut*) several clay sources in the vicinity of Pergamon were examined and samples were taken. The results of these investigations have not been published yet (Schneider and Japp 2009, 292).

14 See Meyer-Schlichtmann 1988, 16–17.

15 Personal communication by D. Hertel, University Cologne.

16 In particular the so called Aiolian Grey Ware and some imitations of

Fig. 2. Pergamenian West Slope Ware Kantharos (S. Japp)

Fig. 3. Pergamenian multi-coloured cup (S. Japp)

Obviously Pergamon started to manufacture pottery again in the 3rd century BC. During the 2nd century BC the production increased and export commenced. Hellenistic vessels from Pergamon are known from sites such as northern Asia Minor and the Black Sea region, while Delos probably served as a transfer site; in the south of Asia Minor or in Greece they are recorded to a lesser extent[17]. This business was intensified in the late 1st century BC. In Roman times Pergamenian pottery was widely spread in the Eastern Mediterranean and the Black Sea region, yet the distribution also extended from South Russia in the north to the Cyrenaica in the south[18].

In 2006 an archaeological-archaeometric programme was initiated by the German Archaeological Institute with the intention to gain more reliability in the identification of locally produced Pergamon wares. Different types of Hellenistic and Roman Table Ware from Pergamon were sampled and examined by X-ray fluorescence (WD-XRF) and neutron activation analysis (NAA)[19]. As a result several chemical groups became apparent although two main groups emerged[20]. The first group included vessel forms such as *kantharoi*, bowls and plates stemming from the 3rd and 2nd centuries BC, early Roman vessels from the early 1st century AD, late Roman Relief Ware and angular bowls from the 2nd to 4th centuries AD. The second group combined undecorated and decorated Hellenistic vessels such as West Slope, Appliqué and White-ground Ware, black-slipped grooved beakers as well as early Roman conical cups and plates with moulded rims, flanged bowls, hemispherical bowls, goblets, beakers, relief decorated drinking vessels and Sanded Ware together with angular bowls from the 1st and 2nd centuries AD. Another chemical group only contained the typical Pergamenian plates of the 3rd and 2nd centuries BC. Moreover, one group seems to hold only early Hellenistic Fine Ware such as carinated bowls, fish plates and West Slope Ware.

Evidently Pergamenian potters did not only use the same clay sources throughout time, but also relatively identical mixtures regarding temper. Clay recipes seem to be used from generation to generation of potters. These recipes were not changed even when new vessel forms or new types of decoration were established.

Pergamenian Vessel Repertoire

In Hellenistic Pergamon different types of Table Ware were produced, drinking vessels such as beakers, bowls, *kantharoi*, *skyphoi* and *kraters* as well as dinner services such as bowls and plates.[21] In general these forms are similar to those that can be found throughout the Hellenistic world, but in addition Pergamenian potters adjusted forms and invented new types.

During the 3rd and 2nd centuries beakers were of conical or hemispherical shape, the latter with or without a small foot[22]. A few hemispherical beakers are decorated with

Greek pottery can be identified as regional or local production: de Luca and Radt 1999, 73–77; Radt 1992, 170–171. 178–180; Schäfer 1968, 29–30; Ziegenaus and de Luca 1975, 95–97.

17 Schäfer 1968, 21–23.

18 Hayes 2008, 49.

19 The NAA analysis was carried out at the Rheinische Friedrich-Wilhelms-Universität Bonn, Helmholtz-Institut für Strahlen- und Kernphysik under the direction of H. Mommsen. The WD-XRF analysis was undertaken at the Freie Universität Berlin under the direction of G. Schneider.

20 Japp 2009; Mommsen and Japp 2009; Schneider and Japp 2009.

21 Publications mentioned in the following should only give an overview of the forms. The list does not claim to be exhaustive.

22 Meyer-Schlichtmann 1988, 76–78 B 1–3.

Fig. 4. Pergamenian hemispherical bowls (S. Japp)

Fig. 5. Pergamenian 'Stülpdeckelschüssel' (S. Japp)

horizontal grooves on the exterior[23]; most of the conical beakers show a few horizontal grooves below the interior rim section[24]. A higher quantity of hemispherical bowls is mould-made and displays a relief decoration on the exterior[25]. Their body is decorated with figural, vegetal and geometric design or combinations, while the rim is equipped with one or two horizontal relief zones. The latter usually depicts Ionic *cymatia*, wavy lines, spirals or rows

[23] Meyer-Schlichtmann 1988, pl. 9 no. 53.

[24] De Luca and Radt 1999, Beilage 2 no. 397–398.

[25] For research on motifs, local production and the question of imitation and originality see G. de Luca to be published in *Pergamenische Forschungen*. See de Luca and Radt 1999, 92–117.

of leave bunches. Pergamenian *kantharoi* are drinking vessels consisting of a profiled foot, a bulbous body, an out-turning rim and two handles[26]. Several are decorated in West Slope Style (**Fig. 2**)[27]. In the late 2nd century BC another kind of drinking vessel became the favourite of the Pergamenian people: cup-like objects with a short profiled food, more or less straight body walls, an out-turning or straight rim and two handles. These Pergamenian *skyphoi* are covered with black, brown and red slip or they are bi-coloured[28]. The shape was simplified during the 1st century BC and remained in common use until the 1st century AD (**Fig. 3**)[29]. West Slope and Appliqué decoration appear on the vessels[30]. Lug-handled *kraters* used for mixing wine and water were mainly extant in the 3rd and 2nd centuries, during the 1st century this form seems to decline. Most of the Pergamenian *kraters* were adorned with motifs in West Slope style on the rim[31].

Between the 3rd and the early 1st century BC hemispherical bowls were the most typical vessel in Pergamon – either used for drinking, eating or as serving vessels as there are bigger and smaller specimen present (**Fig. 4**)[32]. They appear in different qualities regarding workmanship and slip. Huge and deep bowls with down-turning rims were used definitely for dinner services and food storage showing up in the 3rd but especially in the 2nd century BC[33]. As with the hemispherical bowls they display different levels of quality. Small bowls with carinated body, out-turning rim and usually black or grey slip were typical in the 3rd century; however, they are not extant in greater numbers[34]. In the 1st century BC a small amount of *Stülpdeckelschüsseln* with a specific rim shape show up being reminiscent of some *pyxis* types (**Fig. 5**)[35]. Occasionally they were decorated with incised West Slope motifs or only partly covered with slip[36]. Conical cups/bowls with concave vertical rims were produced as part of the Eastern Sigillata C Ware (ESC) offering three main variants: one with an almost straight rim zone[37], one with a convex or concave and finely moulded rim zone[38] and one with a strongly curved rim zone[39]. They were extant during the whole 1st century AD[40]. In the 1st century AD hemispherical cups/bowls with a short vertical rim and a pronounced flange on the exterior wall become evident, also being typical for the ESC production until the 3rd century AD[41]. During the mid-1st century AD angular deep bowls commenced with thickened and projecting rim and heavy short feet[42].

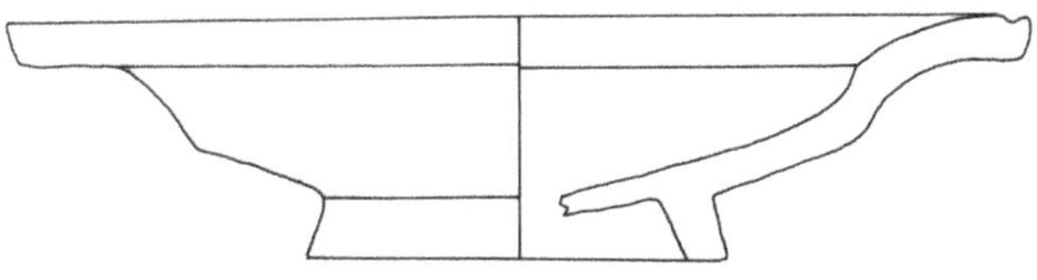

Fig. 6. Typical Pergamenian plate (M 1:2) (Japp 2009, 226 fig. 6 Perga 55)

In the 3rd century BC fishplates[43] and plates with a rolled rim[44] are the most frequent dishes. During the late 3rd and especially in the 2nd century one new type appears which seems to be a unique Pergamenian design and the most common plate in that period (**Fig. 6**)[45]. The rim section is straight out-turning or equipped with a curved lip. It is separated from the body by a groove or ledge on the interior, another groove is situated on the upper part of the lip. Most of these plates belong to the so called *Streifenware*, where a red or reddish brown circle was painted along the interior rim as well as the centre of the vessel. This form was produced until the beginning of the 1st century BC, and then often covered by a dense red slip of good quality. The fish plates lost their characteristic internal depression in that period, and the rim was not vertically but more diagonally down-turning[46]. Not often but in countable numbers, plates with diagonal wall and up-turning rim zone can be distinguished[47]. They were replaced by the typical Roman plates with curved body and straight rim[48]. During the same time a plate variation of the conical cup with moulded rim appears[49]. Plates with diagonally out-turning body walls but without a foot occur in Pergamon occasionally between the 1st century BC and the 2nd century AD[50].

During the Hellenistic period the typical decorated wares were West Slope Ware, White Ground Ware, Appliqué Ware and Lead Glazed Ware. In the early Roman period Sanded Ware and Barbotine Ware were added to that repertoire, replacing it to some extent. West Slope Style was used for

26 Meyer-Schlichtmann 1988, 67–68 S 6; Schäfer 1968, 38.
27 Behr 1988, 113–125.
28 Meyer-Schlichtmann 1988, 65 S 3. 68–71 S 7–9; Schäfer 1968, 47–48.
29 Meyer-Schlichtmann 1988, 63–64 S 1. 66–67 S 5.
30 Behr 1988, 126–143; Hübner 1993.
31 Behr 1988, 155–158; de Luca and Radt 1999, 88 no. 441; Schäfer 1968, 55.
32 De Luca and Radt 1999, 29–39; Meyer-Schlichtmann 1988, 89–92 N 1–3; Schäfer 1968, 37–38.
33 De Luca and Radt 1999, 20–29.
34 De Luca and Radt 1999, 80 no. 384–386; Schäfer 1968, 35–36.
35 Meyer-Schlichtmann 1988, 110–111 N 36. 163–164 Sü 19.
36 Behr 1988, 167–168.
37 Meyer-Schlichtmann 1988, 112–113 N 39b.
38 Meyer-Schlichtmann 1988, 112–113 N 39a. c. d.
39 Meyer-Schlichtmann 1988, 113–114 N 40.
40 The beginning of production as well as the origin of form is still under discussion. See further down.
41 Meyer-Schlichtmann 1988, 107–109 N 33.
42 Meyer-Schlichtmann 1988, 122 Sa 14. 125–129 Sa 24–27.
43 Schäfer 1968, 34–35.
44 De Luca and Radt 1999, 18 Typ IIId; Schäfer 1968, 33–34 C 1–2.
45 De Luca and Radt 1999, 10–15 Typ Ia–d. 16 Typ IIb; Japp 2013, in print; Raeck 2000, 342 no. 3.2 fig. 16; 344 no. 5.2 fig. 17; 354 no. 10.2 fig. 233; 60 no. 13.6–7 fig. 26; 362 no. 16.1 fig. 28. Similar plates have not been published from other sites in Asia Minor. However, I was told by K. Domżalski that in the Black Sea region comparable vessels occur.
46 De Luca and Radt 1999, 19; Meyer-Schlichtmann 1988, 147–148 T 27–28.
47 Meyer-Schlichtmann 1988, 132–134 T 2; Schäfer 1968, 33–34 C 3.
48 Meyer-Schlichtmann 1988, 134–136 T 3–4.
49 Meyer-Schlichtmann 1988, 151–155 T 31–36.
50 Meyer-Schlichtmann 1988, 137–138 T 8.

Fig. 7. Pergamenian thymiaterion lid in White Ground Ware (S. Japp)

Fig. 8. Pergamenian Appliqué skyphos with ivy bunches (S. Japp)

drinking vessels as well as table dishes[51]. Ivy tendrils and garlands, sometimes *palmettes* and dolphins or only one horizontal row of triangles or dots are observable. Three types of decoration techniques can be distinguished: The motifs can be completely painted in white or beige colour or a mixture of painted and incised decoration was used[52]; the majority of finds in Pergamon display this kind. And finally every motif was incised[53]. However, these differing techniques do not have real chronological value. Only the completely incised technique can be given an estimated date, starting in the late 2nd century and becoming especially common during the 1st century BC. A variant of West Slope Ware is the so called football beakers that bear a grid-like motif covering the whole exterior[54]. However, they are rare within the Pergamenian material. The variety of White Ground Ware is not very extensive. Mainly *lagynoi, thymiateria* and *thymiaterion* lids (**Fig. 7**), rarely beakers and plates, were covered with a white ground and decorated with motifs in orange, red or brown colour. The majority of vessels show horizontal strips and bands, simple garlands and irregular dots and spots[55]. This ware was developed at the beginning of the 2nd century and used until the late 1st century BC or even the beginning of the 1st century AD. Decoration with applied reliefs was invented especially for drinking vessels, the Appliqué Ware. The most famous motifs are ivy bunches arranged in garlands along the vessel's body (**Fig. 8**). *Symplegmata* and different kinds of mythological or human figures stemming from the Dionysian or Aphrodisian sphere appear often, with relief pieces placed separately around the body[56]. Appliqué Ware was manufactured between the 2nd quarter of the 2nd century and the early 1st century AD. From the late 1st century BC until the mid-1st century AD the Pergamenian potters made Sanded Ware cups[57]. In Pergamon sand decoration is limited to the exterior of the body while the rim was omitted. Vessels were covered by red or brown slip. Likewise during the early Roman period a small number of drinking vessels were mould-made, for example chalices with pronounced hanging lip or convex moulded lip. The reliefs on the vessel's exterior are often similar to those of the Hellenistic mould-made bowl such as egg-and-dart or a décor made of triangular leaves[58]. Furthermore, garlands and arcades as well as human and animal figures are depicted. From the mid-1st century BC until the late 1st century AD a small number of lead-glazed vessels, often flat bowls, is observable[59]. The mould-made decoration consists of vertical ribs, vine tendrils, oak leave bunches or human figures. The vessels were covered by an olive green, brown or mustard-yellow glaze. It seems to be generally accepted that lead-glazed vessels were manufactured in Pergamon; nevertheless a high quantity of the pieces in Pergamon was imported.

Pergamon was one of the production centres of Sigillata. Indeed it is still under discussion what kind of vessel and surface treatment has to be identified as Sigillata and consequentially the question arises as to when the Sigillata

51 Behr 1988.

52 Behr 1988, 104–105.
53 Behr 1988, 106 '*Westabhangnachfolge*'.
54 De Luca and Radt 1999, 84–85. 88.
55 De Luca and Radt 1999, 91–92; Schäfer 1968, 101–115; Schäfer 1972.
56 Hübner 1993.
57 Meyer-Schlichtmann 1988, 66 S 5.
58 Meyer-Schlichtmann 1988, 191.
59 Pinkwart 1972.

production started in Pergamon. C. Meyer-Schlichtmann classified as 'Pergamenian Sigillata' vessels with typical Hellenistic as well as typical Roman shapes being covered with black, brown, reddish brown or red slip or bi-coloured[60]. This 'Pergamenian Sigillata' was produced between the middle of the 2nd century BC and the middle of the 2nd century AD[61]. In his opinion only the production in Pitane/Çandarlı[62] has to be called ESC, nevertheless Pergamon was the centre influencing the neighbouring workshops. On the other hand ESC or Çandarlı Ware is said to be produced from the early 1st century until the 2nd or late 3rd century AD[63]. Recently Hayes tried to classify the 'Red-Gloss Wares of the Pergamenian region' into two series, one being produced in Pergamon and Pitane/Çandarlı, while the second is said to be known only from the latter site[64]. The archaeometric investigations in Pergamon were able to prove that forms belonging to that second group were produced in Pergamon as well. Notwithstanding these discrepancies it can be stated that Pergamon had an expanded production in Hellenistic times that merged seamlessly into the Roman period[65].

Imports and Local Production

The majority of Table Ware used in Pergamon was produced locally, imports were rare. Only a small number of imported Hellenistic *kantharoi*, mould-made bowls, carinated bowls and fish plates are known, mostly coming from Attica. During the 2nd and 1st centuries BC a few Eastern Sigillata A pieces were brought to Pergamon probably via trade connections. As well in the early Roman period Italian Sigillata came into the city. From the 1st century AD onwards there are imports from the Maeander valley region such as Eastern Sigillata B from Tralleis and perhaps vessels from Sardis. These vessels gave impulses for introducing new forms into the Pergamenian repertoire. The meagre number of imports shows clearly, that local fabrication seems to fulfil the requirements of the inhabitants of Pergamon *in extenso*.

Therefore, networking in Pergamon means less the import of vessels from different production centres than the integration of non-local forms and decorations into the local repertoire and their consequent transformation.

During the 3rd and 2nd centuries BC the typological dependency on Attic models is highly visible especially regarding the simple Table Ware. Surprisingly there are only a few imports. Pure imitations such as pseudo-attic vessels were recorded only briefly which makes it difficult to think of Attic potters working in Pergamon. Perhaps Pergamenian potters were trained in Attica and brought the new forms and types back to their hometown. Or those new forms were not transported via clay vessels but vessels made of other materials. In contrast to this interconnection some vessels such as the plates with profiled rims are solely typical of Pergamenian production. West Slope Ware as well as Hellenistic relief bowls are influenced by Attic models; however, the Pergamenian examples are no imitations, but variations. Originality is observable for the first time during late 2nd century BC with one example being the Appliqué Ware. Since the mid-1st century BC new creations appeared with a dense red slip and a rim zone which was now adorned with mouldings or curves. Some of these vessels are often labelled as *Arretina*-like; nevertheless the original location and transfer of these ideas are not completely clear[66].

Résumé

Pergamon produced a wide variety of Hellenistic and Roman Table Ware while using ideas from other production centres and adopting them into the local repertoire, but also changing them into something independent, fabricating completely new forms and exporting them. The whole production was involved in the Hellenistic-Roman pottery network using it either as a transfer system for ideas or as a distribution centre.

Sarah Japp
Deutsches Archäologisches Institut Orient-Abteilung
Podbielskiallee 69-71
D-14195 Berlin
sarah.japp@dainst.de

Bibliography

Behr, D. 1988. Neue Ergebnisse zur pergamenischen Westabhangkeramik. *Istanbuler Mitteilungen* 38, 97–178.

60 This thesis was already published by J. Schäfer (1962). Vessels with red slip were invented in the Hellenistic East and influenced the Italian pottery. Schäfer named Pergamenian pottery with red, orange red and reddish brown slip *Rote Ware*. In his opinion the production in Pitane/Çandarlı belonged to the Pergamenian production, while Pergamon was the centre of export.

61 Meyer-Schlichtmann 1988, 13–17.

62 Loeschke 1912.

63 For example Crowfoot *et al.* 1957, 283.

64 Hayes 2008, 49–52.

65 These major theses have to be revisited critically. The complex of problems is now treated by the author and members of the *Fundbearbeitung* of the Pergamon excavation. The recent definition of ESC made by the team working on pottery in Pergamon comprises vessels with a dense, red and almost glossy slip covering almost the majority of the surface and intentional bi-coloured vessels. With this definition ESC is not bound to special forms or periods. See Japp, Keweloh and Engels 2012, 251-255.

66 C. Meyer-Schlichtmann (1988, 191–194) assumed that the conical cups/bowls with profiled rim section as well as the similar plates were produced originally in Pergamon since the mid-1st century BC. Those vessels were exported to Italy and adopted into the local Sigillata production. Later on the Italian form was re-transported to Asia Minor and influenced the Pergamenian production. Unfortunately until now there are no sealed complexes, from which the exact starting date of this form in Pergamon could be drawn.

Bohn, R. 1885. *Das Heiligtum der Athena Polias Nikephoros*. Altertümer von Pergamon II. Berlin, de Gruyter.

Bohn, R. 1896. *Die Theater-Terrasse*. Altertümer von Pergamon IV. Berlin, de Gruyter.

Bounegru, O. 2003. La production des ateliers de ceramique de Pergame (vallee de Kestel): Un aperçu general. In C. Abadie-Reynal (ed.), *Les céramiques en Anatolie aux époques Hellénistique et Romaine*, 137–140. Paris, De Boccard.

Bounegru, O. and Erdemgil, S. 1998. Terra Sigillata Produktion aus den Werkstätten von Pergamon-Ketiostal. Vorläufiger Bericht. *Istanbuler Mitteilungen* 48, 263–277.

Conze, A. 1912. *Stadt und Landschaft*. Altertümer von Pergamon I. Berlin, de Gruyter.

Crowfoot, J. W., Crowfoot, G. M. and Kenyon, K. M. 1957. *The Objects from Samaria*, Samaria-Sebaste. Reports of the Work III. London, Palestine Exploration Fund.

De Luca, G. and Radt, W. 1999. *Sondagen im Fundament des Großen Altars*, Pergamenische Forschungen 12. Berlin – New York, de Gruyter.

Erdemgil, S. 1980. Kestel kurtama kazısı. In *II. Kazı Sonuçları Toplantısı*, 103–107. Ankara, Turkish Ministry of Culture.

Erdemgil, S. 1981a. Kestel kazısı 1980 yılı calıçmaları. In *III. Kazı Sonuçları Toplantısı*, 63–66. Ankara, Turkish Ministry of Culture.

Erdemgil, S. 1981b. Kestel, 1980. *Anatolian Studies* 31, 193.

Erdemgil S. and Ozenir, S. 1982. Preliminary Report on the Kilns excavated in Ketios Valley. *Rivista di Archeologia* 6, 109.

Hayes, J. W. 2008. *Roman Pottery. Fine-Ware Imports*. The Athenian Agora XXXII. Princeton, NJ., American School of Classical Studies at Athens.

Hepding, H. 1952. Eine hellenistische Töpferwerkstatt in Pergamon. *Nachrichten der Gießener Hochschulgesellschaft* 21, 49–117.

Hübner, G. 1993. *Die Applikenkeramik von Pergamon: eine Bildersprache im Dienst des Herrscherkultes*. Pergamenische Forschungen 7. Berlin – New York, de Gruyter.

Japp, S. 2009. Archäometrisch-archäologische Untersuchungen an Keramik aus Pergamon und Umgebung. *Istanbuler Mitteilungen* 59, 193–268.

Japp, S. 2013. A Hellenistic Plate of Pergamenian Production – Typological, Chronological and Archaeometric Analysis. In E. Laflı (ed.), *Hellenistic and Roman and Late Roman Ceramics from Anatolia*. Colloquia Anatolica et Aegaea. Acta conferenceus communis omnium gentium Smyrnae III, in print.

Japp, S., Keweloh, A. and Engels, B. 2012. Aktuelle Ergebnisse der Keramikbearbeitung in Pergamon – Eine neue Definition von Eastern Sigillata C/ Pergamenischer Sigillata, in F. Pirson *et al*., Pergamon – Bericht über die Arbeiten in der Kampagne 2011. *Archäologischer Anzeiger*, 251–255.

Kawerau, G. and Wiegand, Th. 1930. *Die Paläste der Hochburg*. Altertümer von Pergamon V 1. Berlin, de Gruyter.

Loeschke, S. 1912. Sigillata-Töpfereien in Tschandarli. *Mitteilungen des Deutschen Archäologischen Instituts, Athenische Abteilung* 37, 344–407.

Mania, U. 2006. Eine neue Werkstatt früher türkischer Keramik. Miletware aus Pergamon. *Istanbuler Mitteilungen* 56, 475–501.

Meyer-Schlichtmann, C. 1988. *Die pergamenische Sigillata aus der Stadtgrabung von Pergamon*. Pergamenische Forschungen 6. Berlin – New York, de Gruyter.

Mommsen, H. and Japp, S. 2009. Neutronenaktivierungs-analyse von 161 Keramikproben mit Fundorten aus der Region Pergamons. *Istanbuler Mitteilungen* 59, 269–286.

Pinkwart, D. 1972. Hellenistisch-römische Bleiglasurkeramik aus Pergamon. In E. Boehringer (ed.), *Pergamon. Gesammelte Aufsätze*. Pergamenische Forschungen 1, 140–163. Berlin, de Gruyter.

Pinkwart, D. and Stammnitz, W. 1984. *Peristylhäuser westlich der unteren Agora*. Altertümer von Pergamon XIV. Berlin, de Gruyter.

Poblome, J., Bounegru, O., Degryse, P., Viaene, W., Waelkens, M. and Erdemgil, S. 2001. The Sigillata manufactories of Pergamon and Sagalassos. *Journal of Roman Archaeology* 14, 143–165.

Radt, W. 1992. Die frühesten Wehrmauern von Pergamon und die zugehörigen Keramikfunde. *Istanbuler Mitteilungen* 42, 163–234.

Radt, W. 1999. *Pergamon, Geschichte und Bauten einer antiken Metropole*. Darmstadt, Wissenschaftliche Buchgesellschaft.

Raeck, W. 2000. Untersuchungen zur Vorgängerbebauung des Traianeums von Pergamon II: Der Bereich westlich des Tempels, untere Hangstufe. *Istanbuler Mitteilungen* 50, 307–364.

Schäfer, J. 1962. Terra Sigillata aus Pergamon. *Archäologischer Anzeiger*, 777–802.

Schäfer, J. 1968. *Hellenistische Keramik aus Pergamon*. Pergamenische Forschungen 2. Berlin, de Gruyter.

Schäfer, J. 1972. Grobe weißgrundige Keramik aus Pergamon. In E. Boehringer (ed.), *Pergamon. Gesammelte Aufsätze*. Pergamenische Forschungen 1, 202–207. Berlin, de Gruyter.

Schneider, G. and Japp, S. 2009. Röntgenfluoreszenz-analysen von 115 Keramikproben aus Pergamon, Çandarlı, Elaia und Atarneus (Türkei). *Istanbuler Mitteilungen* 59, 287–306.

Ziegenaus, O. and de Luca, G. 1975. *Das Asklepieion. Der nördliche Temenosbezirk und angrenzende Anlagen in hellenistischer und frührömischer Zeit*. Altertümer von Pergamon XI,2. Berlin, de Gruyter.

Nets working for Ephesus - Using the example of Pergamenian imports in Ephesus during the Roman occupation period

Asuman Lätzer-Lasar

Abstract

The following paper approaches the domestic material culture of Hellenistic Ephesus through different theories taken from sociology that explore network analysis and exchange theories. 'Social Network Analysis' has only recently become popular in the humanities. The examination of past cultures and the material remains of ancient human activities benefits from the use of network exchange theories to define and reconstruct historical social systems as a way to understand the behaviours that created them. This paper presents a preliminary and loosely sketched case study, in which I try to apply the method of network theory on the material culture of Ephesus. The focus lies on the Hellenistic ceramics that were exchanged between two powerful cities at the West coast of Asia Minor: Ephesus and Pergamon. To concentrate on the specific network connection between Pergamon and Ephesus and the possible sociocultural process that might be indicated, I compared the material of two dated deposits excavated in Ephesus. Hereby ceramics serve as a valuable parameter for analysing social processes, because their shapes and decorations can change quite quickly, as they follow or set the latest fashion. The diachronic analysis of these ceramic deposits gives information about the quality of the network connection and how interaction between these two cities functioned throughout the centuries.

Keywords: Hellenism/Early Roman Imperial Time, Social Network Analysis, Network (Exchange) Theory, Asia Minor, Ephesus, Pergamon, Ceramic Trade

Introduction

In the 1950s, sociologists began to develop 'Social Network Analysis', which aims to examine social relations through the framework of the 'network'. The methodology is still developing, with theories, methods and analysis software helping to understand the social structure of individuals or group entities (nodes), and how they are connected by different interdependencies (ties). Although widely used in other disciplines, social network analysis has only recently become popular in the humanities[1]. Because it has been argued that social structures produce human behaviour[2], it may be that those sciences that examine past cultures and the material remains of ancient human activities will benefit from the use of network exchange theories[3] to define and reconstruct historical social systems as a way to understand the behaviours that created them. Network theory is a useful tool to clarify in what manner human activities affect social processes, so cultural changes can be explained more precisely. In the field of archaeology ceramics serve as a valuable parameter for analysing social processes, because their development reflects current styles and aesthetic taste. Because ceramic material is also preserved in high quantities, pottery statistics are an effective medium for analysis.

The study approaches the domestic material culture of Hellenistic Ephesus through different theories taken from sociology that explore network analysis and exchange theories. This paper presents a preliminary and loosely sketched case study, focussed on the Hellenistic ceramics that were exchanged between Ephesus and another powerful and well-known metropolis in Western Asia Minor: Pergamon. Both cities represent nodes in a widespread trade network that stretches across the Mediterranean and beyond. But I will go further and argue that Ephesus and Pergamon form a network that possesses what is known as a 'short path-length'[4]. The close-knit, interacting clusters that in this case are engaged in the production and distribution of ceramics, are well-defined by group membership: they are potters and traders. These group memberships form what is known in sociological terms as 'strong ties'[5]. They are strong, because they are consistent. In antiquity ceramic production was generally a family business that was carried forward from father to son. If the potters were not the salesmen themselves, they would probably choose a trader to operate on their behalf, and stay with him over a long period. However, strong ties have also a weakness: because the bonds are regular and repeated, they make the circle of people involved smaller,

1 Rutherford 2009, 304.
2 Willer 1999, 1.
3 Cook and Whitmeyer 1992, passim.
4 Collar 2007, 151. I like to thank A. C. F. Collar sincerely for the discussion and helpful advices.
5 Granovetter 1983, passim.

and so it is difficult for new information or innovations to become accepted. So information needs more time to spread than through a network made up of weak ties[6].

To concentrate on the specific network connection between Pergamon and Ephesus and the possible sociocultural process that might be indicated, I will compare the material of two dated deposits excavated in Ephesus diachronically. That will ensure the possible social process to be recognised in small chronological phases.

Political and historical framework

In the Hellenistic period, Ephesus and Pergamon were both very powerful cities, which became rivals after the Romans began their occupation of Asia Minor in the 2nd century BC. In the years after the Roman Empire took over the former Pergamenian kingdom, there was constant political struggle, with hierarchical power and rights shifting from the old capital at Pergamon to the new capital of the Provincia Asia and the seat of the proconsul, Ephesus. It was a period of political unrest, which manifested for example in the Aristonicus revolt, the three Mithridatic Wars and the Ephesian Vesper in 88 BC[7].

Pergamon and Ephesus were involved in a specific and delicate political situation, but were both also part of a unifying Hellenistic culture. Pergamon, as the former capital of the kingdom, retained its strong relationship with typical Hellenistic traditions, as recognisable in urbanisation/architecture, ritual life etc., while Ephesus changed dramatically through the migration of Italians from the 2nd century BC onwards and the possession of a new legislative authority[8]. Although there were huge differences in the political development, it is still possible to see many similarities when it comes to domestic material culture, such as ceramics. Separated by just 180 km, the cities are fairly close, even by ancient standards. Ephesus was connected to the Persian Royal Road to Sardis, but more important for the connection from Ephesus to Pergamon was the highway through the Meander Valley, which is testified to by several Roman milestones. It is likely that Elaia was used as Pergamon's harbour for maritime commerce. In the Hellenistic period both cities were very well-equipped ceramic production centres, with high quality clay resources, outstanding potters and a fully developed infrastructure for the trade of the ceramic goods. Both cities developed their own distinctive ware groups[9], vessel shapes and decorations, e.g. Ionian Reliefbowls[10], Ephesos-type lamps[11], skyphos types[12] etc.

Deposits: Peristyle house in B6 and basilica at the State Agora

For the discussion I want to compare two deposits excavated in Ephesus. As my aim is to analyse the network connection between Pergamon and Ephesus, I will focus on the imported 'Pergamenian' ceramics that appear in these deposits: the White-grounded and Appliqué Ceramic[13] as well as the Pergamenian Sigillata. Several fine wares which occurred in Ephesian contexts have historically been thought to have originated from Pergamon[14], but recent research has shown that some of the ware groups are found in large numbers not only in Pergamon[15], so we may legitimately wonder whether these ware groups being produced in and may even originate from other cities in the Mediterranean. My current PhD-thesis, 'Studies of the Pergamenian import ceramics in Ephesus', is analysing ceramic provenance through archaeometrical methods. In this way I aim to verify which of the ware groups were definitely imported from Pergamon, or whether they were produced locally. I also seek to ascertain whether, if they were imported, to what extent they were being traded with Ephesus. However, as this archaeometrical evidence is not currently available, and for the purposes of the thought experiment in this paper, we will assume that the three ware groups selected are imported from Pergamon. At the very least we may state confidently that the vessels are strongly influenced by a distinct tradition that may be a 'Pergamenian style'.

The first deposit was excavated from under the Terrace House 2, when erecting the pillars for the new roof in 1999[16]. The second deposit comes from the excavations in the basilica at the State Agora, which was published by Mitsopoulous-Leon in 1991. Both deposits have four main layers that are dated to almost the same time periods, making them suitable to compare.

The earliest layer of B6 is a settlement stratum that belongs to a late Hellenistic peristyle house. It contained no Eastern Sigillata A (ESA), but did contain fish-plates. Interesting is the appearance of a Thin-walled beaker with a barbotine dot decoration, which presumably is imported from Sicily[17]. One of the so-called 'Pergamenian ceramics', is

6 Granovetter 1983, 222.
7 Halfmann 2001, 12.
8 Kirbihler 2007, 28–31.
9 I like to thank A. Martin and especially P. Kenrick for the discussion and kindest help with translating the term 'Warengattung' into English. Terminology has always been problematic in the research of ancient ceramics. So it was very important to find an adequate translation that is comprehensible to international scholars and does not create further misunderstandings. The German term 'Warengattung' describes a group of ceramic vessels that share distinctive characteristics, such as a similar fabric, the same slip, as well as decoration system, and also possesses a well-defined typology. The term 'ware' can be used in both narrow and broad definitions, as for example in Eastern Sigillata. But to stress out more that the distinctive characteristics are combining the vessels to a special group I prefer to use the term 'ware group' here.
10 See the researches of C. Rogl.
11 See the researches of A. Giuliani.
12 Meyer-Schlichtmann 1988, S1–S3.
13 Appliqué Ceramic has been considered to be one single ceramic type, but it is more a decoration type which appears on several ware groups, e.g. Slip-Ware, Eastern Sigillata and West Slope Successor.
14 Dereboylu 2001, 28; Hübner 1993, 297.
15 Rotroff 1997, 226.
16 Lätzer 2009, passim.
17 Lätzer 2009, 150, cat. no. 122.

an exceptional finding of a medallion-bowl, which shows the god Asklepios and his daughter Hygeia in the centre[18]. Asklepios was very popular and one of the most important gods in Pergamon. The bowl may have been used for libations, to thank the god after an illness. Bowl and motif are dated to the mid-2nd century BC[19]. In addition there is a typical Hellenistic wide bowl that appeared only in the peristyle houses in Pergamon from the mid-1st century BC–2nd century AD[20]. Finally there is a White-grounded rim of an unknown vessel shape[21].

The next layer is a filling stratum consisting of Pergamenian Sigillata with typical Hellenistic shapes[22]. This includes a well-known skyphos, Meyer-Schlichtmann type S3, with a thick inner lip and an regularly used appliqué called 'Efeublattsträußchen' (ivy leaf bouquet). The bichrome slip where the red colour is shimmering through the black is very characteristic of Pergamenian ceramic. It seems to be a technique that could not be copied easily because, although the black-red bichrome becomes very fashionable during the 1st century BC, evidence of the same technique is lacking in the material found in Ephesus or other cities on the West coast. Four pieces of White-grounded Ceramic are found that belong mostly to the typical Lagynos-type, e.g. a long strap handle.

The third layer shows more variety of shapes and types. There are wide and open shapes of White-grounded Ceramic, but also typical Lagynos mouth rims. Alongside the usual floral and abstract designs in orange through to a brown-red colour, pictures of a plectrum and the right hand side of the face of the god Dionysos stand out as motifs[23]. The decoration of the oinochoe found in this layer shows a combination between white slip with a so-called 'Bommelkette' and appliqué, which is a rarity in both Pergamon and Ephesus. The badge under the lip and on the opposite side to the handle shows the head of a papposilenos[24]. If we compare this with the Ptolemaic jugs from Alexandria with images of Silenus, it must be dated to the 60s of the 1st century BC. The Pergamenian Sigillata shapes consist of common types of bowls, cups and dishes[25].

In the last layer there are many more different types of Pergamenian Sigillata and White-grounded Ceramic. Several bottom rims of lagynoi in differing sizes were found, as well as cup-, beaker- and krater types. However, Appliqué Ceramic is lacking: and I suggest that, at this time, Appliqué Ceramic was replaced by the locally produced Ionian Reliefbowls or the beakers of the Thin-walled Ceramic, both of which are found in large numbers in this layer.

The sherds describe items that were used in an ordinary private household. Some extraordinary pieces that might be primarily used for symposia are present, but the main body of the material is suitable for the daily use. The existence of few western imports in this context, especially in the earliest layer, allow us to assume a house-owner with serious economic power who held regular symposia. At some point he suddenly used beakers instead of the common bowls. Does it mean that he also did change his drinking habits[26]?

The acceptance of goods is namely relevant to the adopters. The parameters for grouping adopters are dependent on age, education, social environment, gender, religion, financial and social status[27].

The earliest layers of the second deposit include a variety of Appliqué Ceramic, for example, cups with shell feet in different colours and qualities. There is also a medallion-bowl with a detailed depiction of Poseidon and Amymone, who has her back to the spectator[28]. It is a scene that appeared on early Hellenistic terracotta altars and also on Ionian Reliefbowls[29]. Another vessel features a lion-shaped spout that remind us of toreutic forerunners. However, due to the fact that this example is not very carefully made, it does not seem to be a direct copy of a metal vessel[30]. Finally we have to state that this layer contains no White-grounded Ceramic or Pergamenian Sigillata.

There is no Pergamenian Sigillata in the next layer either, but diverse types of White-grounded Ceramic do appear: round jugs and a thymiaterion with a lid. Bichrome slips in red and black appear after the mid-2nd century BC. One example of bichrome ceramics found in this layer is the medallion bowl that depicts Eros, who is drinking out of a cornucopia[31].

During the erection of the basilica, which is dated by an inscription between the years 11 and 13 AD, the spectrum does not change. There is still a variety of Appliqué Ceramic present, with a huge range of different qualities. Even the fabric itself changes: we find medallion bowls in ESB-fabric appearing at this stage[32]. Later types of the White-grounded thymiateria appear and show a high and slimmer form than the shapes of the early types[33], but still there is no Pergamenian Sigillata.

After Augustus, when the local production of ESB is at its peak, we find the Pergamenian imports are slowly disappearing. A last piece of Appliqué Ceramic with a garland was found[34], but only the White-grounded Ceramic

18 Lätzer 2009, 141, cat. no. 56.
19 Misopoulos-Leon 1991, 55; Rotroff 1997, 110–117.
20 Lätzer 2009, 200, cat. no. 146.
21 Lätzer 2009, 197, cat. no. 128.
22 Meyer-Schlichtmann 1988, S5b and S8.
23 Lätzer 2009, 152, cat. no. 137.
24 Lätzer 2009, 140, cat. no. 63.
25 Meyer-Schlichtmann 1988, N24, S2 and T2.
26 Lätzer 2009, 168.
27 Collar 2007, 153.
28 Mitsopoulos-Leon 1991, 57, C11.
29 Rotroff 1982, 20.
30 Mitsopoulos-Leon 1991, 62, C29.
31 Mitsopoulos-Leon 1991, 57, C10.
32 Zabehlicky-Scheffenegger 2000, passim.
33 Meriç 2002, 38.
34 Mitsopoulos-Leon 1991, 61, C23.

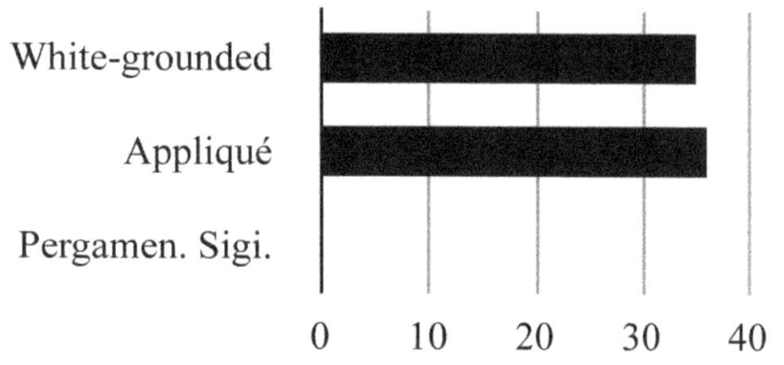

Fig. 1. 'Pergamenian imports', basilica at the State Agora (A. Lätzer-Lasar)

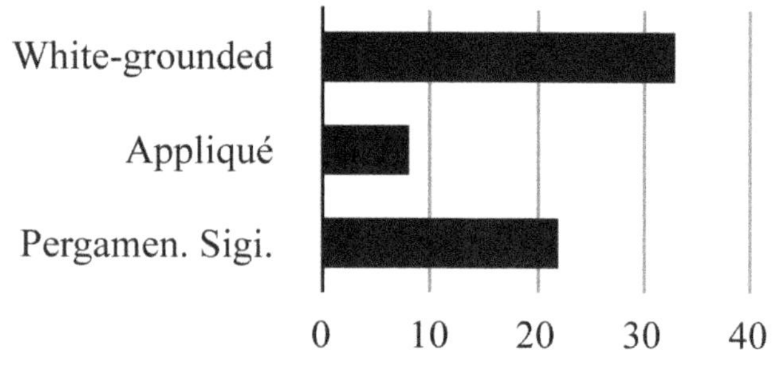

Fig. 2. 'Pergamenian imports', Terrace House 2, sondage B6 (A. Lätzer-Lasar)

stays at a consistent quantity. Alongside the rare figurative decorations, one sherd also has a Greek inscription that gives further information about the contents of the vessel. The epigraphist H. Taeuber (Vienna) read it as 'Leukosin'. This could either indicate the name for a white cosmetic paste that was used by women or in a theatre, or it could also be the name of a medicine for an eye disease. The receipt for the ointment is transmitted through Egyptian papyri[35].

The basilica context shows a limited variety of vessel shapes and types compared to the context of the sondage in B6, as it consists only of drinking cups and thymiateria. However, we should not be too surprised, because the reason lies in the difference of the contextual circumstances. The State Agora was a place where public conventions were held. For sealing a decision concrete rituals had to be performed in which the use of drinking cups and thymiateria was indispensable. Afterwards the ceramics were collectively dumped in a space nearby, e.g. a well[36].

It is not my purpose here to discuss the statistics of the exchanged ceramic cups between the two cities. Instead I will examine whether the statistical data can be used as a tool to explore the theory of networks in relation to the trade activity between the two cities. We can reconstruct the activity of this network and its utility through the physical evidence of goods that were actually exchanged, so in this way, the statistical data will be used to describe the frequency of interaction. Frequency of interaction is a marker of strength of tie in a social network, suggesting that this relationship will exert a significant influence on the nodes when it comes to the transmission of items or ideas[37]. The question here then is if the network connection between Pergamon and Ephesus can be considered to be strong, and if the network structure is manifested in the amount of ceramics that was traded between them.

Statistical comparison and frequency

Fig. 1 and **2** illustrate the distribution of the three ware groups, both from the basilica and sondage B6. Comparing the two deposits, we see approximately the same amount of White-grounded Ceramics in both, while there is a much greater quantity of the highly figurative Appliqué Ceramic in the basilica than in sondage B6. Another difference between the deposits is the striking absence of any Pergamenian Sigillata in the basilica deposit. Is this just a coincidence, or might we propose reasons for this absence in light of the different contexts and the users involved? For example, we may suggest that the consumers in the basilica deposit preferred elaborately decorated vessels and not plain ceramics as Pergamenian Sigillata. However, Eastern Sigillata B forms the major part of the deposit in the basilica. This is due to the fact that the layers of the basilica are dated late into the 1st century AD, at a time when ESB had just started to be extensively produced.

The distribution of the ware groups in sondage B6 is not as balanced as those from the basilica (**Fig. 4**). In B6, typical Hellenistic ceramic with coloured slip forms an extremely high percentage, supplemented with small quantities of other ware groups. Here, we find Pergamenian Sigillata is represented to a much higher degree than other, western Sigillatas. It seems that the owner had no special need for highly decorated vessels.

A diachronic comparison between the two deposits and the relationships between locally produced ceramics, Eastern Sigillata[38] and imported ceramics, as depicted in **Fig. 5** and **6**, makes it clear how eminent imports, especially from Pergamon, were in Ephesus at this time! Even if the single layers are not pure settlement strata, nonetheless the material reflects the general preferences Ephesians had for Pergamenian style vessels, or not. The distribution of the material from the basilica gives us quite a balanced picture, with all ware groups peaking during the period of the erection of the basilica. The imported ceramic

35 Thanks to H. Täuber for this information.
36 Meriç 2002, 17-19.

37 Collar 2007, 151.
38 I counted Eastern Sigillata A and B, although ESA is produced and imported from Syria-Lebanon, but ESB was manufactured around Ephesus. This is because both Sigillata groups represent a new type of ceramics that stands for a Roman influence.

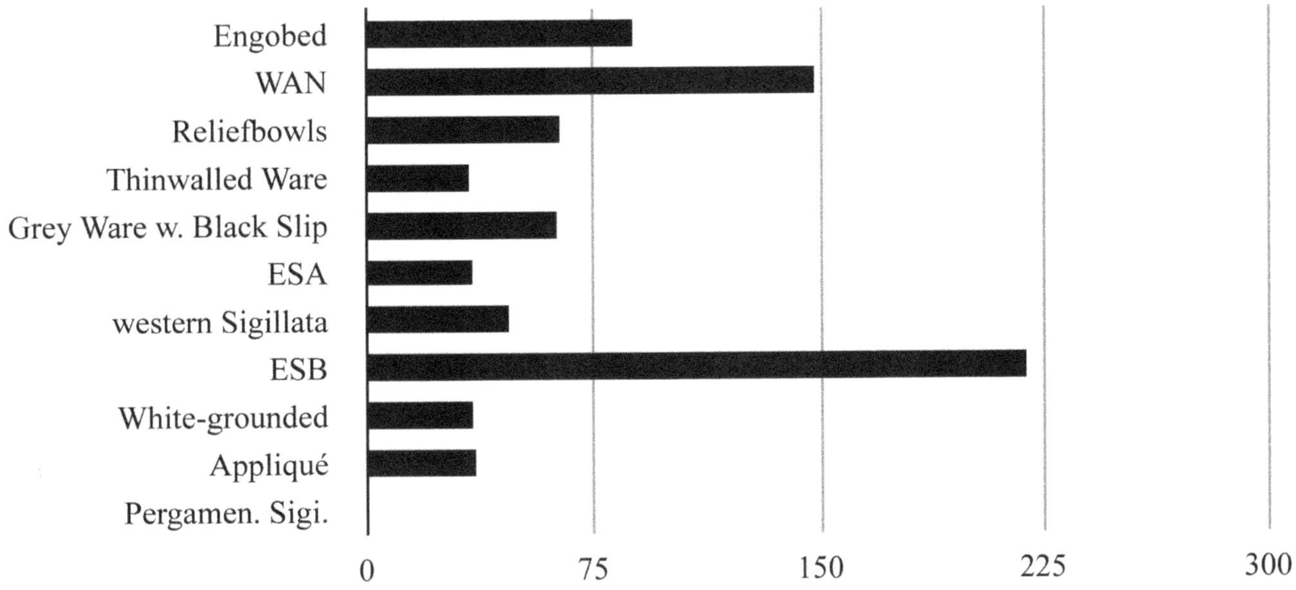

Fig. 3. Ware groups appearing in the basilica at the State Agora (A. Lätzer-Lasar)

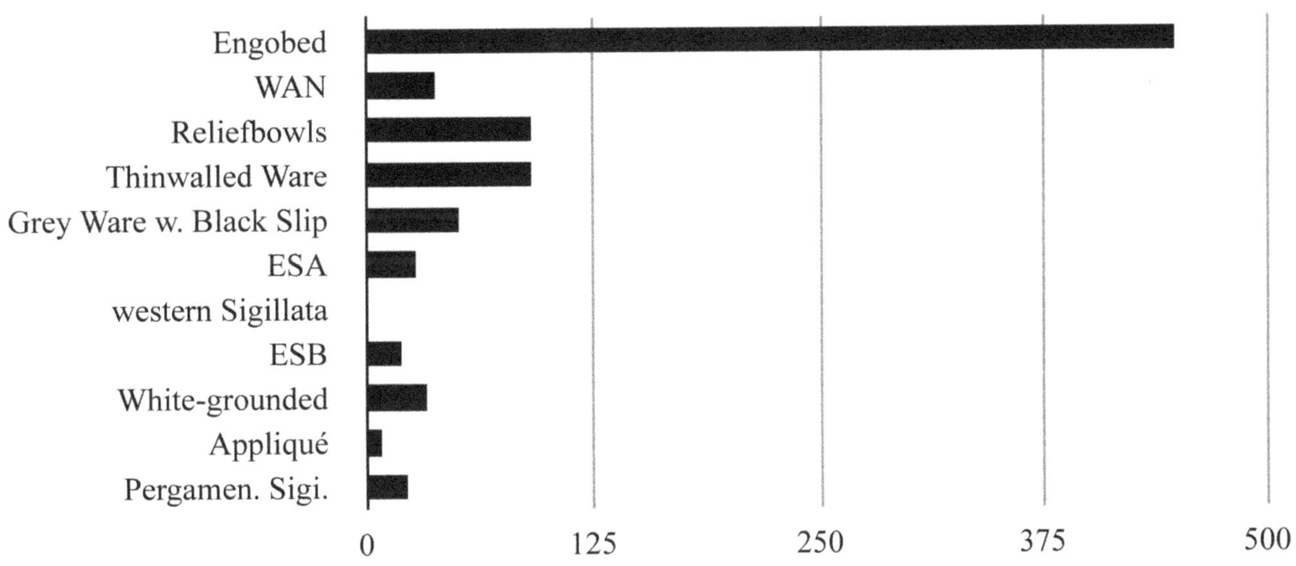

Fig. 4. Ware groups appearing in the Terrace House 2, sondage B6 (A. Lätzer-Lasar)

rises sharply between 11–13 AD, although there was no Pergamenian Sigillata in this context. At the basilica locally produced ceramics were obtained to a greater or lesser extent. Amounts of Eastern Sigillata soared in the last third of the 1st century BC, as production only began around then[39]. However, amounts of imports in the basilica context rose steadily, proportional to the amount of local products.Sondage B6 contained very few imports, alongside the ESA from Syria-Lebanon there were mainly ceramics imported from Pergamon, as well as some from Knidos and Italy. The pattern of increase in the local products is congruent to that from the basilica. We can observe a minor decrease from the 2nd to the 1st century BC, than a peak in the Augustan period and then again a decline during the 1st century AD. The Eastern Sigillata A occurs in Ephesian domestic contexts after the late 2nd century BC. However the Pergamenian imports have a totally different pattern, they increase slowly, but continuously and disproportionately to the other groups. It is difficult to interpret this as an indication for an affinity to the Pergamenians, because the amounts are far too small, especially at that time when Pergamon loses political power. However we might see reasons in increased migration from Pergamon as its political power waned.

[39] Ladstätter 2007, 208.

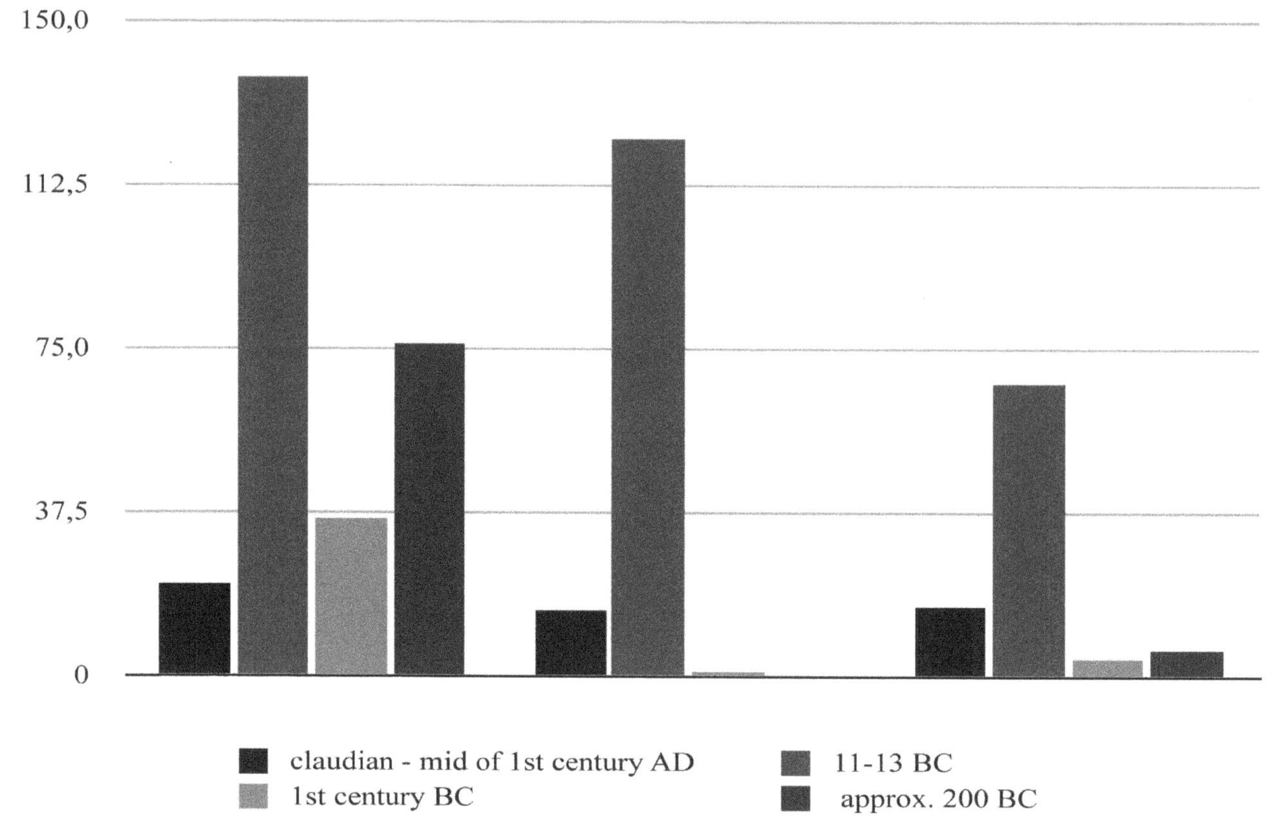

Fig. 5. Local - Eastern Sigillata - Imports, basilica at the State Agora (A. Lätzer-Lasar)

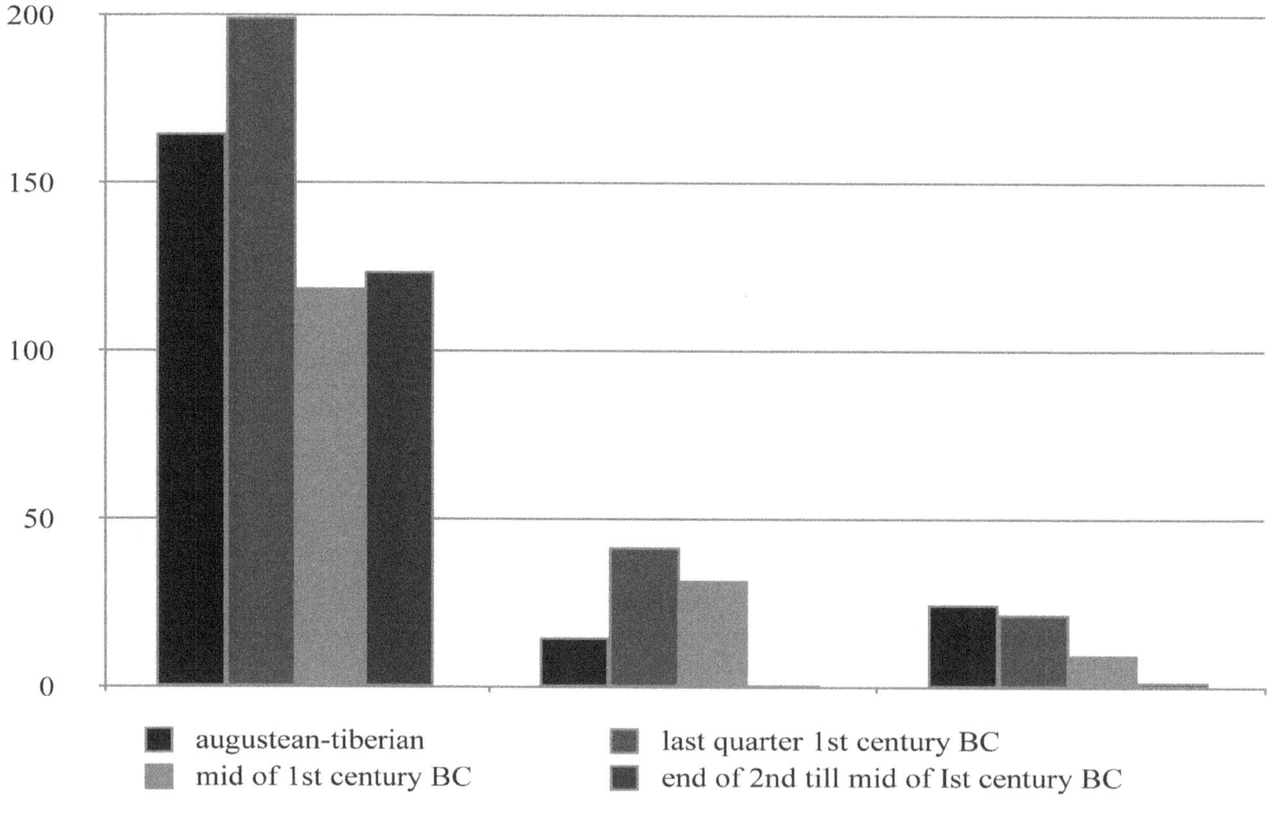

Fig. 6. Local - Eastern Sigillata - imports, Terrace House 2, sondage B6 (A. Lätzer-Lasar)

Summary and conclusions

The aim of this paper was to examine whether social processes occurring as part of a network can be analysed diachronically by comparing the statistical data of the ceramic material of two deposits. We examined the network connection between Ephesus and Pergamon from the early Roman occupation period until the early Imperial period. The focus was on the imported ceramics from Pergamon in Ephesus to see what kind of sociocultural influence the former Hellenistic capital had on the new capital of the Roman Provincia Asia.

Ephesus and Pergamon form a network consisting of strong ties. Networks of strong ties need more time than networks with weak ties (long-distance links) to spread objects or knowledge[40]. The typology of the material of the two deposits persists in the Hellenistic/ Pergamenian tradition throughout the whole occupation period and influenced the local catalogue of shapes. The utility of a cup (drinking habit, ritual performances) naturally remained the same. The vessel shapes did not change very much during the Hellenistic period until the end of the 1st century BC. From this time however, a different ceramic type, in this case Sigillata, and different shapes, such as beakers, are used in Ephesus. We might be able to observe a relationship between the ceramic innovation of Thin-walled beakers in the second half of the 1st century BC and the replacing of traditional Greek symposia with the typical Roman gatherings at collegia in the Augustan period. However, this observation needs further research.

In private contexts we come across what can be considered in sociological terms to be 'early adopters' of innovation[41]. An early adopter is generally a well-known public figure, somebody with social capital and a respected opinion leader. An early adopter is fundamental to the wider diffusion of innovation, because others respect his opinion and wish to emulate his choices. In this case, it might be a Roman wealthy businessman. If he adopts Sigillata – even if it is not western Sigillata but it reminds him of the one used in his home country – and he has a high reputation in society, then others will follow his lead and buy the same products as he does. This social phenomenon is critical to the mechanism of the spread of fashions. Perhaps we can argue that it was in this way that the domestic households in Ephesus adopted Eastern Sigillata and Thin-walled ceramics relatively early. Because this emulation was occurring without any knowledge on the part of the emulators of the original Sigillata that inspired our early adopters, but rather, because of aesthetic reasons or desire to emulate, the transmission of the innovation can be considered horizontal. However, in the public context of the basilica, we see a vertical transmission: within a public context, people refer to symbolic actions, such as when performing rituals. So the equipment they use possesses a deep symbolic meaning for them at this moment.[42] The participants in a ritual have a deep knowledge about the item that was used, and a specific reason for choosing it, probably observed from repeated participation in the ritual or learned as part of their social structure. In Ephesus, it seems that the simple and plain decorated Pergamenian Sigillata did not meet the expectations of the people performing a public ritual at the basilica in the (late-) Hellenistic period. Traditional vessels seem to obtain a more official character. This might be the reason why in the basilica context mostly highly decorated ceramics such as Appliqué and White-grounded Ceramics were found.

The chronology of the two deposits shows us that the ceramics did not change until the end of the 1st century BC. A sociocultural change such as different drinking habits, change of holding conventions or performing rituals can be seen in the private context at least two decades earlier than in the public context.

To apply network theories on material culture diachronically helps to understand, what kind of sociocultural processes might have happened in a society during a specific timeframe. But this method made also clear that exchanging objects in less amounts do not necessarily mean, that the strength of the connection faded. The network connection still can be a stable one with strongties.

Asuman Lätzer-Lasar, M.A.
University of Cologne
Institute of Archaeology/ a.r.t.e.s. Research School/ Center for Advanced Studies MORPHOMATA
laetzera@smail.uni-koeln.de

Bibliography

Collar, A. 2007. Network Theory and Religious Innovation. *Mediterranean Historical Review*, 22:1, 149–162.

Cook, K. S. and Whitmeyer, J. M. 1992. Two Approaches to Social Structure: Exchange Theory and Network Analysis. *Annual Review of Sociology* 18, 109–127.

Dereboylu, E. 2001. Weissgrundige Keramik und hellenistische Reliefbecher aus dem Hanghaus 2 in Ephesos. In F. Krinzinger (ed.), *Studien zur hellenistischen Keramik in Ephesos*. Jahreshefte des Österreichischen Archäologischen Instituts, Ergänzungsheft 2, 21–44. Wien, Phoibos.

40 Granovetter 1983, 212.
41 Collar 2007, 153.
42 Collar 2007, 155.

Granovetter, M. 1983. The Strength of Weak Ties: A Network Theory Revisited. *Sociology Theory* 1, 201–233.

Halfmann, H. 2001. *Städtebau und Bauherren im römischen Kleinasien. Ein Vergleich zwischen Pergamon und Ephesos*. Istanbuler Mitteilungen, Beiheft 43. Tübingen, Wasmuth.

Hübner, G. 1993. *Die pergamenische Applikenkeramik von Pergamon. Eine Bildersprache im Dienst des Herrscherkultes*. Pergamenische Forschungen 7. New York/Berlin, de Gruyter.

Kirbihler, F. 2007. Die Italiker in Kleinasien, mit besonderer Berücksichtigung von Ephesos (133v. Chr. – 1. Jh. n. Chr.). In M. Mayer (ed.), *Neue Zeiten – Neue Sitten. Zu Rezeption und Integration römischen und italischen Kulturguts in Kleinasien*, 19–31. Wien, Phoibos.

Ladstätter, S. 2007. Mode oder politisches Manifest? Überlegungen zur Übernahme römischen Formenguts in der frühkaiserzeitlichen Keramik von Ephesos. In M. Mayer (ed.), *Neue Zeiten – Neue Sitten. Zu Rezeption und Integration römischen und italischen Kulturguts in Kleinasien*, 203–219. Wien, Phoibos.

Lätzer, A. 2009. Studien zu einem späthellenistisch-frührömischen Fundkomplex aus dem Hanghaus 2. *Jahresheft des Österreichischen Archäologischen Instituts* 78, 123–220.

Meriç, R. 2002. *Späthellenistisch-römische Keramik und Kleinfunde aus einem Schachtbrunnen am Staatsmarkt in Ephesos*. Forschungen in Ephesos 9, 3. Wien, Phoibos.

Meyer-Schlichtmann, C. 1988. *Die pergamenische Sigillata aus der Stadtgrabung von Pergamon*. Pergamenische Forschungen 6. New York/Berlin, de Gruyter.

Mitsopoulos-Leon, V. 1991. *Die Basilika am Staatsmarkt in Ephesos. Kleinfunde. 1. Teil: Keramik hellenistischer und römischer Zeit*. Forschungen in Ephesos 9, 2, 2. Wien, Phoibos.

Rotroff, S. I. 1982. *Hellenistic Pottery. Athenian and Imported Moldmade Bowls*. The Athenian Agora XXII. Princeton, NJ., American School of Classical Studies.

Rotroff, S. I. 1997. *Hellenistic Pottery. Athenian and Imported Wheelmade Table Ware and Related Material*. The Athenian Agora XXIV. Princeton, NJ., American School of Classical Studies.

Rutherford, I. 2009. Network Theory and Theoric Networks, in I. Malkin, C. Constantakopoulou and K. Panagopoulou (eds.), *Greek and Roman Networks in the Mediterranean*, 24–38. London/ New York, Routledge.

Willer, D. (ed.) 1999. *Network Exchange Theory*. London, Frederick A. Praeger.

Zabehlicky-Scheffenegger, S. and Schneider, G. 2000. Applikenverzierte Gefäße aus Ephesos. *Rei Cretariae Romanae Fautorum acta* 36, 105–112.

Connections Near and Far: Hellenistic Imported Pottery at Phrygian Gordion

Shannan M. Stewart

Abstract

This paper examines the pottery imported at Gordion in the Hellenistic period, and its implications for the reconstruction of trade networks in Anatolia. In the first phase of the Early Hellenistic period (*c.* 333–275 BC), black slipped imports supplemented the traditional domestic assemblage and were copied in local gray and buff fabrics. Despite the Greek character of these vessels, they most likely came to Gordion from the Black Sea region via an overland route, and call into question their designation as 'Atticizing'. Few imports arrived at the site during the second phase of the Hellenistic period (*c.* 275–235 BC). This interruption in commercial activity was restricted only to table vessels, as objects in other media were still imported. By the Middle Hellenistic period (*c.* 235–189 BC) domestic imported pottery could again be found at Gordion, but only in the homes of a few well-connected individuals who acquired small matching sets of distinctive tableware from exclusive sources. Because the site was abandoned in 189 BC and not soon reoccupied, Gordion provides a rare look at the original distribution pattern of imported pottery among its residents.

Keywords: Gordion, Phrygia, Trade, Network, Black Sea, Atticizing, Hellenization

Standing[1] atop the low occupation mound at Gordion one can see – for many miles in every direction – what Gertrude Bell in 1903 described as 'mountainless, colorless, lifeless, unsubdued'[2] Anatolia (**Fig. 1**). Located high on the Central Anatolian Plateau in a semiarid steppe environment with a continental climate, Gordion is currently surrounded by dry grasslands and irrigated fields, though ancient residents and visitors probably saw more trees nearby, if only scrubby junipers[3]. Anatolia clearly did not meet the aesthetic criteria of Ms Bell, but the monotonous landscape of the Plateau is not completely without advantage, as the absence of significant topographic features facilitates overland movement, trade, and communication across a considerable portion of Asia Minor[4]. Add to this copious springs of potable water, an abundance of arable land, and distant but accessible forests, and it is no surprise that Gordion occupied a prominent place in the settlement history of Anatolia for over three millennia, from the Early Bronze Age until 189 BC.

The Hellenistic period (*c.* 333–189 BC), the chronological focus of this conference, is an eventful but largely unwritten chapter in the history of Gordion, with ancient authors recording only three episodes, all of which feature the same theme: the overland movement of an enormous mass of people who stopped at Gordion. Alexander the Great arrived at Gordion in 333 BC – accompanied by a portion of his sizable army and its hangers-on – and stayed just long enough to rendezvous with the remainder of his land forces, replenish his supplies, and cut his way through the prophecy of the Gordian Knot[5]. In the 260s BC a large tribe of Gauls ended their generations-long migration and settled permanently at Gordion[6], where they and the native population remained until 189 BC, when the site was hastily and thoroughly abandoned at the approach of the Roman legions led by Gn. Manlius Vulso on his Asia Minor military campaign[7].

Written accounts of Hellenistic Gordion are lacunose, uninformed, mired in literary topoi, and generally unconcerned with the site itself. Fortunately, the social, political, and economic history of Gordion is recorded in another format: material evidence. The far-flung proveniences of many finds recovered in the excavation of Gordion confirm that the ancient site – or at least some inhabitants of the ancient site – participated in multiple and changeable networks in every phase of its history. In the Hellenistic period the most abundant category of evidence for external connections is imported ceramic table vessels, the focus of the present study. The pottery under discussion was excavated by Rodney S. Young and his team between 1950 and 1973, under the auspices of the University of Pennsylvania. My examination of the Hellenistic pottery began in 2004 and remains an ongoing

1 I thank Drs Fenn, Römer-Strehl, and Kögler for inviting me to participate in such an excellent conference and for organizing a network of specialists as wonderfully diverse and widely distributed as the material they study.
2 Quoted in Mitchell 1993.
3 Miller 2000, 34.
4 Sams 1979, 45.
5 Arrian 2.3.1–8; Curtius 3.1.11–18; Justin *Historiae Philippicae* 11.7.3–16; Marsyas of Philippi (*FGrHist* 136 F 4); Plutarch *Alexander* 18.1–2.
6 Darbyshire *et al.* 2000, 77–78; Strobel 1996.
7 Grainger 1995; Livy 38.12.3–4.

Fig. 1. View of the Central Anatolian Plateau from the occupation mound at Gordion, pre-Hellenistic burial tumuli in middle distance (S. Stewart)

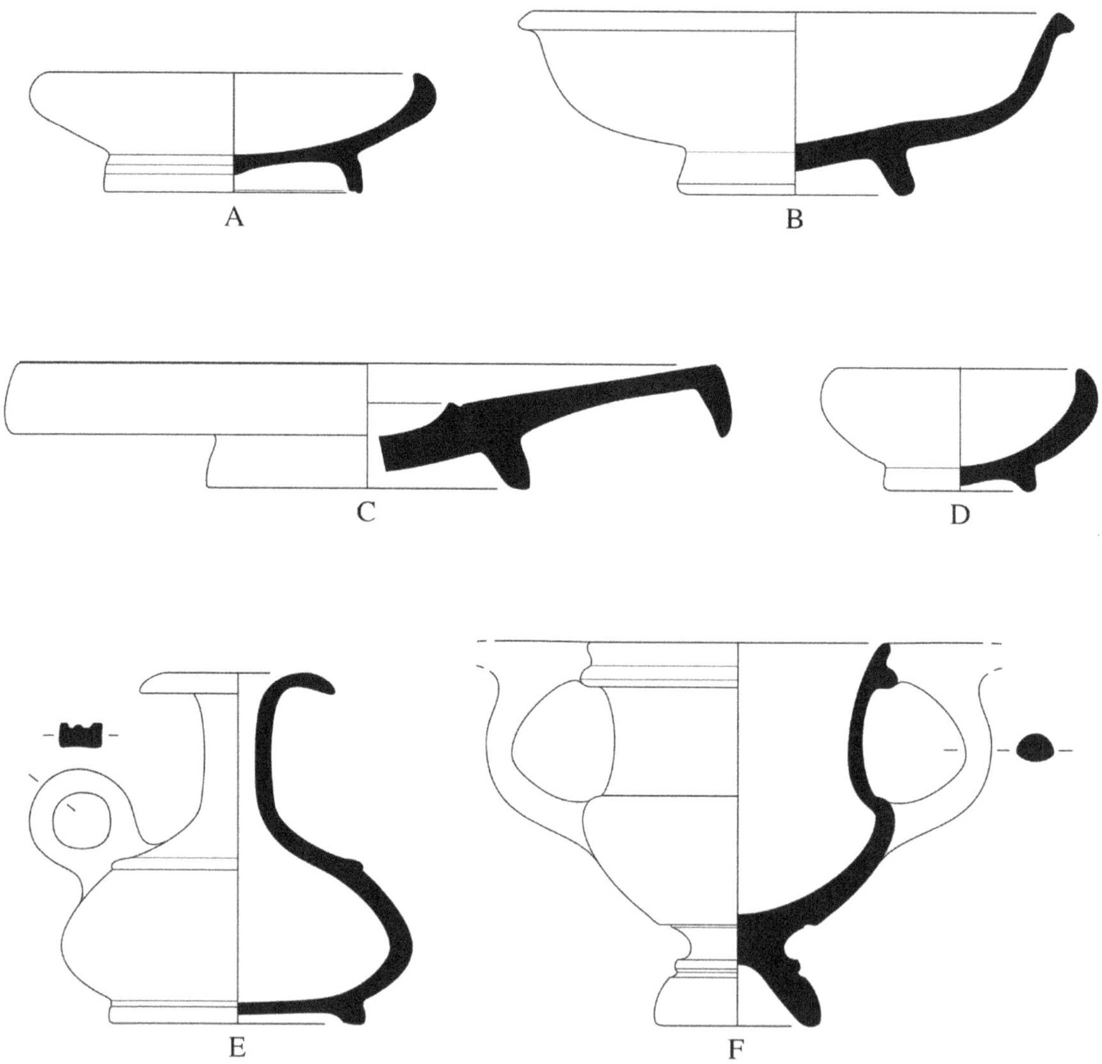

Fig. 2. Early Hellenistic black slipped types found at Gordion. A: shallow echinus bowl. B: outturned rim bowl. C: fishplate. D: salter. E: guttus. F: kantharos (S. Stewart)

Fig. 3. Early Hellenistic shallow echinus bowls: black slipped imports and local versions in Gordion gray and buff fabric (S. Stewart)

Fig. 4. Early Hellenistic gutti: black slipped imports and local versions in Gordion gray fabric (S. Stewart)

project. I here present my interpretations and conclusions to date; continued work at Gordion will no doubt refine our understanding of Hellenistic networks in Anatolia and beyond.

The first phase of the Early Hellenistic period (EHellA, *c.* 333–275 BC) is marked by a sudden and relatively drastic increase in the quantity of Attic-inspired black slipped table vessels imported to the site. Fine Greek wares had supplemented the Gordion assemblage since the early 7th century BC but never constituted more than a fraction of 1% of the total ceramic corpus until the beginning of EHellA, when they make up approximately 3% of entire corpus. Fishplates, shallow echinus bows, outturned rim bowls, salters, gutti, and kantharoi were the most popular shapes among residents of Early Hellenistic Gordion, accounting for approximately 95% of all black slipped vessels imported between *c.* 333 and 275 BC (**Fig. 2**).

Furthermore, these six shapes were all copied by local potters in the standard Gordion gray and buff fabrics (**Figs. 3–4**), suggesting either that the import market alone could not adequately meet demand or that black slipped versions of these vessels were not available to everyone.

At first glance, the presence of so many Greek-looking vessels seems to represent clear evidence of 'Hellenization' in the domestic sphere, but such a simplistic and direct correlation warrants reexamination. What, exactly, were the inhabitants of Gordion importing? Within the restricted range of Greek shapes found in EHellA levels, the vast majority are shallow echinus bowls and outturned rim

Fig. 5. Top row: predominant open shapes in the Early Phrygian local ceramic corpus, c. 800 BC (left: plain-rimmed bowl; right: carinated bowl). Center row: predominant open shapes in the Early Hellenistic local ceramic corpus, c. 333–275 BC (left: plain rim bowl; right: ledge rim dish). Bottom row: predominant Early Hellenistic black slipped shapes (left: shallow echinus bowl; right: outturned rim bowl) (S. Stewart)

bowls. The shallow echinus bowl is simply a dressed up, scaled down version of a plain rim bowl, the most common ceramic shape at Gordion in every phase of habitation, including the Hellenistic period. In the same way, the outturned rim bowl is strongly reminiscent of the ledge rim dish (the Hellenistic incarnation of the Early Phrygian 'carinated bowl'), a shape whose popularity at Gordion is second only to plain rim bowls. The morphological similarities between the most frequently occurring traditional Phrygian shapes and the most frequently imported Greek shapes indicates that they were functionally equivalent despite all superficial differences (**Fig. 5**). Shallow echinus bowls and outturned rim bowls would have held the same kinds of food and facilitated the same mode of dining as plain rim bowls and ledge rim dishes. These two imported shapes do not indicate a new (Greek) behavior, simply a new (Greek) style, and their appeal may have been some combination of familiarity and novelty. On the other hand, salters, gutti, and fishplates have no functional equivalent in the traditional Phrygian assemblage, and their presence in EHellA households indicates the adoption of new dining habits with no precedent at pre-Hellenistic Gordion.

PIXE analysis of the Hellenistic pottery has shown that the black slipped vessels were made of clay with a significantly different chemical composition than the clay used to make local and regional gray and buff wares[8], a conclusion just as easily reached by visual inspection of the pottery. The EHellA black slipped imports, although clearly inspired by types manufactured in Athens, came to Gordion from a variety of production centers, none of which have yet been identified. These vessels are usually classified as 'Atticizing', a modern archaeological term used to describe pots that intentionally imitate (probably contemporary) Attic types. Atticizing vessels can be very similar to their Attic inspirations in shape and size, fabric color and texture, slip color and finish, and production details. Most Atticizing vessels betray their true identity upon close inspection, without the need for scientific analysis. Atticizing vessels were mass produced in the Late Classical and Hellenistic period to satisfy the demand for genuine Attic vessels among those willing to settle for a close second[9].

[8] Williams *et al.* 1987.
[9] Berlin and Lynch 2003.

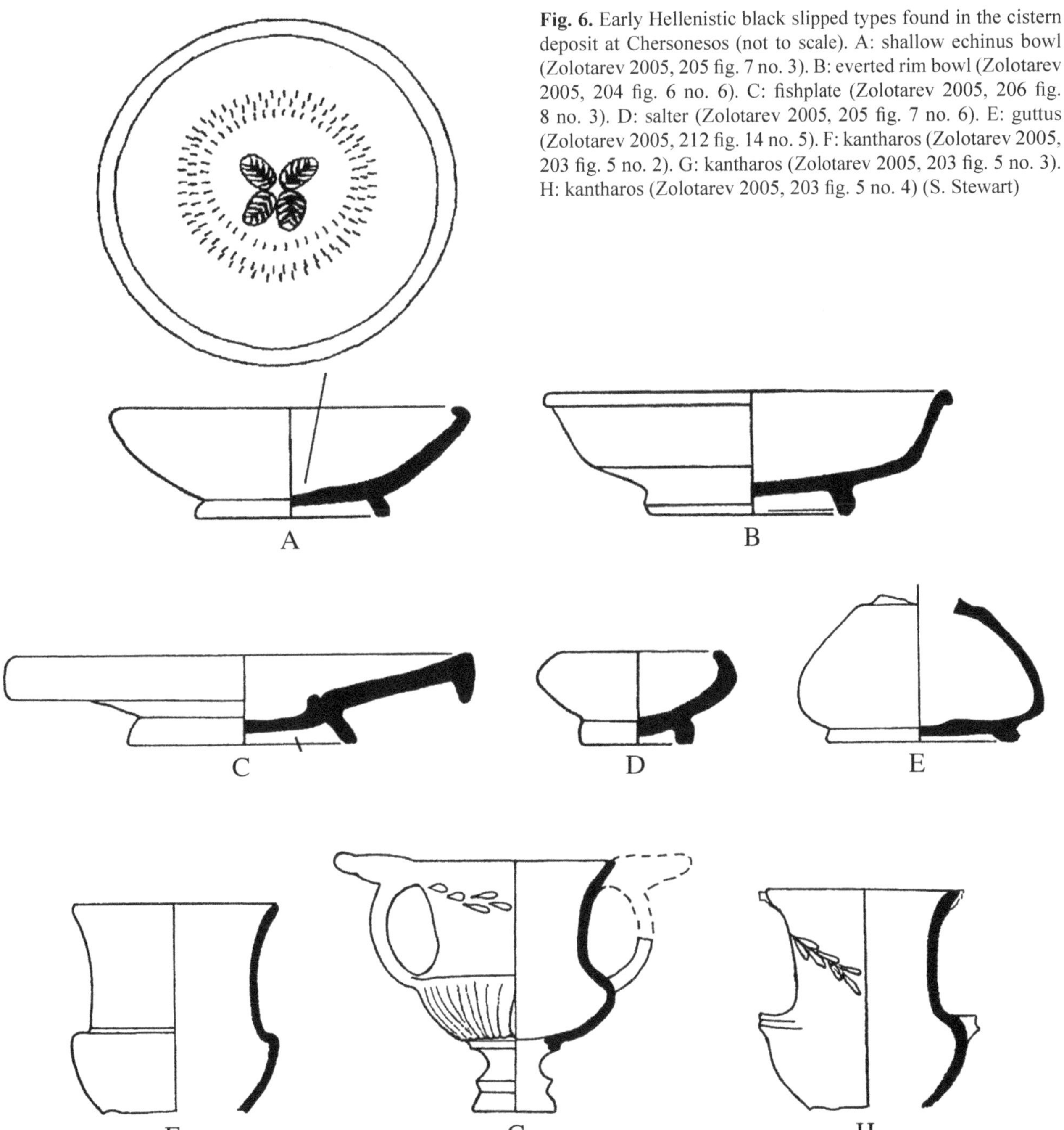

Fig. 6. Early Hellenistic black slipped types found in the cistern deposit at Chersonesos (not to scale). A: shallow echinus bowl (Zolotarev 2005, 205 fig. 7 no. 3). B: everted rim bowl (Zolotarev 2005, 204 fig. 6 no. 6). C: fishplate (Zolotarev 2005, 206 fig. 8 no. 3). D: salter (Zolotarev 2005, 205 fig. 7 no. 6). E: guttus (Zolotarev 2005, 212 fig. 14 no. 5). F: kantharos (Zolotarev 2005, 203 fig. 5 no. 2). G: kantharos (Zolotarev 2005, 203 fig. 5 no. 3). H: kantharos (Zolotarev 2005, 203 fig. 5 no. 4) (S. Stewart)

If these vessels did not come from Athens, whence did they come? The great quantity and wide distribution of contacts represented by Early Hellenistic coins and amphoras recovered at Gordion do not favor any single point of origin for imports. The Persian Royal Road certainly would have facilitated the movement of all manner of goods from the eastern Aegean, where cities along the coast had been participating in Greek culture – or had substantial Greek populations – for centuries. Atticizing vessels were probably manufactured at several Ionian centers to supply the local demand for Greek-style vessels and to accommodate the Hellenic – or at least cosmopolitan – inclinations of native west Anatolians. However, transport amphoras attest to a connection between Gordion and the south coast of the Black Sea, especially Herakleia Pontica[10]. In the Hellenistic period, North Greek amphoras – specifically those from Thasos – were exported to the Black Sea and to Gordion, but fragments of Thasian amphoras are rarely found at archaeological sites in the Aegean, suggesting they arrived at Gordion not from the west coast of Asia Minor by means of the Royal Road, but from the Black Sea via a north-south overland route.

[10] Mark Lawall pers. comm.

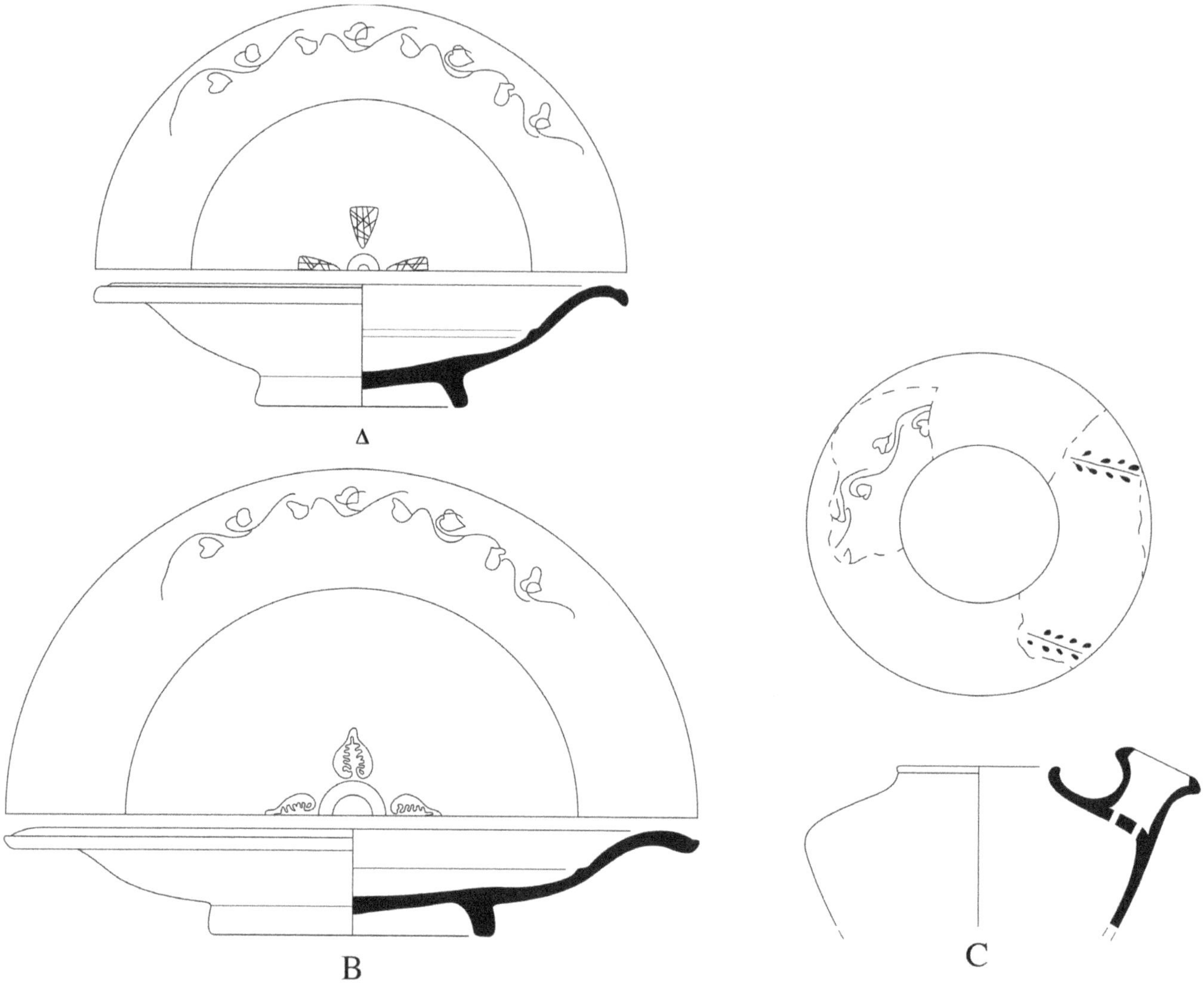

Fig. 7. Types occurring in Mottled Purple Slip Ware. A: small downcurved rim dish. B: large downcurved rim dish. C: strainer askos (S. Stewart)

It is possible, then, that many Atticizing vessels found in Early Hellenistic contexts at Gordion were imported from the Black Sea rather than from Aegean production centers. Additional evidence for a northern provenance has been found in the Black Sea region, at Chersonesos[11]. A cistern excavated in 1991 contained about 3000 fragments of pottery, including transport amphoras from Chersonesos, Sinope, Samos, Thasos, Rhodes, and Herakleia, the same general assortment of transport amphora types found at Gordion in the Late Phrygian and Early Hellenistic periods. Amphora stamps date the deposit to the first half of the third century, but earlier material was also recovered. The limited range of shapes among the black slipped vessels found in the Chersonesos cistern closely matches the equally limited range of shapes among imported vessels from contemporary contexts at Gordion: fishplates, shallow echinus bowls, outturned rim bowls, salters, and kantharoi (**Fig. 6**)[12].

Similarities go beyond general morphological preferences. Shallow echinus bowls at both sites are often adorned with blobby impressed 'palmettes' surrounded by one or more uneven bands of rouletting. Salters at both sites are exclusively of the incurved rim variety, although this was by no means the most popular form of salter at sites in the Aegean[13]. Finally, Early Hellenistic consumers at both sites exhibited no clear preference in kantharos body type (ribbed and plain versions both occur), but among decorative choices there is a clear predilection for opposing olive or myrtle garlands in added beige, one of countless

11 All information about the cistern deposit at Chersonesos is derived from Zolotarev 2005.

12 Zolotarev refers to the black slipped pottery as 'Attic' but offers no evidence for this identification.

13 Berlin 1999, 94.

Fig. 8. Small downcurved rim dish in Mottled Purple Slip Ware (S. Stewart)

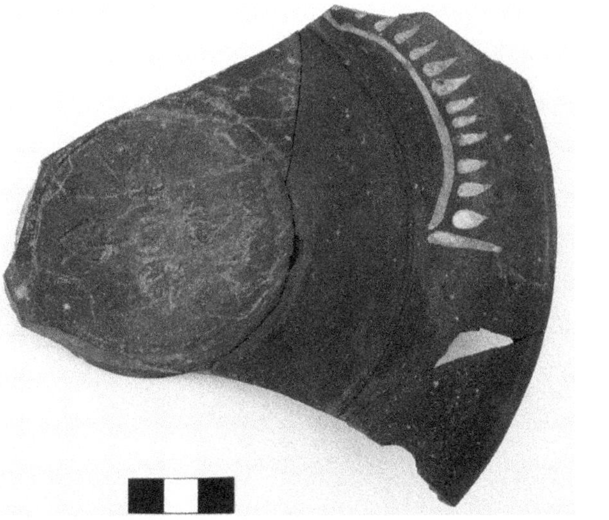

Fig. 10. Small downcurved rim dish in Grainy Brown Ware (S. Stewart)

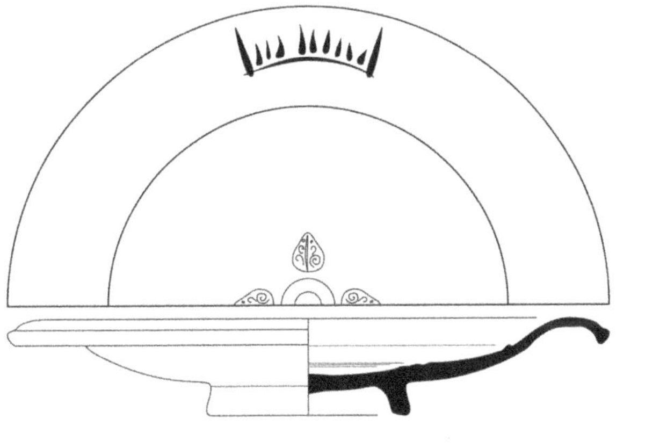

Fig. 9. Type occurring in Grainy Brown Ware: small downcurved rim dish (S. Stewart)

motifs invented at Athens and adopted and developed at productions centers throughout the Mediterranean. Early Hellenistic Chersonesos and Gordion have such strikingly similar black slipped assemblages that the immediate (if not ultimate) sources of the Gordion 'Atticizing' vessels should be sought north of the Plateau, not west. If the inhabitants of Early Hellenistic Gordion imported most of their fancy table ware from the Black Sea, and if they knew the source of these goods (an admittedly shaky assumption), what is the meaning of these vessels? What specific cachet did they encode? The virtual absence of Attic pottery in Hellenistic strata at Gordion suggests that few residents would have known what it looked like. An archaeologist sees the Gordion black slipped imports as cheap imitations of the genuine Attic article, but the residents of Gordion may have seen the same vessels as the genuine Black Sea article. They communicate 'Atticizing' to us, but their original owners may have read 'cosmopolitan,' 'upscale,' or simply 'not from around here' in the fine clays and shiny surfaces of these imported pots. Fragments of EHellA imported wares were found in every trench excavated on the occupation mound at Gordion, with no concentration in any one area. In the context of imported or luxury goods, such a diffuse and seemingly random pattern of distribution could be cited as evidence for the absence of a wealthy quarter or Greek neighborhood, whose residents held a monopoly on imported goods or preferred to use familiar 'motherland' vessels rather than native Phrygian products. However, the imported vessels recovered from houses abandoned in 189 BC (discussed in more detail presently), compel us to rethink this interpretation.

The commercial activities – and probably the attendant political, cultural, and social interactions – conducted via Gordion's various networks abated during the second phase of Hellenistic occupation (EHellB, *c.* 275–235 BC). Black slipped table vessels were no longer imported to the site. More significantly, the production of local gray and buff imitations ceased, suggesting that availability was not the only factor in the disappearance of Greek shapes. Coin hoards accumulated throughout the Early Hellenistic period were added to only sporadically, if at all, between *c.* 275 and 235 BC[14]. Only a few transport amphoras can be assigned to this phase, a small group of Rhodian and Erythraian handle fragments. The most notable feature of the amphora corpus is the absolute absence of Pontic amphoras after *c.* 270 BC, coinciding with the cessation of black slipped imports and lending further support to the premise that the bulk of imported table vessels arrived at Gordion via a north-south overland route between Gordion and the south coast of the Black Sea (although the ultimate origin of the vessels could have been elsewhere). Though

[14] Cox 1966; Mark Lawall pers. comm.

Fig. 11. Rodney's House, excavation of the Pantry and Pithos Room (courtesy Gordion Archive, neg. R 030-042)

Fig. 12. Inventoried vessels from Rodney's House, Pantry (S. Stewart)

imported pottery no longer made its way to Gordion after about 275 BC, the networks and contacts revealed by the numismatic evidence suggest the site remained an active participant in the Hellenistic world.

If connections between Gordion and the outside world were partially severed in the later phases of Early Hellenistic period, they were at least tenuously restored in the Middle Hellenistic period (MHell, *c.* 235–189 BC), and with a special focus on Pergamon. However, the merchants and caravans that transported figurines, amphoras, and coins to Gordion did not bring many table vessels with them: the Middle Hellenistic ceramic assemblage consists almost entirely of locally produced pots with imports making up less than 1% of the total ceramic corpus. Of the 34 MHell regional imports inventoried at Gordion, none has an obvious provenance, and I have assigned descriptive names to the few identifiable wares. Ten pots occur in Mottled Purple Slip Ware (**Figs. 7–8**) and three in Grainy Brown Ware (**Figs. 9–10**); the remaining 21 MHell imports are, for the most part, individual vessels representing the single occurrence of a specific fabric. With the exception of two inventoried cooking pots made of distinctively non-local cooking fabrics, the corpus of regional imports is dominated by drinking and dining forms. The predominantly insular character of the ceramic assemblage

Fig. 13. Inventoried vessels from Roger's House, two imported bowl-kantharoi in foreground (S. Stewart)

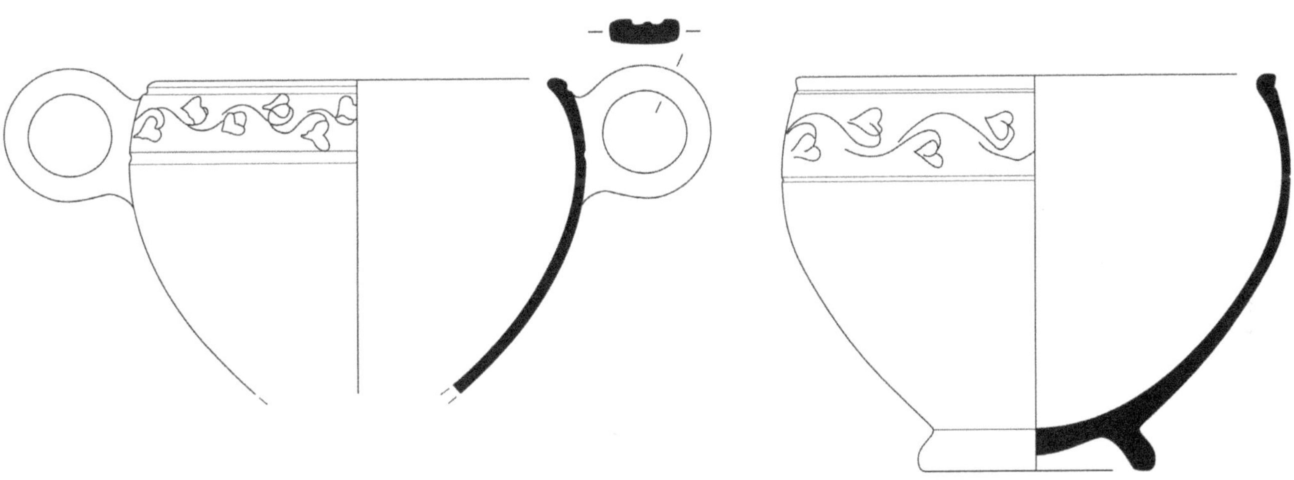

Fig. 14. Profiles of two imported bowl-kantharoi from Roger's House (S. Stewart)

cannot be attributed to limited accessibility or an inward-looking attitude, since other goods were imported to Gordion at this time. Furthermore, the imported vessels are not severely different from the locally produced pots in terms of clay, inclusions, and slip, and in some cases it is difficult to draw the line between a locally manufactured singleton and a real import. I have therefore classified the Middle Hellenistic non-local pottery as 'regional imports' under the assumption that the visible similarities in the physical makeup of the vessel reflect a common (but broad) geological profile and therefore a common (but equally broad) source. 'Regional' should here be understood as 'most likely made in Asia Minor'. The small sample size of Middle Hellenistic imported pottery may restrict its interpretive potential, but the context in which these relatively few vessels were found provides rare information about the original intra-site distribution of imported goods. The final chapter in the history of Hellenistic Gordion was written by Livy, who describes the abandonment of the site and the extermination of its residents at the hands of the Roman consul Gn. Manlius Vulso as part of his campaign against the inhabitants of Galatia (i.e., Phrygia)[15]. When Vulso and his legions arrived at Gordion in 189 BC, they

[15] Livy 38.12.1–38.27.9.

Fig. 15. General view of the Pottery Establishment at the time of excavation, June 1958 (courtesy Gordion Archive, neg. R 398-022)

found the city recently abandoned, everyone having fled eastward to Mount Olympus and Mount Magaba[16]. The Roman legions pursued the refugees, surrounded their encampment, and eventually breeched the defenses. Once the Romans broke through the fortification, the defenders rushed blindly in all directions[17]. Many fell headlong to their deaths[18]. Others were taken prisoner or slaughtered. Livy's dramatic description of the final days of the siege makes it clear that those who had abandoned Gordion were no longer able return[19]. The basic plot of the story is confirmed by archaeological evidence at Gordion: datable coins, pottery, and amphora handles indicate that occupation ended abruptly in 189 BC, and the large number of intact in situ floor deposits leaves no doubt that the site was quickly deserted and not soon repopulated.

Gordion therefore provides valuable evidence for the distribution of imported pottery within an ancient settlement. Imported vessels were found concentrated in just a few 189 BC abandonment deposits excavated by Young and his team. Evidently, these commodities were not equally available to all residents of Middle Hellenistic Gordion but were the privilege of just a few households. The residents that could boast of imports in the pantry were also, probably not coincidently, the most affluent. The residents of Rodney's House (**Figs. 11–12**) owned all known examples of Mottled Purple Slip Ware (five small downcurved dishes, three large downcurved dishes, and one made bowls, dishes, and plates manufactured and procured as large production batches. The domestic inventory of Roger's House (**Figs. 13–14**) included two bowl-kanthroi in an unidentified ware found nowhere else at the site, as well as four cooking pots (the highest concentration in a single house on the mound), seven metal objects, and six glass fragments (none of which belonged to a vessel). The inhabitants of the Pottery Establishment (**Figs. 15–16**), a workshop specializing in the production of figurines, flower-bust thymiateria (incense burners), and small vessels (especially unguentaria), could claim possession of every known vessel in Grainy Brown Ware (all small downcurved rim dishes with a profile nearly identical to those in Mottled Purple Slip Ware), along with a kiln in the courtyard, a pithos and built-in cooking installations in the kitchen, and a substantial quantity of local dining vessels.

Like any exciting and important set of data, the Gordion Hellenistic imported pottery both clarifies and confuses. A close examination of the Early Hellenistic black slipped imports reveals the likely provenance of these vessels, and at the same time undermines the assumed meaning of terms and concepts such as 'Hellenization' and 'Atticizing'. The context of the Middle Hellenistic imported vessels certainly elucidates the character of Gordion's participation in extra-site networks: small sets of dishes and cups were

[16] Livy 38.18.13.
[17] Livy 38.23.1–4.
[18] Livy 38.23.1–2.
[19] Livy 38.21. Livy's sources for the death toll are in conflict: Claudius reports 40,000 casualties while Valerius Antias sets the figure at 10,000.

Fig. 16. Evidence of pottery production from the Pottery Establishment. Top: fired unguentaria (courtesy Gordion Archive, neg. R 405-010). Center left: unfired unguentaria (S. Stewart). Center right: fired scraps of clay used as vessel props in the kiln (S. Stewart). Bottom: vessel finishing tool (S. Stewart)

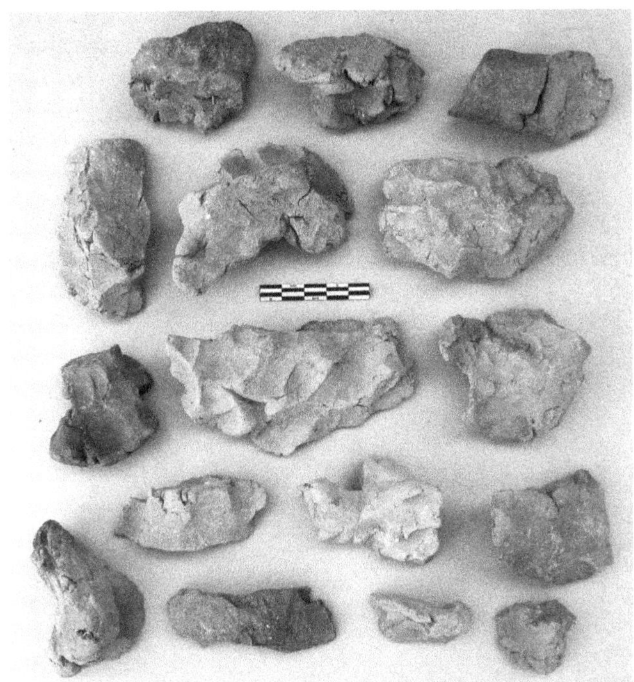

acquired by only a few wealthy, enterprising individuals acting independently. This resolution in the details throws the larger picture out of focus: had Gordion not been abandoned for so long, the contents of the abandoned houses would likely have been scattered across the site and throughout different strata, a situation encountered at virtually every archaeological site with long phases of continuous occupation. Such a small quantity of vessels, when considered in the broad context of the entire site (the most refined context attainable at many archaeological sites), would lead us conclude that MHell Gordion was a poorly-connected place in general. But seen in its original context, the imported pottery reveals the presence of several considerably well-connected individuals living among a larger population. The imported pottery excavated at Gordion sheds light on our view of the intra-site distribution of limited-availability goods, and in so doing it casts doubt on our assumptions about the relationship between original context and archaeological record. The Early Hellenistic black slipped table vessels may be evenly dispersed in excavation trenches, but all were discovered in fills, dumps, and other disturbed deposits. If Gordion had not been abandoned in 189 BC, the distribution pattern of Middle Hellenistic imported vessels would have been indistinguishable from that of most Hellenistic archaeological sites in the Mediterranean.

Shannan M. Stewart
Visiting Assistant Professor
Department of Classics, UIUC
4080 FLB, 707 S. Mathews Avenue
Urbana, IL 61801
stewrt@illinois.edu

Bibliography

Berlin, A. M. and K. M. Lynch. 2003. Going Greek: Atticizing Pottery in an Achaemenid World. *Studia Troica* 12, 167–178.

Cox, D. H. 1966. Gordion Coin Hoards III, IV, V, and VII. *American Numismatic Society Numismatic Notes* 12, 19–55.

Darbyshire, G., Mitchell, S. and Vardar, L. 2000. The Galatian Settlement in Asia Minor. *Anatolian Studies* 50, 75–97.

Miller, N. F. 2000. Plants in the Service of Archaeological Preservation. *Expedition* 42.1, 30–36.

Mitchell, S. 1993. *Anatolia: Land, Men and Gods in Asia Minor*. 2 vols. New York, Oxford University Press.

Sams, G. K. 1979. Patterns of Trade in First Millennium Gordion. *Archaeological News* 8(2/3), 45–53.

Strobel, K. 1996. *Die Galater. Geschichte und Eigenart der keltischen Staatenbildung auf dem Boden des hellenistischen Kleinasien I.* Berlin, Akademie Verlag.

Williams, E. T., Cadet, G., Guardala, N. A., Huang, E. and Winter, F. A. 1987. Analysis of Pottery by PIXE: Late Classical and Hellenistic Imports to Gordion. *Nuclear Instruments and Methods in Physics Research*, 430–432.

Zolotarev, M. I. 2005. A Hellenistic Ceramic Deposit from the North-eastern Sector of hersonesos, in V. F. Stolba and L. Hannestad (eds.), *Chronologies of the Black Sea Area in the Period c. 400–100 BC*, 193–216. Aarhus, Aarhus University Press.

A pottery kiln underneath the Odeon of ancient Sagalassos. The excavation results, the table wares and their archaeometrical analysis

Jeroen Poblome, Dennis Braekmans, Branko Mušič, Mark Van Der Enden, Bert Neyt, Bart De Graeve & Patrick Degryse

Abstract

In 2007, a badly preserved pottery kiln was discovered beneath the remains of the imperial period Roman Odeon at Sagalassos. Geophysical research in the vicinity revealed the possible presence of more such structures. Additionally, recent archaeometrical research is presented in this paper, supporting the case for local production of pottery during the Hellenistic period at Sagalassos. Building on this, the pottery retrieved from the fill layers inside the dismantled Odeon kiln are discussed and attributed to the end of the third century and the (first half of the) second century BC. As no detailed typo-chronological framework for the wares can be constructed yet, the main types are presented and, as much as is already possible, placed in the socio-cultural context of Pisidian Sagalassos.

Keywords: Sagalassos, local pottery production, archaeometry, geophysics, Hellenistic fashion

The badly damaged kiln(s)

Between 2005 and 2008, the remains of the eastern half of the Roman imperial Odeon were excavated at Sagalassos, SW Turkey, by the University of Leuven, Belgium. The concert hall for musical, rhetorical and poetic performances is situated on a terrace to the north of the Lower Agora, partly built into the slope below the Upper Agora. The construction consisted of a covered semi-circular auditorium with a radius of 24m, fronted to the south by a stage building with a façade of *c.* 50m long. Although parts of the eastern entrance hall were still standing to a height of more than 6m, the quality of preservation of the scene, *orchestra* and mainly the *cavea* was of a different nature (**Fig. 1**).

Compared to other monuments at Sagalassos the building period of the Odeon was fairly long. Construction started in Augustan times, the *cavea* was in place by the end of the first century AD, while the building was completed in Severan times with the erection of the columnar façade on the scene (*scaenae frons*). The hall remained in use until the early decades of the sixth century AD.

The excavations revealed a poor state of preservation of the *cavea*. Not only had the benches and seats been removed, possibly already in late antiquity, but also most of the foundation substructures had been dismantled and removed. At several spots, natural bedrock was encountered immediately underneath the erosional and collapse layers, excavated inside the auditorium. In the north-eastern part of the *cavea*, however, the absence of the foundations of the benches led to the discovery in 2007 of a feature predating the Odeon: a kiln (**Fig. 2**) (Locus 79 in sector 2350-2455)[1].

The kiln was partly dug into the natural bedrock of the steep slope situated between the Lower and Upper Agora. The plan of the kiln was hard to reconstruct, appearing in part as an ensemble of heterogeneously coloured spots with some charcoal. The contours of the entrance and combustion chamber could be traced, however, as the ophiolitic bedrock, on top of which the kiln was constructed, was discoloured as a result of radiating heath. The structure could not be entirely excavated as, upon its abandonment and dismantling, the north-eastern part of its remains was overrun by a water channel. The kiln was oriented more or less N/NW-S/SE, with the entrance from the south and the combustion chamber for the larger part situated inside the hill. In this way, the heat could be contained more efficiently. Because of the partial state of preservation, the original dimensions of the kiln could not be determined with certainty. This is the case for the height, but also the diameter could only be estimated. The combustion chamber appeared to have been more or less circular with a maximum length of 1.33m and an estimated width of *c.* 1.30m (1.10m preserved). The stoking channel was 0.90m long, 0.35m wide and preserved to a height of 0.26m. Based on these observations, we consider the kiln to have been originally designed as an updraught structure. Its estimated dimensions are most indicative of a pottery kiln, with the combustion chamber separated from the pot chamber by a pierced floor.

1 For the preliminary excavation report, see Degraeve 2009, 433–434.

Fig. 1. Aerial view of the Roman imperial Odeon at Sagalassos (© Sagalassos Archaeological Research project)

Several fill layers were identified inside the preserved remains of the kiln, up to 0.85m deep in its back part. The stratigraphy was different in the stoking channel compared to the combustion chamber. In each zone three layers had been deposited. The floor of the opening into the kiln was covered by a thin layer (max. 0.15m) of light brown soil (Locus 134), followed by a black ash layer of only 0.05m thick (Locus 87). The upper stratum (Locus 81) was 0.30m thick and contained a lot of stone and brick. At the edge of the combustion chamber, the soil changed and a different stratigraphy was registered. The lowest part of the fill was composed of a very stony soil, 0.20m thick (Locus 129), topped by a silty, dark brown layer of another 0.20 m, containing a considerable quantity of charcoal particles (Locus 110). On top of this, a very heterogeneous red-brown layer was excavated, 0.40m in thickness (Locus 63). The north-western part of this layer was situated in a cavity, dug out into the natural bedrock. The build-up and relative chronology between these layers is not entirely clear, especially as the interface between the northern and southern sequences appeared to be a more or less vertical cut.

Analysis of the pottery contained in these layers pointed out, however, that the lowest strata (Loci 87, 134, 110 and 129) were probably contemporaneous. The material dated from the end of the third and the (first half of the) second century BC (see below). Both upper layers (Loci 81 and 63) also contained a lot of Hellenistic material, but this was mixed with Roman imperial pottery of the end of the first century BC and the first half of the first century AD. Possibly, the upper part of the stratigraphy within the kiln was rearranged at a later stage, in preparation for the construction of the Odeon.

In any case, the kiln had been put out of operation and partially dismantled before the fill layers were deposited in its remains. Therefore, no relationship could be established between the functioning of the kiln and the pottery attested in the fill layers, apart from the fact that the latter should be considered as a *terminus ante quem* for the potting activity. The exact nature of the output of the kiln, as well as its period of activity, thus still remain unknown. Even though the chronological dating of the kiln is indirect, it still represents the oldest artisanal structure identified at Sagalassos thus far. In 2011, the origins of Sagalassos in Classical times were stratigraphically established[2], implying that the kiln could be generally attributed to a period between the fifth (i.e. the origin of the site) and third (i.e. the upper date of the fill material) centuries BC. During the excavation of workshops in the local Potters'

[2] Claeys *et al.*, in preparation.

Fig. 2. The badly preserved pottery kiln underneath the cavea of the Odeon, looking from the remains of the combustion chamber into the stoking channel (© Sagalassos Archaeological Research project)

Quarter, however, we repeatedly noticed that abandoned and dismantled kilns were fairly rapidly levelled with fill layers[3], possibly because the remains of these structures could represent a hindrance in the continued occupation and use of the associated workshop buildings. This practice would suggest that the kiln found underneath the Odeon may be associated with the Hellenistic period, although there is no way to directly prove this point.

Apart from the chronological positioning of the kiln, its topographical location should also be noted. In the context of ancient Sagalassos the latter may be seemingly odd, at first sight, away from the local Potters' Quarter and underneath one of the public monuments – i.e. in the very centre of the Roman town. Obviously, the Hellenistic settlement was of a different organization and smaller in size[4]. So far, the oldest kilns excavated and dated in the Potters' Quarter were Augustan and have been linked to a phase of high-investment in craft production[5]. This could imply another location for the Hellenistic potters of Sagalassos. Actually, recent geophysical research, using ground penetrating radar as well as magnetometry techniques, in the area to the east of the Roman Odeon revealed the presence of five small, yet possibly meaningful anomalies (**Fig. 3**). On the basis of the magnetic results, the surveyed area could be subdivided into two areas.

Area A revealed well preserved architectural remains down to the depth of at least 3 m, possibly forming part of one large building. In Area B no clear indications for walls were picked up, with fairly chaotic anomalies associated with collapse materials. The area also contained some stronger, magnetic anomalies typical for burned clay in any form, such as concentrations of bricks and tiles, or kilns. The shape of the latter anomalies was not as defined as with the geophysical signals of the well preserved kilns in the Potters' Quarter. Perhaps the geophysical anomalies represent badly preserved kilns, as was the case underneath the Odeon. The alternative option that these anomalies result from collapse materials mixed with bricks and tiles cannot be entirely ruled out, however. Apart from their state of preservation, the depth of these features as well as their covering with heterogeneous collapse materials could also explain the less defined nature of the magnetic anomalies. On the other hand, more irregular distortions are usually associated with collapsed materials mixed with brick and tile, whereas the discussed anomalies are somehow isolated, resulting from magnetic responses generated by smaller features, such as kilns. The above argumentation, together with the topographical location of the kiln(?)

[3] Poblome *et al.* 2001.
[4] Waelkens 2004.
[5] Poblome *et al.* 2002a.

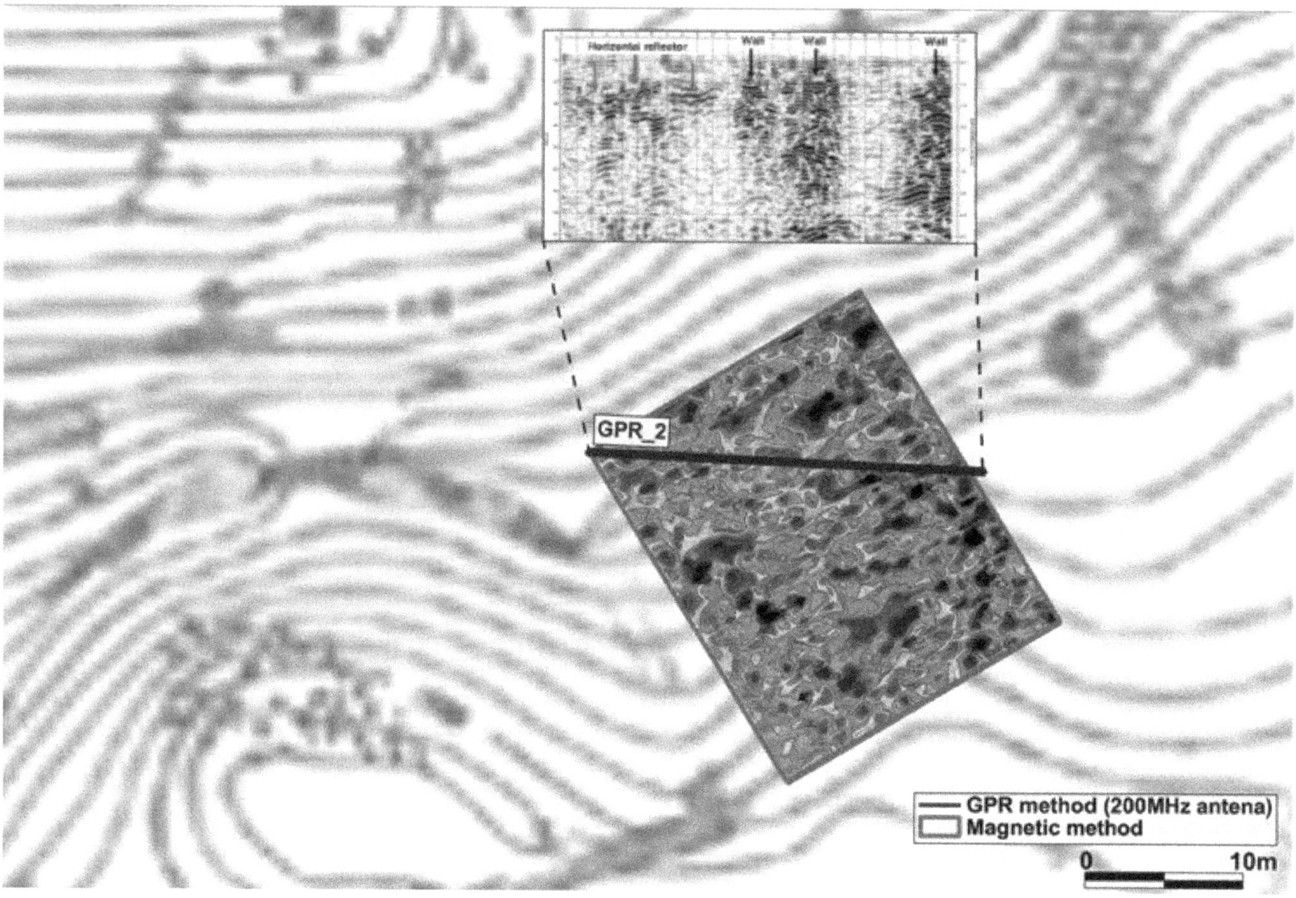

Fig. 3. The area immediately east of the Odeon, surveyed with geophysical methods. The arrows indicate the discussed anomalies (© Sagalassos Archaeological Research project)

anomalies on the same slope and at the same depth as the kiln underneath the Odeon, do not provide direct proof, but fairly substantial evidence for the identification of the Hellenistic potters' quarter of Sagalassos. If its location is to be established by future excavations, the Hellenistic potters' quarter would be located in the (intra-mural) eastern parts of the urban community.

Test tubes, powders and analytical stuff

The remains of the kiln underneath the Odeon, and the possible presence of others, are a first indication for the local production of pottery at (Classical/)Hellenistic(?) Sagalassos. Besides the presence of this structure, the archaeometrical analysis of contemporary pottery is also important to consider in this context. The so-called 'provenance postulate' of archaeological pottery[6] implies that '*differences between distinct sources of raw materials can be recognized analytically*' and that '*compositional variations will be greater between sources than within sources*', making the archaeometrical characterisation of wares an essential step in determining whether or not ceramics were locally or regionally produced and, if so, defining for which classes of pottery this was the case.

Based on analysis of material collected at Kozluca höyük[7] and at Sagalassos[8], local production of Hellenistic table ware at Sagalassos has been established[9]. The fabric and finish of the samples were macroscopically similar at both sites. The slip, on the other hand, was notably different from Roman imperial Sagalassos red slip ware. Based on the specific nature and quality of the slip and shape morphology, the sherds and fabric were attributed to the Hellenistic period. This pottery is usually slipped orange, brownish red or black. Different colour combinations, such as orange brown or reddish brown and blackish grey, also occur frequently. Overall, the slip is thin, sometimes dull and watery in appearance, and it does not always adhere well to the ceramic vessel. Occasionally the exterior lower part is not slipped, while the zone of the rim may be accentuated by a band of darker slip. Compared to Roman imperial Sagalassos red slip ware, the Hellenistic

6 Wiegand *et al.* 1977.

7 Nine samples of material collected during extensive surveying. The site is at *c.* 50 km south-west of Sagalassos.

8 Twelve samples of residual, Hellenistic material in early Roman imperial contexts.

9 Poblome *et al.* 2002b.

fabric tends to be somewhat softer and slightly more buff in colour, but no macroscopic differences are consistently apparent. The paste is very fine and highly microporous, ranging in colour from reddish yellow to brown (7.5 YR 5/4 brown; 5 YR 6/6 reddish yellow). Within this Hellenistic table ware fabric no further chronological distinctions could be made.

The archaeometric analyses indicated that the macroscopically defined Hellenistic table ware fabric actually consisted of two different groups, with different clay compositions and provenances. Half of the material was made from clays collected from the red weathering horizon of the ophiolithic bedrock sampled in the Potters' Quarter of Sagalassos, whereas the other half was made from clays quarried in the north-west part of the nearby Çanaklı valley, which would also serve the production of Roman imperial Sagalassos red slip ware. The fineness of the fabric does not allow these archaeometrical attributions to be replicated macroscopically, however. Nevertheless, as no archaeological indications for pottery production are present in the north-west part of the Çanaklı valley, these clays are considered to have been transported to ancient Sagalassos – fore-shadowing their grand-scale exploitation in Roman times, as the clay raw material for Sagalassos red slip ware. As the Çanaklı clays were used at the same time and for the same type of product as the ophiolitic clays from the Potters' Quarter, we presumed in the cited 2002 publication that the local Hellenistic table ware could already have been produced in the Potters' Quarter, as the area was largely used for this purpose in the Roman period. Since that 2002 publication, various parts of this quarter were intensively studied and excavated[10] and, as stated above, no kiln pre-dating the Augustan period has been identified thus far. The available evidence is not yet substantial enough to entirely rule out production in the Potters' Quarter in Hellenistic times, but the presence of a kiln underneath the Odeon and the geophysical indications for more possible kilns in the immediate area, perhaps suggests other options in the urban landscape.

Even though the location of the Hellenistic workshops remains to be finally resolved, core-drilling in the central depression of the Potters' Quarter provided evidence for the quarrying of the local ophiolitic clays[11]. After quarrying activity, a palaeosol developed in the sediments that accumulated on top of the quarried surfaces. The formation of the paleosol was C14-dated to between 370/60 BC to 50/40 BC[12], providing a *terminus ante quem* for the clay quarrying activities, as well as a general chronological association with the use of the local clays for the local Hellenistic table ware.

Another important observation resulting from the analytical programme is that already by the Hellenistic period, table ware made at Sagalassos was being exchanged, as indicated by the representation of the same fabric compositions at Kozluca Höyük[13]. Macroscopically similar material was collected at other sites within the project's study region, mainly during extensive surveying campaigns[14].

Recently, within the framework of the Leuven Centre for Archaeological Sciences, the clay raw materials available within the 1200km² territory of Roman imperial Sagalassos were mapped and analytically characterized[15], and a substantial collection of Archaic, Classical and Hellenistic pottery found within the project's research region and at Sagalassos were archaeometrically analysed[16].

As to the exploitation of the regional clay raw materials, the greenish grey clays, which had originally accumulated as part of a sequence of lake deposits in the north-west section of the Çanaklı valley, were confirmed as having a consistent and analytically definable geochemical signature in comparison to other clays from the same valley or elsewhere in the study region[17]. The clays are characterized in having higher amounts of chlorite and chlorite/smectite mixed layers. Petrographically, the sherds were made from a fine grained and levigated clay raw material, resulting in a mircoporous fabric with few amphibole and pyroxene minerals evenly distributed in the matrix, suggesting an igneous source rock. Noted differences in composition were mainly related to the calcareous content[18].

Pottery made from this fabric was identified by analysis at the sites of Sagalassos, Düzen Tepe, the Ağlasun Valley, Taşkapı Kale and Hacılar Tekke. Sagalassos and Düzen Tepe were both Classical/Hellenistic community settlements with urban features. The material in the Ağlasun Valley was associated with a contemporary farming estate. Both Taşkapı Kale and Hacılar Tekke were fortified strongholds on a mountain top, originating at least by Archaic times in the case of Hacılar Tekke.

As to products, apart from the Hellenistic table ware defined by Poblome *et al.* 2002, the same ware also appeared with a *West Slope* type of decoration displaying incised lines and applied floral motifs. Additionally, a line of black glazed vessels was made from these clays, a table ware with a whitish cream slip, and tile. The latter were Hellenistic in design. Otherwise, the clay raw material was mostly associated with the higher end of the table ware repertoire, mostly following Hellenistic waves of fashion. The black glazed ware could possibly be somewhat older. In general, this ware is scarce, and when stratigraphically anchored, such as at Düzen Tepe, it appears in secondary fifth to second century BC contexts.

---

10 Murphy and Poblome 2011.
11 Degryse *et al.* 2003.
12 Six 2003–2004.
13 Poblome *et al.* 2002b.
14 Vanhaverbeke and Waelkens 2003, 217– 240.
15 Neyt 2012.
16 Braekmans 2011; Braekmans *et al.* 2011.
17 Neyt 2012, 109–123.
18 Braekmans 2011, 191.

Fig. 4. Fragment of the mould-made bowl from Locus 81 (© Sagalassos Archaeological Research project)

The clays collected from the red weathering horizon of the ophiolithic bedrock in and around the central depression of the Potters' Quarter, on the other hand, proved more difficult to isolate as a typical clay raw material signature. The heterogeneity in the clay samples indicated that ophiolitic clays exhibit a range of signatures, due to the heterogeneous nature of the parent rock, slope activity, mass movements and/or human activity. As a result, the clays collected in the Potters' Quarter are similar to other clay raw materials in the Ağlasun Valley, Dereköy and Düzen Tepe[19]. The petrographic and geochemical analytical results of these Hellenistic sherds found at Sagalassos do not overlap, with clays characterized by a limestone related calcareous signature or, rather containing frequent small chert and volcanic inclusions, in different degrees of fineness[20]. Black glazed wares, as well as Hellenistic shapes with mottled, brown, red brown and grey slips were made from these clays.

Apart from the kiln underneath the Odeon and possibly more kilns in that area, the quarrying of clays in and around the central depression of the Potters' Quarter testifies to pottery production in Hellenistic times at Sagalassos. In these workshops, whose locations still need to be confirmed, clay raw materials from the north-west part of the Çanaklı valley were also processed into quality table wares. Additionally, some other clays from the general surroundings of the site may have been levigated for processing into table ware vessels. A complicating factor in unravelling these details is that Sagalassos and Düzen Tepe[21] originated at the same time during the fifth century BC, and both became active in pottery production. The potters of Düzen Tepe seem to have been manufacturing mostly Classical/Hellenistic wares, whereas only Sagalassos would move on to Hellenistic styles and assemblages. However, some types of tableware, such as black glazed vessels, as well as cooking and storage wares could well have been made either at both places or only at one of them[22].

The pottery in the fill layers of the kiln

Forming part of this research, 14 sherds were sampled from the 2007 excavations in the Odeon. Their analysis fits the picture of a local pottery production at Hellenistic Sagalassos, which made use of various clay resources. Therefore, in presenting the wares found in the fill layers in the kiln beneath the Odeon, we propose in this paper the local production of table wares at Hellenistic Sagalassos. Thus far, only a few Hellenistic deposits have been identified at Sagalassos. In chronological terms, the fill layers of the kiln underneath the Odeon are considered to represent the oldest Hellenistic deposits known from Sagalassos. The pottery from these fill layers is now presented, in an attempt to approach the logic of the morphology of the locally produced wares, as well as their chronological positioning. In what follows, no definite typology, quantification or seriation is attempted, because of the general paucity of deposits and material. A selection of shapes is presented instead, mainly as an overview of types and their chronological positioning, mostly based on external parallels.

In general, a recognizable range of table ware shapes was used throughout the numerous regions of the Hellenistic world (e.g. mouldmade bowls, echinus bowls, outturned rim bowls). However, besides the apparent similarity between the pottery assemblages of widely dispersed sites, there also existed substantial regional and temporal variation in table ware assemblages. Such was the case also at Sagalassos. It is exactly the tension between general trends of similarity in object design and use and the particular details of diverging local production and usagewhich makes the study of past material culture meaningful in highlighting the aspect of choice in the composition and functioning of table ware assemblages. This is an archaeological challenge and task *par excellence*.

Regarding drinking vessels, a fragment of a brown slipped, hemispherical, imbricate mould-made relief bowl has been identified (**Fig. 4**). Upon the invention of mould-made relief bowls in Athens, possibly on the occasion of the first Athenian Ptolemaia in 224 BC and under influence of metal and glass prototypes, their production was initiated in Asia Minor workshops by the end of the third century BC. Imbricate bowls continue in production into the early first century BC. Unfortunately, it is not possible to establish a chronological, stylistic evolution within these centuries[23]. The medallion of the fragment found in

19 Neyt 2012, passim.
20 Braekmans 2011, passim.
21 Vanhaverbeke *et al.* 2010.
22 Poblome *et al.*, in press.
23 Ladstätter and Lang-Auinger 2001, 74; Rotroff 1982, 16–17; Rotroff and Oliver 2003, 91–95.

Locus 81 at the Odeon contained a central floral motif, surrounded by small ribbed leaves and one groove. The wall fragment displayed five rows of rounded lotus petals alternating with smaller leaves, topped by a band with guilloche. The rim is missing. The mould-made bowl was considered an import. In general, the question should be asked how quickly this new fashion of wine drinking was introduced into Hellenistic Sagalassos, when, for instance, mould-made bowls were absent from a deposit at Perge, datable to the end of the third and the beginning of the second century BC[24]. In any case, mould-made bowls were never common at Sagalassos.

So-called mastoi were also registered for the fill layers in the dismantled kiln underneath the Odeon, and these represented the main type of drinking cup at Hellenistic Sagalassos (**Fig. 5, 1**). The execution of these vessels at Sagalassos is fairly simple, having a parabolic body with one or more grooves below the slightly everted rim, slipped orange or red/brown, and sometimes with a shallowly hollowed base. At other sites in Asia Minor, the shape is not common; it did not form part of the local Knidian pottery repertoire, for instance[25], nor was it noted at Perge[26], Gordion[27] or Nagidos[28], to name but a few recently published sites. S. I. Rotroff[29] cites the available, yet few parallels for her Athenian material, which she considered to have been produced during the first quarter of the second century BC. Also at Sardis, its representation is rare and considered as a possible import from Pergamon[30]. Another example in 'Firnisware' formed part of a deposit datable to the second and third quarters of the second century BC at Ephesos[31]. The origins of the type can already be placed in the late sixth century BC[32], although the morphological details were slightly different. The Hellenistic style of mastoi was developed in silver[33] as well as in glass. In the case of glass, parabolic cups formed part of luxury sets of drinking vessels developed in early Hellenistic times, and the shape would later feature as one mass-produced in mould-made glass from the second century BC onwards[34]. Perhaps as a result, they also started in the second century BC to be produced among eastern sigillata A and Pergamene sigillata repertoires[35], but were never common. In contrast to most published sites, their regular presence at Sagalassos is somewhat striking. Admittedly, the finish of the cups at Sagalassos is not as elaborate when compared to other silver, glass or eastern sigillata examples, but mastoi are a standard in Hellenistic deposits at Sagalassos. Moreover, the parabolic cups would become one of the most common shapes produced during the initial stages of Roman imperial Sagalassos red slip ware, as type 1A130 – having implications for the process of romanisation of the local community[36].

A shape with roots in the Near East is the so-called Achaemenid bowl, of which a few sherds were identified in the Odeon kiln fill layers (**Fig. 5, 2**). These bowls are actually handleless cups with a small, shallowly hollowed base, rounded plain body and slightly splayed rim, thinned or simple, springing from a carination at the shoulder. As with the other drinking vessels discussed here, glass and metal examples of this shape are also traditional. In general, the shape forms part of a long line of bowls with everted rims, endemic to southeastern Anatolia and Iran, while the deep version of it can be traced back to the seventh century BC. Especially during Achaemenid times, the shape became popular throughout the empire and beyond[37]. At Sardis, where this wine drinking cup had been particularly popular in Achaemenid times, its use continued at least into the later third century BC[38]. At Perge, the exceptional discovery of the remains of ritual meals discarded in an unfinished cistern or bothros contained an extensive collection of dumped pottery datable to the end of the third and the beginning of the second century BC. The main type of drinking cup found in the cistern was the Achaemenid bowl, presumed to be of local fabrication, highlighting the continuation of regional wine-drinking traditions *à la Perse*[39]. The limited amount of Achaemenid bowl fragments found and made at Sagalassos might well indicate the regional *Nachwirkung* of this shape in south-western Asia Minor. Although never common, Achaemenid bowls were nevertheless continued as type 1A120 in Roman imperial Sagalassos red slip ware.

Considering food serving vessels, various bowls with incurved rim were noted in the deposits (**Fig. 5, 3**). Differences in form execution as well as quality and colour of slip were discernible, but all vessels were similar to the 'deep series' described by S. I. Rotroff[40], regarding Athenian material. Deep echinus bowls became popular in the course of the third century BC, when the shape was also common on sites in Asia Minor[41]. We need to wonder in which ways morphological differentiation in echinus bowls, as described at other sites, were of importance to the potters of Sagalassos in making this shape, especially since deep bowls with incurving rim were already a traditional feature of the Classical/Hellenistic deposits at Düzen Tepe[42]. Also at Perge, comparable material was dated to around 300 BC[43], as well as to around a century later[44]. The origin of bowls with incurving rims has been traced to Iran (Persia) from the late seventh century BC onwards[45], while

24 Çokay-Kepçe and Recke 2007.
25 Kögler 2010.
26 Çokay-Kepçe and Recke 2007; Recke 2003.
27 Stewart 2010.
28 Durukan and Körsulu 2007.
29 Rotroff 1997, 109–110.
30 Rotroff and Oliver 2003, 42.
31 Ladstätter and Lang-Auinger 2001, cat. 37.
32 Schreiber 1999, 195.
33 Strong 1966, 108.
34 von Saldern 2005, 115–118.
35 Hayes 1985, pl. III, 4–5; Meyer-Schlichtmann 1988, 78.
36 Poblome *et al.* 2007.
37 Çokay-Kepçe and Recke 2007; Dusinberre 2003, 176–178.
38 Rotroff and Oliver 2003, 60–62.
39 Çokay-Kepçe and Recke 2007.
40 Rotroff 1997, 161–164.
41 Mitsopoulos-Leon 1991, 18–18; Rotroff and Oliver 2003, 24–25; Kögler 2010, 150–153 and Abb. 72.
42 Poblome *et al.*, in press.
43 Recke 2003, Abb. 4, 10.
44 Çokay-Kepçe and Recke 2007.
45 Dusinberre 2003, 175.

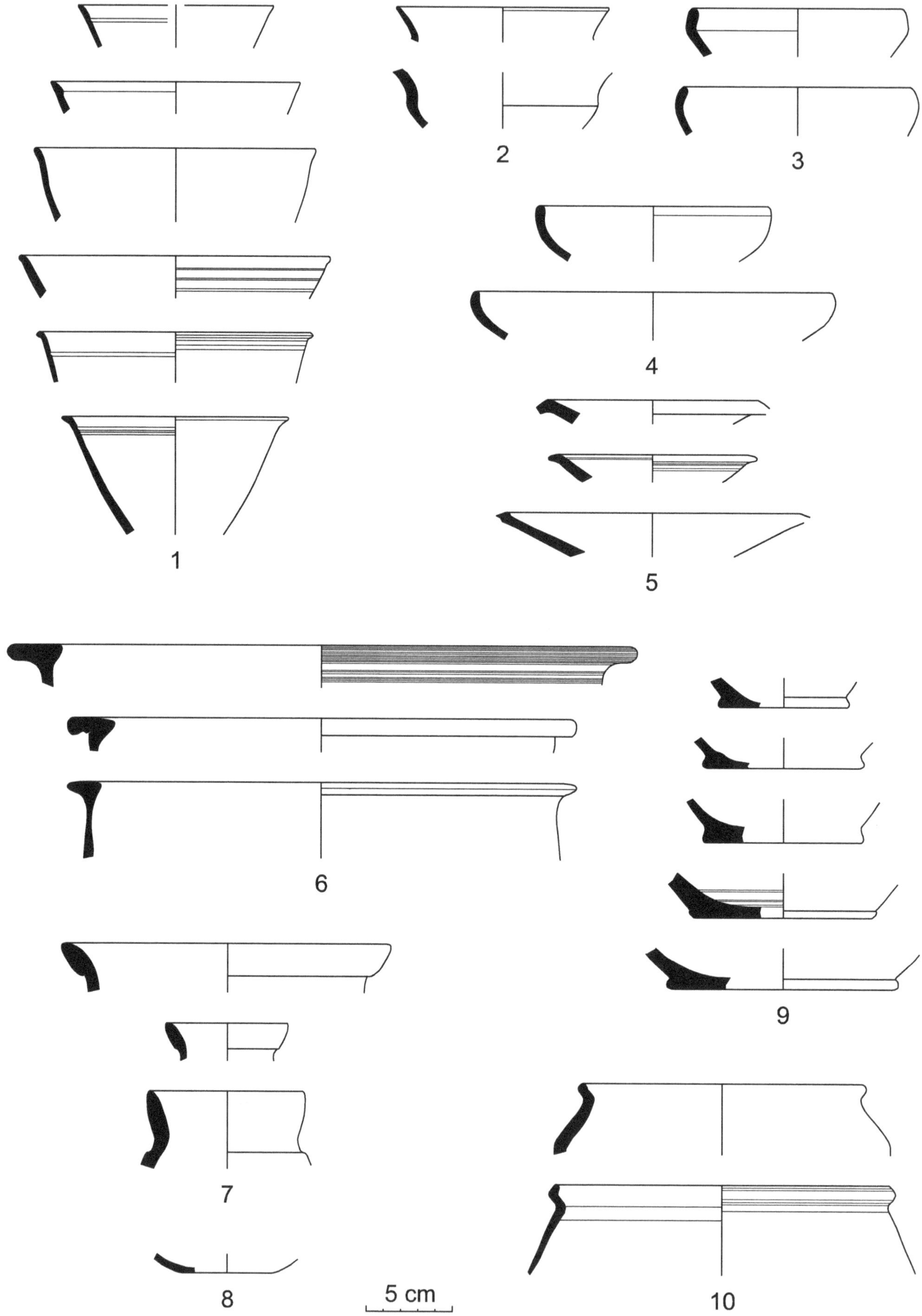

Fig. 5. An overview of the Hellenistic pottery types found at the Odeon (© Sagalassos Archaeological Research project)

Classical examples from the Aegean are also known[46]. In Hellenistic times, the shape is considered to be popular at Anatolian sites, such as Troia, Pergamon, Gordion, Kilise Tepe[47] and Tarsos[48]. Whether or not stylistic associations with other regions are implied for the pottery found at Sagalassos is an open question. Obviously, such stylistic transfers never happened as explicit processes of imitation. We may even wonder whether the potters involved were aware of the socio-cultural origins of the vessel styles. Taking the shapes together, however, does provide us with a general impression of the pottery assemblages attested at Sagalassos and how particular regional Hellenistic assemblages originated. Bowls with incurving rims, for instance, were long-maintained, as their form was to be continued as type 1B170 in Roman imperial Sagalassos red slip ware.

Another type of bowl which was common at Classical/ Hellenistic Düzen Tepe is shallow and hemispherical in design, with walls curving to a vertical position ending in a plain rim (**Fig. 5, 4**). The same type is registered in the Hellenistic fabric described above and occurs frequently in the fill layers of the kiln underneath the Odeon. No genuine parallels can be listed, to our knowledge, however, the type would remain in production as type 1B150 of Roman imperial Sagalassos red slip ware.

Shallow dishes with downturned or projecting rim also formed part of the fill deposits in the kiln beneath the Odeon (**Fig. 5, 5**). In most cases too little of the vessel is preserved to determine whether there was a central depression (typical for fish-plates). Usually the slip is thick and lustrous, mostly orange or red/brown in colour. Most examples are not very shallow but are somewhat deeper, a trend which was discerned for fish-plates from the third century BC onwards by S. I. Rotroff and A. Oliver[49], based on material from Sardis. Simple dishes with downturned rim appear from the later part of the third century BC onwards as well[50]. Dishes with downturned and projecting rims remained popular in Asia Minor throughout the late Hellenistic period.

Some slipped, handleless, deep bowls with projecting or ledge rims were also identified (**Fig. 5, 6**). These could have served in food preparation and/or serving and/or as a krater, or even for washing[51]. The rim is quite wide and extends horizontally, which, in the case of Athenian products, is considered as a third century BC feature[52]. Athenian plain ware lekanai Form 2 and 3 are similar and datable to respectively *c.* 525–215 BC and 275–50 BC[53]. The rim execution of a third century BC krater and lekane found at Perge is comparable[54]. As far as Sagalassos is concerned, we presume the rim and vessel morphology to evolve in the direction of Roman imperial Sagalassos red slip ware type 1F150.

A couple of fragments of jugs with an almond shaped rim was also registered (**Fig. 5, 7**). Possibly in association, some nearly vertical strap handles with a single, central ridge were also noted.

As far as bottom fragments are concerned, flat, shallowly hollowed bases were identified (**Fig. 5, 8**), possibly as parts of (Achaemenid?) bowls, mastoi and jugs, along with so-called disk bases (**Fig. 5, 9**), and a few false ring feet.

Remarkably few sherds of cooking ware were discerned. Two rim fragments of a globular, closed cooking vessel were noted, with a plain rim, folded slightly outwards and with a shallow groove on the inside (**Fig. 5, 10**). The near absence of cooking and plain wares, as well as amphorae, from these deposits and the resulting dominance of slipped table and serving wares might be an indication that the artefacts from the discussed loci did not result from domestic activities. Rather, more specific waste routines can explain this pattern, such as local production (and failure) of the wares in question. In general, Roman imperial and early Byzantine deposits at Sagalassos are heavily dominated by table and serving ware waste, which is considered to be a direct result of the prolific Potters' Quarter to the east of the Theatre. Genuinely misfired pottery was absent from the Hellenistic deposits, but this aspect is also characteristic for the Roman imperial and early Byzantine dumps[55].

Based on the typological and chronological criteria discussed above, we would like to propose a date for these loci ranging between the end of the third century and the (first half of the) second century BC. Some shapes possibly appeared already earlier in the third century BC, while other shapes continued after the (middle of the) second century BC. The amount of available deposits is too limited, however, to build up quantified and seriated sequences and, consequently, independent local shape histories. Admittedly, the proposed date puts little weighton the presence of the discussed fragment of a mould-made bowl, and also does not necessarily take into account the fact that a worn eastern sigillata A body sherd formed part of these deposits. Both fragments were found in the upper fill layer of the dismantled front part and combustion chamber of the kiln. Both these loci also contained some early Roman imperial material datable to the final quarter of the first century BC and the first half of the next one. We cannot prove whether the mould-made bowl fragment and the eastern sigillata A sherd were part of this collection of later material. Both classes of artefact are rarely attested at Sagalassos, but in the few contexts, which have been

46 Edwards 1975, note 15; Rotroff 1997, note 53.
47 Nevett and Jackson 2007, 379–380.
48 Berlin 1999, 94 and note 42; Jones 1950, 156–157; Schäfer 1968, 37–38; Stewart 2010, 170–172 and 195–197.
49 Rotroff and Oliver 2003, 25–26.
50 Kögler 2010, 147–149; Mitsopoulos-Leon 1991, 24; Stewart 2010, 200–201.
51 Berlin 1999, 94.
52 Rotroff 1997, 167–168.
53 Rotroff 2006, 110–112.
54 Recke 2003, fig. 3, 11 and fig. 4, 1.
55 Poblome *et al.* 1998.

excavated, they are known to form part of early Roman imperial deposits. Lacking seriated evidence, the latter deposits are only indicative. In general, however, the methodology applied to the chronological reconstruction of assemblages at Sagalassos does not take full account of outliers and highly representative, yet rare, material, but rather it is based mostly on (seriated) main trends supported by the bulk of the material[56]. In conclusion, the suggested date range for the Odeon deposits under discussion should be open to (criticism and) review, and will need to be reinforced by the excavation, study, and seriation of more contemporary deposits.

Aspects of interpretation

The studied material from the different loci in the Odeon is relatively consistent in its make-up, displaying similar shapes and surface finishing. Especially common are beverage consumption vessels, with the mastos being most represented. The most popular food consumption shape seems to have been the echinus bowl. As a result, the tableware assemblage in use at mid-Hellenistic Sagalassos appears to have been fairly restricted. The predominate mastos and the echinus bowl were augmented by only a handful of other types.

In comparison to other well published contemporary deposits from sites in the Aegean, Anatolia or the Levant, it is also of interest to note what types are conspicuously absent from the discussed Sagalassos deposits. Plates, saucers and dishes seem to have been relatively rare. Widespread Hellenistic shapes, such as the mould-made bowl, fish-plate, rolled rim plate and out-turned rim bowl are only sparsely represented. The kantharos, skyphos and two-handled cup seem to have been absent. Variety in closed vessels and kraters is limited and *West Slope* decoration is scarce. Grey wares and relief decorated wares are all but absent. The deposits presented above obviously cannot be taken to represent Hellenistic Sagalassos as a whole. No domestic contexts have been excavated thus far and the quantity of material currently unearthed is limited. If, however, the data from the above deposits is taken at face value it appears that the variety in tableware in use at Hellenistic Sagalassos was limited, yet functional. Possibly, a limited repertoire was sufficient to fulfil the dining practices of Sagalassos' inhabitants.

Considered at face value, Greek-style eating and drinking had possibly made only a limited impact on Hellenistic Sagalassos. We need to openly question what this 'at face value' means, however. Indeed, there is a tension in interpretation of the Sagalassos Hellenistic material. On the one hand, the presence of certain Greek wares and the popularity of 'doing things Greek' in the eastern Mediterranean is beyond doubt. In the case of the pottery, this is certainly promoted by the excellent standard of publication at sites like Corinth and Athens. Yet how much this effects the preferential publishing of more 'representative' categories of Hellenistic pottery from other sites, is difficult to evaluate. Sagalassos is far from Corinth or Athens, however. Moreover, a more balanced consideration of socio-cultural influences and patterns inherent in the locally-produced material needs to be based on a long-term perspective, taking the Classical/Hellenistic local production of Düzen Tepe and Sagalassos into account, as well as the continued Roman imperial Sagalassos red slip ware production. Based on the study of the presented Odeon material, it is still too early to give a final verdict on the link between the nature of the material culture and the cultural identity of the community that conceived, produced and consumed it.

Acknowledgements

The research for this paper was supported by the Belgian Programme on Interuniversity Poles of Attraction (IAP 7/09), the Research Fund of the University of Leuven (GOA 13/04), Projects G.0788.09 and G.0562.11 of the Fund for Scientific Research-Flanders (FWO), the Hercules Foundation (AKUL/09/16) and a Methusalem Grant from the Flemish Ministry for Science Policy.

The archaeometrical analysis was carried out at the Leuven Centre for Archaeological Sciences. J. Poblome was appointed as Francqui Research Professor for 2011–2014.

Jeroen Poblome
Sagalassos Archaeological Research Project
University of Leuven
Blijde Inkomststraat 21/3314
3000 Leuven, Belgium
jeroen.poblome@arts.kuleuven.be

Dennis Braekmans
Faculty of Archaeology
Leiden University
POBox 9515
2300 RA Leiden, The Netherlands
&
Materials in Art and Archaeology
Laboratory of Materials Science
Delft University of Technology
Mekelweg 2
2628 CD Delft, The Netherlands
d.j.g.braekmans@arch.leidenuniv.nl

Branko Mušič
Univerza V Ljubljani
Filozofska fakulteta
Oddelek za arheologijo
Zavetiška 5
1000 Ljubljana, Slovenia
branko.music@ff.uni-lj.si

[56] Poblome 1999.

Mark Van Der Enden
Graduate School, University of Leicester
University Road, Leicester
LE1 7RH, United Kingdom
mv92@leicester.ac.uk

Bart De Graeve
Sagalassos Archaeological Research Project
University of Leuven
Blijde Inkomststraat 21/3314
3000 Leuven, Belgium

Bert Neyt
Department of Geology
Celestijnenlaan 200e/2408
3001 Heverlee, Belgium
bert.neyt@ees.kuleuven.be

Patrick Degryse
Department of Geology
Celestijnenlaan 200e/2408
3001 Heverlee, Belgium
patrick.degryse@ees.kuleuven.be

Bibliography

Berlin, A. M. 1999. Studies in Hellenistic Ilion: the Lower City. Stratified assemblages and chronology. *Studia Troica* 9, 73–158.

Braekmans, D. 2011. *The Archaic, Classical and Hellenistic ceramics in the later territory of Sagalassos and Düzen Tepe: the petrographic and geochemical evidence*. Unpublished PhD thesis, University of Leuven.

Braekmans, D., Degryse, P., Poblome, J., Neyt, B., Vyncke, K. and Waelkens, M. 2011. Understanding ceramic variability: An archaeometrical interpretation of the Classical and Hellenistic ceramics at Düzen Tepe and Sagalassos (Southwest Turkey). *Journal of Archaeological Science* 38, 2101–2115.

Claeys, J., Poblome, J. and Degryse, P. In preparation. Site F: Sagalassos in a nutshell. Report on excavation activities of 2011 in eastern suburbia. *Adalya*.

Çokay-Kepçe, S. and Recke, M. 2007. Achaemenid bowls in Pamphylia. In I. Delemen (ed.), *The Achaemenid impact on local populations and cultures in Anatolia*, 83–96. Istanbul, Turkish Institute of Archaeology.

Degraeve, B. 2009. The Odeon. In M. Waelkens, Report on the 2006 and 2007 excavation and restoration activities at Tepe Düzen and at Sagalassos, *30. Kazı Sonuçları Toplantısı*, 427–456.

Degryse, P., Poblome, J., Donners, K., Deckers, J. and Waelkens, M. 2003. Geoarchaeological investigations of the "potters' quarter" at Sagalassos, Southwest Turkey. *Geoarchaeology* 18, 255–281.

Durukan, M. and Körsulu, H. 2007. Hellenistik dönem seramikleri. In S. Durugönül (ed.), *Nagidos. Results of an excavation in an ancient city in Rough Cilicia*. Adalya Supplementary Series 6, 155–228. Antalya, Suna & İnan Kıraç Research Institute on Mediterranean Civilizations.

Dusinberre, E. R. M. 2003. *Aspects of empire in Achaemenid Sardis*. Cambridge, Cambridge University Press.

Edwards, G. R. 1975. *Corinthian Hellenistic pottery*. Corinth 7, 3. Princeton, NJ., American School of Classical Studies at Athens.

Hayes, J. W. 1985. Sigillate orientali, in *Atlante delle forme ceramiche 2. Ceramica fine romana nel bacino mediterraneo*, 1–96. Rome, Instituto della Enciclopedia Italiana.

Jones, F. F. 1950. The pottery. In H. Goldman (ed.), *Excavations at Gözlü Kule, Tarsus*, 1. *The Hellenistic and Roman periods*, 149–296. Princeton, NJ., Princeton University Press.

Kögler, P. 2010. *Feinkeramik aus Knidos vom mittleren Hellenismus bis in die mittlere Kaiserzeit*. Wiesbaden, Reichert.

Ladstätter, S. and Lang-Auinger, C. 2001. Zur Datierung und kunsthistorischen Einordnung einer Apollon Kitharodos-Statuette. In F. Krinzinger (ed.), *Studien zur hellenistischen Keramik in Ephesos*. Ergänzungshefte zu den Jahresheften des Österreichischen Archäologischen Institutes in Wien 2, 71–82. Vienna, Österreichisches Archäologisches Institut.

Meyer-Schlichtmann, C. 1988. *Die pergamenische Sigillata aus der Stadtgrabung von Pergamon*. Pergamenische Forschungen 6. Berlin, Walter De Gruyter.

Mitsopoulos-Leon, V. 1991. *Die Basilika am Staatsmarkt in Ephesos. Kleinfunde* 1. *Keramik hellenistischer und römischer Zeit*. Forschungen in Ephesos 9, 2/2. Vienna, Schindler.

Murphy, E. and Poblome, J. 2011. Producing pottery *vs*. producing models: interpreting workshop organization at the Potters' Quarter of Sagalassos, in M. L. Lawall and J. Lund (eds.), *Pottery in the Archaeological Record: a view from the Greek World*. Gösta Enbom Monographs 1, 30–36. Aarhus, Aarhus University Press.

Nevett, L. and Jackson, M. P. C. 2007. Hellenistic ceramics and lamps, in N. Postgate and D. Thomas (eds.), *Excavations at Kilise Tepe, 1994–98. From Bronze Age to Byzantine in western Cilicia*. British Institute at Ankara Monograph 30, 379–386. Cambridge, McDonald Institute for Archaeological Research.

Neyt, B. 2012. *Mineralogical resources for ceramic production in the territory of Sagalassos. A geochemical, mineralogical and petrographical study*. Unpublished PhD thesis, University of Leuven.

Poblome, J., Schlitz, M. and Degryse, P. 1998. Recycling Misfired Pottery. A Standard Practice of the Potters at Ancient Sagalassos?, *Forum Archaeologiae. Zeitschrift für klassische Archäologie* 7, <http://allergy.hno.akh-wien.ac.at/forum/forum0698/07sagalassos.htm>.

Poblome, J. 1999. *Sagalassos red slip ware. Typology and Chronology.* Studies in Eastern Mediterranean Archaeology 2. Turnhout, Brepols.

Poblome, J., Bounegru, O., Degryse, P., Viaene, W., Waelkens, M. and Erdemgil, S. 2001. The sigillata manufactories of Pergamon and Sagalassos. *Journal of Roman Archaeology* 14, 143–165.

Poblome, J., Degryse, P., Viaene, W. and Waelkens, M. 2002a. An Augustan pottery workshop at Sagalassos, in V. Kilikoglou, A. Hein and Y. Maniatis (eds.), *Modern Trends in Scientific Studies on Ancient Ceramics.* British Archaeological Reports. International Series 1011, 335–341. Oxford, BAR Publishing.

Poblome, J., Degryse, P., Viaene, W., Ottenburgs, R., Waelkens, M., Degeest, R. and Naud, J. 2002b. The Concept of a Pottery Production Centre. An Archaeometrical Contribution from Ancient Sagalassos. *Journal of Archaeological Science* 29, 873–882.

Poblome, J., Bes, P. and Lauwers, V. 2007. Winning hearts, minds and stomachs? Artefactual or artificial evidence for Romanization. In M. Meyer (ed.), *Neue Zeiten – Neue Sitten. Zu Rezeption und Integration römischen und italischen Kulturguts in Kleinasien.* Wiener Forschungen zur Archäologie 12, 221–232. Vienna, Phoibos.

Poblome, J., Braekmans, D., Waelkens, M., Fırat, N., Vanhaverbeke, H., Martens, F., Kaptijn, E., Vyncke, K., Willet, R. and Degryse, P. In press. How did Sagalassos come to be? A ceramological survey, in *Festschrift for Levent Zoroğlu.* Antalya, AKMED.

Recke, M. 2003. Die klassische und hellenistische Keramik unter Einfluss der attisch schwarzfigurigen Keramik, in H. Abbasoğlu and W. Martini (eds.), *Die Akropolis von Perge* 1, 103–121. Mainz, Zabern.

Rotroff, S. I. 1982. *Hellenistic pottery. Athenian and imported moldmade bowls.* The Athenian Agora XXII. Princeton, NJ., American School of Classical Studies at Athens.

Rotroff, S. I. 1997. *Hellenistic pottery. Athenian and imported wheelmade table ware and related material.* The Athenian Agora XXIX. Princeton, NJ., The American School of Classical Studies at Athens.

Rotroff, S. I. and Oliver, A. 2003. *The Hellenistic pottery from Sardis: the finds through 1994.* Archaeological Exploration of Sardis Monograph 12. Cambridge, MA, Harvard University Press.

Rotroff, S. I. 2006. *Hellenistic pottery. The plain wares.* The Athenian Agora XXXIII. Princeton, NJ., American School of Classical Studies at Athens.

Schäfer, J. 1968. *Hellenistische Keramik aus Pergamon.* Pergamenische Forschungen 2. Berlin, de Gruyter.

Schreiber, T. 1999. *Athenian vase construction. A potter's analysis.* Malibu, CA, The J. Paul Getty Museum.

Six, S. 2003–2004. *Holocene geomorphological evolution of the territory of Sagalassos. Contribution to the palaeo-environmental reconstruction of Southwest Turkey.* Unpublished PhD thesis, University of Leuven.

Stewart, S. M. 2010. *Gordion After the Knot: Hellenistic Pottery and Culture.* Unpublished PhD thesis, University of Cincinnati.

Strong, D. 1966. *Greek and Roman gold and silver plate.* London, Taylor & Francis.

Vanhaverbeke, H. and Waelkens, M. 2003. *The chora of Sagalassos. The evolution of the settlement pattern from prehistoric until recent times.* Studies in Eastern Mediterranean Archaeology 5. Turnhout, Brepols Publishers.

Vanhaverbeke, H., Waelkens, W., Vyncke, K., De Laet, V., Aydal, S., Mušič, B., De Cupere, B., Poblome, J., Braekmans, D., Degryse, P., Marinova, E., Verstraeten, G., Van Neer, W., Šlapšak, B., Medarič, I., Ekinci, H. A. and Erbay, M. O. 2010. The 'Pisidian' culture? The Classical-Hellenistic site at Düzen Tepe near Sagalassus (southwest Turkey). *Anatolian Studies* 60, 105–128.

von Saldern, A. 2005. *Antikes Glas.* München, C. H. Beck.

Waelkens, M. 2004. Ein Blick von der Ferne. Seleukiden und Attaliden in Pisidien. *Istanbuler Mitteilungen* 54, 435–471.

Wiegand, P. C., Harbottle, G. and Sayre, E. V. 1977. Turquoise sources and source analysis: Mesoamerica and the Southwestern U.S.A., in T. K. Earle and J. E. Ericson (eds.), *Exchange systems in prehistory,* 15–34. New York, Academic Press.

Cradle of ceramics – The emergence of Eastern Sigillata B in the Hellenistic East

Nina Fenn

Abstract

The following paper draws attention to an initial period of the Eastern Sigillata B production in late Hellenistic times, when shapes belonging to the Hellenistic tradition were produced in the fabric of the later well-known ESB. It is important to make this distinction between form and fabric. This observation is not totally new, as very early examples or forerunners of ESB ware have sporadically been put on record from a few places like Priene, Ephesos, Labraunda, Delos and Athens. Despite this, to my knowledge they have not previously been brought together in order to paint a picture of Hellenistic plain as well decorated forms in ESB fabric, and to rethink our notion of the emergence of Eastern Sigillata B. The 'true' sigillata *forms* are generally–and probably rightly–thought to be developed by Italian potters. But I would like to argue that the idea of a sigillata *fabric* originated in the East, without necessarily any links to Italy as early as Hellenistic times.

Keywords: Priene, Eastern Sigillata B, fabric, forerunners, calyces, West Slope succession style, emblem cups, applied relief decoration

The material from Priene

The starting point of our considerations lies on the material from the old and new excavations at Priene, where several examples of early ESB have been found. Examples will also be considered from Ephesos, which must have played a special role in the distribution of ESB, judging from the numerous finds there. In addition, sporadic pieces from a few other excavated sites are brought together.

'Komplex A' is a rich pottery assemblage from late Hellenistic times, excavated in the South Stoa of the Athena Sanctuary at Priene[1]. The material was dumped behind the retaining wall of the terrace on which the Stoa was enlarged towards the East. The terrace fill has a closing date around the middle of the first century BC (Eastern Sigillata A shapes Atlante 3 and 22, thin-walled beakers of type Marabini 1, first Ephesian grey plates and lamps; absence of Italian Sigillata and thin-walled pottery of imperial times).

'Komplex B'[2] comprises material from early Imperial times with which Insula E5 was levelled. An Augustan deposit from insula E5 in the north-west living quarter contains, besides one Italian sigillata plate, thin-walled pottery and the one-handled early Imperial amphora type Peacock- Williams 45 (the so-called micaceous water jar), some pieces in ESB ware.

Plain forms

Calyces

'Komplex A' yielded no ESB of Imperial time but two identical feet of drinking vessels which by first glance are indistinguishable from typical ESB fabric (**Fig. 1**). Their stemmed foot is rather high with ridging on the outside and a dome underneath. Typologically they stand between the black-glazed Classical kantharoi[3] and ESB calyces[4]. The question must remain open what the entire profile of our drinking vessels looked like: with handles or handleless, curved or carinated, kantharoi or calyces? Similarly, one cannot decide whether they are still late Hellenistic or already early Roman in character. We seem to get be dealing with a transitional stage.

Chemical analysis proves that both examples were produced in ESB fabric: In the variation diagram of two characteristic elements–titanium and magnesium–local pottery from Priene is shown by triangular symbols, Ephesian fine pottery by circles and the ESB by square marks (**Fig. 2**). As published ESB reference data we may use an average of Sigillata forms and two samples of medaillon cups[5]. The two calyx feet fall clearly within the ESB group. Therefore the calyces from the late Hellenistic

1 Fenn 2011; Fenn forthcoming.

2 Fenn forthcoming.

3 Rotroff 1997, 83–94 nos 1–149, figs 4–12, pls 1–14 (Classical kantharoi including related shapes of drinking cups); 103 nos. 230. 231 fig. 16 pl. 21 (Hellenistic kantharoi with small foot, modelled on kantharoi of Classical type).

4 See below.

5 Schneider 2000, 532 tab. 3 (average of 29 samples); Zabehlicky-Scheffenegger and Schneider 2000, 110 no F935. F936 tab. 1 (medaillon bowls).

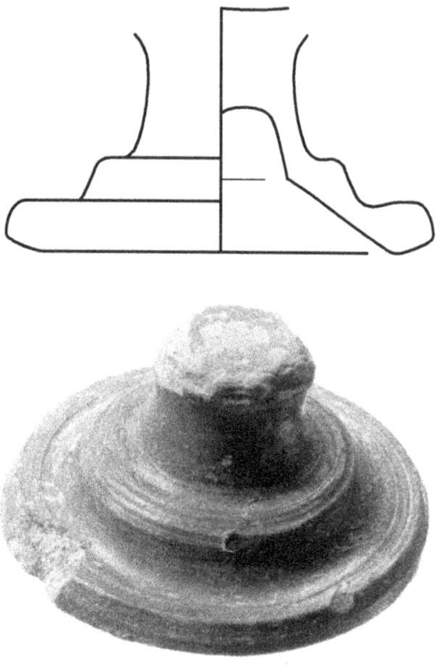

Fig. 1. calyx – Hellenistic form in ESB fabric (drawing M. Brückle; photo A. Ribbeck)

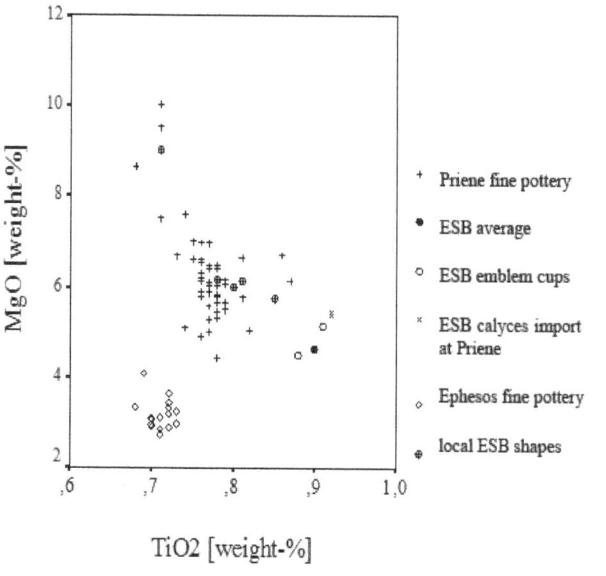

Fig. 2. analysis of ESB fabric and local fabric from Priene (chart N. Fenn)

pottery deposit from the Athena sanctuary were imports to Priene and can be called forerunners of the Imperial ESB production.

A comparison with early Imperial Sigillata from the Ephesian Tetragonos Agora[6] underlines the contrast with our late Hellenistic examples. The calyces' feet with the potter's stamp of Sentius are very sharp in profile. In early Imperial times, the trend is towards low feet, which become more and more profiled. They also demonstrate that the ESB Sigillata shapes undeniably started in the East, not before the Augustan period, under the influence of Italian potters and imports.

Parallels to our two feet come from Delos and Assos. From the final destruction debris of the House of the Actors at Delos a big drinking-vessel with ribbed body and a high stepped foot has long been known[7]. From Assos comes a big ESB kantharos with high foot, for which Michael Zelle proposed a date in Augustan-Claudian times with regard to Italian calices[8]. Possibly the chronological classification could be shifted up a little, but among the examples from Priene, Delos and Assos the last is clearly the youngest. The Delian calyx seems to have been produced in ESB ware, too, like other vessels from Delos from the same context[9].

Other plain forms

It is worth recalling that, besides the calyx, Bruneau published an echinus bowl and a plate with upturned rim in a fabric he calls 'samien ancien'[10]: '… les fragments de Délos représentent pour nous les débuts de la céramique samienne: argile et vernis sont ceux du samien connu jusqu'ici, mais les formes ne sont pas encore celles qu'on trouvera plus tard.'[11] That is, he already advances the hypothesis that there were forerunners to the imperial ESB, which was at that time falsely connected with Samos according to the famous passage of Pliny the Elder. Hellenistic-shaped echinus bowls and plates with upturned rims in ESB fabric were also noted at Ephesos[12]. John Hayes has seen the material on Delos and mentions some more unpublished vessel forms in Hellenistic tradition but ESB fabric[13]: two fragmentary plates of the same shape as the plate with upturned rim, four more plate fragments and one bowl (not described further.) He describes it as a version of the ESB ware with a relatively soft fabric that has a tendency to flake, and notes that this group 'might be considered a forerunner (at some remove in time) of the ESB2 ware'[14]. He also suggests: 'It could, if necessary, be given a separate tag such as "Proto-ESB ware", in order to avoid confusion with existing classifications.'[15] But that term seems problematic as it includes the term 'sigillata'

6 Zabehlicky-Scheffenegger 2003, pl. 76, 2–5.
7 Bruneau 1970, 247 no. D 51 fig. 126. Differing from the Delos exemplar, the underside of the two kantharoi from 'Komplex A' is domed in its upper part and straight in the lowe (the converse is the case on the Delian kantharos).
8 Zelle 1997, 61 no. 133 fig. 13: contrary to the kantharos from Assos (and Delos), the one from Priene shows a massive part between body and foot and no *S*-shaped profile.
9 This should be investigated by means of geochemical analysis; Gerwulf Schneider doubts that the pieces from Delos are in the ESB fabric (pers. comm. at the conference).
10 Bruneau 1970, 247; see Lund 2003, 127, for the current state of research.
11 Bruneau 1970, 247.
12 Mitsopoulos-Leon 1972–1975, 507 figs. 5 a-b; Mitsopoulos-Leon 1991, 94; Gassner 1997, 126, casting doubts on the dating of the Delian contexts.
13 Hayes 2008, 31 with n. 5.
14 Hayes 2008, 31.
15 Hayes 2008, 31 with n. 6.

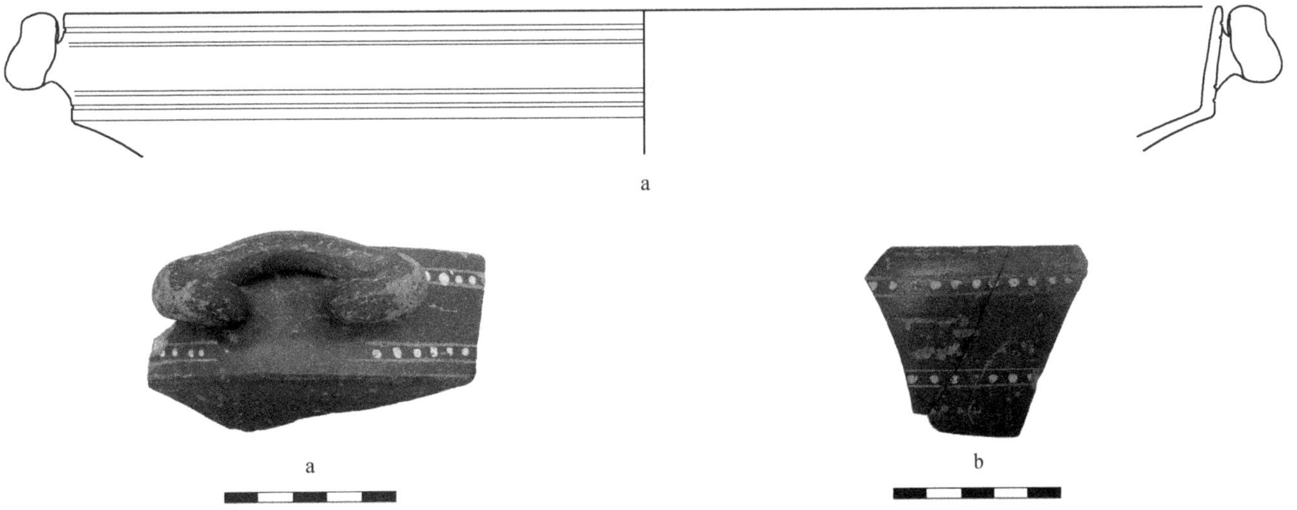

Fig. 3. carinated bowls – Hellenistic form in ESB fabric (drawing after R. Zahn by M. Brückle; photos N. Fenn)

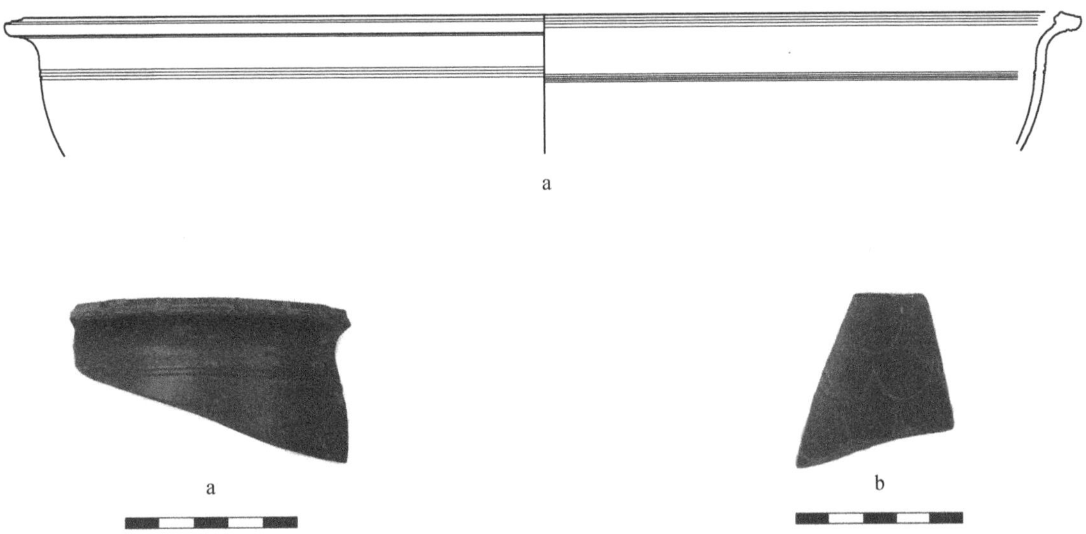

Fig. 4. unknown open Hellenistic forms in ESB fabric (drawing after R. Zahn by M. Brückle; photos N. Fenn)

for a Hellenistic ware, which was, like the ESB, probably produced at Tralleis.

Bowls with incurved profile and plates with upturned rim are a common feature in the East. Besides the Hellenistic colour-coated wares, these shapes were produced in 'Pergamene sigillata', ESA ware, and, as we have seen, in ESB ware too. So the sigillata industry went back to traditional bowls and plate forms; a new element may be seen in their combination to a set. In his publication of the material from Priene, Robert Zahn was one of the first to mention the relation between sigillata and Hellenistic vessels and spoke of forerunners of the profiled ESB forms in Asia Minor[16].

In the west the same bowl and plate shapes occur in Italian pre-Sigillata as well as in Campana A, B, and C wares. As Jeroen Poblome, for instance, already underlined, there were developments taking place in the West as well as in

[16] Zahn 1904, 442. 446.

Fig. 5. closed vessel shape – Hellenistic form in ESB fabric (photo N. Fenn)

the East that lead to a common, so-called 'sigillata concept' from Augustan times[17]. According to that, the 'prototypes' should be seen as a development rather than an invention.

Decorated forms

Decoration in West Slope succession style

There are also Hellenistic shapes in ESB fabric with typical Hellenistic decoration in succession to the West Slope style–that is, with incised patterns and additional painted white decoration. The following examples were found during the 19th-century excavations at Priene and are now stored at the Antikensammlung at Berlin[18]. Two pieces–a rim fragment of 20cm diameter with preserved handle (**Fig. 3a**), and a single rim fragment (**Fig. 3b**)–come from carinated cups[19]. As remote examples we may include the so-called Knidian cups, while their proportions and especially handle forms obviously differ. They are decorated with white dotted lines between incised parallel lines, a feature typical of the West Slope successive style. The quality of the two carinated cups must be brought into connection with the ESB production, as Zahn has already rightly pointed out, in my opinion rightly[20]. Apart from these two carinated cups there are other forms attested from the former excavations at Priene, which are decorated in West Slope successive style. They strengthen the assumption of Hellenistic shapes in ESB ware with West Slope decoration. A drinking vessel with a diameter of about 18cm shows beneath the broken off rim a dotted garland hanging from a group of incised lines (**Fig. 4a**)[21]. Due to firing conditions the slip has turned dark and the fabric grey-brown on one side of the vessel; nevertheless it most probably belongs to ESB ware. A fourth fragment represents an open shape, which cannot be determined more precisely (**Fig. 4b**)[22]: the piece preserves either the carination of the wall or the break of the rim. The outside surface shows a hastily incised scale pattern, which may have been filled with white dots as the shadow in one of the scales indicates. Zahn assumed that another wall fragment belonged to an open shape, too (**Fig. 5**)[23]. But as one part of its interior is without slip, it might be better classified as a closed vessel shape. With a diameter of approximately 12cm it has small dimensions. On the widest part of the body appears an incised tendril. Traces of white are not preserved.

During the new excavations at Priene, several fragments from a lagynos are preserved, with carinated body and decoration in West Slope succession style on the shoulder (**Fig. 6**)[24]. Around the neck are incised garlands, their broad bows and loose hanging ends filled with rows of additional white dots. Although the orange-brown slip is of very good quality and of a high gloss, analysis has shown that this lagynos is of local fabric from Priene. Nevertheless the potter seems to have intended a sigillata-like quality. This phenomenon is probable to occur also at other places.

Finds from other sites strengthen the thesis that there was a pottery production in West Slope successive style at the ESB centre in the late Hellenistic period. In fact there are examples from Ephesos in ESB ware with incised lines and painted white dots. From the basilica at the state market were published body fragments from a jug, a bowl and a lagynos–this time not locally produced but imported[25]. From Labraunda, too, two pieces are recorded; both rim fragments seem to represent the carinated bowl type[26]. Each has a dotted white row beneath the rim with an incised curved line below.

Incidentally, even ESA occurs with West Slope decoration. Again at Labraunda was found the fragment of a plate with a short vertical rim and a white dotted line on its interior[27]. From Tarsos is known a base fragment from a great ESA plate with painted ivy, meander and wavy line[28]. We can understand this as a main trend of a Hellenistic decoration style, common all over the Mediterranean, which lingers on in the ESA and ESB production.

Emblem cups

Cups with interior decoration consisting of painting and incision in West Slope style bear sometimes an additional relief in the middle. These emblem cups have a long Hellenistic tradition, their production starting early in the third century BC, and there are also examples in ESB ware. The Hellenistic cups with interior decoration are

17 Poblome *et al.* 2000.
18 My thanks go to Ursula Kästner for the possibility to study the fragments and judge their fabric.
19 Berlin V.I. 3941 and 3942; see Zahn 1904, 433 no. 134 fig. 550; no. 135 (without figure).
20 Zahn 1904, 433 lists them among the Sigillata sherds whose fabric he describes, clearly the one later known as ESB.
21 Berlin V.I. 3959; see Zahn 1904, 437 no. 154, fig. 551. 553.
22 Berlin V.I. 3958; see Zahn 1904, 437 no. 158, fig. 553.
23 Berlin V.I. 3957; see Zahn 1904, 437 no. 157, fig. 553.
24 From 'Komplex A' see Fenn forthcoming.
25 Mitsopoulos-Leon 1991, 43 and 54 no. B145–147, pl. 63.
26 Hellström 1965, 33. 69 no. 234 (ESB2?). 235 (ESB1?) pl. 13.
27 Hellström 1965, 31. 68 no. 209, pl. 13.
28 Jones 1950, 176. 232 no. 264 a, fig. 157.

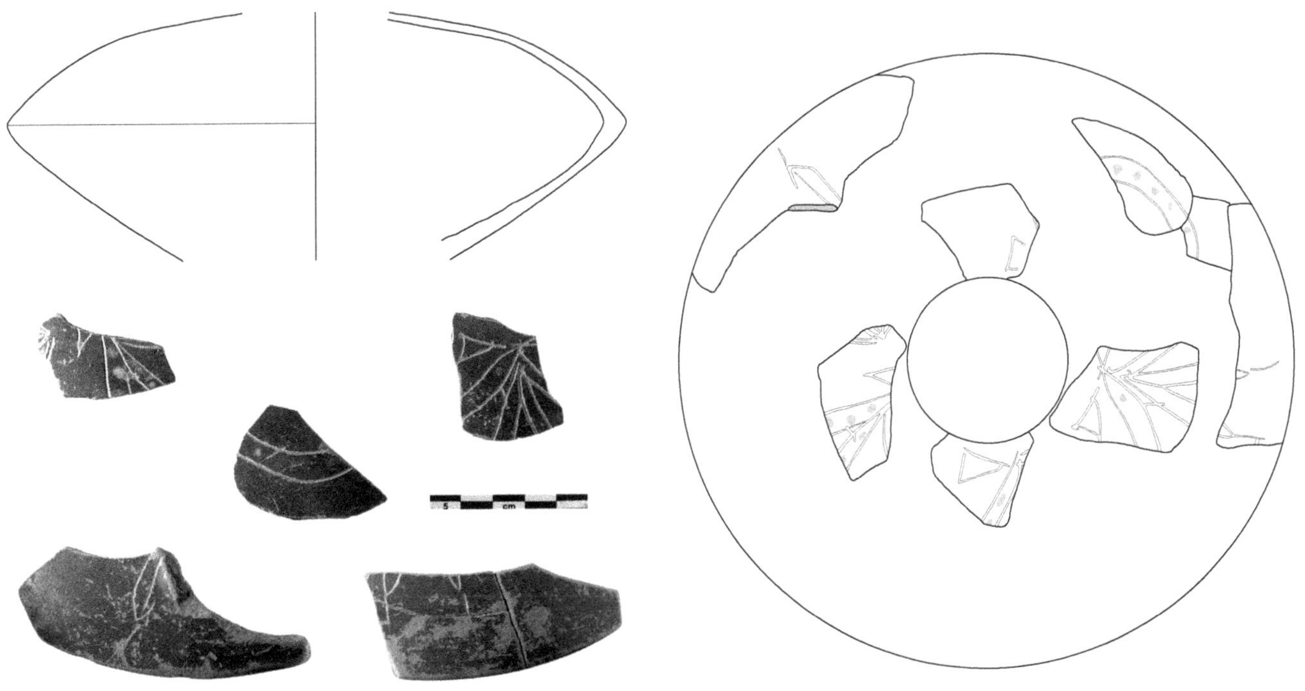

Fig. 6. lagynos – Hellenistic form in local fabric, imitating ESB (drawings M. Brückle; photo B. Schödel)

not a homogeneous group as regards fabric and motifs. Instead they were produced at different centres through the Hellenistic period, among others Athens and Pergamon. In Athenian black-glaze there existed two types, both with glazed grooves on the exterior[29].

ESB examples of emblem cups are known from Ephesos[30] and maybe from Athens[31]. At Ephesos they come from the fill beneath the west stoa at the Tetragonos Agora–the 'Händlerdepot'–dating to the Augustan period. Seven broken bowls bear applied reliefs in their middle, showing Dionysos or single motifs such as a Greek philosopher, a Pan or a floral design. Two of them were analysed with x-ray fluorescence and are clearly grouped with other ESB samples. In contrast to the Hellenistic emblem cups the ESB examples have a wide, rather flat body with a plain surface outside and a small ring-foot. So there are, on the one hand, Hellenistic colour-coated deep emblem cups with ribbing on the outside, and on the other hand, the Roman Imperial type of shallow ESB cups without external grooves.

The missing link may be represented among the finds from the basilica at the state market at Ephesos. Here there are two pieces, which are true Hellenistic, both in shape and in decorative motifs, and probably Eastern Sigillata B in fabric[32]. These deep conical cups have horizontal ribbing on the outside of the vessel and a false ring-foot. One exemplar is decorated with an appliqué male head (Sarapis or Silenus/ satyr?) and the other with a female bust. Veronika Mitsopoulos-Leon describes the fabric of both as cinnamon brown with mica and white inclusions; the orange-brown slip of number C2 as flaking off in round pieces, as is typical for ESB; number C6 with a black soapy slip as a grey variant of ESB fabric.

Unfortunately, there are no examples of ESB emblem bowls from Priene so far. The same may be true for other shapes in ESB ware with appliqué decoration.

Applied relief decoration

Hayes records a solitary fragment of an open vessel shape from the Athenian Agora with an applied knotted

[29] For the conical type 1 with straight rim see e.g. one of the earliest Agora examples from the first half of the third century BC: Rotroff 1997, 111–112. 277 no. 333 fig. 21, pls 33, 36 with the portrait head of a Ptolemaic king surrounded by two incised grooves and painted framework; she suggests an Egyptian influence. – For the hemispherical type 2 with outturned rim see e.g. Rotroff 1997, 114 and 283 no. 386, pl. 37, from the first quarter of the second century BC, which shows the bust of a female figure.

[30] Zabehlicky-Scheffenegger and Schneider 2000, 110–112, figs. 4. 5, chart no. 1 with scientific analysis.

[31] E.g. Athens, Agora Museum P13581: Medallion fragment with head of Euripides in profile to right s. http://www.agathe.gr/id/agora/object/p%2013581, the fabric described on the catalog card as 'dull red glaze, rather flaked'. And Athens, Agora Museum P14992: Medallion with bust of Demosthenes in profile to right s. http://www.agathe.gr/id/agora/object/p%2014992, its fabric described there as 'clay reddish-buff to gray. Dark red glaze partially preserved on bottom; badly flaked black glaze on medallion', probably unevenly fired. Both examples could be of ESB fabric, but no analysis proofs this assumption.

[32] Mitsopoulos-Leon 1991, 56–57; 63 no. C 2, pl. 64 (Sarapis?); C 6, pl. 65 (female bust). Their *terminus ante quem* is 'Bauzeit der Basilika', i.e. Augustan.

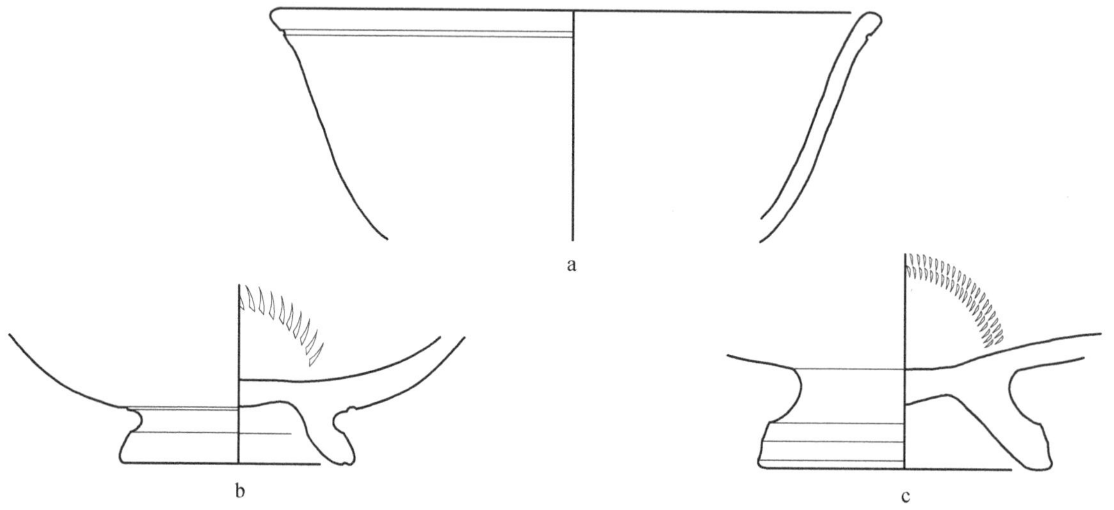

Fig. 7. cups – Augustan (?) forms in ESB fabric (drawings M. Brückle)

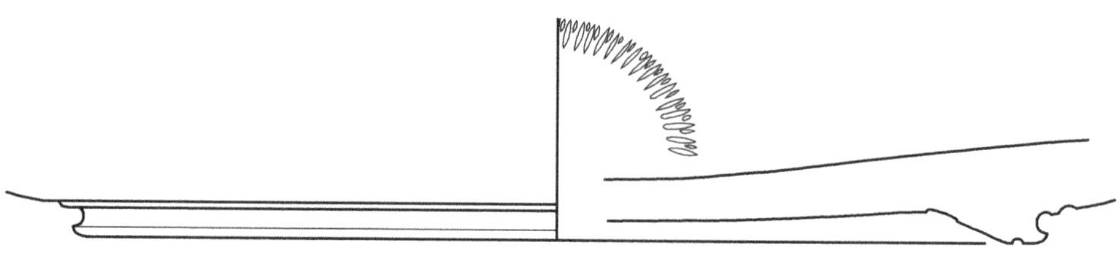

Fig. 8. plate – Augustan form in local fabric, imitating ESB (drawing M. Brückle)

floral motif[33]. He classifies it as 'Proto-ESB ware', but simultaneously notes with a question mark in the catalogue that it may perhaps be Ephesian red-gloss ware. Indeed, there is a production of appliqué ware attested at Ephesos, but in Hellenistic colour coated ware[34]. It would be most interesting to verify the fabric of the example from Athens – whether it is of Ephesian or ESB fabric.

Prosepct: Early Augustan ESB

Imports

Let us take a brief look at the very early Imperial examples in ESB fabric from 'Komplex B' at Priene. With rouletting and no potter's stamps, they still stand in the Hellenistic tradition and hardly find exact parallels among the known ESB spectrum. They may be representatives of the transitional phase from Hellenistic to Roman Imperial/ true Sigillata forms at the production centre of ESB.

The rim fragment of a bell-shaped cup with outturned rim resembles the Augustan shape Atlante 21 except for the ridge below the rim (**Fig. 7a**)[35]. The profile of our example is also still more *S*-shaped. Two feet belonged either to hemispherical cups or to cups with outturned rims. The first has a soft, swinging profile with a ridge on the underside of the foot (**Fig. 7b**). While there is no known ESB type of this form, it has a good parallel among the Ephesian grey ware[36]. The profile of the second foot is comparable to ESB examples from Priene and Ephesos, whereas those bear stamps surrounded by circles (**Fig. 7c**)[37].

Local fabric

From the 'Komplex B' at Priene there also come very early ESB forms in local fabric (**Fig. 2**). Several plates are characterised by a very small outturned foot[38]; one bears still a rouletting (**Fig. 8**). They may show either that the Sigillata forms were developed not only at the production centre of ESB (Tralleis?) but also in the surrounding cities; or that it was not long before the models from the ESB centre were adopted in the Meander region (and beyond?).

[33] Hayes 2008, 31. 161 no. 432 fig. 14 pl. 19.
[34] Zabehlicky-Scheffenegger and Schneider 2000, 105–110 figs. 1–3; p. 112 tab. 1.
[35] Hayes 1985, 57 pl. 12 no. 15.
[36] Rogl 2004, 213. 218 no. K 17 pl. 2.
[37] Priene: Zahn 1904, 436 no. 149 fig. 551; Ephesos: Mitsopoulos-Leon 1991, 102. 113 no. H 80 pl. 139.
[38] Compare Hayes 1985, 53 pl. 11, 8 (Atlante 1) and p. 56 pl. 12, 6 (Atlante 14).

Conclusion

Summing up, there are several hints at Hellenistic forerunners of ESB ware. The spectrum includes plain forms such as calyces, echinus bowls and plates as well as decorated classes. On the one hand, there was an ESB ware production with applied relief decoration–namely medaillon bowls and possibly other shapes–while, on the other hand, there are several examples with decoration in West Slope successive style–among others, carinated bowls, plates, lagynoi and jugs with incised decoration and additional white decoration. The starting period may well be before the middle of the first century BC, as the ware is attested at Delos before 69 BC. The spectrum of the earliest ESB production is still almost unknown and needs intensive further research, including scientific analysis. The sporadic finds from Priene and other places already give important hints. The material from Tralleis and the trading centre of Ephesos could undoubtedly form the backbone of a study of ESB in general. And on any given excavation there is the possibility of turning up previously unknown Hellenistic (as well as Imperial) forms in ESB fabric!

Nina Fenn
Archäologisches Institut
Universität zu Köln
Albertus Magnus Platz
D-50923 Köln
nina.fenn@uni-koeln.de

Bibliography

Bruneau, Ph. 1970. La vaisselle, in Ph. Bruneau, G. Vatin and U. Becerra de Meneses, *L'Îlot de la Maison des Comédiens*. Délos 27, 239–262. Paris, De Boccard.

Fenn, N. 2011. A Late Hellenistic Pottery Deposit from the Athena Sanctuary at Priene, in: *Z' Epistēmonikē Synantēsē gia tēn Ellenistikē Keramikē*. Aigio 2005, 525–532. Athens, TAP.

Fenn, N. forthcoming. *Untersuchungen zu Herkunft und Produktion hellenistischer und kaiserzeitlicher Keramik von Priene (Westtürkei)*. Archäologische Forschungen, Priene. Wiesbaden, Reichert.

Gassner, V. 1997. *Das Südtor der Tetragonos-Agora: Keramik und Kleinfunde*. Forschungen in Ephesos 13, 1, 1. Wien, Verlag der Österreichischen Akademie der Wissenschaften.

Hayes, J. W. 1985. Sigillate orientali, in *Enciclopedia dell'arte antica: Atlante delle forme ceramiche II*, 1–96. Rom, Istituto della Enciclopedia Italiana.

Hayes, J. W. 2008. *Roman Pottery: Fine-ware Imports*. The Athenian Agora XXXII. Princeton, NJ., American School of Classical Studies at Athens.

Hellström, P. 1965. *Pottery of Classical and Later Date: Terracotta Lamps and Glass*. Labraunda 2, 1. Lund, Gleerup.

Mitsopoulos-Leon, V. 1972–1975. Keramik aus Basilika und Prytaneion: ein Überblick. *Österreichische Jahreshefte* 50, Beibl. 495–524.

Mitsopoulos-Leon, V. 1991. *Die Basilika am Staatsmarkt in Ephesos: Kleinfunde I. Keramik hellenistischer und römischer Zeit*. Forschungen in Ephesos 9, 2, 2. Wien, Schindler.

Poblome, J., Brulet, R. and Bounegrou, O. 2000. The Concept of Sigillata : Regionalism or Integration? *Rei Cretariae Romanae Fautorum Acta* 36, 279–283.

Rogl, Ch. 2004. Zu dem Produktionsbeginn schwarzer Sigillata in Ephesos. Die Evidenz der Tetragonos Agora. *Jahreshefte des Österreichischen Archäologischen Institutes in Wien* 73, 207–219.

Rotroff, S. I. 1997. *Hellenistic Pottery : Athenian and Imported Wheelmade Table Ware and Related Material*. The Athenian Agora XXIX. Princeton, NJ., American School of Classical Studies at Athens.

Schneider, G. 2000. Chemical and Mineralogical Studies of Late Hellenistic to Byzantine Pottery Production in the Eastern Mediterranean. *Rei Cretariae Romanae Fautorum Acta* 36, 525–536.

Zabehlicky-Scheffenegger, S., Schneider, G. 2000. Applikenverzierte Gefässe aus Ephesos. *Rei Cretariae Romanae Fautorum Acta* 36, 105–112.

Zabehlicky-Scheffenegger, S. 2003. C. Sentius and his Commercial Connections. In C. Abadie-Reynal (ed.), *Les céramiques en Anatolie aux époques hellénistique et romaine*: Actes de la table ronde d'Istanbul, 22–24 mai 1996, Varia Anatolica 15, 117–119. Paris, Institut Français d'Études Anatoliennes d'Istanbul.

Zahn, R. 1904. Thongeschirr, in T. Wiegand and H. Schrader, *Priene: Ergebnisse der Ausgrabungen und Untersuchungen in den Jahren 1895–1898*, 394–468. Berlin, G. Reimer.

Zelle, M. 1997. *Die Terra Sigillata aus der Westtor-Nekropole in Assos*. Asia Minor Studien 27. Bonn, R. Habelt.

Cyprus

Cypriot Transport Amphorae as Evidence of the Island's Trade Links during the Hellenistic Period

Agata Dobosz

Abstract

The article concerns the question of Cypriot transport amphorae produced during the Hellenistic period, and their distribution on the island and beyond. There are shortly presented Cypriot amphorae of so called Greek type with the characteristics of local production and also the imitations of Knidian and Koan amphorae of Cypriot origin. In the light of recent discoveries and their publication, it is possible to supplement the list of distribution of Cypriot amphorae of the Greek type which was presented by Calvet in 1986[1].

It seems that the predominant centre of the production of the amphorae of the Greek type in Cyprus was Kourion. Probably these amphorae were used mainly on the island itself. However, although they are not very common outside the island, we could state that quite a large amount of them, comparing to the number of those that were left in Kourion, was exported to other places on the island and abroad. Thus, probably for Kourion itself, the trade of locally made amphorae (and of their content) could be significant.

Keywords: Hellenistic Cyprus, Cypriot amphorae, Kourion, Koan, Knidian amphorae imitations

Introduction

The article concerns the question of Cypriot transport amphorae produced during the Hellenistic period, and their distribution on the island and beyond. This subject was undertaken for the first time in literature by V. Grace[2], and was continued by Y. Calvet[3] and H. Meyza[4]. In the light of recent discoveries and their publication, it is possible to supplement the information presented so far. The subject of interest of above mentioned scholars were Cypriot amphorae of so called Greek type with the characteristics of local production[5]. Some of them were stamped. Apart from these amphorae, the imitations of Knidian and Koan amphorae were produced on the island during the Hellenistic period as well. They will also be shortly mentioned below. Observations presented here are based on analysis of the material published so far and also of unpublished fragments of amphorae discovered on the site of Maloutena in Paphos by the Polish Archaeological Mission of Warsaw University[6].

Cypriot amphorae of the Greek type

The most studied and most recognizable group of Cypriot amphorae is this of the Greek type with the characteristics of local production. As one of their production centres V. Grace[7] proposed Kourion, due to the abundance of their fragments found there – she mentioned them as the second largest group of amphorae discovered there after the Rhodian one – and due to the similarity of their clay with the paste of the locally made pottery. Grace[8] describes this clay as follows: 'coarse, usually hard-baked, with many inclusions, in particular large white grits; the colour varies according to the firing, but is often a bright brick red'. This is the most easily recognizable clay of Cypriot amphorae. Data concerning the number of discovered fragments and their distribution presented below applies chiefly to amphorae made with this type of clay, or similar. However, Meyza[9] noted differences between the clay of Kouriote amphorae and cooking ware which were shown as a result of preliminary qualitative petrographic analysis. It could bring into question, in his opinion, the existence of one general Kouriote paste. According to Grace[10], the production of Kouriote amphorae begun at the end of the 4th century BC and seemed to fail during the second half of

1 After this paper was written two very important articles concerning Cypriot amphorae were published: Finkielsztejn 2013: about finds from Israel and Şenol, Şenol 2013: about Cypriot amphorae excavated in Alexandria. The amount of artifacts presented in these papers shows that the distribution of Cypriot amphorae outside the island was much more extended than it is stated in the present article.

2 Grace 1979.

3 Calvet 1986; cf. also Calvet 1972, 1978, 1982, 1993, 2003; Salles 1993.

4 Meyza 2004.

5 Grace (1979, 183) noted, that these amphorae remind her of small-size Chian amphorae produced *c.* 400 BC. She does not define Cypriot amphorae as imitations of this type of Chian ones, but suggests rather, that the manufacturers of Cypriot amphorae were inspired by older Chian production.

6 I would like to express my thanks to the previous and current directors of these excavations, to Professor W. A. Daszewski and Dr H. Meyza, for entrusting to me the studies of Hellenistic amphorae found on this site. I am also very grateful to Professor Z. Sztetyłło for letting me continue her studies of stamped handles and for her help.

7 Grace 1979, 178–179.

8 Grace 1979, 178; cf. Meyza 2004, 274–275.

9 Meyza 2004, 275.

10 Grace 1979, 184–185.

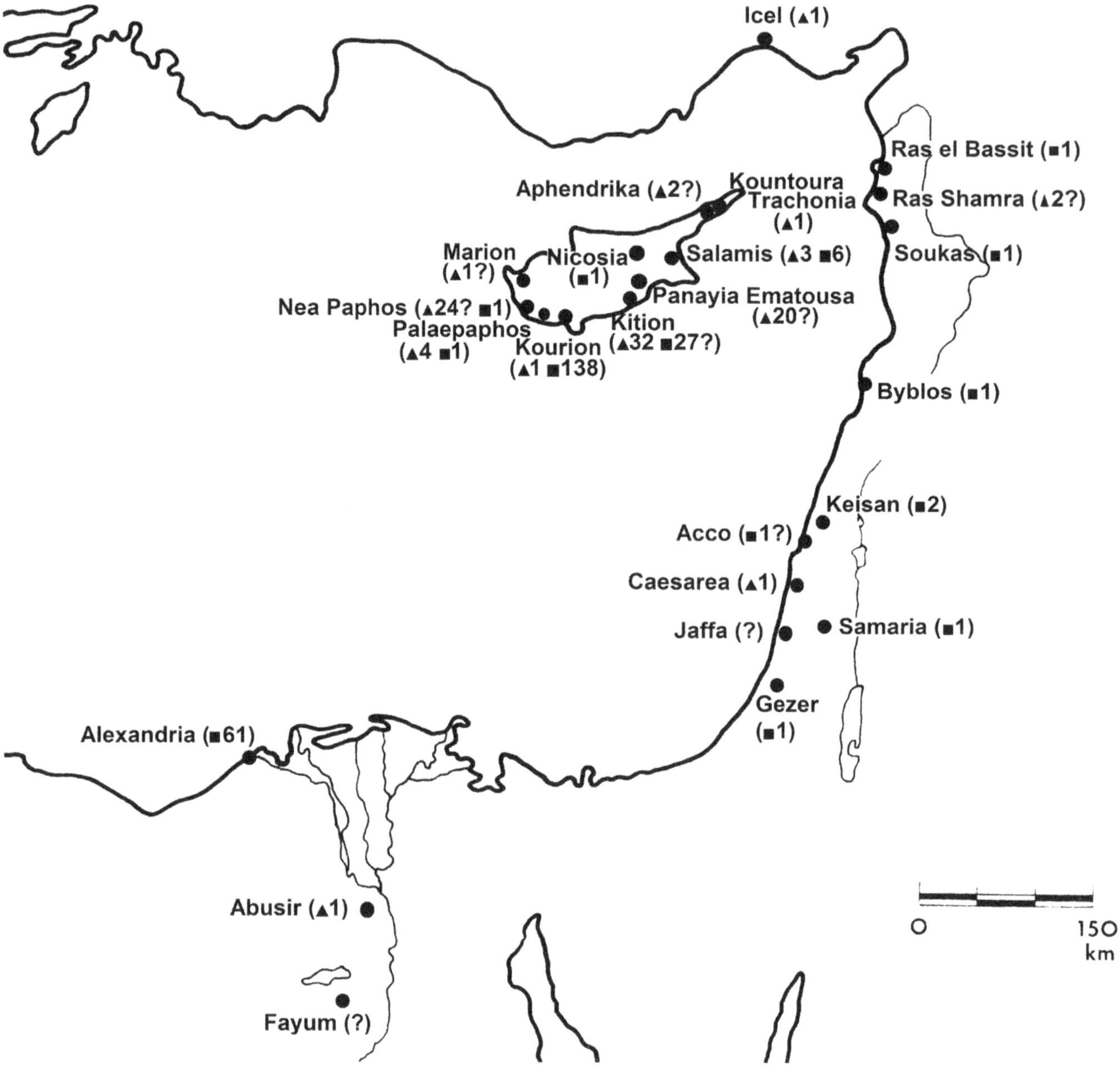

Fig. 1. Distribution of Cypriot Hellenistic amphorae (Drawing by A. Dobosz)

the 2nd century BC. Meyza[11] set their disappearance during the late Hellenistic period. Also Paphos was mentioned by Grace[12] as a centre of the production of amphorae during the Hellenistic time. According to this scholar, a note about Paphian amphorae reused in Egypt in Papyri of Zenon and amphora stamps bearing an inscription *ΠΑ ΦΙ* found in Alexandria[13] and Gezer, could be treated as evidence of it. A clay of an example from Alexandria is described by Grace[14] as follows: 'a pale buff, pinkish at the core, non-micaceous but with dark inclusions'. However, it is necessary to note here the striking fact that only one Cypriot (not necessarily Paphian) amphora stamp has been found in Nea Paphos[15] and one in Palaepaphos[16]. Also, the number of sherds of the amphorae in question which were excavated in these places is much less than those found in Kourion (cf. below and **Fig. 1**). Apart from Kourion and Paphos, Kition[17] (where stamps with the inscription *ke ti*

[11] Meyza 2004, 274.
[12] Grace 1979, 181.
[13] Recently C. Brixhe published a corpus of Pamphylian amphora stamps from the Benaki Collection in Alexandria [non vidi]. He identified stmps with an inscription *ΠΑ ΦΙ* as of Pamphylian origin. The inscription is, in his opinion, a shortform of a personal name. I would like to thank Dr. V. Lungu for this information.
[14] Grace 1949, 188.
[15] Barker 2004, 77.
[16] Lund 1993, 118–119, no. C-354, fig. 52.
[17] Masson 1979, 221–222, fig. 1; Calvet and Masson 1988, 23–25, figs. 1–2.

written in Cypriot syllabary were found) and Salamis(?) are considered as centers of the production of amphorae, too[18]. However, until now no workshops of Hellenistic times producing amphorae in Cyprus have been discovered. Also, petrographic studies of the clay of Hellenistic amphorae produced on the island were very rare and of a preliminary character[19]. The variety of shapes of Cypriot amphorae and the abundance of the types of their stamps, does not make the classification any easier.

Distribution of Cypriot amphorae of the Greek type

Distribution of Cypriot Hellenistic amphorae – including the places shown by Calvet[20] – looks as follows (**Fig. 1**):

Kourion: 38 stamped handles from Kourion and its surroundings noted by Grace[21] and around 100 further examples from Kouriote Acropolis mentioned – and most of them published – by Meyza[22] and also one incomplete amphora[23];
Palaepaphos: The Canadian Palaepaphos Survey Project: one stamped handle and two toes of amphorae [24]; Palaepaphos Skales: two amphorae[25];
Nea Paphos: Ktima: 14? amphorae from Iskender necropolis[26]; Maloutena: six pieces of amphorae of local(?) production, made with clay different from that claimed to be Kouriote – the clay of each fragment differs as well[27], and two fragments of rims of Kouriote(?) origin[28]; Tombs of the Kings: one stamped handle[29]; Ellinospilioi: two whole amphorae[30]; one amphora stored in the Paphos District Museum[31];
Marion: one(?) amphora[32]
Kountoura Trachonia: one(?) amphora[33];
Aphendrika: two(?) amphorae[34];
Salamis: five stamped handles and one that could be of Salamis` production found in the area of the town[35] and also lower part of three amphorae from the necropolis[36];
Kition: Bamboula: 21 stamped fragments and seven further ones of probable Cypriot origin[37] and 34 fragments of amphorae – including two of the clay that is considered as Kouriote one[38]; Kathari: four stamped handles[39]; Larnaca: two stamped handles[40];
Panayia Ematousa: 20 fragments of amphorae made with the clay different from that considered as Kouriote[41].

With the exception of the island itself, Cypriot amphorae are discovered on many sites in Egypt, Levant and Turkey but in extremely small quantities (cf. **Fig. 1**). However, only in Alexandria, 60 stamped handles were recognized by Grace[42] – including few of possible Paphian origin – and Cancardeş-Şenol[43] added one more stamped handle to this group. Calvet[44], listed the places where Cypriot amphorae were found i.e. Egypt: Alexandria, Taposiris Magna, Fayum; Levant: Gezer (a stamp with the *ΠΑ ΦΙ* inscription), Akko, Haïfa, Samaria, Tel Keisan, Byblos, Ras Shamra, Ras el-Bassit, Tell Sukas. We can also add to this list Jaffa[45] and probably southern Turkey, if one amphora published by Şenol and Kerem[46] that is stored in İçel Museum, was found near there.

In the light of the research of Cypriot Hellenistic amphorae and their distribution the following notes can be made: it seems that the predominant centre of their production was Kourion. It also looks as if this was the only place – or one of two places if we also take Kition into consideration –, where these amphorae played a significant role, beside the Rhodian ones, in local markets. From there Kouriote amphorae were exported to the other marketplaces of the island and also further to Egypt – mainly to Alexandria – and in a lesser amount, to the littoral centers in Levant and south Turkey. However, their rarity in the marketplaces here mentioned, let us suppose, that they played a more significant role in Cyprus, especially in Kourion, than abroad. Therefore, we could state that Kouriote amphorae were devoted to local use. On the other hand, if we imply that a large amount of these amphorae, compared to the number of those that were left in Kourion, was exported to other places on the island and abroad, we have to state that for Kourion itself, the trade of locally made amphorae (and of their content) could be significant. In the light of the very general dating of Kouriote amphorae, it is difficult to follow the intensity and variability of their trade during the Hellenistic period. Since our knowledge about amphorae manufactured in Cyprus in other centers beside Kourion and their possible distribution is still rather limited, we are not able to make further conclusions.

18 Masson 1974, 157 no. 2; Calvet 1986, 513.
19 See: Salles 1993, 270; Meyza 2004, 274–275.
20 Calvet 1986.
21 Grace 1979, 179 n. 4; Calvet 1986, 509.
22 Meyza 2004, 275ff.
23 Connelly 1983, 280, no. 10, pl. XLVII: 9,10 fig. 6:9.
24 Lund 1993, 118–119, nos. C-352–C-354, fig. 52.
25 Karageorghis 1983, 96, nos. 1–2 and 99 n. 132.
26 Deshayes 1963, 210–212; Calvet 1986, 509.
27 Papuci-Władyka 1995, 83, no. 11 pl. 1.; 88 no. 22 pl. 3; 116 no. 102 pl. 16; 139 no. 181 pl. 28; 147 no. 200 pl. 30; 161 no. 249 pl. 36.
28 Unpublished, inv. nos. TP 1/93-7 and VT-W 81/94-12. I express my thanks to Professor E. Papuci-Władyka for giving me the permission to continue her studies of partly analysed unstamped pieces of amphorae found on this site which are not published as yet.
29 Barker 2004, 77 tab. 1.
30 Raptou and Marangou 2008, 374 nos. 17–18.
31 Grace 1979, 179; Calvet 1986, 509.
32 Gjerstad *et al.* 1934, Marion, Tomb 22 Pl. XLIV, 1 (tall one, in the middle), after: Deshayes 1963, 211 n. 1.
33 Gjerstad *et al.* 1934, 454 no. 24 pl. LXXV; du Plat Taylor (1937–39, 107 type 6) compares the amphora presented there with the example from Kountoura Trachonia; Salles 1993, 270 recognizes amphorae of the type B of the typology of Deshayes (1963, 210–211) as of Cypriot origin.
34 Dray and du Plat Taylor 1937–39, 107 types 6 and 7; these types were identified by Salles 1993, 270 as of Cypriot origin.
35 Calvet 1972, 52–53 nos. 105–108; Calvet 1978, 225 no. 60 fig. 2:60 pl. LVI; Calvet 1986, 509. 513; Masson 1974, 157 no. 2.
36 Karageorghis 1973, 141 no. 45 pl. CCLXXXVII, 45, 148–149 nos. 197, 220 pl. CCLXXXVIII, 197, 220; Calvet 1986, 509.
37 Calvet 1982, 42–45 nos 114–127; Calvet 1986, 511 nos. 1–7 figs. 4–5; Calvet 1993, 70–73 nos. 100. 102–105.
38 Calvet 1986, 509 nos. 9–13; Salles 1993, 270–271 nos. 539–345.
39 Calvet and Masson 1988; Calvet 2003, 357–358 nos. 55. 57–59.
40 Calvet 2003, 357 no. 56; Masson 1979, 220–222.
41 Winther Jacobsen 1998, 352 no. 95 fig. 40; Winther Jacobsen 2006, 308 nos. A3.9–10 fig. 160.
42 Grace 1979, 179 no. 2.
43 Cancardeş-Şenol 2001, 405 no. 17 fig. 11.22 (sic).
44 Calvet 1986, the full references to the publications are given there.
45 Cypriot amphorae mentioned by Finkielsztejn 2000, 211.
46 Şenol and Kerem 2000, 88 no. 8 pl. 1.

Cypriot imitations of Knidian and Koan amphorae

Apart from amphorae of Greek type with characteristics of Cypriot production, amphorae imitating those of Knidos and Kos were manufactured on the island, too. They were excavated in the House of Dionysos in Paphos and were identified by Hayes[47]. He described the Knidian imitations as: "local or regional counterparts of Knidian amphorae" and dated them from before 150 BC until the late 2nd century BC.

The Koan imitations were found in late 2nd century BC contexts and defined by Hayes as made of "the local fabric". K. Winther Jacobsen[48] also recorded these most probably Cypriot (Paphian?) imitations of Koan amphorae in a large number excavated in Panayia Ematousa. Although these imitations have not been well studied as yet and are still difficult to distinguish because of their complexity and a lack of the petrographic analysis of their clay, it seems that they form a huge group of Hellenistic amphorae found in Cyprus *inter alia* in Nea Paphos[49], Palaepaphos[50] and Panayia Ematousa[51]. With the exception of Cypriot imitations of Knidian and Koan types, probable imitations of Rhodian amphora made in Cyprus were also recorded[52].

It is worth noting that apart from the original Cypriot amphorae of the Greek type and amphorae imitating those of other centres, it seems that the production of basket handled amphorae, known from the Archaic period, also continued on the island during the Hellenistic period[53].

Agata Dobosz
Jagiellonian University
Institute of Archaeology
Gołębia 11, 30-007 Kraków
agata.dobosz@uj.edu.pl, aktaje@gazeta.pl

Bibliography

Barker, C. 2004. The Use of Rhodian Amphorae in Hellenistic Graves at Nea Paphos, Cyprus, in J. Eiring and J. Lund (eds.), *Transport Amphorae and Trade in the Mediterranean.* Acts of the International Colloquium at the Danish Institute at Athens, September 26–29, 2002. Monographs of the Danish Institute at Athens 5, 73–84. Athens, The Danish Institute at Athens.

Brixhe, C. (avec la collaboration de G. Cankardeş Şenol) 2012. *Timbres amphoriques de Pamphylie.* Études Alexandrines 23. Alexandrie, Centre d'Études Alexandrines [non vidi].

Calvet, Y. 1972. *Salamine de Chypre* III. *Les timbres amphoriques (1965–1970).* Paris, De Boccard.

Calvet, Y. 1978. Timbres amphoriques de Salamine (1971–1974). *Report of the Department of Antiquities, Cyprus*, 222–233.

Calvet, Y. 1982. *Kition-Bamboula* I. *Les timbres amphoriques.* Paris, Éditions Recherche sur les civilisations.

Calvet, Y. 1986. Les amphores chypriotes et leur diffusion en Méditerranée orientale, in J.-Y. Empereur and Y. Garlan (eds.), *Recherches sur les amphores greques.* Actes du colloque international organize par le centre national de la recherché scientifique, l'Universitaté de Rennes II et l'École Française d'Athenés. Athénes, 10–12 Septembre 1984. Bulletin de correspondence hellénique Suppl. XIII, 505–514.

Calvet, Y. 1993. Les timbres amphoriques. In J.-F. Salles (ed.) *Kition-Bamboula* IV. *Les niveaux hellénistiques*, 61–80. Paris, Éditions Recherche sur les civilisations.

Calvet, Y. and Masson, O. 1988. Un nouveau timbre amphorique à legend syllabique de Kition. *Centre d'Etudes Chypriotes.* Cahier 10, 1988/2, 23–26.

Cancardeş-Şenol, G. 2001. Stamped amphora handles form the necropolis of Gabbari, in J.-Y. Empereur and M.-D. Nenna (eds.), *Nécropolis* 1. Études alexandrines 5, 397–408.

Cancardeş-Şenol, G. and Şenol, A. K. 2013. Preliminary Remarks on Cypriot Amphorae and Stamps from Alexandria, in M. Lawall and J. Lund (eds.), *The Transport Amphorae and Trade of Cyprus.* Gösta Enbom Monographs 3, 62–83. Aarhus, Aarhus University Press.

Connelly, J. B. 1983. A Hellenistic Deposit on the Kourion Acropolis. In D. Christou, Excavations at Kourion. *Report of the Department of Antiquities, Cyprus* 1983, 266–280.

Deshayes, J. 1963. *La nécropole de Ktima.* Bibliothéque archéologique et historique LXXV. Paris, Librairie orientaliste Paul Geuthner.

Dray, E. and du Plat Taylor, J. 1937–39. Tsambres and Aphendrika. Two Classical and Hellenistic cemeteries in Cyprus. *Report of the Department of Antiquities, Cyprus*, 24–123.

Empereur, J.-Y. and Hesnard, A. 1987. Les amphores hellénistiques du monde égéen, in P. Lévéque and J.-P. Morel (eds.), *Céramiques hellénistiques et*

47 Hayes 1991, 85; cf. Papuci-Władyka 1997.
48 Winther Jacobsen 2006, 319–320.

49 Papuci-Władyka 1995, 73.
50 Lund 1993, 121–124.
51 Winther Jacobsen 2006, 319–320.
52 Calvet 1972, 57 no. 113; Empereur and Hesnard 1987, 13.
53 Winther Jacobsen 2006, 307–308.

romaines II, 9–71. Paris, Annales Littéraires de l'Université de Besançon.

Finkielsztejn, G. 2000. Amphores importees au Levant Sud à l'époque hellénistique et la revision de la chronologie des timbres amphoriques rhodiens. In *E΄ Επιστημονική Συνάντηση για την Ελληνιστική Κεραμική*. Χανιά 1997, 207–220. Athens, TAP.

Finkielsztejn, G. 2013. Cypriot Amphora Stamps of the Hellenistic Period Found in Israel, in M. Lawall and J. Lund (eds.), *The Transport Amphorae and Trade of Cyprus*. Gösta Enbom Monographs 3, 86–100. Aarhus, Aarhus University Press

Gjerstad, E., Lindros, J., Sjöquist, E. and Westholm, A. 1934. *The Swedish Cyprus Expedition. Finds and results of the excavations in Cyprus 1927–1931*. Vol. I–II. Stockholm, The Swedish Cyprus Expedition.

Grace, V. 1949. Standard Pottery Containers of the Ancient Greek World. In *Commemorative Studies in Honor of Theodore Leslie Shear.* Hesperia Suppl. 8, 175–189.

Grace, V. 1979. Kouriaka. In *Studies Presented in memory of Porphyrios Dikaios*, 178–188. Nicosia, The Lions Club of Nicosia.

Hayes, J. W. 1991. *The Hellenistic and Roman Pottery*. Paphos III. Nicosia, Department of Antiquities, Cyprus.

Karageorghis, V. 1983. *Palaepaphos-Skales. An Iron Age cemetery in Cyprus*. Ausgrabungen in Alt-Paphos auf Cypern 3. Konstanz, Universitätsverlag.

Lund, J. 1993. Pottery of the Classical, Hellenistic and Roman Periods, in L. W. Sørensen and D. W. Rupp (eds.), *The Land of the Paphian Aphrodite*. Vol. 2. *The Canadian Palaipaphos Survey Project. Artifact and Ecofactual Studies. Studies in Mediterranean Archaeology*. Vol. CIV: 2, 79–156. Göteborg, Paul Åström Forlag.

Masson, O. 1974. Notes d'onomastique chypriotes. *Report of the Department of Antiquities, Cyprus*, 157–162.

Masson, O. 1979. Variétés chypriotes. *Report of the Department of Antiquities, Cyprus*, 218–222.

Meyza, H. 2004. Kouriaka again: Amphora Stamps from the Kourion Acropolis Excavations, in J. Eiring and J. Lund (eds.), *Transport Amphorae and Trade in the Mediterranean*. Acts of the International Colloquium at the Danish Institute at Athens, September 26–29, 2002. Monographs of the Danish Institute at Athens 5, 273–284, Athens, The Danish Institute at Athens.

Papuci-Władyka, E. 1995. *Nea Pafos. Studia nad ceramiką hellenistyczną z polskich wykopalisk (1965–1991)*. Kraków, Uniwersytet Jagielloński.

Papuci-Władyka, E. 1997. A research report on Hellenistic Pottery: Cos amphoras. *Studies in Ancient Art and Civilisation* 8, 48–54.

Raptou, E. and Marangou, A. 2008. Une Tombe Hellénistique et Romaine à Paphos-Ellinospilioi. *Report of the Department of Antiquities, Cyprus*, 365–387.

Salles, J.-F. 1993. La citerne 198. In J.-F. Salles (ed.), *Kition-Bamboula* IV. *Les niveaux hellénistiques*, 261–284. Paris, Éditions Recherche sur les civilisations.

Şenol, A. K. and Kerem, F. 2000. *İçel müzesinde bulunan bir grup amphora.* Olba III, 81–114.

Winther Jacobsen, K. 2006. Transport amphorae, in L. W. Sørensen and K. Winther Jacobsen (eds.), *Panayia Ematousa* I. *A rural site in south-eastern Cyprus.* Monographs of the Danish Institute at Athens, Vol. 6, 1, 303–337. Athens, The Danish Institute at Athens.

Eastern Cyprus and the Northern Levantine Coast in the Hellenistic Period: The Ceramic Connection

John Lund

Abstract

The paper offers a survey of the scanty available evidence of ceramic exchanges between Eastern Cyprus and the northern Levantine coast in the Hellenistic period. It is concluded that before the middle of the 2nd century BC such exchanges were apparently mainly taking place at the regional level: between the area of Salamis and the plain of Latakia. From the second half of the 2nd century BC onward they seem to have been near inter-regional, and to have mainly involved Eastern Sigillata A from the wider area of Antioch, which not only reached Eastern Cyprus but also South Western Cyprus in great quantities. The reverse flow of goods from Cyprus to North West Syria seems mainly to have comprised archaeologically invisible material, perhaps metal or timber. The changing trade pattern may reflect a corresponding shift of the centre of political and economic gravity in the island towards its new capital, Nea Paphos.

Keywords: Hellenistic Cyprus, the northern Levantine coast, pottery exchange, transport amphorae, 'Persian Bowls', lagynoi, Eastern Sigillata A.

Introduction

The purpose of this paper is to attempt to identify ceramic connections between Eastern Cyprus and the northern Levantine coast with a view to throwing light on the relations between the two areas in the Hellenistic period.

My interest in this subject goes back to a comment made by Jean-François Salles during a discussion at the Second Nieborów conference in Poland in 1993, when he stated that: 'It is true that there are in Paphos strong connections with the rest of Cyprus which we do not have in Kition, but on the other hand, we have in Kition good connections with, let us say, [the] north-east coastal region, which you do not have in Paphos. What is "geographically correct"'[1]. Six years later, I touched on the matter in an article on 'Trade patterns in the Levant from the 1st century BC to the 2nd century AD', which concluded that Southeastern Cyprus was indeed from a ceramic point of view more closely connected with Northwestern Syria and Smooth Cilicia than with Western Cyprus[2]. But the supporting evidence dated mainly from the Roman Imperial period, and it seems appropriate to reconsider the question here for the Hellenistic period.

It may be useful to begin by defining the geographical entities under consideration. For present purposes 'Eastern Cyprus' comprises the area adjoining and to the east of Kition, the territory of Salamis and the eastern part of the fertile Mesaoria Plain, whereas 'The northern Levantine coast' refers to the plain of Latakia in north-western Syria, as well as the Hatay Province of Turkey[3].

Constraints

Several practical and methodological difficulties hamper an inquiry such as the present. There are few adequate publications of Hellenistic pottery at our disposal from both areas, and hardly any available quantified evidence.

Moreover, hardly any Hellenistic pottery kilns have been identified in both areas[4], and scientific clay analyses are few and far between. Our knowledge about the fabrics current in this part of the ancient world is correspondingly restricted, and it is often difficult to identify the geographical source of vessels – in particular when dealing with standard Hellenistic ceramic shapes such as bowls with incurved rim and fish plates[5].

Still, it seems worthwhile to address the problem in order to see where the new evidence, which has emerged over the last two decades, may lead us.

---

1 Salles 1995, 408. I am grateful to Jean-François Salles for having confirmed to me that when referring to the coastal region he was 'clearly thinking of coastal Syria'.

2 Lund 1999.

3 For a survey of the archaeological evidence of Hellenistic date in this area, see Lund 1993.

4 For Cyprus, see Lund 2009; apparently, no ceramic kilns from the Hellenistic period have been detected along the Levantine coastline either.

5 'The Levantine Ceramics Project', which was initiated by Andrea M. Berlin in 2011, will hopefully remedy this situation, see <http://www.levantineceramics.org/> (1st of November, 2012).

Common ground

In the Late Classical and Early Hellenistic period, a ceramic common ground between Eastern Cyprus and the Levantine coast of Syria may be established through the basket handle amphorae and the so-called the 'Persian bowls'. The former go back to the late 8th century in Cyprus and the Levant and had a fairly wide distribution in the Archaic and Classical periods[6], but I am only concerned with the final phase of their existence, the 3rd century BC, when such amphorae were apparently still manufactured and used in Eastern Cyprus, Lebanon and north-western Syria. They may have remained current at some places into the 2nd century BC[7].

The so-called Persian bowls, i.e. large mortaria with a distinctive rim shape, were likewise manufactured at several places in Eastern Cyprus and Phoenicia from the Archaic period onwards[8], and they also occur in Early Hellenistic layers in Eastern Cyprus[9], in the Latakia Plain and in Phoenicia[10].

However, in the absence of scientific clay analyses it is very difficult to distinguish the precise production centers of the late basket-handle amphorae and Persian bowls, and possible exports of the two types from Cyprus to the mainland and *vice versa* cannot be tracked down until such analyses have been performed. Still, the fact that both types were current and presumably produced in Eastern Cyprus as well as on the northern Levantine coast does establish a connection of sorts between the two areas. But this tie was not exclusive to the northern Levantine coast, but extended southwards into Phoenicia, where the bowls and amphorae are also found.

Evidence from Cyprus

Jean-François Salles' comment on the ceramic link between Kition and the northern Levantine coast which is quoted at the outset of this contribution was probably prompted by a group of vessels from 'Well 175' in Kition, in particular two unusual vessel shapes made in the same fabric, which he referred to as 'Hellénistique non-chypriote': 1) a tall skyphos with carinated body and lateral arched handles, and 2) a hemispherical mastoid bowl[11]. The context is dated by its latest datable find: a fragment of an Ionian mould-made bowl from the second half of the 2nd century BC[12]. A slightly earlier context in Kition, dated to the late 3rd or early 2nd century BC, contained a fragment of a plate with a rolled rim in West Slope technique, seemingly of the same fine fabric as the vessels just referred to: hard-fired and relatively thin-walled, made of whitish, beige or orange clay and with a reddish-brown slip[13]. In the near-absence in 1993 of close parallels to these vessels and their fabric from Cyprus, Salles reasonably suggested the coast of Cilicia or southern Turkey as their possible source[14].

However, similar vessels have since then been found in the Danish excavations at Panayia Emathousa/Aradippou[15], as well as among a large group of pottery from the 3rd century to the middle of the 2nd century BC excavated on the Hill of Ayios Georghios in Nicosia in central Cyprus[16]. Similar finds are now also known from elsewhere in the island[17]. In the light of these new discoveries it seems evident that we are not dealing with imports, but with vessels originating in central Cyprus[18].

If we consider the pottery of Hellenistic Cyprus at large, we may associate at least three characteristic products with ceramic workshops in Eastern and South-Eastern Cyprus: 1) a group of zoomorphic rattles in the shape of pigs, which was studied by Hans-Günter Buchholz, who dated them the 3rd and 2nd century BC[19], 2) a lagynos form with a characteristic two-step, funnel-shaped, rim, which was produced from about the middle of the 2nd century to the middle of the 1st century BC[20], and 3) the so-called Aradippou goblet, which seems to have emerged in the 1st century BC and continued to be manufactured in the 1st century AD[21]. As far as I am aware, hardly any exports of these two wares have so far been identified in the northern Levantine area with the exception of four shoulder fragments of lagynoi with painted decoration found in Antioch[22].

Evidence from Northwestern Syria

Three amphorae handles stamped with signs in the Cypriot Syllabic script have been found in the Latakia Plain: at Ras el Basit, Ras Shamra and Tell Sukas[23]. The handles are dated to the late 4th and the 3rd centuries BC, and they are clearly indicative of contacts with Cyprus, but we cannot tell where in the island these amphorae originated, so the three stamped handles cannot be used as evidence of a specific Eastern Cypriot connection with the Latakia plain[24].

---

6 See Jacobsen 2002; Lehmann 1996, 443–445 Form 421 pl. 79–80, and 113; Leidwanger 2005/2006; Salles 1991, 225–231; Wolff 2009.

7 Wolff 2009. See Jacobsen 2006a, 307–308 for references.

8 Lehmann 2005, 73–74; Salles 1991, 221–224 fig. 3.

9 Jacobsen 2006b, 270 UC 49 (Panayia Emathousa/Aradippou); Salles 1991, 219, 221 note 35 (Kition).

10 Berlin 1997, 124–127 nos. PW 341–347 pls. 38, 82 (Tel Anafa); Salles 1991, 219 (Tell Keisan).

11 Salles (ed.) 1993, 184 nos. 201–202 fig. 195 and 184 no. 203 fig. 195.

12 Puppo and Mosca 2000, 464 note 17; Salles (ed.) 1993, 185 no. 206 fig. 195.

13 Salles (ed.) 1993, 187–188 no. 228 figs. 199 and 201.

14 Salles (ed.) 1993, 188.

15 Lund 1998, 333–336 nos. 17–18 fig. 34; Lund 2006a, 190–194.

16 Berlin and Pilacinski 2003 [2004], 204 nos. 64–71 fig. 4.

17 Lund 2005a, 72–73 and 82 figs. 4–5.

18 Lund 1998, 333; Lund 2005a, 72–73; Marquié 2002, 176.

19 Buchholz 1966, 1987, 102 note 510 and 1990, 36 note 36.

20 The type corresponds in part to Borowicz 2005, 32 form L3; Dray and Plat Taylor 1937–1939 [1951], 100 (Type D), Hayes 1991, 18, 20 (Nea Paphos Series 5), and Westholm 1956, 59 and 65 (Type 1). The full documentation for this lagynos type will be published in Lund forthcoming.

21 Lund 2005a; Lund 2006, 35 fig.2.

22 Waagé 1948, 28 fig. 8 nos. 17–20. No such finds occurred at Jebel Khalid according to Tidmarsh 2011, 386 note 229.

23 Calvet 1986, 510–511 notes 21–23. See also the contribution by Agata Dobosz in this volume.

24 Calvet 1986, 510; Meyza 2004, 274 hints at a somewhat longer

Two out of the five stamped amphora handles found at Leukos Limen, the harbour of Ras Shamra, shared the same monogram-stamp consisting of the two Greek letters: Π and O[25]. This stamp is otherwise known from the Athenian Agora, where it occurs in a 3rd century BC context[26], Alexandria[27], Samaria[28], and Salamis, where it occurs twice[29]. Hence, four out of seven known occurrences of this monogram were found in relatively close proximity. Rolf A. Stucky suggested that the amphorae in question might have been produced at Laodicea, which is known from ancient written sources to have been a wine producer of some renown[30]. I wonder, though, whether the letters might not rather be the beginning of the name of a nearby city, Posideion, which is commonly identified with Ras el-Bassit. Among the few published Hellenistic finds from the latter site is a fragmentary amphora handle with the stamp Posidai[eon]. According to a mineralogical analysis this was a local product, but it is so far unique among more than 130 – mainly Rhodian – amphora stamps reported from Ras el-Bassit[31].

Finally, we arrive at Eastern Sigillata A, which emerged in its classic red gloss form about the middle of the 2nd century BC[32], and was probably produced in within the wider area of Antioch, in North Western Syria or Smooth Cilicia[33]. Eastern Sigillata A was widely distributed in the Eastern Mediterranean, and it became the predominating fine ware in both Eastern and Western Cyprus in the 1st century BC[34]. This distribution pattern implies that the ware cannot be construed as evidence of a special connection between the northern Levantine coast and Eastern Cyprus, but it is certainly indicative of contact the wider area of Antioch and Cyprus at large.

Conclusion

In the first century and a half of the Hellenistic period, some sort of link between Eastern Cyprus and the Levantine coast is suggested by the shared use of the basket-handle amphorae and Persian bowls. The presence in Salamis of two Π O monogram stamps from amphorae possibly made at Posideion (or Laodicea) and the three Cypriot amphora stamps found the Latakia plain seem to reflect a mercantile exchange between Cyprus and the Latakia plain. If true, then this would seem mainly to have taken place at a regional level, considering the relatively short sailing distance between Salamis and the Latakia plain.

For the second part of the Hellenistic period, an indisputable trade connection is provided by the Eastern Sigillata A *tsunami*, which not only rolled over the eastern part of Cyprus, but also engulfed the island's western part. This exchange may, however, be said to have happened at a near inter-regional level, seeing that Eastern Sigillata A presumably originated in the *chora* of Antioch, and it may not be coincidental, that a few fragments of Eastern Cypriot lagynoi have been found in that very city. Nonetheless, as far as ceramics are concerned the traffic seems to have been pretty one-sided: moving from Antioch towards Cyprus, which suggests that goods going in the other direction were archaeologically invisible such as copper or timber.

The present evidence for ceramic connections between Eastern Cyprus and the Levantine coast is tenuous, and the picture sketched here may well change as more information becomes available. Still, the preliminary conclusions make sense from a historical point of view, because they reflect the fact that the political and economic centre of gravity in Cyprus shifted from the east to the west during the Hellenistic period, when Salamis and Kition moved to the second rank of cities[35], whereas Nea Paphos, the new capital of the island, expanded rapidly and became a lynchpin in the trade route connecting Alexandria with the Aegean[36].

John Lund
Assistant Keeper, senior researcher
Collection of Classical and Near Eastern Antiquities
The National Museum of Denmark
Frederiksholms Kanal 12
DK-1220 Copenhagen K
John.Lund@natmus.dk

Bibliography

Buchholz, H.-G. 1966. Tönerne Rasseln aus Zypern. *Archäologischer Anzeiger*, 140–151.

Buchholz, H.-G. 1987. Exkurs. In S. Laser, *Sport und Spiel*. Archaeologia Homerica 3 Kapitel T. 100–116. Göttingen, Vandenhoeck & Ruprecht.

Buchholz, H.-G. 1990. Kyprische Eulenrasseln. *Κυπριακή αρχαιολογία. Archaeologia cypria* 2, 33–51.

survival.

25 Stucky 1983, 148–149 nos. 2–3 pl. 48.
26 Grace 1934, 289 no. 269.
27 Stucky 1983, 149 note 7.
28 Reisner *et al.* 1924, 316 VI b no. 15.
29 Calvet 1972, 63–64 nos. 131–132.
30 Stucky 1983, 149.
31 Courbin 1986, 208.
32 Hayes 1985, 9–48; Hayes 2008, 13–30; Lund 2005b; Slane 1997, 269–346; <http://bmcr.bryanmawr.edu/2012/2012-1009.html> (1st of November, 2012).
33 For references, see Lund *et al.* 2006; for another perspective, see Regev 2007, 192–194.
34 Lund 2006b, 41. For Western Cyprus, see Hayes 1991, 32–36.
35 Yon 2006, 61; Yon 2007, 59.
36 Lund 1999; Młynarczyk 1990; Rupp 1997.

Berlin, A. M. 1997. The Plain Wares. In S. C. Herbert (ed.), *The Hellenistic and Roman Pottery.* Tel Anafa II,1. Journal of Roman Archaeology Supplementary Series 10 Part II,1, ix–211 Ann Arbor, Michigan, Kelsey Museum of Archaeology.

Berlin, A. and Pilacinski, J. 2003 [2004]. The pottery of the Early and Middle Hellenistic period. *Report of the Department of Antiquities, Cyprus*, 201–236.

Calvet, Y. 1972. *Salamine de Chypre III: Les timbres amphoriques (1965–1970)*. Paris, De Boccard.

Calvet, Y. 1986. Les amphores chypriotes et leur diffusion en Méditerranée orientale, in J.-Y. Empereur and Y. Garlan (eds.), *Recherches sur les amphores grecques*. Actes du colloque international organisé par le centre national de la recherche scientifique, l'Université de Rennes II et l'École française d'Athènes (Athènes, 10–12 Septembre 1984), Bulletin de Correspondance Hellénique Supplément 13, 505–514. Athènes and Paris, De Boccard.

Courbin, P. 1986. Bassit. *Syria* 63, 175–220.

Diederichs, C. 1980. *Céramiques hellénistiques, romaines et byzantines*. Salamine de Chypre IX. Paris, De Boccard.

Grace, V. R. 1934. Stamped Amphora Handles found in 1931–1932. *Hesperia* 3, 197–310.

Hadjisavvas, S., Lunt, D. A., Parks, D. A., Aviam, M. and Stern, E. J. 1997. *Agia Napa. Excavations at Makronisos and the Archaeology of the Region.* Nicosia, Department of Antiquities, Cyprus.

Hayes, J. W. 1985. Sigillata Orientale A (Eastern Sigillata A), in *EAA, Atlante delle forme ceramiche II*, 1–48. Roma, Istituto dell'arte antica, classica e orientale.

Hayes, J. W. 2008. *Roman Pottery. Fine-Ware Imports*. The Athenian Agora XXXII. Princeton, NJ., American School of Classical Studies at Athens.

Jacobsen, K. W. 2002. Cypriot Transport Amphorae in the Archaic and Classical Period. *Acta Hyperborea* 9, 169–184.

Jacobsen, K. W. 2006a. Transport amphorae, in: L. W. Sørensen and K. W. Jacobsen (eds.), *Panayia Ematousa I. A rural site in south-eastern Cyprus*. Monographs of the Danish Institute at Athens 6, 303–336. Athens, Aarhus University Press.

Jacobsen, K. W. 2006b. Utility ceramics, in: L. W. Sørensen and K. W. Jacobsen (eds.), *Panayia Ematousa I. A rural site in south-eastern Cyprus*. Monographs of the Danish Institute at Athens 6, 244–302. Athens, Aarhus University Press.

Lehmann, G. 1996. *Untersuchungen zur späten Eisenzeit in Syrien und Libanon. Stratigraphie und Keramikformen zwischen ca. 720 bis 300 v.Chr.* Münster, Ugarit-Verlag.

Lehmann, G. 2005. Al Mina and the East: A Report on Research in Progress. In A. Villing (ed.), *The Greeks in the East.* The British Museum Research Publication Number 157, 61–92. London, British Museum.

Leidwanger, J. 2005/2006. The Cypriot Transport Amphora. Notes on Its Development and Distribution. *Skyllis* 7.1–2, 24–31.

Lund, J. 1993. The Archaeological Evidence for the Transition from the Persian Period to the Hellenistic Age in Northwestern Syria. *Transeuphratène* 6, 27–45.

Lund, J. 1998. The ceramic finewares from the Late Classical to the Late Antique period found in 1995 and 1996, in L. W. Sørensen, A. Destrooper-Georgiades, R. Frederiksen, K. W. Jacobsen and J. Lund, *Third Preliminary Report of The Danish Archaeological Excavations at Panayia Ematousa, Aradippou, Cyprus*. Proceedings of the Danish Institute at Athens 2, 332–348.

Lund, J. 1999. Trade patterns in the Levant from *ca.* 100 BC to AD 200 – as reflected by the distribution of ceramic fine wares in Cyprus. *Münstersche Beiträge zur antiken Handelsgeschichte* 18.1, 1–22.

Lund, J. 2005a. Introducing the Aradippou goblet: a case study of regional diversity in Late Hellenistic and Early Roman Cyprus, in L. E. Vaag and M. B. Briese, (eds.), *Trade Relations in the Eastern Mediterranean from Late Hellenistic Period to Late Antiquity: The Ceramic Evidence*. Acts from a Ph. D.-seminar for young scholars, Sandbjerg Manorhouse, 12–15 February 1998. Halicarnassian Studies 3, 68–82. Odense, University Press of southern Denmark.

Lund, J. 2005b. An economy of consumption: the Eastern Sigillata A industry in the late Hellenistic period, in Z. H. Archibald, J. K. Davies and V. Gabrielsen, (eds.), *Making, Moving, and Managing. The New World of Ancient Economies, 323–31 BC*, 233–251. Oxford, Oxford University Press.

Lund, J. 2006a. Ceramic fine wares from the 4th century BC to the 7th century AD, in L. W. Sørensen and K. W. Jacobsen (eds.), *Panayia Ematousa I. A rural site in south-eastern Cyprus*. Monographs of the Danish Institute at Athens 6, 182–230. Athens, Aarhus University Press.

Lund, J. 2006b. On the circulation of goods in Hellenistic and Early Roman Cyprus: the ceramic evidence, in L. W. Sørensen and K. W. Jacobsen (eds.), *Panayia Ematousa I. A rural site in south-eastern Cyprus*. Monographs of the Danish Institute at Athens 6, 31–49. Athens, Aarhus University Press.

Lund, J. 2009. The potters of Hellenistic and Roman Cyprus, Medelhavsmuseet. *Focus on the Mediterranean* 5, 165–170.

Lund, J. forthcoming. *Studies on the circulation of pottery in Cyprus from the 3rd century BC to the 3rd century AD.*

Lund, J., Malfitana, D. and Poblome, J. 2006. *Rhosica vasa mandavi* (Cic., *Att.* 6.1.13): Towards the identification of a major ceramic tableware industry of the Eastern Mediterranean: Eastern Sigillata A. *Archeologia Classica* 57, 491–507.

Marquié, S. 2002. Classical, Hellenistic and Roman Periods, in V. Karageorghis in collaboration with J. Boardman, M. Egetmeyer, M. G. A. Guzzo, M. M.

Mango, S. Marquié, P. H. Merrillees, L. Michaelidou, I. Nicolaou, D. Papanikola-Bakirtzis, D. Z. Pierides, E. Poyiadji, A. T. Reyes, K. Romiopoulou, R. Senff, I. Tassignon and E. Zapiti, *Ancient Art from Cyprus in the collection of George and Nefeli Giabra Pierides*, 176–185. Nicosia, Bank of Cyprus Cultural Foundation.

Meyza, H. 2004. Kouriaka again: Amphora Stamps from the Kourion Acropolis Excavations, in J. Eiring and J. Lund (eds.), *Transport Amphorae and Trade in the Eastern Mediterranean.* Acts of the International Colloquium at the Danish Institute at Athens, September 26–29, 2002. Monographs of the Danish Institute at Athens 5, 273–284. Athens, Aarhus University Press.

Młynarczyk, J. 1990. *Nea Paphos in the Hellenistic Period.* Nea Paphos III. Varsovie, Éditions Géologiques.

Puppo, P. and Mosca, F. 2000. La ceramica megarese a Cipro. Ritrovamenti ed individuazione di officine, in *E΄ Επιστημονική Συνάντηση για την Ελληνιστική Κεραμική.* Χανιά 1997, 461–476. Athens, TAP.

Regev, D. 2007. A New Approach on the Origin of Eastern Sigillata A. In M. Sartre (ed.). *Productions et échanges dans la Syrie grecque et romaine.* Actes du colloque de Tours, juin 2003. Τοποι. Orient-Occident Suppléments 8, 189–200. Lyon, Maison de l'Orient Méditerranéen/Paris, De Boccard.

Reisner, G. A., Fisher, C. S. and Lyon, D. G. 1924. *Harvard Excavations at Samaria 1908 –1910.* Cambridge, Massachusetts, Harvard University Press.

Rupp, D. W. 1997. 'Metro' Nea Paphos: Suburban Sprawl in Southwestern Cyprus in the Hellenistic and Earlier Roman Periods, in W. A. Aufrecht, N. A. Mirau and S. W. Gauley (eds.), *Urbanism in Antiquity From Mesopotamia to Crete.* Journal for the Study of the Old Testament Supplement Series 244, 236–262. Sheffield, University of Sheffield.

Salles, J. F. 1991. Du blé, de l'huile et du vin… Notes sur les échanges commerciaux en Méditerranée orientale vers le milieu du 1er millénaire av. J. C., in H. Sancisi-Werdenburg and A. Kuhrt (eds.), *Asia Minor and Egypt: Old cultures in a new empire.* Proceedings of the Groningen 1988 Achaemenid history workshop. Achaemenid History 6, 207–236. Leiden, The Netherlands Institute for the Near East.

Salles, J.-F. (ed.) 1993. *Les niveaux hellénistiques.* Kition-Bamboula IV. Paris, Éditions Recherches sur les Civilisations, ADPF.

Salles, J.-F. 1995. Céramiques hellénistiques de Kition-Bamboula, in H. Meyza, and J. Młynarczyk, J. (eds.), *Hellenistic and Roman Pottery in the Eastern Mediterranean – Advances in Scientific Studies.* Acts of the II Nieborów Pottery Workshop. Nieborów, 18–20 December 1993. 397–414. Warsaw, Polska Akademia Nauk. Zakład Archeologii Śródziemnomorskiej.

Slane, K. W. 1997. The Fine Wares, in: S. C. Herbert (ed.), *The Hellenistic and Roman Pottery.* Tel Anafa II,1. Journal of Roman Archaeology Supplementary Series 10 Part II,1, 247–393. Ann Arbor, Michigan, Kelsey Museum of Archaeology.

Stucky, R. A. 1983. *Ras Shamra – Leukos Limen, die nachugaritische Besiedlung von Ras Shamra.* Paris, Librairie Orientaliste P. Geuthner.

Tidmarsh, J. 2011. The Imported Fine Wares at Jebel Khalid, in H. Jackson and J. Tidmarsh, *Jebel Khalid on the Euphrates 3: The pottery.* Mediterranean archaeology supplement 7, 279–429. Sydney, Meditarch.

Waagé, F. O. 1948. Hellenistic and Roman Tableware of North Syria. In F. O. Waagé (ed.), *Ceramics and Islamic Coins.* Antioch-on the-Orontes 4.1, 1–60. Princeton, London and The Hague, Princeton University Press.

Wolff, S. R. 2009. Some Notes on Basket-Handled Amphoras. *Eretz-Israel* 29, 137–146 (Hebrew with English summary on p. 287).

Yon, M. 2006. *Kition de Chypre.* Guides archéologiques de l'Institut Français du Proche Orient 4. Paris, Ministère des Affaires Étrangères, Éditions Recherche sur les Civilisations.

Yon, M. 2007. Life and death of a Military Port: Kition 4th-3rd cent. B.C. (political reality and cultural impact). In P. Flourentzos (ed.), *From Evagoras I to the Ptolemies. The transition from the Classical to the Hellenistic Period in Cyprus,* Nicosia 29–30 November 2002, 53–66. Nicosia, Department of Antiquities, Cyprus.

Egypt

Something old, something new: Native cultures under Ptolemaic rule

Andrea M. Berlin

Abstract

At some point in Graeco-Roman antiquity, the traditions of Pharaonic Egypt gave way to a differently constituted culture and society; and such a development did not happen overnight. Here I focus on the Ptolemaic era and try to assess whether and how this foreign dynasty's political and economic control affected native culture by a close examination of the ceramic assemblages from three sites: Naukratis, Coptos, and Elephantine. By assessing and comparing the relative amounts of dining, serving, and cooking vessels within a given assemblage, I suggest that it is possible to recognize a movement away from collective gatherings within the Sanctuary of Khnum at Elephantine. Such a change may mark an initial stage in the transformation away from long-lived patterns of Pharaonic society.

Keywords: Ptolemaic Egypt, pottery, social change, Naukratis, Coptos, Elephantine.

Introduction: Setting the Stage

'Society is a very complex structure, and therefore the study of it cannot be simple. In any country at one time there are many varieties of it in different classes, and probably the contemporary differences are as great as those of many centuries in any one class ... We can at least examine the factors that go to framing the conditions in which a society grows, and try to trace the discoveries without which it had no chance of growing. It is not too much to say that the discoverer is the maker of society.'[1]

From the perspective of the political historian, the centuries leading up to Ptolemaic rule over Egypt were a roller-coaster of conflict: repeated episodes of invasion and foreign take-over punctuated by periods of native rule. From 670 BC, when Esarhaddon made Egypt an Assyrian vassal-state, until 305 BC, when Ptolemy son of Lagos was crowned king of Egypt, rule of the country passed through three native and two foreign dynasties. What effect did this political roller-coaster have on Egyptian society? Here I focus on the Ptolemaic era and the effects of this foreign dynasty's political and economic control. Two theories are possible. The first is that Ptolemaic rule created or inspired a single largely Hellenized cultural sphere. The second is that there were two worlds – a thick layer of traditional Egyptian beliefs, customs, and lifestyles with, on top, a thin Hellenized veneer for government and business elites.

Historians of post-Pharonic Egypt have hardly ignored the question of the effect of foreign rule on Egyptian society[2]. Close study of the evidence of inscriptions, temple building, religious rituals, social organization, and artistic remains have led to widespread agreement on three points: 1) turmoil and upheaval was largely confined to the political sphere; 2) foreign dynasties introduced or inspired few significant cultural changes; and 3) age-old institutions integral to Egyptian culture and identity thrived and in some cases were in fact strengthened. In other words, of the two theories posed above, historians uniformly support the second. Traditional Egyptian culture and society seems to have remained stable and even vibrant throughout Ptolemaic times.

The first category of evidence generally adduced by historians is linguistic – the continuation of the Egyptian language and alphabets as seen in personal documents as well as official inscriptions. Demotic, the popular script developed in the 7th century BC, continued in wide use. Along with demotic, hieroglyphic script also remained viable, as evidenced by official inscriptions such as the Rosetta Stone, which records a temple decree issued by King Ptolemy V in 196 BC.

Temple building and priestly authority continued[3]. Indeed, the Ptolemies devoted more attention and resources to temple buildings, new and old, than in any previous period of Egyptian history. Major new constructions include the temples of Horus at Edfu, Hathor at Denderah, Isis at Philae, Sobek at Kom Ombo and Khnum at Esna. The Ptolemies made so many additions and renovations at the venerable complex of Amon at Karnak that it has been termed 'an almost permanent construction site.' And official support continued for traditional festivals and priestly perquisities within sanctuaries.

1 Petrie 1923, 1.

2 Bowman 1989; Johnson 1986; Johnson 1994; Ray 1987.

3 Baines 1997; Johnson 1986; Kaper 1997; Kurth 1997; Lloyd 1983.

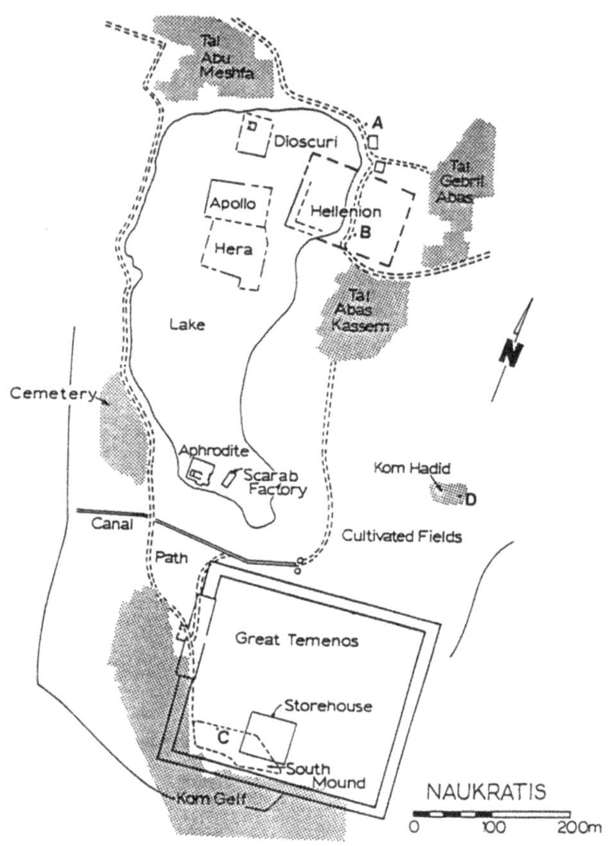

Fig. 1. Naukratis, plan of excavated areas (Berlin 2001)

Animal worship and mummification continued in quantities difficult to take in[4]. In the Fayum villages of Karanis and Tebtunis, thousands of crocodile mummies have been discovered. At Saqqara over four million ibis mummies have been recovered, in huge catacombs inside pots of standard size and manufacture. Records indicate that there were annual mass interments of over 10,000 birds with ritual processions of priests to the burial galleries. In the Serapeum at Memphis there were separate galleries for mummified Apis bulls, baboons, and falcons, the last represented by over half-a-million specimens.

Belief in the family as the most fundamental unit continued. The historian A. B. Lloyd notes that 'the family did not simply consist of its living members but was regarded as a corporation of the living and the dead … [an] attitude expressed through mortuary cult.'[5] Archaeological evidence reveals that this practice continued through Ptolemaic times. In excavations of the catacombs in Alexandria there have been recovered areas for reclining along with multiple small bowls and wine amphoras, all clearly intended for group gathering and drinking in conjunction with a ceremony of mourning or commemoration[6].

Finally, the evidence of that most fundamental component of Egyptian political life: royal portraits. On coins, portable emblems of power as well as an integral part of Mediterranean economic life, Ptolemaic kings and queens appear in the naturalistic guises popular for important people in the classical world – as slightly improved but essentially recognizable individuals. But coins are an obvious example of an official, top-down cultural artifact. In sculptural depictions found in Egypt, on the other hand, the Ptolemaic rulers appear as pharaohs, icons carved in native stone, the medium long preferred for the representation of eternal power[7]. Two different faces, for two different worlds: one looking out, the other in.

This evidence presented above, powerful and widespread, indeed reveals a deeply embedded traditional society. And yet two points must be acknowledged: first, that eventually the traditions of Pharaonic Egypt gave way to a differently constituted culture and society; and second, that such a development did not happen overnight. Since Egyptian society, as indeed all human societies, was a locus of both tradition and change, it is worth pursuing other angles of inquiry with an eye to recognizing and calibrating the stirrings of those changes. To that end, here I present an initial examination of some Ptolemaic-period ceramic assemblages, a body of material not yet studied from this vantage point. It turns out that a look at the pottery adds a different perspective. I close by offering some new ideas for analysis and presentation that are not often pursued but that could make ceramic data more understandable and also relevant to other scholars.

The contribution of ceramic evidence

What can ceramic evidence contribute to the question of how Egyptian society changed under Ptolemaic rule? In order to answer this question, we must first acknowledge the realities and limitations of the data. When we talk about pottery in Ptolemaic Egypt, we are largely talking about quite mundane remains. Ptolemaic period pottery was rarely decorated, so it was not a vehicle for artistic or symbolic representation. It is almost never found outside Egypt, meaning that it was not a trade item that might contribute to studying the economy. In fact most of what is found on excavation is uninspiring – literally and simply ancient dishes and pots and pans. How can such data be organized to answer large historical questions?

I suggest that the answer lies in leveraging three inherent aspects of excavation pottery. First: ***context***. If there is one thing that we usually know about excavation pottery, it's where it comes from. To appreciate what a group of vessels can tell us, we need to take their specific context into account. Second: ***function***. Nothing is more essential to understanding the larger meaning of a group of pottery

4 Bowman 1989, 172–174.
5 Lloyd 1983, 282.
6 Empereur 1998, 205–207. Compare this to a similar array of Old Kingdom material presented by Rzeuska 2006.
7 Bothmar 1962; Bothmar 1996.

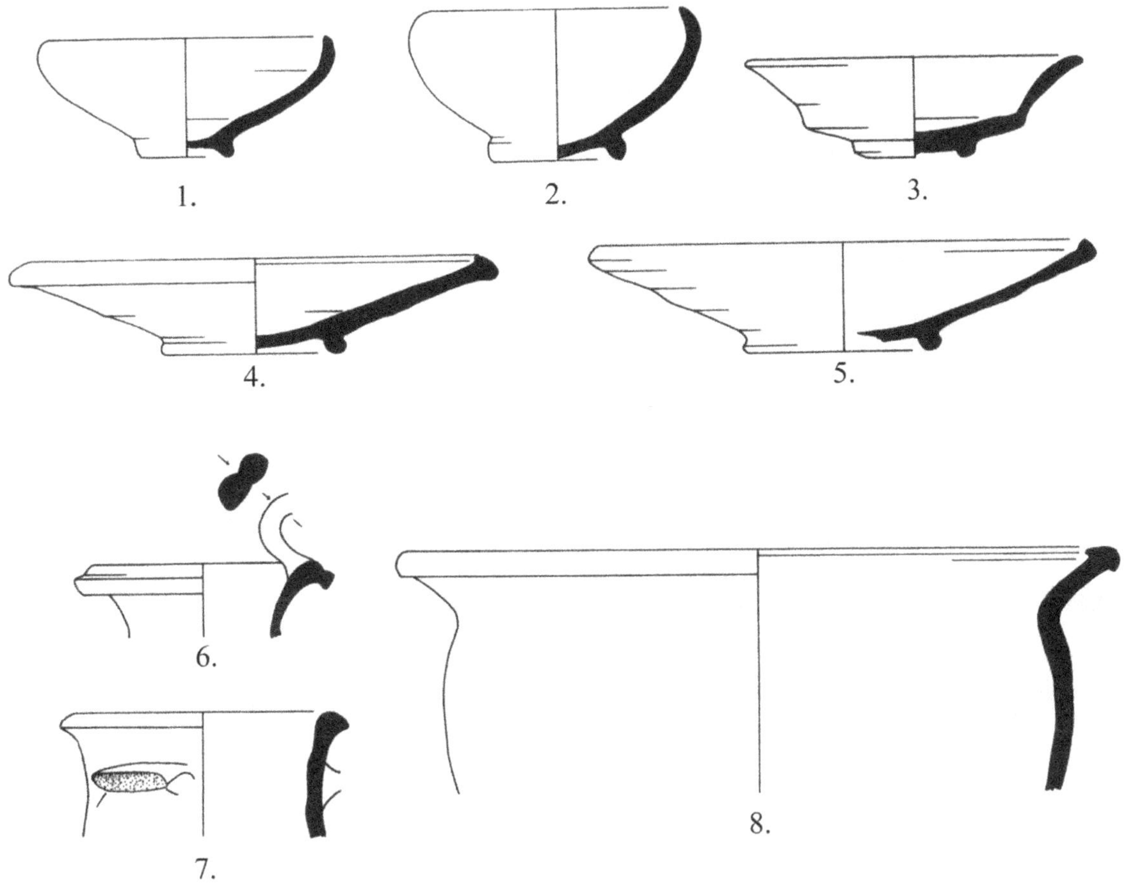

Fig. 2. Naukratis, vessels for individual eating and drinking, and for serving (Berlin 2001)

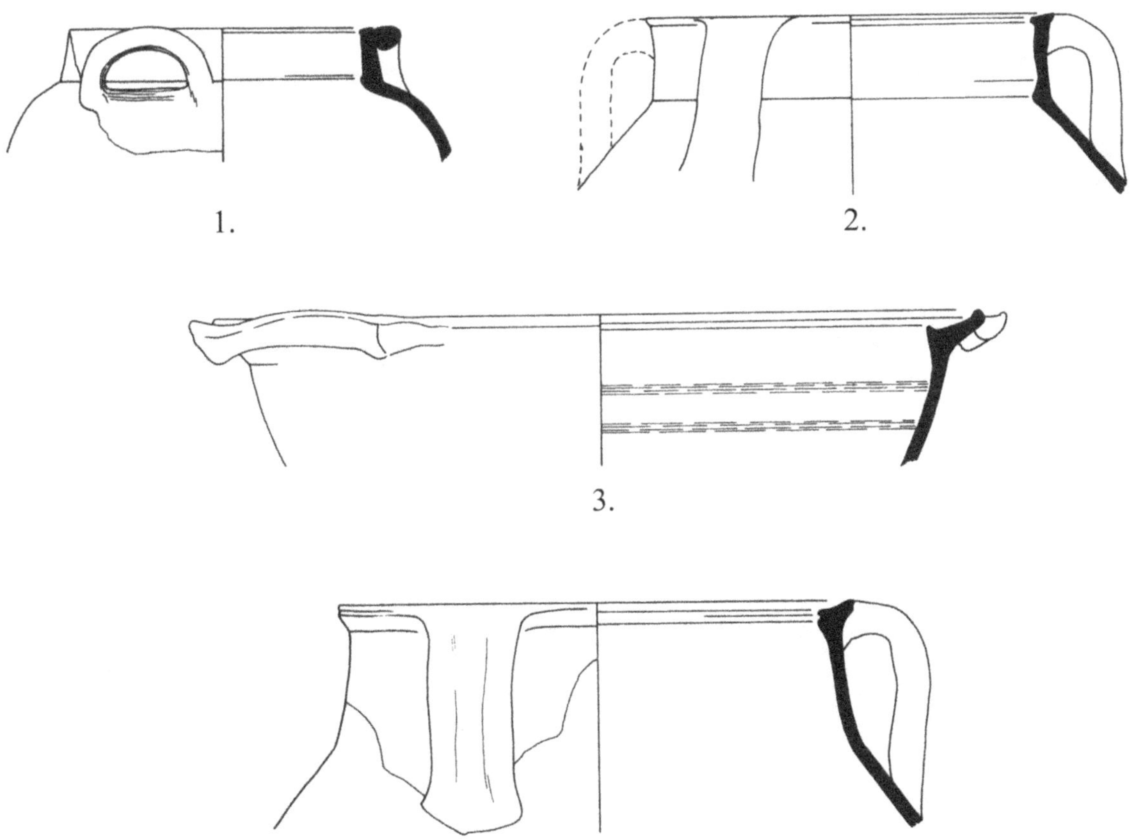

Fig. 3. Naukratis, cooking vessels (Berlin 2001)

Fig. 4. Coptos, view of excavation area (Herbert - Berlin 2003)

than knowing the various uses to which vessels were put. While this is often difficult to determine with precision or certainty, there are clues to help narrow down the options. For example, the kinds of wares and surface finishes, shapes and sizes all tend to differ according to basic functional categories such as table service or kitchen utility wares. The third aspect is ***quantity***. In order to assess an assemblage and compare it with another, we need to know how much of any given item is there. By identifying and adding up items by function, we have a much better chance of understanding how typical or special the assemblage is. Here I deploy the three aspects of **context**, **function**, and **quantity** in order to elevate three typical assemblages of (rather boring!) Ptolemaic period pottery into useful and even interesting historical evidence. I use the published material from three sites: Naukratis in the Delta, Coptos in Upper Egypt, and Elephantine down near the First Cataract.

Focus: Naukratis and Coptos

First, Naukratis. The pottery was excavated between 1977 and 1983, under the direction of Al Leonard, Jr. of the University of Arizona[8]. A number of other excavators preceded him at the site, beginning in 1884 with William Flinders Petrie. Careful correlation of plans and finds of earlier projects allowed Leonard to suggest that his two areas of excavation were most likely private housing on either side of a large Ptolemaic garrison, termed by earlier exavators 'the Great Temenos' (**Fig. 1**)[9].

The great majority of vessels found are items for individual eating and drinking (**Fig. 2.1-5**). Predominant are small bowls with incurved rims; in all there were 388 fragments found of this type, and another 105 of bowls with everted rims. Accompanying the bowls were 247 fragments of nicely sized saucers with thickened rim. For mixing, pouring, and serving food and drink residents of Naukratis used large bowls, either kraters or dinoi, and two types of jugs (**Fig. 2.6-8**). As for cooking, they had three main forms of vessels (**Fig. 3**). Most common were cooking pots. There are several types, but all share a narrow mouth and deep globular body. Second in popularity were casseroles, a broad but more shallow vessel with a rounded bottom. Lastly there were stew pots, which combined the wide mouth of a casserole and the deep body of a cooking pot. Altogether the pottery from Naukratis comprises 740 individual dining vessels, 188 utility and serving vessels, and 575 cooking vessels.

Up the Nile at Coptos is the ancient Sanctuary of Min, already thriving from the early second millennium BC. Here too there have been several excavation projects, again beginning with the indomitable Petrie in 1893. I will use the material excavated between 1987 and 1992, under the direction of Sharon Herbert of the University of Michigan (**Fig. 4**)[10]. Ptolemaic-period remains inside the sanctuary included small rooms with ovens, grinding installations, and a great deal of pottery.

The material breaks down as follows. There were enormous numbers of individual dining vessels, in the same order of popularity as at Naukratis: over 1000 fragments of incurved rim bowls, almost 600 thickened rim saucers, and just 225 everted rim bowls (**Fig. 5.1-5**). As for serving vessels, there were many: large bowls, again either in the shape of a dinos or a krater (**Fig. 5.8**), as well as a third form of large bowl, which I named a grooved rim bowl (**Fig. 5.7**). These are too large for individual dining, but not as big as the kraters and dinoi. I classify them as medium-sized serving vessels. As for jugs, there were a few different types but not that many in total: just 162 – disproportionately fewer vessels for pouring than for mixing and serving (**Fig. 5.6**). (This makes me wonder if some of those big b owls were used for punch, and people just dipped their small bowls or cups inside.) As for cooking vessels, again the same three shapes of cooking pots, casseroles, and stew pots occur, and in the same order of popularity, with cooking pots the most numerous by far (**Fig. 6**).

When the raw figures of pottery by type are tabulated, the Coptos assemblage suddenly looks rather odd. There are enormous numbers of vessels for individual dining

8 Berlin 1997; Berlin 2001.

9 Leonard 1997, 28–30.

10 Herbert and Berlin 2002; Herbert and Berlin 2003.

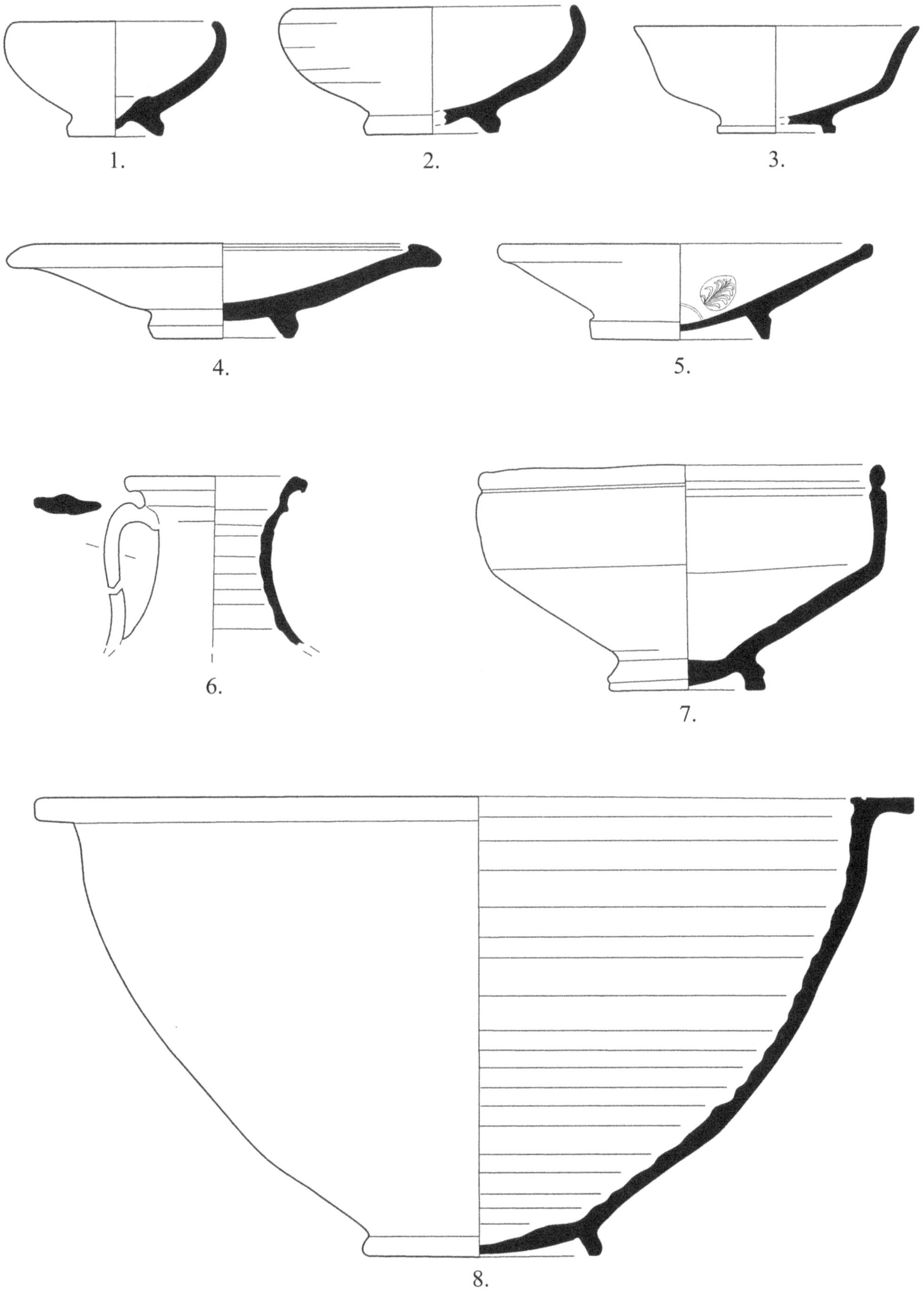

Fig. 5. Coptos, vessels for individual eating and drinking, and for serving (Herbert - Berlin 2003)

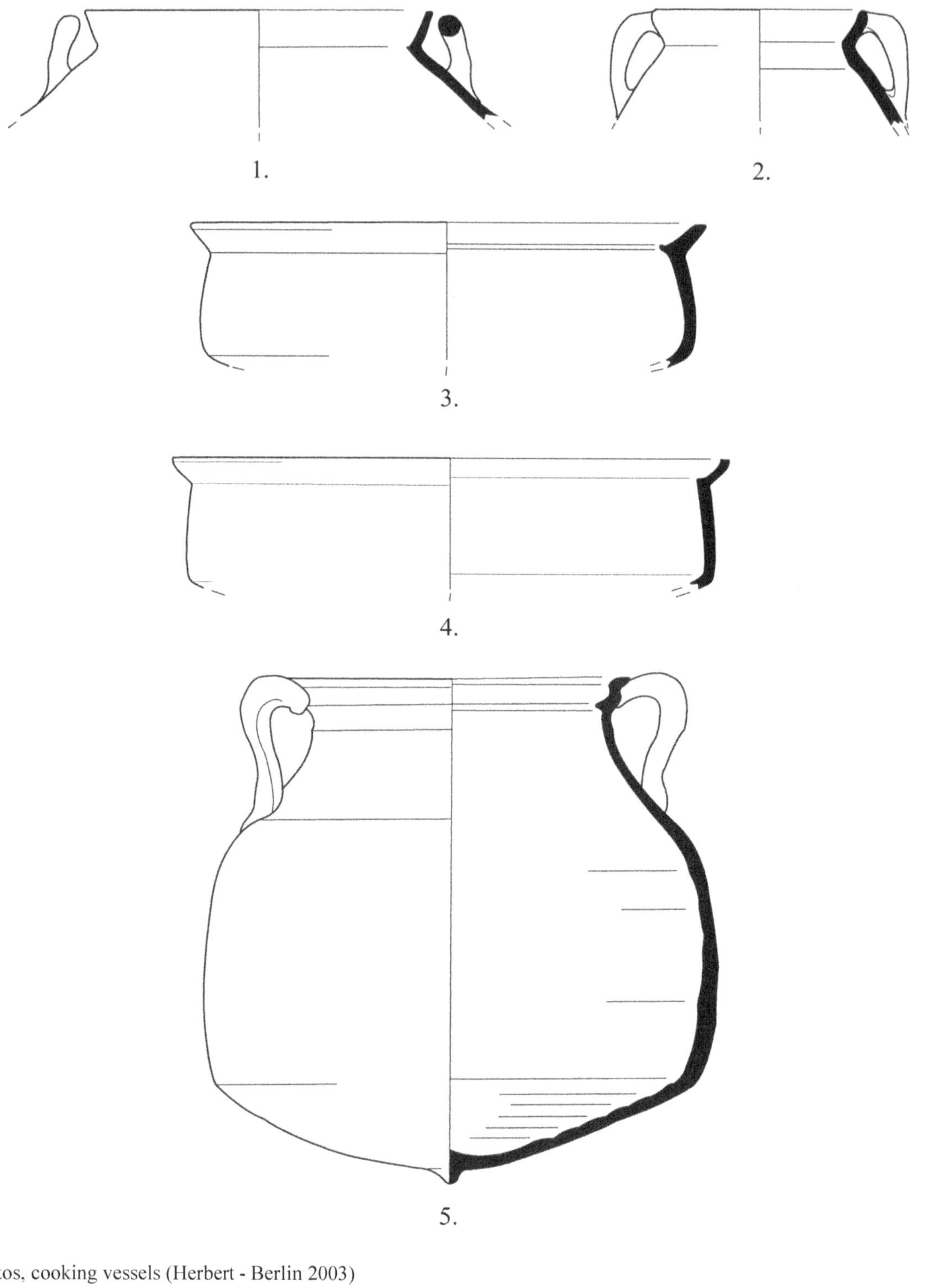

Fig. 6. Coptos, cooking vessels (Herbert - Berlin 2003)

and serving as compared to cooking. Such radically disproportionate numbers led Sharon Herbert and I to interpret the structures not as permanent housing but rather as temporary encampments likely connected with periodic festivals, and their contents as specialized festival assemblages[11].

How do these festival assemblages from Coptos compare to the simple domestic assemblages from Naukratis? While the *types* of pottery from both sites are very similar, the *ratios* between the functional groups differ dramatically (**Fig.** 7). At Coptos, almost half of the entire assemblage (45%) consists of serving vessels: large and medium-sized bowls and jugs. A full third (35%) is made up of small bowls and saucers for individual eating and drinking.

[11] Herbert and Berlin 2003, 24.

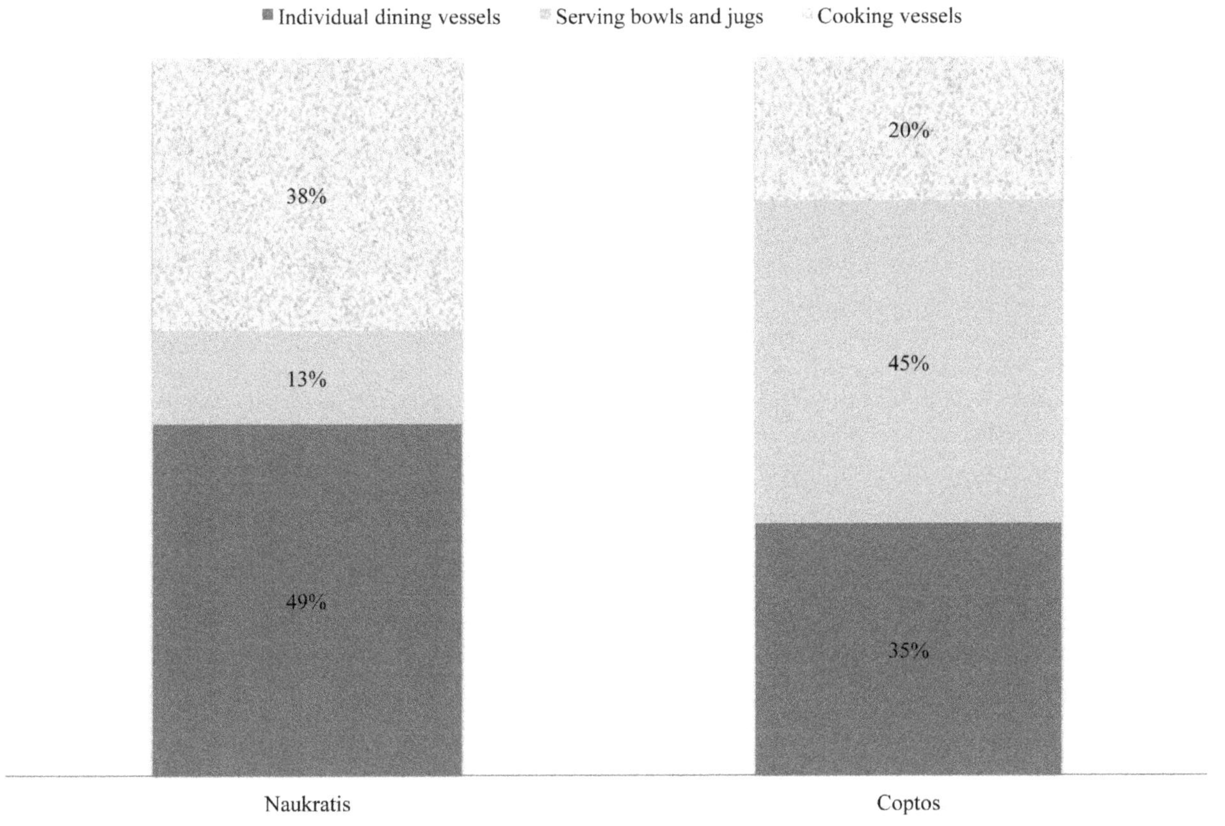

Fig. 7. Chart comparing ratios of pottery from Naukratis and Coptos according to functional groups (Herbert - Berlin 2003)

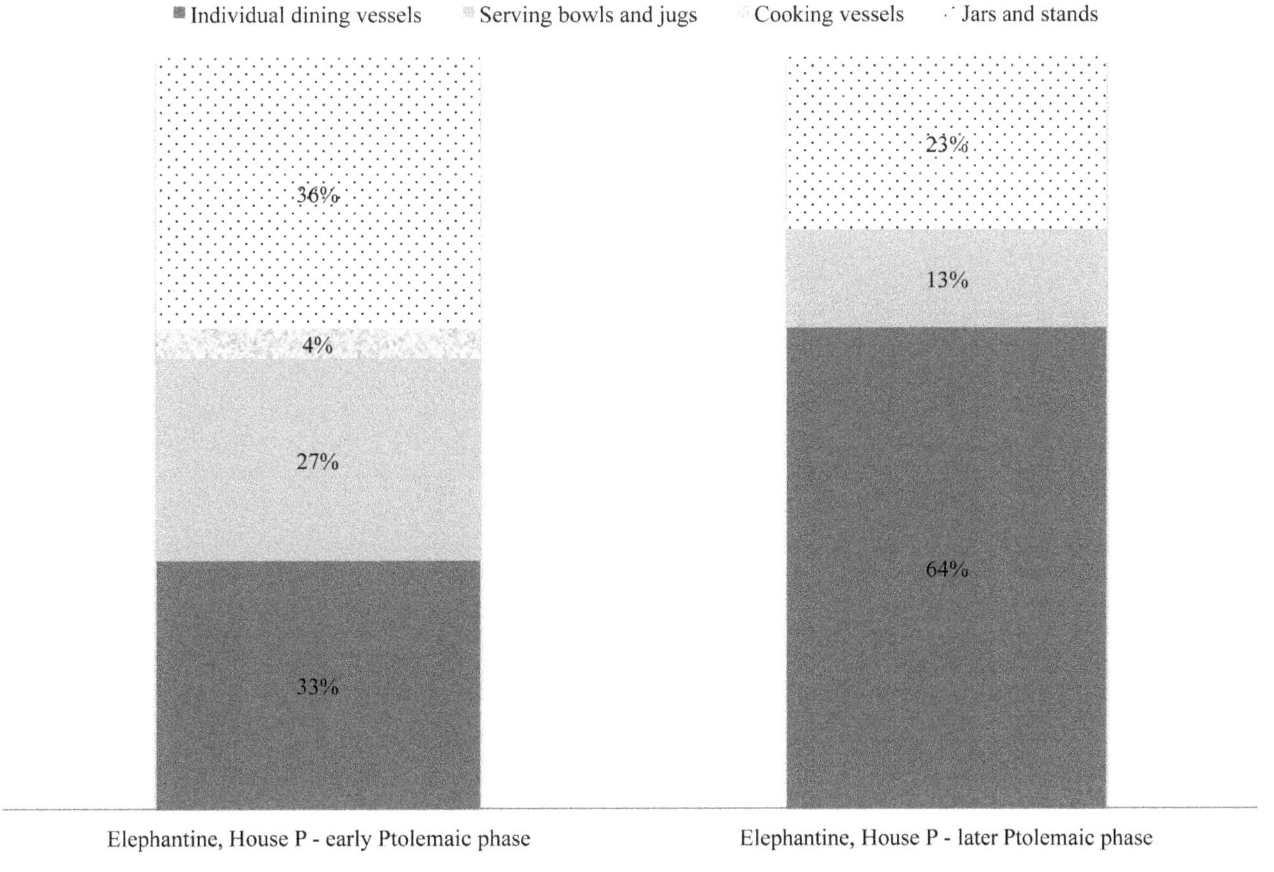

Fig. 8. Chart showing ratios of pottery from House P at Elephantine in the early Ptolemaic (phases 1 and 2) and later Ptolemaic (phases 3 and 4) periods, according to functional groups (Herbert - Berlin 2003)

Only 20% of the assemblage consists of cooking vessels. At Naukratis, on the other hand, almost half of the assemblage is comprised of individual table vessels, a figure in keeping with domestic deposits from other sites in the Hellenistic world. For example, similar ratios are found in the domestic assemblage from Hellenistic Troy, in Turkey and Gamla, in northern Israel[12]. Serving vessels comprise only 13% of the domestic assemblages from Naukratis, one third as many as at Coptos, while cooking vessels make up 38% of the Naukratis assemblages, almost double that at Coptos. In other words, the marked difference in relative amounts of dining, serving, and cooking vessels at Naukratis and Coptos strongly suggest that people were using these vessels under differing circumstances.

Focus: Elephantine

This conclusion is pertinent to an analysis of the Ptolemaic-period ceramics found at Elephantine. Here I investigate the pottery recovered between 1987 and 1992 by the German expedition under the direction of P. Grossman and published by David Aston[13]. The excavations, northwest of the Sanctuary of Khnum, uncovered portions of several seemingly domestic structures, including one which they named House P, in its entirety. House P contained enormous quantities of pottery. Neither the actual function of House P nor its relationship with the sanctuary is clear. Can the pottery help?

Here I rely on David Aston's monumental and thorough publication but in so doing I run up against an issue characteristic of many publications of Egyptian pottery. Aston presents and illustrates every vessel, and assigns each to a fabric and ware group according to the Vienna System, but makes no attempt to classify vessels by functional group nor provides any overall quantification. Rather, every vessel is presented as an end in itself. For the purposes of this analysis, I went through each of House P's Ptolemaic assemblages, grouped the vessels by function, and counted them. While my results are certainly incomplete and likely flawed by such second-hand analysis, I would argue that my general procedure is reliable. First I identified small saucers and bowls for individual dining, then medium and large utility and serving bowls, then cooking vessels, store jars, and finally stands – of which there were an interestingly large number.

The ratios between functional groups varied through time, and in an interesting way (**Fig. 8**). In the earlier part of the Ptolemaic period, there was a roughly even number of vessels for dining and serving. In the later part of the period there are many more vessels for individual dining but the number of serving vessels strongly diminishes. Does this mean anything?

It may. A comparison of the ratios of pottery groups from the earlier and later Ptolemaic phases of House P at Elephantine with that from the households at Naukratis and the festival camps in the sanctuary at Coptos reveals an eye-catching pattern. The early Ptolemaic phase, with many serving vessels, is most similar to the pattern at Coptos. The later Ptolemaic phase, with fewer serving vessels but many individual dining vessels, resembles the pattern at Naukratis.

This discrepancy could suggest a change in the function of Elephantine's House P from the earlier to the later Ptolemaic periods. At first the house could have been the scene of sanctuary-related activities, similar to Coptos. The changing patterns of the later Ptolemaic assemblages, on the other hand, could reflect a decrease in festival activities, or at least suggest that by this time whoever was living here was simply running a regular household. Such a change of function could mean that rituals and activities in the sanctuary itself were also changing.

And changes such as these – fewer festivals or fewer participants in those festivals – are exactly the types of social alterations that need investigating. I began by posing two options for the effect of Ptolemaic rule: one an increasingly unified Hellenic culture and the second a thick layer of native culture topped by a thin Hellenized veneer. Overwhelmingly, the evidence supports the second of these two options – at least at the beginning of the Ptolemaic era. But at some point that native culture must have begun to change in fundamental ways. Capturing the character and trajectory of change is a daunting task, especially since that native culture was comprised of millions of daily lives, each propelled by individual circumstance. One way to capture those changes is by studying pottery. Ceramics derive from and reflect people's lives, which encode and reflect larger developments – away from some traditional activities, perhaps, such as large-scale gatherings in sanctuaries.

After all, while temples and sanctuaries long occupied a fundamental place in Egyptian life and culture, eventually popular participation waned. There came a time when the temples still stood but the festivals that had filled the grounds ceased, when the people who had believed in and animated them turned their energies elsewhere. When and how that happened are questions worth asking. Pottery can provide data that will help find the answers.

Andrea M. Berlin
Department of Archaeology, Boston University

[12] Berlin 2002, 136–137; Berlin 2003, 137–138.
[13] Aston 1999.

Bibliography

Aston, D. A. 1999. *Elephantine* XIX. *Pottery from the Late New Kingdom to the Early Ptolemaic Period.* Mainz, Zabern.

Baines, J. 1997. Temples as symbols, guarontors, and participants in Egyptian civilization. In S. Quirke (ed.), *The Temple in Ancient Egypt*, 216–241. London, British Museum Press.

Berlin, A. M. 1997. The Pottery from the Northwest and North Areas. In A. Leonard, Jr. *Ancient Naukratis. Excavations at a Greek Emporium in Egypt.* Part I. *The Excavations at Kom Ge'if.* Annual of the American Schools of Oriental Research 54, 136–285.

Berlin, A. M. 2001. Naukratis/Kom Hadid: A Ceramic Typology for Hellenistic Lower Egypt. In A. Leonard, Jr. *Ancient Naukratis. Excavations at a Greek Emporium in Egypt*. Part II. *The Excavations at Kom Hadid.* Annual of the American Schools of Oriental Research 55, 26–163.

Berlin, A. M. 2002. Ilion Before Alexander: A Fourth Century B.C. Ritual Deposit. *Studia Troica* 12, 131–165.

Berlin, A. M. 2003. *Gamla. Final Reports*. Vol. 1. *The Pottery of the Second Temple Period.* Israel Antiquities Authority Reports 29. Jerusalem, Israel Antiquities Authority.

Bothmar, B. 1962. A New Field of Egyptian Art: Sculpture of the Late Period. *Connoisseur Year Book*, 34–41. Reprinted in *Egyptian Art. Selected Writings of Bernard V. Bothmer*, 144–156. Oxford, University Press: 2004.

Bothmar, B. 1996. Hellenistic Elements in Egyptian Sculpture of the Late Period. In K. Hamma (ed.), *Alexandria and Alexandrianism:* Papers Delivered at a Symposium Organized by the J. Paul Getty Museum and the Getty Center for the History of Art and the Humanities and Held at the Museum, April 22–25, 1993, 215–230. Malibu: J. Paul Getty Museum. Reprinted in Egypti*an Art. Selected Writings of Bernard V. Bothmer*, 466–493. Oxford, University Press: 2004.

Bowman, A. 1989. *Egypt After the Pharaohs*. Berkeley, University of California Press.

Empereur, J.-Y. 1998. *Alexandria Rediscovered.* New York, George Braziller.

Herbert, S. C. and Berlin, A. M. 2002. Coptos: Architecture and Assemblages in the sacred Temenos from Nectanebo to Justinian. In M.-F. Boussac (ed.), *Autour de Coptos.* Actes du colloque organisé au Musée des Beaux-Arts de Lyon (17–18 mars 2000). Topoi Supplément 3, 73–115.

Herbert, S. C. and Berlin, A. M. 2003. *Excavations at Coptos (Qift) in Upper Egypt, 1987–1992*. Journal of Roman Archaeology supplementary series 53. Portsmouth RI, Journal of Roman Archaeology.

Johnson, J. 1986. The Role of the Egyptian Priesthood in Ptolemaic Egypt. In L. H. Lesko (ed.), *Egyptological Studies in Honor of Richard A. Parker*, 149–159. Hanover, University Press of New England.

Johnson, J. 1994. The Persians and the Continuity of Egyptian Culture, in H. Sancisi-Weerdenburg, A. Kuhrt, and M. C. Root (eds.), *Achaemenid History VIII. Continuity and Change.* Proceedings of the Last Achaemenid History Workshop, 79–95. Leiden, Nederlands Instituut Voor Het Nabije Oosten.

Kaper, O. E. 1997. A painting of the gods of Dakhla in the temple of Ismant el-Kharab. In S. Quirke (ed.), *The Temple in Ancient Egypt,* 204–215. London, British Museum Press.

Kurth, D. 1997. The present state of research into Graeco-Roman temples. In S. Quirke (ed.), *The Temple in Ancient Egypt*, 152–158. London, British Museum Press.

Leonard JR., A. 1997. A History of the Excavations at Naukratis/Kom Ge'if. In A. Leonard, Jr., *Ancient Naukratis. Excavations at a Greek Emporium in Egypt*. Part I. *The Excavations at Kom Ge'if.* Annual of the American Schools of Oriental Research 54, 1–35.

Lloyd, A. B. 1983. The Late Period, 664–323 BC, in B. G. Trigger, B. J. Kemp, D. O'Connor and A. B. Lloyd, *Ancient Egypt: A Social History*, 279–348. Cambridge, Cambridge University Press.

Petrie, W. F. 1923. *Social Life in Ancient Egypt*. Kessinger Publishing reprint 2004.

Ray, J. D. 1987. Egypt: Dependence and Independence (425–343 B.C.). In H. Sancisi-Weerdenburg (ed.), *Achaemenid History I. Sources, Structures and Syntheses.* Proceedings of the Groningen 1983 Achaemenid History Workshop, 79–95. Leiden, Nederlands Instituut Voor Het Nabije Oosten.

Rzeuska, T. 2006. *Saqqara II. Pottery of the Late Old Kingdom. Funerary Pottery and Burial Customs.* Warsaw, Editions Nerito.

Céramiques d'Égypte de la fin IVe siècle av. J.-C. au IIIe siècle av. J.-C.: entre tradition et innovation

Sylvie Marchand

Abstract

Local and imported ceramics of the Ptolemaic Period from the end of the 4th through the 3rd centuries BC illustrate a rare moment in the history of Egyptian material culture. The ceramics of this time period are related to a transitional phase which attests the establishment and evolution of a new local ceramic tradition. This slowly replaces a purely Pharaonic tradition that was inherited from the last indigenous dynasties and strongly influenced by regional cultures and traditions. All of this, taken together, assists in the creation of a new formal repertoire that includes function, form, decoration, and technology that in turn inspires the Greek ceramic tradition. This tradition rapidly evolves, in the second half of the 3rd century, into an Egyptian repertoire that can be dubbed 'classic', with the ceramic tradition of the 2nd century becoming integrated within standard ceramic production throughout the Hellenistic Mediterranean world. Recent archaeological discoveries refresh our knowledge and understanding on this vibrant era of transformation. The ceramic corpus from the villages of Tebtynis in the Fayum and that of Ayn Manawir and Douch in the oasis of Kharga offer us an opportunity to illustrate the nature of the changes that took place in Egypt at the start of the Ptolemaic era.

Keywords: Egypt, Fayoum, Tebtynis, Kharga Oasis, early Ptolemaic period, Pharaonic tradition ceramics, Greek tradition ceramics, egyptian amphoras, *torpedo jars*.

Introduction

L'Égypte du IVe siècle av. J.-C. d'avant la conquête macédonienne est un pays aux traditions céramiques fortes, profondément ancrées dans ses régions, avec une différence entre le Nord et le Sud du pays très marquée dans ses formes céramiques et dans son répertoire décoratif. Ce dernier est particulièrement inventif dans le sud du territoire, dans la région thébaine, à Assouan et dans les grandes oasis du désert Libyque de Kharga et de Dakhla. Les céramiques locales et importées d'époque ptolémaïque de la fin du IVe au IIIe siècle av. J.-C. illustrent un moment privilégié de la culture matérielle égyptienne. On assiste à la mise en place d'une phase de transition qui donne naissance à une nouvelle tradition céramique locale. Elle remplace petit à petit l'héritage pharaonique des dernières dynasties indigènes, avec la création d'un nouveau répertoire formel, fonctionnel, décoratif et technique qui s'inspire largement du vaisselier grec. Cependant, l'ancienne tradition pharaonique persiste dans certaines productions céramiques locales du début de l'époque ptolémaïque au IIIe siècle av. J.-C., notamment dans sa vaisselle culinaire, pour certains conteneurs de transport ou encore dans la vaisselle spécialisée. Cette période de transition débute vraisemblablement vers la fin du IVe siècle av. J.-C., période pendant laquelle l'ancienne et la nouvelle tradition cohabitent, la seconde supplantant l'autre dans le cours de la première moitié du IIIe siècle av. J.-C. Après une phase d' 'assimilation ou d'inspiration' quand le vaisselier grec (amphores, conteneurs, vaisselle culinaire, vaisselle de service et vases à parfum) fait l'objet d'imitations locales plus ou moins fidèles, on assiste dès le milieu du IIIe siècle av. J.-C. mais surtout au IIe siècle av. J.-C. à une seconde phase pendant laquelle les potiers égyptiens réinterprètent les céramiques de tradition grecque de la première génération. Le nouveau répertoire des céramiques égyptiennes continuera alors d'évoluer tout au long de la période ptolémaïque avec des productions originales.

Nous évoquerons quelques données archéologiques récentes qui renouvellent nos connaissances sur cette période. Le mobilier céramique du village de Tebtynis[1] dans le Fayoum et celui des villages d'Ayn Manawir et de Douch dans l'oasis de Kharga[2] offrent l'opportunité d'illustrer par quelques dessins la nature des changements qui s'opèrent au début de l'époque ptolémaïque dans le mobilier céramique, de la vaisselle culinaire aux emballages commerciaux égyptiens et importés.

Données archéologiques nouvelles pour le mobilier céramique d'Égypte du début de l'époque ptolémaïque

Il n'est pas dans notre intention d'établir un inventaire exhaustif des sites égyptiens publiés d'époque ptolémaïque

[1] Fouilles conjointes de l'Ifao et de l'université de Milan sous la direction de Cl. Gallazzi. Les fouilles sont conduites par G. Hadji-Minaglou (Ifao). La mise au net des dessins a été réalisée par Ayman Hussein (Ifao). Une partie du mobilier de la fouille est publié par Ballet et Poludnikiewicz 2012. Voir également pour la céramique ptolémaïque du site de Tebtynis, Marchand 1996, Marangou et Marchand 2007.

[2] Fouilles et prospection de l'Ifao du bassin sud de l'oasis de Kharga sous la direction de M. Wuttmann.

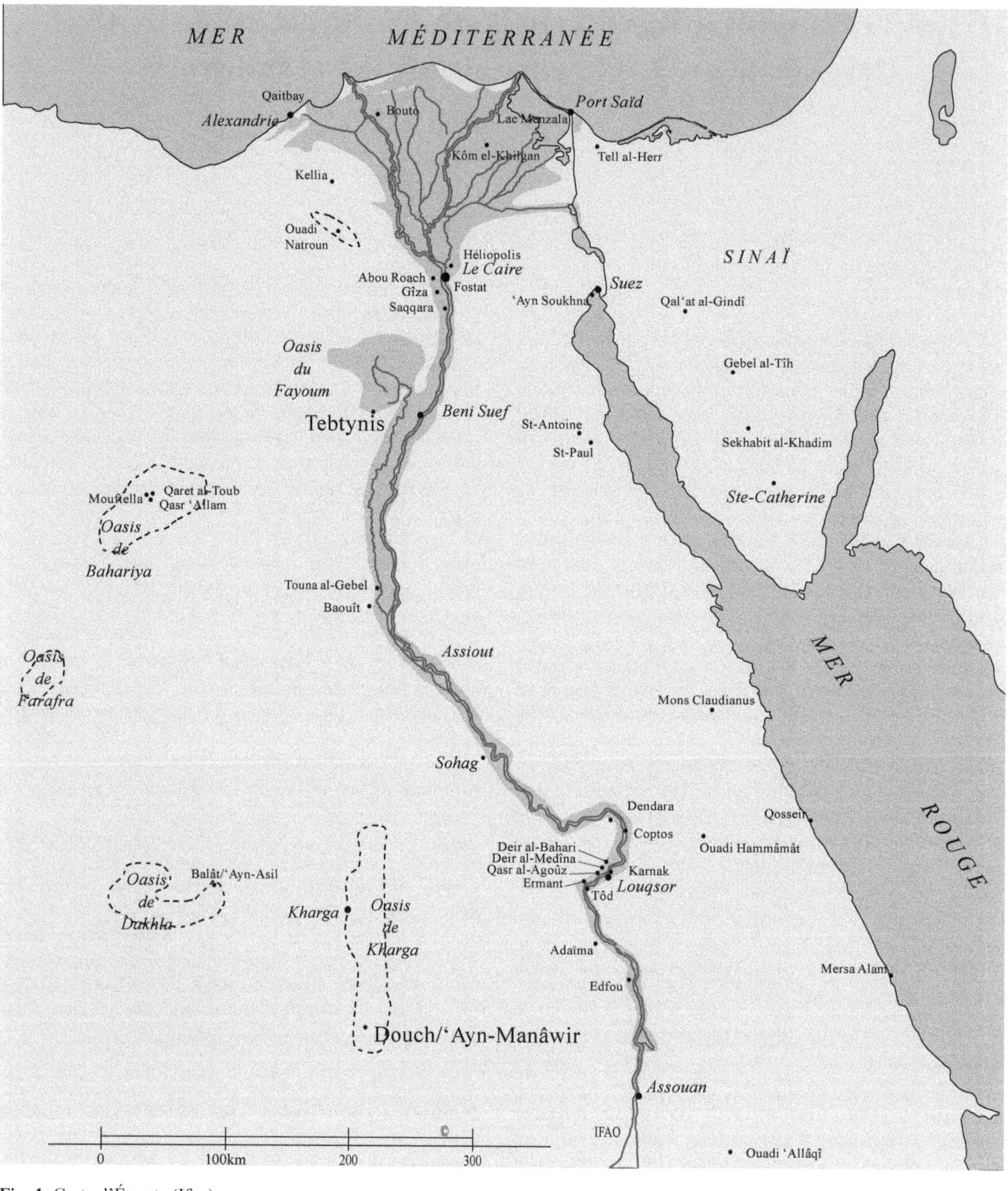

Fig. 1. Carte d'Égypte (Ifao)

ancienne de la fin du IVe au IIIe siècle av. J.-C.[3], mais plus simplement de présenter un état de la recherche sur le mobilier céramique de cette période en évoquant quelques sujets autour desquels la réflexion s'organise depuis quelques années. Nous avons privilégié les corpus des sites qui autorisent une approche culturelle du mobilier céramique recueilli pendant les fouilles au-delà de l'indispensable approche chrono-typologique.

[3] Pour un inventaire récent des sites fouillés en Égypte pour l'époque gréco-romaine, Bagnall et Davoli 2011.

'Les indices de l'hellénisation'[4]

Un sujet continue d'alimenter les débats pour la céramique égyptienne du début de l'époque ptolémaïque, il consiste à identifier et à mesurer les indices de l'hellénisation. Cette recherche a d'abord été conduite sur le mobilier des dernières dynasties indigènes, le résultat après analyses montre que les importations grecques d'amphores et de céramiques fines en Égypte, malgré leur nombre, leur ancienneté et leur diffusion, n'ont eu que peu d'impact sur le catalogue formel des productions égyptiennes jusque dans la première moitié du IVe siècle av. J.-C.[5]. La situation évolue considérablement après la conquête macédonienne, vers la fin du IVe siècle et au début du IIIe siècle av. J.-C., la céramique égyptienne est alors beaucoup plus perméable aux modèles céramiques égéens. En effet, c'est à ce moment que l'on observe sans ambiguïté dans le mobilier céramique des fouilles l'hellénisation des formes du vaisselier égyptien dans toute sa diversité[6]. Au-delà de la forme, on voit également apparaître de nouveaux traitements de surface ou l'emploi de techniques de cuisson spécifique, comme celle qui imite les vernis noirs importés[7]. Le soin apporté au façonnage et à l'épuration des argiles[8] s'ajoutent également à ces changements et évolutions techniques visibles à partir du début de l'époque ptolémaïque.

Fig. 2. Siga locale à décor peint en noir sur engobe blanc du IVe siècle av. J.-C. XXVIIIe–XXXe dynasties. Oasis de Kharga fouilles de Ayn Manawir. Ifao (Photo J.-Fr. Gout. Ifao)

Une fois ce schéma très général établi, il n'est pas évident de situer cette hellénisation dans un cadre géographique qui prenne en compte la diversité des cultures régionales d'Égypte. Pour atteindre ce but il faudrait disposer d'une documentation archéologique plus abondante et moins dispersée géographiquement, mais aussi de contextes archéologiques avec des séquences stratigraphiques clairement établies, et enfin de données statistiques pour chaque catégorie de récipients et d'assemblages de céramiques. Il va sans dire que ce n'est pas le cas, et la liste des sites égyptiens fouillés pour cette période reste partielle et ne couvre pas la totalité du territoire égyptien. Quand on examine la documentation céramique fiable qui répond aux critères archéologiques cités plus haut, on remarque rapidement que la vitesse et les formes de l'hellénisation suivent des chemins différents selon les régions et qu'il n'existe pas un mais plusieurs 'schémas'. Comme nous l'avons déjà signalé plus haut, on distingue une tradition céramique régionale du Nord de celle du Sud, le Sud de l'Égypte offrant des traditions céramiques locales fortement ancrées et résistantes aux innovations. Il est également difficile de comparer en utilisant les mêmes paramètres le mobilier céramique provenant de grands centres urbains comme Alexandrie, de petits villages du terroir comme celui de Tebtynis, ou encore une ferme de l'oasis de Kharga. Selon les régions ou la nature du contexte archéologique, l'adoption par les potiers égyptiens du nouveau répertoire formel et décoratif de tradition grecque peut porter sur tout ou sur une partie seulement de la batterie de cuisine, sur la vaisselle de service ou sur les conteneurs de transport.

Quand et sous quelles formes débute l'hellénisation de la céramique égyptienne? Selon les sites[9], ce phénomène est clairement identifié dès la fin du IVe siècle, au début

4 Terme repris de Ballet 2002.
5 Sur l'adoption de formes grecques dans le répertoire céramique égyptien avant la conquête, voir Ballet 2001, Ballet 2002, Defernez 2001, Defernez 2002, 239, Defernez 2007b, Defernez et Marchand 2006, 71–75, 84–89.
6 Ballet 2002,87, Harlaut 2002, Marchand 2002, 249, Pierrat-Bonnefois 2002.
7 Ballet 2002, 91, Ballet 2011.
8 Voir par exemple le soin apporté par les potiers à l'épuration de pâtes des premières amphores de type grec, Marchand 2002, 249.

9 Les sites de référence pour le mobilier céramique daté de la fin IVe-IIIe siècles av. J.-C.: Alexandrie (Ballet, Boussac et Enklaar 2001, Ballet et Harlaut 2001, 301-318, Élaigne 2002, Harlaut 2002, Senol 2007, 61), Bouto (Ballet 2002, 91, Ballet 2011, Dixneuf et Lecuyot 2007, 136, Dixneuf 2011, 59, 277 Fig. 11), Naucratis (Berlin 1997, 140-143, Berlin 2001, 26-163, Gantès 2007, 150), Tell Atrib (Mysliwiec 2009, 35-51, Poludnikiewicz 1992), Tell el-Herr (Defernez 2007a, Defernez 2007b, 583, Dixneuf 2007), Abou Rawash (Marchand 2007b, 180-181), Saqqâra (Rzeuska 2008, 417-451), Tebtynis (Ballet et Poludnikiewicz 2012, Marchand 1996, Marangou et Marchand 2007, 242-247, 249, 251-263), Hawara (Marchand 2009, 242-247, 249, 251-263), Tôd (Pierrat-Bonnefois 2002), Karnak (Masson 2011b, Marchand 2007a, 373 Fig. 1-6, Scheiber 2003, 63-64), Thèbes ouest-Assasif (Budka 2010, 39 fig. 8), Coptos (Herbert et Berlin 2003, 47-77, Lawall 2003, 158-167), Abydos (Budka 2010, 59 fig. 17), Assouan/ Éléphantine (Aston1999, 247-329, Aston 2007), oasis de Dakhla (Hope 1999, 230, Hope 2000), oasis de Kharga (Marchand 2007c, 492 - 494, Wuttmann et al. 1998, 439 fig. 59a-b), désert Oriental Bérénice (Tomber 1998, 165-169).

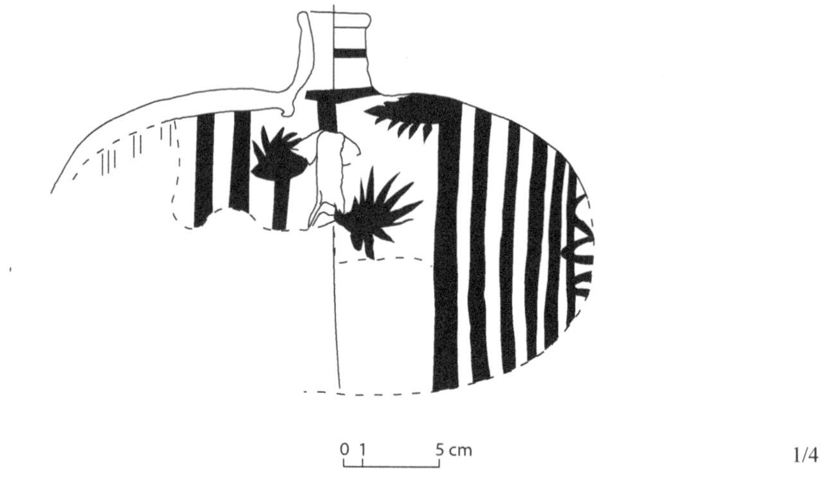

Fig. 3. Siga locale à décor peint en noir sur engobe blanc du IVe siècle av. J.-C. XXVIIIe–XXXe dynasties. Oasis de Kharga fouilles de Ayn Manawir. Ifao (A. Hussein)

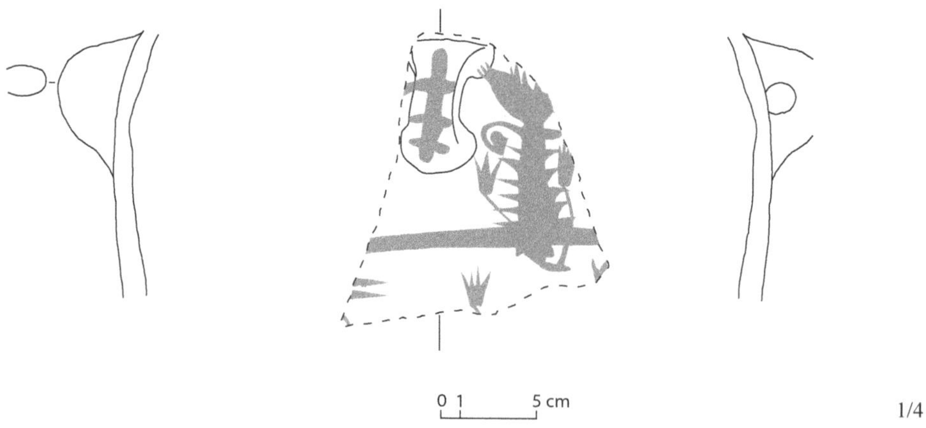

Fig. 4. Conteneur local à anses à décor peint en noir sur engobe blanc. Début de l'époque ptolémaïque de la fin du IVe au IIIe siècle av. J.-C. Oasis de Kharga fouilles de Douch. Ifao (A. Hussein)

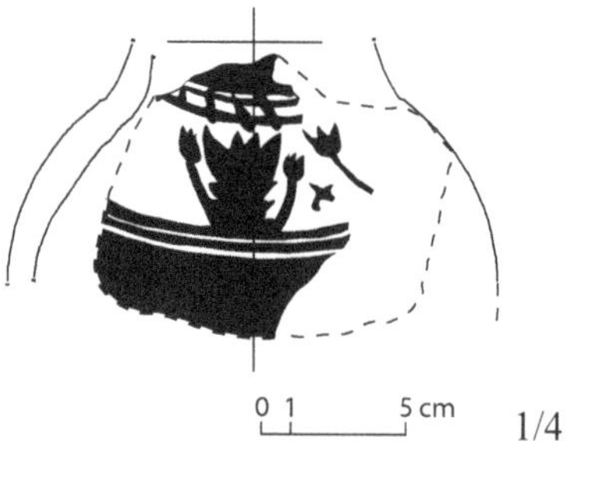

Fig. 5. Jarre à col locale à décor peint en noir sur engobe rouge brillant. Début de l'époque ptolémaïque de la fin du IVe au IIIe siècle av. J.-C. Oasis de Kharga fouilles de Ayn Ziyada. Ifao (A. Hussein)

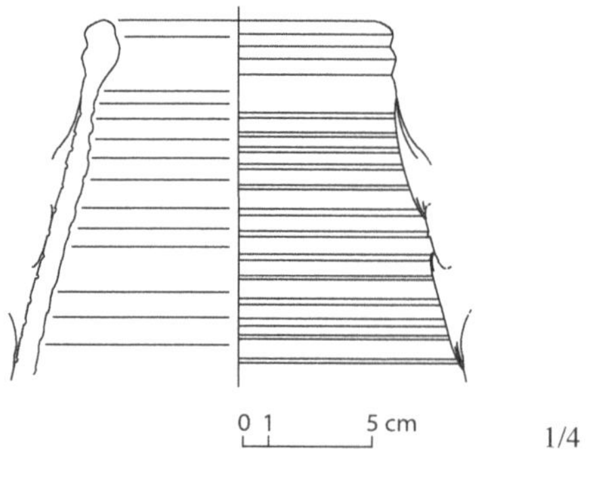

Fig. 6. Conteneur de transport égyptien produit dans la région thébaine en argile calcaire, 'Qena Ware'. Forme attestée à Kharga au Ve siècle av. J.-C. et dans la vallée du Nil du Ve au IIIe siècle av. J.-C. Oasis de Kharga fouilles de Ayn Manawir. Ifao (A. Hussein)

du IIIe siècle ou dans la première moitié du IIIe siècle av. J.-C. Les céramiques touchées par l'hellénisation des formes appartiennent aux grandes familles de récipients connues du répertoire grec, avec la céramique culinaire, la vaisselle de service, les conteneurs, les vases à parfum... Il est hors de notre propos de passer en revue les formes grecques qui renouvellent le vaisselier égyptien au début de l'époque ptolémaïque[10]. Bornons nous à rappeler qu'en les adoptant l'Égypte intègre alors le standard méditerranéen de l'époque hellénistique. L'hellénisation s'étend aux décors de style grec qui sont associés à certaines catégories spécifiques de récipients, il peut s'agir d'impressions, de décors peints (**Fig. 18**), ou plus rarement attesté le décor 'surpeint' apparenté au 'West-Slope'[11].

La forme sans doute la plus emblématique de l'hellénisation est l'amphore égyptienne de type égéen (**Figs. 6–7, Fig. 17**). Ces emballages commerciaux sont l'objet de toutes les attentions et de nombreuses avancées ont été réalisées au cours des dernières années pour améliorer nos connaissances[12]. Leur importance comme outil de mesure pour les échanges, le commerce, et pour la chronologie n'est plus à démontrer. La documentation archéologique la plus fiable et la plus abondante montre que la création de ce nouveau répertoire amphorique égyptien de type égéen, comme un phénomène quantitativement mesurable, est mis en place vers la fin du IVe siècle av. J.-C. Aucun atelier de production n'est recensé pour ce premier répertoire amphorique égyptien, en pâte calcaire rouge ou en pâte alluviale, mais toutes sont diffusées un peu partout le long de la Vallée du Nil. Avant le début de l'époque ptolémaïque, les premières tentatives d'imitations égyptiennes d'amphores grecques voient le jour dans les premières décennies du IVe siècle av. J.-C.[13], elles sont concurrencées par les imitations égyptiennes de conteneurs de tradition chypriote et syro-palestinienne qui apparaissent vers le milieu du IVe siècle av. J.-C. comme les jarres à 'anses de panier' et les *torpedos*. L'arrêt brusque de la fabrication des *torpedos* égyptiennes dans la première moitié du IIIe siècle av. J.-C.[14] (**Fig. 16**) participe à l'hégémonie des amphores égyptiennes de type grec qui deviennent l'unique conteneur de transport pour la production viticole. L'Égypte, comme d'autres contrées du monde méditerranéen comme Chypre[15], a fait le choix de l'amphore de type grec comme principal conteneur de transport. Le processus d'assimilation est acquis au IIIe siècle av. J.-C. avec la création d'un nouveau répertoire amphorique égyptien de tradition grecque. Les raisons de ce choix sont multiples, elles peuvent être d'ordre culturel, technique, économique et commercial. On constate que les amphores de type égéen ont été considérées par la société égyptienne, et par ses négociants, comme le conteneur idéal pour le transport du vin et pour le vendre. Le choix des modèles d'amphores grecques imitées pour constituer le répertoire amphorique égyptien s'est porté sur les amphores importées les plus courantes qui circulent en Égypte à la fin du IVe siècle et au début du IIIe siècle av. J.-C. Elles imitent les amphores de Cnide de Rhodes, ou de Chios[16] qui transportaient les crus les plus réputés du monde égéen dans des conteneurs bien identifiés, la forme bien connue de ces amphores est donc un gage de qualité pour les acheteurs. Une autre raison pour l'adoption de l'amphore de type grec est liée aux contraintes techniques, l'amphore, par sa forme spécifique, est un récipient commode pour le stockage et le transport. Mais une autre raison de ce choix est la nouvelle conjoncture économique et politique qui voit le jour avec la conquête macédonienne et l'établissement de la dynastie Lagide et de Grecs sur le territoire égyptien. La documentation papyrologique abondante donne une image ambitieuse de la politique d'exploitation agricole, particulièrement dans le domaine viticole, en Maréotide, dans le Delta, dans le Fayoum surtout, dès Ptolémée II (285–246 av. J.-C.), avec une mise en valeur du territoire qui s'accompagne de l'introduction de nouvelles plantes, de nouveaux cépages, et la mise en place de vastes systèmes d'irrigation concourant à l'extension de la surface agricole[17]. Ces activités étaient nécessaires pour alimenter de nouveaux marchés urbains dont Alexandrie.

Le maintien de la tradition pharaonique à l'époque ptolémaïque

La résistance des produits égyptiens locaux face aux formes grecques est un sujet passionnant qui alimente le débat pour la caractérisation des céramiques du début de l'époque ptolémaïque. On entend par 'céramiques de tradition pharaonique', le maintien pendant l'époque ptolémaïque de la fin du IVe au IIIe siècle av. J.-C.[18] de récipients appartenant au répertoire de la Basse Époque sur le plan formel, décoratif, technique et fonctionnel.

Pour reconnaître ces formes pharaoniques dans des contextes archéologiques d'époque ptolémaïque, il faut consulter les synthèses chrono-typologiques qui sont à notre disposition pour le IVe siècle av. J.-C. L'examen du mobilier céramique du début au milieu IVe siècle av. J.-C.[19],

10 Poludnikiewicz 1992.
11 Ballet 2011.
12 Sur les amphores égyptiennes et importées d'Égypte, voir la bibliographie de référence dans Marchand et Marangou 2007,765–783. Pour une synthèse sur les amphores égyptiennes de l'époque ptolémaïque au début à l'époque arabe, voir Dixneuf 2011. Voir également les résultats publiés pour certains sites: Alexandrie (Senol 2007, Dixneuf 2011), Tell el-Herr (Defernez et Marchand 2006, Defernez 2007b, Dixneuf 2007), Tebtynis (Marangou et Marchand 2007), Tôd (Pierrat-Bonnefois 2002), Karnak (Masson 2011a, Marchand 2007a), Coptos (Lawall 2003, 156–191), Éléphantine/Assouan (Aston 1999, Aston 2007).
13 Defernez 2007b, Defernez et Marchand 2006, 73.
14 Voir plus loin dans le texte, chapitre 1.4.
15 Voir l'article d'Agata Dobosz dans ce volume.
16 Defernez et Marchand 2006, 91–94, fig. 17–19.
17 Crawford 1979, 138–139, Empereur 1993.
18 Marchand 2002.
19 D. Aston offre la synthèse la plus récente sur ce sujet qui rassemble la bibliographie avec les principaux corpus de sites du Delta. Il donne un développement général du mobilier céramique de la Basse Époque en 4 phases chronologiques, Aston 2010, Phase D du début au milieu du IVe siècle av. J.-C. 183–187 fig. 47–48. Sur la céramique de la fin de la Basse époque au IVe siècle av. J.-C. avant la conquête macédonienne pour les sites du Delta et du Nord Sinaï, voir également Chauvet et Marchand 1998, Defernez et Marchand 2006, Defernez 2001, Defernez 2007b, Roussel et Marchand 1994.

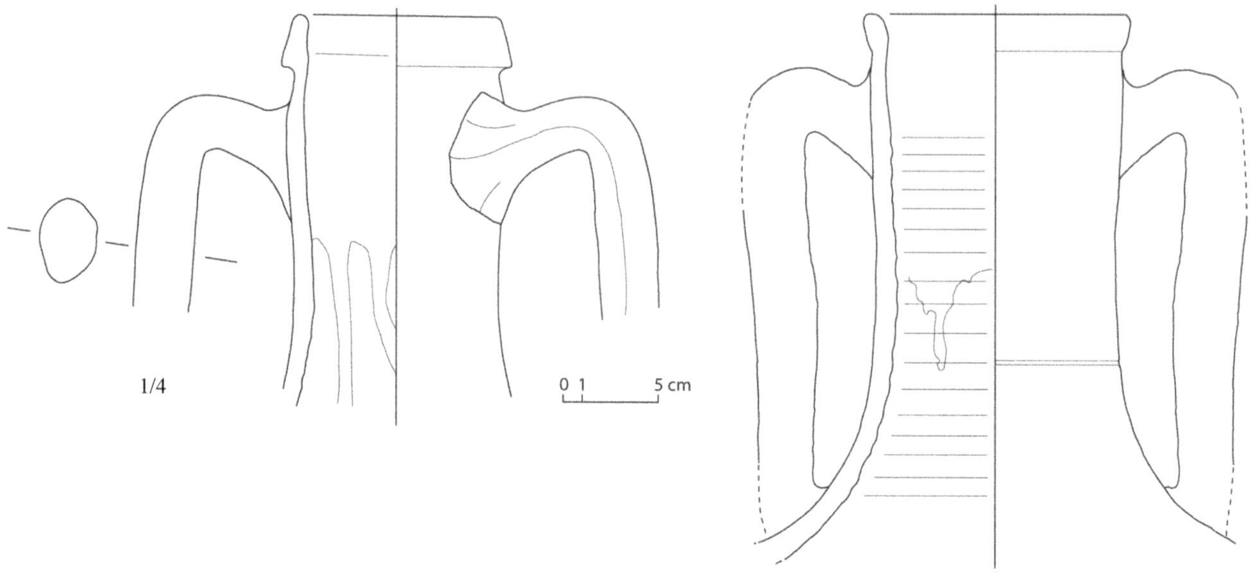

Fig. 7. Tebtynis, Fayoum. Amphores égyptiennes en pâte alluviale de tradition grecque de la première génération d'époque ptolémaïque. Fin de la première moitié du IIIe siècle av. J.-C. Imitation/inspiration de modèles grecs rhodiens et chiotes. (A. Hussein)

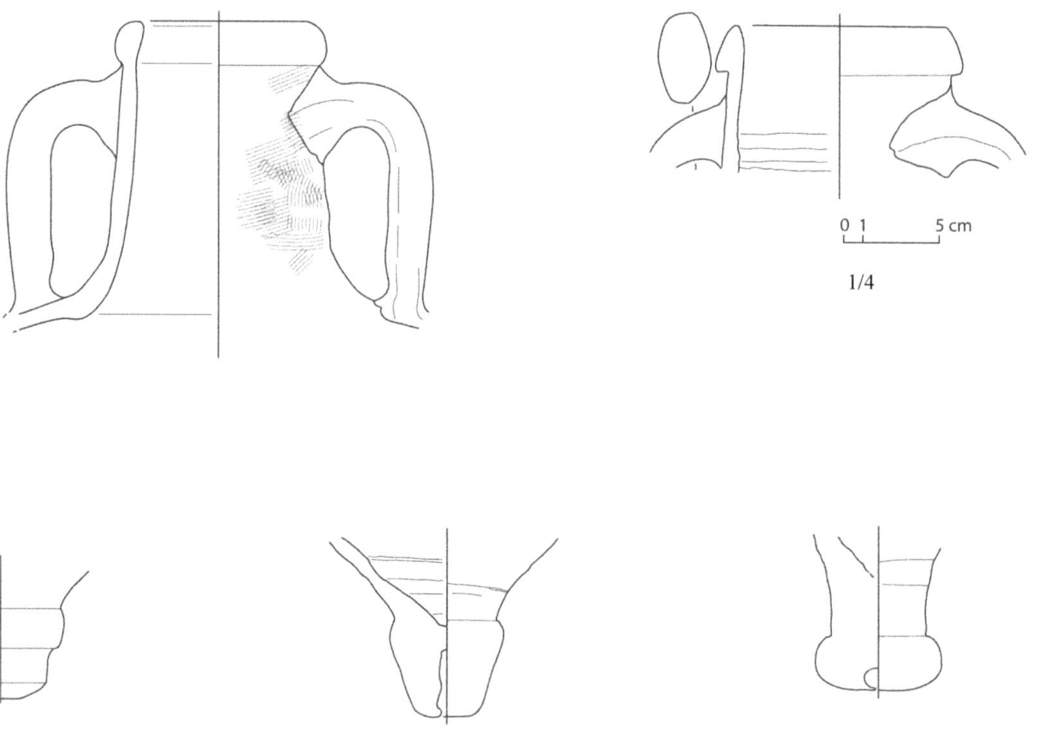

Fig. 8. Tebtynis, Fayoum. Amphores égyptiennes en pâte calcaire de tradition grecque de la première génération d'époque ptolémaïque. Fin de la première moitié du IIIe siècle av. J.-C. Imitation/inspiration de modèles grecs cnidiens, rhodiens ou indéterminés (A. Hussein)

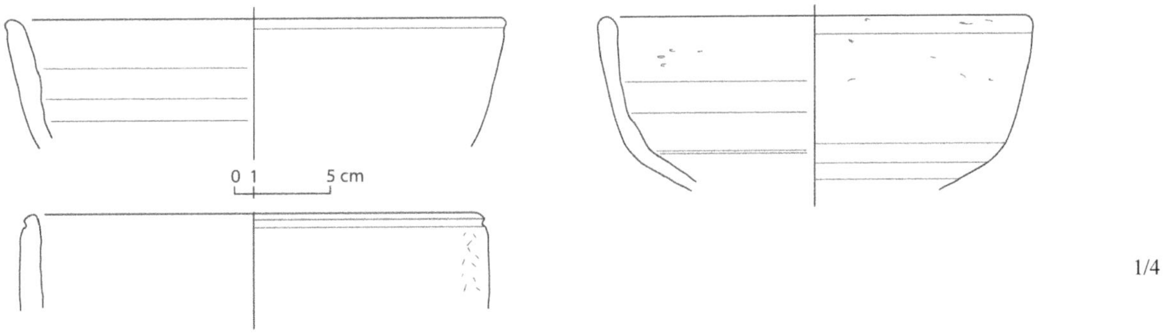

Fig. 9. Tebtynis, Fayoum. Bols de cuisson de tradition pharaonique. IIIe siècle av. J.-C. (A. Hussein)

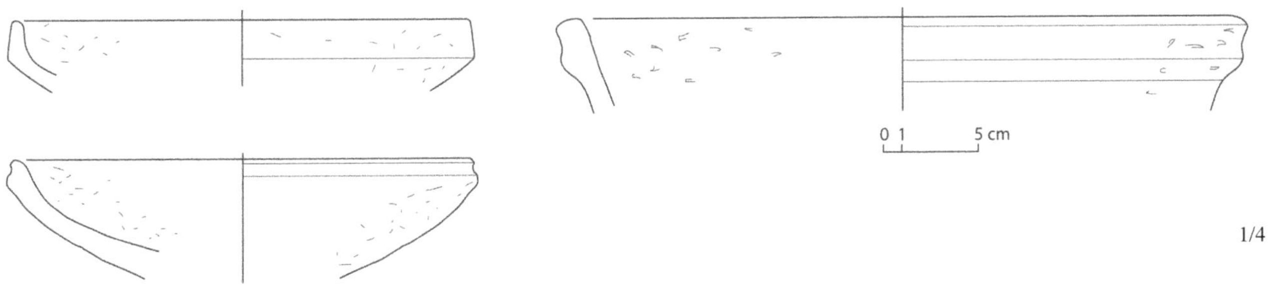

Fig. 10. Tebtynis, Fayoum. Plats creux pour préparations alimentaires de tradition pharaonique. Début du IIIe siècle av. J.-C. (A. Hussein)

montre toute la difficulté qu'il y a de distinguer certaines catégories de récipients découverts dans des niveaux datés de la seconde moitié du IVe de celles qui se poursuivent, parfois sans changement morphologique notab le, pendant le IIIe siècle av. J.-C. Ces derniers permettent de tempérer un schéma uniforme de l'hellénisation des productions égyptiennes locales et mettent en valeur la résistance des cultures régionales égyptiennes héritées des dernières dynasties indigènes.

Le cas du décor peint sur les céramiques d'époque ptolémaïque ne se réduit pas au style grec introduit dans toute l'Égypte, on n'abandonne pas pour autant les répertoires décoratifs locaux anciens. Il est vrai que l'Égypte pharaonique du Nouvel Empire par exemple a créé des œuvres d'art remarquables dans le domaine des céramiques peintes avec des compositions complexes et polychromes. Mais ces réalisations exceptionnelles et innovantes disparaissent totalement à partir de la Troisième Période Intermédiaire sur tout le territoire égyptien. En fait, Il faut attendre la fin de la Basse Époque à partir de la XXVIIIe dynastie au tout début du IVe siècle av. J.-C., pour un retour de la céramique peinte dans le Sud de l'Égypte

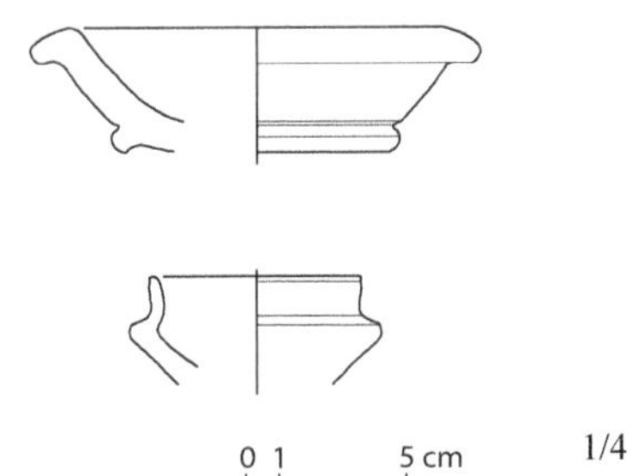

Fig. 11. Tebtynis, Fayoum. Bols et bouteilles de tradition pharaonique. Début du IIIe siècle av. J.-C. (A. Hussein)

qui soit autre chose que de simples décors de bandes noires peintes[20]. Les territoires du Sud dans la première moitié du IVe siècle av. J.-C., de la région thébaine à Éléphantine, ou de l'oasis de Kharga, bénéficient donc avant la conquête macédonienne d'une tradition décorative locale inventive et courante pour de nombreux récipients avec des décors peints de style égyptiens de motifs floraux et géométriques (**Figs. 2–3**)[21]. L'arrivée des Grecs ne met évidemment

Pour le Sud de l'Égypte voir la publication de corpus récents avec la bibliographie pour les autres sites, Aston 1999, Masson 2011a, Masson 2011b.

20 Masson 2011a, 655.

21 Région thébaine (Schreiber 2003), Assouan/ Éléphantine (Aston 1999, 247–329), Oasis de Kharga (Marchand 2007c, 502 fig. 34, 38–41).

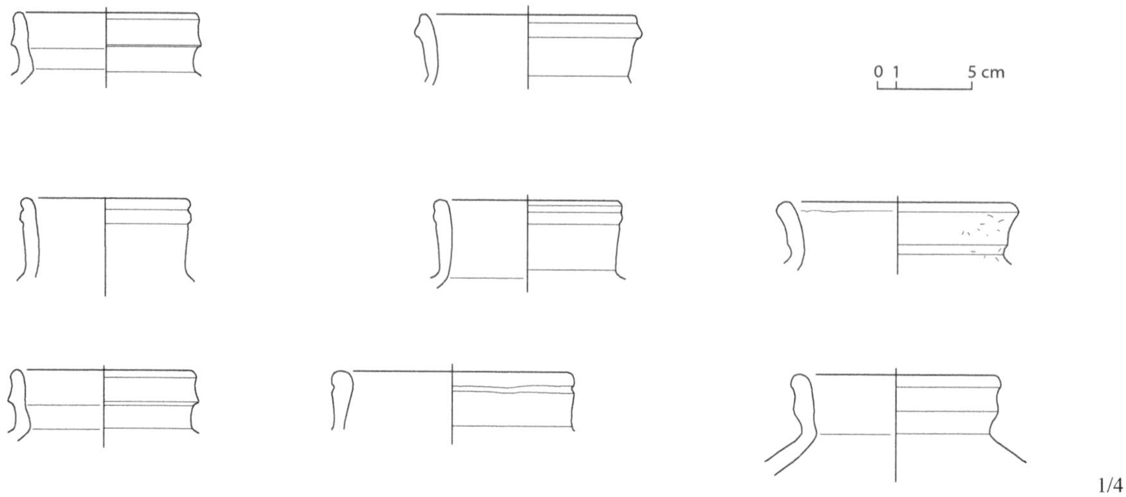

Fig. 12. Tebtynis, Fayoum. Pots de cuisson de tradition pharaonique. IIIe siècle av. J.-C. (A. Hussein)

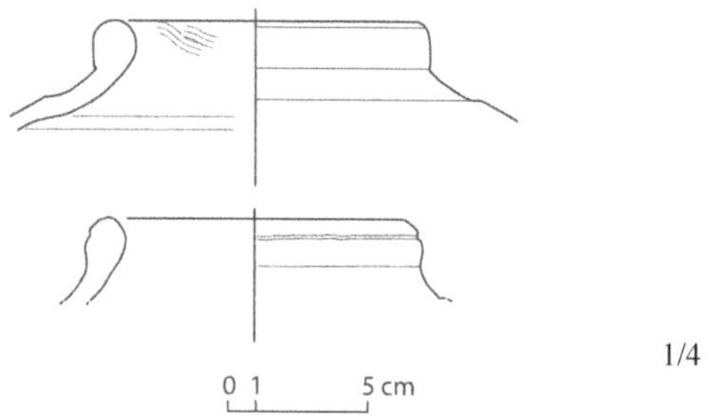

Fig. 13. Tebtynis, Fayoum. Derniers témoins au début de l'époque ptolémaïque d'un courant commercial chypriote représentatif des Ve–IVe siècles av. J.-C. Jarres à 'anses de panier' importées. Début du IIIe siècle av. J.-C. (A. Hussein)

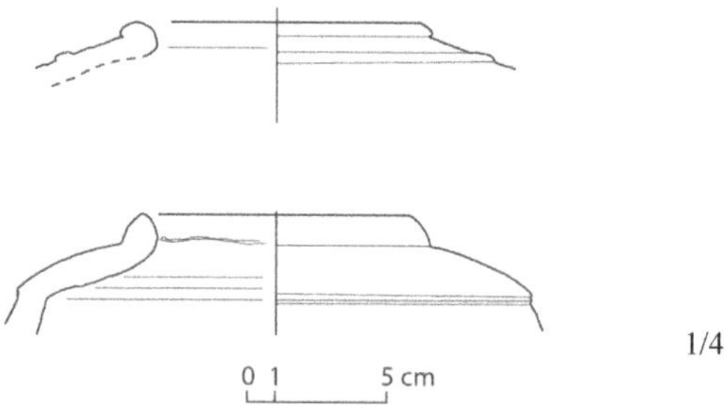

Fig. 14. Tebtynis, Fayoum. Derniers témoins au début de l'époque ptolémaïque d'un courant commercial syro-palestinien représentatif des Ve–IVe siècles av. J.-C. Amphores phéniciennes torpedos importées. Début du IIIe siècle av. J.-C. (A. Hussein)

pas fin à ces styles locaux pendant l'époque ptolémaïque (**Figs. 4–5**)[22] et ils résistent fort bien à la concurrence du style décoratif grec. De fait, l'ancienne tradition décorative locale du Sud ne s'éteindra qu'à la fin du IIe siècle av. J.-C. Dans le Nord de l'Égypte pendant les dernières dynasties indigènes au IVe, on observe à l'inverse du Sud une grande pauvreté des décors peints. Quand les décors de style grec apparaissent au IIIe siècle av. J.-C., ils s'implantent dans un milieu 'vierge' de tout héritage indigène, on assiste au développement original de décors peints d'une réelle qualité esthétique à partir du milieu du IIIe siècle av. J.-C. au Fayoum par exemple (**Fig. 18**)[23].

Les conteneurs de transport locaux résistent également à la vague de l'hellénisation. Les conteneurs égyptiens ne sont pas uniquement créés d'après des modèles de récipients étrangers. Le Sud de l'Égypte avec la région thébaine possède ses propres conteneurs de transport de fabrication locale au début de l'époque ptolémaïque. Les amphores égyptiennes de type grec au début de l'époque ptolémaïque sont abondantes sur les sites du Sud. Néanmoins, les conteneurs de transport locaux en pâte calcaire ou 'Qena-Ware', véritables fossiles vivants d'une production attestée dès la XXVe dynastie, sont encore d'une utilisation courante pendant le IIIe siècle av. J.-C. (**Fig. 6**)[24].

Un autre exemple de persistance du conteneur local peut être donné en examinant la documentation céramique des oasis de Kharga et de Dakhla. On constate que dans ces régions, ce symbole de l'hellénisation qu'est l'amphore de type grec est absent de la production locale pendant toute l'époque ptolémaïque Le conteneur de transport local hérité des XXVIe–XXVIIe dynasties reste la *siga* (**Fig. 3**). Ce conteneur en forme de ballon de rugby continuera de remplir son office pendant l'époque ptolémaïque et pour longtemps puisqu'il est encore fabriqué de nos jours à Al-

22 Région thébaine (Schreiber 2003, Török 1993, Masson 2011, fig. 89–90), Éléphantine/Assouan (Aston 1999, 282–355), Oasis de Dakhla (Hope 1999, 230), Oasis de Kharga (Marchand 2007c, 499 fig. 16–17).

23 Ballet 2002, 96 fig. 6.

24 Région thébaine (Masson 2011b, fig. 24–27, Pierrat-Bonnefois 2002,179.), Éléphantine/Assouan (Aston 2007, 428 fig. 6 Group VI).

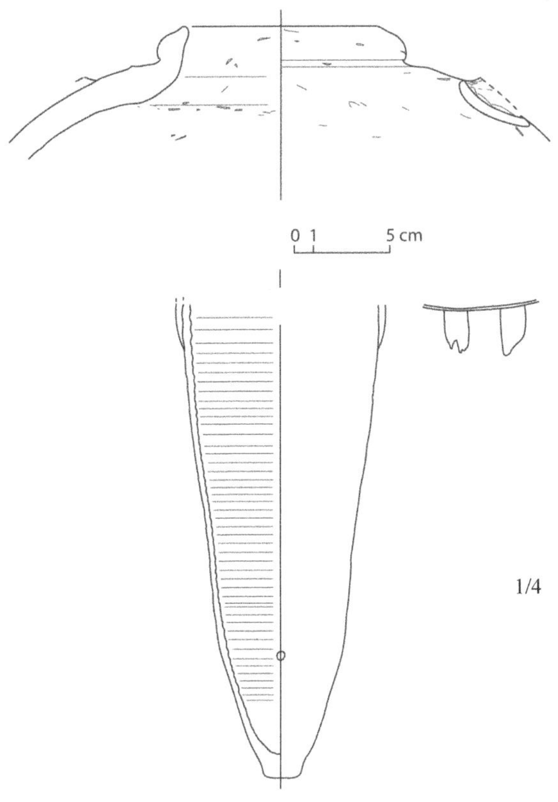

Fig. 15. Tebtynis, Fayoum. Dernières imitations égyptiennes de jarres 'à anses de panier' en pâte alluviale. Début du IIIe siècle av. J.-C. (A. Hussein)

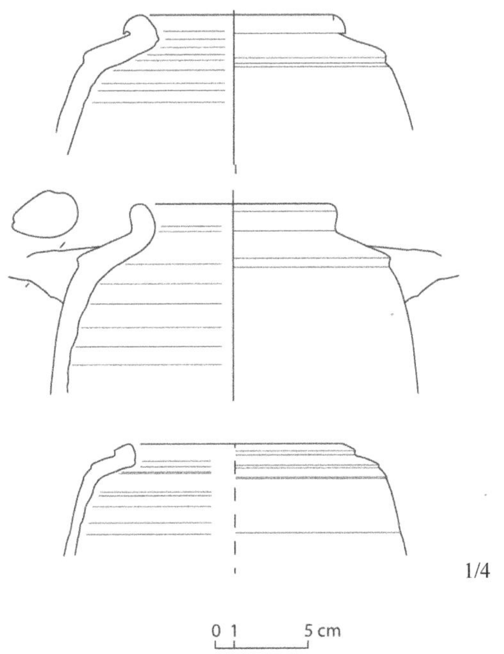

Fig. 16. Tebtynis, Fayoum. Dernières imitations égyptiennes d'amphores torpedos en pâte calcaire et en pâte alluviale. Première moitié du IIIe siècle av. J.-C. (A. Hussein)

Qasr dans l'oasis de Dakhla[25]. Pourtant, quelques rares amphores importées du monde grec et un nombre plus significatif de *torpedos* syro-palestiniennes circulent dans la région depuis le Ve siècle av. J.-C.[26], viennent ensuite à la période suivante, les amphores égyptiennes *AE2* produites dans la Vallée du Nil vers la fin du IIIe au IIe siècle av. J.-C. et des amphores importées chiotes connues à partir de la fin du IVe siècle av. J.-C.[27]. Cependant, dans l'état actuel de nos connaissances, aucune amphore de transport locale de type grec de taille normale n'est fabriquée à Kharga ou à Dakhla[28] pendant l'époque ptolémaïque. Les oasis de Dakhla et de Kharga sont des régions agricoles depuis la plus haute antiquité, elles sont d'ailleurs bien connues pour leur production de vin[29]. On peut supposer que divers produits, dont le vin, continuent d'être exporté dans les *siga* vers la vallée du Nil, de l'époque perse à l'époque ptolémaïque. Ce commerce pendant l'époque ptolémaïque se mesure par la fréquence des *siga* originaires des oasis de Kharga/Dakhla découvertes sur les sites de la vallée du Nil notamment dans la région thébaine et à Assouan[30]. Ailleurs dans le Nord de l'Égypte l'identification des *siga* oasiennes est beaucoup plus rare, on recense quelques exemplaires à Tebynis[31], ou un unique exemplaire à Alexandrie[32].

[25] Marchand 2007c, 492–494.

[26] Marchand 2007c, 496 fig. 1, 4–6. Pour le Ve siècle av. J.-C. à Kharga on note la présence de rares lécythes attiques importés, fig. 2–3.

[27] Amphores égyptiennes de la Vallée du Nil *AE2*: Marchand 2007c, 501 fig. 23. Amphores importées chiotes: Marchand 2007c, 501 fig. 22.

[28] Il faut distinguer une amphore locale de taille normale, c'est à dire un conteneur de transport de taille standard pour transporter des denrées diverses; des amphores miniatures qui ont une tout autre fonction celle de conteneur certes mais pour des cosmétiques. En effet, des amphores miniatures (utilisées comme vase à parfum) sont fabriquées dans l'oasis de Kharga au début de l'époque ptolémaïque à partir de la fin du IVe siècle av. J.-C., cf. Marchand 2007c, 501 fig. 26. Dans l'oasis de Dakhla une amphore de petite taille locale de style grec à décor peint a été découverte dans une tombe datée de l'époque ptolémaïque, cf. Hope 1999, 233 fig. 27.

[29] Sur la production de vin et d'amphores à vin locales à Dakhla à partir de la XVIIIe dynastie au Nouvel Empire, cf. Marchand et Tallet 1999.

[30] Karnak: Masson 2011, fig. 93–95. Éléphantine/Assouan: Aston 1999, 315 n°2754

[31] Marangou et Marchand 2007, 285 fig. 99 *Siga* datée de la fin IVe/première moitié du IIIe siècle av. J.-C.

[32] Matériel inédit étudié par l'auteur en collaboration avec Delphine Dixneuf (fouilles de Fouad dirigées par F. Choël, CEAlex). Siga datée du IIIe siècle av. J.-C.

Fig. 17. Détail d'une scène du tombeau de Pétosiris à Hermopolis/Touna el-Gebel daté de la fin du IVe siècle av. J.-C. Mise du vin dans des amphores égyptiennes de tradition grecque et dans des torpedos égyptiennes de tradition syro-palestinienne (Tiré de Cherpion, Corteggiani, et Gout 2007, 56. Scène 56a (GL. 43–44).

Examinons à présent le cas de la céramique domestique du début de l'époque ptolémaïque. C'est dans cette gamme de récipients que la 'résistance' des potiers locaux va être la plus visible un peu partout sur le territoire égyptien d'Alexandrie à Assouan et dans les oasis. Le problème est de situer précisément le 'curseur chronologique' afin de déterminer précisément la durée de vie des récipients. L'arrêt de la production de ces formes n'est pas toujours clairement établi dans la chronologie interne des sites. Les récipients touchés par la tradition pharaonique (**Figs. 9–12**) comprennent la vaisselle culinaire avec les pots de cuisson, la vaisselle de service, les récipients pour préparations alimentaires et le stockage des denrées. On peut ajouter à cette liste quelques vaisselles spécialisées aux formes souvent peu évolutives comme les pots à pigeonnier par exemple[33] ou encore les petits supports tronconiques, dernier avatar d'une forme spécifiquement pharaonique[34]. Le pot de cuisson (**Fig. 12**) de tradition pharaonique est la forme de tradition pharaonique qui offre le plus de résistance dans la batterie de cuisine égyptienne. Même en présence des nouvelles marmites de tradition grecque qui ont été adoptées très tôt sur la totalité du territoire égyptien, les vieux pots de cuisson égyptiens de tradition pharaonique font de la résistance pour certains types pendant tout le IIIe siècle av. J.-C.

[33] Karnak: Masson 2011, fig. 4–5.
[34] Tebtynis: Marchand 1996, fig. 35. Éléphantine/Assouan: Aston 1999, 337 n 2992–2999.

Les derniers témoins des courants commerciaux orientaux anciens au IIIe siècle av. J.-C: les jarres à 'anses de panier' chypriotes et les torpedos phéniciennes

La période du début du IIIe siècle av. J.-C. voit la fin de courants commerciaux souvent anciens attestés en Égypte dès la Troisième Période Intermédiaire autour du VIIe siècle av. J.-C. et très actifs pendant la Basse Époque aux Ve–IVe siècles av. J.-C., avec des conteneurs de transport et des céramiques fines spécifiques. Le premier est le courant égéen avec les amphores et les céramiques fines importées[35]. Nous n'ouvrirons pas ici le dossier des importations égéennes, rappelons simplement que les derniers vernis noirs attiques, appartenant à une famille de récipients bien connus pendant le IVe siècle av. J.-C., les lécythes trapus, sont découverts dans les niveaux de la seconde moitié du IVe au tout début du IIIe à Tebtynis par exemple[36].

Le deuxième est le courant commercial chypriote. Il est associé aux mortiers ou 'Persian Bowls' qui sont encore attestés au début du IIIe siècle av. J.-C. et à certains emballages commerciaux comme la jarre à 'anses de panier'[37]. Le courant commercial chypriote est toujours

[35] Les céramiques importées égéennes (amphores et céramiques fines) de la fin du VIIe au IVe siècle av. J.-C. en Égypte ont fait l'objet de synthèses récentes, cf. Defernez 2001, Defernez 2002, Defernez 2007b, Smolàrikovà 2002.
[36] Marchand 1996.
[37] Defernez 2001, 391–401.

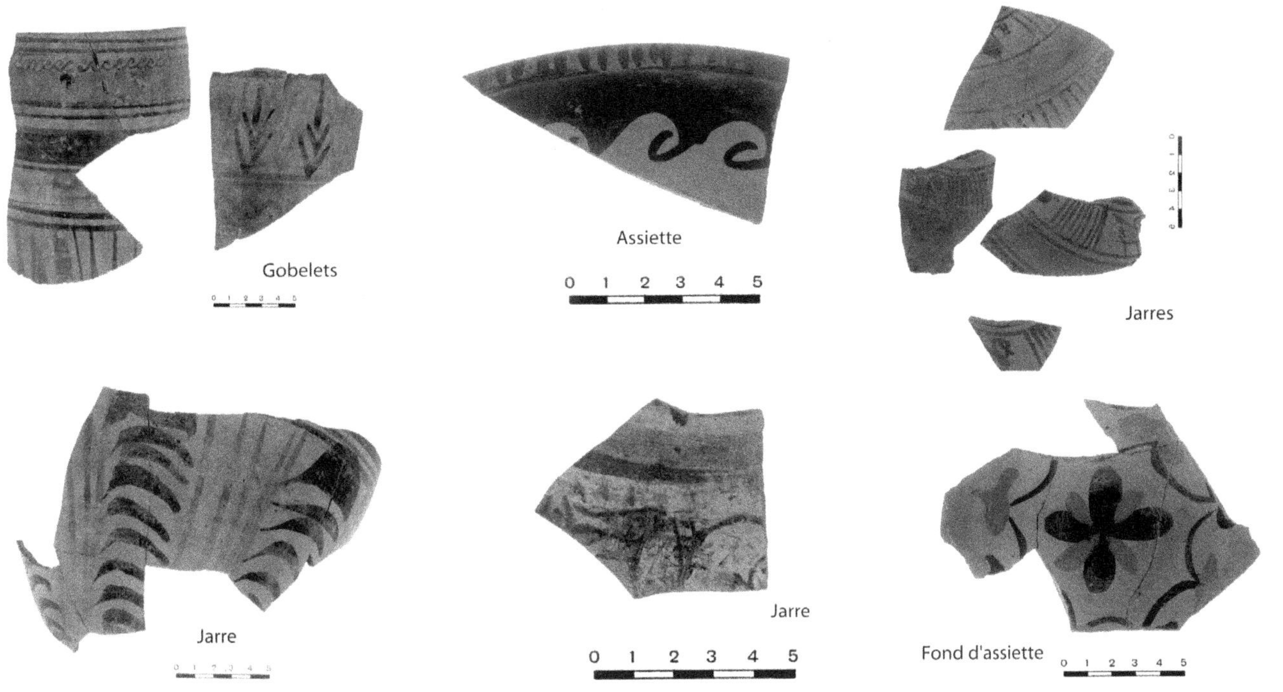

Fig. 18. Tebtynis, Fayoum. Vaisselle de table égyptienne: assiettes, gobelets et jarres, en pâte calcaire fine peinte noire et rouge sur fond clair. Milieu IIIe siècle–IIe siècle av. J.-C. Répertoire décoratif d'inspiration grecque: floral, animalier (cygnes), géométrique et érotique. Le décor érotique est polychrome (vert-jaune-noir et rose réalisé après cuisson sur fond stuqué blanc) (Photo J.-Fr. Gout. Ifao)

très actif au IVe siècle et décroît rapidement, les jarres à 'anses de panier' introduites en Égypte fin VIIe–VIe siècle av. J.-C. disparaissent des couches archéologiques au début du IIIe siècle av. J.-C. (**Fig. 13**).

Le troisième est le courant syro-palestinien avec un conteneur de transport très ancien en Égypte, la *torpedo* originaire de Syrie-Palestine[38]. Héritière des jarres cananéennes diffusées en Égypte pendant le Nouvel Empire, les *torpedos* importées sont trouvées en abondance en Égypte du Delta en Nubie dès la Troisième Période Intermédiaire jusqu'au début de l'époque ptolémaïque (**Fig. 14**). La disparition de ces conteneurs est chose faite dans la première moitié du IIIe siècle av. J.-C.[39]. D'autres conteneurs avec des amphores de tradition punique, d'origine phénicienne, sont diffusés en Méditerranée occidentale en Tunisie et en Espagne à partir du IVe siècle et tout au long du IIIe siècle av. J.-C. Ils sont également attestés en Égypte, à Tebtynis par exemple, à partir du milieu du IIIe et disparaissent des couches archéologiques au début du IIe siècle av. J.-C.[40].

Les derniers conteneurs égyptiens de tradition chypriote et syro-palestinienne au IIIe siècle av. J.-C.

Le dernier point qui reste à examiner est celui du dossier des imitations égyptiennes des conteneurs de transport assimilés aux courants chypriote et syro-palestinien. Elles ne sont courantes en fait qu'à partir du milieu du IVe siècle av. J.-C.[41]. Le phénomène des imitations de ces conteneurs est donc assez tardif et n'est pas contemporain de la vague des prototypes importés en Égypte et qui sont déjà diffusés en Égypte depuis plusieurs siècles. Les imitations égyptiennes des jarres 'à anses de panier' de tradition chypriote vont disparaître très tôt au début du IIIe siècle av. J.-C.[42] (**Fig. 15**). Les imitations égyptiennes des *torpedos* [43] (**Fig.16**) disparaîtront plus tard dans la première moitié du IIIe siècle av. J.-C. On peut supposer l'existence de plusieurs centres de production des *torpedos* en Égypte, par l'examen des pâtes. On distingue au moins deux productions : l'une en pâte calcaire et l'autre en pâte alluviale. La découverte des traces d'un atelier de potier de *torpedos* égyptiennes en pâte calcaire à Tell Atrib[44] dans le Delta dans un niveau archéologique daté la fin du IVe siècle av. J.-C. est exceptionnelle. La fin de vie de cet atelier se situe au moment où s'amorce le déclin de la production, mais surtout c'est le seul atelier identifié à notre connaissance de *torpedos* égyptiennes. Il s'agit d'un conteneur diffusé très largement un peu partout en Égypte comme ses homologues importées. Le plus surprenant dans la disparition brutale des *torpedos* égyptiennes est que leur forme a été sans Après la disparition totale des

38 Beetles 2003, Defernez 2001, 367–386.
39 Marangou et Marchand 2007, 254.
40 Marangou et Marchand 2007, 251.
41 Defernez et Marchand 2006, 66–71.
42 Marangou et Marchand 2007, 253.
43 Marangou et Marchand 2007, 255–256.
44 Mysliwiec 2009, 39, pl. XVII n 1.

Troisième Période intermédiaire **1069-664 av. J.-C.**	XXIe dynastie (1069-944) – Tanis et Thèbes
	XXIIe dynastie (944-736) – Bubastis et Thèbes
	XXIIIe dynastie (736-713) – Tanis
	XXIVe dynastie (725-720) – Saïs
	XXVe dynastie (ca 780-736) dite « kouchite » ou « éthiopienne »
Basse Époque **664-332 av. J.-C.**	XXVIe dynastie (685-525) – Saïs
	XXVIIe dynastie (525-401) – Première domination perse
	XXVIIIe dynastie (405-399)
	XXIXe dynastie (399-380)
	XXXe dynastie (380-342)
	Seconde domination perse (342-332)
Époque grecque **332-30 av. J.-C. – Alexandrie**	Dynastie macédonienne (332-309)
	Dynastie ptolémaïque (304-30)
Époque romaine **(30 av. J.-C - 395 apr. J.-C.)**	
Époque byzantine **(395-642)**	
Époque arabe **(depuis 642)**	

Tab. 1. Chronologie égyptienne

torpedos égyptiennes dans la première moitié du IIIe siècle av. J.-C., les amphores égyptiennes de tradition grecque prendront alors toute leur place. Un document exceptionnel et fort connu, un bas-relief du tombeau de Pétosiris à Hermopolis/Touna el-Gebel[45] daté de la fin du IVe siècle av. J.-C., illustre à merveille ce moment privilégié lorsque les conteneurs égyptiens de type *torpedo* et les amphores égyptiennes de type grec cohabitent encore vers la fin du IVe siècle av. J.-C. (**Fig. 17**). Cette scène montre les vendanges, la mise en amphores du vin et le décompte de la production. Au premier plan, on voit le remplissage d'amphores égyptiennes de tradition grecque de type rhodien ou cnidien avec leur fond en bouton de la fin du IVe et du début du IIIe siècle av. J.-C.[46], et d'amphores égyptiennes *torpedos* de tradition syro-palestinienne dans leur variante tardive avec sa forme allongée connue en Égypte à la fin du IVe siècle av. J.-C.[47].

Conclusion

Au tournant du IIIe au IIe siècle av. J.-C., les céramiques des sites égyptiens nous offrent un faciès bien différent de celui que l'on a pu observer pour celles de la fin du IVe et dans la première moitié du IIIe siècle av. J.-C. Toutes les innovations, avec un vaisselier, formes et décors, d'inspiration grecque, mises en place depuis la fin du IVe siècle av. J.-C., sont alors clairement assumées. On observe au IIe siècle av. J.-C. la création d'un standard égyptien caractérisé par ses propres inspirations.

Sylvie Marchand
Institut français d'archéologie orientale du Caire
37, rue al-Sheikh Aly Youssef, B.P. Qasr al-Ayni 11562
11441 Le Caire. Égypte.
smarchand@ifao.egnet.net

[45] Cherpion, Corteggiani, et Gout 2007, 56. Scène 56a (GL. 43–44).
[46] Cherpion, Corteggiani, et Gout 2007, 2 note 7: communication orale de J.-Y. Empereur. Type d'amphore caractéristique de la fin du IVe et du début du IIIe siècle av. J.-C. Defernez et Marchand 2006, 91–94.
[47] Beetles 2003, Defernez 2001, 387 fig. 4: imitation locale de jarre *torpedo*, datable de la fin du IVe siècle av. J.-C. (Provenance: Tell el-Herr).

Bibliographie

Aston, D. A. 1999. *ELEPHANTINE XIX. Pottery from the Late New Kingdom to the Early Ptolemaic Period.* Archäologische Veröffentlichungen 95. Mainz, Zabern.

Aston, D. A. 2007. Amphorae, Storage jars and Kegs from Elephantine. A brief Survey of Vessels from the Eight-Seventh Centuries BC to the Seventh-Eight Centuries AD., in S. Marchand et A. Marangou, (eds.), *Amphores d'Égypte de la Basse Époque à l'époque arabe.* Cahiers de la Céramique Égyptienne 8, 419–445. Le Caire, IFAO.

Aston, D. A 2010. *Late Period Pottery from the New Kingdom Necropolis at Saqqâra. Egypt Exploration Society.* Excavation Memoir 92. Londres/Leiden Egypt Exploration Society.

Bagnall, R. S. et Davoli, P. 2011. Newsletter. Archaeological Work on Hellenistic and Roman Egypt, 2000–2009. *American Journal of Archaeology* 115, 103–157.

Ballet, P., Boussac, M.-F. et Enklaar, A. 2001. Les hydries de Hadra, in J.-Y. Empereur et M.-D. Nenna (eds.), *Nécropolis* 1. Études Alexandrines 5, 273–290. Le Caire, IFAO.

Ballet, P. et Harlaut, C. 2001. Introduction à la céramique de Gabbari, in J.-Y. Empereur et M.-D. Nenna (eds.), *Nécropolis* 1. Études Alexandrines 5, 295–368. Le Caire, IFAO.

Ballet, P. et Poludnikiewicz, A. 2012. *Études préliminaires: la céramique hellénistique et impériale de Tebtynis (fouilles 1988–1993). Production, consommation et réception dans le Fayoum méridional.* Tebtynis V. Fouilles de l'IFAO 68. Le Caire, IFA.

Ballet, P. 2001. Céramiques hellénistiques et romaines d'Égypte, in P. Lévêque et J.-P. Morel (eds.), *Céramiques hellénistiques et romaines III,* 105–144. Paris, Presses Universitaires Franc-Comtoises.

Ballet, P. 2002. Les productions céramiques d'Égypte à la période hellénistique: les indices de l'hellénisation, in Fr. Blondé, P. Ballet et J.-Fr. Salles (eds.), *Céramiques hellénistiques et romaines. Productions et diffusion en Méditerranée orientale (Chypre, Égypte et côte syro-palestinienne).* Travaux de la Maison de l'Orient n 35, 85–96. Lyon, Maison de l'Orient Méditerranéen-Jean Pouilloux.

Ballet, P. 2011. Les ateliers hellénistiques de Bouto (Tell el-Fara'in) et le «décor surpeint» (Overpainted), in D. A. Aston, B. Bader C. Gallorini, P. Nicholson et S. Buckingham (eds.), *Under the Potter's tree. Studies on Ancient Egypt Presented to Janine Bourriau on the Occasion of her 70th Birthday.* Orientalia Lovaniensia Analecta 204, 189–200. Leuven, Peeters.

Berlin, A. M. 1997. Chapter 6. The pottery from the Northwest and North Areas. In A. Leonard (ed.), *Ancient Naukratis: Excavations at a Greek Emporion in Egypt, Part I: The excavations at Kom Ge'if.* Annual of American Schools of Oriental Research 54, 136–285.

Berlin A. M. 2001. Chapter 2. Naukratis/Kom Hadid: A ceramic typology for Hellenistic Lower Egypt. In A. Leonard (ed.), *Ancient Naukratis: Excavations at a Greek Emporion in Egypt, Part II: The excavations at Kom Hadidf.* Annual of American Schools of Oriental Research 55, 26–163.

Bettles, E. A. 2003. *Phoenician Amphora Production and Distribution in the Southern Levant. A multi-disciplinary investigation into carinated-shoulder amphorae of the Persian period (539–332 BC).* British Archaeological Reports International Series 1183. Oxford, BAR Publishing.

Bourriau, J. 2003. Imported Amphorae in the Third Intermediate and Late Dynastic Periods from the excavations 2000–2001. *Mitteilungen des Deuschen Archäologischen Instituts, Abteilung Kairo* 59, 224–233.

Budka, J. 2010. The use of pottery in funerary contexts during the Libyan and late Period: A view from Thebes and Abydos, in L. Bares, F. Coppens et K. Smolarikova, *Egypt in transition. Social and Religious Development of Egypt during the First Millenium BCE.* Proceedings of an International Conference Prague, September 1-4, 2009, 22–72. Prague, Charles University.

Chauvet, V. et Marchand, S. 1998. Le matériel céramique pré-ptolémaïque des fosses de l'avant-cour du temple d'Amon de Tanisi, in Ph. Brissaud et Chr. Zivie (eds.), *Tanis Travaux récents sur le tell de Sân el-Hagar,* 335–350. Paris, Noésis.

Cherpion, N., Corteggiani, J.-P. et Gout, J.-Fr. 2007. *Le tombeau de Pétosiris à Touna el-Gebel. Relevé photographique.* Bibliothèque générale 27. Le Caire, IFAO.

Crawford D. J. 1979. Food: tradition and change in Hellenistic Egypt. *World Archaeology II/2,* 136–146.

Defernez, C. et Marchand, S. 2006. Imitations égyptiennes de conteneurs d'origine égéenne et levantine (VIe s.–IIe s. av. J.-C.), in B. Mathieu, D. Meeks et M. Wissa (eds.), *L'apport de l'Égypte à l'histoire des techniques. Méthodes, chronologie et comparaisons.* Bibliothèque d'Étude 142, 63–99. Le Caire, IFAO.

Defernez, C. 2001. *La céramique d'époque perse à Tell el-Herr. Etude chrono-typologique et comparative.* Cahier de Recherches de l'Institut de Papyrologie et d'Égyptologie de Lille Supplément 5. Lille, Université Charles de Gaulle Lille 3.

Defernez, C. 2002. Le poids de l'orientalisation et de l'hellénisation dans l'angle Nord-Est du Delta égyptien, in Fr. Blondé, P. Ballet et J.-Fr. Salles (eds.), *Céramiques hellénistiques et romaines. Productions et diffusion en Méditerranée orientale (Chypre, Égypte et côte syro-palestinienne.* Travaux de la Maison de l'Orient n 35, 235–245. Lyon, Maison de l'Orient Méditerranéen-Jean Pouilloux.

Defernez, C. 2007a. Analyse du mobilier céramique de

la nécropole orientale. In D. Valbelle (ed.), *Tell el-Herr les niveaux hellénistiques et du Haut Empire,* 190–204. Paris, Errance.

Defernez, C. 2007b. Le mobilier amphorique provenant d'un édifice monumental découvert sur le site de Tell el-Herr (Nord-Sinaï), in S. Marchand et A. Marangou (eds.), *Amphores d'Égypte de la Basse Époque à l'époque arabe.* Cahiers de la Céramique Égyptienne 8, 419–445. Le Caire, IFAO.

Dixneuf, D. et Lecuyot, G. 2007. Note préliminaire sur les amphores découvertes par la mission « Recherches sur les ateliers hellénistiques et romains de Bouto » (2002–2003), in S. Marchand et A. Marangou (eds.), *Amphores d'Égypte de la Basse Époque à l'époque arabe.* Cahiers de la Céramique Égyptienne 8, 135–141. Le Caire, IFAO.

Dixneuf, D. 2007. La céramique hellénistique de la cave. In D. Valbelle (ed.), *Tell el-Herr les niveaux hellénistiques et du Haut Empire*, 48–79. Paris, Errance.

Dixneuf, D. 2011. *Amphores égyptiennes. Production, typologie, contenu et diffusion (IIIe siècle avant J.-C.–IXe siècle après J.-C.).* Études Alexandrines 22. Le Caire, Sahara.

Élaigne, S. 2002. L'introduction des céramiques fines hellénistiques du bassin oriental de la Méditerranée à Alexandrie. Importations et imitations locales, in Fr. Blondé, P. Ballet et J.-Fr. Salles (eds.), *Céramiques hellénistiques et romaines. Productions et diffusion en Méditerranée orientale (Chypre, Égypte et côte syro-palestinienne).* Travaux de la Maison de l'Orient n 35, 159–173. Lyon, Maison de l'Orient Méditerranéen-Jean Pouilloux.

Empereur, J.-Y. 1993. La production viticole dans l'Égypte ptolémaïque et romaine, in M.-C. Amouretti – J.-P. Brun (eds.), *La production du vin et de l'huile en Méditerranée.* Actes du Symposium international Aix-en-Provence et Toulon, 20–22 novembre 1991. Bulletin de Correspondance Hellénique Supplément 26, 39–47. Paris, De Boccard.

Gantès, L.-Fr., 2007. Les amphores commerciales, grecques, levantines et égyptiennes découvertes à Naucratis: une révision récente, in S. Marchand et A. Marangou (eds.), *Amphores d'Égypte de la Basse Époque à l'époque arabe.* Cahiers de la Céramique Égyptienne 8, 143–155. Le Caire, IFAO.

Harlaut, C. 2002. Productions céramiques égyptiennes d'Alexandrie à l'époque ptolémaïque – évolutions des formes et des fabriques: traditions locales et innovations, in Fr. Blondé, P. Ballet et J.-Fr. Salles (eds.), *Céramiques hellénistiques et romaines. Productions et diffusion en Méditerranée orientale (Chypre, Égypte et côte syro-palestinienne).* Travaux de la Maison de l'Orient n 35, 263–287. Lyon, Maison de l'Orient Méditerranéen-Jean Pouilloux.

Hope, C. A. 1999. Pottery manufacture in the Dakhleh Oasis, in C. S. Churcher et A. J. Mills (eds.), *Reports from the Survey of the Dakhleh Oasis 1977–198.* Dakhla Oasis Project: Monograph 2. 215–250. Oxford, Oxbow Books.

Hope, C. A. 2000 with appendices of Eccleston M. A. J., Kaper, O. E, Marchand, S. and Darnell, D. Kegs and Flasks from the Dakhleh Oasis. *Cahiers de la Céramique Égyptienne* 6, 189–234.

Herbert, S. C. et Berlin, A. 2003. *Excavations at Coptos (Qift) in Upper Egypt, 1987–1992.* Journal of Roman Archaeology Supplementary Series 53. Portsmouth, Rhode Island, Thomson-Shore.

Lawall, M. 2003. Egyptian and imported transport amphoras, in S. C. Herbert, et A. Berlin. *Excavations at Coptos (Qift) in Upper Egypt, 1987–1992.* Journal of Roman Archaeology Supplementary Series 53, 156–191. Portsmouth, Rhode Island, Thomson-Shore.

Marangou, A. et Marchand, S. 2007. Conteneurs importés et égyptiens de Tebtynis (Fayoum) de la deuxième moitié du IVe siècle av. J.-C au Xe siècle apr. J.-C. (1994–2002), in S. Marchand et A. Marangou (eds.), *Amphores d'Égypte de la Basse Époque à l'époque arabe.* Cahiers de la Céramique Égyptienne 8, 239–294. Le Caire, IFAO.

Marangou, A. et Marchand, S. 2009. La contribution des conteneurs commerciaux à l'histoire des échanges entre Chypre et l'Égypte de l'époque archaïque à l'époque romaine tardive, in D. Michaelides, V. Kassianidou et R. S. Merrillees (eds.), *Egypt and Cyprus in Antiquity.* Proceeding of the International Conference Egypt and Cyprus in Antiquity Nicosia 3–6 April 2003, 242–252. Oxford et Oakville, Oxbow Books.

Marchand, S. et Tallet, P. 1999. Ayn Asil et l'Oasis de Dakhla au Nouvel Empire. *Bulletin de l'Institut Français d'Archéologie Orientale* 99, 307–352.

Marchand, S. et Marangou, A. (eds.) 2007, *Amphores d'Égypte de la Basse Époque à l'époque arabe, Cahiers de la Céramique Égyptienne 8.*

Marchand, S. 1996. La céramique du IVe siècle av. J.-C. découverte à Tebtynis. *Cahiers de la Céramique Égyptienne 4*, 171–188.

Marchand, S. 2000. Appendix 3: Les siga des oasis datées de la XXVIIe–XXXe dynastie et de l'époque ptolémaïque ancienne trouvées à 'Ayn Manâwir (oasis de Kharga) et à Tebtynis (Fayoum), 221–226, in C. A. Hope with appendices of M. A. J. Eccleston, O. E. Kaper, S. Marchand and D. Darnell, Kegs and Flasks from the Dakhleh Oasis. *Cahiers de la Céramique Égyptienne* 6, 189–234.

Marchand, S. 2002. Le maintien de la tradition pharaonique pour les productions des céramiques datées de l'époque ptolémaïque en Égypte, in Fr. Blondé, P. Ballet et J.-Fr. Salles (eds.), *Céramiques hellénistiques et romaines. Productions et diffusion en Méditerranée orientale (Chypre, Égypte et côte syro-palestinienne).* Travaux de la Maison de l'Orient n 35, 247–261. Lyon, Maison de l'Orient Méditerranéen-Jean Pouilloux.

Marchand, S. 2007a. Amphores de Karnak (CFEETK secteur du « tombeau d'Osiris ») et de Dendara

(IFAO prospections et sondages sous la basilique), in S. Marchand et A. Marangou (eds.), *Amphores d'Égypte de la Basse Époque à l'époque arabe.* Cahiers de la Céramique Égyptienne 8, 369–376. Le Caire, IFAO.

Marchand, S. 2007b. Les amphores égyptiennes et importées datées de la Basse Époque à l'époque arabe. Abou Rawash (1995–2004), in S. Marchand et A. Marangou (eds.), *Amphores d'Égypte de la Basse Époque à l'époque arabe.* Cahiers de la Céramique Égyptienne 8, 175–188. Le Caire, IFAO.

Marchand, S. 2007c. Les conteneurs de transport et de stockage de l'oasis de Kharga. De la Basse Époque (XXVIIe–XXXe dynasties) à l'époque ptolémaïque, in S. Marchand et A. Marangou (eds.), *Amphores d'Égypte de la Basse Époque à l'époque arabe.* Cahiers de la Céramique Égyptienne 8, 489–502. Le Caire, IFAO.

Marchand, S. 2009. 2. Appendix 2. Hawara 2000. The Pottery from Hawara. In I. Uytterhoeven with an Appendix on the Pottery from Hawara by S. Marchand, *Hawara in the Graeco-Roman Period. Life and Death in a Fayum Village.* Orientalia Lovaniensia Analecta 174, 685–813. Leuven, Peeters.

Marchand, S. 2011. La dernière occupation d'une maison d'époque ptolémaïque du village de Tebtynis (Fayoum). Une céramique de transition tardo-hellénistique. *Cahiers de la Céramique Égyptienne* 9, 215–252.

Masson, A. 2011a. Jarres au décor polychrome du Musée Pouchkine: manisfestations originales de la tendance archaïsante des 25e–26e dynasties? in D. A. Aston, B. Bader C. Gallorini, P. Nicholson et S. Buckingham (eds.), *Under the Potter's tree. Studies on Ancient Egypt Presented to Janine Bourriau on the Occasion of her 70th Birthday.* Orientalia Lovaniensia Analecta 204, 645–678. Leuven, Peeters.

Masson, A. 2011b. Persian and Ptolemaic Ceramics from Karnak: Change and Continuity. *Cahiers de la Céramique Égyptienne 9*, 269–310.

Mysliwiec, K. 2009. *Tell Atrib 1985–1995 II. Contexte archéologique.* Varsovie, Neriton.

Pierrat-Bonnefois, G. 2002. L'hellénisation des productions céramiques en Haute-Égypte: le cas de Tôd, in Fr. Blondé, P. Ballet et J.-Fr. Salles (eds.), *Céramiques hellénistiques et romaines. Productions et diffusion en Méditerranée orientale (Chypre, Égypte et côte syro-palestinienne).* Travaux de la Maison de l'Orient n 35, 175–188. Lyon, Maison de l'Orient Méditerranéen-Jean Pouilloux.

Poludnikiewicz, A. 1992. Local imitations of Greek Pottery found in Tell Atrib. In P. Ballet (ed.), Ateliers de potiers et productions céramiques en Égypte. *Cahiers de la Céramique Égyptienne 3*, 95–101.

Roussel, D. et Marchand, S. 1994. La céramique d'un bâtiment de la XXXe dynastie à Tanis. *Bulletin de liaison de la Céramique Égyptienne* 18, 12–18.

Rzeuska, T.I. 2008. III. The Pottery. In K. Mysliwiec (ed.), *Saqqara III. The Upper Necropolis. Part I : The Catalogue*, 417–451. Varsovie, Neriton.

Schreiber, G. 2003. *Late Dynastic and Ptolemaic Painted Pottery from Thebes (4th–2th c. BC).* Dissertationes Pannonicae Ser. III. Vol. 6. Budapest, Pytheas.

Senol, A. K. 2007. A Statistical Essay on the Distribution of Imported Amphorae Finds of the CEAlex Salvage Excavations, in S. Marchand et A. Marangou (eds.), *Amphores d'Égypte de la Basse Époque à l'époque arabe.* Cahiers de la Céramique Égyptienne 8, 57–76. Le Caire, IFAO.

Smolàrikovà, K. 2002. *Abusir VII Greek imports in Egypt. Graeco-egyptian relations during the first Millenium B.C.* Prague, Charles University.

Tomber, R. 1998. Chapter Six. The pottery, in S. E. Sidebotham et W. Z. Wendrich (eds.), *Berenike 1996. Report of the 1996 Excavations at Berenike (Egyptian Red Sea Coast) and the survey of the Eastern Desert,* 165–169. Leiden, Centre of Non-Western Studies.

Török, L. 1994. Upper Egyptian Pottery Wares with hellenistic decoration and their Impact on Meroitic Vase Painting, in C. Berger, G. Clerc et N. Grimal (eds.), *Hommages à Jean Leclant.* Bibliothèque d'Étude 106/2, 377–387. Le Caire, IFAO.

Wuttman, M., Barakat, H., Bousquet, B., Chauveau, M., Gonon, T., Marchand, S., Robin, M. and Scheitzer, A. 1998. 'Ayn Manâwir (oasis de Kharga). Deuxième rapport préliminaire. *Bulletin de l'Institut Français d'Archéologie Orientale* 98, 367–462.

The Eastern Marmarica (NW-Egypt) - Pottery Production and Networking in a Semiarid Region

Heike Möller & Anna-Katharina Rieger

Abstract

The Marmarica is the semiarid and arid region covering today's north-western Egypt and north-eastern Libya between the Cyrenaica, the Mediterranean Sea, the Nile Valley and the Qattara Depression. Recent research along the coast and on the Tableland in Eastern Marmarica shows that it was, despite its natural prerequisites, a region with a high quantity of pottery production sites and moreover with an unexpected 'surplus'-economic activity based on dry-farming and livestock. Products like barley, wine or vinegar as a preservative agent suited the regional market and were in high demand in the oases, partly even in the Nile Valley[1].

For the latter, foodstuff containers – amphorae – were produced in the region since Ptolemaic times, as evidenced by more than 55 surveyed production sites along the coast from Ras Abu Laho to Ras el-Hekma (**Fig. 1**), in an investigation area of around 1000km^2 (**Fig. 2**).[2]

The reconstruction of a kiln at one of the production sites (Wadi Qasaba) helped to visualise the possible filling capacity that could easily reach 300 containers/amphorae per firing process (**Fig. 3**).[3] This enormous output shows once more the possible economic potential of the semi-arid region.

Amphorae produced in the Eastern Marmarica can be classified according to the Amphores egyptiennes series AE 2-3 with its subtypes.[4] The fabric shows a silty, quartzose, more or less carbonate-rich, slightly ferrous clay. The earliest forms of AE 2 amphora (**Fig. 4**) can be dated by comparison with similar pieces to no later than the Middle of the 2nd century BC.[5] The latest forms of the Roman AE 3 occur probably until the 4th century AD.[6]

Dixneuf[7] already pointed out that the slight difference in the shape of the Roman Egyptian Amphora Type AE 3 is probably based on regional diversity and regionally preferred features. This can be supported by the finds in the Eastern Marmarica: On all investigated production sites the same or highly related forms occur, sometimes different subtypes even coexist at one site[8] and resemble the forms further east, around Lake Mareotis and also those in the Western Marmarica, modern north-eastern Libya[9], but differ to the ones coming from the Delta region and the Nile Valley (**Fig. 5**).

The Marmarica seems to be a zone of transition regarding influences from Tripolitania and those from eastern Egypt – to what extent has to be investigated further. Archaeologically these traces can also be seen by regionally imported wares. Slight differences in Eastern Marmarica to Egypt in general and parallels in Western Marmarica, today´s Libya, show clearly that exchange did exist between the two regions and certainly was stronger than the links with the Delta region and the Nile valley, since hitherto only a few regional imports could be found in the investigated area, and vice versa the export of products from the Marmarica to the Delta region or into the Nile Valley seems to be quite low, as far as known.

However, the Marmarica functioned as a mediator in a broad sense: In the context of clarifying the regional and transregional interactions, the focus had to be turned to the desert routes crossing the Marmarica-Plateau.[10] (**Fig. 6**). By reconstructing the ancient route network in the Eastern Marmarica, concentrating mainly on ancient cistern sites and their archaeological remains, Ptolemaic and Roman amphorae (AE 2 and AE 3) produced at the coastal potters' workshops could be found at the cistern sites on the plateau.[11] Those amphorae reflect an economic interaction between north and south, between the Oasis Siwa and the Marmarican coast, not only in the local, Marmarican, sense, trading foodstuffs and goods, that were either produced at the coast or in the oasis, but also as mediator of imported

1 The research was conducted within the framework of the project 'Der Marmarica-Survey' of A.-K. Rieger, financed by the German Research Foundation (DFG) in collaboration with the Egyptian State Ministry of Antiquities (SMA). The Gerda Henkel Stiftung supported H. Möller with a scholarship. Our thanks go to these institutions for funding and supporting the work.

2 For further reading and there characterisation by large-, medium- and small-scale production sites see: Rieger and Möller 2011

3 Möller in prep.

4 Typology after Empereur 1986, see also: Dixneuf 2011.

5 Dixneuf 2011, AE 2–1.1. (For the production of AE 2 amphorae see: Dixneuf 2011, 87–96.; Coulson et al. 1986, 548; Empereur 1998, 77; Majcherek and Shennawi 1992, 133; Rieger and Möller 2011; Möller in prep.

6 For the production sites, forms and dating in the Mareotis area and the Nile Valley cf. lately Dixneuf 2011, for the Eastern Marmarica cf. Möller in prep.

7 Dixneuf 2011, 97–128

8 Rieger and Möller 2011, Möller in prep.

9 Hulin *et al.* 2009, 181, 184; WMCS 53, Mellaha

10 For further reading see: Vetter et al. in print_a, Rieger *et al.* in prep._a

11 Vetter *et al.* in print_a.

Fig. 1. Large Scale Production Site in Wadi Senab (Photo: H. Möller)

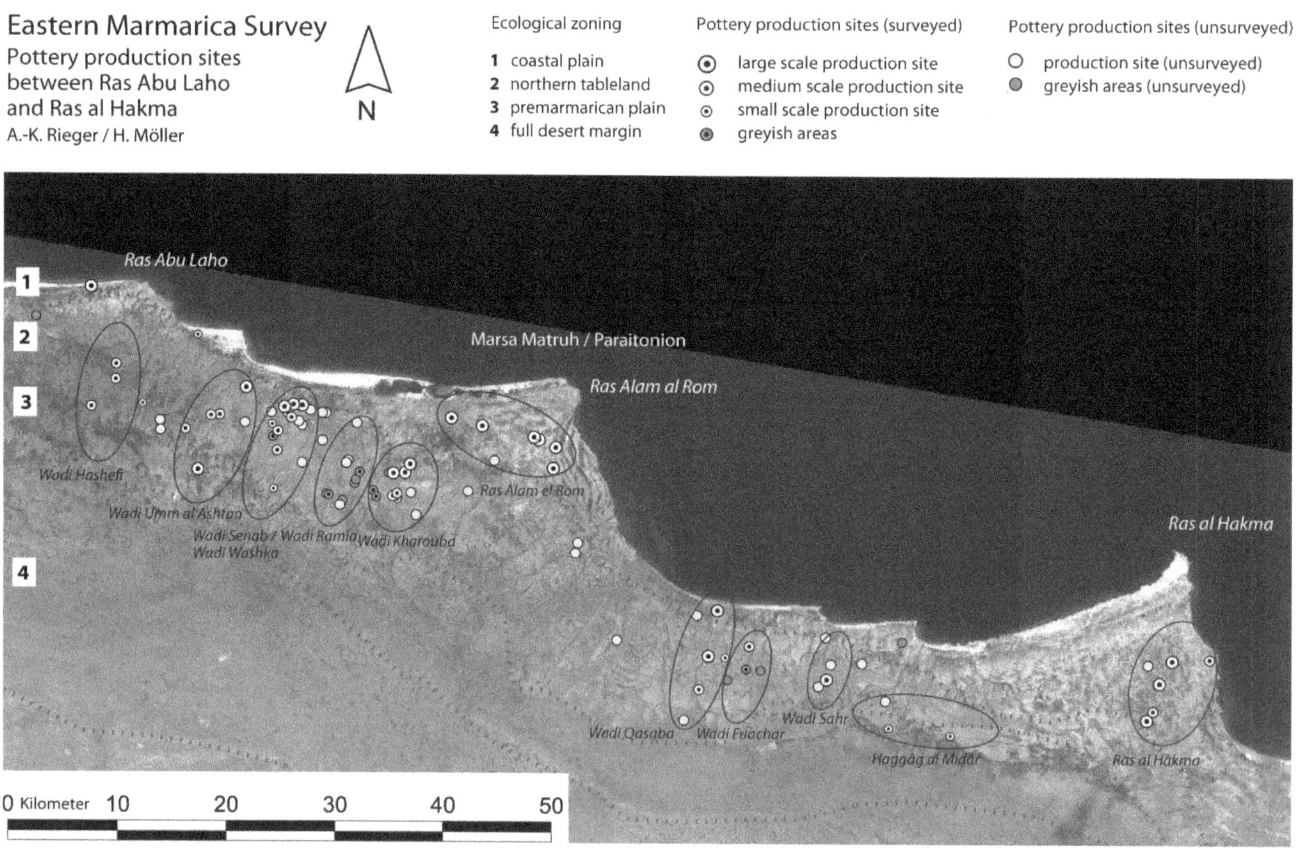

Fig. 2. Pottery production sites in the Eastern Marmarica (Map: A.-K. Rieger, H. Möller)

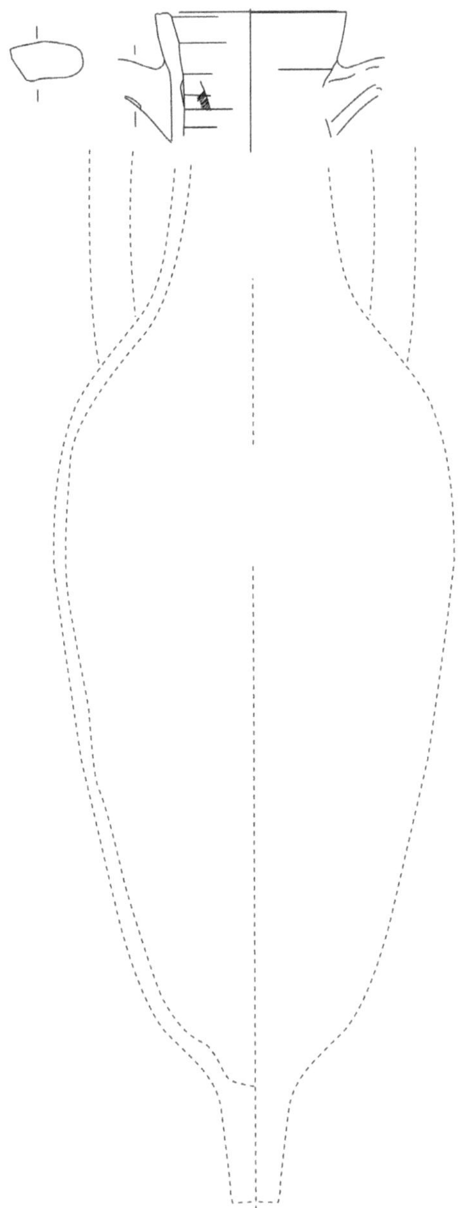

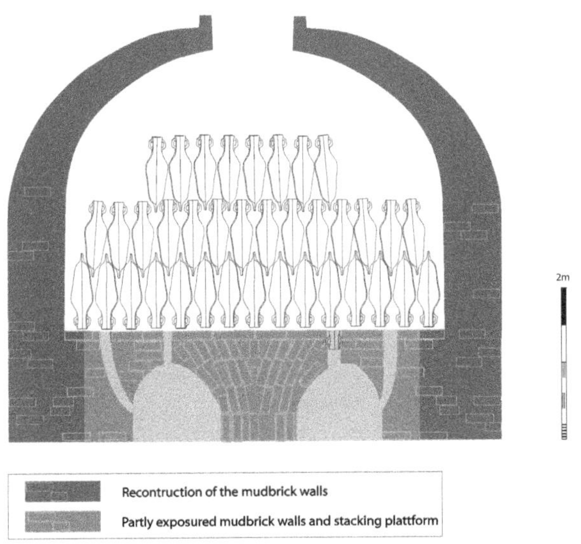

Fig. 3. Roman Amphora Kiln of a Large Scale Production Site in Wadi Qasaba (Reconstruction: H. Möller, A.-K. Rieger)

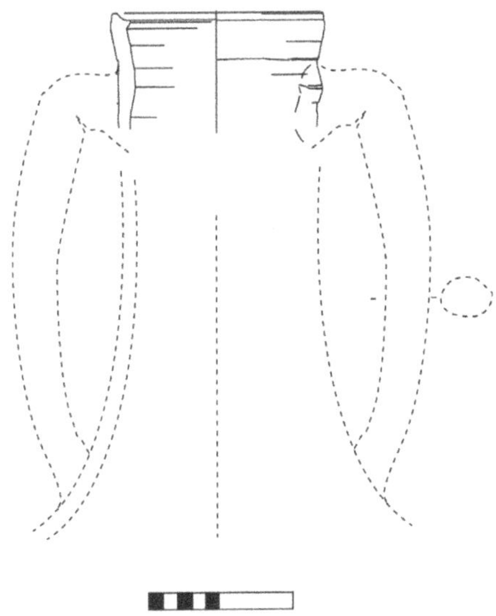

Fig. 4. Eastern Marmarican AE 2-1.1 and AE 2-2.1 Amphorae (after Dixneuf 2011) (Drawings: B. Böhm, H. Möller)

goods of the Western and Eastern Mediterranean since Ptolemaic times, or possibly even earlier.[12]

In summary, the Eastern Marmarica – until a few years ago an archaeologically almost unknown region – reveals remains that are remarkable in many respects: The semi-arid region seems to meet the demand of products by a surplus economy and produces high-quantity containers for the exchange of goods, almost in an 'industrial' sense. Form and fabric of those amphorae show the influence of the neighbouring regions to the east as well as to the west, and the setting of the kiln sites helps to understand their function and production processes, as well as their supply with natural resources. Furthermore, finds along the route network reflect the journey that those containers took and therefore the role that the Marmarica played as a mediator and transition area in all directions in Ptolemaic and Roman times.

Keywords: Eastern Marmarica (northwestern Egypt) – ancient waypoints and routes – Ptolemaic and Roman pottery production sites – amphorae

Heike Möller
Department of Archaeology, University Cologne, Germany.
Email: heike.moeller@uni-koeln.de

Anna - Katharina Rieger
Department of Oriental Art and Archaeology, University of Halle-Wittenberg, Germany.
Email: anna-katharina.rieger@orientarch.uni-halle.de

12 Vetter *et al.* in print_a, Möller in prep.

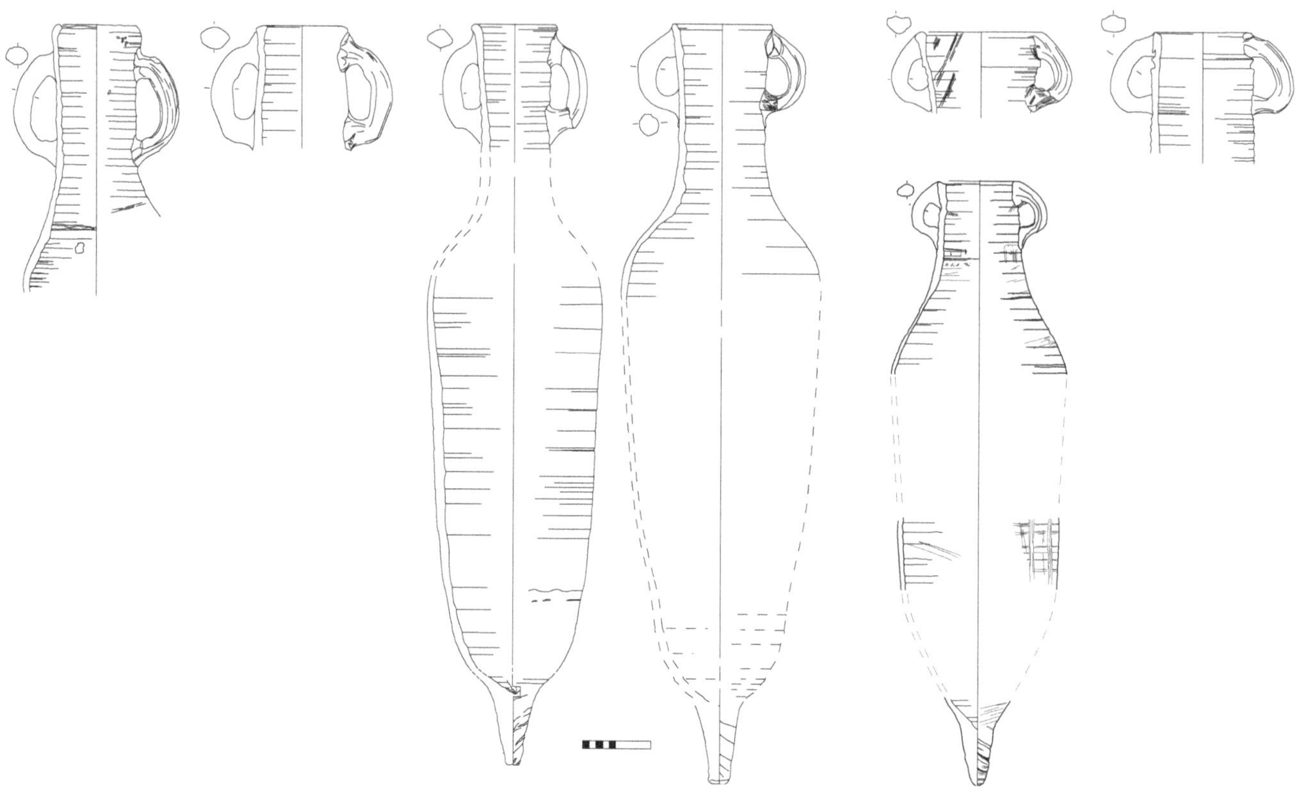

Fig. 5. Eastern Marmarican AE 3-1 and AE 3-2 (after Dixneuf 2011) Amphorae and local variants (Drawings: B. Böhm, H. Möller)

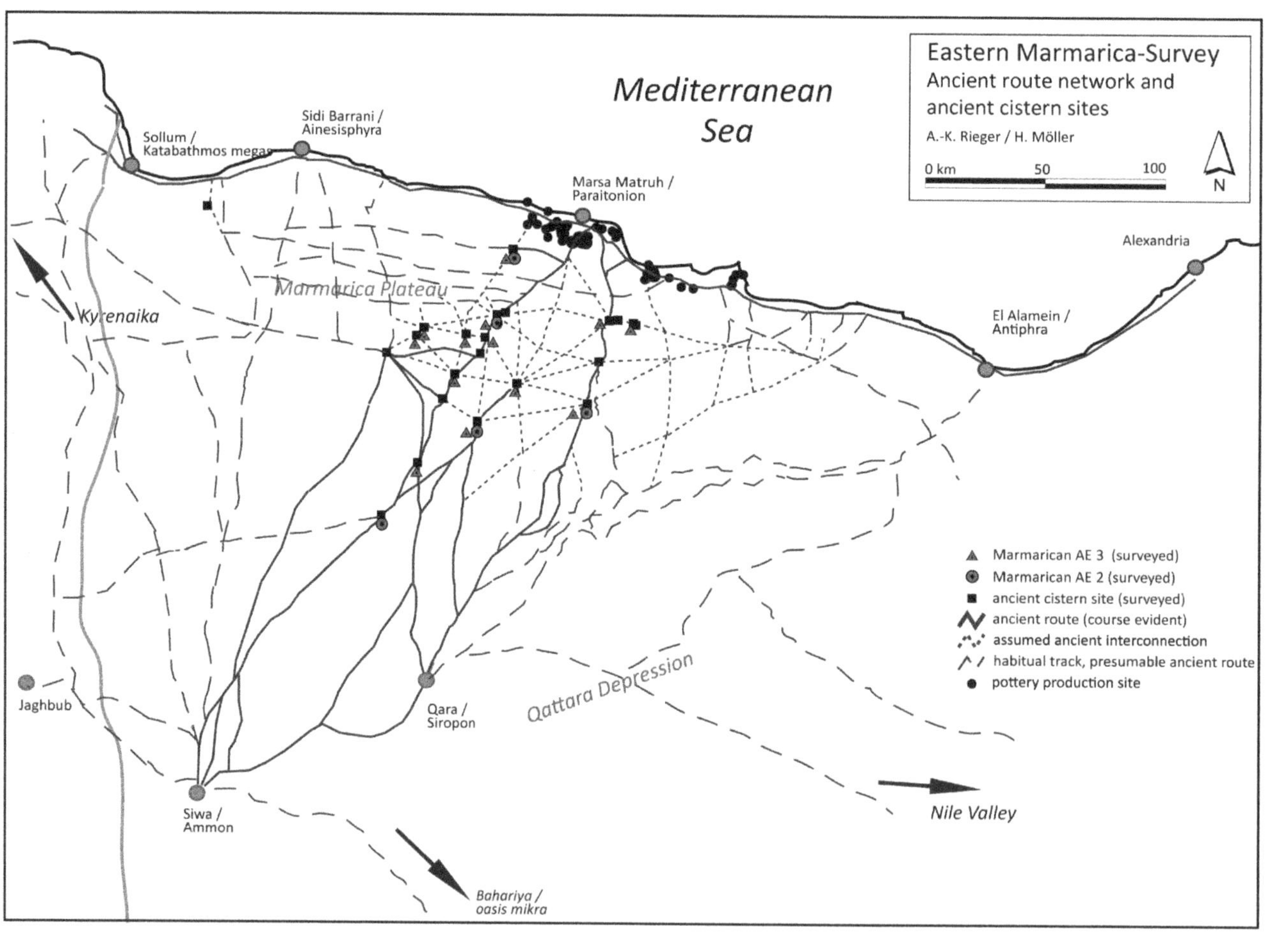

Fig. 6. Ancient Route Network (Map: A.-K. Rieger, H. Möller)

Bibliography

Further reading concerning the Eastern Marmarica:

Bates, O. 1927. Excavations at Marsa Matruh. *Harvard African Studies* 8, 125–97.

Möller, H. in prep. *Ptolemäische und römische Keramik in der antiken Marmarica – Nordwestägyptens Wüstenrandgebiet als Produktionsort und Mittler*, PhD thesis, University of Freiburg im Breisgau.

Rieger, A.-K. 2009. Archäologie eines ariden Raumes: die Strukturierung einer ressourcen- armen Landschaft durch den Menschen am Beispiel der antiken Marmarica (Nordwestägypten), in R. Kath and A.-K. Rieger (eds.), *Raum – Landschaft – Territorium. Zur Konstruktion physischer Räume als nomadischer und sesshafter Lebensraum.* Nomaden und Sesshafte 11, 71–99. Wiesbaden, Reichert.

Rieger, A.-K. and Möller, H. 2011. Kilns, Commodities and Consumers – Greco-Roman Pottery Production in Eastern Marmarica (Northwestern Egypt). *Archäologischer Anzeiger* 2011/1, 141–170.

Rieger, A.-K., Vetter, T. and Möller, H., 2012. The Desert Dwellers of the Marmarica (Western Desert) as a Case Study for the Eastern Desert (?), in H. Barnard and K. Duistermaat (eds.), *The History of the Peoples of the Eastern Desert*, 156–173. Los Angeles, CA, Cotsen Institute of Archeaology Press.

Rieger, A.-K., Möller, H., Valtin, S. and Vetter, T. in print_a for 2012. On the route to Siwa: the ancient roadhouse of Abar el-Kanayis on the Marmarica-Plateau, accepted for *Mitteilungen des Deutschen Archäologischen Instituts, Abteilung Kairo* 68.

Rieger, A.-K. and Möller, H. 2012. Northern Libyan Desert Ware – some news on shell tempered and other hand made pottery from Eastern Marmarica (NW-Egypt). *Libyan Studies* 43, 11–31.

Vetter, T., Rieger, A.-K. and Nicolay, A. 2009. Ancient Rainwater Harvesting System in the north-eastern Marmarica (north-western Egypt). *Libyan Studies* 40, 9–23.

Vetter, T., Rieger, A.-K., Möller, H. and Klammer, O. in print_a. Water, routes and rangelands: Ancient traffic and grazing Infrastructure in the Marmarica (north-western Egypt), in H. Riemer and F. Förster (eds.), *Desert Road Archaeology in Ancient Egypt and Beyond.* Africa Praehistorica 26. Köln, Heinrich-Barth-Institut.

Vetter, T., Rieger, A.-K. and Nicolay, A. in print, Disconnected contributing areas and adapted ancient watershed management in the semi-arid north-eastern Marmarica (NW-Egypt), accepted for *Geomorphology.*

White, D. 2002a. *Marsa Matruh I: The Excavation. The University of Pennsylvania Museum of Archaeology and Anthropology's Excavation on Bates's Island, Marsa Matruh, Egypt 1985–1989.* Prehistory Monographs 1. Philadelphia, Society of Aegean Prehistory.

White, D. 2002b. *Marsa Matruh II: The Objects. The University of Pennsylvania Museum of Archaeology and Anthropology's Excavation on Bates's Island, Marsa Matruh, Egypt 1985–1989.* Prehistory Monographs 2. Philadelphia, Society of Aegean Prehistory.

In general:

Ashmawi, F. el- 1998. Pottery Kiln and Wine-Factory at Burg el-Arab. In J.-Y. Empereur (ed.), *Commerce et artisanat dans l'Alexandrie hellénistique et romain.* Bulletin de Correspondance Hellénique, Supplement 33, 56–64. Athènes, École Française d'Athènes.

Ballet, P. and Dixneuf, D. 2004. Ateliers d'amphores de la *chôra* égyptienne aux époques romaine et byzantine, in J. Eiring and J. Lund (eds.), *Transport Amphorae and Trade in the Eastern Mediterranean.* Acts of the International Colloquium at the Danish Institute at Athens, September 26–29, 2002. Monographs of the Danish Institute at Athens 5, 67–72. Århus, University Press.

Coulson, W. D. E., Wilkie, N. C. and Rehard, J. W. 1986. Amphoras from Naukratis and Environs, in J.-Y. Empereur and Y. Garlan (eds.), *Recherches sur les amphores grecques.* Bulletin de Correspondance Hellénique Supplement 13, 535–550. Athènes, École Française d'Athènes.

Dixneuf, D. 2011. *Amphores égyptiennes. Production, typologie, contenu et diffusion (IIIe siècle avant J.-C. – IXe siècle après J.-C.).* Etudes Alexandrines 22. Alexandria, Centre d'Études Alexandrine.

Empereur, J.-Y. 1986. À la recherche des fours d'amphores, in J.-Y. Empereur and Y. Garlan (eds.), *Recherches sur les amphores grecques.* Bulletin de Correspondance Hellénique Supplement 13, 103–126. Athènes, École Française d'Athènes.

Empereur, J.-Y. 1993. La production viticole dans l'Egypte ptolémaïque et romaine, in M.-C. Amouretti and J.-P. Brun (eds.), *La production du vin et de l'huile en Méditerranée.* Bulletin de Correspondance Hellénique Supplement 26, 9–47. Athènes, École Française d'Athènes.

Empereur, J.-Y. and Picon, M. 1998. Les ateliers d'amphores du Lac Mariout. In J.-Y. Empereur (ed.), *Commerce et artisanat dans l'Alexandrie hellénistique et romain.* Bulletin de Correspondance Hellénique Supplement 33, 75–91. Athènes, École Française d'Athènes.

Hope, C. 1993. Pottery Kilns from the Oasis of el-Dakhla, in D. Arnold and J. Bourriau (eds.), *An Introduction to Ancient Egyptian Pottery,* 121–127. Mainz, Zabern.

Hulin, L., Timby, J. and Mutri, G. 2009. The Western Marmarica Coastal Survey 2009: Preliminary Report. *Libyan Studies* 40, 179–187.

Majcherek, G. and Shennawi, A. el- 1992. Research on Amphorae Production on the Northwestern Coast of Egypt. *Cahiers de la céramique égyptienne* 3, 123–136.

Rodziewicz, M. 1998. Experimental Identification of Pottery from Mareotis. In J.-Y. Empereur (ed.), *Commerce et artisanat dans l'Alexandrie hellénistique et romain.* Bulletin de Correspondance Hellénique Supplement 33, 245–260. Athènes, École Française d'Athènes.

Szymanska, H. and Babraj, K. 2004. Marea Fourth Season of Excavations. *Polish Archaeology in the Mediterranean* 15, 53–62.

Tomber, R. 2006. The Pottery, in V. A. Maxfield and D. P. S. Peacock (eds.), *Survey and Excavations, Mons Claudianus, vol. 3: Ceramic Vessels and Related Objects.* Fouilles de l'Institut français d'archéologie orientale 54, 2006, 1–236.

Exchange of polychromatic painting techniques between Egypt and Greece

Isabella Hodgson

Abstract

In Hellenistic Egypt, as in other areas of the Mediterranean, pottery was painted with tempera colours after firing. The white-ground hydriai form the biggest group within those vases and their production seems to be connected to those of vessels from Rhodes, Cilicia and Cyprus. The emergence of these polychrome vases in Egypt is probably a result of the variety of cultural influences that came into contact with each other in the kingdom of the Ptolemies.

Keywords: tempera painting, polychrome, Egypt, Alexandria, Rhodes, whiteground hydriai, relief ceramics, cinerary vases

Polychrome Ceramics in Egypt

Tempera painted vessels are among the great variety of vases that were used as cinerary urns and grave goods in Hellenistic Egypt. The tempera technique had the advantage of its flexibility and simple execution. This allowed the adoption of other painting styles as well as a fast and easy decoration of clay ground vessels.

Alexandrian white-ground hydriai

About 130 hydriai painted on a white ground with tempera colours were found in Alexandria, half of which are published[1]. All known vessels are from funerary contexts. Their shapes show distinct variations, but generally they are characterised by wide neck diameters, broad shoulders and high handles (**Figs. 1–6**). Most of the hydriai resemble metal vessels quite clearly[2]. Related to the white-ground hydriai in its combination of a Greek shape with a white-ground polychromatic decoration is an oinochoe from the Hadra necropolis[3].

Although archaeometric analyses of Alexandrian clay are missing, the Egyptian origin of these vases is high likely. According to A. Enklaar, white-ground hydriai show a red to greenish coarse clay full of inclusions that also characterizes other Egyptian ceramics[4]. They correspond to descriptions of vases without known context, said to be from Alexandria[5]. Examining a miniature hydria from Alexandria in Bonn, Chr. Römer-Strehl concluded that its rather coarse and micaceous clay could be Egyptian[6]. Finally, Z. Kotitsa found the clay of a hydria in Würzburg to be similar to that of sherds of the Sieglin collection[7].

Most of the Alexandrian hydriai was painted with garlands and ribbons, creating the illusion that they were attached to the neck or handle (**Fig. 1**)[8]. These motives will have been inspired by hydriai in grave contexts that were decorated with real ribbons or garlands[9]. Necklaces serve as neck ornaments, as they did in earlier Attic vase painting, or form the main motif (**Fig. 2**)[10]. Other hydriai are painted with objects connected to the deceased, like attributes of female beauty and elegance or symbols of battle and victory (**Figs. 3–4**)[11]. Grave altars and monuments point directly to the funerary context[12]. A bowl decorated with round objects, and shoes on another vase, are difficult to interpret[13]. Objects of this kind also can be found as separate motifs in Macedonian and Apulian grave paintings[14]. Only one hydria shows the depiction of a figure[15]. The hydriai have been found mostly under grave monuments, in fossa and

---

1 Nenna and Seif El-Din 2000, 144; for the decorated, see below; no preserved or unknown decoration: Adriani 1952, 142 tomb no. 1; Breccia 1909, 23 pl. 11 fig. 11; Breccia 1912, 33. 37 nos. 50. 61–62. 64a pl. 37 fig. 47; Brown 1957, 61 no. 43 pl. 35, 1; CVA Copenhagen 4 pl. 184, 5; Edgar 1911, 49 no. 26254; Edwards 1957, 348 pl. 87.G; Enklaar 1999, 19. 23 fig. 21; New York, Metropolitan Museum, inv. nos. 90.9.59. 90.9.69; Ovidi 1994, 2–3 figs. 2. 5.

2 E.g. cf. Andronikos 1984, 214 fig. 183 with Breccia 1912, 35 nos. 54–55 pl. 39 figs. 50–51; cf. Grammenos 2004, 195 with Adriani 1952, 8. 17 tomb 9 fig. 13.

3 Adriani 1940, 114 pl. 45,5.

4 Enklaar 1986, 41.

5 CVA Copenhagen 4, 143; Edgar 1911, 48–50 nos. 26252-26255; Ovidi 1994, 33 inv. G 594 fn. 10.

6 I owe special thanks to Dr Chr. Römer-Strehl for the kind examination of this hydria (inv. no. 1682).

7 Kotitsa 1998, 88–89; I am grateful to Dr Z. Kotitsa for further information on the clay of this hydria.

8 Adriani 1934, 29 tomb 3 nos. 1–2 pl. 12, 1; Adriani 1952, 8. 17. 25 tomb nos. 9. 42 figs. 13. 20; p. 145 tomb 10; Breccia 1909, 23 pls. 8. 10 figs. 6. 10; Breccia 1912, 33–37 nos. 51–52. 54–60. 63–64 pl. 38, 49; pl. 39, 50–51; Breccia 1930, 118–120 nos. 21887. 21901. 21960. 22015. 22057 pl. 19,1; Edgar 1911, 48–50 nos. 26253. 26255 pl. 19; Hodgson 2010, 66-67 no. 40; Kotitsa 1998, 88–90 no. 70 pl. 37; Parlasca 2010, 283. 288 pl. B, 2; New York, Metropolitan Museum, inv. no. 90.9.55.

9 Andronikos 1984, 214 fig. 183; Breccia 1909, 21–22 figs. 1-2 pls. 7–9; Lohmann 1979, pls. 50, 3; 53, 2.

10 Adriani 1940, 113 pl. 47; Brown 1957, 62 nos. 44–45 pls. 35, 2–36.

11 Breccia 1908, 230; Breccia 1912, 33–35. 37–38 nos. 51–53. 64 b figs. 25–26 pl. 38, 48–49; Breccia 1913, 34 no. 75; Brown 1957, 60–63 nos. 38–41. 44. 46–47 pls. 32–33. 35, 2; pl. 37, 1. 3; New York, Metropolitan Museum, inv. no. 90.9.54.

12 Brown 1957, 60–61 no. 39 pl. 32; Pagenstecher 1913, 47–48 figs. 52–53.

13 Brown 1957, 61 no. 42 pl. 34; Edgar 1911, 48 no. 26252 pl. 19; Parlasca 2010, 282.

14 Brecoulaki 2006, tabs 1. 1; 1. 3; Tinè Bertocchi 1964, 52. 88 figs. 33–34. 68–69.

15 Adriani 1940, 113 fig. 50.

Fig. 1. Breccia 1912, pl. 39 fig. 50

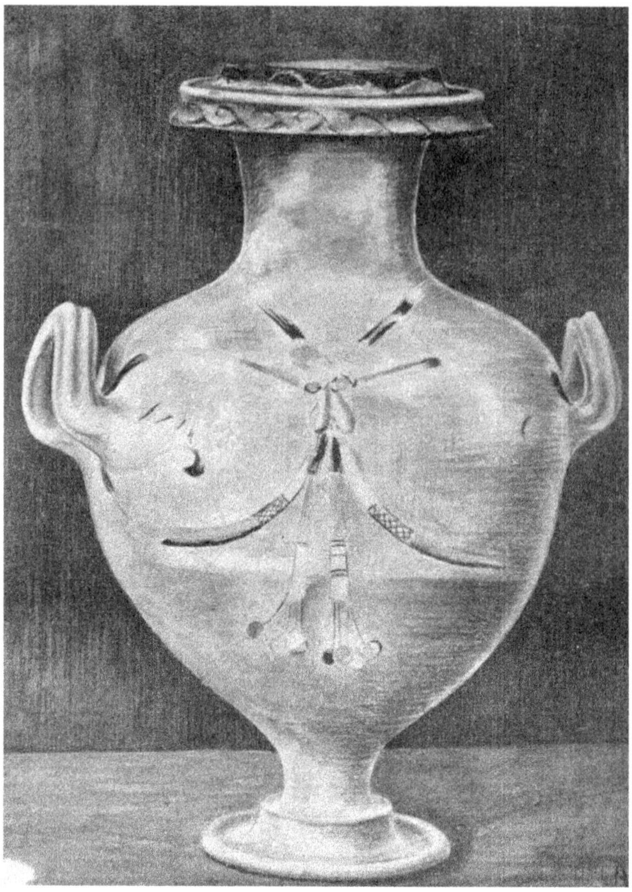

Fig. 2. Adriani 1940, pl. 47 (right fig.)

Fig. 3. Brown 1957, pl. 35, 2

loculus graves that do not allow an internal decoration[16]. Grave goods are often missing as well[17]. The pictures on the vases therefore could be a replacement of both.

There is some evidence for the dating of the vases, but this only allows an approximate chronological ranging. In total, only two find contexts of white-ground hydriai with chronologically significant grave goods have been published. Reasons for this are the laconic documentations of findings, disturbed find contexts and the above-mentioned frequent burying of cinerary urns without grave

16 Adriani 1934, 28–29; Adriani 1952, 8. 17 no. 9; Breccia 1912, XXI–XXII figs. 10–12; LIV no. 12 fig. 17; Breccia 1913, 34 no. 75.
17 Adriani 1952, 15–17. 25 tomb nos. 30–42; Breccia 1912, XXI.

Fig. 4. Breccia 1912, pl. 38 fig. 48

Fig. 5. Enklaar 1999, 23 fig. 21

goods. Fragments of one or more Tanagra figurines in one context can be compared with others dated to the late 4th and early 3rd century BC (**Fig. 9**)[18]. The shape of the two hydriai from this grave especially clearly shows the characteristics described above, i.e. broad shoulders, wide necks, high handles and the proximity to metal vessels (**Fig. 5**). This last feature is emphasized by the simple and low-footed shape of these vases. A bowl from another context shows an angular profile that mostly appears in the 2nd century BC[19]. Sadly, the white-ground polychromatic hydria belonging to this context is unpublished. White-ground and Hadra hydriai are often associated in the graves and their dating will overlap[20]. Decorated Hadra vases were probably produced on Crete from 260 BC until the middle of the 2nd century BC[21]. The vessels of that late stage of development, were presumably no longer exported. Accordingly, A. Enklaar dates the use of these vases in Alexandria between about 260 and 180 BC[22]. Unfortunately, we do not learn exactly which white-ground hydriai were found together with which Hadra vases. Stylistic comparisons with the Hadra hydriai are also not possible, as those vases follow other typologies in shape and decoration. The whiteground polychrome hydriai of Rhodes, on the other hand, show many similarities with those of Alexandria, as will be specified below. Therefore, an exchange with the producers of these vases will have taken place. The Rhodian hydriai date between the early 3rd and the first half of the 2nd century BC (**Figs. 7–8**)[23].

Furthermore, it is known in which necropoleis some of the other vases were found. This would allow us to apply the dating method of A. Enklaar and D. K. Tezgör using the different Alexandrian necropoleis as a horizontal stratigraphy[24]. This approach poses the problem of the long use of these burial places[25]. A. Enklaar partially solves the problem by restricting the datings to special areas within the necropoleis[26]. In the part of the Chatby necropolis which was excavated from 1904 to 1910 mostly

18 Adriani 1934, 29 tomb 3 pls. 11, 1; 12, 2; cf. Besques 1972, 25–26 nos. D 128. D 131. D 134 pl. 28 a. e; pl. 29 a; Burn and Higgins 2001, 55 no. 2082 pls. 16; Jeammet 2003, 182-183 no. 127; Tezgör 2007, 134-135 no. 160 pl. 53-54; Vierneisel-Schlörb 1997, 128 no. 392 pl. 68, 3.

19 Adriani 1952, 142 fig. 70 no. 25; cf. Aston 1999, 340 no. 3029 pl. 115; Giannikourē 1994, 306 pl. 233 ζ; Harlaut 2002, 285 fig. 9 c; 287 fig. 11 d; Lamarche 2003, 141. 174 no. 42; Rappasse 2003, 379. 387 no. 4 fig. 4; Rotroff 1997, 159.

20 Breccia 1913, 30.

21 Englezou 2005, 305–306.

22 Enklaar 1990, 170.

23 Giannikourē 1994, 304.

24 Enklaar 1985, 113; Tezgör 2007, 17–19.

25 Daszewski and Abd-el-Fattah 1990, 441–442; Leclant and Clerc 1988, 310; Leclant and Clerc 1990, 339.

26 Enklaar 1985, 113.

Fig. 6. Adriani 1934, pl. 12, 1

Fig. 7. Giannikourē 1994, pl. 234 β

Fig. 8. Giannikourē 1994, pl. 237 γ

vases from the late 4th and the 3rd century BC were found[27]. Therefore, it might not be a coincidence that the hydriai depicted in the publication of this excavation show rather simple and low feet similar to the two found with fragments of the Tanagra figurines (**Figs. 1. 4. 6**)[28]. Three other comparable vessels found in areas of the Hadra necropolis are dated after the middle of the 3rd century BC (**Figs. 2. 5**)[29]. Those vases show slightly slimmer and higher feet, which could indicate a tendency of development. Altogether, it can be stated that Alexandrian white-ground

27 Rotroff 1997, 29–31.
28 Breccia 1912, 34 fig. 25 pls. 38–39.
29 Adriani 1940, 113 pl. 47; Enklaar 1999, 23–24 fig. 21.

polychrome hydriai were produced in the 3rd and 2nd century BC. Their production will probably not have started long before or after the beginning of the 3rd century, when the first Rhodian hydriai were made.

As to who was buried in those hydriai, we have only a few indications. According to their iconography they will have been used for burials of men and women of a Greek background. Two incised inscriptions mention Chios and Ptolemais as places of origin of the deceased[30]. This suggests that the white-ground hydriai, like the Hadra vases, served as cinerary urns for people of various origins.

Tempera painting of Ptolemaic relief ceramics and figurative vases

Two bowls, two bottles and one alabastron of the Ptolemaic relief ceramics are decorated with polychrome tempera colours (**Fig. 10**)[31]. Also, two Egyptian figurative vessels are polychrome[32]. Those vase types are related to each other in their composition of two mould-cast halves[33]. One figurative vase and an alabastron were dug out in Alexandria, whereas another figurative vase was bought in Zagazig near Bubastis and could have been found close by[34]. A more precise dating of these vases than to the Ptolemaic Period is difficult. Sadly, finds associated with these vessels are unknown and the stylistic comparanda either themselves have an uncertain dating or their chronological range is too wide to be of any relevance[35].

The polychromy of the figurative and relief vessels can be due to the use of coroplastic relief techniques that are strongly related to tempera painting. Another reason for polychromy seems to have been the imitation of fayence vases[36]. Other polychrome Alexandrian vases may also have had an influence.

Small polychromatic vessels from Alexandria

A number of small vases were found in the necropoleis of Moustapha Pasha and Hadra that were painted with polychrome colours after firing. They include an alabastron, a stand, miniature amphoras and a jug (**Fig. 11**)[37]. The decoration consists of geometric motives, branches, leaves, human figures and animals[38]. Some of the vases were painted directly on the clay ground[39]. Presumably

Fig. 9. Adriani 1934, pl. 11, 1

the others also lack priming, as their description mentions white geometric motifs[40]. The shape of the biconical alabastra and the necropoleis in which these vases were found point to the Ptolemaic period[41]. One vessel was associated in a grave with a Megarian bowl of the PAR monogram workshop, active at least from the third to the last quarter of the 2nd century BC[42]. The decoration of this kind of Egyptian vases might also have been inspired by other tempera painted local wares, but there is no sign of external influence. Hellenistic vases decorated directly on the clay ground are comparatively rare, but there are other examples found in Macedonia and Israel[43].

Polychrome vessels related to the white-ground hydriai outside Egypt

Hydriai with related shape and decoration

Like the Alexandrian vases, the Rhodian hydriai show wide neck diameters, high handles and broad shoulders,

30 Brown 1957, 62 no. 45 pl. 36; Edgar 1911, 49 no. 26254.
31 Mandel-Elzinga 1988, 266–267; Pagenstecher 1913, 72. 198–199 nos. 1–2 pl. 24, 1. 2; Wildung and Grimm 1978, no. 119; Schmidt 1997, 116–117 no. 164 pl. 54; Schürmann 1989, 329–330 no. 1247 pl. 206.
32 Adriani 1940, 107 no. 25050 pl. 38,1; Weber 1914, 184–185 no. 308 pl. 29.
33 cf. Fjeldhagen 1995, 198 no. 199; Mandel-Elzinga 1988, 248–249.
34 Adriani 1940, 107 no. 25050; Weber 1914, 185; Wildung and Grimm 1978, no. 119.
35 cf. Mandel-Elzinga 1988, 256–257. 266–267; Nenna and Seif El-Din 2000, 186.
36 Mandel-Elzinga 1988, 256.
37 Adriani 1936, 144–145 fig. 65, 2; Adriani 1940, 113–114 pl. 46, 4; Breccia 1913, 26.
38 Adriani 1936, 145; Adriani 1940, 113–114; Breccia 1913, 26.
39 Breccia 1913, 26.

40 Adriani 1936, 145; Adriani 1940, 113–114.
41 Mandel-Elzinga 1988, 252.
42 Adriani 1936, 144–145 fig. 65,2; Kerschner *et al.* 2002, 197; Rogl 2001, 103–104 fn. 28.
43 Herbert 1980, 29–30 fig. 5; Kotitsa 1996, 142 fn. 1275.

Fig. 10. Wildung and Grimm 1978, no. 119

Fig. 11. Adriani 1940, pl. 46, 4

but generally their necks are more cylindrical and their shoulders more slopping (**Figs. 7–8**)[44]. Furthermore, in contrast to the Alexandrian hydriai, the Rhodian pieces have a largely uniform stepped foot. Like the Alexandrian hydriai, the Rhodian are painted with garlands and ribbons, but unlike them they never show objects[45]. The general similarities are such that a completely independent emergence of both productions seems improbable. On the other hand, the differences point to an independent development. Archaeometric analyses of those vessels have shown that they were made locally[46]. In the Cilician Kelenderis a hydria was found that is painted with ribbons on a white ground. This vase is comparatively slim, but the broad slopping shoulders, high handles, the stepped foot and the painted decoration remind one of the above described Rhodian vases (**Fig. 12**)[47]. Thus, the hydriai of Alexandria, Rhodes and Cilicia seem to be related to each other. Because of the geographical proximity to Egypt, the decoration of a Cypriote Hellenistic jug on a white ground with garlands and ribbons could be inspired by the white-ground polychrome hydriai of Alexandria as well[48].

In recent excavations at Thebes, two hydriai have been found that can also be compared with the Alexandrian and Rhodian ones. First information about those vases was published in the years 1999 and 2000. The first, like the Alexandrian and Rhodian hydriai, has high handles, a wide neck diameter and a voluminous body that expands towards the shoulders[49]. The vase is referred to as a Hadra vase[50]. This term is sometimes used for the white-ground polychrome hydriai of Alexandria, and, according to the shape of this vessel, must apply here as well. Another hydria found at Thebes is decorated with a polychrome garland on a white ground[51]. Its egg-shaped body can be compared to this of a white-ground hydria from the surroundings of Alexandria[52]. This hydria, on the other hand, itself is exceptional among the Alexandrian polychrome vases. The final publication of the hydriai found in Thebes will allow further conclusions about relations between Boeotia and Alexandria or Rhodes.

Imitations of metal hydriai in Tarent

In Tarent, like in Alexandria, clay hydriai covered with a white slip imitated the shape of metal vessels (**Fig. 13**)[53]. These vases will originally have been painted with tempera colours as well. This practice dates to the end of the 4th or in the early 3rd century BC, probably caused by the increase of cremation since the middle of the 4th

44 cf. Giannikourē 1994, pls. 234–245; Kotitsa 1998, 89–90.
45 Giannikourē 1994, 307–309.
46 Giannikourē *et al.* 2008, 569.
47 cf. Giannikourē 1994, pls. 234 β; 237 δ; 239 α. β; 243 α. β; Zoroglu 2004, 305–306 pls. 109, 4; 112 b.
48 Vandenabeele 1998, 216–218 nos. 310.Z-313.Z. 315.Z pls. 131-132.
49 Aravantinos 2000, 382 fig. 4.
50 Aravantinos 2000, 382.
51 Kountourē 1999, 323 fig. 15.
52 Kountourē 1999, 323 fig. 15; Parlasca 2010, 283. 288 pl. B, 2.
53 D'Amicis 1994, 157 pl. 7; Graepler 1997, 48 fn. 82 drawing p. 96 (no. 155.18).

Fig. 12. Zoroglu 2004, pl. 112 b

Fig. 13. D'Amicis 1994, pl. 7

century BC[54]. The Tarentine hydriai, however, adopt the shape of local types of metal vases with spherical bodies[55]. Although no evidence of direct exchange can be detected, the emergence of those vases in both places is due to the same phenomenon, i.e. the demand for prestigious, as well as affordable, cinerary urns. Phenomena like this can explain the sudden increase in popularity experienced by polychrome vessels at the beginning of the Hellenistic Period.

Illusionistic decoration of other shapes

Ribbons, garlands and necklaces can also be found on other Hellenistic tempera painted vessels of the Greek mainland and Italy[56]. However, if their shapes cannot be compared to those of Alexandrian or Rhodian hydriai, the influence of those vases is questionable. Other sources of inspirations existed. K. Parlasca assumes an older Attic tradition of such motives[57]. Indeed, as early as the end of the 5th century BC, the polychrome technique was used to paint ribbons round the necks of white-ground polychrome Attic jugs[58]. Late Classical black glazed vases decorated with golden necklaces and wreaths can also be regarded as precursors of illusionistic vase painting in the Hellenistic period[59]. Overall, the spread of such motifs in the paintings of vases used as grave goods and cinerary urns should not be studied separately from their use in other funerary arts. Illusionistic garlands and ribbons are widespread in the grave paintings of Greece and Italy, and they also appear in those of Alexandria[60]. A main reason for the frequent occurrence of such motives on polychrome vases seems to be the flexibility of the tempera technique, which allows the adoption of elements from various sources.

Forms of exchange

Of particular interest is the connection between the Alexandrian and the Rhodian hydriai. M. D. Nenna and M. Seif El–Din imply that the local origin of the Alexandrian

54 D'Amicis 1994, 152.
55 D'Amicis 1994, 153. 157 fig. 132.
56 Gabrici 1910, 58. 96. 117. 130; Kotitsa 1996, 141–144. 198 nos. HKMIV. SKMI a–c color pl. 2; pls. 35–36; E. Kountourē, 1999, 323 fig. 15; Van der Wielen 1985, 67–68 no. 74 fig. 67.
57 Parlasca 2010, 289.

58 Crosby 1955, 78–81 nos. 1–3 pls. 34a. 35–36 a. 37 b.
59 CVA Berlin 9, pls. 48–54.
60 Adriani 1940, 85 fig. 42; pp. 118–119 figs. 54, 2. 5; Adriani 1952, 98 fig. 58; Breccia, 1912, 19 no. 23 pl. 33, 38; Brecoulaki 2006, pls. 79–80; 82, 2; 88, 4; Brown 1957, 55 no. 37 pl. 30; Steingräber 1991, 18-19 and tabular overview; Tinè Bertocchi 1964, 71. 80. 82. 88-89. 91. 98. 105 figs. 48. 60. 62–63. 68–71. 77. 85.

white-ground hydriai is questionable because of the large number of similar vessels from Rhodes[61]. The above-mentioned differences between the vessels speak in favor of the existence of two independent centers of production. However, it is probable that one group was produced first and inspired the emergence of the other. Although it is impossible to exclude a Rhodian origin, some observations speak in favour of an Alexandrian invention of those vases.

Alexandria, which received settlers from numerous regions of the Mediterranean, saw the confluence of various pottery traditions. As such, in Macedonia the polychrome technique was already being used in the 4th century BC to decorate hydriai used as grave offerings[62]. A Macedonian influence on cinerary urns in Alexandria would not be surprising, as cremation was as widespread in Macedonia as in Alexandria, and members of the Ptolemaic dynasty had been buried in hydriai[63]. Furthermore, the order of the ash layers in an Alexandrian hydria according to A.-M. Guimier-Sorbets and Y. Morizot might show Macedonian influence on the local burial customs[64]. However, not only is the production of polychrome hydriai for Macedonians living in Alexandria possible, other immigrants could have been familiar with such ceramics in the funerary context as well. Attic potters decorated vessels with tempera colours in the last third of the 5th and the first half of the 4th century BC[65]. Such vases were also produced to a limited extent in Classical Boeotia, Locris and Cyprus[66]. Western Greek influence was transmitted by commerce and immigration, and the Egyptian tradition of polychrome vase painting was resumed after an interval in the Late Period[67]. Therefore, the white-ground hydriai could be the product of the fusing of such influences.

In the exchange between productions of Alexandria and Rhodes, Cyprus and Cilicia a *koine* of burial customs could have played an important role. So Rhodians, Cypriotes and Cilicians had cremation burials in cinerary hydriai in Alexandria and were buried in the same way in their home regions[68]. Therefore, migration may have played an important role in the spread of polychrome painted pottery.

My special thanks go to the German Academic Exchange Service (DAAD) for an one-year scholarship that allowed me to study polychrome vases in Greece and Italy.

Isabella Hodgson
Koraka 64
GR-10445 Athens
isabella.hodgson@googlemail.com

Bibliography

Adriani, A. 1934. *Annuario del Museo Greco Romano, 1: 1932–1933*. Alexandria, Société de publications égyptiennes.

Adriani, A. 1936. *Annuaire du Musée Gréco-Romain, 1: 1933–1935*. Alexandria, Société de publications égyptiennes.

Adriani, A. 1940. *Annuaire du Musée Gréco-Romain, 2: 1935–1939*. Alexandria, Société de publications égyptiennes.

Adriani, A. 1952. *Annuaire du Musée Gréco-Romain, 3: 1940–1950*. Alexandria, Société de publications égyptiennes.

Andreiomenou, A. 1985. Βοιωτικά αγγεία του 5ου αι. π.Χ. από το νεκροταφείο της Ακραιφίας, in *Πρακτικά του XII Διεθνούς Συνεδρίου Κλασικής Αρχαιολογία ς, Αθήνα 4–10 Σεπτεμβρίου 1983, 2*, 7–14. Athens, TAP.

Andronikos, M. 1984. *Vergina*. Athens, Εκδοτική θηνών.

Aravantinos, V. 2000. *Αρχαιολογικόν Δελτίον Χρονικα* 55, 377–393.

Aston, D. A. 1999. *Elephantine 19: Pottery from the Late New Kingdom to the Early Ptolemaic Period*. Mainz, Zabern.

Besques, S. 1972. *Catalogue raisonné des figurines et reliefs grecs, étrusques et romains* 3. Paris, Editions des Musées Nationaux.

Breccia, E. 1908. Cronaca del museo e degli scavi e ritrovamenti. *Bulletin de la Société archéologique d'Alexandrie* 10, 35–86.

Breccia, E. 1909. Ghirlandomania Alessandrina. In M. G. Maspero (ed.), *Le Musée Égyptien* 3, 13–25. Cairo, Imprimerie de l'Institut français d'archéologie orientale.

Breccia, E. 1912. *La necropoli di Sciatbi*. Cairo, IFAO.

Breccia, E. 1913. *Rapport sur la marche du Service du Musée d'Alexandrie, en 1912*. Alexandria, Société de publications égyptiennes.

Breccia, E. 1930. Nuovi scavi nelle Necropoli di Hadra. *Bulletin de la Societe archeologique d'Alexandrie* 25, 98–132.

Brecoulaki, H. 2006. *La peinture funéraire de Macédonie*, 2. Athens, Κέντρον Ελληνικής και Ρωμαϊκής Αρχαιότητος του Εθνικού Ιδρύματος Ερευνών.

Brown, B. R. 1957. *Ptolemaic paintings and mosaics*

61 Nenna and Seif El-Din 2000, 144.
62 Kyriakou 2008, 276.
63 Parlasca 2010, 292 (Pol. XV 25, 6; 11).
64 Guimier-Sorbets and Morizot 2005, 144. 148
65 Crosby 1955, 76; Mertens 2006, 191; Trumpf-Lyritzaki 1969, 105; Zervoudaki 1968, 20–21. 32 nos. 17–21. 60 pls. 20, 1; 20, 2.
66 Andreiomenou 1985, 11; Kephalidou 2001, 193–194; Vandenabeele 1998, 45–46.
67 Arnold and Bourriau 1993, 98–99; Breccia 1912, 188–190 nos. 617–624 pls. 81–82; Schmidt 2005, 267.
68 Enklaar 1985, 145–146 fig. 23.

and the Alexandrian style. Cambridge, Mass., Archaeological Institute of America.

Burn, L. and Higgins, R. 2001. *Catalogue of Greek terracottas in the British Museum*, 3. London, British Museum Press.

Crosby, M. 1955. Five Comic Scenes from Athens. *Hesperia* 24, 76–84.

Daszewski, W. A. and Abd-el-Fattah, A. 1990. A hellenistic painting from Alexandria with landscape elements, in *Akten des XIII. Internationalen Kongresses für Klassische Archäologie, Berlin 1988*, 441–442. Mainz, Zabern.

D'Amicis, A. 1994. I sistemi riutali: l'incinerazione, in E. Lippolis (ed.), *Catalogo del Museo Nazionale Archeologico di Taranto*, 3,1, 149–173. Taranto, La Colomba.

Edgar, C. C. 1911. *Greek Vases*. Cairo, IFAO.

Edwards, G. R. 1957. Panathenaics of Hellenistic and Roman Times. *Hesperia* 26, 320–349.

Englezou, M. 2005. *Ελληνιστική Κεραμική Κρήτης*. Athens, TAP.

Enklaar, A. 1985. Chronologie et peintres des hydries de Hadra. *Bulletin antieke beschaving* 60, 106–146.

Enklaar, A. 1986. Les hydries de Hadra, 2. Formes et ateliers. *Bulletin antieke beschaving* 61, 41–63.

Enklaar, A. 1990. Ariadne's thread in the chronology of Hellenistic pottery: The Hadra Vases, in *Β΄ Επιστημονική Συνάντηση για την Ελληνιστική Κεραμεική. Ρόδος 1989*, 167–171. Athens, TAP.

Enklaar, A. 1999. Preliminary report on the pottery found at Hadra Station in 1987, in J.-Y. Empereur (ed.), *Commerce et artisanat dans l'Alexandrie hellénistique et romaine.* Actes du colloque d'Athènes, 11–12 décembre 1988. Bulletin de Correspondance Hellénique Supplementary Volume 33, 15–24. Athens, École Francaise d'Athènes/ Paris, De Boccard.

Fjeldhagen, M. 1995. *Graeco-Roman Terracottas from Egypt*. Copenhagen, Ny Carlsberg Glyptotek.

Gabrici, E. 1910. Necropoli di età ellenistica a Teano dei Sidicini. *Monumenti Antichi* 20, 7–151.

Giannikourē, A. 1994. Υδρίες Hadra με λευκό βάθος από τη Ρόδο. In *Γ΄ Επιστημονική Συνάντηση για την Ελληνιστική Κεραμική. Θεσσαλονίκη 1991*, 302–310. Athens, Archetai.

Giannikourē, A., Sister Daniilia, Andrikopoulos, K., Sotiropoulou, S. and Chryssoulakis, Y. 2008. The Decoration of the "White Ground Hydriai Hadra" from the Rhodian Potters' Workshop: A preliminary study, in G. Phakorellis, N. Zacharias and K. Polikreti (eds.), *Proceedings of the 4th Symposium of the Hellenic Society for Archaeometry*, National Hellenic Research Foundation, Athens, 28–31 May 2003. British Archaeological Reports International series 1746, 569–577. Oxford, BAR Publishing.

Graepler, D. 1997. *Tonfiguren im Grab*. München, Biering und Brinkmann.

Grammenos, D. V. 2004. *Το Αρχαιολογικό Μουσείο Θεσσαλονίκης*. Athens, ΟΛΚΟΣ.

Guimier-Sorbets, A.-M. and Morizot, Y. 2005. Des bûchers de Vergina aux hydries de Hadra: découvertes récentes sur la crémation en Macédoine et à Alexandrie. *Ktèma* 30, 137–152.

Harlaut, C. 2002. Productions Céramiques Égyptiennes d'Alexandrie, in F. Blondé, P. Ballet and J.-F. Salles (eds.), *Céramiques hellénistiques et romaines. Productions et diffusion en Méditerranée orientale*, 263–287. Lyon, Maison de l'Orient Méditerranéen–Jean Pouilloux.

Herbert, S. C. 1980. Tel Anafa, 1980. *Muse* 14, 24–30.

Hodgson, I. 2010. Polychromie, in M. Bentz, W. Geominy and M. Müller (eds.), *TonArt. Virtuosität antiker Töpfertechnik*. Ausstellungskatalog, 60–67. Petersberg, Dr. M. Imhof.

Jeammet, V. 2003. Femme drapée, in *Tanagras, Mythe et archéologie*. Catalogue d'exposition Paris, 182–186. Paris, Éditions de la Réunion des musées nationaux.

Kephalidou, E. 2001. Late archaic polychrome Pottery from Aiani. *Hesperia* 70, 183–219.

Kerschner, M., Mommsen, H., Rogl, Ch. and Schwedt, A. 2002. Die Keramikproduktion von Ephesos in griechischer Zeit. Zum Stand der archäometrischen Forschungen. *Jahreshefte des Österreichischen Archäologischen Institutes in Wien* 71, 189–206.

Kountourē, E. 1999. *Αρχαιολογικόν Δελτίον Χρονικα* 54, 318–323.

Kotitsa, Z. 1996. *Hellenistische Tonpyxiden.* Mainz, Zabern.

Kotitsa, Z. 1998. *Hellenistische Keramik im Martin von Wagner Museum der Universität Würzburg.* Würzburg, Ergon Verlag.

Kyriakou, A. 2008. *Η Στενόμακρη Τούμπα της Βεργίνας.* Thessaloniki, Σφακιανάκη Κορνηλία.

Lamarche, A. 2003. La céramique. Secteur 2 de la Fouille du Pont Gabbari, in J.-Y. Empereur and M.-D. Nenna (eds.), *Nécropolis* 2,1, 111–190. Cairo, IFAO.

Leclant, J. and Clerc, G. 1988. Fouilles et travaux en Égypte et au Soudan, 1986–1987. *Orientalia* 57, 307–404.

Leclant, J. and Clerc, G. 1990. Fouilles et travaux en Égypte et au Soudan, 1988–1989. *Orientalia* 59, 335–439.

Lohmann, H. 1979. *Grabmäler auf unteritalischen Vasen.* Berlin, Gebr. Mann Verlag.

Mandel-Elzinga, U. 1988. Ptolemäische Reliefkeramik. *Jahrbuch des Deutschen Archäologischen Instituts* 103, 247–307.

Mertens, J. R. 2006. Attic White Ground: Potter and Painter. In B. Cohen (ed.), *The Colors of Clay*, 185–238. Los Angeles, J. Paul Getty Museum.

Nenna, M.-D. and Seif El-Din, M. 2000. *La vaisselle en faïence d'époque gréco-romaine*. Cairo, IIFAO.

Ovidi, S. 1994. Un contributo al corpus delle hydriae di Hadra. *Bollettino d'Arte* 79, 1–36.

Pagenstecher, R. 1913. *Expedition Ernst von Sieglin. Ausgrabungen in Alexandria 2. Die griechisch-*

ägyptische Sammlung Ernst von Sieglin 3. Die Gefässe in Stein und Ton, Knochenschnitzereien. Leipzig, Giesecke & Devrient.

Parlasca, K. 2010. Alexandrinische Aschenurnen. *Chronique d'Égypte* 85, 278–294.

Rappasse J. 2003. La Céramique hellénistique. Secteur 5 de la fouille du Pont de Gabbari, in J.-Y. Empereur and M.-D. Nenna (eds.), *Nécropolis* 2, 2, 375–389. Cairo, IFAO.

Rogl, Ch. 2001. Eine Vorschau zu den reliefverzierten Trinkbechern der ephesischen Monogramm-Werkstätte. In F. Krinzinger (ed.), *Studien zur hellenistischen Keramik in Ephesos*. Ergänzungshefte zu den Jahresheften des Österreichischen Archäologischen Instituts 2, 99–111.

Rotroff, S. I. 1997. *Hellenistic Pottery: Athenian and imported wheelmade table ware and related material.* The Athenian Agora XXIX. Princeton, NJ., Princeton Academic Press.

Schmidt, St. 1997. *Katalog der ptolemäischen und kaiserzeitlichen Objekte aus Ägypten im Akademischen Kunstmuseum Bonn.* Munich, Biering und Brinkmann.

Schmidt, St. 2005. Das hellenistische Alexandria als Drehscheibe des kulturellen Austauschs? In H. Beck (ed.), *Ägypten Griechenland Rom. Abwehr und Berührung.* Ausstellungskatalog, 267–278. Frankfurt, Das Städel.

Schürmann, W. 1989. *Katalog der antiken Terrakotten im Badischen Landesmuseum, Karlsruhe*. Göteborg, P. Åström.

Steingräber, St. 1991. Zu Entstehung, Verbreitung und architektonischem Kontext der unteritalischen Grabmalerei. *Jahrbuch des Deutschen Archäologischen Instituts* 106, 1–36.

Tezgör, D. K. 2007. *Tanagréennes d'Alexandrie.* Cairo, IFAO.

Tinè Bertocchi, F. 1964. *La Pittura Funeraria Apula.* Naples, Macchiaroli.

Trumpf-Lyritzaki, M. 1969. *Griechische Figurenvasen des Reichen Stils und der Späten Klassik.* Bonn, Bouvier.

Van der Wielen-van Ommeren, F. 1985. *La céramique à décor polychrome et plastique dite de Canosa.* Unpublished PhD thesis, Université de Genève.

Vandenabeele, F. 1998. *Figurines on Cypriote jugs holding an oinochoe.* Jonsered, P. Åströms Förlag.

Vierneisel-Schlörb, B. 1997. *Die figürlichen Terrakotten.* Kerameikos XV. Munich, Hirmer Verlag.

Weber, W. 1914. *Die ägyptisch-griechischen Terrakotten.* Berlin, K. Curtius.

Wildung, D. and Grimm, G. 1978. *Götter Pharaonen.* Recklinghausen, A. Bongers.

Zervoudaki, E. A. 1968. Attische polychrome Reliefkeramik des späten 5. und des 4. Jahrhunderts v. Chr. *Mitteilungen des Deutschen Archäologischen Instituts, Athenische Abteilung* 83, 1–88.

Zoroglu, L. 2004. Hellenistic Pottery from Kelenderis. In *ΣΤ' Επιστημονική Συνάντηση για την Ελληνιστική Κεραμική*. Βόλος 2000, 299–309. Athens, TAP.

Levant up to Central Asia

Hellenistische Keramik im Nordsyrischen Hinterland - Funde vom Dülük Baba Tepesi

Eva Strothenke

Abstract

On the top of Dülük Baba Tepesi, a hill in the province of Gaziantep and ancient Commagene the primal sanctuary of Iupiter Dolichenus can be located. After the end of the cult a lot of Christian finds and even inscriptions confirm the existence of a monastery on the hill after the pagan cults were gone. The pottery-fragments spread from the Iron Age to the Islamic times. The amount of Hellenistic pottery is in comparison to ceramics from other periods marginal. One can observe that mainly a light brown fine ware with a colored slip from red to brown occurs which seems to be a local/regional fabrication. Shapes like bowls with incurved rims and plates with a central depression reminding of pre-Hellenistic and Hellenistic bowls and fish-plates in black coated ware are common. Therefore it seems that the finds from Dülük Baba Tepesi are local imitations. Another type of Hellenistic pottery is the fusiform unguentarium in a grey fabric. These vessels are very common in the North-Syrian region but a chronological frame in regard to shape and its changes cannot be given. In fact the unguentaria are affected by regional impacts so that only a relative chronology dependent on the shape can be worked out.

Keywords: Südost-Türkei, lokale Ware mit schwarzem Glanzton, Echinus-Schalen, Fischteller, Unguentaria

Einleitung*

Seit 2001 erforscht die 'Forschungsstelle Asia Minor' der Westfälischen Wilhelms-Universität Münster unter der Leitung von Engelbert Winter den Dülük Baba Tepesi in der heutigen Südost-Türkei nahe der Provinzhauptstadt Gaziantep[1]. Der ca. 1200m hohe Hügel ist in der antiken Landschaft Kommagene gelegen und beheimatete das Ursprungsheiligtum des Iupiter Dolichenus, der in römischer Zeit im gesamten Imperium Romanum große Beliebtheit genoss und dessen Kult sich im gesamten Reich etablierte[2]. Die noch andauernden Untersuchungen konnten neben einer Nutzung des Gipfelplateaus in römischer Zeit vor allem eine Kontinuität der Besiedlung von der vorhellenistischen bis in die islamische Zeit belegen. Neuzeitliche Störungen in Form von illegal errichteten Antennen mit tief in den Boden reichenden Betonfundamenten sowie der Einsatz von schweren Baggern zur Planierung des Plateaus, haben jedoch dazu geführt, dass nur selten ungestörte Kontexte zu Tage treten. Eine schematische Kartierung des keramischen Fundmaterials konnte aber dennoch zeigen, dass auf dem Hügel bestimmte Bereiche schwerpunktmäßig in bestimmten Epochen genutzt bzw. in späterer Zeit weniger intensiv neu besiedelt wurden. So lassen sich zwei Arbeitsbereiche klar umreißen, in denen hellenistisches bis späthellenistisch-frührömisches Material den deutlichsten Anteil ausmacht (Arbeitsbereich A und B; **Abb. 1**). Auch die Grabungsergebnisse in Hinblick auf die Befundsituationen, freigelegten Mauerzüge sowie die Kleinfunde unterstützen eine zeitliche Einordnung dieser Bereiche in die hellenistische bis frührömische Besiedlungsphase des Dülük Baba Tepesi.

Ziel dieses Beitrages ist es, das hellenistische Material kurz vorzustellen[3]. Insbesondere Unguentaria, Echinus-Schälchen sowie Fischteller, die sich in ähnlicher Form auch an weiteren Fundplätzen im nordsyrischen Raum finden und vermutlich lokaler bzw. regionaler Produktion sind[4]. Der Großteil dieser Funde wurde in Arbeitsbereich A zu Tage gefördert (**Abb. 1**).

* Ich möchte den Initiatoren der Tagung für die Einladung und Möglichkeit danken, dass ich in diesem Rahmen einen Teil meines Arbeitsgebietes vorstellen kann. Zu Dank verpflichtet bin ich vor allem auch Engelbert Winter (Münster), der mir die Bearbeitung des Keramikmaterials vom Dülük Baba Tepesi anvertraut hat sowie Constanze Höpken (Köln), Werner Oenbrink (Köln) und Michael Blömer (Münster), die mir mit ihrer Kenntnis und Erfahrung stets stützend zur Seite stehen.

1 Zu den Forschungen auf dem Dülük Baba Tepesi: Winter 2011 mit allgemeinen Bemerkungen zu den Grabungsergebnissen sowie Vorberichte zu speziellen Fundgattungen. Vorläufige Berichte zu den laufenden Grabungen wurden in den letzten Jahren zudem zahlreich publiziert. Weitere Informationen finden sich auf der homepage des Forschungsprojektes unter www.doliche.de

2 Zu Iupiter Dolichenus vgl. u.a. Schütte-Maischatz und Winter 2004, bes. 9–12 sowie die Zusammenstellung der Denkmäler des Gottes in Hörig und Schwertheim 1987. Zur Verbreitung des Kultes vgl. Collar 2011, sowie Speidel 1986.

3 Die Ausarbeitung eines vollständigen Waren- und Formenkatalogs ist Gegenstand meiner in Arbeit befindlichen Dissertation über das gesamte Keramikmaterial hellenistischer bis islamischer Zeit vom Dülük Baba Tepesi. Die Untersuchung der wenigen attisch rotfigurigen Fragmente (etwa 15 kleinteilige Fragmente mit qualitätvollem, schwarzem Überzug sowie zwei etwas größeren Stücke, auf denen der Arm eines Aulos-Spielers und zum anderen eine Frauengestalt zu erkennen sind) ist von Werner Oenbrink (Köln) geplant.

4 Von einer eingehenden Betrachtung der Eastern Sigillata A, die vorwiegend und konzentriert im Arbeitsbereich B (**Abb. 1**) anzutreffen ist, musste aus Gründen des Umfangs verzichtet werden. Der Schwerpunkt der Betrachtung soll daher auf das Material gelegt werden, das im Arbeitsbereich A zu Tage gefördert wurde (**Abb. 1**).

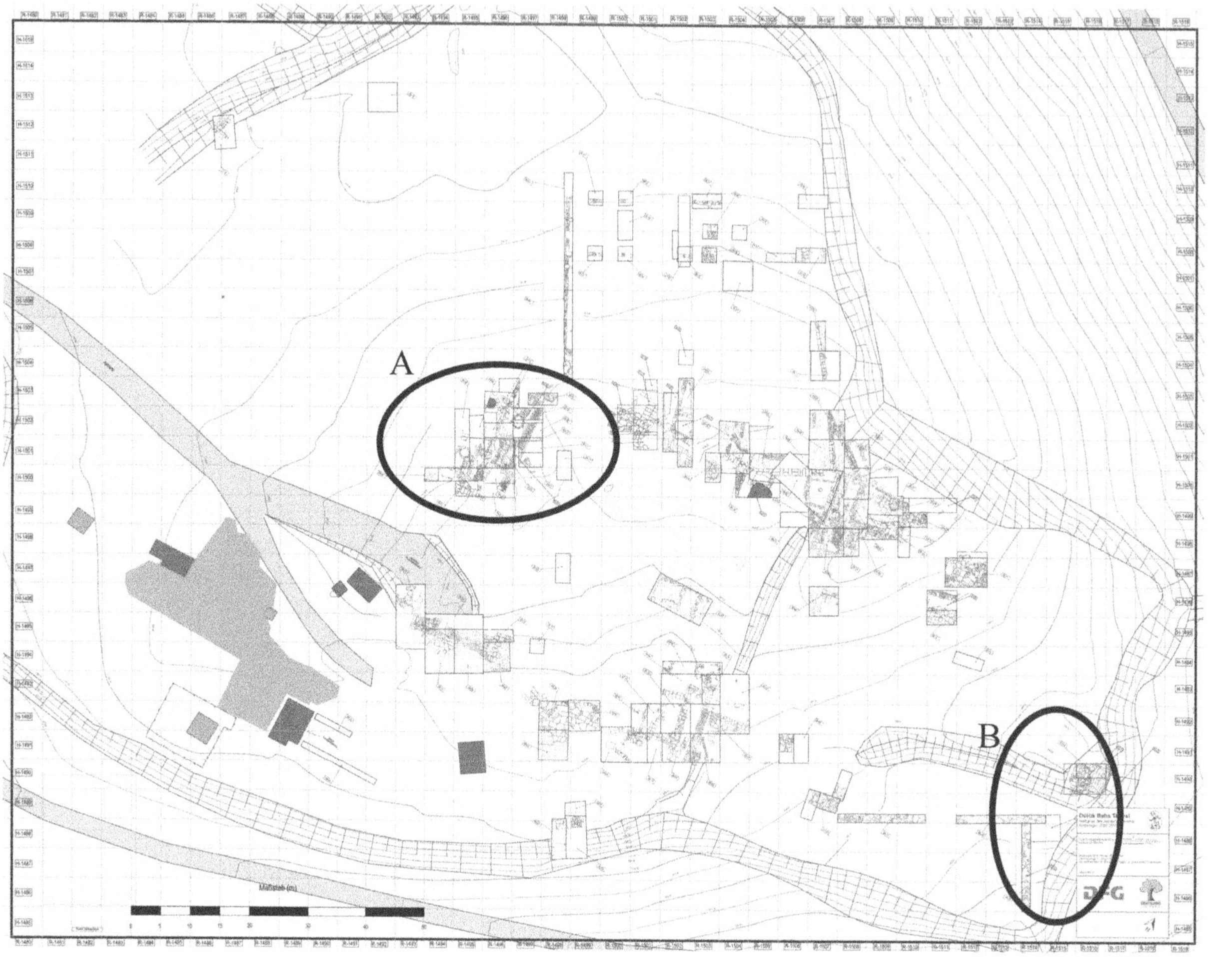

Abb. 1. Gesamtplan des Grabungsareals auf dem Dülük Baba Tepesi mit den eingezeichneten Arbeitsbereichen A und B (Forschungsstelle Asia Minor, Münster)

Auf dem Dülük Baba Tepesi stießen die Ausgräber im Arbeitsbereich A (vgl. **Abb. 1**) auf eisenzeitliche Mauerstrukturen, die später in Baukomplexe der hellenistisch-römischen Zeit integriert wurden (**Abb. 2**). Neben Kleinfunden und Keramik aus der eisenzeitlichen Nutzungsphase des Dülük Baba Tepesi[5], kam in diesem Arbeitsbereich vermehrt Keramik der hellenistischen Zeitstufe zum Vorschein. Den größten Anteil stellen zahlreiche Rand- und Fußfragmente von Unguentaria und Bruchstücke der Echinus-Schalen dar. Weiterhin liegen drei Bodenfragmente mit einer zentralen Vertiefung vor, die als Fischteller angesprochen werden sollen, sowie wenige Fragmente einer hellen Feinware mit glänzend schwarzem Überzug.

Lokal produzierte Feinware mit schwarzem Überzug

In nur geringen Mengen begegnet eine äußerst feine, hellgelb-beige Ware, die einen schwarzen, qualitätvollen Überzug aufweist (**Abb. 3–8**), der glatt und oder auch rau und matt sein kann.

Die Oberflächenbehandlung erinnert an die schwarze Glanzton-Ware aus Griechenland mit dem wichtigsten Herstellungszentrum Athen[6]. Während im Westen diese Keramik einen sehr großen Stellenwert besaß, lässt sich beobachten, dass die Verbreitung im Osten nur gering ist. Zwar stellen anscheinend kleinasiatische Städte eine ähnliche Keramik her, doch erreicht sie dort nie die Beliebtheit – und Qualität – wie im griechischen Raum. In Syrien verdrängte wohl die Eastern Sigillata A mit ihrem leuchtend roten Überzug die Schwarzfirniss-Ware schnell[7]. Dennoch stellten Zentren wie Tarsus oder Antiochia zeitweilig selbst auch schwarz überzogene Gefäße her und exportierten ihre Erzeugnisse in die benachbarten Regionen[8].

Den Unterschied zwischen der im syrischen Raum produzierten Schwarzfirniss-Ware zu der attischen

[5] Die eisenzeitliche Keramik wird von B. Öğüt (München) bearbeitet. Eine erste Vorlage der geborgenen Kleinfunde dieser Phase wie Fibeln, Stempel- und Rollsiegel bietet Schachner 2008 und Schachner 2011.

[6] Thompson 1987, 129–138.

[7] Vgl. dazu den kurzen Überblick bei Kramer 2004, 123.

[8] Zu Tarsus: Jones 1950, 153–158; zu Antiochia: Waagé 1948, 11 f.

Abb. 2. Befundsituation im Grabungsbereich A (Forschungsstelle Asia Minor, Münster)

Importware exakt zu benennen ist schwierig, da mangels objektiver, naturwissenschaftlicher Analysen stets nur auf Waren-Beschreibungen der Bearbeiter anderer Fundplätze Bezug genommen werden kann[9]. Als augenscheinlichsten Unterschied stellt N. Kramer die Scherbenfarbe heraus, die bei attischen Importstücken rot erscheint, während lokale Stücke stets einen hellgelben bis hellbraunen Scherben aufweisen[10]. Betrachtet man die rote Scherbenfarbe als Hauptkriterium zur Erkennung importierter Feinkeramik, so muss für die Exemplare vom Dülük Baba Tepesi eine Produktion in der Region angenommen und die Annahme des Imports aus Attika verworfen werden. Während laut Kramer in Gindaros nur selten Silberglimmerpartikel im Scherben vorkamen[11], ist ein geringer Glimmeranteil bei den lokalen Fragmenten aus Tarsus obligatorisch[12]. Die Fragmente vom Dülük Baba Tepesi weisen keine Glimmerpartikel auf, so dass Tarsus zunächst als Herstellungsort auszufallen scheint und eine engere Verbindung zu den Stücken aus Gindaros gezogen werden sollte. Hierzu passt ebenfalls die Charakterisierung des Überzugs der Stücke aus Gindaros[13].

Aufgrund der geringen Anzahl von Rand- und Bodenfragmenten und wegen des Mangels an exakten Vergleichsstücken im Material der hier erwähnten Fundplätze, gestaltet sich eine zeitliche Einordnung der Keramik vom Dülük Baba Tepesi schwierig[14]. Jones gibt im Allgemeinen für die schwarz gefirnisste Ware eine Zeitspanne vom späten 4. Jh. bis zur Mitte des 2. Jhs. v. Chr.

9 Für Antiochia fehlt eine ausführliche Warenbeschreibung zu der lokal produzierten schwarz überzogenen Ware, auch wenn beispielsweise Christensen – Johansen 1971, 2 ihre Stücke aus Hama trotz allem einer antiochenische Produktion zuschreiben.

10 Kramer 2004, 125 mit Verweis auf Rotroff 1982, 14.

11 Kramer 2004, 125: ‚Der Ton ist stets hervorragend gereinigt und nur selten mit Kalkpartikeln, winzigen Steinchen oder Silberglimmer versehen'.

12 Jones 1950, 153: 'At all times the clay contains small amounts of mica'.

13 Kramer 2004, 125: ‚Der Überzug ist (sonst) matt schwarz (…).'

14 Das ähnlichste Stück zu einem Randfragment vom Dülük Baba Tepesi (**Abb. 3**), stellt eine Form der Eastern Sigillata A dar. Das Fragment kommt einem Teller mit nach oben gebogenem Rand nahe, doch zeigt sich unser Teller erheblich offener gestaltet als die Referenzstücke aus Korinth (Edward 1975, 211 Kat. Nr. 211), oder von der Athener Agora (Rotroff 1997, Kat. Nr. 1641 und 1642). Der Vergleich ist somit nicht nur bezüglich der Form gänzlich unbefriedigend, sondern auch in Bezug auf die abweichende Ware für Rückschlüsse auf einen engeren Datierungsrahmen nicht geeignet. Ebenfalls einer vollkommen anderen Gattung entspricht ein Fragment eines attisch-schwarzfigurigen Deckels aus Ägina (Felten 1982, Kast. Nr. 137 mit Abb. 3 und Taf. 11, 137). Lediglich die Form kommt unserem Fragment am nächsten, so dass ein Nutzen als Deckel in Betracht gezogen werden sollte.

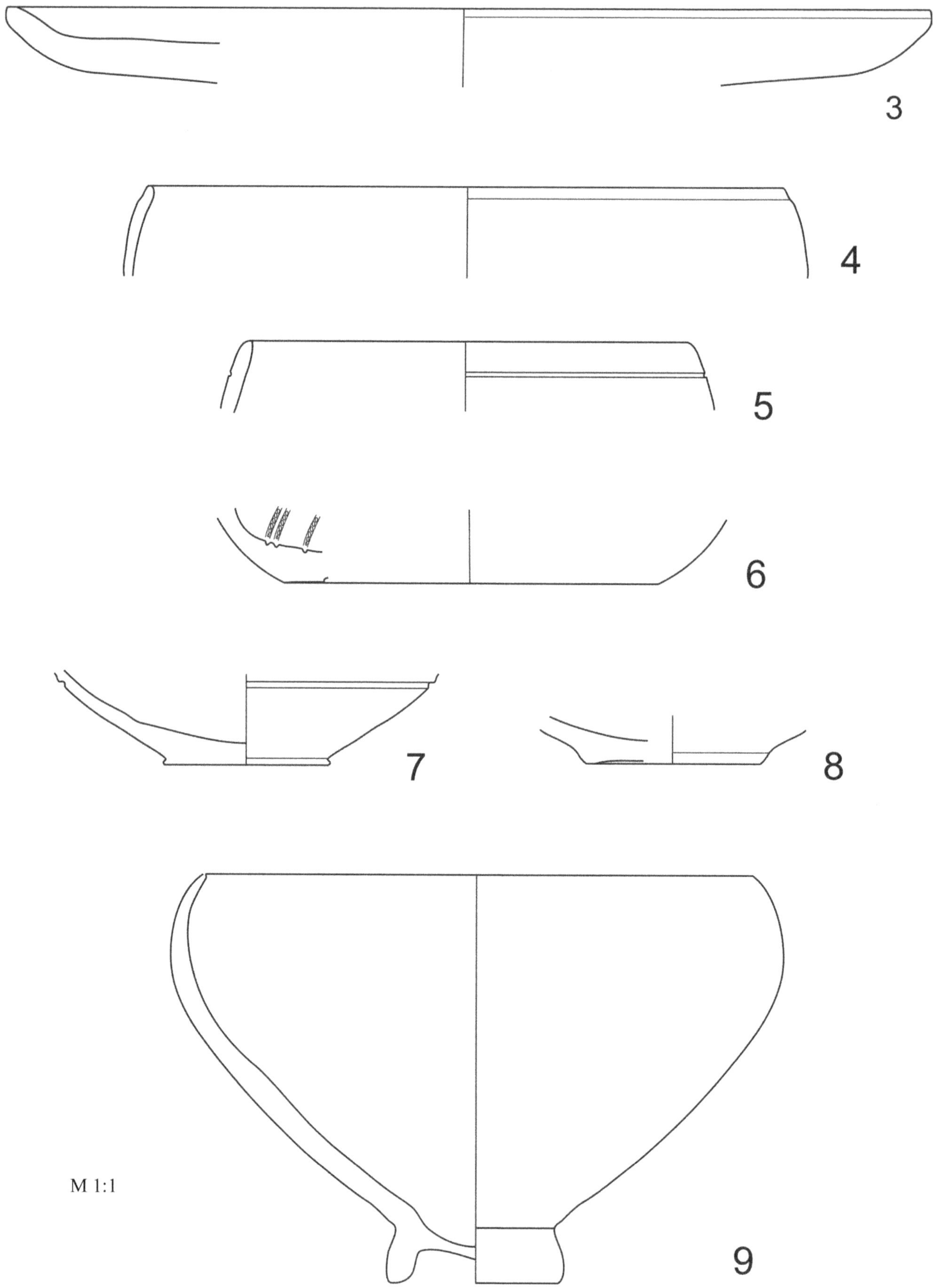

Tafel 1. Abb. 3. Helle Feinware mit schwarzem Überzug (F.-Nr. 09_1801-026) - **Abb. 4.** Helle Feinware mit schwarzem Überzug (F.-Nr. 10_106-007) - **Abb. 5.** Helle Feinware mit schwarzem Überzug (F.-Nr. 09_1901-023) - **Abb. 6.** Helle Feinware mit schwarzem Überzug (F.-Nr. 06_319-042) - **Abb. 7.** Helle Feinware mit schwarzem Überzug (F.-Nr. 08_804-009) - **Abb. 8.** Helle Feinware mit schwarzem Überzug (F.-Nr. 09_1902-011) - **Abb. 9.** Echinus-Schale (F.-Nr. 06_1304-002) (E. Strothenke)

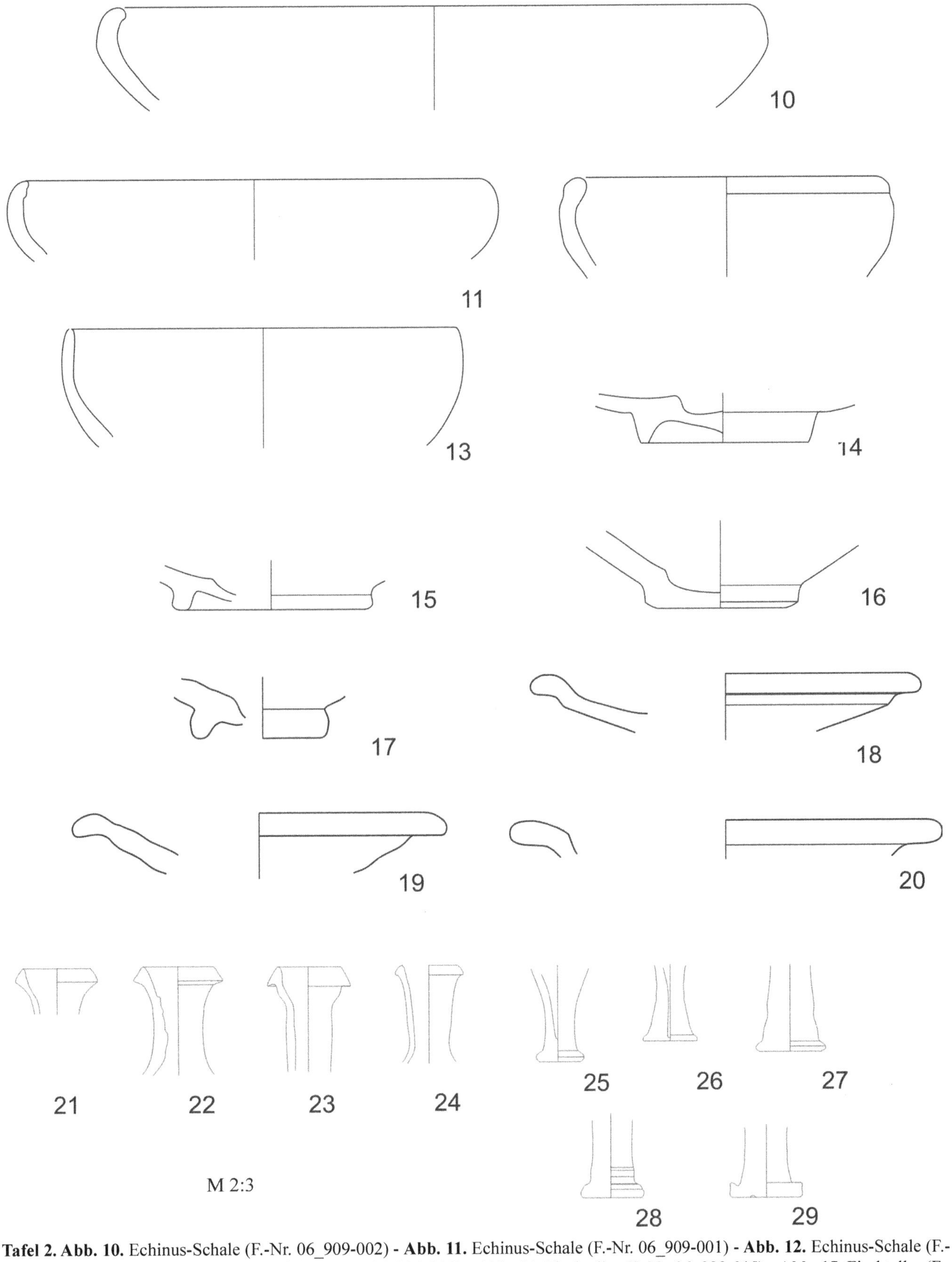

Tafel 2. Abb. 10. Echinus-Schale (F.-Nr. 06_909-002) - **Abb. 11.** Echinus-Schale (F.-Nr. 06_909-001) - **Abb. 12.** Echinus-Schale (F.-Nr. 06_210-006) - **Abb. 13.** Echinus-Schale (F.-Nr. 06_334-012) - **Abb. 14.** Fischteller (F.-Nr. 06_323-015) - **Abb. 15.** Fischteller (F.-Nr. 06_1306-011) - **Abb. 16.** Fischteller (F.-Nr. 09_1804-025) - **Abb. 17.** Fischtelller (F.-Nr. 10_1710-008) - **Abb. 18.** Fischtelller (F.-Nr. 10_1710-015) - **Abb. 19.** Fischtelller (F.-Nr. 10_1710-019) - **Abb. 20.** Fischtelller (F.-Nr. 10_1704-016) - **Abb. 21.** Unguentarium (F.-Nr. 07_211-002) - **Abb. 22.** Unguentarium (F.-Nr. 05_200-001) - **Abb. 23.** Unguentarium (F.-Nr. 08_1505-002) - **Abb. 24.** Unguentarium (F.-Nr. 06_921-003) - **Abb. 25.** Unguentarium (F.-Nr. 06_909-003) - **Abb. 26.** Unguentarium (F.-Nr. 06_902-002) - **Abb. 27.** Unguentarium (F.-Nr. 06_921-002) - **Abb. 28.** Unguentarium (F.-Nr. 06_323-017) - **Abb. 29.** Unguentarium (F.-Nr. 2002-43) (E. Strothenke)

für die in Tarsus bezeichnete ‚Local Undecorated Glazed Ware' an, die ihren Höhepunkt in der Mitte des 3. bis zum Anfang des 2. Jhs. v. Chr. hat[15]. Auch Kramer schließt sich diesem Zeitrahmen in Gindaros größtenteils an[16]. Bei derzeitigem Forschungsstand und da der Dülük Baba Tepesi bislang keine signifikanten Formen zum Vorschein gebracht hat, muss dieser weit gesteckte Zeitrahmen für eine erste Orientierung genügen.

Echinus-Schalen[17] **(Abb. 9–13)**

Bis auf eine nahezu vollständig erhaltene Schale (**Abb. 9**), konnten auf dem Dülük Baba Tepesi zahlreiche Fragmente zu Tage gebracht werden. Hierbei ist allein die Zuordnung von Randbruchstücken mit ihren charakteristischen, nach innen gebogenen Rändern gesichert. Da die Form des Bodens von flachen Standflächen bis hin zu ausgearbeiteten Standfüßen variiert, ist die Zuweisung der Bodenstücke oft unsicher[18]. Der Randdurchmesser dieser Schälchen beträgt von 100mm bis hin zu 250mm, wobei die Wandungsstärke bei den größeren Exemplaren nur unerheblich dicker ist als bei den kleineren Vertretern.

Ein Versuch, eine Entwicklung der Randformen der Schälchen zu erstellen, um sie zeitlich einordnen zu können, wurde bereits an einigen Fundplätzen anhand des dort vorliegenden Materials angestellt. Der anschließende Vergleich der erstellten Typenreihen führte jedoch zu dem Ergebnis, dass unterschiedliche Randgestaltungen wohl nicht chronologisch bedingt sind. Zum einen zeigte sich dies schon an einzelnen Fundplätzen, wo die unterschiedlichen Formen immer miteinander vergesellschaftet auftraten und keine Ablösung der einen Form durch eine andere erkennbar wurde[19]. Zum anderen macht ein Vergleich der Ergebnisse der Fundorte untereinander deutlich, dass die Beobachtungen an einem Fundort sich schon an einem weiteren nicht bestätigen konnten[20]. Dennoch wird eine Einteilung der Randformen in Typen, wie sie beispielsweise auch von H. Jackson durchgeführt wurde, als wichtig erachtet. Die drei von Jackson festgelegten Typen I–III begegnen ebenfalls auf dem Dülük Baba Tepesi. Da sie nicht durch weitere Formabweichungen in der Randgestaltung ergänzt werden können, bestätigen sie Jacksons Einteilung und zeigen durch die Vergesellschaftung der einzelnen Typen in einem Kontext, dass eine chronologische Abfolge anhand der Randgestaltung nicht erschlossen werden kann[21]. Die Echinus-Schalen zeigen sich in ihren einzelnen Variationen in Komplexen an allen hellenistischen Fundplätzen im gesamten östlichen Mittelmeerraum[22]. Sie tauchen hierbei in Schichten auf, die zwischen dem 4. Jh. und 1. Jh. v. Chr. zu datieren sind. Für die Funde vom Dülük Baba Tepesi kann dieser Zeitrahmen mangels weiterer sicher datierbarer Beifunde leider derzeit ebenfalls nicht enger abgesteckt werden.

Die gelb-beige Ware, die mehr oder weniger deutlich mit goldfarbigem Glimmer versehen ist und in der die Echinus-Schalen auf dem Dülük Baba Tepesi scheinbar ausschließlich begegnen, wird in dieser Region allgemeinhin als lokales Produkt angesehen. Wie bereits F. Sarre und G. Herzfeld feststellten, zeigen Tonvorkommen entlang des Euphrats einen deutlichen Goldglimmer-Anteil und M. Gschwind nimmt für Gebrauchskeramik eines frühkaiserzeitlichen Keramik-Komplexes aus Zeugma aus diesem Grund eine Produktion im engeren Umkreis des Stadtgebietes an[23]. Schon F. O. Waagé bezeichnete die Echinus-Schalen aus Antiochia am Orontes als lokale Produkte[24]. Die Vorbilder für die halbkugeligen Schalen mit nach innen gebogenem Rand sind aber wohl Schalen mit glänzend schwarzem Überzug, die in Attika bereits im 5. Jh. v. Chr. hergestellt wurden[25].

Fischteller

Vom Dülük Baba Tepesi liegen drei Bodenfragmente in einer gelb-beigen Ware vor (**Abb. 14–17**). Die zentrale Vertiefung ist charakteristisch für Fischteller. Die Ware der Teller entspricht augenscheinlich dem Fabrikat der oben beschriebenen Echinus-Schalen. Ob es sich bei den hier als Fischtellerböden bezeichneten Fragmente und den Fragmenten der Echinus-Schalen um dieselbe Ware handelt, muss aufgrund augenblicklich noch fehlender naturwissenschaftlicher Analysen offen bleiben. Der Vergleich der Fragmente bei zehnfacher Vergrößerung zeigt eine nur wenig voneinander abweichende Scherbenmatrix, wobei die Fragmente der Fischteller jedoch stärker gemagert und weniger hart gebrannt sind.

---

15 Jones 1950, 152.
16 Kramer 2004, 126.
17 Zur Bezeichnung dieser Schale, deren Form an den Echinus eines dorischen Kapitells erinnert, vgl. Edwards 1975, 29.
18 Vgl. hierzu beispielsweise Jones 1950, 154.
19 In Antiochia beispielsweise zeigen sich nur unerhebliche Veränderungen der Randgestaltungen aus Kontexten, die vom 4. Jh. bis in das 2. Jh. v. Chr. rangieren, vgl. Waagé 1948, Taf. 1 Nr. H 18–20 und Taf. 3 Nr. 78–80.
20 Vgl. z. B. Jones 1959, 156 f., der eine Entwicklung der Echinus-Schalen bereits in hellenistischer Zeit von tiefen hin zu flachen und breiteren Vertretern feststellen konnte, während diese Beobachtungen in anderen Regionen nicht bestätigt werden konnten (vgl. Lapp 1961, 201–202 und Guz-Zilberstein 1995, 290 für Tell Dor/Israel).
21 Jackson 2002, 112 räumt bezüglich der von ihr untersuchten Gräbern ein, dass es sich um gestörte Komplexe handelt bzw. um möglicherweise über einen längeren Zeitraum genutzte Grablegen, so dass sich auch dadurch die Vergesellschaftung der Typen I–III erklären könnte. Meines Erachtens zeigen aber andere Fundkomplexe (vgl. hier Anm. 8 und 9), dass eine zeitliche typologisch-chronologische Unterscheidung nicht getroffen werden kann.
22 Auf die Beliebtheit dieser Schalen im ostmediterranen Raum wurde schon vielfach hingewiesen und ihrem allmählichen Verschwinden ab dem 4. Jh. v. Chr. beispielsweise auf der Athener Agora gegenübergestellt. Vgl. hierzu auch: Guz-Zilberstein 1995, 289; Crowfoot u. a. 1957, 248; Jones 1950, 157 und Waagé 1948, 15–17. Für Parallelen aus dem östlichen Mittelmeerraum: Jackson 2002, 109 und Kramer 2004, Form 1a–b, sowie Jackson 2011, 12 mit Anm. 45.
23 Zu den Goldglimmer-Partikeln siehe Sarre und Herzfeld 1920, 8; zu einer Produktionsstätte von Gebrauchskeramik nahe Zeugma, vgl. Gschwind 2006, 340–341.
24 Vgl. Waagé 1948, 11. 15–17.
25 So auch Kramer 2004, 161.

An der Oberfläche sind vereinzelt Reste von mattem, rotbraunem oder grau-schwarzem Überzug zu erkennen, der offensichtlich weniger gut auf dem Scherben haftet als vergleichsweise der Überzug auf den Fragmenten der Echinus-Schalen.

Da lediglich drei Bodenfragmente vorliegen, kann über die weitere Ausgestaltung der Teller nicht viel gesagt werden. Es sind keine Ränder eindeutig den Fischtellerböden zuzuweisen. Es lassen sich jedoch Randfragmente in gelb-beiger Ware ermitteln (**Abb. 18–20**), die zudem in näherem Fundzusammenhang geborgen werden konnten und von denen zwei Reste eines roten, matten Überzugs aufweisen, die dem Überzug eines der Bodenfragmente entsprechen (**Abb. 15**). Aus Gindaros und Antiochia liegen vollständige Teller-Profile vor, die mit den Funden vom Dülük Baba Tepesi gleichzusetzen sind[26]. Eine Zuordnung der Randfragmente mit Resten von rotem oder braunem Überzug aus benachbarten Fundkomplexen zu den Böden mit zentraler Vertiefung, erscheint daher durchaus vorstellbar.

Die beobachteten goldfarbigen Glimmerpartikel im Scherben unterstützen die Annahme einer Lokalproduktion der Stücke[27]. Das zahlreiche Vorkommen von Bodenfragmenten mit niedrigem und einfachem Standring ohne zentrale Vertiefung, deutet daraufhin, dass vor allem auch einfache Schalen und tiefe Teller in der beschriebenen gelb-beigen Ware produziert wurden. Zudem zeigen die unterschiedlichen Randgestaltungen mutmaßlicher Fischteller im Fundspektrum beispielsweise von Lidar Höyük und Gindaros die Vielfältigkeit des in dieser Ware produzierten Geschirrs[28].

Unguentaria (Abb. 21–29)

Unguentaria-Fragmente zeigen sich auf dem Dülük Baba Tepesi ausschließlich in einer grauen bis dunkelgrauen Ware. Die Außenoberfläche erscheint teils geglättet, selten ist ein hauchdünner, dunkler Überzug zu erkennen. Das Innere ist wohl roh belassen, wobei ein Auftrag von verdichtendem Überzug nicht ausgeschlossen werden kann, um ein Auslaufen von Flüssigkeiten durch den Ton zu vermeiden[29]. Die Ware entspricht nicht nur der von H. Jackson definierten Ware VII, die sie als Hauptware der Unguentaria aus dem Gräberfeld von Jebel Khalid feststellen konnte[30], sondern scheint auch im gesamten Mittelmeergebiet die übliche Ware für Unguentaria darzustellen[31].

Fragmente bauchiger Unguentaria lassen sich auf dem Dülük Baba Tepesi ebenfalls nicht nachweisen[32]. Allein die lang gezogenen, spindelförmigen mit mehr oder weniger massivem Standfuß sind im Fundmaterial vertreten. Ein vollständiges Exemplar konnte nicht geborgen werden.

Als allgemein übliche Form lassen sich bei den Unguentaria zahlreiche Parallelen von Fundplätzen im nordsyrischen Raum nennen. So zeigen sich auch in den Gräbern von Jebel Khalid Unguentaria, die in Ware und Form absolut den Stücken vom Dülük Baba Tepesi gleichkommen[33]. Aus Gindaros[34], Tarsus[35] und Hama[36] wurden ebenfalls derartige Fläschchen vorgelegt. Unpublizierte Stücke aus der näheren Umgebung des Dülük Baba Tepesi, möglicherweise aus Samosata entsprechen voll und ganz unserem Fundmaterial.

Eine zeitliche Einordnung der Unguentaria anhand ihrer Form ist wohl nicht möglich. Der Versuch, eine chronologische Abfolge anhand der Relation von Höhe und Durchmesser der Gefäße zu erhalten, wurde beispielsweise von J. M. Fossey unternommen, der von der Annahme ausgeht, dass bauchige, birnenförmige Exemplare früher anzusetzen sind als die spindelförmigen. Allgemein scheint man diesem Trend in der Formentwicklung der Unguentaria folgen zu können[37], doch zeigen Vergleiche verschiedener Fundplätze untereinander, dass es sich höchstens um ein Merkmal zur Schaffung einer relativen Chronologie handeln kann[38]. H. Jackson schlussfolgert am Ende ihrer Ausführungen daher: 'Obviously regional differences must be taken into account. Agreement seems to be substantial that fusiform unguentaria were most popular in the 2nd century BCE.'[39]

---

26 Zu Antiochia siehe Jones 1950, Taf. 178, 23F. 26. Zu Gindaros vgl. Kramer 2004, 161 f. mit Kat.-Nr. KTÜ 25–63.

27 Vgl. zum Goldglimmer bereits oben Anm. 23.

28 Vgl. Kazenwadle 1996, Taf. 44– 46; Kramer 2004, Taf. 68–69.

29 Vgl. dazu unten Anm. 41.

30 Jackson 2002, 102. 106 Abb. 2 und Jackson 2011, 94–98 Taf. 18 Abb. 84–86.

31 Vgl. dazu Jones 1950, 171; Hellström 1971, 27; Guz-Zilberstein 1995, 306 sowie zusammenfassend Kramer 2004, 213. Fragmente in einer hell-beigen, glimmerhaltigen und wohl lokalen Ware, wie sie N. Kramer in Gindaros beobachten konnten, begegnen auf dem Dülük Baba Tepesi nicht (Kramer 2004, 214). Auch H. Jackson ordnet zwei der 13 Unguentaria-Fragmente ihrer Ware II zu, in der auch die Echinus-Schalen (s.o.) und Fischteller (s.u.) begegnen und der lokalen Ware Kramer zu entsprechen scheinen. Auch sie attestiert dieser Ware eine lokale Herstellung (siehe Jackson 2002, 106 f.).

32 So auch in Gindaros, wobei Kramer 2004, 213 jedoch zurecht darauf hinweist, dass Fragmente dieser bauchigen Exemplare nicht derart ‚markant' sind, dass sie aus dem Fundmaterial mit Sicherheit herausgestellt werden könnten.

33 Persönliche Mitteilung von Heather Jackson, während der ‚Networks in the Hellenistic World. According to the Pottery in the Eastern Mediterranean and Beyond' in Köln vom 23.002–26.02.2011.

34 Kramer 2004, 212–218 Taf. 99–101.

35 Jones 1950, 171 f. Taf. 187, 224E–F. 233. 235. 237.

36 Christensen – Johansen 1971, 45–50 mit Abb. 24. Generell erscheinen die Unguentaria aus Hama bauchiger und noch nicht in dem Maße lang gezogen wie die Fragmente vom Dülük Baba Tepesi.

37 In Athen und Korinth gelten die birnenförmigen Unguentaria als älter, vgl. Pemberton 1985, 285 für Korinth und Thompson 1934, 472–474 für Athen. Ebenso deuten die Beobachtungen von Jones 1950, (Tarsus I) 171 f. in Tarsus und Westholm 1956, 60–61. 73–74 mit Abb. 24, 22–34 auf Zypern darauf hin, dass in hellenistischer Zeit der Trend zu schmalen Fläschchen auf einem hohen und massiven Fuß hinauslief. Eine chronologische und typologische Einteilung versuchte bereits Forti 1962, 143–157, legte jedoch keinerlei Zeichnungen vor. Vgl. weiterhin zur Formentwicklung: Smetana-Scherrer 1982, 88 f. und Anderson-Stojanović 1987, 106–114.

38 Vgl. hierzu die voneinander abweichenden Ansichten von P. W. Lapp (vgl. Lapp 1961, 197 f. und M. Dothan in Ashdod (vgl. Dothan 1971, 57 mit Abb. 18, 3–10 Taf. 17, 1–2). Letzterer kann dem Ergebnis von Lapp aufgrund seines Materials nicht zustimmen, dass dickwandige Unguentaria zwangsläufig früher anzusetzen sind als dünnwandige Exemplare.

39 Jackson 2002, 108; Dotterweich 1999, 3. Zu den regionalen Unterschieden auch schon Anderson-Stojanović 1987, 105, die

Die Frage nach einem möglichen Produktionsort kann bislang nicht beantwortet werden, wenn auch davon ausgegangen werden kann, dass es sich bei den Unguentaria in der hier beschriebenen harten, grauen Ware um lokale Produkte handeln wird. Diese Annahme kann durch die soeben beschriebenen regionalen Unterschiede, die eine chronologische Einordnung der Unguentaria auf Grundlage einer einheitlichen Formentwicklung, nicht ermöglichen, gestützt werden. Weiterhin deuten auch unterschiedliche Verzierungen, die auf bestimmte Regionen beschränkt zu sein scheinen, auf regionale Produktionen hin[40].

Eine Produktionsstätte der grauen, spindelförmigen Unguentaria im nordsyrischen Raum ist somit mit Nachdruck anzunehmen, auch wenn ein Herstellungsort bislang nicht lokalisiert werden kann. Zudem kann aufgrund des geringen Fassungsvermögens der spindelförmigen Unguentaria und der Porosität des Keramikmaterials, das ein Auslaufen von Flüssigkeit über kurz oder lang bedeute, nicht davon ausgegangen werden, dass es sich bei diesen Gefäßen um Transportmittel für feine Öle oder teure Duftwässerchen gehandelt haben könnte[41]. Es ist also vorstellbar, dass Öle und Parfüm beispielsweise als Weihgaben der zu hellenistischer Zeit verehrten Gottheit auf dem Dülük Baba Tepesi in Unguentaria dargebracht wurden[42]. Eine Verwendung der Unguentaria in sepulkralen Kontext[43] ist auf dem Dülük Baba Tepesi aufgrund fehlender Hinweise auf Bestattungen in unmittelbarem Fundzusammenhang der Fragmente zu verwerfen.

Schlussbemerkung

Der Dülük Baba Tepesi fügt sich offensichtlich nicht in ein weitgespanntes Handelsnetz ein, das den Fundplatz in hellenistischer Zeit mit Feinwaren aus Attika oder Korinth versorgt, oder zumindest mit Waren aus dem kleinasiatischen Küstenstädten beliefert. Dies ist sicherlich darauf zurückzuführen, dass der Keramik eine andere Funktion zugeweisen werden muss als es ggf. in Siedlungen zu erwarten ist. Das Heiligtum des Iupiter Dolichenus machte weiterhin in nachhellenistischer Zeit groß angelegte Umbauphasen durch, die zudem dafür sorgten, dass das ohnehin geringe Keramikmaterial dieser Zeitstufe weitestgehend kleinteilig zerstört wurde.

Attische Importe, wie Schwarze Glanztonware, die zumindest an anderen Fundplätzen in Nordsyrien zu einem geringen Prozentsatz begegnen, finden sich nicht auf dem Dülük Baba Tepesi. Allein wohl die ‚Nachahmungen' dieser Ware, produziert in den umliegenden Zentren der Region, erreichen den Hügel; allerdings äußerst spärlich und in ihren Formen ohne exakte Parallelen. Wenige Fragmente attisch rotfiguriger Keramik zeigen andererseits, dass durchaus Importe aus dem ‚entlegenen Westen' auf den Dülük Baba Tepesi gelangten[44]. Keramik jedoch, die in hellenistischen Zentren der kleinasiatischen Westküste durchaus vorkommt, – zu denken sei hierbei an die 'Westabhang-Keramik', die ‚weiße Lagynos-Ware', ‚Schalen des Megarischen Typs' usw. fehlt jedoch. Bewegt man sich in die späthellenistische Zeit und zum Übergang zur frührömischen Zeit, ist zu beobachten, dass gerade im nord-östlichen Bereich des Gipfelplateaus (Arbeitsbereich B; **Abb. 1**) zahlreiche Fragmente der Eastern Sigillata A begegnen, die mehrheitlich der sogenannten frühen hellenistischen Formentradition zugewiesen werden müssen. Dies zeigt wiederum, dass im 1. Jh. v. Chr. Waren bis auf den Hügel, – wenn auch aus der näheren Region, denn für die ESA wird eine Produktion im nordsyrischen Raum angenommen, – hinauf kamen und der Dülük Baba Tepesi durchaus in ein, wenn auch nur kleines regionales Handelsnetz eingeflochten gewesen sein wird.

Die Feststellungen bezüglich der hier in diesem Artikel vorgestellten Keramik, der eine lokale bzw. regionale Produktion wahrscheinlich in eben den gleichen Zentren wie die der ESA zuzuschreiben ist, unterstützt die These, dass der Dülük Baba Tepesi in ein regionales Handelsnetz auch in hellenistischer Zeit eingewoben war, aber 'Übersee-Importe' nicht üblich waren. Es muss dabei bedacht werden, dass es sich beim Dülük Baba Tepesi um einen Platz handelt, der in der frühen Nutzungszeit nicht eine Siedlung, sondern ein Heiligtum beheimatet hat. Gerade die zahlreichen Unguentaria-Funde, vergesellschaftet mit bunten und Stein- und Glasperlen, Stempel- und Rollsiegel sowie die Anhäufung von verbrannten Knochen in Fundzusammenhängen[45], bezeugen die sich auf dem Hügel vollzogenen Opfer- und Kulthandlungen in hellenistischer Zeit bevor der dort verehrte Gott durch die Römer zu Iupiter Dolichenus wurde.

Bezüglich hellenistischer Importware können erste Keramik-Ensembles vom benachbarten Keber Tepe erwartet werden, wo die dem Iupiter Dolichenus

Unguentaria aus Stobi (Makedonien) zum Anlass zusammenfassender Überlegungen nimmt. Ähnlich schon Hellström 1971, 26: 'It may very well have been that more or less contemporary local variations of the unguentarium originated at a number of places without any common source of influence. (…) There are many variations in shape and fabric some of which can be fixed geographically.'

[40] Unguentaria begegnen in Griechenland beispielsweise häufig mit horizontalen weißen Streifen (vgl. Thompson 1987, Kat. Nr. B6–B7. D77–D78 und Smetana-Scherrer 1982, 88), die in Syrien nicht auftauchen; in Palästina sind wiederum Ritzungen üblich, die Stücke aus dem syrischen Raum nicht zeigen (vgl. Berlin1997, 65).

[41] Vgl. dazu den Versuch von S. I. Rotroff zur Durchlässigkeit von Unguentaria, auf den sich Anderson-Stojanović 1987, 116 bezieht. So verloren ungefirnisste, graue Exemplare, die möglicherweise den Stücken vom Dülük Baba Tepesi am nächsten kommen etwa 20% Wasser bzw. 5,5% Öl innerhalb von sieben Tagen. Die Versuchsreihe mit Unguentaria von der Athener Agora kann hier jedoch trotz der Material-Ähnlichkeit der Gefäße untereinander nur als grober Anhaltspukt gewertet werden. Es ist vielmehr anzunehmen, dass der Transport in undurchlässigen Metallgefäßen vorgenommen wurde (dazu überzeugend Hellström 1971, 23 f.).

[42] Für eine Auswahl der Fundplätze mit Unguentaria-Funden in einem nicht-sepulkralen Kontext vgl. neben Smetana-Scherrer 1982, 88–91; Jones 1950, 171 f.; Kramer 2004, 212–218 und vor allem die Zusammenstellung bei Anderson-Stojanović 1987, 106 Anm. 3.

[43] Zur Verwendung der Unguentaria als Grabbeigaben vgl. Hellström 1971, 24.

[44] Zur attisch-rotfigurugen Keramik vgl. oben bereits Anm. 3.

[45] Zu den Knochenfunden vgl. die Untersuchungen von Pöllath und Peters 2011.

namensgebende antike Siedlung Doliche lokalisiert ist, und wo in Zukunft intensive Arbeiten beginnen werden[46]. Der Umstand, dass sich hier eine Siedlung befunden hat, wird in Hinblick auf importierte, hochwertige Tafelware sicherlich weiterreichende Ergebnisse liefern können, so dass man das das 'Netzwerk hellenistischer Keramik' auch im nordsyrischen Hinterland enger knüpfen kann.

Eva Strothenke
Westfälische Wilhelms-Universität Münster
Forschungsstelle Asia Minor im Seminar für Alte Geschichte
Georgskommende 25
D-48143 Münster
eva.strothenke@uni-muenster.de

Bibliographie

Anderson-Stojanovic, V. R. 1987. The Chronology and Function of Ceramic Unguentaria. *American Journal of Archaeology* 91, 105–122.

Berlin, A. M. 1997. The Plain Ware. In S. C. Herbert (Hrsg.), *Tel Anafa II 1: The Hellenistic and Roman Pottery*. Journal of Roman Archaeology Suppl. 10, 1–244. AnnArbor, Kelsey Museum.

Hörig, M. und Schwertheim, E. 1987. *Corpus Cultus Iovi Dolicheni (CCID). Études préliminaires aux religions orientales dans l'Empire romain*. Leiden, Brill.

Christensen, A. P. und Johansen, C. F. 1971. *Les poteries hellénistiques et les Terres Sigillées orientales, Hama III 2, Fouilles et Recherches de la Fondation Carlsberg 1931–1938*. Kopenhagen, Aarhus University Press.

Collar, A. 2011. Military Networks and the Cult of Iupiter Dolichenus, in: Winter 2011, 217–245.

Crowfoot, J. W., Crowfoot, G. M. und Kenyon, K. M. 1957. *Samaria-Sebaste, Reports of the Work of the Joint Expedition in 1931–1933 and of the British Expedition in 1935, vol. III: The Objects from Samaria*. London, Palestine Exploration Fund.

Dothan, M. 1971. *Ashdod II–III. The Second and Third Seasons of Excavations 1963, 1965. Soundings in 1967*. Atiqot 9–10. Jerusalem.

Dotterweich, U. 1999. *Unguentarien mit kuppelförmiger Mündung aus Knidos*. Knidos Studien I. Möhnesee, Bibliopolis.

Edwards, G. R. 1975. *Corinthian Hellenistic Pottery*. Corinth. Results of Excavation VII 3. Princeton, NJ., American School of Classical Studies.

Felten, W. 1982. Attisch-Schwarzfigurige und Rotfigurige Keramik. In H. Walter (Hrsg.), *Alt-Ägina II 1*. 23–55. Mainz, Zabern.

Forti, L. 1962. Gli unguentari del primo periodo ellenistico. *Rendiconti della Accademia di archeologia, lettere e belle arti, Napoli* 37, 143–157.

Guz-Zilberstein, B. 1995. The Typology of the Hellenistic Coarse Ware and Selected Loci of the Hellenistic and Roman periods. In E. Stern (Hrsg.), *Excavations at Dor, Final Report Vol. IB: Areas A and C: The Finds*. Qedem Reports 2, 289–434. Jerusalem, Hebrew University.

Hellström, P. 1971. *Labraunda. Pottery of Classical and Later Date Terracotta, Lamps and Glass*. Lund, Gleerup.

Jackson, H. 2002. The Cemetery Pottery – 1996 and 1997, in G. W. Clarke and P. J. Connor (Hrsg.), *Jebel Khalid on the Euphrates. Report on Excavations 1986–1996, vol. I.* Mediterranean Archaeology Suppl. 5, 101–124. Sydney, Meditarch Publications.

Jackson, H. 2011. The Common Wares from the Housing Insula, in Jackson, H. und Tidmarsh, J. (Hrsg.), *Jebel Khalid on the Euphrates, vol. III.* Mediterranean Archaeology Suppl. 7, 1–261. Sydney, Meditarch Publications.

Jones, F. F. 1950. The Pottery. In H. Goldman (Hrsg.), *Excavations at Gözlü Kule. The Hellenistic and Roman Periods*. Tarsus I, 149–296. Princeton, Princeton University Press.

Kenrick, P. M. 1981. Fine Wares of the Hellenistic and Roman Periods. In J. Matthers (Hrsg.), *The River Qoueiq, Northern Syria, and its Catchment. Studies arising from the Tell Rifa'at Survey 1977–1979*. British Archaeological Reports International Series 98, 439–458. Oxford, Archeopress.

Lapp, P. W. 1961. *Palestinian Ceramic Chronology 200 B.C. – A.D. 70*. New Haven, American Schools for Oriental Research.

Pöllath, N. und Peters, J. 2011. Smoke on the Mountain. In *Winter 2011, 47–68. Bonn, Habelt.*

Rotroff, S. I. 1982. *Hellenistic Pottery : Athenian and Imported Moldmade Bowls*. The Athenian Agora XXII. Princeton, NJ., American School of Classical Studies.

Rotroff, S. I. 1997. *Hellenistic Pottery : Athenian and Imported Wheelmade Table Ware and Related Material*. The Athenian Agora XXIX. Princeton, NJ., American School of Classical Studies.

Schachner, A. 2008. Babylonier und Achämeniden auf dem

[46] Erste Sondagen konnten im Jahr 2010 vom Dülük Baba Tepesi-Grabungsteam unter der örtlichen Leitung des zweiten Grabungsleiters Dr. Mehmet Önal (Şanlıurfa) angelegt werden. Sie brachten neben qualitätvollen Mosaikböden und zahlreichen Tonbullae, auch eine überschaubare Menge an Keramik zu Tage, die zu einem Teil dem vom Dülük Baba Tepesi bekannten Material entsprach, aber auch Keramik – vor allem Feinware – beinhaltete, die nicht den Weg den Hügel hinauf fanden.

Dülük Baba Tepesi: Kulturelle Vielfalt in der späten Eisenzeit im Spiegel der vor-hellenistischen Funde. In E. Winter (Hrsg.), *ΠΑΤΡΙΣ ΠΑΝΤΡΟΦΟΣ ΚΟΜΜΑΓΗΝΗ. Neue Funde und Forschungen zwischen Taurus und Euphrat*. Asia Minor Studien 60, 69–96. Bonn, Habelt.

Schachner, A. 2011. Die Welt des östlichen Mittelmeers in kleinen Bildern – Weitere Beobachtungen zu den Siegeln und Kleinfunden der späten Eisenzeit vom Dülük Baba Tepesi. In: Winter 2011, 19–46.

Schütte-Maischatz, A. und Winter, E. 2004. *Doliche – eine kommagenische Stadt und ihre Götter. Mithras und Iupiter Dolichenus*. Asia Minor Studien 52. Bonn, Habelt.

Smetana-Scherrer, R. 1982. Spätklassische und hellenistische Keramik. In H. Walter (Hrsg.), *Alt-Ägina II 1*. 56–91. Mainz, Zabern.

Speidel, M. 1978. *The Religion of Iuppiter Dolichenus in the Roman Army*. Etudes préliminaires aux religions orientales dans l'empire romain 63. Leiden, Brill.

Thompson, H. A. 1987. Two Centuries of Hellenistic Pottery. In S. I. Rotroff (Hrsg.), *Hellenistic Pottery and Terracottas*, Reprint 11–180. Princeton, NJ., American School of Classical Studies. (= *Hesperia* 3, 1934, 309–480)

Waagé, F. O. 1934. Greek, Hellenistic and Roman Pottery from Alishar. In H. H. von der Osten (Hrsg.), *The Alishar Hüyük Seasons of 1930–1932 III*, 74–88. Chicago, University of Chicago Press.

Waagé, F. O. 1948. Hellenistic and Roman Tableware of North Syria. In F. O. Waagé (Hrsg.), *Antioch on the Orontes IV 1*, 1–60. Princeton, Princeton University Press.

Westholm, A. 1956. Pottery, in O. Vessberg und A. Westholm (Hrsg.), *The Swedish Cyprus Expedition 4, 3: The Hellenistic and Roman Periods in Cyprus*. 53–81. Stockholm, Ohlsson.

Winter, E. (Hrsg.), 2011. *Von Kummuḫ nach Telouch. Historische und archäologische Untersuchungen in Kommagene*. Dolichener und Kommagenische Forschungen 4. Asia Minor Studien 64. Bonn, Habelt.

Überlegungen zur Eastern Sigillata A

Norbert Kramer

Abstract

Based mainly on the material from Gindarus (NW-Syria) and Tel Anafa (N-Israel) this paper deals with the origin and the subgroups of ESA. Two main groups are defined, here referred to as ESA a and b, which are macroscopically distinguishable. According to the available chemical analyses both groups possibly come from a region in NW-Syria. Furthermore it is suggested to distinguish another smaller group, here called ESA c, which is particularly represented in Cilicia. The examination of the manufacturing process and the circulation of an important product such as Eastern Sigillata tableware also provides evidence concerning historical and cultural issues. Especially the boom of ESA in time of the collapse of the Seleucid Empire is still without explanation.

Keywords: Antioch, Ceramics, Eastern Sigillata A, Gindarus, Hellenism, Palestine, Phoenicia, Seleucids, Syria, Tel Anafa

Einleitung

Terra Sigillata in ihren westlichen und östlichen Ausprägungen gehört zum einen aufgrund ihrer nahezu flächendeckenden Verbreitung und zum anderen aufgrund des hohen Grades an chronologischer und herkunftsgeographischer Signifikanz zweifellos zu den wichtigsten materiellen Quellengattungen der Alten Welt. Infolge dieser Eigenschaften dient sie als keramisches 'Leitfossil' zur Datierung von Befunden auf Ausgrabungen ebenso wie als Grundlage der Analyse wirtschaftsgeschichtlicher Bedingungen und zunehmend auch kulturgeschichtlicher Fragestellungen. Nichtsdestoweniger stehen solche weiterführenden Interpretationen unter dem Vorbehalt, dass unser Kenntnisraster zu den einzelnen Sigillaten noch keineswegs geschlossen ist.

Ideale Zustände liegen naturgemäß immer dann vor, wenn die Aussagen zur Herkunft einer Sigillata-Gruppe und der Datierung ihrer Typen auf der sicheren Basis von Funden der Töpferöfen – oder zumindest des Töpferabfalls in Form von Fehlbränden – stehen. Derartige Funde sind für die Westliche Terra Sigillata schon öfter vorgekommen. Für den Bereich der Östlichen Sigillata konnten Produktionsstätten bislang aber nur für die so genannte Eastern Sigillata C (ESC) im Raum Pergamon nachgewiesen werden[1]. Sowohl für die – wohl aus dem Großraum Ephesus stammende – Eastern Sigillata B (ESB)[2] wie für die Eastern Sigillata A (ESA)[3] fehlen noch konkrete Hinweise auf die Herstellungsorte. Im Folgenden soll es kurz um die ESA, ihre möglichen Untergruppen und deren Unterscheidbarkeit sowie damit verbunden die Frage der Herkunft der ESA gehen.

Warengruppen und Herkunft der Eastern Sigillata A

In Hinblick auf die Warenbeschaffenheit der ESA lassen sich immer wieder, etwa für Antiochia, Hama, Samaria und Tel Anafa, Hinweise auf die makroskopische Unterscheidbarkeit von zwei Gruppen finden. Diese Unterscheidung konnte von mir auch anhand des viele Tausend ESA-Fragmente umfassenden, aber leider kaum stratifizierbaren Materiales aus dem nordwestsyrischen Gindarus nachvollzogen werden. Das Zahlenverhältnis liegt hierbei etwa bei fünf zu eins. Die jeweiligen Warenbeschreibungen seien hier wiederholt[4]:

> ESA a (entspricht Samaria / Hama Ware 2):
> *Ton:* sehr fein, manchmal sehr wenig Silberglimmer, sehr selten sehr wenig Kalkpartikel, keine sonstige Magerung, nicht sehr hart, manchmal ‚mehlige' Konsistenz, glatter Bruch; hellbeige-hellbraun (CEC D8–9; Munsell 7,5 YR 6–7/4–6);
> *Überzug:* glatt, leicht glänzend; rotbraun (CEC G12–F11; Munsell 2,5 YR 4–5/6–8; 10 R 4–5/6–8), manchmal violettbraun (CEC H9; Munsell 10 R 4–5/3–4), selten schwarz.
>
> ESA b (entspricht Samaria / Hama Ware 1):
> *Ton:* sehr fein, ohne Einschlüsse, hart, meist leicht körniger Bruch; hellgelblich (CEC C6–7; Munsell 10 YR 6–7/3–4);
> *Überzug:* glatt, leicht glänzend; violett- bis rotbraun (CEC H9–F12; Munsell 10 R 4–5/3–4; 2,5 YR 4/6–8).

---

1 Loeschke 1912 (Çandarlı); nach Funden von Produktionsstätten im Ketiostal von Pergamon konnte von der ESC eine 'Pergamenische Sigillata' abgegrenzt werden, Meyer-Schlichtmann 1988.

2 Hayes 1985, 49 f.; allg. Lund 2003.

3 Zum Stand der Forschung s. Hayes 1985, 13 f.; Slane 1997, 269 f. und Kramer 2004, 173 f., bes. zur verwirrenden Terminologiegeschichte der ESA.

4 Kramer 2004, 178 f., dort auch Diskussion der entsprechenden Unterscheidungen in anderen Publikationen.

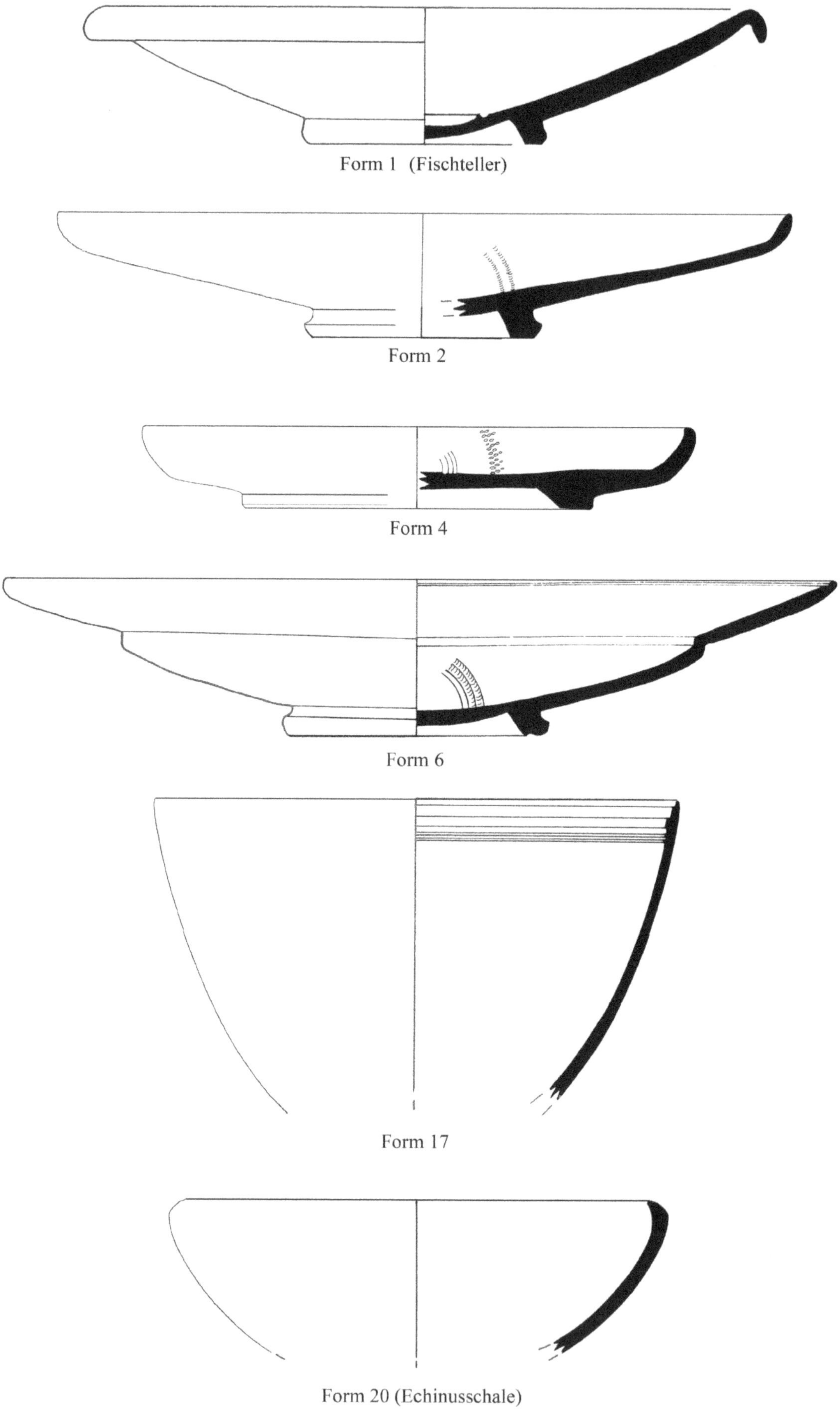

Abb. 1. frühe Formen der ESA / BSP in der Typologie nach Hayes 1985 (Slane 1997, Taf. 1-3, FW 1; 13; 16; 11; 31; 21)

Wie erwähnt, wurden auf vielen Grabungen im ganzen Vorderen Orient über einen langen Zeitraum hinweg und von ganz unterschiedlichen Bearbeitern auffallend übereinstimmende Beobachtungen gemacht, so dass eine solche Gruppierung bei aller Ähnlichkeit doch als gegeben gelten darf. Mit der Unterscheidung dieser Gruppen ist freilich noch nichts zu ihrer Relevanz gesagt. Interessant ist aber nun, dass sich bei ihren Verteilungen geographische Abhängigkeiten abzuzeichnen scheinen: In Antiochia und Hama etwa überwiegt wie in Gindarus die ESA a, während in Samaria und Tel Anafa die ESA b die Mehrheit stellt. Das Material der Grabungen der 1990er Jahre auf dem Tel Anafa in Israel ist dabei aufgrund der Menge der Funde und der erarbeiteten Stratigraphie am Ort von besonderer Bedeutung, so dass auch die entsprechenden Warenbeschreibungen von Kathleen Warner Slane zitiert sein mögen: ‚The biscuit of this ware is normally hard and granular, without visible inclusions; its color varies between very pale brown (10YR8/3) and pink (7,5YR7/4). The slip (...) is usually dark red with a nonreflective sheen. A minority of pieces have a softer, pink biscuit (7,5YR7/4), in which tiny sparkling inclusions are sometimes visible; the slip of such pieces is more orange and may be matte and worn or have a high luster. Pieces with a matte, worn slip have a powdery biscuit, while those with a lustrous slip have a harder fabric, which is nevertheless still softer than the normal, very pale brown fabric.'[5] Fügt man noch Beobachtungen aus weiteren Orten hinzu, so offenbart sich eine Nord-Süd-Aufteilung, nach der die ESA a zahlenmäßig stärker im Großraum Syrien und die ESA b stärker im Großraum Phönizien-Palästina auftritt (vgl. **Abb. 3**). Dies kann als ein Hinweis auf zwei demgemäß zu lokalisierende Produktionszentren gewertet werden[6].

Eine wichtige und zunehmend wichtiger werdende Hilfe bieten die naturwissenschaftlichen Methoden. Angesichts der Bedeutung der Sigillaten hat man sich schon mehrfach um entsprechende Untersuchungen bemüht. Die bislang durchgeführten Arbeiten auf Basis der Neutronenaktivierungsanalyse (NAA) und der Röntgenfluoreszenzanalyse (RFA) konnten nun keine signifikanten Differenzen in der chemischen Zusammensetzung der Tone nachweisen[7]. Insbesondere Gerwulf Schneider spricht sich daher nachdrücklich für eine singuläre Herkunft der ESA aus. Aufgrund der vorliegenden Referenzwerte lassen sich darüber hinaus zunehmend konkretere Aussagen zur Lokalisierung der Tonlagerstätten treffen, wobei für die ESA der nordwestsyrische Raum favorisiert wird[8]. Dieser Ansicht wird auch in vielen Publikationen zum Raum Iudäa / Palästina gefolgt[9].

An dieser Stelle soll der Vorschlag gemacht werden, die beiden Beobachtungen in einer Synthese zusammenzuführen, nach der es zwei Produktionsorte mit makroskopisch unterscheidbaren Produkten gibt, die aber – folgt man den chemischen Analysen – beide in nicht allzu großer Entfernung voneinander in Nordwestsyrien liegen. Eine unverkennbare Leistung einer solchen These des geographischen Zusammenhangs der ESA Werkstätten ist sicher die Erklärbarkeit des dauerhaft absolut identischen Typenspektrums der ESA a und b. Es könnten also bei der ESA ganz ähnliche Verhältnisse wie bei der ESC vorliegen, für die anhand von Werkstattbelegen in Çandarlı (ESC) und Pergamon (Pergamenische Sigillata) zwei Gruppen nachgewiesen werden konnten. Diese sind eng miteinander verwandt, wobei Pergamon das größere und ältere Zentrum war. Das Material ist makroskopisch sehr ähnlich, aber oftmals doch unterscheidbar[10]. Die naturwissenschaftlichen Analysen ergaben für die Stücke aus Çandarlı einen leicht größeren Kalkanteil, allerdings sind die Waren nicht immer voneinander zu trennen[11].

Für die nähere Überprüfung von Thesen zur Herkunft der jeweiligen Sigillaten sind insbesondere die Verteilungen der frühesten und spätesten ihrer Typen wichtig. Dies liegt schlicht daran, dass man sowohl zu Beginn wie auch am Ende der Produktionszeit wohl einen beschränkteren Absatzmarkt annehmen darf. Auch diesbezüglich erscheint der nordwestsyrische Raum um Antiochia als wahrscheinlichster Herstellungsort der ESA[12]. Hinsichtlich der Anfangsphase der Produktion ist aber der Blick noch weiter zurück auf eventuelle Vorläufer zu richten, die gegebenenfalls am gleichen Ort, wenn nicht gar in den gleichen Werkstätten produziert wurden. Eine Beurteilung dieser Fabrikate ist jedoch aufgrund der geringeren Einheitlichkeit wesentlich problematischer, und nur aus wenigen Orten liegen aussagekräftige Vorlagen oder gar chemische Analysen vor.

Als Vorläufer der Östlichen Sigillaten lassen sich in der Regel zwei Gruppen ansprechen, nämlich erstens die hellenistischen Ableger der vor allem aus Athen

[5] Slane 1997, 269.

[6] In dieser Weise wurde es von mir angeregt, Kramer 2004, 179 f. (vgl. auch Kramer 2012, 15 f.), wobei dies auch durch erste chemische Analysen am Material aus Tel Anafa gestützt schien, s. dazu das Folgende; vgl. danach auch Berlin 2005, 442: ‚Eastern Sigillata A was manufactured on the Phoenician coast'.

[7] Gunneweg 1983 (NAA); Slane 1994 und Slane 1997, 394 f. (NAA); Schneider 1995 und Schneider 1996 (RFA). Schneider 1995, 416 deutet nebenbei zwei Untergruppen an; inwieweit diese mit den hier vorgeschlagenen Gruppen ESA a und b korrelieren, kann zur Zeit noch nicht gesagt werden. Insgesamt ist nach wie vor zu bedenken, dass die Zahl der untersuchten Stücke noch nicht repräsentativ ist und auch bei der Interpretation der naturwissenschaftlichen Daten erheblicher Spielraum gegeben ist.

[8] Schneider 1995, 416; Schneider 1996, 131 (zwischen Lattakia und Tarsus).

[9] Rosenthal-Heginbottom 2003, 214 und 220.

[10] Meyer Schlichtmann 1988, 13 f.; vgl. Zelle 1997, 21-24, wo eine dritte Gruppe hinzugefügt wird.

[11] Schneider 2009, 302 f.

[12] Slane 1997, 272. Allerdings kann die jeweilige Zeitspanne der Beschränkung auch sehr kurz sein. Oft ist zu beobachten, dass eine Produktion sich schon von Beginn an auf hohem quantitativen wie qualitativen Niveau gestaltet, was dann auch für die Ausdehnung der Absatzmärkte gelten dürfte. Auf der anderen Seite würde eine abrupt endende Produktion sich kaum an den Verteilungen indizieren lassen. In Hinblick auf die Eastern Sigillata A ist allerdings eher von einer länger andauernden Abnahme der Produktionsraten in mittelrömischer Zeit auszugehen, vgl. Hayes 1985, 38 f.

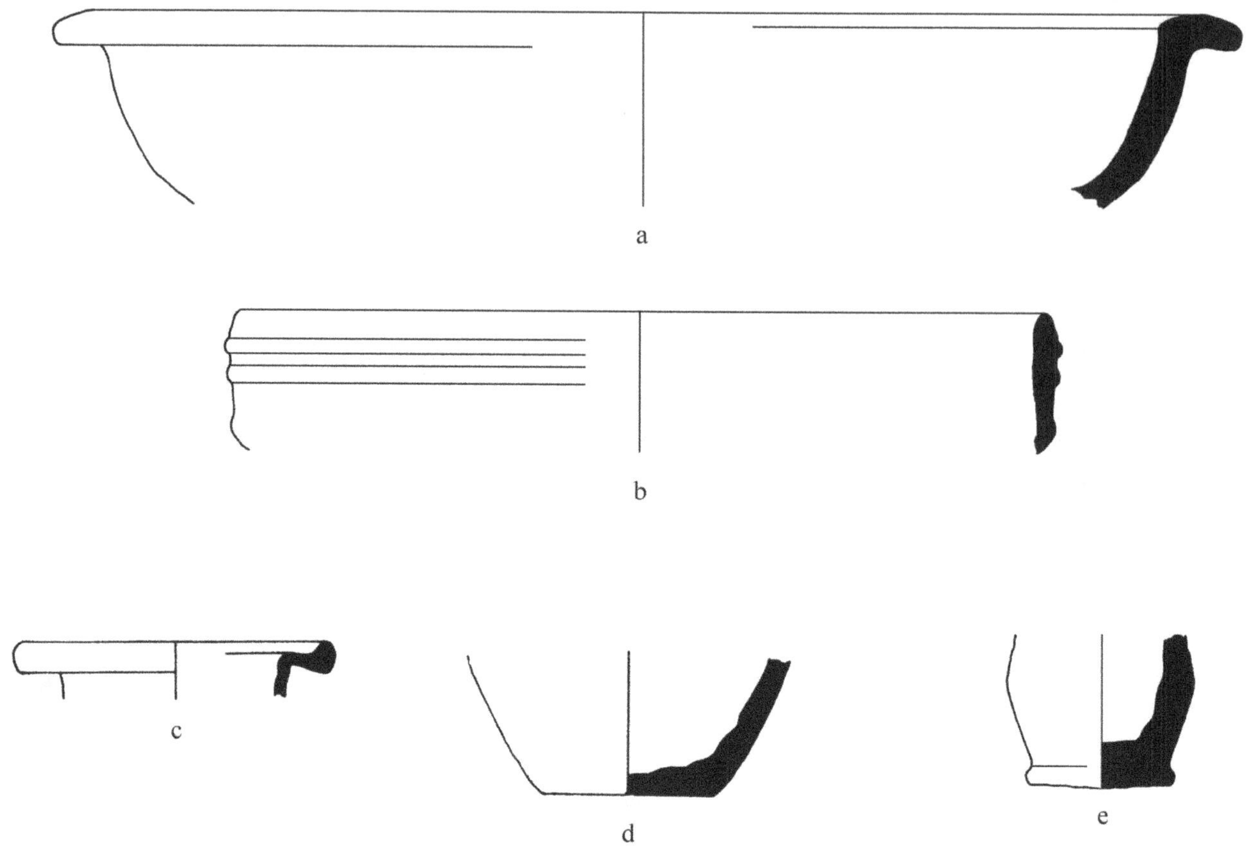

Abb. 2. nicht typologisierte Formen der ESA c (Kramer 2012, Taf. 15 f. 109; 112; 118; Kramer 2004, Taf. 95, ES 2; ES 4)

Abb. 3. Hauptverbreitungsgebiete der Eastern Sigillata A (Talbert 1985, 70, modifiziert)

bekannten Schwarzglanzkeramik und zweitens eine Fein- oder auch ‚Halbfeinkeramik' (Semi Fine Ware), die nicht oder nur teilweise überzogen ist und oftmals auch in den Formen der Schwarzglanzkeramik – oder der frühesten ESA – auftritt. In Bezug auf die erste Gruppe, also die schwarzen Vorläufer der ESA, scheinen die Verhältnisse in Phönizien-Palästina und Nordsyrien auf den ersten Blick unterschiedlich zu sein. Für Tel Anafa wurde ein so genannter Black Slipped Predecessor (BSP) identifiziert, für den chemische Analysen der Warenbeschaffenheit eine direkte Zugehörigkeit zur ESA nahelegen. Die Formen dieser BSP entstammen dem frühesten Typenspektrum der ESA, wobei besonders die schwarzen Fischteller und Echinusschalen zehnmal häufiger seien als ihre roten Pendants[13]. Die Warenidentität mit der ESA und die nordsyrische Herkunft der ESA vorausgesetzt, müsste also auch die BSP aus Nordsyrien stammen, sich dort also auch identische Zustände belegen lassen. Für das nordsyrische Gindarus schien sich aber ein anderes Bild zu ergeben. Hier wurden der ESA nur sehr wenige schwarze Belege (weniger als 1%) zugeordnet, die aber zu denselben frühen Typen wie in Tel Anafa gehören, also vor allem Fischteller und Echinusschalen sowie auch einige markantere Formen (**Abb. 1**)[14]. Über diese schwarzen Belege der ESA hinaus wurde allerdings eine eigenständige gewichtige Schwarzglanzkeramik separiert, die sicher vor der ESA zu datieren ist[15]. Die Ware dieser Stücke aus Gindarus, für die keine chemischen Analysen vorliegen, ist sehr einheitlich und zeigt aufgrund der oft zu beobachtenden Körnigkeit des Bruchs und der normalerweise sehr blassen Farbe mehr Nähe zur ESA b als zur sonst in Gindarus dominanten ESA a. Das Formenrepertoire unterscheidet sich großteils von der ESA. Dies gilt besonders für Knickwandschalen, Skyphoi, Kantharoi und viele andere Typen. Die Mehrheit allerdings stellen wiederum Fischteller und Echinusschalen, die sich – zumal am Fragment und bei der ähnlichen Warenbeschaffenheit – nicht immer sicher anhand von größerer Wandungsstärke, Standringausprägung oder ähnlichen Details von den entsprechenden frühen Typen der ESA abgrenzen lassen. Eingedenk des stets pauschalisierenden und künstlichen Charakters solcher Bezeichnungen, die ja nicht zwangsläufig wirklichen Produktionsgruppen entsprechen, sondern uns zunächst lediglich helfen, das Material zu gliedern, ist es durchaus denkbar, dass in Tel Anafa eine Reihe von Stücken der BSP (=ESA) gemäß der für Gindarus verwendeten Terminologie unter der Schwarzglanzkeramik zu fassen wären[16]. Andersherum könnte eine Reihe von Fischtellern und Echinusschalen der Schwarzglanzkeramik aus Gindarus gemäß der sich aus dem Befund am Ort ergebenden etwas einfacheren Aufteilung aus Tel Anafa auch zur BSP gezählt werden. Unter dieser Annahme könnten Unterschiede, wie etwa das oben angesprochene zahlenmäßige Übergewicht der schwarzen Vertreter der Echinusschalen und Fischteller in der ESA in Tel Anafa, das in Gindarus nicht beobachtet wurde, nachvollziehbar werden.

Die Betrachtung dieser zumeist schwarzen Vorläufer der ESA ließe sich anhand weiterer Arten fortführen. So lassen sich in Nordsyrien zusätzlich Gefäße, die der Westabhangkeramik nachempfunden sind, isolieren, während in Tel Anafa hiervon offenbar nur vereinzelte Belege auftraten, die unter die BSP subsumiert wurden[17]. Dasselbe gilt für die Reliefbecher, die in Gindarus in frühhellenistische Megarische Becher und solche der ESA zu trennen waren, wobei ein ausgesprochen hohes Maß an Ähnlichkeiten der Dekorelemente mit denen aus Antiochia auffiel. In Tel Anafa werden die Reliefbecher wiederum zur ESA / BSP gezählt[18].

Von diesen zumeist schwarz und komplett überzogenen Produkten griechischer Tradition ist ein anderer Vorläufer der ESA zu trennen, der in ähnlicher Weise an den meisten Orten im syrisch-levantinischen Bereich und darüber hinaus zu finden ist. Hauptcharakteristikum dieser Fein- oder Halbfeinkeramik ist ein das Gefäß nur teilweise bedeckender und meist rötlicher Überzug. Darüber hinaus erscheint diese Gattung in Bezug auf Ware, Form und Detailausprägungen des Überzugs weniger einheitlich, so dass eher von einer regional geprägten Produktion als von einem großen Herstellungszentrum auszugehen ist. Es ist möglich, dass die Gestaltungsweise dabei ursprünglich auf eine nichtgriechische, eisenzeitliche Tradition zurückzuführen ist. Jedoch ist sowohl das wiederum durch Echinusschalen und – meist kleinere – Fischteller dominierte Formenspektrum wie auch die Herstellungstechnik des Überzuges durch Eintauchen in einen Schlicker griechischen Praktiken entlehnt. Diese Keramik steht der Sigillata nicht ganz so nahe wie die Schwarzglanzkeramik; es bestehen zum Beispiel Unterschiede in der größeren Wandungsstärke, der weniger scharfen Profilierung, dem raueren Überzug sowie meist im Fehlen von Palmettstempeln und Strichelkränzen. Nichtsdestoweniger könnte die in dieser Keramik weitergeführte Tradition eines rötlichen Überzuges eine wichtige Anregung zum Wechsel auf die rote Überzugstechnik der Sigillaten geliefert haben[19].

In Gindarus liegt auch diese Gattung in außergewöhnlicher Vielfalt und zahlenmäßig fast so stark wie die ESA

[13] Slane 1997, 271.

[14] Dies sind nach der Typologie von Hayes 1985, Abb. 1 f. vor allem die Formen 1 (Fischteller), 2 (schlichter Teller), 6 (markanter großer Teller mit eingeschnürter Wandung), 17 (konischer Becher mit innen profiliertem Rand) und 20 (Echinusschale), Kramer 2004, 178 und 181 f.

[15] Kramer 2004, 122 f.

[16] Darauf könnte auch das sehr viel größere – also vielleicht mehrere Produktionsgruppen umfassende – Spektrum der Anteile der chemisch nachgewiesenen Elemente bei der BSP gegenüber der ESA deuten, selbst wenn die ESA innerhalb dieses Spektrums liegt, s. Slane 1994, 55, Abb. 1.

[17] s. zu Antiochia schon Waagé 1948, Abb. 3; ferner Kramer 2004, 132 f. bzw. Slane 1997, Taf. 4, FW 32.

[18] Kramer 2001, 136 f. und ebd. 187 f. (Form 24); zu Tel Anafa Cornell 1997.

[19] s. zur Abgrenzung einer solchen Keramik Kramer 2004, 159 f.; vgl. Berlin 1997, passim, bes. 7 f. und Römer 1995, 352 zum transeuphratischen Gebiet (‚lokale hellenistische rot engobierte Ware').

vor. Besonders markant dabei ist der regelmäßig an der Außenseite des Gefäßes in Tropfenform auslaufende Überzug, was Anlass zu der Bezeichnung ‚Keramik mit Tropfenüberzug' gab. Ihre Ware erscheint nicht ganz so einheitlich wie die der Schwarzglanzkeramik oder gar der ESA; die feinsten Vertreter sind mit dem bloßen Auge nicht von der ESA zu unterscheiden, die nicht so feinen nähern sich makroskopisch der lokalen Einfachen Keramik an. Auffällig sind immer wieder kleine Brennfehler, die zu Blasen oder grünlichem Ton geführt haben, ohne dass man dabei aber direkt von Fehlbränden sprechen könnte. Alle diese Beobachtungen – vor allem die Nähe der Ware sowohl zur ESA wie auch zur einfachen Gebrauchskeramik – passen gut zusammen, wenn man davon ausgeht, dass die ESA eben aus dieser nordsyrischen Region um Antiochia stammt. Diese Zusammengehörigkeit wird weiter dadurch gestützt, dass die besten Formvergleiche für die Keramik mit Tropfenüberzug aus Gindarus wiederum aus Antiochia stammen, wenn sich auch nicht für alle Formen Parallelen fanden.

Wenn man in Bezug auf diese Halbfeinkeramik / Semi Fine Ware erneut Tel Anafa als Referenzort heranzieht, zeigen sich vielfache Differenzen. So gibt es bei den Formen viele Unterschiede im Detail, und die meisten so benannten Gefäße weisen gar keinen Überzug auf. Dennoch lässt sich auch in Tel Anafa das Phänomen des ungleichmäßigen und teilweisen Überzuges (‚Spatter Painted Ware') beobachten, der aber selten den ausgeprägten Tropfencharakter aufweist. Derartige Gefäße können – anders als in Gindarus – auch Palmettenstempelungen zeigen[20]. Bei Annahme einer lokalen beziehungsweise regionalen Fabrikation dieser Keramik überraschen diese Unterschiede nicht. Etwas verwirrend erscheinen dagegen zunächst die auf Neutronenaktivierungsanalysen basierenden Aussagen zur Tonbeschaffenheit. In der maßgeblichen Publikation von 1997 wird so ein gemeinsames Produktionszentrum vermutlich im phönizischen Küstenbereich vorgeschlagen: ‚The NAA carried out (...) indicated that semi fine and ESA may be from the same manufacturing centers. (...) If semi fine was not produced in Tyre itself, it was certainly produced very close by.'[21] Diese Aussagen gehen unter anderem auf einen Artikel aus dem Jahr 1994 zurück, der sich zunächst mit den – ebenfalls auf NAA gründenden – Thesen Jan Gunnewegs auseinandersetzte, nach der die ESA aus Zypern stammte[22]. In diesem Artikel wurde eine Zusammengehörigkeit von ESA und BSP konstatiert, allerdings die zypriotische Herkunft verworfen. In Bezug auf die Semi Fine Ware wird nun tatsächlich festgestellt, dass sie zum einen ‚almost certainly from a Phoenician coastal source' stammt und zum anderen ‚a tempered variant of ESA' sei[23]. Die Aussage zur Verbindung zur ESA bleibt also vage. Im Falle einer Identität der Waren liefe dies aber darauf hinaus, dass es neben dem ESA Zentrum in Nordsyrien doch mindestens ein weiteres in Phönizien gegeben haben müsste. Allerdings offenbart der Blick auf die Ergebnisdiagramme der chemischen Analysen doch erhebliche Differenzen zwischen der Semi Fine Ware und der ESA[24]. Jedenfalls scheint sich aus diesen Untersuchungen keine zwingende Einheit von phönizischer Semi Fine Ware und ESA und somit eine phönizische Herkunft auch der ESA zu ergeben.

Insgesamt war die Bandbreite und wohl ebenso der quantitative Ausstoß der frühhellenistischen Feinkeramik in Nordwestsyrien überdurchschnittlich groß. Möglicherweise darf man in den entsprechenden Werkstätten – vor allem der Schwarzglanzkeramik – die direkten Vorgänger derjenigen sehen, die dann auf die neue ‚Modeware' ESA umstiegen, welche schnell in größerem Umfang und weiter als je zuvor verhandelt wurde.

Und vielleicht darf man dabei sogar die Untergruppe der ESA b als die ursprüngliche bezeichnen, bedenkt man die größere Nähe der Schwarzglanzkeramik aus Gindarus zur Ware der ESA b. In diesem Zusammenhang ist schließlich die Idee verlockend – wenn auch zum momentanen Zeitpunkt noch nicht zu beweisen –, die in einem Brief Ciceros genannten, offenbar berühmten ‚vasa Rhosica' mit der Eastern Sigillata A zu identifizieren. Rhosus liegt am Golf von Issus, nur etwa 35km von Antiochia entfernt, und würde somit gut zu den bisherigen Kenntnissen des Herstellungsgebietes der ESA passen[25].

Weitere Untergruppen

Jenseits der Lokalisierung der Herstellungszentren der ESA a und ESA b ist davon auszugehen, dass es zusätzlich kleinere Untergruppen gab, zu deren Verbreitung noch kaum etwas gesagt werden kann. Immer wieder gibt es in den Materialvorlagen solche Hinweise auf weitere Serien, die wohl nicht alle als bloße ‚Ausreißer' der Hauptgruppen zu werten sind. Für das nordsyrische Apamea wies Michel Vanderhoeven neben den beiden bekannten, hier als ESA a und b angesprochenen Waren auf weitere Untergliederungen hin, die aber sehr kleinteilige Warendifferenzierungen vornehmen und in der Forschung kaum beachtet wurden[26]. Jennifer Tobin separierte für Issus, also einem Ort wiederum in großer Nähe zu Antiochia, drei Arten der ESA, wobei ihr erster Typ der ESA a entsprechen dürfte[27]. Für Kappadokien stellte Zafer Derin eine weitere Serie vor[28], und selbst für den südlich von Syrien gelegenen

20 Berlin 1997, 7 f. zur ‚Spatter Painted Ware'; Berlin 1997, 75 f. mit PW 145–148 zu den Stempelungen.
21 Berlin 1997, 9 und 10, darauf nimmt im gleichen Band Slane 1997, 272 Bezug.
22 Slane 1994 zu Gunneweg 1983; wie bereitwillig man diese angeblich sicheren naturwissenschaftlichen Ergebnisse annahm, zeigt etwa Herbert 1985, bes. 367.
23 Slane 1994, 63 und 60.
24 Slane 1994, 55, Abb. 1; 61, Abb. 3; 62, Abb. 4.
25 Cic. Att. 6, 1, 13, s. dazu vor allem Lund 2006. Schon vorher wurde versucht, die ‚vasa Rhosica' mit bestimmten Keramikarten in Verbindung zu bringen, wobei in der älteren Literatur meist eine Bleiglasurkeramik favorisiert wurde, s. etwa Hans 1987, bes. 116, Anm. 2 mit weiterer Literatur.
26 Vanderhoeven 1989, 24 f.
27 Tobin 2004, 58.
28 Derin 1994.

Bereich liegen entsprechende Beobachtungen vor, so etwa von Frank Braemer zu Gerasa/Jerash im Nordwesten Jordaniens[29].

An dieser Stelle möchte ich die Isolierung einer weiteren Untergruppe vorstellen, wie ich sie anhand des Surveymateriales aus Diocaesarea im Rauen Kilikien vorgenommen habe und für die leider noch keine chemischen Analysen vorliegen[30]. Diese ESA c, die am Ort etwa 10% der ESA ausmacht, ist hinsichtlich der Ware von der ESA a nur schwer abzugrenzen; die Unterschiede liegen eher in der Art des Überzuges.

> ESA c:
> *Ton:* sehr fein, weich, regelmäßig wenig Glimmer, glatter Bruch; hellgelblich bis hellbräunlich (CEC C7–D8; Munsell 10 YR 6–7/3–4; 7,5 YR 6–7/4–6);
> *Überzug:* glatt, matt, ungleichmäßig dünn und durchscheinend; gelblich oder hellorange, nicht so kräftig rotbräunlich wie die übrige ESA (CEC E9 / Munsell 5 YR 6–7/4–6).

Können diese Merkmale auch des Überzuges durchaus als ‚Ausreißer' der geläufigen ESA auftreten[31], so kommen Besonderheiten im Formenspektrum hinzu, um diese Gruppe zu definieren. Zwar liegen die gängigen ESA Typen in der ESA c vor, jedoch entziehen sich einige Formen dem bekannten Repertoire und finden sich etwa nicht in John Hayes´ Übersicht zur ESA im ‚Atlante delle forme ceramiche'[32] (**Abb. 2**). Parallelen speziell zu diesen gibt es aber gelegentlich in Tarsus im Ebenen Kilikien, wo sich generell – auch in Hinblick auf die Ware – die besten Vergleiche finden[33]. In Gindarus konnte ebenfalls eine kleine bislang nicht bestimmbare Einheit von neun Fragmenten isoliert werden, die sich angesichts der Ware vielleicht zur ESA c schlagen lässt. Allerdings bestehen die Formen hier vor allem aus kleinen Fläschchen mit Flachboden, die in Tarsus oder Diocaesarea bislang ohne Vergleich bleiben[34]. Darüber hinaus beschreibt Rolf Stucky für Ras Shamra - Leukos Limen an der nordsyrischen Küste einige Stücke, die sehr gut zu den skizzierten Kriterien passen[35]. Weiter südlich sind mir bislang keine Vergleichskandidaten aufgefallen. Somit scheint die ESA c vor allem in Kilikien und in geringerem Ausmaß in Nordsyrien verbreitet gewesen zu sein, und möglicherweise wurde sie auch in Kilikien, vielleicht in Tarsus, produziert. Es könnte sich dabei durchaus noch um regelrechte Tochterbetriebe der nordsyrischen ESA-Werkstätten handeln, liegt doch selbst das kilikische Tarsus nur einen Weg von etwa 100km meist an der Küste entlang von Antiochia entfernt.

Ausblick

Die kleinteilige Beschäftigung mit der Eastern Sigillata A bietet auch Erkenntnispotential für zukünftige Untersuchungen zu Wirtschaft und Geschichte des Seleukidenreiches. Einige Perspektiven seien abschließend kurz angedeutet.

1.) Selbst wenn beide große Untergruppen der ESA, wie sie hier vorgestellt wurden, aus Nordwestsyrien stammen, sie vielleicht in großer Nähe zueinander liegen und man möglicherweise gar von Tochterbetrieben sprechen kann, so sind die festgestellten Unterschiede in den Distributionsstrukturen doch bemerkenswert. Wie kommt es, dass einige Werkstätten offenbar langandauernd stärker in den Raum Phönizien-Palästina exportierten als andere mit ihren identischen Produkten? Möglicherweise spielt es eine Rolle, welche Betriebe unmittelbar an der Küste, also an den Seehandelsrouten, lagen.

Dies wird sich aber erst klären lassen, wenn tatsächlich Werkstätten der ESA gefunden werden[36].

2.) Dass das Auftreten von Artefakten ausdünnt, je weiter man sich von ihren Produktionsorten entfernt, überrascht nicht. Vielleicht lassen sich darüber hinaus aber auch Abhängigkeiten der Hauptverbreitungsgebiete der ESA zum politischen Gebilde des Seleukidenreiches ausmachen. Dies gilt natürlich für Nordsyrien mit dem urbanen Schwerpunkt der Tetrapolis inklusive Antiochia am Orontes, aber ebenso für Kilikien, das als letzte Bastion der Seleukiden gelten darf. Besonders spannend sind die Verhältnisse im pausenlos umkämpften Bereich von Südsyrien, Phönizien und Palästina. Nach den Erfolgen Antiochus´ III. im 5. Syrischen Krieg zu Beginn des 2. Jh. v. Chr. gehörte Südsyrien zur Zeit der Etablierung der Eastern Sigillata A in der Mitte des 2. Jh. v. Chr. ebenfalls zu den Seleukiden. Allerdings begann bereits 165 v. Chr. der Makkabäeraufstand, der eine im Laufe der Zeit um sich greifende Abspaltung von Teilen Palästinas vom Seleukidenreich nach sich zog. Hier bietet sich eine ganz eigene kulturhistorische Perspektive, wenn man der Hypothese folgt, dass die in dieser Zeit religiös hochsensibilisierten Juden möglicherweise bewusst die Verwendung dieser nicht-jüdischen Gegenstände ablehnten – obwohl oder gerade weil diese so charakteristisch griechischen Güter so dominant am Markt vertreten waren[37]. Ungeachtet dessen ließe sich aber auch fragen, ob die ansonsten auffallend hohe Dichte an ESA gerade in diesen umstrittenen südlichen Gebieten

29 Braemer 1989.
30 Kramer 2012, 19, Nr. 109–119.
31 Selbst Stücke mit fehlerhaftem Überzug wurden verhandelt, wenn die Gebrauchsfähigkeit nicht eingeschränkt war, s. etwa Mitsopoulos-Leon 1975 zur Sigillata-Ladung aus einem Schiffswrack (300 Stücke geborgen), bes. Taf. 27, 2.
32 Hayes 1985.
33 s. speziell Kramer 2012, 17, Nr. 109, 112 und 118; vgl. allg. Jones 1950, 173 f. In Tarsus ermöglichte mir Azlı Özyar 2003 dankenswerterweise den Zugang zum Magazin der Grabungen auf dem Gözlü Kule, so dass diese Ähnlichkeiten in Autopsie bestätigt werden konnten.
34 Kramer 2004, 181 mit ES 1–6.
35 Stucky 1983, 139. Für diese bringt er – allerdings ohne Begründung – Laodicea als Herkunft ins Gespräch.
36 Die neueren Begehungen in der Amuq- und Orontes-Region haben diesbezüglich keine neuen Erkenntnisse ergeben, s. Yener 2000 und Yener 2005.
37 Zu Jerusalem s. Rosenthal-Heginbottom 2003, 214; zur interpretativen Dimension des Phänomens Berlin 2005, 442 f. und zuletzt Trampedach 2012, 75 f.

des Reiches – die kaum nur eine Folge der intensiven Grabungstätigkeiten im heutigen Israel ist – mehr ist als eine bloße Zufallserscheinung des ungelenkten antiken Handels. Möglicherweise etablierten sich gerade in dieser stets neuralgischen Zone – schon in den 120er Jahren lösten sich etwa auch die phönizischen Städte von der seleukidischen Herrschaft – Strukturen, die den Handel mit dem seleukidischen Kerngebiet belebten. Jedenfalls scheint sich das hohe Aufkommen der ESA südlich von Judäa nicht fortzusetzen, und in Ägypten schließlich ist ihre ohnehin weitgehend auf den Küsten- oder Deltabereich begrenzte Präsenz bemerkenswert gering[38]. Schließlich lässt sich auch an der Ostgrenze des Seleukidenreiches das Aufkommen der Sigillata weiterführend hinterfragen. So wird oftmals angenommen, dass der Euphrat als neue politische Grenze zum in der Mitte des 2. Jh. v. Chr. entstandenen Partherreich kein großes Hindernis für den Warenaustausch gewesen sei. Tatsächlich fallen selbst auf den Grabungen östlich des Euphrats immer wieder Sigillatascherben auf, jedoch ist ihre Zahl im Vergleich zu den Befunden westlich des Flusses auffallend gering. Daher ist meines Erachtens davon auszugehen, dass diese Grenze den Warenfluss doch spürbar beeinträchtigt hat[39]. Derartige Abhängigkeiten zwischen politischen und wirtschaftlichen Grenzen sind für die Antike, der man das Phänomen ‚Wirtschaftspolitik' generell weitgehend abspricht, nach wie vor wenig erforscht. Man muss aber gar keine direkte Wirtschaftspolitik als Steuerungsmechanismus im modernen Sinn postulieren, um entsprechende Abhängigkeiten zu diagnostizieren und sie gegebenenfalls als Indikatoren für andere kulturhistorische Entwicklungen bewerten zu können[40].

3.) In anderer Hinsicht fällt dagegen eine bemerkenswerte Diskrepanz zwischen der Keramikproduktion und den politischen Entwicklungen auf: Es ist erstaunlich, dass sich der Boom der ESA gerade in einer Zeit vollzog, in der das kollabierende, sich schließlich nur noch auf einen kleinen nordsyrischen und kilikischen Restbereich beschränkende Seleukidenreich von endlosen und wahnwitzigen Kämpfen um die Herrschaft erschüttert wurde. Es fragt sich, wie eine solche Zeit des Chaos′ und des Verschleißes aller verbliebenen Ressourcen in fruchtlosen Thronkämpfen zusammengeht mit den ungeheuren Keramikproduktionsraten höchster Qualität inklusive der aufwendigen Rohstoffbeschaffung und -aufbereitung, der kontinuierlichen Ausbildung von Personal, der Beschaffung des Brennmaterials und der Wartung der sicher beeindruckenden Ofenanlagen sowie vor allem der Aufrechterhaltung der Distributionsstrukturen.

Und über diese Fabrikationsbedingungen hinaus ist auch die Fundverteilung im seleukidischen Kerngebiet aufschlussreich. Begehungen in Nordsyrien und der türkischen Antiochene deuten darauf hin, dass die Dichte der besiedelten Tells gerade im späten 2. und 1. Jh. v. Chr. ihr Maximum erreichte. Hier offenbart sich also gerade für die Zeit des politischen Zusammenbruchs eine bemerkenswerte wirtschaftliche und siedlungsgeschichtliche Prosperität. Insbesondere die Zeit der wenig durchschaubaren, ‚barbarischen' Fremdherrschaft des armenischen Königs Tigranes (83–69 v. Chr.) scheint dieser positiven Entwicklung eher dienlich gewesen zu sein[41]. Vermutlich lassen wir uns bei der negativen Bewertung dieser Zeit zu sehr von der römisch geprägten Historiographie verleiten, deren vorrangiges Interesse es war, im Nachhinein die ordnende Hand Roms herauszustellen. Darüber hinaus ging es darum, die griechischen Mächte des Hellenismus und besonders die Seleukiden zunehmend in die Rolle der dekadenten und degenerierten orientalischen Despoten zu schieben, von denen sich Rom positiv abzusetzen hatte. Wie die Dinge im Einzelnen auch zu beurteilen sein mögen, auf jeden Fall erscheint eine Analyse der späten Seleukidenzeit heute nur noch unter Einbeziehung der archäologischen Zeugnisse sinnvoll[42].

Norbert Kramer
Seminar für Alte Geschichte und Epigraphik
Universität Heidelberg
Marstallhof 4
D-69117 Heidelberg
norbert.kramer@zaw.uni-heidelberg.de

Bibliographie

Archibald, Z. H., Davies, J., Gabrielsen, V. und Oliver, G. J. (Hrsg.). 2001. *Hellenistic Economies.* London, New York, Routledge.

Berlin, A. M. 1997. The Plain Wares. In S. C. Herbert (Hrsg.), *Tel Anafa II i: The Hellenistic and Roman Pottery.* Journal of Roman Archaeology Supplement 10 II, i, 1–244. Ann Arbor, Kelsey Museum of the University of Michigan.

Berlin, A. M. 2005. Jewish Life Before the Revolt: The Archaeological Evidence. *Journal for the Study of Judaism* 36, 417–470.

Braemer, F. 1989. Une fabrique (locale?) de céramique fine

[38] Zu Beispielen in Ägypten s. etwa Mieliwodzki 1995 und zum quantitativen Auftreten Malfitana 2002, 152. Interessant ist ferner, dass im ptolemäischen Ägypten kein Konkurrenzprodukt zur kleinasiatischen ESB oder ESC und zur syrischen ESA geschaffen wurde.

[39] s. dazu Kramer 2003, 125 f.

[40] s. zur hellenistischen Wirtschaft Archibald 2001; Davies 2006 und von Reden 2007. Vgl. für die römische Zeit Drexhage 2002, 27 f.

[41] vgl. kurz Kramer 2004, 273 f. mit Quellenangaben.

[42] Auch die seleukidische Münzprägung scheint bis zum Schluss erstaunlich stabil geblieben zu sein, s. etwa Schlösser 1986. Noch Ehling 2008 verzichtet rigoros auf jegliche Berücksichtigung archäologischer Quellen.

à Jerash au tournant de l'ère. *Syria* 66, 153–167.

CEC-Farbkarte, ed. Féderation Européenne des fabricants de carreaux céramiques.

Cornell, L. 1997. A Note on the Molded Bowls. In S. C. Herbert (Hrsg.), *Tel Anafa II i: The Hellenistic and Roman Pottery.* Journal of Roman Archaeology Supplement 10 II, i, 407–416, Ann Arbor, Kelsey Museum of the University of Michigan.

Davies J. K. 2006. Hellenistic Economies. In G. R. Bugh (Hrsg.), *The Cambridge Companion to the Hellenistic World*, 73–92. Cambridge, Cambridge University Press.

Derin, Z. 1994. Aşağı Fırat Havzasındaki (Elazığ - Malatya Bölgesi) Yerleşim Merkezlerinde Ele Geçen "Doğu Sigillatası A Türü Keramikler". *Arkeoloji Dergisi* 2, 149–172.

Drexhage, H. J., Konen, H. und Ruffing, K. 2002. *Die Wirtschaft des Römischen Reiches (1.–3. Jahrhundert)*. Berlin, Akademie-Verlag.

Ehling, K. 2008. *Untersuchungen zur Geschichte der späten Seleukiden (164–163 v. Chr.). Vom Tode des Antiochos IV. bis zur Einrichtung der Provinz Syria unter Pompeius*. Historia Einzelschriften 196. Stuttgart, Franz Steiner-Verlag.

Gunneweg, J. 1983. *The Provenience, Typology and Chronology of Eastern Terra Sigillata.* Qedem 17. Jerusalem, Institute of Archaeology, Hebrew University.

Hans, L.-M. 1987. RHOSICA VASA am Hof Kleopatras VII. *Münstersche Beiträge zur Antiken Handelsgeschichte* 6, 116–121.

Hayes, J. W. 1985. *Atlante delle forme ceramiche II – Ceramica fine romana nel bacino mediterraneo (tardo ellenismo e primo impero).* Enciclopedia dell'Arte Antica. Roma, Istituto della Enciclopedia Italiana.

Herbert, S. 1985. Review Gunneweg 1983. *American Journal of Archaeology* 89, 365–367.

Jones, F. F. 1950. The Pottery. In H. Goldman (Hrsg.), *Excavations at Gözlü Kule.* Tarsus 1, 149–296. Princeton, University Press.

Kramer, N. 2003. Das Itinerar „Stathmoi Parthikoi" des Isidor von Charax – Beschreibung eines Handelsweges? *Klio* 85, 120–130.

Kramer, N. 2004. *Gindaros. Geschichte und Archäologie einer Siedlung im nordwestlichen Syrien von hellenistischer bis in frühbyzantinische Zeit.* Internationale Archäologie 41. Rahden, Verlag Marie Leidorf.

Kramer, N. 2012. *Keramik und Kleinfunde aus Diokaisareia.* Diokaisareia in Kilikien, Ergebnisse des Surveys 2001–2006, Bd. 1. Berlin, De Gruyter.

Loeschke, S. 1912. Sigillata Töpfereien in Tschandarli. *Mitteilungen des Deutschen Archäologischen Instituts, Athenische Abteilung* 37, 344–407.

Lund, J. 2003. Eastern Sigillata B. A Ceramic Fine Ware Industry in the Political and Commercial Landscape of the Eastern Mediterranean. In C. Abadie-Reynal (ed.), *Les céramiques en Anatolie aux époques hellénistique et romaine.* Actes de la Table ronde d'Istanbul, 22–24 mai 1996, 125–136. Paris, De Boccard.

Lund, J., Malfitana, D. und Poblome, J. 2006. Rhosica vasa mandavi (Cic., Att. 6.1.13): Towards the Identification of a Major Ceramic Tableware Industry of the Eastern Mediterranean: Eastern Sigillata A. *Archeologia Classica* 57, 491–507.

Malfitana, D. 2002. Eastern Terra Sigillata Wares in the Eastern Mediterranean. Notes on an Initial Quantitative Analysis, in: F. Blondé, P. Ballet und J.-F. Salles (Hrsg.), *Céramiques héllenistiques et romaines – production et diffusion en Mediterranée orientale (Chypre, Égypte et cote syro-palestinienne)*, 133–157. Lyon, Les belles lettres.

Meyer Schlichtmann, C. 1988. *Die pergamenische Sigillata aus der Stadtgrabung von Pergamon.* Pergamenische Forschungen 6. Berlin, De Gruyter.

Mieliwodzki, P. 1995. Terra Sigillata from Two Seasons of Excavations at Tell Atrib (1991/1992). *Études et Travaux* 17, 121–131.

Mitsopoulos-Leon, V. 1975. Gefäße aus Ostsigillata A von einem gesunkenen Schiff aus dem Golf von Antalya. *Germania* 53, 101–112.

Römer, Ch. 1995. Die rot engobierte Keramik im Unteren Habur-Gebiet, in H. Meyza und J. Młynarczyk (Hrsg.), *Hellenistic and Roman Pottery in the Eastern Mediterranean – Advances in Scientific Studies.* Acts of the II Nieborów Pottery Workshop, 351–363. Warschau, Polska Akademia Nauk.

Rosenthal-Heginbottom, R. 2003. Fine Ware and Lamps from Area A. In H. Geva (Hrsg.), *Jewish Quarter Excavations in the Old City of Jerusalem II: The Finds from Areas A, W and X-2*, 192–223. Jerusalem, Israel Exploration Society.

Schlösser, E. 1986. Gewichte der attischen Tetradrachmen der Seleukiden aus der Münzstätte Antiochia am Orontes. *Schweizer Münzblätter* 36, 62–66.

Schneider, G. 1995. Roman Red and Black Slipped Pottery from NE-Syria and Jordan – First Results of Chemical Analysis, in H. Meyza und J. Mlynarczyk (eds.), *Hellenistic and Roman Pottery in the Eastern Mediterranean – Advances in Scientific Studies.* Acts of the II Nieborów Pottery Workshop, 415–422. Warschau, Polska Akademia Nauk.

Schneider, G. 1996. Chemische und mineralogische Untersuchungen von Keramik der hellenistischen bis frühislamischen Zeit in Nordostsyrien, in K. Bartl und S. R. Hauser (Hrsg.), *Continuity and Change in Northern Mesopotamia from the Hellenistic to the early Islamic Period.* Berliner Beiträge zum Vorderen Orient 17, 127–136. Berlin, Reimer Verlag.

Schneider, G. und Japp, S. 2009. Röntgenfluoreszenzanalysen von 115 Keramikproben aus Pergamon, Çandarlı, Elaia und Atarneus (Türkei). *Istanbuler Mitteilungen* 59, 287–306.

Slane, K. W., Elam, J. M., Glascock, M. D.und Neff, H. 1994. Compositional Analysis of Eastern Sigillata A and Related Wares from Tel Anafa (Israel). *Journal of Archaeological Science* 21, 51–64.

Slane, K. W. 1997. The Fine Wares. In S. C. Herbert (Hrsg.), *Tel Anafa II i: The Hellenistic and Roman Pottery.* Journal of Roman Archaeology Suppl. 10 II, i, 249–406. Kelsey Museum of the University of Michigan. Ann Arbor.

Stucky, R. A. 1983. *Ras Shamra - Leukos Limen.* Mission Archeologique de Ras Shamra 1. Paris, Geuthner.

Talbert, R. J. A. 1985. *Atlas of Classical History.* London, Routledge.

Tobin, J. 2004. *Black Cilicia. A Study of the Plain of Issus During the Roman and Late Roman Periods.* British Archaeological Reports, International Series 1275. Oxford, BAR Publishing.

Trampedach, K. 2012. The War of the Hasmoneans. In G. Signori (Hrsg.), *Dying for the Faith, Killing for the Faith. Old-Testament Faith-Warriors (1 and 2 Maccabees) in Historical Perspective*, 61–78. Leiden, Brill.

Vanderhoeven, M. 1989. *Les terres sigillées.* Fouilles d'Apamée de Syrie 9, 1. Bruxelles, Centre Belge de Recherches Archeologiques à Apamée de Syrie.

von Reden, S. 2007. Wirtschaftliches Wachstum und institutioneller Wandel. In G. Weber (Hrsg.), *Kulturgeschichte des Hellenismus. Von Alexander dem Großen bis Kleopatra*, 177–201. Stuttgart, Klett-Cotta.

Waagé, F. O. 1948. *Ceramic and Islamic Coins.* Antioch on the Orontes 4, 1. Princeton, University Press.

Yener, A. 2000. The Amuq Valley Regional Projects, 1995–1998. *American Journal of Archaeology* 104, 163–220.

Yener, A. 2005. *The Amuq Valley Regional Projects: Surveys in the Plain of Antioch and Orontes Delta, Turkey, 1995–2002*, Bd. 1, Oriental Institute Publication 131. Chicago, Oriental Institute of the University of Chicago.

Zelle, M. 1997. *Die Terra Sigillata aus der Westtor-Nekropole in Assos.* Asia Minor Studien 27. Bonn, R. Habelt.

Hidden in PLAIN Sight: Ceramic Assemblages and Daily Life in the Ptolemaic Southern Levant

P. J. Stone

Abstract

The southern Levant, as a bridge between Egypt and north Syria, Arabia and the Mediterranean Sea, had great strategic and economic importance in the Hellenistic period. We have a wealth of papyrological evidence from the 3rd century BC, the period of Ptolemaic rule in the region. This documentary evidence confirms the importance of the region and furnishes details of local administration, taxation, and economic activities. This detailed historical context combined with archaeological evidence makes it possible to explore how political and economic conditions of Ptolemaic rule affected the lifestyles of people living in the southern Levant. In this paper, I use ceramic evidence to show that people at coastal sites and major inland cities along the Jezreel Valley had ready access to a wide range of regional and imported goods while people at large or important sites with a military or administrative function received a similar range of goods functionally, but with fewer imports, and that people at many small towns and villages had little taste for such goods, whether or not they were available[1].

Keywords: Kedesh, Akko-Ptolemais, Ptolemaic administration, Ancient economy, Household goods

Pottery as a source for history

The papyrological and historical records give us a wealth of evidence for the economy and administration of the Ptolemaic realm. We can speak in some detail about currency standards, the officials appointed to oversee trade and collect taxes, and the specific commodities sought by the royal court. The Zenon Papyri furnish detailed accounts of trade routes, goods exchanged, and duties levied in the southern Levant in the reign of Ptolemy II Philadelphos (283–246 BC). But despite an impressive amount of archaeological excavation in the region that has deliberately or accidentally recovered Hellenistic remains, the 3rd century BC is rather poorly understood from an archaeological standpoint. Without the benefit of securely datable 3rd century BC archaeological evidence in the region, we have little ability to assess how the Ptolemaic policies and priorities that we know so much about affected market routes within the southern Levant, and the lifestyles of the people who lived there.

This is, in large part, a pottery problem[2]. Many standard 3rd century BC ceramic type fossils are frustratingly rare in the Levant. Chronological markers such as 3rd century BC stamped amphora handles, Attic or Atticizing finewares, and as Susan Rotroff has noted fine black slipped vessels from the Aegean decorated in the 'west slope' technique are not attested widely in the region[3]. Even where such vessels are present, it is usually in modest quantities, especially when compared to sites in the Aegean. Aside from coastal sites, where imported finewares do occur with some regularity, 3rd century BC pottery from the southern Levant is hard to recognize. Vessels that could be 3rd century BC occur all over, but the principal shapes are undecorated bowls, saucers, and cooking vessels that could date anywhere from the early 3rd to the middle or end of the 2nd century BC for all we know. As a result, at most inland sites we are dependent upon reliable stratigraphic excavation to allow us to identify 3rd century BC remains. Fortunately, there has been an abundance of such excavation, and attendant publication, in recent years. Here I will draw on the publications of Samaria, Tel Anafa, Bet Yerah, Shechem, and my own work at Akko-Ptolemais and Tel Kedesh[4].

1 I would like to thank the directors of the excavations at Tel Kedesh, Sharon Herbert and Andrea Berlin, for allowing me to work on the material from Kedesh that I refer to in this article. Gratitude is also due to Danny Syon and Moshe Hartal, who permitted me to work on material from Akko and to Oren Tal, for discussing material from Bet-Yerah Philoteira. I thank the United States State Department for an Educational and Cultural Affairs grant that facilitated research at the Albright Institute of Archaeological Research in Jerusalem and the staff of the Israel Antiquities Authority storerooms at Beit Shemesh for their assistance in viewing material.

2 There are no broadly attested and well dated historical horizons like the conquest of Alexander the Great in the 4th century BC or the wars of the Maccabees and Seleucids in the middle of the 2nd century BC that might give us 'fixed points'. To date the only synthetic publication covering Hellenistic pottery from the southern Levant is Paul Lapp's (1961) *Palestinian Ceramic Chronology, 200 B.C. – 70 A.D.*, which left out the 3rd century BC. Since there was no equivalent handbook that incorporated 3rd century BC material, and there is no equivalent class of readily datable import to the Attic pottery of the Persian period in the 3rd century BC Levant, much pottery that likely dated to the 3rd century BC has either been assumed to date to the 4th or 2nd centuries BC on the basis of formal similarities to published pottery.

3 Rotroff 2002, 101–102.

4 Other sites such as Dor (see Guz-Zilberstein 1995; Rosenthal-

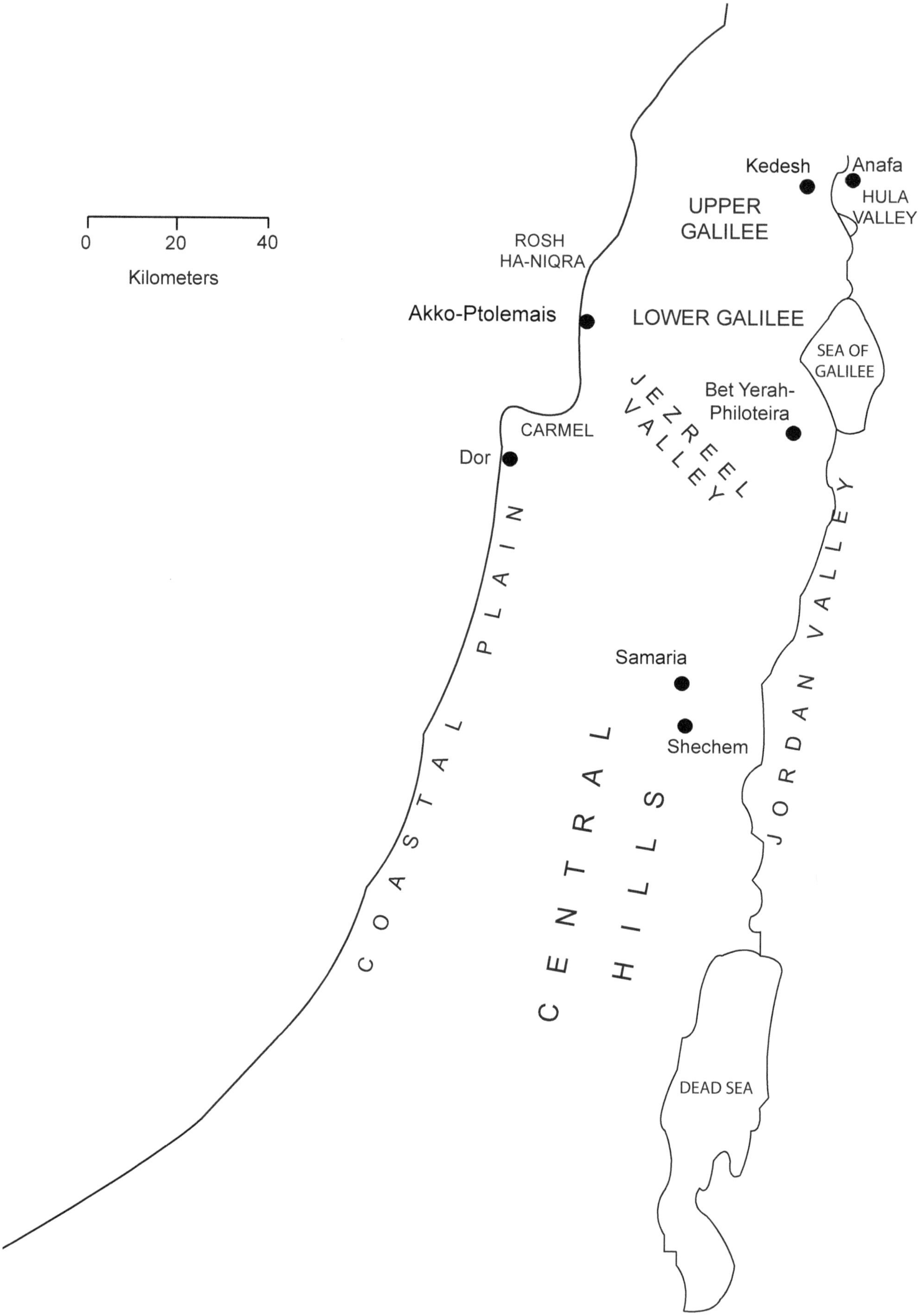

Fig. 1. Map showing southern Levant and sites discussed in the text

Consideration of material from these sites reveals telling patterns in the ceramic record of the region. These patterns give us a window into the economic and social realities of the southern Levant under the Ptolemies.

Historical background

It will be helpful to consider briefly what we know about Ptolemaic administration in the southern Levant and how the region fit into the Ptolemaic kingdom. After Alexander the Great's death in 323 BC the southern Levant was hotly contested. In 301 BC, it was awarded to Seleucos after the Battle of Ipsos, although Ptolemy, the ruler of Egypt, occupied it and was allowed to hold it for the time being. The region would serve as a northern buffer for the Ptolemaic kingdom until 198 BC when the Seleucid Antiochus III finally reclaimed his ancestor's lost province. Since the publication of the Zenon Papyri and the work of Michael Rostovzeff and Victor Tcherikower in the 1930s[5], the Ptolemaic kingdom has been viewed as a tightly controlled economy by ancient standards. For instance, Zenon Papyrus 59012 records duties ranging between 20%–50% on the import and transshipment of goods[6]. Such heavy taxation is generally thought to have suppressed trade and limited imported goods to members of the highest social strata. But the Ptolemaic kings did not want to discourage trade per se. They were interested in acquiring raw materials and luxury goods that were scarce or unavailable in Egypt such as timber, metals, olive oil, Arabian incense, and Aegean wine. For this they would have been dependent on local merchants and traditional trade networks, which they would have had little ability to control directly. Merchants in the coastal cities of the region acted as middlemen who funneled goods such as Arabian incense[7], and Aegean wine, cheese, and honey to Egypt. The coast, at any rate, was the scene of a vibrant exchange of goods.

It may have been in the interests of promoting the trade and transshipment of such goods that Ptolemy II Philadelphos (283–246 BC) founded or refounded several cities in the region (**Fig. 1**). Among these were Akko-Ptolemais, which was already a bustling port town, and Bet Yerah-Philoteira. The latter was situated along the Jordan Valley, the primary north-south route through the region, and near the inland terminus of the Jezreel Valley, which reaches the coast at Akko-Ptolemais and is the best route inland from the coast in the region. The foundations of Ptolemy II were positioned perfectly to convey agricultural produce, dates, and Arabian incense from the Jordan Valley to a coastal outlet, and provide a means for Mediterranean goods to travel inland.

Heginbottom 1995) provide complementary evidence, but I have omitted them here for purposes of clarity and brevity.

5 Rostovzeff 1941, 267–291, 340-357, 384–389; Tcherikower 1937.

6 Edgar 1925, 21–27: P. Cairo Zen. 59012.

7 Edgar 1925, 16–17: P. Cairo Zen. 59009.

Archaeological evidence for trade in the Jezreel Valley

There is ample archaeological evidence from Akko-Ptolemais and Bet Yerah-Philoteira that the Jezreel Valley channeled goods between the coast and Jordan Valley in the 3rd century BC. In the 3rd century BC, potters at Akko-Ptolemais began to produce bowls with incurved and everted rims and saucers with ledge rims in a granular, matte slipped ware that petrographic testing reveals has its origin on the central Levantine coast between the Carmel Range just to the south of Akko-Ptolemais and Rosh Ha-Niqra just to the north (hereafter 'central coastal fine'; **Figs. 1, 2:1–3**)[8]. They also produced cooking pots and casseroles in a distinctive warm red brown cooking fabric with a sandy surface texture (hereafter 'sandy cooking ware') that petrographic testing has also shown originated on the coast at Akko-Ptolemais (**Fig. 2:4–5**). The 3rd century BC ceramic assemblage of Bet Yerah-Philoteira is very similar overall to that of Akko-Ptolemais (for the table assemblage at Akko-Ptolemais see **Fig. 3**), and includes examples of many vessels in both central coastal fine[9] and sandy cooking ware[10]. Clearly people living at sites at the end of the Jezreel Valley were well enough connected with Akko-Ptolemais to rely heavily on coastal suppliers to stock their pantries. They also shared with people on the coast a desire for Greek style cuisine prepared in casseroles – deep cooking pots for soups had a long tradition in the region – and served on saucers.

As I mentioned above, Zenon Papyrus 59012 records the transshipment of Aegean goods through the southern Levant to Egypt, presumably via the agency of local middlemen. Despite this, recognizable Aegean imports are rare in the southern Levant aside from coastal sites such as Dor and Akko-Ptolemais where imported Aegean amphoras[11], baking pans[12], and tablewares[13] occur. This is one of the chief obstacles to identifying 3rd century BC archaeological remains at many inland sites in the region. It is telling then that sites near the end of the Jezreel Valley such as Samaria and Bet Yerah-Philoteira received Aegean amphoras[14] and table vessels[15], presumably shipped inland from Akko-Ptolemais. Imported tablewares from nearby Cyprus, also under Ptolemaic rule, were more common than Aegean tablewares. Cypriote vessels were mostly small bowls and saucers nearly identical to those produced

8 Berlin and Stone, forthcoming; Berlin, Shapiro, and Stone, unpublished report 2010.

9 Ben-Nahum and Getzov 2006, fig. 5.8:1, 13.

10 Ben-Nahum and Getzov 2006, fig. 5.10:7.

11 For Akko-Ptolemais see Finkielszteijn forthcoming; for Dor see Rosenthal Hegginbottom 1995, 202–203.

12 For Akko-Ptolemais see Berlin and Stone forthcoming, fig. 3.2:10–12); for Dor see Guz Zilberstein 1995, fig. 6.23a:4–69.

13 For Akko-Ptolemais see Berlin and Stone forthcoming, figs. 3.1:10; 3.4:2; 3.10:1; 3.20:1–2; for Dor see Marchese 1995, 172; Guz-Zilberstein 1995, fig. 6.3:1–4, 6, 18; Rosenthal-Hegginbottom 1995, fig. 5.8:6–8.

14 For Samaria see Crowfoot and Kenyon 1957, 379; in case of Bet Yerah-Philoteira, personal communication with Oren Tal, December 2009.

15 For Samaria see Crowfoot and Kenyon 1957, figs. 44–45; 47:1–2; 48:3–4; 49:1v2; 51:1–3; Bet Yerah-Philoteira, personal communication with Oren Tal, December 2009.

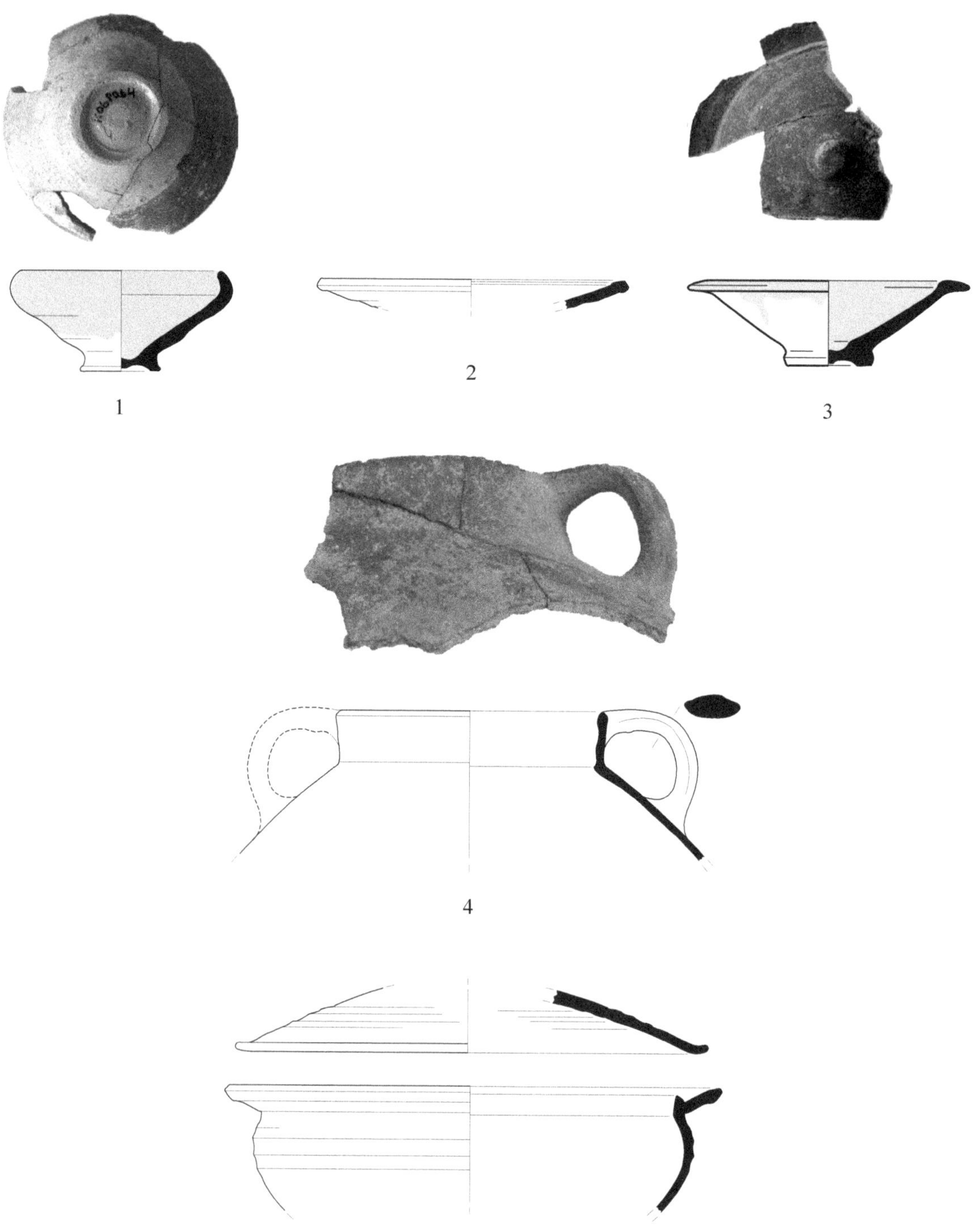

Fig. 2. Typical components of the central coastal fine and sandy cooking ware assemblages

at Akko-Ptolemais, though in a much higher quality clay. Many examples of these bowls and saucers occur at Akko-Ptolemais[16]. Cypriote table vessels occur at both Bet Yerah-Philoteira[17] and Samaria[18]. The same merchants who transported incense and produce across the Jezreel Valley for shipment abroad brought back to Bet Yerah-Philoteira and Samaria Aegean and Cypriote ceramic products for a populace attuned to the wider Mediterranean world and its tastes.

Circulation of goods off the beaten path

Pottery imported from the Aegean and Cyprus is much scarcer once one moves away from the coast or the Jezreel

16 Berlin and Stone forthcoming, figs. 3.1:4; 3.4:4; 3.10:4; 3.6:6–7, 9–10; 3.8:1, 5.
17 Ben-Nahum and Getzov 2006, figs. 5.8:4, 9, 18.
18 Crowfoot and Kenyon 1957, figs. 37:1, 16; 38:5.

Valley. Tel Kedesh, an administrative center and/or Ptolemaic estate in the eastern Upper Galilee, was supplied with matte slipped central coastal fine bowls and saucers from Akko-Ptolemais (**Figs. 2:1–3; 4**) as well as sandy cooking ware cooking pots and casseroles (**Figs. 2:4–5**)[19]. The central coastal fine and sandy cooking vessels were supplemented by very few table and cooking vessels produced in a very coarse, sloppily slipped ware termed spatter painted ware that was produced in the nearby Hula Valley. This evidence that Kedesh was well connected with the coast accords well with the lone papyrological reference to the site.

Kedesh is listed on Zenon Papyrus 59004 as the last place Zenon received flour before he went to Akko-Ptolemais to sail home to Egypt[20]. It is possible that people at Kedesh had access to coastal pottery because it was a royal estate or the estate of a favorite of the Ptolemies, responsible for collecting produce from the Upper Galilee and Hula Valley and sending it to the coast to be traded in the Aegean (or distributing it to official caravans). But this does little to explain why the people living at Kedesh would eschew local pots, many of which were just as serviceable as what they received from the coast. It seems that there was a definite preference for products from the cosmopolitan cities of the coast, vessels that came from a much greater distance. Still, actual Aegean and Cypriote imports of 3rd century BC date, while attested at Kedesh, were not present in the quantities that they were at Akko-Ptolemais or Bet Yerah-Philoteira. The scarcity of imports is perhaps best illustrated by the appearance of only two 3rd century BC stamped Rhodian amphora handles out of 62 recovered from the site and one fragment of a Rhodian amphora in a 3rd century BC context. The residents of Kedesh regularly communicated with the coast and were supplied with much of their pottery from there. They were even comfortable enough with Greek-style cuisine to use casseroles. But the merchants who came through the Upper Galilee apparently brought fewer imported goods from outside the southern Levant than those who traded in the Jezreel Valley.

Much more extreme isolation from the luxuries of the coast can be observed at nearby Tel Anafa in the Hula Valley[21]. In the 3rd century BC Anafa was a small village or farmstead[22] - probably one of the settlements that supplied the administrative center at Kedesh. Unlike Kedesh, almost all pottery used at Anafa was produced locally in the Hula Valley, principally in the spatter painted ware referred to above. Residents of Anafa were also content with a much narrower range of shapes than those of Kedesh or Ptolemaic cities, using nothing but small incurved bowls for dining. They used only globular cook pots for cooking. Casseroles suited for preparing Greek-style dishes are missing along with saucers for eating food prepared in them. The people at Anafa did not enjoy as varied a cuisine as people living on the coast, in the Jezreel Valley, or at the nearby administrative center at Kedesh. They lived very basic lives. Either the merchants that stopped at Kedesh did not bring their wares just a few more kilometers, or the residents of Anafa had no interest in them. Kedesh and Anafa form an intriguing contrast. One is an estate or administrative center off the well-beaten path whose residents nevertheless had access to goods from the coast and a varied assemblage functionally, but few imported goods; the other its satellite with a markedly simple and impoverished material assemblage.

A similar contrast can be seen between the city of Samaria, at the northern end of the Samaritan hills just to the south of the junction between the Jezreel and Jordan Valleys, and the nearby site of Shechem. Alexander established a military colony at Samaria and it remained inhabited as a prosperous city under the Ptolemies. As I mentioned above, the people living at Samaria in the 3rd century BC used incurved and everted rim bowls, and ledge rim saucers, of the same sorts as those used at Akko-Ptolemais, Bet Yerah-Philoteira, and Kedesh. Also like these sites, the residents of Samaria used both cooking pots and casseroles to prepare their meals. Aegean imports at Samaria are most obviously represented by a smattering of west slope style pottery, Attic or Atticizing kantharoi and plates, and an impressive quantity of Rhodian transport amphoras (over 70 3rd century BC handles in the publication)[23]. The people living at Samaria, like those at Kedesh, had access to, and an interest in a varied cooking and dining assemblage, and even regularly consumed imported wine.

Shechem in the 3rd century BC was a much more modest fortified town just to the south of Samaria. Unlike its northern neighbor, it had an extremely pedestrian assemblage. The people living at Shechem ate their meals exclusively from small, locally produced, unslipped bowls with incurved rims and disk feet[24]. Their meals were prepared in deep, globular cooking pots[25], and like at Anafa, casseroles were absent as were Aegean amphoras and imports. The standard of life at Shechem thus mirrors that at Anafa, although it, like Anafa, was not far distant, and possibly in the immediate orbit of a place (here Samaria) with at least some regular connection to coastal suppliers. Shechem was the sort of place that probably supplied Samaria with food. Despite this, the residents of the site did not receive imports, or make use of as wide a range of cooking and dining vessels as their neighbors to the north.

Conclusions: An Ad Hoc Settlement Hierarchy

The picture that emerges from this juxtaposition of sites is a sort of settlement hierarchy. Cities on the coast and cities founded by the Ptolemies near important trade

19 Personal study.
20 Edgar 1925, 7–10, P. Cairo Zen. 59004.
21 Berlin 1997, 18-19, figs. 8–9.
22 Herbert 1994, 12–14.

23 Crowfoot, Crowfoot, and Kenyon 1957, 379.
24 Lapp 2008, pl. 3.27:1–2.
25 Lapp 2008, pls. 3.37:1–7, 10–11.

Fig. 3. 3rd century BC table assemblage from Akko-Ptolemais, central coastal fine and imported vessels

Fig. 4. 3rd century BC table assemblage from Kedesh, central coastal fine vessels

routes like the Jezreel Valley (e.g., Akko-Ptolemais, Bet Yerah-Philoteira) received a wide range of regional and local goods, as well as Mediterranean imports. Clearly there was demand for, and a ready supply of, imported goods. Beneath these were postings with some amount of administrative or military importance, like Kedesh and Samaria, which were in regular contact with the outside world. Their residents had some scruples about what sort of food they ate and how they ate it. They were familiar with and placed an order for casseroles and saucers from the coast. In short, they were with it. But in the case of Kedesh, and perhaps Samaria as well, people at these important sites did not exert enough pull to regularly coax merchants bearing more exotic goods. Perhaps merchants who received imported goods at port were concentrated only along high traffic and high demand routes because these were the only ones profitable enough to warrant paying such high duties (20%–50%). On the lowest rung of this hierarchy were small towns and villages like Anafa and Shechem that depended entirely on local ceramic (and presumably other) products, and whose residents were either unaware of, indifferent to, or ill-disposed towards urbane cuisine and corresponding table settings.

Anafa and Shechem were at a substantial physical distance from each other, and had different cultural backgrounds both before and after the Hellenistic period. This makes it unlikely that their impoverished assemblages are the result of any one specific group's rejection of foreign material culture or practices. It is quite likely that their bland cooking and dining assemblages were in part the unintentional result of an imperial policy that favored trade for the procurement of a specific range of goods and imposed sharp duties on other transactions. They would not have had the opportunity to become comfortable with different sorts of cuisine and table settings if the stuff did not make a regular appearance. However, we should keep in mind that Anafa and Shechem were near sites whose residents used more sophisticated assemblages. There is an element of choice here. It seems that people in many of the towns and villages that fed the Ptolemaic kingdom simply did not care too much about the wider cultural milieu of the early Hellenistic Mediterranean.

Peter J. Stone
Collateral Assistant Professor
Department of History
Virginia Commonwealth University
813 S. Cathedral Place, room 206
Richmond, VA 23284-2001
USA
pjstone@vcu.edu

Bibliography

Ben-Nahum, H. and Getzov, N. 2006. Stratum I-The Hellenistic Period. In N. Getzov (ed.), *The Tel Bet Yerah Excavations 1994–1995*, 133–150. Jerusalem, Israel Antiquities Authority Reports.

Berlin, A. 1997. The Plain Wares. In S. C. Herbert (ed.), *Tel Anafa II: The Hellenistic and Roman Pottery*. Journal of Roman Archaeology Supplementary Series 10, 1–211. Ann Arbor, MI, Kelsey Museum.

Berlin, A. and Stone, P. J. forthcoming. Hellenistic and Early Roman Pottery from the Courthouse Excavations and the Hospitaller Compound, in E. Stern, M. Hartal, and D. Syon (eds.), *Akko, the Excavations of 1991–1998, Vol. 1: The Hellenistic Period*. Jerusalem, Israel Antiquities Authority Reports.

Crowfoot, J. W., Crowfoot, G. M. and Kenyon, K. M. 1957. *The Objects from Samaria*. London, Palestine Exploration Fund.

Edgar, C. C. 1925. *Catalogue général des antiquités Égyptiennes du Musée du Caire, Nos. 59001–59139: Zenon Papyri, Vol. 1*. Cairo, Service des antiquités de l'Égypt.

Finkielsztejn, G. forthcoming. Amphora Stamps from Akko: Hospitaller Compound and Some other Areas, in E. Stern, M. Hartal and D. Syon (eds.), *Akko, the Excavations of 1991–1998, Vol. 1: The Hellenistic Period*. Jerusalem, Israel Antiquities Authority Reports.

Guz-Zilberstein, B. 1995. The Typology of the Hellenistic Coarse Ware and Selected Loci of the Hellenistic and Roman Periods. In E. Stern (ed.), *Excavations at Dor, Final Report Vol. IB: Areas A and C: The Finds*, 289–433. Jerusalem, Institute of Archaeology at Hebrew University.

Lapp, N. 2008. *Shechem IV: The Persian and Hellenistic Pottery of Shechem/Tell Balatah*. Boston, MA, American Schools of Oriental Research.

Lapp, P. 1961. *Palestinian Ceramic Chronology, 200 B.C. –A.D. 70*. New Haven, American Schools of Oriental Research.

Rosenthal-Hegginbottom, R. 1995. Imported Hellenistic and Roman Pottery. In E. Stern (ed.), *Excavations at Dor, Final Report Vol. IB: Areas A and C: The Finds*, 183–288. Jerusalem, Institute of Archaeology at Hebrew University.

Rostovzeff, M. I. 1941. *The Social and Economic History of the Hellenistic World.* Oxford, Clarendon Press.

Rotroff, S. 2002. West Slope in the East, in F. Blondé, P. Ballet and J.-F. Salles (eds.), *Céramiques hellénistiques et romaines: Productions et diffusion in Méditerranée orientale (Chypre, Égypte et côte syro-palestinienne)*, 97–116. Lyon, Maison de l'Orient Méditerranéen-Jean Pouilloix.

Shapiro, A., Berlin, A. and Stone, P. J., Tel Kedesh – Fabrics and Wares. Unpublished report, 2010.

Tcherikover, V. 1937. Palestine under the Ptolemies (A Contribution to the Study of the Zenon Papyri). *Mizraim* IV–V, 9–90.

The Hellenistic pottery from Tall Zirāʿa in northern Jordan - Material from a village within the spheres of influence of the Decapolis cities Gadara, Gerasa and Pella

Frauke Kenkel

Abstract

This paper is based on the Hellenistic pottery from Tall Zirāʿa in northwestern Jordan. The excavations are taking place since 2003 within the 'Gadara Region Project', which is studying the multifaceted cultures from over 5000 years of history in the Wādī al-ʿArab in northern Palestine. The Wadi is situated five kilometres to the southwest of the ancient Decapolis-city Gadara (today Umm Qēs), and in the transition area between the cultural regions of Palestine and Syria.

The Hellenistic pottery; local, regional and imported ware as well as common and table ware, is part of the author's PhD thesis about the Hellenistic, Roman and Byzantine pottery from Tall Zirāʿa, which investigates the development and the character of the settlement for the corresponding time[1]. Although the settlement was located in the hinterland of Gadara during the classical Periods, the high quantity of the imported ware gives evidence that it was an important satellite settlement of the city.

Keywords: Decapolis, Jordan, Tall Zira'a, Gadara, Gerasa, Pella, trade relations

Tall Zirāʿa

The excavations at Tall Zirāʿa form one part of the 'Gadara Region Project'[2], which started with two detailed surveys of the site in 2001 and 2002[3]. Since 2004, the project is a joint venture of the Biblical-Archaeological Institute Wuppertal and the German Protestant Institute, co-directed by Prof. Dr. D. Vieweger and Dr. J. Häser. All results presented in this paper are preliminary, due to the fact that the excavations of the relevant layers on the Tell are not yet completed.

The Wadi al-ʿArab lies roughly five kilometres to the southwest of the ancient Decapolis city of Gadara, today Umm Qēs and was part of an ancient trade route during Bronze and Iron Age. A number of springs, fertile soil and a moderate climate provided excellent living conditions. Over one hundred sites illustrate the dense history of human settlement in the region from the advent of sedentarization to the Islamic period[4]. The frequent cultural developments and political upheavals of the ancient period in Palestine can be observed particularly well in this Wadi.

Tall Zira'a is the most centrally and strategically placed site in the area. It is situated at the confluence of the Wādī al-ʿArab and its largest tributary, the Wādī az-Zahar. Depending on the direction, it rises up to an impressive twenty-two to forty meters above the surrounding countryside. The highest point is situated at 17m below sea level. The settlements from the Bronze Age to the Islamic period were built on top of a natural limestone hill, which is circular-shaped and has a diameter of about 240m at its base and 160m at its plateau. Sheer rock faces on its eastern and northern sides protected the ancient settlements on top of the hill. The cultural layers of these habitation activities are approximately 16m thick[5].

The artesian spring on top of the Tell, and the fact that the land around the settlement is very suitable for agriculture, make this place very important. In addition to this it is located at a strategic position along a highly important trade route in prehistoric and proto-historic times between Egypt and the Mediterranean in the south, and west and Syria and Mesopotamia in the north and east, which was used for thousands of years. In the late Hellenistic period the roads changed and Tall Zirāʿa lay in the hinterland of Gadara. Instead of the Tell, the city of Gadara was then connected to the important trading routes. But Tall Zirāʿa was not deserted, on the contrary, it remained densely settled, probably due to its excellent water supply and fertile soils[6].

As a result of its particular characteristics, the Tell provides perfect conditions for a large-scale pottery study.

1 Frauke Kenkel, Untersuchungen zur hellenistischen, römischen und byzantinischen Keramik des Tall Zirāʿa im Wādī al-'Arab (Nordjordanien) – Handelsobjekte und Alltagsgegenstände einer ländlichen Siedlung im Einflussgebiet der Dekapolisstädte.

2 Vieweger and Häser 2007a, 1–2.

3 Häser and Vieweger 2007, 9.

4 Vieweger and Häser 2007b, 147–167.

5 Vieweger and Häser 2007a, 2.

6 Vieweger *et al.*, 2009, 246.

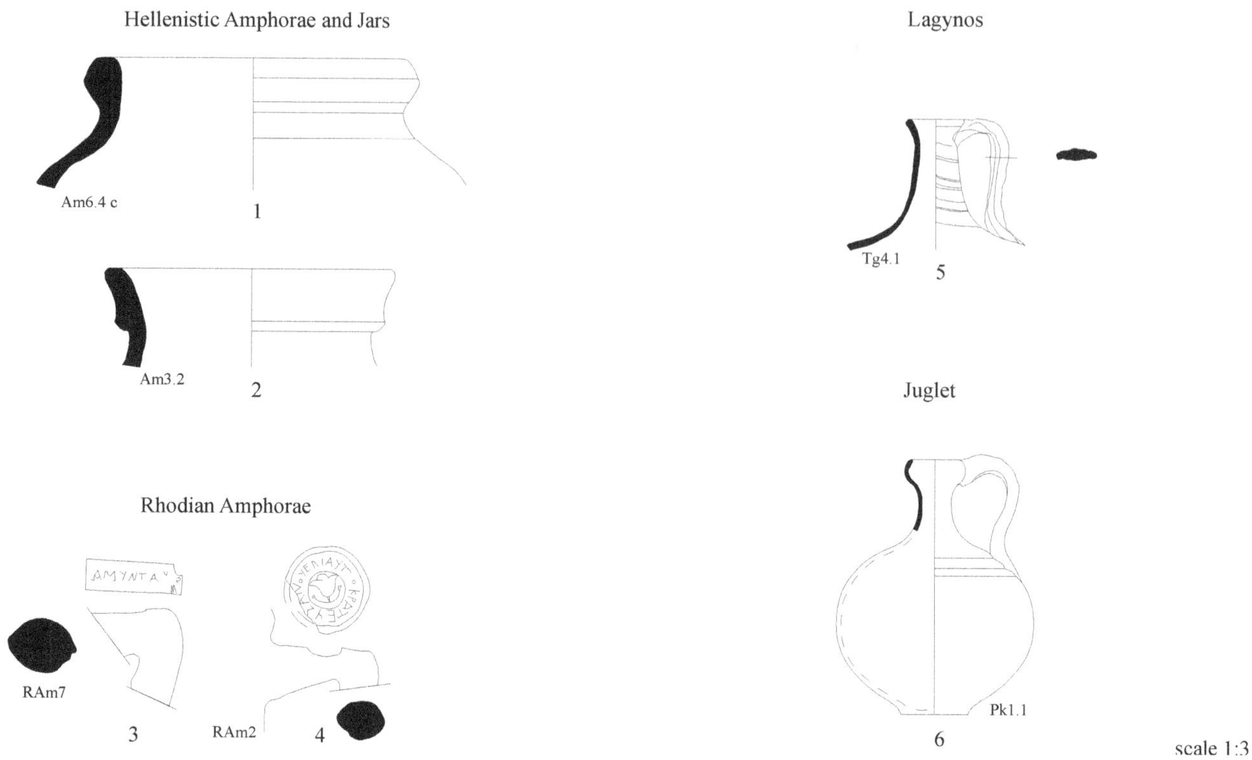

Fig. 1. Hellenistic amphorae (1–4), lagynos (5) and juglet (6). Mainly 2nd to 1st century BC (F. Kenkel)

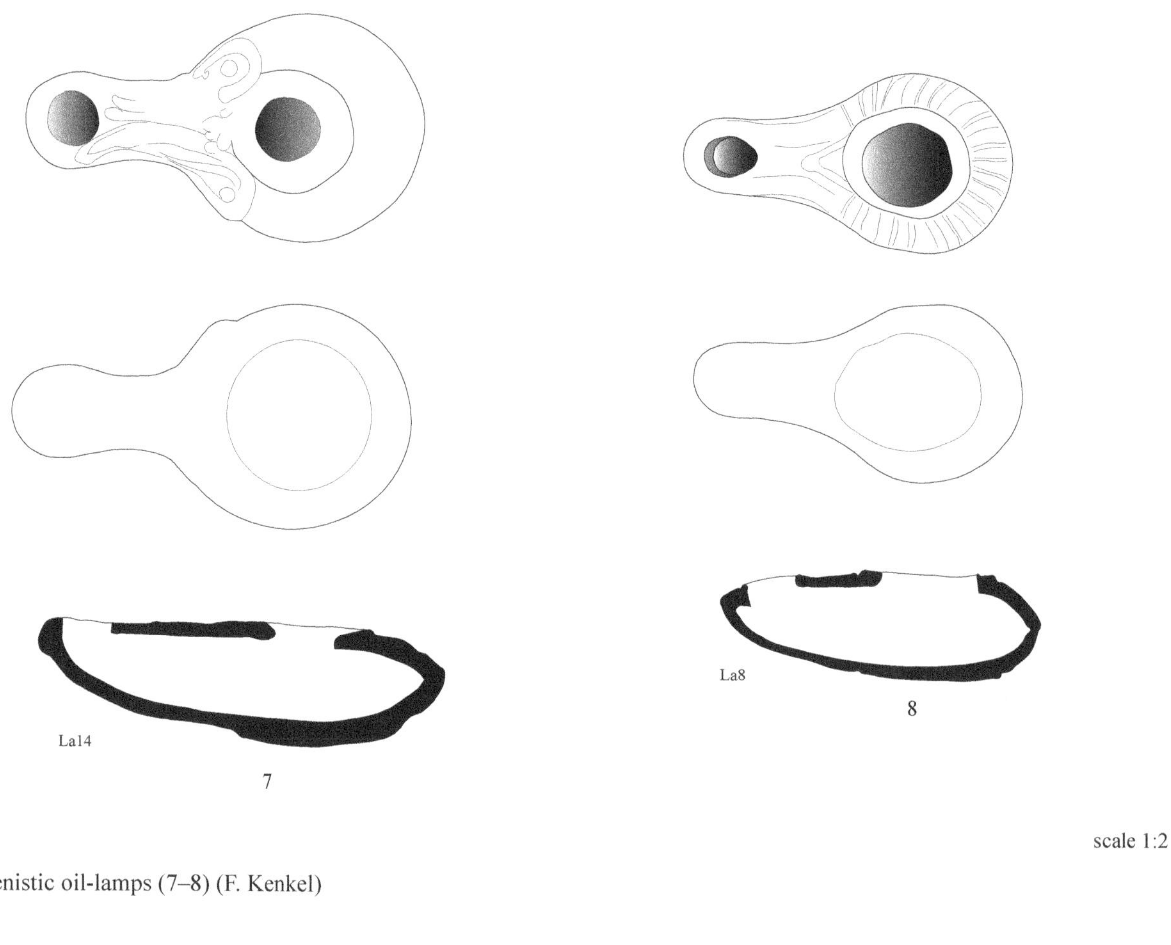

Fig. 2. Hellenistic oil-lamps (7–8) (F. Kenkel)

Decapolis cities

Even so, it is clear today that the Decapolis as a political unit did not exist before the 1st century AD[7], the history of the Decapolis cities began in the Hellenistic period, and until now it is mainly known from Gadara, in lesser parts also from Gerasa and Pella. Therefore the three cities were chosen to work out the position of the Tall Zirāʿa in this region and to underline the high-developed status of this region in Hellenistic times.

Gadara

The ancient city of Gadara is situated at an intersection of the East-West orientated, supra-regional traffic axis, which connected the Mediterranean harbours with the long-distance routes to the northeast (Silk road) and the southeast (Incense road). Because of its exceptional geographical position contrary to other regions, this Area had an extraordinary economic meaning[8]. The earliest but rather scarce archaeological remains come from the second half of the 3rd century BC[9]. As a result of possible urban settlement activities, a waste deposit at the south slope of the Acropolis, which started in this period and existed until the following century was investigated. In the 3rd century BC the city belonged to the Ptolemy region. After 200 BC the Seleucids ruled Gadara, and the city probably got the status of a polis. At the beginning of the 1st century BC, as the Hasmonean Empire expanded into the East of Jordan, Gadara was conquered by Alexander Jannaeus[10].

The pottery found in Gadara spans a period of 2200 years, beginning in the late 3rd century BC and ending with Ottoman pottery from the 18th/19th century AD. Besides the predominantly local coarse ware an astonishingly high rate of imported ware from Egypt, Greece and Italy could be distinguished.

Gerasa

The ruins of Gerasa are situated about 40km north of Amman in a small fertile valley. According to Flavius Josephus Gerasa was conquered by Alexander Jannaeus, too[11]. Gerasa emerged from an older settlement in Hellenistic times, which had existed since at least the 2nd millennium BC[12]. There is a high likelihood that the cities re-establishment took place under a Seleucid ruler. As in Gadara, the Seleucid influence affected its steadily increasing development and status as polis after 200 BC. Excavations on the north side of the Roman city wall revealed a Roman tomb, which contained a collection of Hellenistic pottery from the late 2nd to the early 1st century BC[13].

7 Riedl 2004, 172.
8 Hoffmann 2002, 89.
9 Hoffmann 2002, 101.
10 Hoffmann 2002, 101.
11 Seigne 2002, 6–9.
12 Riedl 2004, 169.
13 Kehrberg 2004, 189–196.

Pella

In Pella one can find indications of the presence of the Ptolemy in the 4th and early 3rd century BC, but there are no actual settlement traces[14].

Polybius reported that Pella was counted among those places, which were already conquered in 218 BC by Antiochos III. Archaeological evidence shows, that life in Pella suddenly flourished again in this time and was mainly supported by a fast expansion of trade in the Near East[15]. The domestic dwellings attained bigger dimensions and were well built: the walls and floors were plastered and decorated. The inhabitants imported expensive goods from the Mediterranean regions, especially Rhodian stamped Amphoras[16]. The archaeological gap in the early Hellenistic period and the cultural bloom and distribution in the late Hellenistic period show the contrast between the administrative practice of the Ptolemaic and Seleucid governments[17]. The city was destroyed in 83–82 BC by Alexander Jannaeus, like Gadara and Gerasa. Literary and archaeological sources show, that Pella was comprehensively Hellenized over some hundred years.

Pottery

As mentioned above, the presented material derives from the excavations in two areas of Tall Zirāʿa and needs to be considered as a preliminary result[18].

Excavation Area I is situated on the northwestern slope of the site. Natural settings and geophysical investigations indicated, that the western slope of the hill was a promising site to rapidly expose the stratigraphy of this place from the Umayyad to the Middle Bronze Age with city walls, residential areas, rural installations and workshops[19]. After the spring campaign of 2010, already 1750m^2 were opened. At first one assumed that Area I was not inhabited in early Hellenistic times, but during the excavations remains of residential buildings were uncovered in parts of this Area[20]. Besides pottery, glass and metal artefacts, many coins were found, which prove the continuous settlement of this area[21].

In 2006, the first excavations were undertaken in Area II. This area is slightly higher than other parts of the site, except the southern one. It is the most well protected place on the Tell since there is a 40m steep front cliff to the north. A sequence of at least ten strata in 1500m^2 was

14 Watson 2002, 62.
15 Watson 2002, 63.
16 Watson 2002, 63.
17 Smith 1990, 123–130.
18 The study of the pottery was possible because of two generously fellowships of the Hugo-Gressmann-foundation and one from the DAAD (German Academic Exchange Service).
19 Häser and Vieweger 2008, 376.
20 Vieweger and Häser 2010, 1–28.
21 Vieweger and Häser 2010, 1–28.

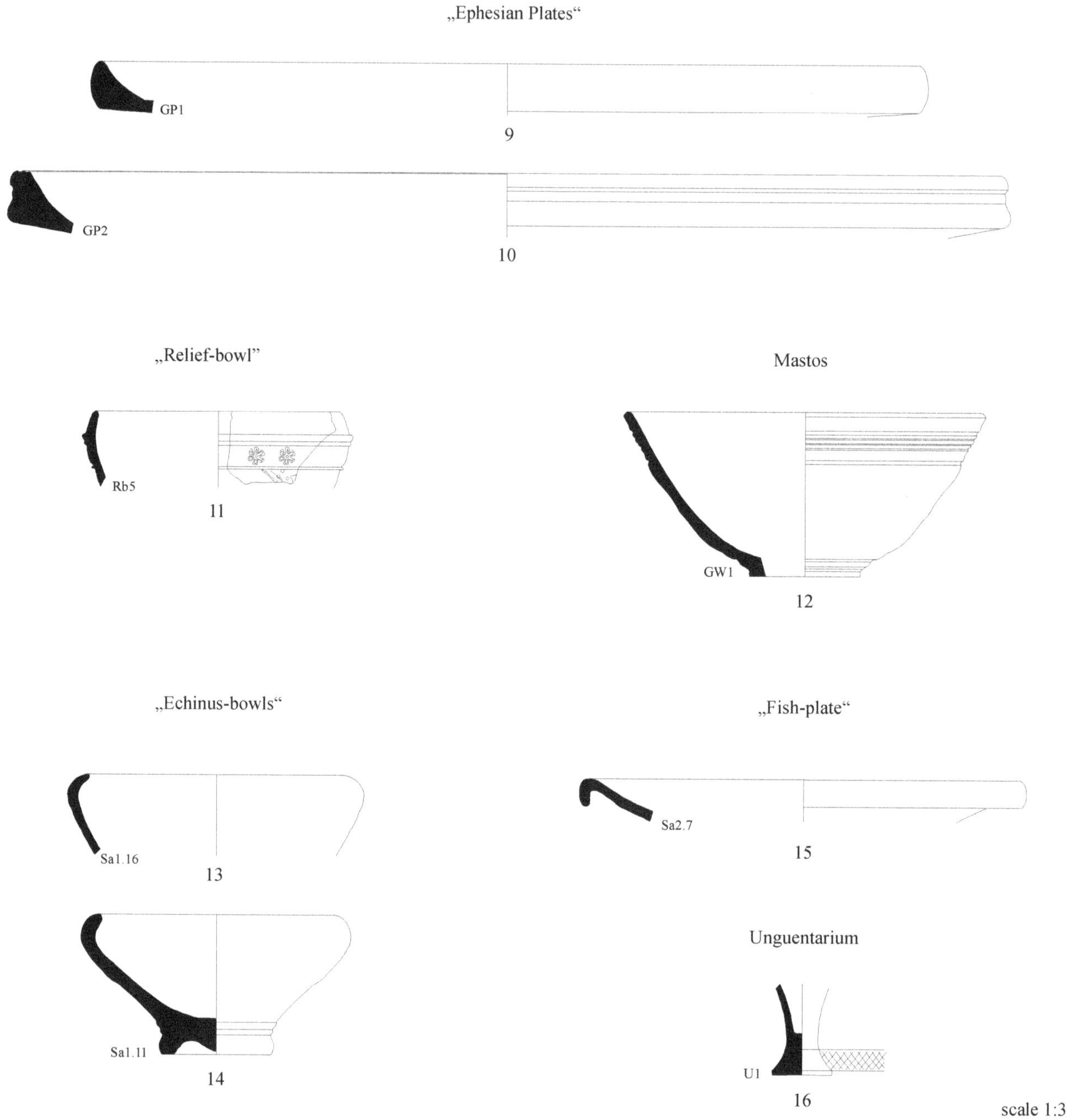

Fig. 3. Hellenistic table ware (9–16). Mainly 2nd to 1st century BC (F. Kenkel)

detected, which can be dated from the Umayyad to the Hellenistic period. The lowermost of the ten strata shelter an early Roman or late Hellenistic wall foundation. The following four strata contain architectural remains from the Roman and Byzantine period[22]. Because of the fact that the Byzantine building program, like in Pella and most of all other excavations in this region, destroyed almost all foundations underneath, the correlation between the architectural remains is very difficult.

All sherds of a certain size were collected. All diagnostic ones, like rims, bases, spouts and decorated pieces, were drawn. As criteria for differentiations, the fabric, the consistency of the sherd, hardness, finish and colour were chosen[23].

The research includes coarse and fine ware, common and cooking ware and the more expensive imported pottery from the Hellenistic to the Byzantine period. From the

[22] Vieweger and Häser 2010, 1–28.

[23] The choosen examples are a small selection of the relevant pieces. The common and cooking wares from the Hellenistic period are presented in the authors PhD thesis, see footnote 1.

excavations at the Tell there are oil lamps (**Fig. 2, 7–8**)[24], Black-Slipped pottery, rhodian *amphorae* (**Fig. 1, 3–4**)[25], Relief-bowls (**Fig. 3, 11**)[26], ephesian plates (**Fig. 3, 9–10**)[27], Eastern Sigillata, *unguentariae* (**Fig. 3, 16**)[28], jugs and juglets (**Fig. 1, 6**)[29], fishplates (**Fig. 3, 15**)[30] and bowls with incurved and outcurved rims (**Fig. 3, 13–14**)[31], mastoi (**Fig. 3, 12**)[32], table *amphorae*, *lagynoi* (**Fig. 1, 5**)[33], *amphoriskoi* and small vessels for unguents from the Hellenistic period, mainly the second and first century BC.

Hellenistic Networks

As a consequence of the conquest of Persia by Alexander the Great and during the period after his death, the Greek influence, which came to the East under the rule of the Macedonians, is pervasive. 198 BC, Jordan was conquered from the Seleucids and Palestine was subject to increased Hellenistic influence through veterans in military colonies. Under the Hasmonean occupation, before Pompey transferred the cities back to their former owners, this impulse was interrupted[34].

Since the relations between East and West were built and fortified through the conquest of Alexander the Great, Jordan was Hellenized[35]. Trade increased and as a result, different interests overlapped. Often the oriental rulers adapted the language of their clients, which made the international contact much easier. Besides Greek education, style and culture, local traditions were held up[36]. Black-Slipped pottery from Greece, storage jars or cooking pots from Cyprus, Rhodian wine amphoras as well as many Ptolemaic and Seleucidian coins show evidence of the trade with the West and the neighbouring countries.

Among the imported pottery, like the Relief-bowls, one can find black and red slipped pottery examples from the Hellenistic period, which appear in the shape of the typical bowls with incurved or outcurved rims and fishplates[37]. They were imitated in local and regional fabrics, but very often without having the same quality like their archetypes. Besides those fine wares, many Amphora fragments were found, which show the widespread trading relations of Gadara and therefore also of Tall Zirāʿa. But the largest proportion of pottery excavated is the common ware, which was probably produced regionally. The Hellenistic examples of Gadara, Gerasa and Pella reflect the known material from Tall Zirāʿa, which was therefore typical for this period. Further research is needed to find the production centres for the vessels of daily use for this region.

Conclusions

The pottery of Tall Zirāʿa is not less comprehensive than the material from the 'bigger' cities in the Decapolis. This site in their hinterland includes the same imported wares, imitations of widespread shapes and Hellenistic forms within the common pottery. Even though it is not as numerous, especially concerning imports, it includes all Hellenistic types we know from this region[38]. Whether the inhabitants of Tall Zirāʿa had direct contact with the traders or obtained the pottery from Gadara, one cannot say. For the record, the total amount of all different wares is not outdone compared to the Decapolis cities. The late Hellenistic material from the cities Gadara, Gerasa and Pella and the settlement on the Tall Zirāʿa includes fabrics, which probably came predominantly from the coast and from local and regional production centres[39]. The majority of the Eastern Sigillata A probably came from the region of Antiochia, Hama and Tel Anafa like the Black-Slipped pottery. The presence of imported pottery gives evidence to the contacts in the Greek and Roman Mediterranean areas and that the inhabitants of northwestern Jordan willingly and easily communicated with the northernmost and coastal regions[40].

---

24 Bailey 1975, pl. 102 Q 509; Stern 1995, 275 fig. 5.16.

25 *RAm7*: Börker 1974, Nr. 23, 30; Börker 1998, Nr. 390–392, 43; Burow 1998, Nr. 49–53, 82; Calvet 1982, Nr. 21, 17; Crowfoot 1957, 382; Grace 1950, 30; Grace 1985, 10; Jöhrens 1999, Nr. 163, 63; Jöhrens 2009, 222; Kramer 2004, AS34–35, 93; Lejpunskaja *et al.* 2010, L-194. L-195, pl. 279; Nicolaou and Empereur 1986, Nr. 3, fig. 2b, 517; Rosenthal-Heginbottom 1995, Nr. 7, 18; *RAm2*: Ariel 2000, Nr. 5, 270; Bleckmann 1912, Nr. 88, 254; Crowfoot 1957, 381; Grace 1970, E7, 304; Jöhrens 1999, Nr. 203, 78; Lejpunskaja *et al.* 2010, L-166 pl. 277.

26 Dereboylu 2001, pl. 13, 60; Hoffmann 2002, fig. 211, 7; Kossatz 1990, fig. 3 M56; fig. 12, 258; fig. 15 M309; Lejpunskaja *et al.* 2010, F-14 pl. 171. F-19 pl. 172; Mitsopoulos-Leon 1991, pl. 81 D33. pl. 87 D55; Rosenthal-Heginbottom 1995, fig. 5.4:19, 20; Smetana-Scherrer 1982, pl. 49, 653.

27 Zabehlicky-Scheffenegger *et al.* 1996, pl. 11, 1–3.

28 Bar-Nathan 2002, pl. 10, 102; Berlin 2006, fig. 2. 29, 11; Briend and Humbert 1980, pl. 14, 20; Jones 1950, 187 E; Lapp 1961, Typ 91.1 A-S, 197; Rotroff 2006, pl. 67, 512; Silberstein 2000, pl. 4, 19.

29 Bar-Nathan 2002, Taf. 6, 15–18; Berlin 2006, Abb. 2.30, 1–5; Crowfoot 1957, Abb. 42, 4; Diez Fernández 1983, T8.1; Fuller 1987, Abb. 69 A–B; Lapp 1961, Typ 31.2 A, 163; Silberstein 2000, pl. 4, 6–8; Tushingham 1985, fig. 21, 27–32.

30 Bar-Nathan 2002, Taf. 16, 267; Crowfoot 1957, fig. 37.1; Edwards 1975, pl. 5, 132; Fortner 2008, pl. 4. 90–104; Guz-Zilberstein 1995, fig. 6.3.11; Hayes 1991, fig. 48, 41; McNicoll *et al.* 1992, pl. 75, 1–5, pl. 77, 7–9; Papanicolaou-Christensen and Friis Johansen 1971, fig. 1; Warner Slane 1997, pl. 1, FW1.

31 *Sal.16*: Bar-Nathan 2002, pl. 1, 9–23; Berlin 1997, pl. 16, PW133–140; Briend and Humbert 1980, pl. 13, 1–7; Crowfoot 1957, fig. 38; Edwards 1975, pl. 2, 15–67; Fortner 2008, Taf. 1–3; Fuller 1987, fig. 76, A–B; Guz-Zilberstein 1995, fig. 6.1.14; Hannestad 1983, pl. 1. 1–17, pl. 47. 464–473; Hayes 1991, fig. 40, 7–11 and 24–25; Jones 1950, 180 D; Kerner 1997, fig.12.1; Lapp 1961, Typ 51.1, 172; Lejpunskaja *et al.* 2010, pl. 117–118; McNicoll *et al.* 1992, pl. 75, 14, pl. 77, 4; Papanicolaou-Christensen and Friis Johansen 1971, fig. 4.44–50 and fig. 5.51–62; Riley 1979, fig. 110.612; Silberstein 2000, pl. 8. 3–5; Vann 1992, fig. 51.6; *Sal.11*: Bar-Nathan 2002, pl. 15, 225; Berlin 1997, pl. 16, PW133–140; Briend and Humbert 1980, pl. 13, 1–7; Crowfoot 1957, fig. 38; Edwards 1975, pl. 2, 15–67; Fortner 2008, pl. 1–3; Fuller 1987, fig. 76, A–B; Hannestad 1983, pl. 1. 1–17, pl. 47. 464–473; Hayes 1991, fig. 40, 7–11 and 24–25; Jones 1950, 180 E; Kerner 1997, fig. 12.1; Krinzinger 2001, pl. 50.33; Lapp 1961, Typ 51.1, 172; Lejpunskaja *et al.* 2010, pl. 117–118; McNicoll *et al.* 1992, pl. 75, 11 and 14; Papanicolaou-Christensen and Friis Johansen 1971, fig. 4.44–50 and 5.51–62; Riley 1979, fig. 110, 614; Silberstein 2000, pl. 8. 3–5.

32 Bar-Nathan 2002, pl.16, 271–278; Gassner 1997, pl. 72 H15; Hannestad 1983, pl. 4, 50; Ladstätter 2005, pl. 154 K134.

33 Guz-Zilberstein 1995, fig. 6.33; Kehrberg 2004, fig. 18; Kehrberg 2006, pl. 37, 4; Rotroff 2006, fig. 16, 18.

34 Riedl 2004, 169.

35 Homès-Frederiq 1986, 178–179.

36 Homès-Frederiq 1986, 178–179.

37 Kerner 1997, 290.

38 Kerner 1997, 290.

39 Schneider 2004, 164.

40 Berlin 2006, 133.

After the Hellenistic period, the local pottery disappeared and more regional, supra-regional and imported wares appeared. The economic conditions of the presented cities and the Tall Zirāʿa document a clear Hellenization from the 2nd century BC on the basis of the increasing imports from Syria, Asia Minor and Greece. Another important fact of this research is that some fabrics from this site could not yet be identified. Similarly, there are some fabrics from Gadara and Pella, which were not found in the material from Tall Zirāʿa. Therefore, there must have been local production centers in the area surrounding the Tell, which 1957. their products to different cities. Further research will hopefully shed some more light on this.

Frauke Kenkel
Deutsches Evangelisches Institut für Altertumswissenschaft des Heiligen Landes
Shari'a Al-Habbab Bin Al-Munthir Nr. 32
P.O. Box 183
JOR-11118 Amman
F.Kenkel@gmx.de

Bibliographie

Ariel, D. T. 2000. Imported Greek Stamped Amphora Handles. In H. Geva (ed.), *Jewish Quarter Excavations in the old city of Jerusalem conducted by Nahman Avigad, 1969–1982*, I, 267–283. Jerusalem, Institute of Archaeology, Hebrew University of Jerusalem.

Bailey, D. M. 1975. *Lamps in the British Museum I – Greek, Hellenistic and early Roman Pottery Lamps*. London, British Museum.

Bar-Nathan, R. 2002, The Pottery. In E. Netzer (ed.), *Hasmonean and Herodian palaces at Jericho, Final Reports of the 1973–1987 Excavations*, III. Jerusalem, Institute of Archaeology, Hebrew University of Jerusalem.

Berlin, A. M. 1997, The Plain Wares. In S. C. Herbert (ed.), *Tel Anafa, Final Report, II, 1, The Hellenistic and Roman Pottery*. Journal of Roman Archaeology Supplement 10. Ann Arbor, Journal of Roman Archaeology.

Berlin, A. M. 2006. *Gamla I, The Pottery of the second Temple Period – The Shmarya Gutmann Excavation, 1976–1989*. Jerusalem, Israel Antiquity Authority.

Biran, A. 1994. *Biblical Dan*. Jerusalem, Israel Exploration Society.

Bleckmann, F. 1912. Zu den rhodischen Eponymen Heliospriestern. *Klio* 12, 249–258.

Börker, Ch. 1974. Griechische Amphorenstempel vom Tell Halaf bis zum Persischen Golf. *Baghdader Mitteilungen* 7, 31–49.

Börker, Ch. 1998. *Die hellenistischen Amphorenstempel aus Pergamon. Der Pergamon-Komplex*. Pergamenische Forschungen 11, part 1, 3–73.

Briend, J. and Humbert, J. P. (eds.) 1980. *Tell Keisan (1971–1976) une cité phénicienne en Galilée*. Paris, Göttingen, Fribourg (Swiss), Gabalda.

Burow, J. 1998. *Die hellenistischen Amphorenstempel aus Pergamon. Die übrigen Stempel aus Pergamon*. Pergamenische Forschungen 11, part 2, 74–159.

Calvet, Y. 1982. *Kition-Bamboula I, Les timbres Amphoriques*. Paris, Éd. Recherche sur les Civilisations.

Crowfoot, J. W., Crowfoot, G. M. and Kenyon, K. M. *Samaria-Sebaste III, The Objects*. London, sold Palestine Exploration Fund.

Dereboylu, E. 2001. Weissgrundige Keramik und hellenistische Reliefbecher aus dem Hanghaus 2 in Ephesos. In F. Krinzinger (ed.), *Studien zur hellenistischen Keramik in Ephesos*, 21–44. Wien, Österreichisches Archäologisches Institut.

Diez Fernández, F. 1983. *Ceramica comun Romana de la Galilea*. Madrid, Escuela Biblica.

Edwards, G. R. 1975. *Corinthian Hellenistic Potters*. Corinth VII 3. Princeton, NJ., American School of Classical Studies at Athens.

Fortner, S. A. 2008. *Die Keramik und Kleinfunde von Bethsaida-Julias am See Genezareth, Israel*. PhD Thesis, University of Munich.

Fuller, M. J. 1987. *Abila of the Decapolis: A Roman-Byzantine City in Transjordan*. PhD thesis, Washington University St. Louis.

Grace, V. R. 1950. The stamped Amphora Handles. In H. Goldman (ed.), *Excavations at Gözlü Kule, Tarsus I, The Hellenistic and Roman Periods*, 135–148. Princeton, NJ., Princeton University Press.

Grace, V. R. and Savvatianou-Pétropoulakou, M. 1970. Les timbres Amphoriques Grecs. In P. Bruneau (ed.), *L'îlot de la maison des comédiens*. Délos XXVII, 277–386. Paris, De Boccard.

Grace, V. R. 1985. The Middle Stoa Dated by Amphora Stamps. *Hesperia* 54, 1–54.

Guz-Zilberstein, B. 1995. The Typology of the hellenistic and roman periods. In E. Stern (ed.), *Excavations at Dor. Final Report, Areas A and C: The Finds*. Qedem Reports 2, 289–313. Jerusalem, The Hebrew University of Jerusalem.

Häser, J. and Vieweger, D. 2007. The 'Gadara Region Project'. Preliminary Report on the Archaeological Excavations on Tall Zir'a in 2005 und 2006. *American Journal of Archaeology* 111/3, 526–530.

Häser, J. and Vieweger, D. 2008. The Tall Zar'a and the Gadara Region Project in the years 2007 and 2008. *Annual of the Department of Antiquities* 52, 375–395.

Hannestad, L. 1983. *The Hellenistic Pottery from Falaika*,

2:1 and 2:2. Copenhagen, Gyldendal.

Hayes, J. W. 1991. *The Hellenistic and Roman Pottery.* Paphos III. Nicosia, Department of Antiquities.

Hoffmann, A. 2002. Topographie und Stadtgeschichte von Gadara/Umm Qais, in A. Hoffman and S. Kerner, S. (eds.), *Gadara-Gerasa und die Dekapolis*, 98–124. Mainz, Zabern.

Homès-Fredericq, D. and Franken, H. J. 1986. *Pottery and Potters, Past and Present – 7000 Years of Ceramic Art in Jordan.* Tübingen, Attempo.

Jöhrens, G. 1999. *Amphorenstempel im Nationalmuseum von Athen: zu den von H. G. Lolling aufgenommenen „unedierten Henkelinschriften“.* Mainz, Zabern.

Jöhrens, G. 2009. Funde aus Milet XXVII. Amphorenstempel aus den Grabungen in Milet 1899–2007. *Archäologischer Anzeiger* 2009/1, 205–235.

Jones, F. F. 1950. The Pottery. In H. Goldman (ed.), *Excavations in Gözlü Kule. Tarsus I, The Hellenistic and Roman Periods*, 149–296. Princeton, NJ., Princeton University Press.

Kehrberg, I. 2004. Late Hellenistic and Early Roman Pottery of Gerasa in View of International Norms in the Eastern Mediterranean. *Studies in the History and Archaeology of Jordan* 8, 189–196.

Kehrberg, I. 2006. A late Hellenistic link between Jordan and Cyprus: A view from Gerasa, in L. Beaumont, C. Barker and E. Bollen (eds.), *Festschrift in Honour of J. Richard Green.* Mediterranean Archaeology 17, 299–306. Sydney, Mediterranean Archaeology.

Kerner, S. 1997. Umm Qays/Gadara: A Preliminary Report 1993–1995. *Annual of the Department of Antiquities in Jordan* 41, 283–302.

Kossatz, A. U. 1990. *Funde aus Milet: Die Megarischen Becher.* Milet V 1. Berlin, De Gruyter.

Ladstätter, S. 2005. Keramik. In H. Thür (ed.), *Hanghaus 2 in Ephesos – die Wohneinheit 4, Baubefund, Ausstattung, Funde*, 230–358. Wien, Verlag der österreichischen Akademie der Wissenschaften.

Kramer, N. 2004. *Gindaros; Geschichte und Archäologie einer Siedlung im nordwestlichen Syrien von hellenistischer bis in frühbyzantinische Zeit.* Rhaden/Westf., Marie Leidorf GmbH.

Krinzinger, F. (ed.), 2001. *Studien zur hellenistischen Keramik in Ephesos.* Wien, Österreichisches Archäologisches Institut.

Lapp, E. C. 1961. *Palestinian Ceramic Chronology. 200 B.C. – A.D. 70.* New Haven, American School of Oriental Research.

Lejpunskaja, N. A., Guldager Bilde, P., Munk Højte, J., Krapivina, V. V. and Kryzickij, S. D. 2010. *The Lower city of Olbia (Sector NGS) in the 6th century BC to the 4th century AD*, 1–2. Aarhus, Aarhus University Press.

McNicoll, A. W., Edwards, P. C., Hanbury-Tension, J., Hennessy, J. B., Potts, T. F., Houston Smith, R., Walmsley, A. and Watson, P. 1992. *Pella in Jordan 2, the second interim report of the joint University of Sydney and College of Wooster excavations at Pella 1982–1985.* Sydney, Mediterranean archaeology.

Mitsopoulos-Leon, V. 1991. *Die Basilika am Staatsmarkt in Ephesos, 1, Keramik hellenistisch und römische Zeit.* Forschungen in Ephesos 9, 2, 2. Wien, Schindler.

Nicolaou, I. and Empereur, J.-Y. 1986. Amphores rhodiennes du musée de Nicosie, in J.-Y. Empereur and Y. Garlan (eds.), *Recherches sur les amphores grecques.* Bulletin de correspondance hellénique, Supplement 13, 515–531.

Papanicolaou-Christensen, A. and Friis Johansen, C. 1971. *Hama, Fouilles et Recherches 1931–1938, III 2. Les poteries hellénistique et les terre sigillées orientales.* Kopenhagen, Fondation Karlsberg.

Riedl, N. 2004. Leben in den »Griechenstädten« der Dekapolis. In *Gesichter des Orients – 10000 Jahre Kunst und Kultur in Jordanien.* Ausstellungskatalog 169–178. Mainz, Zabern.

Riley, J. A. 1979. The Coarse Pottery from Berenice. In J. A. Lloyed (ed.), *Excavations at Sidi Khrebish Benghazi (Berenice) II.1*, 91–467. Tripolis, Department of Antiquities.

Rosenthal, R. and Sivan, R. 1978. *Ancient Lamps in the Schloessinger Collection.* Qedem 8. Jerusalem, The Hebrew University.

Rosenthal-Heginbottom, R. 1995. Imported Hellenistic and Roman Pottery. In E. Stern (ed.), *Excavations at Dor, Final Report, Vol. I B: Areas A and C: The Finds.* Qedem reports 2, 183–288. Jerusalem, Institute of Archaeology, Hebrew University of Jerusalem.

Rotroff, S. I. 2006. *Hellenistic Pottery – The Plain Wares.* The Athenian Agora XXXIII. Princeton, NJ., The American School of Classical Studies at Athens.

Schneider, Ch. 1996. Die Importkeramik, in A. Bignasca, N. Desse-Berset, R. Fellmann Brogli, R. Glutz, S. Karg, D. Keller, B. Kolb, Chr. Kramar, M. Peter, S. G. Schmid, Ch. Schneider, R. A. Stucky, S. Studer and S. Zanoni, *Petra – Ez Zantur I, Ergebnisse der Schweizerisch-Lichtensteinischen Ausgrabungen 1988–1992*, 129–150. Mainz, Zabern.

Schneider, G. 2004. Keramik aus aller Welt – Ergebnisse der Archäometrie. In *Gesichter des Orients – 10000 Kunst und Kultur aus Jordanien.* Ausstellungskatalog 161–165. Mainz, Zabern.

Seigne, J. 2002. Gerasa – Jerash – Stadt der 1000 Säulen, in Hoffman A. and Kerner, S. (eds.), *Gadara-Gerasa und die Dekapolis*, 6–23. Mainz, Zabern.

Silberstein, N. 2000. Hellenistic and Roman Pottery. In Y. Hischfeld (ed.), *Ramat Hanadiv Excavations, Final Report of the 1984–1998 Seasons*, 420–469. Jerusalem, Israel Exploration Society.

Smetana-Scherrer, R. 1982. Spätklassische und hellenistische Keramik. In H. Walter (ed.), *Alt-Ägina II 1*, 56–91. Mainz, Zabern.

Smith, R. H. 1990. The Southern Levant in the Hellenistic period. *Levant* 22, 123–125.

Smith, R. H. and Day, L. P. (eds.) 1989. *Pella of the Decapolis. Vol 2. Final Report on the College of Wooster, Excavations in Area IX, The Civic*

Complex, 1979–1985. Ohio, College of Wooster.

Stern, E. 1995. *Excavations at Dor, Final Report, Vol. Ia und Ib. Areas A and C: the Finds*. Qedem Reports 2. Jerusalem, Israel Exploration Society.

Talgam, R. and Weiss, Z. (eds.) 2004. *The mosaics of the house of Dionysos at Sepphoris*. Jerusalem, The Hebrew University.

Tushingham, A. D. 1985. *Excavations in Jerusalem 1961–1967*, 1. Toronto, Royal Ontario Museum.

Vann, R. (ed.) 1992. *Straton's Tower, Herod's Harbour and Roman Byzantine Caesarea*. Journal of Roman Archaeology Supplement 5. Ann Arbor, Journal of Roman Archaeology.

Vieweger, D. and Häser, J. 2007a. Das 'Gadara-Region Project' Der Tell Zera'a in den Jahren 2005 und 2006. *Zeitschrift des Deutschen Palästina Vereins* 123/1, 1–27.

Vieweger, D. and Häser, J. 2007b. Tall Zira'a – Five Thousand Years of Palestinian History on a Single-Settlement Mound. *Near Eastern Archaeology* 70:3, 147–167.

Vieweger, D. and Häser, J. 2010. Das 'Gadara-Region Project', Der Tell Zera'a in den Jahren 2007 und 2009. *Zeitschrift des Deutschen Palästina Vereins*, 1–28.

Vieweger, D., Auge, W. and Hauptmann, A. 2009. Archaeometry in Archaeological Research; 5000 years of History on Tall Zar'a; Pottery – everyday life, Trade and Technology in Northern Jordan. *Studies in History and Archaeology of Jordan* X, 245–258.

Warner Slane, K. 1997. The Fine Wares. In S. C. Herbert (ed.), *The Hellenistic and Roman Pottery, Tel Anafa II, 1*. Journal of Roman Archaeology Supplement 10, 255–418. Ann Arbor, Journal of Roman Archaeology.

Watson, P. 2002. Pella – Die Stadt am Jordangraben, in A. Hoffman and S. Kerner (eds.), *Gadara-Gerasa und die Dekapolis*. 59–71, Mainz, Zabern.

Zabehlicky-Scheffeneger, S., Sauer, R. and Schneider, G. 1996. Graue Platten aus Ephesos und vom Magdalensberg, in M. Herfort-Koch, U. Mandel and U. Schädler (eds.), *Hellenistische und kaiserzeitliche Keramik des östlichen Mittelmeergebietes*. Kolloquium Frankfurt 24.–25. April 1995, 41–59. Frankfurt a. M., Arbeitskreis Frankfurt und die Antike.

Hellenistic Pottery from Palmyra: Imports and Local Production in a City between cultural and political frontiers

Christiane Römer-Strehl

Abstract

The ceramic material from Palmyra belongs to stratigraphical units and contains pottery from the end of the 3rd century BC until the 3rd/6th century AD. This paper deals only with the Hellenistic material. It is the first time, that we can distinguish Hellenistic pottery in Palmyra.

There are imports like Attic fish-plates or Skyphoi, Rhodian Amphorae and *BSP* – the predecessor *of ESA* – or other regional fabrics from the Orontes-Valley. The local Palmyrene pottery from the 3rd to the middle of the 2nd century BC adapted productions from the eastern Mediterranean area, especially fish plate forms and Echinus bowls. In the second quarter of the 2nd century BC South Mesopotamian influences are visible in the ceramic material for the first time. From the middle of the 1st century BC to the 1st century AD forms, produced in the Eastern Mediterranean area and such imitating these forms in the south of Mesopotamia, were used in parallel in Palmyra. This gives a hint to the importance of this trading place.

Keywords: Palmyra (Syria), lopas, Parthian Glazed Ware, BSP, ESA, fishplates, Rhodian amphoras.

Introduction

Palmyra is located about 300km from the coast of the Eastern Mediterranean and also 300km away from the river Euphrates. In ancient time Palmyra was an important commercial trading point and a buffer state between east and west. At that time and still today all goods had to be brought through this town. The main transport was done by caravans (**Fig. 1**).

In 1998 the first geomagnetic survey has been performed with the help of the Technical University of Munich[1]. One year later the excavation started in the so called 'Hellenistic Area'. A relative stratigraphic sequence from the end of the 3rd century BC to the 4th–6th century AD has been elaborated and building structures from different settlement phases were found. Related to the settlement phases different water installations like water pipes and wells were found on the street[2].

Pottery of the first two settlement phases

In the deepest and therefore oldest Hellenistic layers in trench 1 imported datable pottery has been found. For example: a Skyphos (**Fig. 2a**) and fishplates from Athens (**Fig. 2b-c**). These forms can be dated into the beginning of the 2nd century BC. A Rhodian Amphora stamp from the fabricant of Demothenes was found in the first settlement phase and has to be dated into the time span between 205 to 175 BC (**Fig. 3**)[3]. An untypical relief-sherd belongs to a bottle of red slipped pottery, which was also found in the deepest layers (**Fig. 4**). The quality of this sherd has been proven by chemical analysis as ESA. A man, draped with a himation around the hip and a lance in his hand, is shown[4]. This type of dress is comparable to a presentation of a god and the interpretation of this figure as Zeus is possible. Such a figure has not been found yet on a Sigillata bottle before. This sherd is unique, because of the material and the figure on it. Zeus has been worshiped in the Seleucidian Empire. An interpretation as a ritual flask of the Seleucidian Empire – comparable to the Ptolemaic flasks found in Egypt – is imaginable. All the ceramic material, which was found in the first settlement phase can be dated into the end of the 3rd to the first quarter of the 2nd century BC.

In the second settlement phase there was also found an amphora handle with the eponym of Athanodotos, which after Finkielsteijn can be dated between 170 and 168 BC[5] (**Fig. 5**). The appearance of the Black Slip Predecessor (*BSP)*, which was at first identified by K. W. Slane in the material of Tell Anafa[6], is also visible in Palmyra and can

1 Becker 2000, 77–80 pl. 9–12; Stephani 2000, 74–76 fig. 7–8.

2 Schmidt-Colinet and al-as'Ad 2000, 61-73 fig. 4 pl. 13; Schmidt-Colinet 2003a, 19–22; Schmidt-Colinet and al-As'ad 2003b, 299–302; Schmidt-Colinet and al-As'ad 2008, 452–467 fig. 3–6.

3 Laubenheimer and Schmidt-Colinet 2007, 332 fig. 3; Römer-Strehl 2000, 89–90 fig. 11c; Schmidt-Colinet and al-As'ad 2002, 165 fig. 12; Schmidt-Colinet and al-As'ad 2003b, 302 fig. 2.

4 Römer-Strehl 2000, 87–89 fig. 11a; Schmidt-Colinet and al-As'ad 2002, 165 fig. 11.

5 Finkielsztejn 2001, 192; Laubenheimer and Schmidt-Colinet 2007, 332 fig. 3.

6 Slane 1997, 269–274.

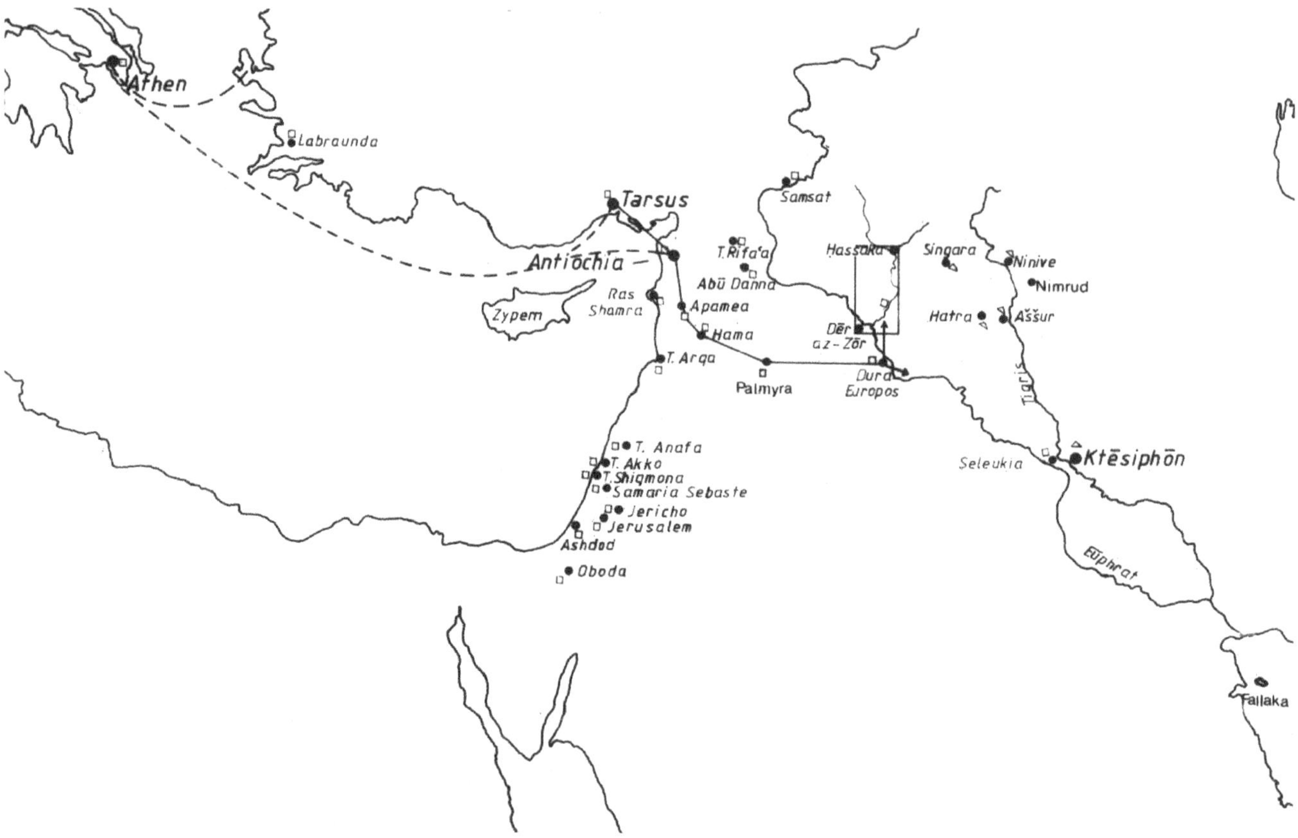

Fig. 1. Map: Overview (Ch. Römer-Strehl)

be dated into the 2nd quarter of the second century BC (**Fig. 6**). Locally made fishplates were already found in the first and second phase but in the second phase they are joined by fishplates from the Orontes Valley with the typical changing from black to red. In addition the first fragments of ESA-fishplates (**Fig. 2d–f**) were found in this phase[7]. This is a new aspect. In Palmyra we find for the first time ESA-fishplate fragments together with BSP-sherds. They coexist in the same settlement phase. This could be an indication that the production of BSP was only made for a very short time. Also is seems to be possible that the production of ESA could have started a little bit earlier than 150 BC. Other typical findings from the second phase are Echinus bowls in different fabrics like BSP, ESA and local or regional Red Slip Pottery.

Another important pottery group are fragments of the so called *Parthian glazed pottery*, which was imported from the South of Mesopotamia and has been found in a small quantity. The forms are amphora bottles (**Fig. 7a**). and fishplates (**Fig. 7b**). In the South of Mesopotamia in places like Seleucia on the Tigris or Larsa the possible place of origin, the production of this kind of ceramic started in the first half of the 2nd century BC[8]. It is possible that in the Susiane-region the production of glazed pottery starts a little bit earlier[9]. In Northern Mesopotamian areas, like the Habur valley[10] or Nimrud[11], the first imports from Seleucia on the Tigris are found not before the middle of the 2nd century BC. Concluding all the dating ceramic material with all its references the second phase is dateable into the second quarter of the 2nd century BC.

Summarizing the results of the pottery examination of the first and second settlement phase, it can be concluded, that the majority of sherds belongs to locally produced pottery. One third of the sherds have been imported from the western Mediterranean like Athens and Rhodes or Antiochia. This picture changes in the second phase. The local products still form the majority, but they are joined by imports from the western Mediterranean. Also the first imports from Mesopotamia are visible. The early notice of *Parthian glazed Pottery* is due to Palmyra's well established commercial network and caravan trade. Therefore sherds from the south of Mesopotamia – assumable Seleucia on the Tigris – can be found there already short after they have been invented in Seleucia. A similar evidence for Palmyra's importance in the ancient trade is the form of the so called Lopas (**Fig. 8**), which is typical for the Greek mainland. As there is no evidence for a local production of cooking

7 Römer-Strehl 2000, 83-85 fig. 9–10.
8 Debevoise 1934, 31–34; Lecompte 1993, 20 f.
9 Boucharlat, 1993, 47 Tab. 5; Finkbeiner 1993b, 283.
10 Römer 1996, 14; Römer-Strehl 2005, 223.
11 Oates 1958, 126.

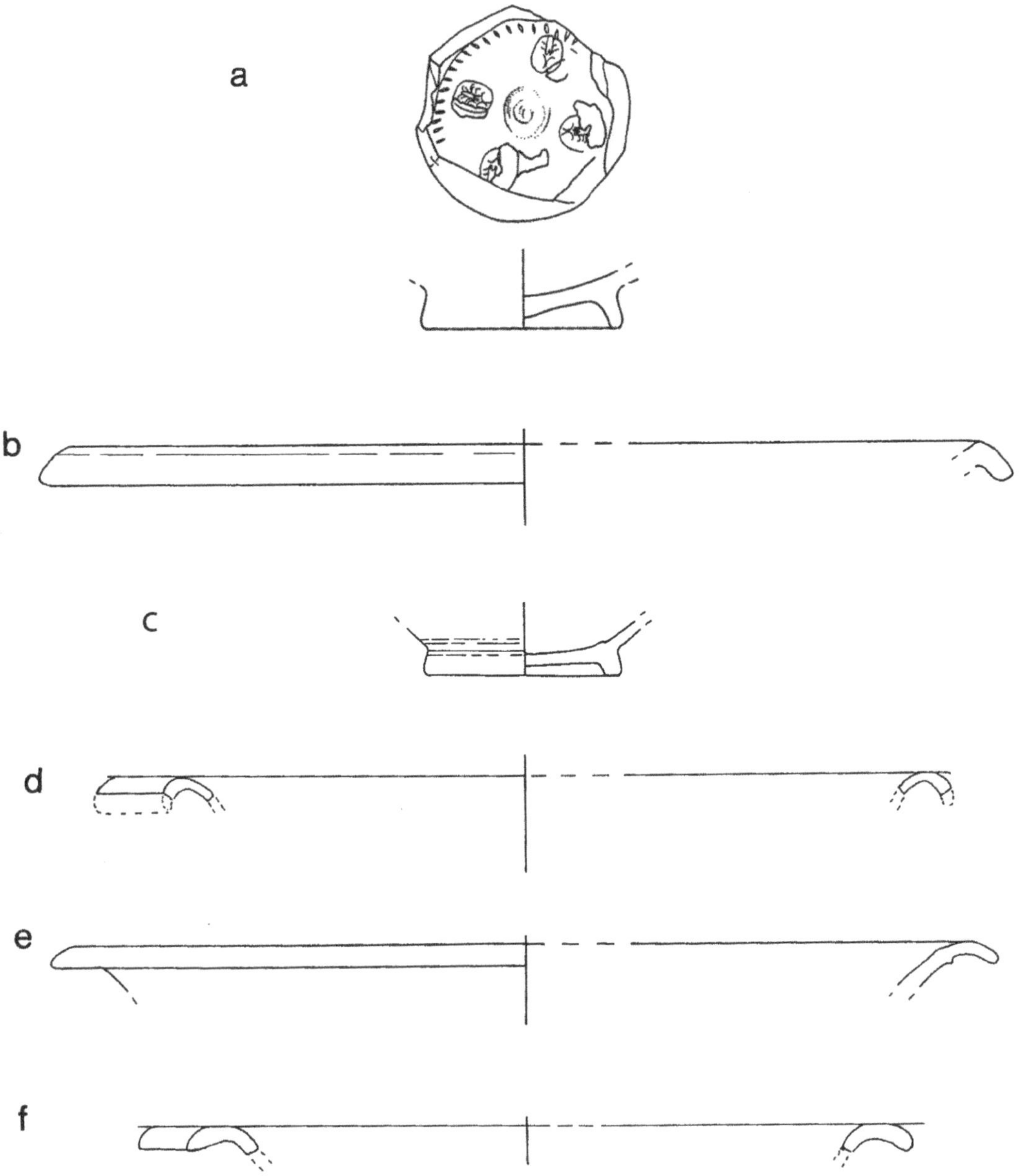

Fig. 2. a: Imported Attic skyphos (Phase 1) - b-c: Imported Attic fishplates (Phase 1) - d-f: ESA fishplates (Phase 2) (Ch. Römer-Strehl)

Fig. 3. Rhodian fabricant stamp (Phase 1) (Ch. Römer-Strehl)

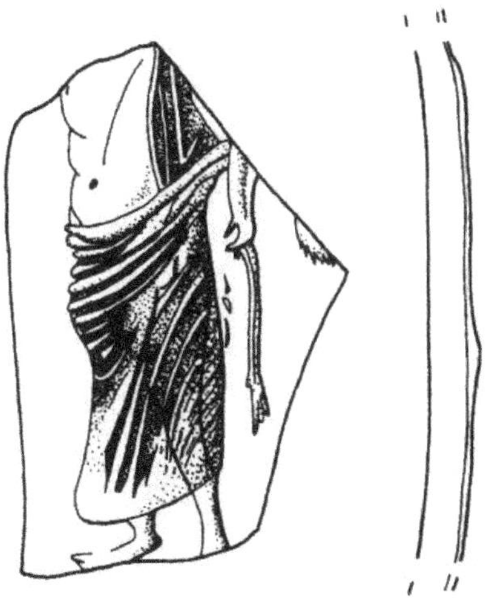

Fig. 4. ESA relief-sherd of a bottle (Phase 1) (Ch. Müller-Hazenbos)

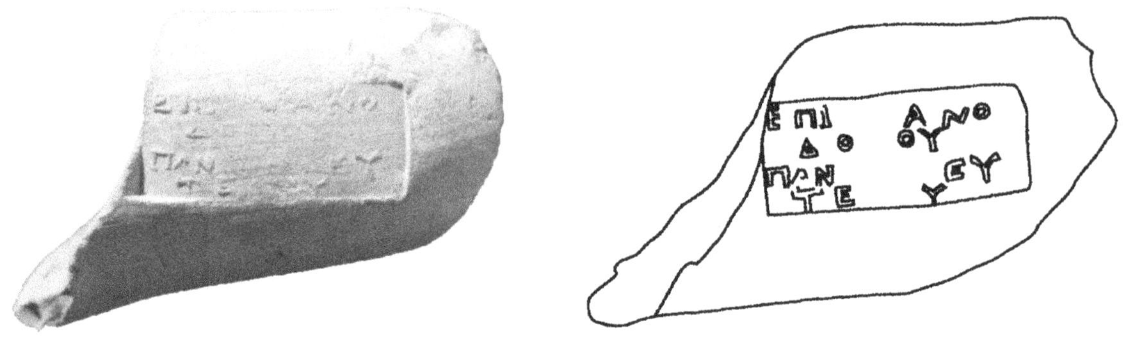

Fig. 5. Rhodian Eponym stamp (Phase 2) (Photo: A. Schmidt-Colinet, drawing: Ch. Römer-Strehl)

Fig. 6. Parthian yellow glazed sherd of an Amphora with the typical finger-dip-decoration together with a BSP ringfoot fragment (Phase 2) (A. Schmidt-Colinet)

pots in Palmyra at that time, all forms must have been imported, and the chemical analysis points without doubt to the Levantine Coast. In the oriental world Greek dining customs were very fashionable. They were so popular that in distant places like Failaka at the Persian Gulf the same type of pottery has been produced locally in that period[12]. Due to the stratigraphic situation in Palmyra the **ESA**-fishplates have to be dated into the same period as **BSP** and therefore a little bit earlier than in other excavations. **ESA**-fishplates in Palmyra obviously were found as early as the 2nd quarter of the 2nd century BC. Recognizing that the production centre is around Antioch on the Orontes, it seems reasonable that places in Syria should get ESA earlier than other regions further.

Pottery of the third and forth settlement phases

The assemblage of pottery of the next two phases are identical in the material: the dominant red slipped fine Ware is **ESA** in different forms like Hama 2, 16 and 17[13], 18 and 20[14] (**Fig. 9**). All fragments have parallels in Antiochia and Hama, also the quality of the **ESA** is comparable with the ESA from these two cities. In addition the number of Parthian glazed pottery became larger. A typological change in the imported cooking pot rims (**Fig. 10**) can be observed. In the third and fourth phase the percentage of imported ceramic again becomes larger compared to the first and second phase. Nevertheless in the third phase it is remarkable how balanced imports from the east and west are. In the fourth phase *ESA* imports clearly dominate the picture.

The pottery of the fifth settlement phase

In the last Hellenistic and early Roman phase for the first time pottery from Asia Minor appears in Palmyra: The so called '*Asia Minor glazed Relief-bowls*' are not very

12 Hannestad 1983, 63–64; Hannestad 1998, 185 fig. 4.7.

13 Papanicolaou-Christensen and Friis Johannsen 1971, 115 pl. 45; s. also Kramer 2004, 181–185.

14 Hayes 1985, 24–25; Papanicolaou-Christensen and Friis Johannsen 1971, 124–159.

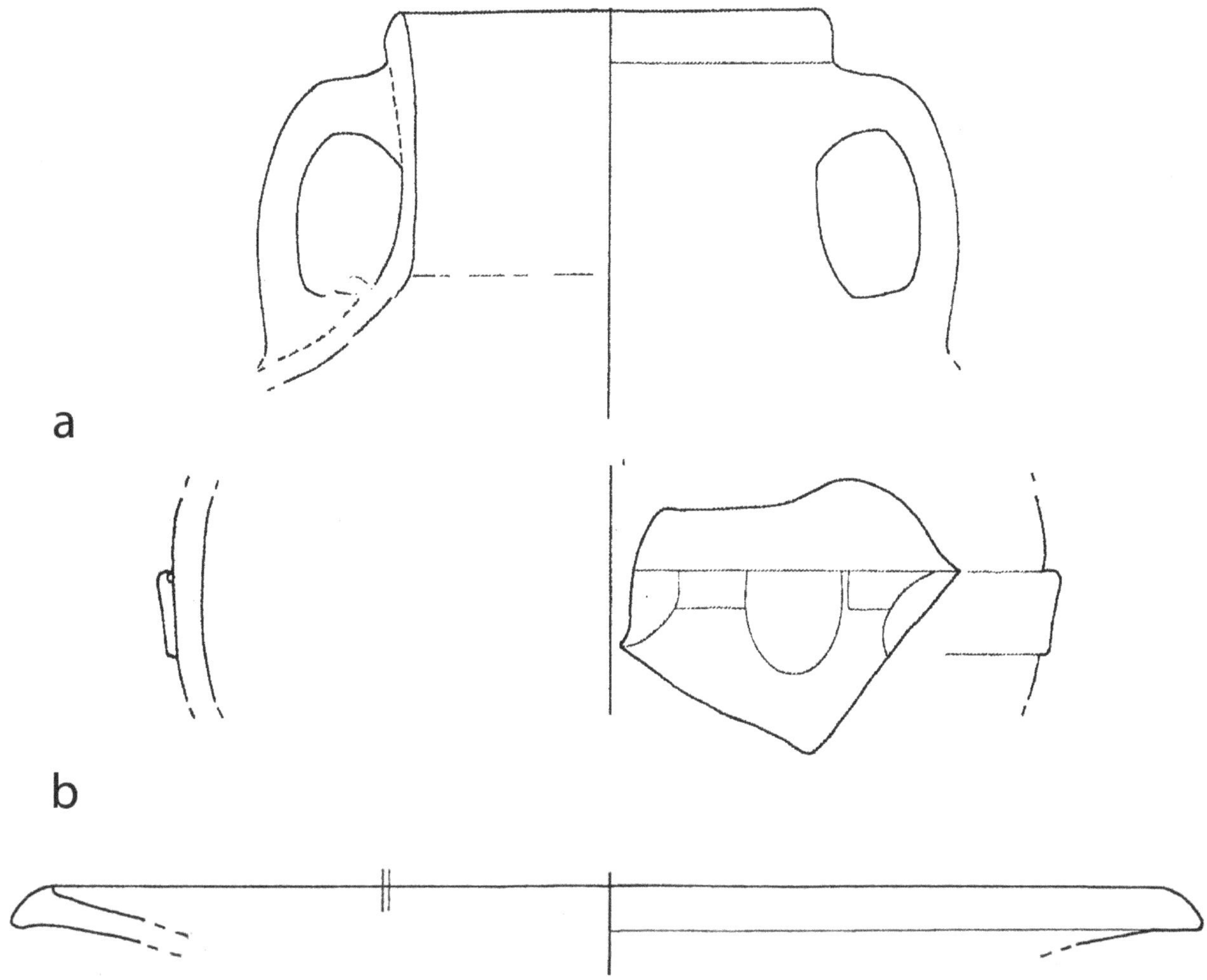

Fig. 7. a: Parthian glazed amphora (Phase 2) - b: Parthian glazed fishplate (Phase 2) (Ch. Römer-Strehl)

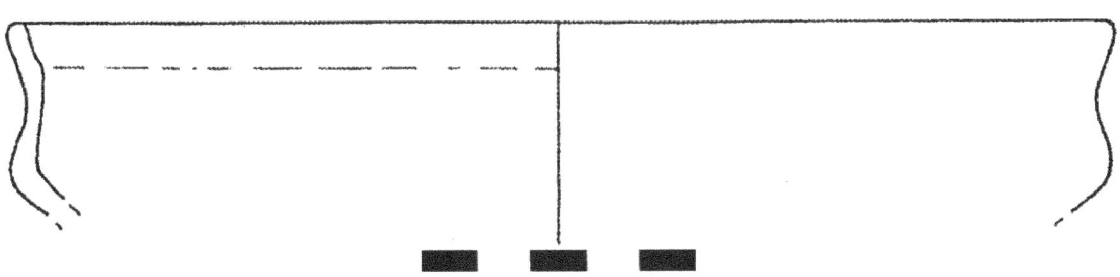

Fig. 8. Imported cooking ware: lopas (Phase 2) (Ch. Römer-Strehl)

common in this region[15] and can be dated into the last quarter of the 1st century BC[16] (**Fig. 11**).

The ESA pieces now belong to a very good quality, with thin walls and a shiny surface. Another important fact is that there are still cooking pots from the Levantine coast with a metallic appearance (**Fig. 12**). In this phase we also find locally produced cooking pots for the first time. They imitate the Levantine imports. Characteristic for this time in Palmyra and in Mesopotamia are ceramic-forms in ESA-fabric imported from the west, and the same form, produced in Parthian Glazed Pottery from southern Mesopotamia[17]. From the point of ceramic distribution

15 Römer-Strehl 2005, 222 f.
16 Hochuli-Gysel 1977, pl. 17, I13; Waagé 1948, 81 fig. 44, 13–14.
17 Hannestad 1983, pl. 18. 193–194; Hauser 1994, 316–317 pl. 18b–d;

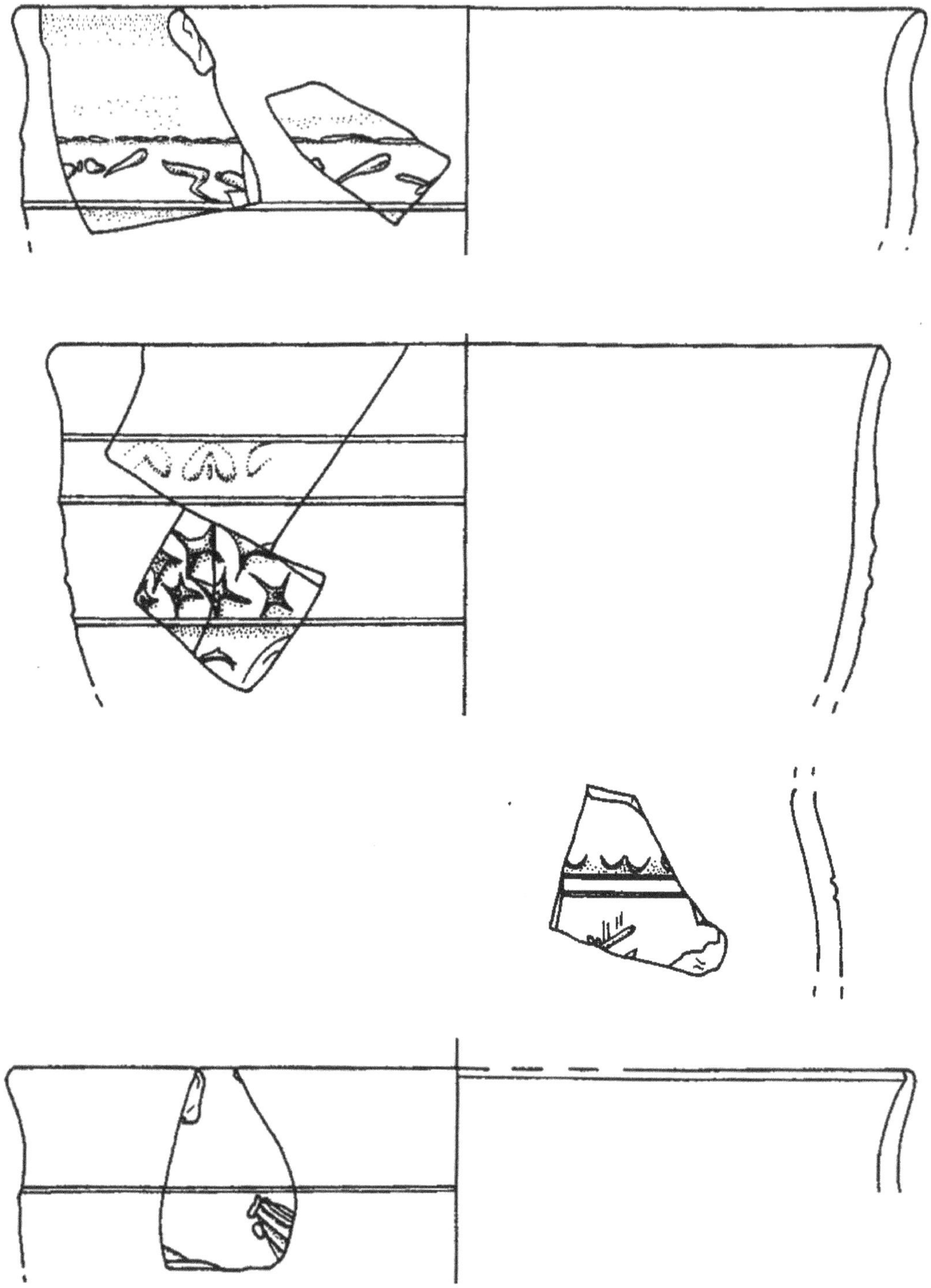

Fig. 9. ESA relief bowls (100 BC Phase 4) (Ch. Müller-Hazenbos)

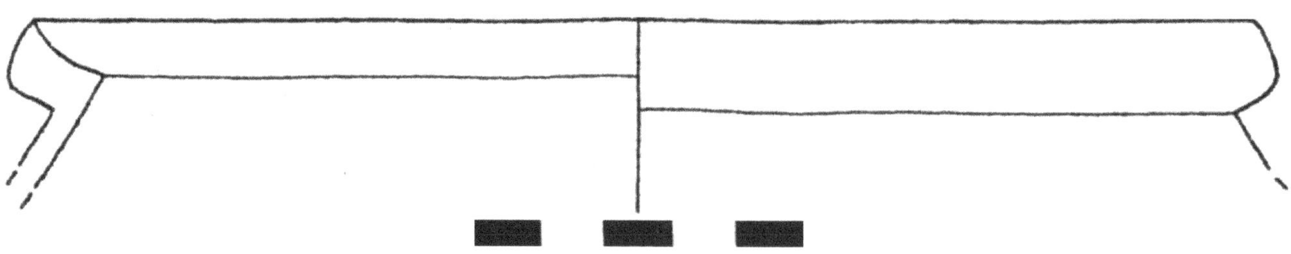

Fig. 10. Imported cooking pot (Phase 4–5) (Ch. Römer-Strehl)

Fig. 11. Imported Asia Minor glazed relief bowl (Phase 5) (A. Schmidt-Colinet)

shares, the local production remains an important factorat the end of the 1st century BC up to the 1st century AD. The increase of imports from Mesopotamia is quite notable. The percentage of imports from the east is at that time larger than that from the west. Now it is the other way round compared to the first two phases.

Conclusion

Summing up all aspects of Hellenistic pottery in Palmyra, it can be noted, that the ceramic production in Palmyra from the very end of the 3rd century BC and in the whole 2nd century BC is orientated to western pottery models. The most important forms are fish-plates[18], relief- and Echinus-bowls. These three forms are well known in whole Mesopotamia including Iran, the Persian Gulf- and Bahrain-region. Hitherto in Palmyra the form of the so called 'Lagynos' is absolutely absence. This is a very famous closed vessel shape in the Greek mainland, Egypt and Asia Minor. The new research seems that this form is only limited to the Persian Gulf- region[19].

In the second quarter of the 2nd century BC one can recognize more South Mesopotamian influence in Palmyra, which is obviously clear in the *Parthian Glazed pottery* with the closed vessel forms like jugs, flask and bottles andtable amphorae.

In the 1st century BC the ceramic production in Palmyra gets a more individual character. This becomes particularly obvious in the production of lamps and cooking pots. Another important point is the distribution of *Eastern Sigillata A*. Only some of the forms in a very good quality reached the city of Palmyra from the second quarter of the 2nd century BC to the middle of the 1st century AD. In Mesopotamia the *ESA* is limited from the middle of the 1st century BC to the middle of the 1st century AD. Also the *ESA* is very rarely represented in Mesopotamia[20]. The most forms of *ESA* are imitated in the glazed ware or the so called BI-Ware[21]. Ceramic exports from Palmyra to other places or cities are rare and extraordinary[22]. However there are trade relations known from epigraphic contexts. In future one should pay more attention to Palmyrene pottery outside of Palmyra.

Acknowledgment

The material has been excavated by A. Schmidt-Colinet and his team in the framework of the project 'Hellenistic Palmyra'. Special thanks to A. Schmidt-Colinet, R. Ployer

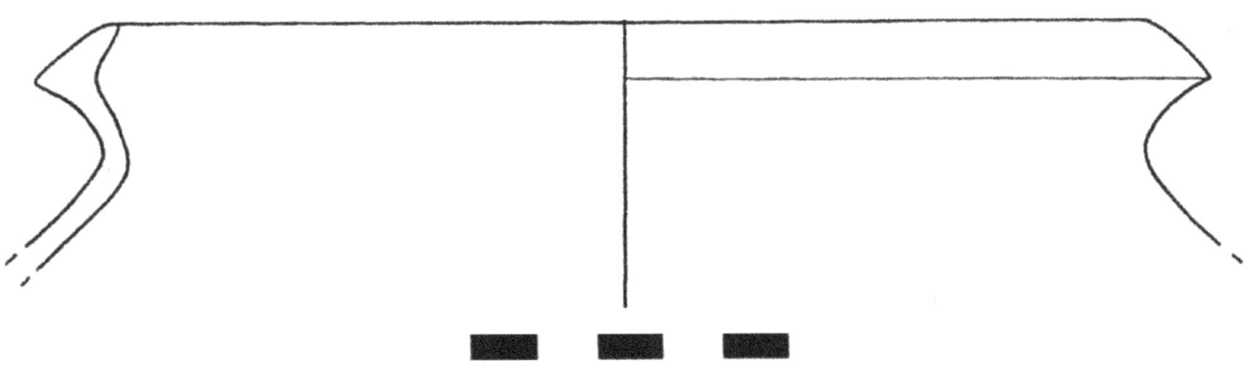

Fig. 12. Imported cooking pot (Phase 5) (Ch. Römer-Strehl)

Lombard and Kervran 1993, 137 fig. 13; Oates and Oates 1958, 114–158. Valtz 1991, 45–56; Valtz 1993, 167–182.

18 Boucharlat 1993, 50 tab. 5; Finkbeiner 1993b, 282; Römer-Strehl 2005, 245 f. fig. 655.
19 Herling and Salles 1993, 169 f. fig. 3.19 and 4.22.
20 Parmeginai 19997, 128; Römer-Strehl 2005, 220; Valtz 1991, 46; Valtz 1993, 176.
21 Gachet and Salles 1993, 70.
22 See Tomber *et al.* 2011, 7–8 fig. 2.5.

and F. Laubenheimer, who supported me with many discussions. A full description of the material can be found in: A. Schmidt-Colinet (ed.), Palmyras Reichtum durch weltweiten Handel. Archäologische Untersuchungen im Bereich der hellenistischen Stadt. Wien, Holzhausen. (in print)

Christiane Römer-Strehl
Institut für Archäologie und Kulturanthropologie der Universität Bonn - Abteilung Klassische Archäologie
Am Hofgarten 21
D-53113 Bonn
Christiane.Roemer-Strehl@gmx.net

Bibliographie

Becker, H. 2000. Geophysikalische Prospektion in Palmyra und ihre Auswertung, in A. Schmidt-Colinet and Kh. al-As'ad, Zur Urbanistik des hellenistischen Palmyra. Ein Vorbericht. *Damaszener Mitteilungen* 12, 77–80.

Boucharlat, R. 1993. Pottery in Susa during the Seleukid, Parthian and early Sasanian periods. In U. Finkbeiner (ed.), *Materialen zur Archäologie der Seleukiden- und Partherzeit im südlichen Babylonien und im Golfgebiet.* Ergebnisse der Symposien 1987 und 1989 in Blaubeuren, 41–58. Tübingen, Wasmuth.

Debevoise, N. C. 1934. *Parthian Pottery from Seleukia on the Tigris.* Ann Arbor, University Press.

Finkbeiner, U. 1993a. Uruk – Warka. Fundstellen der Keramik der Seleukiden- und Partherzeit. In U. Finkbeiner (ed.), *Materialen zur Archäologie der Seleukiden- und Partherzeit im südlichen Babylonien und im Golfgebiet.* Ergebnisse der Symposien 1987 und 1989 in Blaubeuren, 3–16. Tübingen, Wasmuth.

Finkbeiner, U. 1993b. Vergleichende Stratigraphie und Chronologie. In U. Finkbeiner (ed.), *Materialen zur Archäologie der Seleukiden- und Partherzeit im südlichen Babylonien und im Golfgebiet.* Ergebnisse der Symposien 1987 und 1989 in Blaubeuren, 281–288. Tübingen, Wasmuth.

Finkielsztejn, G. 2001. *Chronologie détaillée et revisée des eponyms amphoriques rhodiens de 270 à 108 av. J.-C. environ,* British Archaeological Reports International Series 990. Oxford, BAR Publishing.

Gachet, J and Salles, J.-F. 1993. Failaka, Koweit. In U. Finkbeiner (ed.), *Materialen zur Archäologie der Seleukiden- und Partherzeit im südlichen Babylonien und im Golfgebiet.* Ergebnisse der Symposien 1987 und 1989 in Blaubeuren, 59–85. Tübingen, Wasmuth.

Hannestad, L. 1983. *The Hellenistic Pottery. Ikaros – The Hellenistic settlements 2.* Aarhus, Jutland Archaeological Society Publications.

Hannestad, L. 1990. Change and Conservatism. Hellenistic Pottery on Mesopotamia and Iran, in *Akten des 13. Internationalen Kongresses für Klassische Archäologie Berlin 1988. 24.7 - 30. 7.,* 179–186. Mainz, Zabern.

Hauser, S. R. 1994. *Chronologische und historisch-politische Untersuchungen zur östlichen Gazira in vorislamischer Zeit,* PhD thesis FU Berlin, Microfiche.

Hayes, J. W. 1985. Atlante delle forme ceramiche II - Ceramica fine romana nel bacino mediterraneo (tardo ellenismo e primo impero), *EAA Suppl. Ceramiche II.* Rom, Istituto della Enciclopedia Italiana.

Herling, A. and Salles, J.-F. 1993. Hellenistic Cementries in Bahrain. In U. Finkbeiner (ed.), 161–182.

Hochuli-Gysel, A. 1977. *Kleinasiatische glasierte Reliefbecher 50 v. - 50 n. Chr. und ihre oberitalischen Nachahmungen.* Bern, Stämpfli und Cie AG.

Kramer, N. 2004. *Gindaros. Geschichte und Archäologie einer Siedlung im nordwestlichen Syrien von hellenistischer bis in frühbyzantinische Zeit.* Internationale Archäologie 41. Rahden, Verlag Marie Leidorf.

Laubenheimer, F. and Schmidt-Colinet, A. 2007. Des Amphores à Palmyre. Le matériel des fouilles récente de la mission syro-allemande. *Topoi* 8, 329–255.

Lecomte, O 1993. Stratigraphical Anaylsis and Ceramic Assemblages of the 4th -1st Centuries B.C.E. Babbar of Larsa (Southern Iraq). In U. Finkbeiner (ed.), *Materialen zur Archäologie der Seleukiden- und Partherzeit im südlichen Babylonien und im Golfgebiet.* Ergebnisse der Symposien 1987 und 1989 in Blaubeuren, 17–49. Tübingen, Wasmuth.

Lombard, P. and Kervran, M. 1993. Les Niveaux "Hellenistiques" du Tell de Qal' at al-Bahrain. In U. Finkbeiner (ed.), *Materialen zur Archäologie der Seleukiden- und Partherzeit im südlichen Babylonien und im Golfgebiet.* Ergebnisse der Symposien 1987 und 1989 in Blaubeuren, 127–160. Tübingen, Wasmuth.

Oates, D. and Oates, J. 1958. Nimrud 1957: The Hellenistic Settlement. *Iraq* 20, 114–157.

Papanicolaou-Christensen, A. and Friis Johannsen, C. 1971. *Les poteries hellénistiques et les terres sigillées orientales. Fouilles et recherches 1931–1938.* Hama III 2. Kopenhagen, Fondation Carlsberg.

Parmegiani, N. 1987. The Eastern Sigillata in Tell Barri/Kahat. *Mesopotamia* 22, 113–128.

Römer, C. 1996. A first Glimpse at Glazed Pottery from Tell Shech Hamad, in K. Bartl and S. R. Hauser (eds.), *Continuity and Change in Northern Mesopotamia from the Hellenistic to the Early Islamic Period.* Berliner Beiträge zum Vorderen Orient 17, 13–21. Berlin, Reimer.

Römer-Strehl, C. 2000. Die Keramik, in A. Schmidt-

Colinet and Kh. al-As'ad, Zur Urbanistik des hellenistischen Palmyras. Ein Vorbericht. *Damaszener Mitteilungen* 12, 61–93.

Römer-Strehl, C. 2005. Untersuchungen zur Keramik der seleukidischen und parthisch-römischen Zeit von Tall Seh Hamad. In H. Kühne (ed.), *Magdalu/ Magdala Tall Seh Hamad von der postassyrischen Zeit zur römischen Kaiserzeit*, 197–310. Berlin, Reimer

Schmidt-Colinet, A and al-As'ad, Kh. 2000. Zur Urbanistik des hellenistischen Palmyra. Ein Vorbericht, *Damaszener Mitteilungen* 12, 61–73.

Schmidt-Colinet, A. and al-As'ad, Kh. 2003a. Untersuchungen zur Urbanistik des hellenistischen Palmyra, in K. S. Freyberger, A. Henning and H. v. Hesberg (eds.), *Kulturkonflikte im Vorderen Orient an der Wende vom Hellenismus zur römischen Kaiserzeit.* Orient Archäologie 1, 19–22. Rahden/ Westf, Leidorf GmbH.

Schmidt-Colinet, A. and al-As'ad, Kh. 2003b. Nouvelles données sur Palmyre hellénistique. In M. Sartre (ed.), *La Syrie hellénistique.* Topoi Suppl. 4, 299–302. Paris, De Boccard.

Schmidt-Colinet, A., al-As'ad, Kh. and al-As'ad, W. 2008. Untersuchungen im Areal der Hellenistischen Stadt von Palmyra. Zweiter Vorbericht. *Zeitschrift für Orient-Archäologie* 1, 452–478.

Slane, K. W. 1997. The fine Wares. In S. C. Herbert (ed.), *Tel Anafa II.1: The Hellenistic and Roman Pottery,* 24–406 Ann Arbor, Kelsey Museum.

Stephani, M. 2000. Geodätische und photogrammetrische Datenerfassung in Palmyra und ihre Auswertung, in A. Schmidt-Colinet and Kh. al-As'ad, Zur Urbanistik des hellenistischen Palmyra. Ein Vorbericht. *Damaszener Mitteilungen 12*, 74–76.

Tomber, R., Graf, D., Healy, J. F., Römer-Strehl, C. and Majcherek, G. 2011. Pots with writing, in D. Peacock and L. Blue (eds.), *Myos Hormos – Quseir al-Qadim. Roman and Islamic Ports on the Red Sea. Volume 2: Finds from the Excavations 1999-2003*, 5–10, University of Southampton Series in Archae-ology No. 6. Oxford, BAR Publishing.

Valtz, E. 1991. New Observations on the Hellenistic Pottery from Seleukia on the Tigris, in K. Schippmann, A. Herling and J. -F. Salles (eds.), *Golf-Archäologie. Mesopotamien, Iran, Kuweit, Bahrain, Vereinigte Arabische Emirate und Oman.* Symposium Göttingen 1987. Internationale Archäologie 6, 45–56. Buch am Erlbach, Maria Leidorf.

Valtz, E. 1993. Pottery and Exchanges: Imports and Local Production at Seleukia-Tigris, in A. Invernizzi and J.-F. Salles (eds.), *Arabia Antiqua, Hellenistic Centres around Arabia.* 167–182. Rom, Is. M.E.O.

Waagé, F. O. 1948. (ed.), *Ceramics and Islamic Coins. Antioch-on-the-Orontes IV 1.* Princeton, University Press.

Vaisselles hellénistiques à Europos-Doura: Importations et productions locales

Françoise Alabe

Abstract

A Seleucid foundation (300 BC) in the Middle Euphrates, Europos kept its Macedonian name when it was annexed first to the Parthian Arsacid kingdom (115 BC) then to the Roman Empire (AD 165), until the eve of the city's fall and desertification by the Sassanians (AD 256). Since 1920, the excavations on the site have uncovered an enormous quantity of very fragmentary, locally produced common ware, whose typology is getting better known season after season. Imported ware is rather rare. It consists of container vases (Chios'amphorae, from the city's foundation to the 60s BC) and fine tableware (Attic black-glazed vases, between 300 and 200-175 BC), two categories linked to the consumption of wine. We recognize a few isolated Eastern sigillata vases, a few others of Irano-Mesopotamian tradition (Achaemenid beakers, egg shell or imitations). Glazing does not really appear before the first century BC. Before the Parthian conquest, local potters produced a semi-fineware of Hellenizing repertoire and style: the surfaces are weatherproofed either by buffing (*Grey Ware*), or by a slip, often red, rarely black or brown, but never sintered.

Keywords: Dura-Europos, Seleucid Syria, Parthian kingdom, blade, kiln, grey ware, black slip, red slip.

Présentation

Sur un site déjà amplement dégagé par les fouilles de l'Académie des Inscriptions et Belles-lettres (1920–1923, sous la direction de Frantz Cumont), puis par celles de l'Université de Yale (1931–1938, sous la direction de Mikhaïl Rostovtzeff), les travaux menés par la Mission franco-syrienne dirigée par Pierre Leriche, depuis 1986, visent trois objectifs limités. D'une part, il s'agit de compléter les publications existantes: l'arrêt des fouilles après 1938 n'a mis un terme ni aux études de matériel recueilli, ni aux publications de la série des *Dura Final Reports*, mais il a notablement entravé les recherches, et des monuments importants sont restés inédits. D'autre part, si l'histoire de la ville est connue dans ses grandes lignes depuis plus de 80 ans, certains points essentiels de son histoire urbanistique et monumentale demandaient à être précisés ou vérifiés par une stratigraphie rigoureuse. Enfin, alors que l'enfouissement les avait préservés durant plus d'un millénaire et demi, beaucoup des vestiges exhumés avant la Seconde guerre mondiale se sont gravement dégradés dans les décennies suivantes, sous l'action conjuguée des facteurs atmosphériques, humains et animaux: menés de concert avec la Direction Générale des Antiquités, les travaux récurrents de préservation, de consolidation ou de restauration donnent toujours lieu à des observations archéologiques fines dont les résultats viennent abonder les deux objectifs précédemment évoqués.

En explorant la nécropole aux abords du rempart occidental, les missions précédentes avaient recueilli une proportion importante de vases complets en céramique fine ou semi-fine, déposés en offrande dans les tombes. Au contraire, la vaisselle commune locale, presque toujours dans un état très fragmentaire, représente une écrasante majorité de la céramique découverte depuis 1986 tant dans les sondages stratigraphiques que lors des nettoyages préliminaires aux interventions conservatoires. Or, malgré ce handicap, l'étude de ce matériel – sans être toujours spectaculaire, loin s'en faut – n'est pas totalement désespérée.

Prédominance des fabriques locales

Dès les premières campagnes consacrées à l'examen de la céramique en 1989 et 1990, des observations techniques permirent de caractériser une production considérée comme locale, à travers plusieurs variantes d'aspect et de mise en œuvre[1]. S'il n'a pas été possible de confirmer par des analyses physico-chimiques la provenance exacte de la pâte considérée comme locale, ces observations rejoignent celles faites en 1921 par des pionniers associés à la mission de Fr. Cumont: malgré les décennies écoulées, le diagnostic de F. Massoul garde sa pertinence, et les analyses menées à sa demande par un laboratoire de minéralogie[2] restent valides pour l'essentiel, même si d'autres protocoles sont aujourd'hui souvent préférés. Ses hypothèses sont, dans l'ensemble, corroborées, et ses conclusions affinées dans l'étude menée en 1936 et 1937 par Fr. Matson (1943). D'autre part, l'avancée des travaux sur le terrain a fourni plusieurs arguments à l'appui de cette hypothèse. Parmi les indices archéologiques d'une production locale, on doit citer d'une part la présence de ratés de cuisson, associés

---

1 Alabe 1992, 50.
2 Massoul 1926, 457.

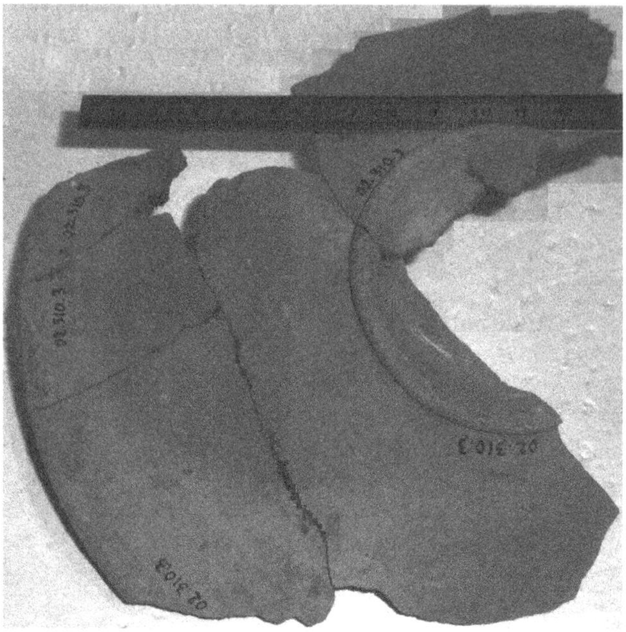

Fig. 1. Coupe rectiligne voilée à la cuisson (MFSED)

dans les remblais à des fragments de vaisselle usagée, et d'autre part les informations fournies par la fouille de fours et d'ateliers céramiques.

Au nombre des ratés de cuisson, le plus remarquable (**Fig. 1**) est une coupe à parois très rectilignes découverte en 2002, dans les couches supérieures du remblai qui comble un front de taille hellénistique au droit de la rue principale[3]. La pâte très dure, légère, rend un son métallique cliquetant; elle a connu un début de vitrification et pris une teinte gris verdâtre assez sombre, d'aspect spongieux, et l'on relève en surface de grands nuages tirant sur un jaune clair très terne: cette poudre se dépose sur les doigts au frottement. Le profil serait archéologiquement complet (seule manque la partie centrale du fond, délimité par un petit pied annulaire rudimentaire dont plus de 55% est préservé), mais le plan de la lèvre n'est pas parallèle au plan de pose, et le pied et la lèvre ne sont pas concentriques. Non seulement il est impossible de repérer une symétrie par rapport à un axe vertical, mais on ne décèle pas non plus d'horizontale. Trop défectueux pour être importé, cet exemplaire est donc bien un produit local: les défauts flagrants de bon nombre de céramiques communes (pâte de piètre qualité, façonnage approximatif, cuisson mal maîtrisée) étaient déjà l'un des arguments invoqués en faveur de leur production locale[4].

Quant aux fours et aux ateliers, sans revenir sur ceux déjà mentionnés dans des publications antérieures[5], je me borne à signaler deux ensembles plus récemment dégagés et dont l'étude est encore en cours, en insistant sur des indications qui concernent la pratique du métier de potier. L'îlot C11, à l'extrême Sud-Est de la ville, abritait un atelier produisant vaisselle de table et céramique glaçurée, comme l'attestent plusieurs fours successifs, des vases incuits et quelques biscuits; exploré depuis 1996 par Justine Gaborit, le secteur a fourni notamment en abondance de la céramique datant de la dernière phase d'occupation avant la prise de la ville par les Sassanides en 256 de notre ère: l'étude et la publication de cette vaisselle romaine ont été confiées à Marie Tuffreau-Libre. Cependant, un mince galet poli, au toucher soyeux, recueilli en 2003 dans une pièce donnant sur la cour, confirme qu'il s'agit bien ici d'un atelier. Tenant parfaitement en main, cet outil de façonnage (estèque) au galbe complexe servait en effet de gabarit pour affiner et régulariser le profil des vases lors des dernières phases du tournage. Dans l'îlot C2, une cinquantaine de mètres plus à l'Ouest, Jacques Thiriot a fouillé en 2010 un four de grande taille (**Fig. 2, Fig. 3**): la vaisselle crue découverte à

Fig. 2. Four en fin de fouille (avril 2010): la chambre de chauffe (MFSED)

Fig. 3. Four en fin de fouille (avril 2010): vue d'ensemble (MFSED)

3 Alabe 2012, 170 n°13.

4 Dyson 1968, 2.

5 Allara 1992; Allara 1994.

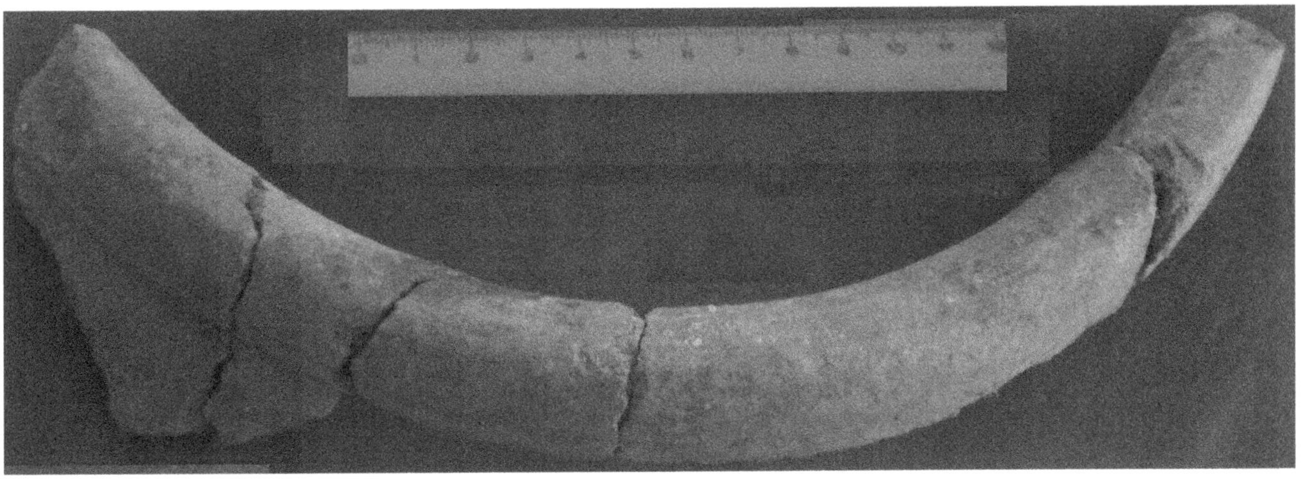

Fig. 4. Vaisselle non cuite découverte dans le four (avril 2010): embouchure de jarre (MFSED)

cette occasion (**Fig. 4**) révèle, malgré son extrême fragilité, un éventail typologique qui recoupe étroitement celui en usage dans les habitations (**Fig. 5**). La parenté observable ici pour l'embouchure de grandes jarres se répète de façon analogue pour de petites formes ouvertes (bols ou jattes) ou fermées (embouchures et fonds de cruchettes).

Vaisselle commune: quelques avancées dans une typologie encore embryonnaire

Pour autant, ces précieuses informations techniques se rapportent encore et toujours à la dernière phase de la ville romaine, et ne font guère progresser le projet d'étudier la colonie séleucide d'Europos-Doura sous un autre prisme que celui des soldats bâtisseurs auxquels nous devons le rempart, formidable, et le plan urbain si scrupuleusement respecté par les Parthes à partir de la fin du IIe siècle av. J.-C. La typologie de la vaisselle commune produite localement reste incomplète. Parmi les formes ouvertes, la présence assurée d'un couvercle[6] (**Fig. 6**) ne rend que plus hasardeuse l'identification de certaines assiettes très évasées[7], dont le profil similaire présentait des lacunes plus accusées. Les petits bols ou coupelles (Diam. ouverture oscillant entre 9,5cm et 12cm) à lèvre redressée ou rentrante[8], toujours fréquents mais assez peu réguliers dans le détail, se distinguent nettement d'un groupe de coupelles un peu plus larges (Diam. ouverture 14cm à 15,5cm)[9] dont le profil rectiligne se résout par un léger épaississement de la lèvre. Ce nouveau type est plus proche de ceux connus dans l'Orient hellénistique, à Failaka (IIe siècle av. J.-C.)[10] ou à Suse[11]. Les deux types sont également attestés dans des modules plus grands (Diam. ouverture 18cm à 24cm), et ceux à paroi rectiligne semblent être plus profonds que ceux à lèvre redressée ou rentrante. Plusieurs fonds de

Fig. 5. Grande jarre bitumée complète de production locale (MFSED)

---

6 Alabe 2012, 172 n°14.
7 Alabe 2005 n°9.
8 Alabe 2005 n°13 et n°20.
9 Alabe 2012, 173 n°19.
10 Bernard, Gachet and Salles 1990, 268–269 n°192.
11 Boucharlat 1987, 200–201; 254–255.

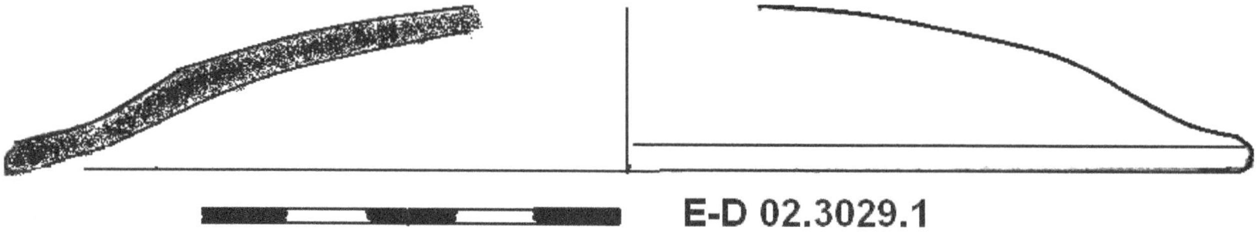

Fig. 6. Vaisselle commune locale: couvercle (MFSED)

jattes, d'assiettes ou de coupelles à dépression centrale[12], lointains dérivés des *Fish Plates* attiques, témoignent d'un façonnage hâtif et peu soigneux: leur plan de pose garde les traces, non ravalées, de la ficelle qui les a détachés du tour, et le creusement de la cupule peut laisser à l'intérieur soit un ombilic central, résidu de cône de tournage imparfaitement rabattu, soit un bourrelet saillant irrégulier dans lequel se sont imprimés les ongles du potier (**Fig.** 7)[13] lorsqu'il a retourné le vase pour le mettre à sécher embouchure en bas. Ces jattes semblent avoir coexisté avec d'autres, de facture plus soignée (pâte moins grossière, pied annulaire), dont le profil à lèvre retombante est conforme au modèle initial[14].

La typologie des formes fermées est plus réduite encore. Cependant, il a récemment été possible de remonter partiellement une cruche piriforme à embouchure large (**Figure 8**) dont la pâte grossière et dure, légèrement surcuite, est marquée de traces d'estèque à mi-panse et à la jonction panse/col. Le pied annulaire, la lèvre évasée arrondie et l'anse en ruban épais témoignent d'une fabrication soignée, les stries indiquent un tournage rapide, et les parois sont assez peu épaisses eu égard au volume de la pièce, dont il manque plus du tiers (les fragments ont été découverts dans les couches de fondation des premiers sols dans le secteur de l'agora par Gaëlle Coqueugniot, que je remercie de m'avoir permis d'en faire état ici). Ce type de pot à une anse verticale devait être assez répandu, si l'on en juge par la fréquence des fragments de pieds annulaires, d'anses et d'embouchures de dimensions voisines, sans parler des tessons de panses atypiques à peine plus épais ou à peine plus minces.

Céramique importée: conteneurs et céramique fine

Tout en étant beaucoup moins nombreuse (selon les contextes envisagés, entre 0,2% et 2,5% des tessons), la céramique importée fournit des informations à la fois plus détaillées et plus sûres. Parallèlement à la céramique fine, où le vernis noir attique est régulièrement présent, une catégorie de vases-conteneurs apparaît dans tous les secteurs, et témoigne d'un courant d'échanges qui paraissait *a priori* improbable. Le vin de Chios était, certes, l'un des crus les plus réputés du bassin égéen, mais il est remarquable que les amphores (et, sans doute, les lagynoi) de Chios soient pour ainsi dire les seuls conteneurs vinaires importés par les Européens de l'Euphrate.

Amphores de Chios

Plusieurs fragments ou tessons atypiques ont déjà été signalés en détail ou plus brièvement[15]. Le rythme de découverte de cette production se maintient à une demi-douzaine de tessons par campagne, tous chantiers confondus. C'est un corpus insuffisant pour raisonner sur la typologie et la chronologie de ces amphores, puisque la moitié environ du total est atypique; les fragments isolés dont la forme est reconnaissable pourraient cependant s'échelonner sur près de deux siècles et demi. Il s'agirait alors d'un courant sporadique, mais récurrent durant toute la période hellénistique; ces arrivées de vin de Chios semblent avoir perduré, pendant quelques décennies au moins, sous l'occupation parthe qui débute, rappelons-le, en 115 av. J.-C. pour se maintenir jusqu'à l'annexion de la ville par l'empire romain au milieu du IIe siècle ap. J.-C. En définitive, ces fragments posent autant de questions qu'ils apportent de réponses – et, avant tout, *qui* buvait ce vin (qui avait ou se donnait les moyens de l'acheter et de le faire acheminer si loin de son terroir), et *comment* le buvait-on (dans quel cadre, en quelle occasion et en quelle compagnie)? Naturellement, on sera tenté de chercher la vaisselle de *symposion* correspondant au rituel social de consommation des grands vins...

Lagynos de Chios

La pâte caractéristique de Chios est identifiable sur des fragments plus rares, semble-t-il, que les fragments d'amphores: deux mètres plus bas dans le comblement déjà évoqué *supra* à propos de l'assiette surcuite, se trouvait un fragment de lèvre ourlée, avec amorce d'un goulot cylindrique de petit diamètre (4cm). En l'absence de décor ou de traitement de surface autre qu'un lissage soigneux à l'éponge, l'hypothèse d'un lagynos-conteneur, dont les Chiotes furent les premiers et longtemps les principaux fournisseurs, est la plus raisonnable[16]. Quant à la carène épaule/panse d'un vase fermé à décor peint en rouge sur

[12] Alabe 2012, 172–173 n°17–18.
[13] Alabe 2012, 172–173 n°18.
[14] Dyson 1968, 5 n°1.
[15] Alabe 1990, 51–52, n°1–3; Alabe 2005, 167, 174 n°5.
[16] Alabe 2012, 170 n°11.

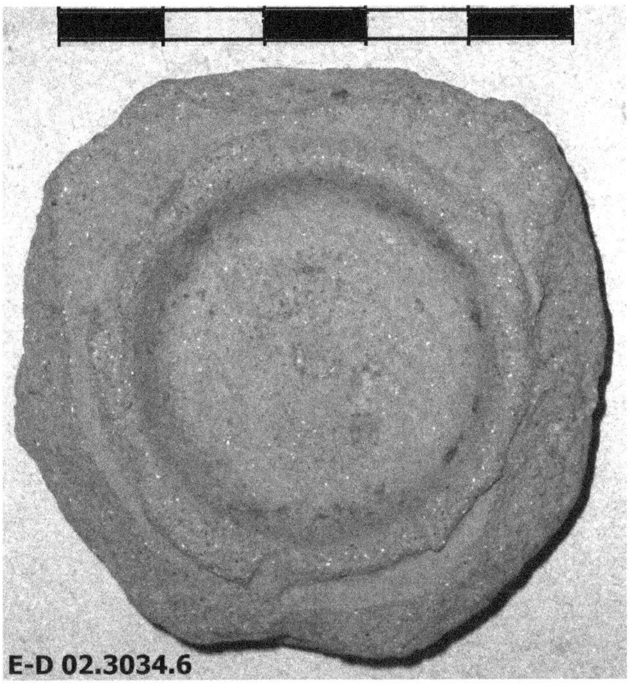

Fig. 7. Vaisselle commune locale: fond d'assiette (ou de coupelle) à dépression centrale (MFSED)

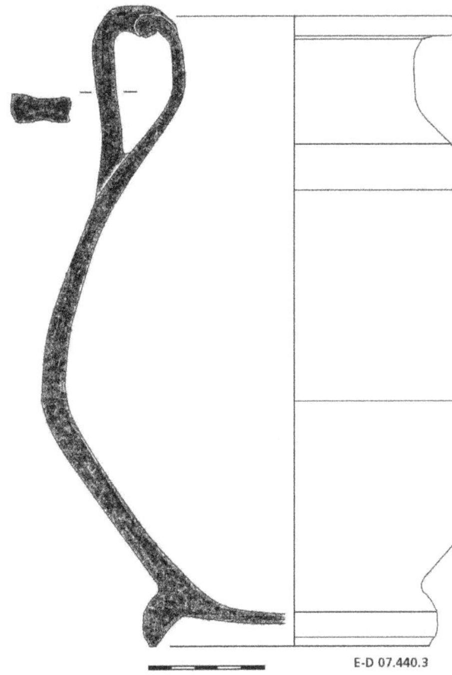

Fig. 8. Vaisselle commune locale: pot à verser (MFSED)

un engobe blanc satiné (Diam. à la carène env. 18cm), recueillie sur les éclats de taille abandonnés au fond de la carrière dans un sondage voisin, elle doit appartenir à un lagynos de table, dont la série est fort abondante dans le monde égéen hellénistique[17]. Le blanc laiteux et opaque de l'engobe recouvrant une pâte plus fine que celle des tessons d'amphore, et un peu plus claire que celle du lagynos-conteneur, invite à rattacher aussi ce fragment à la tradition des ateliers de Chios, dont les calices présentaient dès l'époque archaïque les mêmes qualités.

Céramique attique à vernis noir

Les plus anciens des fragments de céramique attique à vernis noir livrés par le comblement de cette carrière, au droit de la rue principale de la ville[18], semblent remonter au premier quart du IIIe siècle av. J.-C., et les plus récents à la charnière des IIIe et IIe siècles. Les comparaisons avec le corpus de l'Agora d'Athènes permettent de dater les autres vers le milieu du IIIe siècle ou un peu avant. Un canthare de tradition classique[19], dont n'a subsisté que la partie basse, à godrons, pouvait porter sur le haut de la vasque un décor surpeint dans le style *West Slope*[20]. Un très petit fragment de fond – d'assiette ou de kylix? – est décoré d'une palmette qui semble estampée avec le même sceau utilisé pour une assiette d'Athènes[21] vers 275 av. J.-C. Ces deux fragments se trouvaient parmi les éclats de taille, contre le front d'extraction de la carrière. Quant au fond de bol bas à guillochis[22] découvert sur le premier niveau de circulation repéré au-dessus des déchets de taille, sa partie centrale présente un reflet métallique rougeâtre, tandis que son pied annulaire de profil nettement convexe est séparé de la vasque externe par un mince filet réservé sans vernis: ce raffinement ne semble plus guère pratiqué après les années 300–275[23].

Céramique à vernis rouge (Sigillée orientale)

Si répandue en Méditerranée orientale, la sigillée orientale n'apparaît à Europos-Doura qu'exceptionnellement et à titre isolé; le seul fragment identifiable provenant du même contexte, mais quelques dizaines de centimètres plus haut, est la lèvre redressée, à peine renflée, d'une jatte évasée peu profonde dont le profil paraît semblable à un exemplaire plus complet découvert à Doura[24]. Le type se rattache, semble-t-il, aux productions précoces d'*ESA* attestées en Palestine dès le troisième quart du second siècle[25].

Autres importations à engobe grésé

D'autres fabriques du monde égéen oriental sont aussi rares. Ainsi, une seule lampe fragmentaire, recueillie au même niveau dans le comblement de la même carrière[26], appartient à la catégorie des lampes d'Éphèse: la légèreté

17 Bruneau 1970, 251–252; Rotroff 1997, 225–231.
18 Alabe 2012, 166–169 n°1 à n°8.
19 Alabe 2012, 169 n°8.
20 Rotroff 1997, 84–86 et 244–245.
21 Alabe 2012, 168 n°3; Rotroff 1997, 331 n°878.
22 Alabe 2012, 168 n°5.
23 Rotroff 1997, 10–11.
24 Alabe 2012, 169 n°9; Cox 1949, 8 n°39.
25 Slane 1988, 259.
26 Alabe 2012, 169 n°10.

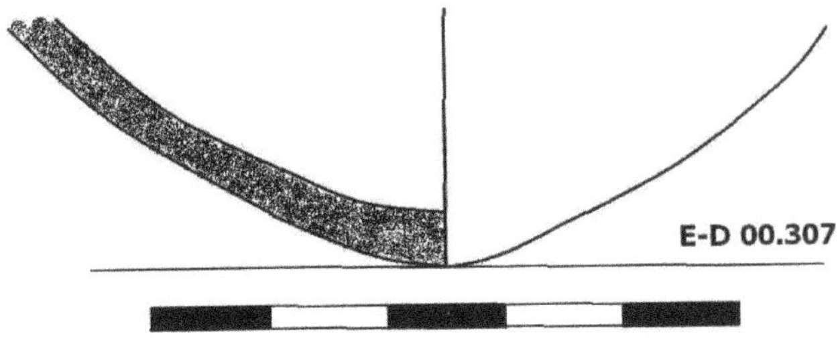

Fig. 9. Faux Egg Shell: fond de bol parabolique (MFSED)

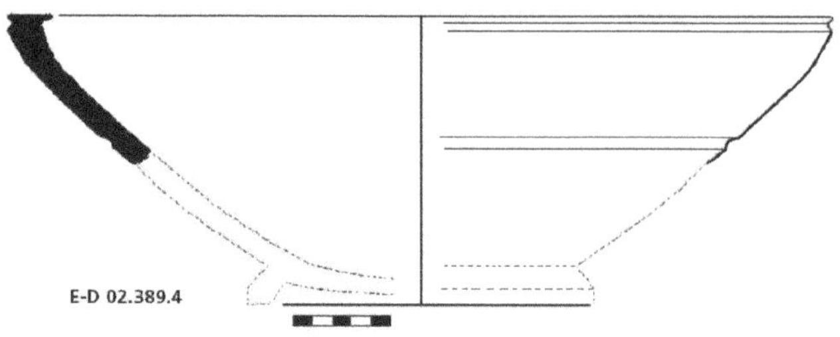

Fig. 11. Grey ware: grande jatte à lèvre horizontale (MFSED)

de la forme, la minceur régulière des parois, la finesse de la pâte grise et l'aspect satiné du vernis noir laissent peu de place au doute. Une lampe à pâte gris jaunâtre trouvée en 1929 au sommet de la citadelle[27] devait déjà se rattacher à la même origine: la publication insiste sur son extrême légèreté, due à des parois très minces. La production de ces lampes et leur diffusion sur les sites grecs datent du premier siècle av. J.-C., et les nombreux exemplaires découverts à Délos[28] correspondent au début de la série.

Importations orientales: 'egg shell' et glaçures

En nombre de tessons décomptés, la catégorie *Egg Shell*, caractérisée par l'extrême minceur des parois (rarement plus de 2mm), la finesse de la pâte, et un répertoire formel dérivant de modèles achéménides, voire néo-babyloniens, représente environ 10% de la céramique découverte dans des niveaux séleucides en Mésopotamie ou dans le Golfe Persique[29]. Elle est au contraire très rare à Europos-Doura,

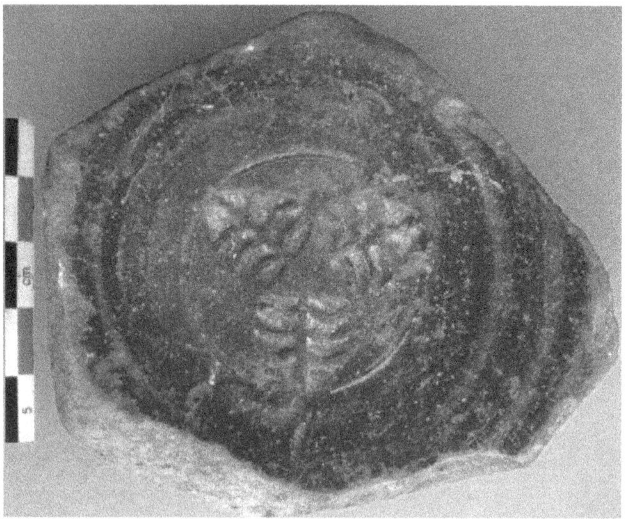

Fig. 10. Grey ware: fond de bol (ou de coupelle) à palmettes estampées (MFSED)

où je n'ai pu en observer qu'une poignée de tessons et de fragments – à peine une quinzaine, au fil de vingt missions…

Ces bribes attestent cependant que les Européens de l'Euphrate n'étaient pas plus coupés du monde oriental que des régions égéennes. Les seules formes récurrentes sont des gobelets coniques[30]: la pâte varie du jaune verdâtre pâle au brun chocolat, passant par le rouge foncé et le beige orangé; tantôt savonneuses, tantôt rugueuses, tantôt poreuses, les surfaces plus ou moins polies sont ravalées à l'estèque, puis lissées à l'éponge humide ou légèrement lustrées. Ces écarts répondent à l'hypothèse[31] de plusieurs centres de fabrication dont les pâtes avaient des caractères distincts.

Le comblement de la carrière de la rue principale a par ailleurs livré le fond (**Fig. 9**) d'un bol parabolique[32] dont le type est, certes, connu par quelques exemplaires à vernis noir du premier quart du IIe siècle av. J.-C. à Athènes et d'autres du début du Ier siècle av. J.-C. à Délos[33]. Mais le bol trouvé à Europos-Doura n'a reçu aucun traitement de surface que le lissage soigneux de l'intérieur à l'éponge humide, tandis que l'extérieur est légèrement rugueux. Ni la pâte, ni le mode de façonnage ne semblent conformes aux routines locales. L'absence d'engobe (et *a fortiori* de vernis) invite à rapprocher ce fond de types analogues bien attestés dans le répertoire de la vaisselle *Egg Shell* à Failaka[34]. Sa paroi trop épaisse (4mm) permettrait d'y reconnaître une production d'imitation, ou 'faux *Egg Shell*', comme celle reconnue à Failaka[35] dans un habitat de la première moitié du second siècle. Quant à la céramique glaçurée, fabriquée dans la ville même lors de la dernière période de vie d'Europos-Doura, elle est presque totalement absente des niveaux les plus anciens. De ce point de vue, les travaux menés depuis 1986 n'ont guère modifié le faciès tracé par nos devanciers. Quelques tessons étaient signalés dans des couches remontant aux années 100–50 av. J.-C., la plupart des vases complets provenant de la nécropole seraient antérieurs aux années 160–165 ap. J.-C., et la majorité des fragments découverts

27 Baur 1947, 6–7 n°4.
28 Rotroff 1997, 511; Bruneau 1965, 71–73.
29 Bernard, Gachet and Salles 1990, 256–257: synthèse des observations disponibles pour Failaka, Séleucie du Tigre et Suse.

30 Alabe 1990, 62–63.
31 Bernard, Gachet and Salles 1990, 257.
32 Alabe 2012, 170 n°12.
33 Bruneau 1970, 248–249; Rotroff 1997, 109–110.
34 Hannestad 1983, 45–47 et n°351.
35 Bernard, Gachet and Salles 1990, 256; 259–260 n°161.

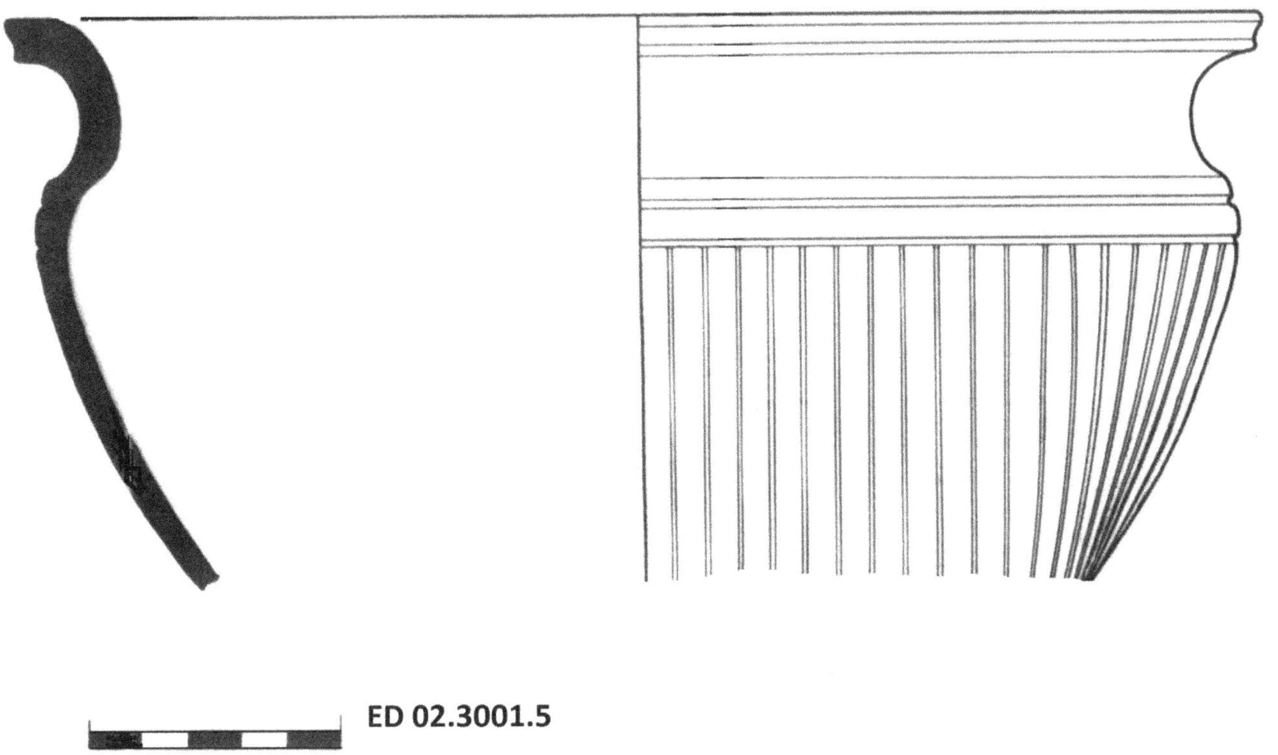

ED 02.3001.5

Figure 12. Vaisselle semi-fine locale à engobe brun: cratérisque (MFSED)

lors des fouilles d'habitations dateraient de la période 150–250 ap. J.-C.[36]. La rareté et l'émiettement de cette vaisselle dans les couches profondes des sondages stratifiés coupent court à toute velléité d'en proposer une évolution typologique plus précise que celle déjà esquissée[37], et rendent sujets à caution les critères qui permettraient de discerner les produits locaux d'éventuelles importations.

Céramiques semi-fines locales

Quelques ateliers produisaient localement une vaisselle 'haut de gamme'[38]. Avec une granulométrie jamais inférieure à 0,5mm et qui atteint souvent 1mm voire 1,5mm, la pâte en est aussi grossière que celle de la poterie commune; de ce fait, sauf quelques lèvres effilées en biseau, l'épaisseur des parois est toujours d'au moins 5 à 7mm: ce ne sont donc pas des céramiques fines. L'usage général des pieds annulaires et le profil complexe de beaucoup de lèvres moulurées dénotent toutefois un façonnage plus soigneux, et le traitement des surfaces permet d'obtenir une meilleure étanchéité en même temps qu'un aspect qui se démarque de la vaisselle ordinaire. Aussi ces séries ont-elles été étudiées et publiées avec les céramiques grecques et romaines importées[39] dont leur répertoire formel est réputé s'inspirer.

'Grey ware'

Cette céramique doit sa couleur grise à une phase finale de cuisson en atmosphère réductrice. C'est le sel (NaCl), présent dans l'eau de façonnage, qui, se combinant à la cuisson en un composé volatil avec le fer contenu dans la pâte[40], provoque son éclaircissement, tout comme on peut lui imputer le pseudo-engobe ou auto-engobe si fréquent sur les poteries communes[41]. La surface lustrée, souvent d'un gris plus sombre que le corps de pâte en cassure, peut porter au fond des petits bols ou assiettes une ornementation de palmettes estampées (**Fig. 10**). Les fragments de cette catégorie recueillis par la MFSED n'en ont guère enrichi la typologie déjà esquissée[42], qui ne comprend que des formes ouvertes. Cependant, les contextes stratigraphiques semblent indiquer que cette production s'est poursuivie bien au-delà de la conquête parthe. De grandes jattes (Diam. 30cm à 35cm), ayant pu servir de cratères dans le cadre de banquets, présentent des profils de lèvres variés (**Fig. 11**). Enfin, quelques fragments appartenant à coup sûr à des formes fermées[43] imposent donc de chercher à préciser, lors de prochaines missions, aussi bien la typologie de cette vaisselle que sa chronologie.

---

36 Toll 1943, 5–6.
37 Toll 1943, 70.
38 Alabe 2005, 170–173.
39 Cox 1949, 16–24.
40 Matson 1943, 85–88.
41 Alabe 2005, 169.
42 Cox 1949, 17–18.
43 Alabe 2012, 164 note 14.

Engobe noir, puis engobe brun?

Jusqu'ici, on n'a observé que deux cas d'engobe noir: le fond d'une assiette à dépression centrale, et une lèvre rentrante de bol[44]. Découverts sous le premier sol de circulation de la rue du rempart, ces fragments ne remettaient pas sérieusement en cause l'assertion selon laquelle '*at Dura, no black slip was ever attempted*'[45]. Le même comblement de carrière a, depuis, livré un vase de production locale (**Fig. 12**) dont l'engobe mat est d'un brun noirâtre. La vasque à godrons, rétrécie en un petit col à ressauts sous une lèvre étalée et moulurée, peut apparaître dès le IVe siècle av. J.-C. (vernis noir imitant la vaisselle métallique), et fait partie du répertoire de l'*ESA* dans des niveaux hellénistiques tardifs à Tel Anafa[46]. La pâte locale étant trop chargée en sable pour autoriser le tournage des détails minutieux de son profil, le façonnage de ce cratérisque[47] fait largement appel à l'estèque, dont les traces sont accusées par l'accumulation d'engobe au fond des creux. Inadapté aux contraintes techniques locales, ce vase hellénisant peut être le fait des premiers colons (première moitié du IIIe siècle av. J.-C.) ou bien s'inscrire dans une réaction plus tardive (milieu du IIe siècle av. J.-C.) revendiquant, contre l'absorption orientale imminente, une identité gréco-macédonienne: le contexte ne permet pas d'en décider. Quoi qu'il en soit, cette recherche de l'aspect noir fut marginale et sans lendemain: l'assiette, le bol et le cratérisque à engobe noir ou brun sont isolés parmi les fragments de près de 150 bols, assiettes et jattes à engobe rouge.

Engobe rouge

Insistant sur l'extrême abondance d'une céramique à engobe rouge (*Red Wash Ware*), la publication de référence ne fait pourtant état que de quelques dizaines de vases[48] dont la description reste très sommaire, et sans mention du contexte. Or, dans le seul sondage mené rue du rempart en 1989 et 1990, le nombre de fragments approchait la centaine, dont plus du tiers se rattachant au même type dont D. Cox signalait neuf exemplaires[49]: aussi cette production est l'objet d'observations détaillées dans une étude précédente, et de remarques complémentaires dans un volume plus récent[50], où l'examen est centré sur le comblement de la carrière déjà évoqué *supra*. La répartition par formes et par variantes techniques y apparaît assez différente de ce qu'elle était sur les ensembles précédemment envisagés. Quatre variantes techniques de cette production à engobe rouge sont en effet distinguées, selon des critères où interviennent la granulométrie, l'aspect et la couleur de la pâte (dure à très dure, très grenue, assez grossière et sableuse, sauf pour la variante 4 plus fine et mieux épurée), mais surtout l'aspect, la solidité et la couleur de l'engobe. En appliquant ces critères à tous les tessons et fragments recueillis, il s'avère que la variante 1 (près de la moitié du premier échantillon) ne compte plus que 39% du total; la proportion de la variante 2 augmente à peine (de 31,5% à 32,5%), et les variantes 3 et 4 (respectivement 10% et 9%) restent minoritaires, mais avec 13% et 14,5% du corpus. Le seul tesson relevant d'un nouveau type est une vasque à godrons qui reprend, dans la variante 4 de l'engobe rouge, la forme du cratérisque à engobe brun: la typologie est donc plutôt confortée, mais à nuancer là encore par l'augmentation relative du nombre d'assiettes, au détriment des bols à lèvre redressée ou rentrante et surtout des grandes jattes à lèvre étalée ou déversée, qui étaient la forme la plus fréquente. Ce dernier type dont la régularité volumétrique était remarquable connaît d'ailleurs quelques écarts modulaires considérables.

D'autre part, la répartition stratigraphique de ces vases est plus diffuse dans ce secteur que dans les sondages des années précédentes: certains fragments étaient au contact des déchets de taille, mais plusieurs exemplaires proviennent des couches médianes et supérieures du comblement, tandis que la plupart de ceux observés jusqu'ici étaient dans des couches contemporaines de la construction du rempart occidental. Cette vaisselle semblait apparaître au milieu du IIe siècle av. J.-C. pour s'estomper dans les décennies suivant la conquête parthe. En fait, des indices plaident pour faire remonter son apparition d'une ou deux décennies avant la mise en place du plan orthogonal. Son usage (et sa production?) semble d'autre part se poursuivre, dans Europos parthe, au moins jusque vers le milieu du Ie siècle av. J.-C., son répertoire fusionnant peu à peu avec une version locale de l'*ESA*, à l'image des aires sous domination attalide, lagide et séleucide. Ces hypothèses, qui devront être étayées par d'autres observations bien stratifiées, pourraient aussi expliquer les écarts typologiques. La production locale à engobe rouge prenant le relais de la vaisselle de table ou de *symposion* importée, il serait naturel que, dans sa phase précoce, les petits vases individuels (coupes et assiettes) soient plus nombreux que les grands vases faisant office de cratères. Puis, au moment où la garnison s'élargit à la dimension urbaine, la consommation du vin a pu reculer face à celle de laitages: destinées au service collectif de la tablée, les grandes jattes seraient alors le fait d'une génération plus perméable aux pratiques régionales, en termes de modes de convivialité et/ou d'habitudes alimentaires.

Bilan

Le nombre restreint de vases importés ne pouvait couvrir les besoins en céramique fine de table de la population urbaine, durant les décennies d'histoire d'Europos-Doura (300 av. J.-C. – 165 ap. J.-C.): un complément indispensable était fourni par une vaisselle semi-fine produite sur place en même temps que la poterie commune. Parmi les différentes

[44] Alabe 2005, 192 n°51; 194 n°58.
[45] Cox 1949, 7.
[46] Slane 1988, 260, FW 250 et FW 251.
[47] Alabe 2012, 164–165; 177 n°38.
[48] Cox 1949, 18–22 (n°105–125, se rapportant à un total de 80 exemplaires).
[49] Cox 1949,21 n°123–124
[50] Alabe 2005, 171–172 et 175 (Tableau 3) puis 191–198 (n°47–74); Alabe 2012, 165–166 puis 179–184 (n°39–56).

séries observées, aux côtés de la vaisselle lustrée *Grey Ware* à peine mieux connue aujourd'hui qu'à la fin des travaux de la Mission de Yale, l'étude stratigraphique reprise depuis 1990 apporte des progrès substantiels concernant la vaisselle engobée qui, en quelques générations, s'ajoute puis se substitue à la céramique à vernis noir importée du bassin égéen. Jamais grésé, rarement poli, l'engobe en est noir ou brun dans quelques cas, et presque toujours rouge. Pour autant, il n'est pas certain que des *Black Slip Predecessors* aient préludé au développement d'une version locale d'*ESA*, comme ce fut le cas en d'autres sites du Proche-Orient, car la technique et le répertoire de la vaisselle à engobe rouge se mettent en place dès le second ou même le premier quart du IIe siècle av. J.-C. – bien avant les premières importations d'*ESA* qui furent toujours, semble-t-il parfaitement sporadiques.

Françoise Alabe
Archéologies d'Orient et d'Occident
CNRS UMR 8546-9
École Normale Supérieure – Paris (France)
CeTHiS – EA 6298
Université François Rabelais – Tours (France)
francoise.alabe@univ-tours.fr

Bibliographie

Alabe, F. 1992. La céramique de Doura-Europos. In P. Leriche (éd.), *Doura-Europos. Etudes 3 – 1990.* Syria 69, 49–63. Paris, Geuthner.

Alabe, F. 2005. Céramiques hellénistiques d'Europos à Doura: hasards ou cohérences? in P. Leriche, A. Dandrau et M. Gelin (éds.), *Doura-Europos. Études 5 – 1994–1997*, 163–198. Paris, Geuthner.

Alabe, F. 2012. Céramique d'Europos hellénistique: la carrière en contrebas de la rue principale et son comblement, in G. Coqueugniot, S. de Pontbriand et P. Leriche (éds.), *Europos-Doura. Varia 1*. Bibliothèque d'Archéologie et d'Histoire n°198, 161–184, Paris et Beyrouth, Institut Français du Proche-Orient.

Allara, A 1992. L'îlot des potiers et les fours à Doura-Europos. In P. Leriche (éd.), *Doura-Europos. Études 3 – 1990*. Syria 69, 101–120. Paris, Geuthner.

Allara, A. 1994. Osservazioni sulle fornaci per ceramica di Dura-Europos sull'Eufrate. *Rivista di Archeologia* 18, 129–134.

Baur, P. V. C. 1947. *The Excavations at Dura-Europos. Final Report IV III. The Lamps.* New Haven, Yale University Press.

Bernard, V., Gachet, J. et Salles, J.-F. 1990. Apostilles en marge de la céramique locale des états IV et V, in Y. Calvet et J. Gachet (éds.), *Failaka. Fouilles françaises 1986–1988*, 241–284, Lyon, Maison de l'Orient Méditerranéen/ Paris, De Boccard.

Boucharlat, R. 1987. Les niveaux post-achéménides à Suse, secteur Nord. Fouilles de l'Apadana-Est et de la Ville Royale-Ouest (1973–1978). *Cahiers de la Délégation Archéologique Française en Iran* 15, 145–312.

Bruneau, Ph. 1965. *Les lampes*. Exploration archéologique de Délos XXVI. Paris, De Boccard.

Bruneau, Ph. 1970. La vaisselle. In Ph. Bruneau (dir.), *L'îlot de la Maison des Comédiens.* Exploration archéologique de Délos XXVII, 239–262. Paris, De Boccard.

Cox, D. H. 1949. *The Greek and Roman Pottery. The Excavations at Dura-Europos. Final Report IV I 2.* New Haven, Yale University Press.

Dyson, S. L. 1968. *The Commonware Pottery. The Brittle Ware. The Excavations at Dura-Europos. Final Report IV I 3.* New Haven, Yale University Press.

Hannestad, L. 1983. *Ikaros. The Hellenistic Settlement 2. The Hellenistic Pottery.* Jutland Archaeological Society Publications XVI:2. Aarhus, Jysk Arkaeologisk Selskab.

Massoul, F. et M. 1926. Appendice sur la céramique de Doura-Europos. In F. Cumont, *Fouilles de Doura-Europos (1922–1923)*, 455–476. Paris, Geuthner.

Matson, F. R. 1943. Technological notes on the pottery. In N. Toll, *The Green Glazed Pottery. The Excavations at Dura-Europos. Final Report IV I 1,* 81–95. New Haven, Yale University Press.

Rotroff, S. I. 1997. *Hellenistic Pottery: Athenian and imported wheelmade Table Ware and related Material.* The Athenian Agora XXIX. Princeton, NJ., American School of Classical Studies in Athens.

Slane, K. W. 1988. The Fine Wares, in A. Berlin et K. W. Slane, *The Hellenistic and Roman Pottery.* Tel Anafa II, i, 247–293. Ann Arbor, Kelsey Museum.

Toll, N. 1943. *The Green Glazed Pottery. The Excavations at Dura-Europos. Final Report IV I 1.* New Haven, Yale University Press.

Pottery imports to Hellenistic Jebel Khalid on the Euphrates

Heather Jackson & John Tidmarsh

Abstract

This paper discusses the range and source of pottery imports to Hellenistic Jebel Khalid on the Euphrates. Apart from transport amphoras, mainly Rhodian, the imported wares consist of tableware vessels in international Hellenistic shapes, with the more-easily transported cups, bowls and plates predominating over jars and jugs. Most imports come from the west, from or through Antioch-on-the-Orontes. A few examples of fine black-glazed ware came from Attica in the earliest phase but most fine black-glazed imports were produced in Antioch. Burnished grey ware arrived from an uncertain source in limited shapes. Eastern Sigillata A was the most prolific import in the second half of the 2nd century BC. West Slope wares were restricted to the early phase, giving way to the import of moulded bowls, again mainly from Antioch. Among rarer imports were a fragment of Gnathia ware, two Campana B plates, 'Ionian' bowls and in the latest phase, a few fragments of Cypriot Sigillata and Pompeian-red Ware. The only import from other than the west were green-glazed wares, probably from down-river. The lack of certain commonware vessels is also discussed, i.e. lagynoi and lopades.

Keywords: fine black-glazed ware, burnished grey ware, West Slope ware, moulded bowls, Eastern Sigillata A, green-glazed ware, amphoras, greyware unguentaria

Introduction

A quarter-century of excavation by an Australian team at Jebel Khalid has produced many tonnes of pottery, 95% of which was locally manufactured[1]. The remaining 5% covers a wide variety of imported wares: Aegean amphoras, fine black-glazed ware, burnished grey ware, West Slope ware, Eastern Sigillata A, green-glazed ware and grey unguentaria. This paper discusses their sources, but first we look at the position of the site and possible trading routes.

Jebel Khalid lies on the west bank of the Euphrates, on a limestone plateau high above the river **(Fig. 1).** A strongly fortified military garrison was settled there in the early 3rd century BC, built on virgin bedrock (**Fig. 2**). This settlement did not have a long life, as it was abandoned *c.* 70 BC and not re-settled by the Romans, thus its Hellenistic status is uniquely preserved. Doubtless its position was primarily to guard and control river traffic and a crossing but it was somewhat south of the best-known land route, which went north-east from Hierapolis towards Zeugma. However, Hierapolis, an important staging post on the route from Antioch and Aleppo, was not far away and could be reached by means of the Wadi Abu Qalqal. The modern version of Hierapolis, Manbij, can easily be reached in 30 minutes by car, representing possibly a half-day on foot. There were also routes along the Euphrates to north and south, as well as the possibility of goods coming by the river itself.

The great majority of imported wares consists of tableware. Transport amphoras and unguentaria are less numerous. Most fragments found were of cups, bowls, and plates in international Hellenistic shapes, with serving and pouring vessels in imported wares being rarer.

Fine Black-glazed Ware

Black-glazed vessels are well represented and after Eastern Sigillata A (see below) constitute the most common class of imported ware. The shapes are those concerned with eating and drinking, in particular plates (mainly fishplates and plates with rolled rim), bowls with out-turned and down-turned rim, and hemispherical and ovoid bowls. Several black-glazed krater fragments have also been recovered.

Although some nine different fabrics can be distinguished, the origin of only four can be pin-pointed. Attic imports, such as a fine early kantharos (c. 290–280 BC) found in the foundations of the temple, are relatively rare and restricted to earlier (3rd century and early 2nd century BC) deposits **(Figs. 3–4).** Neutron Activation Analysis has pointed to Antioch as the source of the two most common black-glazed fabrics with these being of much the same chemical composition as the Eastern Sigillata A discussed below.

Burnished Grey Ware

Another ware occurring early in the life of the site is burnished grey ware, i.e. a grey fabric with a highly burnished surface. Reports of a seemingly similar fabric ('Gris espatulado') come from Tell Khamis, some 30km to the north of Jebel Khalid, and from Dura-Europos further

[1] The pottery, both locally made and imported, has been published in Jackson and Tidmarsh 2011.

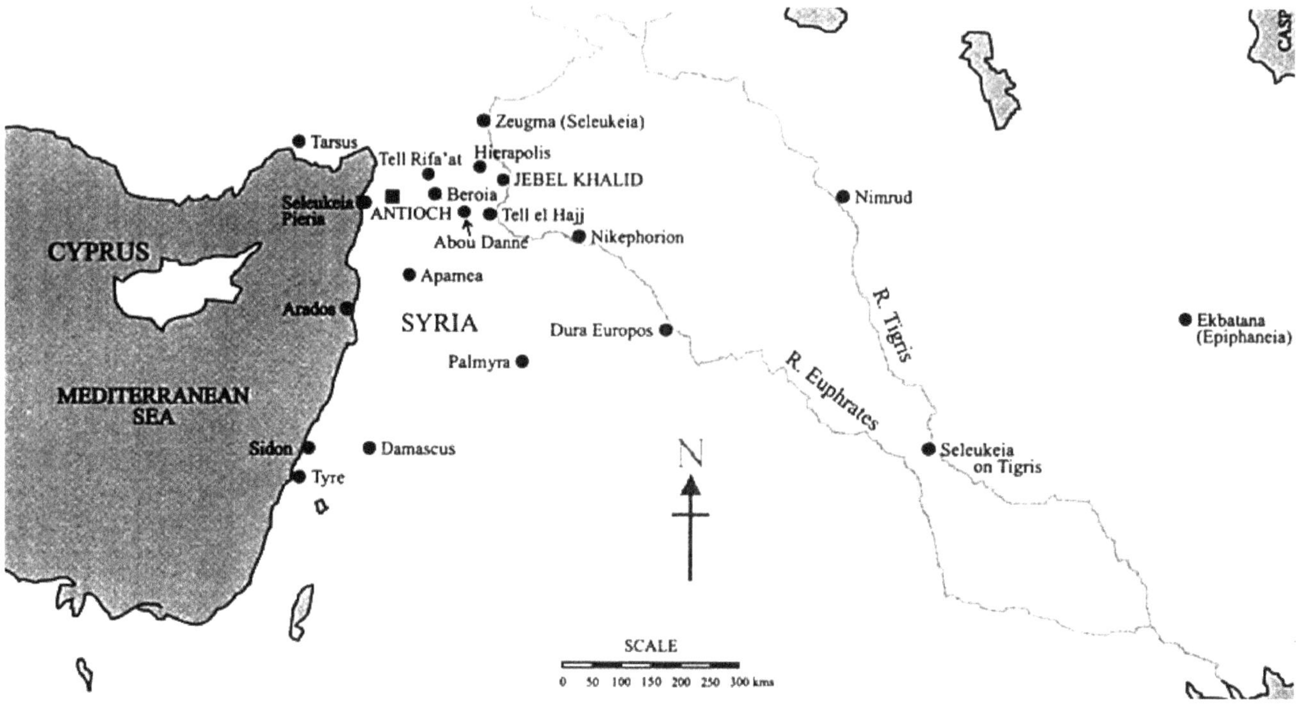

Fig. 1. Map showing position of Jebel Khalid in Hellenistic Syria (Macquarie University, Sydney)

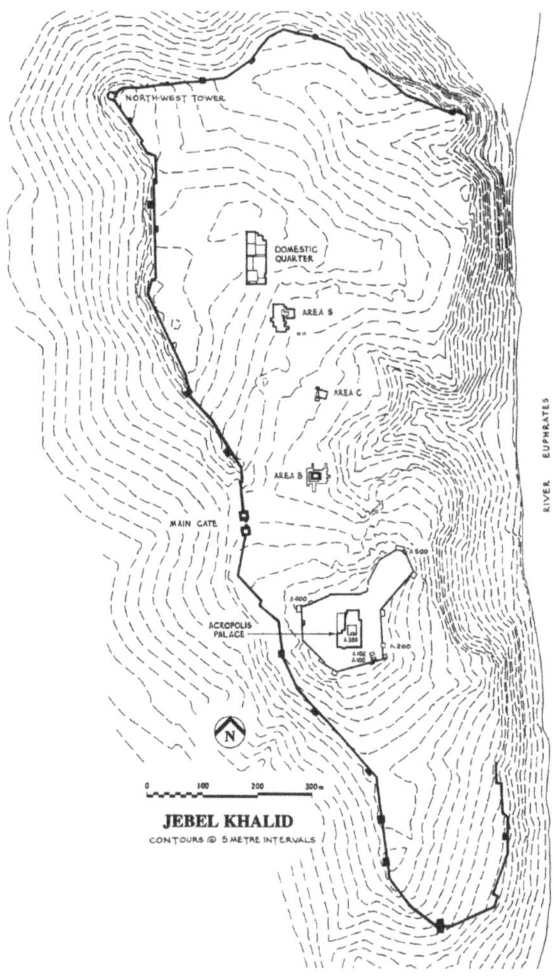

Fig. 2. Contour map of the Jebel Khalid site (B. Rowney)

to the south[2]. At Jebel Khalid, the shape predominantly represented is the rolled-rim plate (which is seen rather less frequently in other wares, either imported or local), but also fishplates, saucers or small plates, bowls or cups of various rims, and, unusually for imported wares, some jugs. The source has not been identified. Results of analysis showed an affinity with the Antiochean black-glazed fabrics but since this ware is not recorded in the Antioch excavations, it seems unlikely that Antioch is the source.

West Slope Ware

A somewhat rarer find in the earlier contexts are fragments of West Slope ware, although the total of 72 fragments surpasses the numbers seen at most other Syro-Palestinian sites. Several of the larger plate fragments belong to the 'Ivy Platter' workshop (location or locations still unclear) with other fragments from Athens (a kantharos of the Dikeras Group), Pergamon (fluted amphoras), and Antioch (simple bowls)[3] (**Fig. 5**). Although the production of West Slope ware at Antioch itself seems to have been limited, the range of (imported) West Slope fabrics and shapes found in that city is very similar to that seen at Jebel Khalid.

2 For Dura-Europos see Cox 1949, 17–18; for Tell Khamis see Séiquer 1999, 210–212.

3 For the 'Ivy Platter' workshop see Rotroff 2002. For the Dikeras Group, Rotroff 1997. For Pergamene West Slope ware see Schäfer 1968, Behr 1988; for West Slope ware from Antioch and the Orontes Valley, Waagé 1948, 28, fig.3, fig. 4:1–4, fig. 5:1–16; For a profile of the Jebel Khalid fragment see Jackson and Tidmarsh 2011, fig,130: 606.

Fig.3: Attic black-glazed kantharos fragment (Inv. No. JK 05.159) (B.Miller)

Fig. 5. Fragment of West Slope ware attributed to the Ivy Platter group (Inv. No. JK 90.091) (B.Miller)

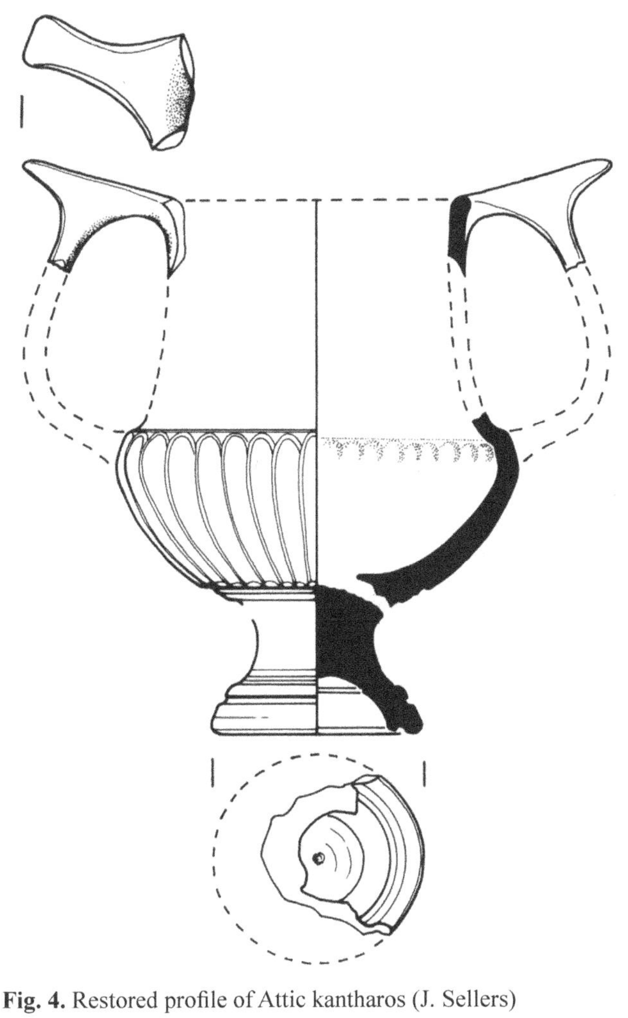

Fig. 4. Restored profile of Attic kantharos (J. Sellers)

Moulded Bowls

Towards the end of the 3rd century or the beginning of the 2nd century BC, moulded ('Megarian') bowls probably replaced any import of cups in West Slope ware. Most of the 167 fragments found so far are of the two commonest fabrics of fine black glaze ware from Antioch, so Antioch is again the main source. No Athenian bowls have been identified, while 'Ionian' bowls, produced by workshops along the west coast of Asia Minor, are rare with only 5 examples identified. A minor local production is suggested by the finding of a mould fragment at Jebel Khalid itself[4].

The imported bowls from Antioch are typically covered in a thick black glaze which, although somewhat glossy, lacks the high sheen or metallic lustre frequently seen on Athenian examples. In some bowls the black glaze has been fired an attractive deep reddish-brown in places while other examples are completely covered in such a glaze.As seen at Antioch, the range of rim decoration is relatively restricted, with egg-and-dart and ovolo (i.e. without the dart) being by far the most common. Pendant drops, usually just below a rim pattern of egg-and-dart or ovolo, and cordate leaves (Waagé's 'floret', characterised by him as 'peculiar to Antioch bowls') are also represented, although not nearly as numerous as the other two. Other rim patterns are seen on a small number of fragments and include the decorative wave and comic (slave) mask.

[4] For the moulded bowls from Antioch see Waagé 1948, 29–31, figs.9–18; for 'Ionian' bowls, Laumonier 1977.

Fig. 6. Moulded bowl fragment (Inv. No. JK 10.808) (S. Hay)

Fig. 7. Moulded bowl fragment (Inv. No. JK 08.058) (B.Miller)

Spirals, guilloche, and meander patterns – all frequently encountered on Athenian and 'Ionian' bowls – are either rare or not seen at Jebel Khalid.

The rim pattern is frequently enclosed and marked off by horizontal beading from the decorative zone on the wall itself. Uncommon on Athenian and 'Ionian' bowls, beading is a standard device on moulded bowls from Antioch, either to frame the rim pattern or to separate an upper and lower wall register[5].

The range of decorative wall patterns includes floral motifs such as palm fronds, acanthus leaves, lotus petals and tendrils. Pine-cone scales are uncommon and long petal bowls, extremely common in Athens (but not Antioch) following their introduction into the former city in the second quarter of the second century, are rare.

Of the figured motifs, Erotes (either singly or in pairs) are relatively popular as are draped females, standing or dancing (**Fig. 6**). One fragment, of typical Antioch fabric and rim decoration, depicts a horse and rider. Amongst the animal motifs, horses, donkeys, cattle, and felines are the most common. Four wall fragments (all from Antioch) depict altars or offering tables. Of these, two support foliage (acanthus?), while a third is surmounted by a comic mask (**Fig. 7**).

Eastern Sigillata Wares

By far the most prolific imports after the mid-2nd century BC are vessels in Eastern Sigillata A (ESA), first produced around the middle of the 2nd century BC[6]. This appears also to be the case at Antioch and the important Orontes Valley cities of Apamea and Hama (Hellenistic Epiphaneia) – in contrast to many Hellenistic sites in the southern Levant (with the exception of Tel Anafa) or further to the east[7]. Not surprisingly for Jebel Khalid, the ware is almost exclusively restricted to those forms of Hellenistic origin – in particular shallow plates with upright rim (Hayes' Forms 3 and 4A), (**Fig. 8**) hemispherical bowls with pedestal foot (Hayes' Form 22), ovoid bowls with moulded rim (Hayes' Form 17B) and hemispherical bowls (Hayes' Forms 18 and 19)[8]. Closed shapes are rare. A small number of Roman forms has been recovered, mainly from the area of the temple (Area B) which continued to be visited both as a sacred area, and later as a source of building material, for several centuries after the settlement had ceased to exist. The precise location of the pottery workshops producing ESA still remains unclear although it is likely that they were situated on the north Syrian littoral—possibly in the region of Antioch itself or somewhat further north[9]. Of the other eastern sigillata wares, only Cypriot Sigillata (both in its grey and red varieties) is seen at Jebel Khalid where it is limited to several fragments of drinking vessels (Hayes forms P33 and P34) produced in the 1st century BC[10] (**Fig. 9**).

Imports from the western Mediterranean are rare and consist of two plates with narrow upright rim of 'Campana B' ware, produced in a variety of locations throughout Italy during the 3rd to 1st centuries BC[11], a small number of Pompeian-red Ware dishes (all from the Acropolis)[12], a Gnathia ware kantharos fragment (**Fig. 10**) of the so-called 'Alexandrian Group' (possibly reaching Jebel

---

5 Callaghan 1996, 372.

6 Hayes 1986, 12; Slane 1997, 274; Herbert–Berlin 2003, 21.

7 For ESA from Apamea, Vanderhoeven 1989; from Hama, Christensen–Johansen 1971; Lund 1995. For ESA from Tel Anafa, Slane 1997.

8 Hayes 1986

9 Schneider 1995, 416; id. 2000, 532; Slane 1997, 272; Lund 2005.

10 Hayes 1991, 44.

11 Morel 1981; id. 1986, 469–70; Cibecchini–Principal 2004.

12 All three belong to Kenrick's Form 382 (Kenrick 1985, 325). See also Peacock 1977; Peña 1990.

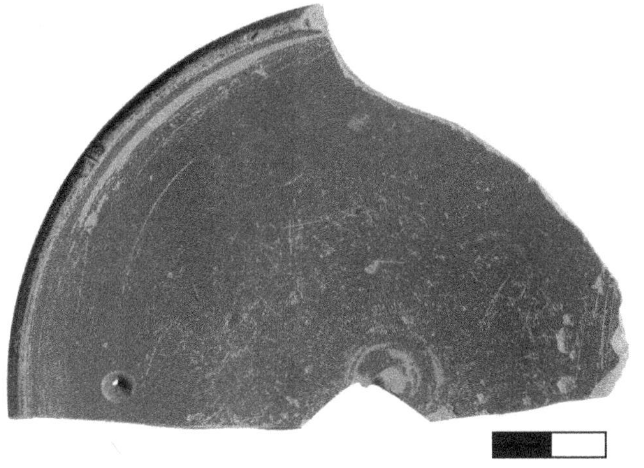

Fig. 8. ESA plate with repair hole (Inv. No. JK 10.309) (B.Miller)

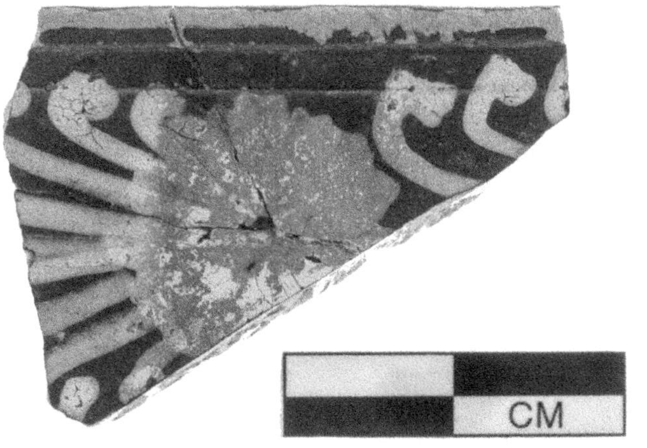

Fig. 10. Fragment of Gnathia ware (Inv. No. JK 88.054) (B.Miller)

Fig. 9. Cypriot Sigillata cup (Inv. No. JK 91.031) (B.Miller)

Khalid via Alexandria where Gnathia ware forms the largest proportion of imported decorated pottery)[13], and a fragment of an Italian-type sigillata plate of mid-1st century AD date from Area B[14].

Green-glazed Ware

The only imported tableware to arrive from any Mesopotamian direction was green-glazed ware. It was not prolific, constituting only 15% of imported wares, but interesting for its purely Hellenistic provenance here at Jebel Khalid, appearing throughout the life of the site[15]. The shapes were designed to please the Hellenistic market as far as plates and bowls were concerned, comprising fishplates, bowls with inturned rim, and bowls with plain, everted rim. The most common small plate profile had a rounded, everted rim with interior groove, common at Failaka in the same ware and also common at Jebel Khalid in the locally-made wares, where it was assumed

13 Green 1976, 12–13; id., 1995.
14 Hayes 1972. The shape seems closest to the shallow plate of Hayes' Form 24.

15 The well-published finds from Dura-Europos (Toll 1943) and Seleucia-on-the-Tigris (Debevoise 1934) are dubiously stratified.

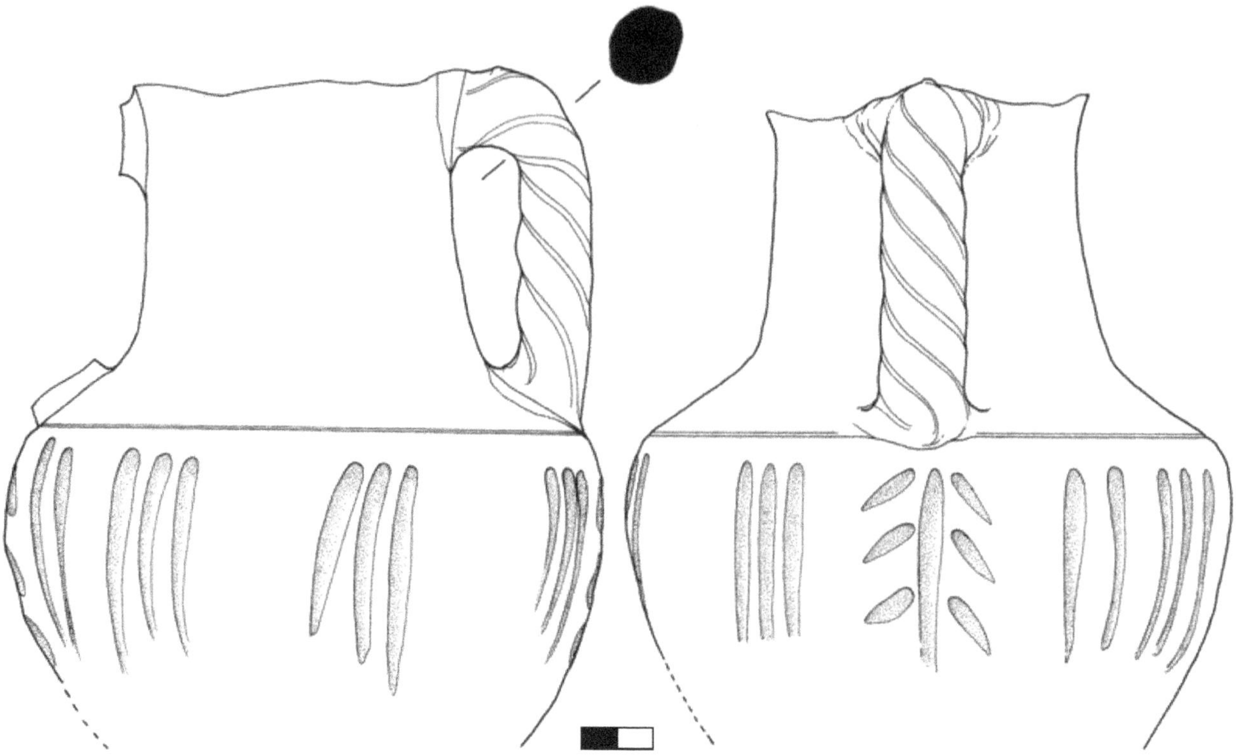

Fig. 11. Green-glazed table amphora (Inv. No. JK 02.884) (J. Sellers)

to replace the plate with rolled rim[16]. Cups were very rare (two fragments only)[17] but table jars were relatively well represented, compared with other imported wares (**Fig. 11**).

The frequently-found twisted jar handles might recall those of West Slope amphorae but some of the jar rim profiles seem more independent of Greek influence[18].

Production centres have not been pinpointed. At Failaka, in the Persian Gulf, and at Seleucia-on-the-Tigris, this is the dominant tableware. In fact, the further one goes down river, the more frequent the occurrence of this ware. Hence the assumption we make that it comes to Jebel Khalid from the south, up the river. In north-east Syria, it is not found in early Hellenistic levels, only in post-150 BC contexts at Tel Beydar and the Upper and Lower Khabur[19]. In contrast, its presence at Jebel Khalid in the early Hellenistic levels argues for a production site further west than those sites that were not receiving it, i.e. somewhere on the Euphrates. There are several possibilities for the place of manufacture. Dura-Europos on the middle Euphrates perhaps produced its own green-glazed wares[20]. Northern Mesopotamia has been regarded as a discrete production area with a possible centre at Assur, where some shapes suggest an 'independent tradition'[21]. Toll also speaks of a possible West Mesopotamian branch of production, with this hypothetical workshop placed at Raqqa[22].

A riverine Euphrates source is supported by analysis of the fabric, which at Jebel Khalid is homogeneous and matches the descriptions of green-glazed fabrics from several different sites[23]. The geochemistry of the clay includes a mafic/ultramafic signature thought to be common to Euphrates riverine clays[24]. The fact that the one sample from Antioch plotted with the Jebel Khalid samples raises an interesting possibility. The corpus of green-glazed ware at Antioch was comparable to that of Jebel Khalid in date, size and types of vessels[25], whereas other coastal sites further south were either devoid of the ware or only received a tiny amount, such as the ten sherds at Tel Anafa[26]. Its relatively strong and early presence at Antioch

16 Jackson and Tidmarsh 2011, 442–445

17 The friable fabric and thick, easily chipped glaze are not really suitable for vertical cup rims.

18 Jackson and Tidmarsh 2011, 493 fig. 148.

19 Galan 2008, 3–4 (Tel Beydar). Dorna-Metzger 1996, 368, places the glazed pottery in the Parthian-Roman period, not the Hellenistic, in spite of the fact that she finds in-turned rim bowls, a truly Hellenistic shape, the most common (Upper Khabur Survey). Römer, 1996, 15–16, dates the earliest showing to the second half of the 1st century BC (Lower Khabur at Tel Seh Hamad). However, at Palmyra, the same author found green-glazed fragments in the lowest Hellenistic levels (C. Römer-Strehl, personal communication).

20 Toll 1943, 6 mentions the discovery of kilns and presumes the heavy green-glazed sarcophagi can only have been made on site. See also Allara 1992, 113 n. 45: 11 kilns were found at Dura-Europos, but dated to the Parthian occupation and later, i.e. none Hellenistic.

21 Toll 1943, 75–76.

22 Toll 1943, 76. For a summary of the argument, see Jackson and Tidmarsh 2011, 480–481; Mallowan 1966, 313 also mentions the likelihood of the Raqqa area being a trading centre.

23 See Jackson and Tidmarsh 2011, 481, especially n. 105.

24 See Appendix III in Jackson and Tidmarsh 2011, 545–554.

25 Waagé 1948, 80–82.

26 Berlin 1997, 169–171.

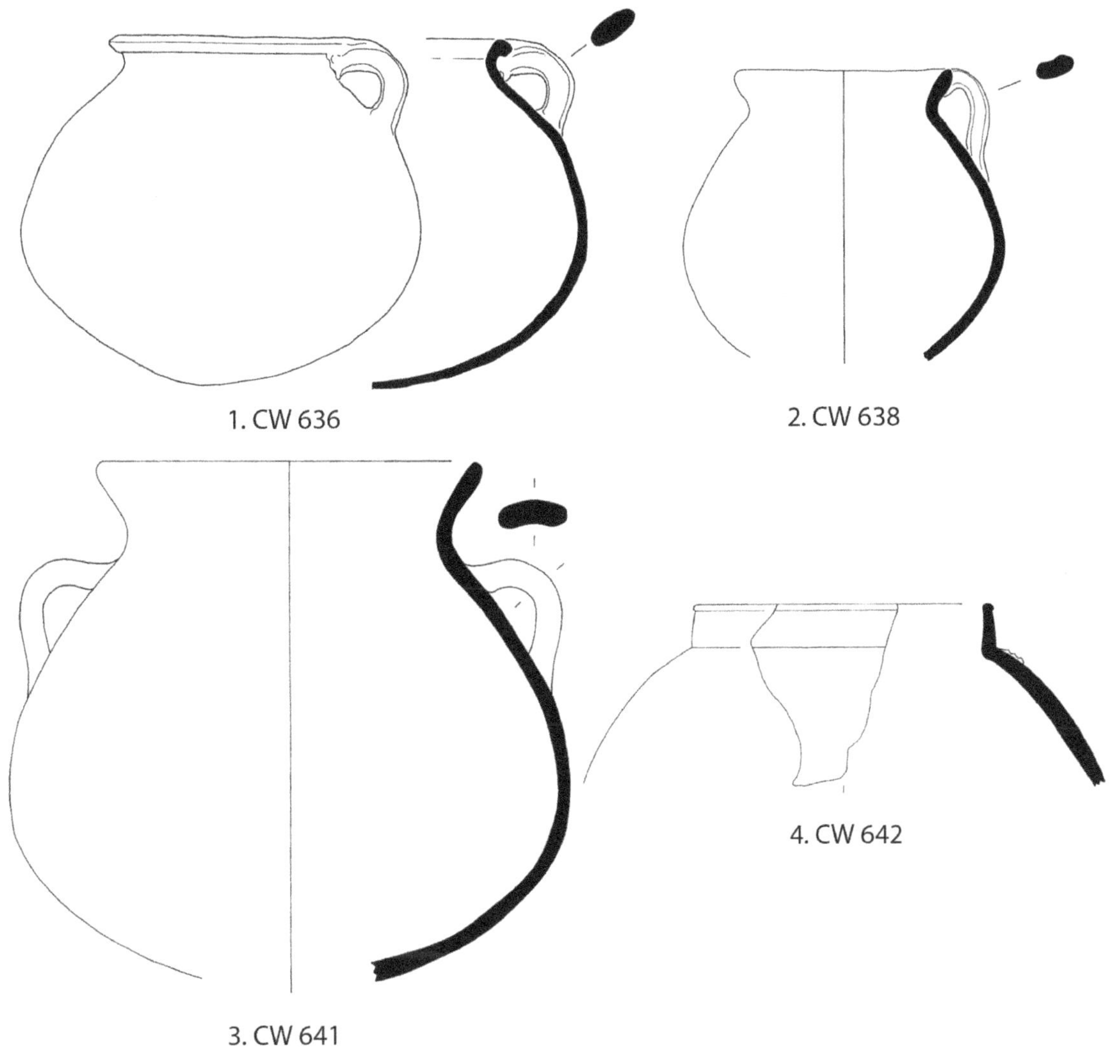

Fig. 12. Cooking pot profiles at Jebel Khalid. (J. Sellers)

suggests that, in this case, the ware was travelling from the Euphrates to Antioch, via Jebel Khalid. Most fine wares were travelling in the opposite direction.

Imported Amphoras

Of the 91 identifiable stamped handles of transport amphoras[27] imported to Jebel Khalid, three were Cypriot, two Knidian, one Thasian and the rest (85) Rhodian. The preponderance of Rhodian imports is well documented at other Levantine and Syrian sites[28]. It is of some interest that this import was largely confined to the early phase of the site, i.e. the 3rd century (total 17) and first half of the 2nd century BC (total 44 up to 146 BC). Finds dated after that were rare, so Clarke has suggested that local production of wine and oil was sufficiently well established by then as to make imports less needed, a suggestion backed by the archaeobotanical evidence of grape pips, olive pips and olive wood used as fuel[29]. The rare later imports were confined to the Governor's Palace on the Acropolis. At the same time, locally- or regionally-made amphoras with Semitic names stamped on the handles began to appear[30].

Greyware Unguentaria

Greyware unguentaria at Jebel Khalid are presumed to be an import to the site, yet their numbers outweigh those of non-greyware unguentaria. Their thin fabric has a bricky-red core, the surface a semi-lustrous grey or grey-brown achieved by firing in a reduced atmosphere[31]. This description matches some of the so-called 'gray unguentaria' found in the Athenian Agora, a fact noted by both Thompson and Rotroff and which prompted Thompson to suggest that Syria was the source of the

27 See Clarke 2002, 2005 and 2008.
28 e.g. Christensen-Johansen 1971, 51 (Hama 100%). See also Berlin 1997, 160–162, for a useful table.
29 See Fairbairn and Asouti, 2005, 190–191.
30 Clarke 2005, 184.
31 Jackson and Tidmarsh 2011, 93–97, figs. 84–86.

Athenian imports[32]. Rotroff is more cautious and notes some shape differences and the lack of purple banding on the Jebel Khalid examples[33]. No positive link can be made without comparative analysis of the Athenian and Jebel Khalid fabrics, but the relative frequency of these vessels at Jebel Khalid compared with other Levantine sites suggests a source close to that site, associated with the manufacture of perfumed unguents.

Lacunae

What was not imported? Lagynoi and lopades. There are no locally-manufactured lagynoi at Jebel Khalid and only a rare few fragments in imported ware – even those are too fragmentary to be sure of their full shape. Lagynoi abound in Hellenistic Cyprus and are well represented at Dor and Anafa[34]. Perhaps Berlin is right when she observes that the vessel is 'common only in areas under Ptolemaic control', ascribing the phenomenon to the Ptolemaic invention of the *lagynophoria* festival of Dionysus[35]. Such an explanation cannot be found for the absence of the *lopas* or casserole from the Jebel Khalid cooking pot corpus, a vessel very familiar at Levantine and Palestinian coastal or near-coastal sites[36]. The only cooking pots found in the housing insula of Jebel Khalid were of the *chytra* type: globular, deep and narrow-mouthed, designed for stews and gruel (**Fig. 12**). This lacuna must reflect a dietary preference, as discussed in a previous publication, which may or may not have something to do with the apparent absence of fish from the diet[37].

Conclusion

Pottery imports to Jebel Khalid mainly came from the West, from or through the portal of Antioch, following the same route as the coins, which are predominantly from the Antioch mint[38]. The dominance of Antioch, capital of the Seleucid Empire, is perhaps not surprising. Traffic was one-way. The paucity of imports from other directions in this huge empire is also reflected in the lack of coinage from eastern mints (only 3% of the identified total). The green-glazed wares came up-river but nothing else did. The dearth of imports from nearby Cyprus (three amphora fragments and a small amount of Cypriot Sigillata) is intriguing—was this due to Antioch rejecting imports from Ptolemaic territories?

These imports gave the Jebel Khalid inhabitants a colourful range of tableware: glossy black-glazed ware, the odd West Slope or Gnathia vessel, masses of bright red/orange Eastern Sigillata A, exotic turquoise and green-glazed ware. Rhodian amphoras, in the early phase at least, brought imported wine from the Aegean. This was not an impoverished lifestyle in this allegedly remote outpost.

Heather Jackson, FSA
Co-Director Jebel Khalid Excavations
Honorary Research Fellow
Centre for Classics and Archaeology
School of Historical and Philosophical Studies
The University of Melbourne
Victoria 3010, Australia
hmjackson@bigpond.com

John Tidmarsh
Co-Director Jebel Khalid Excavations
CCANESA
Madsen Building
University of Sydney
jtid@internode.on.net

Bibliography

Allara, A. 1992. L'îlot des potiers et les fours de Doura-Europos. Étude préliminaire. *Syria* 69, 103–119.

Behr, D. 1988. Neue Ergebnisse zu pergamenischen Westabhangkeramik. *Istanbuler Mitteilungen* 38, 97–178.

Berlin, A. M. 1997. The Plain Wares. In S. Herbert (ed.), *Tel Anafa II, i. The Hellenistic and Roman Pottery*, ix–244. Ann Arbor, Kelsey Museum.

Callaghan, P. J. 1996. An Antiochene Bowl in Cambridge. *Annual of the British School at Athens* 91, 369–375.

Christensen, A. P. and Johansen, C. F. 1971. *Hama: Fouilles et recherches 1931–1938, III, ii: Les poteries hellénistiques et les terres sigillées orientales.* Copenhagen, Fondation Carlsberg.

Cibecchini, F. and Principal, J. 2004. Per Chi Suona La Campana B? in E. C. De Sena and H. Dessales (eds.), *Metodi e approcci archeologici: l'industria*

[32] Thompson 1934, 474.
[33] Rotroff 2006, 142 and n. 49.
[34] Guz-Zilberstein 1995, 309–310 (Dor); Berlin 1997, 42–43 (Anafa).
[35] Berlin 1997, 42–43.
[36] e.g. at Anafa, there were ten different types of casserole and 1437 fragments (Berlin 1997, 94–103); Dor: Guz-Zilberstein 1995, 299–300. At Athens, lopades dominated the Agora cooking corpus, with five forms and 585 vessels represented (Rotroff 2006, 178–186).
[37] On this topic, see Jackson and Tidmarsh 2011, 91–92 and 509. Only one *lopas* fragment was found over the whole site, proving nevertheless that the shape was known. The absence of fish bones may be connected with a taboo on fish-eating associated with the worship of the Syrian goddess, whose temple (and sacred lake with fish) was at nearby Hierapolis.
[38] See Nixon 2002, 2005.

e il commercio nell'Italia antica/Archaeological methods and Approaches: Industry and Commerce in Ancient Italy, 159–172. Oxford, BAR Publishing.

Clarke, G. W. 2002. Stamped Amphora Handles, in G. W. Clarke, P. J. Connor, L. Crewe, B. Frohlich, H. Jackson, J. Littleton, C. E. V. Nixon, M. O'Hea and D. Steele (eds.), *Jebel Khalid on the Euphrates Vol I; Report on Excavations 1986–1996*, 273–290. Sydney, Meditarch.

Clarke, G. W. 2005. Jebel Khalid: Stamped Amphora Handles. *Mediterranean Archaeology* 18, 175–185.

Clarke, G. W. 2008. Jebel Khalid: Stamped Amphora Handles 2006–2008. *Mediterranean Archaeology* 21, 103–114.

Clarke, G. W., Connor P. J., Crewe L., Frohlich, B., Jackson, H., Littleton, J., Nixon, C. E. V., O'Hea, M. and Steele, D. 2002. *Jebel Khalid on the Euphrates Vol I; Report on Excavations 1986–1996*. Sydney, Meditarch.

Cox, D. H. 1949. *The Excavations at Dura-Europos. Final Report IV. Part 1. Fascicle 2. The Greek and Roman Pottery*. New Haven, Yale University Press.

Debevoise, N. C. 1934. *Parthian Pottery from Seleucia-on-the-Tigris*. Ann Arbor, Michigan University Press.

Dorna-Metzger, F. 1996. Hellenistic and Parthian/Roman pottery from the Upper Khabur Survey: A preliminary study, in K. Bartl and S. Hauser (eds.), *Continuity and Change in Northern Mesopotamia from the Hellenistic to the Early Islamic period.* Proceedings of a Colloquium held at the Seminar für Vorderasiatische Altertumskunde, Freie Universität Berlin 6–9 April, 1994. Berliner Beiträge zum Vorderen Orient 17, 363–375. Berlin, Reimer.

Fairbairn, A. and Asouti, E. 2005. Evidence for olive wood and deforestation at Jebel Khalid. *Mediterranean Archaeology* 18, 2005, 190–191.

Galàn, R. 2008. An example of the survival of ancient Mesopotamian architectonical traditions in Northern Jazireh during the Hellenistic period, in J. Cordoba *et al.* (eds.), *Proceedings of the 5th International Congress on the Archaeology of the Ancient Near East. Madrid, April 3–8 2006, Actas del V Congreso Internacional de Arqueología del Oriente Próximo Antiguo Vol III*. Madrid, Universidad Autónoma de Madrid.

Green, J. R. 1976. *Gnathia Pottery in the Akademisches Kunstmuseum Bonn*. Mainz, Zabern.

Green, J. R. 1995. From Taranto to Alexandria, in S. Bourke and J.-P. Descœudres (eds.), *Trade, Contact, and the Movement of Peoples in the Eastern Mediterranean. Studies in Honour of J. Basil Hennessy.* Mediterranean Archaeology Suppl. 3, 271–274. Sydney, Meditarch.

Guz-Zilberstein, B. 1995. The Typology of the Hellenistic Coarse Ware and Selected Loci of the Hellenistic and Roman Periods. In E. Stern (ed.), *Excavations at Dor, Final Report Vol. I B: Areas A and C, The Finds*. Qedem Reports 2, 289–433. Jerusalem, Hebrew University.

Hayes, J. W. 1972. *Late Roman Pottery*. London, British School at Rome.

Hayes, J. W. 1986. Sigillate Orientale. In *Enciclopedia dell'arte antica. Atlante delle forme ceramiche II*, 1–96. Rome, Istituto dell Enciclopedia italiana.

Hayes, J. W. 1991. *The Hellenistic and Roman Pottery.* Paphos III, Nicosia, Report of the Department of Antiquities, Cyprus.

Herbert, S. C. and Berlin, A. 2003. A New Administrative Center for Persian and Hellenistic Galilee: Preliminary Report of the University of Michigan/ University of Minnesota Excavations at Kedesh. *Bulletin of the American School of Oriental Research* 329, 13–59.

Jackson, H. and Tidmarsh, J. 2011. *The Pottery. Jebel Khalid on the Euphrates Vol. III.* Mediterranean Archaeology Supplement 7. Sydney, Meditarch.

Kenrick, P. H. 1985. The Fine Pottery. In *Excavations at Sidi Khrebish Benghazi (Berenice), III,1:* Tripoli, The Dept.

Laumonier, A. 1977. *La céramique hellénistique à reliefs, I, Ateliers 'ioniens'*. Exploration archéologiques de Délos XXXI. Paris, Fontemoing et Cie.

Lund, J. 1995. A Fresh Look at the Roman and Late Roman Fine Wares from the Danish Excavations at Hama, Syria, in H. Meyza and J. Młynarczyk (eds.), *Hellenistic and Roman Pottery in the East Mediterranean – Advances in Scientific Studies. Acts of the II Nieborów Pottery Workshop,* 135–161. Warsaw, Polska Akademia Nauk.

Lund, J. 2005. An Economy of Consumption: the Eastern Sigillata A Industry in the Late Hellenistic Period, in Z. A. Archibald, J. K. Davies and V. Gabrielsen (eds.), *Making, Moving and Managing. The New World of Ancient Economies, 323–31 BC*, 233–252. Oxford, Oxbow Books.

Mallowan, M. 1966. *Nimrud and its Remains, Vol I.* London, Collins.

Morel, J.-P. 1981. *Céramique Campanienne: Les Formes.* Rome, École française de Rome.

Morel, J.-P. 1986. Céramiques à vernis noir d'Italie trouvées à Délos. *Bulletin de Correspondance hellénique* 110, 461–93.

Nixon, C. E. V. 2002. The Coins. In G. W. Clarke, P. J. Connor, L. Crewe, B. Frohlich, H. Jackson, J. Littleton, C. E. V. Nixon, M. O'Hea and D. Steele (eds.), *Jebel Khalid on the Euphrates Vol I; Report on Excavations 1986–1996*, 291–335. Sydney, Meditarch.

Nixon, C. E. V. 2008. Jebel Khalid: Catalogue of the Coins 2000–2006. *Mediterranean Archaeology* 21, 119–161.

Peacock, D. P. S. 1977. Pompeian Red Ware. In D. P. S. Peacock (ed.), *Pottery and early Commerce. Characterisation and Trade in Roman and Later Ceramics*, 147–162. London, New York, Academic Press.

Peña. J. T. 1990. Internal Red-Slip Cookware (Pompeian Red ware) from Cetamura del Chianti, Italy:

Mineralogical Composition and Provenience. *American Journal of Archaeology* 94, 647–661.

Römer, C. 1996. A first glimpse at Glazed Pottery from Tell Šēḫ Ḥamad, in K. Bartl and S. R. Hauser (eds.), *Continuity and Change in Northern Mesopotamia from the Hellenistic to the Early Islamic period.* Proceedings of a Colloquium held at the Seminar für Vorderasiatische Altertumskunde, Freie Universität Berlin 6–9 April, 1994. Berliner Beiträge zum Vorderen Orient 17, 13–22. Berlin, Reimer.

Rotroff, S. I. 1997. *Hellenistic Pottery. Athenian and Wheelmade Table Ware and Related Material.* The Athenian Agora XXIX. Princeton, NJ., American School of Classical Studies at Athens.

Rotroff, S. I. 2002. West Slope in the East, in F. Blondé, P. Ballet and J.-F. Salles, *Céramiques hellénistiques et romaines. Productions et diffusion en Mediterranée orientale (Chypre, Egypte et côte syro-palestinienne)*, 97–115. Lyon, Maison de l'Orient Mediterranéen – Jean Pouilloux.

Rotroff, S. I. 2006. *Hellenistic Pottery. The Plain Wares.* The Athenian Agora XXXIII. Princeton, NJ., American School of Classical Studies at Athens.

Schäfer, J. 1968. *Hellenistische Keramik aus Pergamon.* Pergamenische Forschungen 2. Berlin, de Gruyter.

Schneider, G. 1995. Roman red and black slipped pottery from NE Syria and Jordan. First results of chemical analysis, in H. Meyza and J. Młynarczyk (eds.), *Hellenistic and Roman Pottery in the East Mediterranean – Advances in Scientific Studies. Acts of the II Nieborów Pottery Workshop,* 415–422. Warsaw, Polska Akademia Nauk.

Schneider, G. 2000. Chemical and Mineralogical Studies of Late Hellenistic to Byzantine Pottery Production in the Eastern Mediterranean. *Rei Cretariae Romanae Fautorum Acta* 36, 525–536.

Séiquer, G. M. 1999. Tell Khamīs, in G. del Olmo Lete and J.-L. Montero Fenollós, *Archaeology of the Upper Syrian Euphrates. The Tishrin Dam Area.* Proceedings of the International Symposium held at Barcelona, January 28th–30th, 1998, 205–225. Barcelona, Editorial AUSA.

Slane, K. W. 1997. The Fine Wares. In S. Herbert (ed.) *Tel Anafa II, i. The Hellenistic and Roman Pottery*, Journal of Roman Archaeology Supplementary. Series 10.2, 247–406. Ann Arbor, Michigan, Kelsey Museum of Archaeology.

Thompson, H. A. 1934. Two Centuries of Hellenistic Pottery. *Hesperia* 3, 311–480.

Toll, N. 1943. The Green-Glazed Pottery. *The Excavations at Dura-Europos, Final Report 4.1.1.* New Haven, Yale University Press.

Toll, N. 1946. The Necropolis. *The Excavations at Dura-Europos, Preliminary Report 9, 2.* New Haven, Yale University Press.

Vanderhoeven, M. 1989. Les Terres Sigillées (1966–1972). *Fouilles d'Apamée de Syrie, IX. 1.* Bruxelles, Centre belge de recherches archéologiques à Apamée de Syrie.

Waagé, F. O. 1948. The Glazed Pottery. In F. O. Waagé (ed.), *Antioch-on-the-Orontes Vol. IV, I: Ceramics and Islamic coins,* 80–82. Princeton, University Press.

The Dynamics of Exchange and Innovation in the Oasis City of Merv

Gabriele Puschnigg

Abstract

Comprehensive changes occur in the ceramic production of early Hellenistic Merv (Antiochia in Margiana). Quantitative data demonstrate in particular the increased significance of open vessels for individual serving. Despite the introduction of many new and characteristic shapes, the pottery repertoire is not entirely Hellenistic, but reflects heterogeneous ceramic traditions. At the same time no distinct and independent repertoires are discernible. Merv and its oasis appear to have a consistent ceramic design. The observed transformation suggests a continuous restructuring process taking account of the various currents in cultural behaviour present in the city and its hinterland, rather than the mere import of an already canonical concept of dining habits. Beyond the repercussions expected for the re-organisation of an urban centre, the ceramic evidence from Merv raises the question of the possible impact of imperial policies in a regional context.

Keywords: Merv, Antiochia in Margiana, Central Asia, quantitative analysis

Introduction

The aim of this paper is to explore the potential processes behind the far-reaching transformation in the pottery repertoire of Hellenistic Merv. Starting from a discrete group of vessel forms, the study takes a wider perspective considering the archaeological and historical context of the Merv oasis and looking at implications regarding imperial policies. I will take an analytical approach to the interpretation of the ceramic assemblage using quantitative pottery data. As Merv is situated near the eastern fringe of the Hellenistic world and conventionally outside the focus of pottery studies of this period, I will briefly sketch out some archaeological and methodological issues.

Merv and archaeology

Ancient Merv is characterised by the spectacular remains of its fortifications, which show a progressive urban development from the Achaemenid period onwards into Islamic times. Hellenistic Merv is identified with the square structure of Gyaur Kala, one of the walled parts of the site (**Fig. 1**). On a more detailed scale, there is little historical data on the city's life.

The site bears all the hall-marks of long-term occupation with consecutive adobe structures and their intricate stratigraphy. Naturally, this has direct implications on the composition of finds, including the pottery, which is mostly fragmented and often worn. In archaeological terms, neither the contexts nor the material are of primary quality. As a result, the pottery sequence is still erratic in parts, depending on the available stratigraphic information and additional dating evidence, such as coins. Seleucid or Graeco-Bactrian coins, however, are so scant, that they do not provide reliable dating evidence for pottery assemblages. While the relative chronology is well documented for most vessel types, there is still some uncertainty about the absolute date range of many forms.

Merv and Hellenistic research

Against this background of archaeological uncertainties it seems justified to ask: what can pottery from Merv contribute to the discussion on Hellenistic ceramics? In order to answer this question, we have to consider the state of Hellenistic pottery studies and the specific situation at Merv.

Pottery of the Hellenistic period, in particular the plain wares, only recently became the subject of dedicated studies. The Hellenistic world with its vast extent is not yet understood properly in its everyday functioning. Similarities and differences are noticed across the various regions and are not yet evaluated with regard to their relevance and significance. We are only beginning to deal with the varieties of pottery in the Hellenistic world. At the same time there might be an expectation that Hellenism should lead to visible congruency in its material relics. In search for parallels we depend on the history of archaeological publications. Parts of the Hellenistic East seem particularly under-represented in this respect. While material from Central Asia is generally available, the same cannot be said for Iran. The Hellenistic period was long regarded as an interlude of foreign rule in ancient Iran not worth studying in its own right. Thus, the entry on Achaemenid pottery in Encyclopedia Iranica is immediately followed by the article on Parthian and Sasanian ceramics[1]. Few publications mention Hellenistic

[1] Boucharlat and Haerinck 1991.

Fig. 1. The square city of Gyaur Kala. Excavation areas providing quantitative data are marked in white (Ancient Merz Project)

traditions or focus on characteristic wares and shapes[2]. The scant evidence is, however, unevenly spread over a large geographic area, leaving a considerable gap between the East and the Mediterranean neighbourhood. We have to accept that the results of a comparative study of the pottery will lack in substance. In this regard, it appears to be more important to understand the mechanisms that lie behind adaptations in the local pottery assemblages.

The Merv assemblage fulfils a number of criteria, which make it suitable to address this issue. Firstly, the site was systematically explored since the late 1940s. Material from these old excavations is available through a series of Soviet publications and can be used to ascertain aspects of typology and distribution.

Secondly, material from more recent excavations is quantified, which facilitates a more contextual interpretation of the pottery forms. The use of statistical methods supports an analytical approach with a view to the whole assemblage. In addition, the newly excavated pottery was scientifically analysed. Before taking a closer look at the data, some methodological issues will be considered.

Sampling Hellenistic Merv

Naturally, the impressive size of the walled Hellenistic city, which comprises 330 ha, raises the question how representative the excavated material is in relation to the whole site? The recorded pottery is certainly a minor proportion of the original amount in use at any specific time. In this respect, the constant cycle of re-deposition, which is so characteristic for mud-brick architecture, works to our advantage. As almost all deposits are secondary, functional differences which may have originally existed are minimised in favour of chronological differences. Pottery forms that were found in a specific room do not necessarily reflect any of the activities that might originally have been performed there. Apart from in-built features, such as large storage vessels, the pottery is not found in its primary context. While there is still an element of accident as to which vessels are present in any one context, on a larger scale the complete pottery assemblage is representative of the ceramic repertoire at the site.

Quantity and proportion

It was mentioned before that statistical methods were used for the ceramic analysis and a few issues are reiterated here for a better understanding[3]. The quantitative measure for the ceramic fragments are estimated vessel equivalents (*eves*), which are used to express the amount of pottery. In this study the *eves* are taken from the percentage of rim fragments. A fragment that measures 50% of the original rim equals 0.50 *eves* or half a vessel. In the statistical analysis the ceramic assemblages from individual contexts were compared to each other. One of the applications used for this comparison was correspondence analysis, which helps to assess the differences between ceramic assemblages and their significance. The strength of this approach is that it enables the archaeologist to make an informed evaluation of recognisable patterns in the ceramic material with special regard to their relevance for the whole assemblage. For the discussion of individual forms, more conventional methods are used in addition.

A scientific programme of analyses was run to establish the petrographic and chemical composition of the wares in relation to local clay sources[4]. No imported plain ware fabrics were identified for the pre-Islamic material. Equally, previous publications of pottery from Merv do not mention any visually distinctive plain ware fabric, which would indicate the presence of imported vessel forms in substantial quantities. No stamped amphora fragments have yet been found. These findings suggest that pottery was not imported or traded on a regular basis, neither as a commodity nor in the form of containers.

The data

Major changes within the local pottery repertoire were established for the Hellenistic period[5]. These include the introduction of a series of new vessel forms and manipulations of the colourings of the sherd and surface treatment. The latter were found to be attempts in imitating

---

2 Haerinck 1983; Hannestad 1990.

3 For a detailed discussion of the methodology see Puschnigg 2006, 55–57.

4 Vince, forthcoming.

5 Puschnigg 2008, 111–13.

the appearance of Greek red slip and black table wares. Examples of especially finely mixed versions of the local clay[6] suggest that potters tried to create distinguished fine ware vessels, a hierarchical differentiation not known at Merv for other periods.

Chronological data

Recent excavations of the Gyaur Kala defensive wall (MGK6) established the complete sequence of fortifications and reached down to Hellenistic levels[7]. The pottery forms which are examined here in detail are present in the first three phases of the wall. Most bowl shapes show considerable spatial distribution across Gyuar-Kala and the city's citadel of Erk-Kala. Some forms are distinctive enough to be traced in the literature on excavations conducted during the Soviet period at Merv, which often went down to deeper levels. Other recent excavations in Gyaur Kala (MGK5) and Erk Kala (MEK1) focused on later periods. These, however, still produced large quantities of residual material from much earlier periods, including many of the relevant bowl shapes. For a chronological assessment the data from the Gyaur Kala fortification are most relevant, although it bears some archaeological problems. Deposits from the fortifications are generally less rich in ceramic material compared to those from private housing, and they vary in volume. The contexts of the first two phases of the fortifications are smaller than those of phase 3 leaving some element of uncertainty in the chronological interpretation. At the level of individual pottery types additional information regarding the distribution of wares can be used as supporting evidence for a chronological date. Red slip- or grey ware fragments are particularly important in this respect, as these are newly introduced techniques, which occur only in limited quantities and apparently vanished from the repertoire after a relatively short period of time. The presence of red slip- or dark grey ware in a specific vessel form is therefore taken as indication of its relatively early Hellenistic date. For assessing the ware distribution all quantified recurrences of an individual shape are taken into account.

The vessel forms

One group of early Hellenistic vessels is singled out for examination. These are medium bowls, which form a steady part of Hellenistic repertoires in the literature. They were chosen because they are representative of the new ceramic style and constitute a sizeable quantity. The rim fragments of this group amount to 13.17 *eves,* or roughly 5% of the pre-Islamic pottery assemblage. They show considerable variation in proportion and detail. Each bowl shape is described individually at first, including a summary of descriptive statistics on ware distribution, rim diameters and quantity.

The term 'ware' is used here to designate different colourings of the vessel surface, which were produced intentionally. Despite the lack of variety in plain ware fabrics, there is some diversity in the surface appearance of the pottery resulting from variations in the firing process, including temperature and atmosphere, and surface treatment. Typically for the material at Merv, no shape is produced in only one ware, but occurs in a number of different colourings.

Wares which are particularly relevant for the early Hellenistic pottery are highlighted in the present charts. For vessel shapes counting less than ten recurrences the information is given in words. Some fragments clearly show that the vessels were miss-fired and did not obtain their intended colouring. This group was classified as 'oxid miss-fired' and its proportion is mentioned in the summary statistics for each shape. In the charts it is not shown as a separate group, but is part of the 'oxid, cream' ware group. I have also included the amount of pottery, for which ware identifications are missing, as this is simply part of the archaeological reality. Missing records mostly concern material from the first excavation seasons at Erk Kala (MEK1).

The distribution of rim diameters indicates how well defined and standardised a vessel form is. For the Hellenistic period at Merv open forms play a special role, and the group of medium bowls exemplifies this aspect. As mentioned above, the quantity of individual forms is expressed in *eves*. The values given here reflect the current state of the digital record. They may change in the future, when new material becomes available from excavations.

R1: Rounded bowl with simple rim (**Fig. 2**):
Eves total: 4.37
Miss-fired: 0.34
Record missing: 0.26
Recurrences: 62
Discussion: This bowl type has the highest *eves* value of the entire group. It is well documented from many areas of Merv, including the recent excavations in Erk- and Gyaur Kala, but it was also recorded in previous excavations[8]. In the sequence of the Gyaur Kala fortifications it first appears in phase 2, which is tentatively dated to the Graeco-Bactrian period for historical considerations[9]. The bowl is found in red slip- and grey ware, which suggests a date within the Hellenistic period at Merv. Some of the relatively early fragments are very fine and rather thin-walled.

R304, deep rounded bowl with slightly inturned (incurving) rim (**Fig. 3**):
Eves total: 1.11
Miss-fired: 0
Record missing: 0
Recurrences: 8

6 Joyner, forthcoming; Puschnigg 2006, 105–106.
7 Zavyalov 2007.

8 Usmanova 1963, 195, fig. 24. 26 and 28.
9 Zavyalov 2007, 326.

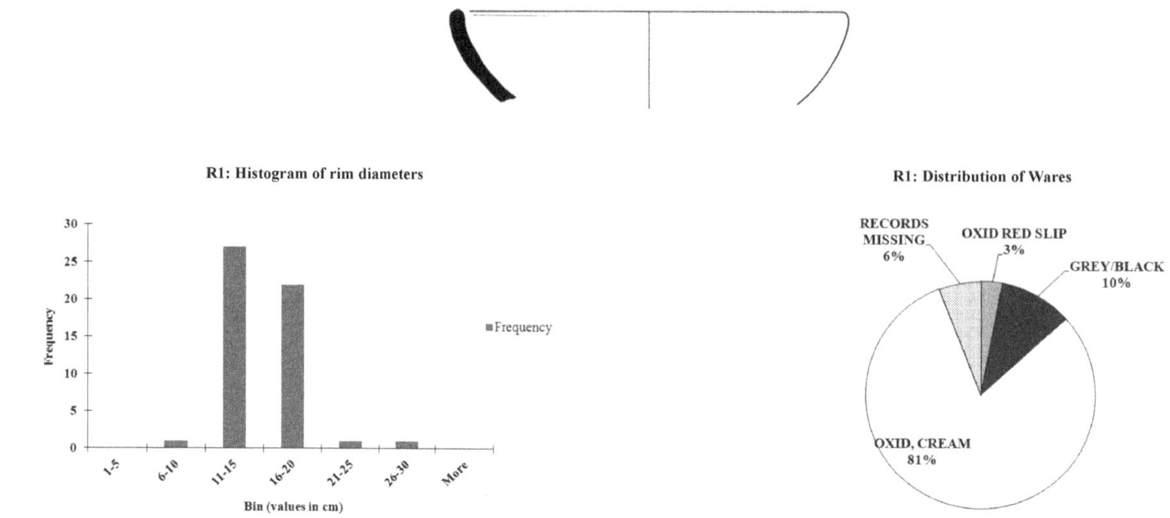

Fig. 2. R1 with distribution charts. The percentage values in the ware distribution chart are calculated from eves values (drawing: K. Morton und F. Vardy, diagrams: G. Puschnigg)

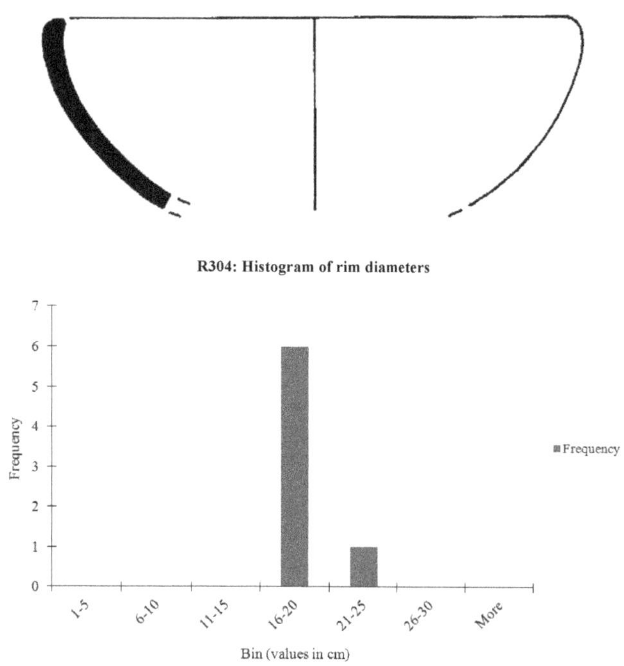

Fig. 3. R304 with histogram of rim diameters (drawing: K. Morton und F. Vardy, diagram: G. Puschnigg)

Discussion: The deep rounded bowl shows a more pronounced rim than the previous form. So far it has only been identified in deposits from the Gyaur Kala fortifications. Fragments of this form possibly occurred in previous excavations in Gyaur Kala[10], but the publisheddrawings do not show enough detail to allow for a precise identification. No red slip- or grey wares are documented for this type. The ware distribution, however, may not yet be representative, as only a relatively small amount of pottery is recorded for this shape. The bowl appears in phase 3 of the Gyaur Kala defensive wall and dominates the shape group associated with this phase.
Phase 3 of the construction work on the Gyaur Kala fortifications istentatively dated to the Early Parthian period[11].

R236, deep rounded bowl with simple rim (**Fig. 4**):
Eves total: 0.30
Miss-fired: 0.03
Record missing: 0.03
Recurrences: 8
Discussion: This form illustrates a slightly larger and deeper bowl. Apart from the Gyaur Kala defensive wall, fragments of this type were also found in MGK5 and in previous excavations in Gyaur Kala[12]. With regard to the small quantity recorded for this shape so far, its distributions of wares and rim diameters are again of preliminary character. No red slip- or grey wares occurred as yet. The deep bowl with simple rim first appears in phase 2 of the Gyaur Kala defensive wall, the phase tentatively attributed to the Graeco-Bactrian period[13].

R85, bowl with flared profile and upright (upturned) simple rim (**Fig. 5**):
Eves total: 0.72
Miss-fired: 0.10
Record missing: 0
Recurrences: 14
Discussion: The bowl appears to be a marginally larger

[10] Usmanova 1963, 187, fig.16. 15.

[11] Zavyalov 2007, 326.
[12] Usmanova 1963, 187, fig.16. 32.
[13] Zavyalov 2007, 326.

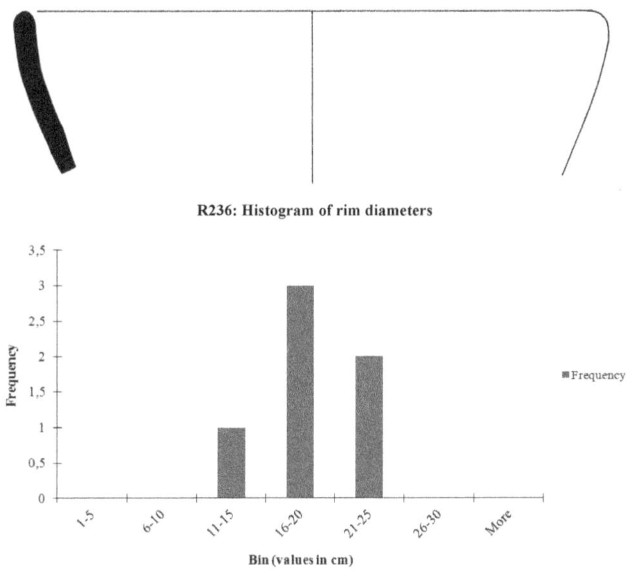

Fig. 4. R236 with histogram of rim diameters (drawing: K. Morton und F. Vardy, diagram: G. Puschnigg)

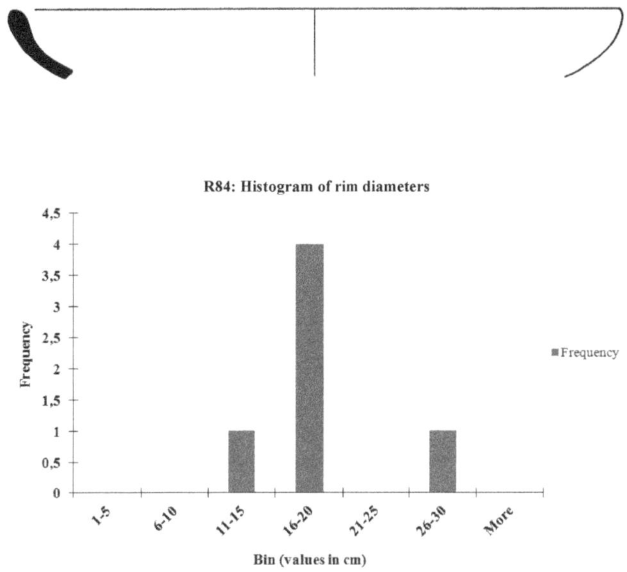

Fig. 6. R84 with histogram of rim diameters (drawing: K. Morton und F. Vardy, diagram: G. Puschnigg)

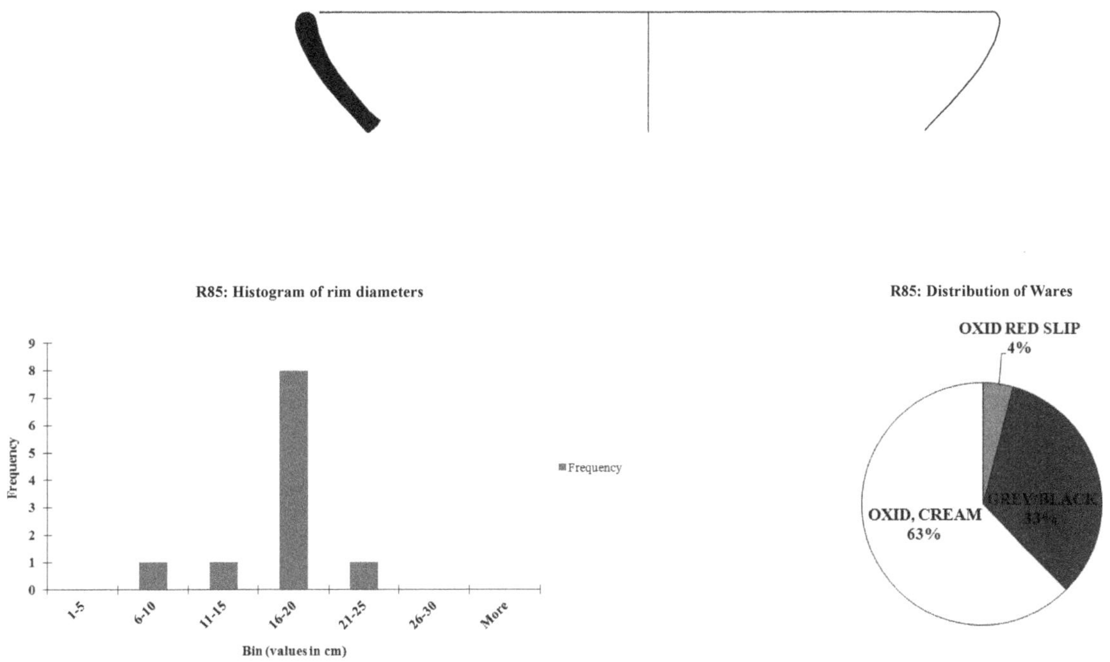

Fig. 5. R85 with distribution charts (drawing: K. Morton und F. Vardy, diagrams: G. Puschnigg)

version of R1. It is well documented in MEK1, MGK5 and also previous excavations in Gyaur Kala[14]. Despite the relatively small amount of pottery recorded for this type, both red slip- and grey wares are documented. The bowl appears in phase 1 of the Gyaur Kala defensive wall, presumed to date back to the Seleucid period[15].

R84, shallow bowl with upright (upturned), slightly thickened rim (**Fig. 6**):
Eves total: 0.41
Miss-fired: 0
Record missing: 0.03
Recurrences: 8
Discussion: This shape represents a shallow bowl. Its ware- and rim diameter distribution may not yet be representative. The shallow bowl occurs in all recent excavation areas. A similar shape is also illustrated for trench 6 of the previous

[14] Usmanova 1963, 187, fig. 16. 31.
[15] Zavyalov 2007, 325.

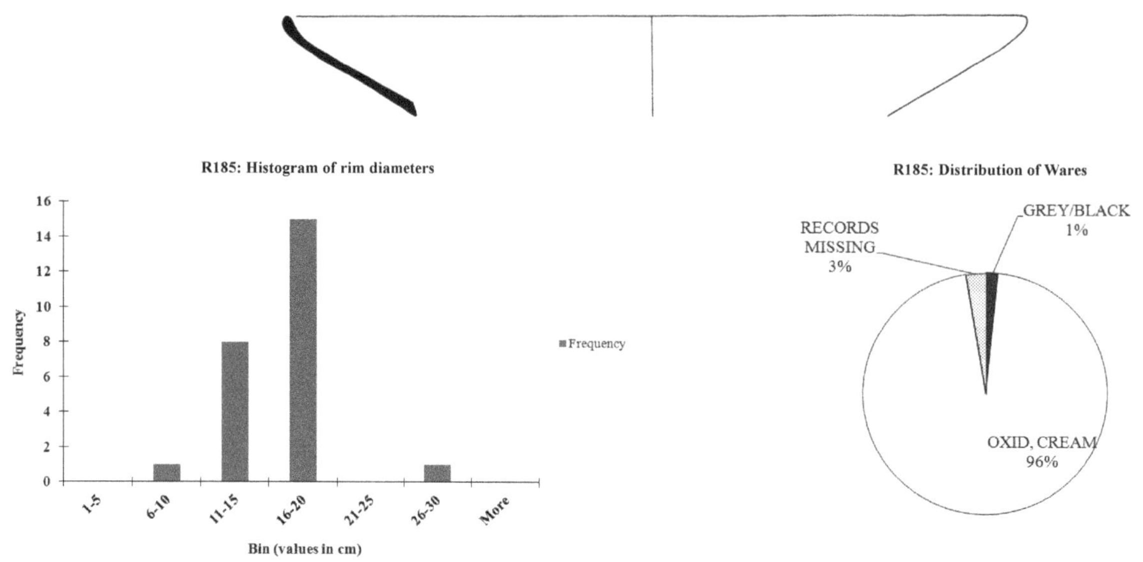

Fig. 7. R185 with distribution charts (drawing: K. Morton und F. Vardy, diagrams: G. Puschnigg)

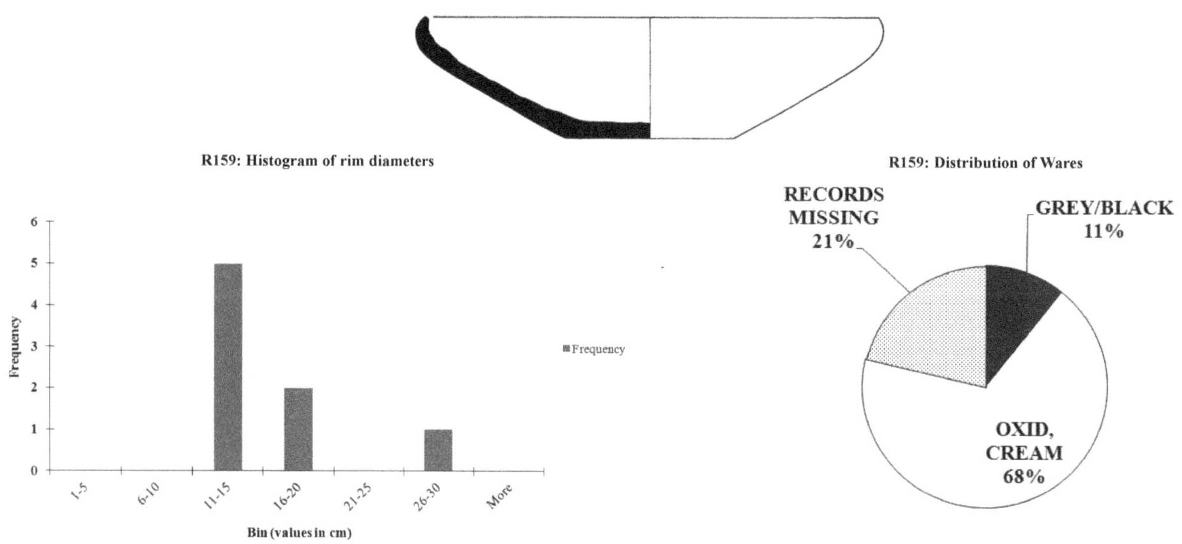

Fig. 8. R159 with distribution charts (drawing: K. Morton und F. Vardy, diagrams: G. Puschnigg)

Fig. 9. R93 (K. Morton und F. Vardy)

Soviet excavations in Gyaur Kala[16]. In the deposits of the Gyaur Kala fortifications, it first appears in phase 3.

R185, flared bowl with upright (upturned), thickened rim **(Fig. 7)**:
Eves total: 1.88
Miss-fired: 0.05
Record missing: 0.05
Recurrences: 28
Discussion: This bowl type is a very fine and thin-walled shape, and might rather be characterised as a plate. A small proportion is documented in grey ware. The bowl occurred in all recent excavation areas. It is, however, difficult to trace in the literature of previous Soviet excavations at Merv, as pottery in general was treated rather summarily and drawings are mainly used to exemplify the character of ceramic assemblages. At the Gyaur Kala defensive walls its first appearance is recorded for phase 3, presumed to be of early Parthian date[17].

[16] Katsuris and Buryakov 1963, 126, fig. 6. 13.

[17] Zavyalov 2007, 326.

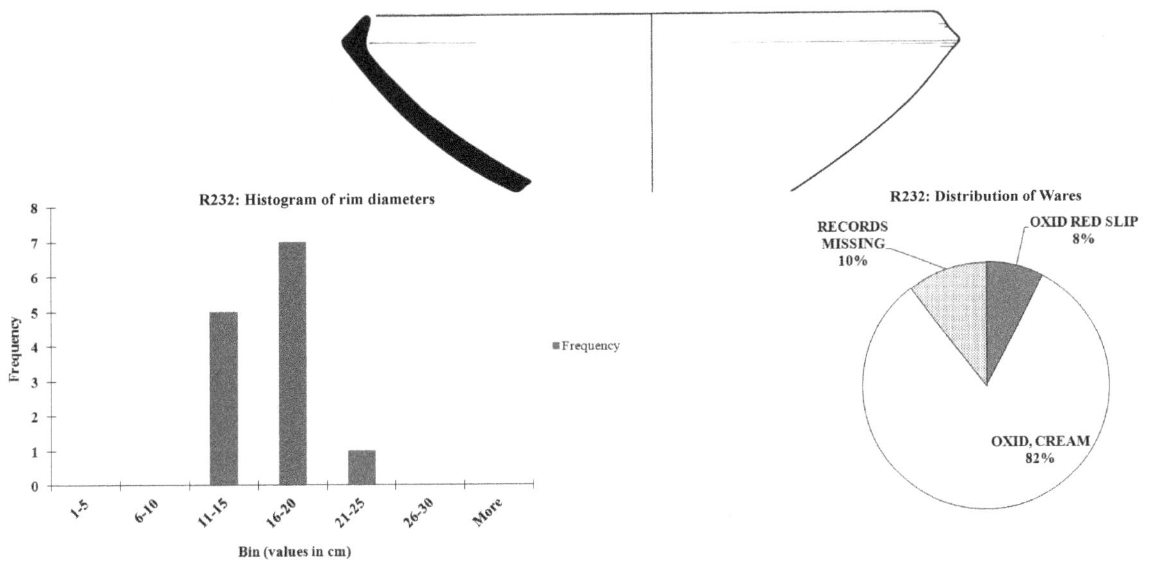

Fig. 10. R232 with distribution charts (drawing: K. Morton und F. Vardy, diagrams: G. Puschnigg)

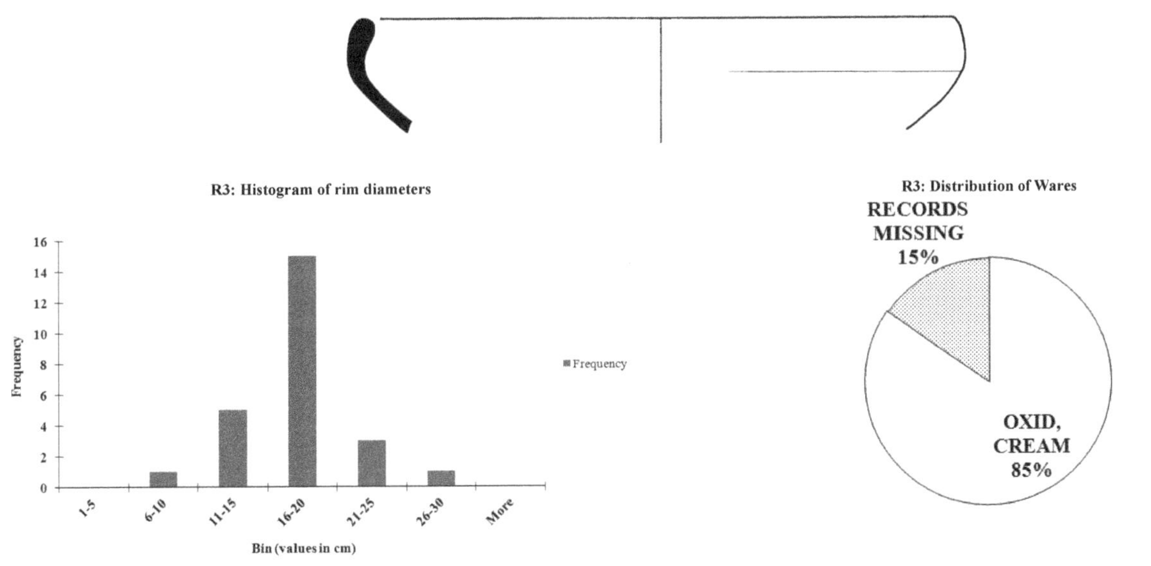

Fig. 11. R3 with distribution charts (drawing: K. Morton und F. Vardy, diagrams: G. Puschnigg)

R159, shallow flared bowl with inturned rim (**Fig. 8**):
Eves total: 0.75
Miss-fired: 0.08
Record missing: 0.16
Recurrences: 13
Discussion: In contrast to the other bowl shapes, one fragment of this type provided a complete vessel profile period at Merv show a flat base, including some of the fish plates and bowls with internally thickened or rolled rim[18]. Fragments of this shape occurred in MEK1 and MGK5. Similar bowls are also recorded from previous excavations at Merv[19]. A relatively large proportion of the shallow bowl with inturned rim is grey ware. At the Gyaur Kala fortifications this shape appears in phase 2, which is tentatively dated to the Graeco-Bactrian era[20].

R93, shallow flared bowl with inturned (incurving) pointed rim (**Fig. 9**):
Eves total: 0.59
Miss-fired: 0
Record missing: 0.31
Recurrences: 9
Discussion: This shape appears to be a slightly larger and more accentuated version of the previous form. Fragments were found in all recent excavations, but the form is not discernible in the Soviet literature. Unfortunately, many of the records are incomplete, and consequently ware- and

[18] Puschnigg 2008, 113–114, figs.3 and 5.
[19] Koshelenko 1985, 383, pl. 95.
[20] Zavyalov 2007, 236.

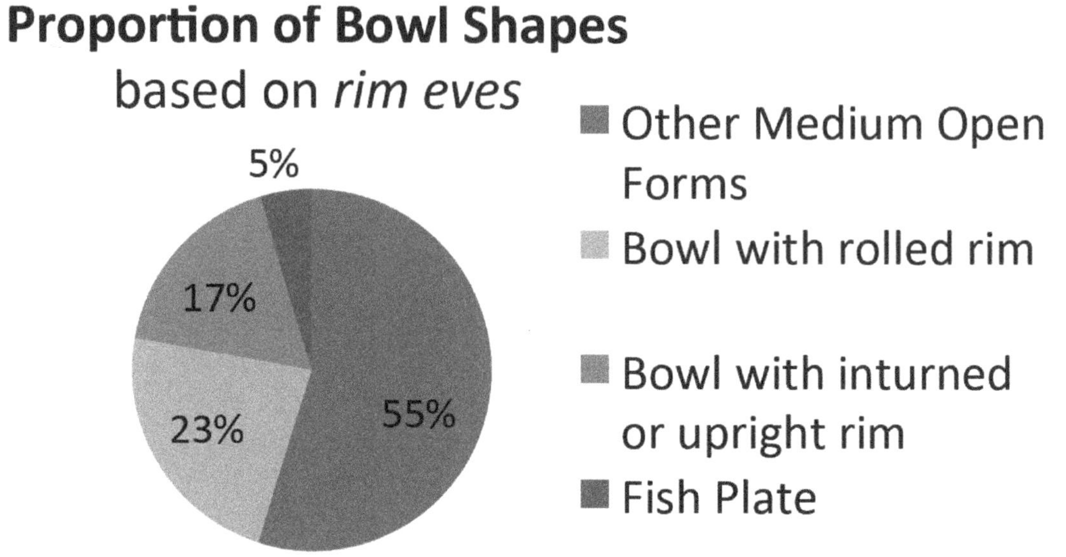

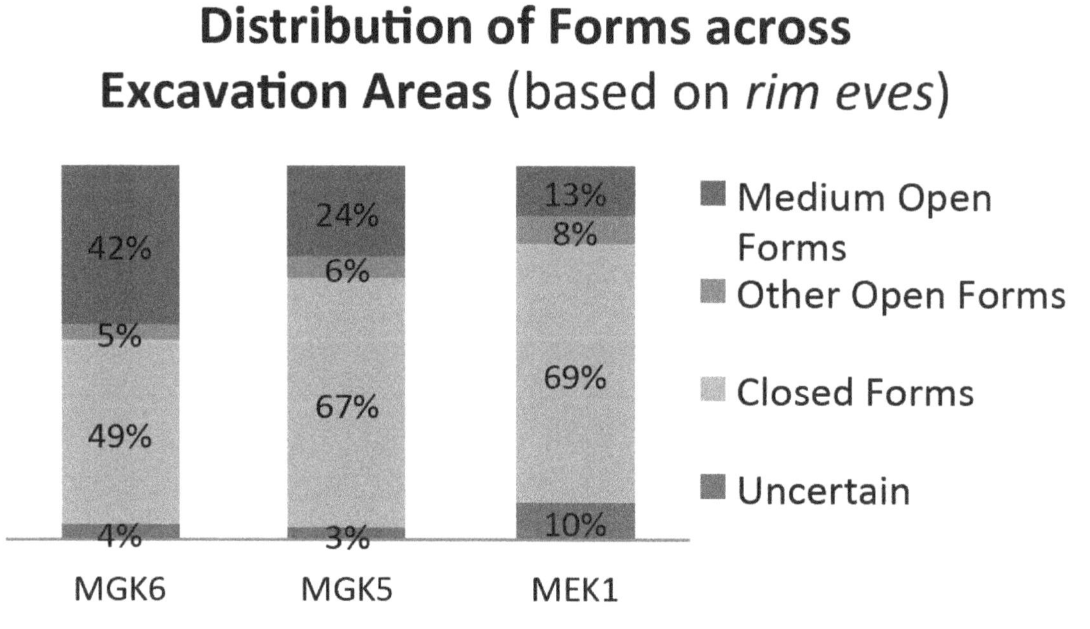

Fig. 12. a: Proportion of the main groups of bowls discussed in this paper in relation to all medium open forms - b: Distribution of open and closed vessel forms across excavation areas: MGK6 (Gyaur Kala fortifications: Hellenistic to early Sasanian levels); MGK5 (Middle Sasanian domestic area); MEK 1 (Late Sasanian private house) (G. Puschnigg)

rim diameter distributions are probably not representative and are therefore not included here. The shape first appears in phase 1 of the Gyaur Kala fortifications, the tentative Seleucid phase[21].

R232, Rounded bowl with sharply inturned (incurving) rim (**Fig. 10**):
Eves total: 1.05
Miss-fired: 0.16
Record missing: 0.11
Recurrences: 15
Discussion: The bowl appears to be a distinctive variant of the bowl with inturned rim. Apart from the fortifications, it was also found in Gyaur Kala, MGK5. A similar bowl shape might be illustrated from previous excavations of trench 6 in Gyaur Kala[22]. Fragments are documented in red slip-, but not in grey ware. The bowl appears in phase 3 of the Gyaur Kala fortifications, the presumed Early Parthian phase[23].

21 Zavyalov 2007, 325.

22 Katsuris and Buryakov 1963, 123, fig. 4. 5.
23 Zavyalov 2007, 326.

R3, rounded bowl with inturned (incurving), thickened rim (**Fig. 11**):
Eves total: 2.09
Miss-fired: 0.13
Record missing: 0.32
Recurrences: 26
Discussion: This type shows a slightly elongated rim profile. The bowl also occurred in MEK1 and MGK5, and is documented in a larger version from previous Soviet excavations at Merv[24]. Fragments from recent excavation areas show a comparatively broad distribution of rim diameters. Despite the relatively large amount of pottery recorded, no red slip- or grey wares occurred. The ware distribution pattern for this shape might indicate a slightly later date, when red slip- and grey wares were no longer produced at Merv. The bowl with inturned thickened rim appears in phase 3 of the Gyaur Kala defensive wall, which is tentatively dated to the Early Parthian period[25].

Interpretation

We have to assess this group of bowls in a larger context to understand their significance.The brief overview suggeststhat the bowls are a regular part of the Hellenistic repertoire at Merv. Most reflect a similar chronological range, although individual forms may be slightly later than others, particularly those without any records on red slip- or grey ware. All exemplify the chronological phase following the transformation of the pottery repertoire, when the new shapes and techniques were already firmly established within the local production. All shapes are more or less variations on the same theme, some show clear affiliations to Echinus bowls. The size of this group, its ware distribution and its presence throughout a considerable chronological period suggest that it played an integral part in the dining routine of the time. Still, the bowl with inturned (incurving) or upright (upturned) rim is only one in a spectrum of medium open bowls, illustrating the new diversity of this form. Prior to the Hellenistic period, medium open vessels did not show such a variety. Now the bowls with inturned rim alone amount to 18% of all medium open forms found at pre-Islamic Merv (**Fig. 12**). Together with the contemporary fish plates and bowls with internally thickened (rolled) rim they reach almost 50% of medium open forms. The significance of medium open forms in this period was also highlighted in the correspondence analysis of the ceramic assemblages fromthe Gyaur Kala fortifications[26]. Although medium bowl shapes are present in earlier phases, the pottery associated with phase 3 of the defensive wall is clearly dominated by open forms. This preponderance also appears to cause the stark contrast to the following phases. Equally, the examination of the form distribution across the recent excavation areas demonstrates that medium open forms decrease in post-Hellenistic phases (**Fig. 12**).

Despite the largely secondary nature of the deposits and the considerable amount of residual material in some contexts, long-term trends are clearly visible in the assemblage comparison of the different areas. Material from the Gyaur Kala fortifications contains the largest proportion of Hellenistic pottery forms, as excavations there reached down to the relevant levels. Other excavation areas in Gyaur- and Erk Kala, MGK5 and MEK1, focused on later, middle and late Sasanian, levels. Hellenistic ceramic shapes from these two excavations are residual.

The introduction of new vessel shapes at Merv was not confined to open forms, although they are the biggest group. Rims of amphoras, jugs and craters are also found. Other forms, goblets and medium to large closed forms, are local. To judge from our data, the Hellenistic pottery repertoire at Merv never consisted entirely of Greek shapes. Drinking vessels, for instance, were apparently not adopted[27]. On the other hand, we cannot identify chronologically parallel repertoires, one Greek and one local. There is not much functional overlap. Possible differences in status may be discernible in the different wares of an individual pottery form, but not in different sets of pottery. Moreover, there is no evidence of a separate ceramic tradition in the oasis outside the city of Gyaur kala. On the contrary, excavations of pottery kilns at Dzhin Depe, about 50km north-west of ancient Merv, revealed Hellenistic vessel forms, including bowls with internally thickened or rolled rim[28]. Samples collected at the site for thin-sectioning and chemical analysis by the Ancient Merv Project contained also fragments of bowls with inturned (incurving) rim, R159 and R185, the first of these in grey ware[29]. The kiln site was dated to the Parthian period according to the kiln structures and the pottery[30]. A detailed evaluation of this dating is impossible at the moment, but the assemblage suggests that Hellenistic open forms were certainly manufactured in the oasis over a considerable period of time and, most importantly, that Greek and local shapes were produced in the same kilns[31].

It is difficult to match the detail and mundane nature of the archaeological evidence with our historical understanding of the Hellenistic period at Merv, which is still obscure. Merv was the administrative centre of the oasis from Achaemenid times onwards. The new square city Gyaur Kala, which is identified as Antiochia in Margiana, the foundation of Antiochus' I[32], incorporated its precursor, Erk Kala, as a citadel (cf. **Fig. 1**). The sheer increase in urban space suggests a substantial re-organisation of the city with possible reverberations for its hinterland, the oasis[33]. With this new urban centre we may expect a large number of new occupants arriving in the oasis. We do not

24 Koshelenko 1985, 384, pl.96.
25 Zavyalov 2007, 236.
26 Puschnigg, forthcoming.

27 Cf. Puschnigg 2008, 125.
28 Merezhin 1962, 31 fig. 18. 13.
29 Williams and Kurbansakhatov 2003, 165.
30 Merezhin 1962, 29, 31–34.
31 Cf. Merezhin 1962, 31 fig. 18.
32 Plinius, Nat.Hist. VI. 18. 46–47.
33 Sherwin-White and Kuhrt 1993, 83–84.

know, however, who they were, but it is likely that they came from a variety of different backgrounds and ethnic groups. Unfortunately, we have no knowledge of the private architecture of Hellenistic Merv.

Doubtlessly, the changes in ceramic forms and techniques that coincide with this period are massive. We cannot reconstruct the exact mechanism of this transformation, be it a limited number of imports or migrant potters, or possibly both. Accompanying this process was most probably a change in dining habits, including the preference of vessels for individual servings, which led to the sharp increase in medium open forms. This should not be understood, however, as a direct transferral of western habits into an eastern environment. With regard to the homogeneity of the ceramic evidence within the oasis, we may assume that the population largely engaged in a common set of culinary practices or at least the repertoire offered all necessary forms to cater for possible variations. To judge from the significance of medium open forms, these practices certainly contained Hellenistic features, but it may have been more multi-facetted and there was probably room for adaptation. I believe that the new style of consumption we see reflected in the ceramic repertoire may be born out of the deliberately cosmopolitan culture promoted in the Seleucid Empire. Historians now agree that the Seleucids tolerated and supported the different cultural traditions of their Empire[34]. We might regard the seemingly eclectic nature of the Hellenistic pottery assemblage as an aspect of this imperial policy. The administration at the city would also have followed a certain etiquette commensurable with court practices, and would have probably influenced some sections of the society. Merv's role as a trading centre is secondary in this assumption. Trade did not stimulate any changes in the ceramic tradition.

Later in the 3rd century BC Merv might have become part of the Graeco-Bactrian Empire[35]. Visible alterations in the pottery repertoire occur only later in the Parthian period, when medium open forms loose their dominant position. Until then, Hellenistic influence is noticeable, especially with regard to open forms[36].

Historical and archaeological evidence show regional variation in the cultural landscapes of the Seleucid Empire[37]. Such patterns are already attested for earlier empires and appear to be part of the inner structure of these complex entities[38]. Against this background we have to question the comparability of Hellenistic pottery repertoires. It is an integral part of ceramic publications to include a list of comparable forms for each vessel type and it is certainly important to know the possible origin or spread of each shape. Many of the open forms from Merv, including the group of bowls discussed above, have analogous shapes across the Hellenistic East from Central Asia[39] to Western Iran and Mesopotamia[40], and further west up to Athens[41]. The interpretation of these findings, however, is problematic for three reasons. Firstly, there is the aforementioned lack of relevant publications, or availability thereof, for many regions in Iran.

Secondly, most of the Greek shapes found in the Hellenistic East are locally produced. Despite the visual similarity, there may still be regional variations in the use and significance of these shapes within their respective assemblage. It seems important therefore to understand each repertoire regarding its practical and social functionality. This will not always be possible, depending on the amount and quality of the surrounding archaeological information, but I believe that a more interpretive approach will be rewarding.

Thirdly, our assessment is hampered by the lack of evidence for other materials, such as glass or metal, which may have contributed in varying degrees to the assemblage of vessels for everyday use. This is, of course, also an unknown factor in the present interpretation.

Considering the Merv pottery assemblage of the early Hellenistic period as a whole, it appears close to contemporary assemblages from Northern Bactrian contexts, especially since local forms, such as the goblets are analogous, too[42]. Ceramic traditions in the two regions were close in the Achaemenid period and close parallels are again visible in late Parthian and early Sasanian times[43]. On the other hand there is also variation. Equally, we find certain parallels in techniques and forms between Merv and north-eastern Iran[44]. More research is needed to evaluate the analogies and differences in the pottery assemblages to understand their cultural implications.

Finally, I would like to briefly refer to the problem of terminology. The description of ceramic forms at Merv, both ancient and Islamic, generally follows the recommendations of the Medieval Pottery Research Group[45]. This was chosen for reasons of consistency within the Merv Project, but descriptions divert in some instances from those used in other publications. I have therefore added the possibly more common expressions in brackets.

Conclusion

One conclusion that should be drawn as a consequence of this analysis is to accept Hellenistic pottery assemblages in their entireness and variability as reflections of the

---

34 Wiesehöfer 2001, 108–109.
35 Polybius, The Histories 10. 49. 1–15.
36 Cf. Puschnigg 2008, 117–119.
37 Hannestad 1990, 186; Sherwin-White and Kuhrt 1993, 141–161.
38 Sherwin-White and Kuhrt 1993, 144.
39 Lyonnet 2000, 78–79 fig. 1.12–15 and fig. 2.17–18.
40 Hannestad 1990, 180–181 fig. 1.1–4 and fig. 2. 6, 9–10; 184–185 fig. 3. 1–4 and fig. 4. 1–5.
41 Rotroff 1997, fig. 62–63.
42 Lyonnet 2000, 75, 78, fig. 1; Rtveladze and Bolelov 2000, 101, 103, fig.1.
43 Cf. Puschnigg 2006, 144–145.
44 Haerinck 1983, 188–190.
45 1998, Occasional Paper No. 1.

daily routines of the respective local population. Singling out typically Greek vessel forms as alien and transient elements relating to only one group in the population stops short of acknowledging the complexity in the cultural life and constitution of different regions and cities. We should look at the pottery assemblages from eastern Hellenistic context aside of a prejudiced concept of Greek colonialism. At Merv many of the changes and new forms in the pottery apparently stayed for a considerable period of time well into the Parthian era. Hellenistic features are noticeable in parts of the ceramic design for many more centuries up to Sasanian times. This may again be peculiar to Merv and other places might show a different history. We should recognise the potential of this highly interesting period in the ceramic development. I believe that the study of pottery assemblages can make a valuable contribution to the understanding of the daily functioning of the empires that followed Alexander's conquest in the East.

Gabriele Puschnigg
Porzellangasse 22/3/13
A-1090 Wien
g.puschnigg@ucl.ac.uk

Bibliography

Boucharlat, R. and Haerinck, E. 1991. Ceramics xi–xii. The Achaemenid Period. The Parthian and Sasanian Periods. *Encyclopedia Iranica online*, http://www.iranicaonline.org/articles/ceramics-xi and -xii.

Haerinck, E. 1983. *La céramique en Iran pendant la période parthe*. Gent, Imprimerie orientaliste.

Hannestad, L. 1990. Change and Conservatism. Hellenistic Pottery in Mesopotamia and Iran. In *Akten des XIII. Internationalen Kongresses für Klassische Archäologie, Berlin 1988,* 179–186. Mainz, Zabern.

Katsuris, K. and Buryakov, Yu. 1963. Izuchenie remeslannogo kvartala antichnogo Merva u severnykh vorot Gyaur-Kaly. *Trudy Yuzhno-Turkmenistanskoi Arkheologicheskoi Kompleksnoi Ekspeditsii* XII, 119–163.

Koshelenko, G. A. 1985. *Drevneishie gosudarstva Kavkaza i Srednei Azii.* Moskva, Izdatel'stvo Nauka.

Lyonnet, B. 2000. Grecheskaya okkupatsiya Sogdiany. Rezul'taty sravnitel'nogo analiza keramiki Afrasiaba i Ai-Khanum. In *Materialy mezhdunarodnoi konferentsii posvyashchennoi 50-letiyu nauchnoi deyatel'nosti G.V. Shishkinoi*, 75–80. Moskva, Gosudarstvennyi Muzei Vostoka.

Joyner, L. forthcoming, Petrographic analysis. In St. J. Simpson (ed.), *A late Sasanian house in Erk Kala.*

Medieval Pottery Research Group 1998. *A Guide to the Classification of Medieval Ceramic Forms*. Occasional Paper 1. Over Wallop, BAS Printers.

Merezhin, L. N. 1962. K kharakteristike keramicheskikh pechei perioda rabovladeniya i rannego srednevekov'ya v Mervskom oazise. *Trudy Yuzhno-Turkmenistanskoi Arkheologicheskoi Kompleksnoi Ekspeditsii* XI, 12–40.

Puschnigg, G. 2006. *Ceramics of the Merv Oasis: recycling the city*. University College London Institute of Archaeology Publications. California, Left Coast Press.

Puschnigg, G. 2008. Hellenistic Echoes in Parthian Merv: Transformation and Adaptation in the Ceramic Repertoire. *Parthica* 10, 109–128.

Puschnigg, G. forthcoming. D. Gilbert and G. Puschnigg with contributions by A. Feuerbach, A. Vince and T. Williams, *The ceramics from Merv.* Volume 1. The Achaemenid to late Sasanian ceramics from Merv c 6th century BC to 7th century AD. Saffron Press.

Rotroff, S. I. 1997. *Hellenistic Pottery. Athenian and Imported Wheelmade Table Ware and Related Material.* The Athenian Agora XXIX. Princeton, NJ., American School of Classical Studies at Athens.

Rtveladze, E. V. and Bolelov, S. B. 2000. Keramicheskii kompleks epokhi ellinizma na Kampyr-Tepe v Severnoi Baktrii. In *Materialy mezhdunarodnoi konferentsii posvyashchennoi 50-letiyu nauchnoi deyatel'nosti G.V. Shishkinoi*, 99–104. Moskva, Gosudarstvennyi Muzei Vostoka.

Sherwin-White, S. M. and Kuhrt, A. 1993. *From Samarkhand to Sardis: a new approach to the Seleucid Empire.* London, Duckworth.

Usmanova, Z. I. 1963. Raskopki masterskoi remeslennika parfyanskogo vremeni na gorodishche Gyaur Kala. *Trudy Yuzhno-Turkmenistanskoi Arkheologicheskoi Kompleksnoi Ekspeditsii* XII, 164–200.

Vince, A. Forthcoming. Pre-7th century pottery fabrics, in D. Gilbert and G. Puschnigg with contributions by A. Feuerbach, A. Vince and T. Williams, *The ceramics from Merv.* Volume 1 The Achaemenid to late Sasanian ceramics from Merv c 6th century BC to 7th century AD. Saffron Press.

Wiesehöfer, J. 2001. *Ancient Persia, from 550 BC to 650 AD.* London, I.B. Tauris.

Williams, T. and Kurbansakhatov, K. 2003. The Ancient Merv Project, Turkmenistan. Preliminary Report on the Second Season (2002). *Iran. Journal of the British Institute of Persian Studies* XLI, 139–170.

Zavyalov, V. A. 2007. The Fortifications of the City of Gyaur Kala, Merv, in J. Cribb and G. Herrmann, (eds.), *After Alexander: Central Asia before Islam,* 313–329. Oxford, Oxford University Press.

La céramique hellénistique en Asie centrale

Bertille Lyonnet

Abstract

After Alexander's difficult conquest over Central Asia, the Greeks maintained their control over the area for only about 150 years but, nevertheless, they left there, and for long, deep influences on the cultures that followed. Unfortunately, most of the Hellenistic cities like Bactra, Merv or Samarkand/Marakanda have been endlessly reoccupied afterwards and only a few give intelligible remains of this period. The site of Aï Khanoum in NE Afghanistan (Bactria) is one of them and several monuments have been excavated, the purpose, decoration and material of which – if not their architecture – is undoubtedly Greek. Almost constant relations with the Mediterranean homeland can be traced out. The article aims at presenting the pottery from this site as well as that of Marakanda (in Sogdiana), both studied by the author, and to date it anew according to the most recent research done about them.

Considering Aï Khanoum, after reviewing the previous dates that had been proposed while the site was being excavated (until 1978), new data is given on the basis of final studies made recently over the material from the House in the SW quarter on the one hand, and from the fill over the first construction level of the Herôon of Kineas – long considered as the most ancient excavated building on the site (AKh I) – on the other hand. This new data shows that the pottery from the Herôon, with already typical Greek shapes like kraterae, fish-plates, and echinus bowls, is most probably contemporaneous with that of the earliest level of the Temple with indented niches (AKh II) and that it cannot be dated earlier than Antiochos I's reign as stressed by numismatic discoveries. It also shows that the House in the SW quarter was not built before 200 BC (AKh IV), and that it is Antiochos III's Anabasis that led to the new impetus of relations with the homeland, with constant introduction of new wares and new fashions until Eucratides' death (AKh VIII), among which the moulded bowls during this last king's reign. As demonstrated long ago, the city was invaded and destroyed around 145 BC by different groups of nomads and only survived after that for a very short period of time.

At Marakanda, only a small part of the rampart and a grain-house have been excavated for this period, called Afrasiab II. Most of the material comes from mixed strata and pits in deep soundings. Our work follows that of previous ones done by our Russian colleagues but has led to a major difference in dates since comparisons with Aï Khanoum show that most of this material (Afrasiab IIA) is contemporaneous with that of the early levels of the Bactrian site (AKh I-III) and predates the innovations seen in Bactria after Antiochos III's Anabasis. Only a few shapes may be related to the time of Eucratides (Afrasiab IIB) but it is difficult to separate this phase from the next Afrasiab III period which lasted until the 1st c. AD. The gap in between IIA and IIB has been considered as a period of independence, contemporary to that of the Graeco-Bactrian kingdom under Diodotus. Recent illegal numismatic discoveries seem to confirm our hypothesis. Further work that we made on the material of another site in the Zeravshan Valley, Koktepe, has also allowed distinguishing a pottery group that can be related to the period of Alexander's conquest. Though still very close to that of the Achaemenid times (Afrasiab I), it is nevertheless different and some specific shapes are introduced like large bowls with a more or less flat horizontal rim, often polished, but it does not contain any kratera, fish plate nor echinus bowl. This material had already been observed by Russian colleagues and mentioned as Afrasiab IA and IB. It further confirms a later date for the introduction of fish plates and echinus bowls in Central Asia, which correlates with a date not anterior to Antiochos I's reign as is proposed now at Aï Khanoum.

Keywords: Central Asia, Aï Khanoum, Afrasiab, Herôon of Kineas, Eucratides, Antiochos I, Antiochos III, Bactria, Sogdiana, Megarian Bowls.

Introduction

Après la conquête particulièrement longue et difficile par Alexandre-le-Grand des territoires d'Asie centrale (**Fig. 1**), en particulier celui de la Sogdiane en 328–327 avant notre ère, la région fut reprise en mains par les Séleucides, connut un mouvement d'indépendance avec le royaume gréco-bactrien, fut reconquise par Antiochos III, puis connut encore des épisodes mouvementés et dissidents pendant la première moitié du 2e siècle avant d'être finalement envahie par plusieurs groupes de nomades venus du nord au milieu du même siècle.

Malgré la relative brièveté de la mainmise des Grecs sur ces territoires, environ 150 ans, les traces qu'ils y ont laissées sont remarquables et leur influence a subsisté pendant de nombreux siècles encore après leur disparition[1].

[1] Schlumberger 1960.

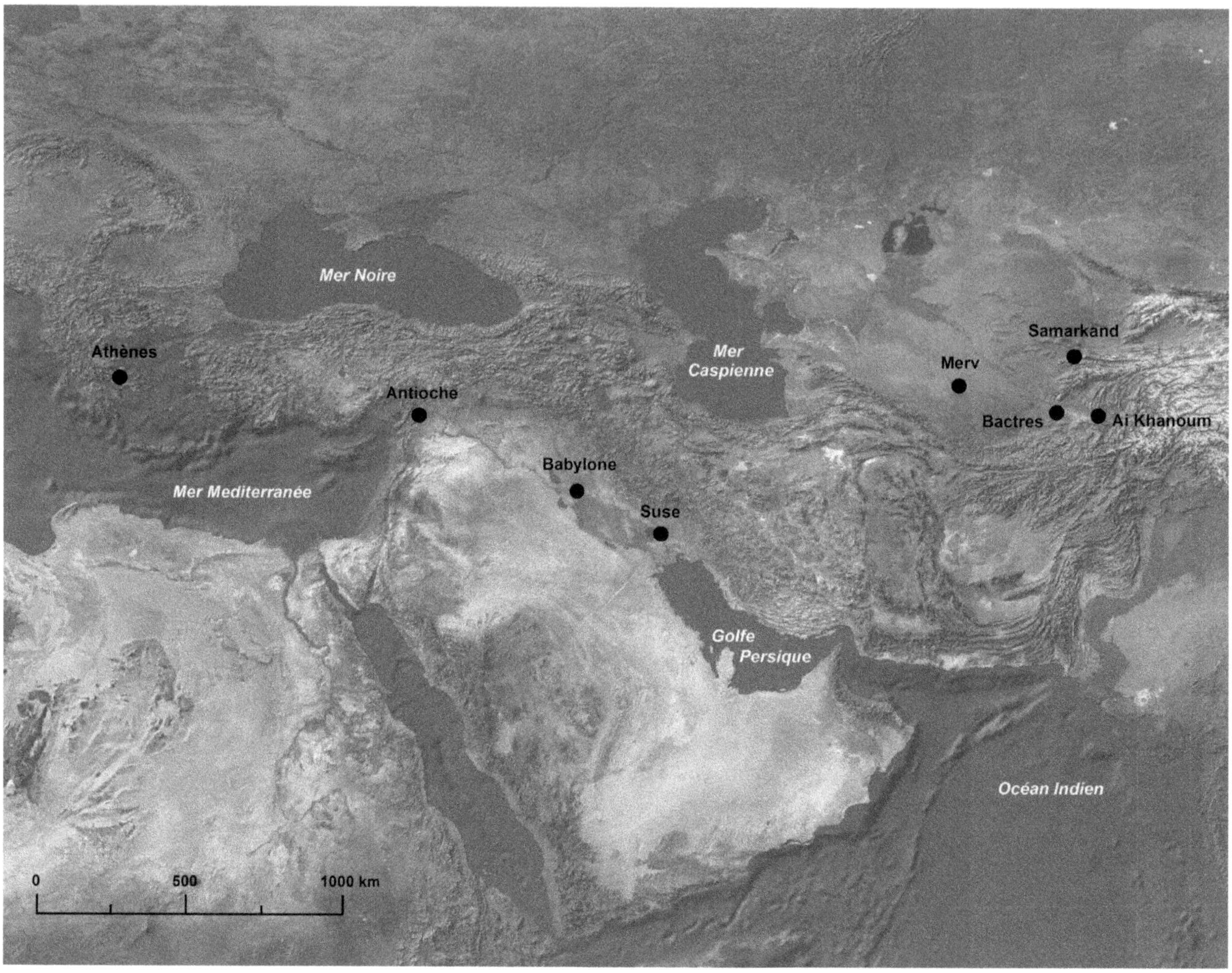

Fig. 1. Carte générale (S. Mantellini)

La ville d'Aï Khanoum, en Afghanistan du N.E., fouillée entre 1964 et 1978 sous la direction de P. Bernard, est l'un des sites qui ont livré les vestiges les plus nombreux de cette époque (Hérôon, temples, palais, théâtre, palestre, arsenal, maisons, rempart, etc.) car elle ne fut réoccupée que très brièvement immédiatement après la prise de la ville autour de 145 avant notre ère, puis fut définitivement abandonnée jusqu'à nos jours: les niveaux grecs y sont donc directement sous la surface. De nombreux autres sites d'Asie centrale ont également révélé des vestiges de cette époque, mais les plus importants comme Bactres ou Merv furent, eux, sans cesse réoccupés par la suite et les niveaux grecs ne peuvent y être atteints que dans des sondages profonds ne permettant guère d'y mettre au jour l'architecture associée et ne donnant qu'un matériel réduit en quantité et souvent mélangé: on connaît, à cet égard, le célèbre découragement d'A. Foucher devant les ruines de Bactres[2]. L'antique Samarkand, capitale de la Sogdiane, fait partie de ces sites majeurs et n'a livré à ce jour, pour cette époque, que quelques dizaines de mètres de remparts et un grenier à grains. Si l'architecture mise au jour n'est souvent pas d'origine grecque mais plutôt du type mésopotamien alors en vigueur, les chapiteaux, sculptures ou inscriptions, de même que la vaisselle utilisée, ne laissent, eux, aucun doute sur les habitants de ces cités. Bien que située à plusieurs milliers de kilomètres des rives de la Méditerranée, la Bactriane a maintenu avec la Grèce et l'Asie mineure des liens très étroits pendant toute la durée de la présence grecque, comme en témoignent l'apport presque constant et immédiat des nouveautés produites dans cette région[3].

L'un des problèmes majeurs qui se posèrent aux archéologues fut de dater avec précision les différentes phases architecturales observées et leur contenu. Les hypothèses ont sans cesse évolué en fonction de l'avancement des connaissances mais beaucoup de zones d'ombre n'ont pas été résolues.

[2] Foucher 1942, 73–75.

[3] Gardin 1985.

Le but de cet article est de présenter une vue générale du matériel céramique hellénistique d'Asie centrale sur la base de celui dont j'ai fait l'étude et qui fut mis au jour à la fois à Aï Khanoum, probablement l'ex-Eucratideia de Bactriane, et à Samarkand/Marakanda, capitale de la Sogdiane, en l'associant aux datations qui lui sont actuellement données sur la base des toutes dernières recherches.

Aï Khanoum

Le site se trouve en Afghanistan du Nord-Est, au confluent du Darya-i Panj, fleuve qui, un peu plus en aval, prend le nom d'Amou Darya, et de la Kokcha. Il fut (re)-découvert en 1961, peu de temps avant que D. Schlumberger, qui dirigeait la Délégation Archéologique Française en Afghanistan (D.A.F.A.), ne quitte le pays et que P. Bernard lui succède. Une première visite et les sondages qu'ils firent ensemble sur le site donnèrent lieu à une étude préliminaire de la céramique[4] qui donnait déjà l'essentiel du matériel.

Les fouilles conduites sous la direction de P. Bernard pendant 14 ans (1965–1978) n'ont jamais permis de connaître avec certitude le nom ancien de la ville ni de savoir dans quelle province, Bactriane ou Sogdiane, se trouvait la cité[5]. On admet, désormais, qu'elle se trouve en Bactriane[6]. Elles ne permirent pas, non plus, d'attribuer avec certitude une date à sa fondation. Une inscription grecque accompagnée d'une maxime delphique trouvée dès le début des fouilles, en 1966, dans un édifice funéraire placé au centre de la ville a seulement permis de considérer qu'il s'agissait là de l'Hérôon d'un certain Kinéas et de le dater du début du 3e siècle av. n. è.[7]. P. Bernard, quant à lui, a souvent considéré que la ville ne pouvait avoir été fondée que par Alexandre ou très peu de temps après[8], même s'il a également avancé la possibilité d'une date plus tardive, sous Séleucos I[9].

La date de la fin de la ville est, quant à elle, restée irrésolue jusqu'à la dernière année des fouilles, en 1978, lorsque fut découverte une inscription peinte sur un vase de la trésorerie mentionnant l'arrivée d'huile d'olive en 24 d'une ère inconnue mais qui ne pouvait être que celle d'Eucratide, le dernier roi attesté dans la ville. Ceci permit de conclure que la prise d'Aï Khanoum datait de l'année 146 ou 145 av. n. è.[10]. Après cette date fatidique, la ville fit l'objet d'une destruction systématique qui dura quelques années sans qu'on puisse en préciser la durée. Les bouleversements occasionnés par le démontage des murs de briques cuites et des colonnes de pierre provoquèrent une importante montée des sols mais le matériel céramique trouvé dans ce niveau de 'réoccupation tardive' est exactement identique à celui du dernier niveau grec, ce qui ne permet pas de proposer plus d'une décennie, voire moins, pour cette période de destruction et de réoccupation.

Des monnaies ont certes été trouvées en abondance au cours des fouilles et auraient dû permettre d'ancrer les divers niveaux fouillés à la chronologie absolue. Toutefois, ces trouvailles ont rarement été faites *in situ* et, de plus, un décalage malheureux entre leur identification et les études du matériel céramique faites sur le terrain n'a pas toujours permis de les mettre en relation en temps voulu. Si certaines monnaies datent de la fin du 4e ou tout début du 3e siècle av. n. è., l'essentiel sont des émissions d'Antiochos I, et le reste se répartit sans hiatus entre ce souverain et Eucratide I, le dernier roi dont les monnaies ont été mises au jour dans la ville[11].

Les fouilles ont livré une énorme quantité de tessons de céramique. Pour les traiter de façon rapide et raisonnée, J.-C. Gardin avait mis au point et appliqué un système typologique rigoureux[12] auquel j'ai participé. Le matériel de chaque monument fut donc systématiquement étudié chaque année et daté sur la base des datations globales adoptées alors pour la ville. Tant la typologie que la chronologie ont évolué d'année en année au fur et à mesure des découvertes[13].

En 1978, dernière année des fouilles, nous avions abouti à un tableau typo-chronologique répartissant le matériel en 8 périodes, depuis la plus ancienne (période I) datée alors entre 320 et 300 av. n. è. et correspondant au matériel trouvé dans un remblai ayant servi à la re-construction de l'Hérôon de Kinéas, jusqu'à la fin de l'occupation (y compris post-grecque) de la ville (période VIII) datée alors entre 160 et 145 av. n. è [14]. En l'absence d'indications précises qu'auraient pu donner des monnaies trouvées en place, ces périodes avaient arbitrairement été considérées d'égale durée (de 20 à 25 ans environ).

Chacune de ces périodes témoignait de l'introduction de nouveaux types grecs, certaines plus que d'autres. Les périodes I–III étaient caractérisées par une céramique essentiellement de couleur claire poursuivant la tradition locale précédente, mais parfois à engobe rouge; d'emblée y étaient attestées des formes typiquement grecques comme les assiettes à poisson, les bols à lèvre rentrante (echinus bowls) ou les cratères (voir **Fig. 2 à 4**). La période IV, quant à elle, témoignait des transformations les plus notoires avec l'introduction massive et soudaine d'une céramique de table gris-noir, de décors de palmettes autour d'un cercle incisé à l'intérieur des bols et des assiettes, et, semblait-il, de bols à décor moulé en relief[15]. D'autres innovations

4 Bernard 1965.
5 Bernard 1978, 3–15; Grenet et Rapin 2001; Lyonnet 1997, 154–155.
6 Grenet et Rapin 2001.
7 Robert 1973.
8 Bernard 1973 (dir),102–107; Bernard 1982.
9 Bernard 1985, 34.
10 Rapin 1983 ; Rapin 1992, 114.
11 Bernard 1985.
12 Gardin 1973.
13 Gardin 1971, Gardin 1985, Gardin et Lyonnet 1976.
14 Tableau publié dans Lyonnet 2001, fig. 1-1 à 1-4.
15 L'apparition de bols dits mégariens dès la période IV a été ensuite mise en doute (Lyonnet 2001). Une étude récente sur le matériel de la maison du quartier sud-ouest (voir *infra*) montre qu'ils n'y sont

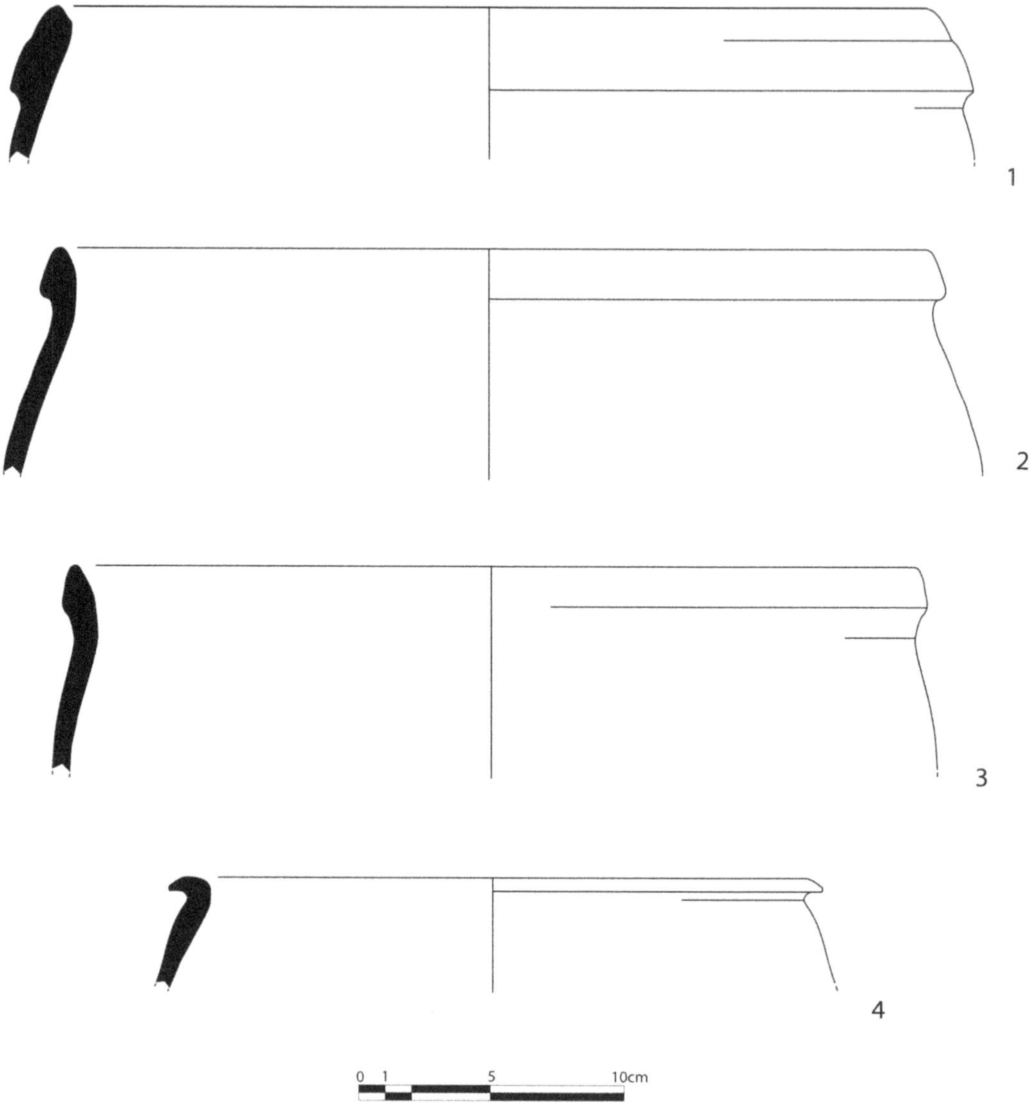

Fig. 2. Aï Khanoum, dans le remblai de reconstruction (2ème état) de l'Hérôon de Kinéas, grands vases fermés (jarres) (J.-B. Houal)

apparaissaient au cours des périodes V à VIII, comme les amphores, les cratères à paroi évasée, les œnochoés, etc. (voir **Fig. 5 à 9**).

En raison de la date alors adoptée pour la période I et du postulat émis sur l'égale durée de chaque période, la période IV était alors datée approximativement entre 260/250 et 240/225 avant notre ère.

Mis à part la première approche du matériel faite par P. Bernard lui-même après sa première visite sur le site et déjà mentionnée ci-dessus, puis une étude typologique sur le matériel des niveaux supérieurs des trois premières campagnes[16], et malgré toutes ces études faites annuellement sur la céramique, ne sont parues ensuite que des notes brèves et non illustrées sur les résultats en cours lors des comptes-rendus des fouilles faits par P. Bernard à l'Académie ainsi qu'une poignée d'autres articles. Une publication définitive était prévue et fut effectivement commencée vers la fin des années 1970 mais elle n'a finalement jamais vu le jour pour des raisons indépendantes de ma volonté. Toute une série de causes ont, ensuite, conduit à l'abandon des études sur ce matériel jusqu'en 2008: d'une part la fin subite des fouilles en raison de la guerre qui avait éclaté en Afghanistan, d'autre part le temps dévolu à la recherche sur le matériel de la prospection faite dans toute la région de Bactriane orientale[17], et, enfin, le retrait de J.-C. Gardin des activités archéologiques tandis que je me consacrais à d'autres lieux dans le monde ainsi qu'à d'autres périodes. Seule ma participation à l'étude du matériel des

attestés que dans le tout dernier état (période VIII).

16 Gardin 1973.

17 Lyonnet 1997.

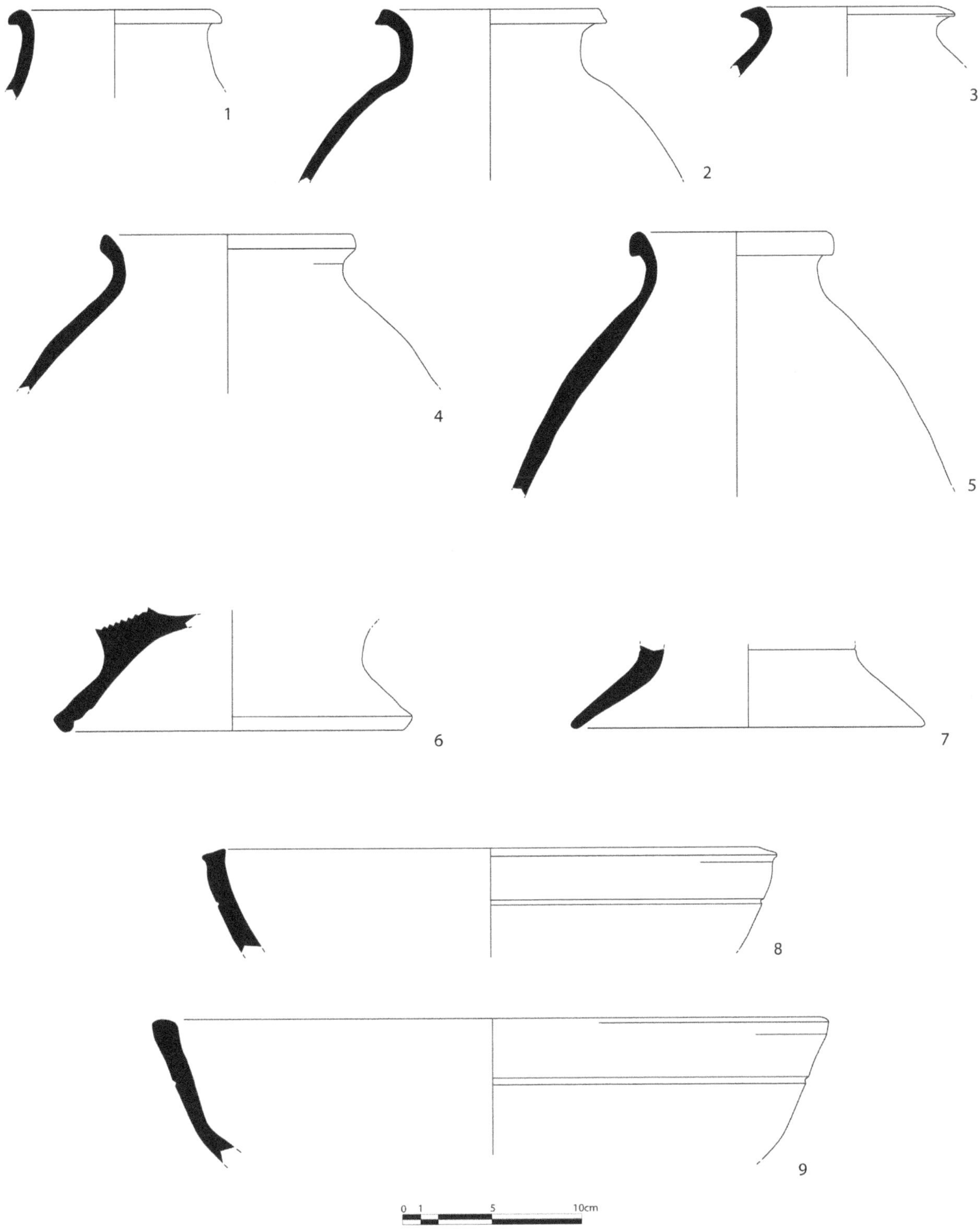

Fig. 3. Aï Khanoum, dans le remblai de reconstruction (2ème état) de l'Hérôon de Kinéas, grands vases fermés (cruches) et ouverts (pieds de cratères, terrines) (J.-B. Houal)

fouilles de l'ancienne Samarkand à partir de 1992 (voir infra) m'ont permis de conserver un lien avec ce matériel.

En 2008, P. Bernard m'a demandé de participer à la publication de la maison du quartier sud-ouest que préparait G. Lecuyot[18]. Il pensait qu'il suffirait de reprendre ce que Gardin avait brièvement publié à ce sujet[19] et de l'illustrer.

[18] Lecuyot, à paraître.
[19] Gardin 1970, 1971.

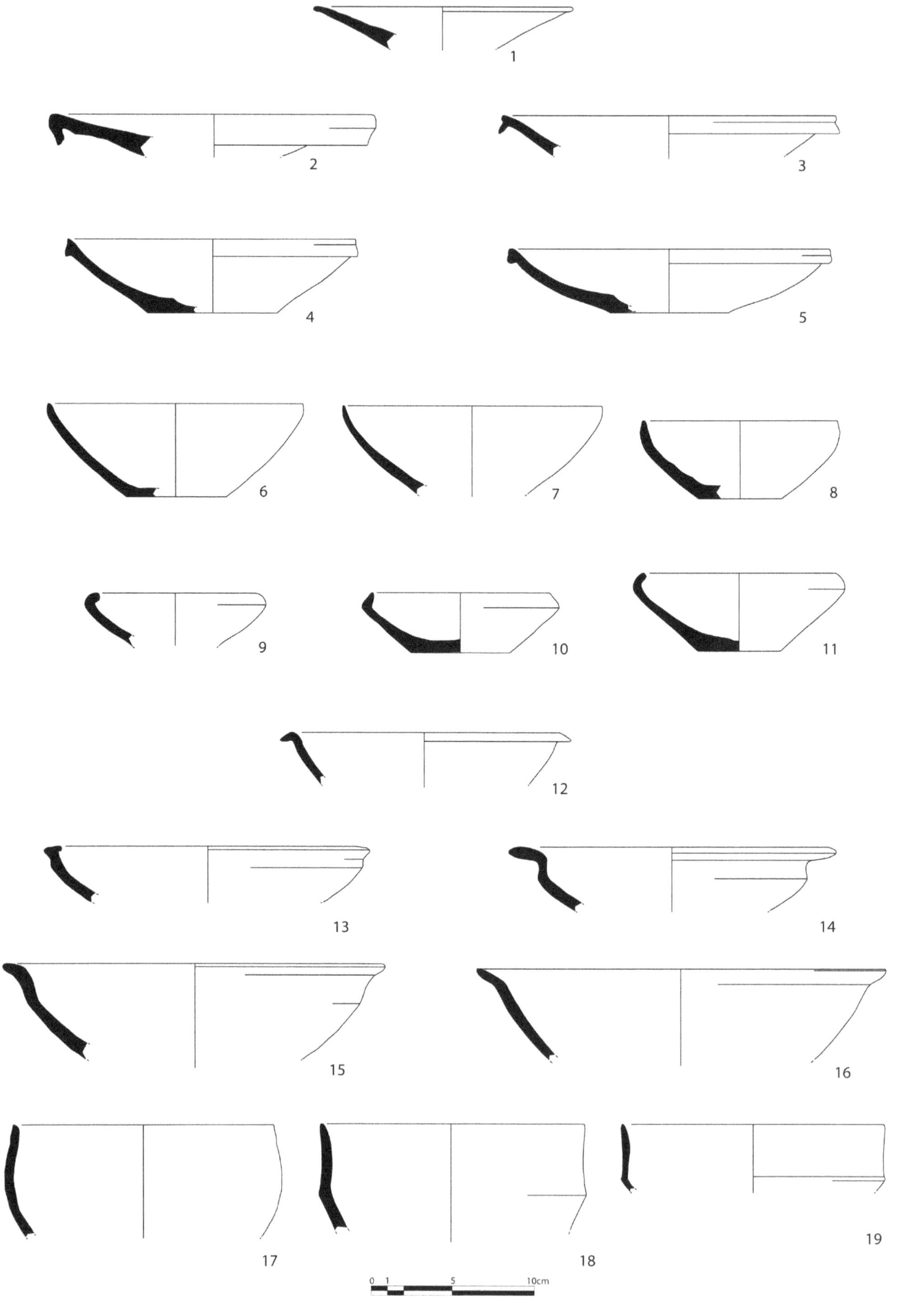

Fig. 4. Aï Khanoum, dans le remblai de reconstruction (2ème état) de l'Hérôon de Kinéas, petite céramique de table. J.-C. (J.-B. Houal)

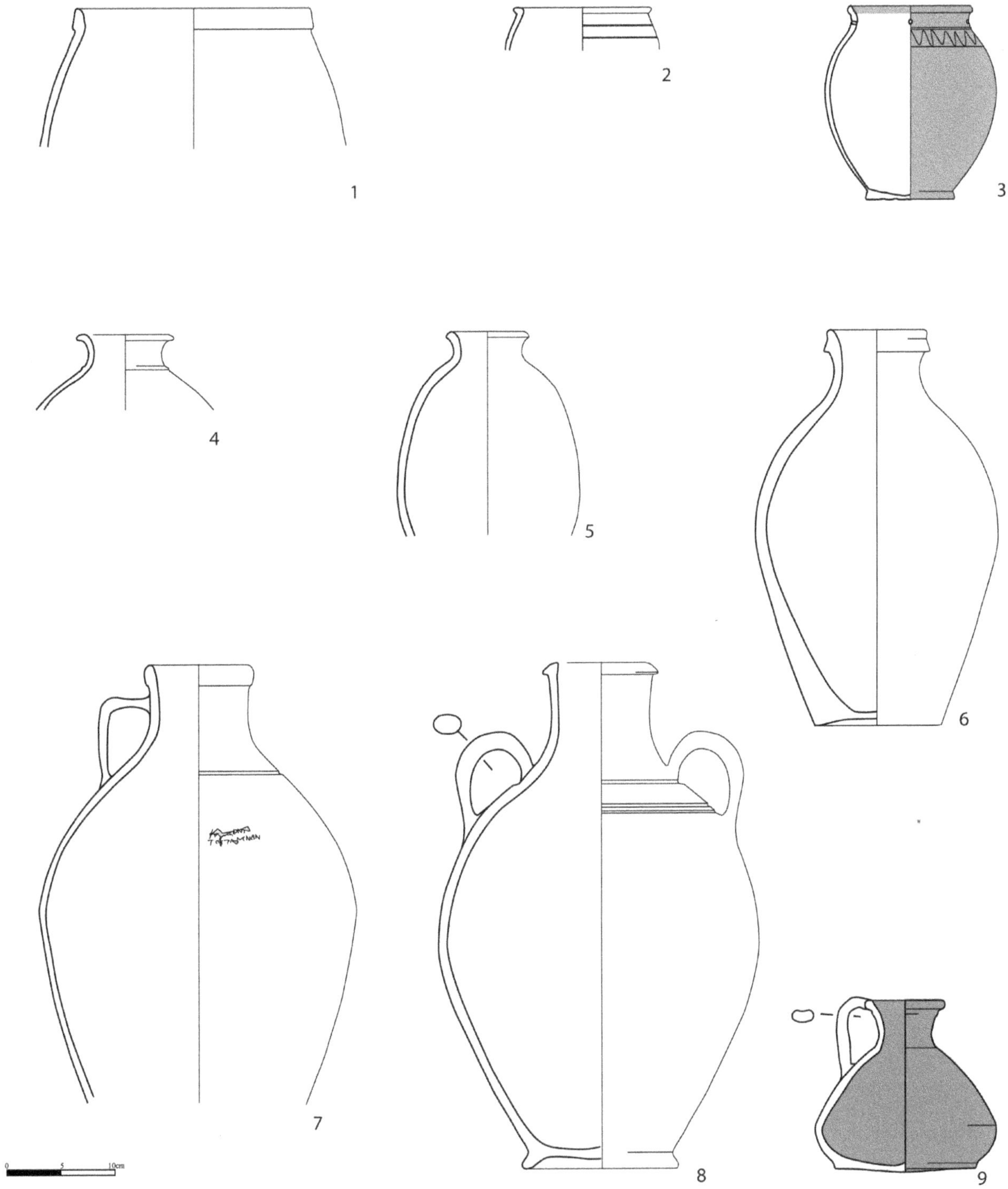

Fig. 5. Aï Khanoum, maison du quartier sud-ouest (tous niveaux confondus), grands vases fermés (J.-B. Houal)

Il apparut très vite, cependant, que le travail devait être revu de façon plus approfondie en fonction des publications parues depuis trente ans, en particulier celles concernant la date d'apparition des bols moulés en relief[20] et celles portant sur les céramiques de table et commune de l'Agora d'Athènes[21]: c'est d'ailleurs aussi ce qu'avaient souligné certaines critiques formulées par J. D. Lerner[22].

Cinq états architecturaux principaux ont été mis au jour dans cette maison, les plus anciens n'ayant été fouillés que

20 Rotroff 1982; Rotroff 2006b.

21 Rotroff 1997; Rotroff 2006a.

22 Lerner 2003–2004; Lerner 2005; Lerner 2010.

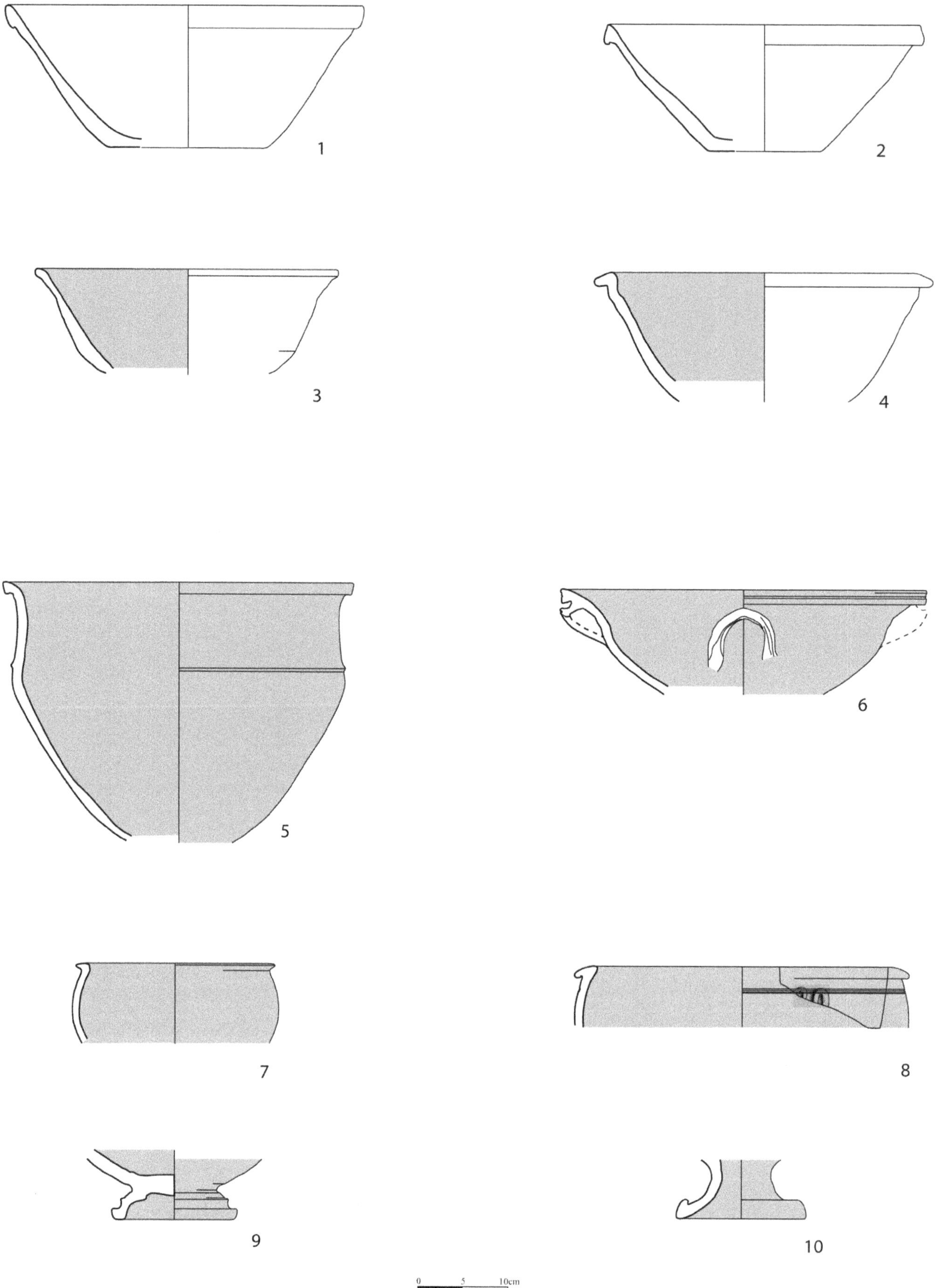

Fig. 6. Aï Khanoum, maison du quartier sud-ouest (tous niveaux confondus), grands vases ouverts (J.-B. Houal)

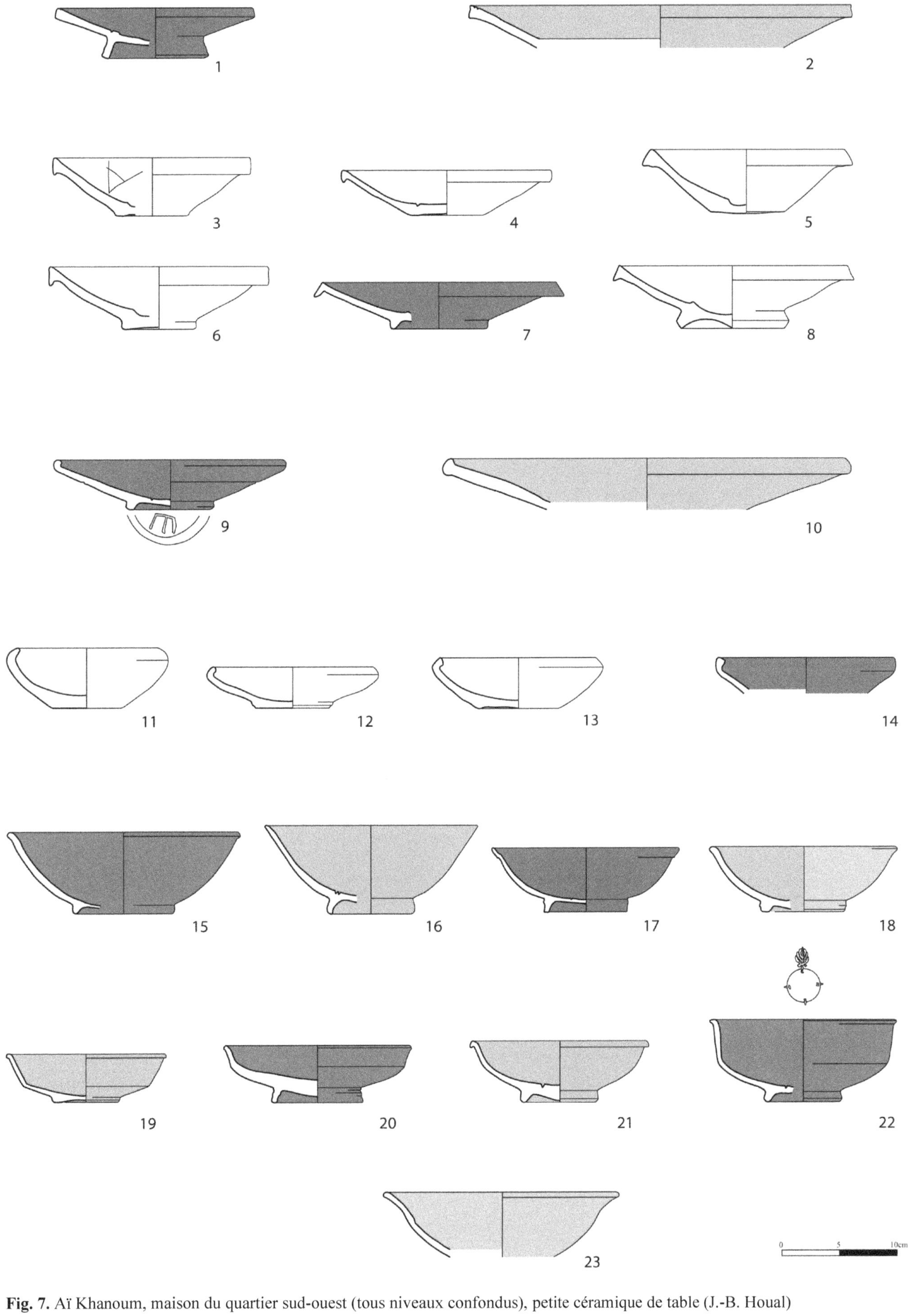

Fig. 7. Aï Khanoum, maison du quartier sud-ouest (tous niveaux confondus), petite céramique de table (J.-B. Houal)

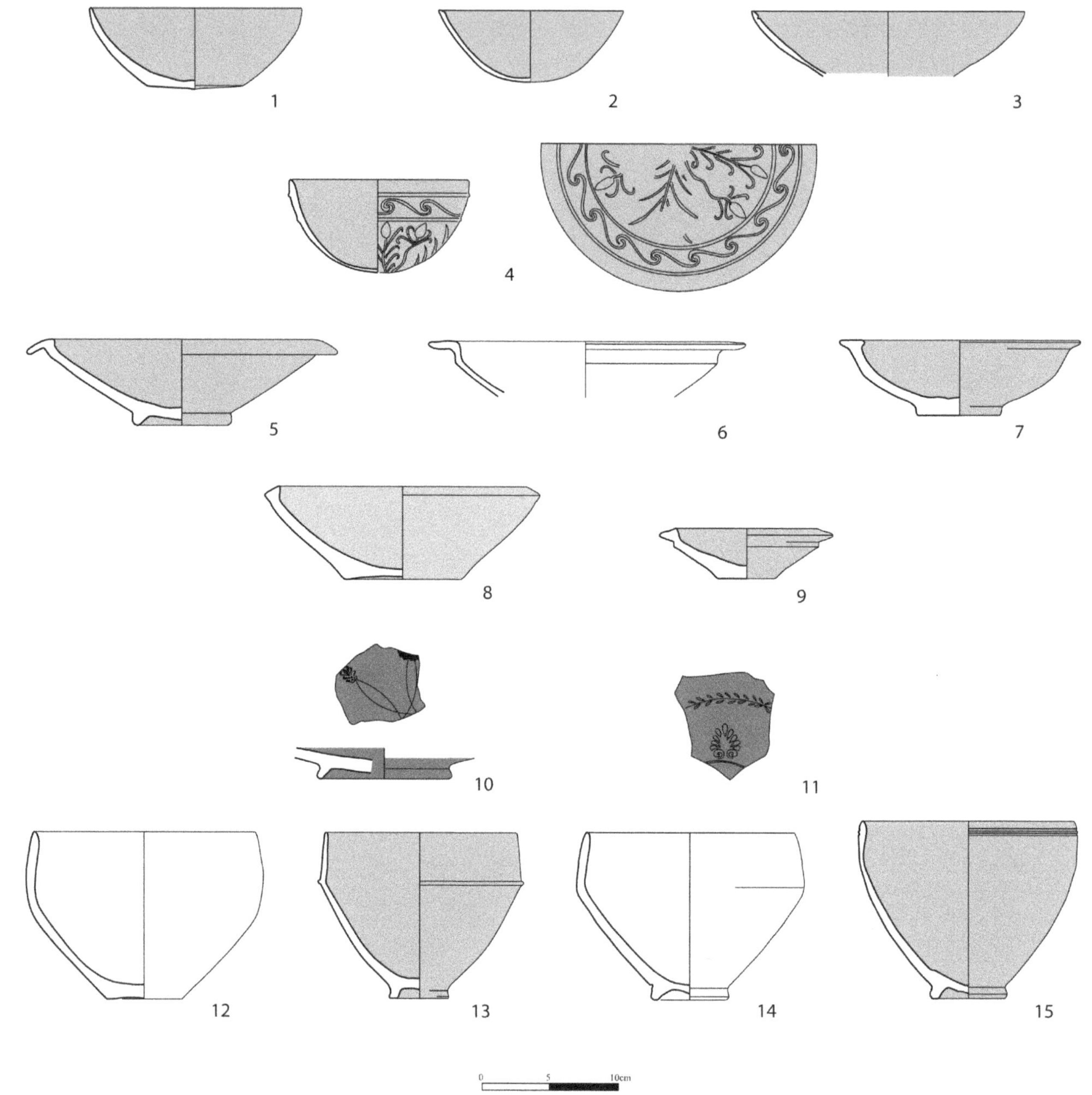

Fig. 8. Aï Khanoum, maison du quartier sud-ouest (tous niveaux confondus), petite céramique de table (suite) (J.-B. Houal)

très partiellement. Dès l'origine, la céramique gris-noir et le décor de palmettes estampés y sont attestés[23], ce qui place cet édifice entre les périodes IV et VIII de la ville.

Un nouvel examen de la provenance des tessons de bols à décor moulé montre qu'ils proviennent tous du dernier état grec.

En me fondant à la fois sur des comparaisons faites avec certaines formes du matériel d'Athènes et sur les propositions de S. I. Rotroff quant à l'apparition et à la diffusion de ces derniers, j'ai été conduite à considérer que l'état le plus ancien de cette maison ne pouvait pas dater d'avant 200 av. n. è. En conséquence, il est très probable, comme l'avait avancé Lerner, que les importantes innovations observées avec la période IV soient dues à la reconquête de la Bactriane par Antiochos III et non à l'installation de colons sous l'impulsion d'Antiochos I comme je l'avais proposé[24]. Certes, ceci implique de placer en un demi-siècle à peine de très nombreuses réfections et reconstructions qui eurent lieu dans cette maison, mais ce cas avait déjà été

[23] Les tessons des figures 5 à 9 proviennent tous de cette maison et sont donc tous datés des périodes IV à VIII.

[24] Lyonnet 1997, 148.

Fig. 9. Aï Khanoum, maison du quartire sud-ouest (tous niveaux confondus), décors sur la céramique de table (DAFA)

soulevé par P. Bernard pour le quartier administratif dès 1967. Cette étude sur la poterie de la maison et le catalogue abondamment illustré qui l'accompagne sont prêts pour publication depuis la fin 2009 mais n'ont pas encore franchi le seuil de l'imprimeur pour des raisons à nouveau indépendantes de ma volonté[25]. Depuis, j'ai également repris le matériel céramique de l'Hérôon de Kinéas qui était fréquemment mentionné, puisque considéré comme le plus ancien du site, mais qui n'avait encore jamais fait l'objet d'une publication détaillée. Cet édifice funéraire, situé au centre de la ville, près du palais, a été l'un des premiers monuments mis au jour à Aï Khanoum. La fouille a montré qu'il avait fait l'objet de plusieurs reconstructions et agrandissement. Trois états grecs y ont été répertoriés, suivis d'une réoccupation (état 4) où le bâtiment est transformé en habitation immédiatement après la chute de la ville. La pierre inscrite mentionnant Kinéas n'a pas été trouvée en place, mais remployée dans l'état 4. Aucune poterie n'était apparemment associée à l'état initial. Celle qui a été étudiée dès 1969 provient d'unremblai installé pour transformer le podium à degré du bâtiment initial en une terrasse (deuxième état).

[25] Lyonnet, à paraître.

Dans la très courte description qu'il donnait dans son article, Gardin[26] parlait d'environ un millier de tessons. Sa remarque essentielle consistait à y souligner d'une part l'absence de céramique gris-noir et de certaines formes caractéristiques de la vaisselle des niveaux supérieurs et, inversement, la présence de formes connues à l'époque achéménide comme les gobelets à flancs verticaux fortement anguleux. Ces deux constats l'avaient conduit, alors, à considérer ce matériel comme étant le plus ancien de la ville, et, en conséquence, à adopter les mêmes dates que celles qui étaient proposées pour le monument funéraire d'après l'inscription (voir ci-dessus). A ce moment de la fouille, un hiatus apparaissait entre ce matériel et celui du niveau inférieur de la maison du quartier sud-ouest, mais celui-ci fut comblé lorsqu'on mit au jour les niveaux inférieurs du temple à redans. Toutefois, une comparaison que j'avais réalisée au cours de la dernière année de fouilles (1978) entre le matériel de l'Hérôon et celui du niveau le plus ancien du temple montrait qu'il n'y avait probablement pas lieu de distinguer chronologiquement les deux assemblages. Cette analyse est malheureusement restée inédite, puis fut oubliée.

La nouvelle étude faite sur ce matériel[27] double le nombre de tessons du remblai en y incluant les fragments atypiques, ce qui ne fait que souligner davantage l'absence de céramique grise[28]. Elle corrige aussi certaines erreurs d'attribution, les tessons pris pour des gobelets à flanc anguleux étant plus probablement des éléments de canalisation à ressaut permettant leur emboîtement, difficiles à dater. Elle confirme surtout qu'il n'y a pas lieu d'attribuer cet ensemble à une période antérieure à celle du niveau inférieur du temple à redans. Or, ce niveau est désormais daté avec certitude du règne d'Antiochos I grâce à l'identification de quatre monnaies de ce souverain[29] qui n'étaient malheureusement pas encore connues à l'époque où nous faisions notre étude. C'est à une conclusion similaire, comme nous allons le voir, que j'avais abouti au même moment grâce à l'étude de la céramique de l'ancienne Samarkand.

Marakanda

Les fouilles du site de l'antique Samarkand, actuellement dénommé Afrasiab, lieu d'un épisode tragique de la vie d'Alexandre puisque c'est là qu'il y a assassiné son ami Cléitos, ont commencé dès la fin du XIXe s.

Cette ville de plus de 200 ha, capitale de la Sogdiane, dont les débuts en tant que ville fortifiée remontent à la période achéménide (Afrasiab I), a vécu sans interruption jusqu'à la conquête mongole en 1220. Les niveaux hellénistiques (Afrasiab II) y sont surtout connus depuis les années 1960[30] et 1970[31]. Seules les fouilles associées au rempart de la citadelle ont fourni du matériel à peu près en place, mais aucune monnaie n'ayant jamais été trouvée associée[32], les datations pour l'occupation hellénistique sont restées imprécises et ont changé au cours du temps: situées entre le 3e et le 1er s. av. n. è. à la fin des années 1960, puis entre la fin du 4e et le 2e s. av. n. è. dans les années 1970, il a ensuite été proposé qu'elle ne puisse dater que du 3e s. av. n. è., car un nouvel assemblage, intermédiaire entre la céramique purement 'achéménide': et la céramique hellénistique, venait d'être mis au jour[33].

Le matériel céramique de la période Afrasiab II découvert par nos collègues est essentiellement en pâte claire, sans décor, et seuls de rares cas sont spécifiés être de couleur gris-noir[34] ou à engobe noir sur pâte rouge[35]. Il comprend des formes typiquement grecques comme les assiettes à poisson à dépression intérieure, les bols à lèvre rentrante (echinus bowl), ou les cratères[36].

Les transformations politiques des années 80, qui ont conduit à la fois à la guerre en Afghanistan et à la chute de l'Union Soviétique, m'ont conduite à travailler sur le matériel des fouilles désormais menées par la Mission Archéologique Française en Ouzbékistan (MAFOuz), sous la direction de F. Grenet.

Pas plus que pour nos prédécesseurs, il ne fut possible de trouver en place des bâtiments de cette époque mis à part le rempart[37] et un vaste grenier incendié contenant encore des graines d'orge et de millet[38]. Néanmoins, le matériel céramique qui fut mis au jour, bien que rarement en place, a permis d'avancer le point de vue d'une période hellénistique répartie en deux phases (Afrasiab IIA et IIB) séparées par un hiatus[39].

La phase IIA fut mise en relation avec les trois premières périodes d'Aï Khanoum en raison de l'absence de céramique gris-noir et de décors autres que l'engobe rouge et le lissage (**Fig. 10, Fig. 11, *1-9*, Fig. 12**). Les similitudes avec le matériel du niveau profond de l'Hérôon furent en particulier soulignées.

26 Gardin 1970.
27 Lyonnet, sous presse. Les figures 2 à 4 donnent les formes principales trouvées dans le remblai de l'état 2 de l'Hérôon.
28 Quelques anomalies ont cependant été notées, dont trois tessons de céramique gris-noir, qui avaient été (et sont) considérés comme erratiques car probablement issus des couches supérieures.
29 Martinez-Sève 2010.

30 Filanovich 1969; Kabanov 1969; Nemtseva 1969.
31 Shishkina 1974; Shishkina 1975; Shishkina 1994.
32 Les monnaies de la période hellénistique sont particulièrement rares sur le site d'Afrasiab. Seules 5 ont été mentionnées dans une publication assez récente – Seleucos I, Antiochos I, Antiochos I ou II, Euthydème I et peut-être Eucratide (Najmark 2005), mais leur provenance est loin d'être assurée. De nouvelles découvertes ont toutefois nettement augmenté le nombre de trouvailles (voir *infra).*
33 Kabanov 1981.
34 Kabanov 1973, 61
35 Shishkina 1975.
36 Un cratère en pâte très cuite, grise, à engobe brun et à décor d'oves estampées sur le bord a été découvert par Kabanov (1981, fig. 23, 18). Il est repris dans Shishkina 1979, fig. 7, 4, et Shishkina 1994, fig. 3, mais le tesson en question n'a jamais pu être retrouvé. Aucun autre fragment de cratère de cette forme ou portant un décor similaire n'a jamais été observé dans la ville, ni lors des fouilles soviétiques, ni dans celles de la Mission Archéologique Française en Ouzbékistan (MAFOuz).
37 Bernard 1996; Rapin et Isamiddinov 1994.
38 Baratin et Martinez-Sève, sous presse.
39 Lyonnet 2001.

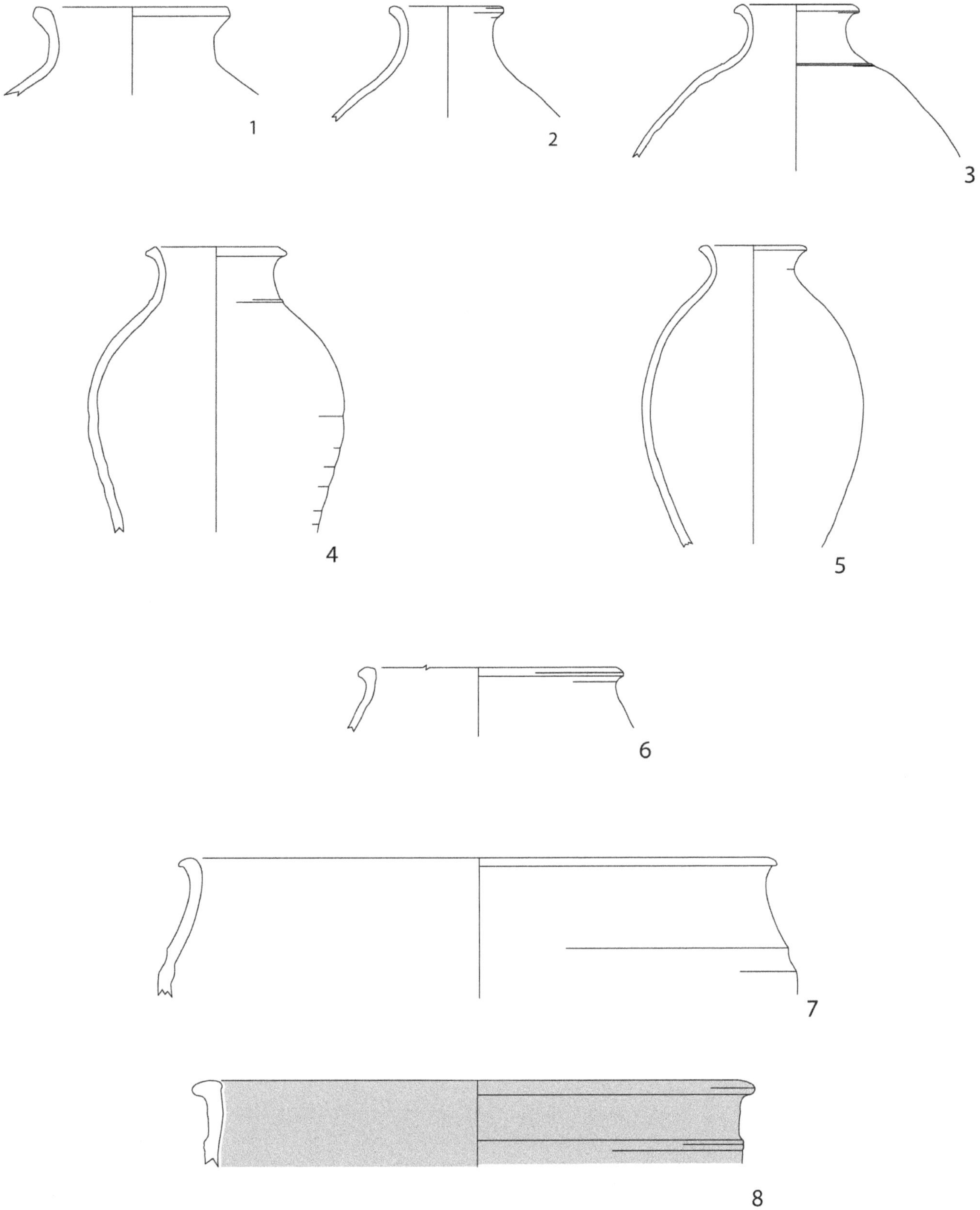

Fig. 10. Afrasiab IIA, grands vases fermés et ouverts (J.-B. Houal)

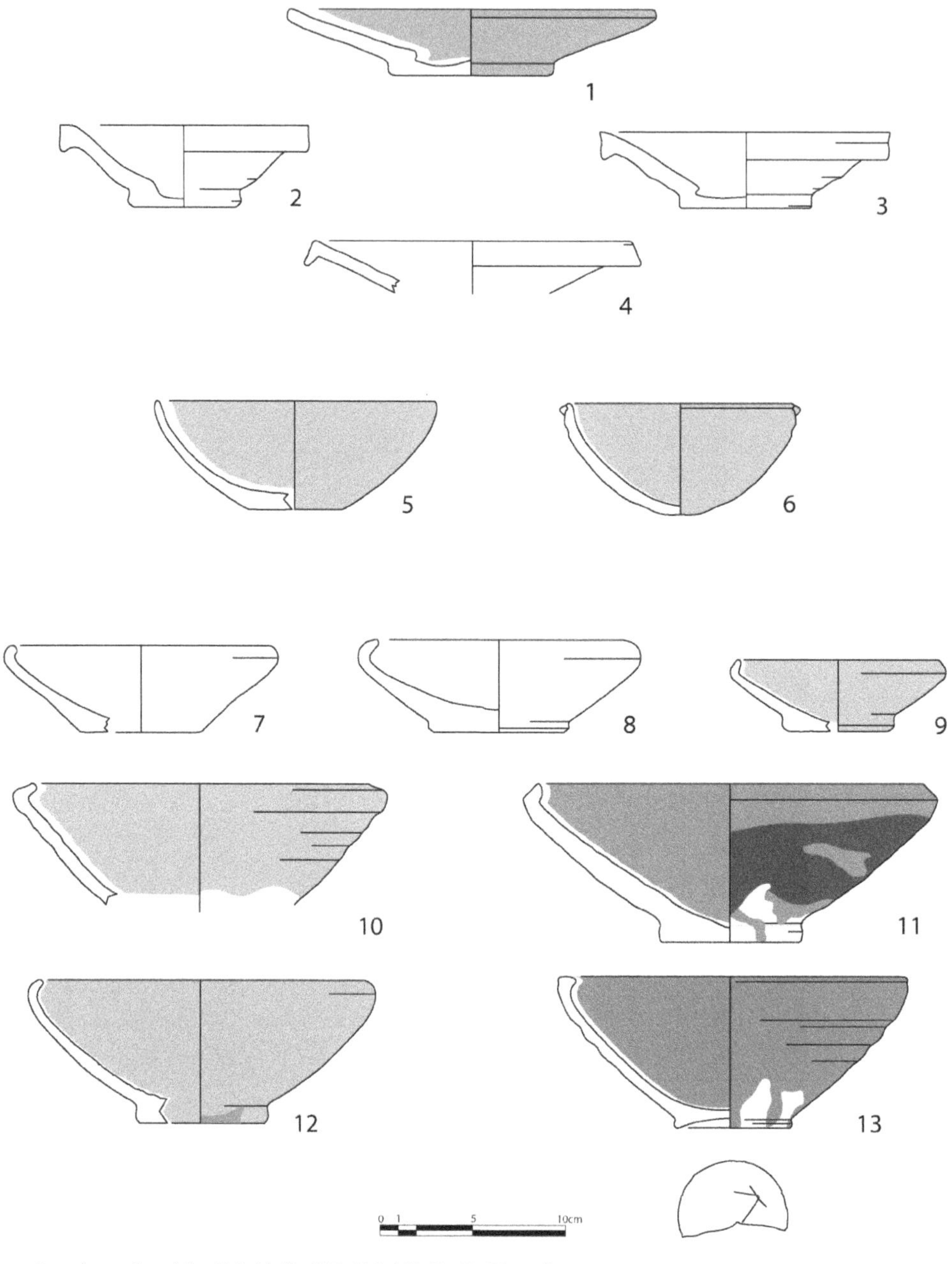

Fig. 11. Afrasiab, petite céramique de table: IIA (1-9), IIB (10-13) (J.-B. Houal)

La phase IIB, quant à elle, semblait de très courte durée, et fut rapprochée de la dernière période d'Aï Khanoum en raison de la présence d'œnochoés, et de bols à bord rentrant de grande taille couverts d'un engobe brun-rouge (**Fig. 11, 10-13**). Toutefois, même dans cette seconde phase, aucune trace de céramique gris-noir n'a été observée et les seuls rares cas de présence de cette céramique semblent ne dater que d'une période ultérieure, Afrasiab III, aux environs de notre ère[40]. Il a également été souligné que les phases IIB et III étaient très difficiles à distinguer, mis à part par l'apparente absence de gobelets sur piédouche dans la première.

Comme pour Aï Khanoum, la question de la date absolue de la phase Afrasiab IIA a évolué entre 2001 et 2010 en fonction des nouvelles recherches. En 2001, je considérais encore possible qu'Afrasiab IIA puisse dater de la période qui suivit immédiatement la conquête d'Alexandre. Toutefois, dans un article paru en 2010, je proposais de reporter cette date au règne d'Antiochos I.

En effet, l'étude finalisée du matériel d'un autre site fouillé par la MAFOuz en Sogdiane, Koktepe, a montré qu'aucune assiette à poisson[41] ni aucun bol à lèvre rentrante n'étaient attestés dans son dernier niveau pourtant considéré comme grec en raison de la taille des briques qui le caractérisaient,

[40] voir Lyonnet 2001, notes 39 et 42.

[41] Un seul cas est attesté.

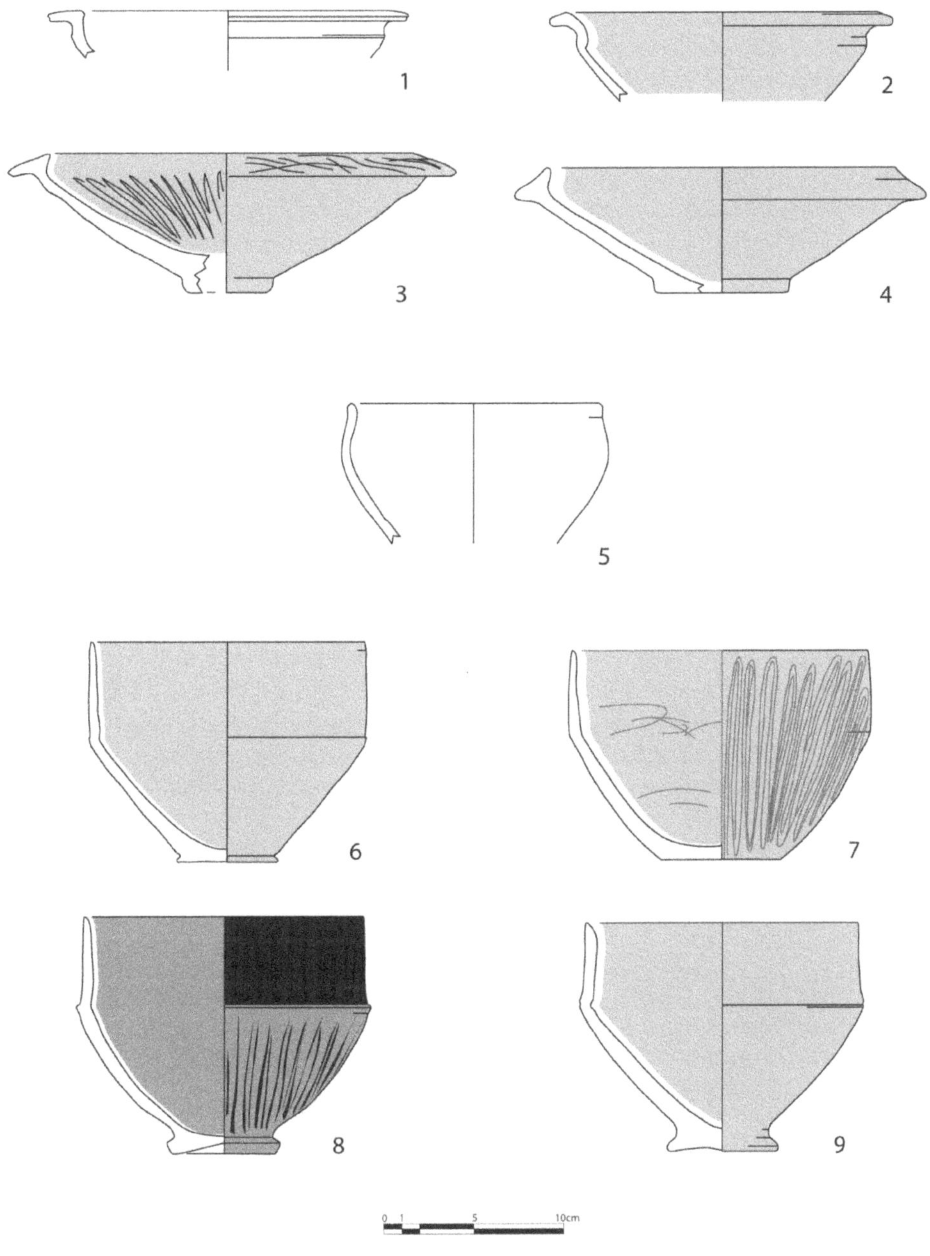

Fig. 12. Afrasiab IIA, petite céramique de table (suite) (J.-B. Houal)

mais qu'on y trouvait, en revanche, des formes qu'il est possible de considérer comme transitionnelles avec la période achéménide précédente. Si cet assemblage n'apparaît pas aussi clairement dans les fouilles franco-ouzbèques faites dans la ville haute d'Afrasiab, un matériel similaire avait pourtant déjà été observé à Afrasiab dans un chantier de la ville basse[42] ainsi que, en périphérie de la ville, sur un établissement de potier[43]. Depuis, il a également été identifié sur la forteresse de Kurganzol considérée comme étant l'une de celles qui ont résisté à Alexandre lors de sa conquête[44]. Dans la mesure où l'on pouvait matérialiser par un assemblage céramique la période qui suivit la conquête d'Alexandre, il devenait donc possible de dater du règne d'Antiochos I celui que j'attribuais à Afrasiab IIA.

La question de l'indépendance de la Sogdiane après son règne et celui de son fils, donc à peu près au moment où la Bactriane s'érigeait en royaume gréco-bactrien sous Diodote I[45], reste d'actualité. En effet, il a été récemment fait état de 26 nouvelles découvertes de monnaies hellénistiques sur le site d'Afrasiab, faites par des méthodes illégales sur tout le site[46] et dont seules quelques-unes ont été publiées à ce jour[47]: 17 se situent entre les règnes d'Alexandre et d'Antiochos I, cinq sont disputées par les numismates

42 Kabanov 1981.
43 Ivanitskij 1992
44 Sverchkov 2008.
45 Lyonnet 2001.
46 Atakhodzhaev, communication personnelle, à paraître.
47 Atakhodzhaev 2005.

entre Antiochos II ou Diodote I, auxquelles s'ajoutent une Diodote I, et trois autres qui pourraient être soit des Antiochos III soit des émissions encore mal connues d'Antiochos I[48]. La monnaie d'Euthydème publiée par Najmark[49] est contestée par Atakhodzhaev[50]. Les imitations des monnaies d'Antiochos I, qui certes ont eu une longue durée de vie dans la région, sont par ailleurs fort nombreuses.

La différence très nette dans le nombre de monnaies grecques découvertes sur Marakanda avant et après le règne des Antiochos est suffisamment claire pour confirmer le point de vue que nous avions avancé, même si l'on peut admettre que l'indépendance ne se soit manifestée qu'au cours du règne des Diodote.

La question de la date précise de notre assemblage IIB reste posée. Il n'y a aucune monnaie d'Eucratide parmi les trouvailles récentes et la provenance de celle qui figure parmi les découvertes anciennes n'est pas du tout assurée. Néanmoins, la reconquête de la Sogdiane sous ce souverain, si elle a bien eu lieu, n'a été que de très courte durée avant l'arrivée des nomades qui mirent définitivement fin à la présence grecque en Asie centrale. Il est donc difficile de trancher et seule la poursuite de l'analyse de la poterie d'Afrasiab en lien avec les données stratigraphiques permettra peut-être de résoudre la question.

Conclusion

Les recherches faites au cours de nombreuses années sur le matériel céramique hellénistique de deux sites majeurs d'Asie centrale, Aï Khanoum en Bactriane, et Marakanda en Sogdiane, n'ont pas permis d'assurer la date précise de l'apparition de certaines innovations. Le dernier état de la question montre que les formes de vaisselle caractéristiques du monde grec comme les assiettes à poisson ou les cratères ne seraient pas apparues immédiatement après la conquête d'Alexandre, mais seulement après quelques décennies, à l'époque du règne d'Antiochos I lorsque des colons commencèrent à investir les lieux. D'autres innovations importantes ne se seraient produites qu'après la reconquête d'Antiochos III. Ce décalage peut se comparer avec les transformations observées dans la poterie d'Asie centrale après la conquête arabe (autour de 720) où, par exemple, ce n'est qu'au début du 9e s. qu'apparaît la céramique à glaçure.

Malgré la brièveté de l'épisode grec dans l'histoire de l'Asie centrale, l'influence qu'il exercera au cours des siècles suivants est remarquable. Si aucune trace n'est plus visible à Aï Khanoum, qui fut détruite et abandonnée peu de temps après la fin d'Eucratide, le matériel mis au jour à Afrasiab et qui caractérise la période III témoigne, lui, d'une influence directe tant dans ses formes que dans ses décors. A cette époque, il est vrai, le commerce circulant le long de la route de la Soie a pu entretenir, voire renouveler, cette influence par l'intermédiaire du monde romain.

Bertille Lyonnet
CNRS
UMR 7192
52 rue du Cardinal Lemoine
75005 Paris
blyonnet@wanadoo.fr

Bibliographie

Atakhodzhaev, A. Kh. 2005. Ranneantichnye monety s gorodishcha Afrasiab (novye nakhodki). In K. A. Abdullaev (ed.), *Materialy po antichnoj kul'ture Uzbekistana. K 70-letiju G.A. Koshelenko*, 33–36. Samarkand, Institute of Ar chaeology.

Baratin, C. and Martinez-Sève, L. sous presse. Le grenier grec de Samarkand. *Cahiers d'Asie Centrale*.

Bernard, P. 1965. Deuxième partie. Les trouvailles. Céramique, vases en pierre, éléments de couverture, autres fragments architecturaux, in D. Schlumberger et P. Bernard, Aï Khanoum. *Bulletin de Correspondance Hellénique* 89, 604–657.

Bernard, P. 1967. Deuxième campagne de fouilles d'Aï Khanoum. *Comptes rendus de l'Académie des Inscriptions et Belles-Lettres*, 306–324.

Bernard, P. (dir.) 1973. *Fouilles d'Aï Khanoum I (campagnes 1965, 1966, 1967, 1967)*. Mémoires de la-Délégation Archéologique Française en Afghanistan 21. Paris, Klincksieck.

Bernard, P. 1978. Le nom de la ville grecque du Tepe Aï Khanoum, in P. Bernard and H.-P. Francfort, *Etude de géographie historique sur la plaine d'Aï Khanoum (Afghanistan)*. Paris, CNRS.

Bernard, P. 1982. Alexandre et Aï Khanoum, *Journal des Savants*, Avril-Juin, 125–138.

Bernard, P. 1985. *Fouilles d'Aï Khanoum IV. Les monnaies hors trésors. Questions d'histoire gréco-bactrienne.* Mémoires de la Délégation Archéologique Française en Afghanistan 28. Paris, De Boccard.

Bernard, P. 1996. Maracanda-Afrasiab, colonie grecque de Sogdiane. In *La Persia et l'Asia Centrale da Allessandro al X Secolo, Atti dei Convegni Lincei* 127, 331–365. Roma, Accademia Nazionale dei Lincei.

Filanovich, M. 1969. K kharakteristike drevnejshego poselenija na Afrasiabe. In Ja. G. Guljamov (ed.),

[48] Information de F. Grenet, que je remercie.
[49] *Supra*, note 31.
[50] Voir Lyonnet, sous presse, note 42.

Afrasiab I, 206–220. Tashkent, Fan.
Foucher, A. 1942. *La vieille route de l'Inde de Bactres à Taxila*, vol. I. Mémoires de la Délégation Archéologique Française en Afghanistan 1. Paris, Éd. d'Art et d'Histoire.
Gardin, J.-C. 1970. La céramique. In P. Bernard, Campagne de fouilles 1969 à Aï Khanoum. *Comptes rendus de l'Académie des Inscriptions et Belles-Lettres*, 347–349.
Gardin, J.-C. 1971. Céramique. In P. Bernard, La campagne de fouilles 1970 à Aï Khanoum. *Comptes rendus de l'Académie des Inscriptions et Belles-Lettres*, 447–452.
Gardin, J.-C. 1973. Les céramiques. In P. Bernard (ed.), *Fouilles d'Aï Khanoum I (campagnes 1965, 1966, 1967, 1968)*. Mémoires de la Délégation Archéologique Française en Afghanistan 21, 121–188 et pl. 113–143. Paris, Klincksieck.
Gardin, J.-C. 1985. Les relations entre la Méditerranée et la Bactriane dans l'antiquité, d'après des données céramologiques inédites, in J.-L. Huot, M. Yon et Y. Calvet (ed.), *De l'Indus aux Balkans, Recueil à la mémoire de J. Deshayes*, 447–460. Paris, ERC.
Gardin, J.-C. et Lyonnet, B. 1976. La céramique, in P. Bernard, H.-P. Francfort, J.-C. Gardin, J.-C. Liger, B. Lyonnet et S. Veuve, Fouilles d'Aï Khanoum. Campagne de 1974. *Bulletin de l'Ecole Française d'Extrême-Orient* 63, 45–51.
Grenet, F. et Rapin, C. 1998 [2001]. Alexander, Aï Khanum, Termez: remarks on the spring campaign of 328. *Bulletin of the Asia Institute* 12, 79–89.
Ivanitskij, I. D. 1992. Saratepe 2- Poselenie keramikov serediny I tysjacheletija do n. e. pod Samarkandom. *Istorija Material'noj Kul'tury Uzbekistana* 26, 22–41.
Kabanov, S. K. 1969. Izuchenie stratigrafii gorodishcha Afrasiab. *Sovetskaja Arkheologija* 1, 183–198.
Kabanov, S. K. 1981. Osvoenie zapadnykh rajonov goroda na rannikh etapakh ego zhizni. In Ju. F. Burjakov (ed.), *K istoricheskoj topografii drevnego i srednevekovogo Samarkanda*, 23–59. Tashkent, Fan.
Lecuyot, G. à paraître. *Fouilles d'Aï Khanoum. L'habitat*. Mémoires de la Délégation Archéologique Française en Afghanistan. Paris.
Lerner, J. 2003–2004. Correcting the Early History of Ay Khanom. *Archäologische Mitteilungen aus Iran und Turan* 35–36, 373–410.
Lerner, J. 2005. Greek Ceramic Period IV of Aï Khanoum. *Tsentral'naja Azija. Istochniki, istorija, kul'tura. Materialy mezhdunarodnoj nauchnoj konferentsii posvjashchennoj 80-letiju Dr. E. A. Davidovich i Akad. Dr. B. A. Litvinskogo*, 464–476. Moscou, Vostochnaja Literatura RAN.
Lerner, J. 2010. Revising the Chronologies of the Hellenistic Colonies of Samarkand-Marakanda (Afrasiab II-III) and Aï Khanoum (Northeastern Afghanistan). *Anabasis* 1, 58–79.
Lyonnet, B. 1997. *Prospections archéologiques en Bactriane orientale (1974–1978)*, sous la direction de J.-C. Gardin, vol. 2, *Céramique et peuplement, du Chalcolithique à la conquête arabe*. Paris, ERC.
Lyonnet, B. 2001. Les Grecs, les Nomades et l'indépendance de la Sogdiane, d'après l'occupation comparée d'Aï Khanoum et de Marakanda au cours des derniers siècles avant notre ère. *Bulletin of the Asia Institute* 12, 141–159.
Lyonnet, B. 2010. D'Aï Khanoum à Koktepe. Questions sur la datation absolue de la céramique hellénistique d'Asie centrale. In K. Abdullaev (ed.), *Traditsii Vostoka i Zapada v antichnoj kul'ture Srednej Azii, Sbornik statej v chest' Polja Bernara*, 141–153. Tashkent, Noshirlik yog'dusi.
Lyonnet, B. à paraître. La céramique de la Maison du quartier sud-ouest d'Aï Khanoum, in G. Lecuyot, avec des contributions de P. Bernard, H.-P. Francfort, B. Lyonnet et L. Martinez-Sève, *Fouilles d'Aï Khanoum. L'habitat.* Mémoires de la Délégation Archéologique Française en Afghanistan. Paris.
Lyonnet, B. sous presse. Ellinisticheskaja keramika iz Geroona Kinea v Aj Khanum (Afganistan), in S. Bolelov et O. Inevatkina (ed.), *Drevnie tsivilizatsii na Srednem Vostoke*, Moscou.
Martinez-Sève, L. 2010. A propos du temple aux niches indentées d'Aï Khanoum: quelques observations, in P. Carlier et C. Lerouge-Cohen (eds.), *Paysage et religion en Grèce antique*. Travaux de la Maison R. Ginouvès 10, 195–207. Paris, De Boccard.
Najmark, A. I. 2005. Nakhodki grecheskikh monet v Sogdiane. *Numizmatika i epigrafika* 17, 116–138.
Nemtseva, N. B. 1969. Stratigrafija juzhnoj okrainy gorodishcha Afrasiab. In Ja. G. Guljamov (ed.), *Afrasiab I*, 153–205.Tashkent, Fan.
Rapin, C. 1983. Les inscriptions économiques de la trésorerie hellénistique d'Aï Khanoum (Afghanistan). *Bulletin de Correspondance Hellénique* 107, 315–372.
Rapin, C. 1992. *Fouilles d'Aï Khanoum VIII. La trésorerie du palais hellénistique d'Aï Khanoum. L'apogée et la chute du royaume grec de Bactriane*. Mémoires de la Délégation Archéologique Française en Afghanistan 33. Paris, De Boccard.
Rapin, C. et Isamiddinov, M. 1994. Fortifications hellénistiques de Samarcande (Samarkand-Afrasiab). *Topoi* 4/2, 547–565.
Robert, L. 1973. Les inscriptions. In P. Bernard, *Fouilles d'Aï Khanoum I (campagnes 1965, 1966, 1967, 1968)*. Mémoires de la Délégation Archéologique Française en Afghanistan 21, 207–237. Paris, Klincksieck.
Rotroff, S. I. 1982. *Hellenistic Pottery. Athenian and imported moldmade bowls*. The Athenian Agora XXII. Princeton, NJ., American School of Classical Studies at Athens.
Rotroff, S. I. 1997. *Hellenistic Pottery. Athenian and imported wheelmade table ware and related material*. The Athenian Agora XXIX. Princeton, NJ., American School of Classical Studies at Athens.

Rotroff, S. I. 2006a. The Introduction of the Moldmade Bowl Revisited: Tracking a Hellenistic Innovation. *Hesperia* 75.3, 357–378.

Rotroff, S. I. 2006b. *Hellenistic Pottery. The Plain Wares*. The Athenian Agora XXXIII. Princeton, NJ., American School of Classical Studies at Athens.

Shishkina, G. V. 1974. Keramika kontsa IV–II vv. do n. e. (Afrasiab II). In Ja. G. Guljamov (ed.), *Afrasiab* III, 28–51. Tashkent, Fan.

Shishkina, G. V. 1975. Ellinisticheskaja keramika Afrasiaba. *Sovetskaja Arkheologija* 2, 60–78.

Shishkina, G. V. 1994. Ancient Samarkand: Capital of Soghd. *Bulletin of the Asia Institute* 8, 81–99.

Schlumberger, D. 1960. Descendants non-méditerranéens de l'art grec. *Syria* 37, 131–166 et 253–318.

Sverchkov, L. 2008. The Kurganzol Fortress (on the History of Central Asia in the Hellenistic Era). *Ancient Civilizations from Scythia to Siberia* 14, 123–191.

Perspectives

Hellenistic Pottery in a Wider Perspective – On the Use and Misuse of the Application of Network Theory to Material Culture

Stefan Riedel

Abstract

The study of pottery offers the opportunity to illuminate the interrelations and connections within the Hellenistic Eastern Mediterranean since it is by far the most abundant and widely distributed kind of material preserved in the archaeological record. In order to attain a more structured view of the underlying patterns of these interrelations, the paper considers and combines different aspects of network theory and analysis with special regard to their application to antiquity. Emanating from the diversity of networks which are often interwoven, the network theoretical approach towards the study of pottery unveils its potential to track down these interrelations and their operation. Hence, pottery does not merely depict economic networks but illuminates many aspects of social interactions between and within ancient societies. One possibility closely linked to network theory is the study of diffusion processes which often demonstrates the involvement of lower social strata into larger networks and their exposure to it, e.g. in the case of adaption or local imitation of foreign pottery. Thus, the study of pottery in many respects reveals patterns of interrelations of almost every group within ancient societies, leading to a more sophisticated view of human interactions in the past[1].

Keywords: network theory, material culture, pottery, Eastern Mediterranean, diversity of networks, process of diffusion

Introduction

In 2007 Konstantinos Vlassopoulos argued for a shift in Greek history towards the study of its different networks incorporating both Greeks and non-Greeks, and thus to deviate from the polis-centred approaches in favour of a more global view of ancient interconnections[2]. He generally emphasises the significance of the mobilisation of goods, people, ideas, and technologies in antiquity and its major contribution to the formation of wide-ranging networks of different character[3]. These underlying social networks[4] are the result of various human interactions through time and space. But the comprehension and reconstruction of any ancient network's specific character faces particular problems[5]. Basically, there is no ancient network – regardless whether of social, economic, political character, and the like – completely comprehensible in all its facets and details. Nevertheless, the study of the material which is preserved in the archaeological record offers the opportunity to reconstruct and visualise at least parts of the underlying social relations and their functioning. Therefore, in many respects the study of pottery – by far the most abundant kind of material culture preserved – comes with the potential to illuminate different kinds of networks comprising their emergence, maintenance, and vanishing as well as their functioning. Due to these considerations the following paper attempts to fathom the application of network theory to Hellenistic pottery in order to reveal its opportunities and drawbacks for the understanding of human interactions in the past.

Networks in the Hellenistic World – New Avenues of Pre-existing Connections

From a Hellenocentric point of view the anabasis of Alexander and the fall of the Achaemenid Empire increased

1 I am deeply grateful to the organizers of the conference and editors of the proceedings to present this paper here although I did not present it at the conference in Cologne/Bonn. Moreover, I would like to thank Constance von Rüden and Christoph Kremer very much for discussing many of the theoretical issues concerning this paper and giving useful advice and inspiring impulses. I am also obliged to both of them and Anne Heselhaus for critically reading and commenting on an earlier draft of this paper.

2 Vlassopoulos 2007.

3 Vlassopoulos 2007, 93–95.

4 The simplifying but often used term of social networks is not to be regarded as self-contained since in many cases it is very difficult to distinguish social aspects from other ones concerning networks. Political and economic networks for example in most cases include social components – beside the fact, that they are often interwoven themselves. Nevertheless, the term social networks is used in this paper to describe networks whose character primarily focuses on social aspects which cannot be subsumed under other structures such as political and economic ones. But one always has to remind oneself of the role of social aspects in almost every kind of network – especially in antiquity.

5 During the last years different methods from network analysis were also adopted in the range of classical antiquity, demonstrating the possibilities inherent in this theoretical approach. Thus Shawn Graham works on the network of Antonine itineraries (Graham 2006), Ian Rutherford combines parts of network theory with his study of religious delegations (Rutherford 2007), Anna Collar uses network theory to explain the spread of the religion of Theos Hypsistos (Collar 2007) and Tom Brughmans applies network analysis to the distribution of table ware in the Roman East (Brughmans 2010).

the Greek sphere of influence to an unprecedented dimension covering many different ethnicities and cultures. During the last years of Alexander himself and the reigns of his successors the Greeks respectively Macedonians as the new potentates had to arrange themselves with the particular existing societies. Such arrangements certainly had to take place in every social stratum and area of life in order to guarantee a more or less peaceful co-existence. Of course reciprocal connections between different Greek poleis, institutions, and individuals with their counterparts in the later realm of Alexander existed before, but with the conquest and incorporation of those areas and their division among the Diadochi these interrelations certainly became more intensified or transformed, new ones must have emerged and others vanished. The pre-existing interconnections within the Eastern Mediterranean have been subject of studies especially concerning the Bronze and Early Iron Age[6]. They concentrate on various matters such as trade and transfer of motives respectively knowledge[7]. These early relations of different societies within the Eastern Mediterranean are well attested in the archaeological record and more recent studies on the so called Dark Ages showed that also during those times connections between different groups existed although they were probably much smaller in scale and not that wide-ranging as they were before[8]. With what is called the Orientalizing Period in Greek Art the influence of the East becomes again very apparent and at the latest with the foundation of settlements abroad the Greeks became again interconnected with many societies in the Eastern Mediterranean.

Therefore, it is not to question that some kinds of networks existed before the Age of Alexander between Greeks and the East, but how they developed in a time of political and social changes since the functioning of networks mostly becomes apparent when changes occur. Such changes might be new shapes or types of pottery but also new political, economic or religious powers. In general new challenges accrue to a network from many different sources but just a few are able to trigger major changes[9]. Especially in the cases of the encounter of preliminarily more or less independent social systems the respective influences lead to the development of a kind of new conglomerate networks.

Mediterranean Interconnections in the Light of Network Theoretical Approaches

By retracing the route of an Achaemenid glass bowl up to Ihringen in South-Eastern Germany, Erich Kistler recently demonstrated how far-ranging ancient networks had been[10]. But he also correctly emphasises that the object underwent social and contextual changes on its way through different societies[11] which indicates that the Achaemenid King and the Celtic potentate were not directly linked to one another.

This aspect of interrelation is due to the idea of the small-world theory[12] which basically regards a network as a number of nodes connected to one another in different ways. In such a network some nodes are closely linked to their neighbouring nodes thus forming a cluster. Neighbours in this case is not necessarily to be in a spatial sense of meaning but also covers social closeness[13] e.g. in spatially separated but nevertheless interrelated elite groups. Additionally some nodes of a cluster are linked to nodes which are themselves part of other clusters. In terms of network theory the connections are distinguished between strong and weak ties, whereupon the close links within a cluster are usually the strong ones, which are frequently used and trusted, whereas the weak ones are the long-range connections which establish a node's connection to a node of a remote cluster[14]. Therefore, the sum of the clusters taken together basically forms a network. The character, i.e. the value of the ties is crucial when it comes to any kind of diffusion within the network – regardless whether goods, ideas, people, or the like are objects of transmission. Diffusion via strong ties is of course important but concerns primarily the local level, whereas the long-ranging weak ties exhibit shortcuts to

6 e.g. Knapp 2006 who discusses the issue of Orientalization respectively Orientalism within the Eastern Mediterranean and especially Cyprus in Late Bronze and Early Iron Age or Knappett and Evans and Rivers 2008 who use network analysis to investigate the interrelations of 34 sites in Bronze Age Aegean.

7 cf. von Rüden 2011 who studies the wall paintings of the palace of Qaṭna in Western Syria from the mid-second millennium BC in consideration of a transfer of motives within the Eastern Mediterranean.

8 e.g. Fantalkin 2006 who summarizes the contacts between the Greeks and the Southern Levant during the first half of the first millennium BC especially in the light of a suggested changing hegemony in the Eastern Mediterranean and the agency of the Phoenicians.

9 On this matter of fact see e.g. Watts 2003, 220–252.

10 Kistler 2010. His case study refers to the elites but might of course be extended towards other social strata.

11 Kistler 2010, 63–64. Although it must be kept in mind that an object's connotations might also change if the parties who are involved in its transfer are directly linked to each other. Therefore, the social and contextual changes of exchanged objects depends on various aspects concerning their original purpose as well as the social background of their new environment.

12 The small-world theory was first formalized by Watts and Strogatz 1998 but the idea to track down connections between two random participants in a social network derives from Stanley Milgram's experiments in the 1960s (Milgram 1967; Travers and Milgram 1969). His conclusion that only six steps are necessary to connect two randomly chosen people within the United States (the five intermediates connecting the two people stated by Milgram 1967, 65 and Travers and Milgram 1969, 431 lead to the number of six concerning the connections itself) led to the popular urban legend of the so called six degrees of separation which was staged by John Guare in 1990 (Guare 1990). The supposed assumption that only six steps are needed to connect any two people in the world is of course just appropriate in the sense of mathematics (for these mathematical suggestions see e.g. Barabási 2003, 35 and already Milgram 1967, 67 was aware of this matter of fact).

13 To express the opposite of closeness in a small-world network where an indirect connection between two nodes exists, Milgram 1967, 67 uses the term 'psychological distance'.

14 The idea to distinguish between strong and weak ties originates from the sociologist Mark S. Granovetter (Granovetter 1973. For a definition of which aspects are important in the measuring of the strength of ties see Granovetter 1973, 1361–1363).

remote nodes and clusters thus guaranteeing the better functioning of the network as a whole[15].

Another obvious but crucial aspect about effective networks is the matter of fact that some nodes possess much more links than others. These nodes are referred to as hubs. In a network which underlies dynamic changes these hubs are even of higher relevance because newcomers to a network tend to connect to the well-connected nodes instead of to those with just a few links. This circumstance is due to the so called power law which generally speaking formalizes the preference to place new links[16]. Beside that it seems to be a corollary since a new participant joins the network in order to gain some profit from it, which is easier if he is at least connected to an important node with access to many others.

The example of the Achaemenid glass bowl already indicates a wide-ranging interconnectedness in the Ancient World covering large parts of the Mediterranean although in its last usage the bowl must merely have been a symbol of exotic luxury[17]. Basically, this interrelations have always been recognized in the archaeological record but only little attempt was made to investigate the factors and mechanisms behind these connections in classical antiquity except for mere trade relations. But economy is just one of the various fields in which networks play an important role[18]. Apart from biological, natural networks, and the like there are four main areas of human interaction where networks appear and whose study is of particular interest: the political, economic, religious, and social sector. A major problem concerning antiquity is that these sectors respectively their networks are in many cases interwoven and not to be separated. Taking into account that a network consists of different interlocked clusters it would basically be possible to regard the whole giant network with all its various connections as the sum of all different networks, too[19]. But in most cases such a global view would fail to explain the detailed functioning. Therefore, it is necessary to consider 'the social system as a network of networks overlapping and interacting in various ways'[20] and to investigate single networks on a micro-level which in turn must be merged to explain the superior one. Thus some nodes need not to be just hubs within one network but can also act as mediators between different networks, i.e. being a kind of inter-network-hubs. The interacting and interlocking of different networks is naturally manifold. On the one hand a network might be influenced by another one, e.g. connections of a political network might directly influence an economic one, whereas on the other hand there are networks whose initial existences and functioning depends on an older network. To stick to the same picture, certain trading networks might just have been possible to establish because within a political one the course has been set before through e.g. an intergovernmental treaty.

The Role of Pottery in Ancient Networks

From the matter of fact that various forms of networks exist the question arises, which kinds of networks pottery may depict. Beside the four main sectors mentioned above there are two basic kinds of networks due to the material culture which could be defined as material and non-material networks.

At this juncture material networks are those in which the material itself is the integral part of the interconnection, i.e. the reason for its emergence and maintenance. This is most notably the case in economic networks such as trade. Non-material on the contrary are those networks which are also depicted in the material but the material itself is not the primarily object of diffusion. The latter is more about the transmission of technological knowledge, habits, and the like which often become apparent in local imitations of foreign imports but also might be connected with the transfer of ideas and practices which could not have been obtained from the material itself but required some kind of personal instruction[21]. Non-material networks are not as easy to trace in the archaeological record as material ones but their study offers a promising opportunity to illuminate different aspects of the social formation and functioning of ancient societies. But as the different sectors which networks become manifest in, these two kinds of networks are also often overlapping and interwoven. As Robin Osborne points out, apart from being object of trade[22], Greek pottery also conveyed sort of Hellenic culture like drinking habits and mythology. However, he also emphasises that the pottery itself did not generate this philhellenism but reflects it since the pottery was imported because e.g. the Etruscans knew Greek life-style and not because they wanted to learn about it[23]. Nevertheless, the pottery displays the merging of material and non-material

15 Watts and Strogatz 1998, 440–441.

16 Hubs and especially the power law are basic elements of another model in network theory which is called the scale-free network (see Barabási 2003, especially 79–92). This is basically to be seen as a further development out of the small-world model which does not reject the former one but makes important additions to it. Nevertheless, for promising applications of network theory to archaeology the combination and alteration of several theories is needed and further additions must be made (see also Brughmans 2010, 278–280).

17 See Kistler 2010, 64.

18 See Ulf 2009, 102.

19 Ulf 2009, 101–102 regards the 'network of society' as the overarching giant network, which is interconnected with all other social networks. Although he argues from the perspective of the individual and the question of multiple identities, the idea can also be transferred to other networks focusing on groups, places, and the like.

20 Wellman 1983, 168.

21 cf. MacDonald 1981, who argues that the 'imitations' of Athenian vases in Italy, mainland Greece, and probably parts of Asia Minor during the late 5th and early 4th century BC is not just due to the copying of Athenian imports but that Athenian potters emigrated to the regions in question and certainly taught their techniques to local artisans.

22 On the relation of Hellenistic pottery and trade see e.g. Guldager Bilde 1993, 192–195 who coherently states that pottery never was the main cargo in ancient trading relations. A sophisticated study of the relation especially between fine pottery and the 'main commodities' of trade concerning Athenian decorated pottery is given by Gill 1991 who comes to the same conclusion.

23 Osborne 2007, especially 87–90.

networks since it is object of trade and alongside depicts networks of knowledge transfer and adaption, whether it generates them or not.

Therefore, Hellenistic pottery does not differ from the one of earlier periods. Although society in general had changed, the kinds of networks and the sectors where they become apparent remained the same. But the changed political structure which could be called a Greek supremacy extended the possibilities for exchanges and relations between formerly more or less independent societies. Hence, one major question of interest which might be illuminated by the application of network theory is how people in Hellenistic times dealt with foreign influences which are reflected in the archaeological record. But first of all foreign influence has to be attested in the place or society in question. As already stated before, trade is the most obvious but not the only possibility in which cultural contact becomes apparent in the archaeological record. Other contact zones[24] with a material component which are all well attested for Hellenistic times are military conflicts and mercenaries, gift exchange, foundations of new settlements and the general mobility of people, travelling artisans, and the transfer of goods in a religious connotation such as dedications to sanctuaries. Furthermore, especially the mobility of people must also have resulted in some kind of reflow of foreign goods and ideas respectively their transformation into the societies the moving people originated from.

Considering the four main sectors in which networks emerge, it is to analyse whether the study of pottery offers a promising opportunity to depict those networks and leverage the understanding of their functioning. Since foreign imports must somehow have been brought to the place they were found about two millennia afterwards, particularly trade has ever been regarded as the main factor. And indeed, the study of economic interrelations provides a better understanding of how societies in the Hellenistic times were connected. It helps identifying centres of production and visualizing the distribution of shapes and wares. This also might lead to a reconstruction of trading-routes which in return sharpen our view for the nodal points respectively hubs playing a basic role in the distribution. Therefore, in many respects the reconstruction and investigation of economic networks sets up the framework for researching other types of networks because it already allows to identify structures such as hubs which are crucial not only in terms of economy but also play a major role within other networks. Furthermore, the distribution of any good also provides the geographical space in which a network is to be traced through the study of the material. Political and religious networks on the contrary are not easy to reconstruct via the study of pottery alone. But in certain circumstances pottery mirrors such networks, and thus can contribute to some of their aspects, e.g. the population's awareness and acceptance of sanctuaries[25] or political relations[26]. The latter is the case with the Hellenistic mouldmade bowls and their introduction in Athens. Susan Rotroff coherently argues that the first of these bowls alluded to Ptolemaic metal vessels which were on display in the polis in a time when Ptolemy III. Euergetes maintained good relationships with the city[27]. Therefore, and due to the dating of the earliest deposits on the Agora where mouldmade bowls were found in as well as in comparison to the chronology of Rhodian amphorae, she suggests an introduction in Athens around 224/3 BC[28]. Hence, the political situation in Hellenistic Athens at that time offered the Athenian potters the opportunity to create a new kind of vessel which afterwards – independently from the possible political connotations of the first bowls – was adapted in many parts of the Mediterranean making it a key class of datable Hellenistic pottery to modern scholars[29]. This example again shows quite plainly that one network influenced other ones – here the Athenian political connections were the impetus for the invention and distribution of the mouldmade bowl, and thus influenced economic and social networks which could be called networks of preference of style[30].

Furthermore, the emergence of this new class of pottery, its spread, and acceptance is closely related to another aspect of network theory – the process of diffusion. Due to this, the material reveals whether an innovation evolved into a successful cascade, was accepted by parts of the network or neglected a short time after its emergence. Rotroff applied Spratt's model of the different stages within the process of innovation to the case of the mouldmade bowl showing that the different stages and their temporal distance are visible in the archaeological record[31].

Using the related model of Everett Rogers, this theory can be extended towards the study of the diffusion of an innovation respectively a certain type of pottery which is closely related to the study of networks within the social sector. Rogers classified five categories due to the attitude towards an innovation and the point of its acceptance:

[24] For the term itself and the different kinds of contact zones see Ulf 2009, especially 91–101 who considers them under the aspect of the use of different kinds of power.

[25] Dedications to a sanctuary might indicate its sphere of influence, although it must be taken into account that in most cases the dedicator, especially of a vessel, is not known. Since there is no special type of pottery exclusively reserved for certain religious rituals, pottery is therefore not a good indicator for the functioning of religious networks (the hypothesis brought forward by Crown 1994, 198–203 concerning her studies of the Salado pottery in 13th century Southwest Northern and Central America, that certain decorations and types of pottery are associated with the spread of religious imaginations is a logic idea but cannot be verified for antiquity).

[26] The political relations are not evident from the material itself but emanate from other sources, most notably literary ones.

[27] Rotroff 1982, 6–13.

[28] Rotroff 1982, especially 9–13; Rotroff 2006, especially 360–367. 373–376.

[29] On the distribution of the mouldmade bowl, its production centres, and the relation of exports and local imitations see Guldager Bilde 1993.

[30] Osborne 2005, 91 talks about 'a network of aesthetic preferences' concerning the Greek-non-Greek relations in earlier periods.

[31] Rotroff 2006, 367–373. Spratt 1982, 80–85 categorizes six stages within the process of innovation: discovery – invention – development – investment – production, distribution and sale – obsolescence.

Innovators – Early Adopters – Early Majority – Late Majority – Laggards[32]. By this means, the participants in a network might be categorized which also gives insight into the valuation of an innovation and even the hierarchy within the network. The latter touches upon the idea of different thresholds of each participant, i.e. how a node is influenced by others concerning its decision-making. Hence, a node's threshold in a social network is usually rated by these external influences, i.e. the number of acquaintances who necessarily adopted the innovation before in order to make a particular node to adopt is as well[33]. Beside that an individual's threshold depends on her or his attitude towards the innovation[34]. Therefore, to create a successful cascade the threshold is a crucial factor especially concerning the hubs of a network because these are the nodal points not only in the process of diffusion[35]. Therefore, the presence of the pottery in question in relation to its probable date of introduction at different places, but also the absence in certain areas reveals a networks functioning and hierarchy. If e.g. a certain type of pottery is to be found at a nodal point such as Alexandria in Egypt, but is not distributed any further, this indicates the position of Alexandria in the network. But furthermore, the absence of specific shapes and wares also illuminates the taste and habits of local societies, for it must not have been the case that a hub refused to distribute but that in the local societies there was no need to use the import. Due to this, local imitations depend on whether a new shape, decoration or the like fits the habits of the society or advanced them[36]. Thus the import, adaption or transformation of foreign types of pottery[37] indicate changes on a local level which might result in a change of habits, as it is often postulated in the case of the so called Hellenization. But it must also be considered that specific shapes of pottery underwent changes in usage when they were transferred to another group or society which was not familiar with it before[38].

Aspects of Network Theory and the Study of Antiquity – Concluding Remarks

As indicated in this paper, the application of network theory to material culture in general and pottery in particular inheres in the potential of a better understanding of human interactions in the past – especially in the cases where we lack other sources, most notably concerning the lower social strata. It might reveal patterns of functioning and habits of ancient societies in a more detailed way than the mere study of the material itself. But it must be emphasized that the application of network theory to material culture cannot substitute the study of the material itself. Nevertheless, it might give new insights into the chosen field of study which would otherwise be not that obvious. Therefore, it is a worthy and promising approach towards a better understanding of human interrelations in the past and could in many cases be used as a decisive assisting tool in addition to the necessary study of the material itself. However, network theory provides ideas and models on a theoretical base which should give impulses towards a more structured thinking about the formation and functioning of ancient interrelations.

Stefan Riedel
Zentrum für Mittelmeerstudien
Konrad-Zuse-Straße 16
D-44801 Bochum
stefan.riedel-j8h@rub.de

Bibliography

Barabási, A.-L. 2003. *Linked. How Everything Is Connected to Everything Else and What It Means for Business, Science, and Everyday Life*. New York, Plume.

Boardman, J. 2004. Copies of Pottery: By and for Whom? In K. Lomas (ed.), *Greek Identity in the Western Mediterranean. Papers in Honour of Brian Shefton*, 149–162. Leiden and Boston, Brill.

Brughmans, T. 2010. Connecting the Dots: Towards Archaeological Network Analysis. *Oxford Journal of Archaeology* 29, 3, 277–300.

Collar, A. 2007. Network Theory and Religious Innovation. *Mediterranean Historical Review* 22, 1, 149–162.

Crown, P. L. 1994. *Ceramics and Ideology. Salado Polychrome Pottery*. Albuquerque, University of New Mexico Press.

Fantalkin, A. 2006. Identity in the Making: Greeks in the

32 Rogers 2003, especially 272–285.

33 Granovetter 1978, 1422; Valente 1996, 69–71.

34 Thus at least one of the Early Adopters must be convinced by the innovator or the innovation itself to create a successful cascade, because if every node is just willing to adopt it if two or more of its acquaintances already did, the innovation would fizzle out right after its emergence (cf. Granovetter 1978, 1424–1425).

35 Network theorists often disregard the strength of influence of different nodes probably because it is not easy to grasp. Nevertheless, it must be taken into account that some nodes are more influential than others which impacts the thresholds, too. This matter of fact is similar to the power law, which concerns the connections within a network (cf. Barabási 2003, 67–72).

36 cf. Boardman 2004, 149–150.

37 This issue also alludes to the aspect of knowledge transfer through travelling artisans and the like, which cannot be considered here in detail. But especially when it comes to the imitation of ceramics which need more specialized methods of production, the imitators might in some cases have become aware of the needed knowledge to produce similar vessels themselves which they could not have become aware of just by looking at the imports.

38 cf. Kistler 2010 for the social and contextual changes of the Achaemenid glass bowl. Therefore, the suggestion of Osborne 2005, 87–90 that the import of Greek pottery followed a basic knowledge of Greek life-style is to doubt, although it might be possible in some cases (like the Etruscans who he choose as subject of that particular study).

Eastern Mediterranean during the Iron Age, in A. Villing and U. Schlotzhauer (eds.), *Naukratis: Greek Diversity in Egypt. Studies in East Greek Pottery and Exchange in the Eastern Mediterranean*, 199–208. London, The British Museum Press.

Gill, D. W. J. 1991. Pots and Trade: Spacefillers or Objets d'Art? *The Journal of Hellenic Studies* 111, 29–47.

Graham, S. 2006. Networks, Agent-Based Models and the Antonine Itineraries: Implications for Roman Archaeology. *Journal of Mediterranean Archaeology* 19, 1, 45–64.

Granovetter, M. S. 1973. The Strength of Weak Ties. *American Journal of Sociology* 78, 6, 1360–1380.

Granovetter, M. S. 1978. Threshold Models of Collective Behavior. *American Journal of Sociology* 83, 6, 1420–1443.

Guare, J. 1990. *Six Degrees of Separation. A Play*. New York, Vintage.

Guldager Bilde, P. 1993. Mouldmade Bowls, Centres and Peripheries in the Hellenistic World, in P. Bilde, T. Engberg-Pedersen, L. Hannestad, J. Zahle and K. Randsborg (eds.), *Centre and Peripheries in the Hellenistic World*, 192–209. Aarhus, Aarhus University Press.

Kistler, E. 2010. Großkönigliches *symbolon* im Osten – exotisches Luxusgut im Westen: Zur Objektbiographie der achämenidischen Glasschale aus Ihringen, in R. Rollinger, B. Gufler, M. Lang and I. Madreiter (eds.), *Interkulturalität in der Alten Welt. Vorderasien, Hellas, Ägypten und die vielfältigen Ebenen des Kontaktes*, 63–95. Wiesbaden, Harrassowitz.

Knapp, A. B. 2006. Orientalization and Prehistoric Cyprus: The Social Life of Oriental Goods, in C. Riva and N. C. Vella (eds.), *Debating Orientalization. Multidisciplinary Approaches to Change in the Ancient Mediterranean*, 48–65. London and Oakville, Equinox.

Knappett, C., Evans, T. and Rivers, R. 2008. Modelling Maritime Interaction in the Aegean Bronze Age. *Antiquity* 82, 1009–1024.

MacDonald, B. R. 1981. The Emigration of Potters from Athens in the Late Fifth Century B.C. and its Effect on the Attic Pottery Industry. *American Journal of Archaeology* 85, 2, 159–168.

Milgram, S. 1967. The Small-World Problem. *Psychology Today* 1, 1, 61–67.

Osborne, R. 2007. What Travelled with Greek Pottery? *Mediterranean Historical Review* 22, 1, 85–95.

Rogers, E. M. 2003. *Diffusion of Innovations*. 5th Edition. New York, Free Press.

Rotroff, S. I. 1982. *Hellenistic Pottery. Athenian and Imported Moldmade Bowls*. The Athenian Agora XXII. Princeton, NJ., American School of Classical Studies at Athens.

Rotroff, S. I. 2006. The Introduction of the Mouldmade Bowl Revisited: Tracking a Hellenistic Innovation. *Hesperia* 75, 3, 357–378.

Rutherford, I. 2007. Network Theory and Theoric Networks. *Mediterranean Historical Review* 22, 1, 23–37.

Spratt, D. A. 1982. The Analysis of Innovation Process. *Journal of Archaeological Science* 9, 79–94.

Travers, J. and Milgram, S. 1969. An Experimental Study on the Small World Problem. *Sociometry* 32, 4, 425–443.

Ulf, C. 2009. Rethinking Cultural Contacts. *Ancient West and East* 8, 81–132.

Valente, T. W. 1996. Social Network Thresholds in the Diffusion of Innovations. *Social Networks* 18, 69–89.

Vlassopoulos, K. 2007. Between East and West: The Greek *Poleis* as Part of a World-System. *Ancient West and East* 6, 91–111.

von Rüden, C. 2011. *Die Wandmalereien aus Tall Mišrife/Qaṭna im Kontext überregionaler Kommunikation*. Qaṭna Studien. Forschungsergebnisse und vergleichende Untersuchungen des deutsch-syrischen archäologischen Projekts auf dem Tall Mišrife 2. Wiesbaden, Harrassowitz.

Watts, D. J. 2003. *Six Degrees. The Science of a Connected Age*. London, Vintage.

Watts, D. J. and Strogatz, S. H. 1998. Collective Dynamics of 'Small-World' Networks. *Nature* 393, 440–442.

Wellman, B. 1983. Network Analysis: Some Basic Principles. *Social Theory* 1, 155–200.

Concluding Remarks

Nina Fenn & Christiane Römer-Strehl

The preceding papers bear out the statement that ‚Hellenistic pottery is a language with lots of dialects' (Kotitsa). Here we offer a summary and some conclusions[1].

Disciplines

The contributions in this volume, which represent participants' specific areas of reseach, demonstrate the diversity of Hellenistic pottery and also reveal a variety of approaches and methods of investigation. Each offers valuable clues about historical contexts and networks. Advances in our understanding of this subject require the cooperation of archaeologists, historians, and numismatists working throughout the Mediterranean, the Near East, Egypt, and even the Roman west. Unfortunately in some areas, for example in the German-speaking countries, study of these disciplines and geographic areas are still separated. The contributions of this conference reflect an attempt to unite different approaches and their subject-specific aspects.

An aspect specific to Hellenistic pottery is a characteristic range of forms and decoration that occur simultaneously across a wide geographic area. This means that it is extremely important to investigate issues of fabric composition and provenance, and this requires close co-operation between archaeology and scientific disciplines. G. Schneider and M. Daszkiewicz (Berlin-Warschau) in particlar have worked throughout the Eastern Mediterranean, including Albania, Greece, Asia Minor, Cyprus, Levantine and the Near East. Such fruitful co-operation provides new evidence for the interpretation of economic, political and historical processes across the Hellenistic world.

Results of the conference sections

Greece

In comparison to other regions in the Eastern Mediterranean, in Greece research on Hellenistic pottery is well advanced. Conference papers focused on Athens, the Peloponnesos, Euboia and Macedonia. These contributions revealed that Athens remained the ‚epicenter' of innovation in pottery design as late as the third century BC. Attic ceramics were traded all over Greece and functioned as trendsetters for local productions. We have long understood that Athenian mouldmade relief bowls with their distinctive motifs fulfilled this role (s. Rotroff). But in addition Attic black glazed drinking vessels, especially those with West Slope decoration, dominated everywhere, both as exports and as inspirational sources setting the tone for local reproductions (s. Seilheimer). Some regions did also receive small amounts of imports from other places, e.g., Macedonian, Ionian and Corinthian pottery in Euboia (s. Ackermann). In remote areas conservative styles in drinking vessels prevailed (s. Langridge-Noti). For example, Langridge-Noti showed that in Laconia the traditional ‚one-handled mug' was still the most popular drinking vessel in Hellenistic times. The mouldmade bowls found here were mostly local products with a small capacity similar to the volume of the mugs. The ceramics suggest that Laconia had only a loose connection to Athens and weak trade relations with the Northern Peloponnesos.

Albania

In the past several years Albania has come more to the fore in archaeological research. Earlier perceptions of Albania as a fringe area should be revised; it may now be seen as a transfer zone due to its position along the Adriatic Sea, which connected the Aegean and Italy. Conference papers presented material from the north, the middle and the south of Albania. The example of Lissos was very instructive, because both the range of fine wares and amphorae from the port area were presented. An overview of these functionally diverse ceramic categories revealed astonishing differences. From the second century BC onwards amphorae were no longer imported from the Aegean but instead came from Italy (s. Lahi). Fine ware imports, by contrast, still originated in the Eastern Mediterranean (s. Kögler). From the harbour city of Durres red-figured lekythoi from a third century BC sanctuary-complex are decorated with an abridged version of Italiote scenes (s. Shehi and Tichit); these clearly reflect influences from South Italy, in particular Apulia. It would be interesting to see the full array of finds from the sanctuary published in order to be able to assess influences in both functional and chronological terms and to compare this with settlement material.

In southern Albania there are rich oil resources, and one byproduct is bitumen, which has been identified in the pottery of Apollonia (s. Fiedler and Döhner). The authors demonstrate that close examination of the inner vessel surfaces can offer new insights relating to life span and

[1] Andrea Berlin and Gabriele Puschnigg helped us with the linguistic revision of the following pages.

storage of foodstuffs. They also suggest that scientific methods should be used to identify the different sources of the petroleum springs in the Eastern and Western Mediterranean; in such ways the commerce of bitumen from Apollonia and other places could be followed.

Aegean islands

The Aegean islands were the intermediaries between Greece and Asia Minor. Of these the most important was Delos, whose geographical position within the trading network can be likened to that of a spider in her web. The conference contributions illuminate two different time horizons (s. Gros; Peignard-Giros). Initially Delos was within the realm of Athens; in the course of changing political conditions the island's inhabitants seemed to have taken on a new role as agents between East and West.

Research suggests that the residents of Delos concentrated on long-distance trade. We are uninformed about local Delian pottery production, as no supporting archaeological evidence has been found to date. We also do not know about connections between Delos and the surrounding islands. Was there regional exchange? More investigations on the islands in the immediate vicinity of Delos could further clarify the situation in the Aegean.

Asia Minor

Going further East we arrive at the West coast of Asia Minor. The conference proceedings touched upon the important cities of Pergamon (s. Japp) and Ephesos (s. Lätzer-Lasar). Few cities along this coast can match these two in significance regarding pottery production and its impact on the region of Asia Minor and beyond during the Hellenistic period. At first potters in Pergamon and Ephesos assimilate themselves to Attic styles, but soon become independent and by the later part of the period they themselves are ‚style-setters' (Berlin). While the authors investigate the relationship between the two cities—Pergamenian pottery in Ephesos and Ephesian pottery in Pergamon—we are still in the dark about competition and communication between workshops in these two cities.

Moving farther East shows us a different picture. At Sagalassos in Pisidia, Hellenistic shapes replace older forms in the wake of Alexander's campaign; this might be regarded as evidence of development towards a Hellenistic identity (s. Poblome). In the city of Perge on the South coast, on the other hand, we see the persistence of older traditional Achaemenid bowls, although one would have expected a stronger effect from the city's open position towards the sea. Once beyond Asia Minor, some portions of the coast and the hinterland seem to be cut off. Not everywhere however: Gordion, in the former Phrygian kingdom in central Anatolia, is comparable with Sagalassos. Here the ‚idea of having tableware' did not exist before the Hellenistic period; only after Alexander did local potters begin producing it (s. Stewart).

Cyprus

On Cyprus, local production of fine wares ceased in the face of the ‚tsunami' of ESA (Eastern Sigillata) washing in from the East. By late Hellenistic and early Roman times, though, local production of fine wares resumed in western Cyprus (s. Lund). By contrast, Cypriot transport amphoras are found widely moving east and south from Cyprus towards Turkey, the Levant, and Egypt (s. Dobosz). Cypriot sites along the seacoast received imports of Rhodian amphoras, while local products were also inspired by the forms of Phoenician, Koan, and Knidian transport jars.

Egypt

In terms of geography, Egypt should hold an important position in terms of networks in the Hellenistic world. Against our expectations, however, conference papers showed that position was limited in scope, with more effects coming in than going out. Third century BC fine wares indicate very little outside influence, either from Greece (Athens and/or Macedonia) or the Levant. New forms such as the krater or fish plate were accepted into the repertoire only sporadically; instead, Egyptian potters confined themselves to local and regional products with distinct concepts for each site. The fine wares of the Ptolemaic period were rarely decorated and are hardly ever found outside Egypt. Except for the so-called Egyptian faience (the correct technical term is silica ceramics) other fine local products were not meant for export but were exchanged within Egypt (s. Berlin). This marks a strong contrast to the situation in Greece, Asia Minor and Cyprus.

Local coarse wares appear in traditional Egytian forms (s. Marchand). Interestingly, Greek influences in cooking ware forms do appear from the third century BC onwards (chytrai, lopades)—not as imports, however, but as local products made in Greek cooking ware designs. In Upper Egypt these Greek-inspired forms linger on until the second century BC, and in Lower Egypt apparently even longer.

Imported Aegean transport amphoras from Rhodes, Chios and Cyprus appear on the Egyptian market together with local imitations. In Ptolemaic times Egyptian amphoras were produced at sites along the coast and traveled to the southern oases along traditional caravan routes (s. Möller). The evidence gathered here characterises Egypt as a ‚Hellenistically inspired sphere under Ptolemaic rule' (Berlin).

Levant up to Central Asia

Even in remote places in the northern part of the Levant, such as Dülük Baba Tepesi (s. Strothenke), Hellenistic forms such as fish plates and mouldmade bowls appear in the local ceramic spectrum. Surprisingly, however, relations to neighbouring areas, e.g., Antiochia, seem to have been limited. By contrast, the Hellenistic material from Jebel Khalid seems to reflect the character of a metropolis (s. Jackson). Assemblages here contain imports from Athens, Asia Minor and Cyprus as well as regional products from Antiochia while the local pottery production reflects features of all these various sources.

Eastern Sigillata A plays a particular role in the pottery research of the Levant (s. Kramer). While the main production site(s) of ESA still cannot be identified with certainty, the ware's distribution can be traced along established routes north and south along the Levantine coast. The point at which production began is also in discussion, though the latest research points to a date around or only very shortly before 150 BC.

Inland in the southern Levant Aegean imports are uncommon. At Tel Kedesh in northern Israel Cypriote imports outnumber those from the Aegean and the character of the locally produced pottery is Hellenistic (s. Stone). At smaller cities in the region of the Decapolis, such as Tell Ziraa, the picture resembles that elsewhere in the southern Levant (s. Kenkel); whereas a higher amount of imports, especially from the West, reached major places such as Gadara.

The cities of Palmyra (s. Römer-Strehl), a caravan stop-over, and Dura-Europos (s. Alabe) are situated on a major trading route from the Levant to Central Asia. At both sites imports from the West are attested from the end of the third century BC. The range of imports is more varied at Dura-Europos than at Palmyra in consequence of the former city's position at the river Euphrates. But the lion's share of the pottery repertoires at both cities consists of vessel shapes that are widespread throughout the Mesopotamian region around 200 BC. Thus, both cities may be said to represent a Mesopotamian sphere in the Hellenistic period.

In Central Asia Attic imports appear; their presence in a region so far away from mainland Greece is striking. At the same time at places such as Merv we see local production of Hellenistic fine wares, in grey fabric or with red slip, and in characteristic Hellenistic forms including echinus bowls and fish plates (s. Puschnigg). In Bactria the change from earlier traditions to Greek forms begins with Antiochos I, when networks with the West seem to be reflected in the vessel shapes (s. Lyonnet). Here the military probably played a part in the introduction of Mediterranean forms like kraters, mouldmade bowls, and fish plates.

Types of networks

In the cooperation of the different research directions it is important to be aware of the type(s) of network(s) we are talking about (s. Riedel). From a ‚ceramological' point of view it is apparent how pottery can illuminate various networks: the distribution of pottery may indicate individual, technological, cultural, economic, military, and political networks, some of which will overlap.

Individual aspect

Personal relationships can be verified: the potter Bion is a good example of this aspect (s. Rotroff). By means of potters' stamps the family and workshop connections (son, brother) are evident. Relying on his personal relations as well as his family workshop organization Bion built up his network in different places like an international entrepreneur. He stands for the spread of ideas and represents the potter as businessman with economic interests. This specific instance makes different networks apparent.

Potters were in a position to create trends and fashions, as can be seen, e.g., by Macedonian potters in Pydna or other potters in Ephesos. In these places and probably elsewhere as well, ‚some individuals kick it off' (Berlin) and launched styles that became popular and typical.

Technological aspect

Often Hellenistic pottery provides evidence for the transfer of technical fashions, for example via moulds. We do not see the export of pots but the spread of manufacturing know-how. Decorated mouldmade relief bowls, West slope-style decoration or white ground technique (s. Hodgson) exemplify this phenomenon. It is no longer the individual potter who forms the networks. The network is defined by the spread of technology.

Cultural aspect

Similarities within the pottery assemblages for dining and cooking reflect shared cultural habits and attitudes. During the Hellenistic period styles and social behaviour in drinking and dining were adopted in the Aegean and beyond. This may be connected with a feeling of identity, which we are familiar with today as well. The most significant indications for this type of network are vessel forms and specific wares that appear nearly everywhere.

Among table wares the fish plate and the relief bowl are characteristic of Hellenistic culture. Both are tied to the dining habits of the symposium. As serving and drinking vessels they became the symbol of the Hellenistic—or Macedonian—lifestyle. The idea of having similarly beautiful sets of dishes for feasting may reflect an ongoing exchange of ideas over long distances. In the early part of the period there were only imports but local versions soon appear. These were clearly influenced by the imported wares though they are not merely imitations but retain some local flavor. The fishplates and relief bowls in ESA may function as a link between the black and red glazed pottery.

In a similar way the cooking wares reflect the adoption of Greco-Hellenistic cooking customs. Typical Greek shapes like the lopas and chytra are found from the eastern Mediterranean to the Persian Gulf. As with the fine wares, so too with the cooking wares there are imported vessels as well as local productions of similar forms. This suggests that a general idea of a typical cooking assemblage could have existed. In fact the form probably did not always define the function, e.g., the lopas may not have been used only for stewing fish even if the form was connected with 'Greek style' cooking. Similarly, if we glance in our own kitchens we may see an 'Asian wok' used for stir fried meals even such meals do not follow an original Asian recipe.

Transport amphoras are a third category suitable to trace networks. They were not traded for their own sake, however, but as containers for wine, olives, and other commodities. Research in this field generally depends on study by specialists; our proceedings contain one examplary contribution (s. Dobosz).

Economic/ Commercial aspect

Certainly pottery is connected with trade, although this is a complex and layered phenomenon. While a single vessel may have been made far from the place it was found, there can be different reasons for its final location. Perhaps it was a result of international trade; perhaps it was a result of diplomatic exchange within an ‚elite network‘ (Berlin); perhaps it was a souvenir from a journey, etc. In all instances there is an overlap between personal and cultural networks.

In some contexts foreign wares appear only in small quantities, e.g., Attic pottery in Central Asia or Ephesian relief bowls in Palmyra. These few pieces may have reached these places as accidental cargo of merchant ships or caravans. They are indicators of trade routes but not direct evidence for intensive trade relations. In general pottery does not represent one-to-one trade. Taking the literature sources into consideration one should ask what was taken on board as an exchange value for the ceramics: most likely money, grain, building materials etc.

Unsurprisingly the same specific wares appear at other places in huge quantities. In such cases we may assume commercial trading links, by which supra-regional widespread wares were exchanged as goods on their own. As an example shipwrecks off the southern coast of Turkey showed that there had been piles of ESA cups and plates on board, whose traces were then dispersed on land. Normally such trade will have begun over sea routes and then, depending on natural conditions, continued on land. And of course it is most intriguing to wonder about traded wares absent at some places and those wares that were not traded at all.

Military and political aspects

Military and political networks are related, and both can be glimpsed through the movement of pottery to foreign or distant territories. In some conference papers as well as in parts of the final discussion it was suggested that pottery could be seen somehow as a byproduct of military and political activities. Military forces often required standardised supplies at home as well as abroad, and both local products and imports could be consigned to meet the needs of soldiers. Closely connected with the conquest of new territories would be the installation of a new administration. Dura-Europos and Merv are two examples of administrative centres. Both functioned as natural stop-overs along a trade route (the later Silk Road) as well as military outposts for Hellenistic, Roman, and Parthian rulers.

It is sometimes tempting to link pottery to political events, but again this is complicated. The Macedonian shield bowls are a prime example. The design was originally developed in Macedonia and became widespread. Possibly after the battle of Pydna (168 BC) in Macedonia the type came to stand as a commemoration of earlier Macedonian victories. But in Asia Minor, locally produced shield bowls probably did not convey any such message. Customers there would not have understood the design as Macedonian message, so its meaning was lost. Another complicated connection may be seen with Mithridates' destruction of the free port of Delos and the beginning of imitations in the East. It is strange yet true that there is a 'happy pottery trade between fighting parties like Rhodes and Pergamon' (Rotroff).

Here we widen our perspective to ask how, or even if, a long-term political administration has an impact on coin circulation (s. Noeske). Did the Macedonian occupation stop Athenian exports? Were trade connections affected as places changed from Ptolemaic to Seleucid control? Such questions have to be treated carefully, as there is no necessary link between politics and trade: ‚material and politic are not the same' (Stewart).

A 'picture' of Hellenistic networks – according to the pottery in the Eastern Mediterranean and beyond

In the discussions different global and regional markets were clarified. Some markets emited influences and other markets absorbed them. In this resumé we ask how the flow of merchandise and commodities works. Where are the starting points of specific pottery products? Where are the nodes (in the sense of connecting points)? Where are the endpoints and extremities?

Starting points of long distance/supra-regional networks

In the development of supra-regional networks, military campaigns and colonies must have played an important role. At many places we find Greek prototypes only with the first Greek or Macedonian soldiers. These people likely provided the first impetus, which afterwards led to the sprouting of a new connection. Alexander built new towns and, it seems, new identities. One can trace the edges of the Hellenistic ‚worldwide web' of influence by the occurence of fish plates, mold made relief bowls and the use of specific cooking vessels.

In the late third century BC Athens was detached and replaced by other centres such as Ephesos and Pergamon, which in turn became the starting points of new supraregional networks. Ephesos was well positioned for the export of her pottery products, with her own harbour supporting the distribution. Although only marginal in mainland Greece, the typical Ephesian mouldmade bowl was a market leader in many places, and especially in high numbers in the Black Sea region. There Ephesian bowls captured 60% of the market, while Knidian and Attic bowls took up only 2% each and bowls from Pergamon only 1% at most.

On the evidence of the pottery, Pergamenian influence seems to have been weaker than that of Ephesos, and oriented in a different direction. Products from Pergamon have been found predominantly in Asia Minor and in the Aegean islands of Lesbos, Delos and Samos, however in smaller numbers in the southern and western Aegean. Meanwhile ESA with her production centre(s) presumably in northern Syria had a wide distribution radius beyond a core area of the Levant and Cyprus, extending in diminishing numbers west to the Adriatic Sea, east to Central Asia, north to the Black Sea, and south to Egypt.

Web nodes

Delos and Cyprus hold exceptional positions as trading centres within the networks of import and export, which underlines the importance of the sea routes (s. above). Since the middle of the second century BC Delos played an outstanding role by taking in commodities from Asia Minor and sending them out west, south and north. Documentated are ties with Athens (imports of black gloss and west slope decorated pottery), Rhodes (amphoras), Italy (amphoras, thin-walled pottery), Ephesos (mouldmade bowls), Phocaia (cooking ware), north Syria (ESA), Knidos (rouletted bowls), and Pergamon (appliqué ware). Within the networks in the Eastern Mediterranean Cyprus is a relatively important node. Her connections range from Cilicia and the northern Levant to Egypt (especially Alexandria) and Rhodes as well as Greece and the Black Sea region.

Smaller networks and passing points

During the conference regional networks have become clear for Greece: the Pelponnesos appears to be diveded in different zones, within which Corinth and Laconia had contacts with Alexandria, and Messene was in relation with Italy. Within nothern Greece close relations existed between Macedonia and Thessaly on the one hand and with Epirus on the other hand. Epirus in turn had a close connection to the northwestern Peloponnesos. We can see an internal Greek network in which single regions are overlapping.

Looking from the perspective of the eastern Mediterranean Albania lies at a periphery. But the conference contributions have shown that this region was a transfer zone on the trading routes to northern Italy. For example Ephesian mould made bowls, white ground lagynoi and gray ware plates did not stop at Albania but made their way through North Italy up to Magdalensberg in modern-day Austria. The actual route will have used the Adriatic Sea, with the Albanian coastal sites acting only as passing points.

In modern-day Turkey we can distinguish well-defined zones: the export-oriented Asia Minor coast with its metropolises Ephesos, Pergamon and Knidos as well as Tralles; and the more confined southern coast with its hinterland, acting as a transfer zone via searoutes to Cyprus, other Aegean islands and the Levant but apparently not on landroutes to the West.

In the Levant Mediterranean imports at inland sites reveal east-west routes emerging from cities on the coast. Places in the east far away from the seaside such as Jebel Khalid, Palmyra, and Dura-Europos were connected to Mediterranean networks due to their position on important landroutes, which also fostered interregional exchange.

Endpoints

Gordion is an example of an endpoint. In the material there are only a few sherds that can be named as network indicators explained by the remote location of the city far away from the main routes and metropolises. Gordion's connections to the Black Sea still have to be investigated. In the Black Sea region we glimpse the final destination of Attic bell kraters found in south Russian tombs. In a fortified farmhouse on the Crimea almost all vessels have been repaired (personal information Pia Guldager Bilde), which might suggest a site at the end of a trading network. And yet according to S. Rotroff in the Athenian Agora many ESA vessels show mend-holes. Since Athens can hardly be considered an endpoint, this feature might suggest instead either extreme thrift or second-hand purchases. The question of where the networks end remains open. Is it in Central Asia? in Uzbeskistan?

The future

We aimed high with the goals of this conference. It has shown us that we are only at the beginning in the research of networks in the Hellenistic world and the contribution of Hellenistic pottery. Despite the wealth of excavated and published material the overall picture is still very incomplete. It would be especially desirable to fill in gaps in several regions. For example Kos, Lesbos, Thasos, Rhodes, Amorgos, and the southern and eastern coasts of the Black Sea are still largely unknown. There remain many questions regarding Mesopotamia and the North African coast. There are even still difficulties in determining the origin of well-known Hellenistic forms, e.g., the braziers.

Other points of view could be gained by statistical approaches. We still have difficulty calculating the amount of pottery in a house, a residential quarter, or a whole area of one city. We must fine-tune our chronologies so that we will be able to recognize when stylistic innovations reach other centers, and when they inspire local versions. One possible major project would be an internet platform where everybody working on Hellenistic pottery could feed in his/her database. Chronologically differentiated maps would allow us to track the export and imports of specific wares and so visualize networks.

We are happy that this conference inspired the formation of a new research group: ‚International Association for Research on Pottery of the Hellenistic period (IARPOTHP)' (http://iarpothp.org/). We hope that future meetings will carry on the spirit of investigation that we began with this conference on 'Networks in the Hellenistic World– according to the pottery'.

Nina Fenn
Christiane Römer-Strehl

www.ingramcontent.com/pod-product-compliance
Ingram Content Group UK Ltd.
Pitfield, Milton Keynes, MK11 3LW, UK
UKHW061844041026
15591UKWH00015B/899

9 781407 311579